AF901354

New Perspectives

Microsoft® 365®
Office 2021

Introductory

Cengage

Australia • Brazil • Canada • Mexico • Singapore • United Kingdom • United States

Cengage

New Perspectives Series® Microsoft® Office 365® & Office 2021 Introductory
Jennifer Campbell, Patrick Carey, Ann Shaffer

SVP, Product: Erin Joyner

VP, Product: Thais Alencar

Product Director: Mark Santee

Senior Product Manager: Amy Savino

Product Assistant: Ciara Horne

Learning Designer: Zenya Molnar

Content Manager: Christina Nyren

Digital Delivery Quality Partner: Jim Vaughey

Developmental Editors: Robin Romer, Michael Sanford, Mary Pat Shaffer

VP, Product Marketing: Jason Sakos

Director, Product Marketing: Danaë April

Executive Product Marketing Manager: Jill Staut

IP Analyst: Ann Hoffman

IP Project Manager: Anjali Kambli

Production Service: Lumina Datamatics Ltd.

Designer: Erin Griffin

Cover Image Source: Artur Debat/Getty Images

Mac Users: If you're working through this product using a Mac, some of the steps may vary. Additional information for Mac users is included with the Data files for this product.

Disclaimer: This text is intended for instructional purposes only; data is fictional and does not belong to any real persons or companies.

Disclaimer: The material in this text was written using Microsoft Windows 10 and Office 365 Professional Plus and was Quality Assurance tested before the publication date. As Microsoft continually updates the Windows 10 operating system and Office 365, your software experience may vary slightly from what is presented in the printed text.

Library of Congress Control Number: 2022935104

Student Edition ISBN: 978-0-357-67208-2
K12 ISBN: 978-0-357-67210-5
Looseleaf ISBN: 978-0-357-67209-9*
*Looseleaf available as part of a digital bundle

Cengage
200 Pier 4 Boulevard
Boston, MA 02210
USA

Cengage is a leading provider of customized learning solutions with employees residing in nearly 40 different countries and sales in more than 125 countries around the world. Find your local representative at **www.cengage.com.**

To learn more about Cengage platforms and services, register or access your online learning solution, or purchase materials for your course, visit **www.cengage.com.**

Printed in the United States of America
Print Number: 01 Print Year: 2022

BRIEF CONTENTS

TABLE OF CONTENTS

EXCEL MODULES

ACCESS MODULES

POWERPOINT MODULES

Getting to Know Microsoft Office Versions

Cengage is proud to bring you the next edition of Microsoft Office. This edition was designed to provide a robust learning experience that is not dependent upon a specific version of Office.

Microsoft supports several versions of Office:

- **Office 365:** A cloud-based subscription service that delivers Microsoft's most up-to-date, feature-rich, modern productivity tools direct to your device. There are variations of Office 365 for business, educational, and personal use. Office 365 offers extra online storage and cloud-connected features, as well as updates with the latest features, fixes, and security updates.
- **Office 2021:** Microsoft's "on-premises" version of the Office apps, available for both PCs and Macs, offered as a static, one-time purchase and outside of the subscription model.
- **Office Online:** A free, simplified version of Office web applications (Word, Excel, PowerPoint, and OneNote) that facilitates creating and editing files collaboratively.

Office 365 (the subscription model) and Office 2021 (the one-time purchase model) had only slight differences between them at the time this content was developed. Over time, Office 365's cloud interface will continuously update, offering new application features and functions, while Office 2021 will remain static. Therefore, your onscreen experience may differ from what you see in this product. For example, the more advanced features and functionalities covered in this product may not be available in Office Online or may have updated from what you see in Office 2021.

For more information on the differences between Office 365, Office 2021, and Office Online, please visit the Microsoft Support site.

Cengage is committed to providing high-quality learning solutions for you to gain the knowledge and skills that will empower you throughout your educational and professional careers.

Thank you for using our product, and we look forward to exploring the future of Microsoft Office with you!

Using SAM Projects and Textbook Projects

SAM Projects allow you to actively apply the skills you learned live in Microsoft Word, Excel, PowerPoint, or Access. Become a more productive student and use these skills throughout your career.

To complete SAM Textbook Projects, please follow these steps:

SAM Textbook Projects allow you to complete a project as you follow along with the steps in the textbook. As you read the module, look for icons that indicate when you should download **sam** ↓ your SAM Start file(s) and when to upload **sam** ↑ the final project file to SAM for grading.

Everything you need to complete this project is provided within SAM. You can launch the eBook directly from SAM, which will allow you to take notes, highlight, and create a custom study guide, or you can use a print textbook or your mobile app. Download IOS or Download Android.

To get started, launch your SAM Project assignment from SAM, MindTap, or a link within your LMS.

Step 1: Download Files

- Click the "Download All" button or the individual links to download your **Start File** and **Support File(s)** (when available). You must use the SAM Start file.
- Click the Instructions link to launch the eBook (or use the print textbook or mobile app).
- Disregard any steps in the textbook that ask you to create a new file or to use a file from a location outside of SAM.
- Look for the SAM Download icon **sam** ↓ to begin working with your start file.
- Follow the module's step-by-step instructions until you reach the SAM Upload icon **sam** ↑.
- Save and close the file.

Step 2: Save Work to SAM

- Ensure you rename your project file to match the Expected File Name.
- Upload your in-progress or completed file to SAM. You can download the file to continue working or submit it for grading in the next step.

Step 3: Submit for Grading

- Upload the completed file to SAM for immediate feedback and to view the available Reports.
  - The **Graded Summary Report** provides a detailed list of project steps, your score, and feedback to aid you in revising and re-submitting the project.
  - The **Study Guide Report** provides your score for each project step and links to the associated training and textbook pages.
- If additional attempts are allowed, use your reports to assist with revising and resubmitting your project.
- To re-submit the project, download the file saved in step 2.
- Edit, save, and close the file, then re-upload and submit it again.

For all other SAM Projects, please follow these steps:

To get started, launch your SAM Project assignment from SAM, MindTap, or a link within your LMS.

Step 1: Download Files

- Click the "Download All" button or the individual links to download your **Instruction File**, **Start File**, and **Support File(s)** (when available). You must use the SAM Start file.
- Open the Instruction file and follow the step-by-step instructions. Ensure you rename your project file to match the Expected File Name (change _1 to _2 at the end of the file name).

Step 2: Save Work to SAM

- Upload your in-progress or completed file to SAM. You can download the file to continue working or submit it for grading in the next step.

Step 3: Submit for Grading

- Upload the completed file to SAM for immediate feedback and to view available Reports.
  - The **Graded Summary Report** provides a detailed list of project steps, your score, and feedback to aid you in revising and resubmitting the project.
  - The **Study Guide Report** provides your score for each project step and links to the associated training and textbook pages.
- If additional attempts are allowed, use your reports to assist with revising and resubmitting your project.
- To re-submit the project, download the file saved in step 2.
- Edit, save, and close the file, then re-upload and submit it again.

For additional tips to successfully complete your SAM Projects, please view our Common Student Errors Infographic.

Module 1

Creating and Editing a Document

Writing a Business Letter and Formatting a Flyer

Objectives

Session 1.1
- Create and save a document
- Enter text and correct errors as you type
- Use AutoComplete and AutoCorrect
- Select text and move the insertion point
- Undo and redo actions
- Adjust paragraph spacing, line spacing, and margins
- Preview and print a document
- Create an envelope

Session 1.2
- Open an existing document
- Use the Editor pane
- Change page orientation, font, font color, and font size
- Apply text effects and align text
- Copy formatting with the Format Painter
- Insert a paragraph border and shading
- Delete, insert, and edit a photo
- Add a page border
- Create bulleted and numbered lists
- Use Microsoft Word Help

Case | Water Resources Department

David Alzacar is the communications director for the Water Resources Department in Portland, Oregon. As part of his outreach efforts, he has produced a set of brochures promoting the city's water conservation efforts. David has asked you to create a cover letter to accompany the brochures he is sending to the organizers of a national sustainability conference. He has also asked you to create an envelope for sending a water quality report to an environmental engineering publication. Next, he wants your help creating a flyer encouraging community members to join a citizen advisory panel. Finally, he would like to add bulleted and numbered lists to the minutes of a recent advisory panel meeting.

You will create the letter and flyer using **Microsoft Word 365** (or simply **Word**), a full-featured word processing app that lets you create professional-looking documents and revise them easily. You'll start by opening Word and saving a new document. Then you'll type the text of the cover letter and print it. In the process of entering the text, you'll learn several ways to correct typing errors and how to adjust paragraph and line spacing. When you create the envelope, you'll learn how to save it as part of a document for later use. As you work on the flyer, you will learn how to open an existing document, change the way text is laid out on the page, format text, add a page border, and insert and resize a photo. Finally, you'll add bulleted and numbered lists to a document, and then learn how to use Microsoft Word Help.

Starting Data Files

Word1 →

Module
NP_WD_1-1.docx
NP_WD_1-2.docx
Support_WD_1_Water.png

Review
NP_WD_1-3.docx
NP_WD_1-4.docx
Support_WD_1_Glass.png

Case1
(none)

Case2
NP_WD_1-5.docx
Support_WD_1_Sign.jpg

Session 1.1 Visual Overview:

The **Quick Access Toolbar** is a collection of buttons that provides one-click access to commonly used commands, such as Save, Undo, and Repeat; you might see additional buttons here.

Each **tab** includes commands related to particular activities or tasks. The Home tab includes options for formatting and editing text.

The **title bar** displays the name of the open file and the program.

The **ribbon** is the main set of buttons and other tools you can use to complete tasks. It is organized into tabs and groups.

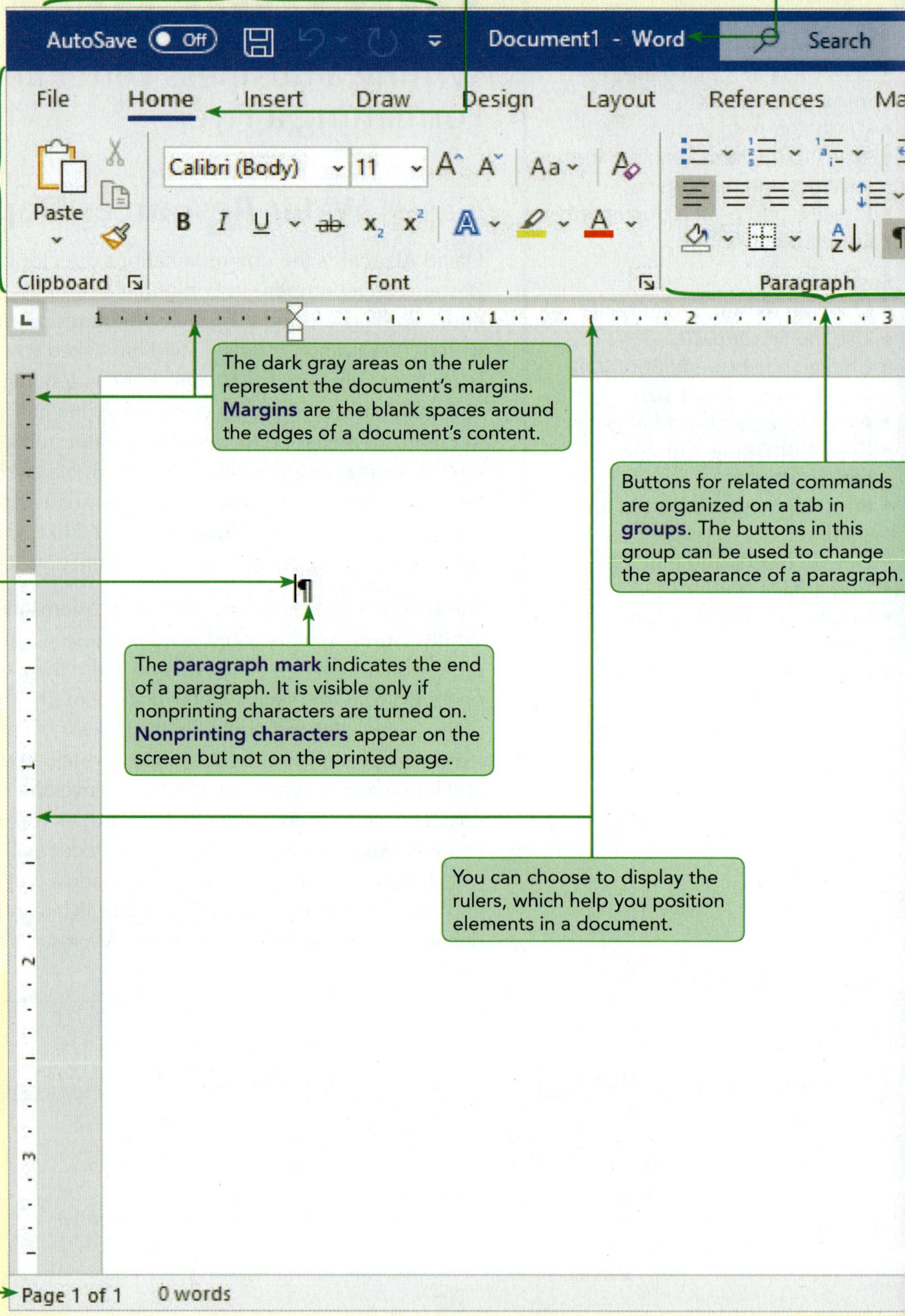

The dark gray areas on the ruler represent the document's margins. **Margins** are the blank spaces around the edges of a document's content.

Buttons for related commands are organized on a tab in **groups**. The buttons in this group can be used to change the appearance of a paragraph.

The **insertion point** shows where characters will appear when you start typing.

The **paragraph mark** indicates the end of a paragraph. It is visible only if nonprinting characters are turned on. **Nonprinting characters** appear on the screen but not on the printed page.

You can choose to display the rulers, which help you position elements in a document.

The **status bar** provides information about the current document, such as the current page and number of words in the document; it also contains buttons and other controls for working with the document.

The Word Window

The Show/Hide button is selected, meaning that nonprinting characters are displayed in the document.

You can click the Ribbon Display Options button to display a menu with options for how the ribbon looks. If the ribbon is hidden, click Show Tabs and Commands in this menu to redisplay it.

You use the Minimize button to reduce the Word window to an icon in the taskbar, which you can click later to display the Word window again.

You use the Restore Down button to reduce the Word window to a smaller size; the Restore Down button is then replaced with the Maximize button, which you can click to restore the Word window to its full size.

If you are signed in, your name appears here as a link that you can click to access information about your Microsoft account.

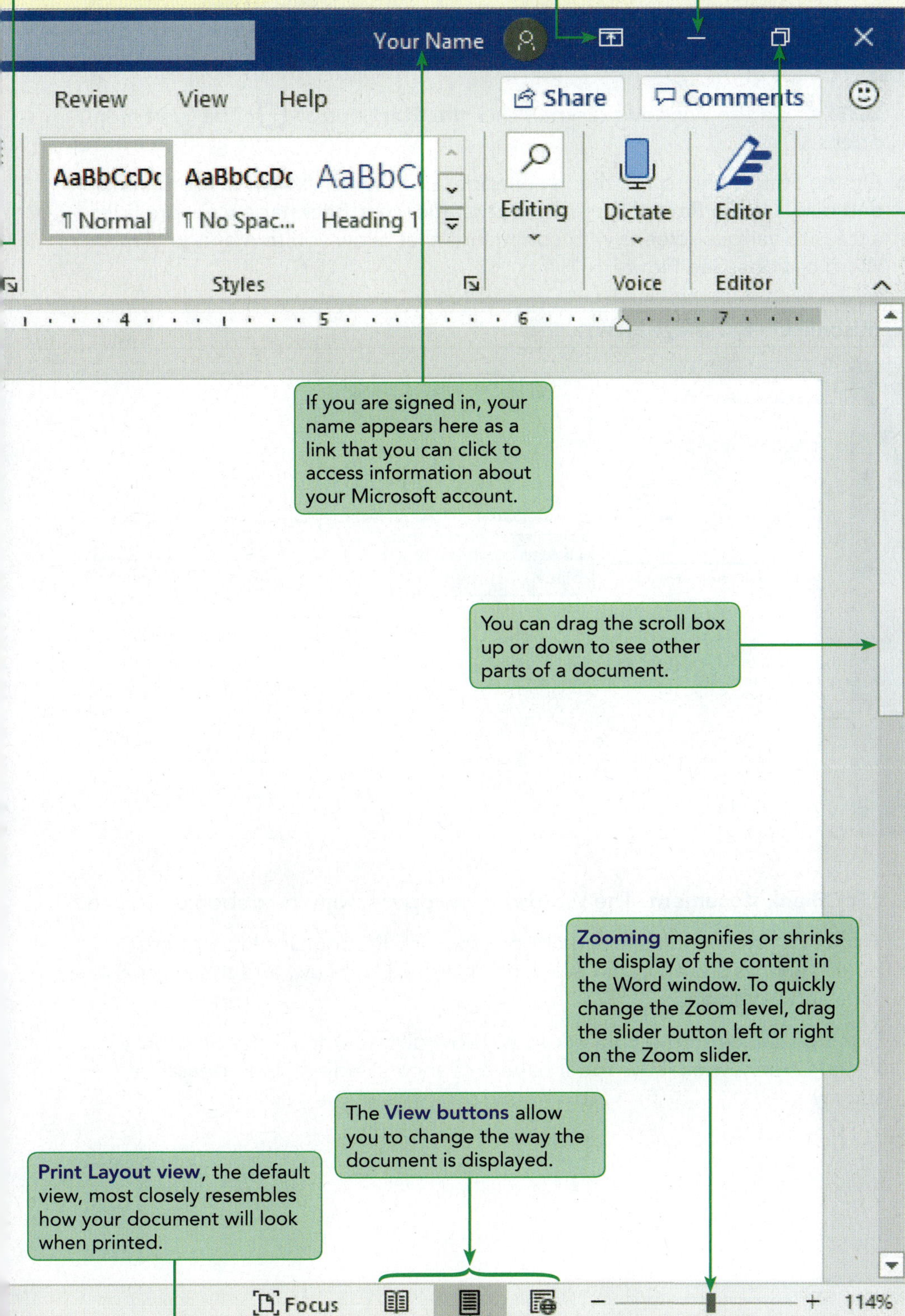

You can drag the scroll box up or down to see other parts of a document.

You can click the scroll arrows to scroll up or down one line, or hold the mouse button to scroll up or down more quickly.

Zooming magnifies or shrinks the display of the content in the Word window. To quickly change the Zoom level, drag the slider button left or right on the Zoom slider.

The **View buttons** allow you to change the way the document is displayed.

Print Layout view, the default view, most closely resembles how your document will look when printed.

Starting Word

With Word, you can quickly create polished, professional documents. You can type a document, adjust margins and spacing, create columns and tables, add graphics, and then easily make revisions and corrections. In this session, you will create one of the most common types of documents—a block-style business letter.

To begin creating the letter, you first need to start Microsoft Word and then set up the Word window.

To start Word:

1. sam On the Windows taskbar, click the **Start** button. The Start menu opens.
2. On the Start menu, scroll the list of apps, and then click **Word**. Word starts and displays the Recent screen in Backstage view. Backstage view provides access to various screens with commands that allow you to manage files and Word options. See Figure 1–1.

Figure 1–1 Recent screen in Backstage view

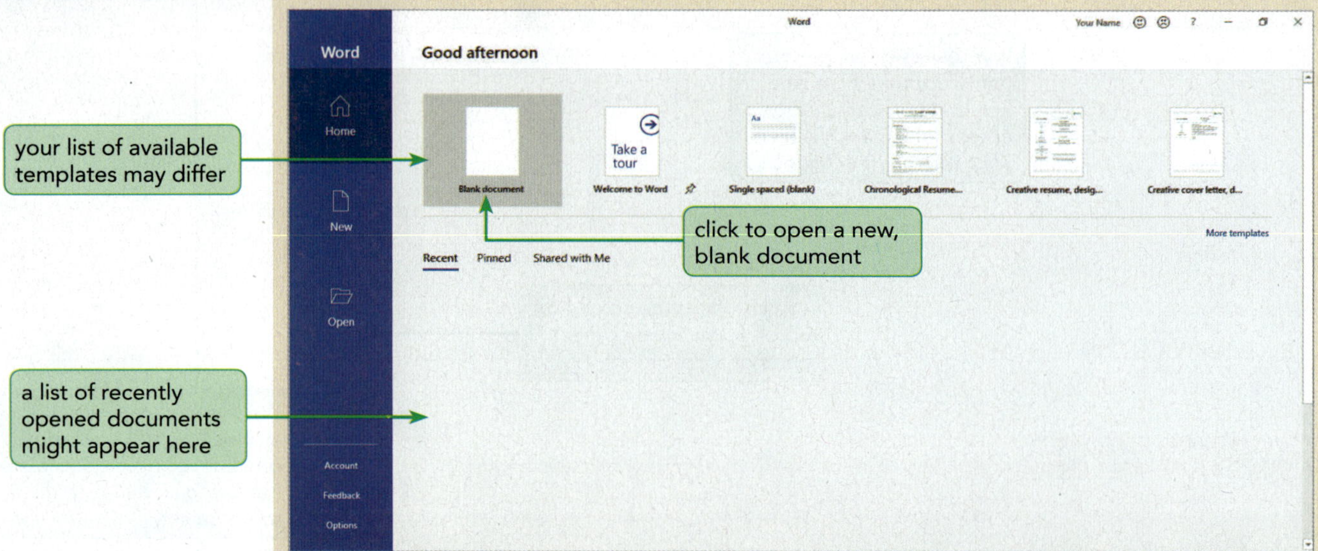

3. Click **Blank document**. The Word window opens, with the ribbon displayed.

   Trouble? If you don't see the ribbon, click the Ribbon Display Options button, as shown in the Session 1.1 Visual Overview, and then click Show Tabs and Commands.

   Don't be concerned if your Word window doesn't match the Session 1.1 Visual Overview exactly. You'll have a chance to adjust its appearance shortly.

Working in Touch Mode

You can interact with the Word screen using a mouse, or, if you have a touchscreen, you can work in Touch Mode, using a finger instead of the pointer. In **Touch Mode**, extra space around the buttons on the ribbon makes it easier to tap the specific button you need. The figures in this text show the screen with Mouse Mode on, but it's helpful to learn how to switch back and forth between Touch Mode and Mouse Mode.

Note: The steps in this module assume that you are using a mouse. If you are instead using a touch device, please read these steps but don't complete them so that you remain working in Touch Mode.

To switch between Touch and Mouse Mode:

1. On the Quick Access Toolbar, click the **Customize Quick Access Toolbar** button to open the menu. The Touch/Mouse Mode command near the bottom of the menu does not have a checkmark next to it, indicating that it is currently not selected.

   Trouble? If the Touch/Mouse Mode command has a checkmark next to it, press ESC to close the menu, and then skip to Step 3.

2. On the menu, click **Touch/Mouse Mode**. The menu closes, and the Touch/Mouse Mode button appears on the Quick Access Toolbar.
3. On the Quick Access Toolbar, click the **Touch/Mouse Mode** button. A menu opens with two options—Mouse and Touch. The icon next to Mouse is shaded gray to indicate it is selected.

   Trouble? If the icon next to Touch is shaded gray, press ESC to close the menu and skip to Step 5.

4. On the menu, click **Touch**. The menu closes, and the ribbon increases in height so that there is more space around each button on the ribbon. See Figure 1–2.

Figure 1–2 Word window in Touch Mode

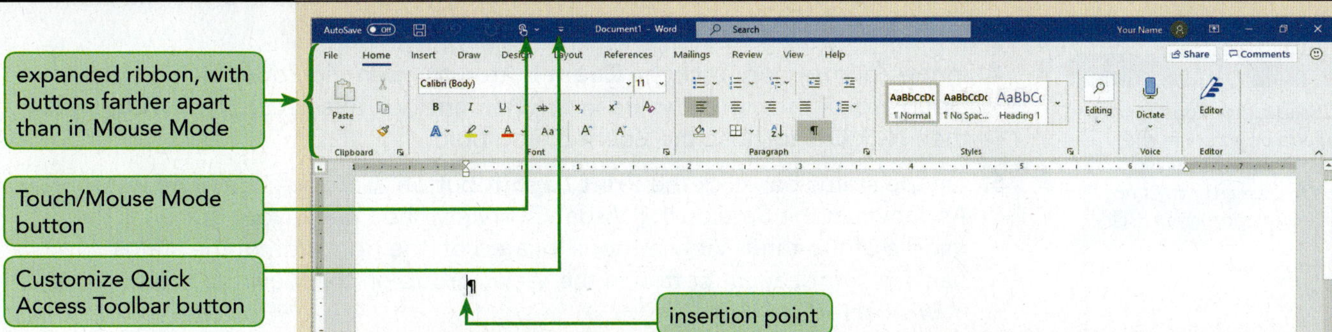

   Trouble? If you are working with a touchscreen and want to use Touch Mode, skip Steps 5 and 6.

5. On the Quick Access Toolbar, click the **Touch/Mouse Mode** button, and then click **Mouse**. The ribbon changes back to its Mouse Mode appearance, as shown in the Session 1.1 Visual Overview.

6. On the Quick Access Toolbar, click the **Customize Quick Access Toolbar** button, and then click **Touch/Mouse Mode** to deselect it. The Touch/Mouse Mode button is removed from the Quick Access Toolbar.

Setting Up the Word Window

Before you start using Word, you should make sure you can locate and identify the different elements of the Word window, as shown in the Session 1.1 Visual Overview. In the following steps, you'll make sure your screen matches the Visual Overview.

To set up your Word window to match the figures in this book:

1. If the Word window does not fill the entire screen, click the **Maximize** button in the upper-right corner of the Word window.

   The insertion point on your computer should be positioned about an inch from the top of the document, as shown in Figure 1–2, with the top margin visible.

   Trouble? If the insertion point appears at the top of the document, with no white space above it, position the pointer between the top of the document and the horizontal ruler, until it changes to , double-click, and then scroll up to top of the document.

2. On the ribbon, click the **View** tab. The ribbon changes to show options for changing the appearance of the Word window.

3. In the Show group, click the **Ruler** check box to insert a checkmark, if necessary. If the rulers were not displayed, they are displayed now.

   Next, you'll change the Zoom level to a setting that ensures that your Word window will match the figures in this book. To increase or decrease the screen's magnification, you could drag the slider button on the Zoom slider in the lower-right corner of the Word window. But to choose a specific Zoom level, it's easier to use the Zoom dialog box.

Tip

Changing the Zoom level affects only the way the document is displayed on the screen; it does not affect the document itself.

4. In the Zoom group, click the **Zoom** button to open the Zoom dialog box. Double-click the current value in the **Percent** box to select it, type **120**, and then click **OK** to close the Zoom dialog box.

5. On the status bar, click the **Print Layout** button to select it, if necessary. As shown in the Session 1.1 Visual Overview, the Print Layout button is the middle of the three View buttons located on the right side of the status bar. The Print Layout button in the Views group on the View tab is also now selected.

Before typing a document, you should make sure nonprinting characters are displayed. Nonprinting characters provide a visual representation of details you might otherwise miss. For example, the (¶) character marks the end of a paragraph, and the (•) character marks the space between words.

To verify that nonprinting characters are displayed:

1. On the ribbon, click the **Home** tab.
2. In the blank Word document, look for the paragraph mark (¶) in the first line of the document, just to the right of the blinking insertion point.

   Trouble? If you don't see the paragraph mark, click the Show/Hide ¶ button ¶ in the Paragraph group.

   In the Paragraph group, the Show/Hide ¶ button should be highlighted in gray, indicating that it is selected, and the paragraph mark (¶) should appear in the first line of the document, just to the right of the insertion point.

Saving a Document

Tip

To save a document to OneDrive for the first time, you can click the Save button on the Quick Access Toolbar.

Before you begin working on a document, you should save it with a new name. When you click the File tab and then click Save to save a document for the first time, Word displays the Save As screen in Backstage view. On the Save As screen, you can select the location where you want to store your document. After that, you can click the Save button on the Quick Access Toolbar to save your document to the same location you specified earlier and with the same name.

To save the document:

1. Click the File tab on the ribbon, and then click Save. Word switches to the Save As screen in Backstage view, as shown in Figure 1–3.

Figure 1–3 Save As screen in Backstage view

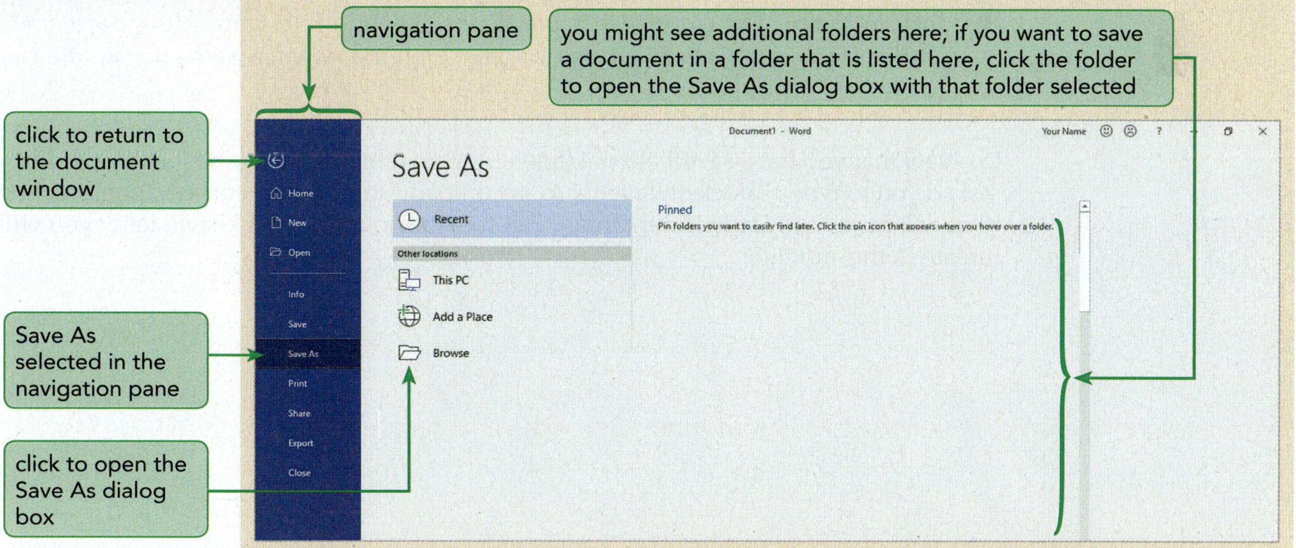

Because a document is now open, more commands are available in Backstage view than when you started Word. The **navigation pane** on the left contains commands for working with the open document and for changing settings that control how Word works.

2. Click the **Browse** button. The Save As dialog box opens.

Trouble? If your instructor wants you to save your files to your OneDrive account, click OneDrive, and then log in to your account.

3. Navigate to the location specified by your instructor. The default file name, "Doc1," appears in the File name box. You will change that to something more descriptive. See Figure 1–4.

Figure 1–4 **Save As dialog box**

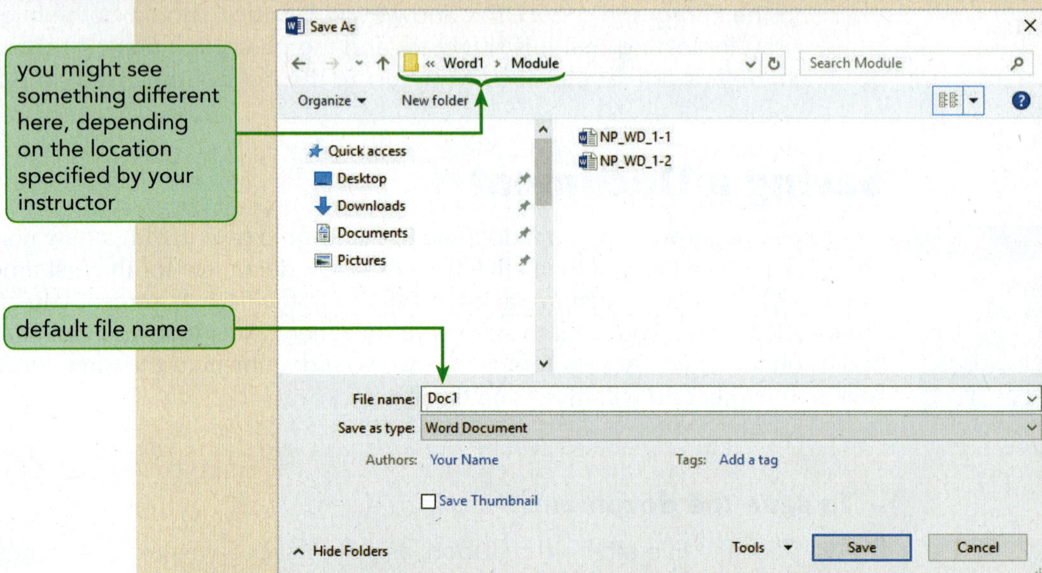

4. Click the **File name** box, and then type **NP_WD_1_Letter**. The text you type replaces the selected text in the File name box.

5. Click **Save**. The file is saved, the dialog box and Backstage view close, and the document window appears again, with the new file name in the title bar.

Now that you have saved the document, you can begin typing the letter. David has asked you to type a block-style letter to accompany some water conservation brochures that will be sent to Carla Zimmerman. Figure 1–5 shows the block-style letter you will create in this module.

Figure 1–5 Completed block-style letter

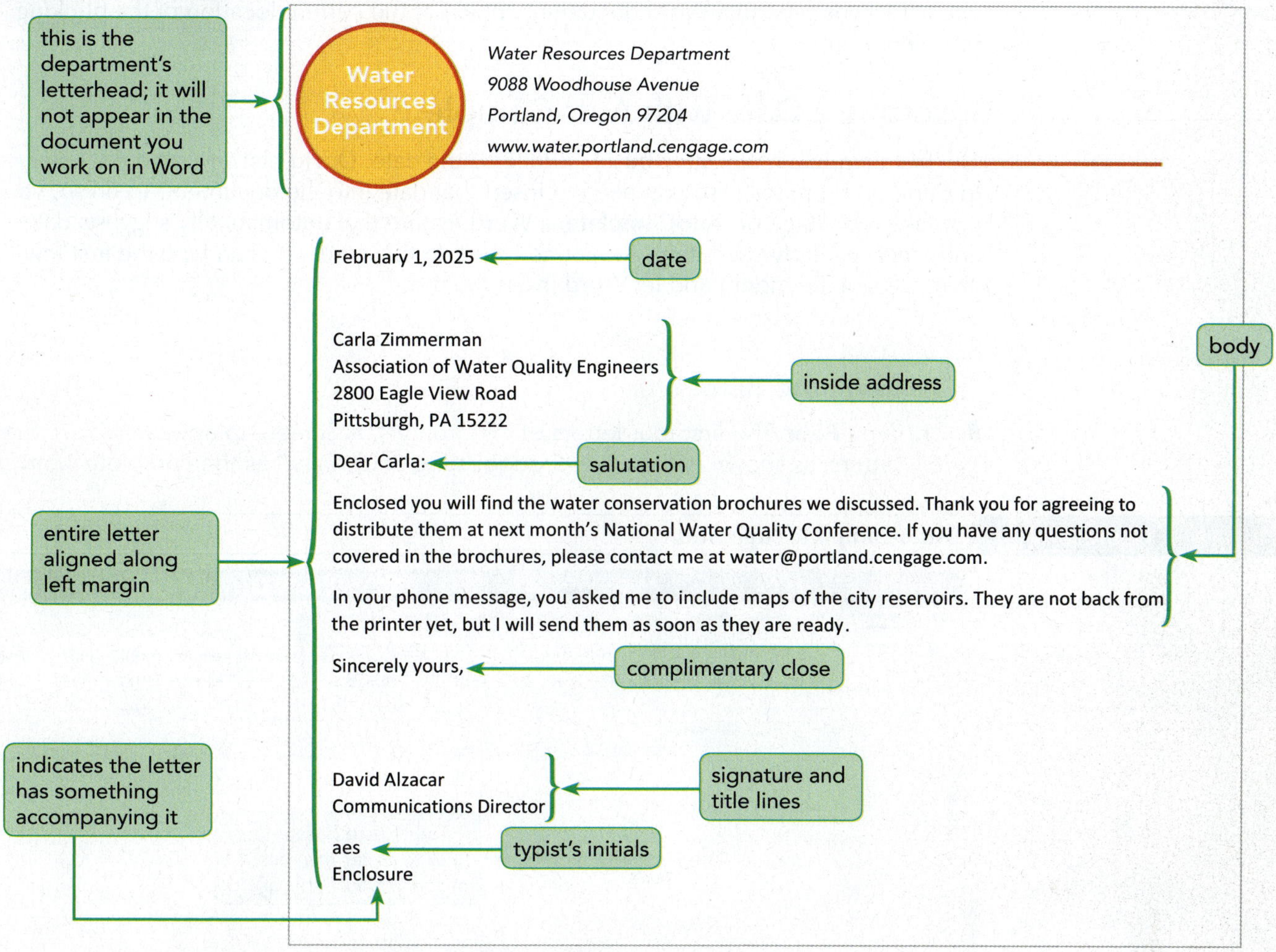

Proskills

Written Communication: Creating a Business Letter

Several styles are considered acceptable for business letters. The main differences among the styles have to do with how parts of the letter are indented from the left margin. In the block style, which you will use in this module, each line of text starts at the left margin. In other words, nothing is indented. Another style is to indent the first line of each paragraph. The choice of style is largely a matter of personal preference, or it can be determined by the standards used in a particular business or organization. To further enhance your skills in writing business correspondence, you should consult an authoritative book on business writing that provides guidelines for creating a variety of business documents, such as *Business Communication: Process & Product* by Mary Ellen Guffey and Dana Loewy.

Entering Text

The letters you type in a Word document appear at the current location of the blinking insertion point.

Inserting a Date with AutoComplete

The first item in a block-style business letter is the date. David plans to send the letter to Carla on February 1, so you need to insert that date into the document. To do so, you can take advantage of **AutoComplete**, a Word feature that automatically suggests dates and other regularly used items for you to insert. In this case, you can type the first few characters of the month and let Word insert the rest.

To insert the date:

1. Type **Febr** (the first four letters of "February"). A ScreenTip appears above the letters, as shown in Figure 1–6, suggesting "February" as the complete word.

Figure 1–6 AutoComplete suggestion

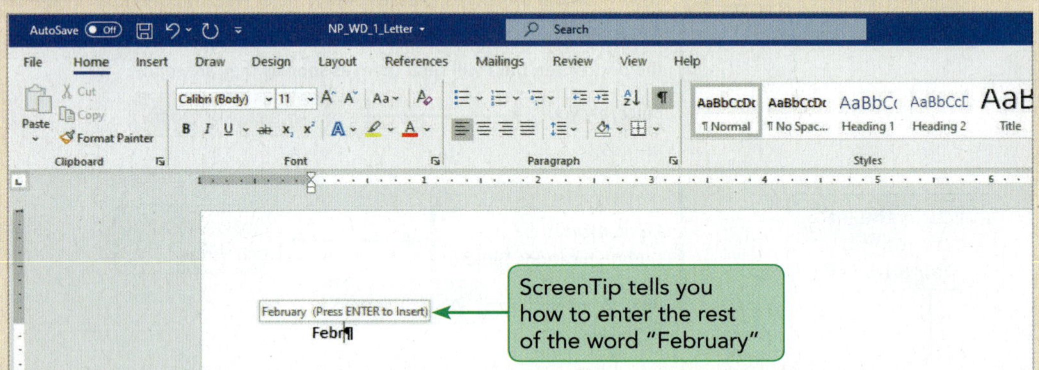

A **ScreenTip** is a label with descriptive text or an explanation about what to do next.

If you wanted to type something other than "February," you could continue typing to complete the word. In this case, you want to accept the AutoComplete suggestion.

2. Press **ENTER**. The rest of the word "February" is inserted in the document. Note that AutoComplete works for long month names like February but not shorter ones like May, because "Ma" could be the beginning of many words besides "May."

3. Press **SPACEBAR**, type **1, 2025** and then press **ENTER** twice, leaving a blank paragraph between the date and the line where you will begin typing the inside address, which contains the recipient's name and address. Notice the nonprinting character (•) after the word "February" and before the number "1," which indicates a space. Word inserts this nonprinting character every time you press SPACEBAR.

Trouble? If February happens to be the current month, you will see a second AutoComplete suggestion displaying the current date after you press SPACEBAR. To ignore that AutoComplete suggestion, continue typing the rest of the date, as instructed in Step 3.

Note that you can also insert the current date (as well as the current time) by using the Insert Date and Time button in the Text group on the Insert tab. This opens the Date and Time dialog box, where you can select from a variety of date and time formats. If you want Word to update the date or time automatically each time you reopen the document, select the Update automatically check box. In that case, Word inserts the date and time as a special element called a field, which you'll learn more about as you become a more experienced Word user. However, for typical correspondence, it makes more sense to deselect the Update automatically check box so the date and time are inserted in the document as ordinary text.

Continuing to Type the Block-Style Letter

In a block-style business letter, the inside address appears below the date, with one blank paragraph in between. Some style guides recommend including even more space between the date and the inside address. But in the short letter you are typing, more space would make the document look out of balance.

To insert the inside address:

1. Type the following information, pressing **ENTER** after each item:

   Carla Zimmerman

   Association of Water Quality Engineers

   2800 Eagle View Road

   Pittsburgh, PA 15222

   Remember to press ENTER after you type the zip code. Your screen should look like Figure 1–7. Don't be concerned if the lines of the inside address seem too far apart. You'll use the default spacing for now, and then adjust it after you finish typing the letter.

Figure 1–7 Letter with inside address

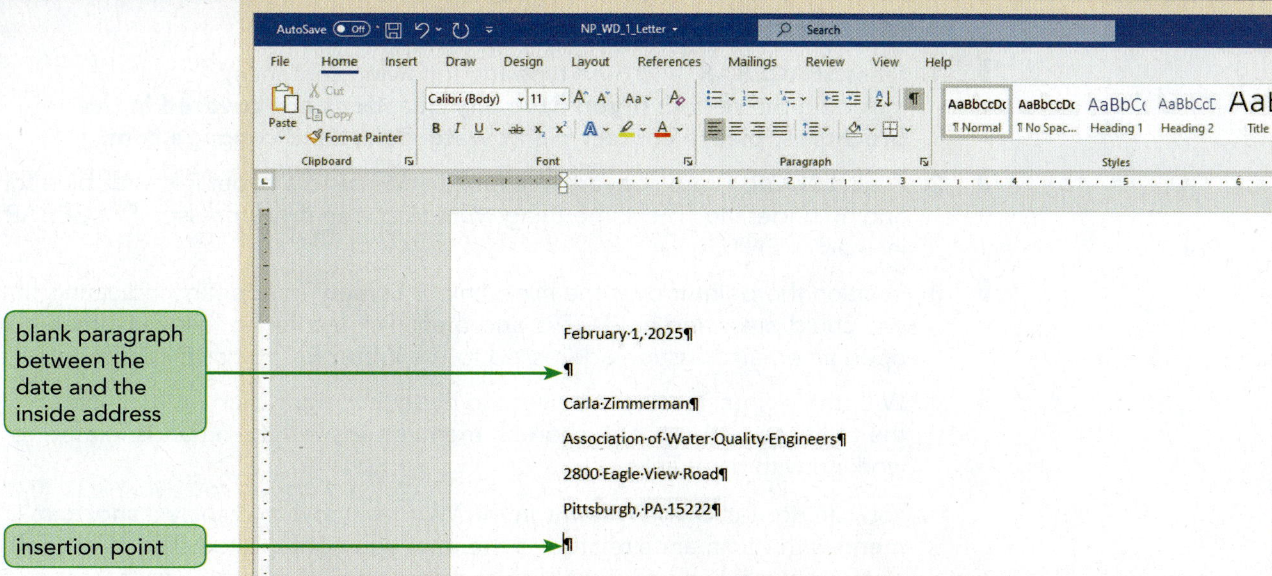

Trouble? If you make a mistake while typing, press BACKSPACE to delete the incorrect character, and then type the correct character.

Now you can move on to the salutation and the body of the letter. As you type the body of the letter, notice that Word automatically moves the insertion point to a new line when the current line is full.

To type the salutation and the body of the letter:

1. Type **Dear Carla:** and then press **ENTER** to start a new paragraph for the body of the letter.
2. Type the following sentence, including the period: **Enclosed you will find the sustainability brochures we discussed.**
3. Press **SPACEBAR**. Note that you should only include one space between sentences.
4. Type the following sentence, including the period: **Thank you for agreeing to distribute them at next month's National Water Quality Conference.**
5. On the Quick Access Toolbar, click the **Save** button. Word saves the document as **NP_WD_1_Letter** to the same location you specified earlier.

Tip

The obsolete practice of pressing SPACEBAR twice at the end of a sentence dates back to the age of typewriters, when the extra space made it easier to see where one sentence ended and another began.

The next sentence you need to type includes David's email address.

Typing a Hyperlink

When you type an email address and then press the SPACEBAR or ENTER, Word converts it to a hyperlink, with blue font and an underline. A **hyperlink** is a specially formatted word, phrase, or graphic that, when clicked or tapped, lets you display a webpage on the Internet, another file, an email, or another location within the same file; it is sometimes called hypertext or a link. Hyperlinks are useful in documents that you plan to distribute via email. In printed documents, where blue font and underlines can be distracting, you'll usually want to convert a hyperlink back to regular text.

To add a sentence containing an email address:

1. Press **SPACEBAR**, and then type the following sentence, including the period: **If you have any questions not covered in the brochures, please contact me at water@portland.cengage.com.**
2. Press **ENTER**. Word converts the email address to a hyperlink, with blue font and an underline. The same thing would happen if you pressed SPACEBAR instead of ENTER.
3. Position the pointer over the hyperlink. A ScreenTip appears, indicating that you could press and hold CTRL and then click the link to follow it—that is, to open an email message addressed to the Water Resources Department.
4. With the pointer positioned over the hyperlink, right-click—that is, press the right mouse button. A shortcut menu opens with commands related to working with hyperlinks.

   You can right-click many items in the Word window to display a **shortcut menu** with commands related to the item you right-clicked. The **Mini toolbar** also appears when you right-click or select text, giving you easy access to the buttons and settings most often used when formatting text. See Figure 1–8.

Figure 1–8 Shortcut menu

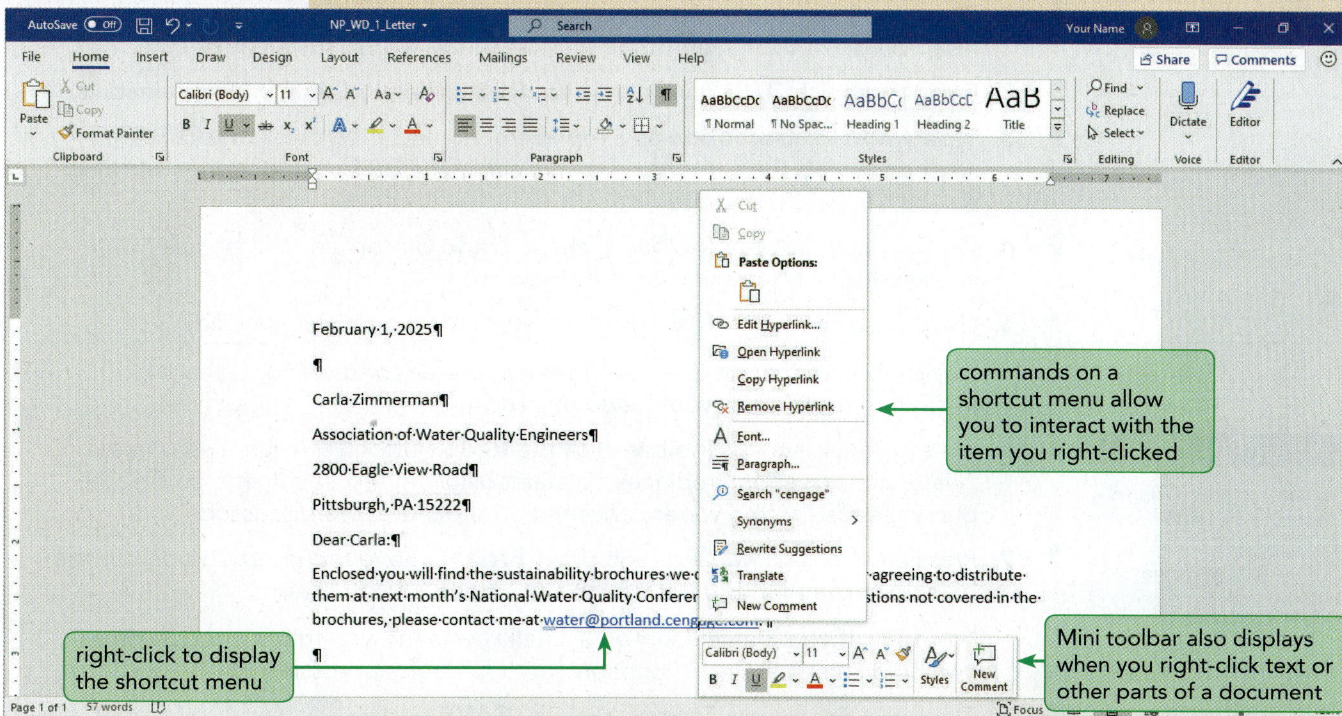

5. Click **Remove Hyperlink** in the shortcut menu. The shortcut menu and the Mini toolbar are no longer visible. The email address is now formatted in black, like the rest of the document text.
6. On the Quick Access Toolbar, click the **Save** button.

Using the Undo and Redo Buttons

When you first open Word, you see the Undo button and the Repeat button in the Quick Access Toolbar. To undo (or reverse) the last thing you did in a document, you can click the Undo button on the Quick Access Toolbar. Once you click the Undo button, the Repeat button is replaced with the Redo button. To restore your original change, click the Redo button, which reverses the action of the Undo button (or redoes the undo). To undo more than your last action, you can continue to click the Undo button, or you can click the Undo arrow on the Quick Access Toolbar to open a list of your most recent actions. When you click an action in the list, Word undoes every action in the list up to and including the action you clicked.

David asks you to change "sustainability" to "water conservation" in the first sentence you typed. You'll make the change now. If David decides he doesn't like it after all, you can always undo it. To delete a character, space, or blank paragraph to the right of the insertion point, you press DEL, or to delete an entire word, you can press CTRL+DEL. To delete a character, space, or blank paragraph to the left of the insertion point, you press BACKSPACE, or to delete an entire word, you can press CTRL+BACKSPACE.

To change the word "sustainability":

1. Press the ↑ key twice and then press the ← key as necessary to move the insertion point to the left of the first "s" in the word "sustainability."
2. Press and hold **CTRL**, and then press **DEL** to delete the word "sustainability."
3. Type **water conservation** as a replacement, and then press **SPACEBAR**. After reviewing the sentence, David decides he prefers the original wording, so you'll undo the change.
4. On the Quick Access Toolbar, click the **Undo** button. The phrase "water conservation" is removed from the sentence.
5. Click the **Undo** button again to restore the word "sustainability."

   David decides that he does want to use "water conservation" after all. Instead of retyping it, you'll redo the undo.
6. On the Quick Access Toolbar, click the **Redo** button twice. The phrase "water conservation" replaces "sustainability" in the document, so that the phrase reads "... the water conservation brochures we discussed."
7. Press and hold **CTRL**, and then press **END** to move the insertion point to the blank paragraph at the end of the document.

   Trouble? If you are working on a small keyboard, you might need to press and hold a key labeled "Function" or "FN" before pressing END.
8. On the Quick Access Toolbar, click the **SAVE** button. Word saves your letter with the same name and to the same location you specified earlier.

Tip

You can also press CTRL+Z to execute the Undo command, and press CTRL+Y to execute the Redo command.

In the previous steps, you used the arrow keys and a key combination to move the insertion point to specific locations in the document. For your reference, Figure 1–9 summarizes the most common keystrokes for moving the insertion point in a document.

Figure 1–9 Keystrokes for moving the insertion point

To Move the Insertion Point	Press
Left or right one character at a time	← or →
Up or down one line at a time	↑ or ↓
Left or right one word at a time	CTRL+ ← or CTRL+ →
Up or down one paragraph at a time	CTRL+ ↑ or CTRL+ ↓
To the beginning or to the end of the current line	HOME or END
To the beginning or to the end of the document	CTRL+HOME or CTRL+END
To the previous screen or to the next screen	PAGE UP or PAGE DOWN
To the top or to the bottom of the document window	ALT+CTRL+PAGE UP or ALT+CTRL+PAGE DOWN

Correcting Errors as You Type

As you have seen, you can press BACKSPACE or DEL to remove an error, and then type a correction. In many cases, however, the AutoCorrect feature will do the work for you. Among other things, **AutoCorrect** automatically detects and corrects common typing errors, such as typing "adn" instead of "and." For example, you might have noticed AutoCorrect at work if you forgot to capitalize the first letter in a sentence as you typed the letter. After you type this kind of error, AutoCorrect automatically corrects it when you press SPACEBAR, TAB, or ENTER.

Word draws your attention to other potential errors by marking them with underlines. If you type a word that doesn't match the correct spelling in the Word dictionary, or if a word is not in the dictionary at all, a wavy red line appears beneath it. A wavy red underline also appears if you mistakenly type the same word twice in a row. Misused words (for example, "you're" instead of "your") are underlined with a double blue line, as are problems with punctuation and potential grammar errors, such as a singular verb used with a plural subject. Possible wordiness is marked with a dotted purple underline, although keep in mind that this feature does not produce consistent results. Word might mark a phrase as wordy in one document, but then not mark the same phrase in a different document. This feature can be a helpful guide, but ultimately you'll need to make your own decisions about whether a phrase could be more concise.

You'll see how this works as you continue typing the letter and make some intentional typing errors.

To learn more about correcting errors as you type:

1. Type the following sentence, including the errors: **in you're phone mesage, you asked me me to include maps of teh city reservoirres. They are not back from the printer yet, but I will send them as soon as they are actually ready.**

   As you type, AutoCorrect changes the lowercase "i" at the beginning of the sentence to uppercase. It also changes "mesage" to "message" and "teh" to "the." Also, the incorrectly used word "you're" is marked with a double blue underline. The second "me" and the spelling error "reservoirres" are marked with wavy red underlines.

2. Press **ENTER**. One additional error is now visible—the phrase "actually ready" is marked with a dotted purple underline, indicating a lack of conciseness. See Figure 1–10.

Figure 1–10 **Errors marked in the document**

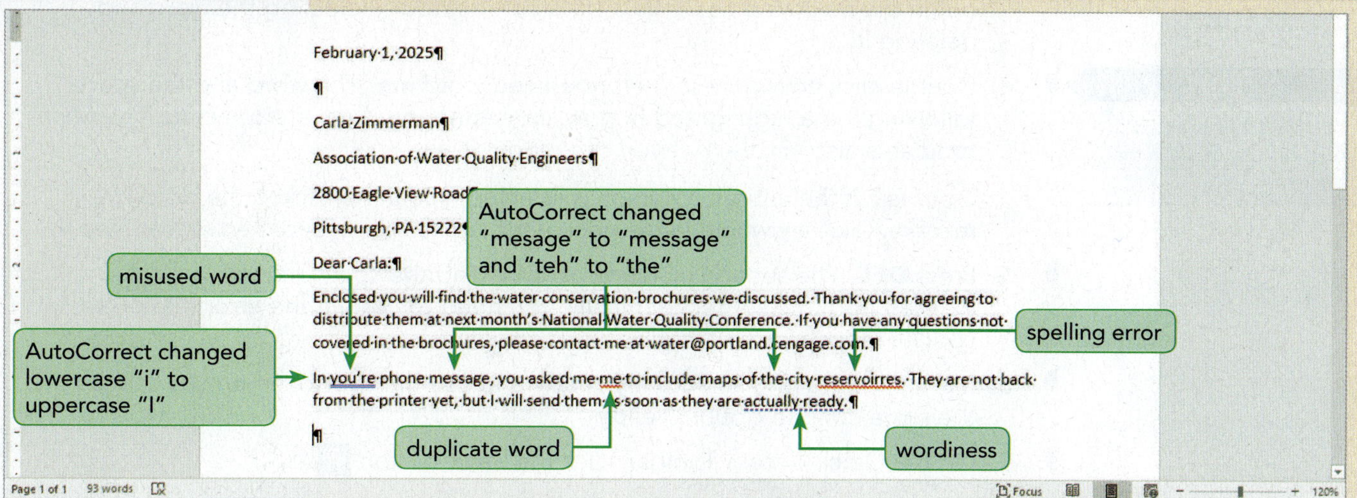

To correct an error marked with an underline, you can right-click the error and then click a replacement in the shortcut menu. If you don't see the correct word in the shortcut menu, click anywhere in the document to close the menu, and then type the correction yourself. You can also bypass the shortcut menu entirely and simply delete the error and type a correction.

To correct the spelling, grammar, and wordiness errors:

1. Right-click **you're** to display the shortcut menu shown in Figure 1–11.

Figure 1–11 Shortcut menu with suggested spelling

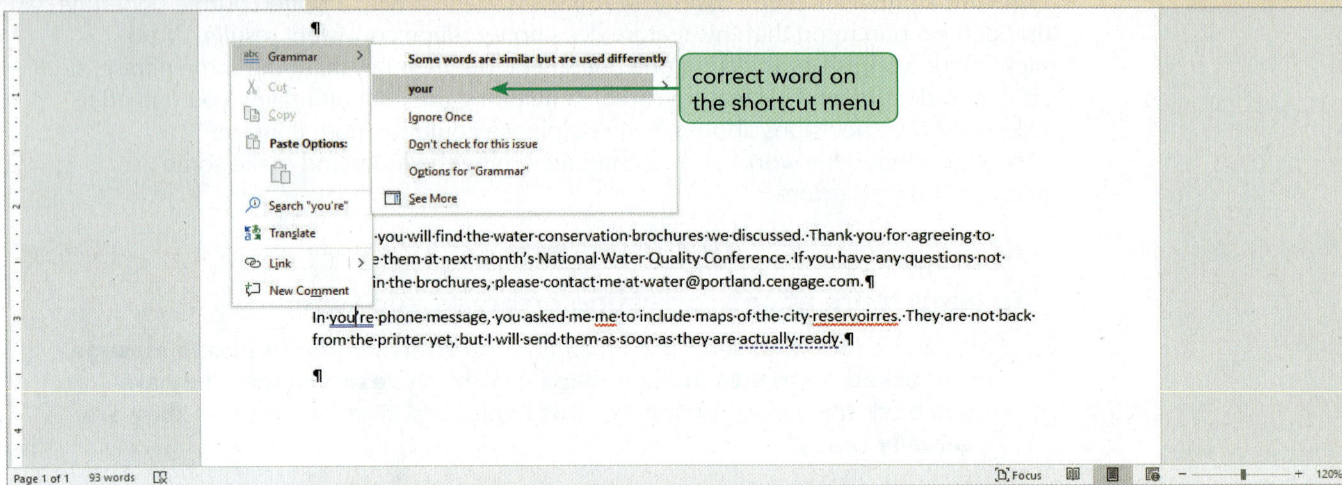

Trouble? If you see a shortcut menu other than the one shown in Figure 1–11, you didn't right-click exactly on the word "you're." Press ESC to close the menu, and then repeat Step 1.

2. On the shortcut menu, click **your**. The correct word is inserted into the sentence, and the shortcut menu closes.

3. Use a shortcut menu to replace the spelling error "reservoirres" with the correct word "reservoirs."

   You could use a shortcut menu to remove the second instance of "me," but in the next step you'll try a different method—selecting the word and deleting it.

Tip

To deselect highlighted text, click anywhere in the document.

4. Double-click anywhere in the underlined word **me**. The word and the space following it are highlighted in gray, indicating that they are selected. The Mini toolbar is also visible, but you can ignore it.

   Trouble? If the entire paragraph is selected, you triple-clicked the word by mistake. Click anywhere in the document to deselect it, and then repeat Step 4.

5. Press **DEL**. The second instance of "me" and the space following it are deleted from the sentence. Finally, you need to correct the error related to concise language.

6. Right-click the phrase **actually ready** and use the shortcut menu to choose the more concise option, **ready**.

7. On the Quick Access Toolbar, click the **Save** button.

You can see how quick and easy it is to correct common typing errors with AutoCorrect and the multicolored underlines, especially in a short document that you are typing yourself. If you are working on a longer document or a document typed by someone else, you'll also want to have Word check the entire document for errors. You'll learn how to do this in Session 1.2.

Next, you'll finish typing the letter.

To finish typing the letter:

1. Press **CTRL+END**. The insertion point moves to the end of the document.
2. Type **Sincerely yours,** (including the comma).
3. Press **ENTER** three times to leave space for the signature.
4. Type **David Alzacar** and then press **ENTER**. Because David's last name is not in the Word dictionary, a wavy red line appears below it. You can ignore this for now.
5. Type your first, middle, and last initials in lowercase, and then press **ENTER**. AutoCorrect wrongly assumes your first initial is the first letter of a new sentence and changes it to uppercase. If your initials do not form a word, a red wavy underline appears beneath them. You can ignore this for now.
6. On the Quick Access Toolbar, click the **Undo** button. Word reverses the change, replacing the uppercase initial with a lowercase one.
7. Type **Enclosure** so your screen looks like Figure 1–12.

Tip

You need to include your initials in a letter only if you are typing it for someone else.

Figure 1–12 Letter to Carla Zimmerman

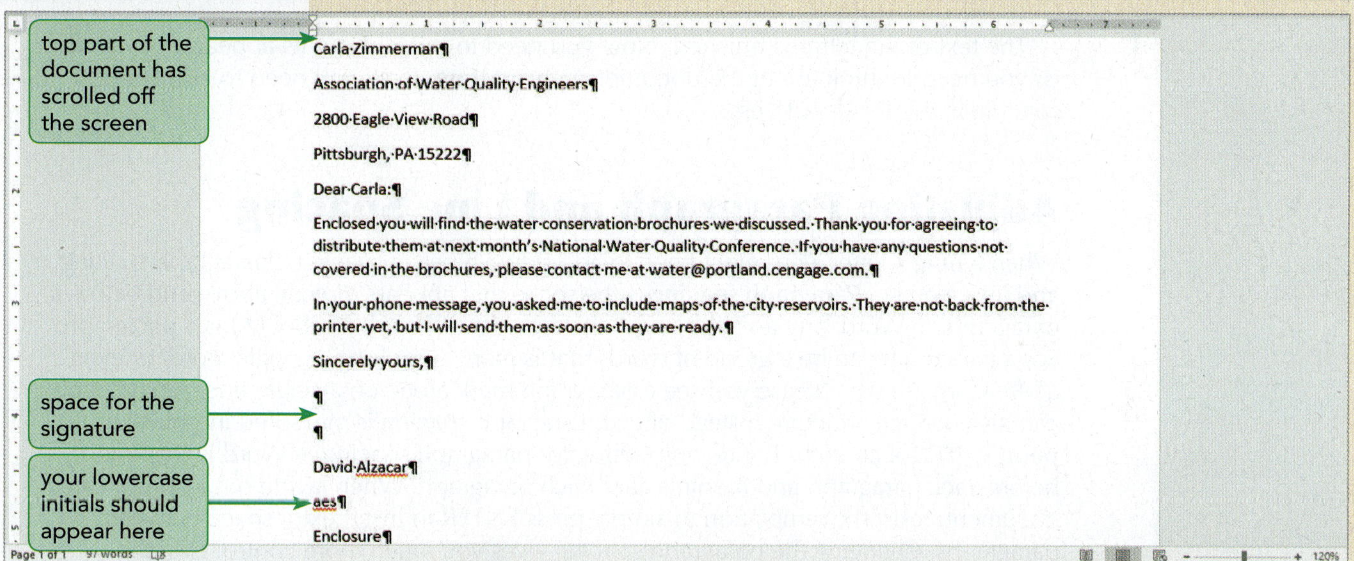

Notice that as you continue to add lines to the letter, the top part of the letter scrolls off the screen. For example, in Figure 1–12, you can no longer see the date. Don't be concerned if more or less of the document has scrolled off the screen on your computer.

8. Save the document.

Now that you have finished typing the letter, you need to proofread it.

Proofreading a Document

After you finish typing a document, you need to proofread it carefully from start to finish. Part of proofreading a document in Word is removing all wavy underlines, either by correcting the text or by telling Word to ignore the underlined text because it isn't really an error. For example, David's last name is marked as an error, when in fact it is spelled correctly. You need to tell Word to ignore "Alzacar" wherever it occurs in the letter. You need to do the same for your initials.

To proofread and correct the remaining marked errors in the letter:

1. Right-click **Alzacar**. A shortcut menu opens.
2. On the shortcut menu, click **Ignore All** to indicate that Word should ignore the word "Alzacar" each time it occurs in this document. (The Ignore All option can be particularly helpful in a longer document.) The wavy red underline disappears from below David's last name.
3. If you see a wavy red underline below your initials, right-click your initials. On the shortcut menu, click **Ignore All** to remove the red wavy underline. To choose to ignore something just once in a document, you could click See More in the shortcut menu, and then click Ignore Once in the Editor pane. You'll learn how to use the Editor pane in Session 1.2.
4. Read the entire letter to proofread it for typing errors. Correct any errors using the techniques you have just learned.
5. Scroll up, if necessary, so you can see the complete inside address, which you'll work on next, and then save the document.

The text of the letter is finished. Now you need to think about its appearance—that is, you need to think about the document's **formatting**. First, you need to adjust the spacing in the inside address.

Adjusting Paragraph and Line Spacing

When typing a letter, you might need to adjust two types of spacing—paragraph spacing and line spacing. **Paragraph spacing** is the space that appears directly above and below a paragraph. In Word, any text that ends with a paragraph mark symbol (¶) is a paragraph. So, a **paragraph** can be a group of words that is many lines long, a single word, or even a blank line, in which case you see a paragraph mark alone on a single line. A paragraph can also contain a picture instead of text. Paragraph spacing is measured in points; a **point** is 1/72 of an inch. The default setting for paragraph spacing in Word is 0 points before each paragraph and 8 points after each paragraph. When laying out a complicated document, resist the temptation to simply press ENTER to insert extra space between paragraphs. Changing the paragraph spacing gives you much more control over the final result.

Line spacing is the space between lines of text within a paragraph. Word offers a number of preset line spacing options. The 1.0 setting, which is often called **single-spacing**, allows the least amount of space between lines. All other line spacing options are measured as multiples of 1.0 spacing. For example, 2.0 spacing (sometimes called **double-spacing**) allows for twice the space of single-spacing. The default line spacing setting is 1.08, which allows a little more space between lines than 1.0 spacing.

Now consider the line and paragraph spacing in the letter. The four lines of the inside address are too far apart. That's because each line of the inside address is actually a separate paragraph. Word inserted the default 8 points of paragraph spacing after each of these separate paragraphs. See Figure 1–13.

Figure 1–13 Line and paragraph spacing in the letter to Carla Zimmerman

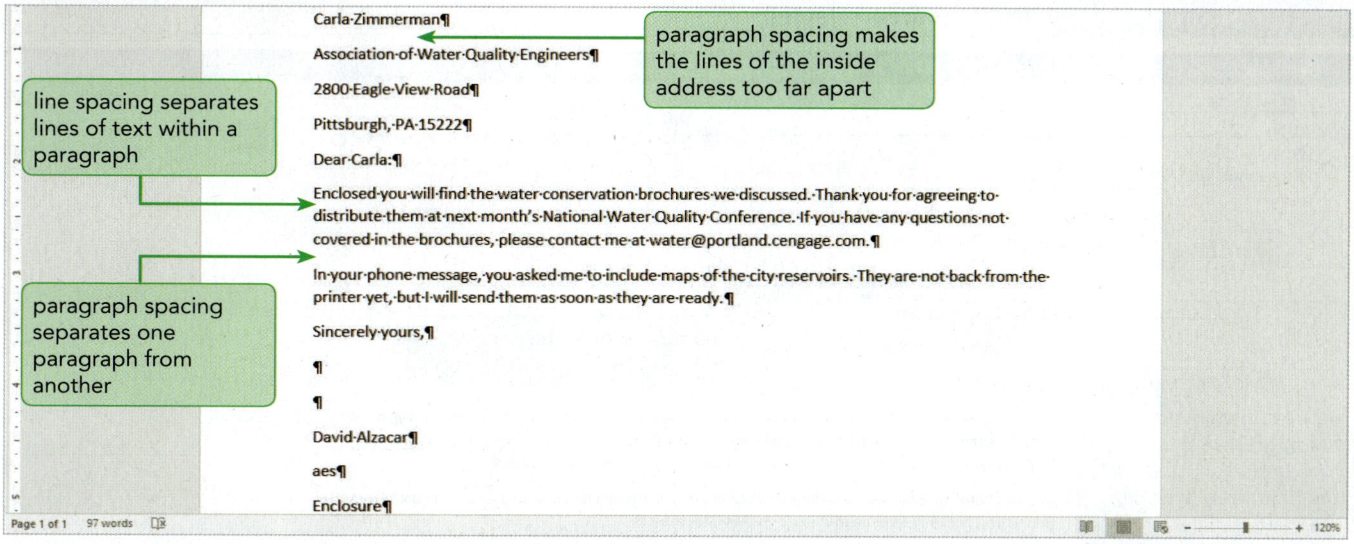

To follow the conventions of a block-style business letter, the four paragraphs that make up the inside address should have the same spacing as the lines of text within a single paragraph—that is, they need to be closer together. You can accomplish this by removing the 8 points of paragraph spacing after the first two paragraphs in the inside address. To conform to the block-style business letter format, you also need to close up the spacing between your initials and the word "Enclosure" at the end of the letter.

To adjust paragraph and line spacing in Word, you use the Line and Paragraph Spacing button in the Paragraph group on the Home tab. Clicking this button displays a menu of preset line spacing options (1.0, 1.15, 2.0, and so on). The menu also includes two paragraph spacing options that allow you to add 12 points before a paragraph or remove the default 8 points of space after a paragraph.

Next you'll adjust the paragraph spacing in the inside address and after your initials. In the process, you'll also learn some techniques for selecting text in a document.

To adjust the paragraph spacing in the inside address and after your initials:

1. Move the pointer to the white space just to the left of "Carla Zimmerman" until it changes to a right-pointing arrow.

2. Click the mouse button. The entire name, including the paragraph symbol after it, is selected.

Trouble? If the Mini toolbar obscures your view of Carla's name, move the pointer away from the address to close the Mini toolbar.

3. Press and hold the mouse button, drag the pointer down to select the next two paragraphs of the inside address as well, and then release the mouse button.

Carla's name, the name of her organization, and the street address are selected as well as the paragraph marks at the end of each paragraph. You did not select the paragraph containing the city, state, and zip code because you do not need to change its paragraph spacing. See Figure 1–14.

Tip

The white space in the left margin is sometimes referred to as the selection bar because you can click it to select text.

Figure 1–14 Inside address selected

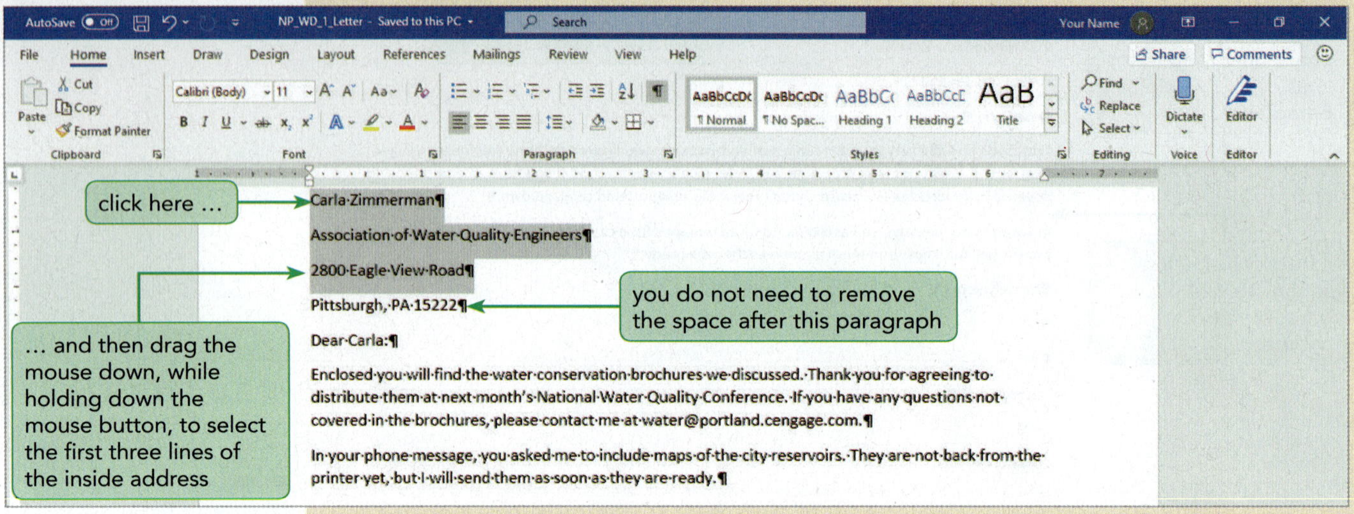

4. Make sure the Home tab is selected on the ribbon.
5. In the Paragraph group on the Home tab, click the **Line and Paragraph Spacing** button. A menu of line spacing options appears, with two paragraph spacing options at the bottom. See Figure 1–15.

Figure 1–15 Line and paragraph spacing options

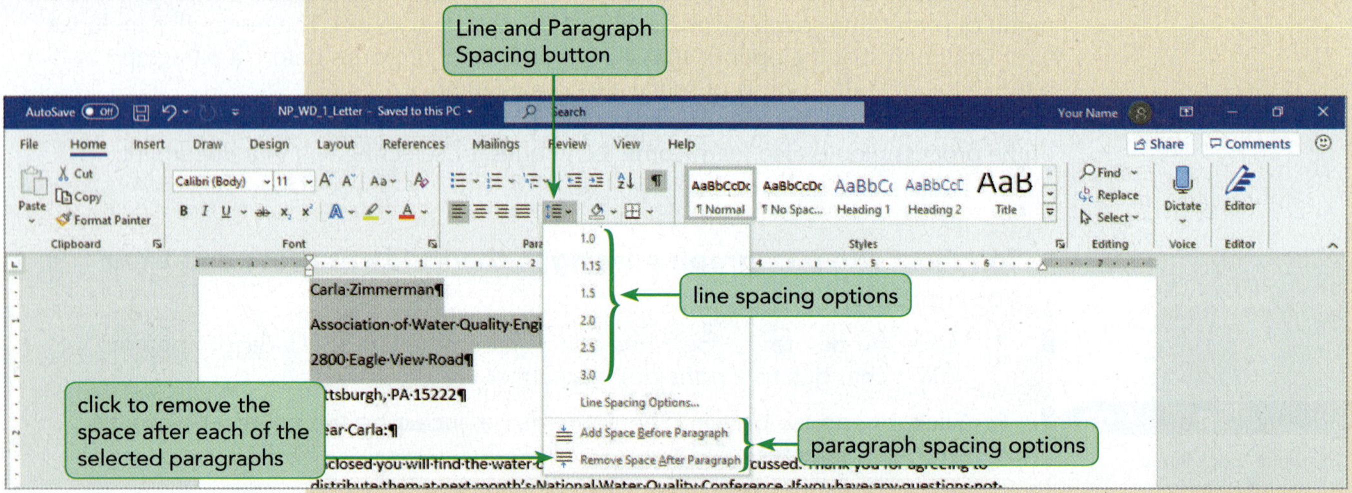

At the moment, you are interested only in the paragraph spacing options. Your goal is to remove the default 8 points of space after the first two paragraphs in the inside address.

6. Click **Remove Space After Paragraph**. The menu closes, and the paragraphs are now closer together.
7. Double-click your initials to select them and the paragraph symbol after them.
8. In the Paragraph group, click the **Line and Paragraph Spacing** button, click **Remove Space After Paragraph**, and then click anywhere in the document to deselect your initials.

Another way to compress lines of text is to press SHIFT+ENTER at the end of a line. This inserts a **manual line break**, also called a **soft return**, which moves the insertion point to a new line without starting a new paragraph. You will use this technique now as you add David's title below his name in the signature line.

To use a manual line break to move the insertion point to a new line without starting a new paragraph:

1. Click to the right of the "r" in "Alzacar."
2. Press **SHIFT+ENTER**. Word inserts a small arrow symbol ↵, indicating a manual line break, and the insertion point moves to the line below David's name.
3. Type **Communications Director**. David's title now appears directly below his name with no intervening paragraph spacing, just like the lines of the inside address.
4. Save the document.

Insight

Understanding Spacing between Paragraphs

When discussing the correct format for letters, many business style guides talk about single-spacing and double-spacing between paragraphs. In these style guides, to single-space between paragraphs means to press ENTER once after each paragraph. Likewise, to double-space between paragraphs means to press ENTER twice after each paragraph. With the default paragraph spacing in Word, however, you need to press ENTER only once after a paragraph. The space Word adds after a paragraph is not quite the equivalent of double-spacing, but it is enough to make it easy to see where one paragraph ends and another begins. Keep this in mind if you're accustomed to pressing ENTER twice; otherwise, you could end up with more space than you want between paragraphs.

As you corrected line and paragraph spacing in the previous set of steps, you used the mouse to select text. Word provides multiple ways to select, or highlight, text as you work. Figure 1–16 summarizes these methods and explains when to use them most effectively. Note that there are multiple ways to select each element in a document. Three especially useful options are: (1) selecting an entire paragraph by triple-clicking it; (2) selecting nonadjacent text by pressing and holding CTRL, and then dragging the mouse pointer to select multiple blocks of text; and (3) selecting an entire document by pressing CTRL+A.

Figure 1–16 **Methods for selecting text**

To Select	Mouse	Keyboard	Mouse and Keyboard
A word	Double-click the word	Move the insertion point to the beginning of the word, press and hold CTRL+SHIFT, and then press →	
A line	Click in the white space to the left of the line	Move the insertion point to the beginning of the line, press and hold SHIFT, and then press ↓	
A sentence	Click at the beginning of the sentence, then drag the pointer until the sentence is selected		Press and hold CTRL, then click any location within the sentence
Multiple lines	Click and drag in the white space to the left of the lines	Move the insertion point to the beginning of the first line, press and hold SHIFT, and then press ↓ until all the lines are selected	
A paragraph	Double-click in the white space to the left of the paragraph, or triple-click at any location within the paragraph	Move the insertion point to the beginning of the paragraph, press and hold CTRL+SHIFT, and then press ↓	
Multiple paragraphs	Click in the white space to the left of the first paragraph you want to select, and then drag to select the remaining paragraphs	Move the insertion point to the beginning of the first paragraph, press and hold CTRL+SHIFT, and then press ↓ until all the paragraphs are selected	
An entire document	Triple-click in the white space to the left of the document text	Press CTRL+A	Press and hold CTRL, and click in the white space to the left of the document text
A block of text	Click at the beginning of the block, then drag the pointer until the entire block is selected		Click at the beginning of the block, press and hold SHIFT, and then click at the end of the block
Nonadjacent blocks of text			Press and hold CTRL, then drag the mouse pointer to select multiple blocks of nonadjacent text

Adjusting the Margins

Another important aspect of document formatting is the amount of margin space between the document text and the edge of the page. You can check the document's margins by changing the Zoom level to display the entire page.

To change the Zoom level to display the entire page:

1. On the ribbon, click the **View** tab.
2. In the Zoom group, click the **One Page** button. The entire document is now visible in the Word window. See Figure 1–17.

Figure 1–17 Document zoomed to show entire page

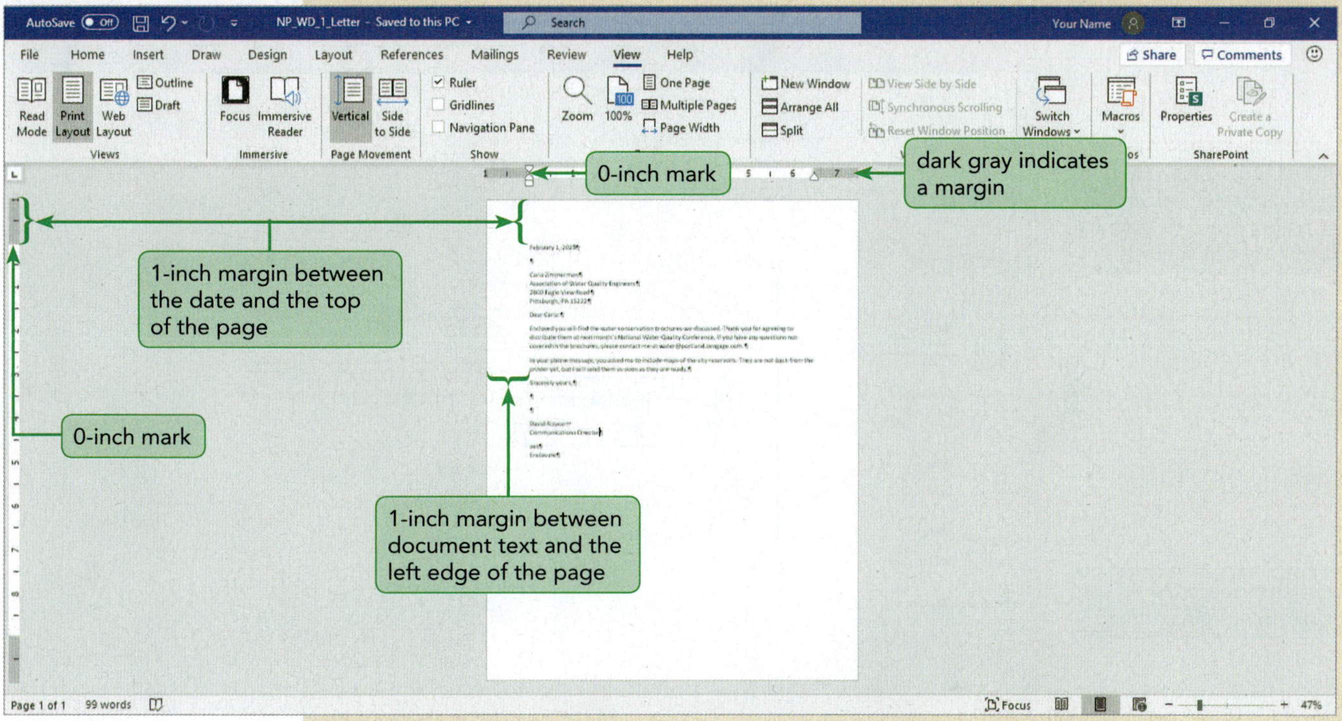

On the rulers, the margins appear dark gray. By default, Word documents include 1-inch margins on all sides of the document. By looking at the vertical ruler, you can see that the date in the letter, the first line in the document, is located 1 inch from the top of the page. Likewise, the horizontal ruler indicates the document text begins 1 inch from the left edge of the page.

Reading the measurements on the rulers can be tricky at first. On the horizontal ruler, the 0-inch mark is like the origin on a number line. You measure from the 0-inch mark to the left or to the right. On the vertical ruler, you measure up or down from the 0-inch mark.

David plans to print the letter on the Water Resources Department letterhead, which includes a graphic and the department's address. To allow more blank space for the letterhead, and to move the text down so that it doesn't look so crowded at the top of the page, you need to increase the top margin. The settings for changing the page margins are located on the Layout tab on the ribbon.

To change the page margins:

1. On the ribbon, click the **Layout** tab. The Layout tab displays options for adjusting the layout of your document.
2. In the Page Setup group, click the **Margins** button. The Margins gallery opens, as shown in Figure 1–18.

Figure 1–18 Margins gallery

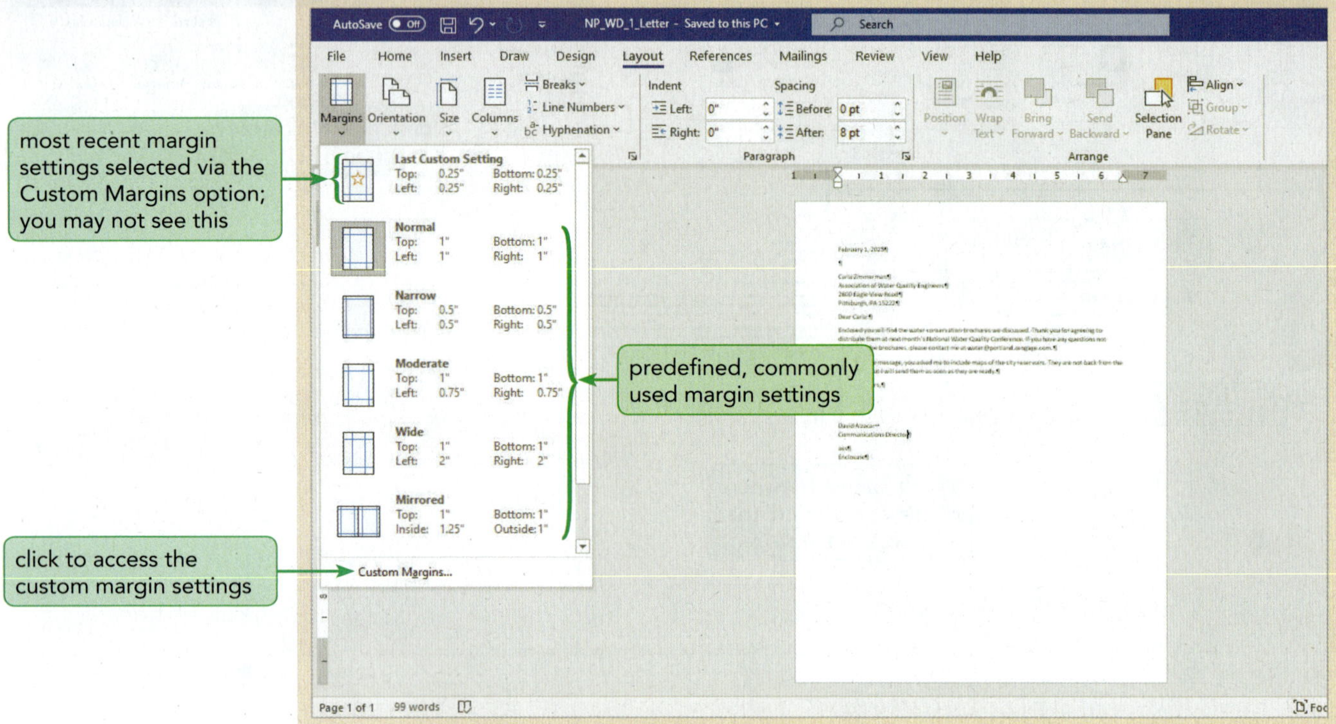

In the Margins gallery, you can choose from a number of predefined margin options, or you can click the Custom Margins command to select your own settings. After you create custom margin settings, the most recent set appears as an option at the top of the menu. For the current document, you will create custom margins.

3. Click **Custom Margins**. The Page Setup dialog box opens with the Margins tab displayed. The default margin settings are displayed in the boxes at the top of the Margins tab. The top margin of 1" is already selected, ready for you to type a new margin setting.
4. In the Top box in the Margins section, type **2.5**. You do not need to type an inch mark ("). See Figure 1–19.

Figure 1–19 **Creating custom margins in the Page Setup dialog box**

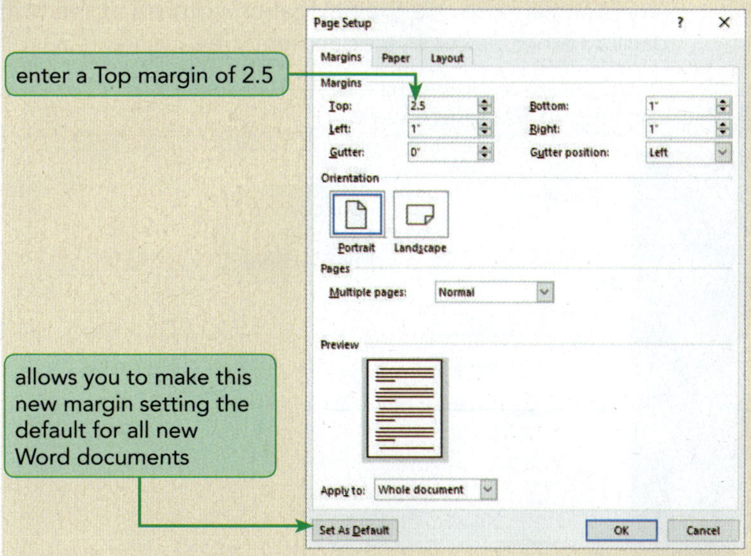

5. Click **OK**. The text of the letter is now lower on the page. The page looks less crowded, with room for the company's letterhead.
6. Change the Zoom level back to **120%**, and then save the document.

For most documents, the Word default of 1-inch margins is fine. In some professional settings, however, you might need to use a particular custom margin setting for all your documents. In that case, define the custom margins using the Margins tab in the Page Setup dialog box, and then click the Set As Default button to make your settings the default for all new documents. Keep in mind that most printers can't print to the edge of the page; if you select custom margins that are too narrow for your printer's specifications, Word alerts you to change your margin settings.

Previewing and Printing a Document

To make sure the document is ready to print, and to avoid wasting paper and time, you should first review it in Backstage view to make sure it will look right when printed. Like the One Page zoom setting you used earlier, the Print option in Backstage view displays a full-page preview of the document, allowing you to see how it will fit on the printed page. However, you cannot actually edit this preview. It simply provides one last opportunity to look at the document before printing.

To preview the document:

1. Proofread the document one last time and correct any remaining errors.
2. Click the **File** tab to display Backstage view.
3. In the navigation pane, click **Print**.

   The Print screen displays a full-page version of your document, showing how the letter will fit on the printed page. The Print settings to the left of the preview allow you to control a variety of print options. For example, you can change the number of copies from the default setting of "1." The 1 Page Per

Sheet button opens a menu where you can choose to print multiple pages on a single sheet of paper or to scale the printed page to a particular paper size. You can also use the navigation controls at the bottom of the screen to display other pages in a document. See Figure 1–20.

Figure 1–20 Print settings in Backstage view

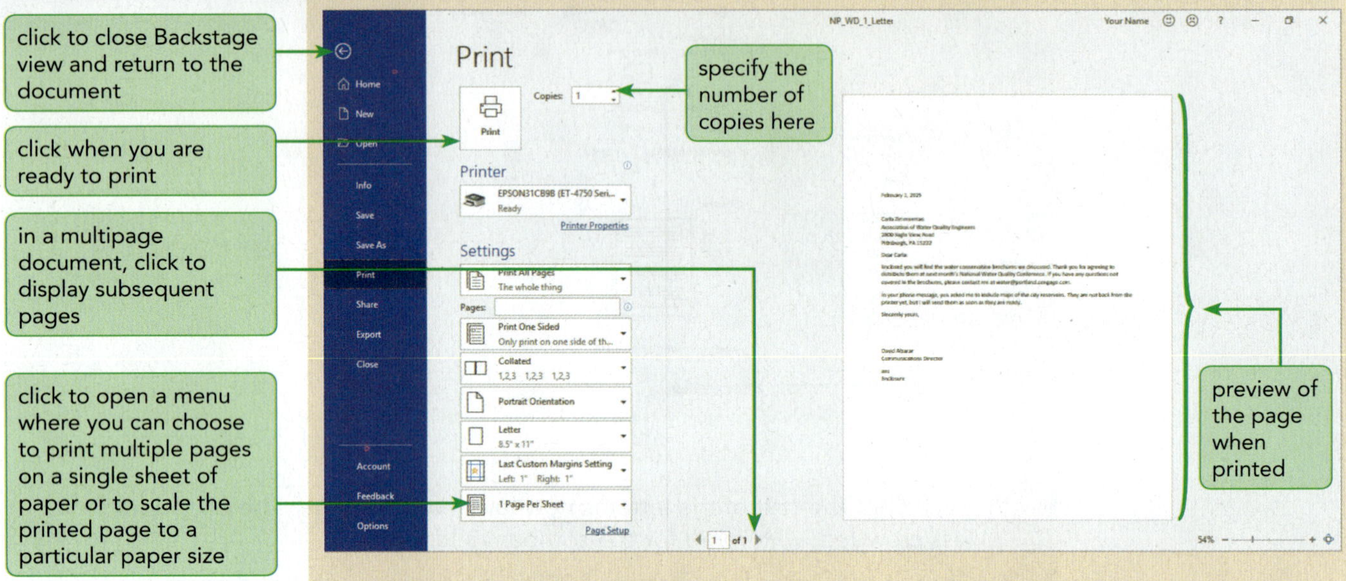

4. Review your document and make sure its overall layout matches that of the document in Figure 1–20. If you notice a problem with paragraph breaks or spacing, click the **Back** button at the top of the navigation pane to return to the document, make any necessary changes, and then start again at Step 2.

At this point, you can print the document or you can leave Backstage view and return to the document in Print Layout view. In the following steps, you should print the document only if your instructor asks you to. If you will be printing the document, make sure your printer is turned on and contains paper.

To leave Backstage view or to print the document:

1. Click the **Back** button at the top of the navigation pane to leave Backstage view and return to the document in Print Layout view, or click the **Print** button. Backstage view closes, and the letter prints if you clicked the Print button.
2. sam Click the **File** tab, and then click **Close** in the navigation pane to close the document without closing Word.

Next, David asks you to create an envelope he can use to send a water quality report to an environmental engineering publication.

Creating an Envelope

Before you can create the envelope, you need to open a new, blank document. To create a new document, you can start with a blank document—as you did with the letter to Carla Zimmerman—or you can start with one that already contains formatting and generic text commonly used in a variety of professional documents, such as a fax cover sheet or a memo. These preformatted files are called **templates**. You could use a template to create a formatted envelope, but to create a basic envelope for a business letter, it's better to start with a new, blank document.

To create a new document for the envelope:

1. Click the **File** tab, and then click **New** in the navigation pane. The New screen is similar to the one you saw when you first started Word, with a blank document in the upper-left corner, along with a variety of templates. See Figure 1–21.

Figure 1–21 New options in Backstage view

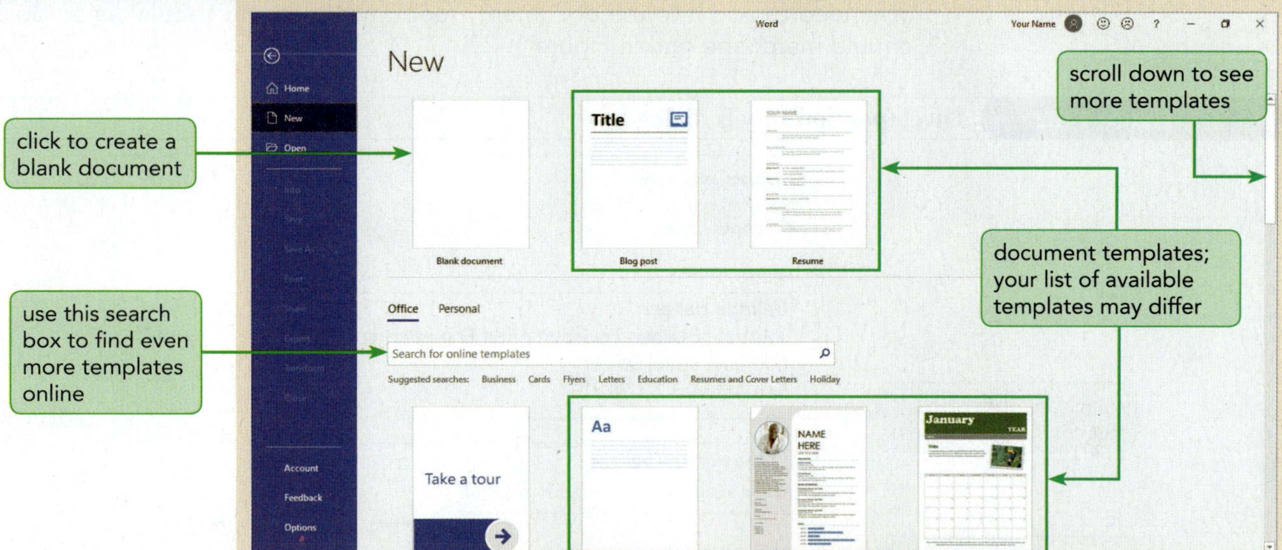

2. Click **Blank document**. A new document named Document2 opens in the document window, with the Home tab selected on the ribbon.
3. If necessary, change the Zoom level to **120%**, and display nonprinting characters and the rulers.
4. Save the new document as **NP_WD_1_Envelope** in the location specified by your instructor.

To create the envelope:

1. On the ribbon, click the **Mailings** tab. The ribbon changes to display the various Mailings options.
2. In the Create group, click the **Envelopes** button. The Envelopes and Labels dialog box opens, with the Envelopes tab displayed. The insertion point appears in the Delivery address box, ready for you to type the recipient's address. Depending on how your computer is set up, and whether you are

working on your own computer or a school computer, you might see an address in the Return address box.

3. In the Delivery address box, type the following address, pressing **ENTER** to start each new line:

Belinda Harper

Journal of Urban Environmental Engineering

600 East Kelda Street

San Antonio, TX 78205

Because David will be using the department's printed envelopes, you don't need to print a return address on this envelope.

4. Click the **Omit** check box to insert a checkmark, if necessary.

At this point, if you had a printer stocked with envelopes, you could click the Print button to print the envelope. To save an envelope for printing later, you need to add it to the document. Your Envelopes and Labels dialog box should match the one in Figure 1–22.

Figure 1–22 **Envelopes and Labels dialog box**

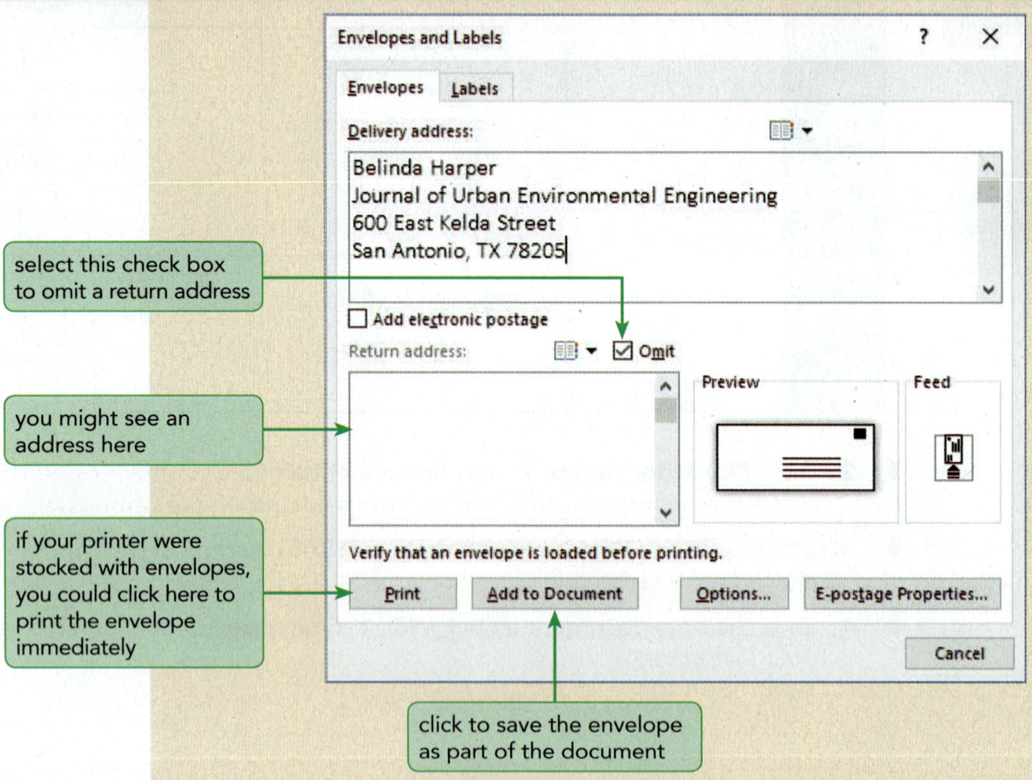

5. Click **Add to Document**. The dialog box closes, and you return to the document window. The envelope is inserted at the top of your document, with 1.0 line spacing. The double line with the words "Section Break (Next Page)" is related to how the envelope is formatted and will not be visible when you print the envelope. The envelope will print in the standard business envelope format. In this case, you added the envelope to a blank document, but you could also add an envelope to a completed letter, in which case Word adds the envelope as a new page before the letter.

6. Save the document. David will print the envelope later, so you can close the document now.
7. Click the **File** tab, and then click **Close** in the navigation pane. The document closes, but Word remains open.

You're finished creating the cover letter and the envelope. In the next session, you will modify a flyer by formatting the text and adding a photo.

Insight

Creating Documents with Templates

Microsoft offers predesigned templates for all kinds of documents, including calendars, reports, and thank-you cards. You can use the scroll bar on the right of the New screen (shown earlier in Figure 1–21) to scroll down to see more templates, or you can use the Search for online templates box in the New screen to search among thousands of other options available at Office.com. When you open a template, you actually open a new document containing the formatting and text stored in the template, leaving the original template untouched. A typical template includes placeholder text that you replace with your own information.

Templates allow you to create stylish, professional-looking documents quickly and easily. To use them effectively, however, you need to be knowledgeable about Word and its many options for manipulating text, graphics, and page layouts. Otherwise, the complicated formatting of some Word templates can be more frustrating than helpful. As you become a more experienced Word user, you'll learn how to create your own templates.

Review

Session 1.1 Quick Check

1. What Word feature automatically inserts dates and other regularly used items for you?
2. Explain how to display nonprinting characters.
3. In a block-style letter, does the inside address appear above or below the date?
4. Explain how to use a hyperlink in a Word document to open a new email message.
5. Define the term "paragraph spacing."
6. Explain how to display a shortcut menu with options for correcting a word with a wavy red underline.

Session 1.2 Visual Overview:

Alignment buttons control the text's **alignment**—that is, the way it lines up horizontally between the left and right margins. Here, the Center button is selected because the text containing the insertion point is center-aligned.

You can click the Clear All Formatting button to restore selected text to the default font, font size, and color.

Clicking the Format Painter button displays the Format Painter pointer, which you can use to copy formatting from the selected text to other text in the document.

The Font group on the Home tab includes the Font box and the Font size box for setting the font and the font size, respectively. A **font** is a set of characters that uses the same typeface.

You click the Shading arrow to apply a colored background to a selected paragraph.

You use the Borders arrow to apply an outline to the selected paragraph. The image on the Borders button reflects the most recently used Border option.

This document has a landscape orientation, meaning it is wider than it is tall.

You can insert a photo or another type of picture in a document by using the **Pictures button** located on the Insert tab of the ribbon. After you insert a photo or another picture, you can format it with a style that adds a border or a shadow or changes its shape.

The white font color used on this text is an example of **character formatting** because it affects individual characters.

The boldface and blue font color applied to this text are examples of formatting that you should use sparingly to draw attention to a specific part of a document.

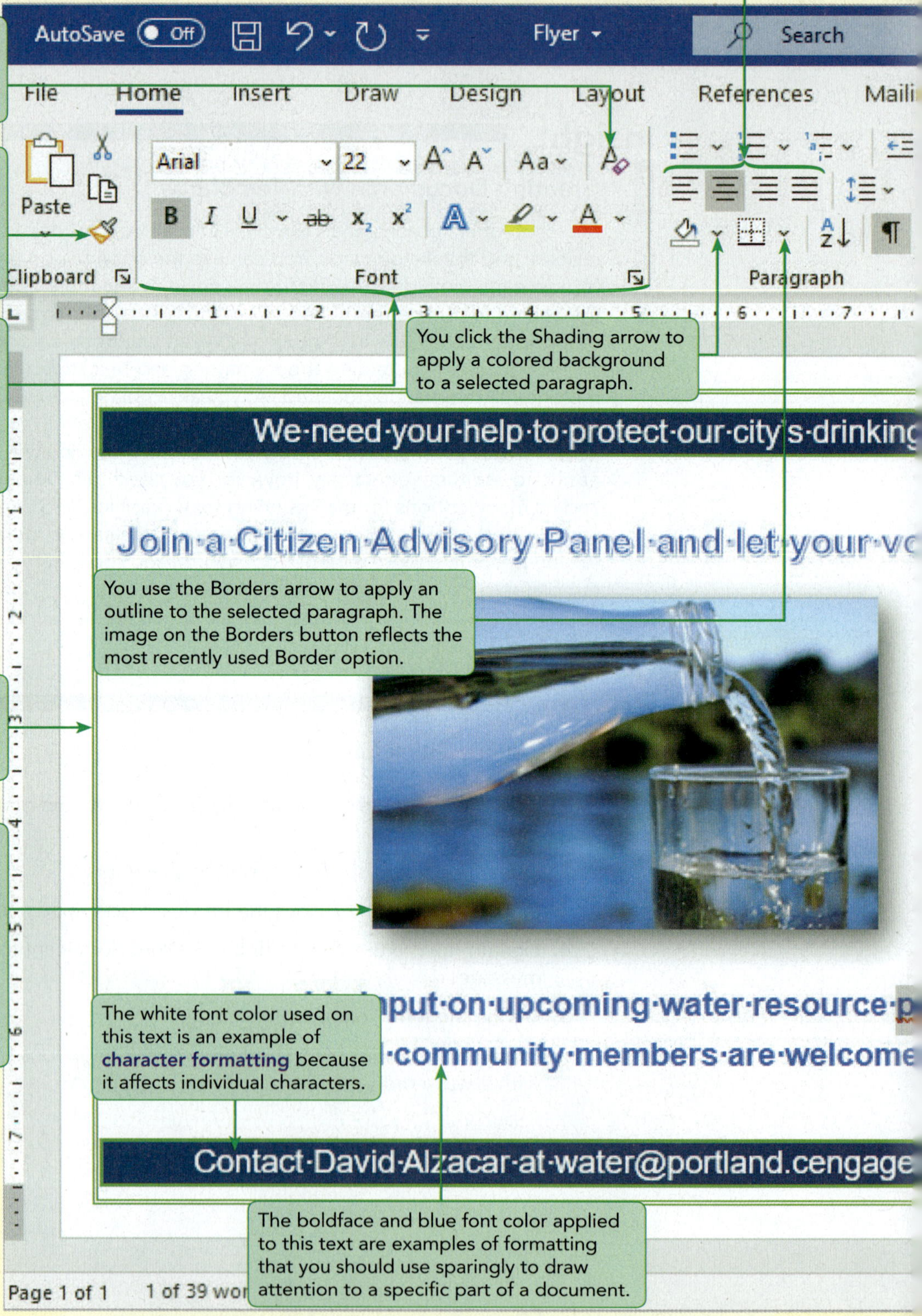

iStock.com/LazingBee

Formatting a Document

You can enter a keyword in the Search box and get access to Word features and commands; you can also look up information in **Microsoft Word Help**.

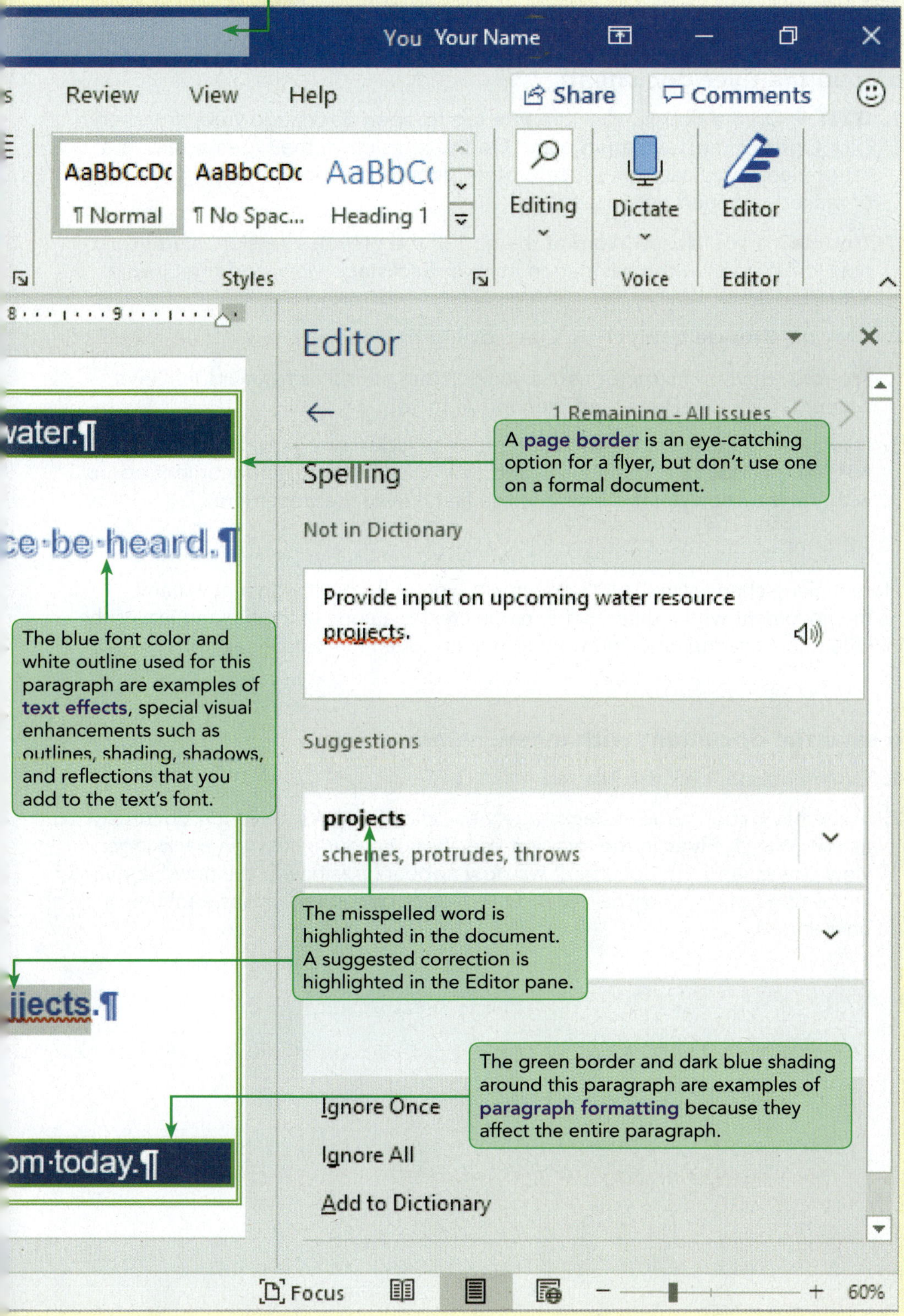

A **page border** is an eye-catching option for a flyer, but don't use one on a formal document.

The blue font color and white outline used for this paragraph are examples of **text effects**, special visual enhancements such as outlines, shading, shadows, and reflections that you add to the text's font.

The misspelled word is highlighted in the document. A suggested correction is highlighted in the Editor pane.

The green border and dark blue shading around this paragraph are examples of **paragraph formatting** because they affect the entire paragraph.

A **pane** is a window that helps you navigate through a complex task or feature. This one, the **Editor pane**, opens when you click the Editor button in the Editor group on the Home tab or the Proofing group on the Review tab. You can use it to correct spelling and grammar errors.

Opening an Existing Document

In this session, you'll complete a flyer encouraging community members to join a citizen advisory panel. David has already typed the text of the flyer, inserted a photo into it, and saved it as a Word document. He would like you to check the document for spelling and grammar errors, format the flyer to make it eye-catching and easy to read, and then replace the current photo with a new one. You'll start by opening the document.

To open the flyer document:

1. sam On the ribbon, click the **File** tab to open Backstage view, and then click **Open** in the navigation pane. On the left side of the Open screen is a list of places you can go to locate other documents, and on the right is a list of recently opened documents.

   Trouble? If you closed Word at the end of the previous session, start Word now, click Open in the navigation pane in Backstage view, and then begin with Step 2.

2. Click the **Browse** button. The Open dialog box opens.

   Trouble? If your instructor asked you to store your files to your OneDrive account, click OneDrive, and then log in to your account.

3. Navigate to the **Word1 > Module** folder included with your Data Files, click **NP_WD_1-1.docx** in the file list, and then click **Open**. The document opens with the insertion point blinking in the first line of the document.

Before making changes to David's document, you will save it with a new name. Saving the document with a different file name creates a copy of the file and leaves the original file unchanged in case you want to work through the module again.

To save the document with a new name:

1. On the ribbon, click the **File** tab.
2. In the navigation pane in Backstage view, click **Save As**. Save the document as **NP_WD_1_Flyer** in the location specified by your instructor. Backstage view closes, and the document window appears again with the new file name in the title bar. The original NP_WD_1-1.docx document closes, remaining unchanged.

Proskills

Decision Making: Creating Effective Documents

Before you create a new document or revise an existing document, take a moment to think about your audience. Ask yourself these questions:

- Who is your audience?
- What do they know?
- What do they need to know?
- How can the document you are creating change your audience's behavior or opinions?

Every decision you make about your document should be based on your answers to these questions. To take a simple example, if you are creating a flyer to announce an upcoming seminar on college financial aid, your audience would be students and their parents. They probably all know what the term "financial aid" means, so you don't need to explain that in your flyer. Instead, you can focus on telling them what they need to know—the date, time, and location of the seminar. The behavior you want to affect, in this case, is whether your audience will show up for the seminar. By making the flyer professional looking and easy to read, you increase the chance that they will.

You might find it more challenging to answer these questions about your audience when creating more complicated documents, such as corporate reports. But the focus remains the same—connecting with the audience. As you are deciding what information to include in your document, remember that the goal of a professional document is to convey the information as effectively as possible to your target audience.

Before revising a document for someone else, it's a good idea to familiarize yourself with its overall structure.

To review the document:

1. Verify that the document is displayed in Print Layout view and that nonprinting characters and the rulers are displayed. For now, you can ignore the wavy underlines that appear in the document.
2. Change the Zoom level to **120%**, if necessary, and then scroll down, if necessary, so that you can read the last line of the document.

   At this point, the document is very simple. By the time you are finished, it will look like the document shown in the Session 1.2 Visual Overview, with the spelling and grammar errors corrected. Figure 1–23 summarizes the tasks you will perform.

Figure 1–23 Formatting changes requested by David

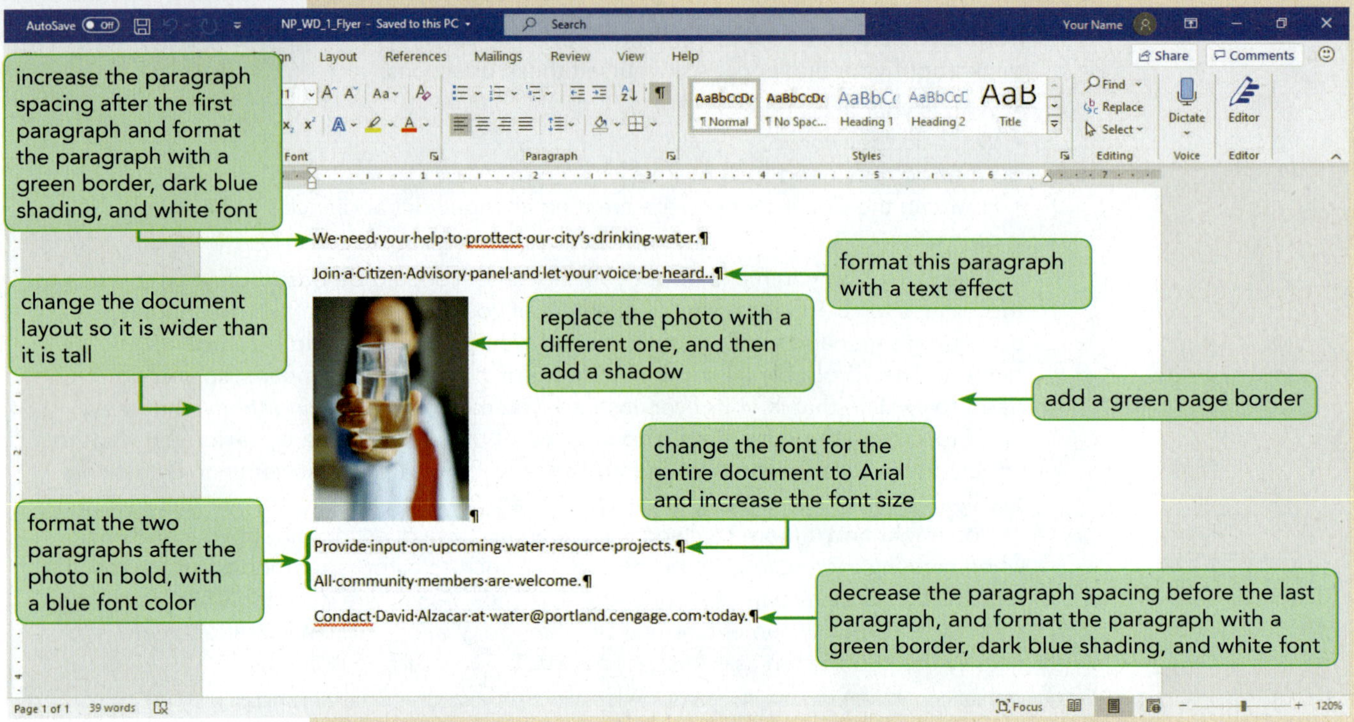

iStock.com/laflor

You will start by correcting the spelling and grammar errors.

Using the Editor Pane

As you type, Word marks possible spelling and grammatical errors, as well as wordiness, with underlines so you can quickly go back and correct those errors. A more thorough way of checking the spelling in a document is to use the Editor pane to check a document word by word for a variety of errors. You can customize the spelling and grammar settings to add or ignore certain types of errors.

David asks you to use the Editor pane to check the flyer for mistakes. Before you do, you'll review the various Spelling and Grammar settings.

To review the Spelling and Grammar settings:

1. On the ribbon, click the **File** tab, and then click **Options** in the navigation pane. The Word Options dialog box opens. You can use this dialog box to change a variety of settings related to how Word looks and works.
2. In the left pane, click **Proofing**.

   Note the four selected options in the "When correcting spelling and grammar in Word" section. These options tell you that Word will check for misspellings, grammatical errors, and frequently confused words as you type, marking them with wavy underlines as necessary.
3. In the "When correcting spelling and grammar in Word" section, click **Settings**. The Grammar Settings dialog box opens. Here you can control the

types of grammar errors Word checks for. All of the boxes in the Grammar section are selected by default, which is what you want. See Figure 1–24.

Figure 1–24 Grammar Settings dialog box

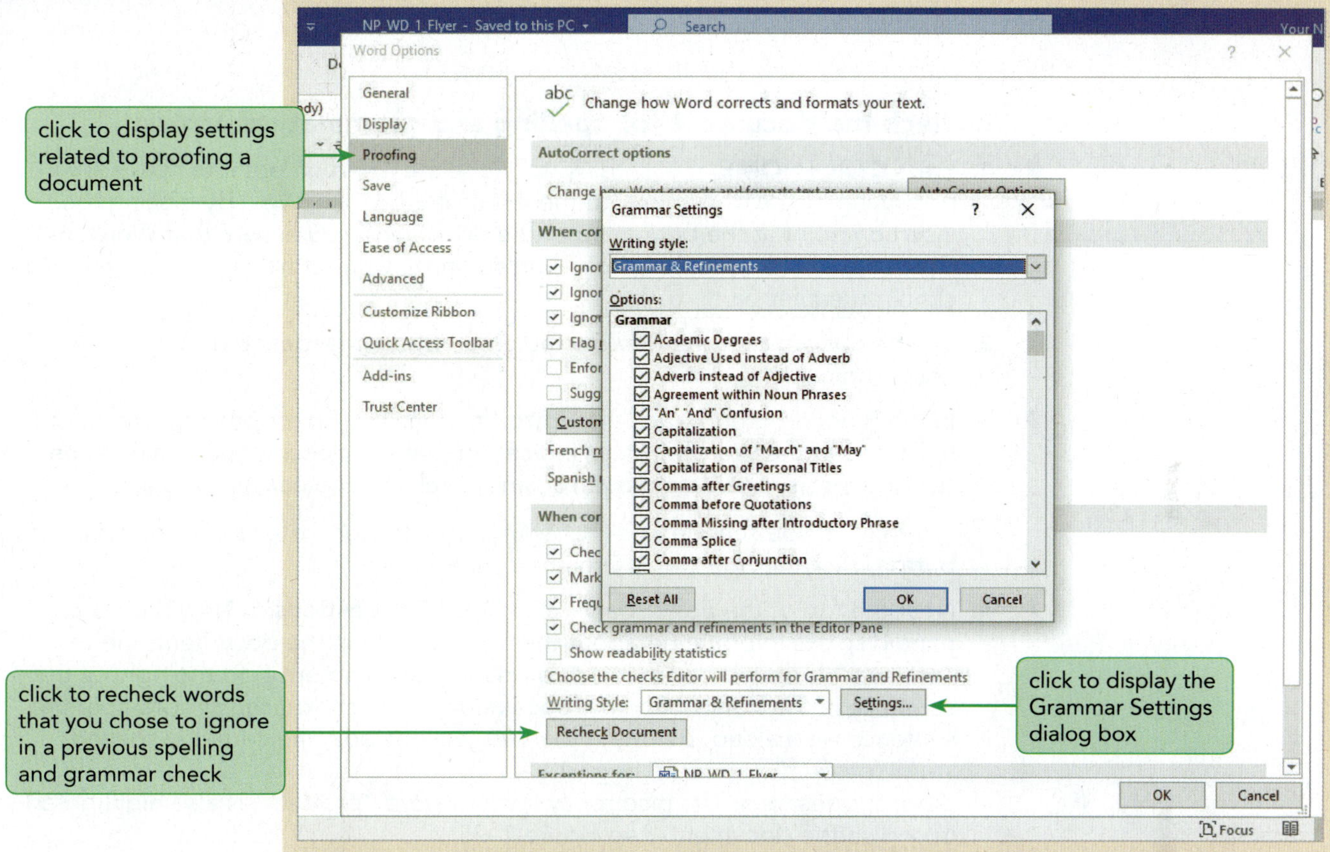

4. Scroll down in the Grammar Settings dialog box to display the Conciseness settings. By default, only Nominalizations and Wordiness are selected.

5. Click **Cancel** to close the Grammar Settings dialog box and return to the Word Options dialog box.

   Note that the results of the Spelling and Grammar checker are sometimes hard to predict. For example, in some documents Word will mark a misused word or duplicate punctuation as an error and then fail to mark the same items as errors in another document. Also, if you choose to ignore a misspelling in a document and then, without closing Word, type the same misspelled word in another document, Word will probably not mark it as an error. Sometimes, if you change a document's line or paragraph spacing, Word will mark text as errors that it previously did not. These issues can be especially problematic when working on a document typed by someone else. So to ensure that you get the best possible results, it's a good idea to click Recheck Document in the Word Options dialog box before you use the Spelling and Grammar checker.

6. Click the **Recheck Document** button, and then click **Yes** in the warning dialog box.

7. In the Word Options dialog box, click **OK** to close the dialog box. You return to the document.

Now you are ready to check the document's spelling and grammar. All errors marked with red underlines are considered spelling errors, while all errors marked with blue underlines are considered grammatical errors. Errors marked with purple dotted underlines are considered errors related to a lack of conciseness. To begin checking the document, you'll use the Editor button in the Proofing group on the Review tab. Note that in some installations of Word, this button might be called the "Spelling & Grammar" button instead.

To check the document for spelling and grammatical errors:

1. Press **CTRL+HOME**, if necessary, to move the insertion point to the beginning of the document, to the left of the "W" in "We." By placing the insertion point at the beginning of the document, you ensure that Word will check the entire document from start to finish, without having to go back and check an earlier part.
2. On the ribbon, click the **Review** tab. The ribbon changes to display reviewing options.
3. In the Proofing group, click the **Editor** button. The Editor pane opens on the right side of the Word window, indicating that the document contains three spelling errors, one grammar error, and no clarity and conciseness errors.

   Trouble? If you see the Spelling & Grammar button instead of the Editor button, click the Spelling & Grammar button.
4. Near the top of the Editor pane, click **Total Suggestions 4**. Now the Editor pane displays information about the first error. As in the document, the word "prottect" is underlined in red as a possible spelling error. To the right of the sentence in the Editor pane is a speaker icon, which you can click to hear the sentence read aloud. Below, in the Suggestions box, the correctly spelled word "protect" appears along with its definition. You might also see some other suggestions. The incorrectly spelled word "prottect" is also highlighted in gray in the document. See Figure 1–25.

Figure 1–25 Editor pane

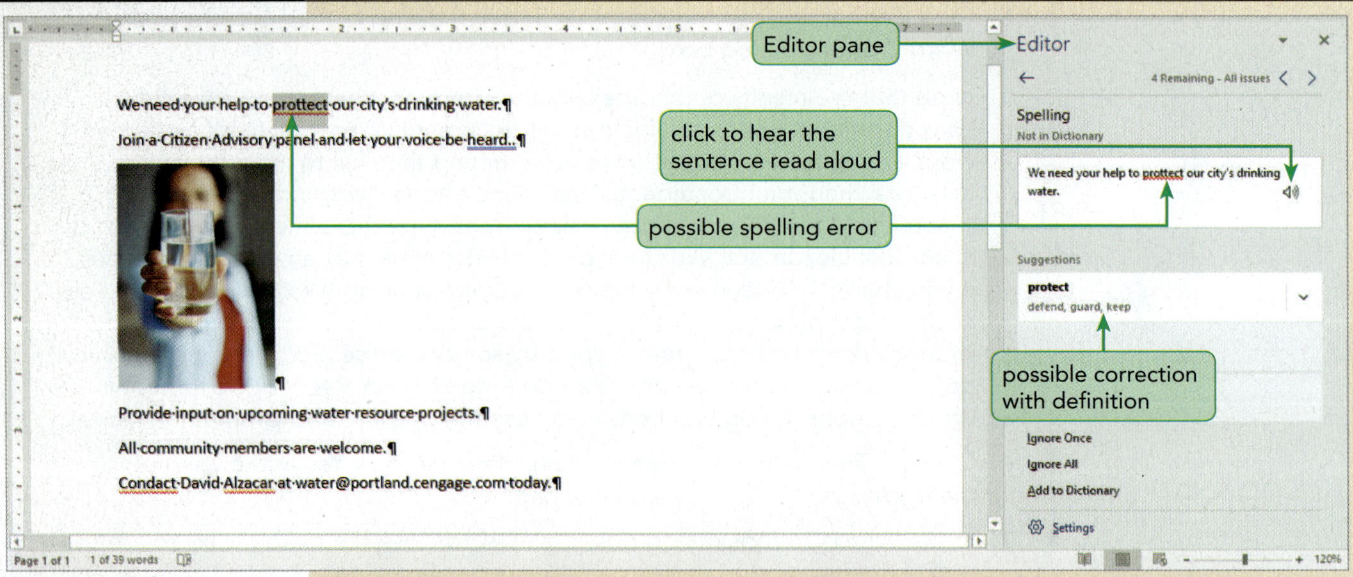

iStock.com/laflor

Trouble? If you don't see "Total Suggestions 4" at the top of the Editor pane, that's fine. Everything else in Step 4 should still match what you see on your screen.

5. In the Editor pane, click the **protect** suggestion. The misspelled word "prottect" is replaced with "protect."

   Next Word highlights the last word in the second sentence, indicating another possible error. The explanation near the top of the pane indicates that Word has detected a redundant punctuation mark—that is, an extra period.

6. In the Suggestions list, click **heard.** (with one period).

   The first word of the last sentence is now highlighted in the document.

7. In the Editor pane, click the **Contact** suggestion. (Make sure to click "Contact" with an uppercase "C.") David's last name is now highlighted in the document. Although the Editor pane doesn't recognize "Alzacar" as a word, it is spelled correctly, so you can ignore it. Note that if his name appeared repeatedly in the document, you could click Ignore All to ignore all instances of it.

   Trouble? If you see "Resume" in the Editor pane instead of "Resume checking all results," click "Resume" instead.

8. In the Editor pane, click **Ignore Once**. A dialog box opens, indicating that the spelling and grammar check is complete.

   Trouble? If you do not see the dialog box mentioned in Step 8, skip Step 9.

9. Click **OK** to close the dialog box.
10. Close the Editor pane.

Proskills

Written Communication: Proofreading Your Document

Although the Editor pane is a useful tool, it won't always catch every error in a document, and it sometimes flags "errors" that are actually correct. This means there is no substitute for careful proofreading. Always take the time to read through your document to check for errors the Editor pane might have missed. Keep in mind that the Editor pane cannot pinpoint inaccurate phrases or poorly chosen words. You'll have to find those yourself. To produce a professional document, you must read it carefully several times. It's a good idea to ask one or two other people to read your documents as well; they might catch something you missed.

You still need to proofread the document. You'll do that next.

To proofread the document:

1. Review the document text for any remaining errors. In the second paragraph, change the lowercase "p" in "panel" to an uppercase "P."
2. In the last line of text, replace "David Alzacar" with your first and last names, and then save the document. Including your name in the document will make it easier for you to find your copy later if you print it on a shared printer.

Now you're ready to begin formatting the document. You will start by turning the page so it is wider than it is tall. In other words, you will change the document's **orientation**.

Changing Page Orientation

Portrait orientation, with the page taller than it is wide, is the default page orientation for Word documents because it is the orientation most commonly used for letters, reports, and other formal documents. However, David wants you to format the flyer in **landscape orientation**—that is, with the page turned so it is wider than it is tall—to better accommodate the photo. You can accomplish this task by using the Orientation button located on the Layout tab on the ribbon. After you change the page orientation, you will select narrower margins so you can maximize the amount of color on the page.

To change the page orientation:

1. Change the document Zoom level to **One Page** so that you can see the entire document.
2. On the ribbon, click the **Layout** tab. The ribbon changes to display options for formatting the overall layout of text and images in the document.
3. In the Page Setup group, click the **Orientation** button, and then click **Landscape** on the menu. The document changes to landscape orientation.
4. In the Page Setup group, click the **Margins** button, and then click the **Narrow** option on the menu. The margins shrink from 1 inch to .5 inch on all four sides. See Figure 1–26.

Figure 1–26 Document in landscape orientation with narrow margins

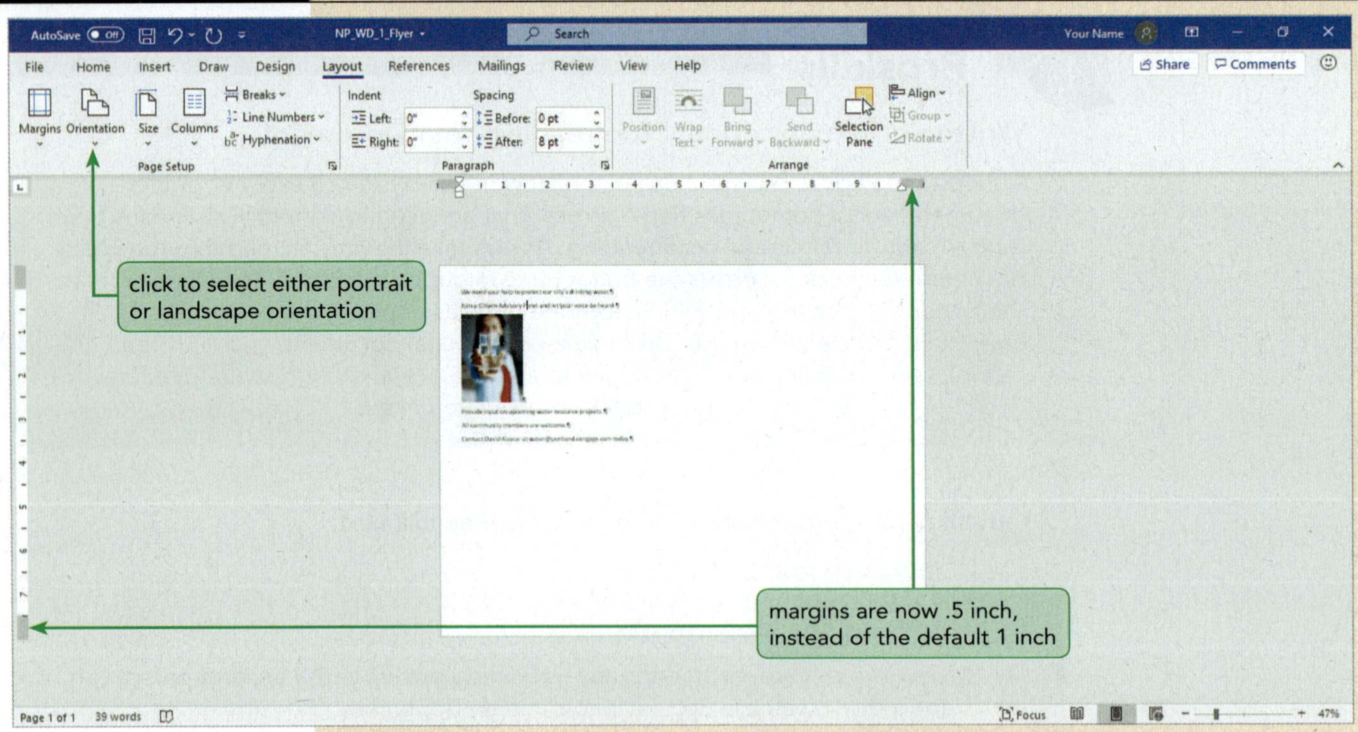

iStock.com/laflor

Changing the Font and Font Size

David typed the document in the default font size, 11 point, and the default font, Calibri, but he would like to switch to the Arial font instead. Also, he wants to increase the size of all five paragraphs of text. To apply these changes, you start by selecting the text you want to format. Then you select the options you want in the Font group on the Home tab.

To change the font and font size:

1. Change the document Zoom level to **120%**.
2. On the ribbon, click the **Home** tab.
3. To verify that the insertion point is located at the beginning of the document, press **CTRL+HOME**.
4. Press and hold **SHIFT**, and then click to the right of the second paragraph marker, at the end of the second paragraph of text. The first two paragraphs of text are selected, as shown in Figure 1–27.

Figure 1–27 **Selected text, with default font displayed in Font box**

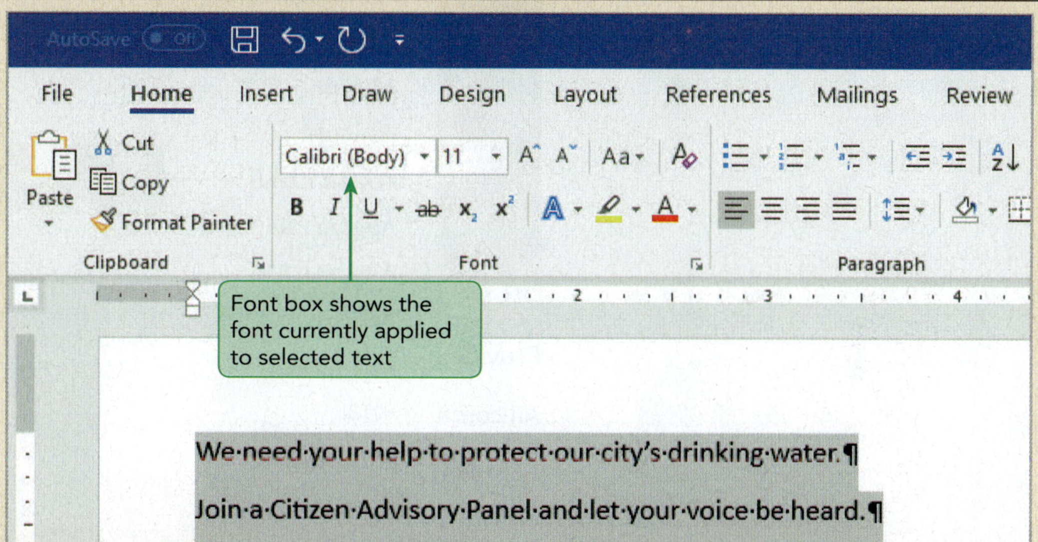

iStockPhoto.com/laflor

The Font box in the Font group displays the name of the font applied to the selected text, which in this case is Calibri. The word "Body" next to the font name indicates that the Calibri font is intended for formatting body text. **Body text** is ordinary text, as opposed to titles or headings.

5. In the Font group on the Home tab, click the **Font arrow**. A list of available fonts appears, with Calibri Light and Calibri at the top of the list. Calibri is highlighted in gray, indicating that this font is currently applied to the selected text. The word "Headings" next to the font name "Calibri Light" indicates that Calibri Light is intended for formatting headings.

   Below Calibri Light and Calibri, you might see a list of fonts that have been used recently on your computer, followed by a complete alphabetical list of all available fonts. (You won't see the list of recently used fonts if you just installed Word.) You need to scroll the list to see all the available fonts. Each name in the list is formatted with the relevant font. For example, the name "Arial" appears in the Arial font. See Figure 1–28.

Figure 1–28 Font list

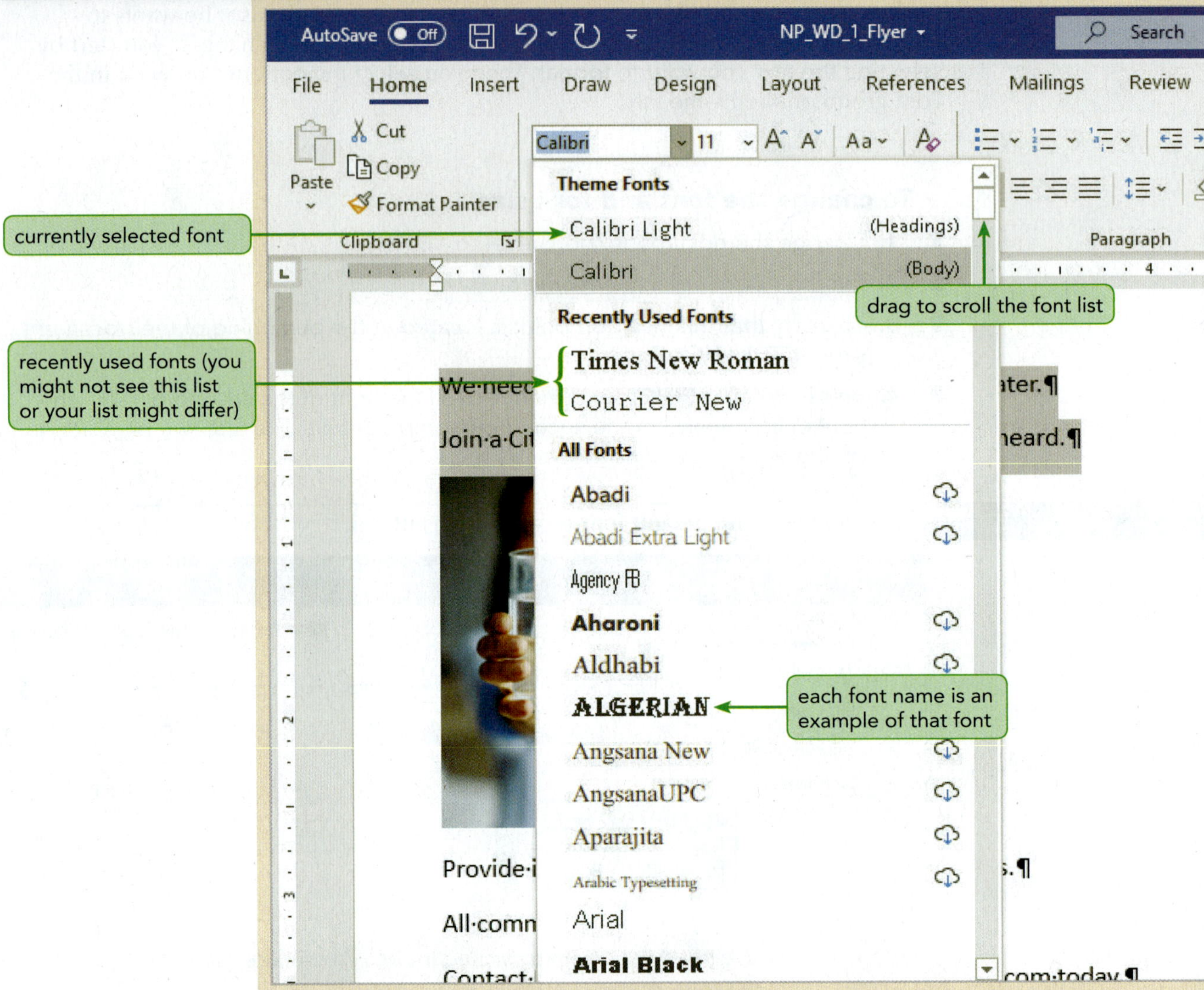

iStock.com/laflor

6. Without clicking, move the pointer over a dramatic-looking font in the font list, such as Algerian or Arial Black, and then move the pointer over another font.

   The selected text in the document changes to show a Live Preview of the font the pointer is resting on. **Live Preview** shows the results that would occur in your document if you clicked the option you are pointing to.

7. When you are finished reviewing the Font list, click **Arial**. The Font menu closes, and the selected text is formatted in Arial.

   Next, you will make the text more eye-catching by increasing the font size. The Font Size box currently displays the number "11," indicating that the selected text is formatted in 11-point font.

8. Verify that the first two paragraphs are still selected, and then click the **Font Size arrow** in the Font group to display a menu of font sizes. As with the Font menu, you can move the pointer over options in the Font Size menu to see a Live Preview of that option.

9. On the Font Size menu, click **22**. The selected text increases significantly in size, and the Font Size menu closes.
10. Select the three paragraphs of text below the photo, format them in the Arial font, and then increase the paragraph's font size to 22 points.
11. Click a blank area of the document to deselect the text, and then save the document.

Keep in mind that to restore selected text to its default appearance, you can click the Clear All Formatting button in the Font group on the Home tab.

David examines the flyer and decides he would like to apply more character formatting, which affects the appearance of individual characters, in the middle three paragraphs. After that, you can turn your attention to paragraph formatting, which affects the appearance of the entire paragraph.

Applying Text Effects, Font Colors, and Font Styles

For formal, professional documents, you typically only need to use **bold** or *italic* to make a word or paragraph stand out. Occasionally you might need to underline a word. To apply these forms of character formatting, select the text you want to format, and then click the Bold, Italic, or Underline button in the Font group on the Home tab. To really make text stand out, you can use text effects. You access these options by clicking the Text Effects and Typography button in the Font group on the Home tab. Keep in mind that text effects can be very dramatic.

David suggests applying text effects to the second paragraph.

To apply text effects to the second paragraph:

1. Scroll up, if necessary, to display the beginning of the document, and then click in the selection bar to the left of the second paragraph. The entire second paragraph is selected.
2. In the Font group on the Home tab, click the **Text Effects and Typography** button.

   A gallery of text effects appears. Options that allow you to fine-tune a particular text effect, perhaps by changing the color or adding an even more pronounced shadow, are listed below the gallery. A **gallery** is a menu or grid that shows a visual representation of the options available when you click a button.
3. In the middle of the bottom row of the gallery, place the pointer over the blue letter "A." This displays a ScreenTip with the text effect's full name: Fill: Blue, Accent color 5; Outline: White, Background color 1; Hard Shadow: Blue, Accent color 5. A Live Preview of the effect appears in the document. See Figure 1–29.

Figure 1–29 Live Preview of a text effect

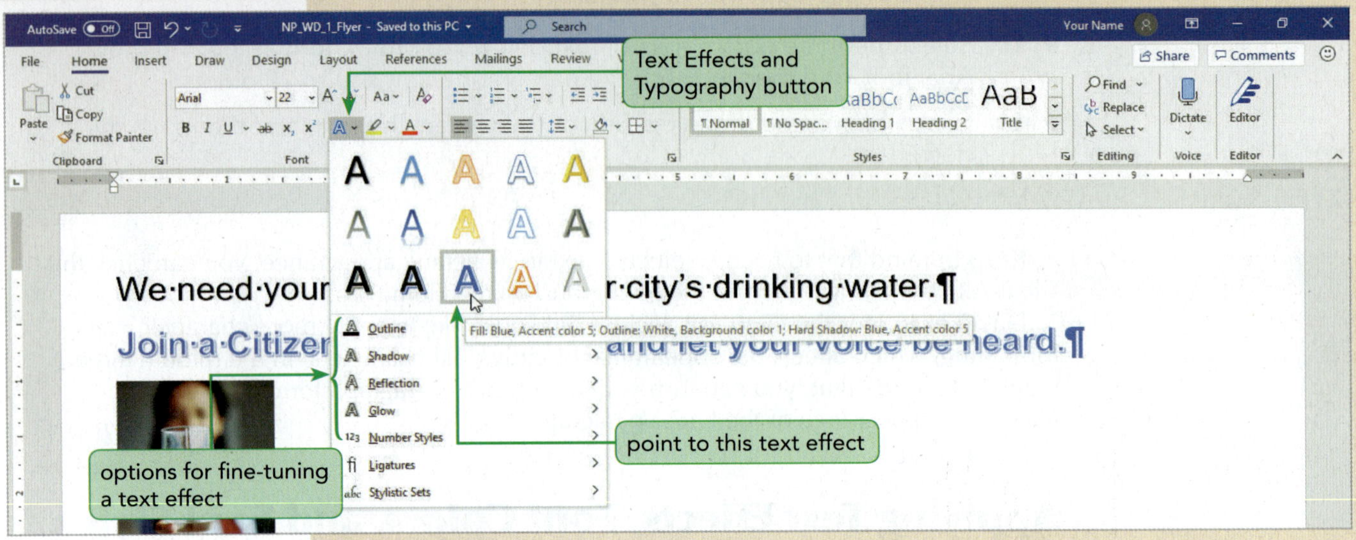

iStock.com/laflor

4. In the bottom row of the gallery, click the blue letter "A." The text effect is applied to the selected paragraph, and the Text Effects gallery closes. The second paragraph is formatted in blue, as shown in the Session 1.2 Visual Overview. On the ribbon, the Bold button in the Font group is now highlighted because bold formatting is part of this text effect.

   Next, to make the text stand out a bit more, you'll increase the font size. This time, instead of using the Font Size button, you'll use a different method.

5. In the Font group, click the **Increase Font Size** button. The font size increases from 22 points to 24 points, which is the next higher font size on the Font menu.

6. Click the **Increase Font Size** button again. The font size increases to 26 points, which is the next higher font size on the Font menu. If you need to decrease the font size of selected text, you can use the Decrease Font Size button. Each time you click the Decrease Font Size button, the font decreases to the next lower font size on the Font menu.

David asks you to emphasize the third and fourth paragraphs by adding bold and a blue font color.

To apply a font color and bold:

1. Select the third and fourth paragraphs of text, which contain the text "Provide input on upcoming water resource projects. All community members are welcome."

2. In the Font group on the Home tab, click the **Font Color arrow**. A gallery of font colors appears. Black is the default font color and appears at the top of the Font Color gallery, with the word "Automatic" next to it.

   The options in the Theme Colors section of the menu are complementary colors that work well when used together in a document. The options in the Standard Colors section are more limited. For more advanced color options, you could use the More Colors or Gradient options. David prefers a simple blue.

Trouble? If the third and fourth paragraphs turned red, you clicked the Font Color button instead of the arrow next to it. On the Quick Access Toolbar, click the Undo button, and then repeat Step 2.

3. In the Theme Colors section, place the pointer over the square that's second from the right in the top row. A ScreenTip with the color's name, "Blue, Accent 5," appears. A Live Preview of the color appears in the document, where the text you selected in Step 1 now appears formatted in blue. See Figure 1–30.

Figure 1–30 Font Color gallery showing a Live Preview

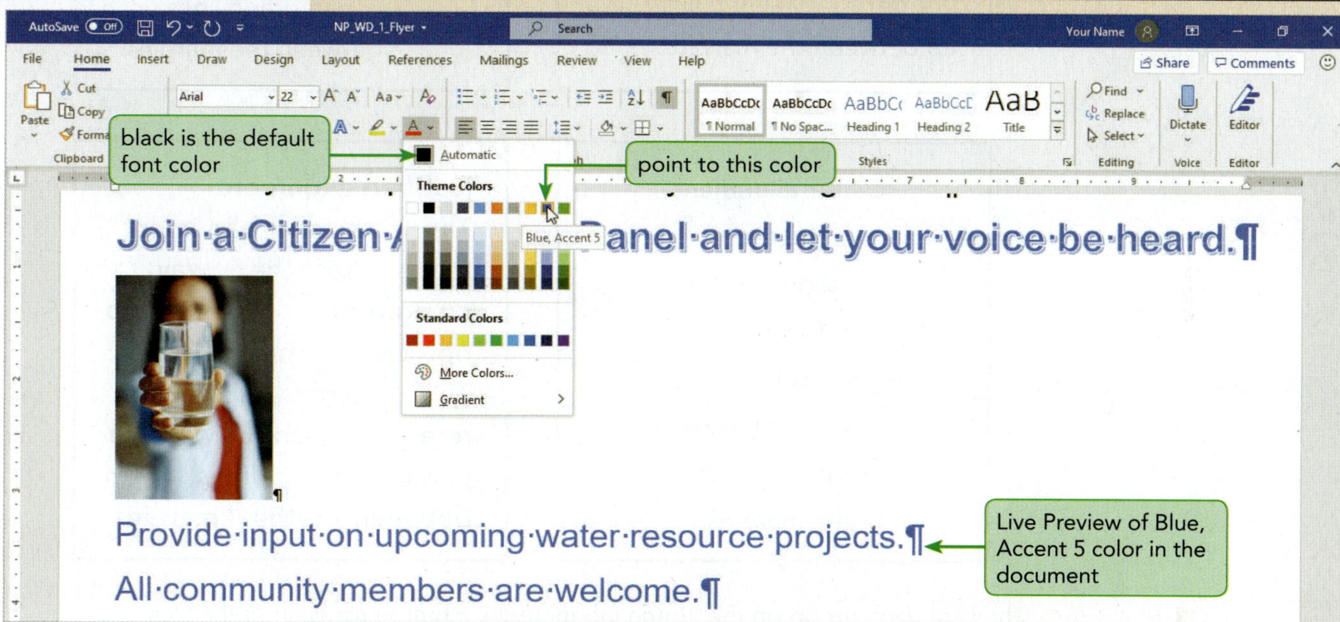

iStock.com/laflor

4. Click the **Blue, Accent 5** square. The Font color gallery closes, and the selected text is formatted in blue. On the Font Color button, the bar below the letter "A" is now blue, indicating that if you select text and click the Font Color button, the text will automatically change to blue.
5. In the Font group, click the **Bold** button B. The selected text is now formatted in bold, with thicker, darker lettering.

Next, you will complete some paragraph formatting, starting with paragraph alignment.

Aligning Text

Alignment refers to how text and graphics line up between the page margins. By default, text is **left-aligned** in Word. That is, the text is flush with the left margin, with the text along the right margin **ragged**, or uneven. By contrast, **right-aligned** text is aligned along the right margin and is ragged along the left margin. **Centered** text is positioned evenly between the left and right margins and is ragged along both the left and right margins. Finally, with **justified alignment**, full lines of text are spaced between both the left and the right margins, and no text is ragged. Text in newspaper columns is often justified. See Figure 1–31.

Figure 1-31 **Varieties of text alignment**

left alignment
The term "alignment" refers to the way a paragraph lines up between the margins. The term "alignment" refers to the way a paragraph lines up between the margins.

right alignment
The term "alignment" refers to the way a paragraph lines up between the margins. The term "alignment" refers to the way a paragraph lines up between the margins.

center alignment
The term "alignment" refers to the way a paragraph lines up between the margins.

justified alignment
The term "alignment" refers to the way a paragraph lines up between the margins. The term "alignment" refers to the way a paragraph lines up between the margins.

The Paragraph group on the Home tab includes a button for each of the four major types of alignment described in Figure 1-31: the Align Left button, the Center button, the Align Right button, and the Justify button. To align a single paragraph, click anywhere in that paragraph, and then click the appropriate alignment button. To align multiple paragraphs, select the paragraphs first, and then click an alignment button.

You need to center all the text in the flyer now. You can center the photo at the same time.

Use CTRL+A to select the entire document, instead of dragging the pointer. It's easy to miss part of the document when you drag the pointer.

To center-align the text:

1. Make sure the Home tab is still selected, and press **CTRL+A** to select the entire document.
2. In the Paragraph group, click the **Center** button, and then click a blank area of the document to deselect the selected paragraphs. The text and photo are now centered on the page, similar to the centered text shown earlier in the Session 1.2 Visual Overview.
3. Save the document.

Adding a Paragraph Border and Shading

A **paragraph border** is an outline that appears around one or more paragraphs in a document. You can choose to apply only a partial border—for example, a bottom border that appears as an underline under the last line of text in the paragraph—or an entire box around a paragraph. You can select different colors and line weights for the border as well, making it more or less prominent as needed. You apply paragraph borders using the Borders button in the Paragraph group on the Home tab. **Shading** is background color that you can apply to one or more paragraphs and that can be used in conjunction with a border for a more defined effect. You apply shading using the Shading button in the Paragraph group on the Home tab.

Now you will apply a border and shading to the first paragraph, as shown earlier in the Session 1.2 Visual Overview. Then you will use the Format Painter to copy this formatting to the last paragraph in the document.

To add shading and a paragraph border:

1. Scroll up if necessary and select the first paragraph. Be sure to select the paragraph mark at the end of the paragraph.
2. On the Home tab, in the Paragraph group, click the **Borders arrow**. A gallery of border options appears, as shown in Figure 1–32. To apply a complete outline around the selected text, you use the Outside Borders option.

Figure 1–32 Border gallery

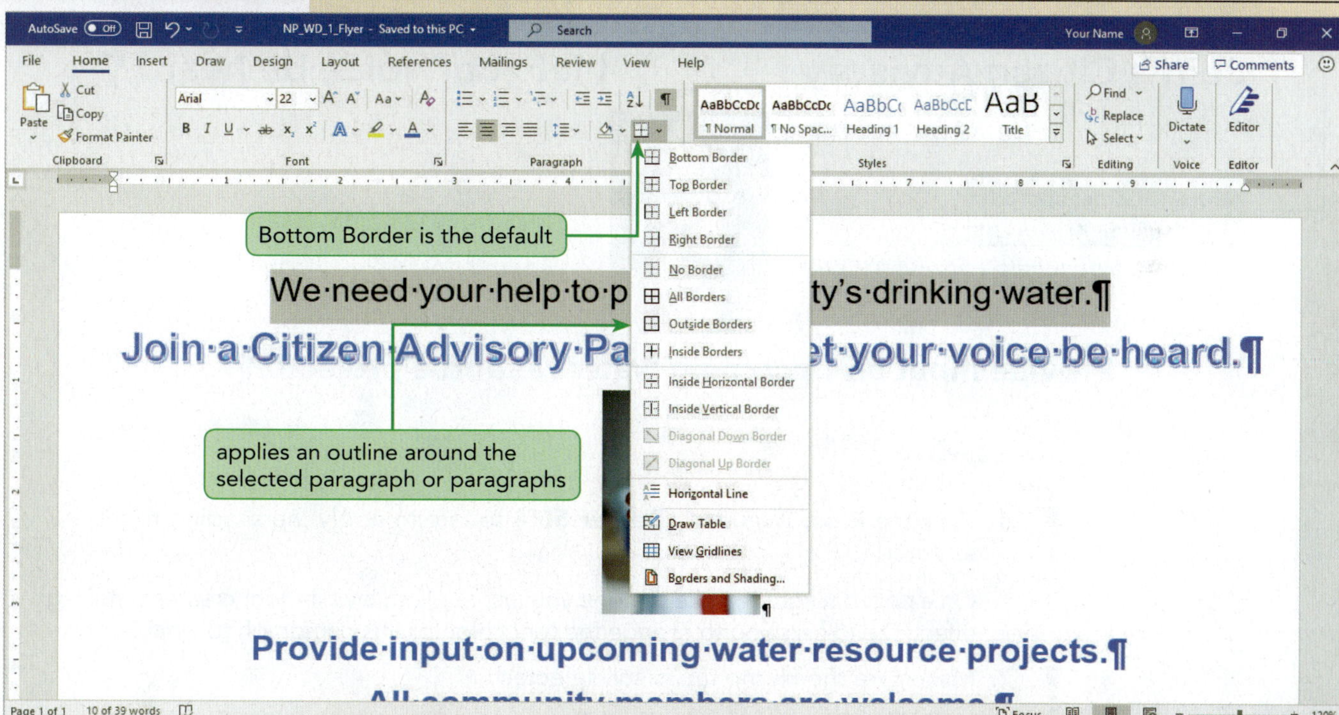

iStock.com/laflor

Trouble? If the gallery does not open and instead the paragraph becomes underlined with a single underline, you clicked the Borders button instead of the arrow next to it. On the Quick Access Toolbar, click the Undo button, and then repeat Step 2.

3. In the Border gallery, click **Outside Borders**. The menu closes and a black border appears around the selected paragraph, spanning the width of the page. In the Paragraph group, the Borders button changes to show the Outside Borders option.

Trouble? If the border around the first paragraph doesn't extend all the way to the left and right margins and instead encloses only the text, you didn't select the paragraph mark as directed in Step 1. Click the Undo button repeatedly to remove the border, and begin again with Step 1.

4. In the Paragraph group, click the **Shading arrow**. A gallery of shading options opens, divided into Theme Colors and Standard Colors. You will use a shade of dark blue in the fifth column from the left.
5. In the bottom row in the Theme Colors section, move the pointer over the square in the fifth column from the left to display a ScreenTip that reads "Blue, Accent 1, Darker 50%." A Live Preview of the color appears in the document. See Figure 1–33.

Figure 1–33 Shading gallery with a Live Preview displayed

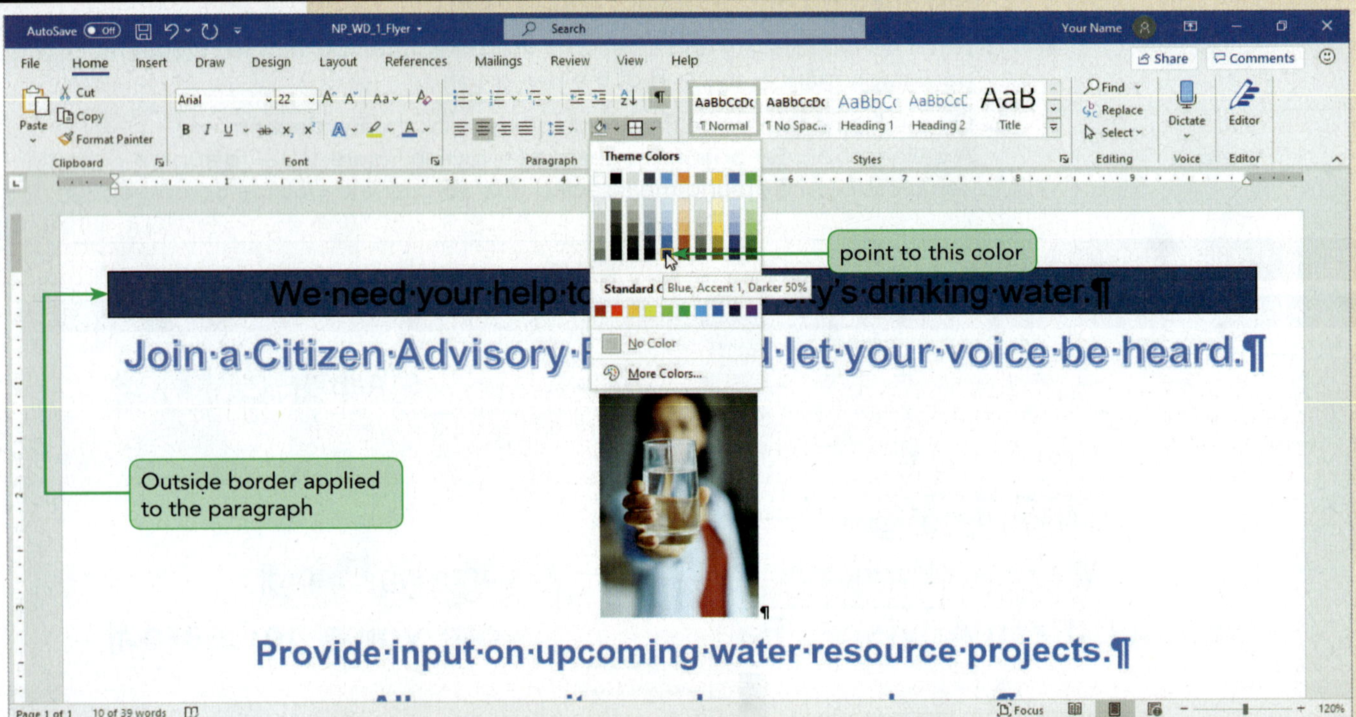

iStock.com/laflor

6. Click the **Blue, Accent 1, Darker 50%** square to apply the shading to the selected text.

   On a dark background like the one you just applied, a white font creates a striking effect. David asks you to change the font color for this paragraph to white.
7. Make sure the Home tab is still selected.
8. In the Font group, click the **Font Color arrow** to open the Font Color gallery, and then click the **white** square in the top row of the Theme Colors. The Font Color gallery closes, and the paragraph is now formatted with white font.

   The black paragraph border is hard to see with the dark blue shading, so you will change the border to a different color. To make more advanced changes to borders or paragraph shading, you need to use the Borders and Shading dialog box.
9. Click the **Borders arrow** and then, at the bottom of the menu, click **Borders and Shading**. The Borders and Shading dialog box opens with the Borders tab displayed.

Tip

If you select an extremely dark shading color, Word will automatically change the font color to white.

10. Click the **Color arrow** to open the Color gallery, and then click the **Green, Accent 6** square, which is the right-most square in the top row of the Theme Colors section.

Next, to make the border more noticeable, you will increase its width.

11. Click the **Width arrow**, and then click **3 pt**. At this point, the settings in your Borders and Shading dialog box should match the settings in Figure 1–34.

Figure 1–34 Borders and Shading dialog box

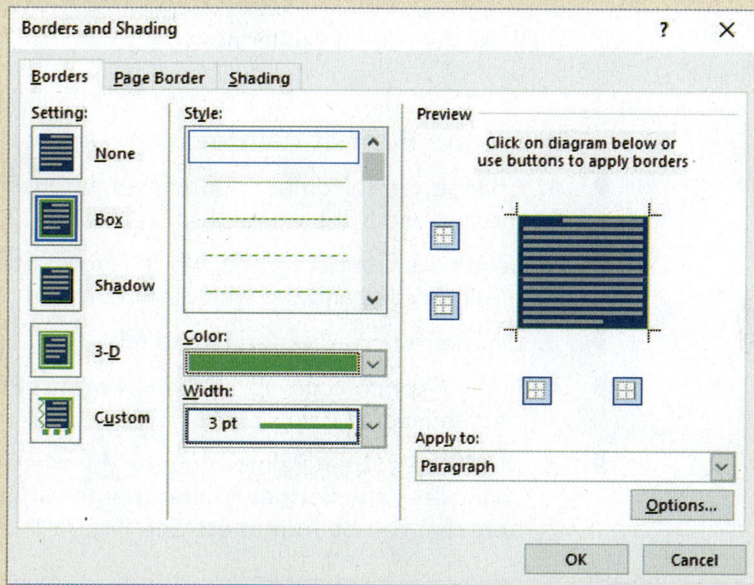

12. Click **OK** to close the Borders and Shading dialog box and return to the document.

13. Click a blank area of the document to deselect the text, review the change, and then save the document. The first paragraph is now formatted with a green border, a dark blue background, and white text as shown in the Session 1.2 Visual Overview.

To add balance to the flyer, David suggests formatting the last paragraph in the document with the same shading, border, and font color as the first paragraph. You'll do that next.

Copying Formatting with the Format Painter

You could select the last paragraph and then apply the border, shading, and font color one step at a time. But it's easier to copy all the formatting from the first paragraph to the last paragraph using the Format Painter button in the Clipboard group on the Home tab.

Reference

Using the Format Painter

- Select the text whose formatting you want to copy.
- On the Home tab, in the Clipboard group, click the Format Painter button, or to copy formatting to multiple sections of nonadjacent text, double-click the Format Painter button.
- The pointer changes to the Format Painter pointer, the I-beam pointer with a paintbrush.
- Click the words you want to format, or drag to select and format entire paragraphs.
- When you are finished formatting the text, click the Format Painter button again to turn off the Format Painter.

You'll use the Format Painter now.

To use the Format Painter:

1. Change the document Zoom level to One Page so you can easily see both the first and last paragraphs.
2. Select the first paragraph, which is formatted with the dark blue shading, the green border, and the white font color.
3. On the ribbon, click the **Home** tab.
4. In the Clipboard group, click the **Format Painter** button to activate, or turn on, the Format Painter.
5. Move the Format Painter pointer over the document. The pointer changes to the Format Painter pointer when you move the pointer near an item that can be formatted. See Figure 1–35.

Figure 1–35 Format Painter

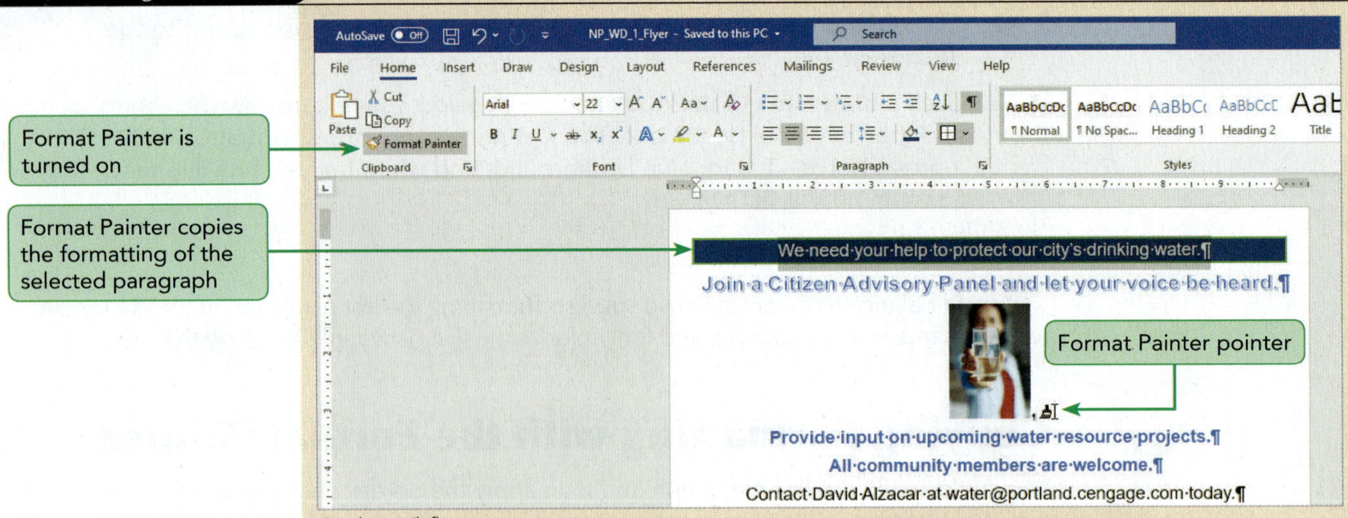

iStock.com/laflor

Tip

To turn off the Format Painter without using it, press ESC.

6. Click and drag the Format Painter pointer to select the last paragraph in the document. The paragraph is now formatted with dark blue shading, a green border, and white font. The pointer returns to its original I-beam shape.

   Trouble? If the text in the newly formatted paragraph wrapped to a second line, replace your full name with your first name, or, if necessary, use only your initials so the paragraph is only one-line long.

7. Click anywhere in the document to deselect the text, review the change, and then save the document.

Your next task is to increase the paragraph spacing below the first paragraph and above the last paragraph. This will give the shaded text even more weight on the page. To complete this task, you will use the settings on the Layout tab, which offer more options than the Line and Paragraph Spacing button on the Home tab.

To increase the paragraph spacing below the first paragraph and above the last paragraph:

1. Click anywhere in the first paragraph, and then click the **Layout** tab. On this tab, the Paragraph group contains settings that control paragraph spacing. Currently, the paragraph spacing for the first paragraph is set to the default 0 points before the paragraph and 8 points after.
2. In the Paragraph group, click the **After** box to select the current setting, type **42**, and then press **ENTER**. The added space causes the second paragraph to move down 42 points.
3. Click anywhere in the last paragraph.
4. On the Layout tab, in the Paragraph group, click the **Before** box to select the current setting, type **42**, and then press **ENTER**. The added space causes the last paragraph to move down 42 points.

Insight

Formatting Professional Documents

In more formal documents, use color and special effects sparingly. The goal of letters, reports, and many other types of documents is to convey important information, not to dazzle the reader with fancy fonts and colors. Such elements only serve to distract the reader from your main point. In formal documents, it's a good idea to limit the number of colors to two and to stick with left alignment for text. In a document like the flyer you're currently working on, you have a little more leeway because the goal of the document is to attract attention. However, you still want it to look professional.

Next, David wants you to replace the photo with one that will look better in the document's new landscape orientation. You'll replace the photo, and then you'll resize it so that the flyer fills the entire page.

Inserting a Picture and Adding Alt Text

A **picture** is a photo or another type of image that you insert into a document. To work with a picture, you first need to select it. Once a picture is selected, a contextual tab—the Picture Format tab—appears on the ribbon, with options for editing the picture and adding effects such as a border, a shadow, a reflection, or a new shape. A **contextual tab** appears on the ribbon only when an object is selected. It contains commands related to the selected object so that you can manipulate, edit, and format the selected object. You can also use the mouse to resize or move a selected picture. To insert a new picture, you use the Pictures button in the Illustrations group on the Insert tab.

To delete the current photo and insert a new one:

1. Click the photo to select it.

   The circles, called **sizing handles**, around the edge of the photo indicate the photo is selected. The Layout Options button, to the right of the photo, gives you access to options that control how the document text flows around the photo. You don't need to worry about these options now. Finally, note that the Picture Format tab appeared on the ribbon when you selected the photo. See Figure 1–36.

Figure 1–36 Selected photo

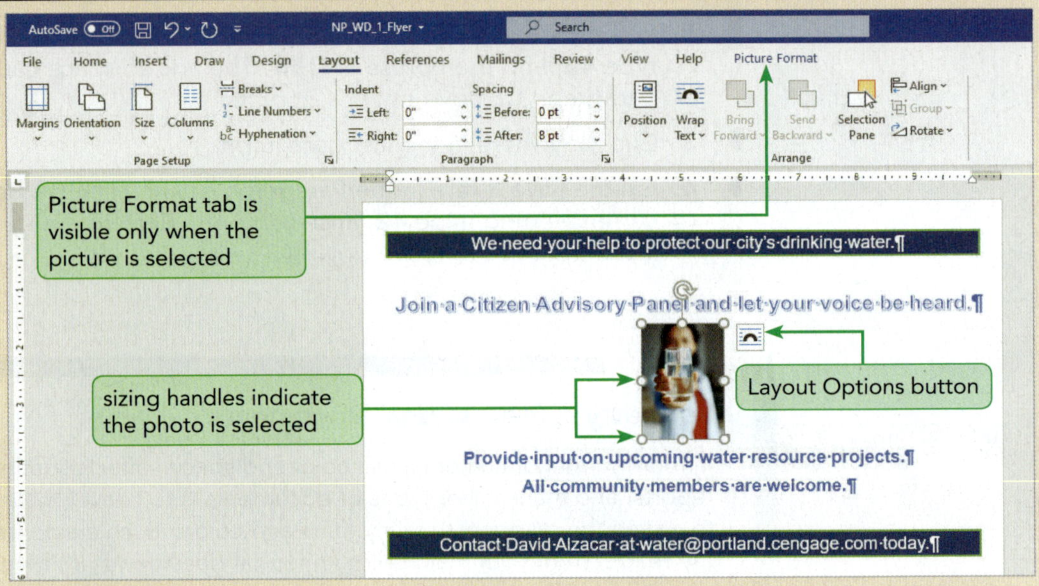

iStock.com/laflor

2. Press **DEL**. The photo is deleted from the document. The insertion point blinks next to the paragraph symbol.

   Now you are ready to insert the new photo in the paragraph containing the insertion point. When you do, you will briefly see a gray box at the bottom of the photo containing a description of the image. This description, which is called **alternative text** (or **alt text**, for short), makes it possible for a screen-reading device to read a description of the image aloud. This is useful for people with vision impairment, who would otherwise find it difficult or impossible to read a document.

   Word automatically creates alt text for most photos, although it is often too generic to be really helpful (for example, "Two people"). To refine alt text created by Word so that it accurately describes an image, click the Alt Text button in the Accessibility group on the Picture Format tab. This opens the Alt Text pane, where you can edit the existing alt text. As you become a more experienced Word user, you'll have the chance to create new alt text for charts, tables, and other items. Before you can use automatic alt text, you need to be using Word 365 and make sure the automatic alt text option is turned on in the Word Options dialog box.

To turn on automatic alt text, insert a new photo, and edit its alt text:

1. Click **File**, and then click **Options** to open the Word Options dialog box with the General tab displayed.
2. In the navigation pane, click **Ease of Access**. In the "Automatic Alt Text" section, click the **Automatically generate alt text for me** check box to insert a checkmark, if necessary, and then click **OK** to close the Word Options dialog box.
3. On the ribbon, click the **Insert** tab. The ribbon changes to display the Insert options.
4. In the Illustrations group, click the **Pictures** button. The Insert Picture From gallery opens.
5. Click **This Device**. The Insert Picture dialog box opens.
6. Navigate to the **Word1 > Module** folder included with your Data Files, and then click **Support_WD_1_Water.png** to select the file. The name of the selected file appears in the File name box.
7. Click the **Insert** button to close the Insert Picture dialog box and insert the photo. An image of water pouring from a bottle into a glass appears in the document, below the second paragraph. The photo is selected, as indicated by the sizing handles on its border, and the Picture Format tab is displayed. After a pause, a gray box with the text "Alt Text: A picture containing . . ." appears as shown in Figure 1–37, remains on the screen for about five seconds, and then disappears.

Tip

To swap one picture for another while retaining the formatting and size of the original, right-click the picture, click Change Picture, click From File, and then select the photo you want to insert.

Figure 1–37 Newly inserted photo with alt text visible

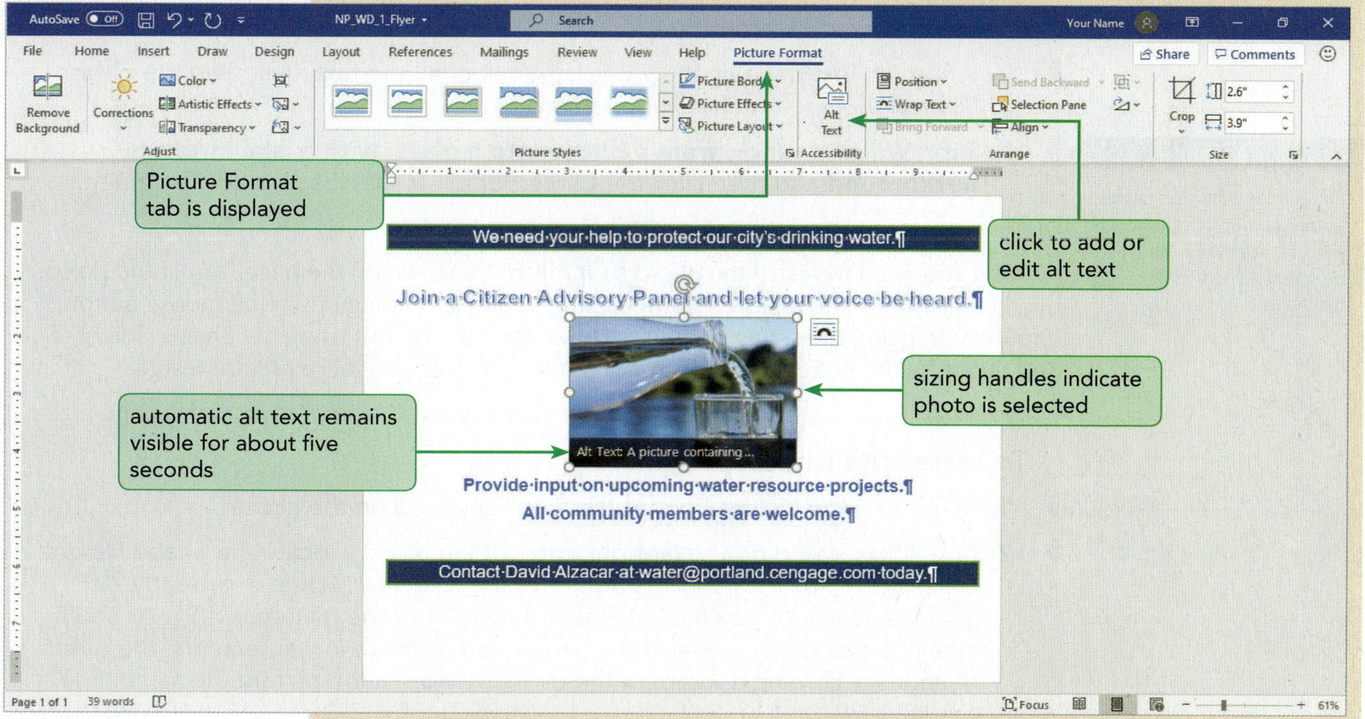

iStock.com/LazingBee

Trouble? If you see a blue message box explaining how alt text works, click Got It to close the message box.

8. In the Accessibility group on the ribbon, click the **Alt Text** button to display the Alt Text pane, which displays the current alt text, as well as a note indicating the description was automatically generated. See Figure 1–38.

Figure 1–38 **Alt Text pane**

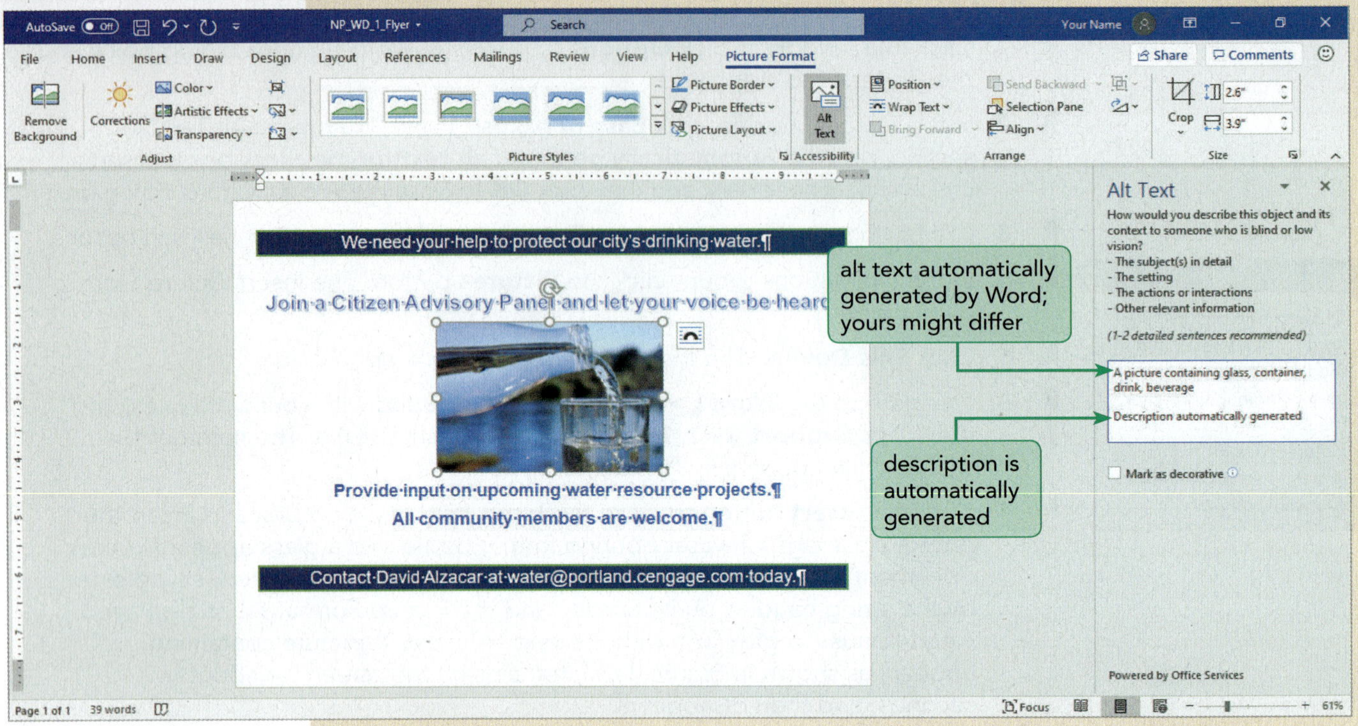

iStock.com/LazingBee

Trouble? If the Alt Text pane does not contain alt text, click the Generate a description for me button.

9. In the Alt Text pane, in the white box, select all the text, including the phrase "Description automatically generated."
10. Type **Water pouring from a bottle into a glass, with a lake in the background** and then click the **Close** button ☒ to close the Alt Text pane.

Tip

For images that require no screen reader narration, you can select the Mark as decorative check box in the Alt Text pane.

Now you need to resize the photo so it fills more space on the page. You could do so by clicking one of the picture's corner sizing handles, holding down the mouse button, and then dragging the sizing handle to resize the picture. But using the Shape Height and Shape Width boxes on the Picture Format tab gives you more precise results.

To resize the photo:

1. Make sure the Picture Format tab is still selected on the ribbon.
2. In the Size group on the far-right edge of the ribbon, locate the Shape Height box, which indicates that the height of the selected picture is currently 2.6". The Shape Width box indicates that the width of the picture is 3.9". As you'll see in the next step, when you change one of these measurements, the other changes accordingly, keeping the overall shape of the picture the same. See Figure 1–39.

Figure 1–39 **Shape Height and Shape Width boxes**

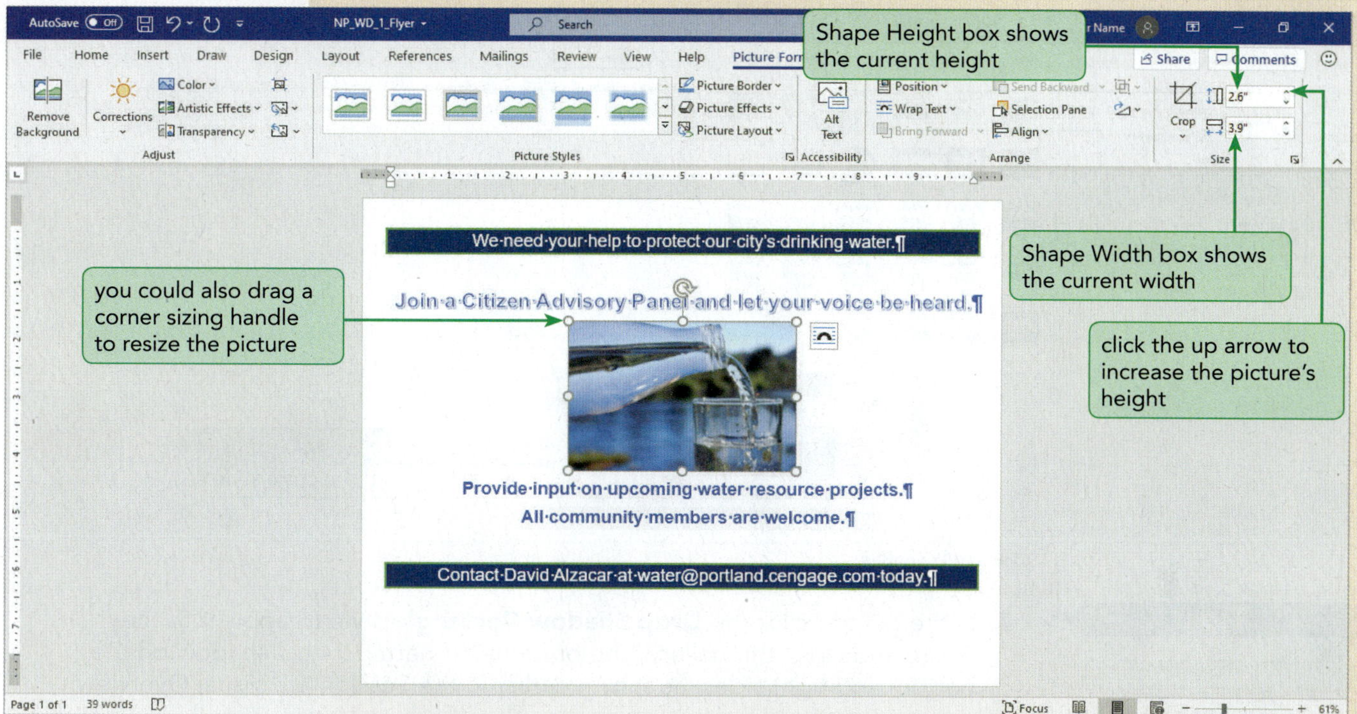

iStock.com/LazingBee

3. Click the **up arrow** in the Shape Height box in the Size group. The photo increases in size slightly. The measurement in the Shape Height box increases to 2.7", and the measurement in the Shape Width box increases to 4.05".
4. Click the **up arrow** in the Shape Height box repeatedly until the picture is 3.2" tall and 4.8" wide.

Finally, to make the photo more noticeable, you can add a **picture style**, which is a collection of formatting options, such as a frame, a rounded shape, and a shadow. You can apply a picture style to a selected picture by clicking the style you want in the Picture Styles gallery on the Picture Format tab. Note that to return a picture to its original appearance, you can click the Reset Picture button in the Adjust group on the Picture Format tab. In the following steps, you'll start by displaying the Picture Styles gallery.

To add a style to the photo:

1. Make sure the Picture Format tab is still selected on the ribbon.
2. In the Picture Styles group, click the **More** button to the right of the Picture Styles gallery to open the gallery and display more picture styles. Some of the picture styles simply add a border, while others change the picture's shape. Other styles combine these options with effects such as a shadow or a reflection.
3. Place the pointer over various styles to observe the Live Previews in the document, and then place the pointer over the Drop Shadow Rectangle style, which is the middle style in the top row. See Figure 1–40.

Figure 1–40 Previewing a picture style

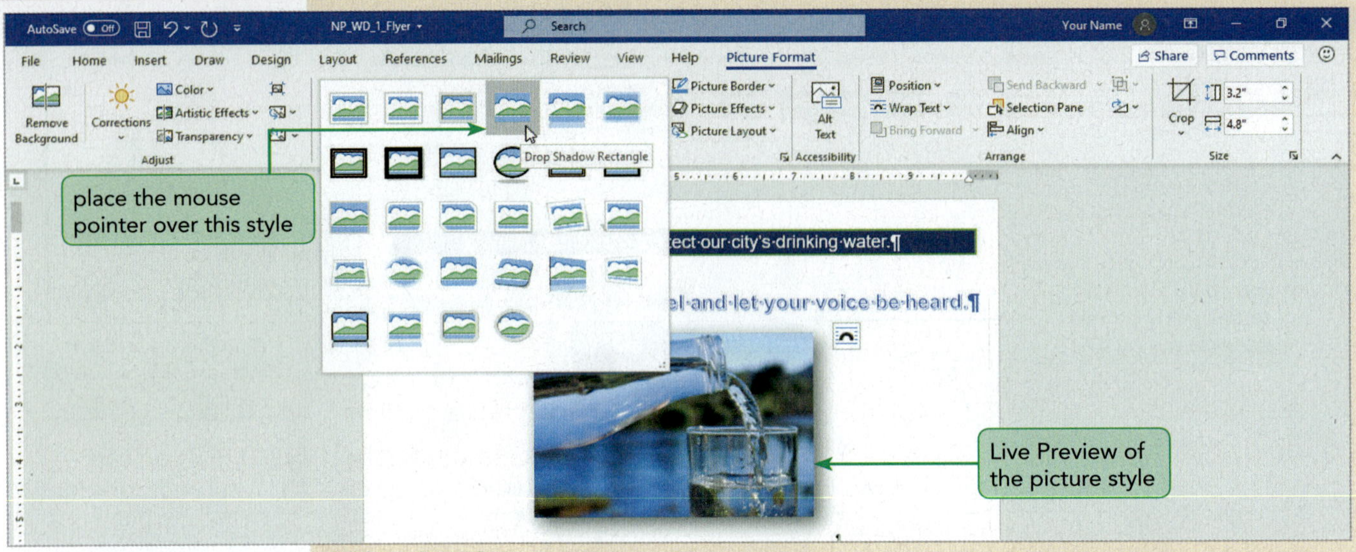

iStock.com/LazingBee

Tip

To return a picture to its original appearance, click the Reset Picture button in the Adjust group on the Picture Format tab.

4. In the gallery, click the **Drop Shadow Rectangle** style to apply it to the photo and close the gallery. The photo is formatted with a shadow on the bottom and right sides, as shown earlier in the Session 1.2 Visual Overview.
5. Click anywhere outside the photo to deselect it, and then save the document.

Insight

Working with Inline Pictures

By default, when you insert a picture in a document, it is treated as an inline object, which means its position changes in the document as you add or delete text. Also, because it is an inline object, you can align the picture just as you would align text, using the alignment buttons in the Paragraph group on the Home tab. Essentially, you can treat an inline picture as just another paragraph.

When you become a more advanced Word user, you'll learn how to wrap text around a picture so that the text flows around the picture—with the picture maintaining its position on the page no matter how much text you add to or delete from the document. The alignment buttons don't work on pictures that have text wrapped around them. Instead, you can drag the picture to the desired position on the page.

To complete the flyer, you need to add a border around the page.

Adding a Page Border

As with a paragraph border, the default style for a page border is a simple black line that forms a box around each page in the document. However, you can choose more elaborate options, including a dotted line, double lines, and, for informal documents, a border of graphical elements, such as stars or trees.

To insert a border around the flyer:

1. On the ribbon, click the **Design** tab.
2. In the Page Background group, click the **Page Borders** button. The Borders and Shading dialog box opens with the Page Border tab displayed. You can use the Setting options on the left side of this tab to specify the type of border you want. Because a document does not normally have a page border, the default setting is None. The Box setting is the most professional and least distracting choice, so you'll select that next.

   It's important to select the Box setting before you select other options for the border. Otherwise, when you click OK, your document won't have a page border, and you'll have to start over.
3. In the Setting section, click the **Box** setting. Selecting this option would add a simple line page border, but David prefers a different line style.
4. In the Style box, scroll down and click the **double-line style**. Now you can select a different line color, just as you did when creating a paragraph border.
5. Click the **Color arrow** to open the Color gallery, and then click the **Green, Accent 6** square, which is the right-most square in the top row of the Theme Colors section. The Color gallery closes and the Green, Accent 6 color is displayed in the Color box. At this point, you could change the line width as well, but David prefers the default setting. See Figure 1–41.

Figure 1–41 Adding a border to the flyer

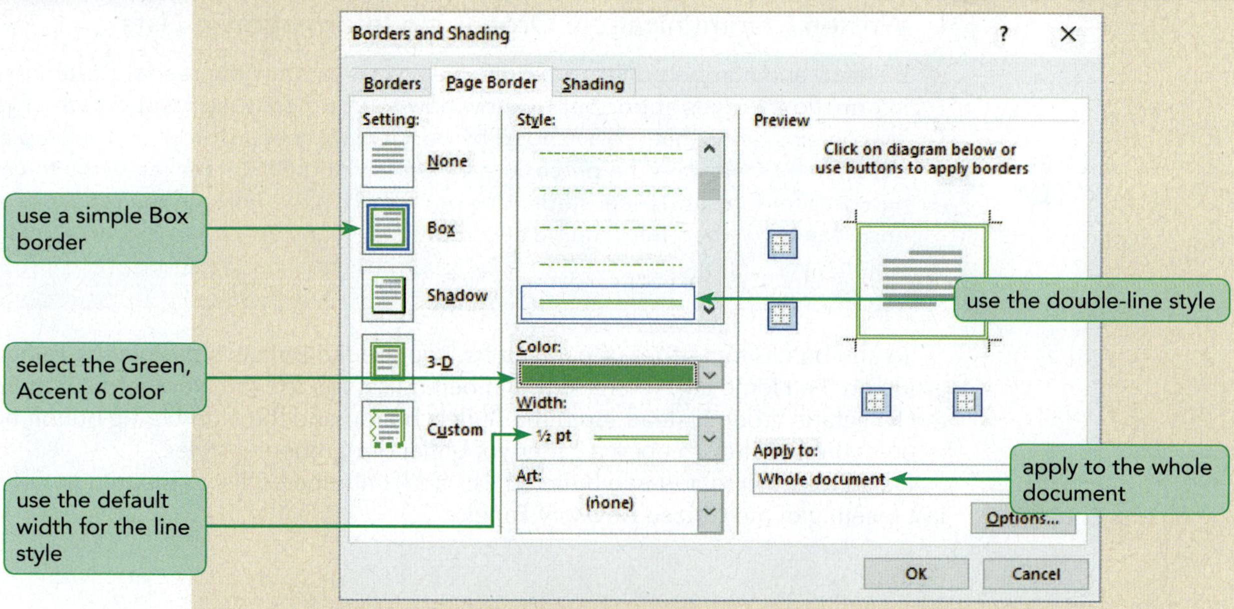

6. In the lower-right corner of the Borders and Shading dialog box, click the **Options** button. The Border and Shading Options dialog box opens.

   By default, the border is positioned 24 points from the edges of the page. If you plan to print your document on an older printer, it is sometimes necessary to change the Measure from setting to Text, so that the border is positioned relative to the outside edge of the text rather than the edge of the page. Alternatively, you can increase the settings in the Top, Bottom, Left, and Right boxes to move the border closer to the text. For most modern printers, however, the default settings are fine.

7. In the Border and Shading Options dialog box, click **Cancel**, and then click **OK** in the Borders and Shading dialog box. The flyer now has a double-line green border, as shown earlier in the Session 1.2 Visual Overview.
8. Save the document.
9. Close the document without closing Word.

David needs your help with one last task—adding bulleted and numbered lists to a document containing the minutes of the Citizen Advisory Panel's May meeting. After you finish formatting the document, David can make the minutes available to the public through the department's website.

Creating Bulleted and Numbered Lists

A **bulleted list** is a group of related paragraphs with a black circle or other character to the left of each paragraph. For a group of related paragraphs that have a particular order (such as steps in a procedure), you can use consecutive numbers instead of bullets to create a **numbered list**. If you insert a new paragraph, delete a paragraph, or reorder the paragraphs in a numbered list, Word adjusts the numbers to make sure they remain consecutive.

Proskills

Written Communication: Organizing Information in Lists

Bulleted and numbered lists are both great ways to draw the reader's attention to information. But it's important to know how to use them. Use numbers when your list contains items that are arranged by priority in a specific order. For example, in a document reviewing the procedure for performing CPR, it makes sense to use numbers for the sequential steps. Use bullets when the items in the list are of equal importance or when they can be accomplished in any order. For example, in a resume, you could use bullets for a list of professional certifications.

To add bullets to a series of paragraphs, you use the Bullets button in the Paragraph group on the Home tab. To create a numbered list, you use the Numbering button in the Paragraph group instead. Both the Bullets button and the Numbering button have arrows you can click to open a gallery of bullet or numbering styles.

David asks you to add two bulleted lists and a numbered list to the minutes of the last meeting of the Citizen Advisory Panel.

To apply bullets to paragraphs:

1. Open the document **NP_WD_1-2.docx** located in the Word1 > Module folder, and then save the document as **NP_WD_1_Minutes** in the location specified by your instructor.
2. Verify that the document is displayed in Print Layout view and that the rulers and nonprinting characters are displayed. Make sure the Zoom level is set to **120%**.
3. On page 1, select the complete list of members in attendance, starting with Tomeka Newcomb and concluding with Jeffrey Holmes.

4. On the ribbon, click the **Home** tab, if necessary.
5. In the Paragraph group, click the **Bullets** button. Black circles appear as bullets before each item in the list. Also, the bulleted list is indented, and the paragraph spacing between the items is reduced.

   After reviewing the default, round bullet in the document, David decides he would prefer square bullets.

6. In the Paragraph group, click the **Bullets arrow**. A gallery of bullet styles opens. See Figure 1–42.

Figure 1–42 Bullets gallery

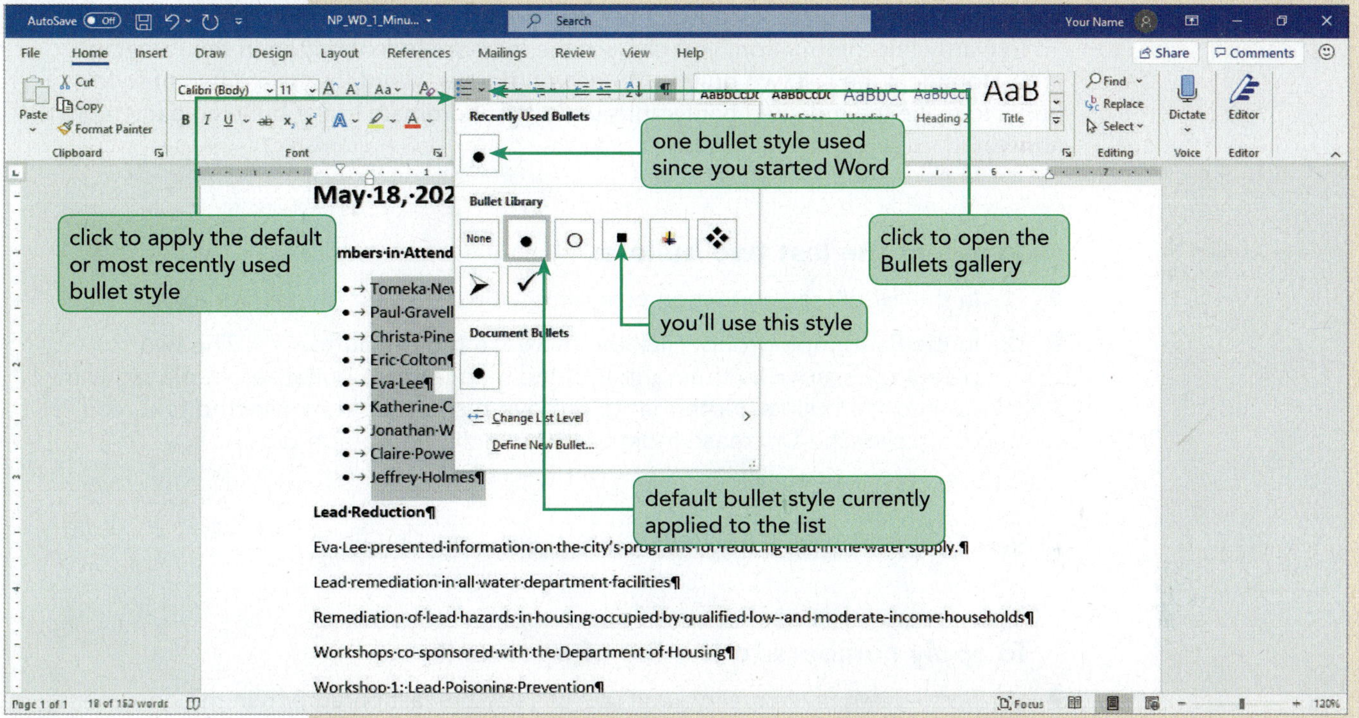

The Recently Used Bullets section appears at the top of the gallery of bullet styles; it displays the bullet styles that have been used since you started Word, which, in this case, is just the round black bullet style that was applied by default when you clicked the Bullets button. The **Bullet Library**, which offers a variety of bullet styles, is shown below the Recently Used Bullets. To create your own bullets from a picture file or from a set of predesigned symbols including diamonds, hearts, or Greek letters, click Define New Bullet, and then click Symbol or Picture in the Define New Bullet dialog box.

7. Move the pointer over the bullet styles in the Bullet Library to see a Live Preview of the bullet styles in the document. David prefers the black square style.
8. In the Bullet Library, click the **black square**. The round bullets are replaced with square bullets.

Next, you need to format the list of lead-reduction programs with square bullets. When you first start Word, the Bullets button applies the default, round bullets you saw earlier. But after you select a new bullet style, the Bullets button applies the last bullet style you used. So, to add square bullets to the lead-reduction programs list, you just have to select the list and click the Bullets button.

To add bullets to the list of lead-reduction programs:

1. Scroll down in the document, and select the paragraphs describing the department's lead-reduction programs, starting with "Lead remediation in all water department facilities" and ending with "Workshop 2: Children and Lead Paint Hazards."
2. In the Paragraph group, click the **Bullets** button. The list is now formatted with square black bullets.

The list is finished except for one issue. Below "Workshops co-sponsored with the Department of Housing" are two subordinate items listing the workshop titles. However, that's not clear because of the way the list is currently formatted.

To clarify this information, you can use the Increase Indent button in the Paragraph group to indent the last two bullets. When you do this, Word inserts a different style bullet to make the indented paragraphs visually subordinate to the bulleted paragraphs above.

To indent the last two bullets:

1. In the list of lead-reduction programs, select the last two paragraphs.
2. In the Paragraph group, click the **Increase Indent** button. The two paragraphs move to the right, and the black square bullets are replaced with open circle bullets. Note that to remove the indent from selected text, you could click the Decrease Indent button in the Paragraph group.

Next, you will format the agenda items as a numbered list.

To apply numbers to the list of agenda items:

1. Scroll down, if necessary, until you can see the last paragraph in the document.
2. Select all the paragraphs below the "Agenda for Next Meeting" heading, starting with "Opening remarks, public comments, and minutes" and ending with "Report on upcoming projects . . . ."
3. In the Paragraph group, click the **Numbering** button. Consecutive numbers appear in front of each item in the list. See Figure 1–43.

Figure 1–43 Numbered list

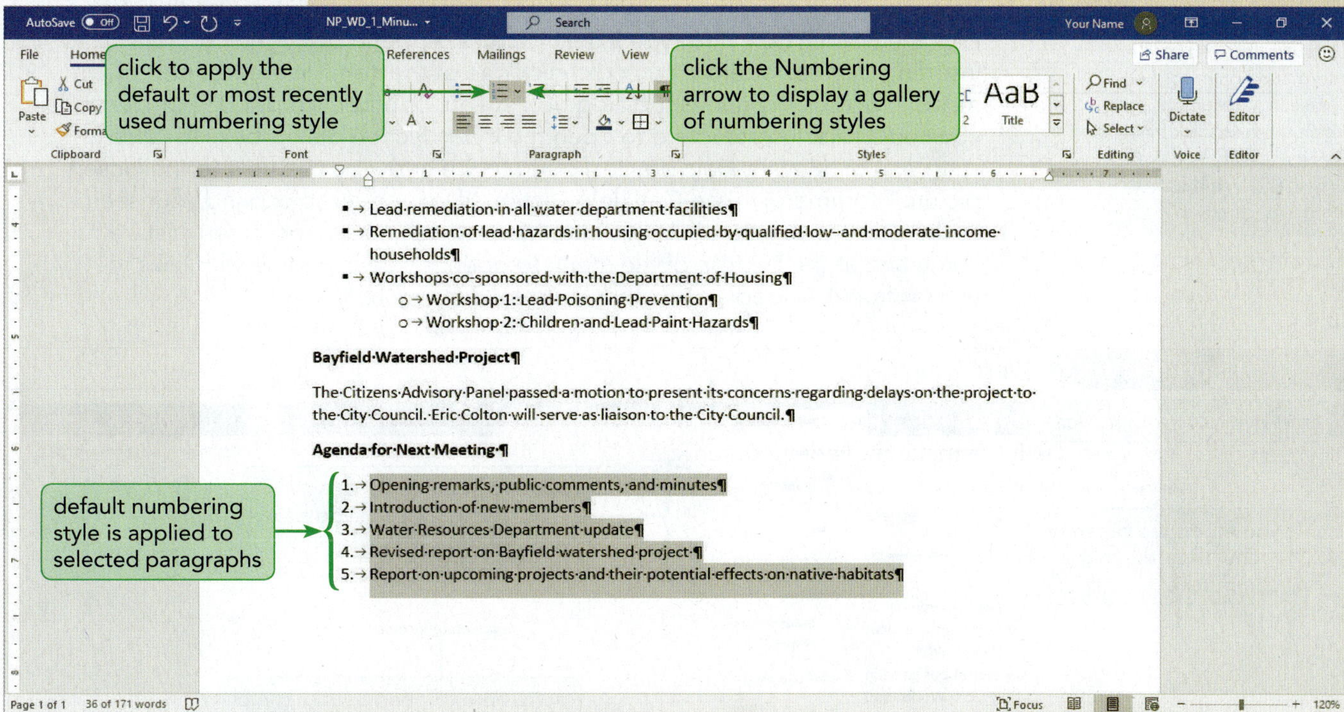

4. Click anywhere in the document to deselect the numbered list.
5. sam Save the document.

As with the Bullets arrow, you can click the Numbering arrow, and then select from a library of numbering styles. You can also indent paragraphs in a numbered list to create an outline, in which case the indented paragraphs will be preceded by lowercase letters instead of numbers. To apply a different list style to the outline (for example, with Roman numerals and uppercase letters), select the list, click the Multilevel List button in the Paragraph group, and then click a multilevel list style. Keep in mind that you can always add items to a bulleted or numbered list by moving the insertion point to the end of the last item in the list and pressing ENTER. The Bullets button is a **toggle button**, which means you can click it to add or remove bullets from selected text. The same is true of the Numbering button.

The document is complete and ready for David to post to the department's website. Because David is considering creating a promotional brochure that would include numerous photographs, he asks you to look up more information about inserting pictures. You can do that using Word Help.

Getting Help

Tip

To display a menu of recent and suggested Help topics, click the Search box and wait for the menu to appear.

To get the most out of Word Help, your computer must be connected to the Internet so it can access the reference information stored at Office.com. The quickest way to look up information is to use the Search box on the ribbon. You can also use the Search box to quickly access Word features.

Tip

To search the web for information on a word or phrase in a document, select the text, click the References tab, and then click the Search button in the Research group.

To look up information in Word Help:

1. Verify that your computer is connected to the Internet, and then, on the ribbon, click the **Search** box, and type **insert picture**. A menu of Help topics related to inserting pictures opens. You could click one of the items in the top part of the menu to access the relevant dialog box, menu, or other Word tool. For example, you could click Insert Picture to open the Insert Picture dialog box. To open a submenu of relevant Help articles, point to the arrow button next to the "insert picture" command in the Get Help section. If you prefer to expand your search to the entire web, you could click the More search results for "insert picture" command at the bottom of the menu to open the Search pane with links to articles from Wikipedia and other sources. See Figure 1–44.

Figure 1–44 **Word Help menu**

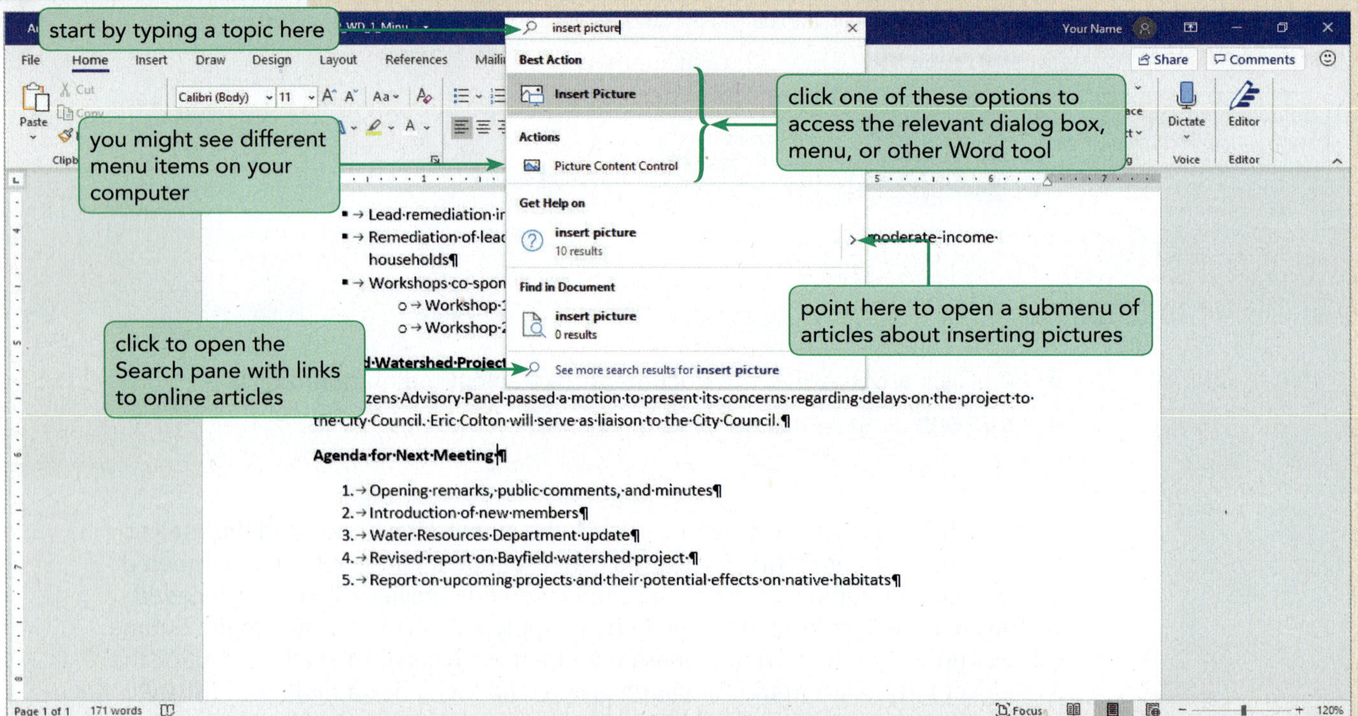

2. Point to the **arrow button** next to "insert picture" in the Get Help on section. A menu of articles about inserting pictures appears.
3. Click the first item in the menu to open the Help pane with information about inserting pictures.
4. Scroll down in the Help pane to read all the information. Note that you can use the Search help box at the top of the Help pane to look up information on other topics.
5. Click the **Close** button in the upper-right corner to close the Help pane.
6. Click the **File** tab, and then click **Close** in the navigation pane to close the document without closing Word.

Word Help is a great way to learn about and access Word's many features. Articles and videos on basic skills provide step-by-step guides for completing tasks, while more elaborate, online tutorials walk you through more complicated tasks. Be sure to take some time on your own to explore Word Help so you can find the information and features you want when you need it.

Review

Session 1.2 Quick Check

1. Explain how to accept a spelling correction suggested by the Editor pane.
2. What orientation should you choose if you want your document to be wider than it is tall?
3. What is the default font size?
4. What is a gallery?
5. What is the default text alignment?
6. Explain two important facts about a picture inserted as an inline object.
7. What is the default shape for bullets in a bulleted list?

Practice

Review Assignments

Data Files needed for the Review Assignments: NP_WD_1-3.docx, NP_WD_1-4.docx, Support_WD_1_Glass.png

David asks you to write a cover letter to Roberto Campos at the New Day Neighborhood Center to accompany a pamphlet on water quality that will be used in an upcoming workshop. After that, he wants you to create an envelope for the letter, and then format a flyer announcing free educational tours of Portland's water resource facilities. Finally, he needs you to add bulleted and numbered list to the minutes for the Citizen Advisory Panel's July meeting. Change the Zoom level as necessary while you are working. Complete the following steps:

1. Open a new, blank document and then save the document as **NP_WD_1_CamposLetter** in the location specified by your instructor.
2. Type the date **February 15, 2025** using AutoComplete for "February."
3. Press ENTER twice, and then type the following inside address, using the default paragraph spacing and pressing ENTER once after each line:

   Roberto Campos

   New Day Neighborhood Center

   6690 Sullivan Circle

   Portland, OR 97203
4. Type **Dear Roberto:** as the salutation, press ENTER, and then type the following two paragraphs as the body of the letter:

   Enclosed you will find the water quality pamphlet we discussed. I hope the young people taking part in your sustainability workshop find this information useful. Additional data on our city's water supply is available at www.water.portland.cengage.com.

   Keep in mind that we also offer free educational tours of our water resources facilities. We can accommodate groups as large as thirty.
5. Press ENTER, type **Sincerely yours,** as the complimentary closing, press ENTER three times, type **David Alzacar** as the signature line, insert a manual line break, and type **Communications Director** as his title.
6. Press ENTER, type your initials, insert a manual line break, and then use the Undo button to make your initials all lowercase, if necessary.
7. Type **Enclosure** and save the document.
8. Scroll to the beginning of the document and proofread your work. Remove any wavy underlines by using a shortcut menu or by typing a correction yourself. Remove the hyperlink formatting from the web address.
9. Remove the paragraph spacing from the first three lines of the inside address.
10. Change the top margin to 2.75 inches. Leave the other margins at their default settings.
11. Save your changes to the letter, preview it, print it if your instructor asks you to, and then close it.
12. Create a new, blank document, and then create an envelope. Use Roberto Campos's address (from Step 3) as the delivery address. Use your school's name and address for the return address. Add the envelope to the document. If you are asked if you want to save the return address as the new return address, click No.
13. Save the document as **NP_WD_1_CamposEnvelope** in the location specified by your instructor, and then close the document.
14. Open the document **NP_WD_1-3.docx**, located in the Word1 > Review folder included with your Data Files, and then check your screen to make sure your settings match those in the module.
15. Save the document as **NP_WD_1_DrinkingWater** in the location specified by your instructor.

16. Use the Recheck Document button in the Word Options dialog box to reset the Spelling and Grammar checker, and then use the Editor pane to correct any errors. Ignore any items marked as errors that are in fact correct, and accept any suggestions regarding clarity and conciseness. If the Editor pane does not give you the opportunity to correct all the errors marked in the document, close the Editor pane and correct the errors using shortcut menus.
17. Proofread the document and correct any other errors. Be sure to change "Today" to "**today**" in the last paragraph.
18. Change the page orientation to Landscape and the margins to Narrow.
19. Format the document text in 22-point Times New Roman font.
20. Center the text and the photo.
21. Format the first paragraph with an outside border using the default style, and change the border color to Gold, Accent 4, and the border width to 1½ pt. Add blue shading to the paragraph, using the Blue, Accent 5 color in the Theme Colors section of the Shading gallery. Format the paragraph text in white.
22. Format the last paragraph in the document using the same formatting you applied to the first paragraph.
23. Increase the paragraph spacing after the first paragraph to 42 points. Increase the paragraph spacing before the last paragraph in the document to 42 points.
24. Format the second paragraph with the Gradient Fill: Gold, Accent color 4; Outline: Gold, Accent color 4 text effect. Increase the paragraph's font size to 26 points.
25. Format the text in the third and fourth paragraphs (the first two paragraphs below the photo) using the Blue, Accent 5 font color, and then add bold and italic.
26. Delete the photo and replace it with the **Support_WD_1_Glass.png** photo, located in the Word1 > Review folder.
27. Delete the existing alt text and the text indicating that the description was automatically generated, and then type **Water pouring into a glass**. (Do not include the period after "glass.")
28. Resize the new photo so that it is 3.8" tall, and then add the Soft Edge Rectangle style in the Pictures Styles gallery.
29. Add a page border using the Box setting, a double-line style, the default width, and the Gold, Accent 4 color.
30. Save your changes to the flyer, preview it, and then close it.
31. Open the document **NP_WD_1-4.docx**, located in the Word1 > Review folder, and then check your screen to make sure your settings match those in the module.
32. Save the document as **NP_WD_1_JulyMinutes** in the location specified by your instructor.
33. Format the list of members in attendance as a bulleted list with square bullets, and then format the list of lawn-care initiatives with square bullets (starting with "Alternate-day watering . . ." and ending with "Workshop 2: Drought-Tolerant Gardening"). Indent the paragraphs for Workshop 1 and Workshop 2 so they are formatted with open circle bullets.
34. Format the five paragraphs below the "Agenda for Next Meeting" heading as a numbered list.
35. Use Word Help to look up the topic **work with pictures**. Read the first article, return to the Help home page, and then close Help.

Apply

Case Problem 1

There are no Data Files needed for this Case Problem.

Laufer Commercial Real Estate You are a real estate agent at Laufer Commercial Real Estate, in St. Louis, Missouri. You recently sold a building and need to forward an extra key to the building's new owner. Create a cover letter to accompany the key by completing the following steps. Because your office is currently out of letterhead, you'll start the letter by typing a return address. As you type the letter, remember to include the appropriate number of blank paragraphs between the various parts of the letter. Complete the following steps:

1. Open a new, blank document, and then save the document as **NP_WD_1_Kettering** in the location specified by your instructor. If necessary, change the Zoom level to 120%.
2. Type the following return address, using the default paragraph spacing and replacing [Your Name] with your first and last names:
   [Your Name]
   Laufer Commercial Real Estate
   3996 Pepperdine Avenue, Suite 10
   St. Louis, MO 63105
3. Type **November 9, 2025** as the date, leaving a blank paragraph between the last line of the return address and the date.
4. Type the following inside address, using the default paragraph spacing and leaving the appropriate number of blank paragraphs after the date:
   Sam Kettering
   Marshall-Hempstead Properties
   4643 Jillian Drive
   Columbia, MO 65201
5. Type **Dear Mr. Kettering:** as the salutation.
6. To begin the body of the letter, type the following two paragraphs: **Enclosed please find the extra office key for the apartment building you recently purchased at 362 Neuhauser Road. The previous owner found it when he was cleaning out his desk and asked me to send it to you.**
   It was a pleasure working with you. In order to improve our service, I would be grateful if you would review the following questions, and then email me your answers at kettering@laufer.cengage.com.
7. Remove the hyperlink formatting from the email address.
8. Add the following questions as separate paragraphs, using the default paragraph spacing:
   Did you find our staff helpful and well-informed?
   Were you satisfied with the service provided during your real estate transaction?
   Would you recommend Laufer Commercial Real Estate to others?
   Can you suggest any ways to improve our service?
9. Insert a new paragraph after the last question, and then type the complimentary closing **Sincerely,** (including the comma).
10. Leave the appropriate amount of space for your signature, type your full name, insert a manual line break, and then type **Licensed Real Estate Agent**.
11. Type **Enclosure** in the appropriate place.
12. Use the Editor pane to correct any errors. Ignore any items marked as errors that are in fact correct (such as the word "Neuhauser"), and accept any suggestions regarding clarity and conciseness. Instruct the Editor pane to ignore the recipient's name. If the Editor pane does not give you the opportunity to correct all the errors marked in the document, close the Editor pane and correct the errors using shortcut menus.

13. Italicize the four paragraphs containing the questions.
14. Format the list of questions as a bulleted list with square bullets.
15. Remove the paragraph spacing from the first three lines of the return address. Do the same for the first three paragraphs of the inside address.
16. Center the four paragraphs containing the return address, format them in 16-point font, and then add the Fill: Blue, Accent color 1; Shadow text effect.
17. Deselect any selected text, and then create an envelope in the current document. Use Sam Kettering's address (from Step 4) as the delivery address. Edit the delivery address as necessary to remove any incorrect text. Use the return address shown in Step 2. Add the envelope to the NP_WD_1_Kettering.docx document. If you are asked if you want to save the return address as the default return address, click No.
18. Save the document, preview it, and close it.

Create

Case Problem 2

Data Files needed for this Case Problem: NP_WD_1-5.docx, Support_WD_1_Sign.jpg

Newland Health Care You work as a marketing coordinator for Newland Health Care. You need to create a flyer promoting the weekly flu shot clinics that will be held in November. Complete the following steps:

1. Open the document **NP_WD_1-5.docx** located in the Word1 > Case2 folder included with your Data Files, and then save the document as **NP_WD_1_Flu** in the location specified by your instructor.
2. In the document, replace "Student Name" with your first and last names.
3. Use the Editor pane to correct any errors. Instruct the Editor pane to ignore your name if Word marks it with a wavy underline. If the Editor pane does not give you the opportunity to correct all the errors marked in the document, close the Editor pane and correct the errors using shortcut menus.
4. Change the page margins to Narrow.
5. Complete the flyer as shown in Figure 1–45. Use the photo **Support_WD_1_Sign.jpg** located in the Word1 > Case2 folder. Use the default line spacing and paragraph spacing unless otherwise specified in Figure 1–45.

Figure 1–45 **Formatted Newland Health Care flyer**

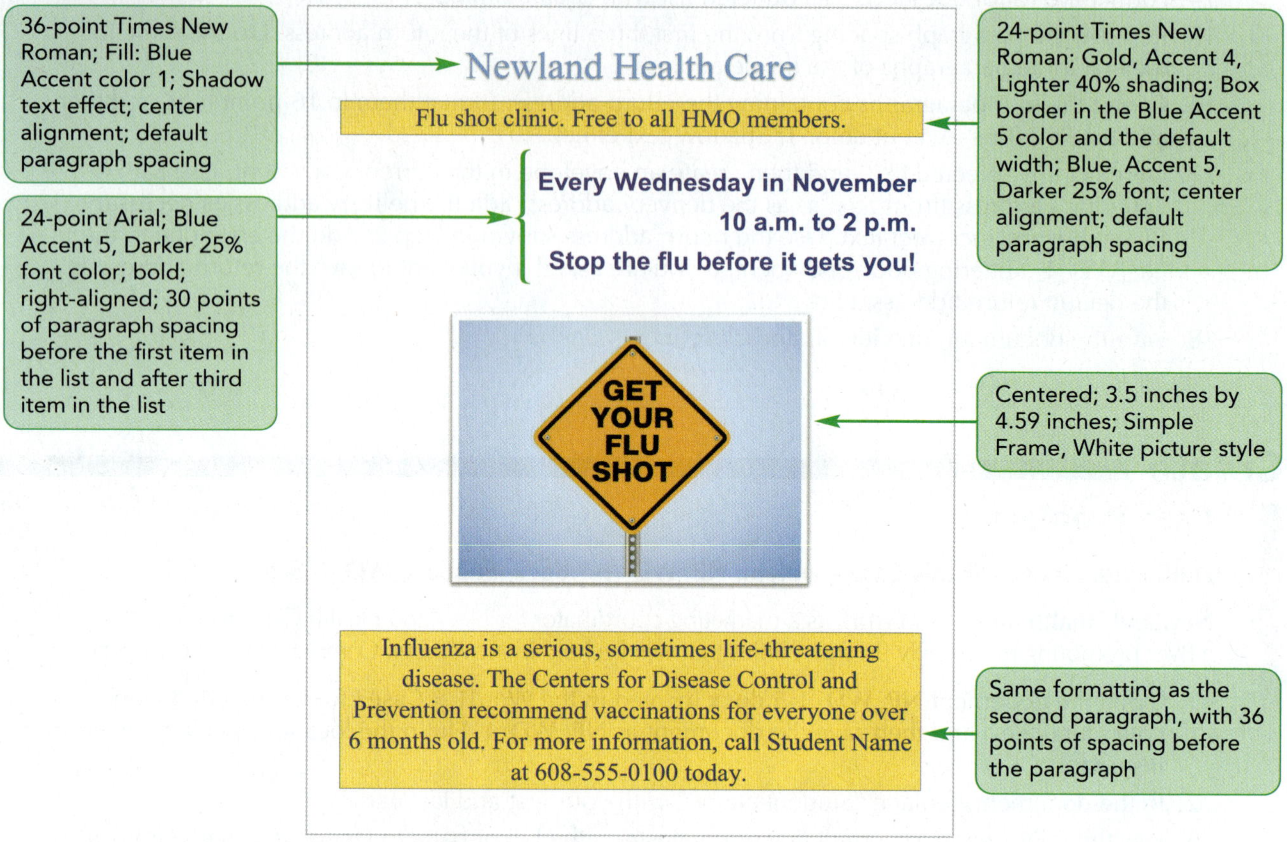

iStock.com/chokkicx

6. Delete the existing alt text and the text indicating that the description was automatically generated, and then type **A sign with the message "GET YOUR FLU SHOT"**. (Do not include the period after the quotation mark.)
7. Save the document, preview it, and then close it.

Module 2

Navigating and Formatting a Document

Editing an Academic Document According to MLA Style

Objectives

Session 2.1

- Read, reply to, delete, and add comments
- Move text using drag and drop
- Cut and paste text
- Copy and paste text
- Navigate through a document using the Navigation pane
- Find and replace text
- Format text with styles

Session 2.2

- Review the MLA style for research papers
- Indent paragraphs
- Insert and modify page numbers
- Create footnotes and endnotes
- Create citations
- Create and update a bibliography
- Modify a source

Case | Cedar Hills Community College

Sabrina Desantes, a student at Cedar Hills Community College, is doing a student internship at Prairie Savings and Loan. She has written a handout for first-time homebuyers that explains the process of getting a mortgage. She asks you to help her finish the handout. The text needs some reorganization and other editing, as well as some formatting so the finished document looks professional and is easy to read.

Sabrina is also taking an American history class and is writing a research paper on Alexander Hamilton, the first Secretary of the Treasury and the founder of the Bank of the United States. To complete the paper, she needs to follow a set of very specific formatting and style guidelines for academic documents.

Sabrina has asked you to help her edit these two very different documents. In Session 2.1, you will review and respond to some comments in the handout and then revise and format that document. In Session 2.2, you will review the MLA style for research papers and then format Sabrina's research paper to match the MLA specifications.

Starting Data Files

Word2 → Module: NP_WD_2-1.docx, NP_WD_2-2.docx

Review: NP_WD_2-3.docx, NP_WD_2-4.docx

Case1: NP_WD_2-5.docx

Case2: NP_WD_2-6.docx

Session 2.1 Visual Overview:

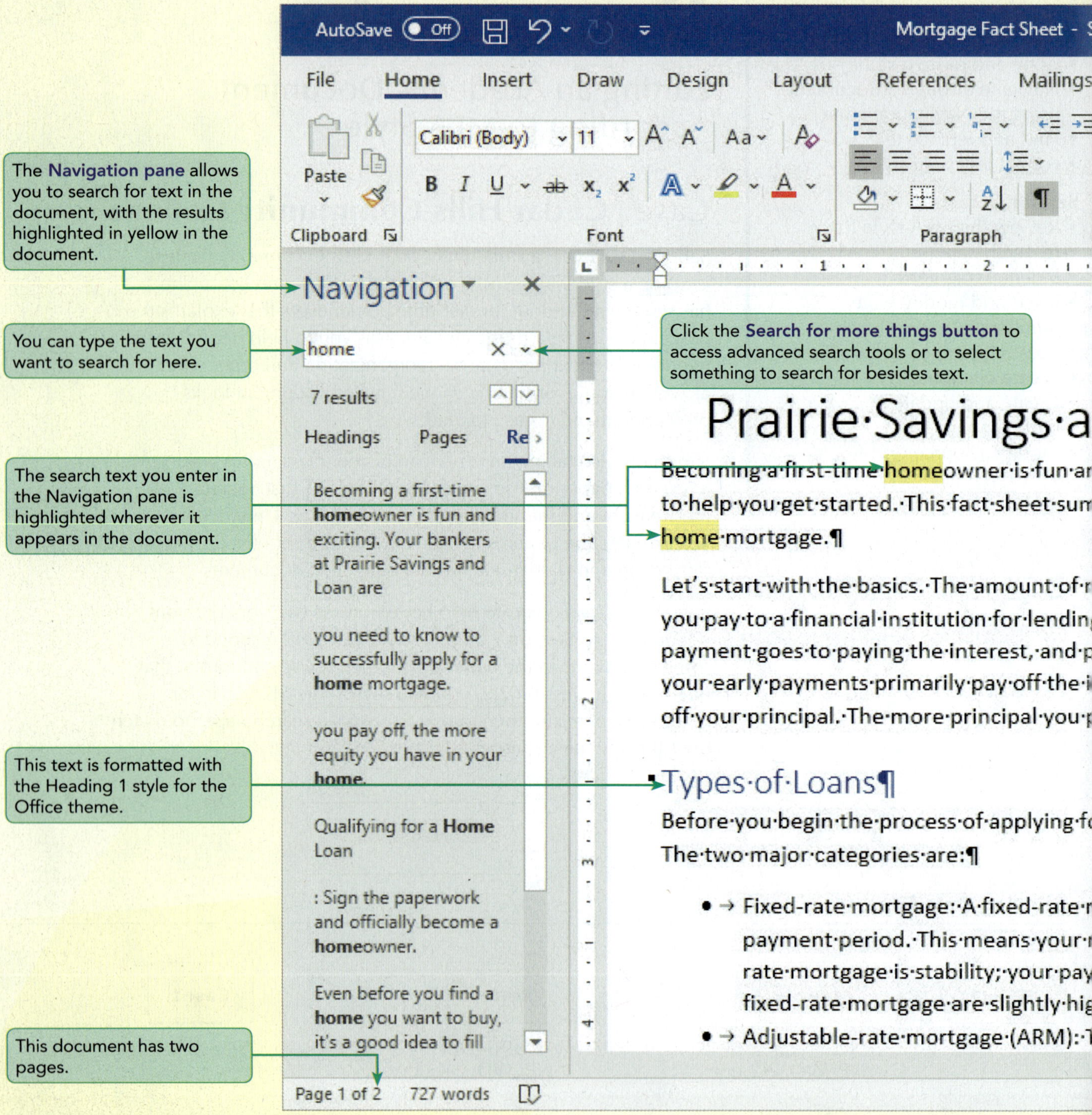

The Navigation Pane and Styles

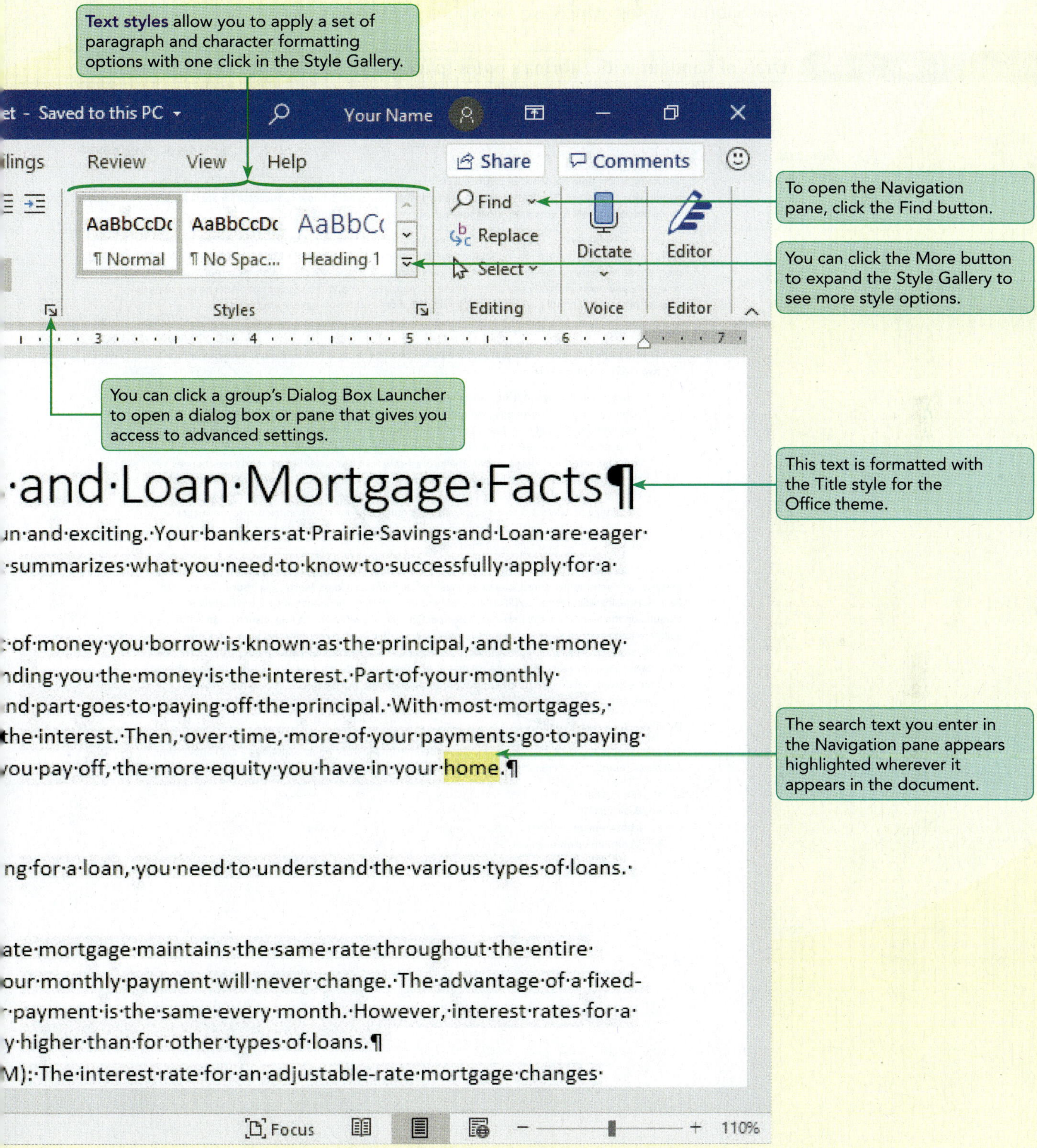

Reviewing the Document

Before revising a document for someone else, it's a good idea to familiarize yourself with its overall structure and the revisions that need to be made. Take a moment to review Sabrina's notes, which are shown in Figure 2–1.

Figure 2–1 Draft of handout with Sabrina's notes (page 1)

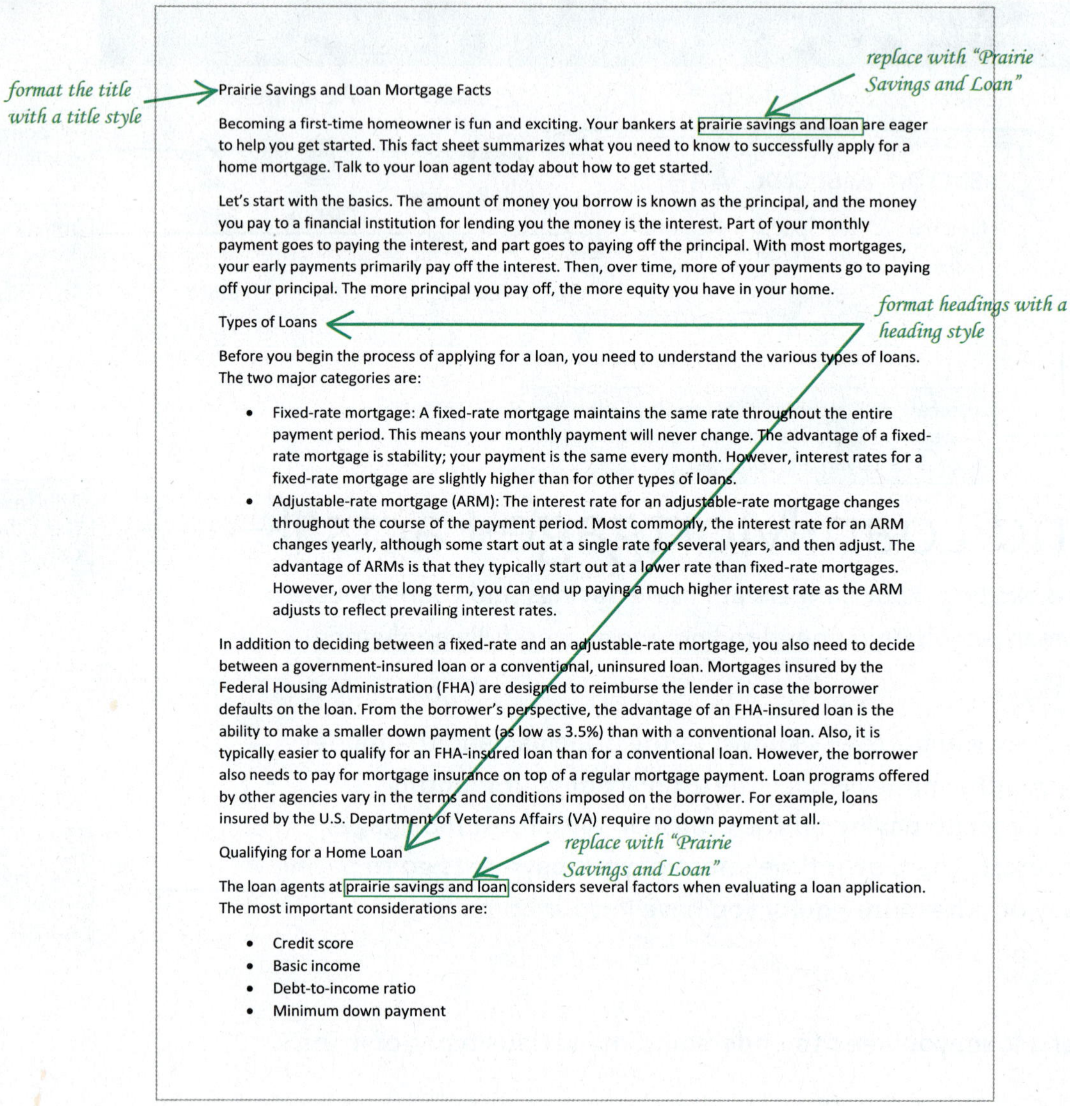

Prairie Savings and Loan Mortgage Facts

Becoming a first-time homeowner is fun and exciting. Your bankers at prairie savings and loan are eager to help you get started. This fact sheet summarizes what you need to know to successfully apply for a home mortgage. Talk to your loan agent today about how to get started.

Let's start with the basics. The amount of money you borrow is known as the principal, and the money you pay to a financial institution for lending you the money is the interest. Part of your monthly payment goes to paying the interest, and part goes to paying off the principal. With most mortgages, your early payments primarily pay off the interest. Then, over time, more of your payments go to paying off your principal. The more principal you pay off, the more equity you have in your home.

Types of Loans

Before you begin the process of applying for a loan, you need to understand the various types of loans. The two major categories are:

- Fixed-rate mortgage: A fixed-rate mortgage maintains the same rate throughout the entire payment period. This means your monthly payment will never change. The advantage of a fixed-rate mortgage is stability; your payment is the same every month. However, interest rates for a fixed-rate mortgage are slightly higher than for other types of loans.
- Adjustable-rate mortgage (ARM): The interest rate for an adjustable-rate mortgage changes throughout the course of the payment period. Most commonly, the interest rate for an ARM changes yearly, although some start out at a single rate for several years, and then adjust. The advantage of ARMs is that they typically start out at a lower rate than fixed-rate mortgages. However, over the long term, you can end up paying a much higher interest rate as the ARM adjusts to reflect prevailing interest rates.

In addition to deciding between a fixed-rate and an adjustable-rate mortgage, you also need to decide between a government-insured loan or a conventional, uninsured loan. Mortgages insured by the Federal Housing Administration (FHA) are designed to reimburse the lender in case the borrower defaults on the loan. From the borrower's perspective, the advantage of an FHA-insured loan is the ability to make a smaller down payment (as low as 3.5%) than with a conventional loan. Also, it is typically easier to qualify for an FHA-insured loan than for a conventional loan. However, the borrower also needs to pay for mortgage insurance on top of a regular mortgage payment. Loan programs offered by other agencies vary in the terms and conditions imposed on the borrower. For example, loans insured by the U.S. Department of Veterans Affairs (VA) require no down payment at all.

Qualifying for a Home Loan

The loan agents at prairie savings and loan considers several factors when evaluating a loan application. The most important considerations are:

- Credit score
- Basic income
- Debt-to-income ratio
- Minimum down payment

Figure 2-1 Draft of handout with Sabrina's notes (page 2)

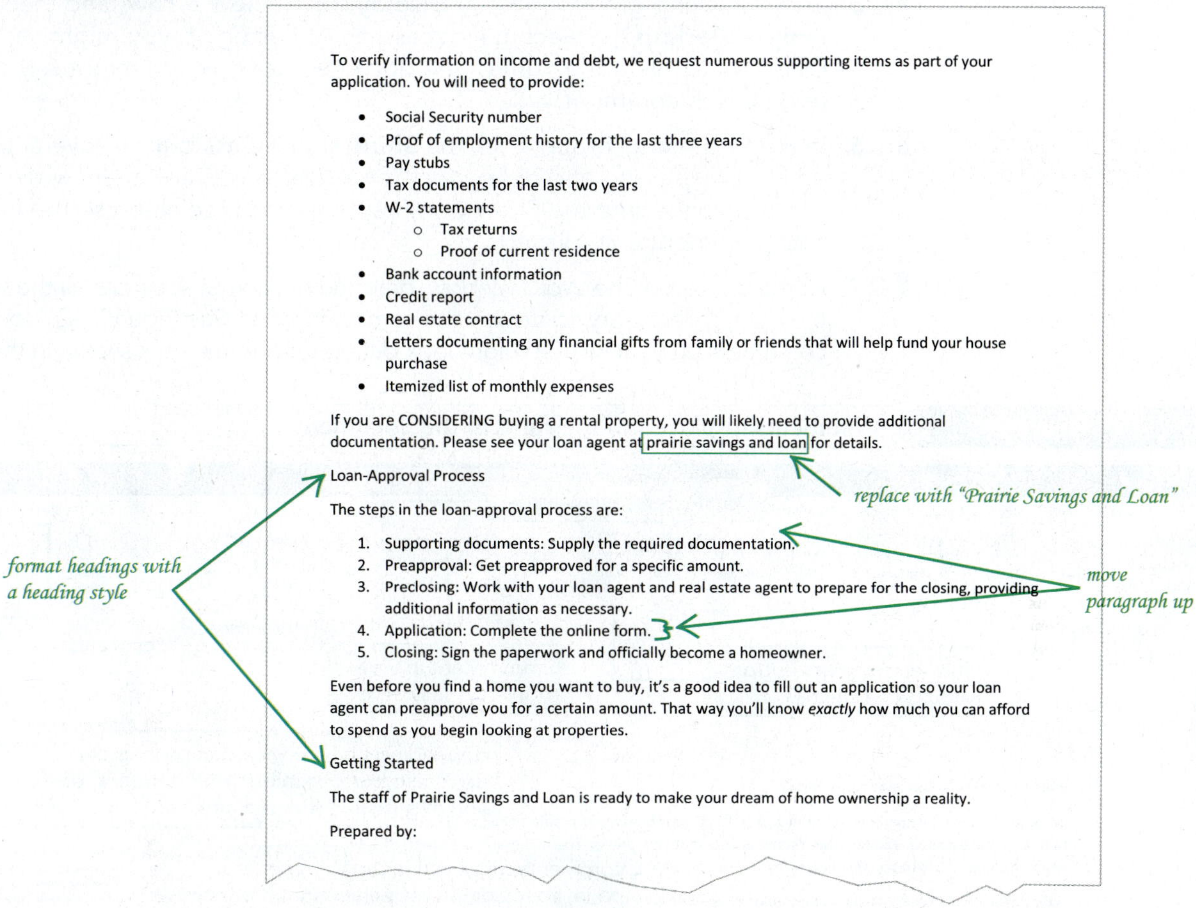
To verify information on income and debt, we request numerous supporting items as part of your application. You will need to provide:

- Social Security number
- Proof of employment history for the last three years
- Pay stubs
- Tax documents for the last two years
- W-2 statements
  - Tax returns
  - Proof of current residence
- Bank account information
- Credit report
- Real estate contract
- Letters documenting any financial gifts from family or friends that will help fund your house purchase
- Itemized list of monthly expenses

If you are CONSIDERING buying a rental property, you will likely need to provide additional documentation. Please see your loan agent at prairie savings and loan for details.

Loan-Approval Process

The steps in the loan-approval process are:

1. Supporting documents: Supply the required documentation.
2. Preapproval: Get preapproved for a specific amount.
3. Preclosing: Work with your loan agent and real estate agent to prepare for the closing, providing additional information as necessary.
4. Application: Complete the online form.
5. Closing: Sign the paperwork and officially become a homeowner.

Even before you find a home you want to buy, it's a good idea to fill out an application so your loan agent can preapprove you for a certain amount. That way you'll know *exactly* how much you can afford to spend as you begin looking at properties.

Getting Started

The staff of Prairie Savings and Loan is ready to make your dream of home ownership a reality.

Prepared by:

Sabrina also included additional guidance in some comments she added to the document file. A **comment** is like an electronic sticky note attached to a word, phrase, or paragraph in a document. Comments appear in the Comments pane, along with the name of the person who added them. Within a single document, you can add new comments, reply to existing comments, and delete comments.

You will open the document now, save it with a new name, and then review Sabrina's comments in Word.

To open and rename the document:

1. **sam** Open the document **NP_WD_2-1.docx** located in the Word2 > Module folder included with your Data Files.
2. Save the document as **NP_WD_2_Mortgage** in the location specified by your instructor.
3. Verify that the document is displayed in Print Layout view, that the Zoom level is set to **120%**, and that the rulers and nonprinting characters are displayed.
4. On the ribbon, click the **Review** tab to display the tools used for working with comments. Comments can be displayed in several different ways, so your first step is to make sure the comments in the document are displayed to match the figures in this book—using Simple Markup view.

5. In the Tracking group, click the **Display for Review arrow**, and then click **Simple Markup** to select it, if necessary. At this point, you might see comment icons to the right of the document text, or you might see the full text of each comment.

6. In the Comments group, click the **Show Comments** button several times to practice displaying and hiding the Comments pane, and then, when you are finished, make sure the Show Comments button is selected so the full text of each comment is displayed.

7. At the bottom of the Word window, drag the horizontal scroll bar all the way to the right, if necessary, to display the comment icons. See Figure 2–2. Note that the comments on your screen might look different from the ones shown in the figure.

Figure 2–2 Comments displayed to the right of the document

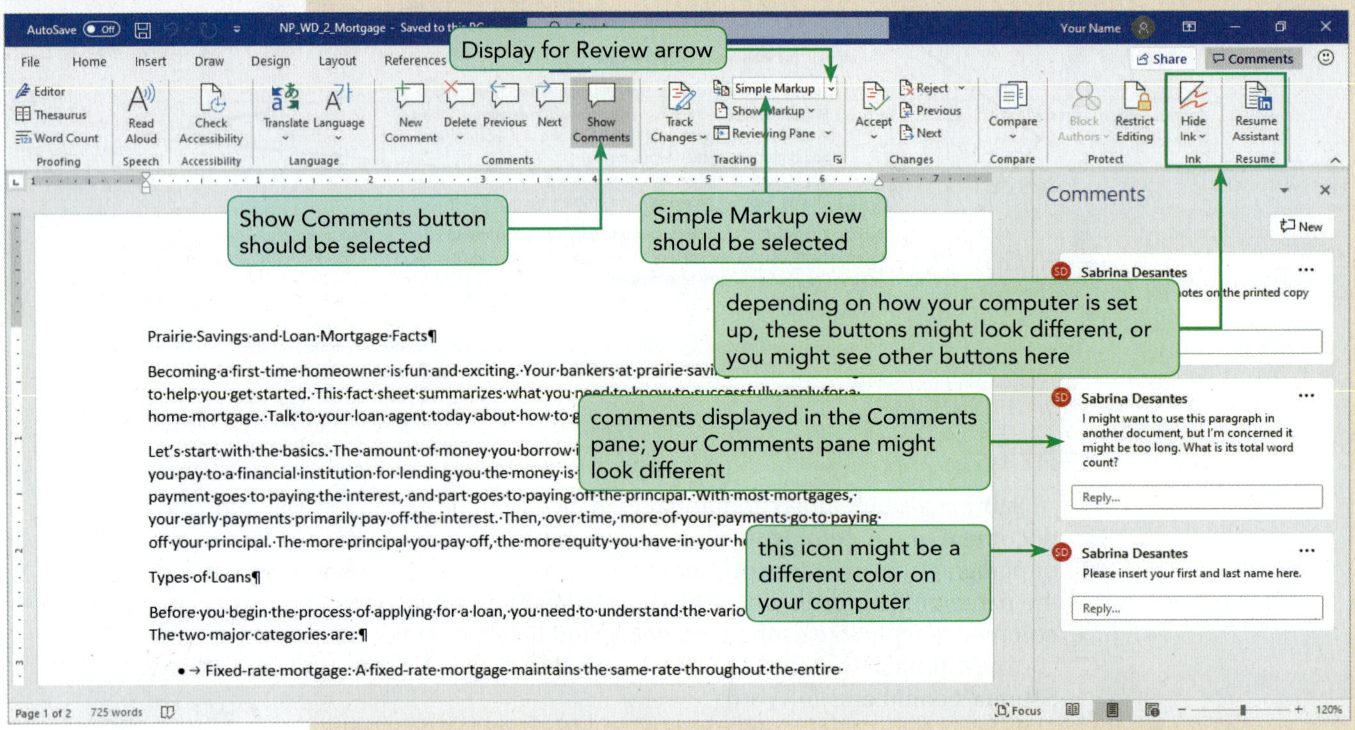

Trouble? Don't be concerned if your Comments pane looks different than the Comments pane in the figures. You can still complete the steps.

Keep in mind that when working on a small monitor, it can be helpful to switch the document Zoom level to Page Width, in which case Word automatically reduces the width of the document to accommodate the Comments pane.

8. Read the document, including the comments. The handout includes the title "Prairie Savings and Loan Mortgage Facts" at the top, as well as headings (such as "Types of Loans" and "Qualifying for a Home Loan") that divide the document into parts. Right now, the headings are hard to spot because they don't look different from the surrounding text. Sabrina used the default font size, 11-point, and the default font, Calibri (Body), for all the text in the document.

9. Scroll down until you can see the first line on page 2 (which begins "To verify information…"), and then click anywhere in that sentence. The message "Page 2 of 2" in the status bar, in the lower-left corner of the Word window, tells you that the insertion point is currently located on page 2 of the two-page document. The shaded space between the first and second pages of the document indicates a page break. To hide the top and bottom margins in a document, as well as the space between pages, you can double-click the shaded space between any two pages.

10. Position the pointer over the shaded space between page 1 and page 2 until the pointer changes to the hide white space pointer, and then double-click. The shaded space disappears. Instead, the two pages are now separated by a gray, horizontal line.

Trouble? If the Header & Footer contextual tab appears on the ribbon, you double-clicked the top or bottom of one of the pages, instead of in the space between them. Click the Close Header and Footer button on the Header & Footer tab, and then repeat Step 10.

11. Use the show white space pointer to double-click the gray horizontal line between pages 1 and 2. The shaded space between the two pages is redisplayed.

Working with Comments

Now that you are familiar with Sabrina's handout, you can review and respond to her comments. The Comment group on the Review tab includes helpful tools for working with comments.

Reference

Working with Comments

- On the ribbon, click the Review tab.
- To display comments in an easy-to-read view, in the Tracking group, click the Display for Review arrow, and then click Simple Markup.
- Use the Show Comments button in the Comments group to display or hide the text of the comments.
- To move the insertion point to the next or previous comment in the document, click the Next button or the Previous button in the Comments group.
- To delete a comment, click anywhere in the comment, and then click the Delete button in the Comments group.
- To delete all the comments in a document, click the Delete arrow in the Comments group, and then click Delete All Comments in Document.
- To add a new comment, select the document text you want to comment on, click the New Comment button in the Comments group, type the comment text, and then click the Post comment button.
- To reply to a comment, click the Reply box in the comment, type your reply, and then click the Post reply button.
- To indicate that a comment and all of its replies are no longer a concern, click the More thread actions button, and then click Resolve thread.
- To respond to a resolved comment, click Reopen in the comment, and then type your reply.

To review and respond to the comments in the document:

1. Press **CTRL+HOME** to move the insertion point to the beginning of the document.
2. On the Review tab, in the Comments group, click the **Next** button. The first comment now has an outline, indicating that it is selected. See Figure 2–3.

Figure 2–3 Comment attached to document text

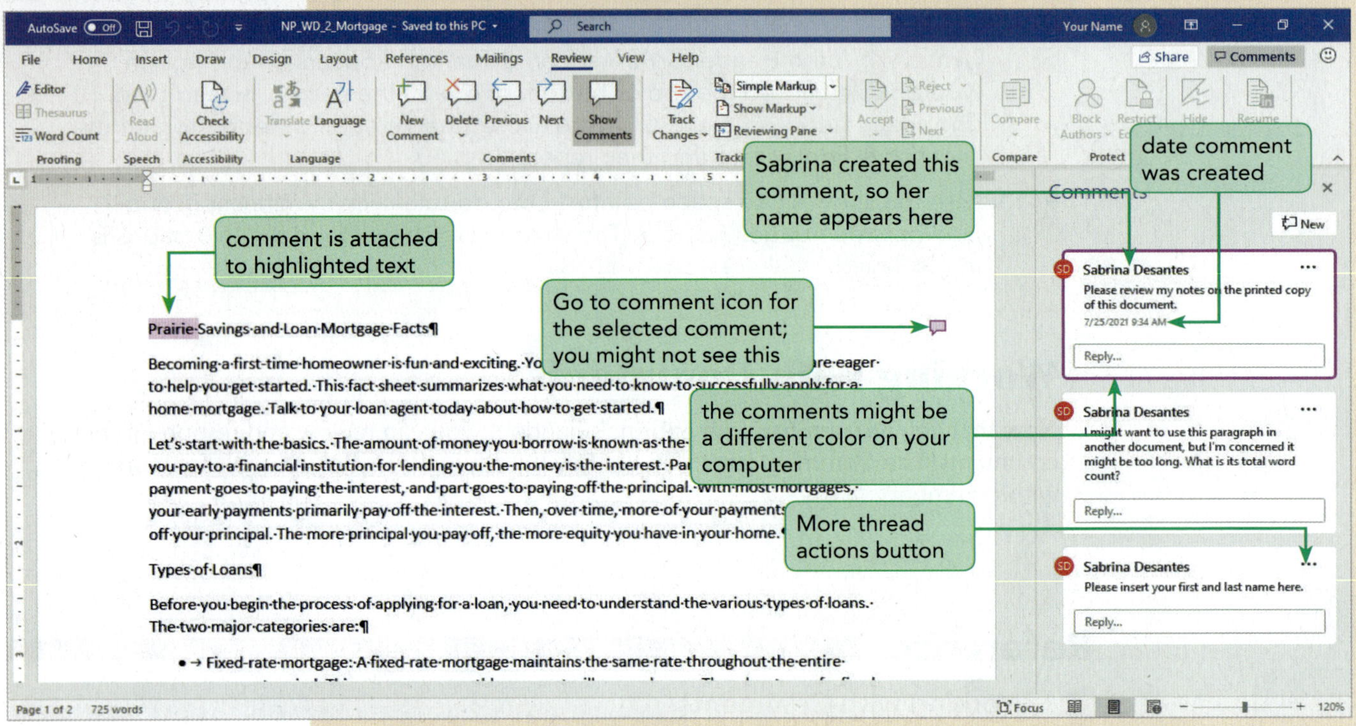

In the document, the text "Prairie" is highlighted. Because Sabrina created the comment, her name appears at the beginning of the comment. In the Comments pane, the current comment has a colored outline.

3. Read the comment, and then in the Comments group, click the **Next** button to select the next comment. According to this comment, Sabrina wants to know the total word count of the paragraph the comment is attached to. You can get this information by selecting the entire paragraph and locating the word count in the status bar.
4. Triple-click anywhere in the second paragraph of the document (which begins "Let's start with the basics...") to select the paragraph. In the status bar, the message "89 of 725 words" tells you that 89 of the document's 725 words are currently selected. So the answer to Sabrina's question is 89.

   Trouble? Don't be concerned if you see a slightly different word count in the status bar. No matter what you see, type the number indicated in Step 5.
5. Click the second comment to select it again, click the **Reply** box, type **89**, and then click the **Post reply** button in the comment if you see it on your screen. Your reply appears below Sabrina's original comment.

If you are logged in, the name that appears in your reply comment is the name associated with your Microsoft account. If you are not logged in, the name in the Reply comment is taken from the User name box on the General tab of the Word Options dialog box.

6. In the Comments group, click the **Next** button to select the next comment, which asks you to insert your name after "Prepared by:" at the end of the document.
7. Click after the colon in "Prepared by:", press **SPACEBAR**, and then type your first and last names. To indicate that you have complied with Sabrina's request by adding your name, you could click the comment in the Comments pane, click the More thread actions button, and then click Resolve thread. However, in this case, you'll simply delete the comment. Sabrina also asks you to delete the first comment.
8. Click anywhere in the final comment, and then in the Comments group, click the **Delete** button.
9. In the Comments group, click the **Previous** button multiple times until the comment at the beginning of the document is selected, and then click the **Delete** button to delete the comment. Note that to delete all the comments in the document, you could click the Delete arrow in the Comments group, and then click Delete All Comments in Document.

Insight

Changing the Username

To change the username associated with your copy of Word, click the Dialog Box Launcher in the Tracking group on the Review tab, and then click Change User Name. From there, you can change the username and the initials associated with your copy of Word. To override the name associated with your Microsoft account and use the name that appears in the User name box in the Word Options dialog box instead, select the "Always use these values regardless of sign in to Office" check box. However, there is no need to change these settings for this module, and you should never change them on a shared computer at school unless specifically instructed to do so by your instructor.

As you reviewed the document, you might have noticed that, on page 2, a word appears in all uppercase letters. This is probably just a typing mistake. You can correct it and then add a comment that points out the change to Sabrina.

To correct the mistake and add a comment:

1. Scroll down to the middle of page 2, and then, in the paragraph above the "Loan Approval Process" heading, select the text **CONSIDERING**.
2. On the ribbon, click the **Home** tab.
3. In the Font group, click the **Change Case** button Aa▾, and then click **lowercase**. The text changes to read "considering." Note that you could select Capitalize Each Word to make the first letter in each word you have selected uppercase.
4. Verify that the text is still selected, and then click the **Review** tab on the ribbon.

- **5.** In the Comments group, click the **New Comment** button. A new comment appears, with the insertion point ready for you to begin typing.
- **6.** In the new comment, type **I assumed you didn't want this in all uppercase letters, so I changed it to lowercase.** (including the period) and then click the **Post comment** button in the comment if you see it on your screen. Save the document.

  You can now close the Comments pane because you are finished working with comments.
- **7.** In the Comments group, click the **Show Comments** button. The "Go to comment" icon alerts you to the presence of a comment without taking up all the space required to display the Comments pane. You can point to highlighted text to read a particular comment without displaying the Comments pane.
- **8.** Point to the word "considering" on page 2. The word is highlighted, and the full comment is displayed, as shown in Figure 2–4.

Figure 2–4 **Document with the Go to comment icon**

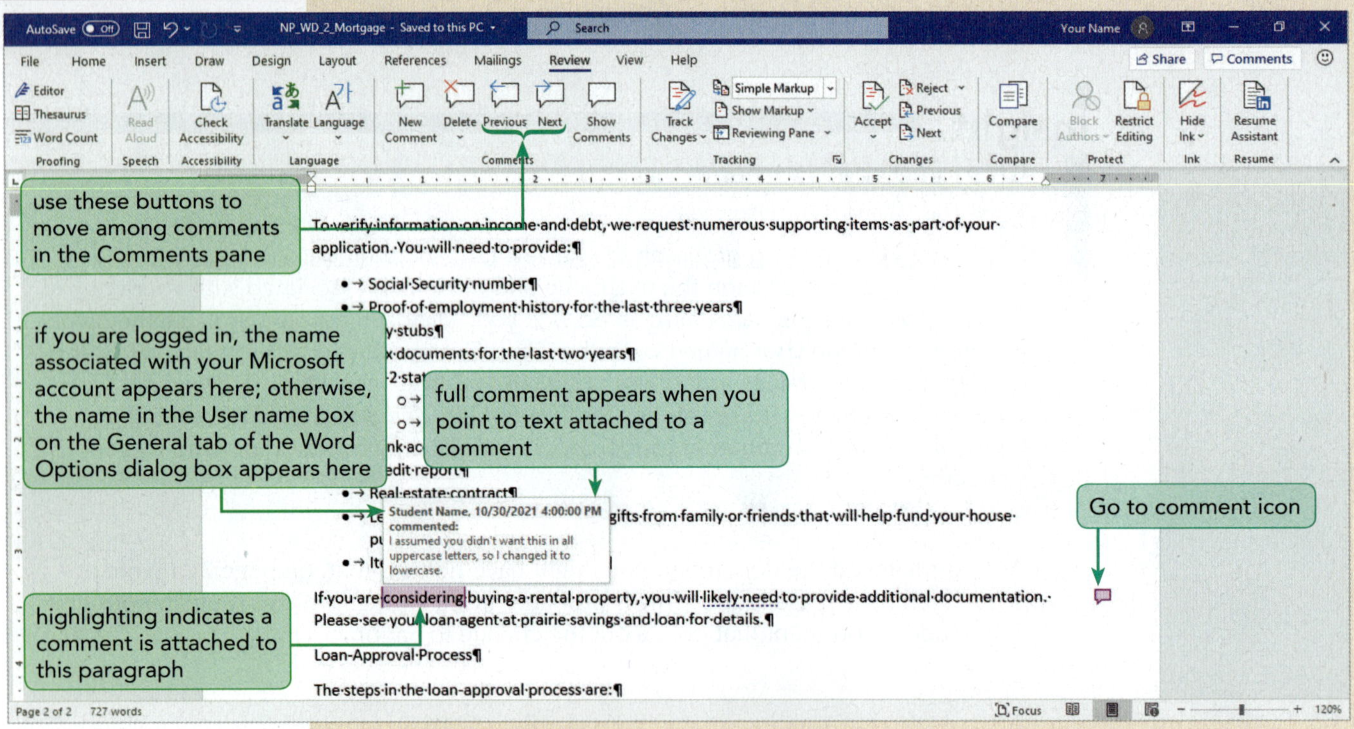

- **9.** Click anywhere outside the comment to close it.

Moving Text in a Document

One of the most useful features of a word-processing program is the ability to move text easily. For example, Sabrina wants to reorder the information in the numbered list on page 2. You could do this by deleting a paragraph and then retyping it at a new location. However, it's easier to select and then move the text. Word provides several ways to move text—drag and drop, cut and paste, and copy and paste.

Dragging and Dropping Text

To move text with **drag and drop**, you select the text you want to move, press and hold the mouse button while you drag the selected text to a new location, and then release the mouse button.

In the numbered list on page 2, Sabrina wants you to move up the paragraph that reads "Application: Complete the online form" so it is the first item in the list.

To move text using drag and drop:

1. Scroll down to display the numbered list on page 2.
2. Triple-click to select the fourth paragraph in the numbered list, "Application: Complete the online form." Take care to include the paragraph marker at the end. The number 4 remains unselected because it's not actually part of the paragraph text.
3. Position the pointer over the selected text. The pointer changes to a left-pointing arrow.
4. Press and hold the mouse button, and move the pointer slightly until the drag-and-drop pointer appears. A dark black insertion point appears within the selected text.
5. Without releasing the mouse button, drag the pointer to the beginning of the list until the insertion point is positioned to the left of the first "S" in "Supporting documents: Supply the required documentation." Use the insertion point, rather than the pointer, to guide the text to its new location. See Figure 2–5.

Figure 2–5 Moving text with the drag-and-drop pointer

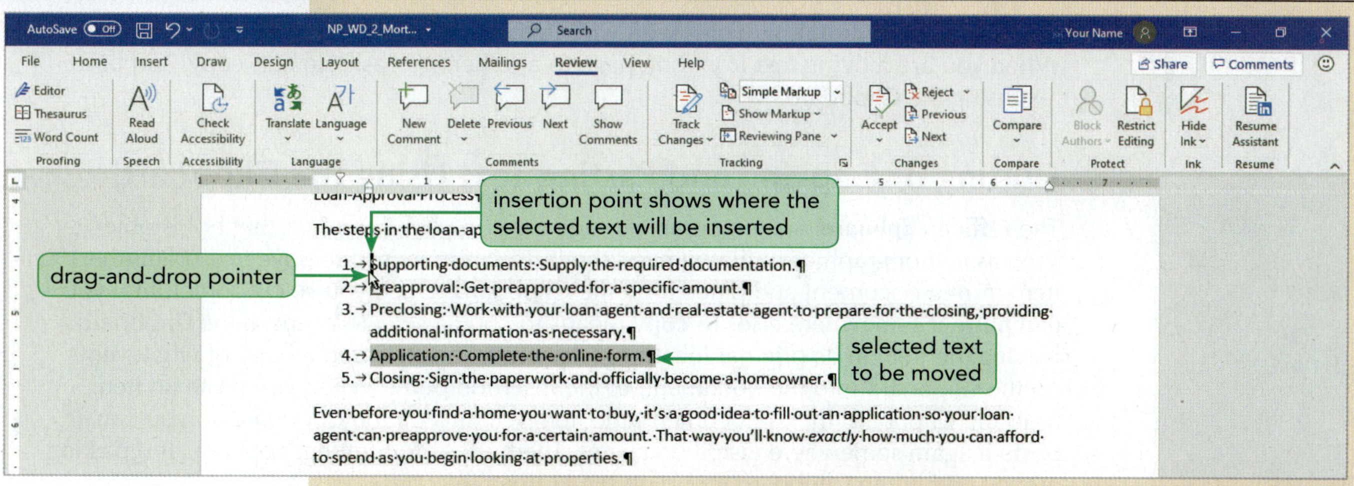

6. Release the mouse button, and then click a blank area of the document to deselect the text. The first item in the list is now "Application: Complete the online form." The remaining paragraphs have been renumbered as paragraphs 2 through 5. See Figure 2–6.

Figure 2–6 **Text in new location**

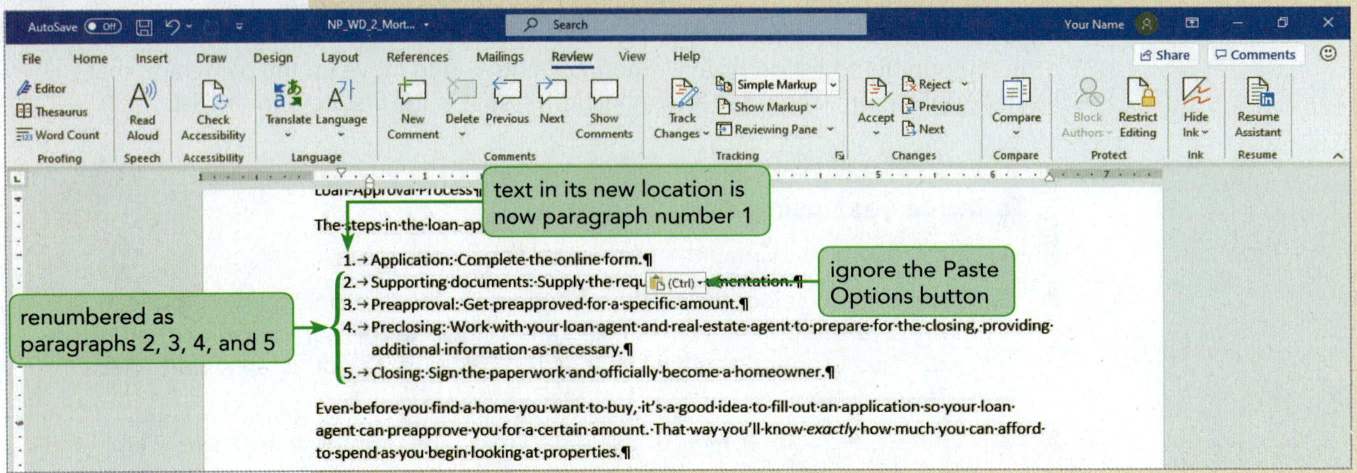

The Paste Options button appears near the newly inserted text, providing access to more advanced options related to pasting text. You don't need to use the Paste Options button right now; it will disappear when you start performing another task.

Trouble? If the selected text moves to the wrong location, click the Undo button on the Quick Access Toolbar, and then repeat Steps 3 through 6.

7. Save the document.

Dragging and dropping works well when you are moving text a short distance. When you are moving text from one page to another, it's easier to cut, copy, and paste text using the Clipboard.

Cutting or Copying and Pasting Text Using the Clipboard

The **Office clipboard** is a temporary storage area on your computer that holds objects such as text or graphics until you need them. To **cut** means to remove text or another item from a document and place it on the Clipboard. Once you've cut something, you can paste it somewhere else. To **copy** means to copy a selected item to the Clipboard, leaving the item in its original location. To **paste** means to insert a copy of whatever is on the Clipboard into the document, at the insertion point. When you paste an item from the Clipboard into a document, the item remains on the Clipboard so you can paste it again somewhere else if you want. The buttons for cutting, copying, and pasting are located in the Clipboard group on the Home tab.

By default, Word pastes text in a new location in a document with the same formatting it had in its old location. To select other ways to paste text, you can use the Paste Options button, which appears next to newly pasted text, or the Paste arrow in the Clipboard group. Both buttons display a menu of paste options. Two particularly useful paste options are Merge Formatting, which combines the formatting of the copied text with the formatting of the text in the new location, and Keep Text Only, which inserts the text using the formatting of the surrounding text in the new location.

When you need to keep track of multiple pieces of cut or copied text, it's helpful to open the **Clipboard pane**, which displays the contents of the Clipboard. You open the Clipboard pane by clicking the Clipboard Dialog Box Launcher in the Clipboard group on the Home tab. When the Clipboard pane is displayed, the Clipboard can store up to 24 text items. When the Clipboard pane is not displayed, the Clipboard can hold only the most recently copied item.

Sabrina would like to move the last sentence in the second paragraph (the paragraph below the title "Prairie Savings and Loan Mortgage Facts"). You'll use cut and paste to move this sentence to a new location.

To move text using cut and paste:

1. Make sure the Home tab is selected on the ribbon.
2. Scroll up until you can see the second paragraph in the document, just below the "Prairie Savings and Loan Mortgage Facts" title.
3. Press and hold **CTRL**, and then click anywhere in the last sentence of the second paragraph, which reads "Talk to your loan agent today about how to get started." The entire sentence is selected, but not the space before it.
4. In the Clipboard group, click the **Cut** button. The selected text is removed from the document and copied to the Clipboard. The space that originally appeared before the sentence remains, so you have to delete it.
5. Press **BACKSPACE** to delete the space.
6. Scroll down to the bottom of page 2, and then click at the end of the second-to-last paragraph in the document, just to the right of the period after "reality."
7. In the Clipboard group, click the **Paste** button. The sentence appears in the new location. Note that Word also inserts a space before the sentence. The Paste Options button appears near the newly inserted sentence.

   Trouble? If a menu opens below the Paste button, you clicked the Paste arrow instead of the Paste button. Press ESC to close the menu, and then repeat Step 7, taking care not to click the arrow below the Paste button.
8. Save the document.

Tip

You can also press CTRL+X to cut selected text. Press CTRL+V to paste the most recently copied item.

Sabrina explains that she'll be using some text from the mortgage fact sheet as the basis for another department handout. She asks you to copy that information and paste it into a new document. You can do this using the Clipboard pane.

To copy text to paste into a new document:

1. In the Clipboard group, click the **Clipboard Dialog Box Launcher**. The Clipboard pane opens on the left side of the document window, as shown in Figure 2–7.

Figure 2–7 **Clipboard pane**

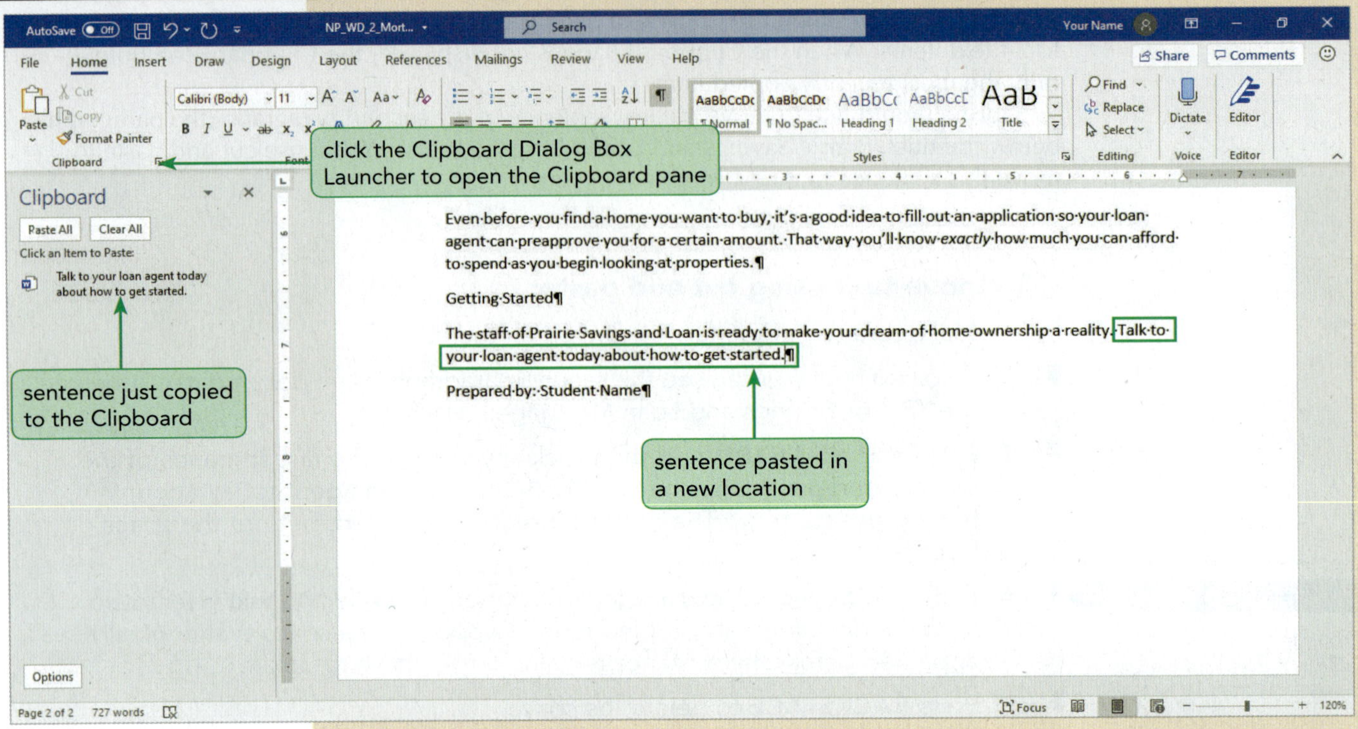

Notice the Clipboard contains the sentence you copied in the last set of steps. Now you can copy another sentence to the Clipboard.

2. Scroll up slightly, if necessary, and then locate the last sentence in the paragraph above the "Getting Started" heading.
3. Press and hold **CTRL**, and then click anywhere in the sentence, which begins "That way you'll know *exactly* how much...." The sentence and the space following it are selected. Notice that the word "exactly" is italicized for emphasis.
4. In the Clipboard group, click the **Copy** button. The sentence appears at the top of the Clipboard pane, as shown in Figure 2–8. You can also copy selected text by pressing CTRL+C.

Figure 2–8 **Items in the Clipboard pane**

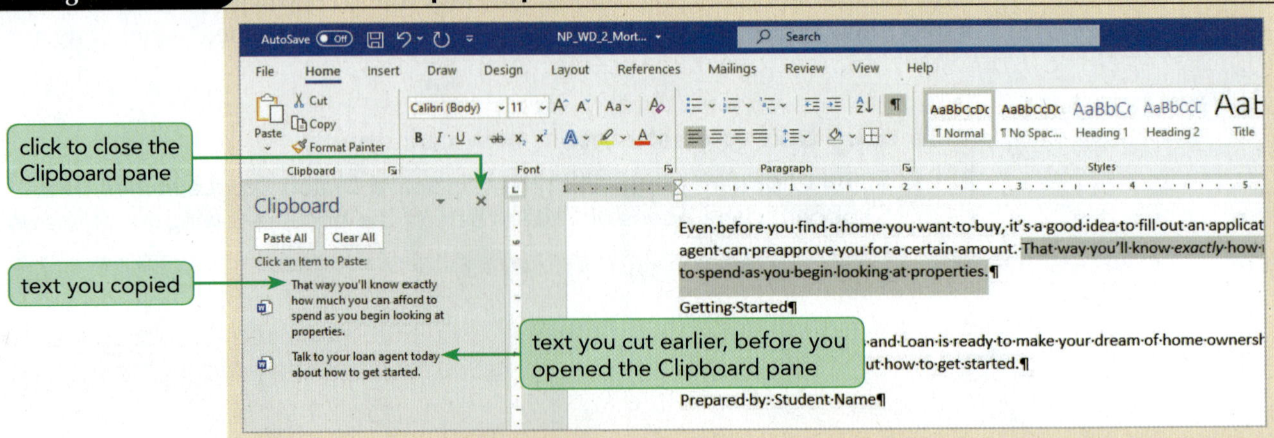

Now you can use the Clipboard pane to insert the copied text into a new document.

To insert the copied text into a new document:

1. Open a new, blank document. Open the Clipboard pane, if necessary. At this point, you could click the Paste All button in the Clipboard pane to paste the entire contents of the Clipboard into the document, but Sabrina wants to paste one item at a time.
2. In the Clipboard pane, click the first item in the list of copied items, which begins "That way you'll know exactly how much...." The text is inserted in the document and the word "exactly" retains its italic formatting.

   Sabrina doesn't want to keep the italic formatting in the newly pasted text. You can remove this formatting by using the Paste Options button, which is visible just below the pasted text.
3. Click the **Paste Options** button (Ctrl) in the document. The Paste Options menu opens, as shown in Figure 2–9.

Figure 2–9 Paste Options menu

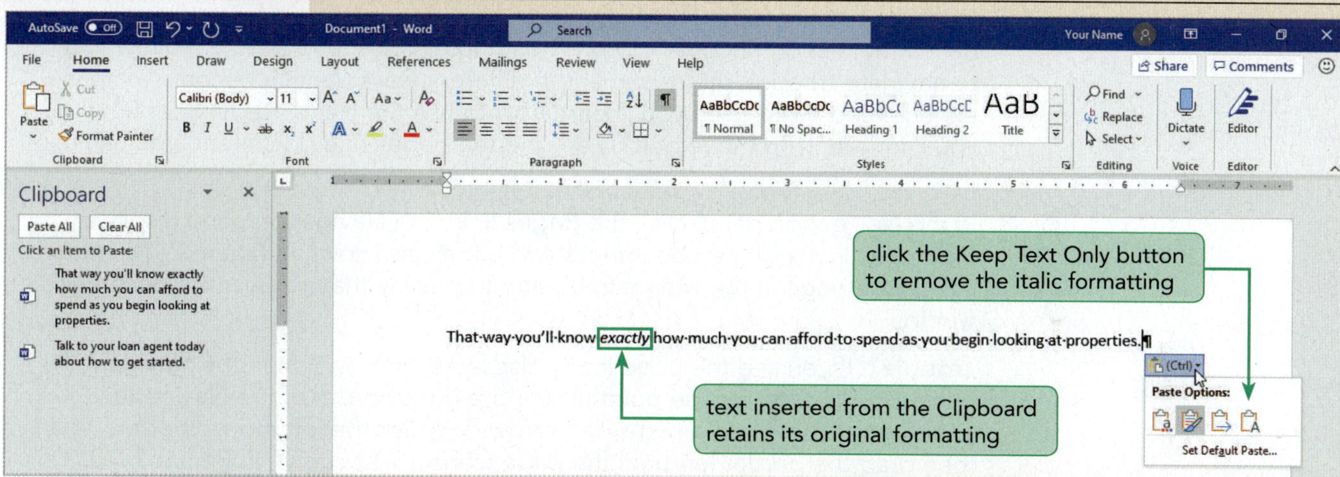

To paste the text without the italic formatting, you can click the Keep Text Only button.

4. Click the **Keep Text Only** button. Word removes the italic formatting from "exactly."
5. Press **ENTER** to start a new paragraph, and then click the second item in the Clipboard pane, which begins "Talk to your loan agent...." The text is inserted as the second paragraph in the document.
6. Save the document as **NP_WD_2_Handout** in the location specified by your instructor, and then close it. You return to the NP_WD_2_Mortgage.docx document, where the Clipboard pane is still open.
7. In the Clipboard pane, click the **Clear All** button. The copied items are removed from the Clipboard.
8. In the Clipboard pane, click the **Close** button. The Clipboard pane closes.
9. Click anywhere in the document to deselect the paragraph, and then save the document.

Tip

To select a paste option before pasting an item, click the Paste arrow in the Clipboard group, and then click the paste option you want.

Using the Navigation Pane

The Navigation pane simplifies the process of moving through a document page by page. You can also use the Navigation pane to locate a particular word or phrase. You start by typing the text you're searching for—the **search text**—in the Search box at the top of the Navigation pane. As shown in the Session 2.1 Visual Overview, Word highlights every instance of the search text in the document. At the same time, a list of the **search results** appears in the Navigation pane. You can click a search result to go immediately to that location in the document.

To become familiar with the Navigation pane, you'll use it to navigate through the document page by page. You'll start by moving the insertion point to the beginning of the document.

To navigate through the document page by page:

1. Press **CTRL+HOME** to move the insertion point to the beginning of the document, making sure the Home tab is still selected on the ribbon.
2. In the Editing group, click the **Find** button. The Navigation pane opens on the left side of the Word window.

   In the box at the top, you can type the text you want to find. The three links below the Search document box—Headings, Pages, and Results—allow you to navigate through the document in different ways. As you become a more experienced Word user, you'll learn how to use the Headings link; for now, you'll ignore it. To move quickly among the pages of a document, you can use the Pages link.
3. In the Navigation pane, click the **Pages** link. The Navigation pane displays thumbnail icons of the document's two pages, as shown in Figure 2–10. You can click a page in the Navigation pane to display that page in the document window.

   Trouble? If you see the page icons displayed side by side in the Navigation pane, position the mouse pointer over the right border of the Navigation pane until it turns into a two-sided arrow ⇔, click the left mouse button, and then drag the border left until the page icons are as shown in Figure 2–10.

Figure 2–10 Document pages displayed in the Navigation pane

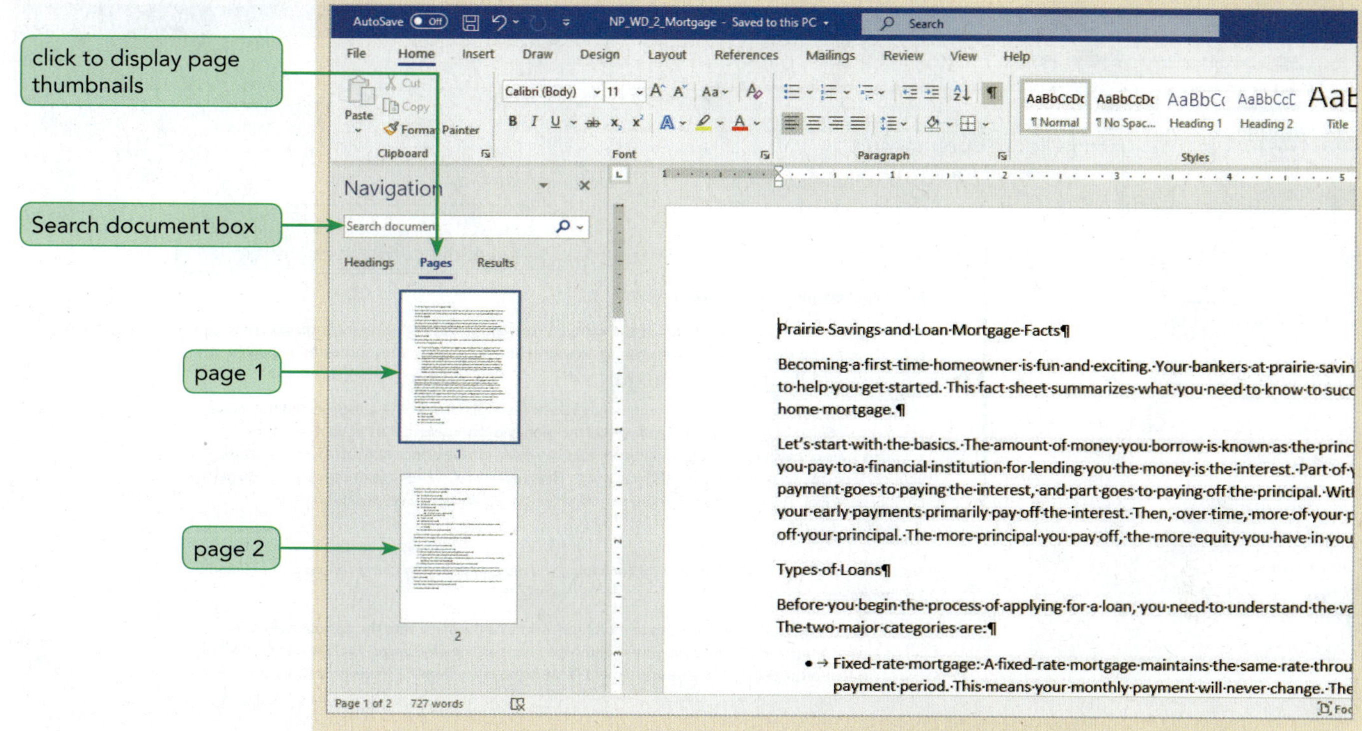

4. In the Navigation pane, click the **page 2** thumbnail. Page 2 is displayed in the document window, with the insertion point blinking at the beginning of the page.
5. In the Navigation pane, click the **page 1** thumbnail to move the insertion point back to the beginning of the document.

Sabrina thinks she might have mistakenly used "prairie savings and loan" in some parts of the document when she actually meant to use "Prairie Savings and Loan." She asks you to use the Navigation pane to find all instances of "prairie savings and loan."

To search for "prairie savings and loan" in the document:

1. In the Navigation pane, click the **Results** link, click the **Search document** box, and then type **prairie savings and loan**. You do not have to press ENTER.

   Every instance of the text "prairie savings and loan" is highlighted in yellow in the document. The yellow highlight is only temporary; it will disappear as soon as you begin to perform any other task in the document. A full list of the five search results is displayed in the Navigation pane. Some of the search results contain "Prairie Savings and Loan" (with "P," "S," and "L" in uppercase letters), while others contain "prairie savings and loan" (with all lowercase letters). To narrow the search results, you need to tell Word to match the case of the search text.
2. In the Navigation pane, click the **Search for more things** button . This displays a two-part menu. In the bottom part, you can select other items to search for, such as graphics or tables. The top part provides more advanced search tools. See Figure 2–11.

Figure 2–11 **Navigation pane with Search for more things menu**

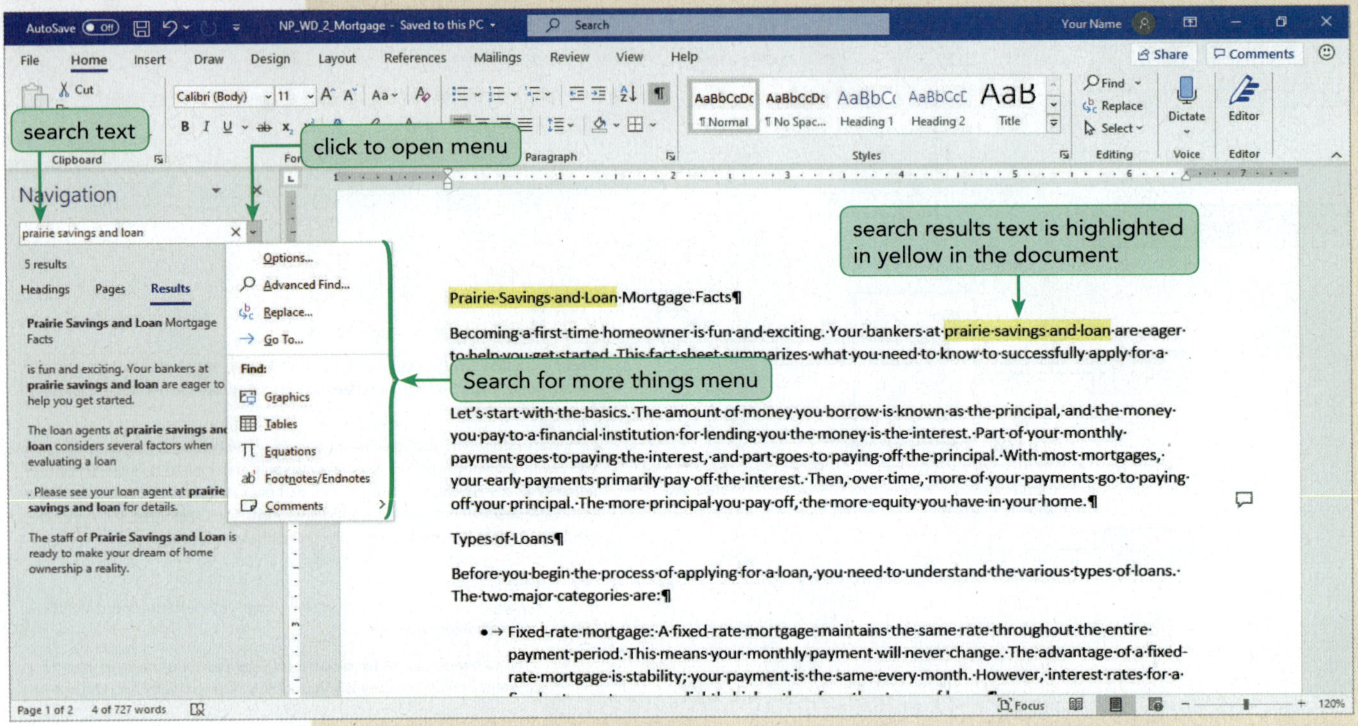

3. At the top of the Search for more things menu, click **Options** to open the Find Options dialog box.

   The check boxes in this dialog box allow you to fine-tune your search. For example, to ensure that Word finds the search text only when it appears as a separate word and not when it appears as part of another word, you could select the Find whole words only check box. Right now, you are concerned only with making sure the search results have the same case as the search text.

4. Click the **Match case** check box to select it, and then click **OK** to close the Find Options dialog box. Now you can search the document again.

5. Press **CTRL+HOME** to move the insertion point to the beginning of the document, click the **Search document** box in the Navigation pane, and then type **prairie savings and loan**. This time, only three search results appear in the Navigation pane, and they contain the lowercase text "prairie savings and loan."

   To move among the search results, you can use the up and down arrows in the Navigation pane.

6. In the Navigation pane, click the **down arrow** button. Word selects the first instance of "prairie savings and loan" in the Navigation pane, as indicated by a blue outline. Also, in the document, the first instance has a gray selection highlight over the yellow highlight. See Figure 2–12.

Figure 2–12 Navigation pane with the first search result selected

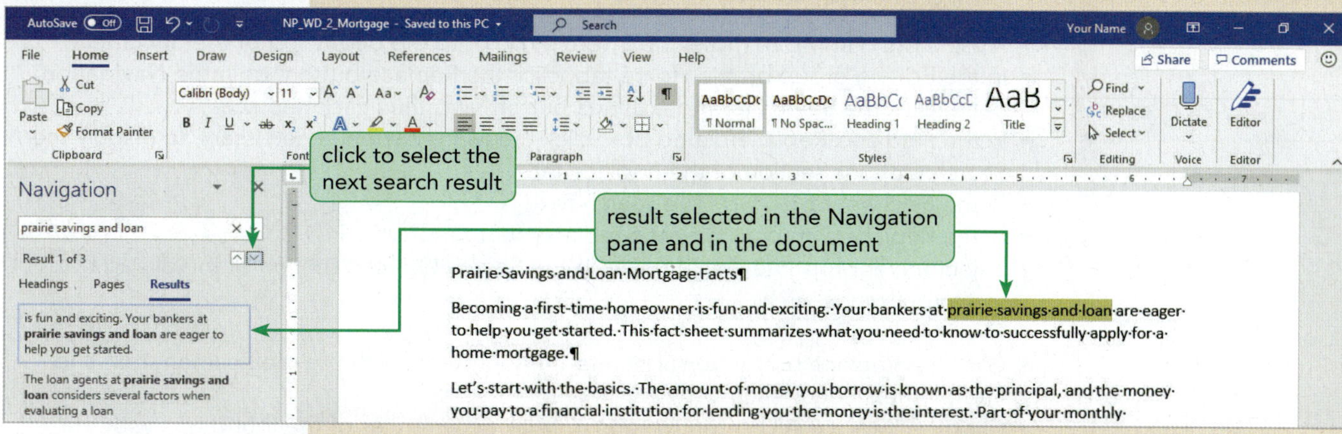

Trouble? If the second instance of "prairie savings and loan" is selected in the Navigation pane, then you pressed the ENTER key after typing "prairie savings and loan" in Step 5. Click the up arrow button to select the first instance.

7. In the Navigation pane, click the **down arrow** button. Word selects the second instance of "prairie savings and loan" in the document and in the Navigation pane.
8. Click the **down arrow** button again to select the third search result, and then click the **up arrow** button to select the second search result again.

   You can also select a search result in the document by clicking a search result in the Navigation pane.
9. In the Navigation pane, click the third search result (which begins ". Please see..."). The third search result is selected in the document and in the Navigation pane.

After reviewing the search results, Sabrina decides she would like to replace the three instances of "prairie savings and loan" with "Prairie Savings and Loan." You can do that by using the Find and Replace dialog box.

Finding and Replacing Text

To open the Find and Replace dialog box from the Navigation pane, click the Search for more things button, and then click Replace. This opens the **Find and Replace dialog box**, with the Replace tab displayed by default. The Replace tab provides options for finding a specific word or phrase in the document and replacing it with another word or phrase. To use the Replace tab, type the search text in the Find what box, and then type the text you want to substitute in the Replace with box. You can also click the More button on the Replace tab to display the Search Options section, which includes the same options you saw earlier in the Find Options dialog box, including the Find whole words only check box and the Match case check box.

After you have typed the search text and selected any search options, you can click the Find Next button to select the first occurrence of the search text; you can then decide whether to substitute the search text with the replacement text.

Reference

Finding and Replacing Text

- Press CTRL+HOME to move the insertion point to the beginning of the document.
- In the Editing group on the Home tab, click the Replace button, or in the Navigation pane, click the Search for more things button, and then click Replace.
- In the Find and Replace dialog box, click the More button, if necessary, to display the Search Options section of the Replace tab.
- In the Find what box, type the search text.
- In the Replace with box, type the replacement text.
- Select the appropriate check boxes in the Search Options section of the dialog box to narrow your search.
- Click the Find Next button.
- Click the Replace button to substitute the found text with the replacement text and find the next occurrence.
- Click the Replace All button to substitute all occurrences of the found text with the replacement text without reviewing each occurrence. Use this option only if you are absolutely certain that the results will be what you expect.

You'll use the Find and Replace dialog box now to replace three instances of "prairie savings and loan" with "Prairie Savings and Loan."

To replace three instances of "prairie savings and loan" with "Prairie Savings and Loan":

1. Press **CTRL+HOME** to move the insertion point to the beginning of the document.
2. In the Navigation pane, click the **Search for more things** button ▾ to open the menu, and then click **Replace**. The Find and Replace dialog box opens with the Replace tab on top.

   The search text you entered earlier in the Navigation pane, "prairie savings and loan," appears in the Find what box. If you hadn't already conducted a search, you would need to type your search text now. Because you selected the Match case check box earlier in the Find Options dialog box, "Match Case" appears below the Find what box.
3. In the lower-left corner of the dialog box, click the **More** button to display the search options. Because you selected the Match case check box earlier in the Find Options dialog box, it is selected here.

   Trouble? If you see the Less button instead of the More button, the search options are already displayed.
4. Click the **Replace with** box, and then type **Prairie Savings and Loan**.
5. Click the **Find Next** button. Word highlights the first instance of "prairie savings and loan" in the document. See Figure 2–13.

Figure 2–13 Find and Replace dialog box

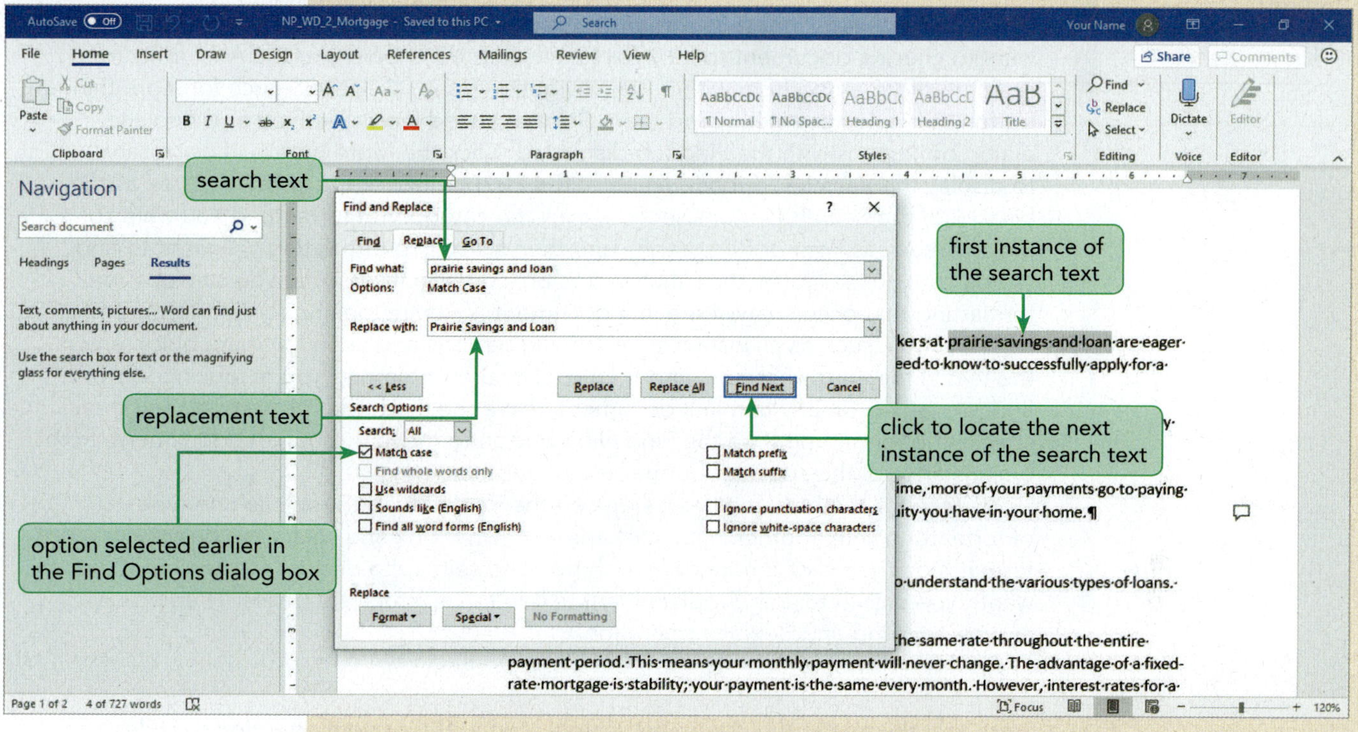

6. Click the **Replace** button. Word replaces "prairie savings and loan" with "Prairie Savings and Loan" and then selects the next instance of "prairie savings and loan." If you do not want to make a replacement, you can click the Find Next button to skip the current instance of the search text and move on to the next. In this case, however, you do want to make the replacement.
7. Click the **Replace** button. Word selects the last instance of "prairie savings and loan."
8. Click the **Replace** button. Word makes the substitution and then displays a message box telling you that Word has finished searching the document.
9. Click **OK** to close the message box, and then in the Find and Replace dialog box, click **Close**.

You are finished with the Navigation pane, so you can close it. But first you need to restore the search options to their original settings. It's a good practice to restore the original search settings so that future searches are not affected by any settings you used for an earlier search.

To restore the search options to their original settings:

1. In the Navigation pane, open the **Find Options** dialog box, deselect the **Match case** check box, and then click **OK** to close the Find Options dialog box.
2. Click the **Close** button ☒ in the upper-right corner of the Navigation pane.
3. Save the document.

Insight

Searching for Formatting

You can search for formatting just as you can search for text. For example, you might want to check a document to look for text formatted in bold and the Arial font. To search for formatting from within the Navigation pane, click the Search for more things button to display the menu, and then click Advanced Find. The Find and Replace dialog box opens with the Find tab displayed. Click the More button, if necessary, to display the Search Options section of the Find tab. Click the Format button at the bottom of the Search Options section, click the category of formatting you want to look for (such as Font or Paragraph), and then select the formatting you want to find.

You can look for formatting that occurs only on specific text, or you can look for formatting that occurs anywhere in a document. If you're looking for text formatted in a certain way (such as all instances of "Prairie Savings and Loan" that are bold), enter the text in the Find what box, and then specify the formatting you're looking for. To find formatting on any text in a document, leave the Find what box empty, and then specify the formatting. Use the Find Next button to move through the document, from one instance of the specified formatting to another.

You can follow the same basic steps on the Replace tab to replace one type of formatting with another. First, click the Find what box and select the desired formatting. Then click the Replace with box and select the desired formatting. If you want, type search text and replacement text in the appropriate boxes. Then proceed as with any Find and Replace operation.

Now that the text in the document is final, you will turn your attention to styles, which affect the look of the entire document.

Working with Styles

A style is a set of formatting options that you can apply by clicking an icon in the Style gallery on the Home tab. Each style is designed for a particular use. For example, the Title style is intended for formatting the title at the beginning of a document.

All the text you type in a document has a style applied to it. By default, text is formatted in the Normal style, which applies 11-point Calibri font, left alignment, 1.08 line spacing, and a small amount of extra space between paragraphs. In other words, the Normal style applies the default formatting you learned about when you first began typing a Word document.

There are two types of styles—character and paragraph. A **paragraph style** is a named set of paragraph and character format settings, such as line spacing, text alignment, and borders, that can be applied to a paragraph to format it all at once. The Normal, Heading, and Title styles all apply paragraph-level formatting. A **character style** is a named group of character format settings; character styles are set up to format only individual characters or words (for example, emphasizing a phrase by adding italic formatting and changing the font color).

One row of the Style gallery is always visible on the Home tab. To display the entire Style gallery, click the More button in the Styles group. After you begin applying styles in a document, the visible row of the Style gallery changes to show the most recently used styles.

You are ready to use the Style gallery to format the document title.

To display the entire Style gallery and then format the document title with a style:

1. Make sure the Home tab is still selected and locate the More button in the Styles group, as shown earlier in the Session 2.1 Visual Overview.
2. In the Styles group, click the **More** button. The Style gallery opens, displaying styles arranged in rows and columns, as shown in Figure 2–14. If your screen is set at a lower resolution than the screenshots in this book, the Style gallery on your screen might contain less than three rows.

Figure 2–14 Displaying the Style gallery

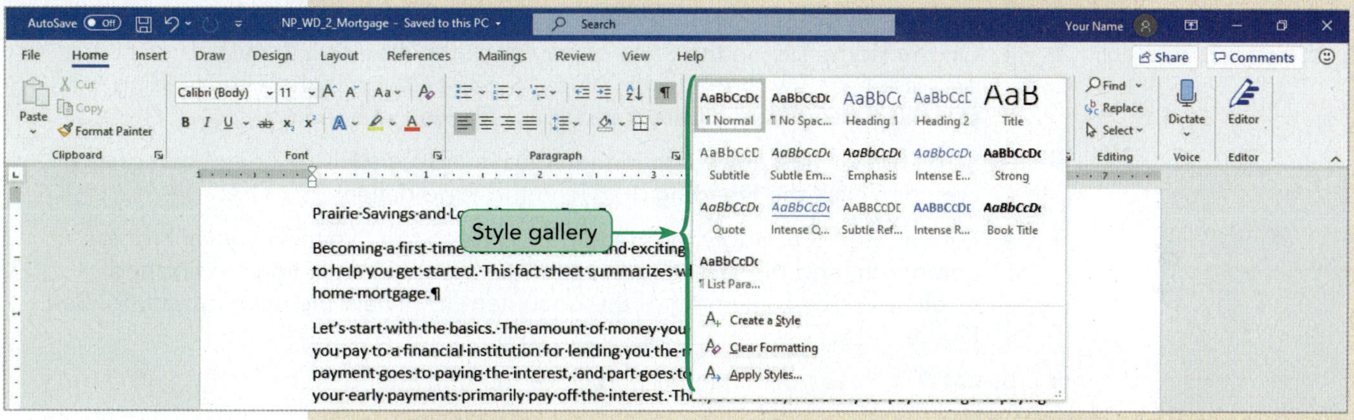

You don't actually need any of the styles in the bottom row now, so you can close the Style gallery.

3. Press **ESC** to close the Style gallery.
4. Scroll up, if necessary, and click anywhere in the first paragraph, "Prairie Savings and Loan Mortgage Facts," if necessary, and then point to (but don't click) the **Title** style, which is the fifth style from the left in the top row of the gallery. The ScreenTip "Title" is displayed, and a Live Preview of the style appears in the paragraph containing the insertion point, as shown in Figure 2–15. The Title style changes the font to 28-point Calibri Light.

Figure 2–15 Title style in the Style gallery

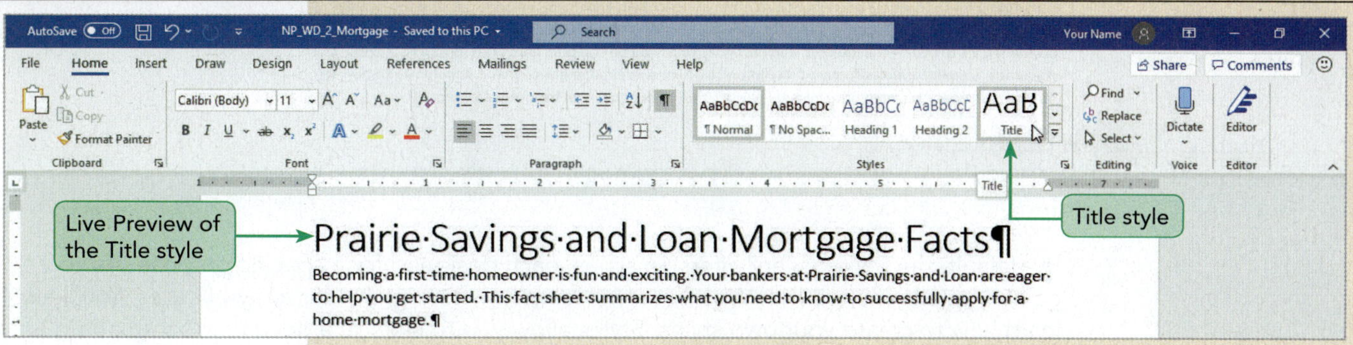

5. Click the **Title** style. The style is applied to the paragraph. After you apply a style, you can always add additional formatting. In this case, Sabrina would like you to center the title.
6. In the Paragraph group, click the **Center** button. The title is centered in the document.

Next, you will format the document headings using the heading styles, which have different levels. The highest level, Heading 1, is used for the major headings in a document, and it applies the most noticeable formatting using a larger font than the other heading styles. (In heading styles, the highest, or most important, level has the lowest number.) The Heading 2 style is used for headings that are subordinate to the highest level headings; it applies slightly less dramatic formatting than the Heading 1 style.

The handout only has one level of headings, so you will apply only the Heading 1 style.

To format text with the Heading 1 style:

1. Click anywhere in the "Types of Loans" paragraph.
2. On the Home tab, in the Style gallery, click the **Heading 1** style. The paragraph is now formatted in blue, 16-point Calibri Light. The Heading 1 style also inserts some paragraph space above the heading.
3. Scroll down, click anywhere in the "Qualifying for a Home Loan" paragraph, and then click the **Heading 1** style in the Style gallery.
4. Repeat Step 3 to apply the Heading 1 style to the "Loan Approval Process" paragraph, and the "Getting Started" paragraph. When you are finished, scroll up to the beginning of the document to review the new formatting. See Figure 2–16.
5. **sam** Save your changes and close the document.

Figure 2–16 Document with Title and Heading 1 styles

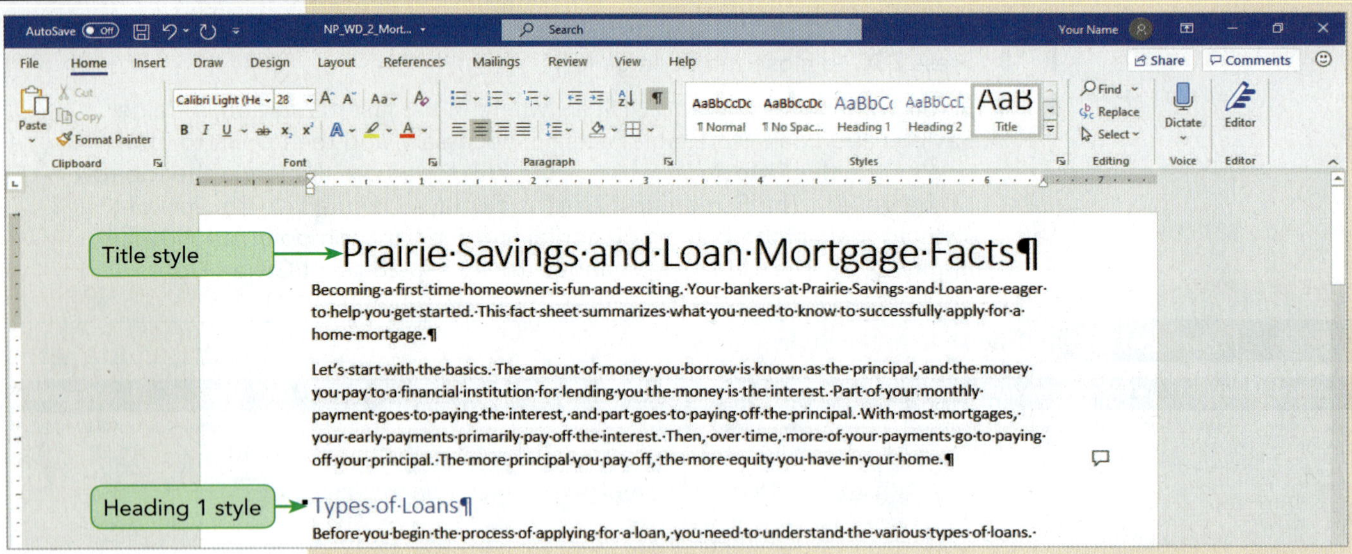

By default, the Style gallery offers 16 styles, each designed for a specific purpose. As you gain more experience with Word, you will learn how to use a wider array of styles. You'll also learn how to create your own styles. Styles allow you to change a document's formatting in an instant. But the benefits of heading styles go far beyond attractive formatting. Heading styles allow you to reorganize a document or generate a table of contents with a click of the mouse. Also, heading styles are set up to keep a heading and the body text that follows it together, so a heading is never separated from its body text by a page break. Each Word document includes nine levels of heading styles, although only the Heading 1 and Heading

2 styles are available by default in the Style gallery. Whenever you use the lowest heading style in the Style gallery, the next-lowest level is added to the Style gallery. For example, after you use the Heading 2 style, the Heading 3 style appears in the Styles group in the Style gallery.

Insight

Creating a Resume with the Resume Assistant

Word Styles are particularly useful when formatting a resume. For additional help in creating a resume, you can use the Resume Assistant pane, which allows you to look for ideas on what to include in your resume. If Word detects that you are working on a document that is formatted like a resume, you might see a suggestion box with the heading "Working on a Resume?" If so, you can click See resume suggestions to open the Resume Assistant. Otherwise, to open it manually, click the Resume Assistant button in the Resume group on the Review tab. This opens the Resume Assistant pane, where you can click Get started to search for tips and examples provided by LinkedIn.

On the first line, type the name of the job (role) you are looking for, and then enter the industry that interests you. For example, you might type "Loan Agent" on the first line and "Banking" on the second line. As you type text in the Resume Assistant, a menu appears where you can click possible search terms. After you've entered your role and industry, you'll see a list of examples. (You might have to click See examples first.) Click Read more in any example to display the full resume. To look for resumes for different jobs, click the Back button, delete the role and industry you entered previously, and type new ones. You can scroll down in the Resume Assistant pane to see a list of top skills for the role you searched on, as well as suggested jobs and articles about resume writing.

Sabrina's mortgage fact sheet is now finished. She will review it, delete the comments, and have copies printed for new homebuyers.

Review

Session 2.1 Quick Check

1. Explain how to insert a comment in a document.
2. Which paste option inserts copied text using the formatting of the surrounding text?
3. How can you ensure that the Navigation pane will find instances of "Prairie Savings and Loan" instead of "prairie savings and loan"?
4. Which style is applied to all text in a new document by default?
5. What are the two types of styles?

Session 2.2 Visual Overview:

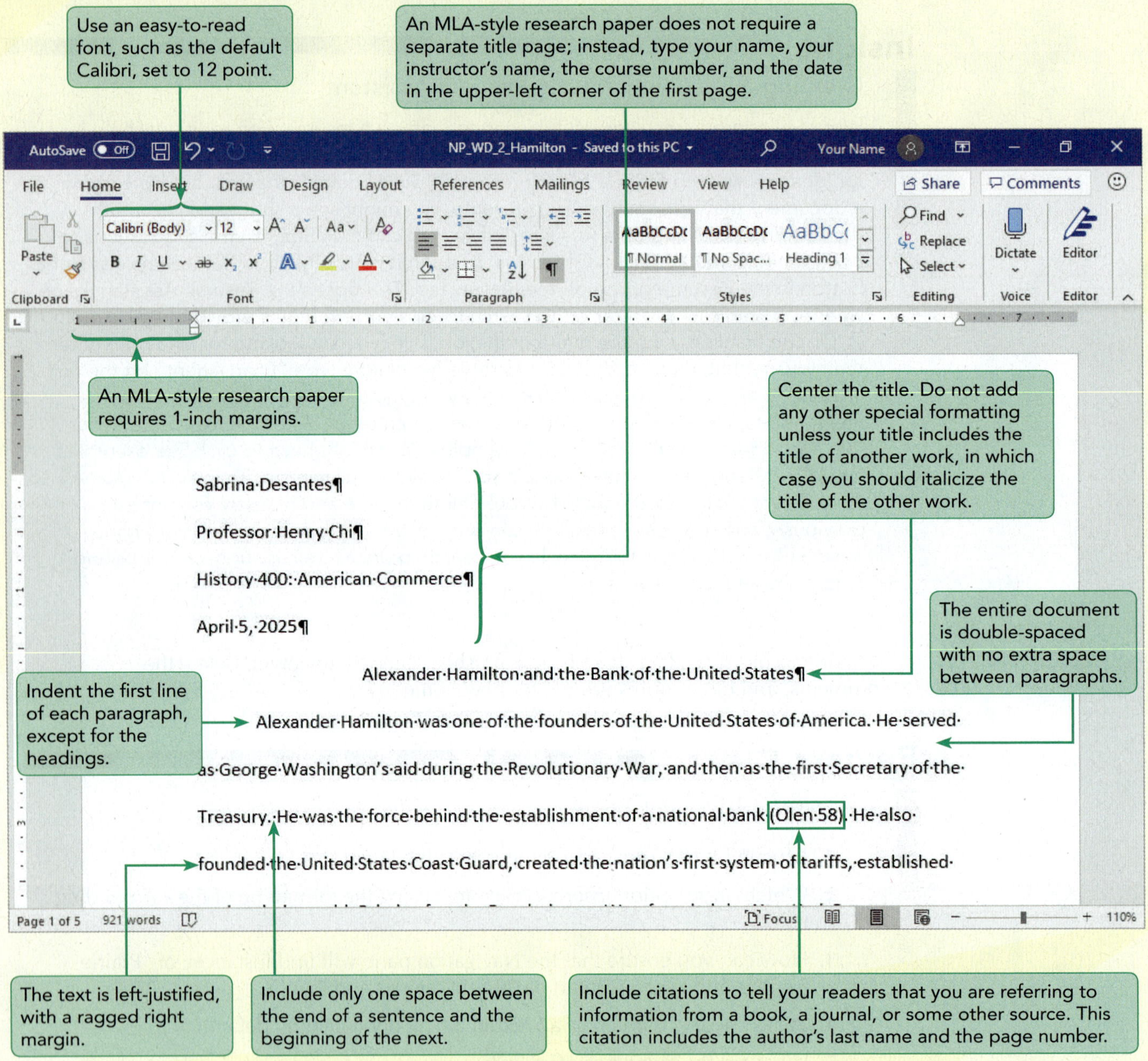

MLA Formatting Guidelines

The References tab includes options that help you create a research paper.

In the Style box, specify the style of research paper you are creating. For college research papers, the MLA style is commonly used.

After you create all the citations, click the Bibliography button to create a list of all the sources mentioned in your citations. This list is known as a **bibliography** or, in the MLA style, a **works cited list**.

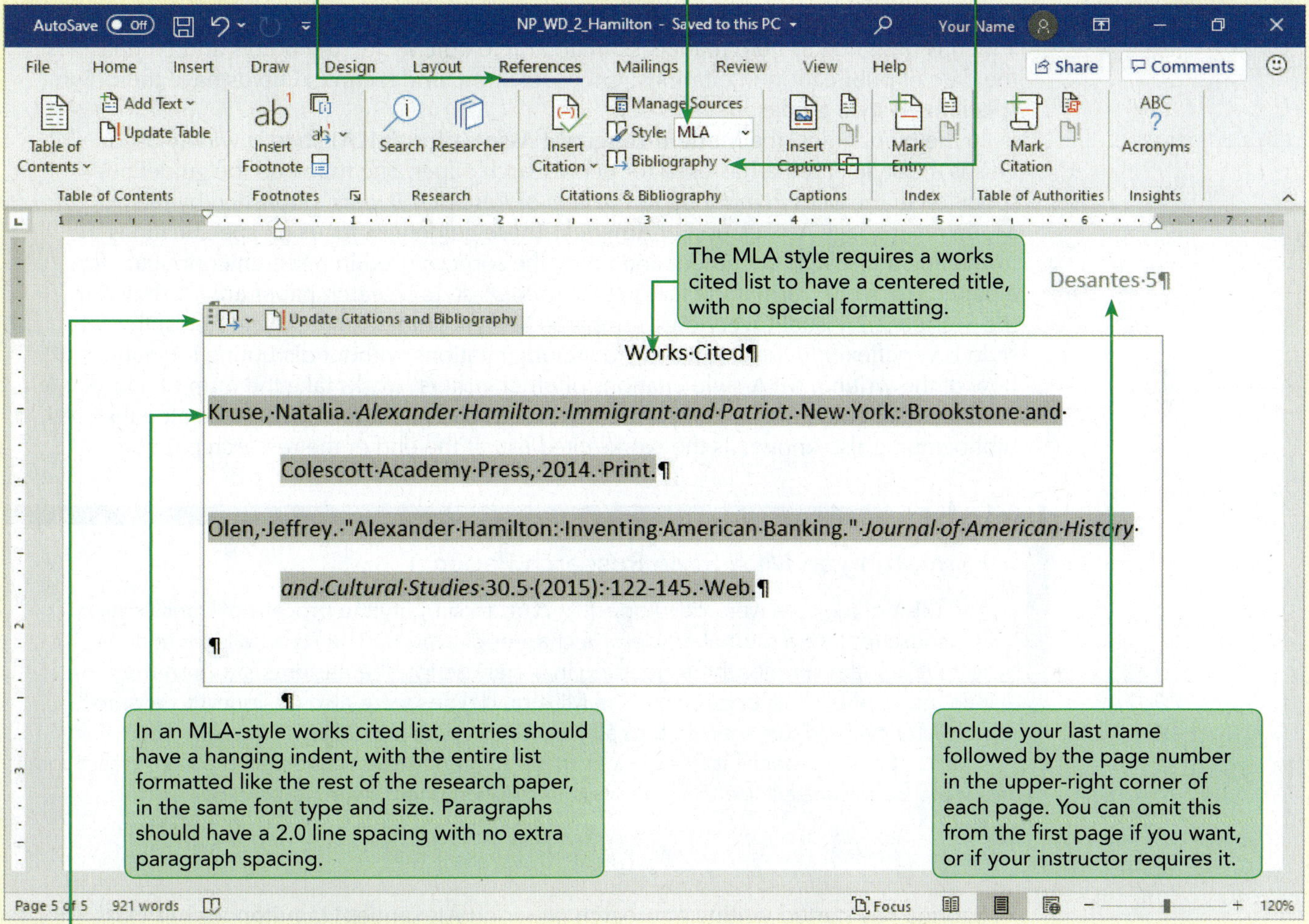

The MLA style requires a works cited list to have a centered title, with no special formatting.

In an MLA-style works cited list, entries should have a hanging indent, with the entire list formatted like the rest of the research paper, in the same font type and size. Paragraphs should have a 2.0 line spacing with no extra paragraph spacing.

Include your last name followed by the page number in the upper-right corner of each page. You can omit this from the first page if you want, or if your instructor requires it.

Word inserts a bibliography, or works cited list, contained in a special feature, known as a **content control**, used to display information that is inserted automatically and that may need to be updated later. You can use the buttons in the content control tab to make changes to material inside the content control.

Reviewing the MLA Style

A **style guide** is a set of rules that describe the preferred format and style for a certain type of writing. People in different fields use different style guides, with each style guide designed to suit the needs of a specific discipline. For example, journalists commonly use the *Associated Press Stylebook*, which focuses on the concise writing style common in magazines and newspapers. In the world of academics, style guides emphasize the proper way to create a **citation**, which is a formal reference to the work of others that appears in parentheses at the end of a sentence. Researchers in the social and behavioral sciences use the **American Psychological Association (APA) style**, which is designed to help readers scan an article quickly for key points and emphasizes the date of publication in citations. Other scientific and technical fields have their own specialized style guides.

In the humanities, the **Modern Language Association (MLA) style** is widely used. This is the style Sabrina has used for her research paper. She followed the guidelines specified in the *MLA Handbook for Writers of Research Papers*, published by the Modern Language Association of America. These guidelines focus on specifications for formatting a research document and citing the sources used in research conducted for a paper. The major formatting features of an MLA-style research paper are illustrated in the Session 2.2 Visual Overview. Compared to style guides for technical fields, the MLA style is very flexible, making it easy to include citations without disrupting the natural flow of the writing. MLA-style citations of other writers' works take the form of a brief parenthetical entry, with a complete reference to each item included in the alphabetized bibliography, also known as the works cited list, at the end of the research paper.

Insight

Formatting an MLA-Style Research Paper

The MLA guidelines were developed, in part, to simplify the process of transforming a manuscript into a journal article or a chapter of a book. The style calls for minimal formatting; the simpler the formatting in a manuscript, the easier it is to turn the text into a published document. The MLA guidelines were also designed to ensure consistency in documents, so that all research papers look alike. Therefore, you should apply no special formatting to the text in an MLA-style research paper. Headings should be formatted like the other text in the document, with no bold or heading styles.

Sabrina has started writing a research paper on Alexander Hamilton for her class. You'll open the draft of Sabrina's research paper and determine what needs to be done to make it meet the MLA style guidelines for a research paper.

To open the document and review it for MLA style:

1. sam Open the document **NP_WD_2-2.docx** located in the Word2 > Module folder included with your Data Files, and then save the document as **NP_WD_2_Hamilton** in the location specified by your instructor.
2. Verify that the document is displayed in Print Layout view and that the rulers and nonprinting characters are displayed. Make sure the Zoom level is set to **120%**.
3. Review the document to familiarize yourself with its structure. First, notice the parts of the document that already match the MLA style. Sabrina

included a block of information in the upper-left corner of the first page, giving her name, her instructor's name, the course name, and the date. The title at the top of the first page also meets the MLA guidelines in that it is centered and does not have any special formatting. The headings ("Early Life," "Revolutionary War," "The Federalist Papers," and "Building a New Economy") have no special formatting, but unlike the title, they are left-aligned. Finally, the body text is left-aligned with a ragged right margin, and the entire document is formatted in the same font, Calibri, which is easy to read.

What needs to be changed in order to make Sabrina's paper consistent with the MLA style? Currently, the entire document is formatted using the default settings, which are the Normal style for the Office theme. To transform the document into an MLA-style research paper, you need to complete the checklist shown in Figure 2–17.

Figure 2–17 **Checklist for formatting a default Word document to match the MLA style**

- ✓ Double-space the entire document.
- ✓ Remove extra paragraph spacing from the entire document.
- ✓ Increase the font size for the entire document to 12 points.
- ✓ Indent the first line of each body paragraph .5 inch from the left margin.
- ✓ Add the page number (preceded by your last name) in the upper-right corner of each page. If you prefer, you can omit this from the first page.

You'll take care of the first three items in the checklist now.

To begin applying MLA formatting to the document:

1. Press **CTRL+A** to select the entire document.
2. Make sure the Home tab is selected on the ribbon.
3. In the Paragraph group, click the **Line and Paragraph Spacing** button and then click **2.0**.
4. Click the **Line and Spacing** button again, and then click **Remove Space After Paragraph**. The entire document is now double-spaced, with no paragraph spacing, and the entire document is still selected.
5. In the Font group, click the **Font Size arrow**, and then click **12**. The entire document is formatted in 12-point font.
6. Click anywhere in the document to deselect the text.
7. In the first paragraph of the document, replace Sabrina's name with your first and last names, and then save the document.

Now you need to indent the first line of each body paragraph.

Indenting a Paragraph

Word offers a number of options for indenting a paragraph. You can move an entire paragraph to the right, or you can create specialized indents, such as a **hanging indent**, where all lines except the first line of the paragraph are indented from the left margin. As you saw in the Session 2.2 Visual Overview, all the body paragraphs (that is, all the paragraphs except the information in the upper-left corner of the first page, the title, and the headings) have a first-line indent in MLA research papers. Figure 2–18 shows some examples of other common paragraph indents.

Figure 2–18 Common paragraph indents

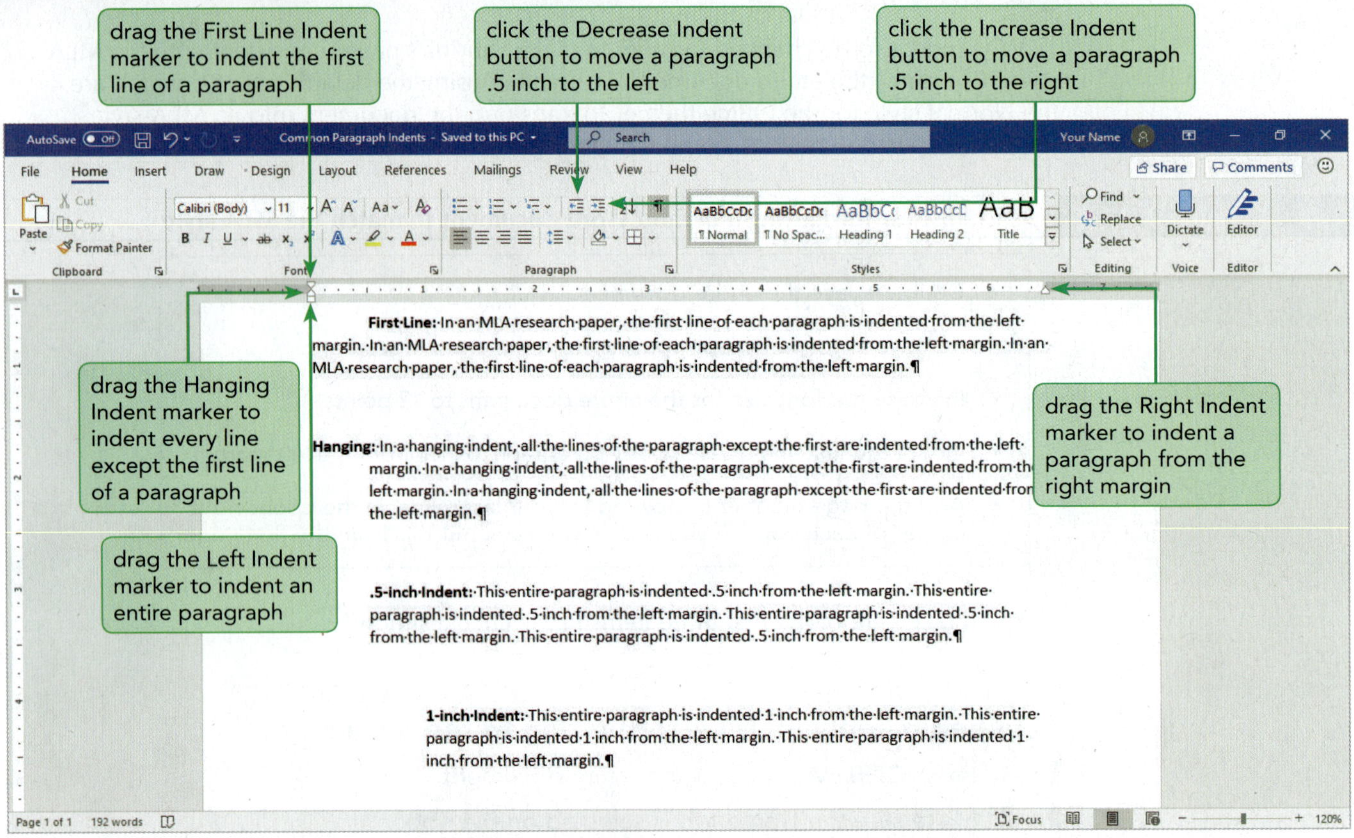

To quickly indent an entire paragraph .5 inch from the left, position the insertion point in the paragraph you want to indent, and then click the Increase Indent button in the Paragraph group on the Home tab. You can continue to indent the paragraph in increments of .5 inch by repeatedly clicking the Increase Indent button. To move an indented paragraph back to the left .5 inch, click the Decrease Indent button.

To create first-line, hanging, or right indents, you can use the indent markers on the ruler. First, click in the paragraph you want to indent or select multiple paragraphs. Then drag the appropriate indent marker to the left or right on the horizontal ruler. The indent markers are small and can be hard to see. As shown in Figure 2–18, the **First Line Indent marker** is triangle-shaped and looks like the top half of an hourglass; the **Hanging Indent marker** looks like the bottom half. The rectangle below the Hanging Indent marker is the **Left Indent marker**. The **Right Indent marker** looks just like the Hanging Indent marker except that it is located on the far-right side of the horizontal ruler.

Note that when you indent an entire paragraph using the Increase Indent button, the three indent markers move as a unit along with the paragraphs you are indenting. If you prefer, instead of dragging indent markers to indent a paragraph, you can click the Dialog Box Launcher in the Paragraph group on the Home tab, and then adjust the Indentation settings in the Paragraph dialog box.

In Sabrina's paper, you will indent the first lines of the body paragraphs .5 inch from the left margin, as specified by the MLA style.

To indent the first line of each paragraph:

1. On the first page of the document, just below the title, click anywhere in the first main paragraph, which begins "Alexander Hamilton was...."
2. On the horizontal ruler, position the pointer over the First Line Indent marker . When you see the ScreenTip that reads "First Line Indent," you know the mouse is positioned correctly.
3. Press and hold the mouse button as you drag the **First Line Indent** marker to the right, to the .5-inch mark on the horizontal ruler. As you drag, a vertical guideline appears over the document, and the first line of the paragraph moves right. See Figure 2–19.

Figure 2–19 Dragging the First Line Indent marker

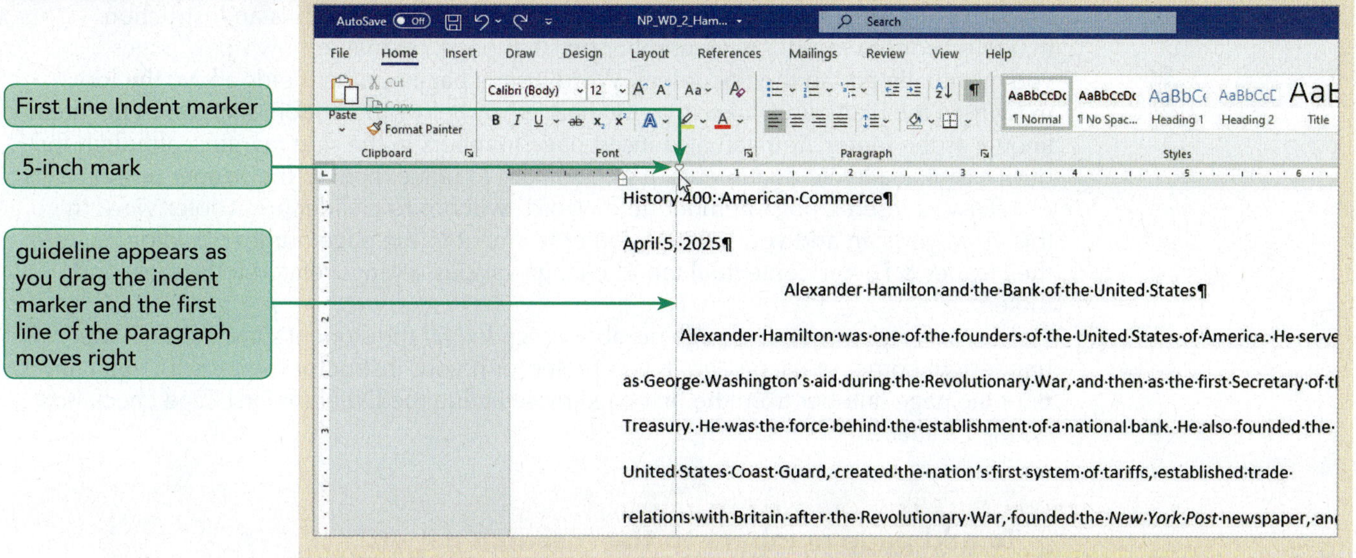

4. When the First Line Indent marker is positioned at the .5-inch mark on the ruler, release the mouse button. The first line of the paragraph containing the insertion point indents .5 inch, and the vertical guideline disappears.
5. Scroll down, if necessary, click anywhere in the next paragraph in the document (which begins "All told, Alexander Hamilton..."), and then drag the **First Line Indent** marker to the right, to the .5-inch mark on the horizontal ruler. As you move the indent marker, you can use the vertical guideline to ensure that you match the first-line indent of the preceding paragraph.

   You could continue to drag the indent marker to indent the first line of the remaining body paragraphs, but it's faster to use the Repeat button on the Quick Access Toolbar.

6. Scroll down and click in the paragraph below the "Early Life" heading, and then on the Quick Access Toolbar, click the **Repeat** button . Note that, on most computers, you can press F4 instead to repeat an action, if you prefer.

7. Click in the next paragraph, at the top of page 2 (which begins "He soon began to desire..."), and then click the **Repeat** button.
8. Continue using the **Repeat** button to indent the first line of all of the remaining body paragraphs, including the paragraph on page 4. Take care not to indent the headings, which in this document are formatted just like the body text.
9. Scroll to the top of the document, verify that you have correctly indented the first line of each body paragraph, and then save the document.

Next, you need to insert page numbers.

Inserting and Modifying Page Numbers

When you insert page numbers in a document, you don't have to type a page number on each page. Instead, you can insert a **page number field**, which is an instruction that tells Word to insert a page number on each page, no matter how many pages you eventually add to the document. Word inserts page number fields above the top margin, in the blank area known as the **header**, or below the bottom margin, in the area known as the **footer**. You can also insert page numbers in the side margins, although for business or academic documents, it's customary to place them in the header or footer.

After you insert a page number field, Word switches to Header and Footer view. In this view, you can add your name or other text next to the page number field or use the Header & Footer contextual tab to change various settings related to headers and footers.

The MLA style requires a page number preceded by the student's last name in the upper-right corner of each page. If you prefer (or if your instructor requests it), you can omit the page number from the first page by selecting the Different First Page check box on the Header & Footer tab.

To add page numbers to the research paper:

1. Press **CTRL+HOME** to move the insertion point to the beginning of the document.
2. On the ribbon, click the **Insert** tab. The ribbon changes to display the Insert options, including options for inserting page numbers.
3. In the Header & Footer group, click the **Page Number** button to open the Page Number menu. Here you can choose where you want to position the page numbers in your document—at the top of the page, at the bottom of the page, in the side margins, or at the current location of the insertion point. To remove page numbers from a document, you can click the Remove Page Numbers command on the Page Number menu.
4. Point to **Top of Page**. A gallery of page number styles opens. You can scroll the list to review the many styles of page numbers. Because the MLA style calls for a simple page number in the upper-right corner, you will use the Plain Number 3 style. See Figure 2–20.

Figure 2–20 Gallery of page number styles

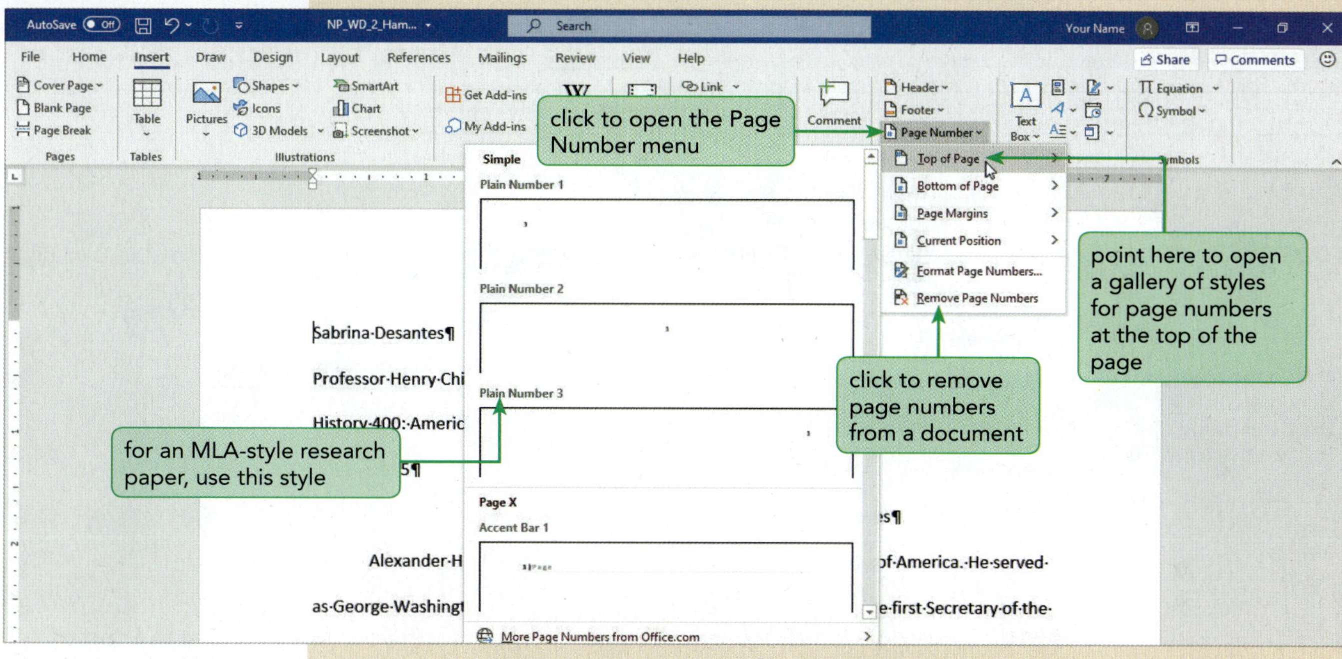

5. In the gallery, click the **Plain Number 3** style. The Word window switches to Header and Footer view, with the page number for the first page in the upper-right corner. The page number has a gray background, indicating that it is actually a page number field and not simply a number that you typed.

   The Header & Footer tab is displayed on the ribbon, giving you access to a variety of formatting options. The insertion point blinks to the left of the page number field, ready for you to add text to the header if you wish. Note that in Header and Footer view, you can type only in the header or footer areas. The text in the main document area is a lighter shade of gray, indicating that it cannot be edited in this view.

6. Type your last name, and then press **SPACEBAR**. If you see a wavy red line below your last name, right-click your name, and then click **Ignore All** on the Shortcut menu.
7. Select your last name and the page number field.
8. In the Mini toolbar, click the **Font Size arrow**, click **12**, and then click anywhere in the header to deselect the text. Now the header's font size matches the font size of the rest of the document. This isn't strictly necessary in an MLA research paper, but some instructors prefer it. The page number no longer has a gray background, but it is still a field, which you can verify by clicking it.
9. Click the **page number field** to display its gray background. See Figure 2–21.

Figure 2–21 Last name inserted next to the page number field

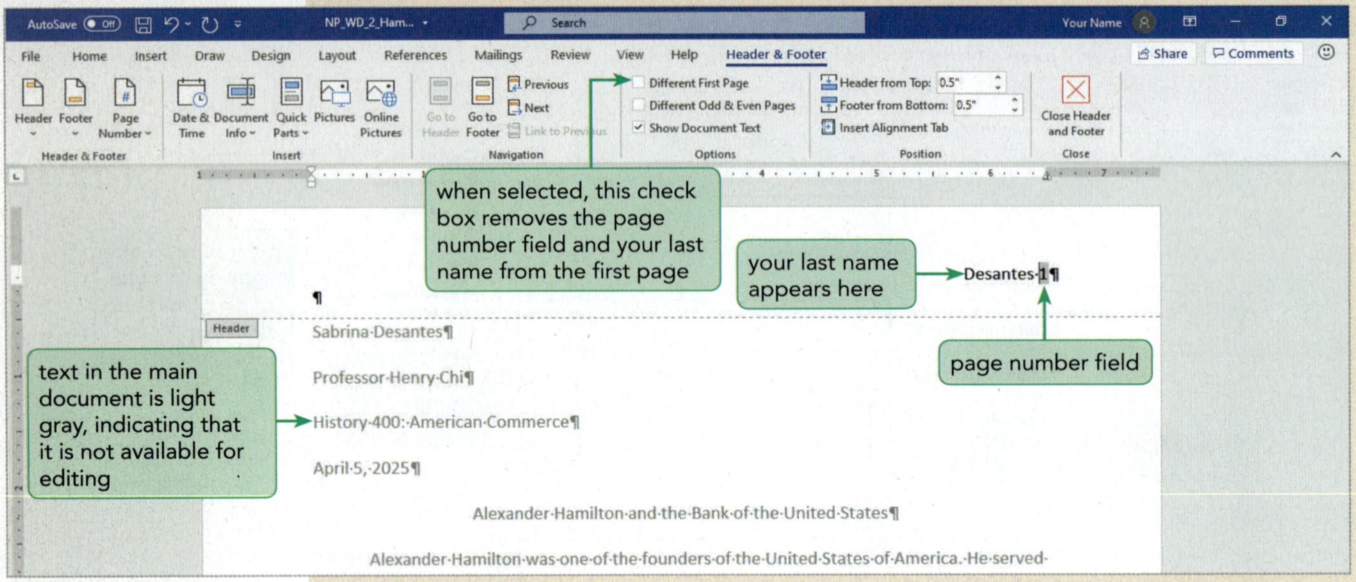

10. Scroll down and observe the page number (with your last name) at the top of pages 2, 3, and 4. As you can see, whatever you insert in the header on one page appears on every page of the document by default.
11. Scroll up to return to the header on the first page.
12. On the Header & Footer tab, in the Options group, click the **Different First Page** check box to insert a check. The page number field and your last name are removed from the first page header. The insertion point blinks at the header's left margin in case you want to insert something else for the first page header. In this case, you don't.
13. In the Close group, click the **Close Header and Footer** button. You return to Print Layout view, and the Header & Footer tab is no longer displayed on the ribbon.
14. Scroll down to review your last name and the page number in the headers for pages 2, 3, and 4. In Print Layout view, the text in the header is light gray, indicating that it is not currently available for editing.

Tip

After you insert page numbers, you can reopen Header and Footer view by double-clicking a page number in Print Layout view.

You have finished all the tasks related to formatting the MLA-style research paper. Now Sabrina would like to add a footnote to provide some extra information.

Creating a Footnote

A **footnote** is an explanatory comment or reference that appears at the bottom of a page. When you create a footnote, Word inserts a small, superscript number (called a **reference marker**) in the text. The term **superscript** means that the number is raised slightly above the line of text. Word then inserts the same number in the page's bottom margin and positions the insertion point next to it so you can type the text of the footnote. **Endnotes** are similar, except that the text of an endnote appears at the end of a document. By default, the reference marker for an endnote is a lowercase Roman numeral, and the reference marker for a footnote is an ordinary, Arabic numeral.

Word automatically manages the reference markers for you, keeping them sequential from the beginning of the document to the end, no matter how many times you add, delete, or move footnotes or endnotes. For example, if you move a paragraph containing footnote 4 so that it falls before the paragraph containing footnote 1, Word renumbers all the footnotes in the document to keep them sequential.

Reference

Inserting a Footnote or an Endnote

- Click the location in the document where you want to insert a footnote or an endnote.
- On the ribbon, click the References tab.
- In the Footnotes group, click the Insert Footnote button or the Insert Endnote button.
- Type the text of the footnote in the bottom margin of the page, or type the text of the endnote at the end of the document.
- When you are finished typing the text of a footnote or an endnote, click in the body of the document to continue working on the document.

Sabrina asks you to insert a footnote that provides additional information about Alexander Hamilton's writing skills.

To add a footnote to the research paper:

1. Use the Navigation pane to find the phrase "made him invaluable" on page 2, and then click to the right of the period after "invaluable."
2. Close the Navigation pane.
3. On the ribbon, click the **References** tab.
4. In the Footnotes group, click the **Insert Footnote** button. A superscript "1" is inserted to the right of the period after "invaluable." Word also inserts the number "1" in the bottom margin below a separator line. The insertion point is now located next to the number in the bottom margin, ready for you to type the text of the footnote.
5. Type **A digital archive of his letters maintained by the New York Public Library testifies to his excellent handwriting.** See Figure 2–22.

Figure 2–22 Inserting a footnote

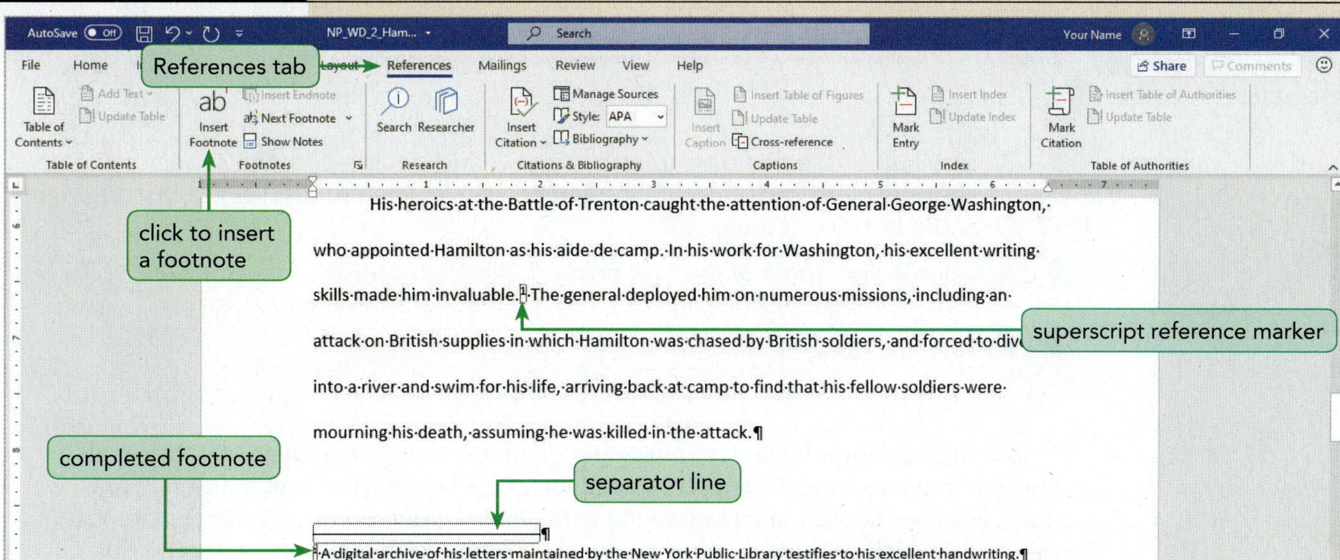

Now, Sabrina would like you to insert a second footnote.

To insert a second footnote:

1. Scroll up to the third line of page 2, locate the phrase "send Hamilton to New York to be educated" and then click to the right of the period after "educated."
2. In the Footnotes group, click the **Insert Footnote** button, and then type **The letter impressed a local newspaper owner, who decided to publish it.** Because this footnote is placed earlier in the document than the one you just created, Word inserts a superscript "1" for this footnote and then renumbers the other footnote as "2." See Figure 2–23. You can easily move back and forth between superscript footnote numbers and footnote text, as you'll see in the next two steps.

Figure 2–23 **Inserting a second footnote**

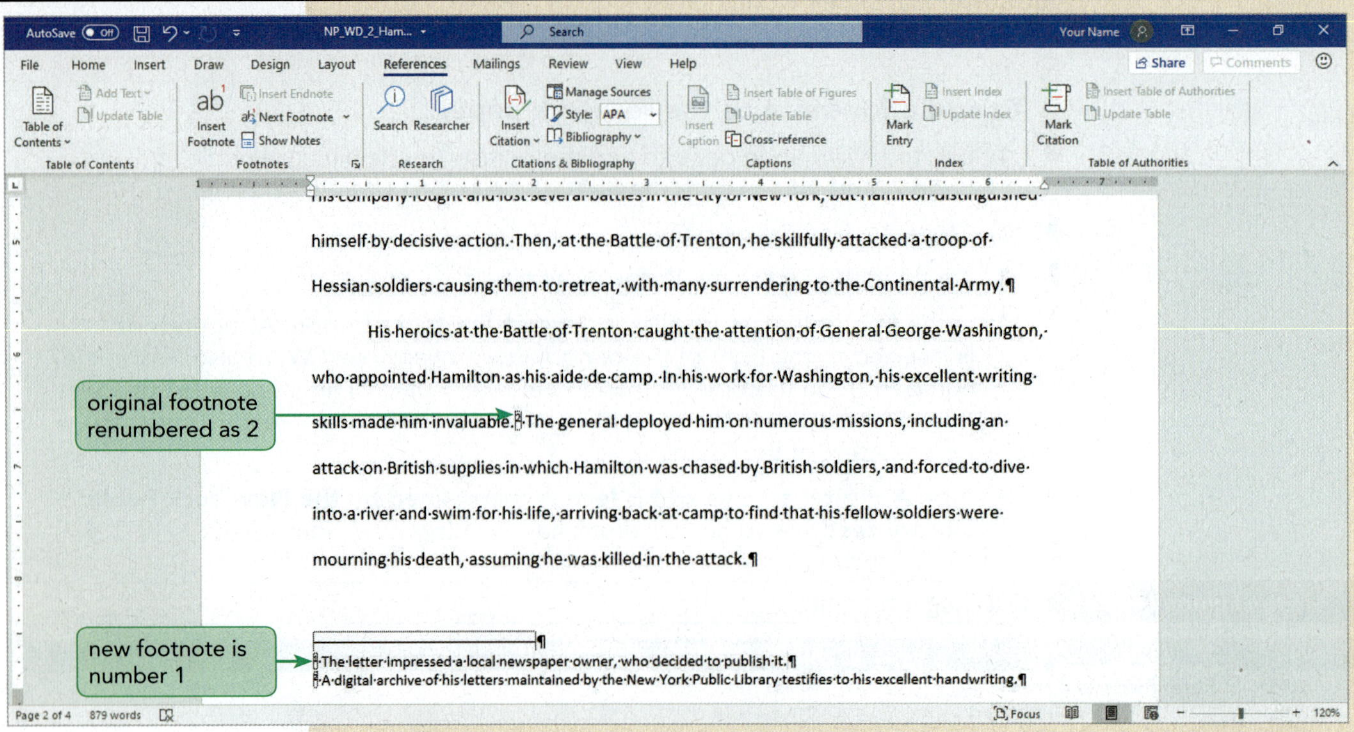

3. Scroll up to the first paragraph of page 2 and double-click the superscript **1** after the word "educated." The screen scrolls down to display the footnote at the bottom of the page.
4. Double-click the **1** at the beginning of the footnote. The screen scrolls up to display the superscript number 1 in the first paragraph on page 2.
5. Save the document.

Inserting endnotes is similar to inserting footnotes, except that the notes appear at the end of the document. To insert an endnote, click where you want to insert it, and then click the Insert Endnote button in the Footnotes group on the References tab. You can double-click endnote numbers to move back and forth between the superscript numbers in the document and the notes at the end of the document.

Next Sabrina wants your help with creating the essential parts of any research paper—the citations and the bibliography.

Creating Citations and a Bibliography

A bibliography (or, as it is called in the MLA style, the works cited list) is an alphabetical list of all the books, magazine articles, websites, movies, and other works referred to in a research paper. The items listed in a bibliography are known as **sources**. The entry for each source includes information such as the author, the title of the work, the publication date, and the publisher.

Within the research paper itself, you include a parenthetical reference, or citation, every time you summarize, quote, or refer to a source. Every source included in your citations then has a corresponding entry in the works cited list. A citation should include enough information to identify the quote or referenced material, so the reader can easily locate the source in the accompanying works cited list. The exact form for a citation varies depending on the style guide you are using and the type of material you are referencing.

Some style guides are very rigid about the form and location of citations, but the MLA style offers quite a bit of flexibility. Typically, though, you insert an MLA citation at the end of a sentence in which you quote or refer to material from a source. For books or journals, the citation itself usually includes the author's last name and a page number. However, if the sentence containing the citation already includes the author's name, you need to include only the page number in the citation. Figure 2–24 provides some sample MLA citations; the format shown could be used for books or journals. For detailed guidelines, you can consult the *MLA Handbook, Eighth Edition*.

Figure 2–24 **MLA guidelines for citing a book or journal**

Citation Rule	Example
If the sentence includes the author's name, the citation should only include the page number.	Peterson compares the opening scene of the movie to a scene from Shakespeare (188).
If the sentence does not include the author's name, the citation should include the author's name and the page number.	The opening scene of the movie has been compared to a scene from Shakespeare (Peterson 188).

Note that Word's citation and bibliography tools correspond to the seventh edition of the *MLA Handbook*, which is not the most recent edition. Here's a link to the Modern Language Association website, where you can learn about the latest edition, which includes guidance on citing digital sources: www.mla.org.

Word greatly simplifies the process of creating citations and a bibliography. You specify the style you want to use, and then Word takes care of setting up the citation and the works cited list appropriately. Every time you create a citation for a new source, Word prompts you to enter the information needed to create the corresponding entry in the works cited list. If you don't have all of your source information available, Word also allows you to insert a temporary, placeholder citation, which you can replace later with a complete citation. When you are finished creating your citations, Word generates the bibliography automatically. Note that placeholder citations are not included in the bibliography.

Proskills

Written Communication: Acknowledging Your Sources

A research paper is a means for you to explore the available information about a subject and then present this information, along with your own understanding of the subject, in an organized and interesting way. Acknowledging all the sources of the information presented in your research paper is essential. If you fail to do this, you might be subject to charges of plagiarism, or trying to pass off someone else's thoughts as your own. Plagiarism is an extremely serious accusation for which you could suffer academic consequences ranging from failing an assignment to being expelled from school.

To ensure that you don't forget to cite a source, you should be careful about creating citations in your document as you type. In this module, you will insert citations into completed paragraphs as practice, but in real life you should insert citations as you type your document. It's easy to forget to go back and cite all your sources correctly after you've finished typing a research paper. Failing to cite a source could lead to accusations of plagiarism and all the consequences that entails. If you don't have the complete information about a source available when you are typing your paper, you should at least insert a placeholder citation. But take care to go back later and substitute complete citations for any placeholders.

Creating Citations

Before you create citations, you need to select the style you want to use, which in the case of Sabrina's paper is the MLA style. Then, to insert a citation, you click the Insert Citation button in the Citations & Bibliography group on the References tab. If you are citing a source for the first time, Word prompts you to enter all the information required for the source's entry in the bibliography or works cited list. If you are citing an existing source, you simply select the source from the Insert Citation menu.

By default, an MLA citation includes only the author's name in parentheses. However, you can use the Edit Citation dialog box to add a page number. You can also use the Edit Citation dialog box to remove, or suppress, the author's name, so only the page number appears in the citation. However, in an MLA citation, Word will replace the suppressed author name with the title of the source, so you need to suppress the title as well, by selecting the Title check box in the Edit Citation dialog box.

Reference

Creating Citations

- On the ribbon, click the References tab. In the Citations & Bibliography group, click the Style arrow, and then select the style you want.
- Click in the document where you want to insert the citation. Typically, a citation goes at the end of a sentence, before the ending punctuation.
- To add a citation for a new source, click the Insert Citation button in the Citations & Bibliography group, click Add New Source, enter information in the Create Source dialog box, and then click OK.
- To add a citation for an existing source, click the Insert Citation button, and then click the source.
- To add a placeholder citation, click the Insert Citation button, click Add New Placeholder, and then, in the Placeholder Name dialog box, type placeholder text, such as the author's last name, that will serve as a reminder about which source you need to cite. Note that a placeholder citation cannot contain any spaces.
- To add a page number to a citation, click the citation in the document, click the Citation Options button, click Edit Citation, type the page number, and then click OK.
- To display only the page number in a citation, click the citation in the document, click the Citation Options button, and then click Edit Citation. In the Edit Citation dialog box, select the Author and Title check boxes to suppress this information, and then click OK.

So far, Sabrina has referenced information from two different sources in her research paper. You'll select a style and then begin adding the appropriate citations.

To select a style for the citation and bibliography:

1. On the ribbon, click the **References** tab. The ribbon changes to display references options.
2. In the Citations & Bibliography group, click the **Style arrow**, and then click **MLA Seventh Edition** if it is not already selected.

Be sure to select the correct citation and bibliography style before you begin.

3. Press **CTRL+F** to open the Navigation pane.
4. Use the Navigation pane to find the phrase "However, as at least one historian," which appears on page 3, and then click in the document at the end of that sentence (between the end of the word "him" and the closing period).
5. Close the **Navigation** pane, and then click the **References** tab on the ribbon, if necessary. You need to add a citation that informs the reader that historian Natalia Cruz made the observation described in the sentence. See Figure 2–25.

Figure 2–25 **MLA style selected and insertion point positioned for new citation**

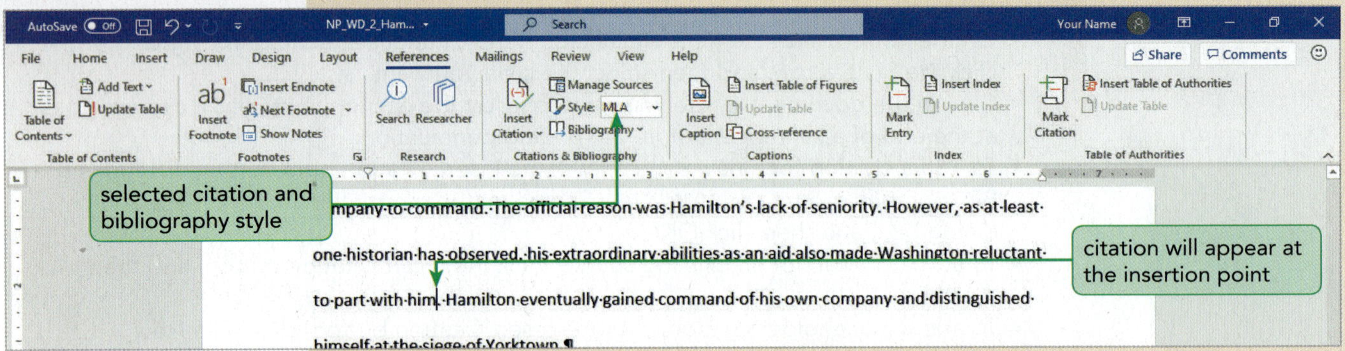

6. In the Citations & Bibliography group, click the **Insert Citation** button to open the menu. At this point, you could click Add New Placeholder on the menu to insert a temporary, placeholder citation. However, because you have all the necessary source information, you can go ahead and create a complete citation.
7. On the menu, click **Add New Source**. The Create Source dialog box opens, ready for you to add the information required to create a bibliography entry for Natalia Cruz's book.
8. If necessary, click the **Type of Source arrow**, scroll up or down in the list, and then click **Book**.
9. In the Author box, type **Natalia Cruz**.
10. Click in the **Title** box, and then type **Alexander Hamilton: Immigrant and Patriot**.
11. Click in the **Year** box, and then type **2014**. This is the year the book was published. Next, you need to enter the name and location of the publisher.
12. Click the **City** box, type **New York**, click the **Publisher** box, and then type **Brookstone and Colescott Academy Press**.

    Finally, you need to indicate the medium used to publish the book. In this case, Sabrina used a printed copy, so the medium is "Print." For books or journals published online, the correct medium would be "Web."
13. Click the **Medium** box, and then type **Print**. See Figure 2–26.

Tip

When entering information in a dialog box, you can press TAB to move the insertion point from one box to another.

Figure 2–26 **Create Source dialog box with information for the first source**

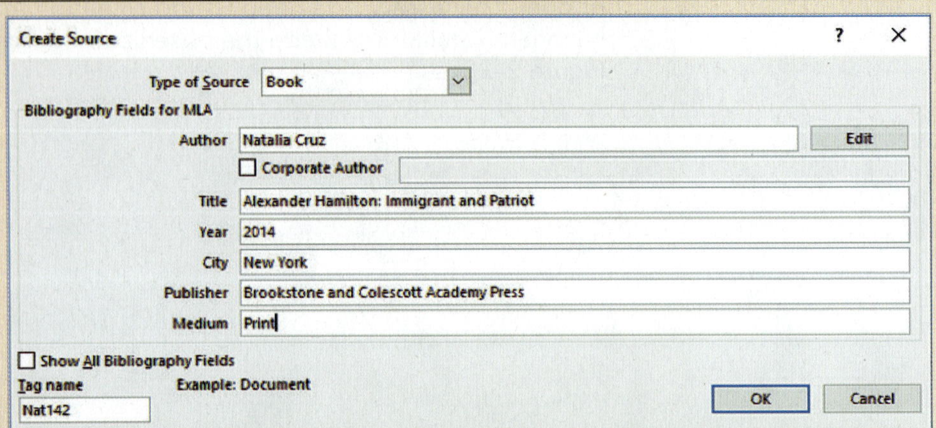

14. Click **OK**. Word inserts the parenthetical "(Cruz)" at the end of the sentence in the document.

Trouble? If the Researcher pane opens, close it.

Although the citation looks like ordinary text, it is actually contained inside a content control, a special feature used to display information that is inserted automatically and that may need to be updated later. You can see the content control itself only when it is selected. When it is unselected, you simply see the citation. In the next set of steps, you will select the content control and then edit the citation to add a page number.

To edit the citation:

1. In the document, click the citation **(Cruz)**. The citation appears in a content control, which is a box with a tab on the left and an arrow button on the right. The arrow button is called the Citation Options button.

2. Click the **Citation Options** button. A menu of options related to editing a citation opens, as shown in Figure 2–27.

Figure 2–27 Citation Options menu

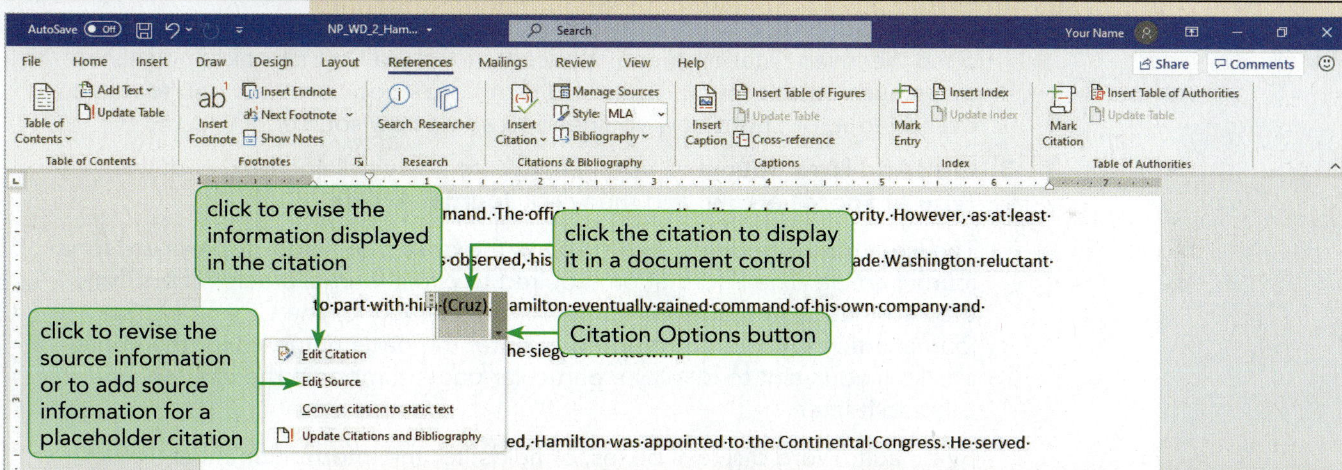

To edit the information about the source, you click Edit Source. To change the information that is displayed in the citation itself, you use the Edit Citation option.

3. On the Citation Options menu, click **Edit Citation**. The Edit Citation dialog box opens, as shown in Figure 2–28.

Figure 2–28 Edit Citation dialog box

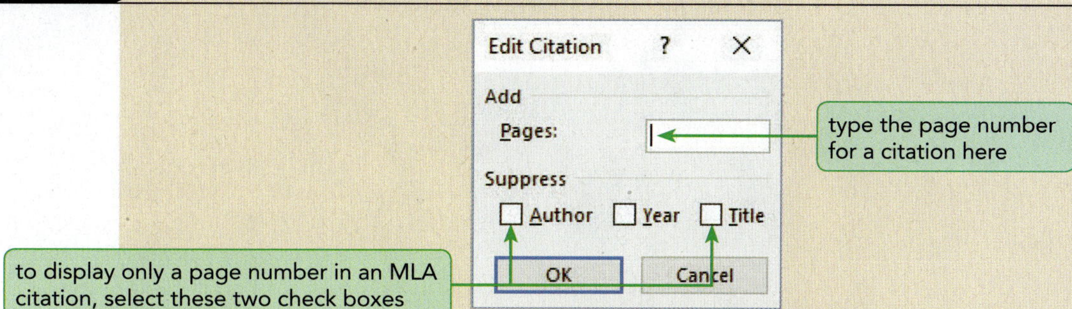

To add a page number for the citation, you type the page number in the Pages box. If you want to display only the page number in the citation (which would be necessary if you already mentioned the author's name in the same sentence in the text), then you would also select the Author and Title check boxes in this dialog box to suppress this information.

4. Type **37** to insert the page number in the Pages box, click **OK** to close the dialog box, and then click anywhere in the document outside the citation content control. The revised citation now reads "(Cruz 37)."

Note that if you need to delete a citation, you can click the citation to display the content control, click the tab on the left side of the content control, and then press DEL. Next, you will add two more citations, both for the same journal article.

To insert two more citations:

1. Scroll down to the second-to-last paragraph on page 3, and then click at the end of the last sentence in that paragraph (which begins "According to historian Jeffrey Olen..."), between the word "powers" and the period. This sentence mentions historian Jeffrey Olen; you need to add a citation to one of his journal articles.
2. In the Citations & Bibliography group, click the **Insert Citation** button to open the Insert Citation menu. Notice that Natalia Cruz's book is now listed as a source on this menu. You could click Cruz's book on the menu to add a citation to it, but right now you need to add a new source.
3. Click **Add New Source** to open the Create Source dialog box, click the **Type of Source arrow**, and then click **Journal Article**.

   The Create Source dialog box displays the boxes, or fields, appropriate for a journal article. The information required to cite a journal article differs from the information you entered earlier for the citation for the Cruz book. For journal articles, you are prompted to enter the page numbers for the entire article. If you want to display a particular page number in the citation, you can add it later.

   By default, Word displays boxes, or fields, for the information most commonly included in a bibliography. In this case, you also want to include the volume and issue numbers for Jeffrey Olen's article, so you need to display more fields.
4. In the Create Source dialog box, click the **Show All Bibliography Fields** check box to select this option. The Create Source dialog box expands to allow you to enter more detailed information. Red asterisks highlight the fields that are recommended, but these recommended fields don't necessarily apply to every source.

5. Enter the following information, scrolling down to display the necessary boxes:

   Author: **Jeffrey Olen**

   Title: **Alexander Hamilton: Inventing American Banking**

   Journal Name: **Journal of American History and Cultural Studies**

   Year: **2015**

   Pages: **122–145**

   Volume: **30**

   Issue: **5**

   Medium: **Web**

   When you are finished, your Create Source dialog box should look like the one shown in Figure 2–29.

Figure 2–29 Create Source dialog box with information for the journal article

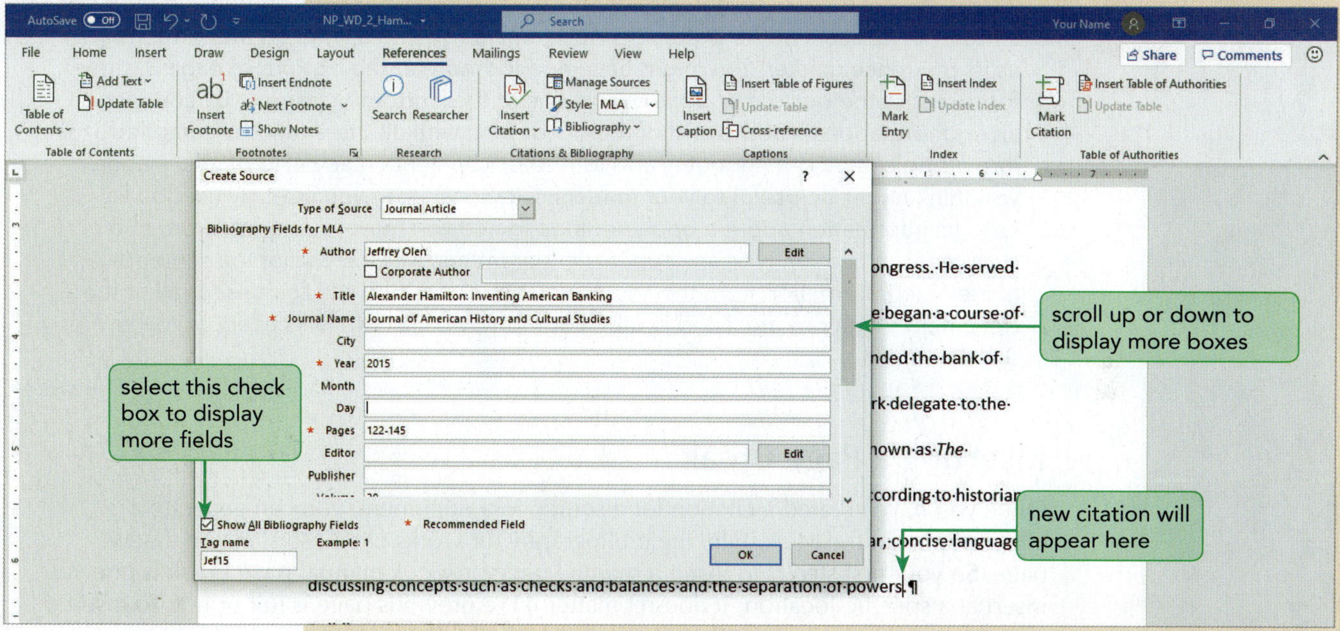

6. Click **OK**. The Create Source dialog box closes, and the citation "(Olen)" is inserted in the text. Because the sentence containing the citation already includes the author's name, you will edit the citation to include the page number and suppress the author's name.
7. Click the **(Olen)** citation to display the content control, click the **Citation Options** button, and then click **Edit Citation** to open the Edit Citation dialog box.
8. In the Pages box, type **142**, and then click the **Author** and **Title** check boxes to select them. You need to suppress both the author's name and the title because otherwise Word will replace the suppressed author name with the title. When using the MLA style, you don't ever have to suppress the year because the year is never included as part of an MLA citation. When working in other styles, however, you might need to suppress the year.

9. Click **OK** to close the Edit Citation dialog box, and then click anywhere outside the content control to deselect it. The end of the sentence now reads "...separation of powers (142)."
10. Scroll down to the last sentence in the document. Click at the end of the sentence, to the left of the period after "1811."
11. On the References tab, in the Citations & Bibliography group, click the **Insert Citation** button, and then click the **Olen, Jeffrey** source in the menu. You want the citation to refer to the entire article instead of just one page, so you will not edit the citation to add a specific page number.
12. Save the document.

You have entered the source information for two sources.

Insight

Understanding Endnotes, Footnotes, and Citations

It's easy to confuse footnotes with endnotes, and endnotes with citations. Remember, a footnote appears at the bottom, or foot, of a page and always on the same page as its reference marker. You might have one footnote at the bottom of page 3, three footnotes at the bottom of page 5, and one at the bottom of page 6. By contrast, an endnote appears at the end of the document, with all the endnotes compiled into a single list. Both endnotes and footnotes can contain any kind of information you think might be useful to your readers. Citations, however, are only used to list specific information about a book or other source you refer to or quote from in the document. A citation typically appears in parentheses at the end of the sentence containing information from the source you are citing, and the sources for all of the document's citations are listed in a bibliography, or a list of works cited, at the end of the document.

Inserting a Page Break

Once you have created a citation for a source in a document, you can generate a bibliography. In the MLA style, the bibliography (or works cited list) starts on a new page. So your first step is to insert a manual page break. A **manual page break** is one you insert at a specific location; it doesn't matter if the previous page is full or not. To insert a manual page break, use the Page Break button in the Pages group on the Insert tab.

To insert a manual page break:

1. Press **CTRL+END** to move the insertion point to the end of the document.
2. On the ribbon, click the **Insert** tab.
3. In the Pages group, click the **Page Break** button. Word inserts a new, blank page at the end of the document, with the insertion point blinking at the top. Note that you could also use the CTRL+ENTER keyboard shortcut to insert a manual page break. To insert a new, blank page in the middle of a document, you would use the Blank Page button in the Pages group instead.
4. Scroll up to see the dotted line with the words "Page Break" at the bottom of the text on page 4. You can delete a manual page break just as you would delete any other nonprinting character, by clicking immediately to its left and then pressing DEL. See Figure 2–30.

Figure 2–30 Manual page break inserted into the document

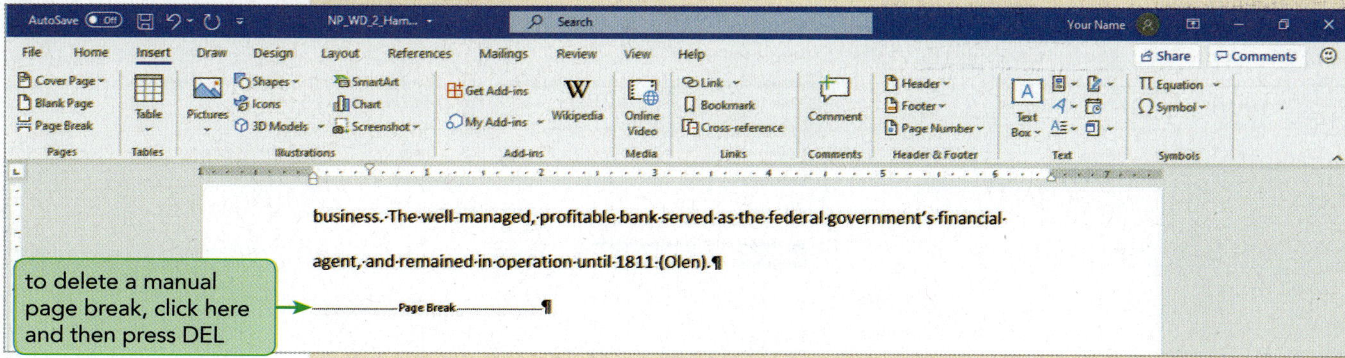

Now you can insert the bibliography on the new page 5.

Generating a Bibliography

When you generate a bibliography, Word scans all the citations in the document, collecting the source information for each citation, and then it creates a list of information for each unique source. The format of the entries in the bibliography will reflect the style you specified when you created your first citation, which in this case is the MLA style. The bibliography itself is a **field**, similar to the page number field you inserted earlier in this session. In other words, it is really an instruction that tells Word to display the source information for all the citations in the document. Because it is a field and not actual text, you can easily update the bibliography later to reflect any new citations you might add.

You can choose to insert a bibliography as a field directly in the document, or you can insert a bibliography enclosed within a content control that also includes the heading "Bibliography" or "Works Cited." Inserting a bibliography enclosed in a content control is best because the content control includes a useful button that you can use to update your bibliography if you make changes to the sources.

To insert the bibliography:

1. Scroll down so you can see the insertion point at the top of page 5.
2. On the ribbon, click the **References** tab.
3. In the Citations & Bibliography group, click the **Bibliography** button. The Bibliography menu opens, displaying three styles with preformatted headings—"Bibliography," "References," and "Works Cited." The Insert Bibliography command at the bottom inserts a bibliography directly in the document as a field, without a content control and without a preformatted heading. See Figure 2–31.

Figure 2–31 **Bibliography menu**

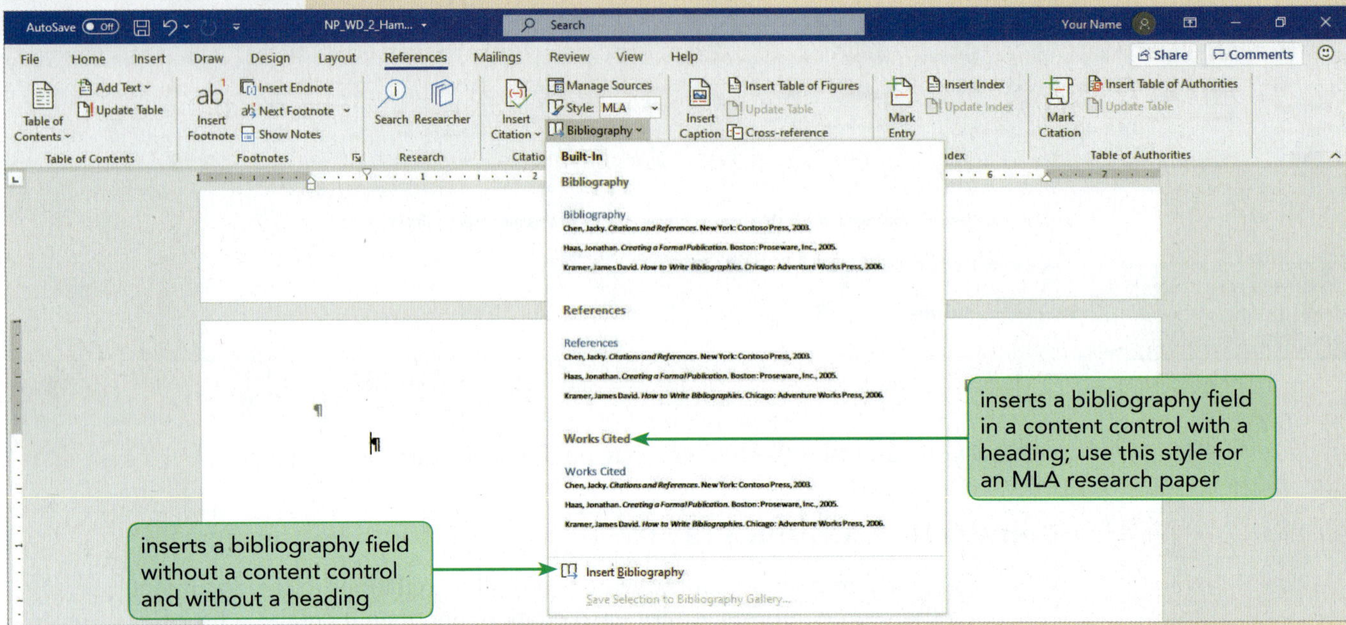

4. Click **Works Cited**. Word inserts the bibliography, with two entries, below the "Works Cited" heading. The bibliography text is formatted in Calibri, the default font for the Office theme. The "Works Cited" heading is formatted with the Heading 1 style.

   To see the content control that contains the bibliography, you need to select it.

5. Click anywhere in the bibliography. Inside the content control, the bibliography is highlighted in gray, indicating that it is a field and not regular text. The content control containing the bibliography is also now visible in the form of a rectangular border and a tab with two buttons. See Figure 2–32.

Figure 2–32 **Bibliography displayed in a content control**

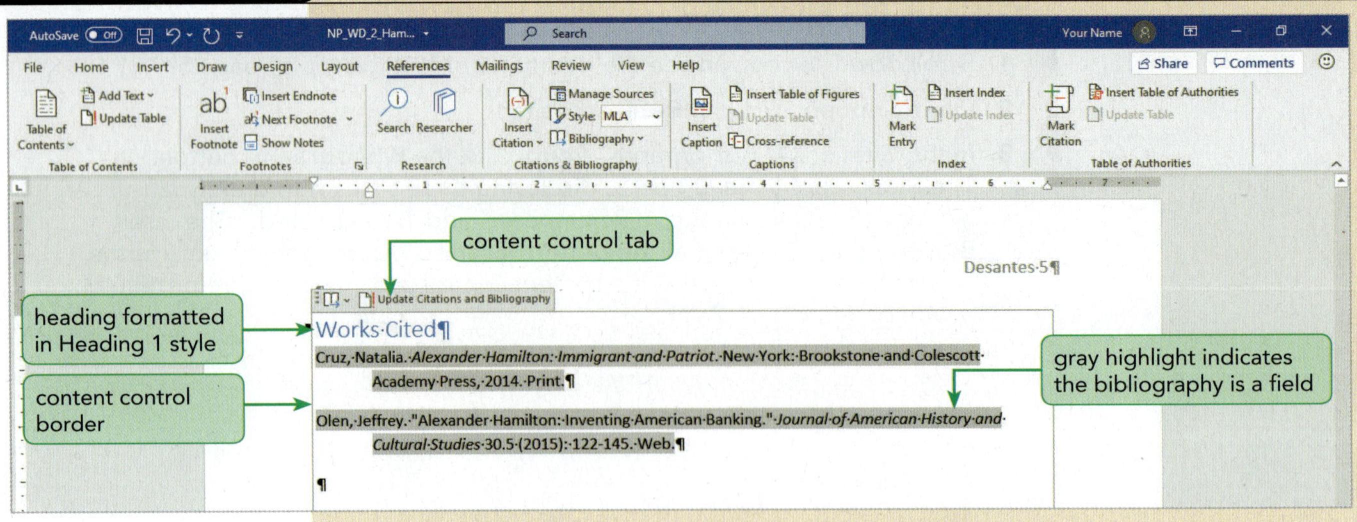

As Sabrina looks over the works cited list, she realizes that she misspelled the last name of one of the authors. You'll correct the error now and then update the bibliography.

Insight

Managing Sources

When you create a source, Word adds it to a Master List of all the sources created on your computer. Word also adds each new source to the Current List of sources for that document. Both the Master List and the Current List are accessible via the Source Manager dialog box, which you open by clicking the Manage Sources button in the Citations & Bibliography group on the References tab. Using this dialog box, you can copy sources from the Master List into the Current List and vice versa. As you begin to focus on a particular academic field and turn repeatedly to important works in your chosen field, you'll find this ability to reuse sources very helpful.

Modifying an Existing Source

Tip

To transform a placeholder citation into a regular citation, click the Citation Options button, click Edit Source, and then enter source information.

To modify information about a source, you click a citation to that source in the document, click the Citation Options button on the content control, and then click Edit Source. Depending on how your computer is set up, after you are finished editing the source, Word may prompt you to update the Master List and the source information in the current document. In almost all cases, you should click Yes to ensure that the source information is correct in all the places it is stored on your computer.

To edit a source in the research paper:

1. Click in the blank paragraph below the bibliography content control to deselect the bibliography.
2. Scroll up to display the top of page 3, and then click the **(Cruz 37)** citation you entered earlier in the sixth line from the top of the page. The content control appears around the citation.
3. Click the **Citation Options** button, and then click **Edit Source**. The Edit Source dialog box opens. Note that Word displays the author's last name first in the Author box, just as it would appear in a bibliography.
4. In the **Author** box, double-click **Cruz** to select the author's last name, and then type **Kruse**. The author's name now reads "Kruse, Natalia."
5. Click **OK**. The revised author name in the citation now reads "(Kruse 37)." A message dialog box appears, asking if you want to update the master source list and the current document. You need to click Yes so that Word makes the change both in the list of sources for the current document and in the master list of all sources created in your copy of Word.
6. Click **Yes** to close the message box and return to the document.
7. Click anywhere on the page to deselect the citation content control.
8. Save the document.

You've edited the document text and the citation to include the correct spelling of "Kruse," but now you need to update the bibliography to correct the spelling.

Updating and Finalizing a Bibliography

The bibliography does not automatically change to reflect edits you make to existing citations or to show new citations. To incorporate the latest information stored in the citations, you need to update the bibliography. To update a bibliography in a content control, click the bibliography, and then, in the content control tab, click Update Citations and Bibliography. To update a bibliography field that is not contained in a content control, right-click the bibliography, and then click Update Field on the shortcut menu.

To update the bibliography:

1. Scroll down to page 5, and click anywhere in the works cited list to display the content control.
2. In the content control tab, click **Update Citations and Bibliography**. The works cited list is updated, with "Cruz" changed to "Kruse" in the first entry.

Sabrina still has a fair amount of work to do on her research paper. After she finishes writing it and adding all the citations, she will update the bibliography again to include all her cited sources. At that point, you might think the bibliography would be finished. However, a few steps remain to ensure that the works cited list matches the MLA style. To finalize Sabrina's works cited list to match the MLA style, you need to make the changes shown in Figure 2–33.

Figure 2–33 Steps for finalizing a Word bibliography to match MLA guidelines for the works cited list

1. Format the "Works Cited" heading to match the formatting of the rest of the text in the document.
2. Center the "Works Cited" heading.
3. Double-space the entire works cited list, including the heading, and remove extra space after the paragraphs.
4. Change the font size for the entire works cited list to 12 points.

To format the bibliography as an MLA-style works cited list:

1. Click in the **Works Cited** heading, and then click the **Home** tab on the ribbon.
2. In the Styles group, click the **Normal** style. The "Works Cited" heading is now formatted in Calibri body font like the rest of the document. The MLA style for a works cited list requires this heading to be centered.
3. In the Paragraph group, click the **Center** button.
4. Select the entire works cited list, including the heading. Change the font size to **12** points, change the line spacing to **2.0**, and then remove the paragraph spacing after each paragraph.
5. Click below the content control to deselect the works cited list, and then review your work. See Figure 2–34.

Figure 2–34 MLA-style Works Cited list

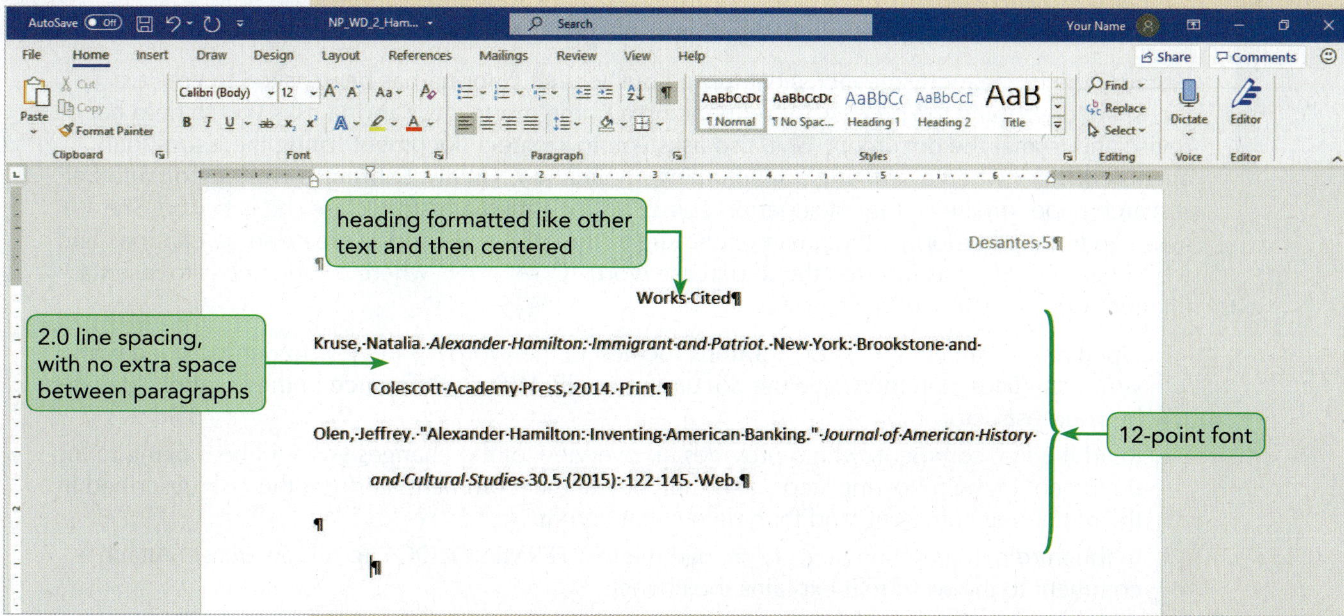

6. **sam** Save the document and close it.

Sabrina's research paper now meets the MLA style guidelines.

Review

Session 2.2 Quick Check

1. List the five tasks you need to perform to make a default Word document match the MLA style.
2. How can you quickly repeat the action you just performed?
3. Explain how to remove a page number from the first page of a document.
4. What is the default form of an MLA citation in Word?
5. Explain how to edit a citation to display only the page number.
6. Explain how to generate a works cited list.

Practice

Review Assignments

Data Files needed for the Review Assignments: NP_WD_2-3.docx, NP_WD_2-4.docx

Because the home mortgage fact sheet turned out so well, Sabrina has been asked to create a fact sheet describing the process for refinancing a home mortgage. Sabrina asks you to help her revise and format the document. She also asks you to create a document listing the issues loan agents consider when evaluating a refinancing application. Finally, Sabrina is working on another research paper on the history of situation comedies for a media history class she is taking. She asks you to help her format the paper according to the MLA style and to create some citations and a bibliography. She has inserted the uppercase word "CITATION" wherever she needs to insert a citation. Complete the following steps:

1. Open the document **NP_WD_2-3.docx** located in the Word2 > Review folder included with your Data Files, and then save the document as **NP_WD_2_Refinance** in the location specified by your instructor.
2. Read the first comment, which provides an overview of the changes you will be making to the document in the following steps, and then delete that comment. Perform the task described in the remaining comment, and then delete that comment.
3. In the third paragraph on page 1, change the text TERMINOLOGY to all lowercase. Attach a comment to the word that explains the change.
4. In the numbered list on page 2, move the first item in the list ("Prepare for closing.") down to make it the fourth item in the list.
5. Replace all three instances of "Mortgage" with "mortgage"—making sure to match the case.
6. Format the title "Refinancing at Prairie Savings and Loan" using the Title style. Format the following headings with the Heading 1 style: "Choosing a Type of Loan," "Qualifying to Refinance," and "Refinancing Process."
7. Display the Clipboard pane. On page 1, copy the bulleted list of the three major considerations (which begins "Credit score") to the Clipboard, and then copy the "Qualifying to Refinance" heading to the Clipboard. To ensure that you copy the heading formatting, be sure to select the paragraph mark after "Qualifying to Refinance" before you click the Copy button.
8. Open a new, blank document, and then save the document as **NP_WD_2_Qualify** in the location specified by your instructor.
9. At the beginning of the document, paste the "Qualifying to Refinance" heading and then, from the Paste Options menu, apply the Keep Text Only option. Below the heading, paste the list of considerations. If necessary, reapply the bulleted list formatting to the last item in the list.
10. At the end of the document, type **Prepared by:** followed by your first and last names.
11. Save the NP_WD_2_Qualify.docx document and close it.
12. In the NP_WD_2_Refinance.docx document, clear the contents of the Clipboard pane, close the Clipboard pane, save the document, and then close it.
13. Open the document **NP_WD_2-4.docx** located in the Word2 > Review folder.
14. Save the document as **NP_WD_2_Comedy** in the location specified by your instructor.
15. In the first paragraph, replace Sabrina's name with your own.
16. Adjust the font size, line spacing, paragraph spacing, and paragraph indents to match the MLA style.
17. Insert your last name and a page number on every page except the first. Use the same font size as in the rest of the document.
18. On page 2, locate the third sentence after the "Physical Comedy" heading, which begins "The term 'slapstick' derives from...." Insert a footnote at the end of the sentence that reads: **Many images of slapsticks are available on the web. Search for the term "wooden slapstick noisemaker."**
19. If necessary, select MLA Seventh Edition as the citations and bibliography style.

20. Use the Navigation pane to highlight all instances of the uppercase word "CITATION." Keep the Navigation pane open so you can continue to use it to find the locations where you need to insert citations in Steps 21–25.
21. Delete the first instance of "CITATION" and the space before it, and then create a new source with the following information:
    Type of Source: **Book**
    Author: **Cleo Jantsch**
    Title: **Modern Comedy: A History in Words and Photos**
    Year: **2018**
    City: **Cambridge**
    Publisher: **New Media Press**
    Medium: **Print**
22. Edit the citation to add **106** as the page number. Display only the page number in the citation.
23. Delete the second instance of "CITATION" and the space before it, and then create a new source with the following information:
    Type of Source: **Journal Article**
    Author: **Frieda Robbins**
    Title: **Physical Comedy in Early American Television**
    Journal Name: **Media Signpost Quarterly: Criticism and Comment**
    Year: **2016**
    Pages: **68–91**
    Volume: **10**
    Issue: **2**
    Medium: **Web**
24. Edit the citation to add **75** as the page number.
25. Delete the third instance of "CITATION" and the space before it, and then insert a citation for the book by **Cleo Jantsch**.
26. At the end of the document, start a new page and insert a bibliography in a content control with the heading "Works Cited."
27. In the second source you created, change "**Robbins**" to "**Robbinson**" and then update the bibliography.
28. Finalize the bibliography to create an MLA style works cited list.
29. Save the document and close it.
30. Close any other open documents.

Apply

Case Problem 1

Data File needed for this Case Problem: NP_WD_2-5.docx

Paralegal Ester Ashkan has more than a decade of experience as a paralegal. After moving to New Mexico, she is looking for a job at one of the many law firms in Albuquerque. She has asked you to edit and format her resume. As part of the application process, she will have to upload her resume to employee recruitment websites. Because these sites typically request a simple page design, Ester plans to rely primarily on heading styles to organize her information. When the resume is complete, she wants you to remove any color applied by the heading styles. She also needs help beginning a separate document that lists some of her current affiliations and certifications. Complete the following steps:

1. Open the document **NP_WD_2-5.docx** located in the Word2 > Case1 folder included with your Data Files, and then save the file as **NP_WD_2_Resume** in the location specified by your instructor.

2. If you see a box at the top of the Word window with the heading "Working on a resume?", click See resume suggestions, and review some examples in the Resume Assistant pane. If you do not see the box at the top of the Word window, open the Resume Assistant and review some examples in the Resume Assistant pane. When you are finished, close the Resume Assistant pane.
3. Read the comment included in the document, and then perform the task it specifies.
4. Respond to the comment with the response **If you like, I can show you how to remove hyperlink formatting the next time we meet.**, and then mark Ester's comment as resolved.
5. Replace all occurrences of "SarasotaFlorida" with **Sarasota, Florida**.
6. Format the document with styles as follows:
   - Ester's name:
     - Title style
   - Ester's address, phone number, and email address:
     - Subtitle style, 0 points of paragraph spacing
   - The "Summary," "Experience," "Education," and "Affiliations and Certifications" headings:
     - Heading 1 style; Black, Text 1 font color; all uppercase
   - The paragraphs containing the names of the three law firms where Ester used to work:
     - Heading 2 style; Black, Text 1 font color
7. In the bulleted list for Beckett, Hunter, and Lawrence, move the bullet that begins "Managed documents for cases…" up to make it the second bullet in the list.
8. Copy the "AFFILIATIONS AND CERTIFICATIONS" heading to the Clipboard, and then copy the last two bullets in the list of affiliations and certifications to the Clipboard.
9. Open a new, blank document, and then save the document as **NP_WD_2_Affiliations** in the location specified by your instructor.
10. Paste the heading in the document as text only, and then paste the bulleted list.
11. At the end of the document, type **Prepared by:** followed by your first and last names.
12. Save the NP_WD_2_Affiliations.docx document and close it.
13. In the **NP_WD_2_Resume.docx** document, clear the contents of the Clipboard pane, and close the Clipboard pane.
14. In the email address, replace "ester_ashkan" with your first and last names in all lowercase, separated by an underscore, and then save the document and close it.
15. Save and close the document.

Challenge

Case Problem 2

Data File needed for this Case Problem: NP_WD_2-6.docx

Albertine State College Xavier Jackson is a student at Albertine State College. He's working on a research paper about modern architecture for an history of architecture course, taught by Professor Linda Liu. The research paper is only partly finished, but before he does more work on it, he asks you to help format this early draft to match the MLA style. He also asks you to help create some citations, add a placeholder citation, and manage his sources. Complete the following steps:

1. Open the document **NP_WD_2-6.docx** located in the Word2 > Case2 folder included with your Data Files, and then save the document as **NP_WD_2_Modern** in the location specified by your instructor.
2. Revise the paper to match the MLA style, seventh edition. Instead of Xavier's name, use your own. Also, use the current date. Use the same font size for the header as for the rest of the document.

3. Locate the sentences in which the authors Thomas Cohn and Haley Bowerman are mentioned. At the end of the appropriate sentence, add a citation for page 123 in the following book and one for page 140 in the following journal article:

   Cohn, Thomas. *Frank Lloyd Wright: Wisconsin Boy, Titan of Modernism*. New York: Domicile Academy Press, 2010. Print.

   Bowerman, Haley. "Bauhaus Style and Structure in the Western World." Journal of Modernist Architecture and Domestic Arts (2018): 133–155. Web.

4. At the end of the second-to-last sentence in the document, insert a placeholder citation that reads "Wesley." At the end of the last sentence in the document, insert a placeholder citation that reads "Zhang."

Explore 5. Use Word Help to look up the topic "Add citations in a Word document," and then, within that article, read the section titled "Find a source." Then read the section "Edit a source," which includes a note about editing a placeholder.

Explore 6. Open the Source Manager, and search for the name "Cohn." From within the Current List in the Source Manager, edit the Thomas Cohn citation to change "Titan" to "King" so the book title reads "Frank Lloyd Wright: Wisconsin Boy, King of Modernism." After you make the change, update the source in both lists. When you are finished, delete "Cohn" from the Search box to redisplay all the sources in both lists.

Explore 7. From within the Source Manager, copy a source not included in the current document from the Master List to the Current List. Examine the sources in the Current List, and note the checkmarks next to the two sources for which you have already created citations and the question marks next to the placeholder sources. Sources in the Current list that are not actually cited in the text have no symbol next to them. For example, if you copied a source from the Master List into your Current List, that source has no symbol next to it in the Current List.

8. Close the Source Manager, create a bibliography on a new page with a "Works Cited" heading, and note which works appear in it.

Explore 9. Open the Source Manager, and then edit the Wesley placeholder source to include the following information about a journal article:

   Wesley, Jamal. "Le Corbusier and the International Style." Modernism International Journal (2018): 72–89. Web.

10. Update the bibliography.

Explore 11. Open Microsoft Edge, and use the web to research the difference between a works cited list and a works consulted list. If necessary, open the Source Manager, and then delete any uncited sources from the Current List to ensure that your document contains a true works cited list, as specified by the MLA style, and not a works consulted list. (Xavier will create a full citation for the "Zhang" placeholder later.)

12. Update the bibliography, finalize it so it matches the MLA style, save the document, and close it.

Module 3

Creating Tables and a Multipage Report

Writing a Recommendation

Objectives

Session 3.1

- Review document headings in the Navigation pane
- Reorganize document text using the Navigation pane
- Collapse and expand body text in a document
- Create and edit a table
- Sort rows in a table
- Modify a table's structure
- Format a table
- Merge cells and add a formula

Session 3.2

- Set tab stops
- Turn on automatic hyphenation
- Divide a document into sections
- Create a SmartArt graphic
- Create headers and footers
- Insert a cover page
- Change the document's theme
- Review a document in Read Mode

Case | Spruce & Cooper

Eboni Wheatley is the new IT manager at Spruce & Cooper, an online gourmet gift basket business that is expanding rapidly.

She has written a multiple-page report for the company's leadership team summarizing basic information about wireless site surveys. She has asked you to finish formatting the report. Eboni also needs your help with adding a table and a diagram to the end of the report.

In this module, you'll use the Navigation pane to review the document headings and reorganize the document. You will also insert a table and modify it by changing the structure and formatting, merging table cells, and adding a formula. Next, you'll set tab stops, hyphenate the document, and insert a section break. In addition, you'll create a SmartArt graphic and add headers and footers. Finally, you will insert a cover page, change the theme, and review the document in Read Mode.

Starting Data Files

Word3 → Module
NP_WD_3-1.docx
NP_WD_3-2.docx

Review
NP_WD_3-3.docx

Case1
NP_WD_3-4.docx

Case2
(none)

Session 3.1 Visual Overview:

You can organize text or numerical data in a document using the Table button in the Tables group on the Insert tab.

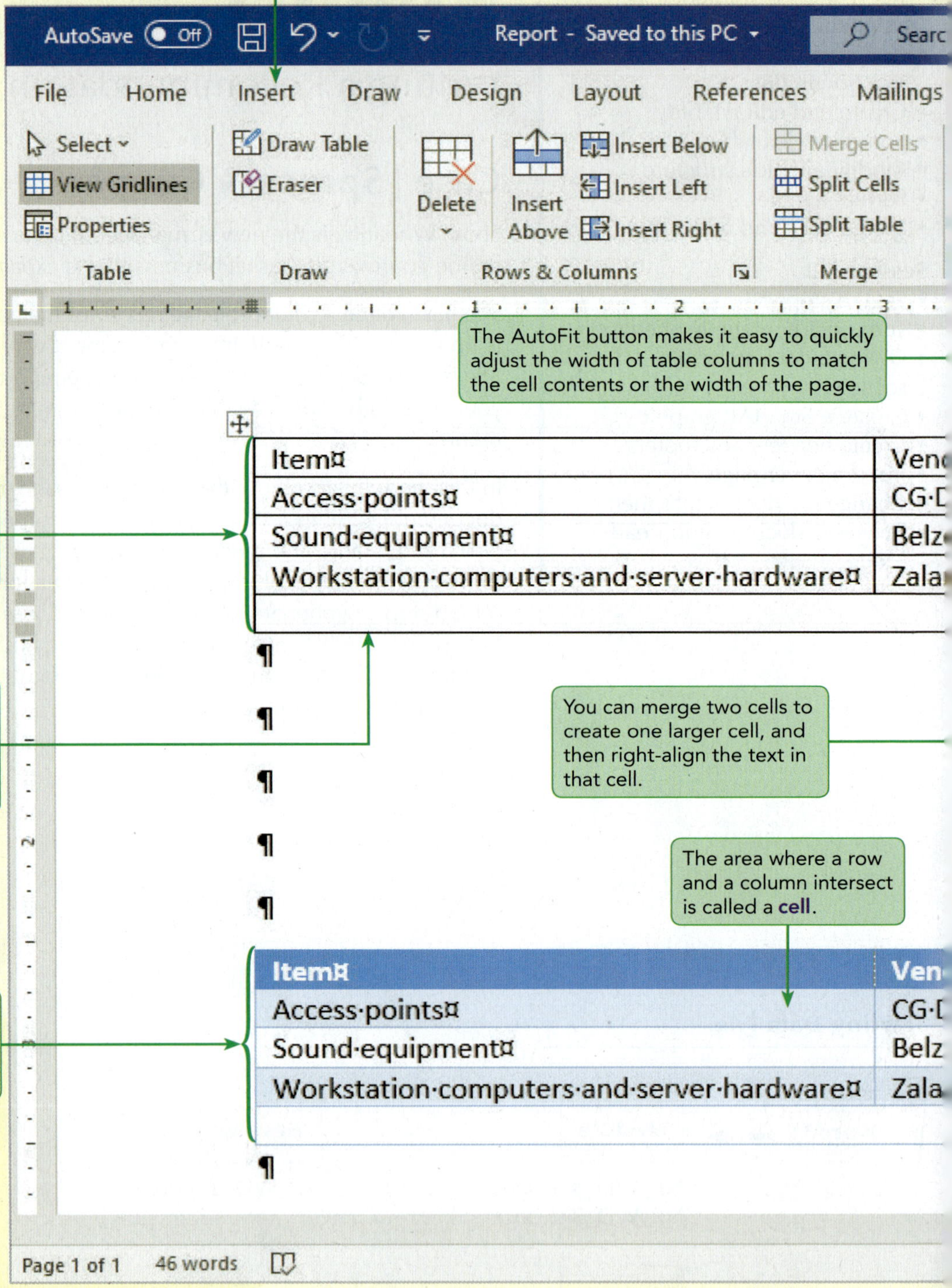

The AutoFit button makes it easy to quickly adjust the width of table columns to match the cell contents or the width of the page.

A **table** consists of information arranged in a grid made up of horizontal rows and vertical columns.

When you first insert a table into a document, it looks like this, with black **borders** defining the rows and columns.

You can merge two cells to create one larger cell, and then right-align the text in that cell.

The area where a row and a column intersect is called a **cell**.

This table has been formatted with one of the table styles available on the Table Design tab.

Organizing Information in Tables

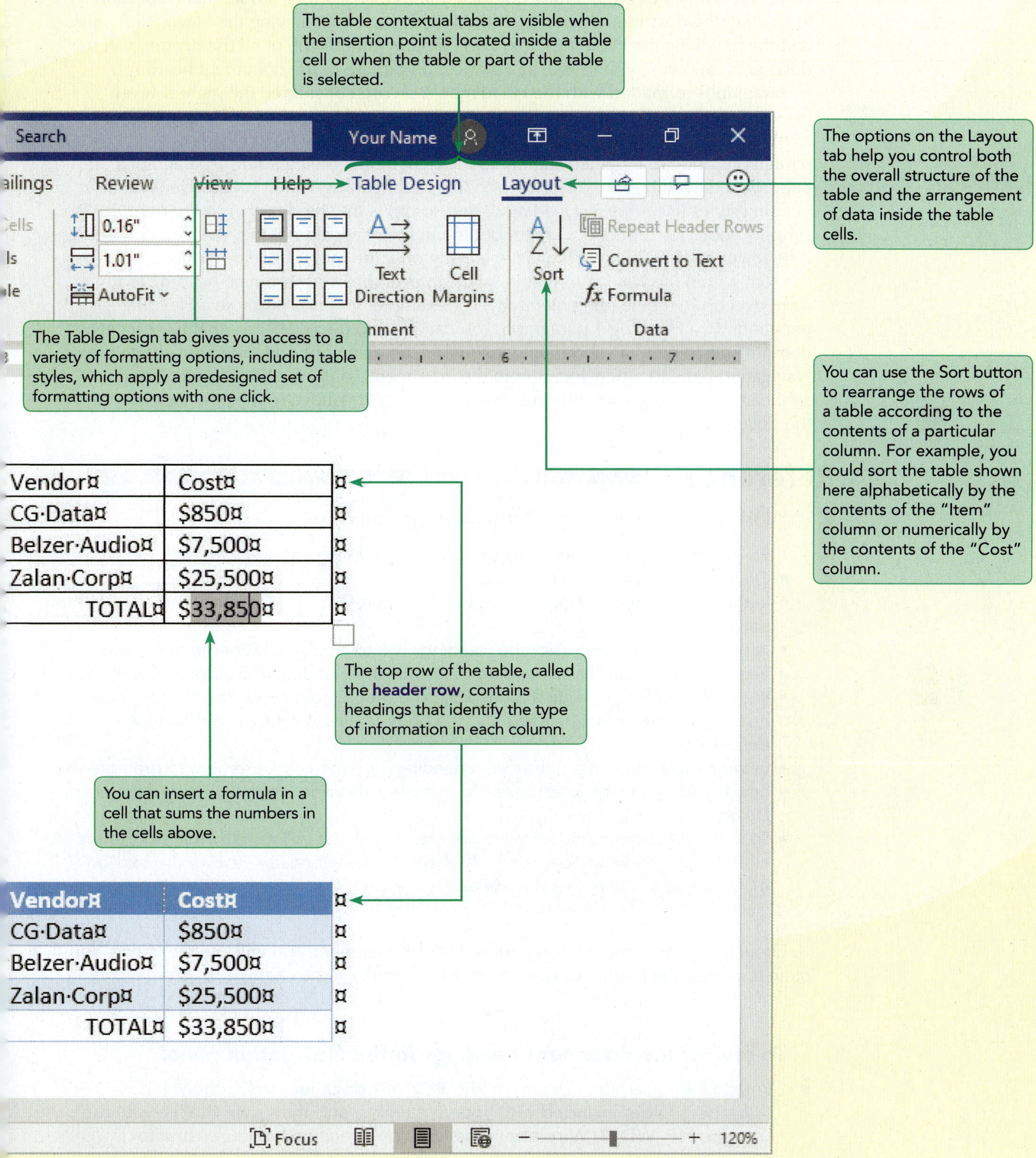

Working with Headings in the Navigation Pane

When used in combination with the Navigation pane, Word's heading styles make it easier to navigate through a long document and to reorganize a document. You start by formatting the document headings with heading styles, displaying the Navigation pane, and then clicking the Headings link. This displays a hierarchy of all the headings in the document, allowing you to see, at a glance, an outline of the document headings.

Paragraphs formatted with the Heading 1 style are considered the highest-level headings and are aligned at the left margin of the Navigation pane. Paragraphs formatted with the Heading 2 style are considered subordinate to Heading 1 paragraphs and are indented slightly to the right below the Heading 1 paragraphs. Subordinate headings are often referred to as **subheadings**. Each successive level of heading styles (Heading 3, Heading 4, and so on) is indented farther to the right. To simplify your view of the document outline in the Navigation pane, you can choose to hide lower-level headings from view, leaving only the major headings visible.

From within the Navigation pane, you can **promote** a subordinate heading to the next level up in the heading hierarchy. For example, you can promote a Heading 2 paragraph to a Heading 1 paragraph. You can also do the opposite—that is, you can **demote** a heading to a subordinate level. You can also click and drag a heading in the Navigation pane to a new location in the document's outline. When you do so, any subheadings—along with their subordinate body text—move to the new location in the document.

Reference

Working with Headings in the Navigation Pane

- Format the document headings using Word's heading styles.
- On the ribbon, click the Home tab.
- In the Editing group, click the Find button, or press CTRL+F, to display the Navigation pane.
- In the Navigation pane, click the Headings link to display a list of the document headings, and then click a heading to display that heading in the document window.
- In the Navigation pane, click a heading, and then drag it up or down in the list of headings to move that heading and the body text below it to a new location in the document.
- In the Navigation pane, right-click a heading, and then click Promote to promote the heading to the next-highest level. To demote a heading, right-click it, and then click Demote.
- To hide subheadings in the Navigation pane, click the collapse triangle next to the higher level heading above them. To redisplay the subheadings, click the expand triangle next to the higher-level heading.

Eboni saved the draft of her report as a Word document. You will use the Navigation pane to review the outline of Eboni's report and make some changes to its organization.

To review the document headings in the Navigation pane:

1. sam Open the document **NP_WD_3-1.docx** located in the Word3 > Module folder included with your Data Files, and then save the file with the name **NP_WD_3_Wireless** in the location specified by your instructor.

2. Verify that the document is displayed in Print Layout view and that the rulers and nonprinting characters are displayed.
3. Make sure the Zoom level is set to **120%**, and that the Home tab is selected on the ribbon.
4. Press **CTRL+F**. The Navigation pane opens to the left of the document.
5. In the Navigation pane, click the **Headings** link. The document headings are displayed in the Navigation pane, as shown in Figure 3–1. The blue highlighted heading ("Summary") indicates that part of the document currently contains the insertion point.

Figure 3–1 **Headings displayed in the Navigation pane**

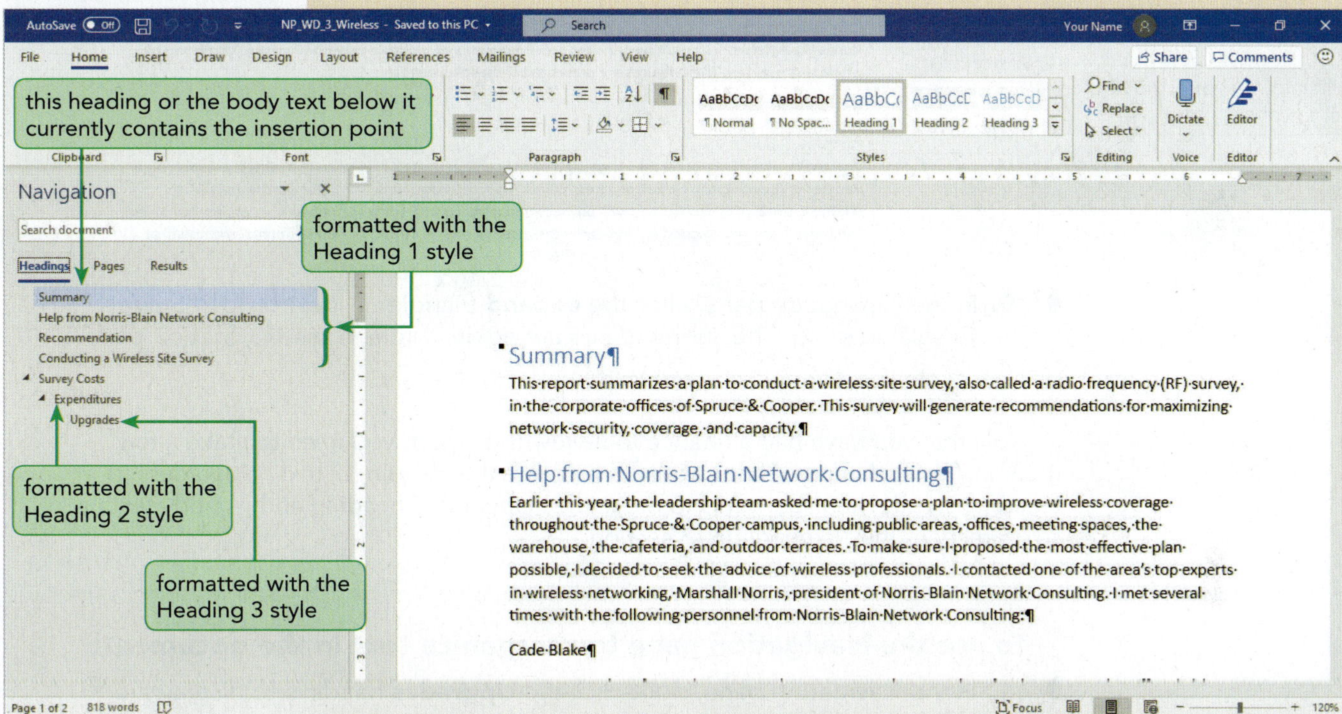

6. In the Navigation pane, click the **Recommendation** heading. Word displays the heading in the document window, with the insertion point at the beginning of the heading. The "Recommendation" heading is highlighted in blue in the Navigation pane.
7. In the Navigation pane, click the **Survey Costs** heading. Word displays the heading in the document window. In the Navigation pane, you can see that there are subheadings below this heading.
8. In the Navigation pane, click the **collapse** triangle next to the "Survey Costs" heading. The subheadings below this heading are no longer visible in the Navigation pane. This has no effect on the text in the actual document. See Figure 3–2.

Figure 3–2 **Heading 2 and Heading 3 text hidden in Navigation pane**

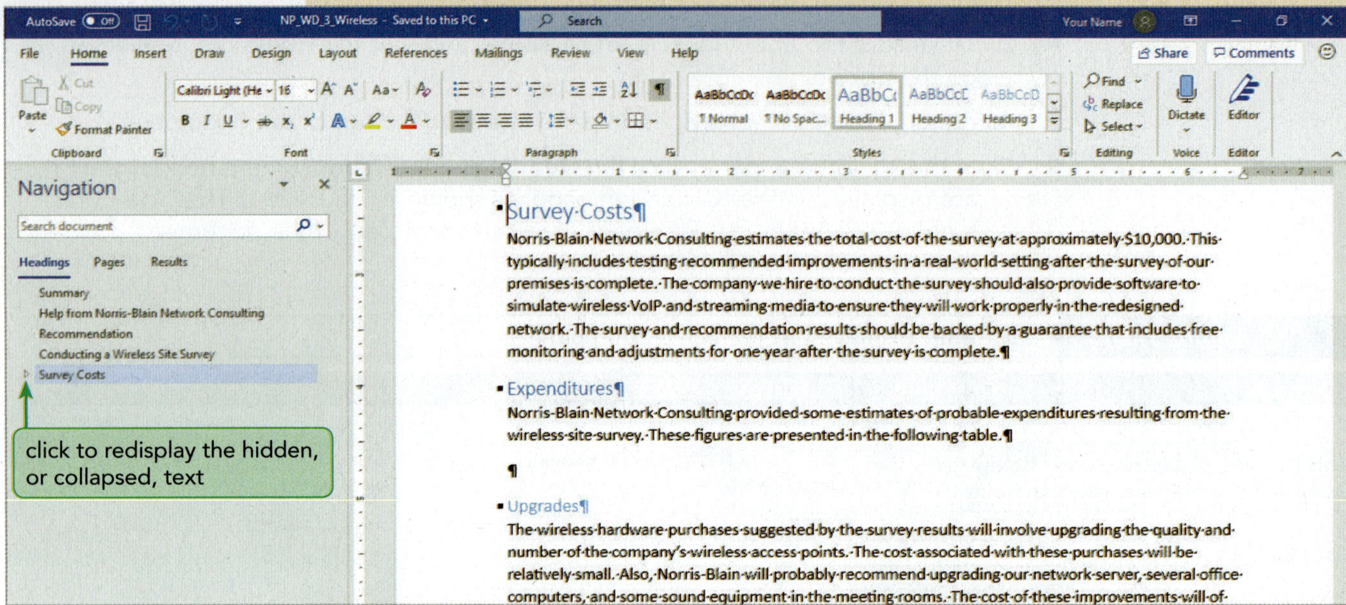

9. In the Navigation pane, click the **expand** triangle ▷ next to the "Survey Costs" heading. The subheadings are again visible in the Navigation pane.

Now that you have had a chance to review the report, you need to make a few organizational changes. Eboni wants to promote the Heading 3 text "Upgrades" to Heading 2 text. Then she wants to move the "Upgrades" heading and its body text up, so it precedes the "Expenditures" section.

To use the Navigation pane to reorganize text in the document:

1. In the Navigation pane, right-click the **Upgrades** heading to display the shortcut menu.
2. Click **Promote**. The heading moves to the left in the Navigation pane, aligning below the "Expenditures" heading. In the document window, the text is now formatted with the Heading 2 style, with its slightly larger font.
3. In the Navigation pane, click and drag the **Upgrades** heading up. As you drag the heading, the pointer changes to a drag pointer, and a blue guideline is displayed. You can use the guideline to position the heading in its new location.
4. Position the guideline directly below the "Survey Costs" heading, as shown in Figure 3–3.

Figure 3–3 **Moving a heading in the Navigation pane**

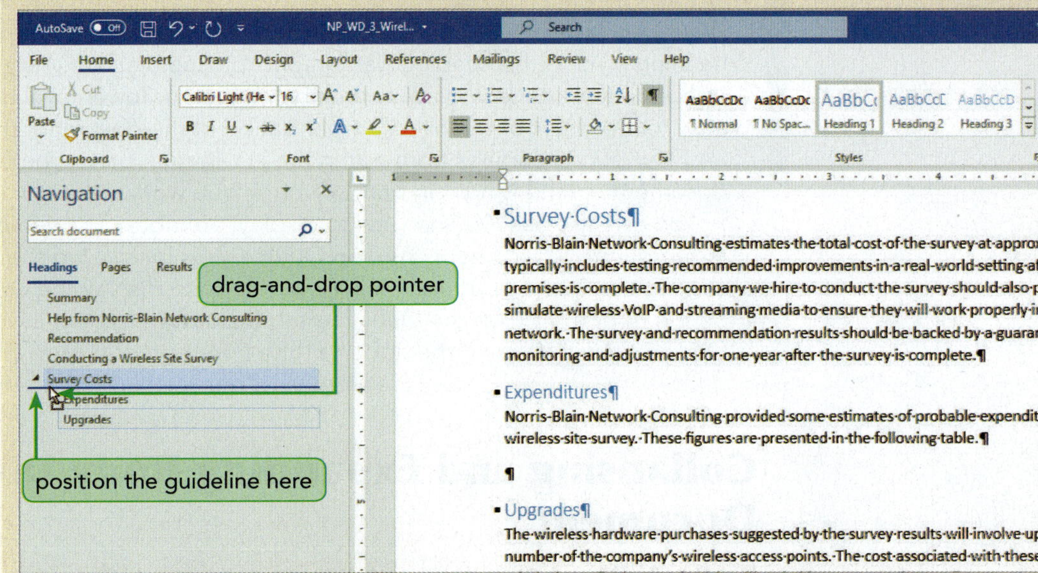

5. Release the mouse button. The "Upgrades" heading is displayed in its new position in the Navigation pane, as the second-to-last heading in the outline. The heading and its body text are displayed in their new location in the document, before the "Expenditures" heading. See Figure 3–4.

Figure 3–4 **Heading and body text in new location**

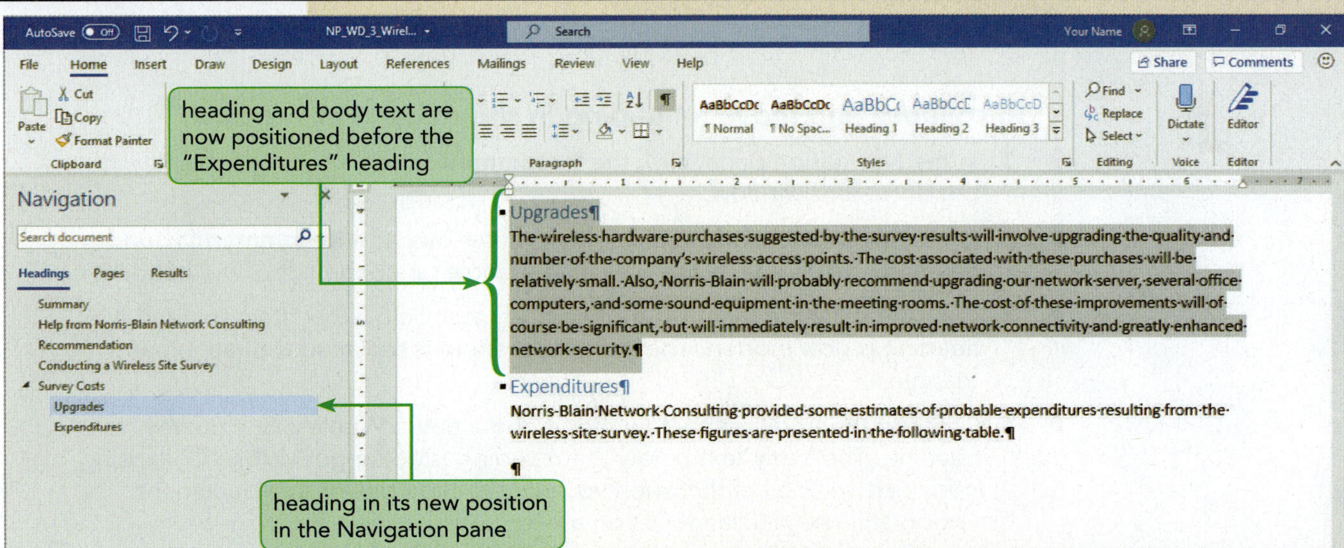

6. Click anywhere in the document to deselect the text, and then save the document.

Eboni also wants you to move the "Recommendation" heading and its accompanying body text. You'll do that in the next section, using a different method.

Insight

Promoting and Demoting Headings

When you promote or demote a heading, Word applies the next higher- or lower-level heading style to the heading paragraph. You could accomplish the same thing by using the Style gallery to apply the next higher- or lower-level heading style, but it's easy to lose track of the overall organization of the document that way. By promoting and demoting headings from within the Navigation pane, you ensure that the overall document outline is right in front of you as you work.

You can also use Outline view to display, promote, and demote headings and to reorganize a document. Turn on Outline view by clicking the View tab, and then clicking the Outline button in the Views group to display the Outlining contextual tab on the ribbon. To hide the Outlining tab and return to Print Layout view, click the Close Outline View button on the ribbon or the Print Layout button in the status bar.

Collapsing and Expanding Body Text in the Document

Because the Navigation pane gives you an overview of the entire document, dragging headings within the Navigation pane is the best way to reorganize a document. However, you can also reorganize a document from within the document window, without using the Navigation pane, by first hiding, or collapsing, the body text below a heading in a document. After you collapse the body text below a heading, you can drag the heading to a new location in the document. When you do, the body text moves along with the heading, just as if you had dragged the heading in the Navigation pane. You'll use this technique now to move the "Recommendation" heading and its body text.

To collapse and move a heading in the document window:

1. In the Navigation pane, click the **Recommendation** heading to display it in the document window.
2. In the document window, place the pointer over the **Recommendation** heading to display the gray collapse triangle ◢ to the left of the heading.
3. Click the **collapse** triangle ◢. The body text below the "Recommendation" heading is now hidden. The collapse triangle is replaced with an expand triangle.
4. Collapse the body text below the "Conducting a Wireless Site Survey" heading. The body text below that heading is no longer visible. Collapsing body text can be helpful when you want to hide details in a document temporarily, so you can focus on a particular part. See Figure 3–5.

Figure 3–5 **Body text collapsed in the document**

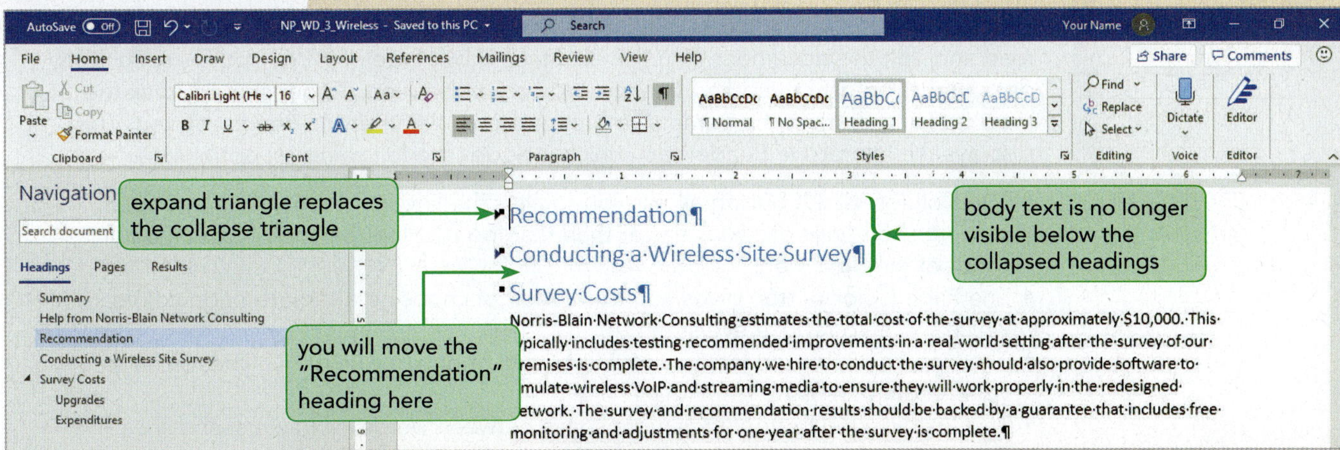

5. In the document, select the **Recommendation** heading, including the paragraph mark at the end of the paragraph.
6. Click and drag the heading down. As you drag, a dark black insertion point moves along with the pointer.
7. Position the dark black insertion point to the left of the "S" in the "Survey Costs" heading, and then release the mouse button. The "Recommendation" heading and its body text move to the new location, before the "Survey Costs" heading.

   Finally, you need to expand the body text below the two collapsed headings.

8. Click anywhere in the document to deselect the text.
9. Click the **expand** triangle ▷ to redisplay the body text below the heading.
10. Click to the **expand** triangle ▷ to the left of the "Conducting a Wireless Site Survey" heading to redisplay the body text below the heading.
11. Save the document.

The document is now organized the way Eboni wants it. Next, you need to create a table summarizing her data on probable expenditures.

Insight

Using the Immersive Reader

Hiding body text in a document makes it easy to focus on important material as you read and edit the document. You can also take advantage of Word options specifically designed to help with reading fluency and comprehension. To get started, click the View tab, and then, in the Immersive group, click the Immersive Reader button. This displays the Immersive Reader tab, which includes the following six options:

- The Column Width button allows you to alter the line length. For some people, reading short lines of text is easier than reading text that extends across the full width of the document.
- The Page Color button gives you the option of choosing alternate page colors, which can help reduce eye strain.
- The Line Focus button lets you highlight sets of one, three, or five lines to narrow your reading focus.
- The Text Spacing button adds more space between words, characters, and lines. Depending on your needs, you might find that this makes a block of text easier to read.
- The Syllables button inserts breaks between syllables, making it easier to pronounce unfamiliar words.
- The Read Aloud button begins an automated reading of the document text. As each word is pronounced, it is highlighted in the text.

The Immersive Reader tab stays visible as long as the current document is open. To hide it, click the Close Immersive Reader button.

The Dictate button in the Voice group on the Home tab is an accessibility option that can increase writing fluency for some people. If a microphone is installed on your computer, you can use the Dictate button to add text to a document by speaking rather than typing.

To get started, click the Dictate button, and wait for the button icon to change into white microphone with a red circle next to it. Then speak clearly into your computer's microphone. The sentences you speak are immediately translated into document text. Note that you'll probably need to edit the text when you are finished dictating, but with practice, you can learn how to dictate in a way that produces fewer and fewer errors. Exactly how fast you need to talk, and how precisely, will vary from one microphone to another.

Inserting a Blank Table

Tip

The terms "table," "field," and "record" are also used to refer to information stored in database programs, such as Microsoft Access.

A table is a useful way to present information that is organized into categories, or **fields**. For example, you could use a table to organize contact information for a list of clients. For each client, you could include information in the following fields: first name, last name, street address, city, state, and zip code. The complete set of information about a particular client is called a **record**. In a typical table, each column is a separate field, and each row is a record. A header row at the top contains the names of each field.

The sketch in Figure 3–6 shows what Eboni wants the table in her report to look like.

Figure 3–6 **Table sketch**

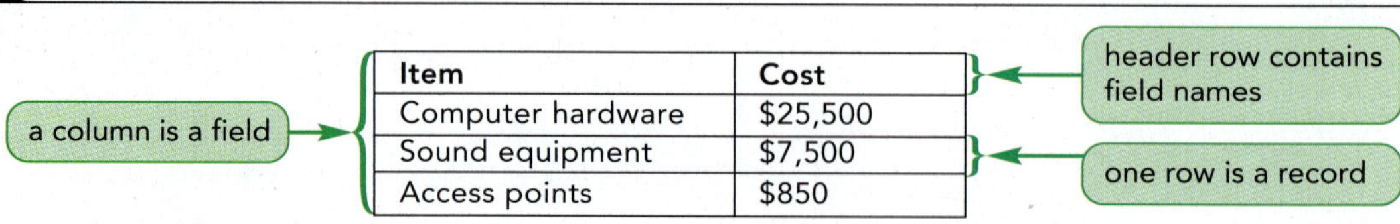

Eboni's table includes two columns, or fields: "Item" and "Cost." The header row contains the names of these two fields. The three rows below contain the records.

Creating a table in Word is a three-step process. First, you use the Table button on the Insert tab to insert a blank table structure. Then you enter information into the table. Finally, you format the table to make it easy to read.

Before you begin creating the table, you'll insert a page break before the "Expenditures" heading. This will move the heading and its body text to a new page, with plenty of room below for the new table. As a general rule, you should not use page breaks to position a particular part of a document at the top of a page. If you add or remove text from the document later, you might forget that you inserted a manual page break, and you could end up with a document layout you didn't expect. By default, Word heading styles are set up to ensure that a heading always appears on the same page as the body text paragraph below it, so you'll never need to insert a page break just to move a heading to the same page as its body text. However, in this case, a page break is appropriate because you need the "Expenditures" heading to be displayed at the top of a page with room for the table below.

To insert a page break and insert a blank table:

1. In the Navigation pane, click **Expenditures** to display the heading in the document, with the insertion point to the left of the "E" in "Expenditures."
2. Close the Navigation pane, and then press **CTRL+ENTER** to insert a page break. The "Expenditures" heading and the body text following it move to a new, third page.
3. Scroll to position the "Expenditures" heading at the top of the Word window, and then press **CTRL+END** to move the insertion point to the blank paragraph at the end of the document.
4. On the ribbon, click the **Insert** tab.
5. In the Tables group, click the **Table** button. A table grid opens, with a menu at the bottom.
6. Use the pointer to point to the **upper-left cell** of the grid, and then move the pointer down and across the grid to highlight two columns and four rows. (The outline of a cell turns orange when it is highlighted.) As you move the pointer across the grid, Word indicates the size of the table (columns by rows) at the top of the grid. A Live Preview of the table structure is displayed in the document. See Figure 3–7.

Tip

You can use the Quick Tables option to choose from preformatted tables that contain placeholder text.

Figure 3–7 Inserting a blank table

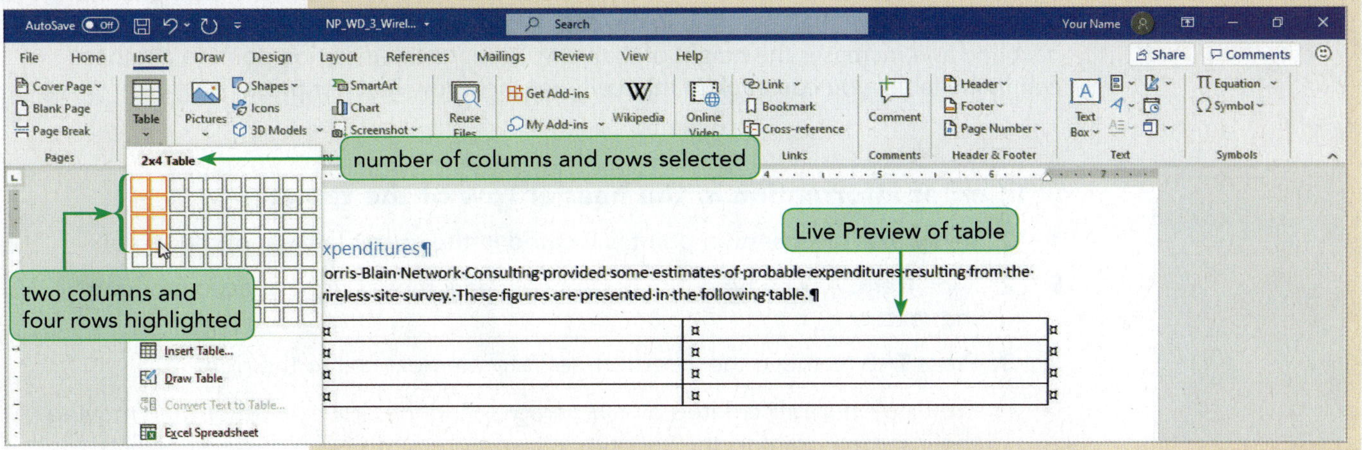

7. When the table size is 2×4, click the lower-right cell in the block of selected cells. An empty table consisting of two columns and four rows is inserted in the document, with the insertion point in the upper-left cell. See Figure 3–8.

Figure 3–8 Blank table inserted in document

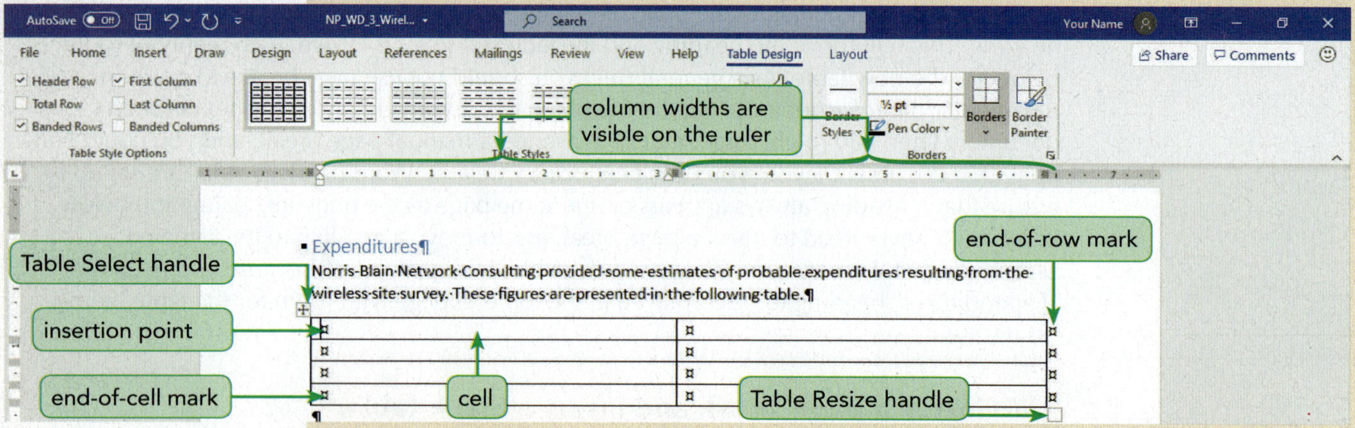

The two columns are of equal width. Because nonprinting characters are displayed in the document, each cell contains an end-of-cell mark, and each row contains an end-of-row mark, which are important for selecting parts of a table. The Table Select handle is displayed at the table's upper-left corner. You can click the Table Select handle to select the entire table, and you can drag it to move the table. You can drag the Table Resize handle, which is displayed at the lower-right corner, to change the size of the table. The Table Design and Layout contextual tabs are displayed on the ribbon.

Trouble? If you inserted a table with the wrong number of rows or columns, click the Undo button on the Quick Access Toolbar to remove the table, and then repeat Steps 4 through 7.

The blank table is ready for you to begin entering information.

Entering Data in a Table

You can enter data in a table by moving the insertion point to a cell and typing. If the data takes up more than one line in the cell, Word automatically wraps the text to the next line and increases the height of that row. To move the insertion point to another cell in the table, you can click in that cell, use the arrow keys, or press TAB.

To enter information in the header row of the table:

1. Verify that the insertion point is located in the upper-left cell of the table.
2. Type **Item**. As you type, the end-of-cell mark moves right to accommodate the text.
3. Press **TAB** to move the insertion point to the next cell to the right.

   Trouble? If Word created a new paragraph in the first cell rather than moving the insertion point to the second cell, you pressed ENTER instead of TAB. Press BACKSPACE to remove the paragraph mark, and then press TAB to move to the second cell in the first row.

4. Type **Cost** and then press **TAB** to move to the first cell in the second row.

You have finished entering the header row—the row that identifies the information in each column. Now you can enter the information about the various expenditures.

To continue entering information in the table:

1. Type **computer hardware** and then press **TAB** to move to the second cell in the second row. Notice that the "c" in "computer" is capitalized, even though you typed it in lowercase. By default, AutoCorrect capitalizes the first letter in a cell entry.
2. Type **$25,500** and then press **TAB** to move the insertion point to the first cell in the third row.
3. Enter the following information in the bottom two rows, pressing **TAB** to move from cell to cell:

   Sound equipment; **$7,500**

   Access points; **$850**

At this point, the table consists of a header row and three records. Eboni realizes that she needs to add one more row to the table. You can add a new row to the bottom of a table by pressing TAB when the insertion point is in the rightmost cell in the bottom row.

To add a row to the table:

1. Verify that the insertion point is in the lower-right cell (which contains the value "$850"), and then press **TAB**. A new, blank row is added to the bottom of the table.
2. Type **Servers**, press **TAB**, type **$15,000**, and then save the document. When you are finished, your table should look like the one shown in Figure 3–9.

Figure 3–9 Table with all data entered

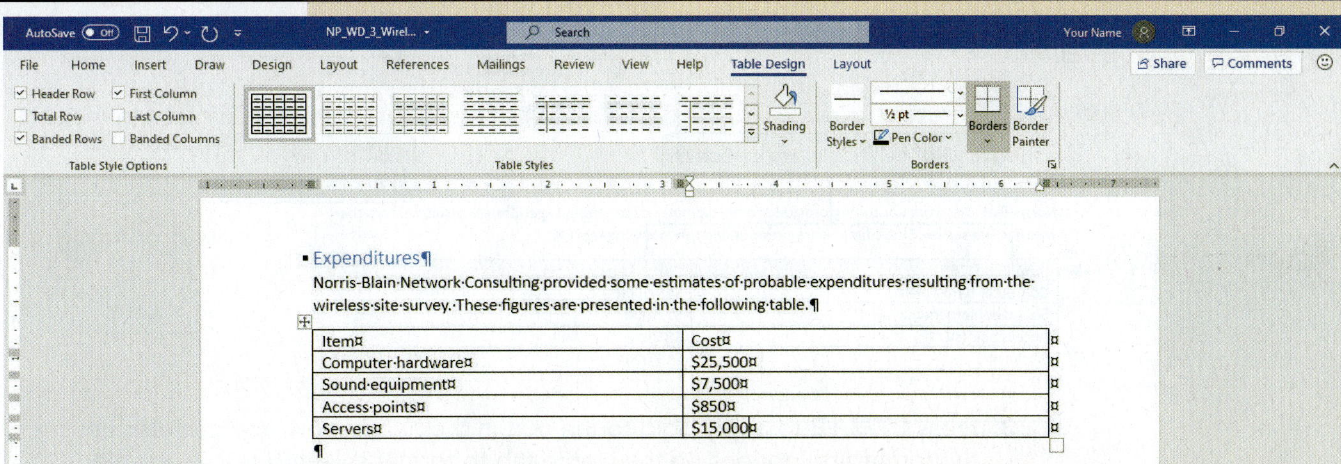

Trouble? If a new row is added to the bottom of your table, you pressed TAB after entering "$15,000". Click the Undo button on the Quick Access Toolbar to remove the extra row from the table.

The table you've just created presents information about expenditures in an easy-to-read format. To make it even easier to read, you can format the header row in bold so it stands out from the rest of the table. To do that, you need to first select the header row.

Selecting Part of a Table

When selecting part of a table, you need to make sure you select the end-of-cell mark in a cell or the end-of-row mark at the end of a row. If you don't, the formatting changes you make next might not have the effect you expect. The foolproof way to select part of a table is to click in the cell, row, or column you want to select; click the Select button on the Layout contextual tab; and then click the appropriate command—Select Cell, Select Column, or Select Row. Or click Select Table to select the entire table. To select a row, you can also click in the left margin next to the row. Similarly, you can click just above a column to select it. After you've selected an entire row, column, or cell, you can drag the mouse to select adjacent rows, columns, or cells.

Note that in the following steps, you'll position the pointer until it takes on a particular shape so that you can then perform the task associated with that type of pointer. Pointer shapes are especially important when working with tables and graphics; in many cases, you can't perform a task until the pointer is the right shape. It takes some patience to get accustomed to positioning the pointer until it takes on the correct shape, but with practice you'll grow to rely on the pointer shapes as a quick visual cue to the options currently available to you.

To select and format the header row:

1. Position the pointer in the selection bar, to the left of the header row. The pointer changes to a right-pointing arrow.
2. Click the mouse button. The entire header row, including the end-of-cell mark in each cell and the end-of-row mark, is selected. See Figure 3–10.

Figure 3–10 Header row selected

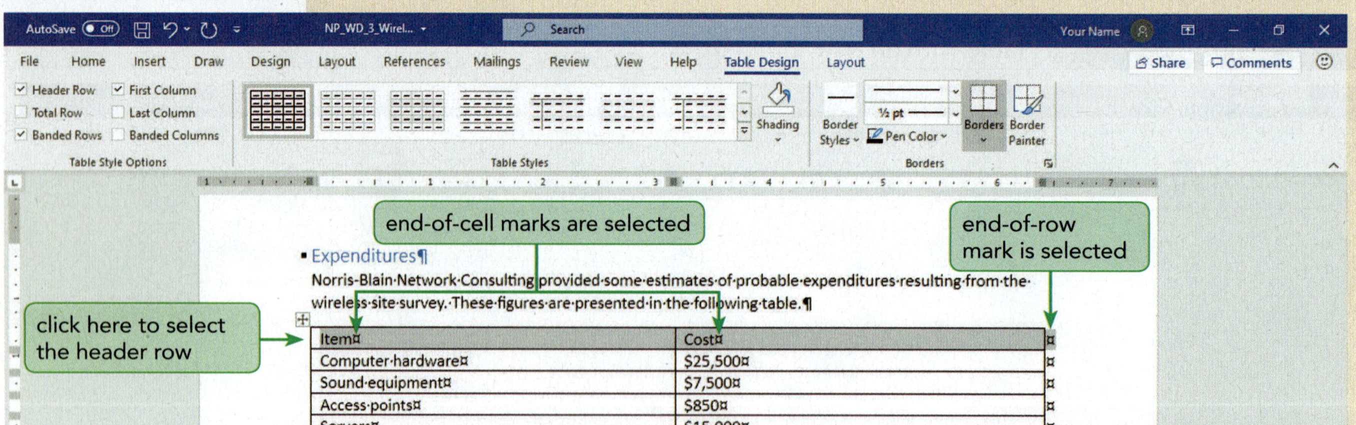

3. Press **CTRL+B** to apply bold to the text in the header row. You can also use the formatting options on the Home tab to format selected text in a table, including adding italic formatting, changing the font, aligning text within cells, or applying a style. However, text in a table that is formatted with a heading style will not show up as a heading in the Navigation pane.
4. Click anywhere in the table to deselect the header row, and then save the document.

Note that, in some documents, you might have a long table that extends across multiple pages. To make a multipage table easier to read, you can format the table header row to appear at the top of every page. To do so, click in the header row, click the Layout tab, and then click the Properties button in the Table group. In the Table Properties dialog box, click the Row tab, and then select the "Repeat as header row at the top of each page" check box.

Now that you have created a very basic table, you can sort the information in it and improve its appearance.

Sorting Rows in a Table

The term **sort** refers to the process of rearranging information in alphabetical, numerical, or chronological order. You can sort a series of paragraphs, including the contents of a bulleted list, or you can sort the rows of a table.

When you sort a table, you arrange the rows based on the contents of one of the columns. For example, you could sort the table you just created based on the contents of the "Item" column—either in ascending alphabetical order (from A to Z) or in descending alphabetical order (from Z to A). Alternatively, you could sort the table based on the contents of the "Cost" column—either in ascending numerical order (lowest to highest) or in descending numerical order (highest to lowest).

Clicking the Sort button in the Data group on the Layout tab opens the Sort dialog box, which provides a number of options for fine-tuning the sort, including options for sorting a table by the contents of more than one column. This is useful if, for example, you want to organize the table rows by last name and then by first name within each last name. By default, Word assumes your table includes a header row that should remain at the top of the table—excluded from the sort.

Reference

Sorting the Rows of a Table

- Click anywhere within the table.
- On the ribbon, click the Layout contextual tab.
- In the Data group, click the Sort button.
- In the Sort dialog box, click the Sort by arrow, and then select the header for the column you want to sort by.
- In the Type box located to the right of the Sort by box, select the type of information stored in the column you want to sort by; you can choose Text, Number, or Date.
- To sort in alphabetical, chronological, or numerical order, verify that the Ascending option button is selected. To sort in reverse order, click the Descending option button.
- To sort by a second column, click the Then by arrow, and then select a column header. If necessary, specify the type of information stored in the Then by column, and then confirm the sort order.
- At the bottom of the Sort dialog box, make sure the Header row option button is selected. This indicates that the table includes a header row that should not be included in the sort.
- Click OK.

Eboni would like you to sort the contents of the table in ascending numerical order based on the contents of the "Cost" column.

To sort the information in the table:

1. Make sure the insertion point is located somewhere in the table.
2. On the ribbon, click the **Layout** contextual tab.
3. In the Data group, click the **Sort** button. The Sort dialog box opens. Take a moment to review its default settings. The leftmost column in the table, the "Item" column, is selected in the Sort by box, indicating the sort will be based on the contents in this column. Because the "Item" column contains text, "Text" is selected in the Type box. The Ascending option button is selected by default, indicating that Word will sort the contents of the "Item" column from A to Z. The Header row option button is selected in the lower-left corner of the dialog box, ensuring the header row will not be included in the sort.

   You want to sort the column by the contents of the "Cost" column, so you need to change the Sort by setting.
4. Click the **Sort by arrow**, and then click **Cost**. Because the "Cost" column contains numbers, the Type box now displays "Number". The Ascending button is still selected, indicating that Word will sort the numbers in the "Cost" column from lowest to highest. At this point, if you wanted to sort by a second column, you could click the Then by arrow, and then select the Item header. See Figure 3–11.

Figure 3–11 Sort dialog box

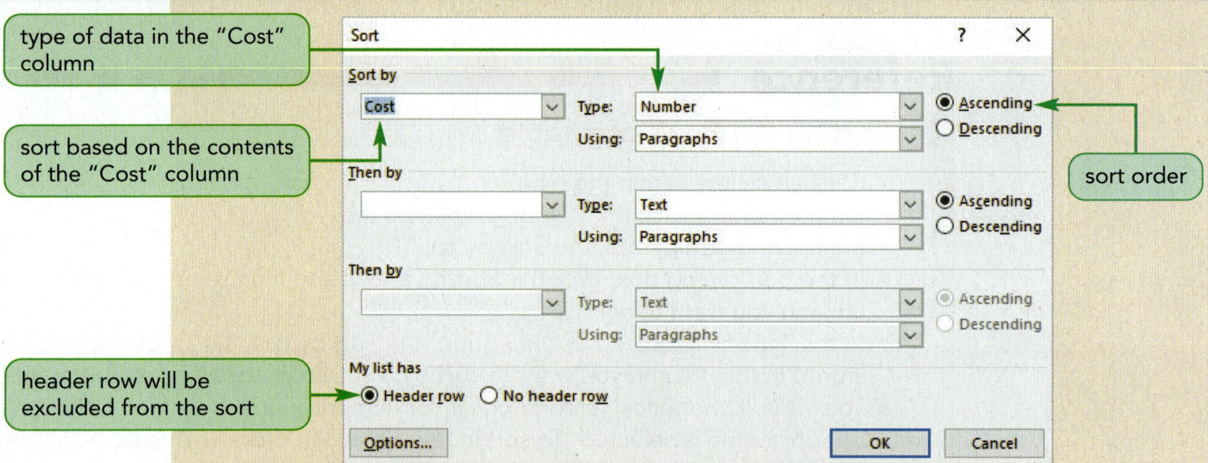

5. Click **OK** to close the Sort dialog box, and then click anywhere in the table to deselect it. Rows 2 through 5 are now arranged numerically from lowest to highest, according to the numbers in the "Cost" column, with the "Computer hardware" row at the bottom. See Figure 3–12.

Figure 3–12 Table after being sorted

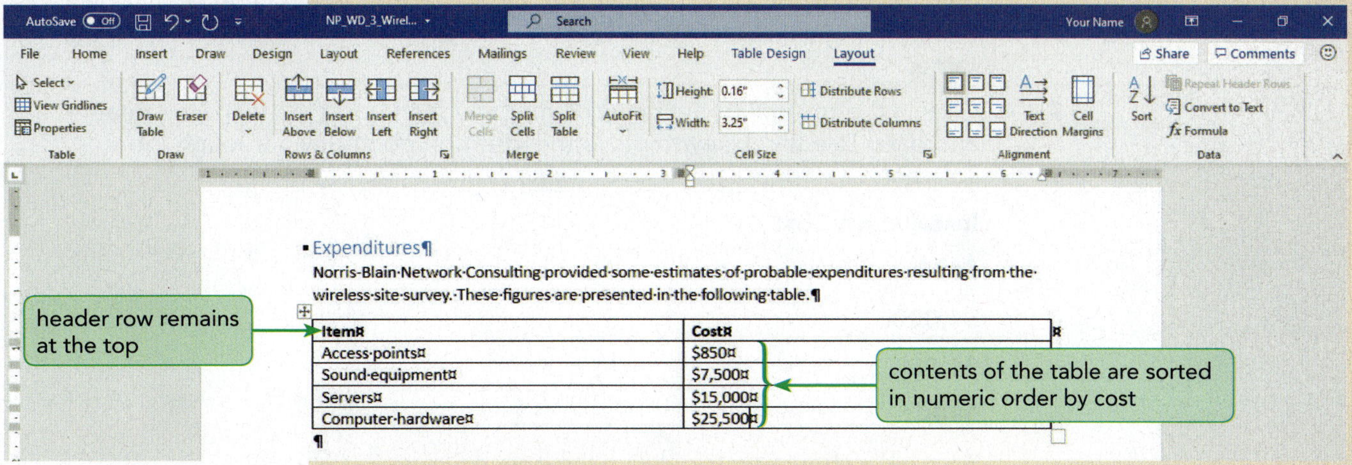

6. Save the document.

Eboni decides that the table should also include the cost for installing each item. She asks you to insert an "Installation Cost" column.

Inserting Rows and Columns in a Table

To add a column to a table, you can use the tools in the Rows & Columns group on the Layout tab, or you can use the Add Column button in the document window. To use the Add Column button, make sure the insertion point is located somewhere within the table. When you position the pointer at the top of the table, pointing to the border between two columns, the Add Column button is displayed. When you click that button, a new column is inserted between the two existing columns.

To insert a column in the table:

1. Verify that the insertion point is located anywhere in the table.
2. Position the pointer at the top of the table, so that it points to the border between the two columns. The Add Column button ⊕ appears at the top of the border. A blue guideline shows where the new column will be inserted. See Figure 3–13.

Figure 3–13 Inserting a column

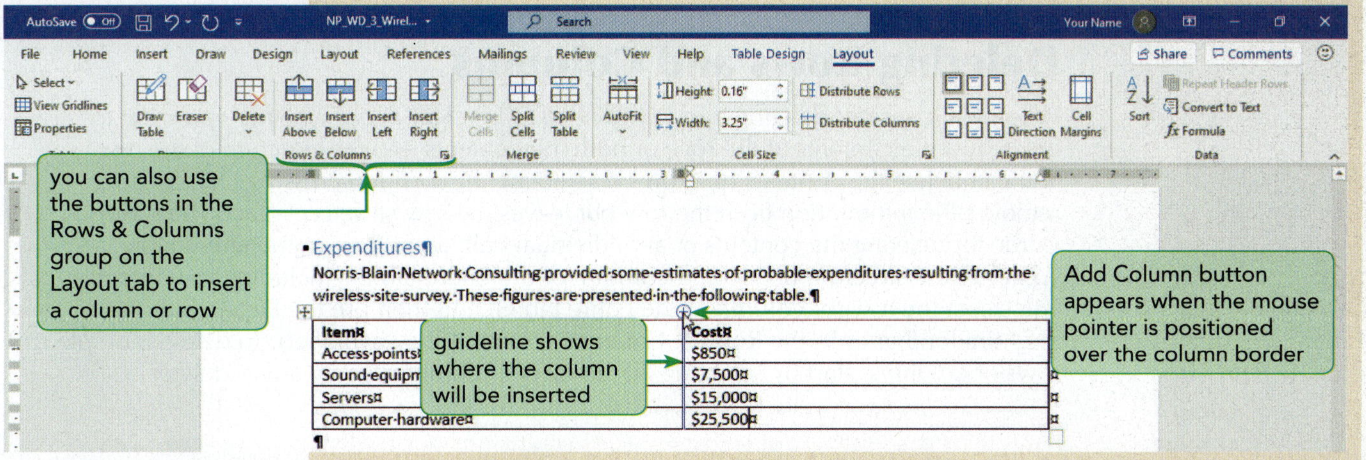

3. Click the **Add Column** button. A new, blank column is inserted between the "Item" and "Cost" columns. The three columns in the table are narrower than the original two columns, but the overall width of the table remains the same.

4. Click in the top cell of the new column, and then enter the following header and data. Use the ↓ key to move the insertion point down through the column.

   Installation Cost

   $600

   $1,000

   $1,250

   $900

   Your table should now look like the one in Figure 3–14.

Figure 3–14 New "Installation Cost" column

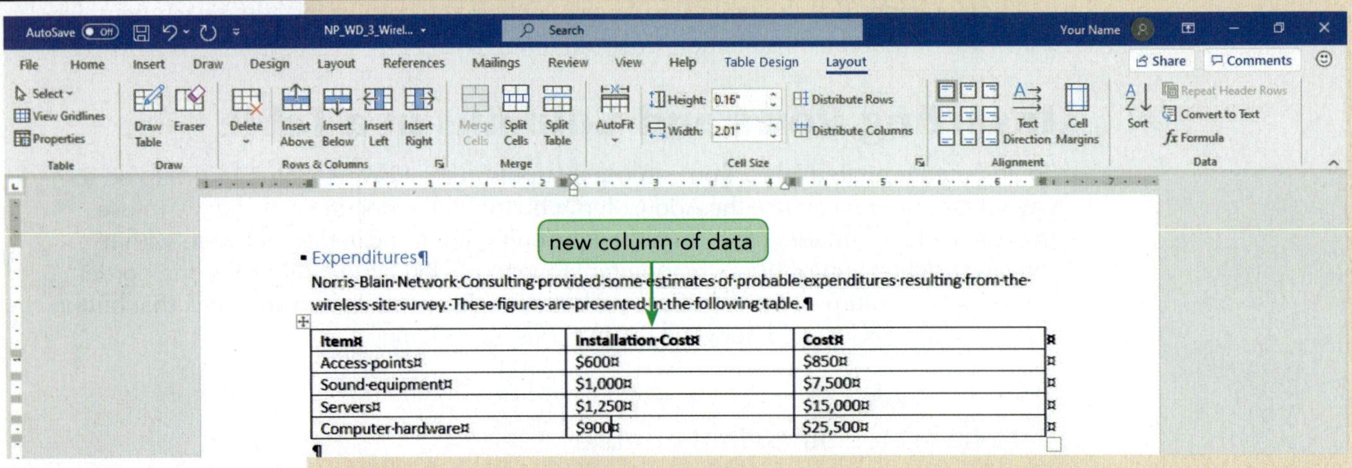

Because you selected the entire header row when you formatted the original headers in bold, the newly inserted header, "Installation Cost," is also formatted in bold.

Eboni just learned that the costs listed for computer hardware actually cover both ordinary work station computers and new servers. Therefore, she would like you to delete the "Servers" row from the table.

Deleting Rows and Columns

When you consider deleting a row, you need to be clear about whether you want to delete just the contents of the row, or both the contents and the structure of the row. You can delete the contents of a row by selecting the row and pressing DEL. This removes the information from the row but leaves the row structure intact. The same is true for deleting the contents of an individual cell, a column, or the entire table. To delete the structure of a row, a column, or the entire table—including its contents—you select the row (or column or the entire table), and then use the Delete button on the Mini toolbar or in the Rows & Columns group on the Layout tab. To delete multiple rows or columns, start by selecting all the rows or columns you want to delete.

Before you delete the "Servers" row, you need to edit the contents in the last cell of the first column to indicate that the items in that row include servers.

To delete the "Servers" row:

1. Triple-click the cell containing the text "Computer hardware" to select it and type **Workstation computers and server hardware**. Part of the text wraps to a second line within the cell. Note that you could also click anywhere in a cell, and then use BACKSPACE or DEL to delete text, and then type new text. In other words, you can edit text in a table just as you would edit ordinary text in a document.

   Next, you can delete the "Servers" row, which is no longer necessary.

2. Click in the selection bar to the left of the **Servers** row. The row is selected, with the Mini toolbar displayed on top of the selected row.
3. On the Mini toolbar, click the **Delete** button. The Delete menu opens, displaying options for deleting cells, columns, rows, or the entire table. See Figure 3–15.

Figure 3–15 Deleting a row

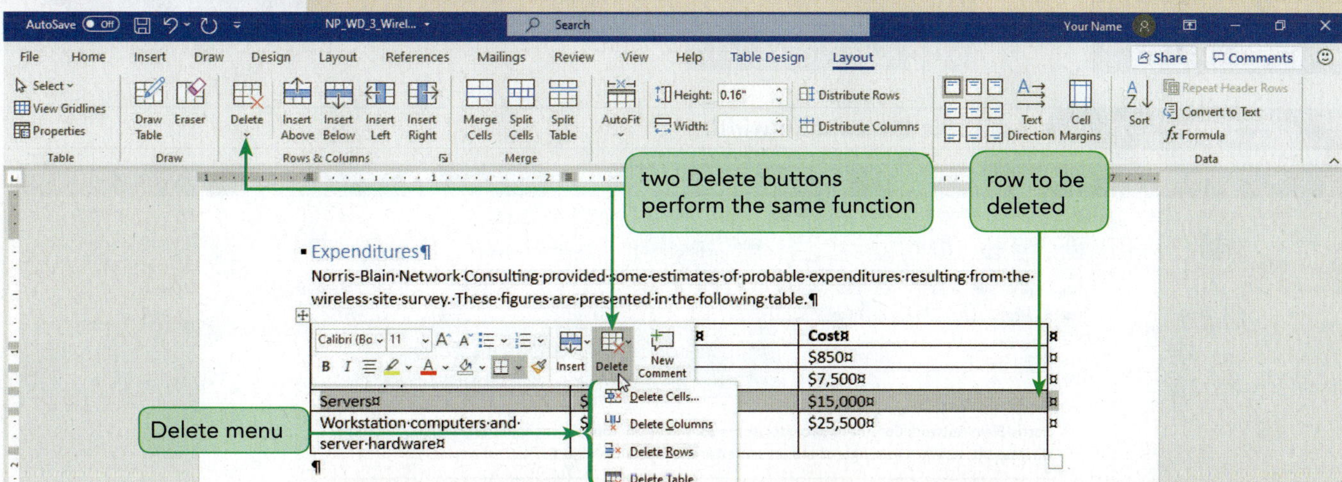

4. Click **Delete Rows**. The "Servers" row is removed from the table, and the Mini toolbar disappears.
5. Save your work.

The table now contains all the information Eboni wants to include. Next, you'll adjust the widths of the three columns.

Changing Column Widths and Row Heights

Word offers many ways to change the size of columns and rows. While it's good to know how to adjust row heights, in most cases, you'll only need to focus on column widths, because columns that are too wide for the material they contain can make a table hard to read.

You can change a column's width by dragging the column's right border to a new position. Or, if you prefer, you can double-click a column border to make the column width adjust automatically to accommodate the widest entry in the column. A more precise option is to click in the column you want to adjust, click the Layout tab, and then change the setting in the Width box, just as you would adjust the width of a picture. To adjust the width of all the columns to match their widest entries, click anywhere in the table, click the AutoFit button in the Cell Size group on the Layout tab, and then click AutoFit Contents.

You can also adjust the height of rows and the width of the entire table. To change the height of a row, position the pointer over the bottom row border and drag the border up or down, or click in the row and change the setting in the Height box on the Layout tab. You can change the width of the entire table by changing the width of all the columns and the height of all the rows at one time. To do this, drag the Table Resize handle (shown in Figure 3–8) or select the entire table and then adjust the settings in the Height and Width boxes on the Layout tab. As a final option, you can adjust the width of the entire table to span the width of the page by clicking the AutoFit button and then clicking AutoFit Window.

You'll adjust the columns in Eboni's table by double-clicking the right column border. You need to start by making sure that no part of the table is selected. Otherwise, when you double-click the border, only the width of the selected part of the table will change.

When resizing a column, be sure that no part of the table is selected. Otherwise, you'll resize just the selected part.

To change the width of the columns in the table:

1. Verify that no part of the table is selected, and then position the pointer over the right border of the "Installation Cost" column until the pointer changes to +||+. See Figure 3–16.

Figure 3–16 Adjusting the column width

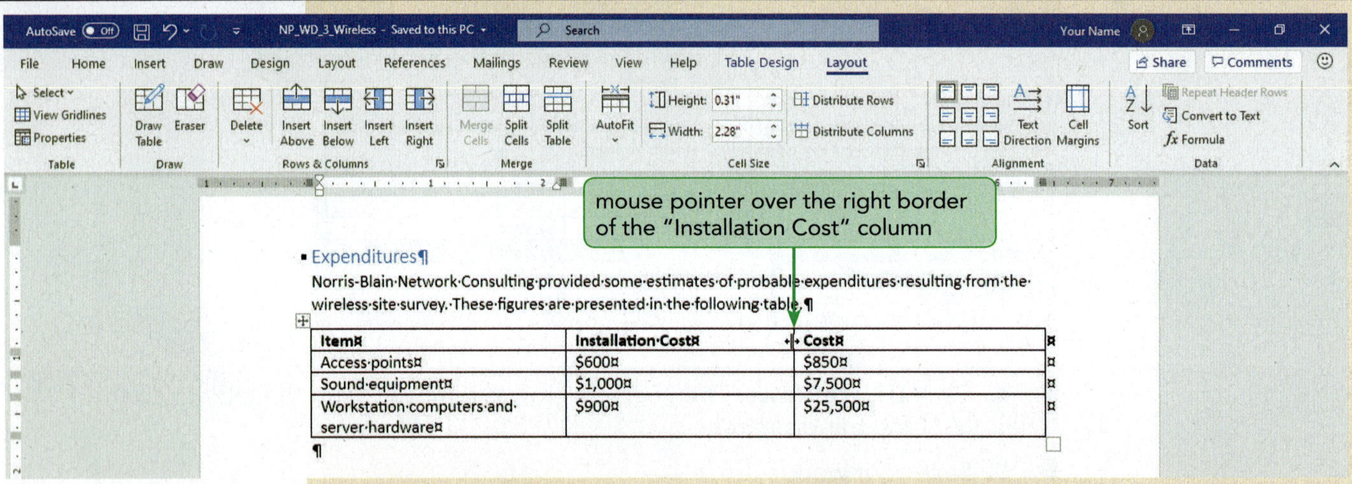

2. Double-click the mouse button. The right column border moves left so that the "Installation Cost" column is just wide enough to accommodate the widest entry in the column.
3. Verify that no part of the table is selected and that the insertion point is located in any cell in the table.
4. Make sure the Layout contextual tab is selected on the ribbon.
5. In the Cell Size group, click the **AutoFit** button, and then click **AutoFit Contents**. All of the table columns adjust so that each is just wide enough to accommodate its widest entry. The text "Workstation computers and server hardware" in row 4 no longer wraps to a second line.
6. Save the document.

To finish the table, you will add some formatting to improve the table's appearance.

Formatting Tables with Styles

To adjust a table's appearance, you can use any of the formatting options available on the Home tab. To change a table's appearance more dramatically, you can use table styles, which allow you to apply a collection of formatting options, including shading, color, borders, and other design elements, with a single click.

By default, a table is formatted with the Table Grid style, which includes only black borders between the rows and columns, no paragraph spacing, no shading, and the default black font color. You can select a more colorful table style from the Table Styles group on the Table Design tab. Whatever table style you choose, you'll give your document a more polished look if you use the same style consistently in all the tables in a single document.

Some table styles format rows in alternating colors, called **banded rows**, while others format the columns in alternating colors, called **banded columns**. You can choose a style that includes different formatting for the header row than for the rest of the table. Or, if the first column in your table is a header column—that is, if it contains headers identifying the type of information in each row—you can choose a style that instead applies different formatting to the first column.

Reference

Formatting a Table with a Table Style

- Click in the table you want to format.
- On the ribbon, click the Table Design tab.
- In the Table Styles group, click the More button to display the Table Styles gallery.
- Position the pointer over a style in the Table Styles gallery to see a Live Preview of the table style in the document.
- In the Table Styles gallery, click the style you want.
- To apply or remove style elements (such as special formatting for the header row, banded rows, or banded columns), select or deselect check boxes as necessary in the Table Style Options group.

Eboni wants to use a table style that emphasizes the header row with special formatting, does not include column borders, and uses color to separate the rows.

To apply a table style to the Expenditures table:

1. Click anywhere in the table, and then scroll to position the table at the very bottom of the Word window. This will make it easier to see the Live Preview in the next few steps.
2. On the ribbon, click the **Table Design** tab. In the Table Styles group, the plain Table Grid style is highlighted, indicating that it is the table's current style.
3. In the Table Styles group, click the **More** button . The Table Styles gallery opens. The default Table Grid style now appears under the heading "Plain Tables." The more elaborate styles appear below, in the "Grid Tables" section of the gallery.

4. Use the gallery's vertical scroll bar to view the complete collection of table styles. When you are finished, scroll up until you can see the "Grid Tables" heading again.

5. Move the pointer over the style located in the fourth row of the Grid Tables section, first column on the right. See Figure 3–17.

Figure 3–17 Table styles gallery

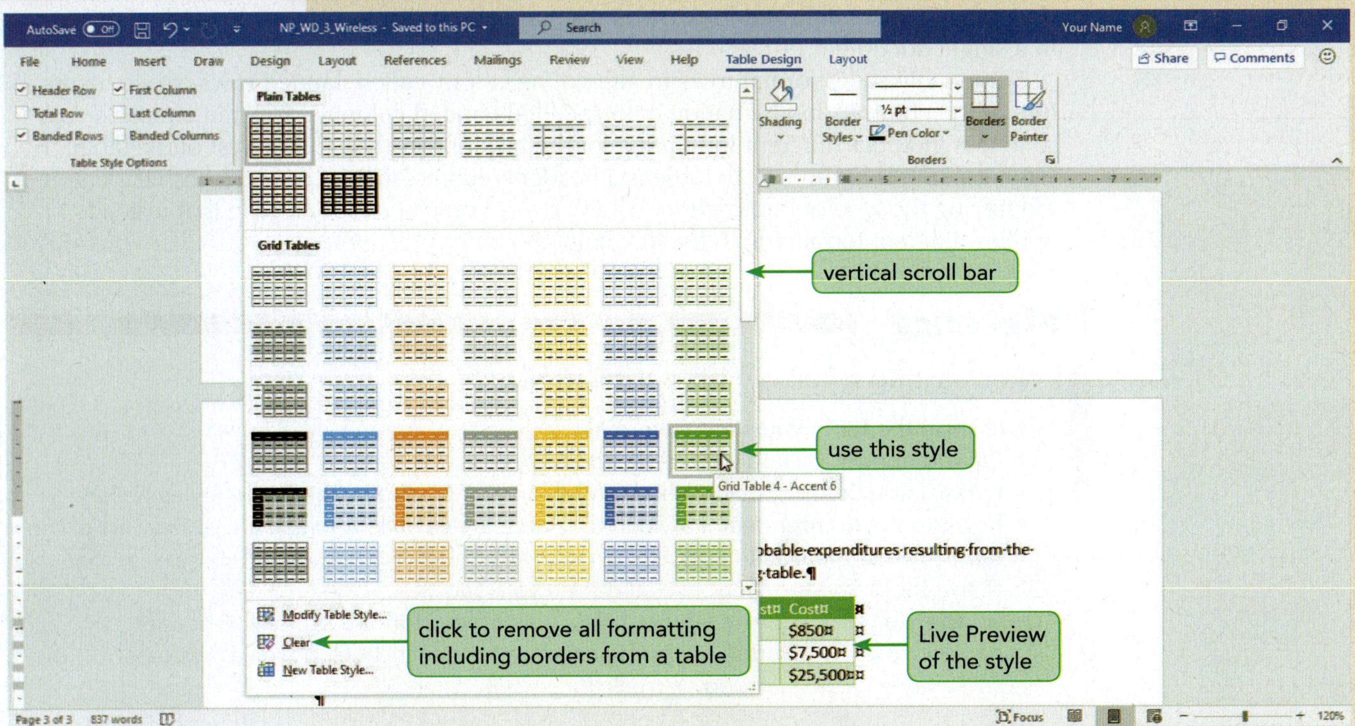

A ScreenTip displays the style's name, "Grid Table 4 - Accent 6." The style consists of a dark green heading row, with alternating rows of light green and white below. A Live Preview of the style is visible in the document.

6. Click the **Grid Table 4 - Accent 6** style. The Table Styles gallery closes.

7. Scroll to position the table at the top of the Word window, so you can review it more easily. The table's header row is formatted with dark green shading and white text. The rows below appear in alternating colors of light green and white.

The only problem with the newly formatted table is that the text in the first column is formatted in bold. In tables where the first column contains row headers, bold would be appropriate—but this isn't the case with Eboni's table. You'll fix this by deselecting the First Column check box in the Table Style Options group on the Table Design tab.

To remove the bold formatting from the first column:

1. In the Table Style Options group, click the **First Column** check box to deselect this option. The bold formatting is removed from the entries in the "Item" column. Note that the Header Row check box is selected. This indicates that the table's header row is emphasized with special formatting (dark green shading with white text). The Banded Rows check box is also selected because the table is formatted with banded rows of green and white. To remove the banded rows, you could deselect the Banded Rows checkbox. To apply or remove banded columns, you could select or deselect the Banded Columns checkbox. Figure 3–18 shows the finished table.

Figure 3–18 Completed table

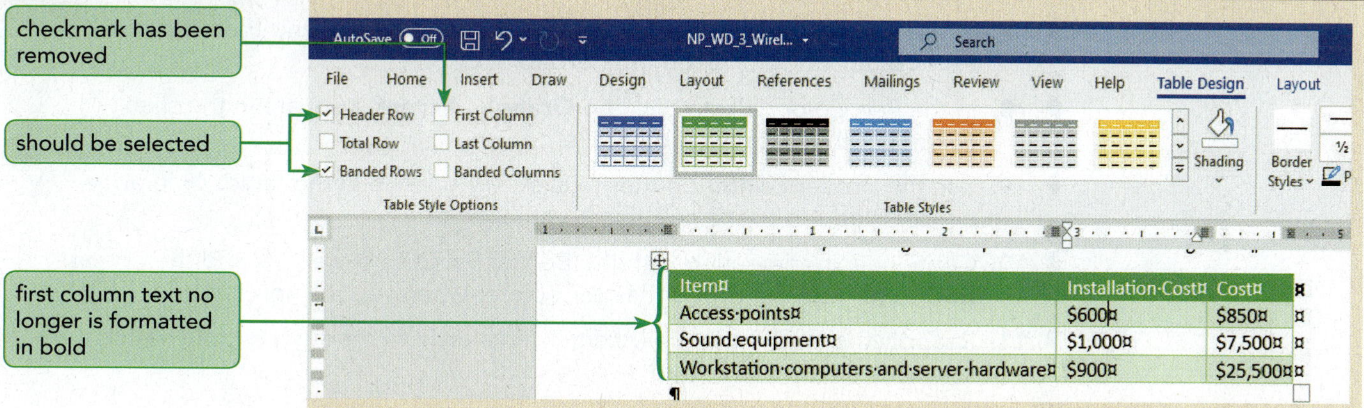

2. Save the document.

After you apply a table style, it's helpful to know how to remove it in case you want to start over from scratch. The Clear option on the menu below the Table Styles gallery removes the current style from a table, including the borders between cells. When a table has no borders, the rows and columns are defined by **gridlines**, which are useful as guidelines but do not appear when you print the table.

In the following steps, you'll experiment with clearing the table's style, displaying and hiding the gridlines, and removing the table's borders.

To experiment with table styles, gridlines, and borders:

1. In the Table Styles group, click the **More** button, and then click **Clear** in the menu below the gallery. The green shading and borders are removed from the table. Next, you need to make sure the table gridlines are displayed.
2. On the ribbon, click the **Layout** contextual tab.
3. In the Table group, click the **View Gridlines** button, if necessary, to select it. The table now looks much simpler, with no shading or font colors. Instead of the table borders, dotted gridlines separate the rows and columns. The text in the table is spaced farther apart because removing the table style restored the default paragraph and line spacing of the Normal style. The bold formatting that you applied earlier, which is not part of a table style, is visible again.

   It is helpful to clear a table's style and view only the gridlines if you want to use a table to lay out text and graphics on a page, but you want no visible indication of the table itself.

Another option is to remove only the table borders, leaving the rest of the table style applied to the table. To do this, you have to select the entire table. But first you need to undo the style change.

4. On the Quick Access Toolbar, click the **Undo** button to restore the Grid Table 4 - Accent 6 style, so that your table looks like the one in Figure 3–18.
5. In the upper-left corner of the table, click the **Table Select** handle to select the entire table, and then click the **Table Design** tab.
6. In the Borders group, click the **Borders arrow** to open the Borders gallery, click **No Border**, and then click anywhere in the table to deselect it. The borders are removed from the table, leaving only the nonprinting gridlines to separate the rows and columns. To add borders of any color to specific parts of a table, you can use the Border Painter.
7. In the Borders group, click the **Border Painter** button, and then click the **Pen Color** button to open the Pen Color gallery.
8. In the Pen Color gallery, click the **Orange, Accent 2** square in the sixth column of the first row of the gallery.
9. Use the Border Painter pointer to click any gridline in the table. An orange border is added to the cell where you clicked.
10. Continue experimenting with the Border Painter pointer, and then press **ESC** to turn off the Border Painter pointer when you are finished.
11. Reapply the Grid Table 4 - Accent 6 table style to make your table match the one shown earlier in Figure 3–18.
12. Save the document and then close it.

Proskills

Problem Solving: Fine-Tuning Table Styles

After you apply a table style to a table, you might like the look of the table but find that it no longer effectively conveys your information or is not quite as easy to read. To solve this problem, you might be inclined to go back to the Table Styles gallery to find another style that might work better. Another method to correct problems with a table style is to identify the table elements with problematic formatting and then manually make formatting adjustments to only those elements using the options on the Table Design tab. For example, you can change the thickness and color of the table borders using the options in the Borders group, and you can add shading using the Shading button in the Table Styles group. Also, if you don't like the appearance of table styles in your document, consider changing the document's theme (as explained later in this module) and previewing the table styles again. The table styles have a different appearance in each theme. When applying table styles, remember there are many options for attractively formatting the table without compromising the information being conveyed.

Adding Formulas

Now that the Expenditures table is finished, Eboni would like your help finishing a table containing her estimates for the cost of the servers and workstations. She might add it to the report later, but for now it's stored in a separate document. The table is almost complete, but she still needs to add a formula field that calculates and displays the total cost of the new hardware.

The Formula button in the Data group on the Layout tab allows you to insert a field that performs mathematical operations such as addition, subtraction, or division. By default, it inserts a formula field that sums the numbers in the rows above the cell containing the formula field. You'll see how that works in the following steps. In the process, you'll learn how to insert formulas that perform other operations.

To open the document and add a formula:

1. Open the document **NP_WD_3-2.docx** located in the Word3 > Module folder, and then save the file with the name **NP_WD_3_Hardware** in the location specified by your instructor.
2. Verify that the document is displayed in Print Layout view and that the rulers and nonprinting characters are displayed.
3. Make sure the Zoom level is set to 120%. Eboni wants you to insert a formula that sums the three dollar amounts in the right-hand column.
4. Click the blank cell below "$14,000."
5. Click the **Layout** contextual tab, and then click the **Formula** button in the Data group. The Formula dialog box opens. By default, the Formula box contains =SUM(ABOVE), which tells Word to add together all the numbers in the cells above the cell that contains the insertion point, and then display the result of that calculation in the cell that contains the insertion point. You can use the Number format arrow to determine how the result of the formula will look in the cell. For example, you can choose to display it with no decimal places, with or without a dollar sign, or with a percentage sign. In this case, Eboni wants the result of the calculation to display with no decimal places to match the dollar amounts in the cells above.
6. Click the **Number format arrow**, and then click **#,##0**. If you wanted to perform a calculation other than summing numbers, you could type a new formula in the Formula box, or you could select an option using the Paste function arrow. Using formulas other than the default SUM formula is an advanced skill, but you can learn how to incorporate them into your documents by searching Help for information on adding formulas to tables. See Figure 3–19.

Figure 3–19 Formula dialog box

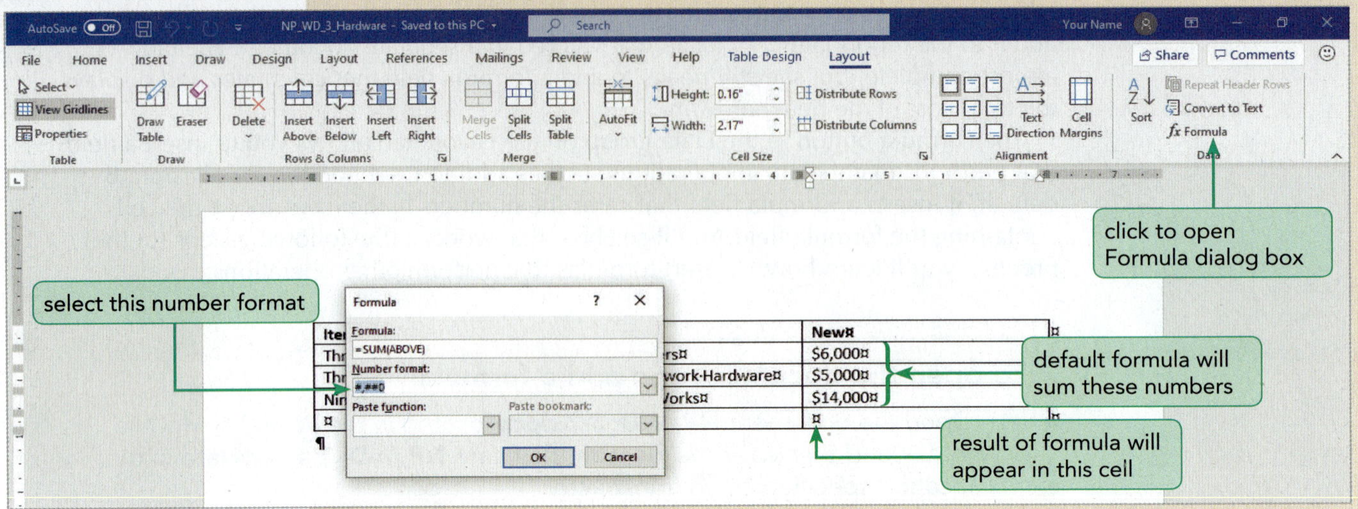

7. Click **OK**. The Formula dialog box closes, and the result of the calculation, 25,000, appears in the right-most cell in the bottom row. Next, you need to add a dollar sign to match the entries in the cells above.
8. Click to the left of the "2" in "25,000" and type **$**. When you click in the cell, gray shading appears behind the result of the formula. The shading indicates that the value is actually the result of a formula field rather than plain text.
9. Save the document.

The beauty of a formula field is that you can edit the numbers in a table, and then quickly update the result of the calculation. In this case, Eboni wants to change the cost of the new workstations from $14,000 to $14,500.

To change the cost of the new workstations and then update the formula:

1. Click the cell containing "$14,000," use the → or ← keys to move the insertion point to the left of the first "0," press DEL, and then type **5** to change the amount to $14,500. Now you need to update the formula to reflect the higher cost.
2. Right-click the cell containing the formula field, which currently displays the value $25,000. A shortcut menu opens, as shown in Figure 3–20. If the gray shading around the value $25,000 did not appear earlier, it appears now.

Figure 3–20 Updating the formula

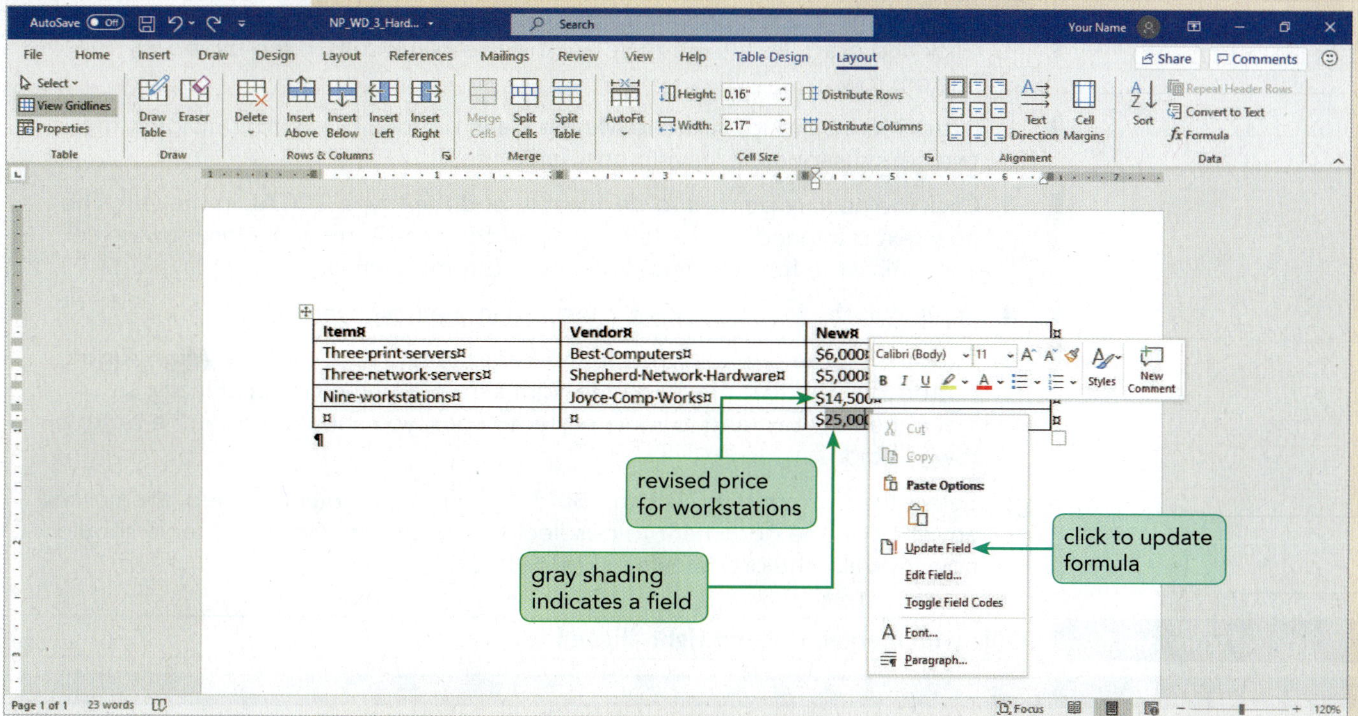

3. Click **Update Field** in the shortcut menu. The shortcut menu closes, and the value displayed in the cell changes to $25,500.

To finish the table, Eboni would like to add "TOTAL" next to the cell containing the formula field.

Merging Cells

Currently, the table contains two blank cells in the bottom row. Eboni could insert "TOTAL" in the cell next to the one containing the formula, but the table will look more polished if she combines, or **merges**, the two blank cells, and then inserts the text in the resulting new, larger cell. To merge one or more cells, select the cells, and then click the Merge Cells button in the Merge group on the Layout tab. Note that you can also split one cell into multiple cells by clicking the cell you want to split, clicking the Split Cells button in the Merge group to open the Split Cells dialog box, and then specifying the desired number of rows and columns you want to divide the cell into.

To merge the two blank cells and insert new text in the resulting cell:

1. Click and drag the mouse to select the two blank cells in the table's bottom row.
2. In the Merge group, click the **Merge Cells** button. The border dividing the two cells disappears, leaving one, larger cell.
3. Click the new, larger cell to deselect it, and then type **TOTAL** in the cell. The new text is aligned on the left border of the cell. To move it closer to the cell containing the formula field, you need to right-align it.
4. Verify that the insertion point is located in the new, merged cell.
5. Click the **Home** tab, and then in the Paragraph group, click the **Align Right** button. The text moves to the right side of the merge cell. Finally, to make the new text and formula easier to spot, you should format the bottom row in bold.
6. Select the bottom row, click the **Bold** button **B** in the Font group, then click anywhere in the document to deselect the row. Your completed table should now look like the one shown in Figure 3–21.

Figure 3–21 **Table with merged cell and right-aligned text**

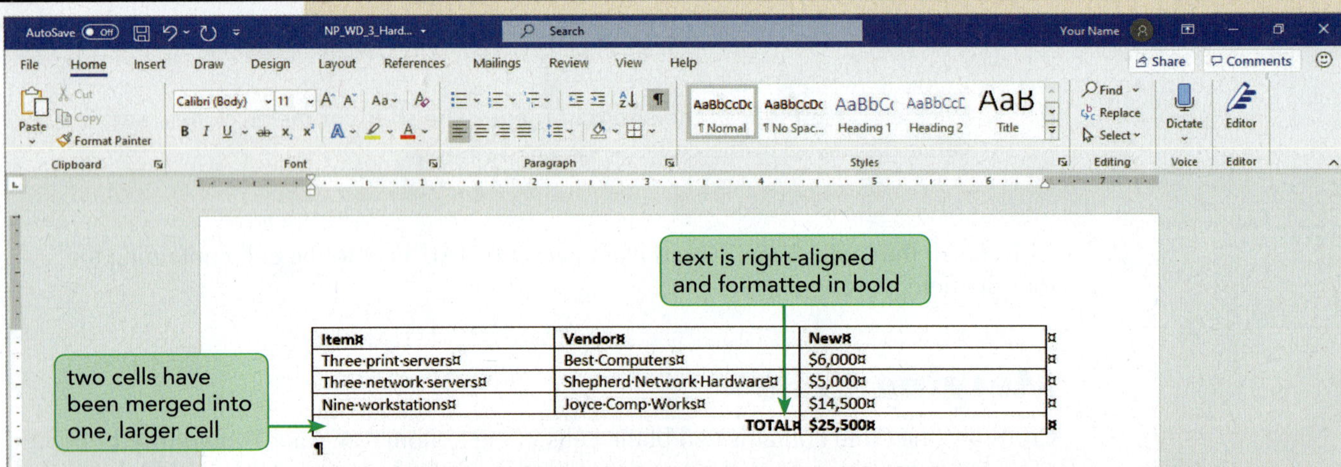

7. Save the document and then close it.

Insight

Using the Draw Table Pointer

Instead of inserting a blank table grid as a starting point, you can draw a table structure using the Draw Table pointer. This is especially useful when you want to use a table as a way to lay out the contents of a flyer or other specially formatted documents. You can insert titles, graphics, and other elements in the table cells, apply formatting to the cells, and then, when you are finished, remove all borders and hide the gridlines.

To get started, click the Insert tab, click the Table button in the Tables group, and then click Draw Table. This displays the Draw Table pointer, which looks like a pencil. You can click the mouse button and drag the Draw Table pointer to draw horizontal and vertical lines on the page. You can put row and column borders anywhere you want; there's no need to make all the cells in the table the same size. When you are finished drawing the table, turn off the Draw Table pointer by pressing ESC. To delete a border, click the Eraser button in the Draw group on the Layout tab, and click anywhere on the border you want to erase. Click the Eraser button again to turn it off.

In the next session, you'll complete the rest of the report by organizing information using tab stops, dividing the document into sections, inserting headers and footers, inserting a cover page, and, finally, changing the document's theme.

Review

Session 3.1 Quick Check

1. What kind of style must you apply to a paragraph to make the paragraph appear as a heading in the Navigation pane?
2. What are the three steps involved in creating a table in Word?
3. Explain how to insert a new column in a table.
4. After you enter data in the last cell in the last row in a table, how can you insert a new row?
5. When sorting a table, is the header row included by default?
6. To adjust the width of a table's column to span the width of the page, would you use the AutoFit Contents option or the AutoFit Window option?

Session 3.2 Visual Overview:

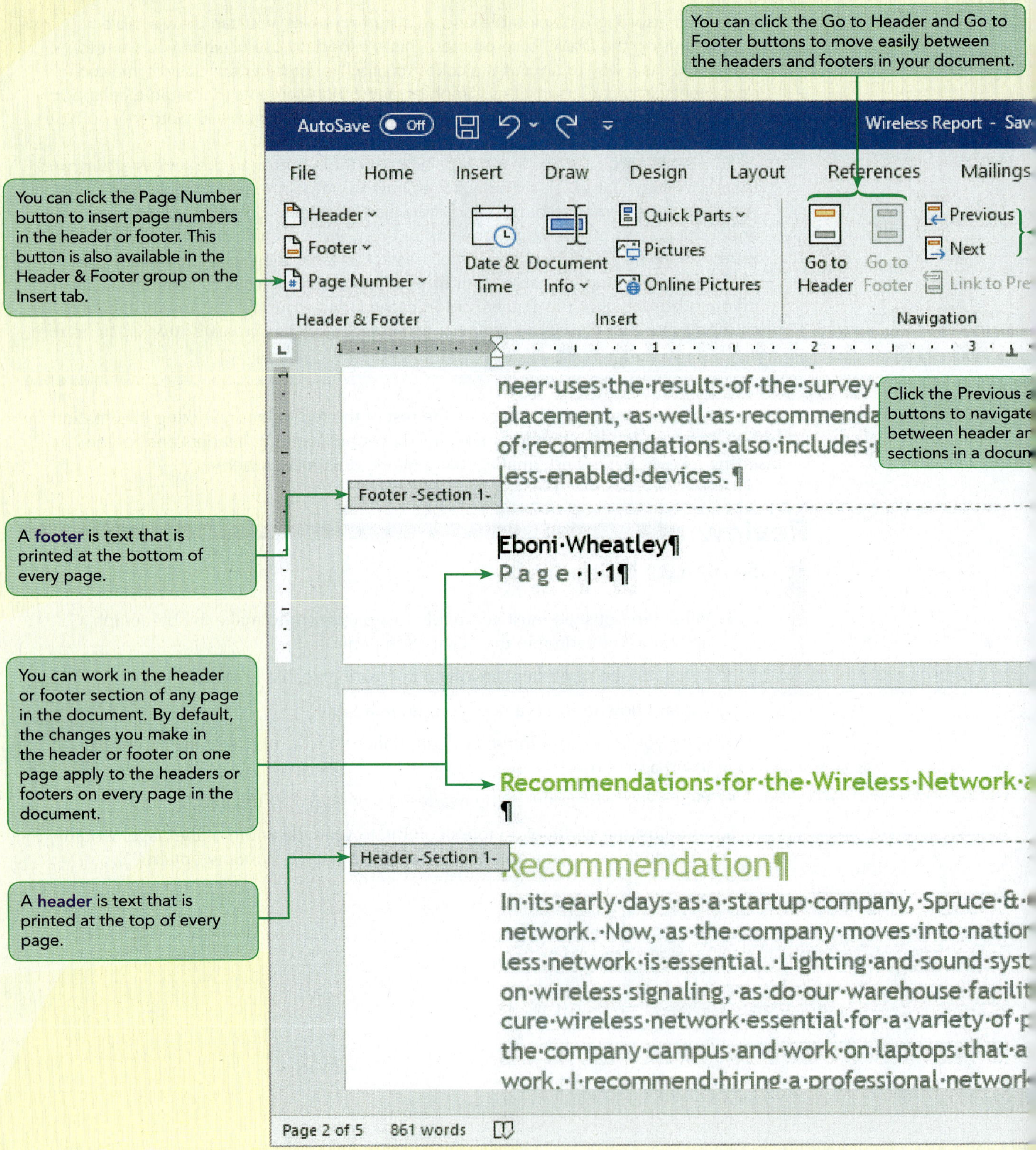

Working with Headers and Footers

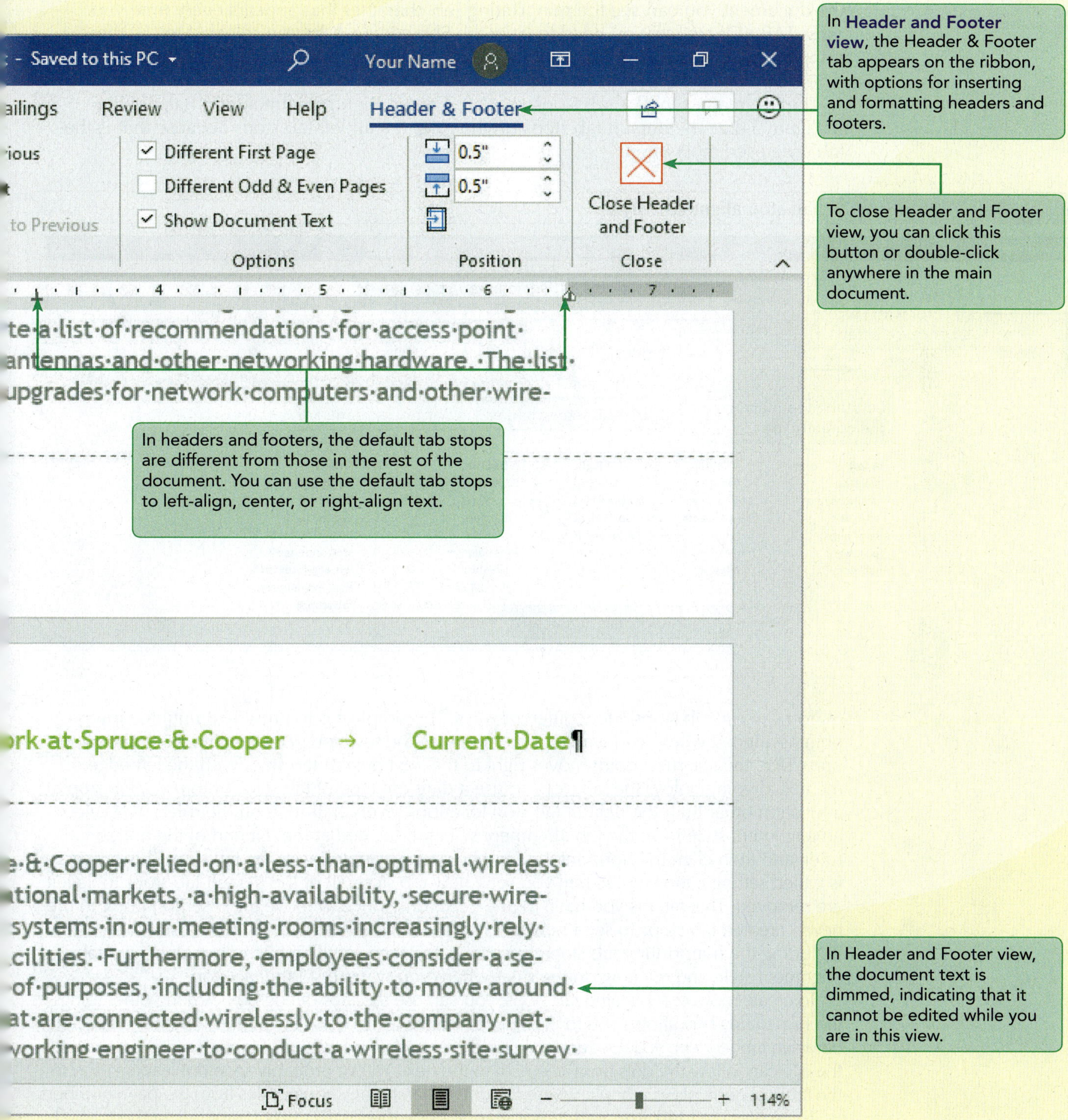

Setting Tab Stops

A **tab stop** (often called a **tab**) is a location on the horizontal ruler where the insertion point moves when you press TAB. You can use tab stops to align small amounts of text or data. By default, a document contains tab stops every one-half inch on the horizontal ruler. There's no mark on the ruler indicating these default tab stops, but in the document you can see the nonprinting Tab character that appears every time you press TAB. (Of course, you need to have the Show/Hide ¶ button selected to see these nonprinting characters.) A nonprinting tab character is just like any other character you type; you can delete it by pressing BACKSPACE or DEL.

The five major types of tab stops are Left, Center, Right, Decimal, and Bar, as shown in Figure 3–22. The default tab stops on the ruler are all left tab stops because that is the tab style used most often.

Figure 3–22 Tab stop alignment styles

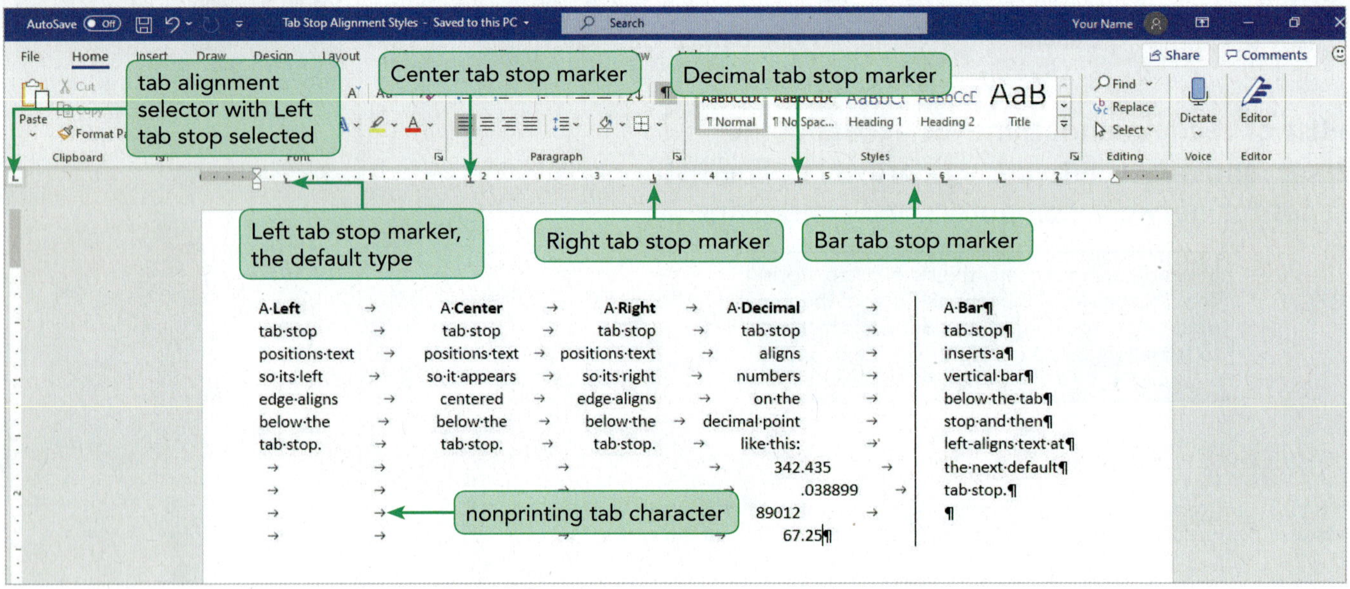

You can use tab stops a few different ways. The simplest is to press TAB until the insertion point is aligned where you want it, and then type the text you want to align. Each time you press TAB, the insertion point moves right to the next default tab stop, with the left edge of the text aligning below the tab stop. To use a different type of tab stop, or to use a tab stop at a location other than the default tab stop locations (every half-inch on the ruler), first select an alignment style from the tab alignment selector, located at the left end of the horizontal ruler, and then click the horizontal ruler where you want to insert the tab stop. This process is called setting a tab stop. When you set a new tab stop, all of the default tab stops to its left are removed. This means you have to press TAB only once to move the insertion point to the newly created tab stop. To set a new tab stop in text you have already typed, select the text, including the nonprinting tab stop characters, and then set the tab stop by selecting a tab alignment style and clicking on the ruler where you want to set the tab stop.

To create more complicated tab stops, you can use the Tabs dialog box. Among other things, the Tabs dialog box allows you to insert a **dot leader**, which is a row of dots (or other characters) between tabbed text. A dot leader makes it easier to read a long list of tabbed material because the eye can follow the dots from one item to the next. You've probably seen dot leaders used in the table of contents in a book, where the dots separate the chapter titles from the page numbers.

To create a left tab stop with a dot leader, click the Dialog Box Launcher in the Paragraph group on the Home tab, click the Indents and Spacing tab, if necessary, and then click the Tabs button at the bottom of the dialog box. In the Tab stop position box in the Tabs dialog box, type the location on the ruler where you want to insert the tab. For example, to insert a tab stop at the 4-inch mark, type 4. Verify that the Left option button is selected in the Alignment section, and then, in the Leader section, click the option button for the type of leader you want. Click the Set button, and then click OK.

Reference

Setting, Moving, and Clearing Tab Stops

- To set a tab stop, click the tab alignment selector on the horizontal ruler until the appropriate tab stop alignment style is displayed, and then click the horizontal ruler where you want to position the tab stop.
- To move a tab stop, drag it to a new location on the ruler. If you have already typed text that is aligned by the tab stop, select the text before dragging the tab stop to a new location.
- To clear a tab stop, drag it off the ruler.

In the report you have been working on for Eboni, you need to type the list of consultants and their titles. You can use tab stops to quickly format this small amount of information in two columns. As you type, you'll discover whether Word's default tab stops are appropriate for this document or whether you need to set a new tab stop. Before you get started working with tabs, you'll take a moment to explore Word's Resume Reading feature.

To enter the list of consultants using tabs:

1. Open the **NP_WD_3_Wireless.docx** document. The document opens with the "Summary" heading at the top of the Word window. In the lower-right corner, a "Welcome back!" message is displayed briefly and is then replaced with the Resume Reading button.
2. Point to the **Resume Reading** button to expand its "Welcome back!" message. See Figure 3–23.

Figure 3–23 "Welcome back!" message displayed in reopened document

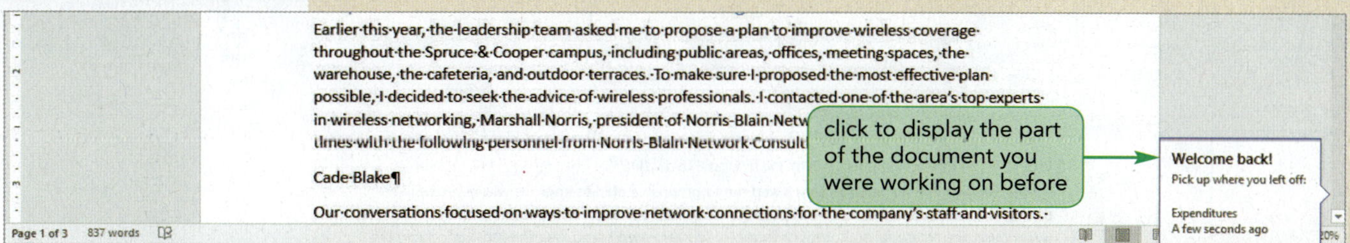

3. Click the **Welcome back!** message. The document window scrolls down to display the table, which you were working on just before you closed the document.
4. Scroll up to display the "Help from Norris-Blain Network Consulting" heading on page 1.
5. Confirm that the ruler and nonprinting characters are displayed, and that the document is displayed in **Print Layout** view, zoomed to **120%**.
6. Click to the right of the last "e" in "Cade Blake."
7. Press **TAB**. An arrow-shaped tab character appears, and the insertion point moves to the first tab stop after the last "e" in "Blake." This tab stop is the default tab located at the 1-inch mark on the horizontal ruler. See Figure 3–24.

Figure 3–24 **Tab character**

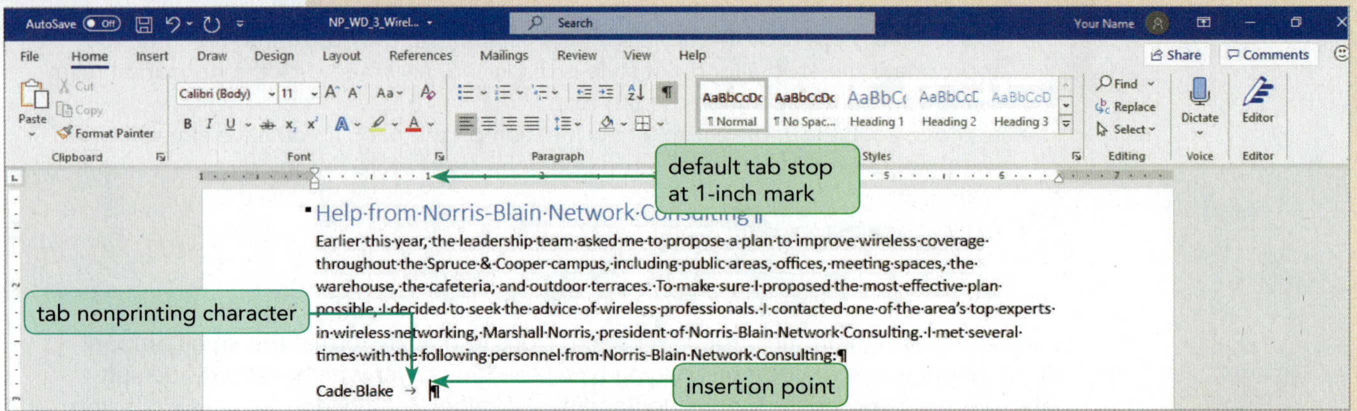

8. Type **Senior Consultant**, and then press **ENTER** to move the insertion point to the next line.
9. Type **Samuel J. Iglesias**, and then press **TAB**. The insertion point moves to the next available tab stop, this time located at the 1.5-inch mark on the ruler.
10. Type **Senior Consultant**, and then press **ENTER** to move to the next line. Notice that Samuel J. Iglesias's title does not align with Cade Blake's title on the line above it. You'll fix this after you type the last name in the list.
11. Type **Beverly Sheffield-McCoy**, press **TAB**, and then type **Project Manager**. See Figure 3–25.

Figure 3–25 **List of consultants**

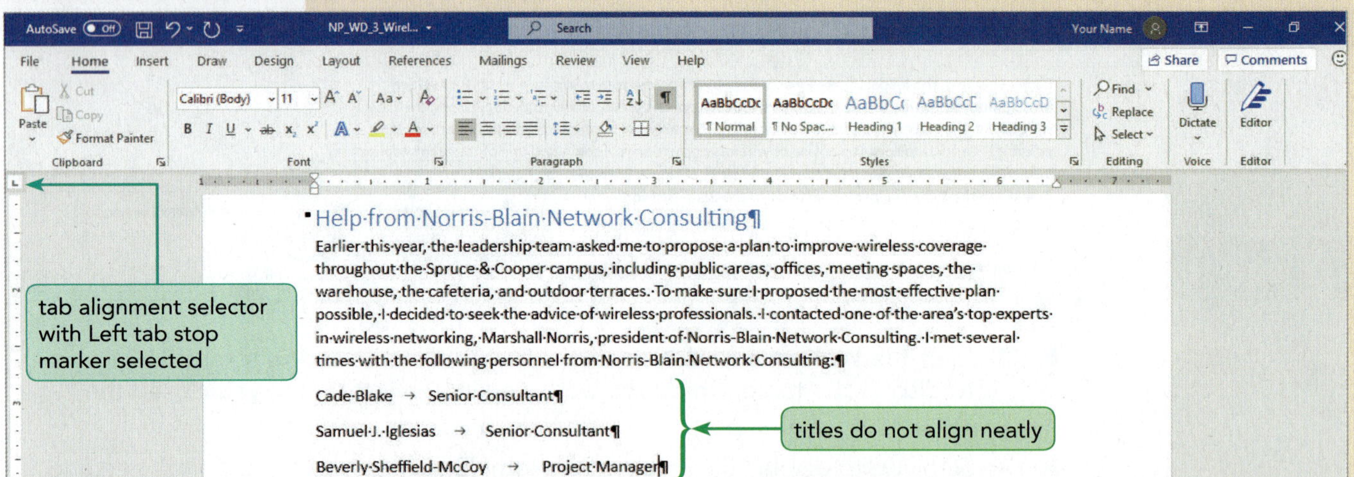

The list of names and titles is not aligned properly. You could fix this by dragging a tab stop to a new location. However, you would have to select the list of names and positions before dragging the tab stop. In this case, it's easier to insert a new tab stop.

To add a new tab stop to the horizontal ruler:

1. Make sure the Home tab is displayed on the ribbon, and then select the list of consultants and their titles.
2. On the horizontal ruler, click at the 2.5-inch mark. Because the current tab stop alignment style is Left tab, Word inserts a left tab stop at that location.

Remember that when you set a new tab stop, all the default tab stops to its left are removed. The column of titles shifts to the new tab stop. Note that if you needed to remove a tab stop, you could drag it off the ruler. See Figure 3–26.

Figure 3–26 **Titles aligned at new tab stop**

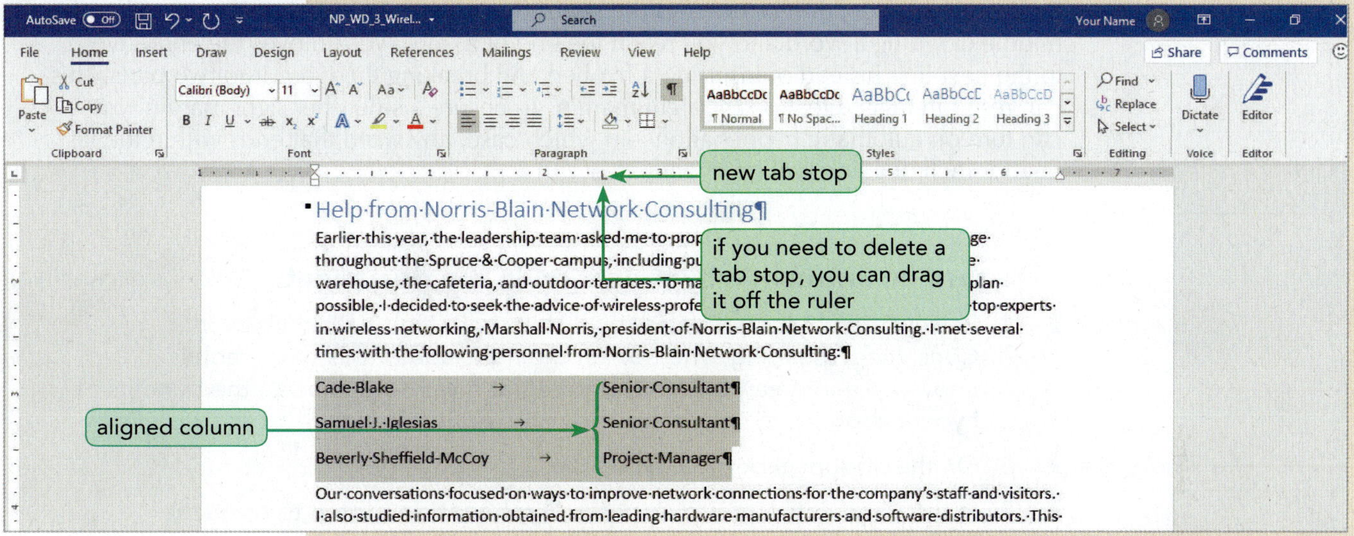

To complete the list, you need to remove the paragraph spacing after the first two paragraphs in the list, so the list looks like it's all one paragraph. You can quickly reduce paragraph and line spacing to 0 points by clicking the No Spacing style in the Styles group. In this case, you want to reduce only the paragraph spacing to 0 points, so you'll use the Line and Paragraph Spacing button instead.

3. Select the first two paragraphs in the list, which contain the names and titles for Cade and Samuel.
4. In the Paragraph group, click the **Line and Paragraph Spacing** button, and then click **Remove Space After Paragraph**.
5. Click anywhere in the document to deselect the list, and then save your work.

Proskills

Decision Making: Choosing Between Tabs and Tables

When you have information that you want to align in columns in your document, you need to decide whether to use tabs or tables. Whatever you do, don't try to align columns of data by adding extra spaces by pressing SPACEBAR. Although the text might seem precisely aligned on the screen, it probably won't be aligned when you print the document. Furthermore, if you edit the text, the spaces you inserted to align your columns will be affected by your edits; they get moved just like regular text, ruining your alignment.

So what is the most efficient way to align text in columns? It depends. Inserting tabs works well for aligning small amounts of information in just a few columns and rows, such as two columns with three rows, but tabs become cumbersome when you need to organize a lot of data over multiple columns and rows. In that case, using a table to organize columns of information is better. Unlike with tabbed columns of data, it's easy to add data to tables by inserting columns. You might also choose tables over tab stops when you want to take advantage of the formatting options available with table styles. As mentioned earlier, if you don't want the table structure itself to be visible in the document, you can clear its table style and then hide its gridlines.

Now you're ready to address some other issues with the document. First, Eboni has noticed that the right edges of most of the paragraphs in the document are uneven, and she'd like you to try to smooth them out. You'll correct this problem in the next section.

Hyphenating a Document

By default, hyphenation is turned off in Word documents. That means if you are in the middle of typing a word and you reach the end of a line, Word moves the entire word to the next line instead of inserting a hyphen and breaking the word into two parts. This can result in ragged text on the right margin. To ensure a smoother right margin, you can turn on automatic hyphenation—in which case, any word that ends within the last quarter-inch of a line will be hyphenated.

To turn on automatic hyphenation in the document:

1. Review the paragraph below the "Help from Norris-Blain Network Consulting" heading. The text on the right side of this paragraph is uneven. Keeping an eye on this paragraph will help you see the benefits of hyphenation.
2. On the ribbon, click the **Layout** tab.
3. In the Page Setup group, click the **Hyphenation** button to open the Hyphenation menu, and then click **Automatic**. The Hyphenation menu closes. The document text shifts to account for the insertion of hyphens in words that break near the end of a line. For example, in the paragraph below the "Help from Norris-Blain Network Consulting" heading, the words "throughout" and "networking" are now hyphenated. See Figure 3–27.

Figure 3–27 Hyphenated document

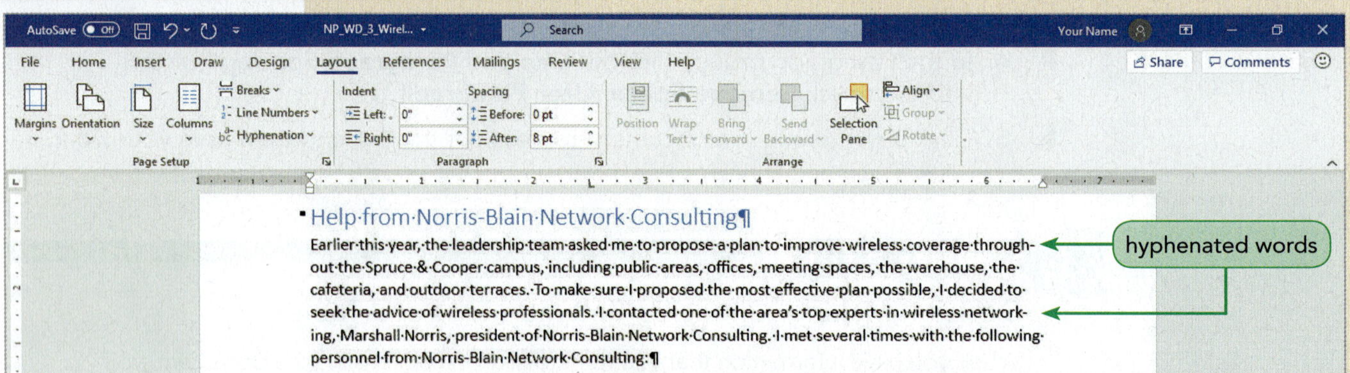

4. Save the document.

Eboni plans to post a handout in the company dining room to illustrate the benefits of improving the corporate network, and she wants to include a sample handout in the report. Before you can add the sample handout, you need to divide the document into sections.

Formatting a Document into Sections

> **Tip**
>
> If you insert an endnote in a document with sections, the endnote will appear at the end of the section containing the superscript endnote number, not at the end of the document.

A **section** is a part of a document that can have its own page orientation, margins, headers, footers, and so on. In other words, each section is like a document within a document. To divide a document into sections, you insert a **section break**. You can select from a few different types of section breaks. One of the most useful is a Next page section break, which inserts a page break and starts the new section on the next page. Another commonly used kind of section break, a Continuous section break, starts the section at the location of the insertion point without changing the page flow. To insert a section break, you click the Breaks button in the Page Setup group on the Layout tab and then select the type of section break you want to insert.

Eboni wants to format the handout in landscape orientation, but the report is currently formatted in portrait orientation. To format part of a document in an orientation different from the rest of the document, you need to divide the document into sections.

To insert a section break below the table:

1. Press **CTRL+END** to move the insertion point to the end of the document, just below the table.
2. In the Page Setup group, click the **Breaks** button. The Breaks gallery opens, as shown in Figure 3–28.

Figure 3–28 Breaks gallery

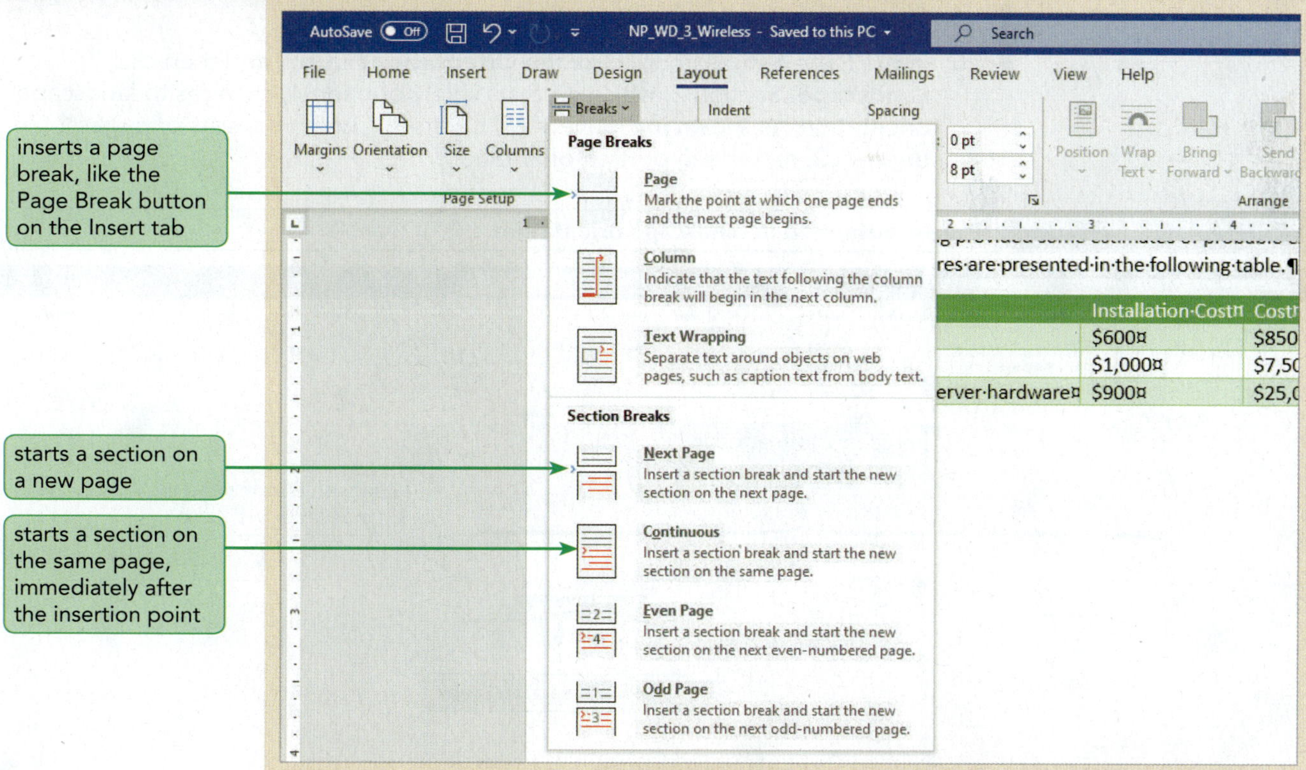

The Page Breaks section of the gallery includes options for controlling how the text flows from page to page. The first option, Page, inserts a page break. It has the same effect as clicking the Page Break button on the Insert tab or pressing CTRL+ENTER. The Section Breaks section of the gallery includes four types of section breaks. The two you'll use most often are Next Page and Continuous.

Tip

To delete a section break, click to the left of the line representing the break, and then press DEL.

3. Under "Section Breaks," click **Next Page**. A section break is inserted in the document, and the insertion point moves to the top of the new page 4.
4. Scroll up, if necessary, until you can see the double dotted line and the words "Section Break (Next Page)" below the table on page 3. This line indicates that a new section begins on the next page.
5. Save the document.

You've created a new page that is a separate section from the rest of the report. The sections are numbered consecutively. The first part of the document is section 1, and the new page is section 2. Now you can format section 2 in landscape orientation without affecting the rest of the document.

To format section 2 in landscape orientation:

1. Scroll down and verify that the insertion point is positioned at the top of the new page 4.
2. On the ribbon, click the **View** tab.
3. In the Zoom group, click the **Multiple Pages** button, and then change the Zoom level to **30%** so you can see all four pages of the document displayed side by side.
4. On the ribbon, click the **Layout** tab.
5. In the Page Setup group, click the **Orientation** button, and then click **Landscape**. Section 2, which consists solely of page 4, changes to landscape orientation, as shown in Figure 3–29. Section 1, which consists of pages 1 through 3, remains in portrait orientation.

Figure 3–29 Page 4 formatted in landscape orientation

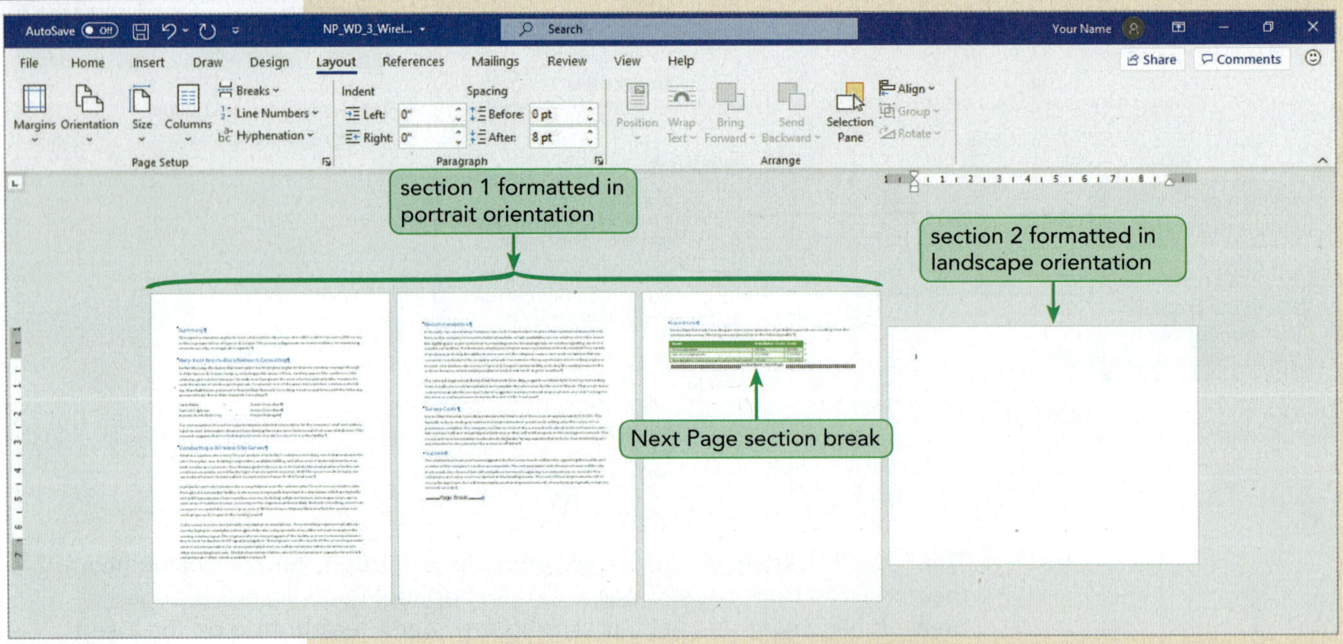

6. Change the Zoom level back to **120%**, and then save the document.

Page 4 is now formatted in landscape orientation, ready for you to create Eboni's handout, which will consist of a graphic that shows the benefits of improving the company's wireless network. You'll use Word's SmartArt feature to create the graphic.

Creating SmartArt

A **SmartArt** graphic is a diagram of shapes, such as circles, squares, or arrows. A well-designed SmartArt graphic can illustrate concepts that might otherwise require several paragraphs of explanation. To create a SmartArt graphic, you switch to the Insert tab and then, in the Illustrations group, click the SmartArt button. This opens the Choose a SmartArt Graphic dialog box, where you can select from eight categories of graphics, including graphics designed to illustrate relationships, processes, and hierarchies. Within each category, you can choose from numerous designs. Once inserted into your document, a SmartArt graphic contains placeholder text that you replace with your own text. When a SmartArt graphic is selected, the SmartArt Design and Format tabs appear on the ribbon.

To create a SmartArt graphic:

1. Verify that the insertion point is located at the top of page 4, which is blank.
2. On the ribbon, click the **Insert** tab.
3. In the Illustrations group, click the **SmartArt** button. The Choose a SmartArt Graphic dialog box opens, with categories of SmartArt graphics in the left panel. The middle panel displays the graphics associated with the category currently selected in the left panel. The right panel displays a larger image of the graphic that is currently selected in the middle panel, along with an explanation of the graphic's purpose. By default, All is selected in the left panel.
4. Explore the Choose a SmartArt Graphic dialog box by selecting categories in the left panel and viewing the graphics displayed in the middle panel.
5. In the left panel, click **Relationship**, and then scroll down in the middle panel and click the **Converging Radial** graphic (in the first column, seventh row from the top), which shows three rectangles with arrows pointing to a circle. In the right panel, you see an explanation of the Converging Radial graphic. See Figure 3–30.

Figure 3–30 Selecting a SmartArt graphic

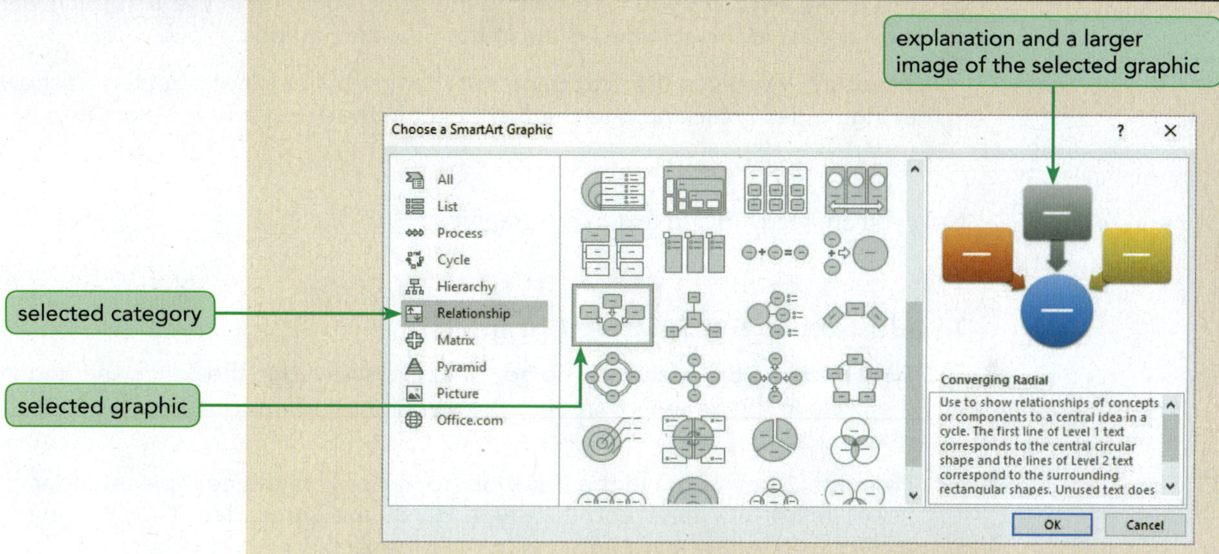

6. Click **OK**. The Converging Radial graphic, with placeholder text, is inserted at the top of page 4. The graphic is surrounded by a rectangular border, indicating that it is selected. The SmartArt contextual tabs appear on the ribbon. To the left of the graphic, you also see the Text pane, a small window with a title bar that contains the text "Type your text here." See Figure 3–31.

Figure 3–31 SmartArt graphic with text pane displayed

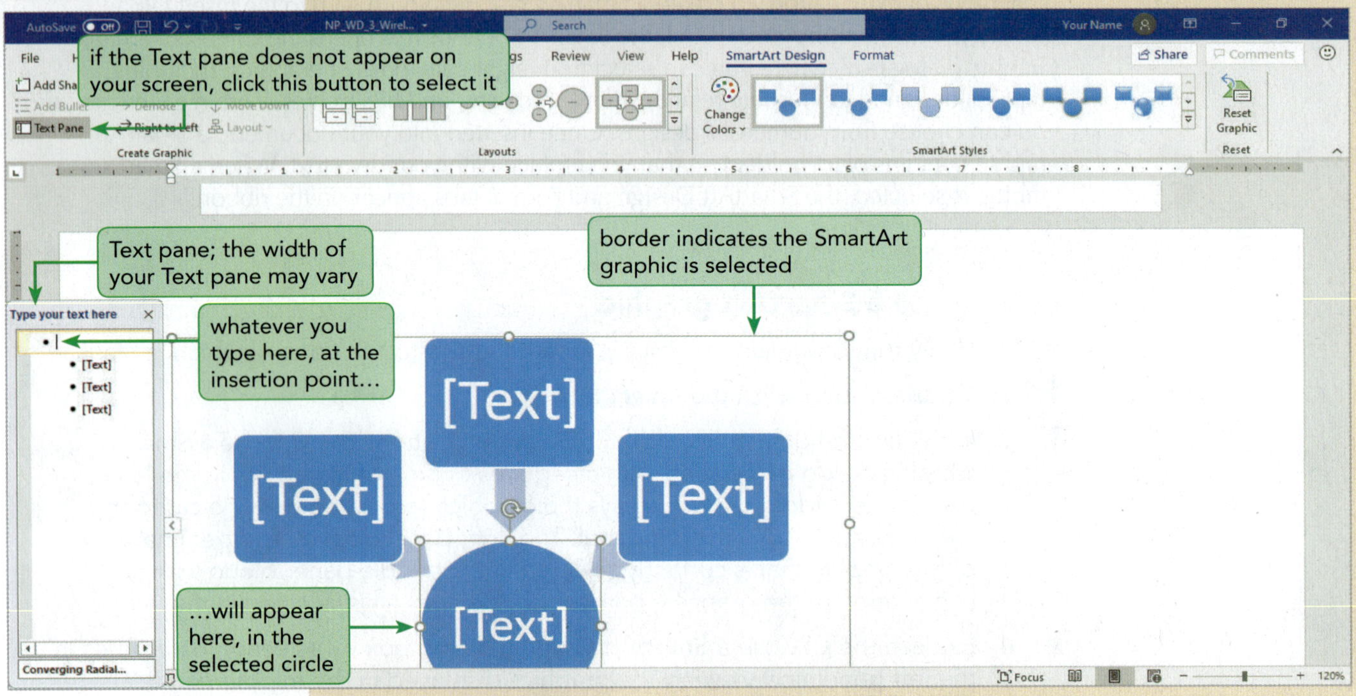

Trouble? If you do not see the Text pane, click the Text Pane button in the Create Graphic group on the SmartArt Design tab to select it.

The insertion point is blinking next to the first bullet in the Text pane, which is selected with an orange rectangle. The circle at the bottom of the SmartArt graphic is also selected, as indicated by the border with sizing handles. At this point, anything you type next to the selected bullet in the Text pane will also appear in the selected circle in the SmartArt graphic.

Trouble? If you see the Text pane but the first bullet is not selected as shown in Figure 3–31, click next to the first bullet in the Text pane to select it.

Now you are ready to add text to the graphic.

To add text to the SmartArt graphic:

1. Type **Better Connectivity**. The new text is displayed in the Text pane and in the circle in the SmartArt graphic. Now you need to insert text in the three rectangles.
2. Press the ↓ key to move the insertion point down to the next placeholder bullet in the Text pane, and then type **Hardware Upgrades**. The new text is displayed in the Text pane and in the blue rectangle on the left. See Figure 3–32.

Figure 3–32 New text in Text pane and in SmartArt graphic

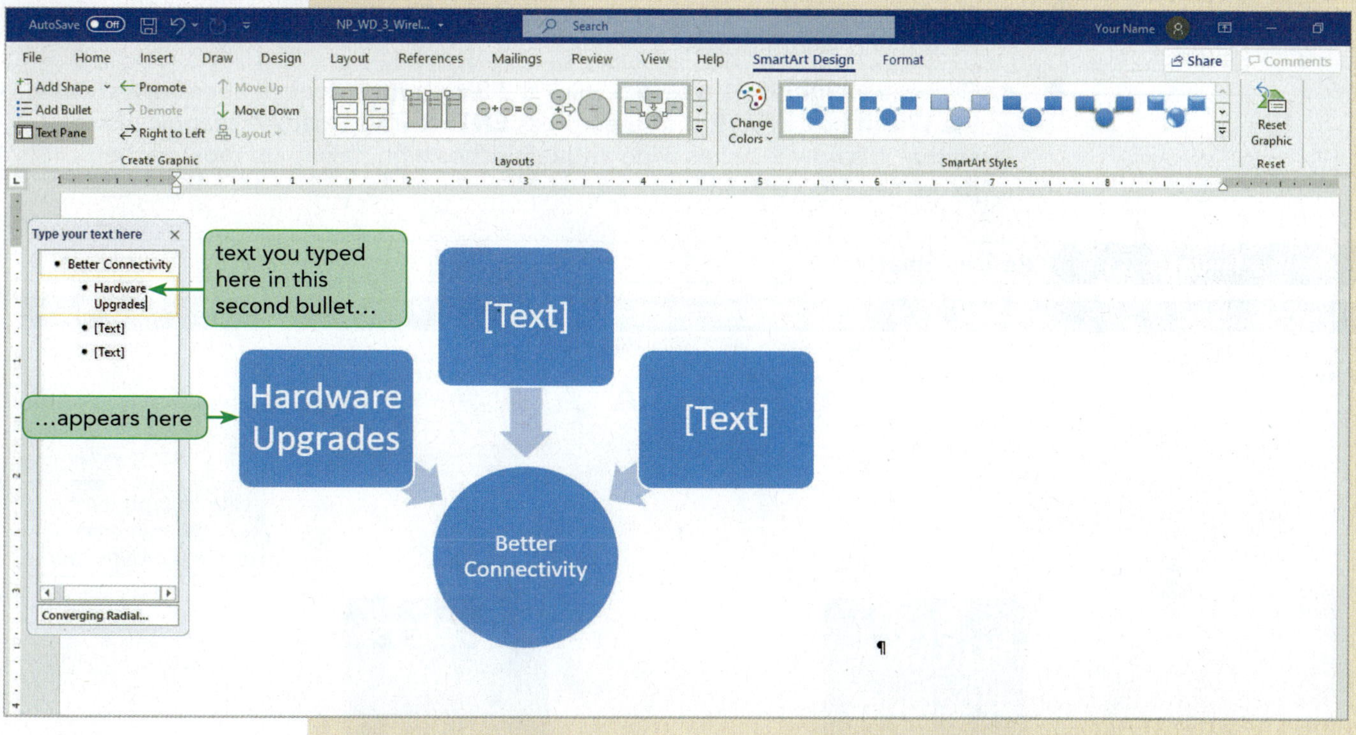

3. Press the ↓ key to move the insertion point down to the next placeholder bullet in the Text pane, and then type **Wireless Site Survey**. The new text appears in the middle rectangle and in the Text pane. You don't need the third rectangle, so you'll delete it.
4. Click the blank rectangle, on the right side of the SmartArt image, to select it. Make sure to click in the blue area and not on any letters. Then, press DEL. The rectangle on the right is deleted from the SmartArt graphic. The two remaining rectangles and the circle enlarge and shift position. Note that if you wanted to add a shape to the diagram, you could click a shape in the SmartArt graphic, click the Add Shape arrow in the Create Graphic group on the SmartArt Design tab, and then click a placement option.
5. Make sure the SmartArt Design tab is still selected on the ribbon.
6. In the Create Graphic group, click the **Text Pane** button to deselect it. The Text pane closes.
7. Click the white area inside the SmartArt border to ensure that none of the individual shapes are selected.

Next, you need to resize the SmartArt graphic so it fills the page.

To adjust the size of the SmartArt graphic:

1. Zoom out so you can see the entire page. As you can see on the ruler, the SmartArt is currently 6 inches wide. You could drag the SmartArt border to resize it, just as you can with any graphic, but you will get more precise results using the Size button on the Format tab.

2. On the ribbon, click the **Format** tab.
3. On the right side of the Format tab, click the **Size** button to display the Height and Width boxes.
4. Click the **Height** box, type **6.5**, click the **Size** button again if necessary, click the **Width** box, type **9**, and then press **ENTER**. The SmartArt graphic resizes, so that it is now 9 inches wide and 6.5 inches high, taking up most of the page. See Figure 3–33.

Figure 3–33 Resized SmartArt

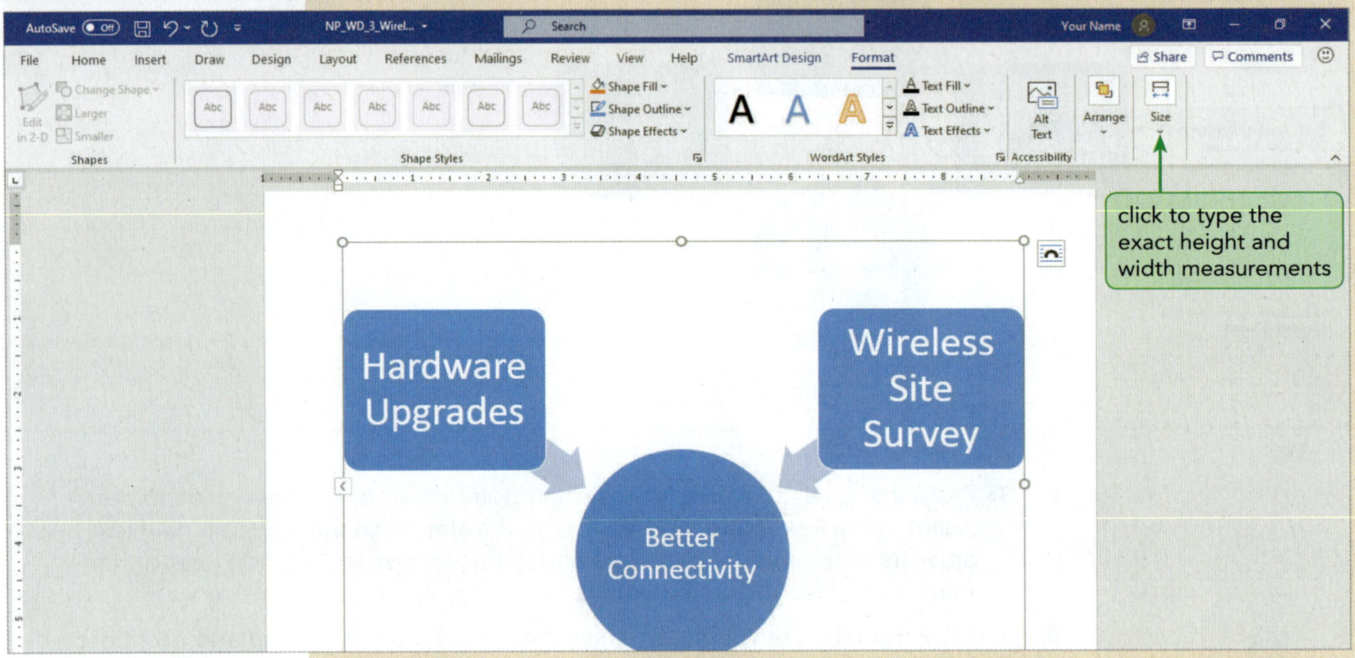

Trouble? If one of the shapes in the SmartArt graphic was resized, rather than the entire SmartArt graphic, the insertion point was located within the shape rather than in the white space. On the Quick Access Toolbar, click the Undo button, click in the white area inside the SmartArt border, and then repeat Steps 3 and 4.

5. Click outside the SmartArt border to deselect it, and then review the graphic centered on the page.

Tip

To add a border to a SmartArt graphic, click the Format tab, click the Shape Outline button in the Shape Styles group, and select an outline color.

Next, you need to insert a header at the top of each page in the report and a footer at the bottom of each page in the report.

Adding Headers and Footers

The first step to working with headers and footers is to open Header and Footer view. You can do that in three ways: (1) insert a page number using the Page Number button in the Header & Footer group on the Insert tab; (2) double-click in the header area (in a page's top margin) or in the footer area (in a page's bottom margin); or (3) click the Header button or the Footer button on the Insert tab.

By default, Word assumes that when you add something to the header or footer on any page of a document, you want the same text to appear on every page of the document. To create a different header or footer for the first page, you select the Different First Page check box in the Options group on the Header & Footer tab. When a document is divided into sections, like Eboni's report, you can create a different header or footer for each section.

For a simple header or footer, double-click the header or footer area, and then type the text you want directly in the header or footer area, formatting the text as you would any other text in a document. To choose from a selection of predesigned header or footer styles, use the Header and Footer buttons on the Header & Footer tab (or on the Insert tab). These buttons open galleries that you can use to select from a number of header and footer styles, some of which include page numbers and graphic elements such as horizontal lines or shaded boxes.

Some styles also include document controls that are similar to the kinds of controls that you might encounter in a dialog box. Any information that you enter in a document control is displayed in the header or footer as ordinary text, but it is also stored in the Word file so that Word can easily reuse it in other parts of the document. For example, later in this module, you will create a cover page for Eboni's report. Word's predefined cover pages include document controls similar to those found in headers and footers. So if you use a document control to enter the document title in the header, the same document title will show up on the cover page; there's no need to retype it.

In the following steps, you'll create a footer for the whole document (sections 1 and 2) that includes the page number and your name. As shown in Eboni's plan in Figure 3–34, you'll also create a header for section 1 only (pages 1 through 3) that includes the document title and the date. You'll leave the header area for section 2 blank.

Figure 3–34 **Plan for headers and footers in Eboni's report**

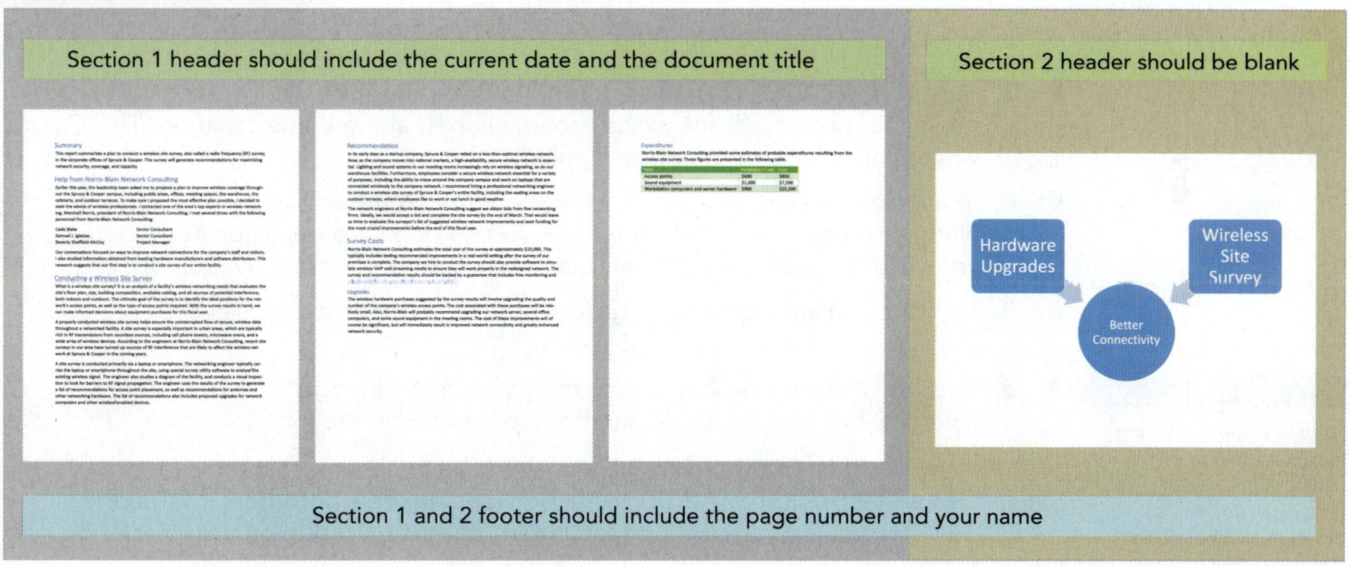

First you will create the footer on page 1.

To create a footer for the entire document:

1. Change the Zoom level to **120%**, and then scroll up until you can see the bottom of page 1 and the top of page 2.
2. Double-click in the white space at the bottom of page 1. The document switches to Header and Footer view. The Header & Footer tab is displayed on the ribbon. The insertion point is positioned on the left side of the footer area, ready for you to begin typing. The label "Footer -Section 1-"

tells you that the insertion point is located in the footer for section 1. The document text is gray, indicating that you cannot edit it in Header and Footer view. The header area for section 1 is also visible at the top of page 2. The default footer tab stops (which are different from the default tab stops in the main document) are visible on the ruler. See Figure 3–35.

Figure 3–35 Creating a footer

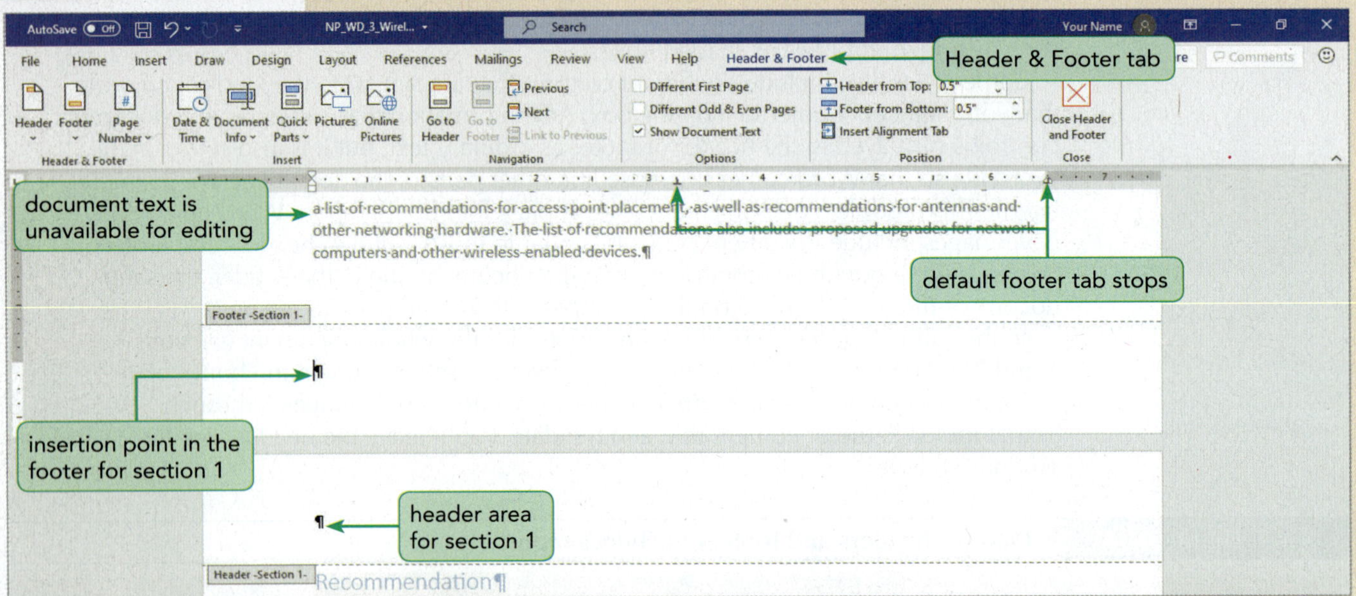

3. Type your first and last names, and then press **ENTER**. The insertion point moves to the second line in the footer, aligned along the left margin. This is where you will insert the page number.
4. In the Header & Footer group, click the **Page Number** button. The Page Number menu opens. Because the insertion point is already located where you want to insert the page number, you'll use the Current Position option.
5. Point to **Current Position**. A gallery of page number styles opens. Eboni wants to use the Accent Bar 2 style.
6. Click the **Accent Bar 2** style (the third style from the top). The word "Page," a vertical bar, and the page number are inserted in the footer.

   Next, you'll check to make sure that the footer you just created for section 1 also appears in section 2. To move between headers or footers in separate sections, you can use the buttons in the Navigation group on the Header & Footer tab.
7. In the Navigation group, click the **Next** button. Word displays the footer for the next section in the document—that is, the footer for section 2, which appears at the bottom of page 4. The label at the top of the footer area reads "Footer -Section 2-" and contains the same text (your name and the page number) as in the section 1 footer. Word assumes, by default, that when you type text in one footer, you want it to appear in all the footers in the document.

Tip

To change the numbering style or to specify a number to use as the first page number, click the Page Number button in the Header & Footer group, and then click Format Page Numbers.

Now you need to create a header for section 1. Eboni does not want to include a header in section 2 because it would distract attention from the SmartArt graphic. So you will first separate the header for section 1 from the header for section 2.

To separate the headers for section 1 and section 2:

1. Verify that the insertion point is located in the section 2 footer area at the bottom of page 4 and that the Header & Footer tab is selected on the ribbon. To switch from the footer to the header in the current section, you can use the Go to Header button in the Navigation group.
2. In the Navigation group, click the **Go to Header** button. The insertion point moves to the section 2 header at the top of page 4. See Figure 3–36.

Figure 3–36 Section 2 header is currently the same as the previous header, in section 1

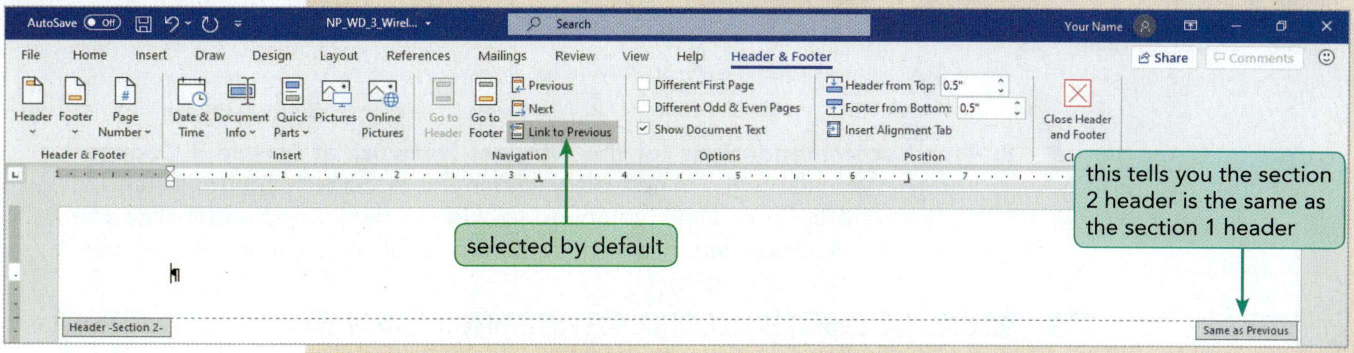

Notice that in the Navigation group, the Link to Previous button is selected. In the header area in the document window, the gray tab on the right side of the header border contains the message "Same as Previous," indicating that the section 2 header is set up to display the same text as the header in the previous section, which is section 1. To make the section 2 header a separate entity, you need to break the link between the section 1 and section 2 headers.

Tip

When you create a header for a section, it doesn't matter what page you're working on as long as the insertion point is located in a header in that section.

3. In the Navigation group, click the **Link to Previous** button to deselect it. The Same as Previous tab is removed from the right side of the section 2 header border.
4. In the Navigation group, click the **Previous** button. The insertion point moves up to the nearest header in the previous section, which is the section 1 header at the top of page 3. The label "Header -Section 1-" identifies this as a section 1 header.
5. In the Header & Footer group, click the **Header** button. A gallery of header styles opens.
6. Scroll down and review the various header styles, and then click the **Grid** style (eighth style from the top). The placeholder text "[Document title]" is aligned at the left margin. The placeholder text "[Date]" is aligned at the right margin.
7. Click the **[Document title]** placeholder text. The placeholder text is now selected within a document control. See Figure 3–37.

Figure 3–37 **Adding a header to section 1**

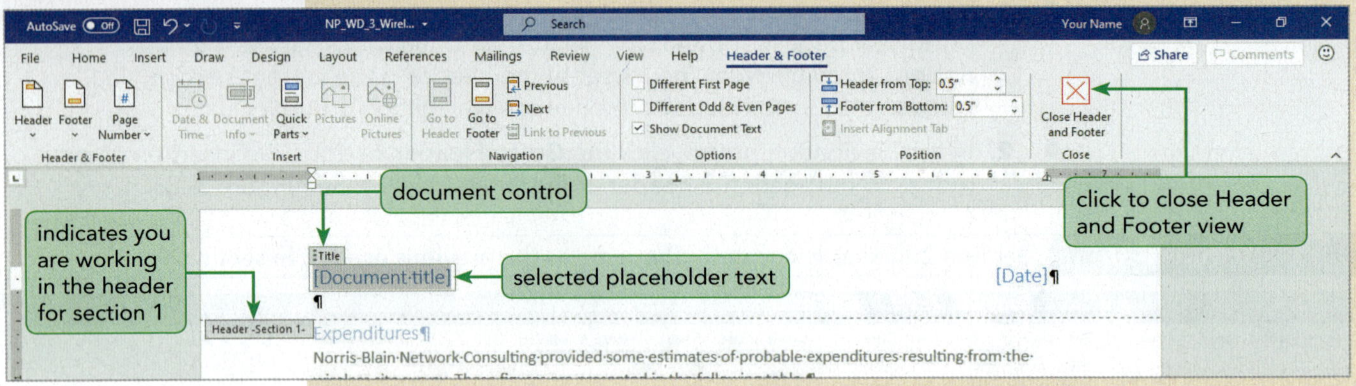

8. Type **Recommendations for the Wireless Network at Spruce & Cooper**. The text you just typed is now displayed in the document control instead of the placeholder text. Next, you need to add the date. The header style you selected includes a date picker document control, which allows you to select the date from a calendar.

9. Click the **[Date]** placeholder text to display an arrow in the document control, and then click the arrow. A calendar for the current month appears, as shown in Figure 3–38. In the calendar, the current date is outlined in dark blue.

Figure 3–38 **Adding a date to the section 1 header**

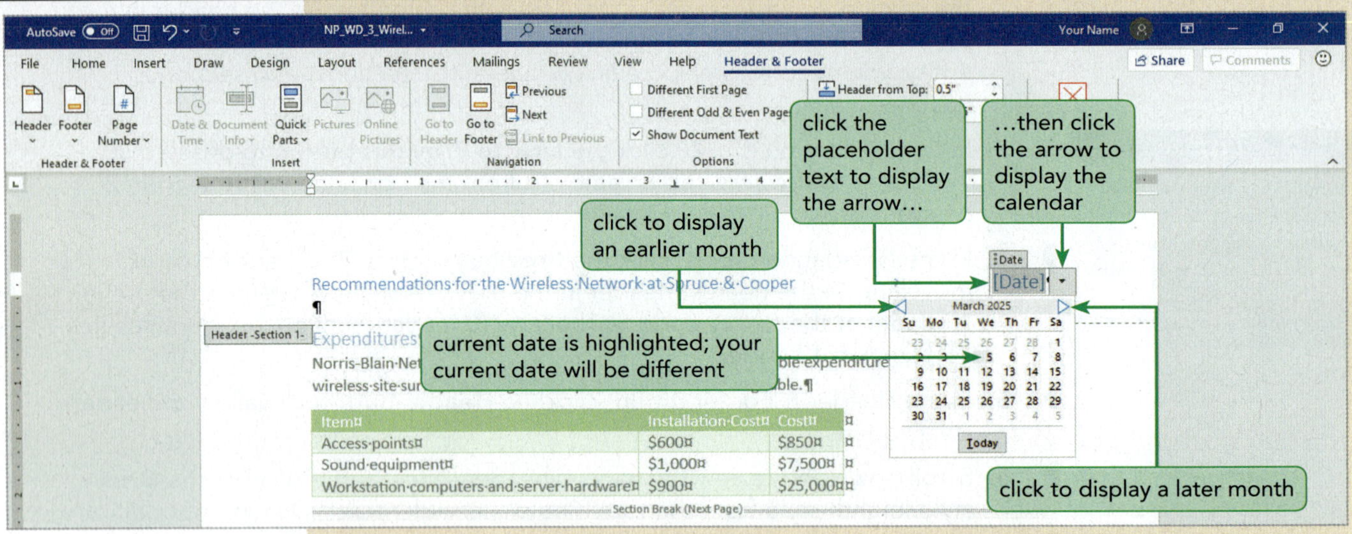

10. Click the current date. The current date, including the year, is inserted in the document control.

11. Scroll up slightly and click anywhere in the section 1 footer (on the preceding page) to deselect the date document control. You are finished creating the header and footer for Eboni's report, so you can close Header and Footer view and return to Print Layout view.

12. In the Close group, click the **Close Header and Footer** button, or double-click anywhere in the main document, and then save your work.

13. On the ribbon, click the **View** tab.

14. In the Zoom group, click the **Multiple Pages** button, and then change the Zoom level to **30%** so you can see all four pages of the document, including the header at the top of pages 1 through 3 and the footer at the bottom of pages 1 through 4. Take a moment to compare your completed headers and footers with Eboni's plan for the headers and footers shown earlier in Figure 3–34.

Next, you need to insert a cover page for the report.

Inserting a Cover Page

A report's cover page typically includes the title and the name of the author. Some people also include a summary of the report on the cover page, which is commonly referred to as an abstract. In addition, you might include the date, the name and possibly the logo of your company or organization, and a subtitle. A cover page should not include the document header or footer.

To insert a preformatted cover page at the beginning of the document, you use the Cover Page button on the Insert tab. You can choose from a variety of cover page styles, all of which include document controls in which you can enter the document title, the document's author, the date, and so on. These document controls are linked to any other document controls in the document. For example, you already entered "Recommendations for the Wireless Network at Spruce & Cooper" into a document control in the header of Eboni's report. So if you use a cover page that contains a similar document control, "Recommendations for the Wireless Network at Spruce & Cooper" will be displayed on the cover page automatically. Note that document controls sometimes display information entered when either Word or Windows was originally installed on your computer. If your computer has multiple user accounts, the information displayed in some document controls might reflect the information for the current user. In any case, you can easily edit the contents of a document control.

To insert a cover page at the beginning of the report:

1. Verify that the document is still zoomed so that you can see all four pages, and then press **CTRL+HOME**. The insertion point moves to the beginning of the document.

2. On the ribbon, click the **Insert** tab.

3. In the Pages group, click the **Cover Page** button. A gallery of cover page styles opens.

Notice that the names of the cover page styles match the names of the preformatted header styles you saw earlier. For example, the list includes a Grid cover page, which is designed to match the Grid header used in this document. To give a document a uniform look, it's helpful to use elements with the same style throughout.

4. Scroll down the gallery to see the cover page styles, and then locate the Grid cover page style.

Tip

To delete a cover page that you inserted from the Cover Page gallery, click the Cover Page button in the Pages group, and then click Remove Current Cover Page.

5. Click the **Grid** cover page style. The new cover page is inserted at the beginning of the document.
6. Change the Zoom level to **120%**, and then scroll down to display the report title in the middle of the cover page. The only difference between the title "Recommendations for the Wireless Network at Spruce & Cooper" here and the title you entered in the document header is that here the title is displayed in all uppercase letters. The entire title is right-aligned. The cover page also includes document controls for a subtitle and an abstract. See Figure 3–39.

Figure 3–39 Newly inserted cover page

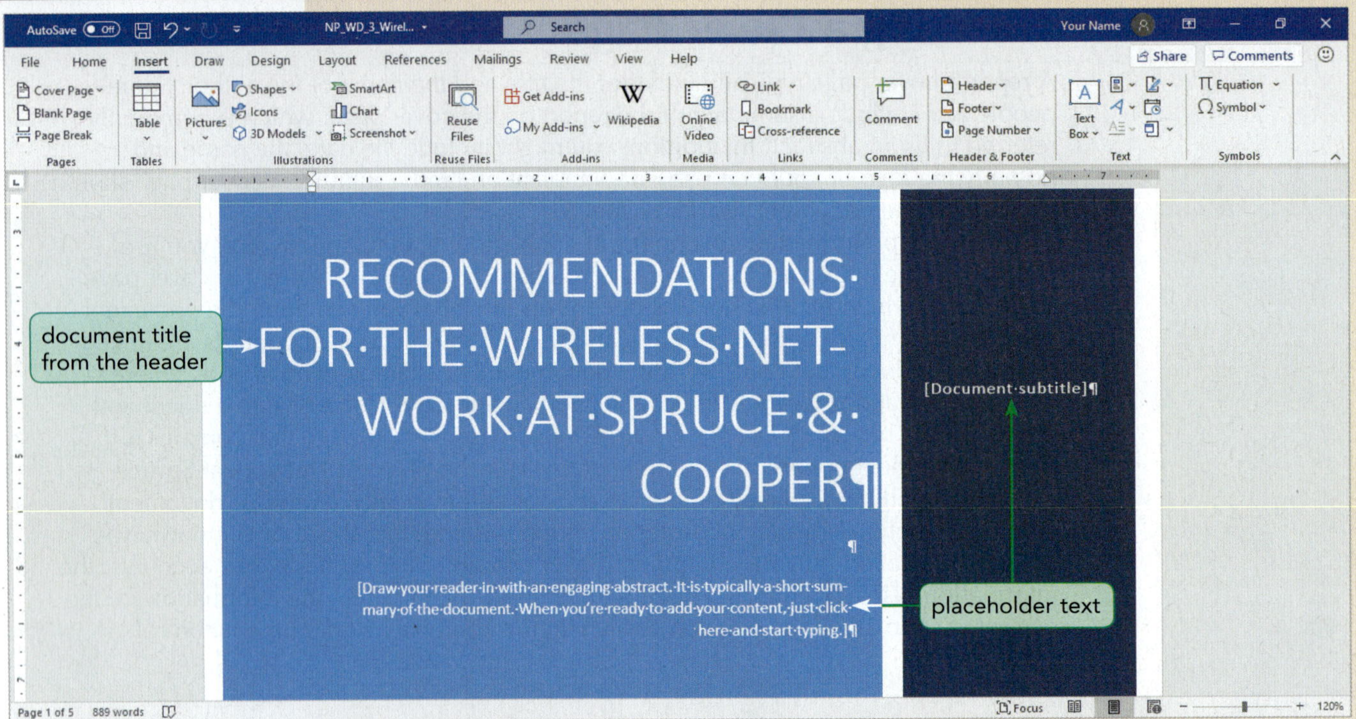

The word "NETWORK" is hyphenated, which looks awkward in a title that is formatted in all capital letters. You can fix that by changing the document's hyphenation settings.

7. On the ribbon, click the **Layout** tab.
8. In the Page Setup group, click the **Hyphenation** button, and then click **Hyphenation Options**.
9. In the Hyphenation dialog box, click the **Hyphenate words in CAPS** check box to remove the checkmark, and then click **OK**. The word "NETWORK" moves to the third line, so the hyphen is no longer necessary.

   Next, you need to type a subtitle in the subtitle document control on the right side of the page.
10. Click the **[Document subtitle]** placeholder text, and then type **Prepared by Eboni Wheatley**. Next, you will remove the abstract document control because you do not need an abstract for this report.
11. Below the document title, right-click the placeholder text that begins **[Draw your reader in...** to display the shortcut menu, and then click **Remove Content Control**. The content control is removed from the cover page.
12. Save the document.

Working with Themes

A **theme** is a coordinated collection of fonts, colors, and other visual effects designed to give a document a cohesive, polished look. A variety of themes are installed with Word, with more available online at Templates.office.com. When you open a new, blank document in Word, the Office theme is applied by default. To change a document's theme, you click the Themes button, which is located in the Document Formatting group on the Design tab, and then click the theme you want. Pointing to the Themes button displays a ScreenTip that tells you what theme is currently applied to the document.

Tip

Each document theme is designed to convey a specific look and feel. The Office theme is designed to be appropriate for standard business documents. Other themes are designed to give documents a flashier look.

The **theme colors** are the colors you see in the Theme Colors section of any color gallery, such as the Font Color gallery. Theme colors are used in the document's styles to format headings, body text, and other elements. When applying color to a document, you usually have the option of selecting a color from a palette of colors designed to match the current theme or from a palette of standard colors. For instance, recall that the colors in the Font Color gallery are divided into Theme Colors and Standard Colors. When you select a Standard Color, such as Dark Red, that color remains the same no matter which theme you apply to the document. But when you click one of the Theme Colors, you are essentially telling Word to use the color located in that particular spot on the Theme Colors palette. Then, if you change the document's theme later, Word substitutes a color from the same location on the Theme Colors palette. This ensures that all the colors in a document are drawn from a group of colors coordinated to look good together. So as a rule, if you are going to use multiple colors in a document (perhaps for paragraph shading and font color), it's a good idea to stick with the Theme Colors.

A similar substitution takes place with fonts when you change the theme. However, to understand how this works, you need to understand the difference between headings and body text. Eboni's document includes the headings "Summary," "Help from Norris-Blain Network Consulting," "Conducting a Wireless Site Survey," "Recommendation," "Survey Costs," "Upgrades," and "Expenditures"—all of which are formatted with heading styles. The text below the headings is considered body text. For example, the paragraph below the "Summary" heading is body text.

To ensure that your documents have a harmonious look, each theme assigns a font for headings and a font for body text. These two fonts are known as the document's **theme fonts**. They are used in the document's styles and appear at the top of the font list when you click the Font arrow in the Font group on the Home tab.

Typically, in a given theme, the same font is used for both headings and body text, but not always. In the Office theme, for instance, they are slightly different; the heading font is Calibri Light, and the body font is Calibri. These two fonts appear at the top of the Font list as "Calibri Light (Headings)" and "Calibri (Body)" when you click the Font arrow in the Font group on the Home tab. When you begin typing text in a new document with the Office theme, the text is formatted as body text with the Calibri font by default.

When applying a font to selected text, you can choose one of the two theme fonts at the top of the Font list, or you can choose one of the other fonts in the Font list. If you choose one of the other fonts and then change the document theme, that font remains the same. But if you use one of the theme fonts and then change the document theme, Word substitutes the appropriate font from the new theme. When you paste text into a document that has a different theme, Word applies the theme fonts and colors of the new document. To retain the original formatting, use the Keep Source Formatting option in the Paste Options menu.

Figure 3–40 compares elements of the default Office theme with the Integral theme. The Integral theme was chosen for this example because, like the Office theme, it has different heading and body fonts.

Figure 3–40 Comparing the Office theme to the Integral theme

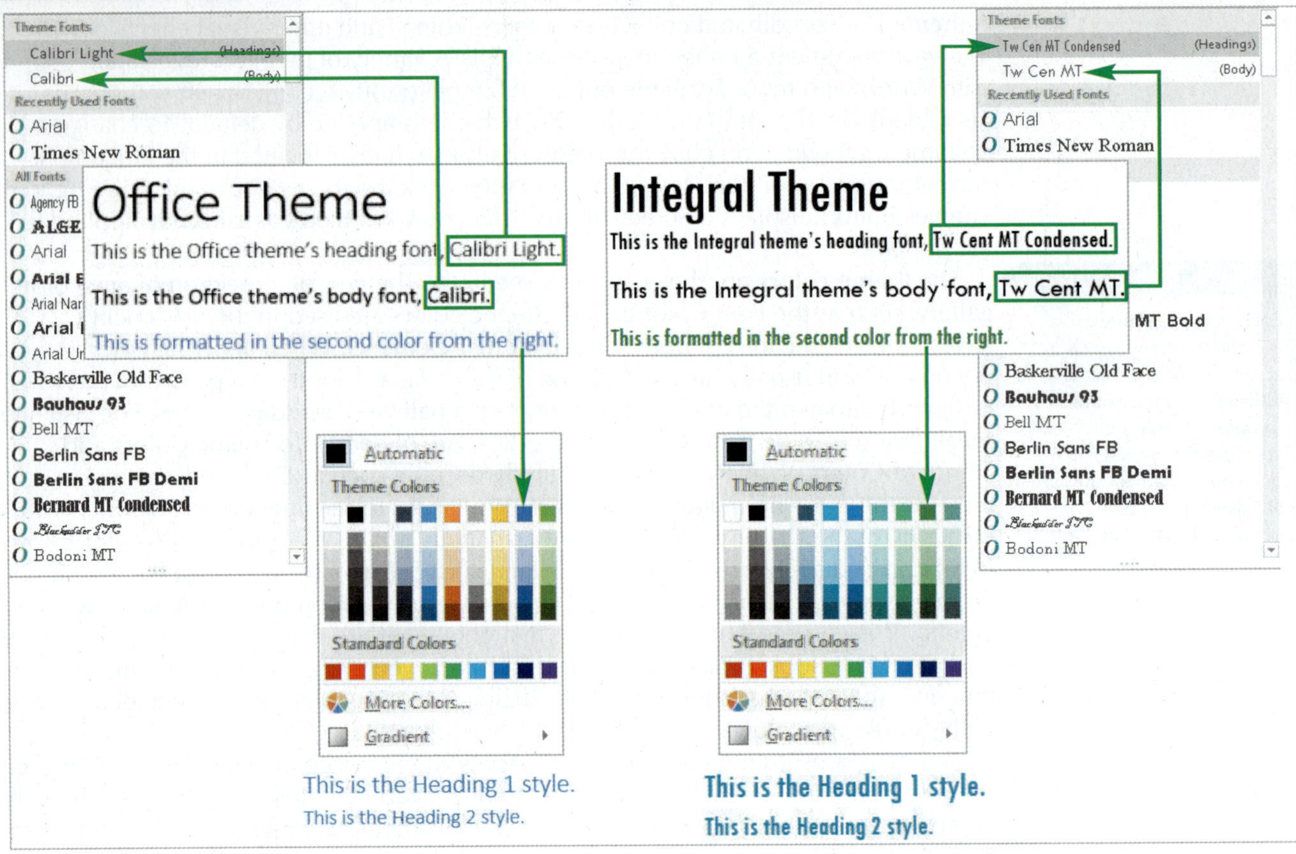

Because Eboni has not yet selected a new theme, the Office theme is currently applied to the document. However, she thinks the Facet theme might be more appropriate for the document. She asks you to apply it now.

To change the document's theme:

1. If necessary, scroll to display the title on the cover page. This will allow you to quickly see how the document changes when you change the theme. Note that currently one section of the cover page is formatted with a blue background and the other is formatted with a blue-gray background.
2. On the ribbon, click the **Design** tab.
3. In the Document Formatting group, point to the **Themes** button. A ScreenTip appears containing the text "Current: Office Theme" as well as general information about themes.
4. In the Document Formatting group, click the **Themes** button. The Themes gallery opens. Because Microsoft occasionally updates the available themes, you might see a different list than the one shown in Figure 3–41.

Figure 3–41 Themes gallery

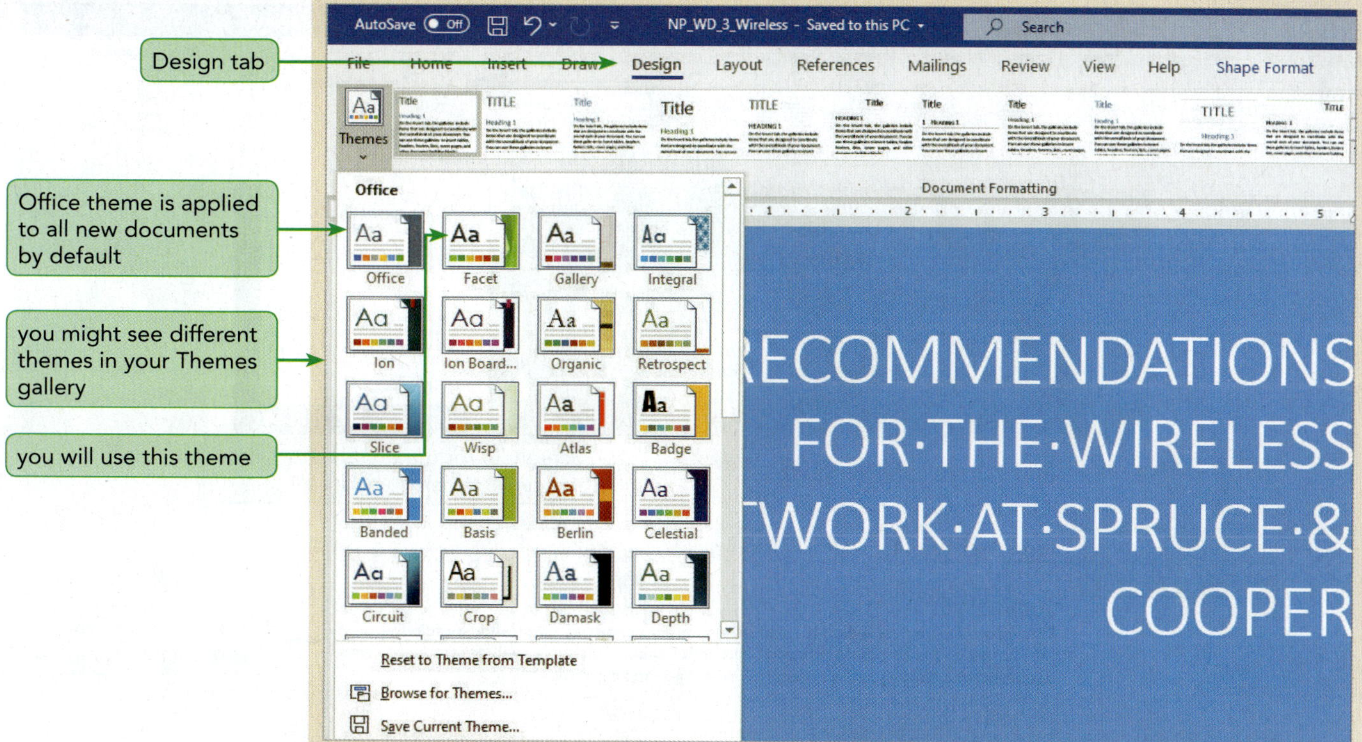

5. Move the pointer (without clicking it) over the various themes in the gallery to see a Live Preview of each theme in the document. The heading and body fonts as well as the heading colors change to reflect the fonts associated with the various themes.

6. In the Themes gallery, click the **Facet** theme, and then scroll down to review the document's new look. One section of the cover page now has a green background, and the other has a dark gray background. The table is formatted in shades of brown, and the SmartArt is green. The document text is now formatted in the body and heading fonts of the Facet theme, with the headings formatted in green.

   Trouble? If you do not see the Facet theme in your Themes gallery, click a different theme.

7. In the Document Formatting group, point to the **Fonts** button. A ScreenTip appears, listing the currently selected theme (Facet), the heading font (Trebuchet MS), and the body font (Trebuchet MS). See Figure 3–42.

Figure 3–42 **Fonts for the Facet theme**

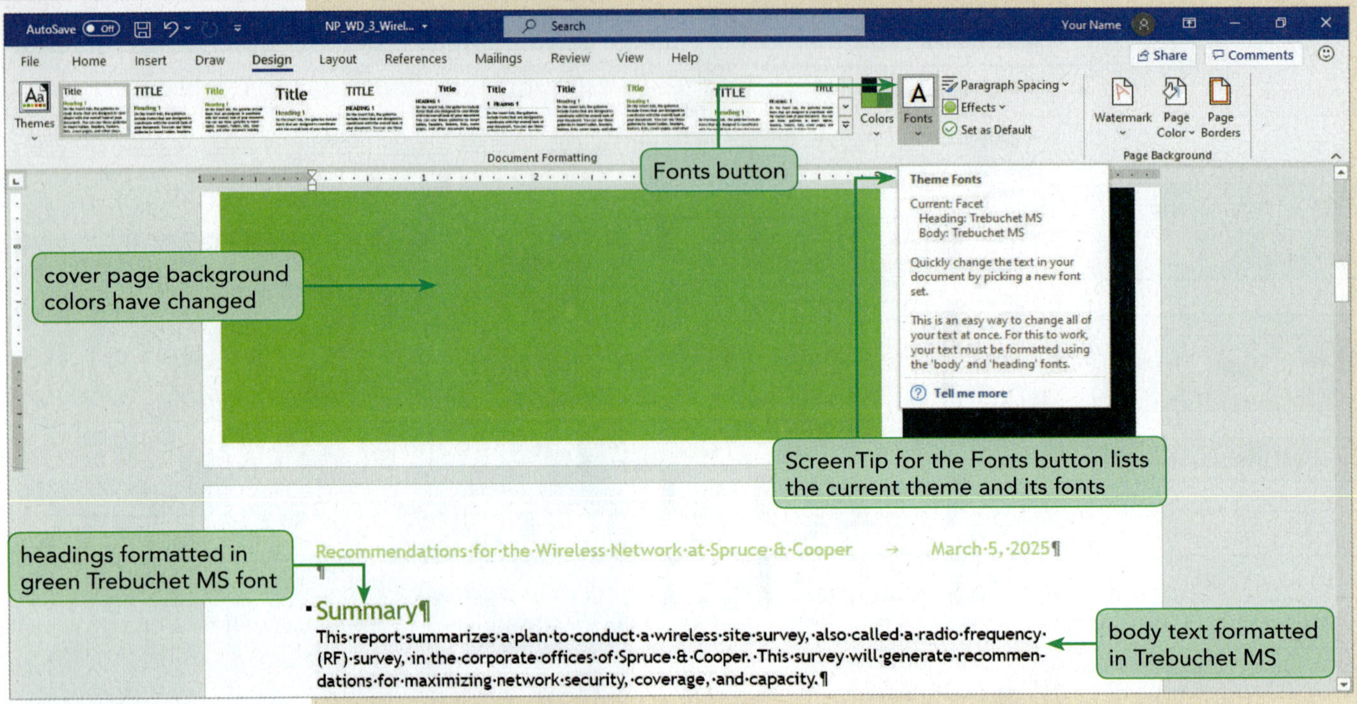

Trouble? If a menu appears, you clicked the Fonts button instead of pointing to it. Press ESC, and then repeat Step 7.

Note that if you wanted to select a different set of theme fonts, you could click the Fonts button and then select a set of fonts. You could also click the Colors button and select a different set of theme colors. However, the fonts and colors in a theme have been paired by designers who have a lot of experience selecting options that, together, create a coherent look. So for professional documents, you should avoid changing the theme fonts and colors.

8. **sam** Save your changes.

Insight

Personalizing the Word Interface

The Word Options dialog box allows you to change the look of the Word interface. For starters, you can change the Office Theme from the default setting (Colorful) to Dark Gray, Black, or White. Note that in this context, "Office Theme" refers to the colors of the Word interface, and not the colors and fonts used in a Word document. You can also use the Office Background setting to add graphic designs, such as clouds or stars, to the Word interface. To get started, click the File tab, click Options in the navigation pane, make sure the General tab is displayed, and then select the options you want in the Personalize your copy of Microsoft Office section of the Word Options dialog box.

Your work on the report is finished. You should preview the report before closing it.

To preview the report:

1. On the ribbon, click the **File** tab.
2. In the navigation pane, click the **Print** tab. The cover page of the report is displayed in the document preview in the right pane.
3. Examine the document preview, using the arrow buttons at the bottom of the pane to display each page.
4. If you need to make any changes to the report, return to Print Layout view, edit the document, preview the document again, and then save the document.
5. Display the document in Print Layout view.
6. Change the Zoom level back to **120%**, and then press **CTRL+HOME** to make sure the insertion point is located on the first page.

Reviewing a Document in Read Mode

The members of Spruce & Cooper's leadership team could choose to print the report, but some might prefer to read it on their computers instead. In that case, they can take advantage of **Read Mode**, a document view designed to make reading on a screen as easy as possible. Unlike Print Layout view, which mimics the look of the printed page with its margins and page breaks, Read Mode focuses on the document's content. Read Mode displays as much content as possible on the screen at a time, with buttons that allow you to display more. Note that you can't edit text in Read Mode. To do that, you need to switch back to Page Layout view.

Tip

You can also use Focus mode to focus only on document content. Click the Focus button on the status bar or on the View tab in the Immersive group to hide everything in the Word window except for the document. To exit Focus mode, press ESC.

To display the document in Read Mode:

1. In the status bar, click the **Read Mode** button. The document switches to Read Mode, with a reduced version of the cover page on the left and the first part of the document text on the right. On the left edge of the status bar, the message "Screens 1–2 of 9" explains that you are currently viewing the first two screens out of a total of 9.

   Trouble? If your status bar indicates that you have a different number of screens, you may be using a computer with a different screen resolution than the resolution used to create the figures in this book. Change the Zoom level as needed so that the document is split into 9 screens.

   The title page on the left is screen 1. The text on the right is screen 2. To display more of the document, you can click the arrow button on the right. See Figure 3–43.

Figure 3–43 Document displayed in Read Mode

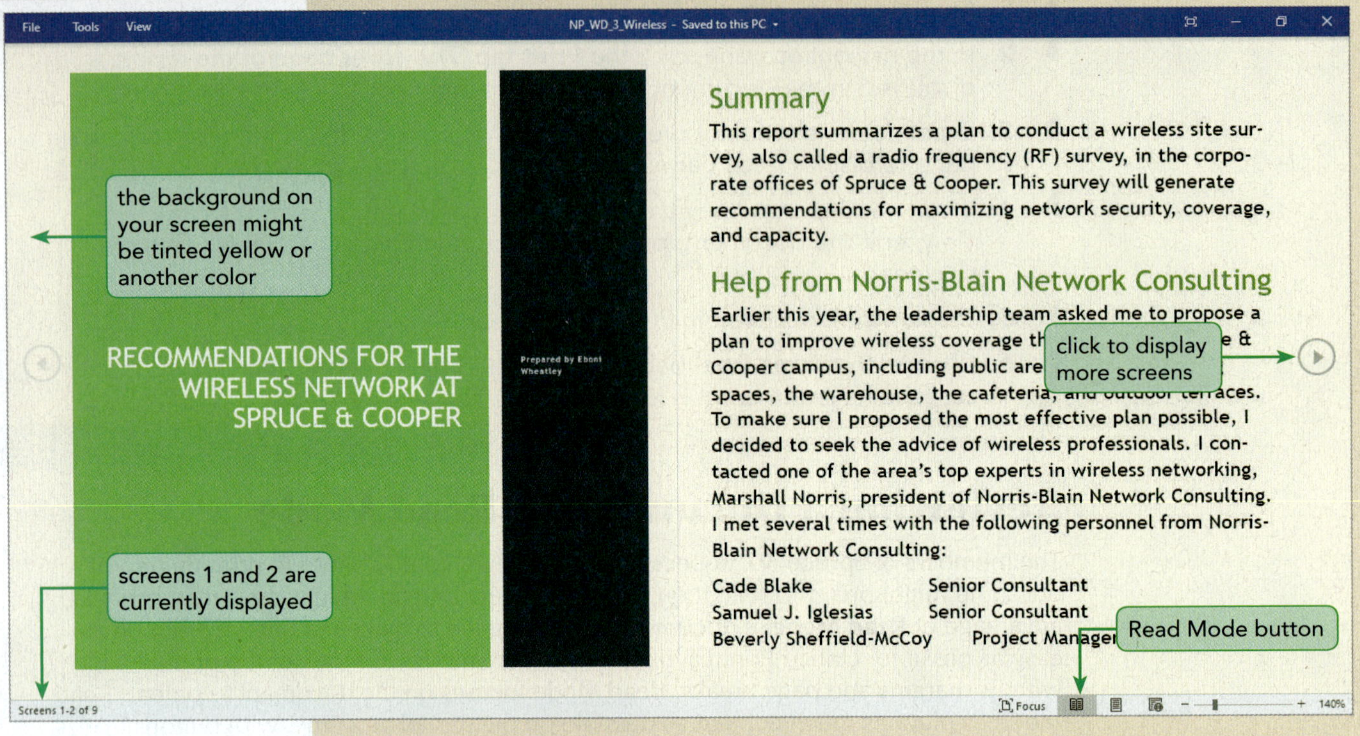

Trouble? If the pages on your screen are not laid out as shown in Figure 3–43, click View on the menu bar, point to Layout, and then click Column Layout.

2. Click the **right arrow** button on the right to display screens 3 and 4. A left arrow button is now displayed on the left side of the screen. You could click it to move back to the previous screens.
3. Click the **right arrow** button to display screens 5 and 6, then screens 7 and 8, and then screen 9.
4. Click the **left arrow** button on the left as necessary to return to screens 1 and 2, and then click the **Print Layout** button in the status bar to return to Page Layout view.
5. Close the document.

Tip

To zoom in on a SmartArt graphic, you can double-click it. Click anywhere outside the object zoom window to return to the Read Mode screens.

You now have a draft of the document, including a cover page, the report text, a nicely formatted table, and the SmartArt graphic (in landscape orientation).

Proskills

Written Communication: Taking Notes

The process of writing a report or other long document usually involves taking notes. It's essential to organize your notes in a way that allows you to write about your topic logically and coherently. It's also important to retain your notes after you finish a first draft, so that you can incorporate additional material from your notes in subsequent drafts.

Clicking the Linked Notes button on the Review tab opens the Microsoft OneNote desktop app in a window on the right side of the screen. (If you don't see the Linked Notes button and are using the OneNote desktop app, click the File tab to display Backstage view. Click Options in the navigation pane, and then click Add-ins. Click the arrow button in the Manage box, select Com Add-ins, if necessary, and then click the Go button. In the Com Add-ins dialog box, select OneNote Linked Notes Add-In, and then click OK.) In the Microsoft OneNote window, you can take notes that are linked to your Microsoft Word account. Every time you start Word and click the Linked Notes button, your notes are displayed in the OneNote window. You can copy material from a Word document and paste it in OneNote, and vice versa.

To get started, open a Word document, save it, make sure you are logged into your Microsoft account, click the Review tab, and then, in the OneNote group, click the Linked Notes button. This opens the Select Location in OneNote dialog box, where you can select a notebook. OneNote works best if you use a notebook stored on OneDrive, so unless you have a compelling reason to do otherwise, select a notebook stored on OneDrive. Now you're ready to take notes. Start by typing a title for your notebook page at the insertion point, then click in the blank space below the title, and start taking notes. To display the OneNote ribbon, with a selection of tools for working with notes, click the ellipses at the top of the OneNote window. Click the Close button in the upper-right corner of the OneNote window pane when you are finished.

Review

Session 3.2 Quick Check

1. What is the default tab stop style?
2. Explain how to configure Word to hyphenate a document automatically.
3. What is the first thing you need to do if you want to format part of a document in an orientation different from the rest of the document?
4. Explain how to create separate headers for a document with two sections.
5. Explain how to insert a preformatted cover page.
6. What is the default theme in a new document?

Practice

Review Assignments

Data File needed for the Review Assignments: NP_WD_3-3.docx

The wireless site survey has been completed, and the Spruce & Cooper wireless network has been upgraded. Now Eboni Wheatley is focusing on the second phase of her work on the network—improving security. She has begun working on a report for the leadership team that outlines information about conducting security training classes and installing network security software. You need to format the report, add a table at the end containing a preliminary schedule, add a formula to another table that summarizes costs associated with subscriptions for network security protection, and create a sample graphic that Eboni could use in a handout announcing the security training.

Complete the following steps:

1. Open the document **NP_WD_3-3.docx** located in the Word3 > Review folder included with your Data Files, and then save it as **NP_WD_3_Security** in the location specified by your instructor.
2. Promote the "Schedule" and "Planning for Level 1 Sessions" headings from Heading 2 text to Heading 1 text, and then move the "Planning for Level 1 Sessions" heading and its body text up above the "Schedule" heading.
3. Insert a page break before the "Schedule" heading. On the new page 2, in the blank paragraph before the "Network Security Subscription Costs" heading, insert a table using the information shown in Figure 3–44. Format the header row in bold.

Figure 3–44 Level 1 training schedule

Date	Topic
8/6/2025	Social engineering
5/21/2025	Introduction to cybersecurity
10/5/2025	Mobile security
7/20/2025	Cloud-based threats
6/16/2025	Data protection

4. Sort the table by the contents of the "Date" column in ascending order.
5. In the appropriate location in the table, insert a new row for an **Endpoint security** class on **9/3/2025**.
6. Delete the "Mobile security" row from the table.
7. Modify the widths of both columns to accommodate the widest entry in each.
8. Apply the Grid Table 4 - Accent 4 style to the table, and then remove the special formatting for the first column.
9. Locate the table in the "Network Security Subscription Costs" section of the document. In the table's lower-right cell, add a formula field that sums the total cost per month and displays the result in a format that matches the other numbers in the table, including a dollar sign ($).
10. Change the cost for DNS Protection to **$650.00** and then update the formula.
11. Merge the two blank cells, insert **TOTAL** in the new, merged cell, right-align the text in the cell, and then format the contents of the bottom row in bold.
12. Apply the Grid Table 4 - Accent 4 style to the table, and then remove the special formatting for the first column.
13. On page 1, replace the text "[instructor names]" with a tabbed list of instructors and their specialties, using the following information: **Suzette Carrington-Brewster**, **Malware**; **Lia Kim**, **Server security**; **Leopold R. Coia**, **Social engineering**. Insert a tab after each name, and don't include any punctuation in the list.

14. Use a left tab stop to align the instructors' specialties 2.5 inches from the left margin, and then adjust the list's paragraph spacing so it appears to be a single paragraph.
15. Turn on automatic hyphenation.
16. After the second table on page 2, insert a section break that starts a new, third page, and then format the new page in landscape orientation.
17. Insert a SmartArt graphic that illustrates the two parts of upgrading Spruce & Cooper's network security. Use the Circle Process graphic from the Process category, and, from left to right, include the following text in the SmartArt diagram: **Security Training**, **Web Secure Portal Plus**, and **Secure Network**. Do not include any punctuation in the SmartArt. Size the SmartArt graphic to fill the page.
18. Create a footer for sections 1 and 2 that aligns your first and last names at the left margin. Insert the page number, without any design elements and without the word "Page," below your name.
19. Separate the section 2 header from the section 1 header, and then create a header for section 1 using the Retrospect header style. Enter **IMPROVING NETWORK SECURITY AT SPRUCE & COOPER** as the document title, and select the current date. Note that the document title will be displayed in all uppercase no matter how you type it.
20. Insert a cover page using the Retrospect style. If you typed the document title in all uppercase in the header, it will be displayed in all uppercase here. If you used a mix of uppercase and lowercase in the header, you'll see a mix here. Revise the document title if necessary to make it all uppercase, change the hyphenation options so "NETWORK" is no longer hyphenated, and then add the following subtitle: **PREPARED BY *YOUR NAME***, replacing *YOUR NAME* with your first and last name. Delete the Author document control. Also delete the Company Name and Company Address document controls, as well as the vertical bar character between them.
21. Change the document theme to Slice, then save and preview the report. Eboni will be adding more text to page 3, so don't be concerned that most of that page is blank.
22. Close the document.

Apply

Case Problem 1

Data File needed for this Case Problem: NP_WD_3-4.docx

LEED Landscape Design Association You are the business manager of the LEED Landscape Design Association, a professional organization for LEED landscape designers in Atlanta, Georgia, and the surrounding area. LEED, which is short for Leadership in Energy and Environmental Design, is a certification system designed to encourage environmentally friendly construction and design, as well as sustainable landscape design. Landscapers join the LEED Landscape Design Association to make professional contacts with like-minded vendors and customers. You have been asked to help prepare an annual report for the board of directors. The current draft is not complete, but it contains enough for you to get started.

Complete the following steps:

1. Open the document **NP_WD_3-4.docx** located in the Word3 > Case1 folder included with your Data Files, and then save it as **NP_WD_3_LEED** in the location specified by your instructor.
2. Adjust the heading levels so that the "LEED Sustainable Landscape Fair" and "LEED Tech Fest" headings are formatted with the Heading 2 style.
3. Move the "New Members" heading and its body text down to the end of the report.
4. Format the Board of Directors list using a left tab stop with a dot leader at the 2.2-inch mark. (*Hint:* Use the Dialog Box Launcher in the Paragraph group on the Layout tab to open the Paragraph dialog box, and then click the Tabs button at the bottom of the Indents and Spacing tab to open the Tabs dialog box.)
5. Insert a page break that moves the "New Members" heading to the top of a new page, and then, below the body text on the new page, insert a table consisting of three columns and four rows.
6. In the table, enter the information shown in Figure 3–45. Format the column headings in bold.

Figure 3-45 **Information for membership table**

Type	Fee	Members
Vendor	$500	225
Enterprise	$200	125
Individual	$175	200

7. Sort the table in ascending order by type.
8. In the appropriate location in the table, insert a row for a **Student** membership type, with a **$25** fee, and **170** members.
9. Adjust the column widths so each column accommodates the widest entry.
10. Add a new row to the bottom of the table, and then insert a formula that sums the total number of members. Make sure the formula displays the result in the appropriate format.
11. Merge the two blank cells, add the right-aligned text **TOTAL** to the new, merged cell, and then format the bottom row in bold.
12. Format the table using the Grid Table 4 - Accent 3 table style without banded rows or bold formatting in the first column.
13. Turn on automatic hyphenation.
14. Insert a Blank footer, and then type your name to replace the selected placeholder text in the footer's left margin. In the right margin, insert a page number using the Large Color style. (*Hint*: Press TAB twice to move the insertion point to the right margin before inserting the page number, and then insert the page number at the current location.)
15. Insert a cover page using the Semaphore style. Select the current date. Enter the document title, **LEED LANDSCAPE DESIGN ASSOCIATION** in the appropriate document control. If necessary, change the Hyphenation options so "ASSOCIATION" appears on one line. In the subtitle document control, enter **Prepared by [Your Name]**, but replace "[Your Name]" with your first and last names). (Note that the text you type is formatted in a special font format called small caps.) Delete the remaining document controls.
16. Change the document theme to Facet.
17. Save, preview, and then close the document.

Create

Case Problem 2

There are no Data Files needed for this Case Problem.

York Pickup and Delivery Rory York owns a small pickup and delivery company in Birmingham, Alabama. A professional contact has just emailed him a list of potential corporate customers. Rory asks you to create and format a table containing the list of customers. When you're finished with that project, you'll create a table detailing some of his recent repair expenses in the garage where he houses his fleet of trucks.

Complete the following steps:

1. Open a new, blank document, and then save it as **NP_WD_3_Corporate** in the location specified by your instructor.
2. Create the table shown in Figure 3-46.

Figure 3–46 Corporate customers table

Company	Contact	Phone
Walnut Springs Coffee Imports	Krystal Winford	205-555-0100
CDX Creative Partners	Tobias Forster	205-555-0107
Blue Diamond Construction Supply	Layla Jordan	205-555-0114
Cornerstone and Woodward Partners Incorporated	Mohammed Khan	205-555-0121
Carbon Wear Unlimited	Huey McGrath	205-555-0128

For the table style, start with the Grid Table 4 - Accent 4 table style, make any necessary changes, and then change the theme to a theme that uses TW Cen MT (Condensed) for the heading font and TW Cen MT for the body font, and that formats the heading row with the Green, Accent 4 shading color. (Note that the text in the heading row is formatted with the theme's body font, which means it is displayed in TW CEN MT after you change the theme.) The final table should be about 5 inches wide and about 2.5 inches tall, as measured on the horizontal and vertical rulers. (*Hint*: Remember that you can drag the Table Resize handle to increase the table's overall size.)

3. Replace "Huey McGrath" with your first and last names.
4. Add a new blank paragraph below the corporate customers table, and then, in that new paragraph, create the table shown in Figure 3–47, using the same table style and modifications you used for the corporate customers table. Use a formula for the total with a number format that includes a dollar sign but no decimal places. (*Hint*: You can edit the number format in the Formula dialog box to delete both instances of a decimal place with two trailing zeros.) The final table should be about 5.5 inches wide and about 2 inches tall, as measured on the horizontal and vertical rulers.

Figure 3–47 Garage repair table

Repair	Completion Date	Cost
Install new overhead lights	3/4/2025	$450
Replace deadbolts on front and back doors	3/15/2025	$125
Fix broken screens	3/21/2025	$50
	TOTAL	$ 625

5. Save, preview, and then close the document.

Module 4

Enhancing Page Layout and Design

Creating a Newsletter

Objectives

Session 4.1

- Use continuous section breaks for page layout
- Format text in columns
- Insert symbols and special characters
- Distinguish between inline and floating objects
- Wrap text around an object
- Insert and format text boxes
- Insert drop caps

Session 4.2

- Create and modify WordArt
- Crop a picture
- Search for online pictures and 3D models
- Rotate and adjust a picture
- Remove a picture's background
- Insert and format an icon
- Balance columns
- Add a page border
- Save a document as a PDF
- Open a PDF in Word

Case | **Metropolitan Library System**

Vassily Gogol is a librarian for the Metropolitan Library System in Indianapolis, Indiana. He has decided to begin publishing a monthly newsletter with articles about the latest events at the system's many branches. He has already written the text of the first newsletter. Now he needs you to transform the text into an eye-catching publication with a headline, pictures, drop caps, and other desktop-publishing elements. Vassily's budget doesn't allow him to hire a professional graphic designer to create the document using desktop-publishing software. But there's no need for that because you can do the work for him using the formatting, graphics, and page layout tools in Word. After you finish the newsletter, Vassily wants you to save the newsletter as a PDF so he can email it to the printing company. You also need to review a document that is currently available only as a PDF.

Starting Data Files

Word4 →

Module
NP_WD_4-1.docx
Support_WD_4_Bookmobile.png
Support_WD_4_Cupcakes.png
Support_WD_4_Festival.docx
Support_WD_4_Hours.docx
Support_WD_4_Listening.pdf

Review
NP_WD_4-2.docx
Support_WD_4_Island.png
Support_WD_4_Retirement.png
Support_WD_4_Schedule.docx
Support_WD_4_Volunteers.docx

Case1
NP_WD_4-3.docx
Support_WD_4_Bins.docx
Support_WD_4_Earth.png
Support_WD_4_Sorting.png

Case2
(none)

Session 4.1 Visual Overview:

This picture is an example of an **object**—that is, something you can manipulate independently of the text. The bookmobile picture, the headphone icon, the WordArt headline, and the text boxes are also objects. To edit an object, you first have to click it to select it.

This specially formatted text is an example of **WordArt**, which is created using the WordArt button in the Text group on the Insert tab.

These are examples of text boxes, which are like mini documents within a document.

This bookmobile picture was inserted from a file, but you can also use the Online Pictures command on the Pictures menu to search for photos and other illustrations on the web.

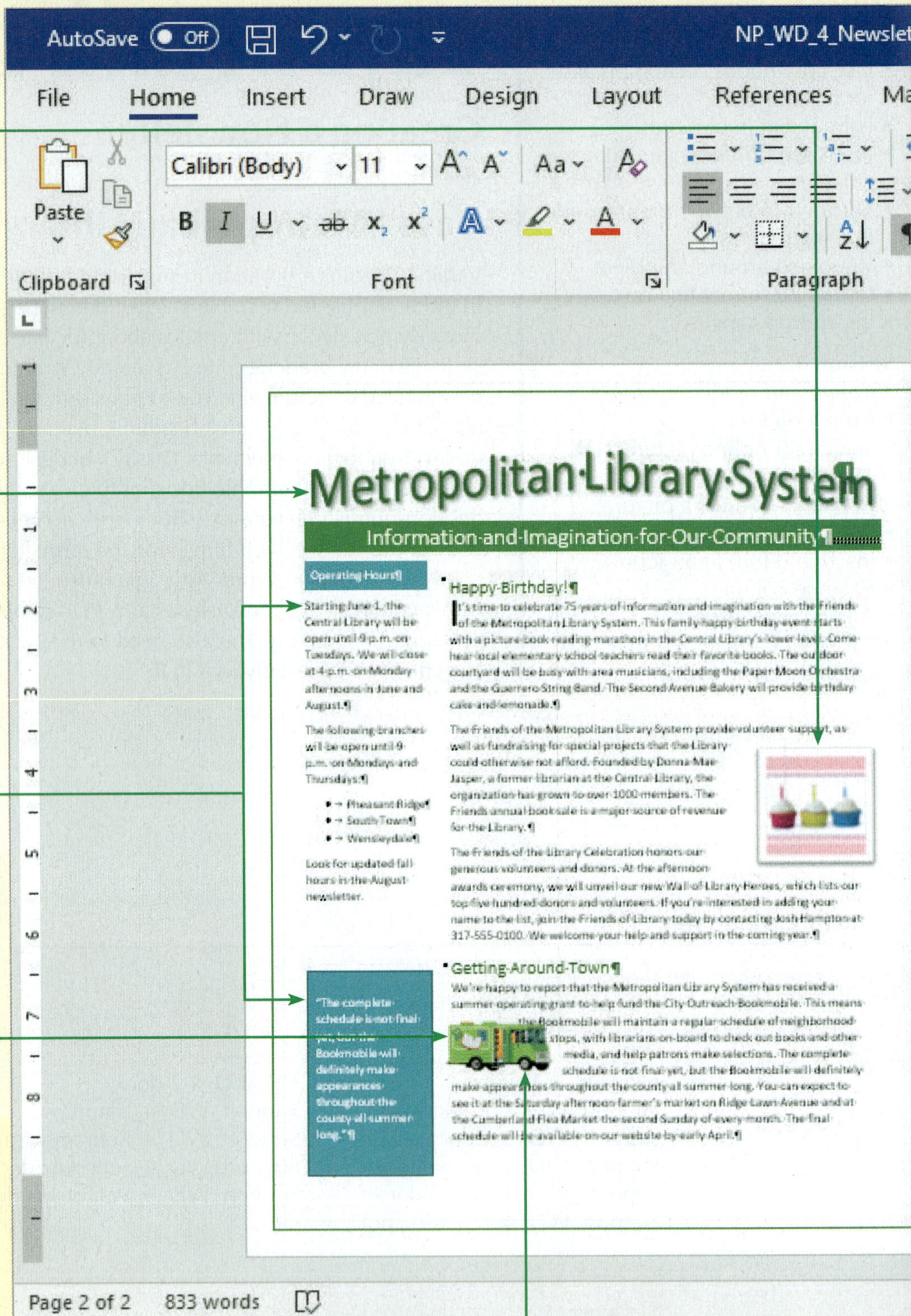

Mascha Tace/Shutterstock.com; Ruth Black/Shutterstock.com

Pictures and text boxes are separate from the document text; you need to adjust the way text flows, or **wraps**, around those elements. Here, the Tight text wrap option is used to make text flow as closely as possible around the shape of the bookmobile.

Elements of Desktop Publishing

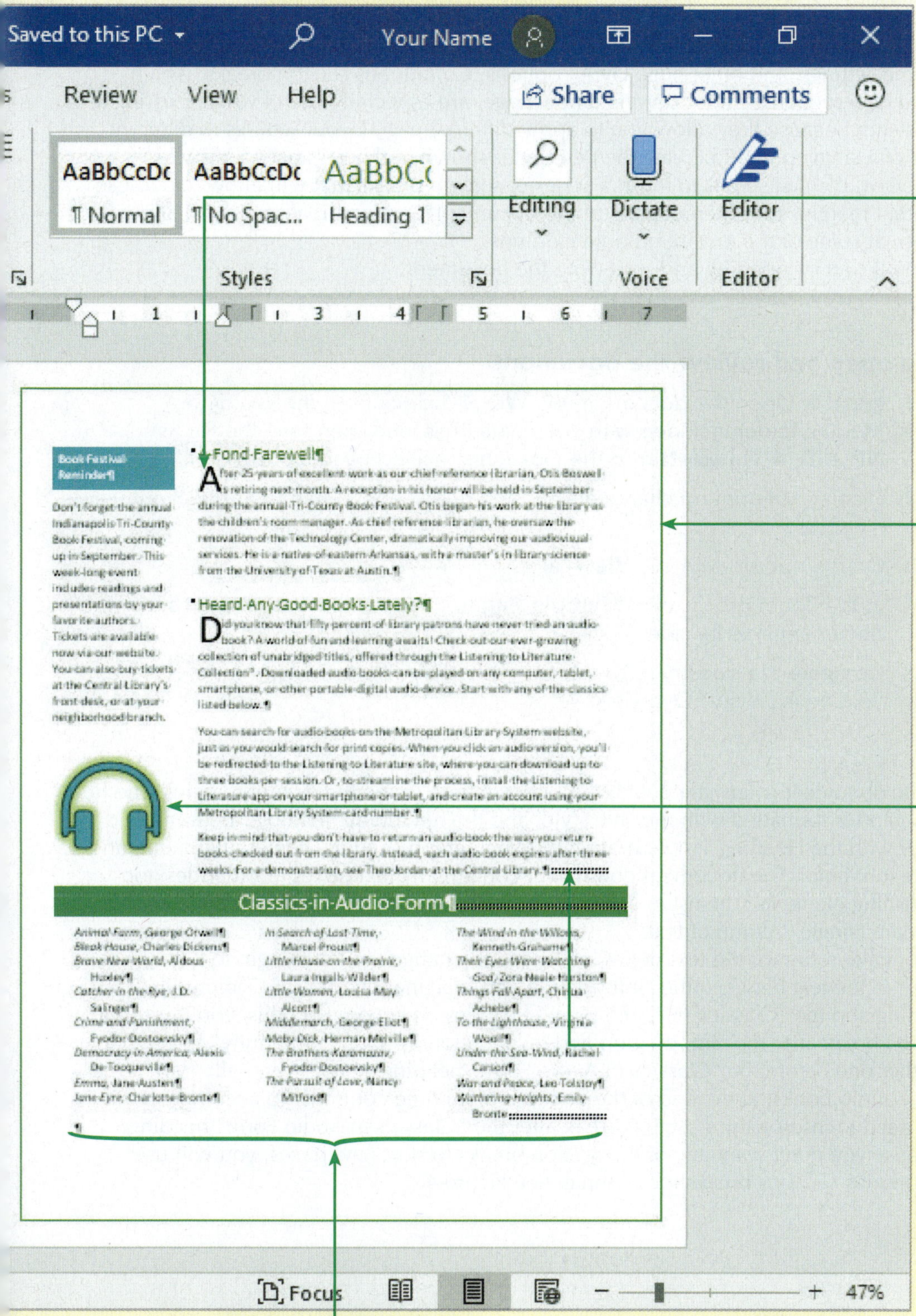

A **drop cap** is a large, decorative letter at the beginning of a paragraph. Word treats a drop cap like a picture, which means you can click it to select it, and then resize the drop cap by dragging its sizing handles.

Desktop publishing is the process of preparing commercial-quality printed material, such as the newsletter shown here, using a desktop or laptop computer. Using Word, you can create documents that have elements of desktop publishing, such as special font treatments, graphics, and page layout options, as well as design elements such as page borders.

The headphones image is an example of an icon, which you can insert using the Icons button in the Illustrations group on the Insert tab.

A **continuous section break** starts a new section at the insertion point without starting a new page. Section breaks allow you to format parts of a document in columns and use different margins in different parts of the document.

In desktop-published documents, text is commonly arranged in two or more **columns**.

Using Continuous Section Breaks to Enhance Page Layout

Newsletters and other desktop-published documents often incorporate multiple section breaks, with the various sections formatted with different margins, page orientations, column settings, and other page layout options. Continuous section breaks, which start a new section without starting a new page, are especially useful when creating a newsletter because they allow you to apply different page layout settings to different parts of a single page. To create the newsletter shown in the Session 4.1 Visual Overview, the first step is to insert a series of section breaks that will allow you to use different margins for different parts of the document. Section breaks will also allow you to format some of the text in multiple columns.

You'll start by opening and reviewing the document.

To open and review the document:

1. sam Open the document **NP_WD_4-1.docx** from the Word4 > Module folder included with your Data Files, and then save the file as **NP_WD_4_Newsletter** in the location specified by your instructor.
2. Display nonprinting characters and the rulers, and switch to Print Layout view, if necessary.
3. On the ribbon, click the **View** tab.
4. In the Zoom group, click **Multiple Pages** so you can see both pages of the document side by side.
5. Compare the document to the completed newsletter shown in the Session 4.1 Visual Overview.

The document is formatted with the Office theme, using the default margins. The first paragraph is formatted with the Title style, and the remaining headings are formatted either with the Heading 1 style or with blue paragraph shading, center alignment, and white font color. The document doesn't yet contain any text boxes or other desktop-publishing elements. The list of audio books at the end of the document appears as a standard, single column of text.

To make room for the text boxes, you need to change the left margin to 2.5 inches for all of the text between the "Information and Imagination for Our Community" heading and the "Classics in Audio Form" heading. To accomplish this, you'll insert a section break after the "Information and Imagination for Our Community" heading and another before the "Classics in Audio Form" heading. You'll eventually format the list of audio books, at the end of the document, in three columns. To accomplish that, you need to insert a third section break after the "Classics in Audio Form" heading. Because you don't want any of the section breaks to start new pages, you will use continuous sections breaks for all three. See Figure 4–1.

Figure 4–1 Newsletter document before adding section breaks

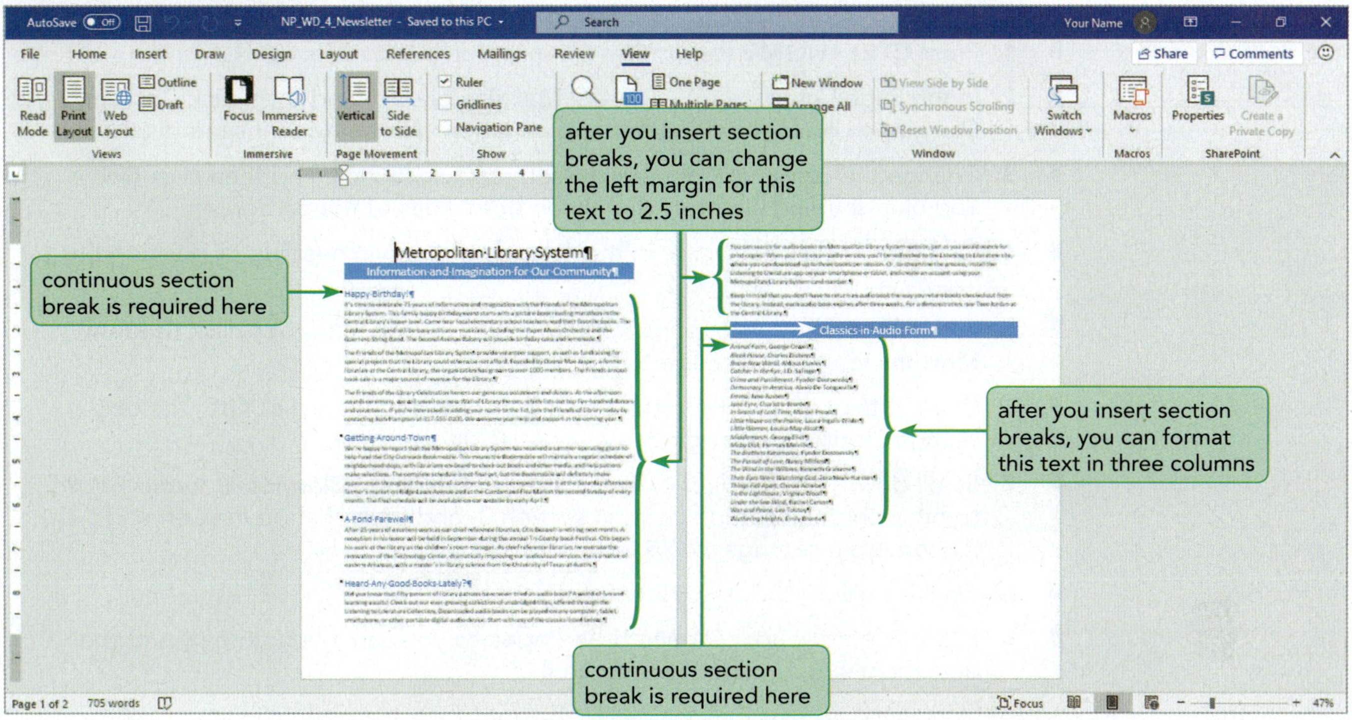

To insert continuous section breaks in the document:

1. Change the Zoom level to **120%**.
2. In the document, click at the beginning of the third paragraph, which contains the heading "Happy Birthday!"
3. On the ribbon, click the **Layout** tab.
4. In the Page Setup group, click the **Breaks** button, and then click **Continuous**. A short dotted line, indicating a continuous section break, appears in the blue shading at the end of the preceding paragraph, although you might find it hard to see. If there was more white space to the right of the line of text, you would see a longer line with the words "Section Break (Continuous)." You'll be able to see the section break text more clearly when you insert the next one.
5. Scroll down to page 2, click at the beginning of the shaded paragraph "Classics in Audio Form," and then insert a continuous section break. A dotted line with the words "Section Break (Continuous)" appears at the end of the preceding paragraph.
6. Click at the beginning of the next paragraph, which contains the text "*Animal Farm*, George Orwell," and then insert a continuous section break. A dotted line with the words "Section Break (Continuous)" appears in the blue shading at the end of the preceding paragraph.

Now that you have created sections within the newsletter document, you can format the individual sections as if they were separate documents. In the following steps, you'll format the first and third sections by changing their left and right margins to .75 inch. You'll also format the second section by changing its left margin to 2.5 inches.

To set custom margins for sections 1, 2, and 3:

1. Press **CTRL+HOME** to position the insertion point in section 1.
2. In the Page Setup group, click the **Margins** button, and then click **Custom Margins** to open the Page Setup dialog box with the Margins tab displayed.
3. Change the Left and Right margin settings to **.75** inch, and then click **OK**. The blue shading expands slightly on both sides of the paragraph.
4. On page 1, click anywhere in the "Happy Birthday!" heading to position the insertion point in section 2.
5. In the Page Setup group, click the **Margins** button, and then click **Custom Margins** to open the Page Setup dialog box.
6. Change the Left margin setting to **2.5** inches, and then click **OK**. The text in section 2 shifts to the right.
7. Scroll down to page 2, click in the shaded heading "**Classics in Audio Form**" to position the insertion point in section 3, and then change the Left and Right margin settings to **.75** inch.
8. On the ribbon, click the **View** tab.
9. In the Zoom group, click **Multiple Pages** so you can see both pages of the document side by side. See Figure 4–2.

Figure 4–2 Sections 1, 2, and 3 with new margins

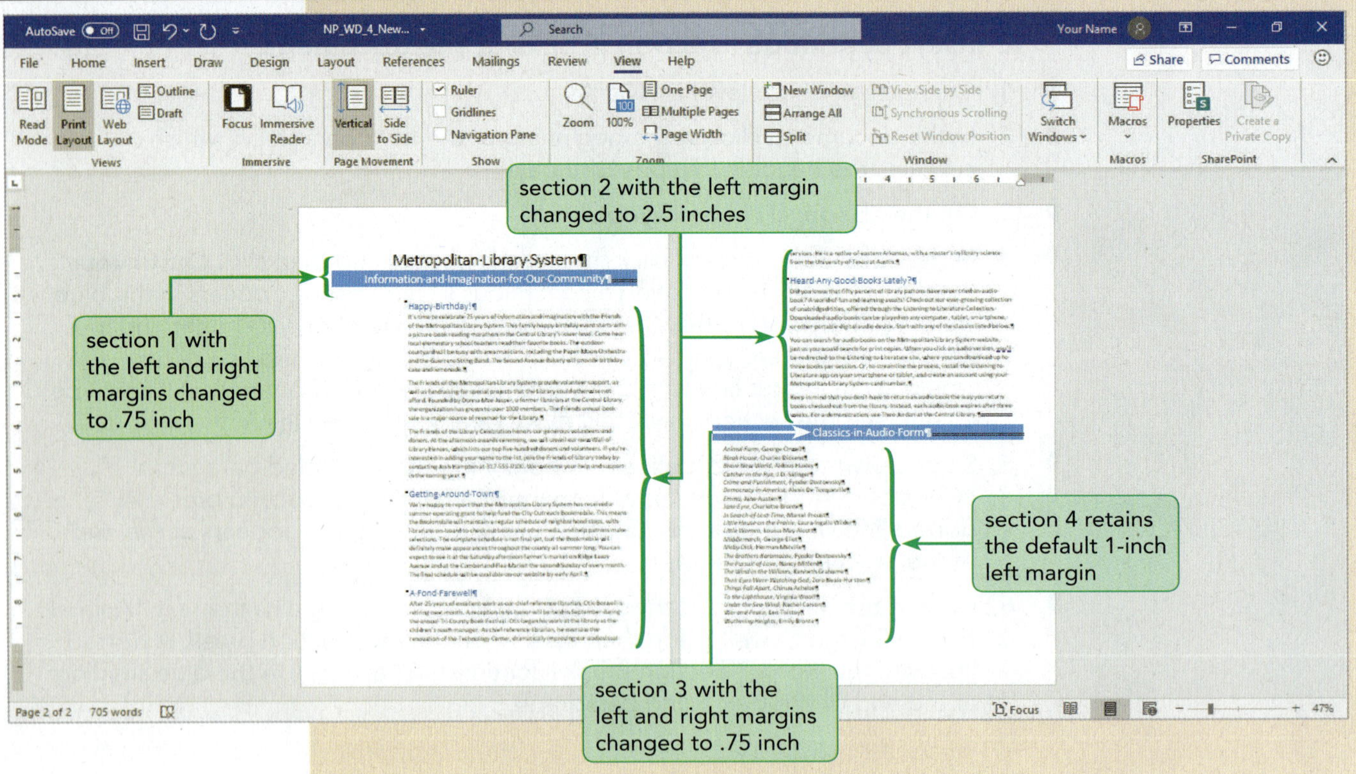

10. Save the document.

In addition to allowing you to format parts of a document with different margins, section breaks allow you to format part of a document in columns. You'll add some columns to section 4 next.

Formatting Text in Columns

Tip

When working with large amounts of text formatted in columns, it's helpful to hyphenate the document to avoid excessive white space caused by short lines.

Text meant for quick reading is often laid out in columns, with text flowing down one column, continuing at the top of the next column, flowing down that column, and so forth. To get started, click the Columns button in the Page Setup group on the Layout tab, and then click the number of columns you want in the Columns gallery. For more advanced column options, you can use the More Columns command to open the Columns dialog box. In this dialog box, you can adjust the column widths and the space between columns and choose to format either the entire document in columns or just the section that contains the insertion point.

As shown in the Session 4.1 Visual Overview, Vassily wants section 4 of the newsletter document, which consists of the audio books list, to be formatted in three columns.

To format section 4 in three columns:

1. Click anywhere in the list of audio books at the end of the document to position the insertion point in section 4.
2. On the ribbon, click the **Layout** tab.
3. In the Page Setup group, click the **Columns** button to display the Columns gallery. At this point, you could click Three to format section 4 in three columns of equal width. However, it's helpful to take a look at the columns dialog box so you can get familiar with some more advanced column options.
4. Click **More Columns** to open the Columns dialog box, and then in the Presets section, click **Three**. See Figure 4–3.

Figure 4–3 Columns dialog box

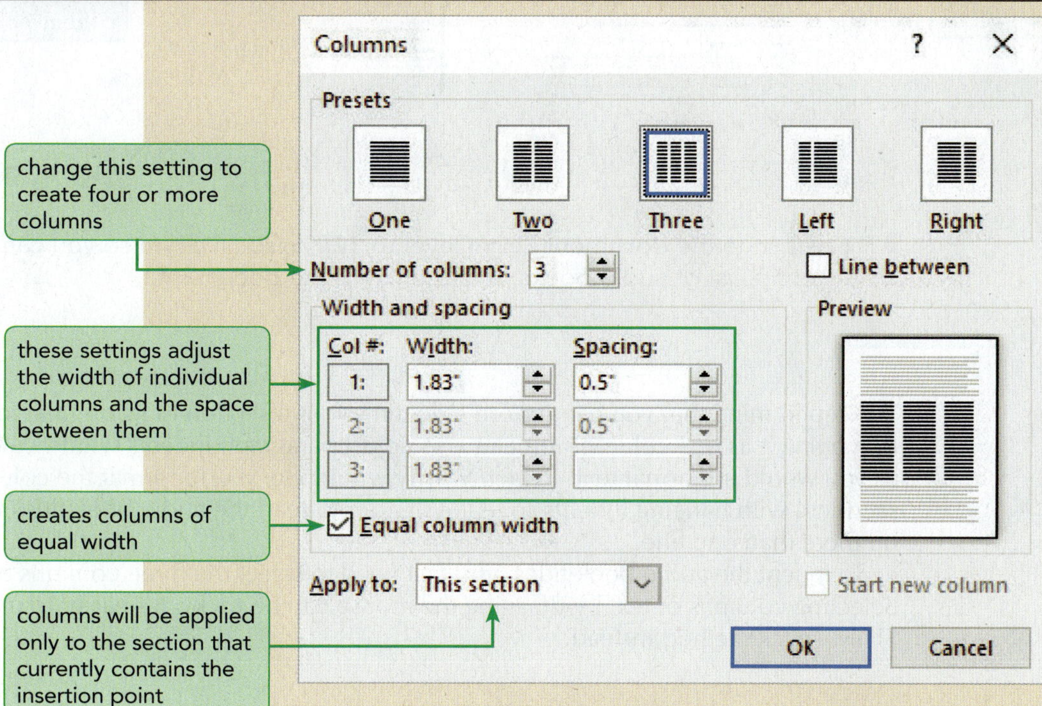

To format text in four or more columns, you can change the setting in the Number of columns box instead of selecting an option in the Presets section. By default, the Apply to box, in the lower-left corner, displays "This section," indicating that the three-column format will be applied only to the current section. To apply columns to the entire document, you could click the Apply to arrow and then click Whole document. To change the width of the individual columns or the spacing between the columns, you can use the settings in the Width and spacing section of the Columns dialog box.

5. Click **OK**. Section 4 is now formatted in three columns of the default width, although the third column is currently blank. This will change when you add more formatting elements to the newsletter. See Figure 4–4.

Figure 4–4 **Section 4 formatted in three columns**

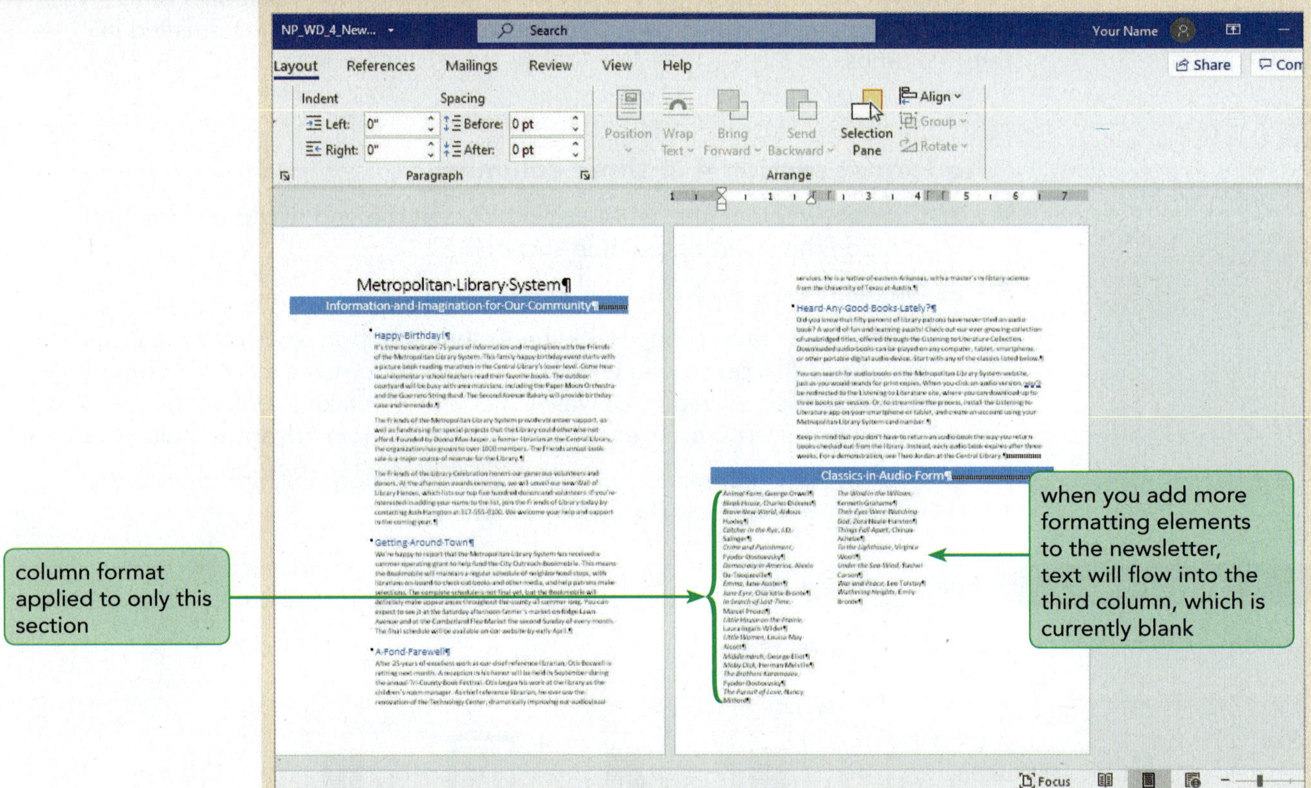

6. Change the document Zoom level to **120%**, scroll down so you can see the entire list of audio books, and then save the document.

Keep in mind that you can restore a document or a section to its original format by formatting it as one column. You can also adjust paragraph indents within columns, just as you would in normal text. In fact, Vassily would like you to format the columns in section 4 with hanging indents so that it's easier to read the audio book titles that take up more than one line.

To indent the audio book titles, you first need to select the three columns of text. Selecting columns of text by dragging the mouse can be tricky. It's easier to use the SHIFT+click method instead.

To format the columns in section 4 with hanging indents:

1. Make sure the **Layout** tab is selected on the ribbon.
2. Click at the beginning of the first audio book title and author name ("*Animal Farm*, George Orwell"), press and hold **SHIFT**, and then click at the end of the last audio book title and author name ("*Wuthering Heights*, Emily Bronte"). The entire list of audio books is selected.
3. In the Paragraph group, click the **Paragraph Dialog Box Launcher** to open the Paragraph dialog box with the Indents and Spacing tab displayed.
4. In the Indentation section, click the **Special** arrow, click **Hanging**, and then change the By setting to **0.2"**.
5. Click **OK** to close the Paragraph dialog box, and then click anywhere in the list to deselect it. The list of audio books and authors is now formatted with a hanging indent, so the second line of each paragraph is indented .2 inches. See Figure 4–5.

Figure 4–5 Text formatted in columns with hanging indent

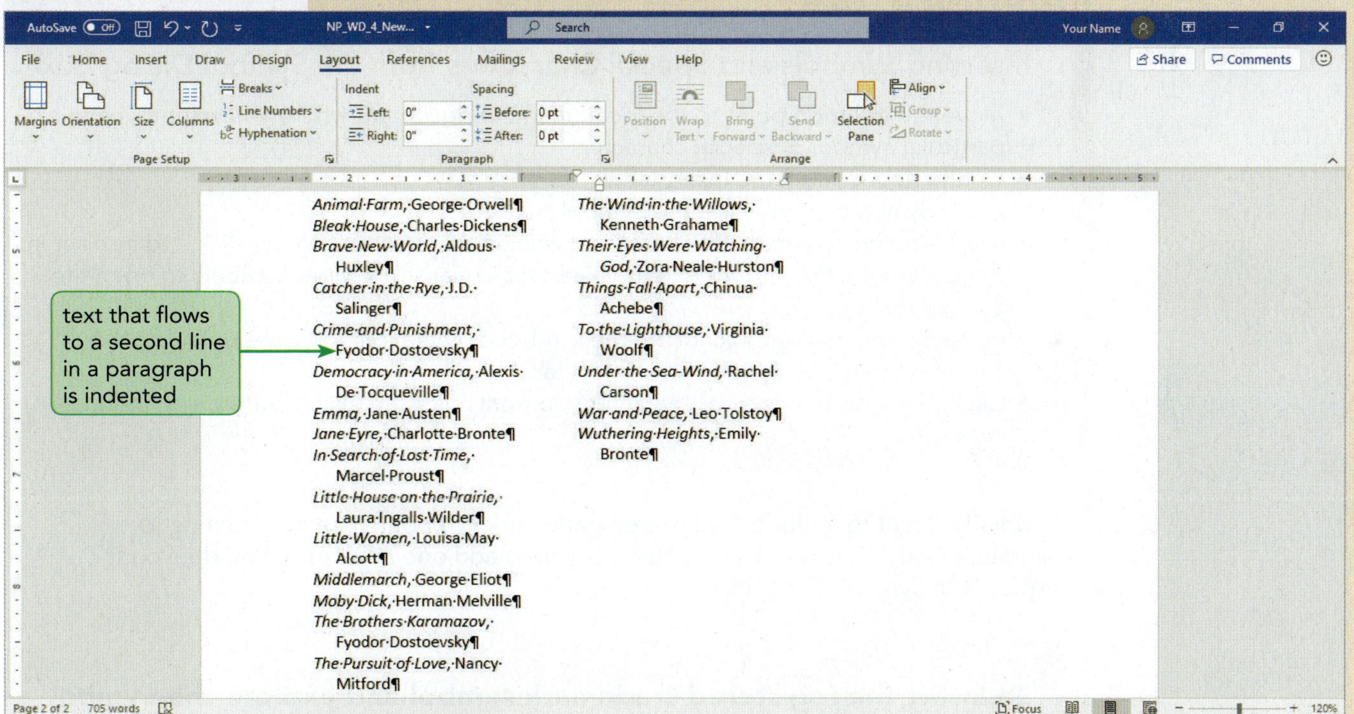

Inserting Symbols and Special Characters

When creating documents in Word, you can change some of the characters available on the standard keyboard into special characters or symbols called **typographic characters**. The AutoCorrect feature in Word automatically converts some standard characters into typographic characters as you type. In some cases, you need to press SPACEBAR and type more characters before Word inserts the appropriate typographic character. If Word inserts a typographic character that you don't want, you can click the Undo button to revert to the characters you originally typed. See Figure 4–6.

Figure 4–6 Common typographic characters

To Insert This Symbol or Character	Type	Word Converts To
Em dash	word--word	word—word
Smiley face	:)	😊
Copyright symbol	(c)	©
Trademark symbol	(tm)	™
Registered trademark symbol	(r)	®
Fractions	1/2, 1/4	½, ¼
Arrows	<-- or -->	← or →

Most of the typographic characters in Figure 4–6 can also be inserted using the Symbol button on the Insert tab, which opens a gallery of commonly used symbols, and the More Symbols command, which opens the Symbol dialog box. The Symbol dialog box provides access to all the symbols and special characters you can insert into a Word document.

Reference

Inserting Symbols and Special Characters from the Symbol Dialog Box

- Move the insertion point to the location in the document where you want to insert a particular symbol or special character.
- On the ribbon, click the Insert tab.
- In the Symbols group, click the Symbol button.
- If you see the symbol or character you want in the Symbol gallery, click it to insert it in the document. For a more extensive set of choices, click More Symbols to open the Symbol dialog box.
- In the Symbol dialog box, locate the symbol or character you want on either the Symbols tab or the Special Characters tab.
- Click the symbol or special character you want, click the Insert button, and then click Close.

Vassily forgot to include a registered trademark symbol (®) after "Listening to Literature Collection" on page 2. He asks you to add one now. After you do, you'll explore the Symbol dialog box.

To insert the registered trademark symbol and explore the Symbol dialog box:

1. Use the Navigation pane to find **the Listening to Literature Collection** in the document, and then close the Navigation pane.
2. Click at the end of the word "Collection" to position the insertion point between the "n" at the end of "Collection" and the period.
3. Type **(r)**. AutoCorrect converts the "r" in parentheses into the superscript ® symbol.

   If you don't know which characters to type to insert a symbol or special character, you can review the AutoCorrect replacements in the AutoCorrect: English (United States) dialog box.
4. On the ribbon, click the **File** tab.
5. In the navigation pane, click **Options** to open the Word Options dialog box.

6. In the left pane, click **Proofing**, and then click the **AutoCorrect Options** button. The AutoCorrect: English (United States) dialog box opens, with the AutoCorrect tab displayed.
7. Review the table at the bottom of the AutoCorrect tab. The column on the left shows the characters you can type, and the column on the right shows what AutoCorrect inserts as a replacement. See Figure 4–7.

Figure 4–7 AutoCorrect: English (United States) dialog box

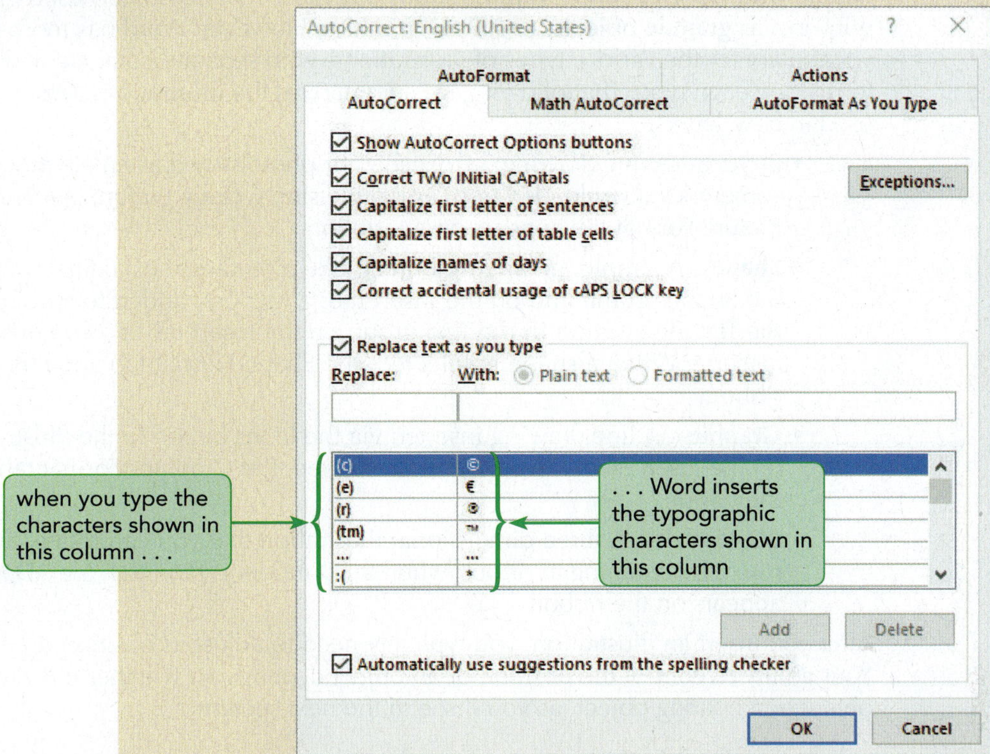

8. Scroll down to review the AutoCorrect replacements, click **Cancel** to close the AutoCorrect: English (United States) dialog box, and then click **Cancel** to close the Word Options dialog box.

   Now you can explore the Symbol dialog box, which offers another way to insert symbols and special characters.
9. On the ribbon, click the **Insert** tab.
10. In the Symbols group, click the **Symbol** button, and then click **More Symbols**. The Symbol dialog box opens with the Symbols tab displayed.
11. Scroll down the gallery of symbols on the Symbols tab to review the many symbols you can insert into a document. To insert one, you would click it, and then click the Insert button.
12. Click the **Special Characters** tab. The characters available on this tab are often used in desktop publishing. Notice the shortcut keys that you can use to insert many of the special characters.
13. Click **Cancel** to close the Symbol dialog box.

Introduction to Working with Objects

An object is something that you can manipulate independently of the document text. In desktop publishing, you use objects to illustrate the document or to enhance the page layout. To complete the newsletter for Vassily, you'll need to add some text boxes, drop caps, and pictures. These are all examples of objects in Word.

Inserting Graphic Objects

The Insert tab is the starting point for adding all types of illustrations to a document. People who work in online or print publishing often refer to objects used for illustration purposes as **graphic objects**, or simply **graphics**. However, Word has more specific vocabulary for the various types of illustrations, with separate contextual tabs for formatting each type. The following list summarizes the illustrations most commonly used in newsletters:

- **Picture**—A line drawing, screenshot, or photo stored as an electronic file, and sometimes downloaded from an online site; when a picture is selected, the Picture Format tab appears on the ribbon.
- **Shape**—A simple, geometric object, like a rectangle or a circle, created using the Shapes command on the Insert tab; a text box added to a document via the Text Box button in the Text group on the Insert tab is also considered a shape. When a shape is selected, the Shape Format tab appears on the ribbon.
- **Graphic**—A line drawing inserted via the Icons button in the Illustrations group on the Insert tab; when an icon is selected, the Graphics Format tab appears on the ribbon.
- **3D Models**—A three-dimensional illustration that you can rotate, and also resize by zooming in or out; when a 3D model is selected, the 3D Model tab appears on the ribbon.

After you insert an illustration, you typically need to adjust its position on the page. Your ability to control the position of an object depends on whether it is an inline object or a floating object, as you'll see in the next section.

Distinguishing Between Inline and Floating Objects

An **inline object** behaves as if it were text. Like an individual letter, it has a specific location within a line of text, and its position changes as you add or delete text. You can align an inline object just as you would align text, using the alignment buttons in the Paragraph group on the Home tab. In a simple document like a letter, inline objects are a good choice. However, in more complicated documents, inline objects are difficult to work with because every time you add or remove paragraphs of text, the object moves to a new position.

In contrast, you can position a **floating object** anywhere on the page, with the text flowing, or wrapping, around it. Unlike an inline object, which has a specific position in a line of text, a floating object has a more fluid connection to the document text. It is attached, or **anchored**, to an entire paragraph—so if you delete that paragraph, you will also delete the object. However, you can also move the object independently of that paragraph. An anchor symbol next to an object tells you that the object is a floating object rather than an inline object, as illustrated in Figure 4–8. As a general rule, you'll usually want to transform inline objects into floating objects, because floating objects are far more flexible.

Figure 4–8 **An inline object compared to a floating object**

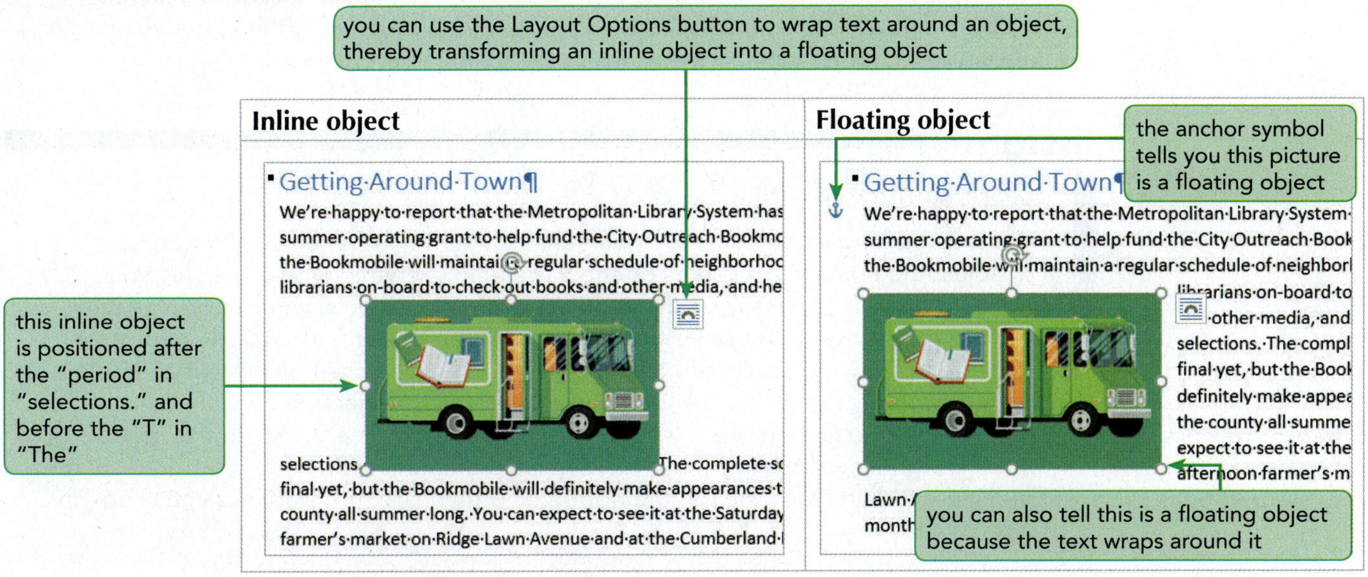

Mascha Tace/Shutterstock.com

Wrapping Text Around an Object

To transform an inline object into a floating object, you apply a **text wrapping setting** to it. First, click the object to select it, click the Layout Options button next to the object, and then click an option in the Layout Options gallery. For example, you can select Square text wrapping to make the text follow a square outline as it flows around the object, or you can select Tight text wrapping to make the text follow the shape of the object more exactly. Figure 4–9 describes the different types of wrapping. Note that you can also transform a floating object into an inline object by selecting the Inline with Text option in the Layout Options gallery.

Figure 4–9 **Text wrapping options in the Layout Options gallery**

Menu Icon	Type of Wrapping	Description
	Inline with Text	The object behaves as if it were text, and has a specific position within a paragraph. You can align inline objects using the alignment buttons on the Home tab, just as you would align text.
	Square	Text flows in a square outline around the object, regardless of the shape of the object; by default, Square text wrapping is applied to preformatted text boxes inserted via the Text Box button on the Insert tab.
	Tight	Text follows the exact outline of the object; if you want the text to flow around an object, this is usually the best option.
	Through	Text flows through the object, filling up any open areas; this type is similar to Tight text wrapping.
	Top and Bottom	Text stops above the object and then starts again below the object.
	Behind Text	The object is layered behind the text, with the text flowing over it.
	In Front of Text	The object is layered in front of the text, with the text flowing behind it; if you want to position an object in white space next to the text, this option gives you the greatest control over its exact position. By default, In Front of Text wrapping is applied to any shapes inserted via the Shapes button in the Illustrations group on the Insert tab.

Most graphic objects, including photos and SmartArt, are inline by default; however, all text boxes and shapes are floating by default. Objects that are inserted as floating objects by default have a specific text wrapping setting assigned to them, but you can change the default setting to any text wrapping setting you want.

Insight

Displaying Gridlines

When formatting a complicated document such as a newsletter, you'll often have to adjust the position of objects on the page until everything looks the way you want. To make it easier to see the relative position of objects, you can display the document's gridlines. These vertical and horizontal lines are not actually part of the document. They are simply guidelines you can use when positioning text and objects on the page. By default, when gridlines are displayed, objects align with, or snap to, the nearest intersection of a horizontal and vertical line. The figures in this module do not show gridlines because they would make the figures difficult to read. To display gridlines, click the View tab on the ribbon, and then click the Gridlines check box to insert a check.

Inserting Text Boxes

You can choose to add a preformatted text box to a document, or you can create your own text box from scratch and adjust its appearance. To insert a preformatted text box, you use the Text Box button in the Text group on the Insert tab. Text boxes inserted this way include placeholder text that you can replace with your own text. Preformatted text boxes come with preset font and paragraph options that are designed to match the text box's overall look. However, you can change the appearance of the text in the text box by using the options on the Home tab, just as you would for ordinary text. The text box, as a whole, is designed to match the document's current theme. You could alter its appearance by using the Shape Styles options on the Shape Format tab, but there's typically no reason to do so.

Because the preformatted text boxes are so professional looking, they are usually a better choice than creating your own. However, if you want a very simple text box, you can use the Shapes button in the Illustrations group to draw a text box. After you draw the text box, you can adjust its appearance by using the Shape Styles options on the Shape Format tab. You can type any text you want inside the text box at the insertion point. When you are finished, you can format the text using the options on the Home tab. Note that you can actually use any shape as a text box. To get started, draw a shape (for example, a star) in the document, and then, while the shape is selected, type any text you want. You can format text inside a shape just as you would format ordinary text.

Reference

Inserting a Text Box

To insert a preformatted, rectangular text box, click in the document where you want to insert the text box.

- On the ribbon, click the Insert tab.
- In the Text group, click the Text Box button to open the Text Box gallery, and then click a text box style to select it.
- In the text box in the document, delete the placeholder text, type the text you want to include, and then format the text using the options on the Home tab.

or

- To insert and format your own rectangular text box, click the Insert tab on the ribbon.
- In the Illustrations group, click the Shapes button to open the Shapes gallery, and then click Text Box.
- In the document, position the pointer where you want to insert the text box, press and hold the mouse button, and then drag the pointer to draw the text box.
- In the text box, type the text you want to include, and then format the text using the options on the Home tab.
- Format the text box using the options in the Shape Styles group on the Shape Format tab.

Inserting a Preformatted Text Box

Vassily's newsletter requires three text boxes. You need to insert the first text box on page 1, to the left of the "Happy Birthday!" heading. For this text box, you'll insert one that is preformatted to work as a sidebar. A **sidebar** is a text box designed to look good positioned to the side of the main document text. A sidebar is typically used to draw attention to important information.

To insert a preformatted text box in the document:

1. Scroll up to the top of page 1, and then click anywhere in the "Happy Birthday!" heading.
2. Change the Zoom level to **Multiple Pages** so you can see both pages of the document.
3. On the ribbon, click the **Insert** tab.
4. In the Text group, click the **Text Box** button to display the Text Box gallery, and then use the scroll bar to scroll down the gallery to locate the Ion Sidebar 1 text box.
5. Click **Ion Sidebar 1**. The text box is inserted in the left margin of page 1. See Figure 4–10.

Figure 4–10 **Text box inserted on page 1**

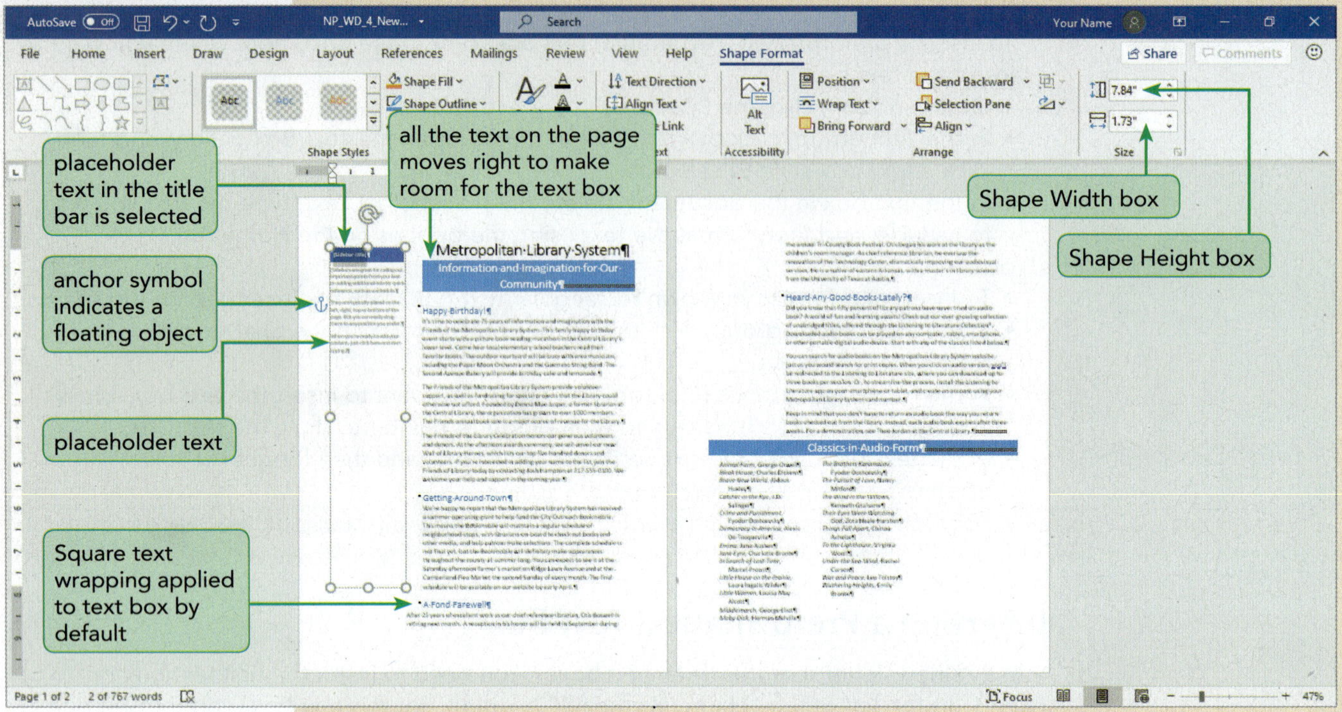

Most of the text on page 1 moves right to make room for the text box because Square text wrapping is applied to the text box by default. Later, after you resize and move the text box, the first two paragraphs will resume their original positions, centered at the top of the page. The anchor symbol next to the text box tells you it is a floating object.

The text box consists of a blue title bar at the top that contains placeholder text, with additional placeholder text below the title bar. The dotted outline with sizing handles indicates the borders of the text box. When you first insert a text box, the placeholder text in the title bar is selected, ready for you to type your own title. In this case, however, before you add any text, you'll resize and reposition the text box.

6. On the ribbon, click the **Shape Format** tab, if necessary.
7. In the Size group, click the **Shape Height** box, type **4.3**, click the **Shape Width** box, type **1.5**, and then press **ENTER**. The text box is now shorter and narrower.
8. Change the Zoom level to **120%**.

   Next, you need to drag the text box down below the first two paragraphs. To make this easier, you will make use of Word's alignment guides to help you position the text box. You will verify that those guides are turned on next.

9. In the Arrange group, click the **Align** button, and then click **Use Alignment Guides**, if necessary, to insert a check, or, if it is already checked, press **ESC** to close the menu. Now you are ready to move the text box, but first you need to select the entire text box. Currently, only the placeholder text in the text box title bar is selected.
10. Position the pointer somewhere over the text box border until the pointer changes to .

11. Click the **text box border** to select the entire text box. The text box border changes from dotted to solid, and the Layout Options button appears to the right of the text box.

12. With the pointer positioned over the border, press and hold the **mouse button**, and then drag the text box down so that the top of the text box aligns with the first line of text below the "Happy Birthday!" heading. The left edge of the text box should align with the left edge of the blue-shaded heading "Information and Imagination for Our Community." A green alignment guide appears when you have the text box aligned with the left edge of the blue-shaded heading. Alignment guides appear when you move an object close to a margin. The anchor symbol will likely remain in its original position, next to the blue-shaded paragraph, although on your computer it might move to a different location, or not be visible at all as you drag the text box. When you are sure the text box is positioned as shown in Figure 4–11, release the mouse button.

Figure 4–11 Resized and repositioned text box

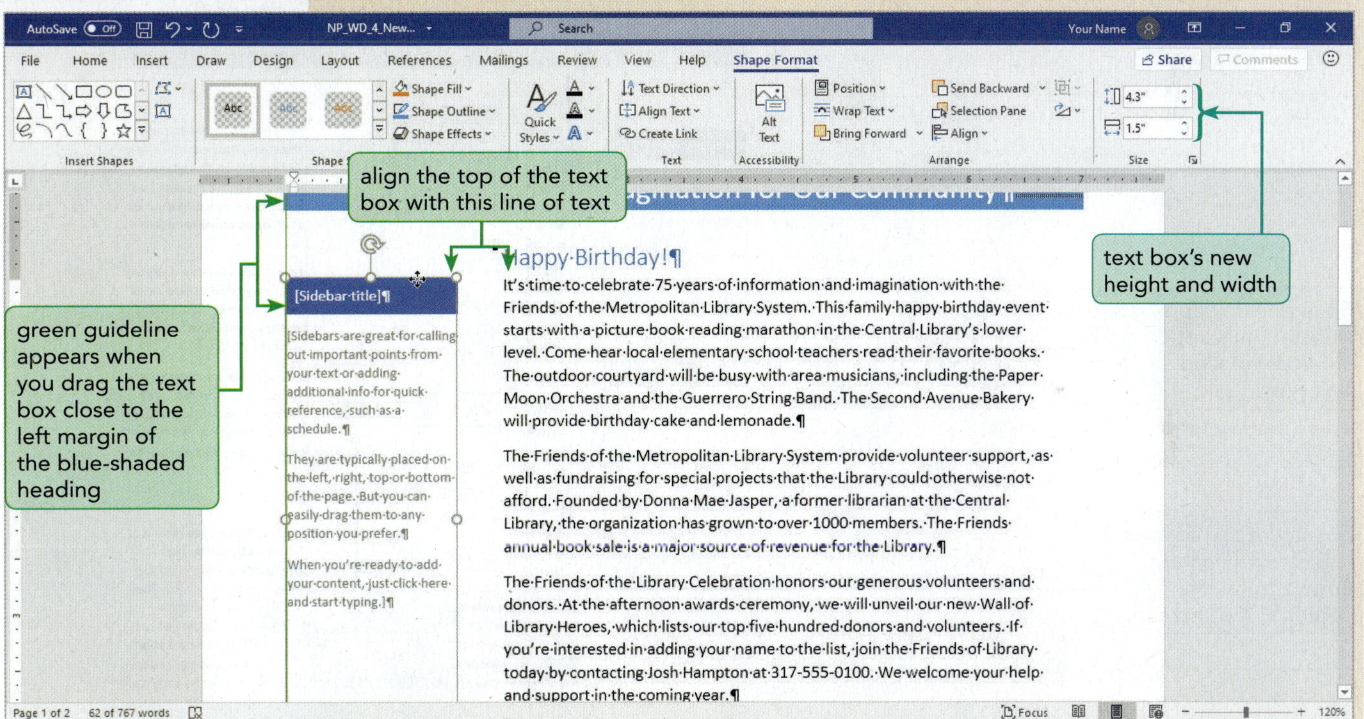

13. If necessary, drag the anchor icon to position it to the left of the blue-shaded paragraph.

After you insert a text box or other object, you usually need to adjust its relationship to the surrounding text; that is, you need to adjust its text wrapping setting.

Changing the Text Wrapping Setting for the Text Box

A preformatted text box inserted via the Text Box button on the Insert tab is, by default, a floating object formatted with Square text wrapping. You will verify this when you open the Layout Options gallery in the following steps. Then you'll select the In Front of Text option instead to gain more control over the exact position of the text box on the page.

To open the Layout Options gallery and change the wrapping option:

1. Change the Zoom level to **70%** so you can see the text box's position relative to the text on page 1.
2. Click the **Layout Options** button. The Layout Options gallery opens with the Square option selected. See Figure 4–12.

Figure 4–12 Square text wrapping currently applied to text box

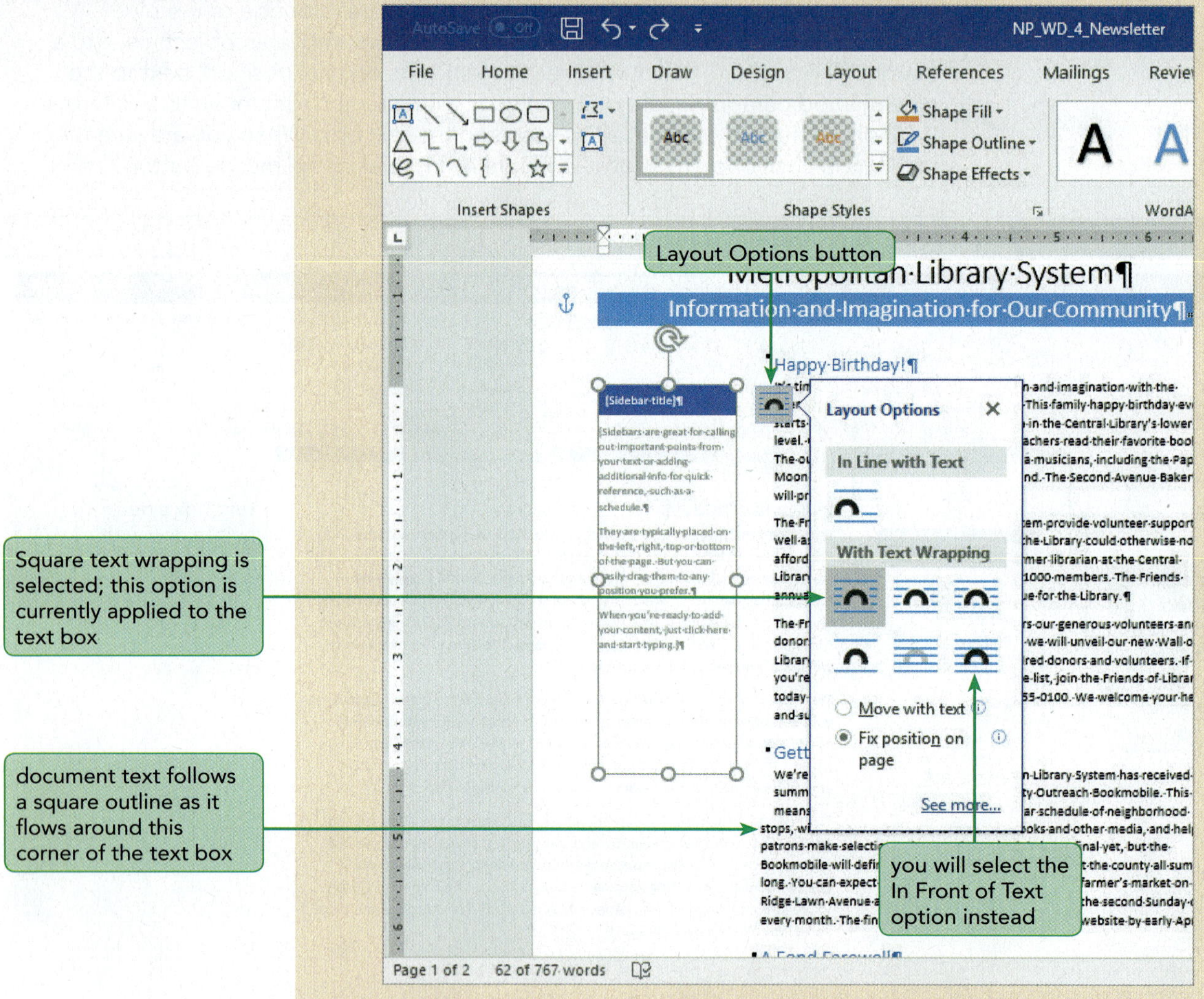

Square text wrapping is currently applied to the text box. You can see evidence of Square text wrapping where the document text flows around the lower-right corner of the text box. You'll have a chance to see some more dramatic examples of text wrapping later in this module, but it's important to be able to identify subtle examples of it.

3. Click any of the other options in the Layout Options gallery, and observe how the document text and the text box shift position. Continue exploring the Layout Options gallery, trying out several of the options.
4. Click the **In Front of Text** option, and then click the **Close** button in the upper-right corner of the Layout Options gallery to close the gallery. The document text shifts so that it now flows directly down the left margin, without wrapping around the text box.

Your next formatting task is to make sure the text box is assigned a fixed position on the page. You could check this setting using the Layout Options button, but you'll use the Wrap Text button in the Arrange group on the Shape Format tab instead.

5. On the ribbon, click the **Shape Format** tab, if necessary.
6. In the Arrange group, click the **Wrap Text** button. The Wrap Text menu gives you access to all the options in the Layout Options gallery, plus some more advanced settings.
7. Verify that **Fix Position on Page** has a checkmark next to it. This setting helps ensure that the text box will remain in its position on page 1, even if you add text above the paragraph it is anchored to. However, if you add so much text that the paragraph moves to page 2, then the text box will also move to page 2, but it will be positioned in the same location on the page that it occupied on page 1. To avoid having graphic objects move around unexpectedly on the page as you add or delete other elements, it's a good idea to check this setting either in the Wrap Text menu or in the Layout Options menu for every graphic object.
8. Click anywhere in the document to close the gallery, and then save the document.

Adding Text to a Text Box

Tip

If you want to work on a document's layout before you've finished writing the text, you can insert placeholder text by inserting a new paragraph, typing =lorem() and then pressing ENTER.

Now that the text box is positioned where you want it, with the correct text wrapping, you can add text to it. In some documents, text boxes are used to present new information, while others highlight a quote from the main document. A direct quote from a document formatted in a text box is known as a **pull quote**. To create a pull quote text box, you can copy the text from the main document, and then paste it into the text box, or instead you can type text in a text box. You can also insert text from another Word document by using the Object arrow on the Insert tab.

To insert text in the text box:

1. Change the Zoom level to **120%**, and then scroll as necessary so you can see the entire text box.
2. In the text box's title bar, click the placeholder text **[Sidebar title]** to select it, if necessary, and then type **Operating Hours** as the new title
3. Click the placeholder text below the title bar to select it. See Figure 4–13.

Figure 4–13 Text box with placeholder text selected

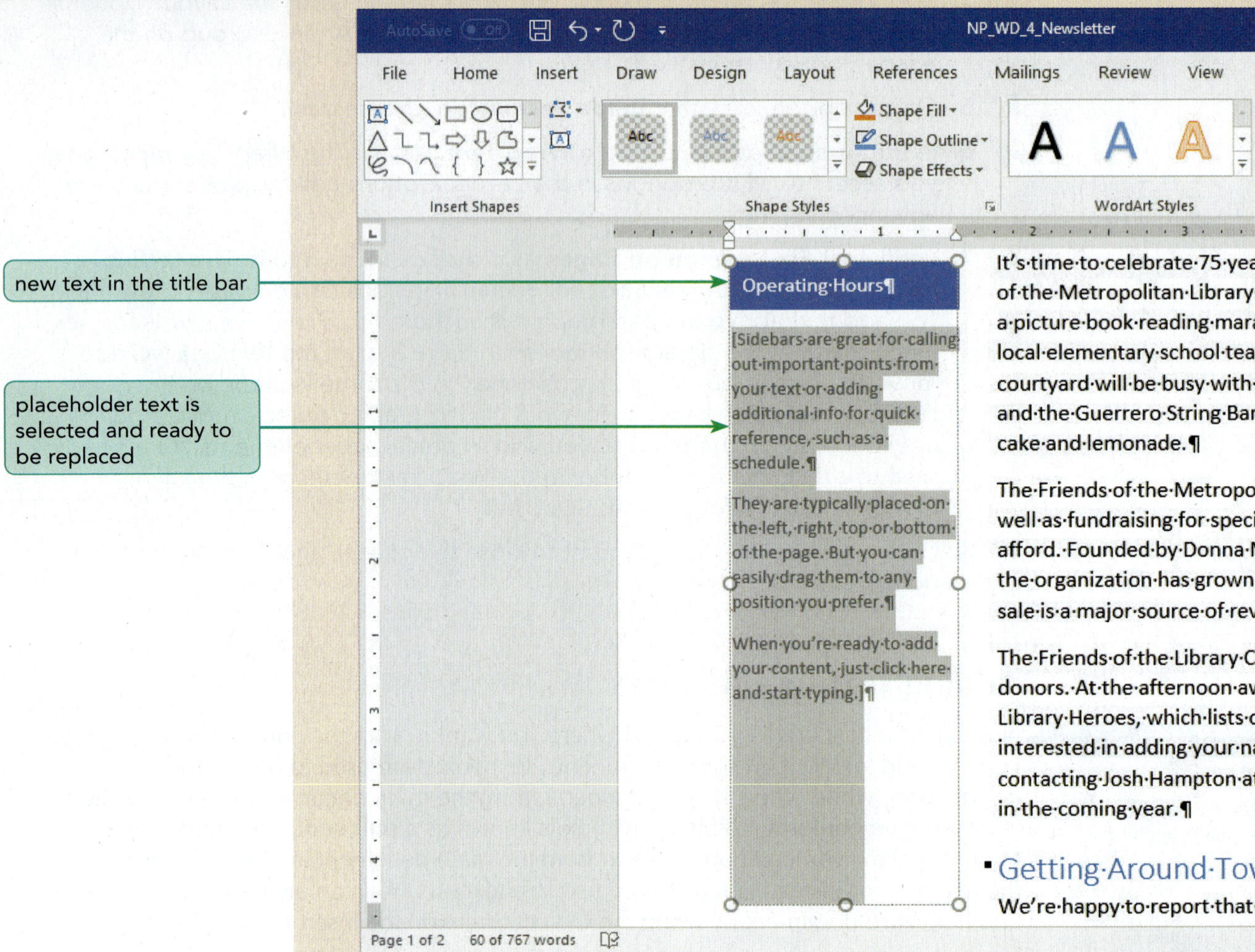

4. Press **DEL** to delete the placeholder text. Now you can insert new text from another Word document.
5. On the ribbon, click the **Insert** tab.
6. In the Text group, click the **Object arrow** to open the Object menu, and then click **Text from File**. The Insert File dialog box opens. Selecting a Word document to insert is just like selecting a document in the Open dialog box.
7. Navigate to the **Word4 > Module** folder, click **Support_WD_4_Hours .docx** to select the file, and then click the **Insert** button. The operating hours information is inserted directly into the text box. The inserted text was formatted in 9-point Calibri in the Support_WD_4_Hours.docx document, and it retains that formatting when you paste it into the newsletter document. To make the text easier to read, you'll increase the font size to 11 points.
8. With the insertion point located in the last paragraph in the text box (which is blank), press **BACKSPACE** to delete the blank paragraph, and then click and drag the pointer to select all the text in the text box, including the title in the shaded title box.
9. On the ribbon, click the **Home** tab.
10. In the Font group, click the **Font Size** arrow, and then click **11**. The size of the text in the text box increases to 11 points. See Figure 4–14.

Figure 4–14 **Operating hours information inserted in text box**

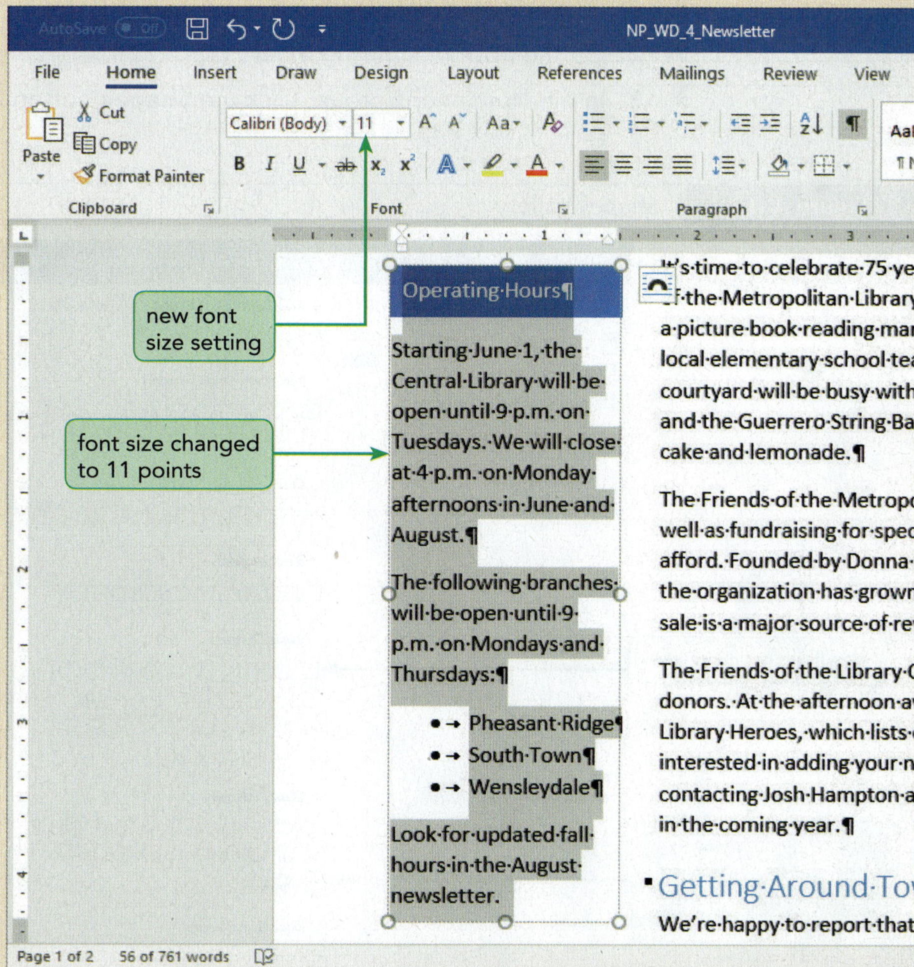

Trouble? Don't be concerned if the text in your text box wraps slightly differently from the text shown in Figure 4–14. The same fonts can vary slightly from one computer to another, causing slight differences in the way text wraps within and around text boxes.

11. Click anywhere outside the text box to deselect it, and then save the document.

The first text box is complete. Now you need to add one more on page 1 and another on page 2. Vassily wants the second text box on page 1 to have a different look from the first one, so he asks you to use the Shapes button to draw a text box.

Drawing and Formatting a Text Box Using the Shapes Menu

A text box is considered a shape, just like the other shapes you can insert via the Shapes button on the Insert tab. This is true whether you insert a text box via the Text Box button or via the Shapes button. While text boxes are typically rectangular, you can turn any shape into a text box. Start by using the Shapes button to draw a shape of your choice, and then, with the shape selected, type any text you want. You won't see an insertion point inside the shape, but you can still type text inside it and then format it. You can format the shape itself by using the Shape Styles options on the Shape Format tab.

To draw and format a text box:

1. Scroll down to display the bottom half of page 1.
2. On the ribbon, click the **Insert** tab.
3. In the Illustrations group, click the **Shapes** button to display the Shapes gallery. See Figure 4–15.

Figure 4–15 Shapes gallery

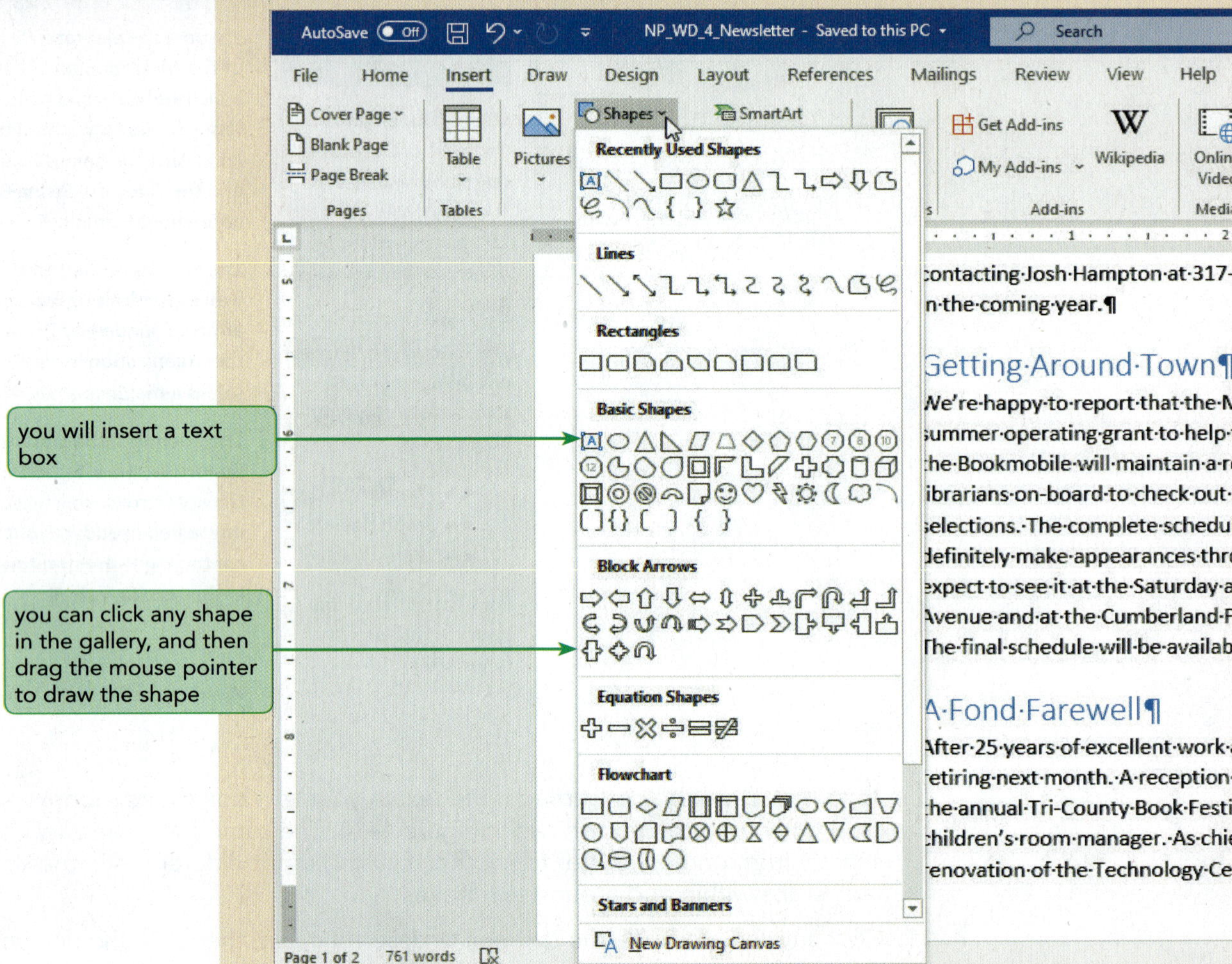

At this point, you could click any shape in the gallery, and then drag the pointer in the document to draw that shape. Then, after you finish drawing the shape, you could start typing in the selected shape to insert text.

4. In the Basic Shapes section of the Shapes gallery, click the **Text Box** icon. The gallery closes, and the pointer turns into a black cross +.
5. Position the pointer in the blank area in the left margin at about the 6-inch mark (according to the vertical ruler), and then click and drag down and to the right to draw a text box approximately 1.5 inches wide and 2.5 inches tall. When you are satisfied with the text box, release the mouse button.

   Don't be concerned about the text box's exact dimensions or position on the page. For now, just make sure it fits in the blank space to the left of the last two paragraphs on the page.

The new text box is selected, with sizing handles on its border and the insertion point blinking inside. The Layout Options button is visible, and the text box's anchor symbol is positioned to the left of the paragraph below the "Getting Around Town" heading. By default, a shape is always anchored to the nearest paragraph that begins above the shape's top border. It doesn't matter where the insertion point is located.

6. Use the Shape Height and Shape Width boxes on the Shape Format tab to set the height to **2.5** inches and the width to **1.5** inches.
7. Drag the text box as necessary to align its bottom border with the last line of text on the page and its left border with the left edge of the text box above. See Figure 4–16.

Figure 4–16 **Text box created using the Shapes button**

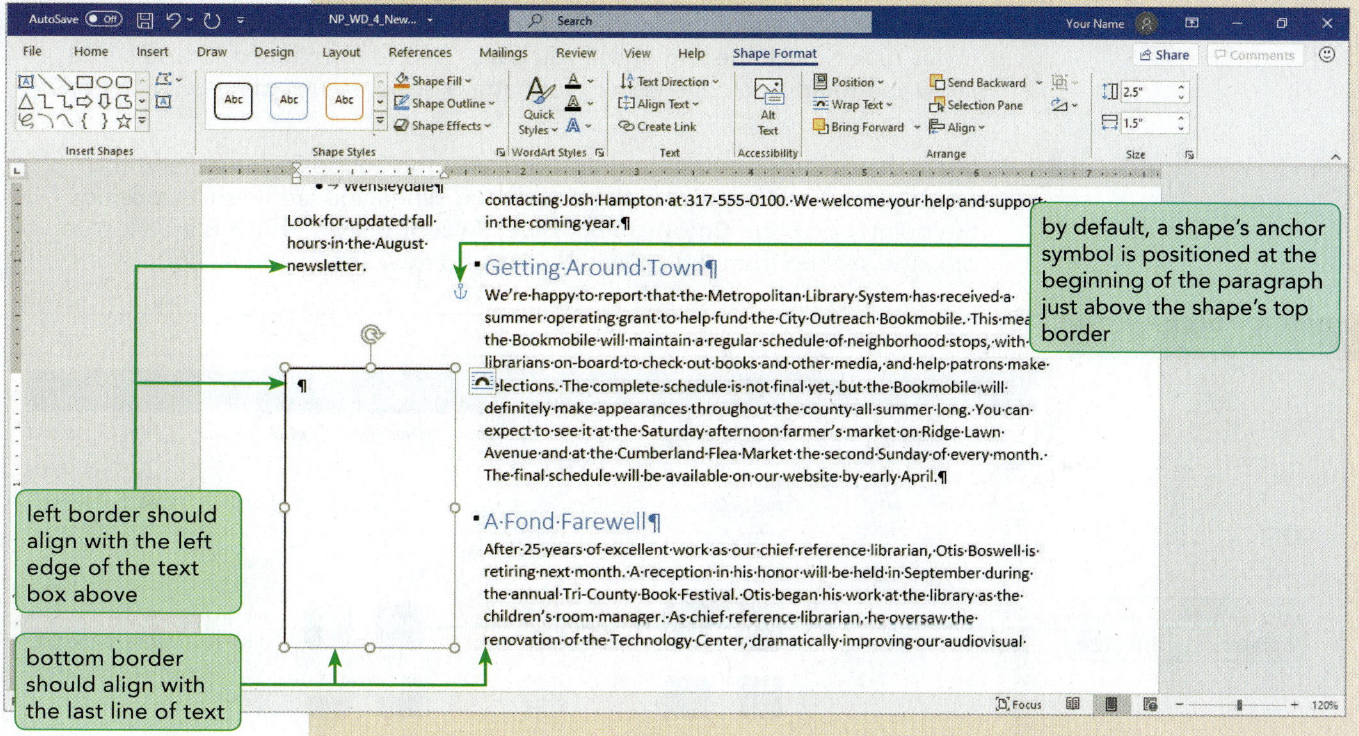

Now you need to add some text to the blank text box. Instead of inserting text from another Word document, you will copy a sentence from the newsletter and paste it into the text box to create a pull quote. After you add the text, you'll format the text box to make it match the one shown earlier in the Session 4.1 Visual Overview.

To copy text from the newsletter and paste it into the text box:

1. Select the third sentence after the "Getting Around Town" heading (which begins "The complete schedule is not final yet . . ."), and then press **CTRL+C** to copy it to the Office Clipboard.
2. Click in the blank text box, and then press **CTRL+V** to paste the copied sentence into the text box. The newly inserted sentence is formatted in 11-point Calibri, just as it was in the main document.

3. Add quotation marks at the beginning and end of the sentence, so it's clear the text box is a pull quote. Your next task is to center the sentence between the top and bottom borders of the text box. Then you'll add some color.
4. On the ribbon, click the **Shape Format** tab, if necessary.
5. In the Text group, click the **Align Text** button to display the Align text menu, and then click **Middle**. The text is now centered between the top and bottom borders of the text box. Note that you can use also the Text Direction button in the Text group to rotate text within a text box. Next, you need to change the text's font color and add a background color. But first you'll make sure the text box is positioned so that you can see a Live Preview when you open the Shape Styles gallery.
6. Scroll down, if necessary, so that the bottom of the text box is positioned just above the bottom of the Word screen.
7. In the Shape Styles group, click the **More** button to display the Shape Styles gallery. Like the text styles you have used to format text, shape styles allow you to apply a collection of formatting options, including font color and shading, with one click.
8. Move the pointer over the various options in the Shape Styles gallery, and observe the Live Previews in the document. When you are finished, position the pointer over the **Colored Fill - Blue, Accent 5** style, which is a dark blue box, the second from the right in the second row. See Figure 4–17.

Figure 4–17 Shape Styles gallery

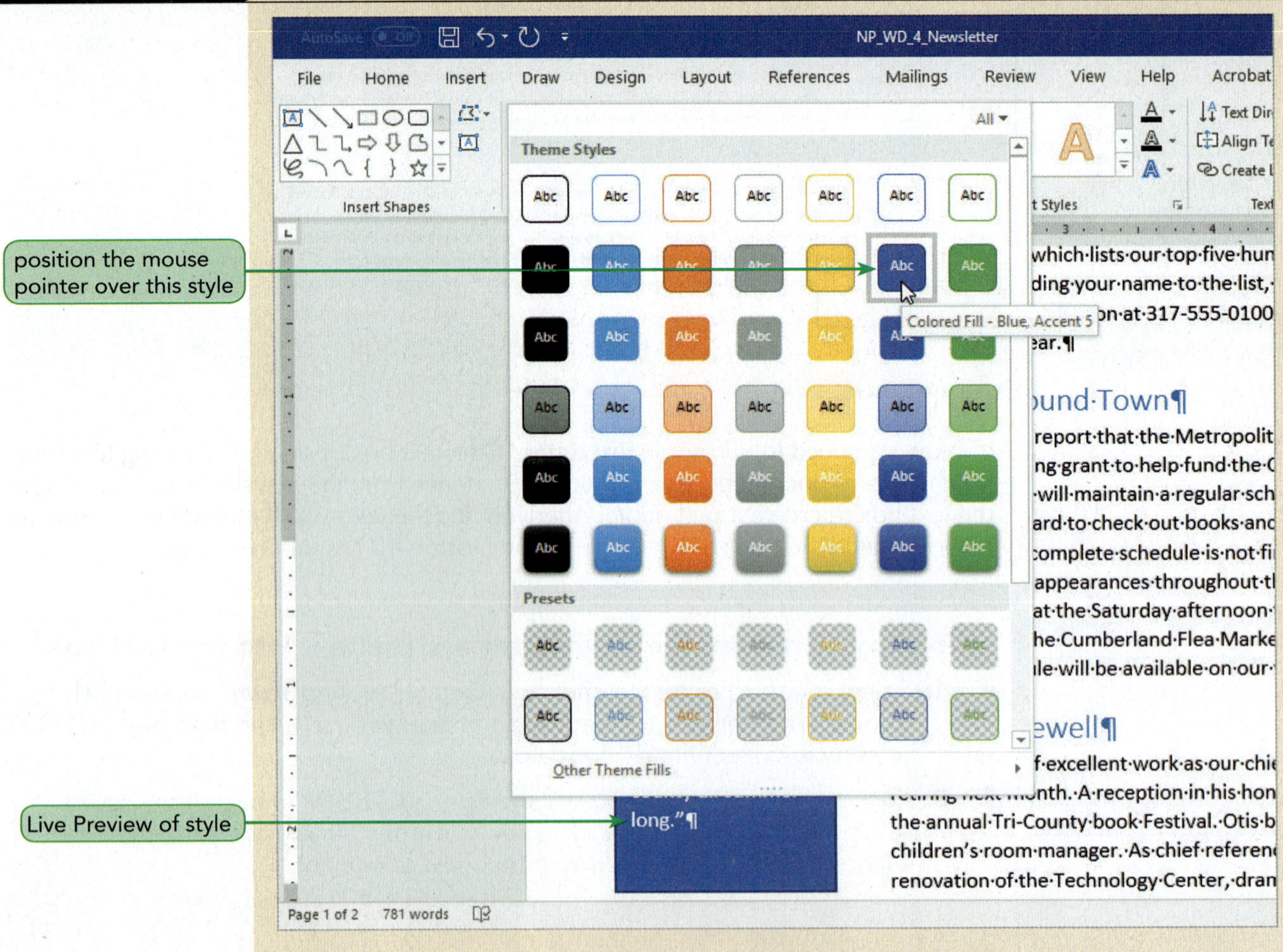

9. In the Shape Styles gallery, click the **Colored Fill - Blue, Accent 5** style. The style is applied to the text box, and the Shape Styles gallery closes.

Now, you need to make sure the text box is located in a fixed position on the page. In the following steps, you'll also experiment with the text box's anchor symbol. It's important to understand the role the anchor symbol plays in the document's overall layout.

To fix the text box's position on the page and experiment with the anchor symbol:

1. Verify that the text box is still selected, with the Shape Format tab displayed on the ribbon.
2. In the Arrange group, click the **Wrap Text** button. A checkmark appears next to Move with Text because that is the default setting for shapes.
3. Click **Fix Position on Page** to add a checkmark and close the Wrap Text menu.

   If you select the entire paragraph to which the text box is anchored, you will also select the text box, as you'll see in the next step.
4. Triple-click the paragraph below the "Getting Around Town" heading. The entire paragraph and the text box are selected. If you pressed DEL at this point, you would delete the paragraph of text and the text box. If you ever need to delete a paragraph but not the graphic object that is anchored to it, you should first drag the anchor to a different paragraph.
5. Click anywhere in the document to deselect the text and the text box, and then save the document.

You've finished creating the second text box on page 1. Vassily wants you to add a third text box at the top of page 2. For this text box, you'll again use the preformatted Ion Side Bar 1 text box.

To insert another preformatted text box:

1. Scroll down to display the top half of page 2, and then click in the first line on page 2.
2. On the ribbon, click the **Insert** tab.
3. In the Text group, click the **Text Box** button to display the menu, scroll down, and then click **Ion Sidebar 1**.
4. Click the **text box border** to select the entire text box and display the Layout Options button.
5. Click the **Layout Options** button, click the **In Front of Text** option, if necessary, verify that the **Fix position on page** button is selected, and then close the Layout Options gallery.
6. Drag the text box left so its left side aligns with the left edge of the blue-shaded paragraph below, with the top of the text box aligned with the first line of text on page 2. A green alignment guide might appear if you try to position the right border of the text box too close to the document text.
7. Change the text box's height to **3.5** inches and the width to **1.5** inches.

8. In the title bar, replace the placeholder text with **Book Festival Reminder**.
9. In the main text box, click the **placeholder text** to select it, and then press **DEL**.
10. On the ribbon, click the **Insert** tab.
11. In the Text group, click the **Object arrow**, and then click **Text from File**.
12. Navigate to the **Word4 > Module** folder, if necessary, and then insert the document named **Support_WD_4_Festival.docx**.
13. Delete the extra paragraph at the end of the text box, increase the font size for the text and title to **11** points, click anywhere inside the text box to deselect the text, and then make sure your text box is positioned like the one shown in Figure 4–18.

Figure 4–18 **Completed text box on page 2**

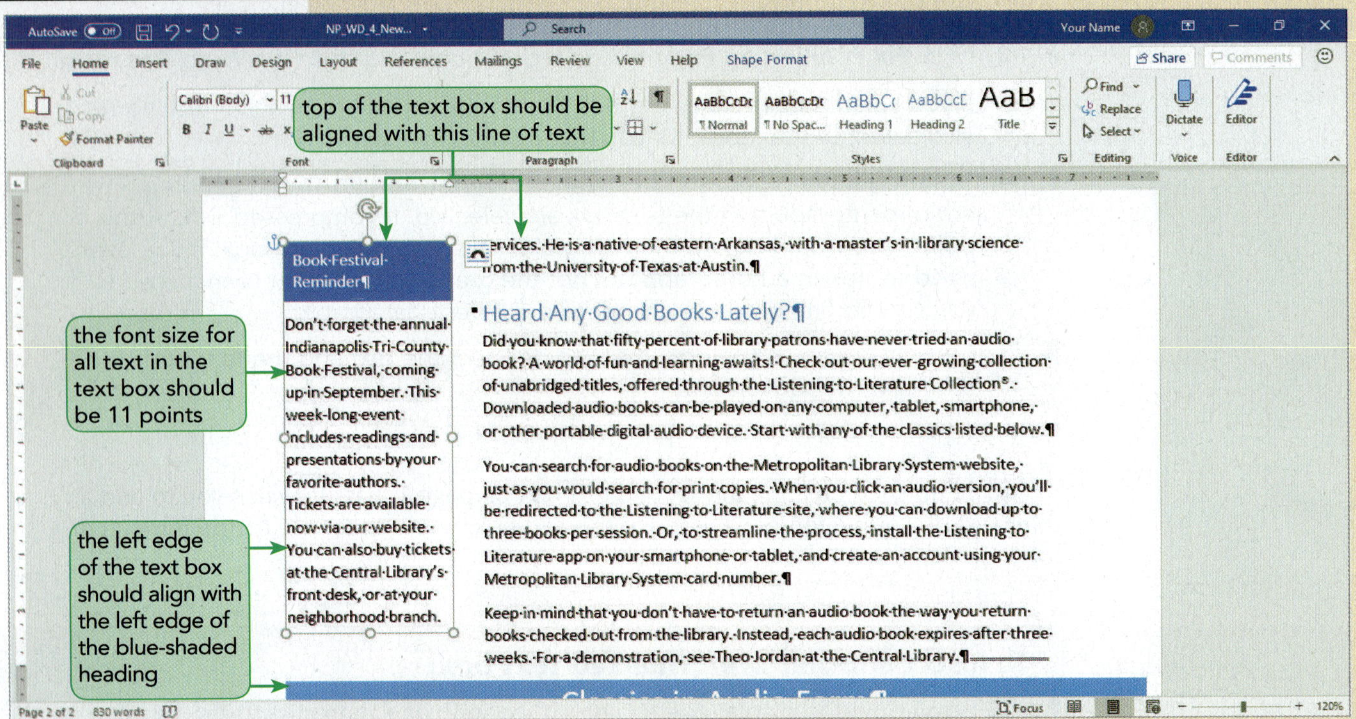

14. Click anywhere in the document to deselect the text box, and then save the document.

Insight

Linking Text Boxes

If you have a large amount of text that you want to place in different locations in a document, with the text continuing from one text box to another, you can use linked text boxes. For example, in a newsletter, you might have an article that starts in a text box on page 3 of the newsletter and continues in a text box on page 4. To flow the text automatically from one text box to a second, blank text box, click the first text box to select it (this text box should already contain some text). Next, on the ribbon, click the Shape Format tab, click the Create Link button in the Text group, and then click the empty text box. The text boxes are now linked. You can resize the first text box without worrying about how much text fits in the box. The text that no longer fits in the first text box is moved to the second text box. Note that you'll find it easier to link text boxes if you use simple text boxes without title bars.

To make the main document text look more polished, you will add some drop caps.

Inserting Drop Caps

As you saw in the Session 4.1 Visual Overview, a drop cap is a large decorative letter that replaces the first letter of a paragraph. Drop caps are commonly used in newspapers, magazines, and newsletters to draw the reader's attention to the beginning of an article. You can place a drop cap in the margin or next to the paragraph, or you can have the text of the paragraph wrap around the drop cap. By default, a drop cap extends down three lines, but you can change that setting in the Drop Cap dialog box.

Vassily asks you to create a drop cap for some of the paragraphs that follow the headings. He wants the drop cap to extend two lines into the paragraph, with the text wrapping around it.

To insert drop caps in the newsletter:

1. Scroll up to page 1, and then click anywhere in the paragraph below the "Happy Birthday!" heading.
2. On the ribbon, click the **Insert** tab.
3. In the Text group, click the **Add a Drop Cap** button. The Drop Cap gallery opens.
4. Move the pointer over the **Dropped** option and then the **In margin** option, and observe the Live Preview of the two types of drop caps in the document. The default settings applied by these two options are fine for most documents. Clicking Drop Cap Options, at the bottom of the menu, allows you to select more detailed settings. In this case, Vassily wants to make the drop cap smaller than the default. Instead of extending down through three lines of text, he wants the drop cap to extend only two lines.
5. Click **Drop Cap Options**. The Drop Cap dialog box opens.
6. Click the **Dropped** icon, click the **Lines to drop** box, and then change the setting to **2**. See Figure 4–19.

Figure 4–19 Drop Cap dialog box

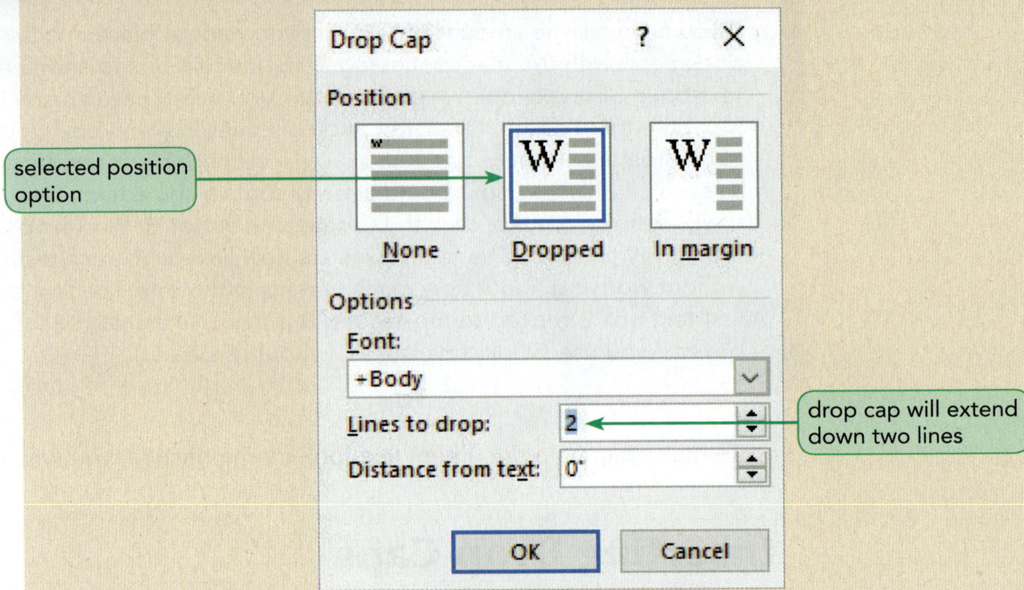

> **Tip**
>
> To delete a drop cap, click the paragraph that contains it, open the Drop Cap dialog box, and then click None.

7. Click **OK**. Word formats the first character of the paragraph as a drop cap "I," as shown in the Session 4.1 Visual Overview. The dotted box with selection handles around the drop cap indicates it is selected.
8. Near the bottom of page 1, insert a similar drop cap in the paragraph following the "A Fond Farewell" heading. You skipped the paragraph following the "Getting Around Town" heading because you'll eventually insert a graphic there. Including a drop cap there would make the paragraph look too cluttered.
9. On page 2, insert a similar drop cap in the paragraph following the "Heard Any Good Books Lately?" heading.
10. Click anywhere in the text to deselect the drop cap, and then save your work.

Proskills

Written Communication: Writing for a Newsletter

Pictures, WordArt, and other design elements can make a newsletter very appealing to readers. They can also be a lot of fun to create and edit. But don't let the design elements in your desktop-published documents distract you from the most important aspect of any document—clear, effective writing. Because the newsletter format feels less formal than a report or letter, some writers are tempted to use a casual, familiar tone. If you are creating a newsletter for friends or family, that's fine. But in most other settings—especially in a business or academic setting—you should strive for a professional tone, similar to what you find in a typical newspaper. Avoid jokes; you can never be certain that what amuses you will also amuse all your readers. Worse, you risk unintentionally offending your readers. Also, space is typically at a premium in any printed document, so you don't want to waste space on anything unessential. Finally, keep in mind that the best writing in the world will be wasted in a newsletter that is overburdened with too many design elements. You don't have to use every element covered in this module in a single document. Instead, use just enough to attract the reader's attention to the page, and then let the text speak for itself.

Review

Session 4.1 Quick Check

1. Explain how to format a document in three columns of the default width.
2. What should you do if you don't know which characters to type to insert a symbol or special character?
3. What does the anchor symbol indicate?
4. How do you convert an inline object into a floating object?
5. What is a pull quote?
6. How many lines does a drop cap extend by default?

Session 4.2 Visual Overview:

You can use the Remove Background button to remove a picture's background.

You can click the Crop button arrow to access more advanced cropping options, including cropping to a shape such as an oval or an arrow.

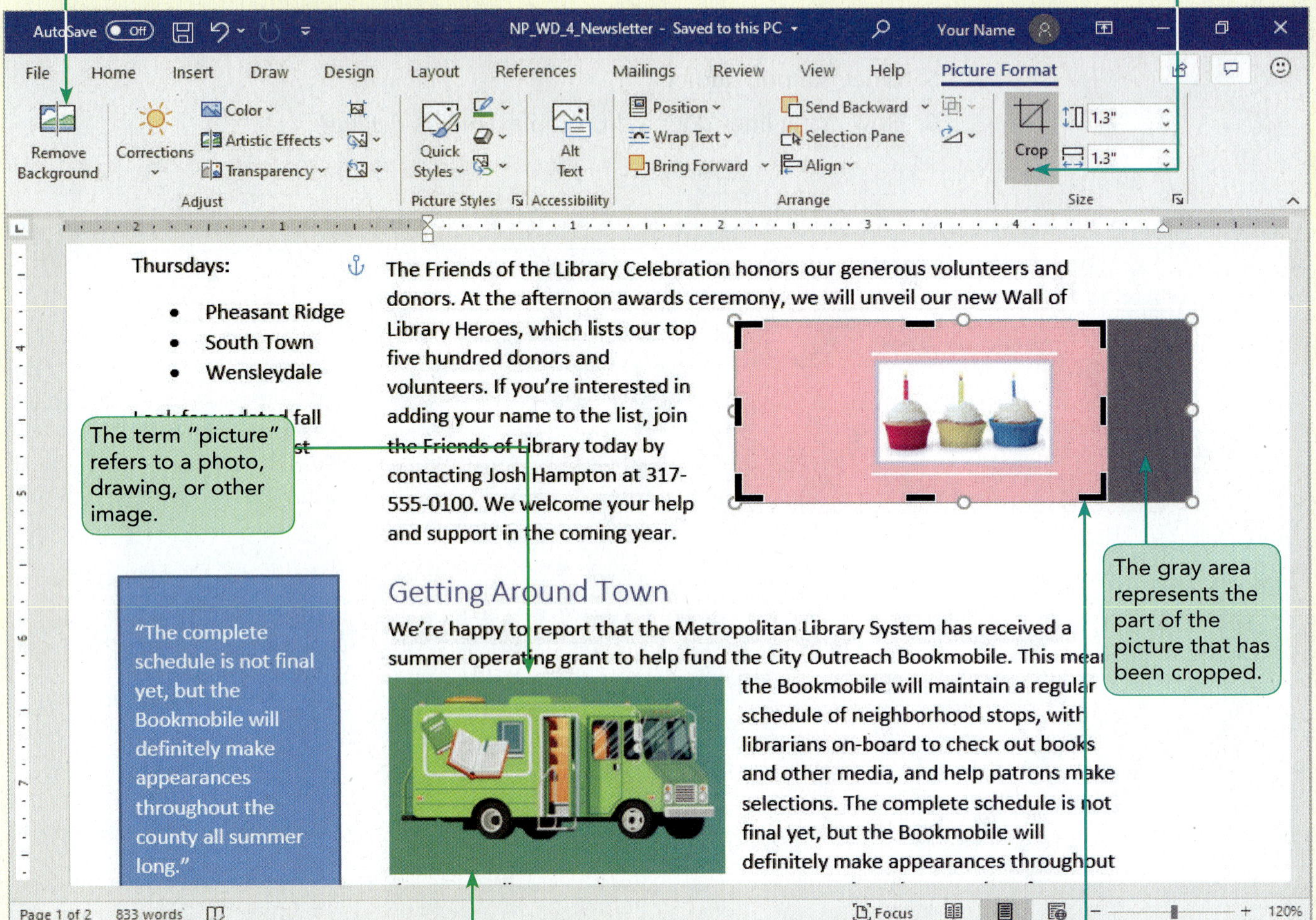

The term "picture" refers to a photo, drawing, or other image.

The gray area represents the part of the picture that has been cropped.

Mascha Tace/Shutterstock.com; Ruth Black/Shutterstock.com

This picture of the bookmobile was inserted into the document, with the text wrapping around its rectangular, green background.

You can **crop**, or cut off, part of a picture by clicking the Crop button in the Size group on the Picture Format tab, and then dragging a black handle on the picture border.

Editing Pictures

Clicking the Remove Background button in the Adjust group on the Picture Format tab displays the Background Removal tab, with tools for removing a picture's background.

You can use these buttons to mark areas in the picture that you want to keep and to mark areas that you want to remove along with the rest of the picture's background.

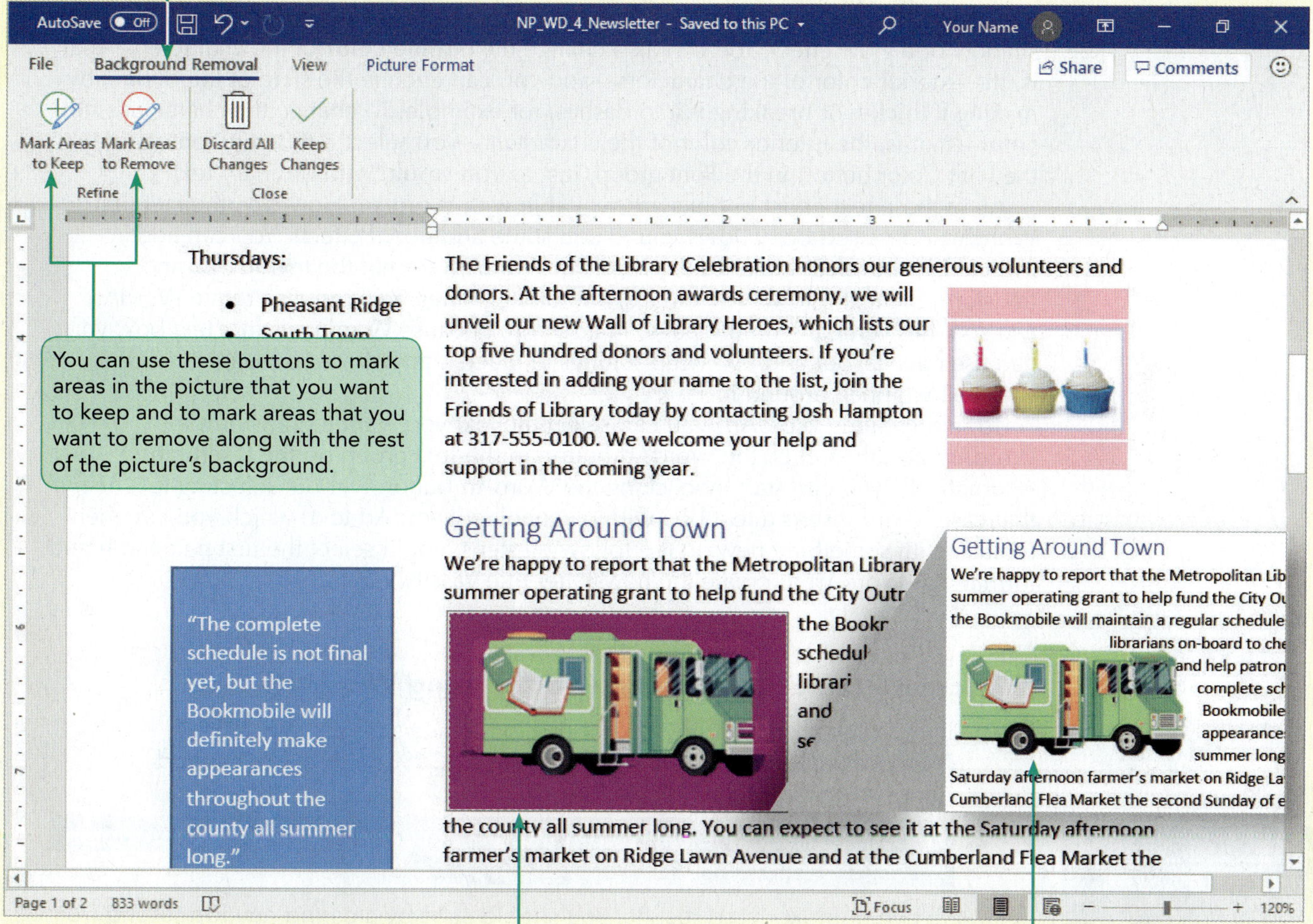

Mascha Tace/Shutterstock.com; Ruth Black/Shutterstock.com

The purple area is the part of the picture that Word considers part of the background.

The picture of the bookmobile is displayed here with its background removed, which allows the text to wrap around the shape of the bookmobile itself.

Formatting Text with WordArt

To create special text elements such as a newspaper headline, you can use decorative text known as WordArt. Essentially, WordArt is text in a text box that is formatted with a text effect. Before you move on to learning about WordArt, it's helpful to review the formatting options available with text effects.

To begin applying a text effect, you select the text you want to format. Then you can choose from several preformatted text effects via the Text Effects and Typography button in the Font group on the Home tab. You can also modify a text effect by choosing from the options on the Text Effects and Typography menu. For example, you can add a shadow or a glow effect. You can also change the **outline color** of the characters—that is, the exterior color of the characters—and you can change the style of the outline by making it thicker or breaking it into dashes, for example. To change the character's **fill color**—that is, the interior color of the characters—you select a different font color via the Font Color button in the Font group, just as you would with ordinary text.

All of these text effect options are available with WordArt. However, the fact that WordArt is in a text box allows you to add some additional effects. You can add rounded, or **beveled**, edges to the letters in WordArt, format the text in 3D, and transform the text into waves, circles, and other shapes. You can also rotate WordArt text so it lies vertically on the page. In addition, because WordArt is in a text box, you can use page layout and text wrap settings to place it anywhere you want on a page, with text wrapped around it.

To start creating WordArt, you can select the text you want to transform into WordArt, and then click the WordArt button in the Text group on the Insert tab. Alternatively, you can start by clicking the WordArt button without selecting text first. In that case, Word inserts a text box with placeholder WordArt text, which you can then replace with something new. In the following steps, you'll select the first paragraph and format it as WordArt to create the newsletter title Vassily wants.

To create the title of the newsletter using WordArt:

1. If you took a break after the last session, make sure the **NP_WD_4_ Newsletter.docx** is open and zoomed to **120%**, with the rulers and nonprinting characters displayed.
2. On page 1, select the entire paragraph containing the "Metropolitan Library System" heading, including the paragraph mark.

   To avoid unexpected results, you should start by clearing any formatting from the text you want to format as WordArt, so you'll do that next.

> Be sure to select the paragraph mark so the page layout in your newsletter matches the figures.

3. On the ribbon, click the **Home** tab, if necessary.
4. In the Font group, click the **Clear All Formatting** button. The paragraph reverts to the Normal style. Now you can convert the text into WordArt.
5. On the ribbon, click the **Insert** tab.
6. In the Text group, click the **Insert WordArt** button. The WordArt gallery opens.
7. Position the pointer over the WordArt style that is second from the left in the top row. A ScreenTip describes some elements of this WordArt style—"Fill: Blue, Accent color 1; Shadow." See Figure 4–20.

Figure 4–20 **WordArt gallery**

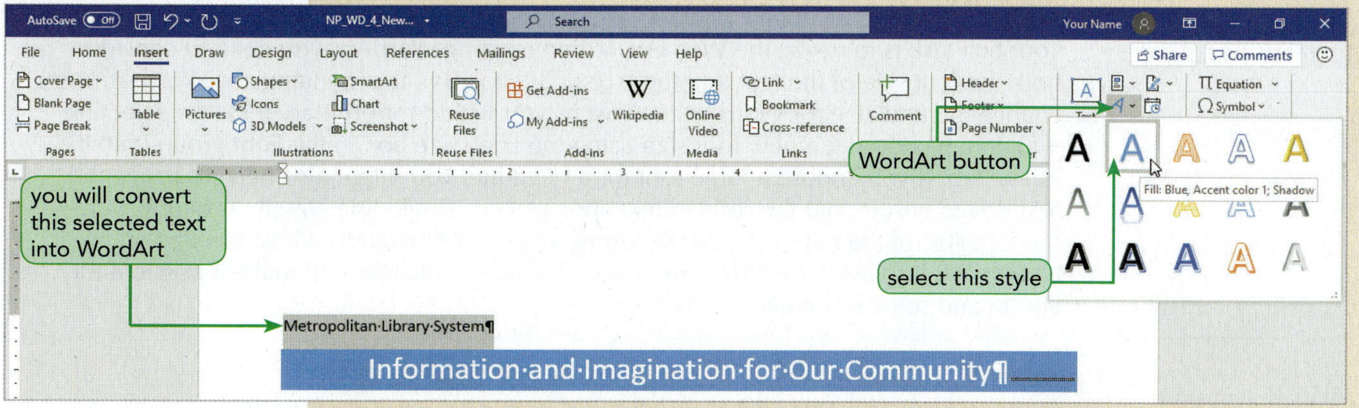

8. Click the WordArt style **Fill: Blue, Accent color 1; Shadow**. The gallery closes, and a text box containing the formatted text is displayed in the document. See Figure 4–21.

Figure 4–21 **WordArt text box inserted in document**

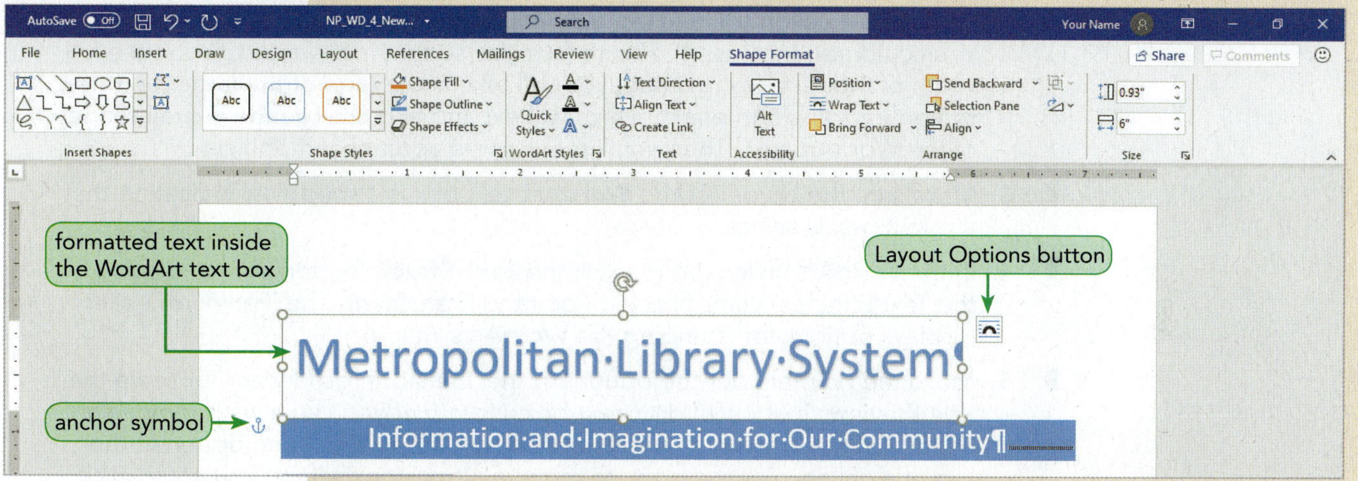

The Shape Format tab appears as the active tab on the ribbon, displaying a variety of tools that you can use to edit the WordArt. Before you change the look of the WordArt, you need to fix its position on the page and change its text wrap setting. You will use the Top and Bottom option, which is only available via the Wrap Text button in the Wrap Text group.

9. Make sure the **Shape Format** tab is selected on the ribbon.
10. In the Arrange group, click the **Wrap Text** button to open the Wrap Text menu, then click **Top and Bottom**. Note that for a WordArt text box that contains fewer characters, you might find that the Square text wrap option works better. When wrapping text around an object on a page, it's often necessary to experiment until you find the best option.
11. Click the **Wrap Text** button again and then click **Fix Position on Page** to insert a check.
12. If necessary, drag the WordArt text box up to position it above the shaded paragraph, using the top and left green guidelines as necessary.
13. Save the document.

Next, you will modify the WordArt in several ways.

Modifying WordArt

Your first task is to resize the WordArt. When resizing WordArt, you need to consider both the font size of the text and the size of the text box that contains the WordArt. You change the font size for WordArt text just as you would for ordinary text—by selecting it and then choosing a new font size using the Font Size box in the Font group on the Home tab. If you choose a large font for a headline, you might also need to resize the text box to ensure that the resized text appears on a single line. Vassily is happy with the font size of the new WordArt headline, so you only need to adjust the size of the text box so it spans the width of the page. The larger text box will make it possible for you to add some more effects.

To resize the WordArt text box and add some effects:

1. Make sure the **Shape Format** tab is selected on the ribbon.
2. Change the width of the text box to **7** inches. The text box height should remain at the default 0.93 inches.

   By default, the text is centered within the text box, which is what Vassily wants. Note, however, that you could use the alignment buttons on the Home tab to align the text any way you wanted within the text box borders. You could also increase the text's font size so that it expands to span the full width of the text box. Instead, you will take advantage of the larger text box to apply a transform effect, which will expand and change the overall shape of the WordArt text. Then you'll make some additional modifications.
3. Make sure the border of the **WordArt** text box is a solid line, indicating that the text box is selected.
4. In the WordArt Styles group, click the **Text Effects** button to display the Text Effects gallery, and then point to **Transform**. The Transform gallery displays options for changing the WordArt's shape.
5. Move the pointer over the options in the Transform gallery and observe the Live Previews in the WordArt text box. Note that you can always remove an effect that has been previously applied by clicking the None option at the top of a gallery. For example, to remove a transform effect, you could click the None option in the No Transform section at the top of the gallery. When you are finished, position the pointer over the **Chevron: Up** effect. See Figure 4–22.

Figure 4–22 Applying a transform text effect

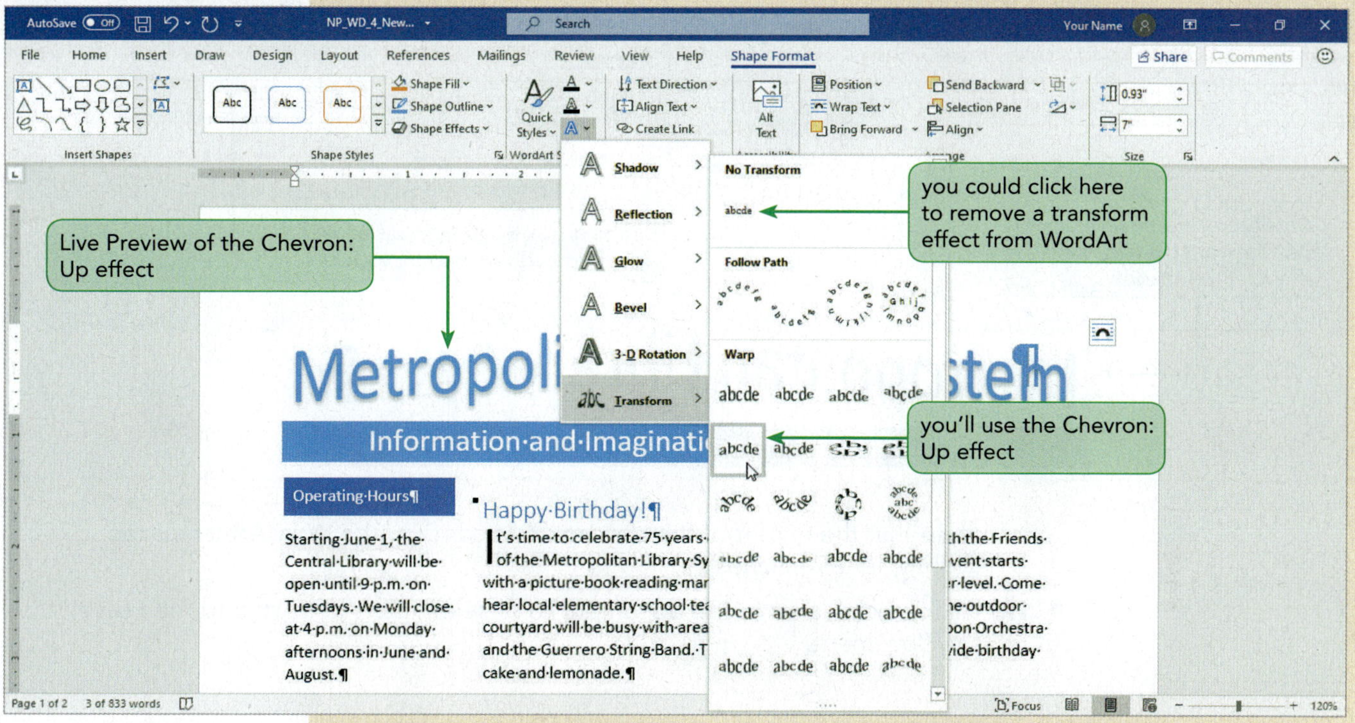

6. Click the **Chevron: Up** effect. The Transform menu closes, and the effect is applied to the WordArt. Now you will make some additional changes using the options in the WordArt Styles group. You'll start by changing the fill color.
7. In the WordArt Styles group, click the **Text Fill arrow** to display the Text Fill color gallery.
8. In the Theme Colors section of the gallery, click the square that is fifth from the left in the second row from the bottom to select the **Blue, Accent 1, Darker 25%** color. The Text Fill gallery closes, and the WordArt is formatted in a darker shade of blue. Next, you'll add a shadow to make the headline more dramatic.
9. In the WordArt Styles group, click the **Text Effects** button to display the Text Effects gallery, and then point to **Shadow** to display the Shadow gallery, which is divided into several sections.
10. In the Outer section, point to the top-left option to display a ScreenTip that reads "Offset: Bottom Right."
11. Click the **Offset: Bottom Right** shadow style. A shadow is added to the WordArt text. See Figure 4–23.

Figure 4–23 **Completed WordArt headline**

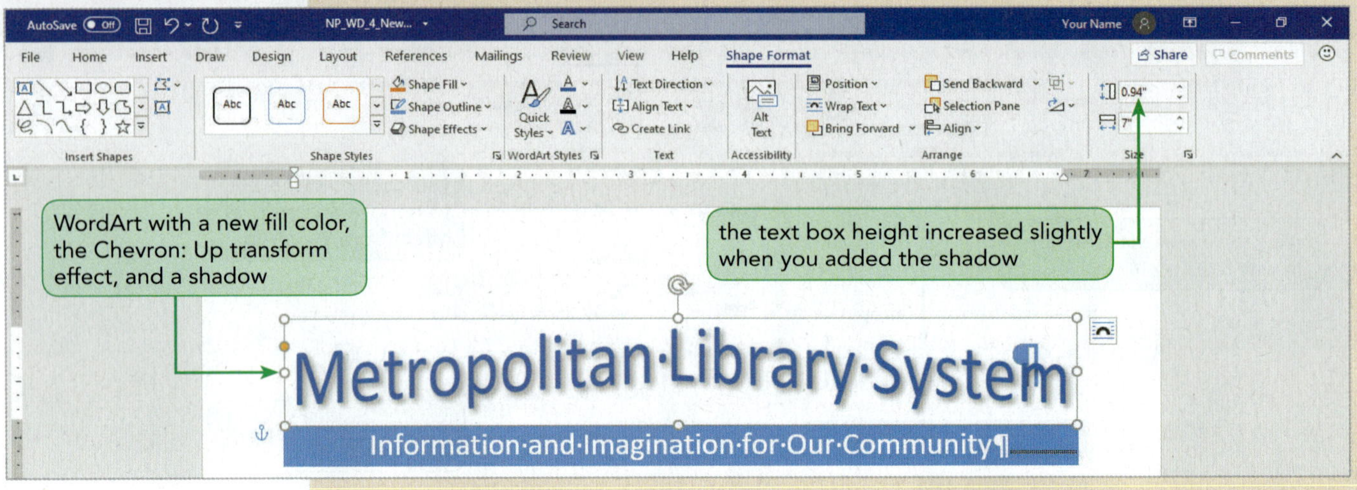

Note that the height of the text box that contains the WordArt increased slightly, to 0.94 inches.

12. Click a blank area of the document to deselect the WordArt, and then save the document.

The WordArt headline is complete. Your next job is to add some pictures to the newsletter.

Working with Pictures

In Word, a picture is a photo, drawing, icon, or other image. Although you can copy and paste pictures into a document from other documents, you'll typically insert pictures using the Pictures button in the Illustrations group on the Insert tab. Click the Pictures button and then click This Device to insert a picture from a file stored on your computer. Click Online Pictures on the Pictures menu to insert images that you find online using Bing Image Search or that you have stored on OneDrive. As you saw in the Session 4.1 Visual Overview, the final version of the newsletter will contain a photograph, a drawing, and an icon.

After you insert a picture into a document, it functions as an object that you can move, resize, wrap text around, and edit in other ways using the appropriate contextual tab on the ribbon. In general, the skills you used when modifying text boxes apply to pictures as well.

Note that you can also use the Online Video button in the Media group on the Insert tab to insert an online video into your document from YouTube or elsewhere on the web. However, you should use videos sparingly in professional documents.

And be aware that inserting an online video introduces code that hackers could manipulate to import malware into your computer.

Proskills

Written Communication: Understanding Copyright Laws

The ownership of all forms of media, including text, drawings, photographs, and video, is governed by copyright laws. You should assume that anything you find on the web is owned by someone who has a right to control its use. It's your responsibility to make sure you understand copyright laws and to abide by them. The U.S. Copyright Office maintains a Frequently Asked Questions page that should answer any questions you might have: www.copyright.gov/help/faq.

Generally, copyright laws allow a student to reuse a photo, drawing, or other item for educational purposes, on a one-time basis, without getting permission from the owner. However, to avoid charges of plagiarism, you need to acknowledge the source of the item in your work. You don't ever want to be accused of presenting someone else's work as your own. Businesses face much more stringent copyright restrictions. To reuse any material, you must request permission from the owner, and you will often need to pay a fee.

When you search for images by clicking the Pictures button in the Illustrations group on the Insert tab, and then clicking Online Pictures, all of the images that initially appear as a result of your search will be licensed under a Creative Commons license. (You'll learn more about using the Online Pictures command later in this module.) There are several types of Creative Commons licenses. One type allows you to use an image for any reason, including commercial use, and to modify the image, as long as the photographer is credited or attributed (similar to the credits under the photos in some figures in this book). Another type of license allows you to use an image with an attribution as long as it is not for commercial purposes and as long as you do not modify the image. Even if an image has a Creative Commons license, you must still review the exact license on the website on which the image is stored. When you point to an image in the search results in the Online Pictures window, the More information and actions button appears in the lower-right corner of the image. Click the icon to display more information about the image, including its website. Note that you can also click the Learn more here link, at the bottom of the Online Pictures dialog box, to read an in-depth explanation of copyright regulations.

Cropping a Picture

Vassily wants to insert a photo of cupcakes into the newsletter on page 1. He has the illustration saved as a PNG file named Support_WD_4_ Cupcakes.png, so you can insert it using the Pictures button in the Illustrations group. Keep in mind that whenever you insert a picture in a document, you should add alt text, or revise the default alt text, as necessary.

To insert the picture on page 1:

1. On page 1, click at the end of the first paragraph below the "Happy Birthday" heading to position the insertion point between " . . . and lemonade." and the paragraph mark. Normally, there's no need to be so precise about where you click before inserting a picture, but doing so here will ensure that your results match the results described in these steps exactly.
2. On the ribbon, click the **Insert** tab.
3. In the Illustrations group, click the **Pictures** button to display the Pictures menu.
4. Click **This Device** to open the Insert Picture dialog box.
5. Navigate to the **Word4 > Module** folder included with your Data Files, and then insert the picture file named **Support_WD_4_Cupcakes.png**. The picture is inserted in the document as an inline object. It is selected, and the

Picture Format tab is displayed on the ribbon. For a few seconds, the default alt text appears at the bottom of the picture. It is not correct, so you need to create new alt text.

6. In the Accessibility group, click the **Alt Text** button to open the Alt Text pane, delete the alt text and the sentence below it, type **Three cupcakes with candles**, and then close the Alt Text pane.
7. Scroll down if necessary so you can see the entire picture.

The picture is wider than it needs to be and would look better as a square. So you'll need to cut off, or crop, part of it. In addition to being able to crop part of a picture, Word offers several more advanced cropping options. One option is to crop to a shape, which means trimming the edges of a picture so it fits into a star, an oval, an arrow, or another shape. You can also crop to a specific ratio of height to width.

Whatever method you use, once you crop a picture, the part you cropped is hidden from view. However, it remains a part of the picture in case you change your mind and want to restore the cropped picture to its original form.

Before you crop off the sides of the picture, you'll try cropping it to a specific shape.

To crop the picture:

1. In the Size group, click the **Crop arrow** to display the Crop menu, and then point to **Crop to Shape**. A gallery of shapes is displayed, similar to the gallery you saw in Figure 4–15.
2. In the Basic Shapes section of the gallery, click the **Lightning Bolt** shape (third row down, sixth from the right). The picture takes on the shape of a lightning bolt, with everything outside the lightning bolt shape cropped off.

   This isn't a useful option for the picture, but cropping to shapes can be very effective with pictures in informal documents, such as party invitations or posters, especially if you then use the Behind Text wrapping option, so that the document text flows over the picture.
3. Press **CTRL+Z** to undo the cropping.
4. In the Size group, click the **Crop** button (not the Crop arrow). Dark black sizing handles appear around the picture borders.
5. Position the pointer directly over the middle sizing handle on the right border. The pointer changes to ⊢.
6. Press and hold down the mouse button, and drag the pointer slightly left. The pointer changes to +.
7. Drag the pointer toward the left until the picture border aligns with the 4-inch mark on the horizontal ruler, as shown in Figure 4–24.

Figure 4–24 **Cropping a picture**

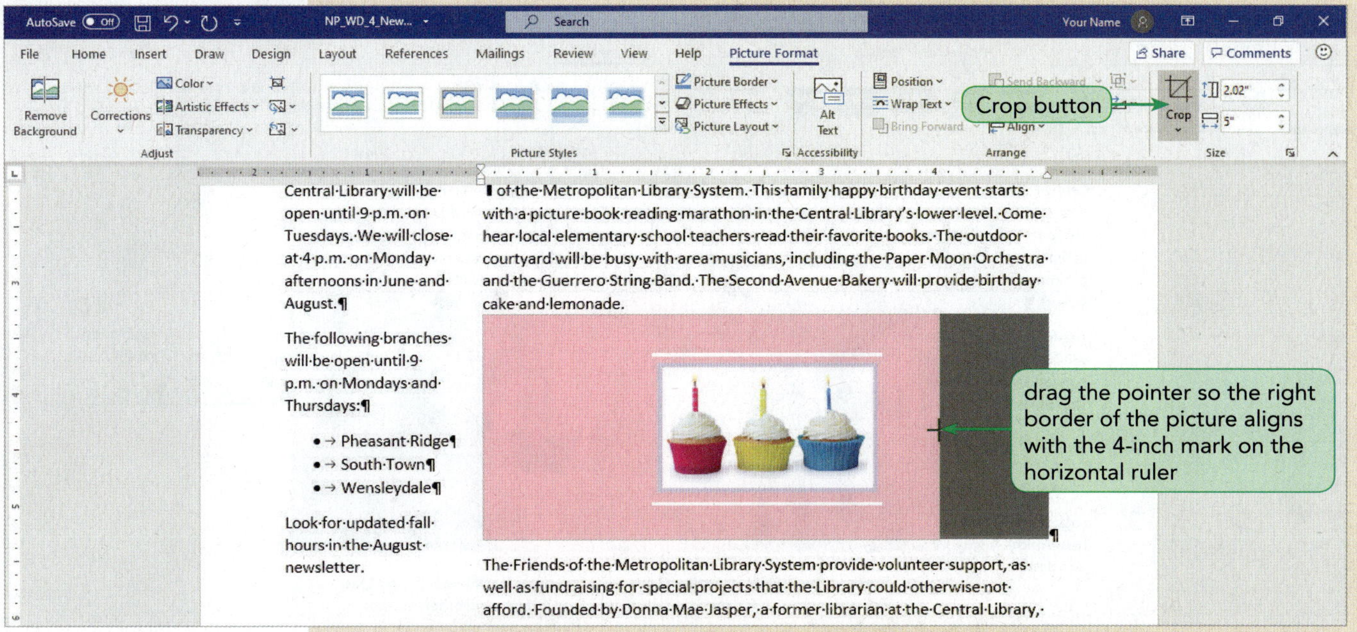

Ruth Black/Shutterstock.com

8. When the picture looks like the one shown in Figure 4–24, release the mouse button. The right portion of the picture is no longer visible. You can ignore the text wrapping for now. The original border remains, indicating that the cropped portion is still saved as part of the picture in case you want to undo the cropping.

9. Drag the middle sizing handle on the left border to the right until the left border aligns with the 1.5-inch mark on the horizontal ruler.

The picture now takes up much less space, but it's not exactly a square. To ensure a specific ratio, you can crop the picture by changing its **aspect ratio**—that is, the ratio of width to height. You'll try that next. But first, you'll restore the picture to its original state.

Tip

If you aren't sure what formatting has been applied to a picture, and you want to start over, use the Reset Picture button in the Adjust group.

10. In the Adjust group, click the **Reset Picture arrow** to display the Reset Picture menu, and then click **Reset Picture & Size**. The picture returns to its original state.

11. In the Size group, click the **Crop arrow**, and then point to **Aspect Ratio** to display the Aspect Ratio menu, which lists various ratios of width to height. A square has a 1-to-1 ratio of width to height.

12. Under "Square," click **1:1**. The picture is cropped to a square shape. See Figure 4–25.

Figure 4–25 Picture cropped to a 1:1 aspect ratio

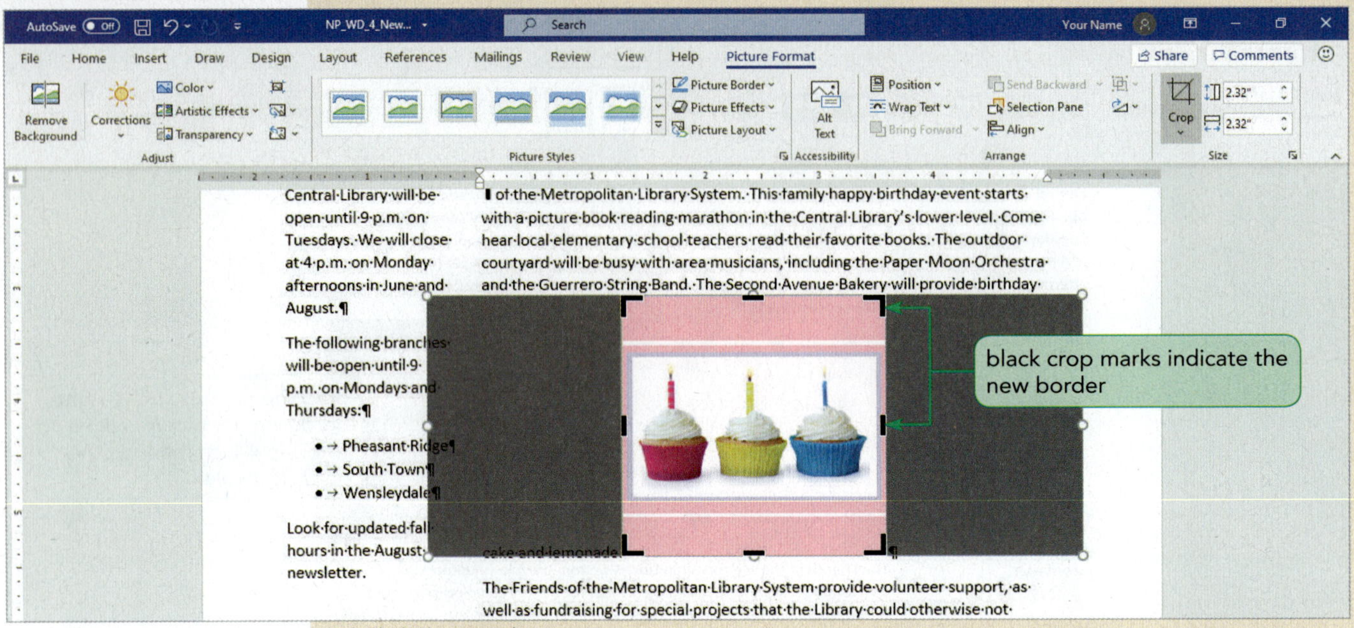

Ruth Black/Shutterstock.com

13. Click anywhere outside the picture to deselect it and complete the cropping procedure.

Next, you need to change the picture from an inline object to a floating object by wrapping text around it. You also need to position it on the page. You can complete both of these tasks at the same time by using the Position button in the Arrange group.

To change the picture's position and wrapping:

1. Change the Zoom level to **One Page**, and then click the **picture** to select it.
2. On the ribbon, click the **Picture Format** tab.
3. In the Arrange group, click the **Position** button to display the Position gallery. You can click an icon in the "With Text Wrapping" section to move the selected picture to one of nine preset positions on the page. As with any gallery, you can see a Live Preview of the options before you actually select one.
4. Move the pointer over the various icons, and observe the changing Live Preview in the document, with the picture moving to different locations on the page and the text wrapping around it.
5. Point to the icon in the middle row on the far right side to display a ScreenTip that reads "Position in Middle Right with Square Text Wrapping," and then click the **Position in Middle Right with Square Text Wrapping** icon. The picture moves to the middle of the page along the right margin. By default, it is formatted with Square text wrapping, so the text wraps to its left, following its square outline. Next, you'll add a picture style.
6. In the Pictures Styles group, click the **Simple Frame, White** style, which is the left-most style in the visible row of the Picture Styles gallery. A frame and a shadow are applied to the picture. See Figure 4–26.

Tip

When you select an option in the Position gallery, Fix Position on Page is also selected on the Wrap Text menu by default.

Tip

To add a simple border without adding a style, click the Picture Border button, and then click a color in the color gallery.

Figure 4–26 **Picture style added to cupcake picture**

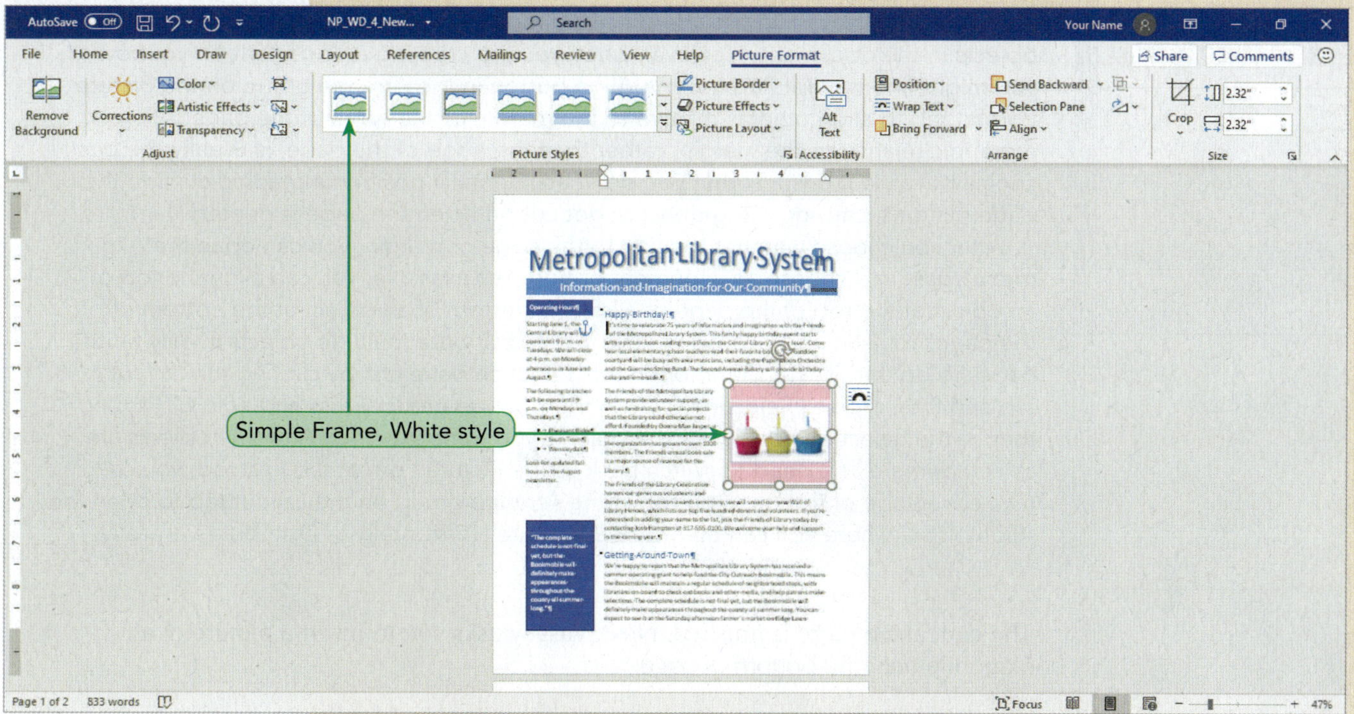

Ruth Black/Shutterstock.com

Your final step is to resize the picture to make it a bit smaller.

7. In the Size group, click the **Shape Height** box, type **1.3**, and then press **ENTER**. The settings in both the Shape Height and Shape Width boxes change to 1.3 inches. For most types of graphics, the aspect ratio is locked, meaning that when you change one dimension, the other changes to match. In this case, because the aspect ratio of the picture is 1:1, when you changed the height to 1.3 inches, the width also changed to 1.3 inches, ensuring that the picture retained its square shape.
8. Click anywhere in the document to deselect the picture, and then save the document.

Insight

Aligning Graphic Objects and Using the Selection Pane

The steps in this module provide precise directions about where to position graphic objects in the document. However, when you are creating a document on your own, you might find it helpful to use the Align button in the Arrange group on the Picture Format tab to align objects relative to the margin or the edge of the page. Aligning a graphic relative to the margin, rather than the edge of the page, is usually the best choice because it ensures that you don't accidentally position a graphic outside the page margins, causing the graphic to get cut off when the page is printed.

After you choose whether to align to the page or margin, you can open the Align menu again and choose an alignment option. For example, you can align the top of an object at the top of the page or align the bottom of an object at the bottom of the page. You can also choose to have Word distribute multiple objects evenly on the page. To do this, it's helpful to open the Selection pane first by clicking the Layout tab and then clicking Selection Pane in the Arrange group. Press and hold CTRL, and then in the Selection pane, click the objects you want to select. After the objects are selected, there's no need to switch back to the Picture Format tab. Instead, you can take advantage of the Align button in the Arrange group on the Layout tab to open the Align menu, where you can then click Distribute Horizontally or Distribute Vertically.

The cupcake picture is finished. Next, Vassily asks you to insert a picture of a bookmobile near the bottom of page 1.

Searching for and Inserting Online Pictures and 3D Models

Tip

Be mindful of copyright restrictions for online pictures. For more on this, see the ProSkills box "Written Communication: Understanding Copyright Laws."

If you don't already have the pictures you need for a document stored as image files, you can look for pictures online. You can also look for **3D models**, which are illustrations created using 3D animation techniques that you can rotate in three dimensions. The first step in using online pictures or 3D models is finding the picture or model you want. Most image websites include a search box where you can type some descriptive keywords to help you narrow the selection down to a smaller range. To search for images from within Word, click the Pictures button in the Illustrations group on the Insert tab, and then click Online Pictures. This opens the Online Pictures dialogue box, shown in Figure 4–27, where you can use the Search Bing box at the top to look for images, or click categories such as "Animals" to see a collection of related images.

Figure 4–27 **Inserting an online picture**

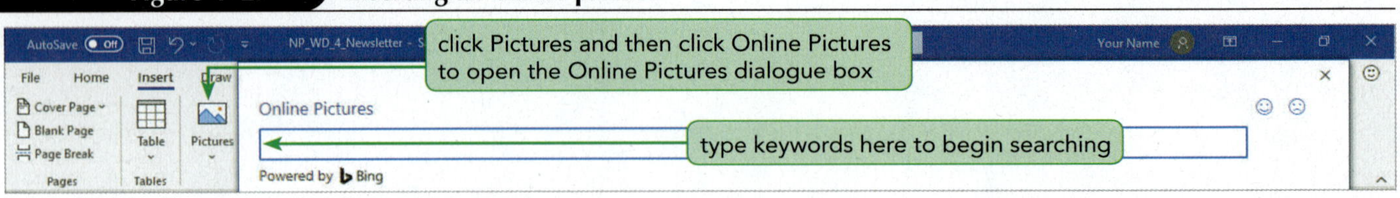

To start a search, you would type keywords, such as "walking a dog," in the search box, and then press ENTER. Images from all over the web that have the keywords "walking a dog" and that are licensed under Creative Commons would appear below the search box. Typically, the search results include photos and premade pictures known as **clip art**, which can be used to illustrate a wide variety of publications. To insert one of those images, you would click it, and then click the Insert button. To widen your search to all the images on the web (the vast majority of which are subject to strict copyright restrictions), you could click the Creative Commons only check box to deselect it.

To insert a 3D model in a document, click the 3D Models button in the Illustrations group on the Insert tab. This opens the Online 3D Models dialog box, where you can type some key words, or click categories such as "Animals" to see a collection of related 3D models. Click the model you want, click the Insert button, and then use the handles on the image in the document to resize or rotate it. You can wrap text around a 3D model just as you would wrap text around any type of picture. Like other pictures, 3D models are typically copyright protected. After you insert a 3D model, you can use the tools on the 3D Model tab to select other options and to add alt text. You can use the More button in the 3D Model Views group to choose from a variety of views for your model. For example, you could choose to display an astronaut 3D model as seen from above or below.

Because results from an online search are unpredictable, in the following steps you will insert a picture included with your Data Files.

Tip

If you use Word 365, you can access a library of royalty-free stock images by clicking the Pictures button in the Illustrations group on the Insert tab, and then clicking Stock images.

To insert a picture in the newsletter:

1. Zoom in so you can read the document text at the bottom of page 1, and then click at the end of the paragraph below the "Getting Around Town" heading to position the insertion point between "early April." and the paragraph mark.
2. Change the Zoom level to **Multiple Pages** so you can see the entire document.
3. On the ribbon, click the **Insert** tab.
4. In the Illustrations group, click the **Pictures** button, click **This Device** to display the Insert Picture dialog box, and then navigate to the **Word4 > Module** folder.
5. Click the image **Support_WD_4_Bookmobile.png**, and then click the **Insert** button. The dialog box closes, and the picture of a bookmobile is inserted as an inline object at the current location of the insertion point. The picture has a vertical orientation, so it looks like it is driving up the page. See Figure 4–28.

Figure 4–28 Picture inserted as inline object

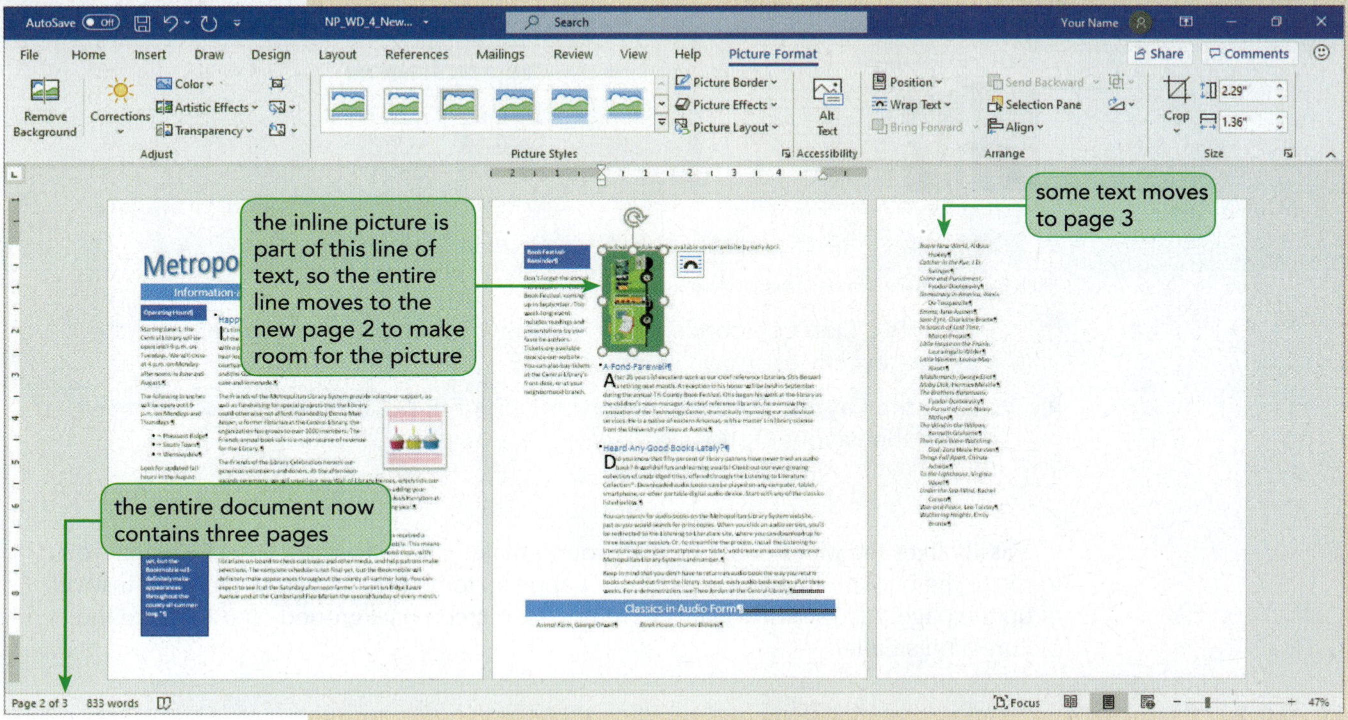

Ruth Black/Shutterstock.com; Mascha Tace/Shutterstock.com

6. Change the alt text for the image to **Bookmobile**, and then close the Alt Text pane.

   Because the picture is too large to fit on page 1, the line that contains the insertion point jumps to page 2, with the picture displayed below the text. The rest of the document text starts below the picture on page 2 and flows to page 3. The picture is selected, as indicated by its border with handles. The Picture Format tab is displayed on the ribbon. Now you can wrap text around the picture, and position it on the page.

7. In the Arrange group, click the **Wrap Text** button, and then click **Tight**. The picture is now a floating object and has moved back to page 1.

8. Drag the picture to the bottom of page 1, and position it so the "Getting Around Town" heading wraps above the picture and the text below the heading wraps to the right of the picture. See Figure 4–29. The anchor symbol for the picture is only partially visible because it's covered by the blue text box.

Figure 4–29 Resized picture as a floating object

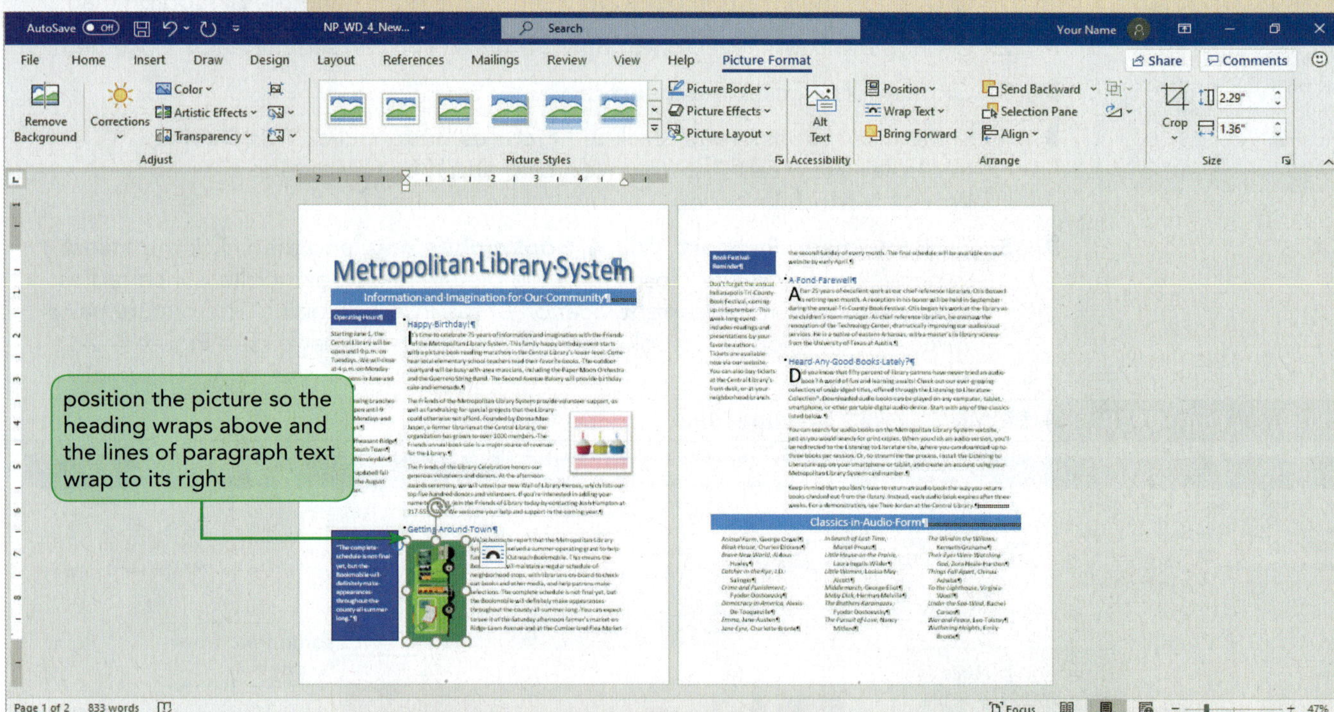

Ruth Black/Shutterstock.com; Mascha Tace/Shutterstock.com

Trouble? Don't be concerned if you can't get the text to wrap around the picture exactly as shown in Figure 4–29.

9. Click the **Layout Options** button, click **Fix position on page**, and then close the Layout Options gallery.

Vassily likes the picture, but he asks you to make a few changes. First, he wants you to rotate the bookmobile to the right, so it appears to be driving across the page instead of up the page. Also, Vassily wants to remove the green background, and to make the picture a bit smaller.

Insight

Using the Draw Tab

You can use the tools on the Draw tab to draw on a touch screen, using your finger or a stylus. If you do not have a touch screen, you can use the mouse instead. When the Draw with Touch button is selected, you can choose to draw with a pen, a pencil, or a highlighter. For each drawing tool, you can choose from different colors, and you can adjust any of the drawing tools to create a wider or more narrow line. You can select different effects, such as Galaxy, which creates a glitter effect. To begin selecting an effect, click a pen in the Pens group on the Draw tab, and then click the down arrow button on the pen's icon in the Pens group to display a menu of options. The Ink-to-Shape button lets you incorporate hand-drawn text edits (including common copy-editing symbols such as an inverted V to indicate an insertion) into regular document text. Likewise, you can use the Ink to Math button to convert hand-drawn mathematical equations into document text, which you can then edit using the Equation tab. After you have finished drawing, you can "replay" the drawing action and watch the characters and shapes you drew get redrawn in the document. To hide anything you have drawn in a document, click the Hide Ink button in the Ink group on the Review tab.

Rotating a Picture

You can quickly rotate a picture by dragging the Rotation handle that appears on the picture's border when the picture is selected. To access some preset rotation options, you can click the Rotate Objects button in the Arrange group on the Picture Format tab to open the Rotate menu. To quickly rotate a picture 90 degrees, click Rotate Right 90° or Rotate Left 90° in the Rotate menu. You can also flip a picture, as if the picture were printed on both sides of a card and you wanted to turn the card over. To do this, click Flip Vertical or Flip Horizontal in the Rotate menu.

Vassily only wants to rotate the picture 90 degrees to the right. You could do that quickly by clicking the Rotate Objects button in the Arrange group, and then clicking Rotate Right 90°. But it's helpful to know how to rotate a picture by dragging the Rotation handle, so you'll use that method in the following steps.

To rotate the picture:

1. Change the document Zoom level to **120%**, and then scroll down so you can see the bottom half of page 1.
2. Click the **bookmobile picture**, if necessary, to select it, and then position the pointer over the circular rotation handle above the middle of the picture's top border. The pointer changes to .
3. Drag the pointer down and to the right, until the bookmobile rotates to a horizontal position. Release the mouse button. The picture is displayed in the new, rotated position, but, depending on where you positioned it earlier, part of the picture might overlap the blue text box. See Figure 4–30.

Figure 4–30 **Dragging the Rotation handle**

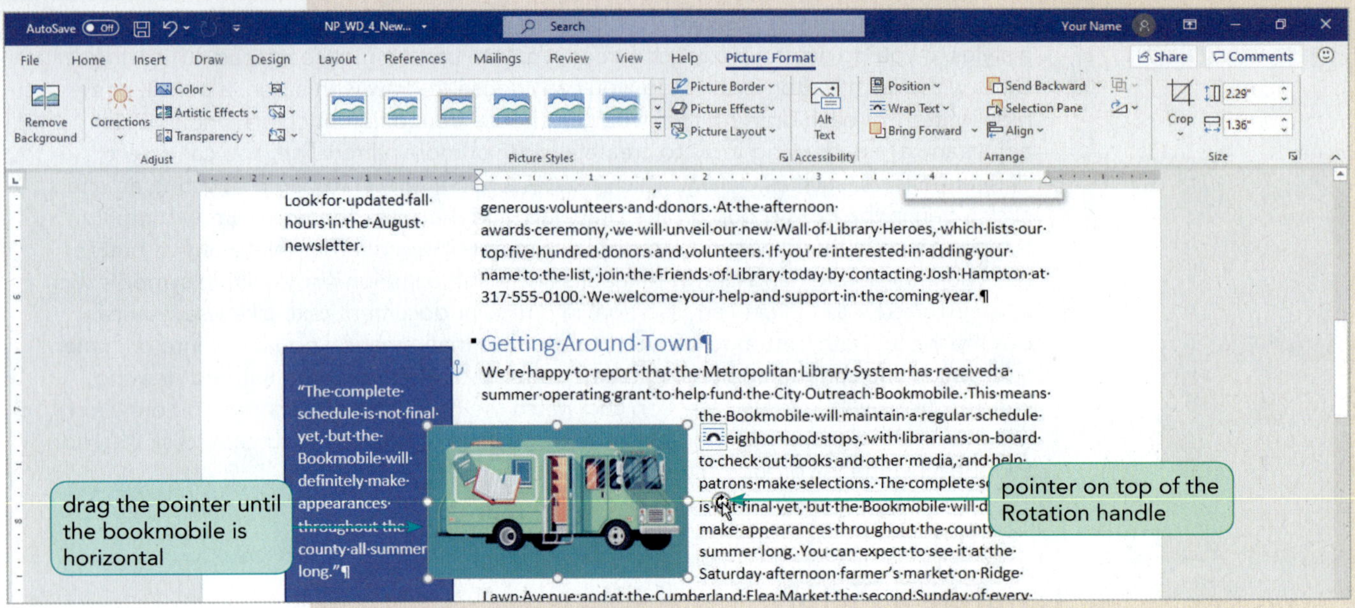

Mascha Tace/Shutterstock.com

4. Drag the bookmobile picture right, so its left edge aligns below the left edge of the "Getting Around Town" heading, and two lines of paragraph text wrap above it.
5. Save the document.

You're almost finished editing the bookmobile picture. Your next task is to remove its background, but first you'll explore the options in the Adjust group.

Adjusting a Picture

The Adjust group on the Picture Format tab provides several tools for adjusting a picture's overall look. You'll explore some of these options in the following steps.

To try out some options in the Adjust group:

1. Make sure that the **bookmobile picture** is still selected, and that the **Picture Format** tab is selected on the ribbon.
2. In the Adjust group, click the **Corrections** button, and then move the pointer over the various options in the Corrections gallery and observe the Live Preview in the document. You can use the Corrections gallery to sharpen or soften a picture's focus or to adjust its brightness.
3. Press **ESC** to close the Corrections gallery.
4. In the Adjust group, click the **Color** button, and then move the pointer over the options in the Color gallery, and observe the Live Preview in the document. You can adjust a picture's color saturation and tone. You can also use the Recolor options to completely change a picture's colors.
5. Press **ESC** to close the Color gallery.

6. In the Adjust group, click the **Artistic Effects** button, and then move the pointer over the options in the Artistic Effects gallery, and observe the Live Preview in the document.
7. Press **ESC** to close the Artistic Effects gallery.
8. In the Adjust group, click the **Compress Pictures** button to open the Compress Pictures dialog box. In the Resolution portion of the dialog box, you can select the option that reflects the purpose of your document. Compressing pictures reduces the file size of the Word document but can result in some loss of detail. To compress all the pictures in a document, deselect the Apply only to this picture check box.
9. Click **Cancel** to close the Compress Pictures dialog box.

Now you are ready to remove the green background from the bookmobile picture.

Removing a Picture's Background

Removing a picture's background can be tricky, especially if you are working on a photo with a background that is not clearly differentiated from the foreground image. For example, you might find it difficult to remove a white, snowy background from a photo of an equally white snowman. Removing a background from a drawing, like the bookmobile picture, is usually much easier than removing a background from a photo. You start by clicking the Remove Background button in the Adjust group, and then making changes to help Word distinguish between the background that you want to exclude and the image you want to keep.

Reference

Removing a Picture's Background

- Select the picture, and then on the Picture Format tab, in the Adjust group, click the Remove Background button.
- To mark areas to keep, click the Mark Areas to Keep button in the Refine group on the Background Removal tab, and then use the drawing pointer to select areas of the picture to keep.
- To mark areas to remove, click the Mark Areas to Remove button in the Refine group on the Background Removal tab, and then use the drawing pointer to select areas of the picture to remove.
- Click the Keep Changes button in the Close group.

You'll start by zooming in so you can clearly see the picture as you edit it.

To remove the green background from the bookmobile picture:

1. On the Zoom slider, drag the slider button to change the Zoom level to **180%**, and then scroll as necessary to display the selected bookmobile picture.
2. In the Adjust group, click the **Remove Background** button. See Figure 4–31.

Figure 4–31 **Removing a picture's background**

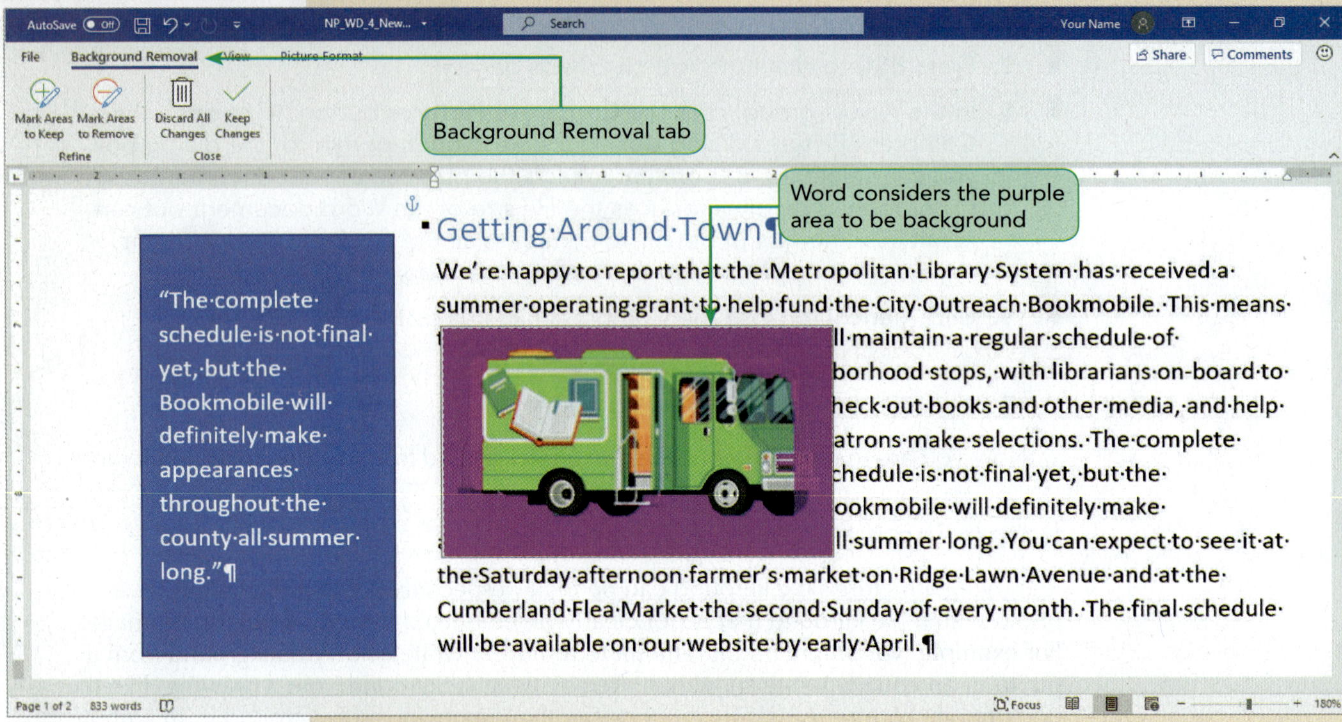

Mascha Tace/Shutterstock.com

The part of the picture that Word considers to be the background turns purple, and the Background Removal tab appears on the ribbon. Notice that the front and back ends of the bookmobile are purple, indicating that Word considers them to be part of the background. If you have trouble distinguishing colors, note that the front and back ends of the bookmobile are obscured by shading. The shading indicates that Word considers that part of the bookmobile to be background.

3. On the Background Removal tab, click the **Mark Areas to Keep** button in the Refine group to select it, if necessary, and then move the drawing pointer over the bookmobile. You can use this pointer to click any areas you want to keep.

4. Move the pointer over a purple area on the left side of the bookmobile. See Figure 4–32.

Figure 4–32 Marking an area to keep

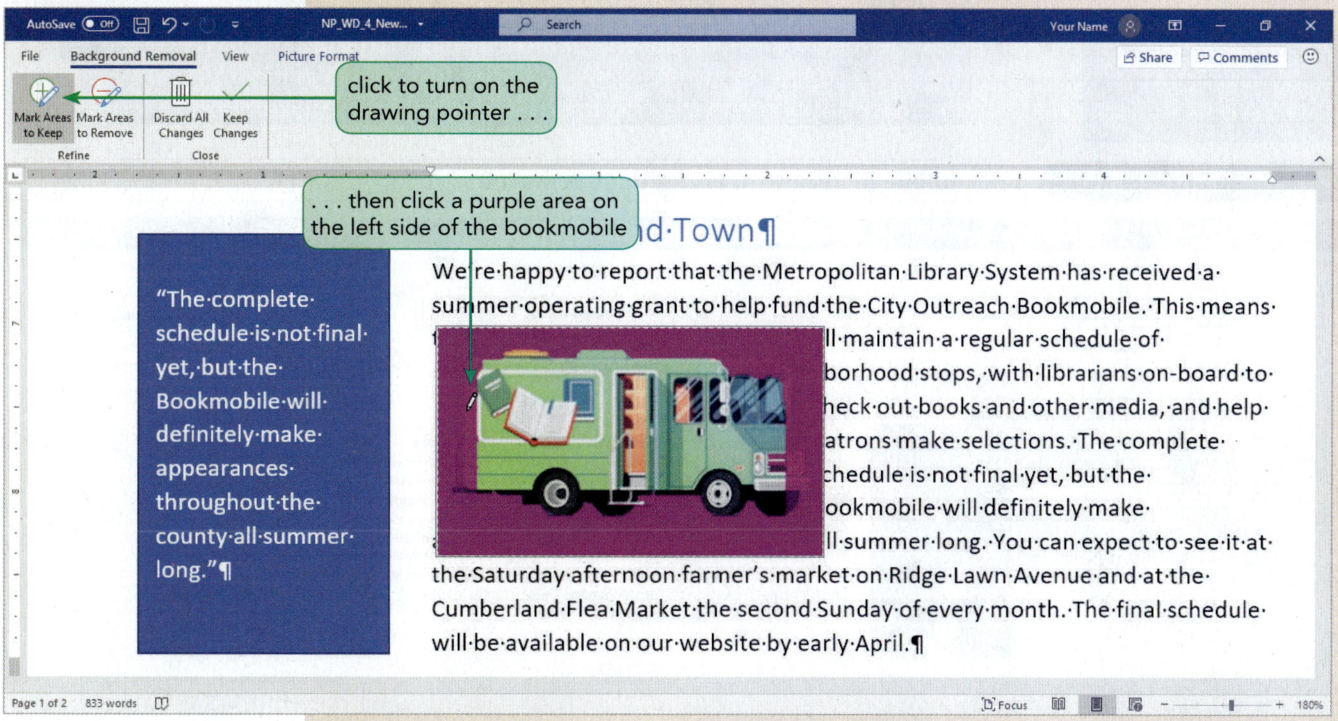

Mascha Tace/Shutterstock.com

5. Click the mouse button. The area you clicked loses the shading, so you can see the bookmobile clearly. To give the image a clean line on the left, do not click the bump at the back of the bookmobile.

6. Click the other major shaded spots on the right side of the bookmobile, including the front bumper and the headlight. You might need to click once, or you might need to click multiple times to convert all of the bookmobile from background to foreground. Also click the step below the door. It's fine if a little of the green background is visible here and there. Feel free to use CTRL+Z to undo changes and start again as necessary. Removing a picture's background can be tricky, and it often takes several tries to get it right.

   Note that you could click the Mark Areas to Remove button and then use the pointer in a similar way to mark parts of the picture that you want to remove, rather than retain. In an image with a larger background, you could also click and drag the Mark Areas to Remove pointer or the Mark Areas to Keep pointer to select a larger area of the picture for deletion or retention.

   Now you will accept the changes you made to the picture.

7. In the Close group, click the **Keep Changes** button. The background is removed from the picture, leaving only the image of the bookmobile, with no green background. Now the text wrapping follows the curved shape of the bookmobile, although the bookmobile might overlap some letters. Depending on exactly where you positioned the bookmobile, some of the text might now wrap to its left.

Position the bookmobile picture carefully, so it doesn't overlap any text

8. Change the Zoom level to **100%** so that you can see the entire bookmobile, as well as the top of page 2.
9. Change the picture's height to 1.4 inches, and then drag the bookmobile as necessary so the text wraps similarly to the text shown in Figure 4–33, and then click anywhere in the document to deselect the bookmobile picture.

Figure 4–33 Bookmobile picture with background removed

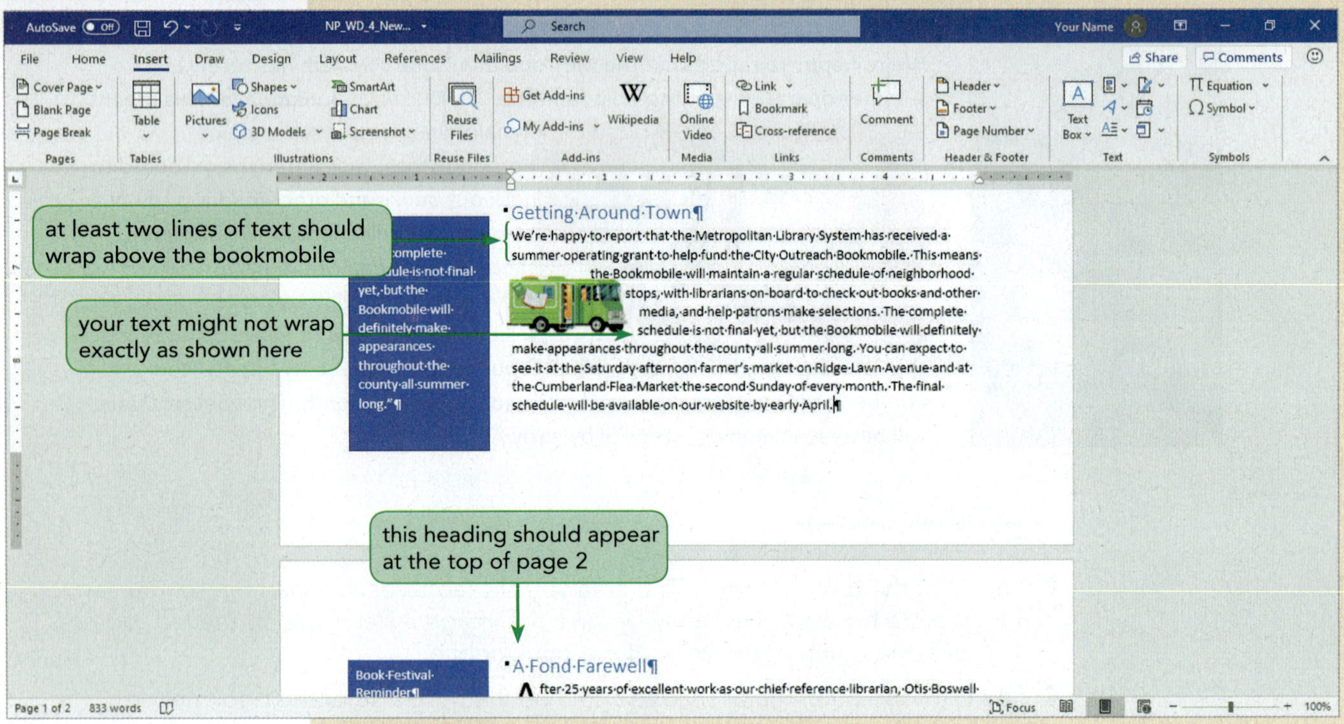

Mascha Tace/Shutterstock.com

Don't be concerned if you can't get the text wrapping to match exactly. The most important thing is that when you are finished, the heading "A Fond Farewell" should be positioned at the top of page 2. Also, at least two lines of text should wrap above the bookmobile. Finally, you might need to adjust the bookmobile's position slightly so it doesn't overlap any text.

10. Click outside the picture to deselect it, and then save the document.

You're finished with your work on the bookmobile picture. Now Vassily asks you to add a picture illustrating the article about audio books.

Adding an Icon

Vassily doesn't have a particular image in mind for the audio books article. You could search for an illustration online, but sometimes it's easier to use the streamlined drawings, known as icons, available via the Icons button in the Illustrations group on the Insert tab. After you add an icon to a document, you can fine-tune it by changing its fill and outline colors. Note that to work with icons, your computer must be connected to the Internet.

To insert an icon:

1. Change the Zoom level to **120%**, and then scroll to display the middle of page 2. You'll insert the icon in the blank space in the margin, below the text box.
2. Click at the end of the paragraph below the "Heard Any Good Books Lately?" heading to position the insertion point between ". . . listed below." and the paragraph mark.
3. On the ribbon, click the **Insert** tab.
4. In the Illustrations group, click the **Icons** button. The Insert Icons dialog box opens, displaying a row of icon categories and a gallery of popular icons.
5. Explore the options in the Insert Icons gallery, using the arrows to scroll to the right and left to view additional icon categories.
6. In the category list, click **Technology And Electronics**, and then click the headphones icon in the fourth row. A checkmark indicates that the icon is selected, as shown in Figure 4–34.

   Trouble? Don't be concerned if the layout of your Insert Icons dialog box is different from the one shown in Figure 4–34. If you don't see a headphones icon, click another option.

Figure 4–34 Icon selected in the Insert Icons dialog box

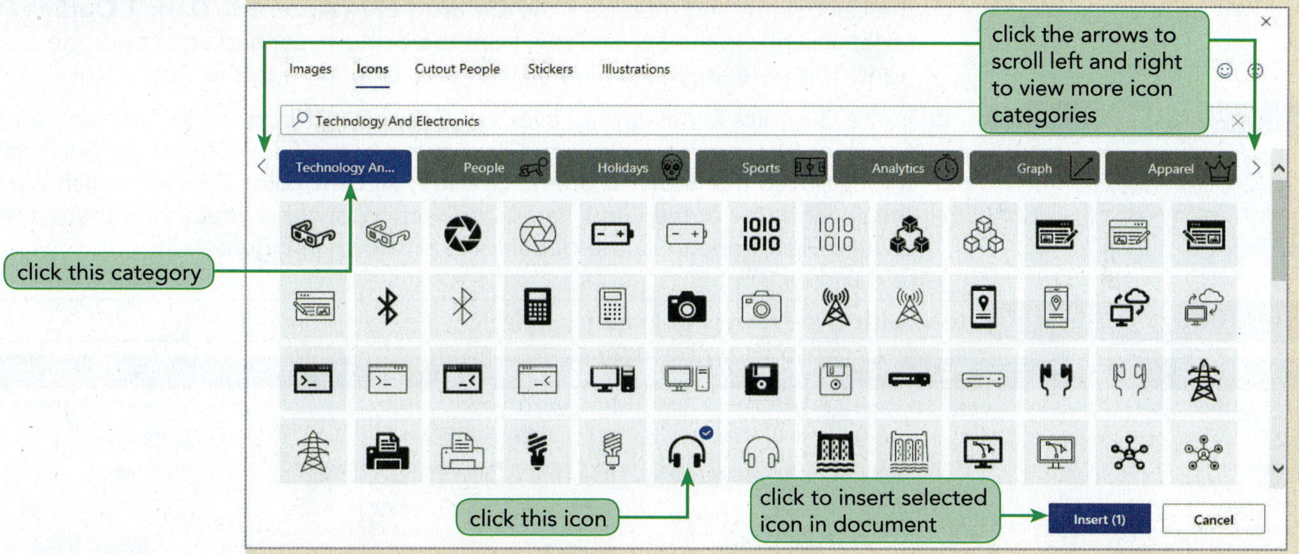

Tip

To edit an icon using the tools on the Shape Format tab, select the icon, click the Convert to Shape button in the Change group on the Graphic Format tab, and then click the icon or one of its shapes.

7. Click the **Insert** button. The headphones icon is inserted as an inline object at the end of the paragraph, with the Graphics Format tab displayed. The alt text indicates that the icon shows headphones (the exact text will vary), so you don't need to change it.

   Next, you need to wrap text around the icon, and position it on the page.
8. In the Arrange group, click the **Wrap Text** button to open the Wrap Text menu. The In Line with Text option is selected. Because the icon is still an inline picture, the Move with Text and Fix Position on Page options are grayed out, indicating that they are not available.
9. Click **In Front of Text** to select it.

10. Click the **Wrap Text** button again, and then click **Fix Position on Page**. The picture appears layered on top of the document text. Keep in mind that even though you selected Fix Position on Page, the picture is not stuck in one place. You can drag it anywhere you want. The point of the Fix Position on Page setting is that it prevents the picture from moving unexpectedly as you make changes to other parts of the document.
11. Drag the icon to the left, to center it in the white space below the text box in the margin.

To make the icon more eye-catching, Vassily would like to change its fill and outline colors. You could do that by using the Graphics Fill button and the Graphics Outline button in the Graphics Styles group on the Graphics Format tab. You can also change both options at once by applying a graphics style. You'll try that option next, and then you'll enlarge the icon to make it more noticeable.

To apply a graphics style and enlarge the icon:

1. In the Graphics Styles group, click the **More** button to open the Graphics Styles gallery, point to some of the style icons and view the Live Previews in the document, and then click the **Colored Fill - Accent 5, Dark 1 Outline** style, which is in the second row from the bottom, second style from the right. The style applies a blue fill with a black outline to the icon.
2. In the Graphics Styles group, click the **Graphics Effects** button to open the Graphics Effects menu, point to **Glow** to open the Glow Effects gallery, and then point to the **Glow: 8 point; Orange, Accent color 2** effect, which is in the second row of the Glow Variations section, second effect from the left. A Live Preview appears in the document, as shown in Figure 4–35.

Tip

You can use the 3-D Rotation effects to rotate an icon in three dimensions.

Figure 4–35 Icon with Live Preview of graphics style

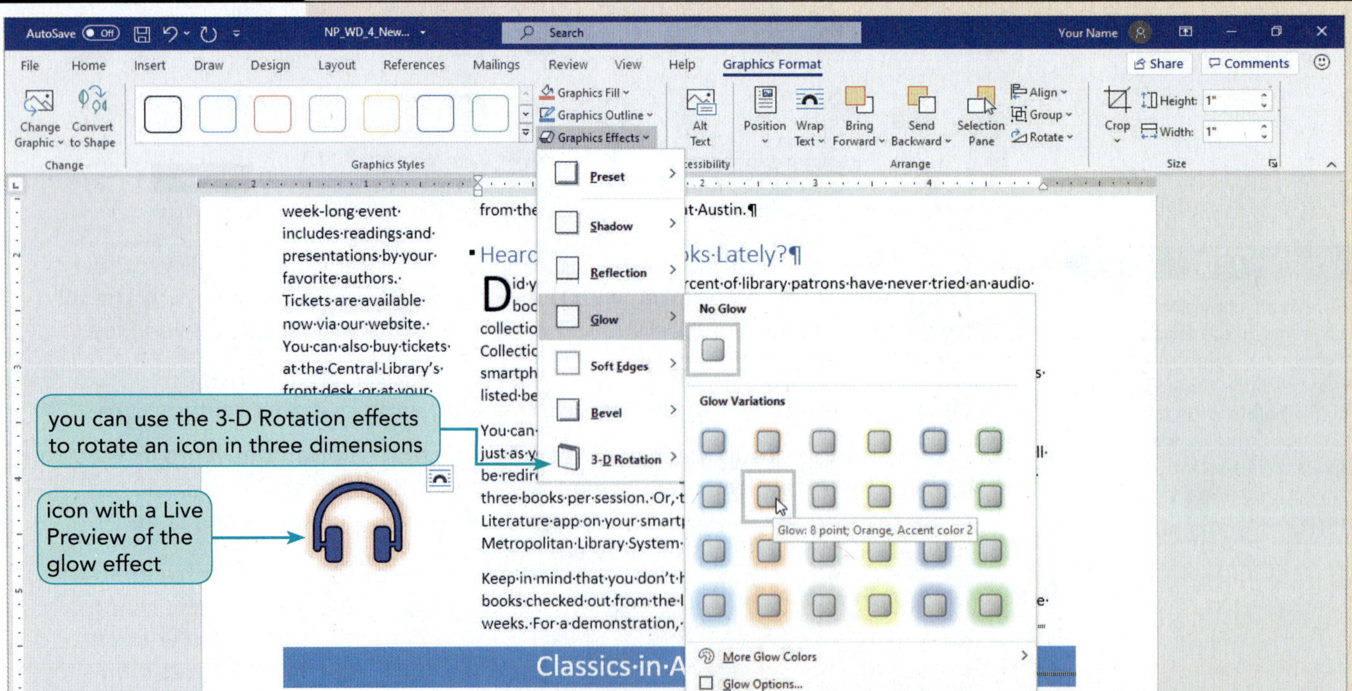

3. Click the **Glow 8 point: Orange; Accent color 2** effect. An orange glow appears around the icon in the document.
4. In the Size group, change the icon's height to 1.5 inches. Because the icon has a square aspect ratio, its width also changes to 1.5 inches.
5. Drag the icon as necessary to make sure it is centered in the white space below the text box in the margin, click anywhere in the document to deselect the icon, and then save the document.

Insight

Working with Digital Picture Files

Digital picture files come in two main types—vector graphics and raster graphics. A vector graphics file stores an image as a mathematical formula, which means you can increase or decrease the size of the image as much as you want without affecting its overall quality. Vector graphics are often used for line drawings and, because the file sizes tend to be small, are widely used on the web. File types for vector graphics are often proprietary, which means they work only in specific graphics programs. In Word, you will sometimes encounter files with the .wmf file extension, which is short for Windows Metafiles. A WMF file is a type of vector graphics file created specifically for Windows. In most cases, though, you'll work with raster graphics, also known as bitmap graphics. A **bitmap** is a grid of square colored dots, called **pixels**, that form a picture. A bitmap graphic, then, is essentially a collection of pixels. The most common types of bitmap files are as follows:

- **BMP**—These files, which have the .bmp file extension, tend to be very large, so it's best to resave them in a different format before using them in a Word document.
- **EPS**—These files, which have the .eps file extension, are created by Adobe Illustrator and can contain text as graphics.
- **GIF**—These files are suitable for most types of simple line art, without complicated colors. A GIF file is compressed, so it doesn't take up much room on your computer. A GIF file has the file extension .gif.
- **JPEG**—These files are suitable for photographs and drawings. Files stored using the JPEG format are even more compressed than GIF files. A JPEG file has the file extension .jpg. If conserving file storage space is a priority, use JPEG graphics for your document.
- **PNG**—These files are similar to GIF files but are suitable for art containing a wider array of colors. A PNG file has the file extension .png.
- **TIFF**—These files are commonly used for photographs or scanned images. TIFF files are usually much larger than GIF or JPEG files but smaller than BMP files. A TIFF file has the file extension .tif.

Now that you are finished inserting and formatting the graphic elements in the newsletter, you need to make sure the columns are more or less the same length.

Balancing Columns

To **balance** columns on a page—that is, to make them equal length—you insert a continuous section break at the end of the last column. Word then adjusts the flow of content between the columns so they are of equal or near-equal length. The columns remain balanced no matter how much material you remove from any of the columns later. The columns also remain balanced if you add material that causes the columns to flow to a new page; the overflow will also be formatted in balanced columns.

To balance the columns:

1. Press **CTRL+END** to move the insertion point to the end of the document.
2. Insert a continuous section break. See Figure 4–36.

Figure 4–36 **Newsletter with balanced columns**

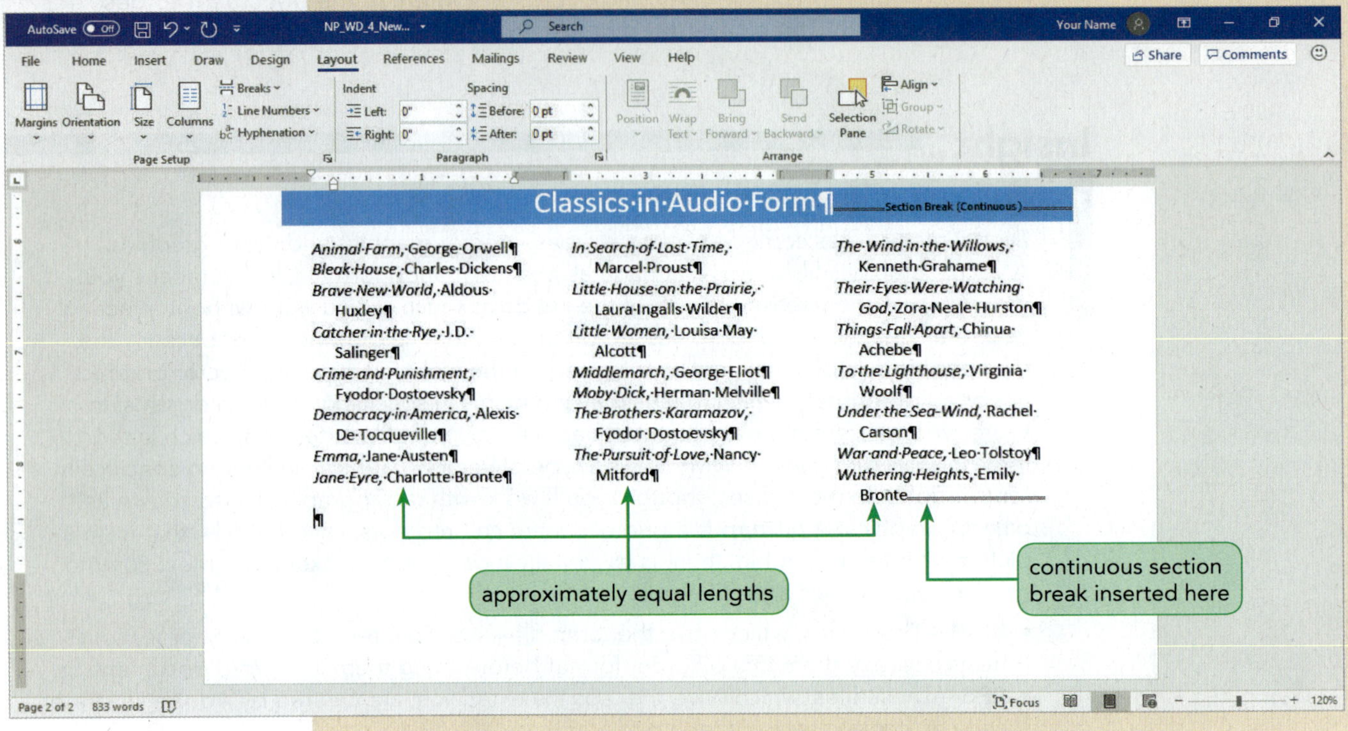

Word balances the text between the three columns, moving some text from the bottom of the left column to the middle column, and from the middle column to the right column, so the three columns are approximately the same length.

Note that you can also adjust the length of a column by inserting a column break using the Breaks button in the Page Setup group on the Layout tab. A column break moves all the text and graphics following it to the next column. Column breaks are useful when you have a multipage document formatted in three or more columns, with only enough text on the last page to fill some of the columns. In that case, balancing columns on the last page won't work. Instead, you can use a column break to distribute an equal amount of text over all the columns on the page. However, as with page breaks, you need to be careful with column breaks because it's easy to forget that you inserted them. Then, if you add or remove text from the document, or change it in some other significant way, you might end up with a page layout you didn't expect.

Enhancing the Newsletter's Formatting

A newsletter is a good opportunity to take advantage of some of Word's flashier formatting options, such as adding a page border and changing the theme colors. Vassily asks you to do both in order to make the newsletter even more eye-catching.

To change the theme colors and insert a border around both pages of the newsletter:

1. Change the Zoom level to **Multiple Pages**.
2. On the ribbon, click the **Design** tab.
3. In the Document Formatting group, click the **Colors** button, scroll down, and then click **Green**. The colors of the various document elements—such as the text boxes, the icon, and headings—change to reflect the new theme colors. See Figure 4–37.

Figure 4–37 Newsletter with new theme colors

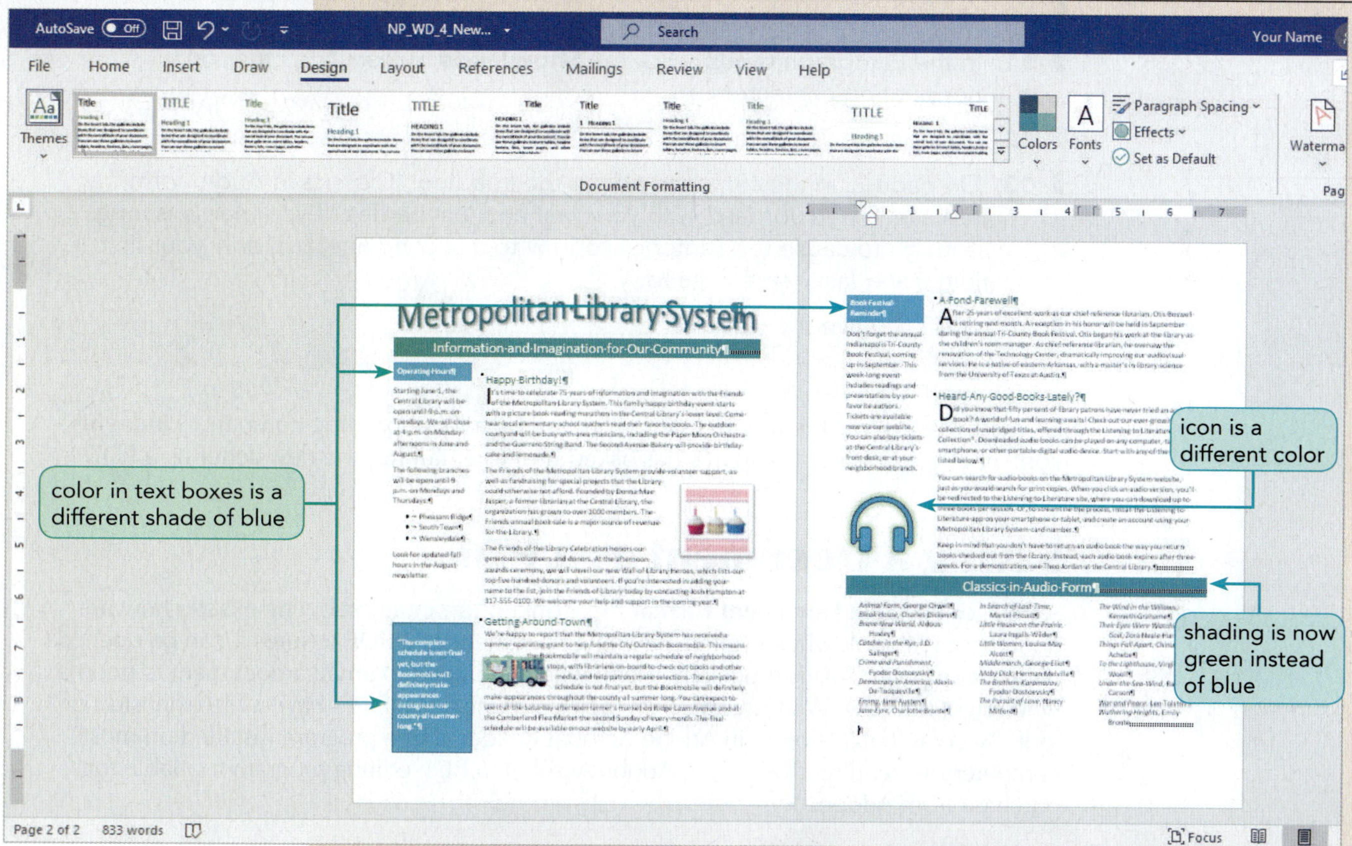

Ruth Black/Shutterstock.com; Mascha Tace/Shutterstock.com

4. In the Page Background group, click the **Page Borders** button. The Borders and Shading dialog box opens with the Page Border tab displayed.
5. In the Setting section, click the **Box** setting.

   Vassily is happy with all the default page border settings, except one; he wants to change the border color to green.

6. Click the **Color** arrow to open the Color gallery, and then click the **Green, Accent 1** square, which is the fifth square from the left in the top row of the Theme Colors section. The Color gallery closes, and the Green, Accent 1 color is displayed in the Color box.
7. Click **OK**. The newsletter now has a simple, green border, as shown earlier in the Session 4.1 Visual Overview.

8. Compare the newsletter to the Session 4.1 Visual Overview, and adjust the position of the various elements as necessary, to make your newsletter match the Visual Overview as closely as possible. Note that you can click a text box or graphic object to select it, and then use the arrow keys on your keyboard to nudge the item up, down, left, or right. Don't be concerned with trying to get the text to wrap around the bookmobile image exactly as it does in the Session 4.1 Visual Overview. Just make sure at least two lines of text wrap above it, and that the heading "A Fond Farewell" appears at the top of page 2.
9. Save the document. Finally, to get a better sense of how the document with complicated formatting will look when printed, it's a good idea to review it with nonprinting characters turned off.
10. On the ribbon, click the **Home** tab.
11. In the Paragraph group, click the **Show/Hide** button ¶ to turn off nonprinting characters.
12. Change the Zoom level to **120%**, and then scroll to display page 2.
13. On page 2, in the sentence above the heading "Classics in Audio form," replace "Theo Jordan" with your first and last names. If your name is long enough to cause the sentence to flow to a second line, use only your first initial and last name instead.
14. sam Save the document.

Vassily plans to have the newsletter printed by a local printing company. Linda, his contact at the printing company, has asked him to email her the newsletter as a PDF.

Saving a Document as a PDF

A **PDF**, or **Portable Document Format file**, contains an image showing exactly how a document will look when printed. Saving a document as a PDF ensures it can be opened on any computer. This is especially useful when you need to email a document to people who might not have Word installed on their computers. All PDFs have a file extension of .pdf. By default, PDFs open in Adobe Acrobat Reader, a free program installed on most computers for reading PDFs, or in Adobe Acrobat, a PDF-editing program available for purchase from Adobe.

Tip

To save a document as a PDF and attach it to an email message in Outlook, click the File tab, click Share in the navigation pane, click Email, and then click Send as PDF.

To save the newsletter document as a PDF:

1. On the ribbon, click the **File** tab to open Backstage view.
2. In the navigation pane, click **Export** to display the Export screen with Create PDF/XPS Document selected.
3. Click the **Create PDF/XPS** button. The Publish as PDF or XPS dialog box opens.
4. If necessary, navigate to the location specified by your instructor for saving your files, and then verify that "NP_WD_4_Newsletter" appears in the File name box. Below the Save as type box, verify that the "Open file after publishing" check box is selected. The "Standard (publishing online and printing)" button might be selected by default. This generates a PDF suitable for printing. If you plan to distribute a PDF only via email or over the web, you should select the "Minimum size (publishing online)" button instead. See Figure 4–38.

Figure 4–38 **Publish as PDF or XPS dialog box**

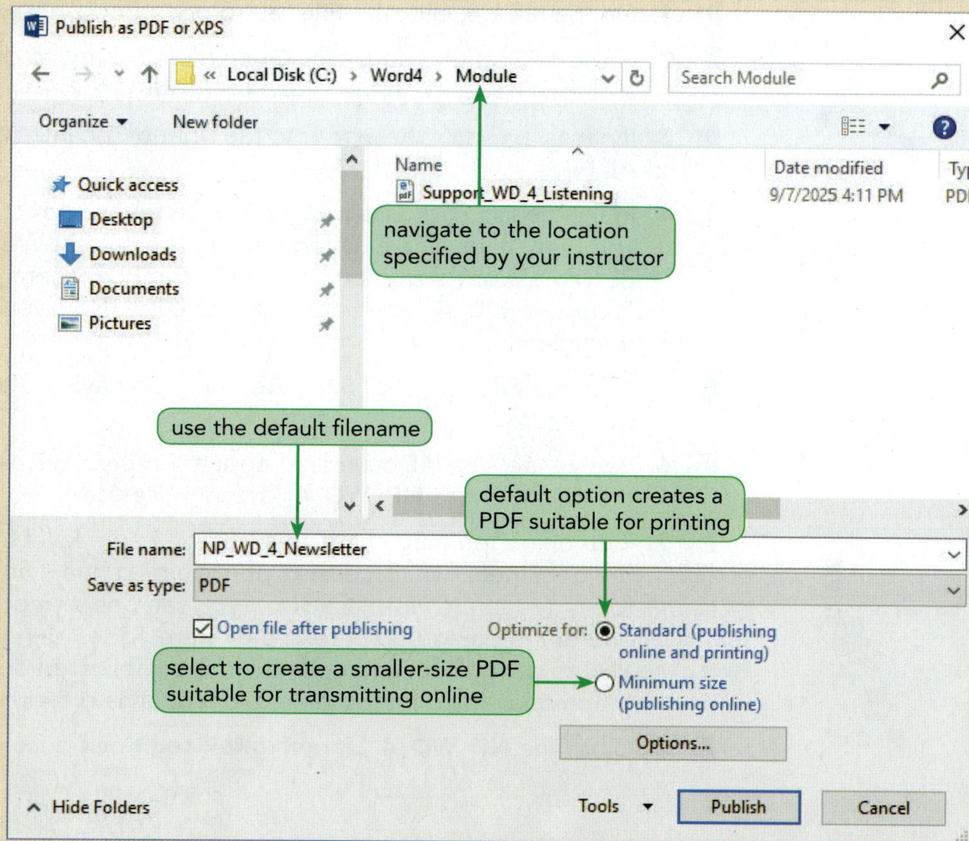

5. Click the **Publish** button. The Publish as PDF or XPS dialog box closes, and, after a pause, Adobe Acrobat Reader, Adobe Acrobat, or Microsoft Edge opens with the NP_WD_4_Newsletter.pdf file displayed.
6. Scroll down and review the PDF, and then close Adobe Acrobat Reader or Adobe Acrobat.
7. In Word, close the document, saving changes if necessary, but keep Word running.

In addition to saving a Word document as a PDF, you can convert a PDF to a Word document.

Converting a PDF to a Word Document

Tip

If the PDF's creator restricted the file's security using settings available in Adobe Acrobat, you will not be able to copy text from the PDF or convert it to a Word document.

You may sometimes need to use text from a PDF in your own Word documents. Before you can do this, of course, you need to make sure you have permission to do so. Assuming you do, you can open the PDF in Acrobat or Acrobat Reader, drag the pointer to select the text you want to copy, press CTRL+C, return to your Word document, and then press CTRL+V to paste the text into your document. If you need to reuse or edit the entire contents of a PDF, it's easier to convert it to a Word document. This is a very useful option with PDFs that consist mostly of text. For more complicated PDFs, such as the NP_WD_4_Newsletter.pdf file you just created, the results are less predictable.

Vassily has a PDF containing some text about the Listening to Literature app. He asks you to open it in Word and convert it back to a Word document file.

To open the PDF in Word:

1. On the ribbon, click the **File** tab to open Backstage view.
2. In the navigation pane, click **Open**, if necessary, to display the Open screen, and then navigate to the **Word4 > Module** folder.
3. If necessary, click the **arrow** to the right of the File name box, and then click **All Files**.
4. In the file list, click **Support_WD_4_Listening.pdf**, click the **Open** button, and then, if you see a dialog box explaining that Word is about to convert a PDF to a Word document, click **OK**. The PDF opens in Word, with the name "Support_WD_4_Listening" in the title bar. Now you can save it as a Word document.
5. Click the **File** tab, click **Save As**, and then navigate to the location specified by your instructor.
6. Verify that "Word Document" appears in the Save as type box, and then save the document as **NP_WD_4_ListeningRevised**.
7. Turn on nonprinting characters, set the Zoom level to **120%**, and then review the document, which consists of a WordArt headline and a paragraph of text formatted in the Normal style. If you see one or more extra spaces at the end of the paragraph of text, they were added during the conversion from a PDF to a Word document. In a more complicated document, you might see graphics overlaid on top of text, or columns broken across multiple pages.
8. Close the **NP_WD_4_ListeningRevised.docx** document.

Review

Session 4.2 Quick Check

1. What term refers to the interior color of the characters in WordArt?
2. Name six types of bitmap files.
3. What kind of laws govern the use of media, including text, line drawings, photographs, and video?
4. When cropping a picture, how can you maintain a specific ratio of width to height?
5. What should you do if you need to ensure that your document can be read on any computer?

Practice

Review Assignments

Data Files needed for the Review Assignments: NP_WD_4-2.docx , Support_WD_4_Island.png, Support_WD_4_Retirement.png, Support_WD_4_Schedule.docx, Support_WD_4_Volunteers.docx,

Vassily is working on another newsletter. This one is for employees of the Indianapolis Public Library system. He has already written the document's text, and he asks you to transform it into a professional-looking newsletter. He also asks you to save the newsletter as a PDF so he can email it to the printer and to edit some text currently available only as a PDF. The finished newsletter should match the one shown in Figure 4–39.

Figure 4–39 Completed employee newsletter

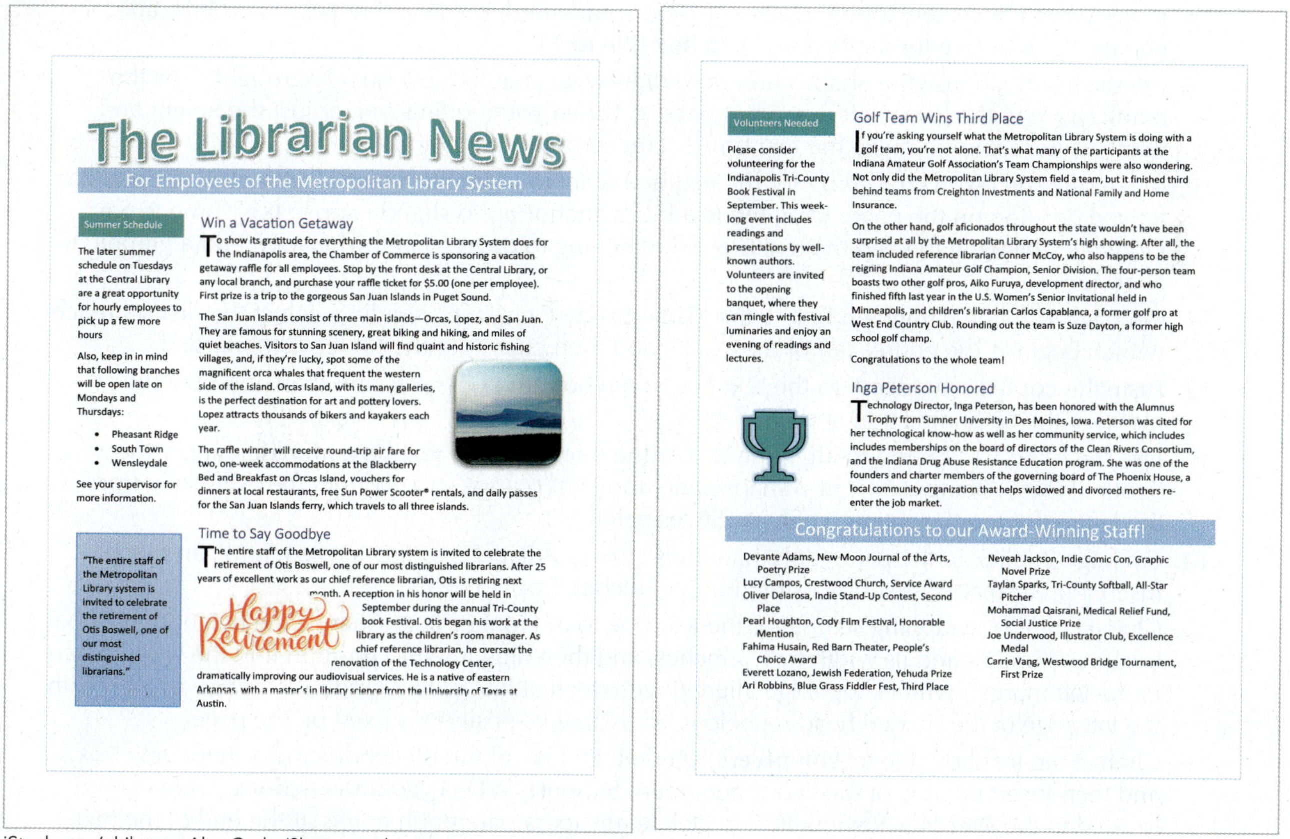

The Librarian News

For Employees of the Metropolitan Library System

Summer Schedule

The later summer schedule on Tuesdays at the Central Library are a great opportunity for hourly employees to pick up a few more hours

Also, keep in in mind that following branches will be open late on Mondays and Thursdays:

- Pheasant Ridge
- South Town
- Wensleydale

See your supervisor for more information.

Win a Vacation Getaway

To show its gratitude for everything the Metropolitan Library System does for the Indianapolis area, the Chamber of Commerce is sponsoring a vacation getaway raffle for all employees. Stop by the front desk at the Central Library, or any local branch, and purchase your raffle ticket for $5.00 (one per employee). First prize is a trip to the gorgeous San Juan Islands in Puget Sound.

The San Juan Islands consist of three main islands—Orcas, Lopez, and San Juan. They are famous for stunning scenery, great biking and hiking, and miles of quiet beaches. Visitors to San Juan Island will find quaint and historic fishing villages, and, if they're lucky, spot some of the magnificent orca whales that frequent the western side of the island. Orcas Island, with its many galleries, is the perfect destination for art and pottery lovers. Lopez attracts thousands of bikers and kayakers each year.

The raffle winner will receive round-trip air fare for two, one-week accommodations at the Blackberry Bed and Breakfast on Orcas Island, vouchers for dinners at local restaurants, free Sun Power Scooter® rentals, and daily passes for the San Juan Islands ferry, which travels to all three islands.

"The entire staff of the Metropolitan Library system is invited to celebrate the retirement of Otis Boswell, one of our most distinguished librarians."

Time to Say Goodbye

The entire staff of the Metropolitan Library system is invited to celebrate the retirement of Otis Boswell, one of our most distinguished librarians. After 25 years of excellent work as our chief reference librarian, Otis is retiring next month. A reception in his honor will be held in September during the annual Tri-County book Festival. Otis began his work at the library as the children's room manager. As chief reference librarian, he oversaw the renovation of the Technology Center, dramatically improving our audiovisual services. He is a native of eastern Arkansas, with a master's in library science from the University of Texas at Austin.

Happy Retirement

Volunteers Needed

Please consider volunteering for the Indianapolis Tri-County Book Festival in September. This week-long event includes readings and presentations by well-known authors. Volunteers are invited to the opening banquet, where they can mingle with festival luminaries and enjoy an evening of readings and lectures.

Golf Team Wins Third Place

If you're asking yourself what the Metropolitan Library System is doing with a golf team, you're not alone. That's what many of the participants at the Indiana Amateur Golf Association's Team Championships were also wondering. Not only did the Metropolitan Library System field a team, but it finished third behind teams from Creighton Investments and National Family and Home Insurance.

On the other hand, golf aficionados throughout the state wouldn't have been surprised at all by the Metropolitan Library System's high showing. After all, the team included reference librarian Conner McCoy, who also happens to be the reigning Indiana Amateur Golf Champion, Senior Division. The four-person team boasts two other golf pros, Aiko Furuya, development director, and who finished fifth last year in the U.S. Women's Senior Invitational held in Minneapolis, and children's librarian Carlos Capablanca, a former golf pro at West End Country Club. Rounding out the team is Suze Dayton, a former high school golf champ.

Congratulations to the whole team!

Inga Peterson Honored

Technology Director, Inga Peterson, has been honored with the Alumnus Trophy from Sumner University in Des Moines, Iowa. Peterson was cited for her technological know-how as well as her community service, which includes includes memberships on the board of directors of the Clean Rivers Consortium, and the Indiana Drug Abuse Resistance Education program. She was one of the founders and charter members of the governing board of The Phoenix House, a local community organization that helps widowed and divorced mothers re-enter the job market.

Congratulations to our Award-Winning Staff!

Devante Adams, New Moon Journal of the Arts, Poetry Prize
Lucy Campos, Crestwood Church, Service Award
Oliver Delarosa, Indie Stand-Up Contest, Second Place
Pearl Houghton, Cody Film Festival, Honorable Mention
Fahima Husain, Red Barn Theater, People's Choice Award
Everett Lozano, Jewish Federation, Yehuda Prize
Ari Robbins, Blue Grass Fiddler Fest, Third Place
Neveah Jackson, Indie Comic Con, Graphic Novel Prize
Taylan Sparks, Tri-County Softball, All-Star Pitcher
Mohammad Qaisrani, Medical Relief Fund, Social Justice Prize
Joe Underwood, Illustrator Club, Excellence Medal
Carrie Vang, Westwood Bridge Tournament, First Prize

iStock.com/philotera; Alex Gorka/Shutterstock.com

Complete the following steps:

1. Open the file **NP_WD_4-2.docx** from the Word4 > Review folder included with your Data Files, and then save the document as **NP_WD_4_Employees** in the location specified by your instructor.
2. Insert continuous section breaks in the following locations:
   a. On page 1, at the beginning of the "Win a Vacation Getaway" heading, to the left of the "W" in "Win"
   b. On page 2, at the beginning of the shaded heading "Congratulations to our Award-Winning Staff!" to the left of the "C" in "Congratulations"
   c. On page 2, at the beginning of the first name, to the left of the "D" in "Devante"
3. In sections 1 and 3, change the left and right margins to .75 inches. In section 2, change the left margin to 2.5 inches.

4. Format section 4 in two columns of equal width, and then format the entire list of names and awards with a 0.2-inch hanging indent.
5. Search for the term **Sun Power Scooter** in the newsletter, and then add the ® symbol to the right of the final "r."
6. On page 1, click anywhere in the "Win a Vacation Getaway" heading, and then insert a preformatted text box using the Ion Sidebar 1 option.
7. Change the text wrapping setting for the text box to In Front of Text. Change the height of the text box to 4.3 inches and its width to 1.5 inches, and then drag it to position it in the white space in the left margin, with its top edge aligned with the "Win a Vacation Getaway" heading. The left border of the text box should align with the left edge of the shaded paragraph above. Verify that the text box's position is fixed on the page.
8. Change the text box title to **Summer Schedule**. Delete all the placeholder text in the text box, and then insert the text of the Word document **Support_WD_4_Schedule.docx**, which is located in the Word4 > Review folder. Delete any extra paragraph marks at the end of the text, and change the font size for the text and text box title to 11.
9. On the Insert tab, use the Shapes button to draw a rectangular text box that roughly fills the blank space in the lower-left margin of page 1. When you are finished, adjust the height and width as necessary to make the text box 2.5 inches tall and 1.5 inches wide.
10. Make sure the text wrap setting for the text box is set to In Front of Text and that the text box has a fixed position on the page. Drag the text box's anchor up to slightly above the "Time to Say Goodbye" heading to keep the text box from moving to page 2 later, when you add a graphic to page 1.
11. On page 1, in the paragraph below the "Time to Say Goodbye" heading, select the first sentence (which begins "The entire staff of the . . . "), and then copy it to the Office Clipboard.
12. Paste the copied sentence into the text box at the bottom of page 1, and then add quotation marks at the beginning and end.
13. Use the Align Text button to align the text in the middle of the text box, and then apply the Subtle Effect - Orange, Accent 2 shape style (the light orange style option, the third style from the left in the fourth row of the Shape Styles gallery).
14. On page 2, click in the paragraph that reads "Congratulations to the whole team!" and then insert a preformatted text box using the Ion Sidebar 1 option.
15. Change the text wrapping setting for the text box to In Front of Text. Change the height of the text box to 3.8 inches and its width to 1.5 inches, and then drag it left to position it in the white space in the left margin, with its top edge aligned with the first line of text, and its left edge aligned with the left edge of the shaded heading below. Verify that its position is fixed on the page.
16. Change the text box title to **Volunteers Needed**. Delete all the placeholder text in the text box, and then insert the text of the Word document **Support_WD_4_Volunteers.docx**, which is located in the Word4 > Review folder. Delete any extra paragraph marks at the end of the text, and change the font size for the text and text box title to 11.
17. In the first line of text after each of the four headings formatted with blue font, insert a drop cap that drops two lines.
18. On page 1, select the entire first paragraph, "The Librarian News," including the paragraph mark. Clear the formatting from the paragraph, and then format the text as WordArt, using the Fill: Blue, Accent color 5; Outline: White, Background color 1; Hard Shadow: Blue, Accent color 5 style (the middle option in the bottom row).
19. Change the WordArt text box width to 7 inches, and retain the default height.
20. Retain the Square text wrapping, and make sure the WordArt has a fixed position on the page. Drag the WordArt text box up above the shaded paragraph if necessary, so it appears at the top of the page.
21. Apply the Chevron: Up transform text effect, and then add a shadow using the Offset: Bottom Right style (the first option in the top row of the Outer section).
22. Click at the end of the paragraph below the "Win a Vacation Getaway" heading, and then insert the picture file named **Support_WD_4_Island.png** from the Word4 > Review folder. If necessary, edit the alt text so it describes the picture.

23. Practice cropping the photo to a shape, and then try cropping it by dragging the cropping handles. Use the Reset Picture button as necessary to restore the picture to its original appearance. When you are finished, crop the picture using a square aspect ratio, and then change its height and width to 1.5 inches. Use the Position button to place the picture in the middle of the right side of page 1 with square text wrapping, and then add the Bevel Rectangle picture style.
24. On page 1, click at the end of the "Time to Say Goodbye" heading, and then insert the picture **Support_WD_4_Retirement.png** from the Word4 > Review folder.
25. Change the alt text to read **The words "Happy Retirement" written in calligraphy** and then rotate the picture so the words are positioned horizontally.
26. Change the photo's height to 2.5 inches, and retain the default width. Apply Tight text wrapping, position it in the paragraph below the "Time to Say Goodbye" heading, with two lines of text wrapped above it, fix its position on the page, and then remove the picture's background. Readjust the picture so the paragraph text wraps around it as shown in Figure 4–39. Take care not to let the picture overlap any text.
27. On page 2, click at the end of the paragraph below the "Inga Peterson Honored" heading, and then insert the trophy icon from the Celebration category. The alt text is correct, so you don't need to change it.
28. Apply Tight text wrapping, fix its position on the page, change the icon's height and width to 1.2 inches, then drag the icon to center it in the white space below the text box.
29. Apply the Colored Fill – Accent 5, Dark 1 Outline graphics style (third row, second from the right in the Graphics style gallery).
30. Add the Glow: 5 point; Orange, Accent color 2 graphics effect (top row, second from the left in the Glow Variations gallery).
31. Balance the columns at the bottom of page 2.
32. Change the theme colors to Blue Warm.
33. Insert a simple box outline of the default style and width for the entire document. For the border color, use Blue, Accent 2, Lighter 60% (third row, sixth from the left in the Theme Colors palette). Make any additional adjustments necessary to ensure that your newsletter matches the one shown in Figure 4–39. You will probably need to adjust the position of the text boxes on page 1 to ensure that their left edges align with the left edge of the blue-shaded heading above. Likewise, on page 2, you might need to adjust the position of the text box to ensure that its left edge aligns with the left edge of the blue-shaded heading below. Also, on page 1, position the bottom text box so its bottom border aligns with the last line of text on the page.
34. In the second to last line on page 2, replace "Carrie Vang" with your first and last names.
35. Save the document, and then save it again as a PDF named **NP_WD_4_Employees** in the location specified by your instructor. Wait for the PDF to open, review it, and then close the program in which it opened. Close the **NP_WD_4_Employees.docx** document, but leave Word open.
36. In Word, open the **NP_WD_4_Employees.pdf** file, save it as a Word document named **NP_WD_4_EmployeesRevised**, review its appearance, note the problems with the formatting that you would have to correct if you actually wanted to use this new DOCX file, and also note that alt text is no longer associated with the three images. Close the document.

Apply

Case Problem 1

Data Files needed for this Case Problem: NP_WD_4-3.docx, Support_WD_4_Bins.docx, Support_WD_4_Earth.png, Support_WD_4_Sorting.png

Solana Homes Malika Foster is the sales manager for Solana Homes, a gated community in suburban Chicago. She wants to emphasize the community's commitment to environmentally friendly practices, such as recycling, so she has written a flyer to include in the packet of information she gives each potential home buyer. Now she needs your help to finish it. The finished flyer should match the one shown in Figure 4–40.

Figure 4–40 **Completed recycling flyer**

Solana Homes: Creating a Sustainable Community

Recycle, Reuse, Renew

Recycling Bins

Each household is entitled to one recycling bin for curbside pickup. You can recycle an unlimited amount of materials.

Solana Builds Recycling Pavilion

We're happy to announce that the Solana Homes community will include a recycling pavilion offering state-of-the art collection facilities, with bi-weekly pickups. The pavilion is designed to make recycling easy in all kinds of weather. The Solana architects were motivated by numerous studies demonstrating that community support and accessible facilities greatly increase the number of families committed to recycling.

Recycling bins will also be installed throughout the grounds, and residents can schedule curbside pickups at no extra cost. Solana Homes has contracted with Mason Waste Disposal and Recycling to handle trash and recycling pickups. Company owner Ella Fortman has been recognized numerous times as an innovator in co-mingling reuse and recycling.

Hazardous Waste Collection

Many household hazardous wastes can be recycled cleanly and effectively by recycling professionals. Aren't sure what's considered hazardous waste? The labels of most products will provide helpful clues. Look for the following words: caution, danger, toxic, pesticide, keep away from children, flammable, and warning. Acceptable materials include antifreeze, brake fluid, kerosene, oil-based paint, furniture polish, pesticides, herbicides, household batteries, pool chemicals, and fertilizers.

Many hazardous wastes can be recycled

Hazardous waste collection will be handled by the city Sanitation Department, which has a robust hazardous waste treatment program. Sanitation workers will retrieve the items from the curb next to your trash bins on your usual trash pickup day.

Winners of the Solana Green Award

Casey Ann Ramirez-Bosco
Michael Paul Berners
Becky Cade
Elina Compere
Jose Carmela
Layla Carrington
Bruce Butler
Roger Kent Erickson
Henry Douglas
Tomas Carrico
Clarita Carrico
Kelly Dowell
Seamus Dante Dolan
Clarissa Fey-Esperanza
Haiyan Jiang
Tory Jeschke
Jacques Lambeau
Tia Morello-Jimenez
Mario Ruffolo
Eileen Jasper-Schwartz
Helena Pentakota Smith
Sigrid Del Rio
Harriet Schaefer
Jonas Jones
Sandra Jane Carmel
Christina Chamberlain
Boris Andre Nesaule

Voin_Sveta/Shutterstock.com; lesia_g/Shutterstock.com

Complete the following steps:

1. Open the file **NP_WD_4-3.docx** located in the Word4 > Case1 folder included with your Data Files, and then save it as **NP_WD_4_Flyer** in the location specified by your instructor.
2. Change the document margins to Narrow, and then, where indicated in the document, insert continuous section breaks. Remember to delete each instance of the highlighted text "[Insert SECTION BREAK]" before you insert a section break.
3. In section 2, change the left margin to 3 inches, and then format section 4 in four columns.
4. Format the second paragraph in the document ("Recycle, Reuse, Renew") as WordArt, using the Gradient Fill: Dark Green, Accent color 5; Reflection style (second from the left in the middle row of the WordArt gallery). Change the text box height to 0.7 inches and the width to 7 inches. Change the text wrapping setting to Top and Bottom and fix its position on the page.

If necessary, drag the WordArt down below the first paragraph ("Solana Homes: Creating a Sustainable Community"). Don't be concerned if the WordArt overlaps and is positioned below the section break line.

5. Insert drop caps that drop two lines in the first paragraph after the "Solana Builds Recycling Pavilion" heading and in the first paragraph after the "Hazardous Waste Collection" heading.
6. Click in the fourth paragraph in the document (the one with the drop cap "W"), and then insert a preformatted text box using the Grid Sidebar option. Change the text wrapping setting for the text box to In Front of Text, and then change its height to 2.8 inches and its width to 2.3 inches.
7. Drag the text box to position it in the white space on the left side of the page, and then align its top border with the "Solana Builds Recycling Pavilion" heading.
8. Delete the title placeholder text in the text box, and type **Recycling Bins**. Delete the placeholder paragraphs, and insert the text of the Word document **Support_WD_4_Bins** from the Word4 > Case1 folder. Delete any extra blank paragraphs.
9. In the blank space below the text box, draw a rectangular text box. When you are finished, adjust the height and width to make the text box 1.3 inches tall and 2 inches wide. Apply the Moderate Effect – Turquoise, Accent 1 shape style (second from the left in the second row from the bottom in the Themes Styles section), and then position the text box as shown in Figure 4–40, leaving room for the graphic you will add later.
10. In the text box, type **Many hazardous wastes can be recycled.** Align the text in the middle of the text box, and then use the Center button on the Home tab to center the text between the text box's left and right borders.
11. At the end of the fifth paragraph (which begins "Recycling bins will also be installed . . . "), insert the picture **Support_WD_4_Earth.png** from the Word4 > Case1 folder.
12. Change the alt text to **Recycle logo** and crop the picture to an oval shape.
13. Apply Square text wrapping, fix its position on the page, and then change its height to 1 inch. Drag the picture to position it so the first line of the fifth paragraph wraps above it, as shown in Figure 4–40.
14. At the end of the first paragraph below the "Hazardous Waste Collection" heading, insert the picture **Support_WD_4_Sorting.png** from the Word4 > Case1 folder.
15. Change the alt text to **Recycling bins** and then change the picture's height to 1.3 inches.
16. Apply In Front of Text text wrapping, add the Center Shadow Rectangle picture style, and then position the picture in the left margin, centered between the two text boxes, with a fixed position on the page, as shown in Figure 4–40.
17. Balance the columns at the end of the flyer.
18. In the last line of the document, replace "Boris Andre Nesaule" with your first and last names. Take care not to delete the section break by mistake.
19. Make any adjustments necessary so that your newsletter matches the one shown in Figure 4–40, and then save the document.
20. Save the document as a PDF named **NP_WD_4_FlyerPDF** in the location specified by your instructor. Review the PDF, and then close the program in which it opened.
21. In Word, open the PDF named **NP_WD_4_FlyerPDF.pdf**, save it as **NP_WD_4_FlyerFromPDF**, review its contents, note the corrections you would have to make if you actually wanted to use this document, and also note that alt text is no longer associated with the two images. Close any open documents.

Create

Case Problem 2

There are no Data Files needed for this Case Problem.

Ocotillo Health Care You are a public relations specialist at Ocotillo Health Care in Tempe, Arizona. As part of your training, your supervisor asks you to review online examples of flyers encouraging healthy eating and then re-create the first page of a flyer on healthy eating as a Word document. Instead of writing the complete text of the flyer, you can use placeholder text. Complete the following steps:

1. Open a new, blank document, and then save it as **NP_WD_4_Healthy** in the location specified by your instructor.
2. Open your browser and search online for images of flyers by searching for the keywords **healthy eating flyer image**. Review at least a dozen images of flyers before picking a style that you want to re-create in a Word document. The style you choose should contain at least two pictures. Keep the image of the flyer visible in your browser so you can return to it for reference as you work.
3. In your Word document, create the first page of the flyer. Compose your own WordArt headlines and other headings, or replicate the headlines and headings in the sample flyer. To generate text that you can use to fill the space below the headings, type **=lorem()** and then press ENTER. Change the document theme, theme fonts, and theme colors as necessary to replicate the colors and fonts in the flyer you are trying to copy. Don't worry about the flyer's background color; white is fine.
4. Add at least two pictures, using pictures that you find online. Rotate or flip pictures, and remove their backgrounds as necessary to make them work in the flyer layout. Revise the image's alt text if necessary.
5. Add at least one 3D model to the flyer. Revise the model's alt text if necessary.
6. Make any other changes necessary so that the layout and style of your document match the flyer example that you found online.
7. Somewhere in the document, attach a comment that reads **I used the following webpage as a model for this flyer design:**, and then include the URL for the flyer image you used as a model. To copy a URL from a browser window, click the URL in the browser's Address bar, and then press CTRL+C.
8. Save the document, close it, and then close your browser.

Module 1

Getting Started with Excel

Tracking Miscellaneous Expenses for a Conference

Objectives

Session 1.1
- Open and close a workbook
- Navigate through a workbook and worksheet
- Select cells and ranges
- Plan and create a workbook
- Insert, rename, and move worksheets
- Enter text, dates, and numbers
- Undo and redo actions
- Resize columns and rows

Session 1.2
- Enter formulas and the SUM and COUNT functions
- Copy and paste formulas
- Move or copy cells and ranges
- Insert and delete rows, columns, and ranges
- Create patterned text with Flash Fill
- Add cell borders and change font size
- Change worksheet views
- Prepare a workbook for printing

Case | MedIT

Carmen Estrada is an event coordinator for MedIT, a company that develops information technology for hospitals and clinics. Carmen is planning the upcoming regional conference for MedIT customers and vendors in Boston, Massachusetts. An important aspect of event planning is reviewing budget data and supplying additional expense information for the conference. Carmen wants you to review the conference planning documents and then create a document that she can use to detail miscellaneous expenses for the conference event.

Starting Data Files

Excel1 →

Module
NP_EX_1-1.xlsx

Review
(none)

Case1
NP_EX_1-2.xlsx

Case2
NP_EX_1-3.xlsx

Session 1.1 Visual Overview:

The ribbon is organized into tabs. Each **tab** has a group of related commands for particular activities or tasks.

Buttons for related commands are organized on a tab in **groups**.

Excel stores a collection of sheets within a single file called a **workbook**. The name of the current workbook appears in the title bar.

The **ribbon** contains grouped command buttons that you click to interact with Excel and execute commands.

The **Name box** displays the cell reference of the active cell. In this case, the active cell is cell K16.

The area above the worksheet grid is the **formula bar** where you can enter or edit data in the active cell.

A group of cells in a rectangular block is called a **cell range** (or **range**). If the blocks are not connected, as shown here, it is a **nonadjacent range**.

The **row headings** are numbers in boxes along the left side of the workbook window that identify the worksheet rows.

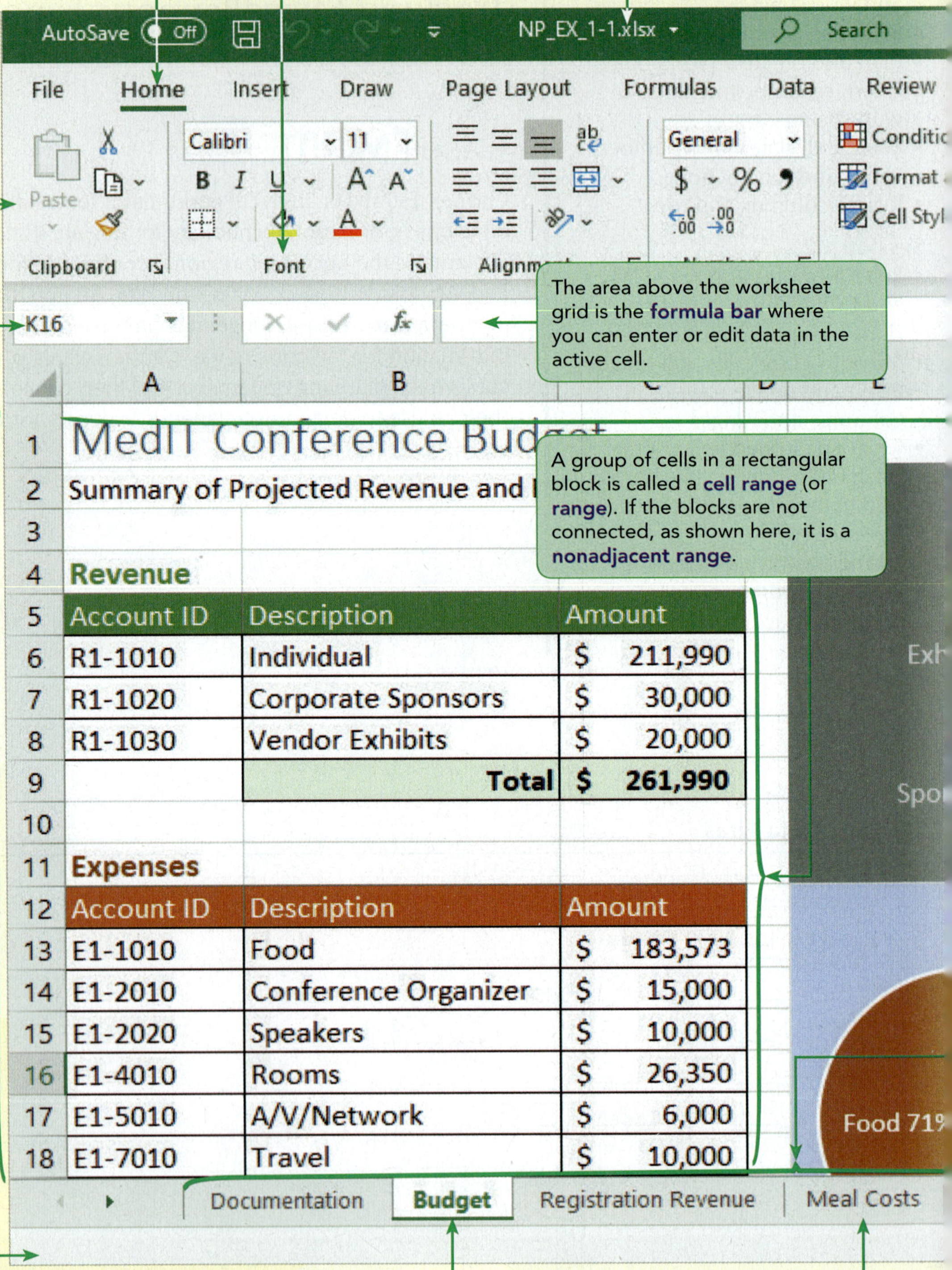

The **status bar** is a bar at the bottom of the Excel window that shows information about the current worksheet as well as view buttons and Zoom controls.

The sheet currently displayed in the workbook window is the **active sheet**. Its sheet tab is underlined, and the sheet name is green and bold.

Inactive sheets are not visible in the workbook window. Their sheet tabs are not underlined, and their sheet names are black.

The Excel Workbook

The Search box in the title bar is used to find a command or access the Office Help system.

The **Ribbon Display Options button** is used to hide or show the ribbon and its tabs and commands.

The **Minimize button** reduces a window so that only its program icon is visible on the taskbar.

The **Restore Down button** returns a window to its previous size. If the **Maximize button** appears, it expands the window to fill the entire screen.

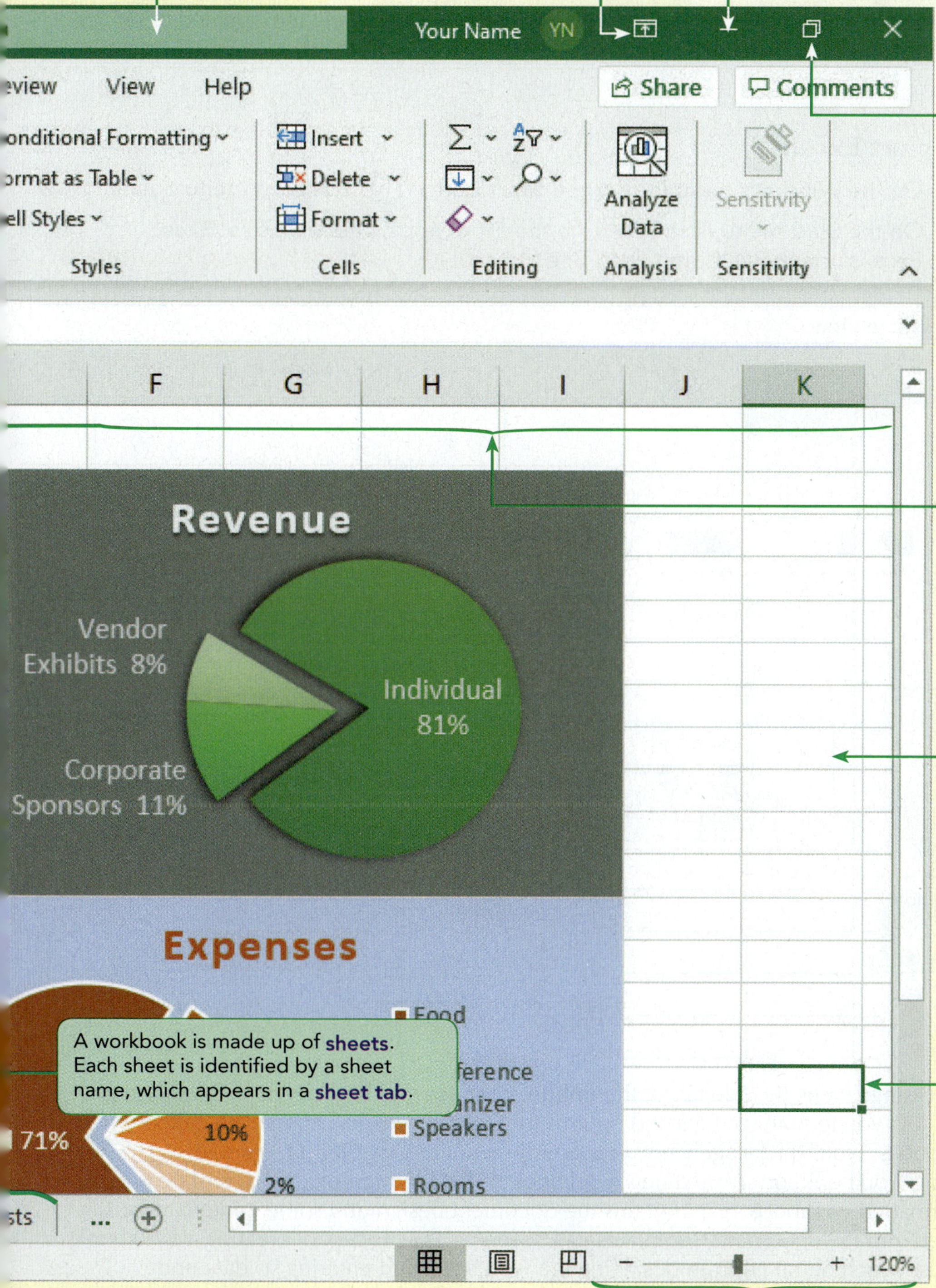

The **column headings** are letters in boxes along the top of the workbook window that identify the worksheet columns.

A single sheet in a workbook file that is laid out in a grid of rows and columns is called a **worksheet**. It appears in the **workbook window**, which displays part of the current sheet.

A workbook is made up of **sheets**. Each sheet is identified by a sheet name, which appears in a **sheet tab**.

Each intersection of a row and column forms a box or **cell** where you enter and store data. The currently selected cell in the active worksheet is the **active cell**.

controls increase or the magnification of the content. These modules sheets zoomed to 120%.

Introducing Excel and Spreadsheets

Microsoft Excel (or just **Excel**) is a program to record, analyze, and present data arranged in the form of a spreadsheet. A **spreadsheet** is a grouping of text and numbers in a rectangular grid or table. Spreadsheets are often used in business for budgeting, inventory management, and financial reporting because they unite text, numbers, and charts within one document. They can also be employed for personal use in planning a family budget, tracking expenses, or creating a list of personal items. The advantage of an electronic spreadsheet is that the content can be easily edited and updated to reflect changing financial conditions.

To start Excel:

1. On the Windows taskbar, click the **Start** button. The Start menu opens.
2. On the Start menu, scroll through the list of apps, and then click **Excel**. Excel starts in Backstage view. See Figure 1–1.

Figure 1–1 Backstage view

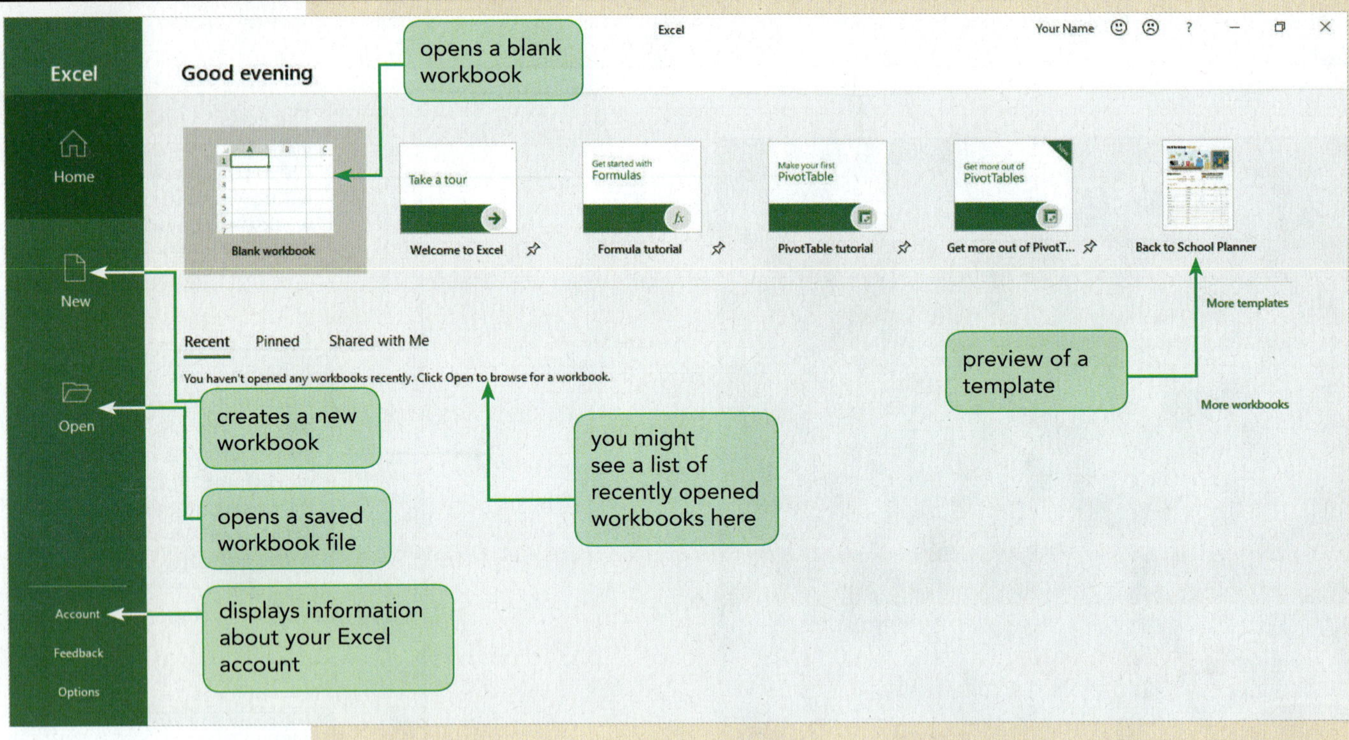

Backstage view, the File tab of the ribbon, contains various screens with commands that allow you to manage files and options for Excel. Excel documents are called workbooks. From Backstage view, you can open a blank workbook, open an existing workbook, or create a new workbook based on a template. A **template** is a preformatted workbook that contains the document design and some content already entered into the document. Templates can speed up the process of creating a workbook because much of the effort in designing the workbook and entering its data and formulas is already done for you.

Carmen created an Excel workbook containing information on the budget for the upcoming Boston conference. You'll open that workbook now.

To open the Conference workbook:

1. In the navigation bar in Backstage view, click **Open**. The Open screen is displayed and provides access to different locations where you might store files.
2. Click **Browse**. The Open dialog box appears.
3. Navigate to the **Excel1 > Module** folder included with your Data Files.

   Trouble? If you don't have the starting Data Files, you need to get them before you can proceed. Your instructor will either give you the Data Files or ask you to obtain them from a specified location (such as a network drive). If you have any questions about the Data Files, see your instructor or technical support person for assistance.
4. Click **NP_EX_1-1.xlsx** in the file list to select it.

   If your instructor wants you to submit your work as a SAM Project for automatic grading, you must download the Data File in Step 4 from the assignment launch page.
5. Click the **Open** button. The workbook opens in Excel.

   Trouble? If you don't see the full ribbon as shown in the Session 1.1 Visual Overview, the ribbon may be partially or fully hidden. To pin the ribbon so that the tabs and groups are fully displayed and remain visible, click the Ribbon Display Options button, and then click Show Tabs and Commands.
6. If the Excel window doesn't fill the screen, click the **Maximize** button in the upper-right corner of the title bar. See Figure 1–2.

Figure 1–2 Conference workbook

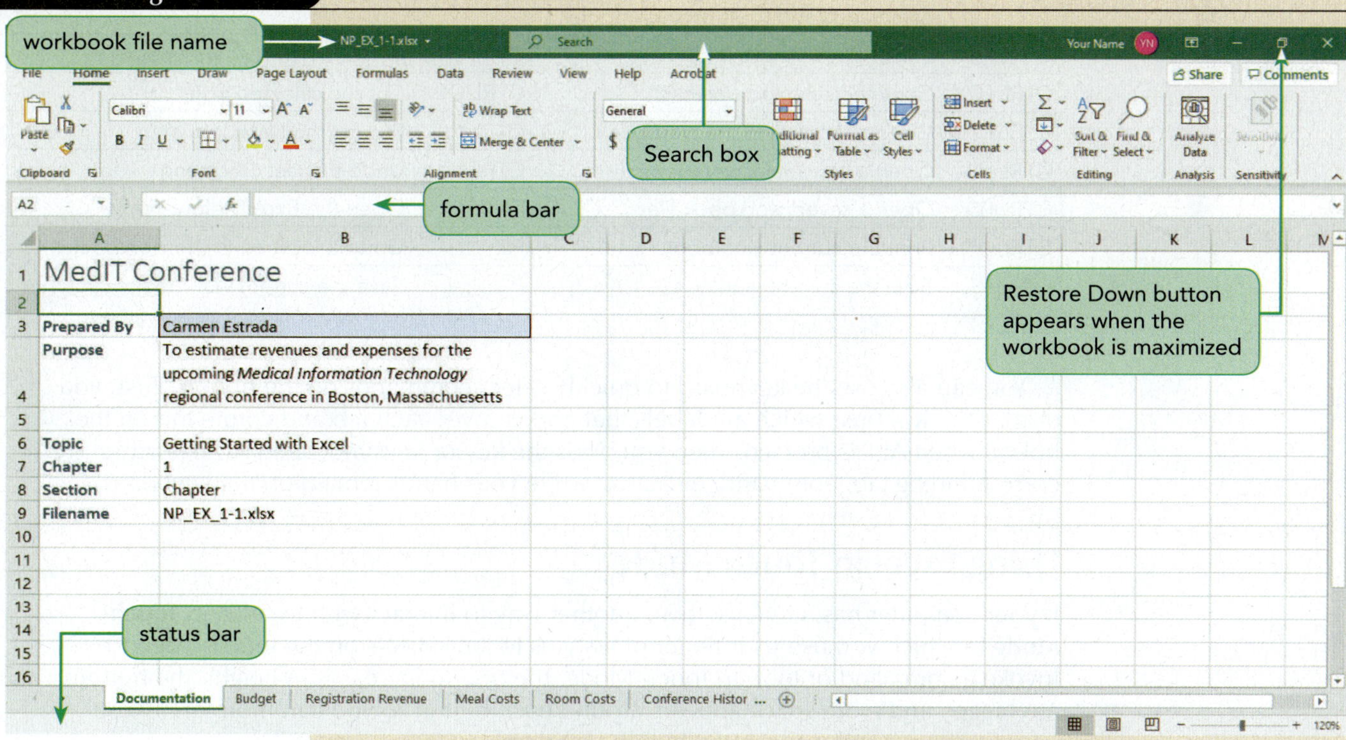

Before reviewing the contents of this workbook, you first should understand how to work with the Excel interface.

Getting Help

Excel is an extensive and powerful program supporting a wide variety of commands and tools. If you are unsure about the function of an Excel command or you want information about how to accomplish a task, you can use the Help system. To access Excel Help, you press F1. You can also enter a phrase or keyword into the Search box next to the file name in the title bar. From this box, you can get quick access to detailed information on all of the Excel features.

Using Keyboard Shortcuts to Work Faster

There are several ways of accessing an Excel command. Perhaps the most efficient method is entering the command through your device's keyboard through the use of keyboard shortcuts. A **keyboard shortcut** is a key or combination of keys that you press to access a feature or perform a command. Excel provides keyboard shortcuts for many commonly used commands. For example, CTRL+S is the keyboard shortcut for the Save command, which means you hold down CTRL while you press S to save the workbook. (Note that the plus sign is not pressed; it is used to indicate that an additional key is pressed.) When available, a keyboard shortcut is listed next to the command's name in a ScreenTip. A **ScreenTip** is a label that appears next to an object, providing information about that object or giving a link to associated help topics. Figure 1–3 lists some of the keyboard shortcuts commonly used in Excel.

Figure 1–3 Excel keyboard shortcuts

Press	To	Press	To
ALT	Display the Key Tips for the commands and tools on the ribbon	CTRL+V	Paste content that was cut or copied
CTRL+A	Select all objects in a range	CTRL+W	Close the current workbook
CTRL+C	Copy the selected object(s)	CTRL+X	Cut the selected object(s)
CTRL+G	Go to a location in the workbook	CTRL+Y	Repeat the last command
CTRL+N	Open a new blank workbook	CTRL+Z	Undo the last command
CTRL+O	Open a saved workbook file	F1	Open the Excel Help window
CTRL+P	Print the current workbook	F5	Go to a location in the workbook
CTRL+S	Save the current workbook	F12	Save the current workbook with a new name or to a new location

You can also use the keyboard to quickly select commands on the ribbon. First, you display the **KeyTips**, which are labels that appear over each tab and command on the ribbon when ALT is pressed. Then you press the key or keys indicated to access the corresponding tab, command, or button while your hands remain on the keyboard.

Using Excel in Touch Mode

If your computer has a touchscreen, another way to interact with Excel is in **Touch Mode** in which you use your finger or a stylus to tap objects on the touchscreen to invoke a command or tool. In Touch Mode, the ribbon increases in height, the buttons are bigger, and more space appears around each button so you can more easily use your finger or a stylus to tap the button you need.

The figures in these modules show the screen in **Mouse Mode**, in which you use a computer mouse to interact with Excel and invoke commands and tools. If you plan on doing some of your work on a touch device, you'll need to switch between Touch Mode and Mouse Mode. You should turn Touch Mode on only if you are working on a touch device.

To switch between Touch Mode and Mouse Mode:

1. On the Quick Access Toolbar, click the **Customize Quick Access Toolbar** button. A menu opens, listing buttons you can add to the Quick Access Toolbar as well as other options for customizing the toolbar.

   Trouble? If the Touch/Mouse Mode command on the menu has a checkmark next to it, press ESC to close the menu, and then skip Step 2.

2. From the Quick Access Toolbar menu, click **Touch/Mouse Mode**. The Quick Access Toolbar now contains the Touch/Mouse Mode button, which you can use to switch between Mouse Mode and Touch Mode.

3. On the Quick Access Toolbar, click the **Touch/Mouse Mode** button. A menu opens listing Mouse and Touch, and the icon next to Mouse is shaded to indicate that it is selected.

   Trouble? If the icon next to Touch is shaded, press ESC to close the menu and continue with Step 5.

4. Click **Touch**. The display switches to Touch Mode with more space between the commands and buttons on the ribbon. See Figure 1–4.

Figure 1–4 Excel displayed in Touch Mode

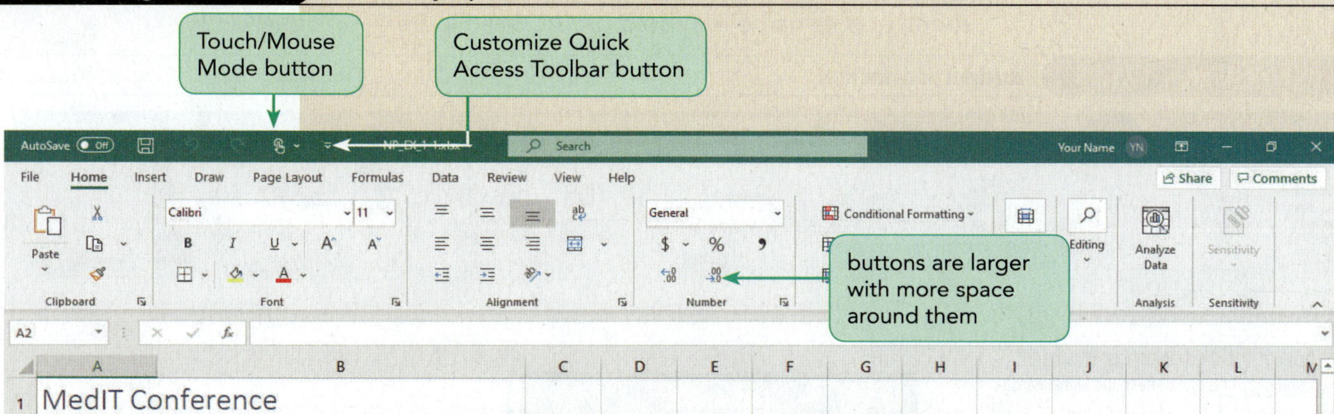

Next, you will switch back to Mouse Mode. If you are working with a touchscreen and want to use Touch Mode, skip Steps 5 and 6.

5. On the Quick Access Toolbar, click the **Touch/Mouse Mode** button, and then click **Mouse**. The ribbon returns to Mouse Mode, as shown earlier in Figure 1–2.

6. On the Quick Access Toolbar, click the **Customize Quick Access Toolbar** button, and then click **Touch/Mouse Mode** to deselect it. The Touch/Mouse Mode button is removed from the Quick Access Toolbar.

Now that you've seen how to interact with the Excel program, you ready to explore the workbook that Carmen has prepared.

Exploring a Workbook

The contents of a workbook are shown in the workbook window, which is below the ribbon. Workbooks are organized into separate pages called sheets. Excel supports two types of sheets: worksheets and chart sheets. A worksheet contains a grid of rows and columns into which you can enter text, numbers, dates, and formulas. Worksheets can also contain graphical elements such as charts, maps, and clip art. A **chart sheet** is a sheet that contains only a chart that is linked to data within the workbook. A chart sheet can also contain other graphical elements like clip art, but it doesn't contain a grid for entering data values.

Changing the Active Sheet

Worksheets and chart sheets are identified by the sheet tabs at the bottom of the workbook window. The workbook for the MedIT conference in Boston contains eight sheets labeled Documentation, Budget, Registration Revenue, Meal Costs, Room Costs, Conference History, Budget History, and Registration List. The sheet currently displayed in the workbook window is the active sheet, which in this case is the Documentation sheet. The sheet tab of the active sheet is highlighted, and the sheet tab name appears in bold.

If a workbook contains more sheet tabs than can be displayed in the workbook window, the list of tabs will end with an ellipsis (...), indicating the presence of additional sheets. You can use the sheet tab scrolling buttons, located to the left of the sheet tabs, to scroll through the tab list. Scrolling through the sheet tab list does not change the active sheet; it changes only which sheet tabs are visible within the workbook window.

You will view the contents of the Conference workbook by clicking the tabs for each sheet.

Tip

Some Excel documents have hidden sheets, which are still part of the workbook but do not appear within the workbook window.

To change the active sheet:

1. Click the **Budget** sheet tab. The Budget worksheet becomes the active sheet, and its name is in bold green. See Figure 1–5.

Figure 1–5 **Budget worksheet**

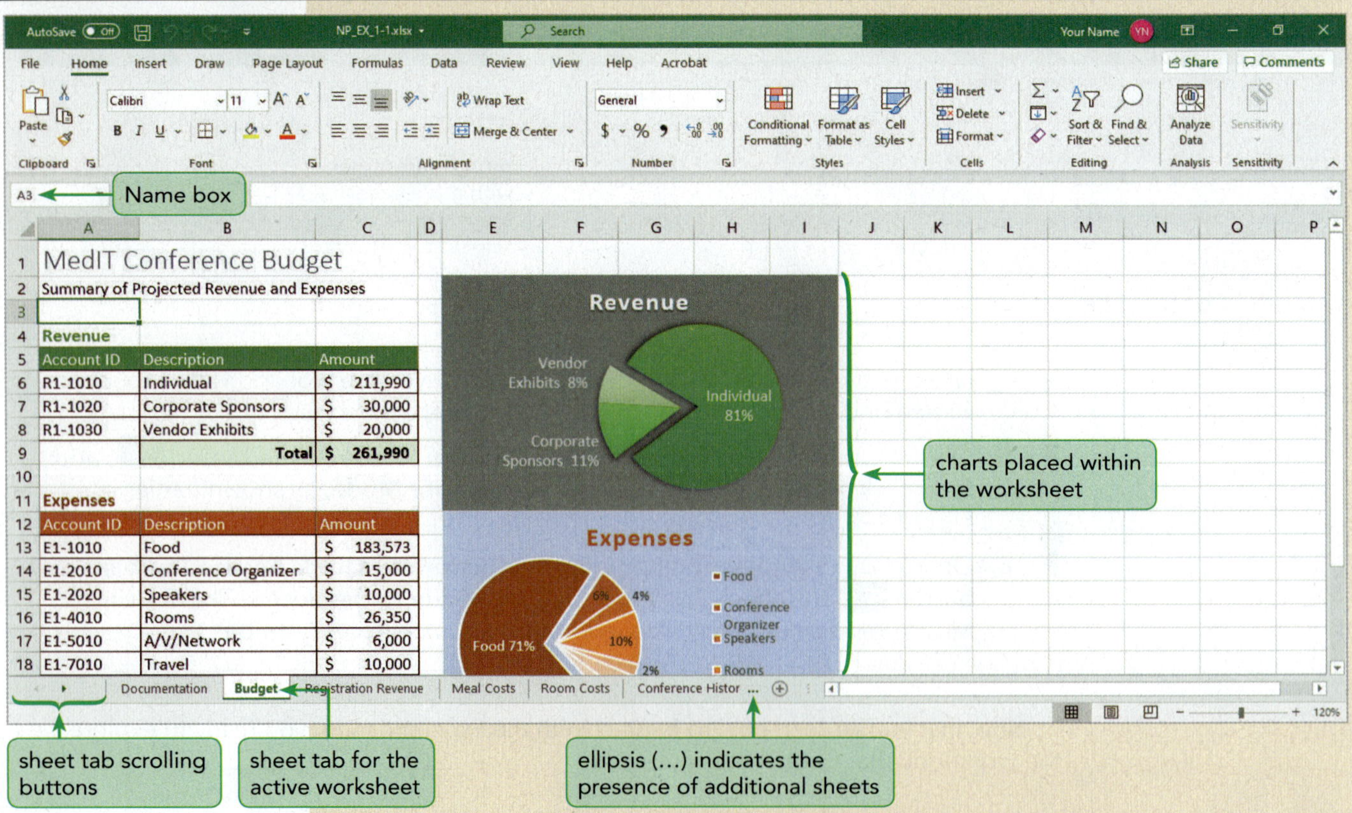

The Budget sheet contains estimates of the conference's revenue and expenses. The sheet also contains charts of the revenue and expense categories. From the charts, it's easily apparent that the major source of revenue for the conference comes from individual registrations and the major expense comes from feeding all the attendees over the three conference days.

2. Click the **Registration Revenue** sheet tab to make it the active sheet. The Registration Revenue tab provides a more detailed breakdown of the revenue estimates for the conference.

3. Click the **Meal Costs**, **Room Costs**, and **Conference History** sheet tabs to view each worksheet. Figure 1–6 shows the contents of the Conference History chart sheet. Because this is a chart sheet, it contains only the Excel chart and not the rows and columns of text and numbers you saw in the worksheets.

Figure 1–6 **Conference History chart sheet**

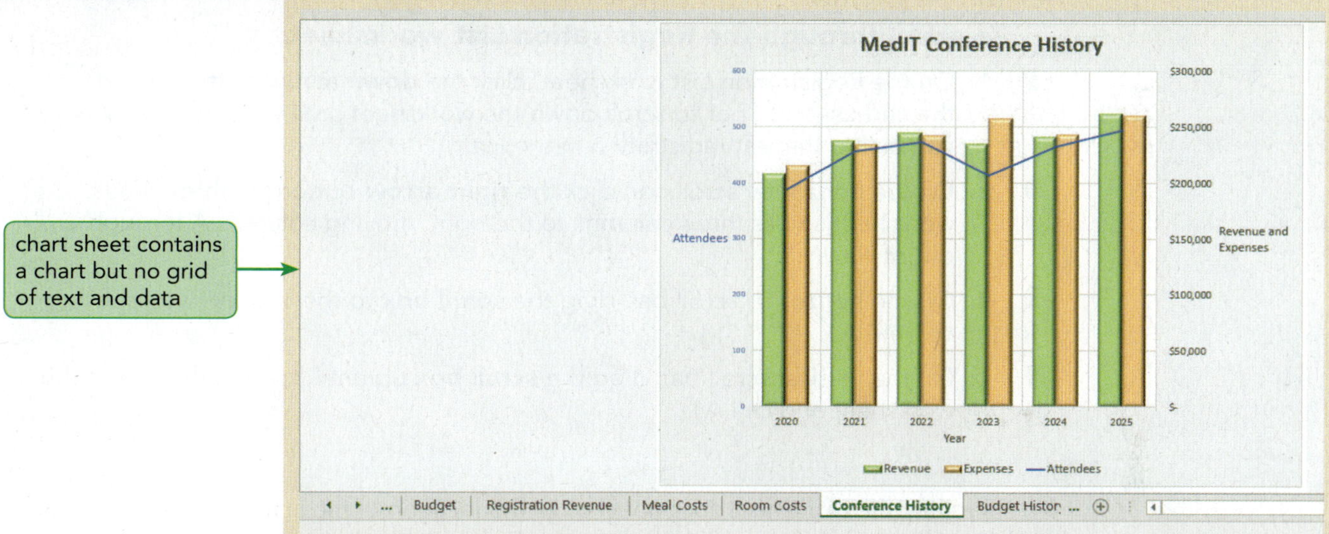

4. Click the **Budget History** and **Registration List** sheet tabs to view the remaining two worksheets in the workbook.

Trouble? If you can't see the sheet tabs for the last few sheets in the workbook, click the sheet tab scrolling buttons to scroll through the tab list.

Now you know how to switch between the eight sheets in the workbook. Next, you will move around the individual worksheets so you can review their contents.

Navigating Within a Worksheet

A worksheet is organized into a grid of cells, which are formed by the intersection of rows and columns. Rows are identified by numbers, and columns are identified by letters. Row numbers range from 1 to 1,048,576. Column labels start with the letters A to Z. After Z, the next column headings are labeled AA, AB, AC, and so forth. The last possible column label is XFD, which means there are 16,384 columns available in a worksheet. The total number of possible cells in a single Excel worksheet is more than 17 billion, providing an extremely large worksheet for reports.

Each cell is identified by a **cell reference**, which indicates the column and row in which the cell is located. For example, as shown in Figure 1–5, the total expected revenue from the conference, $261,990, is displayed in cell C9. Cell C9 is the intersection of column C and row 9. The column letter always appears before the row number in any cell reference.

The cell that is currently selected in the worksheet is the active cell and has a thick green border. The corresponding column and row headings for the active cell are also highlighted. The cell reference of the active cell appears in the Name box, located just below the left side of the ribbon. The active cell in Figure 1–5 is cell A3.

To move different parts of the worksheet into view, you can use the horizontal and vertical scroll bars located at the bottom and right edges of the workbook window, respectively. A scroll bar has arrow buttons that you can click to shift the worksheet one column or row in that direction, and a scroll box that you can drag to shift the worksheet larger amounts in the direction you choose.

You will scroll the active worksheet so you can review the rest of the Registration List worksheet.

To scroll through the Registration List worksheet:

1. On the Registration List worksheet, click the **down arrow** button ▼ on the vertical scroll bar to scroll down the worksheet until you see row 496 containing the last registration in the list.
2. On the horizontal scroll bar, click the **right arrow** button ▶ three times. The worksheet scrolls three columns to the right, moving columns A through C out of view.
3. On the horizontal scroll bar, drag the **scroll box** to the left until you see column A.
4. On the vertical scroll bar, drag the **scroll box** up until you see the top of the worksheet and cell A1.

Scrolling the worksheet does not change the location of the active cell. Although the active cell might shift out of view, you can always see the location of the active cell in the Name box. To make a different cell active, you can either click a new cell or use keyboard shortcuts to move between cells, as described in Figure 1–7.

Figure 1–7 **Excel navigation keyboard shortcuts**

Press	To move the active cell
↑↓←→	Up, down, left, or right one cell
HOME	To column A of the current row
CTRL+HOME	To cell A1
CTRL+END	To the last cell in the worksheet that contains data
ENTER	Down one row or to the start of the next row of data
SHIFT+ENTER	Up one row
TAB	One column to the right
SHIFT+TAB	One column to the left
PGUP, PGDN	Up or down one screen
CTRL+PGUP, CTRL+PGDN	To the previous or next sheet in the workbook

Keyboard shortcuts are especially useful in worksheets in which the data is spread across many rows or columns. For example, some financial worksheets can have tens of thousands of rows of data. You will use these shortcuts to move through the Registration List worksheet.

To change the active cell using keyboard shortcuts:

1. On the Registration List worksheet, move the pointer over cell **C10** and then click the mouse button. The active cell moves from cell A2 to cell C10. A green border appears around cell C10 to indicate that it's now the active cell. The labels for row 10 and column C are highlighted, and the cell reference in the Name box is C10.
2. Press **RIGHT ARROW**. The active cell moves one column to the right to cell D10.
3. Press **PGDN**. The active cell moves down one full screen.
4. Press **PGUP**. The active cell moves up one full screen, returning to cell D10.
5. Press **CTRL+END**. The active cell is cell H496, the last cell containing data in the worksheet.
6. Press **CTRL+HOME**. The active cell returns to the first cell in the worksheet, cell A1.

To change the active cell to a specific cell location, you can use the Go To dialog box or the Name box. These methods are especially helpful when you are working in worksheets with many rows or columns. You'll try both these methods now.

To change the active cell using the Go To dialog box and Name box:

1. On the Home tab, in the Editing group, click the **Find & Select** button, and then click **Go To** on the menu that opens (or press **CTRL+G** or **F5**). The Go To dialog box opens.
2. Type **A100** in the Reference box. See Figure 1–8.

Figure 1–8 Go To dialog box

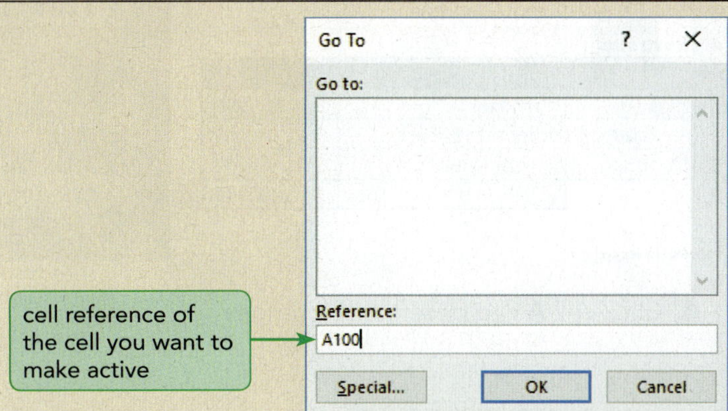

3. Click **OK**. Cell A100 becomes the active cell showing the registration information for Anjali Cunha of New Bedford, Massachusetts.
4. Click the Name box, type **A3**, and then press **ENTER**. Cell A3 becomes the active cell in the worksheet.

Selecting a Cell Range

Many tasks in Excel require you to work with a group of cells. A group of cells in a rectangular block is called a cell range (or simply a range). Each range is identified with a **range reference** that includes the cell reference of the upper-left cell of the rectangular block and the cell reference of the lower-right cell separated by a colon. For example, the range reference A1:G5 refers to all the cells in the rectangular block from cell A1 through cell G5.

As with individual cells, you can select cell ranges using your mouse, the keyboard, or commands. You will select a range in the Budget worksheet.

To select a cell range in the Budget worksheet:

1. Click the **Budget** sheet tab. The Budget worksheet becomes the active sheet.
2. Click cell **A5** to select it and, without releasing the mouse button, drag down and right to cell **C8**.
3. Release the mouse button. The range A5:C8 is selected. The selected cells are highlighted and surrounded by a green border. The first cell you selected in the range, cell A5, is the active cell in the worksheet. The Quick Analysis button appears next to the selected range, providing options for working with the range. See Figure 1–9.

Tip

You can also select a cell range by typing its range reference in the Name box and pressing ENTER.

Figure 1–9 Range A5:C8 selected

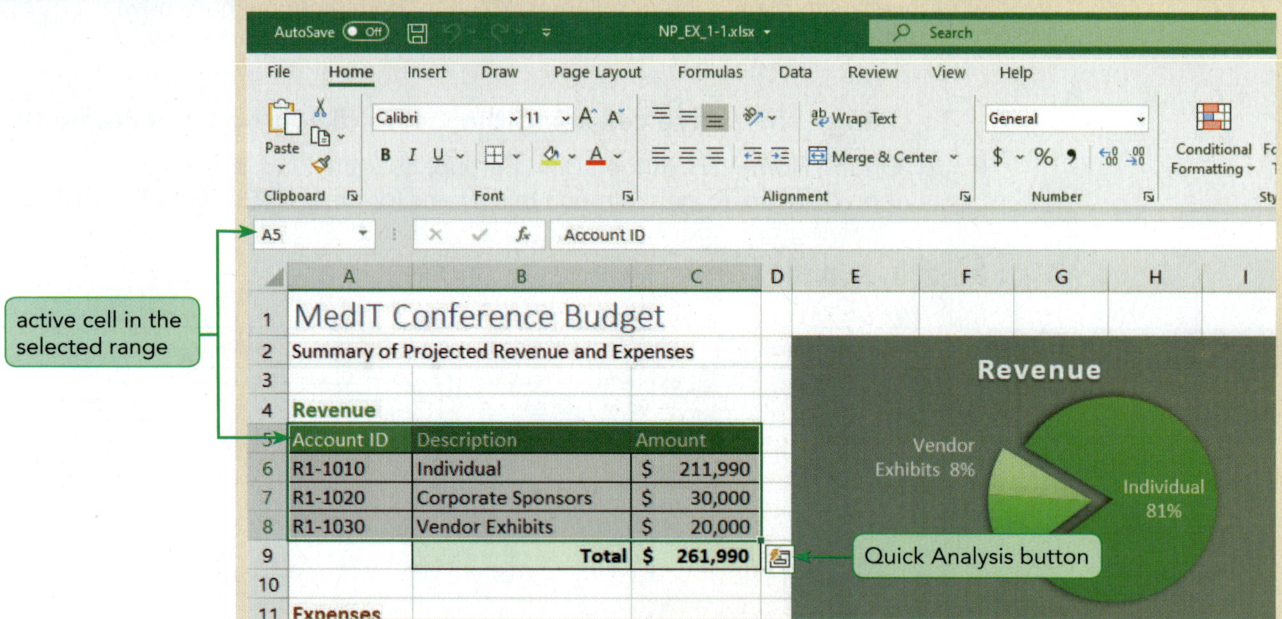

4. Click cell **A1** to deselect the range.

Another type of range is a nonadjacent range, which is a collection of separate rectangular ranges. The range reference for a nonadjacent range includes the range reference to each range separated by a comma. For example, the range reference A1:G5,A10:G15 includes two ranges—the first range is the rectangular block of cells from cell A1 to cell G5, and the second range is the rectangular block of cells from cell A10 to cell G15.

You will select a nonadjacent range in the Budget worksheet.

Tip

You can also select a range by opening the Go To dialog box and entering the cell reference in the Reference box.

To select a nonadjacent range in the Budget worksheet:

1. Click cell **A5**, hold down **SHIFT** as you click cell **C8**, and then release **SHIFT** to select the range A5:C8.
2. Scroll down the worksheet using the vertical scroll bar and then hold down **CTRL** as you drag to select the range **A12:C19** and then release **CTRL**. The two separate blocks of cells in the nonadjacent range A5:C8,A12:C19 are selected. See Figure 1–10.

Figure 1–10 Range A5:C8,A12:C19 selected

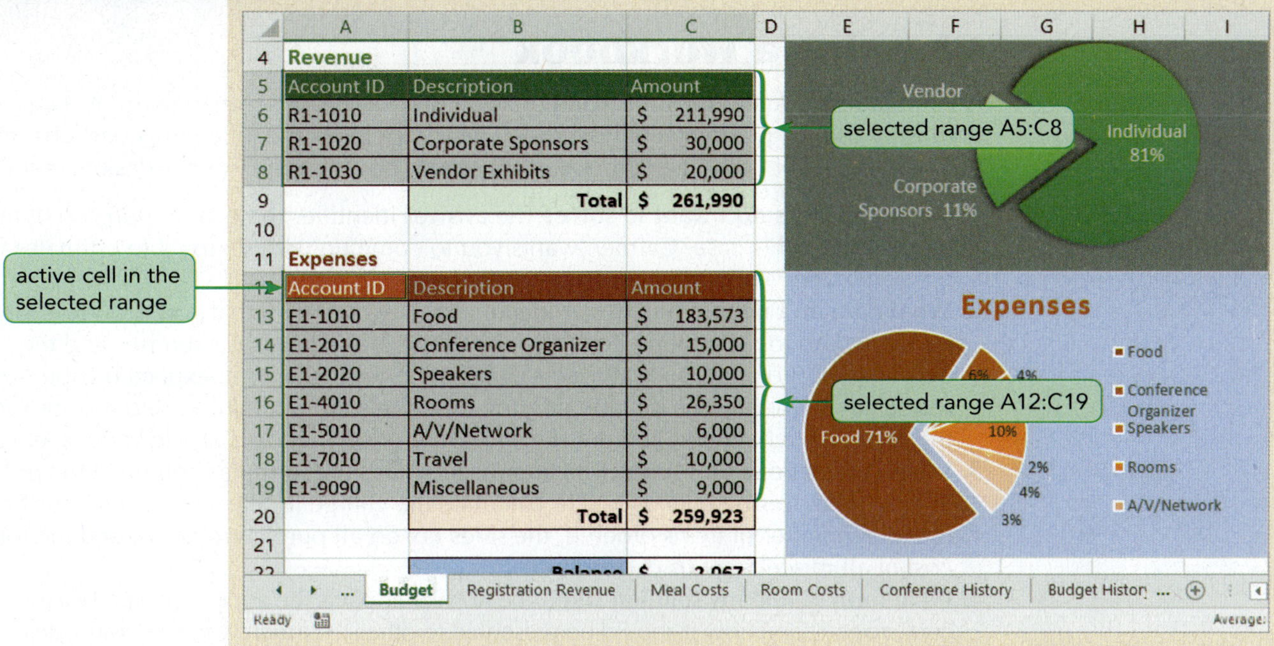

You can also use the Name box and Go To dialog box to select entire columns or rows. Just enter the column letters or row numbers as the reference separated by a colon. For example, the range reference E:E selects all cells in column E and the range reference 5:5 selects all cells in row 5.

Closing a Workbook

Once you are finished with a workbook, you can close it. When you close a workbook, a dialog box might appear, asking whether you want to save any changes you may have made to the workbook. If you have made changes that you want to keep, you should save the workbook. Because you have finished reviewing Carmen's workbook for MedIT, you will close the workbook without saving any changes you may have inadvertently made to its contents.

To close Carmen's workbook:

1. On the ribbon, click the **File** tab to display Backstage view, and then click **Close** in the navigation bar (or press **CTRL+W**).
2. If a dialog box opens, asking whether you want to save your changes to the workbook, click **Don't Save**. The workbook closes without saving any changes. Excel remains opens, ready for you to create or open another workbook.

Now that you've reviewed Carmen's workbook estimating the revenues and expenses for the upcoming conference in Boston, you are ready to create a new workbook. Carmen wants you to create a workbook in which you will estimate the miscellaneous expenses from the conference.

Planning a Workbook

A good practice is to plan your workbooks before you begin creating them. You can do this by using a planning analysis sheet, which includes the following questions that help you think about the workbook's purpose and how to achieve your desired results:

1. **What problems do I want to solve?** The answer identifies the goal or purpose of the workbook. In this case, Carmen wants you to come up with reasonable estimates for the conference's miscellaneous expenses.
2. **What data do I need?** The answer identifies the type of data that you need to collect for the workbook. Carmen needs a list of all the miscellaneous expenses and the estimated cost of each so that MedIT will not be surprised by unexpected expenses. Miscellaneous expenses include printing brochures and schedules, decorations for the conference banquet, and gifts for the conference attendees and keynote speakers.
3. **What calculations do I need?** The answer identifies the formulas you need to apply to your data. Carmen needs you to calculate the charge for each miscellaneous item, the total number of items ordered, the sales tax on all purchased items, and the total cost of all miscellaneous expenditures.
4. **What form should my solution take?** The answer impacts the appearance of the workbook content and how it should be presented to others. Carmen wants the estimates stored in a single worksheet that is easy to read and prints clearly.

You will create a workbook based on this plan. Carmen will then incorporate your projections for miscellaneous expenses into her full budget to ensure that the conference costs will not exceed the projected revenue.

Proskills

Written Communication: Creating Effective Workbooks

Workbooks convey information in written form. As with any type of writing, the final product creates an impression and provides an indicator of your interest, knowledge, and attention to detail. To create the best impression, all workbooks—especially those you intend to share with others such as coworkers and clients—should be well planned, well organized, and well written.

A well-designed workbook should clearly identify its overall goal and present information in an organized format. The data it includes—both the entered values and the calculated values—should be accurate. The process of developing an effective workbook includes the following steps:

1. Determine the workbook's purpose, content, and organization before you start.
2. Create a list of the sheets used in the workbook, noting each sheet's purpose.
3. Insert a documentation sheet that describes the workbook's purpose and organization. Include the name of the workbook's author, the date the workbook was created, and any additional information that will help others to track the workbook to its source.
4. Enter all the data in the workbook. Add labels to indicate what the values represent and, if possible, where they originated so others can view the source of your data.
5. Enter formulas for calculated items rather than entering the calculated values into the workbook. For more complicated calculations, provide documentation explaining them.
6. Test the workbook with a variety of values; edit the data and formulas to correct errors.
7. Save the workbook and create a backup copy when the project is completed. Print the workbook's contents if you need to provide a hard-copy version to others or for your files.
8. Maintain a history of your workbook as it goes through different versions, so that you and others can quickly see how the workbook has changed during revisions.

By including clearly written documentation, explanatory text, a logical organization, and accurate data and formulas, you will create effective workbooks that others can easily use.

Starting a New Workbook

You create new workbooks from the New screen in Backstage view. The New screen includes templates that you can use to preview different types of workbooks you can create with Excel. You will create a new workbook from the Blank workbook template, and then add all the content that Carmen wants for the miscellaneous expenses workbook.

To start a new, blank workbook for miscellaneous expenses:

1. **sam** On the ribbon, click the **File** tab to display Backstage view.
2. Click **New** in the navigation bar to display the New screen, which includes access to templates for a variety of workbooks.
3. Click **Blank workbook**. A blank workbook opens.

   In these modules, the workbook window is zoomed to 120% for better readability. If you want to zoom your workbook window to match the figures, complete Step 4. If you prefer to work in the default zoom of 100% or at another zoom level, read but do not complete Step 4; you might see more or less of the worksheet on your screen, but this will not affect your work in the modules.

Tip

You can also create a new blank workbook by pressing CTRL+N.

4. If you want your workbook window zoomed to 120% to match the figures, on the Zoom slider at the lower-right of the program window, click the **Zoom In** button [+] twice to increase the percentage to **120%**. The 120% magnification increases the size of each cell but reduces the number of worksheet cells visible in the workbook window. See Figure 1–11.

Figure 1–11 Blank workbook

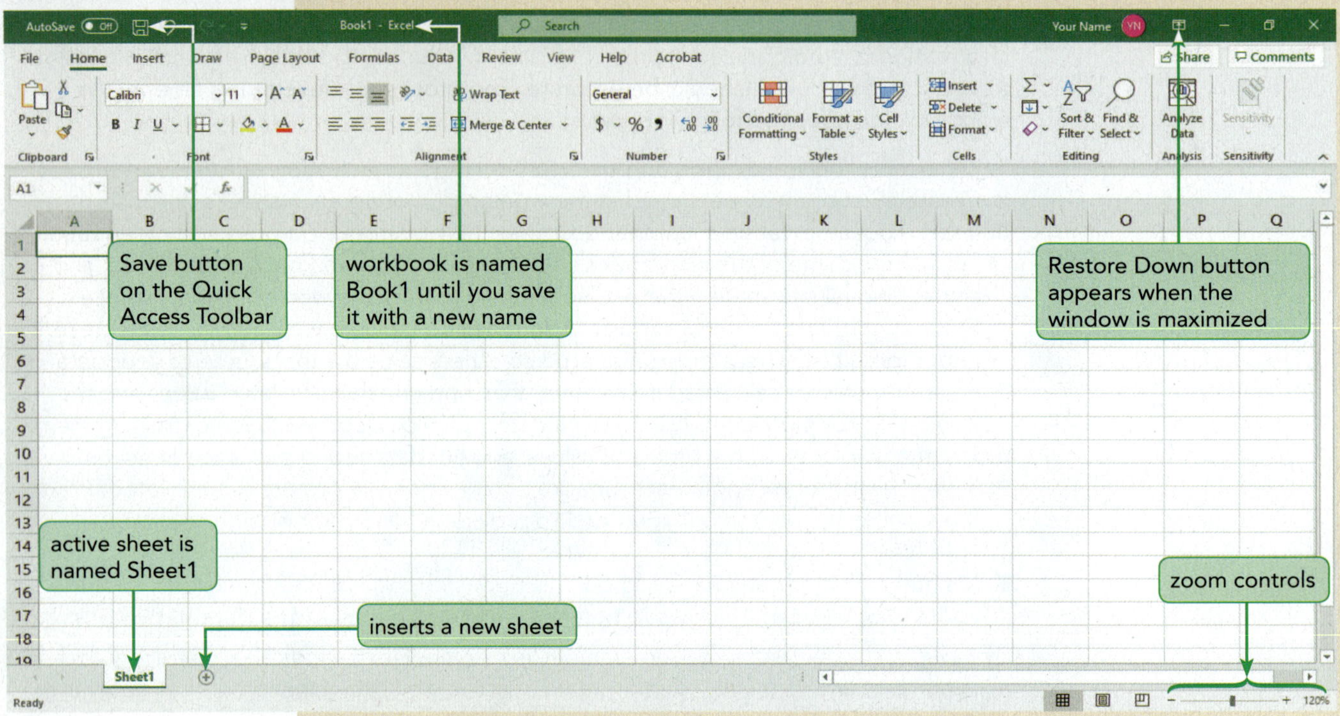

The name of the active workbook, Book1, appears in the title bar. If you open multiple blank workbooks, they are named Book1, Book2, Book3, and so forth until you save them with a more descriptive name.

Renaming and Inserting Worksheets

Blank workbooks open with a single blank worksheet named Sheet1. It's a good practice to give your sheets more descriptive names that indicate the purpose and content of the sheet. Sheet names cannot exceed 31 characters, but they can contain blank spaces and include uppercase and lowercase letters.

Because Sheet1 is not a very descriptive name, Carmen wants you to rename the worksheet as Miscellaneous Expenses.

To rename the Sheet1 worksheet:

1. Double-click the **Sheet1** tab to select the text of the sheet name.

2. Type **Miscellaneous Expenses** as the new name, and then press **ENTER**. The width of the sheet tab expands to fit the longer sheet name.

Many workbooks include multiple sheets so that data can be organized in logical groups. A common business practice is to include a documentation worksheet that contains a description of the workbook, the name of the person who prepared the workbook, and the date it was created.

Carmen wants you to create two new worksheets. You will rename one worksheet as Documentation and the other worksheet as Site Information. The Site Information worksheet will be used to store information about the convention center that is hosting the conference.

To insert and name the Documentation and Site Information worksheets:

1. To the right of the Miscellaneous Expenses sheet tab, click the **New sheet** button ⊕. A new sheet named Sheet2 is inserted to the right of the Miscellaneous Expenses sheet.
2. Double-click the **Sheet2** sheet tab, type **Documentation** as the new name, and then press **ENTER**. The worksheet is renamed.
3. To the right of the Documentation sheet, click the **New sheet** button ⊕ and then rename the inserted Sheet3 worksheet as **Site Information**.
4. If you want these worksheets zoomed to 120% to match the figures, go to each worksheet, and then on the Zoom slider, click the **Zoom In** button + twice to increase the percentage to **120%**.

Moving Worksheets

Another good practice is to place the most important sheets at the beginning of the workbook (the leftmost sheet tabs) and the least important sheets at the end (the rightmost sheet tabs). To change the placement of sheets in a workbook, you drag them by their sheet tabs to the new location.

Carmen wants you to move the Documentation worksheet to the front of the workbook, so that it appears before the Miscellaneous Expenses sheet.

To move the Documentation worksheet:

1. Point to the **Documentation** sheet tab. The sheet tab name changes to bold.
2. Press and hold the mouse button. The pointer changes to the drag pointer, and a small arrow appears in the upper-left corner of the tab.
3. Drag to the left until the small arrow appears in the upper-left corner of the Miscellaneous Expenses sheet tab, and then release the mouse button. The Documentation worksheet is now the first sheet in the workbook.

You can copy a worksheet by holding down CTRL as you drag and drop the sheet tab. Copying the worksheet duplicates all of the worksheet data and its structure.

Deleting Worksheets

In some workbooks, you will want to delete an existing sheet. The easiest way to delete a sheet is by using a **shortcut menu**, which is a list of commands related to an object that opens when you right-click the object. Carmen asks you to include site information on the Miscellaneous Expenses worksheet so all the information about the conference site and the miscellaneous expenses is on one sheet.

To delete a worksheet:

1. Right-click the **Site Information** sheet tab. A shortcut menu opens.
2. Click **Delete**. The Site Information worksheet is removed from the workbook.

When you delete a sheet, you also delete any text and data it contains. So be careful that you do not remove important and irretrievable information.

Saving a Workbook

Tip

To save a new workbook to OneDrive, click the Save button on the Quick Access Toolbar, enter a file name, and then select a OneDrive folder. The AutoSave button in the title bar can save the workbook as it is edited.

As you modify a workbook, you should save it regularly—every 10 minutes or so is a good practice. The first time you save a workbook, the Save As dialog box opens so you can name the file and choose where to save it. You can save the workbook on your computer or network or to your account on OneDrive.

You will save the miscellaneous expenses workbook that you just created.

To save the miscellaneous expenses workbook for the first time:

1. On the Quick Access Toolbar, click the **Save** button (or press **CTRL+S**). The Save this file dialog box opens.
2. Click **More options**. The Save As screen in Backstage view opens.
3. Click the **Browse** button. The Save As dialog box opens.
4. Navigate to the location specified by your instructor.
5. In the File name box, select **Book1** (the default name assigned to your workbook) if it is not already selected, and then type **NP_EX_1_Misc** as the new name.
6. Verify that **Excel Workbook** appears in the Save as type box.
7. Click **Save**. The workbook is saved, the dialog box closes, and the workbook window reappears with the new file name in the title bar.

As you modify the workbook, you will need to resave the file. Because you already saved the workbook with a file name, the next time you save, the Save command saves the changes you made to the workbook without opening the Save As dialog box.

Tip

You can save the workbook to your OneDrive account by clicking the file name in the title bar and then clicking Upload.

Sometimes you will want to save a current workbook under a new file name. This is useful when you want to modify a workbook without losing its content and structure or when you want to save a copy of the workbook to a new location. To save a workbook with a new name, click the File tab to return to Backstage view, click Save As on the navigation bar, specify the new file name and location, and then click Save.

Entering Text, Dates, and Numbers

Worksheet cells can contain text, numbers, dates, and times. **Text data** is any combination of letters, numbers, and symbols. A **text string** is a series of text data characters. **Numeric data** is any number that can be used in a mathematical operation. **Date data** and **time data** are values displayed in commonly recognized date and time formats. For example, Excel interprets the cell entry April 15, 2025, as a date and not as text. By default, text is left-aligned within worksheet cells, and numbers, dates, and times are right-aligned.

Entering Text

Text is often used in worksheets as labels for the numeric values and calculations displayed in the workbook. Carmen wants you to enter text content into the Documentation sheet.

To enter text in the Documentation sheet:

1. Go to the **Documentation** sheet, and then press **CTRL+HOME** to make sure cell A1 is the active cell.
2. Type **MedIT** in cell A1. As you type, the text appears in cell A1 and in the formula bar.
3. Press **ENTER** twice. The text is entered into cell A1, and the active cell moves down two rows to cell A3.
4. Type **Author** in cell A3, and then press **TAB**. The text is entered and the active cell moves one column to the right to cell B3.
5. Type your name in cell B3, and then press **ENTER**. The text is entered and the active cell moves one cell down and to the left to cell A4.
6. Type **Date** in cell A4, and then press **TAB**. The text is entered, and the active cell moves one column to the right to cell B4, where you would enter the date you created the worksheet. For now, you will leave the cell for the date blank.
7. Press **ENTER** to make cell A5 the active cell, type **Purpose** in the cell, and then press **TAB**. The active cell moves one column to the right to cell B5.
8. Type **To estimate expenses at the MedIT convention** in cell B5, and then press **ENTER**. Figure 1–12 shows the text entered in the Documentation sheet.

Figure 1–12 Text entered in the Documentation sheet

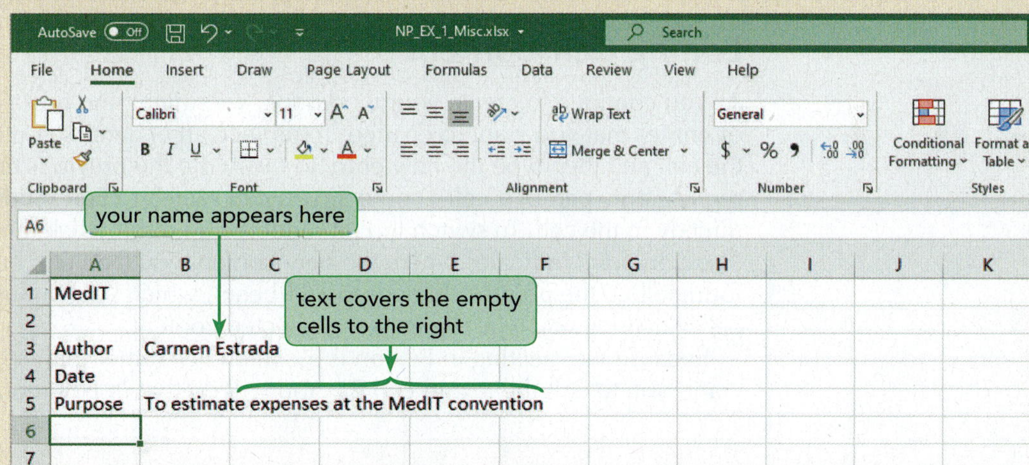

The text strings you entered in cells B3 and B5 are so long that they cover the adjacent cells. Any text that doesn't fit within a cell will cover the adjacent cells to the right if they are empty. If the adjacent cells contain data, only the text that fits into the cell is displayed and the rest of the text string is hidden. The complete text is still stored in the cell; it is just not displayed. (You will learn how to display all text in a cell in the next session.)

Undoing and Redoing an Action

As you enter data in a workbook, you might need to undo a previous action. Excel maintains a list of the actions you performed in the workbook during the current session, so you can undo most of your actions. You can use the Undo button on the Quick Access Toolbar or press CTRL+Z to reverse your most recent actions one at a time. If you want to undo more than one action, you can click the Undo arrow and then select the earliest action you want to undo—all actions after that initial action will also be undone.

You will undo the most recent change you made to the Documentation sheet—the text you entered into cell B5. Then you will enter a different description of the workbook's purpose in cell B5.

To undo the text entry in cell B5:

1. On the Quick Access Toolbar, click the **Undo** button (or press **CTRL+Z**). The last action is reversed, removing the text you entered in cell B5.
2. Type **To estimate miscellaneous expenses at the MedIT convention in Boston** in cell B5, and then press **ENTER**. The new purpose statement is entered in cell B5.

If you want to restore actions you have undone, you can redo them. To redo one action at a time, you can click the Redo button on the Quick Access Toolbar or press CTRL+Y. To redo multiple actions at once, you can click the Redo arrow and then click the earliest action you want to redo. After you undo or redo an action, Excel continues the action list starting from any new changes you make to the workbook.

Editing Cell Content

As you continue to create your workbook, you might find mistakes you need to correct or entries that you want to change. To replace all of a cell's content, you simply select the cell and then type the new entry to overwrite the previous entry. If you want to replace only part of a cell's content, you can switch to **Edit mode** to make the changes directly in the cell. To switch to Edit mode, you double-click the cell. A blinking insertion point indicates where the new content you type will be inserted. In the cell or formula bar, the pointer changes to an I-beam, which you can use to select text in the cell. Anything you type replaces the selected content.

Because the meeting in Boston is a conference rather than a convention, Carmen wants you to edit the text in cell B5. You will do that in Edit mode.

To edit the text in cell B5:

1. Double-click cell **B5** to select the cell and switch to Edit mode. A blinking insertion point appears within the text of cell B5. The status bar displays Edit instead of Ready to indicate that the cell is in Edit mode.
2. Press **LEFT ARROW** or **RIGHT ARROW** as needed to move the insertion point directly to the right of the word "convention" in the cell text.
3. Press **BACKSPACE** 10 times to delete the word "convention," and then type **conference** in the entry. See Figure 1–13.

Figure 1–13 Edited text in the Documentation sheet

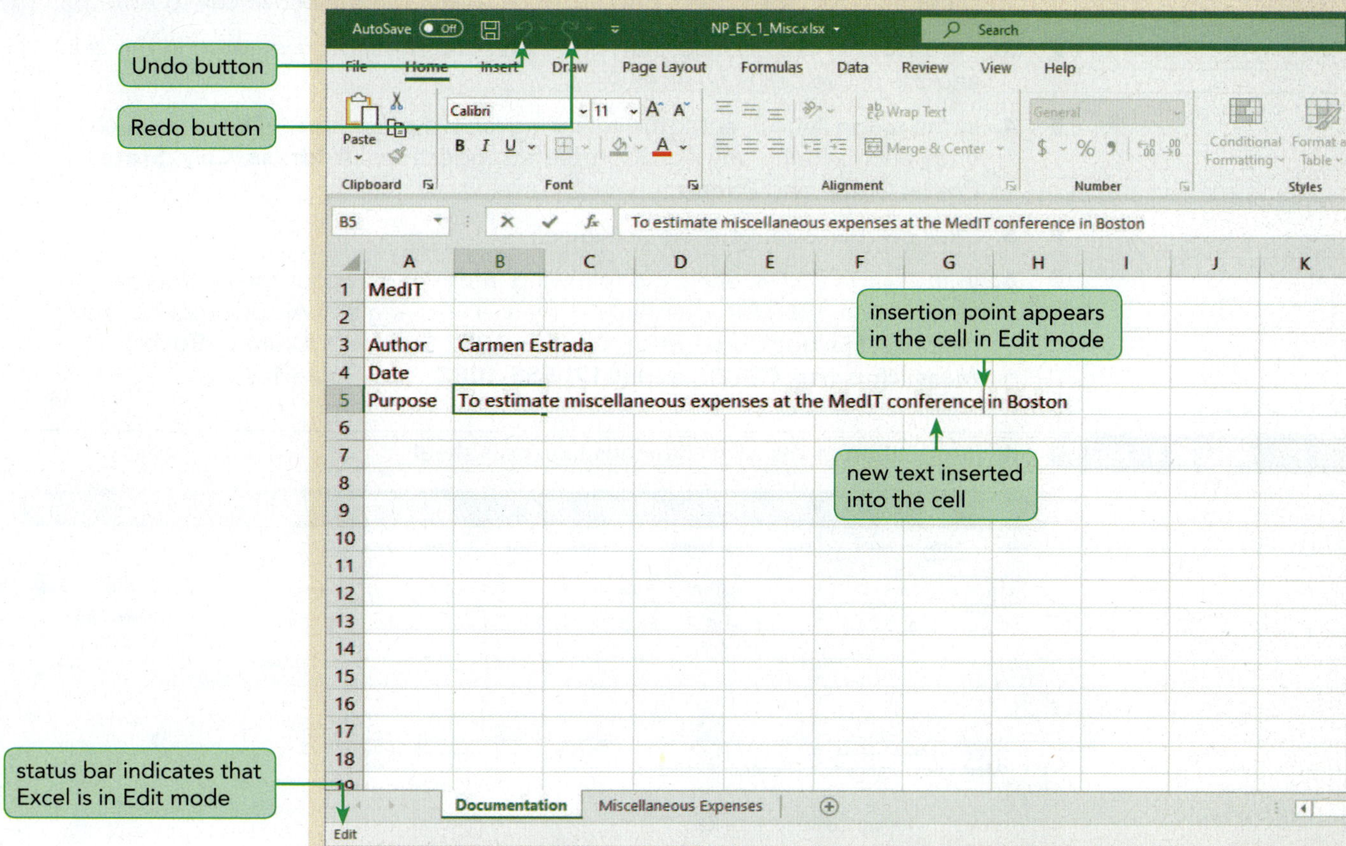

4. Press **ENTER** to exit the cell and return to Ready mode.

Now that you have returned to Ready mode, you can continue to insert and edit content from other cells and sheets in the workbook.

Understanding AutoComplete

As you type text in the active cell, Excel tries to anticipate the remaining characters by displaying text that begins with the same letters as a previous entry in the same column. This feature, known as **AutoComplete**, helps make entering repetitive text easier and reduces data entry errors. To accept the suggested text, press TAB or ENTER. To override the suggested text, continue to type the text you want to enter in the cell. AutoComplete does not work with dates or numbers or when a blank cell is positioned between the previous entry and the text you are typing.

You will see AutoComplete entries as you enter descriptive text about the Boston conference in the Miscellaneous Expenses worksheet.

To enter information about the conference site:

1. Click the **Miscellaneous Expenses** sheet tab to make Miscellaneous Expenses the active sheet.

2. In cell A1, type **MedIT Conference Miscellaneous Expenses** as the worksheet title, and then press **ENTER** twice to change the active cell to A3.
3. Type **Host** in cell A3, and then press **ENTER**. The label is entered in the cell and the active cell is now cell A4.
4. In the range A4:A8, enter the following labels, pressing **ENTER** after each entry and ignoring any AutoComplete suggestions: **Address**, **City**, **State**, **Postal Code**, and **Phone**.
5. Click cell **B3** to make it the active cell.
6. In the range B3:B8, enter the following information about the conference site, pressing **ENTER** after each entry and ignoring any AutoComplete suggestions: **Harbor Convention Center**, **1082 Suncrest Avenue**, **Boston**, **Massachusetts**, **02128**, and **(617) 555-1082**. See Figure 1–14.

Figure 1–14 **Site information in the Miscellaneous Expenses sheet**

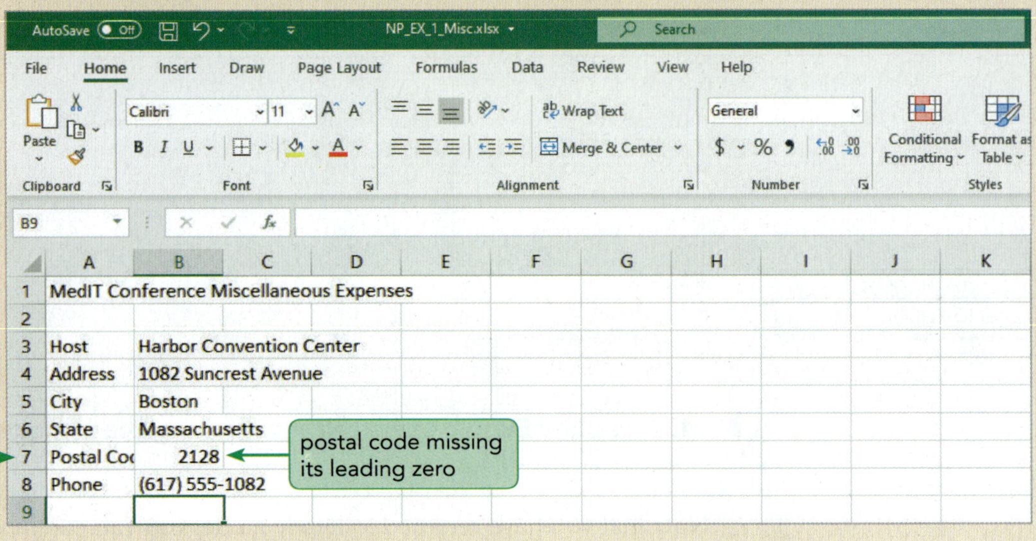

The postal code value in cell B7 is missing its leading zero, you will fix that problem next.

Displaying Numbers as Text

When you enter a number in a cell, Excel removes leading zeroes from integer values. So a number like 02128 that you entered in cell B7 is changed to 2128. Because the number you entered in cell B7 is actually a postal code, it needs the leading zero. In these instances, you can instruct Excel to treat a number as text so that the leading zero is not dropped. You'll make this change the for the postal code in cell B7.

Tip

You can also display a number as text by typing an apostrophe (') before the number.

To display the postal code as text:

1. Click cell **B7** to select it. The number is right-aligned in the cell.
2. On the Home tab, in the Number group, click the **Number Format arrow**. A list of number display options appears.

3. Scroll down the list, and then click **Text**. Anything entered in the cell will now be considered text.

4. Type **02128** in cell B7, and then press **ENTER**. The leading zero remains in the entry, and the entry is left-aligned in the cell just like other text. See Figure 1–15.

Figure 1–15 Number displayed as text

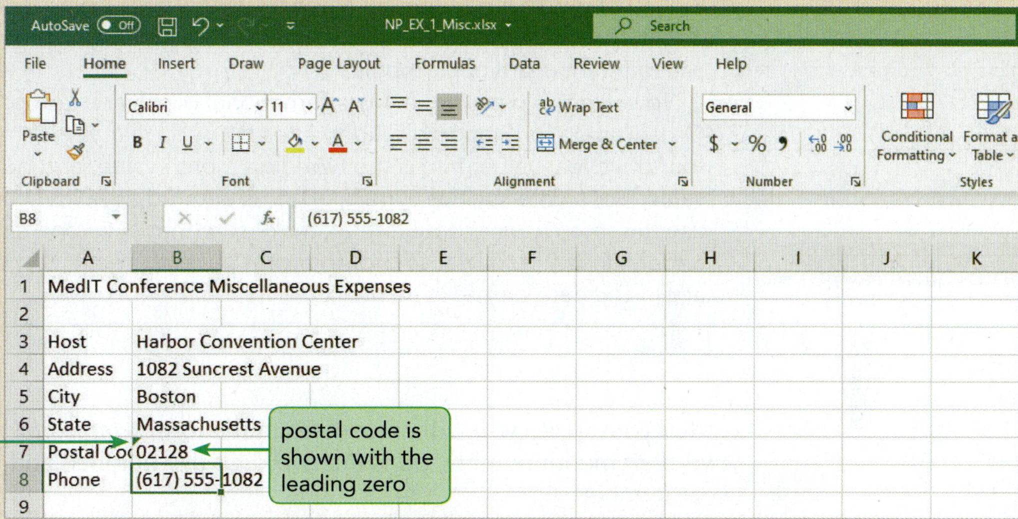

Tip

To remove a green triangle, click the cell, click the icon that appears, and then click Ignore Error.

Notice that a green triangle appears in the upper-left corner of cell B7. Excel uses green triangles to flag potential errors in cells. In this case, it is simply a warning that you displayed a number as text. Because this is intentional, you do not have to edit the cell to fix the "error."

Entering Dates

Excel recognizes dates in any standard date formats. For example, in Excel, all the following entries represent the same date:

- 4/6/2025
- 4/6/25
- 4-6-2025
- April 6, 2025
- 6-Apr-25

Even though dates are entered as text, Excel stores the date as a number equal to the number of days between the specified date and January 0, 1900. Times are also entered as text and stored as fractions of a 24-hour day. For example, a date and time of April 15, 2025, 6:00 PM is stored as the number 45,762.75, which is 45,762 days after January 0, 1900, plus 3/4 of one day. Excel stores dates and times as numbers so they can be used for date and time calculations, such as determining the elapsed time between one date and another.

Based on how your computer displays dates, Excel might change the appearance of a date after you type it. For example, if you enter the date 4/15/25 into the active cell, Excel might display the date with the four-digit year value, 4/15/2025. If you enter the text April 15, 2025, Excel might change the date format to 15-Apr-25. Changing how the date or time is displayed does not affect the underlying date or time value.

Insight

International Date Formats

For international business transactions, you may need to adopt international standards for expressing dates, times, and currency values in your workbooks. For example, a worksheet cell might contain the date 06/05/25, which could be interpreted as either the 5th of June 2021, or the 6th of May 2021.

The interpretation depends on which country the workbook has been designed for. You can avoid this problem by entering the full date, as in June 5, 2025. However, this might not work with documents written in foreign languages, such as Japanese, that use different character symbols.

To solve this problem, many international businesses adopt ISO (International Organization for Standardization) dates in the format *yyyy-mm-dd*, where *yyyy* is the four-digit year value, *mm* is the two-digit month value, and *dd* is the two-digit day value. So, a date such as June 5, 2025, is entered as 2025/06/05. If you choose to use this international date format, make sure that everyone else using your workbook understands this format so they interpret dates correctly. You can include information about the date format in the Documentation sheet.

For your work, you will enter dates in the format *mm/dd/yyyy*, where *mm* is the two-digit month number, *dd* is the two-digit day number, and *yyyy* is the four-digit year number.

To enter a date into the Documentation sheet:

1. Click the **Documentation** sheet tab to make the Documentation sheet the active worksheet.
2. Click cell **B4** to make it the active cell, type the current date in the *mm/dd/yyyy* format, and then press **ENTER**. The date is entered in the cell.

   Trouble? Depending on your system configuration, Excel might change the date to the date format *dd-mmm-yy*. This difference will not affect your work.
3. Click the **Miscellaneous Expenses** sheet tab to return to the Miscellaneous Expenses worksheet.

The next part of the Miscellaneous Expenses worksheet will list the miscellaneous expenses that will be tracked in the conference budget. As shown in Figure 1–16, the list includes each expense's category, subcategory, description, number of units, and the cost per unit.

Figure 1–16 Miscellaneous expenses

Expense Category	Subcategory	Description	Units	Cost per Unit
E2	9010	printing of brochures and conference materials	1600	$2.45
E2	9030	transportation shuttles	3	$335.75
E2	9020	decorations for banquet	1	$850.55
E2	9040	gift bags for conference attendees	525	$6.25
E2	9045	gifts for banquet speakers	6	$55.25

You will enter the first three columns of this table into the worksheet.

To enter the first part of the table of miscellaneous expenses:

1. In the Miscellaneous worksheet, click cell **A10** to make it the active cell, type **Expense Category** as the column label, and then press **TAB** to move to cell B10.
2. Type **Subcategory** in cell B10, press **TAB** to move to cell C10, type **Description** in cell C10, and then press **ENTER**.
3. In the range A11:C15, enter the Expense Category, Subcategory, and Description text for the five miscellaneous expenses listed in Figure 1–16, pressing **TAB** to move from one cell to the next, and pressing **ENTER** to move to a new row. Note that the text in some cells will be partially hidden; you will fix that problem shortly. See Figure 1–17.

Figure 1–17 Miscellaneous expense categories, subcategories, and descriptions

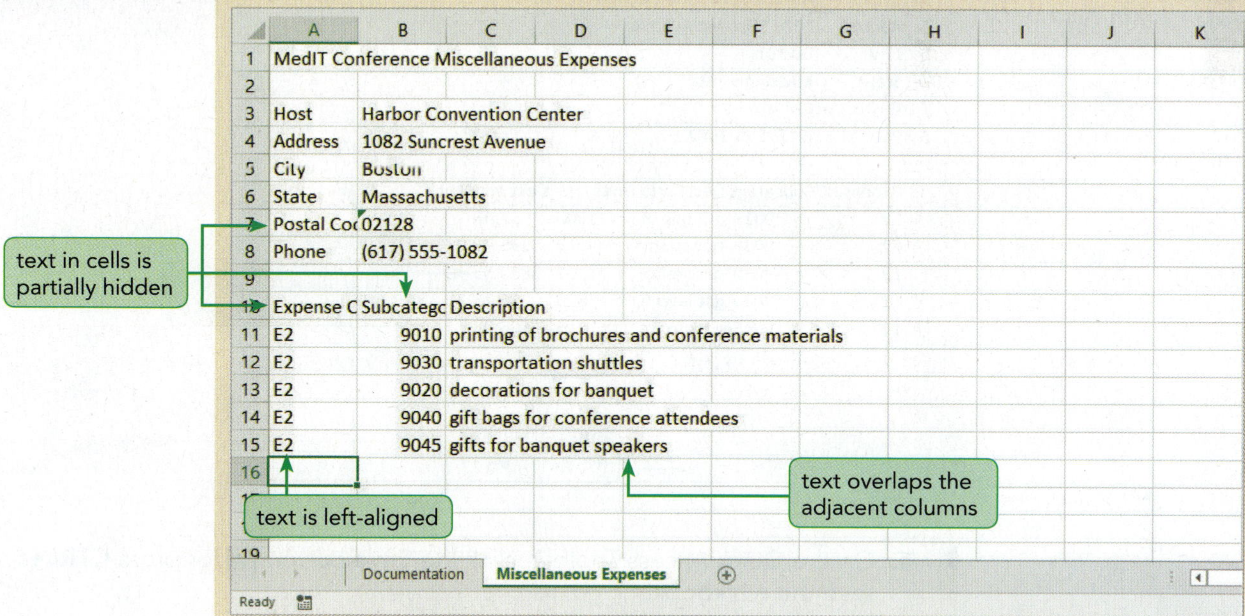

Next you will enter the miscellaneous expenses.

Entering Numbers

Tip

The text string ##### appears in a cell when the complete number cannot be displayed. To display the number, increase the cell width.

In Excel, numbers can be integers such as 378, decimals such as 1.95, or negative values such as –5.2. In the case of currency and percentages, you can include the currency symbol or the percent sign when you enter the value. Excel treats a currency value such as $87.25 as the number 87.25, and a percentage such as 95% as the decimal 0.95. Much like dates, currency and percentages are displayed with their symbols but stored as numbers.

You will complete the list of miscellaneous expenses by inserting their number of units and costs per unit.

To enter the miscellaneous expenses:

1. Click cell **D10**, type **Units** as the label, and then press **TAB**. Cell E10 becomes the active cell.
2. Type **Cost per Unit** in cell E10, and then press **ENTER**. Cell D11 becomes the active cell.
3. Type **1600** in cell D11, press **TAB** to make cell E11 the active cell, type **$2.45** in cell E11, and then press **ENTER**. Cell D12 becomes the active cell.
4. In the range D12:E15, enter the number of units and cost per unit for the remaining four expense categories shown in Figure 1–16. See Figure 1–18.

Figure 1–18 Miscellaneous expense units and costs per unit

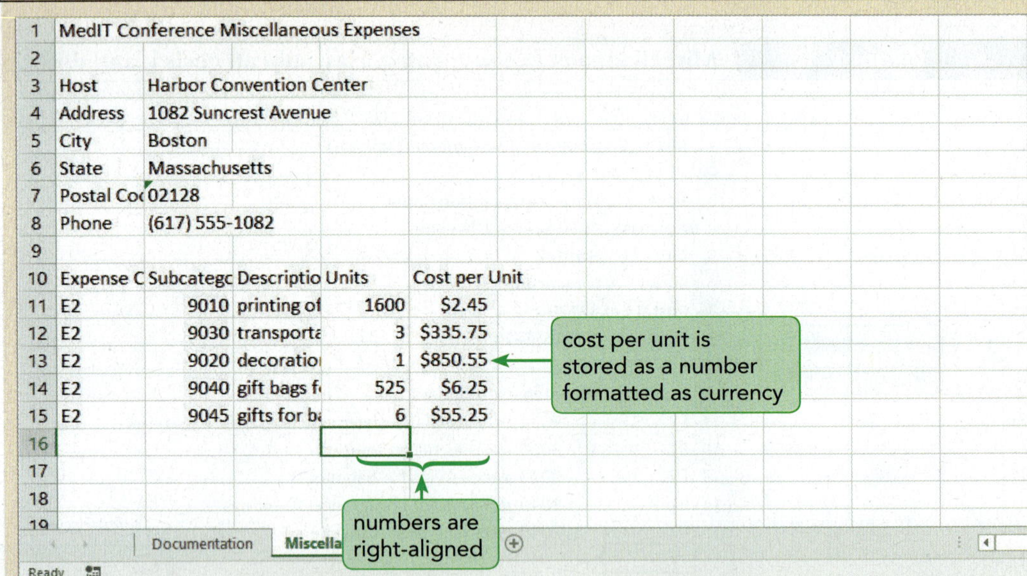

5. On the Quick Access Toolbar, click the **Save** button (or press **CTRL+S**) to save the workbook.

Much of the information from the miscellaneous expenses table is difficult to read because of the hidden text. You can display all the cell contents by changing the size of the columns and rows in the worksheet.

Resizing Columns and Rows

There are several ways to resize columns and rows, including changing column widths, wrapping text within cells, and changing row heights. You can use a combination of these in a worksheet to create the best fit for your data.

Setting a Column Width

Column widths are expressed as the number of characters the column can contain. The default column width is 8.43 standard-sized characters. In general, this means that you can type eight characters in a cell. Any additional text is hidden or overlaps the adjacent cell. Column widths are also expressed in terms of pixels. A **pixel** is an individual point on a computer monitor or printout. A column width of 8.43 characters is equivalent to 64 pixels.

Insight

Setting Column Widths

On a computer monitor, pixel size is based on screen resolution. As a result, cell content that looks fine on one screen might appear differently when viewed on a screen with a different resolution. If you work on multiple computers or share your workbooks with others, you should set column widths based on the maximum number of characters you want displayed in the cells rather than pixel size. This ensures that everyone sees the cell contents the way you intended.

You will increase the width of column A so that all of the text labels within that column are completely displayed.

To increase the width of column A:

1. Point to the **right border** of the column A heading until the pointer changes to ↔.
2. Click and drag to the right until the width of the column heading reaches **18** characters, but do *not* release the mouse button. The ScreenTip that appears as you resize the column shows the new column width in characters and in pixels. See Figure 1–19.

Figure 1–19 **Width of column A increased to 18 characters**

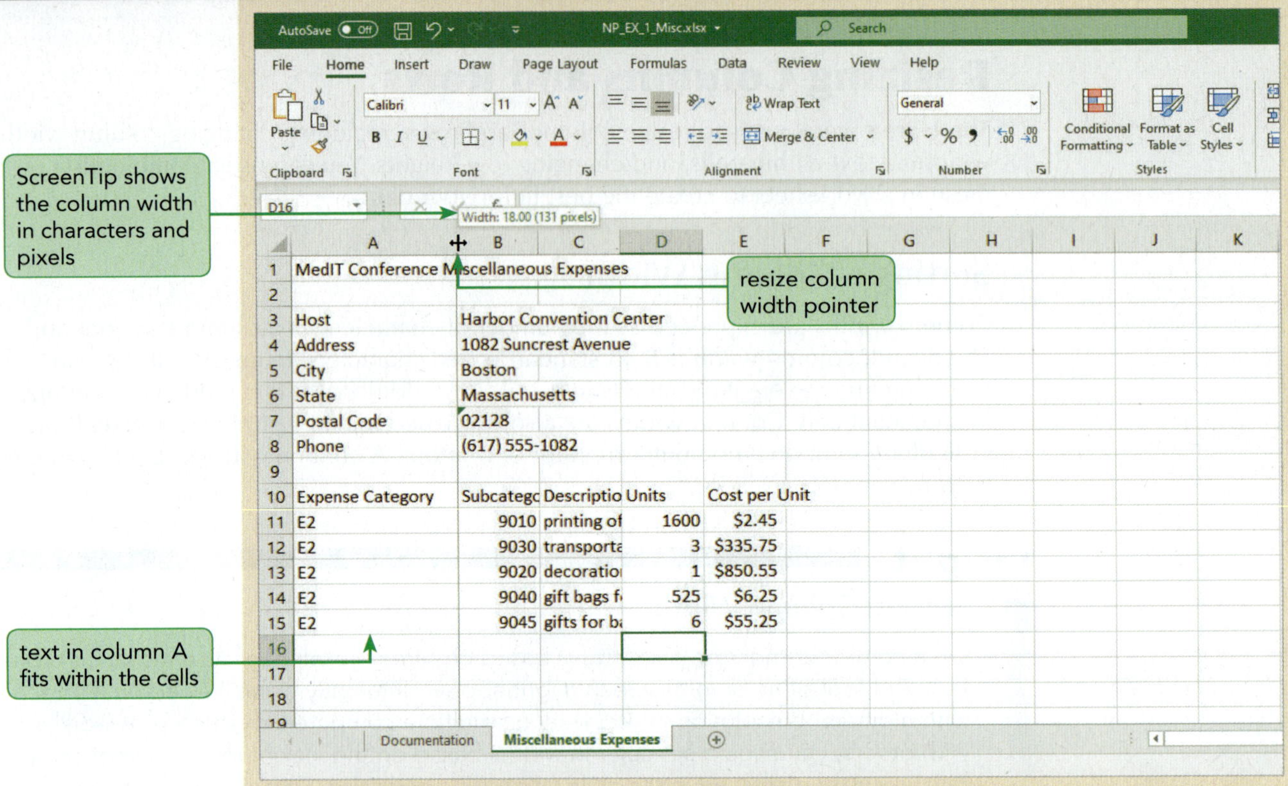

3. Release the mouse button. The width of column A expands to 18 characters, and all the text within that column is visible within the cells.

You can change the width of multiple columns at once. To select a range of columns, click the first column heading in the range, hold down SHIFT, and then click the heading of the last column or click and drag the pointer over the column headings. To select nonadjacent columns, hold down CTRL and click the heading of each column you want to select. When you change the width of one column, the widths of all the other columns that are selected also change.

Using the mouse to resize columns can be imprecise and a challenge to some users with special needs. The Format command on the Home tab gives you precise control over column width and row height settings. You will use the Format command to set the width of column B to exactly 12 characters so that the hidden text in cell B10 is completely visible.

To set the width of column B using the Format command:

1. Click the **column B** heading. The entire column is selected.
2. On the Home tab, in the Cells group, click the **Format** button, and then click **Column Width**. The Column Width dialog box opens.
3. Type **12** in the Column width box to specify the new column width.
4. Click **OK**. The width of column B is set to exactly 12 characters.
5. Click cell **A2** to deselect column B. See Figure 1–20.

Figure 1–20 Width of column B set to 12 characters

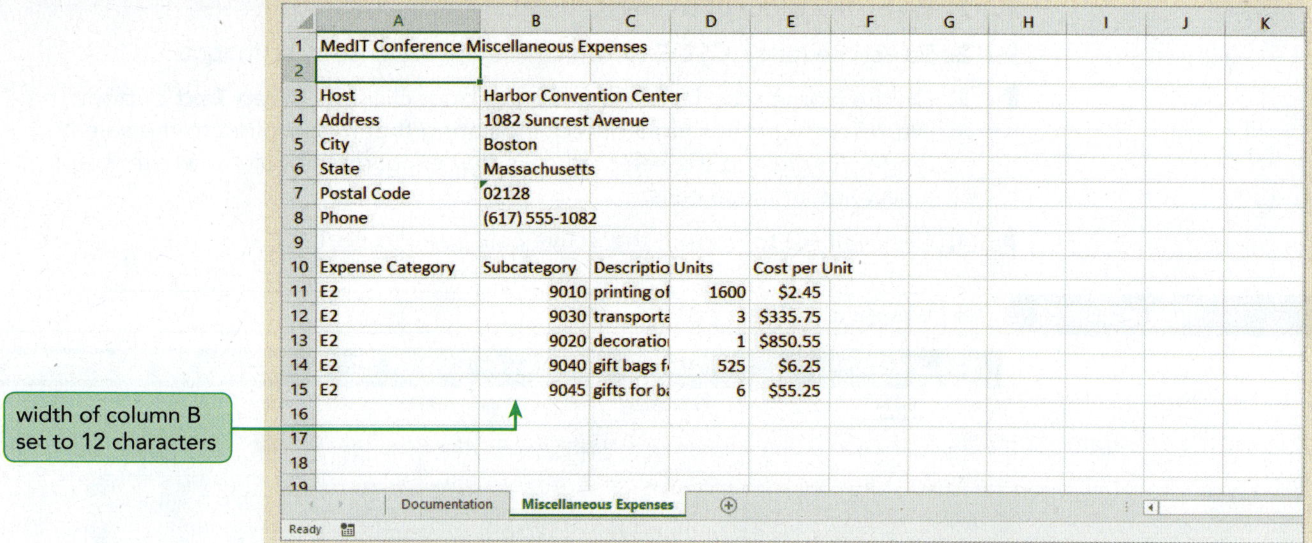

You can also use the **AutoFit** feature to automatically adjust a column width or row height to accommodate its widest or tallest entry. To AutoFit a column to the width of its contents, double-click the right border of the column heading. You'll use AutoFit to resize columns C and E so that all the content is fully displayed.

To use AutoFit to display all the contents of columns C and E:

1. Point to the **right border** of column C until the pointer changes to the resize column width pointer ↔.
2. Double-click the **right border** of the column C heading. The width of column C increases to about 43 characters so that the longest item description is completely visible.
3. Double-click the **right border** of the column E heading. The width of column E increases to about 12 characters.

Sometimes when you use AutoFit, the column becomes wider than you want. Another way to display long text entries is to wrap the text within each cell.

Wrapping Text Within a Cell

When you wrap text within a cell, any content that doesn't fit on the first line is displayed on a new line in the cell. Wrapping text increases the row height to display any additional new lines added in the cell. You can wrap only text within a cell; numbers, dates, or times do not wrap.

You'll reduce the width of column C to 30 characters, and then wrap the category descriptions so all of the text is visible.

To wrap text in column C:

1. Resize the width of column C to **30** characters.
2. Select the range **C11:C15**, which has the expense descriptions.
3. On the Home tab, in the Alignment group, click the **Wrap Text** button. The Wrap Text button is highlighted, indicating that it is applied to the selected range. Any text in the selected cells that exceeds the column width wraps to a new line in those cells.
4. Click cell **A2** to make it the active cell. See Figure 1–21.

Figure 1–21 Text wrapped within a cell

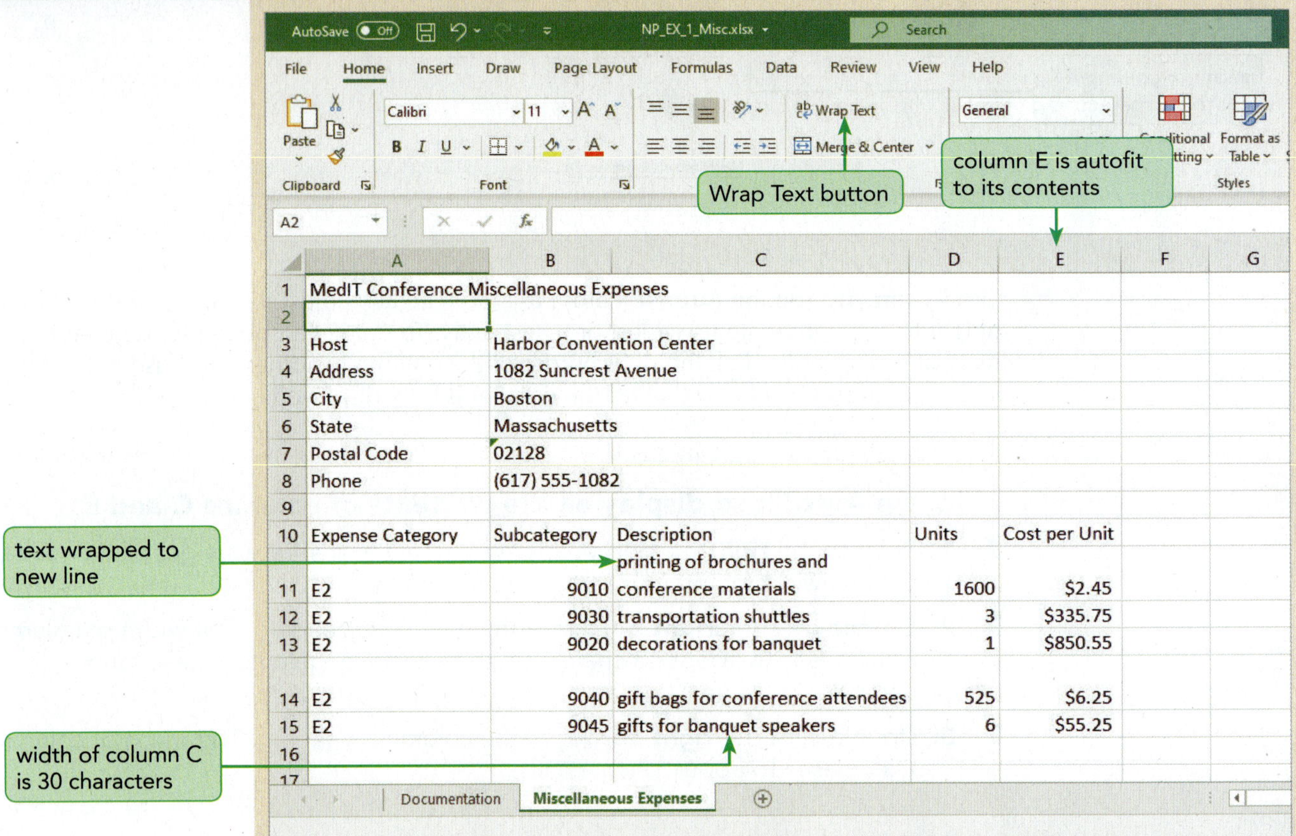

Another way to create a new line within a cell is to press ALT+ENTER where you want the new line to start. Subsequent characters will be on a new line.

Changing Row Heights

Row heights are measured in points or pixels. A **point** is approximately 1/72 of an inch. The default row height is 15 points or 20 pixels. There are several ways to set row heights. You can drag the bottom border of the row heading. You can click the Format button in the Cells group on the Home tab, and then click Row Height. Or, you can double-click the bottom border of the row heading to AutoFit a row to its tallest cell.

The height of row 14 is a too tall for its contents. Carmen asks you to reduce it.

To change the height of row 14:

1. Point to the **bottom border** of the row 14 heading until the pointer changes to the resize row height pointer ‡.
2. Drag the bottom border up until the height of the row is equal to **18** points (or **24** pixels), and then release the mouse button. The height of row 14 better matches its contents.
3. Press **CTRL+S** to save the workbook.

You have entered the table of miscellaneous expenses for the Boston conference. In the next session, you will use formulas and functions to calculate the total cost of all of those expenses.

Review

Session 1.1 Quick Check

1. How are chart sheets different from worksheets?
2. What is the cell reference for the cell located in the third column and fourth row of a worksheet?
3. What is the range reference for the block of cells D3 through E10?
4. What is the range reference for cells A1 through C5 and cells A8 through C12?
5. How is text aligned within a worksheet cell by default?
6. How would the number 00514 appear in a cell?
7. Cell B2 contains the entry May 3, 2025. Why doesn't Excel consider this a text entry?
8. How do you autofit a column to match its longest cell entry?

Session 1.2 Visual Overview:

The **font size** specifies the size of text characters measured in units called points.

The Page Layout tab is used to specify how the worksheet will be arranged and printed.

In Excel, every formula begins with an equal sign (=).

When the active cell contains a formula, the formula appears in the formula bar and the result of the formula appears in the cell.

The worksheet cells are surrounded by **gridlines**, which are horizontal and vertical lines in a worksheet or chart that make it easier to read.

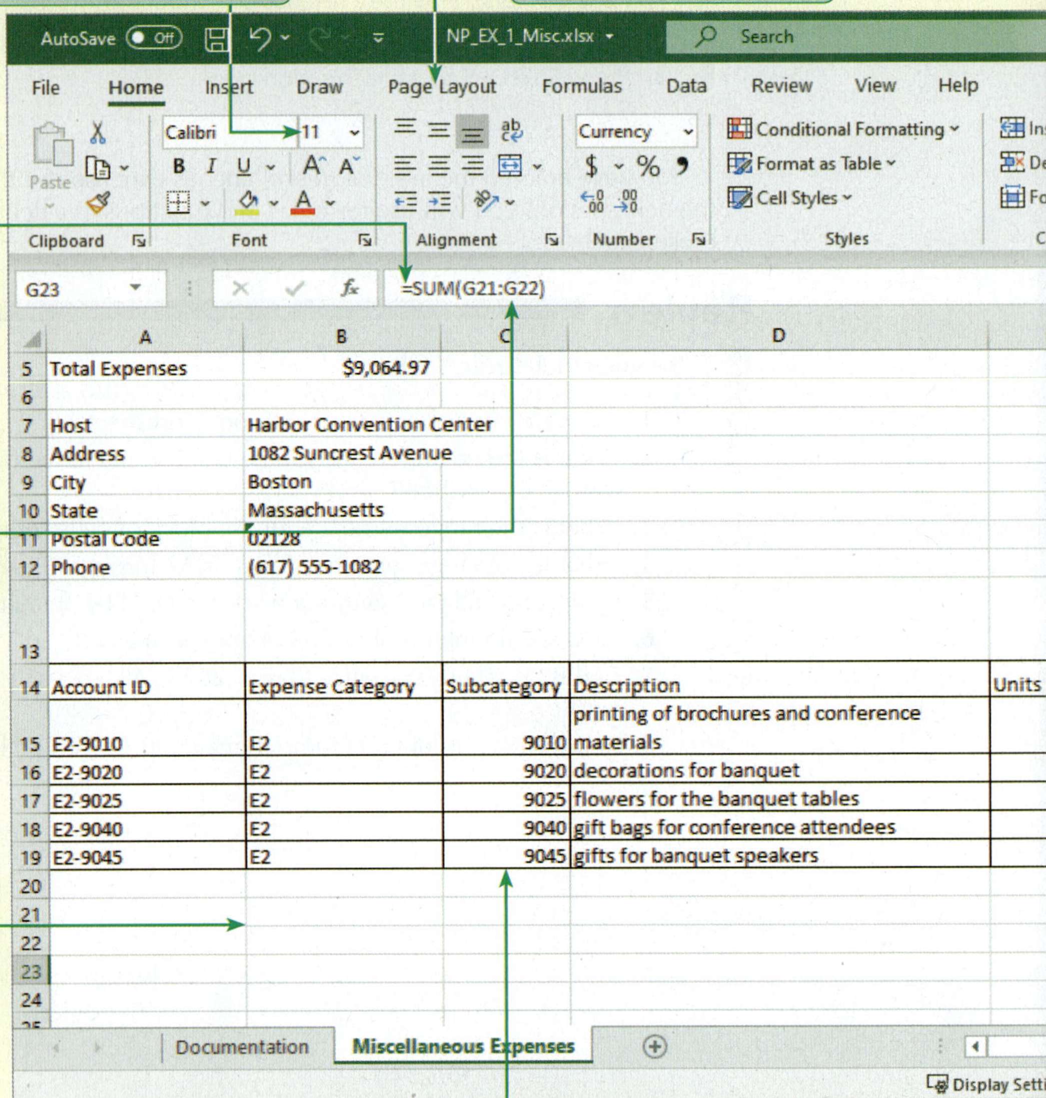

A border is a line added along the edge of a cell, row, column, or table.

Excel Formulas and Functions

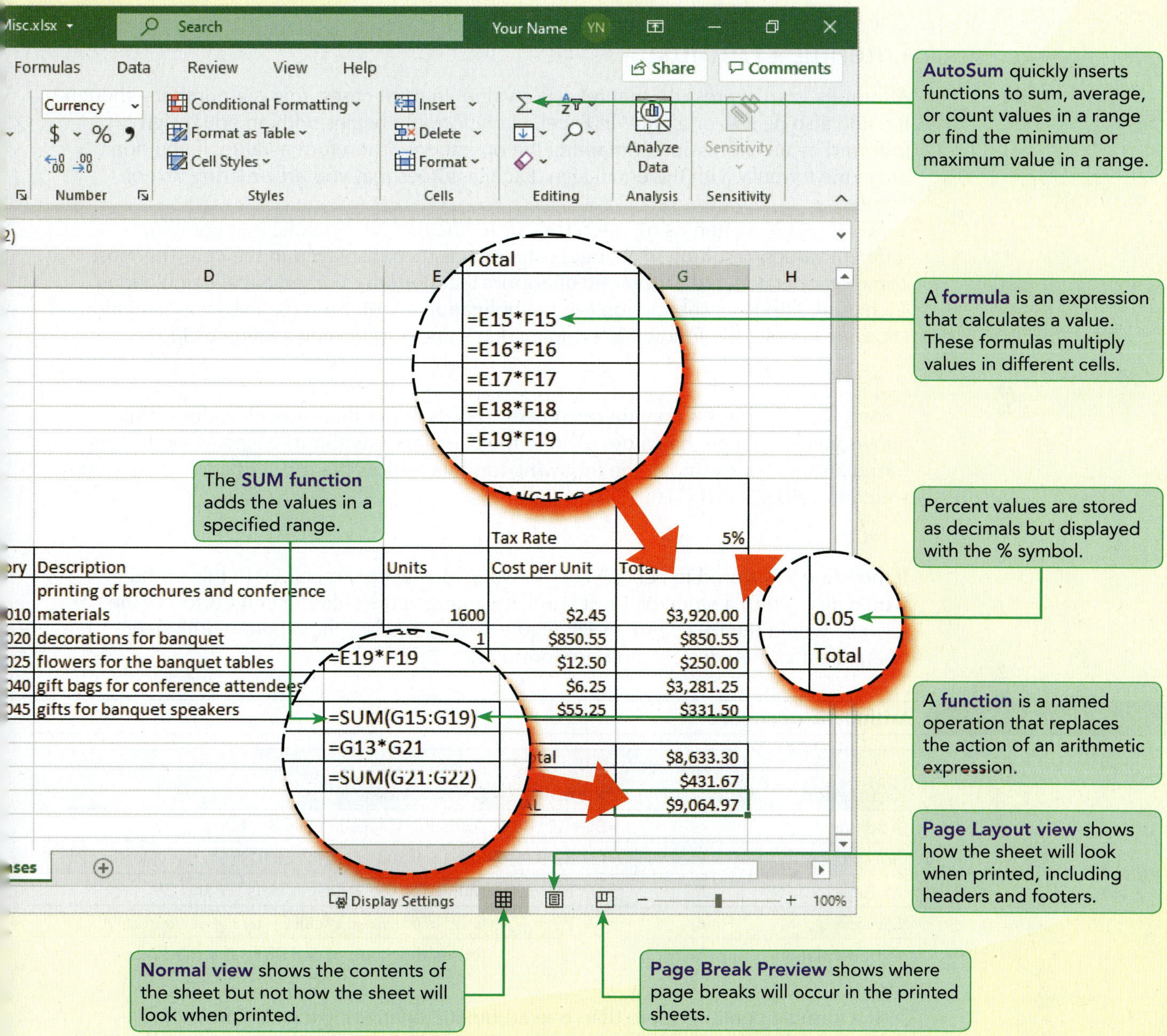

Calculating with Formulas

So far you have entered text, numbers, and dates in the worksheet. However, the main reason for using Excel is to perform calculations and analysis on data. For example, Carmen wants the workbook to calculate the number of items in the miscellaneous expense category and the total cost of those items. Such calculations are added to a worksheet using formulas and functions.

Entering a Formula

A formula is an expression that returns a value. In most cases, this is a number—though it could also be text or a date. In Excel, every formula begins with an equal sign (=) followed by an expression containing the operations that return a value. If you don't begin the formula with the equal sign, Excel assumes that you are entering text or numbers.

A formula is written using **operators**, or mathematical symbols, that combine different values, resulting in a single value that is then displayed in the cell. The most common operators are **arithmetic operators** that perform mathematical calculations such as addition (+), subtraction (–), multiplication (*), division (/), and exponentiation (^). For example, the following formula adds 3 and 8, returning a value of 11:

```
=3+8
```

Most Excel formulas contain references to cells rather than specific values. This allows you to change the values used in the calculation without having to modify the formula itself. For example, the following formula returns the result of adding the values stored in cells C3 and D10:

```
=C3+D10
```

If the value 3 is stored in cell C3 and the value 8 is stored in cell D10, this formula would also return a value of 11. If you later changed the value in cell C3 to 10, the formula would return a value of 18. Figure 1–22 describes the different arithmetic operators and provides examples of formulas.

Figure 1–22 **Arithmetic operators**

Operation	Arithmetic Operator	Example	Description
Addition	+	=B1+B2+B3	Adds the values in cells B1, B2, and B3
Subtraction	–	=C9-B2	Subtracts the value in cell B2 from the value in cell C9
Multiplication	*	=C9*B9	Multiplies the values in cells C9 and B9
Division	/	=C9/B9	Divides the value in cell C9 by the value in cell B9
Exponentiation	^	=B5^3	Raises the value of cell B5 to the third power

If a formula contains more than one arithmetic operator, Excel performs the calculation based on the following order of operations, which is the sequence in which operators are applied in a calculation:

1. Calculate any operations within parentheses
2. Calculate any exponentiations (^)
3. Calculate any multiplications (*) and divisions (/)
4. Calculate any additions (+) and subtractions (–)

For example, the following formula returns the value 23 because multiplying 4 by 5 is done before adding 3:

```
=3+4*5
```

If a formula contains two or more operators with the same level of priority, the operators are applied in order from left to right. In the following formula, Excel first multiplies 4 by 10 and then divides that result by 8 to return the value 5:

```
=4*10/8
```

When parentheses are used, the value inside them is calculated first. In the following formula, Excel calculates (3+4) first, and then multiplies that result by 5 to return the value 35:

```
=(3+4)*5
```

Figure 1–23 shows how changes in a formula affect the order of operations and the result of the formula.

Figure 1–23 **Order of operations applied to formulas**

Formula	Order of Operations	Result
=50+10*5	10*5 calculated first and then 50 is added	100
=(50+10)*5	(50+10) calculated first and then 60 is multiplied by 5	300
=50/10–5	50/10 calculated first and then 5 is subtracted	0
=50/(10–5)	(10–5) calculated first and then 50 is divided by that value	10
=50/10*5	Two operators at same precedence level, so the calculation is done left to right with 50/10 calculated first and that value is then multiplied by 5	25
=50/(10*5)	(10*5) is calculated first and then 50 is divided by that value	1

Carmen wants the miscellaneous expenses workbook to calculate the total cost of each item. The total cost is equal to the number of units ordered multiplied by the cost per unit. You already entered this information in columns D and E. Now you will enter a formula in cell F11 to calculate the total cost of printing for the conference.

To enter a formula that calculates the total cost of printing:

1. If you took a break after the previous session, make sure the NP_EX_1_Misc.xlsx workbook is open and the Miscellaneous Expenses worksheet is active.
2. Click cell **F10**, type **Total** as the label, and then press **ENTER**. The label is entered in cell F10 and cell F11 is the active cell.
3. Type **=D11*E11** (the number of units multiplied by the cost per unit). As you type the formula, a list of Excel function names appears in a ScreenTip, which provides a quick method for entering functions. The list will close when you complete the formula. You will learn more about Excel functions shortly. Also, Excel color codes each cell reference and its corresponding cell with the same color. See Figure 1–24.

Figure 1–24 **Formula being entered in cell F11**

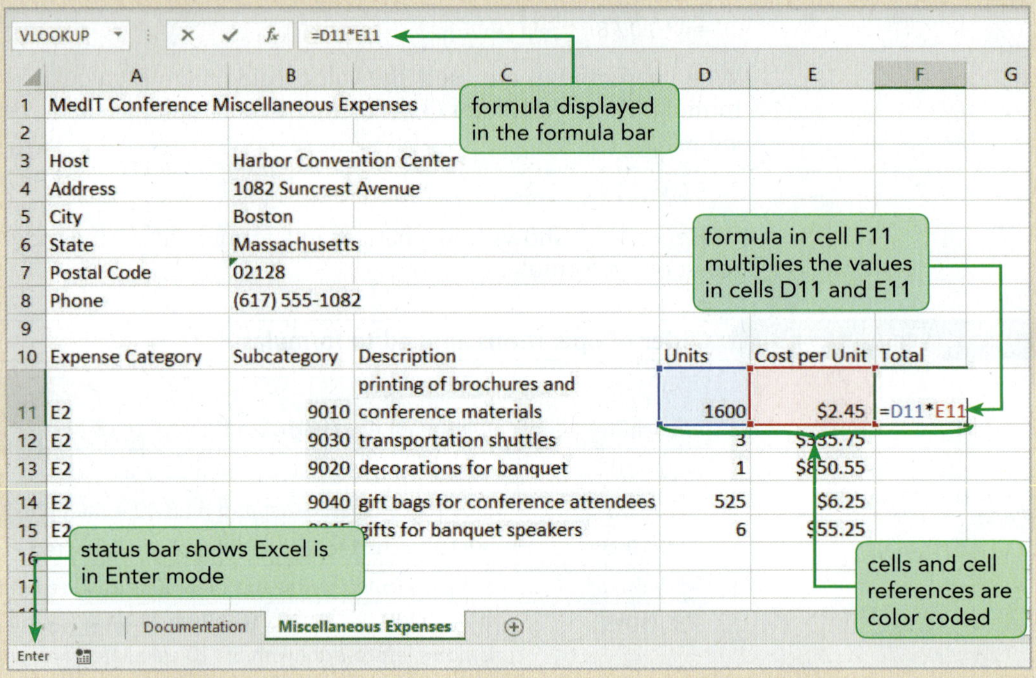

4. Press **ENTER**. The formula result $3,920.00 appears in cell F11. This value is the total cost of printing 1600 brochures and other conference materials. The result is displayed as currency because cell D11, which is referenced in the formula, contains a currency value.
5. Click cell **F11** again to make it the active cell. The cell displays the result of the formula, but the formula bar displays the formula you entered so that you can see at a glance both the formula and its value.

For the first item, you entered the formula by typing each cell reference in the expression. You can also insert a cell reference by clicking the cell as you type the formula. This technique reduces the possibility of error caused by typing an incorrect cell reference. You will use this method to enter the formula to calculate the charge for renting vans to shuttle conference attendees between the airport and the hotel.

To enter a formula to calculate the cost of shuttle using the mouse:

Be sure to type = first; otherwise, Excel will not recognize the entry as a formula.

1. Click cell **F12** to make it the active cell.
2. Type = to indicate that you are entering a formula. Any cell you click from now on inserts the cell reference of the selected cell into the formula until you complete the formula by pressing Enter or Tab.
3. Click cell **D12**. The cell reference is inserted into the formula in the formula bar. At this point, any cell you click changes the cell reference used in the formula. The cell reference isn't locked until you type an operator.
4. Type * to enter the multiplication operator. The cell reference for cell D12 is locked in the formula, and the next cell you click will be inserted after the operator.

5. Click cell **E12** to enter its cell reference in the formula. The formula, =D12*E12, is complete.

6. Press **ENTER**. Cell F12 displays the value $1,007.25, which is the cost of renting vans to transport attendees to and from the conference.

Next, you will enter formulas to complete the calculations of the remaining miscellaneous expenses.

Copying and Pasting Formulas

Many worksheets have the same formula repeated across several rows or columns. Rather than retyping the formula, you can copy a formula from one cell and paste it into another cell. When you copy a formula, Excel places the formula onto the **Clipboard**, which is a temporary storage area for selections you copy or cut. When you **paste**, Excel retrieves the formula from the Clipboard and places it into the selected cell or range.

The cell references in the copied formula change to reflect the formula's new location in the worksheet. For example, consider a formula from a cell in row 12 that adds other values in row 12. When that formula is copied to row 15, the formula changes to add the corresponding values in row 15. By automatically updating the formula based on its new location, Excel makes it easy to quickly enter the same general formula throughout a worksheet.

You will calculate the costs of the remaining expense categories by copying the formula you entered in cell F12 and pasting it to the range F13:F15.

To copy and paste the formula in cell F12:

1. Click cell **F12** to select the cell that contains the formula you want to copy.

2. On the Home tab, in the Clipboard group, click the **Copy** button (or press **CTRL+C**). Excel copies the formula to the Clipboard. A blinking green box surrounds the cell being copied.

3. Select the range **F13:F15**. You want to paste the formula into these cells.

4. In the Clipboard group, click the **Paste** button (or press **CTRL+V**). Excel pastes the formula into the selected cells, adjusting each formula so that the total cost of each item is based on the Units and Cost per Units values in that row. A button appears below the selected range, providing options for pasting formulas and values. See Figure 1–25.

Figure 1–25 Copied and pasted formulas

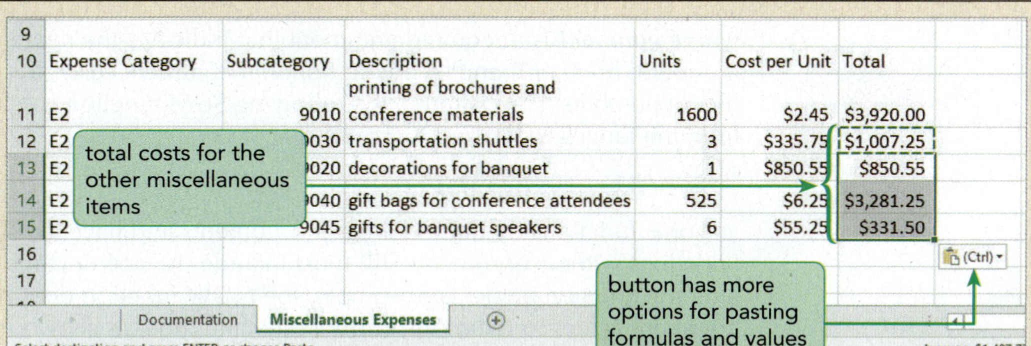

5. If necessary, click cell **F13** to make it the active cell. The formula =D13*E13 appears in the formula bar. Notice that the cell references in the formula were updated to reflect its current position of the cell in the worksheet.
6. Click cell **F14** to verify that the formula =D14*E14 appears in the formula bar, and then click cell **F15** to verify that the formula =D15*E15 appears in the formula bar.

Another way of performing calculations is to use functions.

Calculating with Functions

A function is a named operation that replaces the arithmetic expression in a formula. Functions are used to simplify long or complex formulas. For example, to add the values from cells A1 through A10, you could enter the following long formula:

```
=A1+A2+A3+A4+A5+A6+A7+A8+A9+A10
```

Or, you could use the SUM function to calculate the sum of those cell values by entering the following formula:

```
=SUM(A1:A10)
```

In both instances, Excel adds the values in cells A1 through A10, but the SUM function is faster and simpler to enter and less prone to a typing error. You should always use a function, if one is available, in place of a long, complex formula. Excel supports more than 300 functions from the fields of finance, business, science, and engineering, including functions that work with numbers, text, and dates.

Understanding Function Syntax

Every function follows a set of rules, or **syntax**, which specifies how the function should be written. The general syntax of all Excel functions is

FUNCTION(***arg1***,***arg2***,[*arg3*],[*arg4*],…)

where *FUNCTION* is the function name, and ***arg1***, ***arg2***, and so forth are arguments. An **argument** is information that the function uses to calculate an answer. Arguments can be required or optional. Required arguments, shown in bold, are needed by the function to operate. Optional arguments, enclosed in square brackets, are not required but may be used by the function. Optional arguments are always placed at the end of the argument list. In this case, ***arg1***, ***arg2***, are required arguments and *arg3*, *arg4* are optional arguments.

The SUM function shown earlier has the syntax

SUM(***number1***,[*number2*],[*number3*],…)

where ***number1*** is a required argument that indicates the range of values to sum and *number2*, *number3*, and so on are optional arguments used for nonadjacent ranges or lists of numbers. For example, the following SUM function calculates the sum of values from the ranges A1:10 and A21:A30:

```
SUM(A1:A10,A21:A30)
```

Some functions do not require any arguments and have the syntax *FUNCTION*( ). Functions without arguments still must include the opening and closing parentheses after the function name. For example, the NOW function does not require any argument values to return the current date and time, as shown in the following formula:

```
=NOW()
```

You can learn more about function syntax using Excel Help.

Inserting Functions with AutoSum

A fast and convenient way to enter commonly used functions is with AutoSum. The AutoSum button, located on the Home tab of the ribbon, includes options to insert the following functions into a selected cell or cell range:

- SUM—Sum of the values in the specified range
- AVERAGE—Average value in the specified range
- COUNT—Total count of numeric values in the specified range
- MAX—Maximum value in the specified range
- MIN—Minimum value in the specified range

After you select one of the AutoSum options, Excel determines the most appropriate range from the available data and enters it as the function's argument. You should always verify that the range included in the AutoSum function matches the range that you want to use.

You will use AutoSum to enter the SUM function to add the total cost from all miscellaneous expense categories.

To use AutoSum to sum the miscellaneous expense values:

1. Click cell **E16** to make it the active cell, type **Subtotal** as the label, and then press **TAB** to make cell F16 the active cell.
2. On the Home tab, in the Editing group, click the **AutoSum arrow**. The button's menu opens and displays five common functions: Sum, Average, Count Numbers, Max (for maximum), and Min (for minimum).
3. Click **Sum** to enter the SUM function. The formula =SUM(F11:F15) is entered in cell F16. The cells being summed are selected and highlighted on the worksheet so you can quickly confirm that Excel selected the appropriate range from the available data. A ScreenTip appears below the formula describing the function's syntax. See Figure 1–26.

Tip

You can quickly insert the SUM function by clicking the worksheet cell where the sum should be calculated and pressing ALT+=.

Figure 1–26 SUM function entered using the AutoSum button

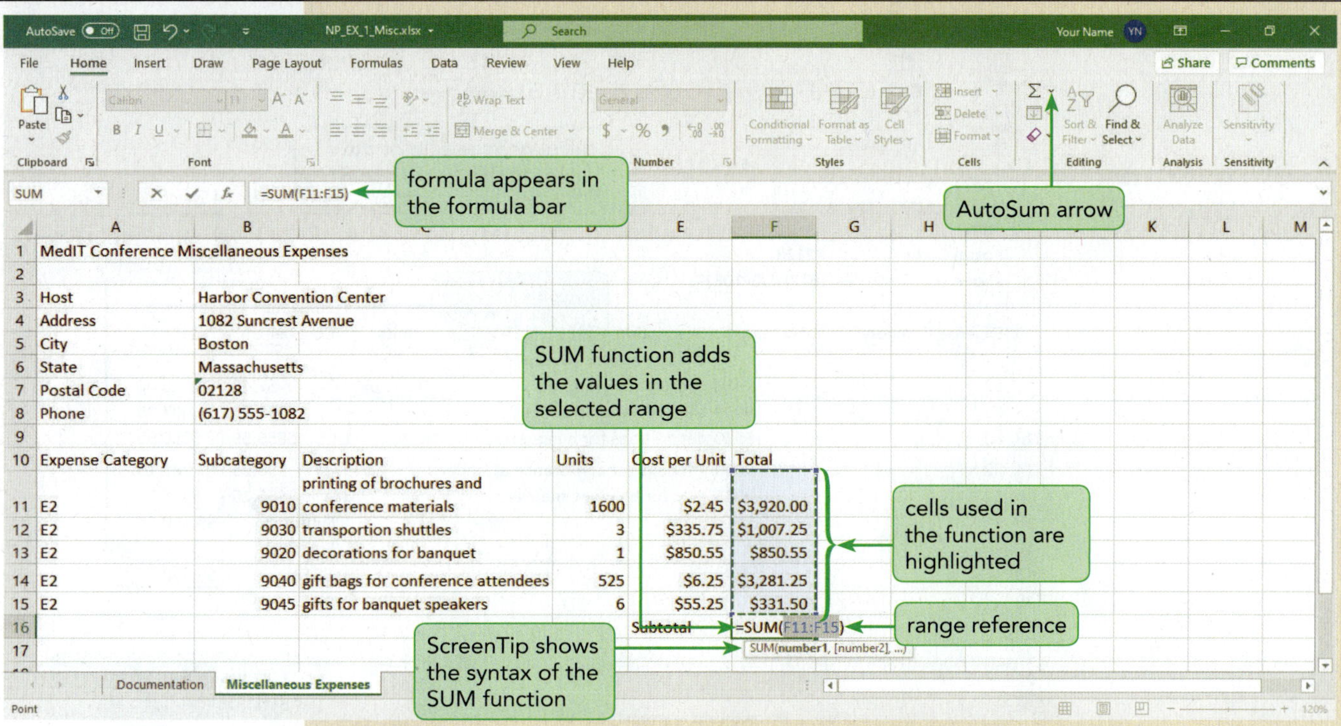

4. Press **ENTER** to accept the formula. The sum of the miscellaneous expenses is $9,390.55.

Carmen wants you to include a 5% sales tax on the miscellaneous expenses. You will calculate the tax, and then add the subtotal value to the tax.

To calculate the sales tax and total expenses:

1. Click cell **E9**, type **Tax Rate** as the label and then press **TAB** to make cell F9 the active cell.
2. Type **5%** in cell F9, and then press **ENTER**. The 5% value is displayed in cell F9, but the stored value is 0.05. Percentages are displayed with the % symbol but stored as the decimal value.
3. Click cell **E17** to make it the active cell, type **Est. Tax** as the label, and then press **TAB** to make F17 the active cell.
4. Type the formula **=F9*F16** in cell F17 to calculate the sales tax on all of the miscellaneous expenditures, and then press **ENTER**. The formula multiplies the sales tax in cell F9 by the order subtotal in cell F16. The estimated taxes of $469.53, which is 5% of the subtotal value of $9,390.55, is displayed in cell F17.
5. In cell E18, type **TOTAL** as the label, and then press **TAB** to make cell F18 the active cell.
6. Type the formula **=SUM(F16:F17)** in cell F18 to calculate the total cost of the miscellaneous expenditures plus tax, and then press **ENTER**. The overall total is $9,860.08.
7. Click cell **F18** to view the formula in the cell. See Figure 1–27.

Figure 1–27 **Total miscellaneous expenses**

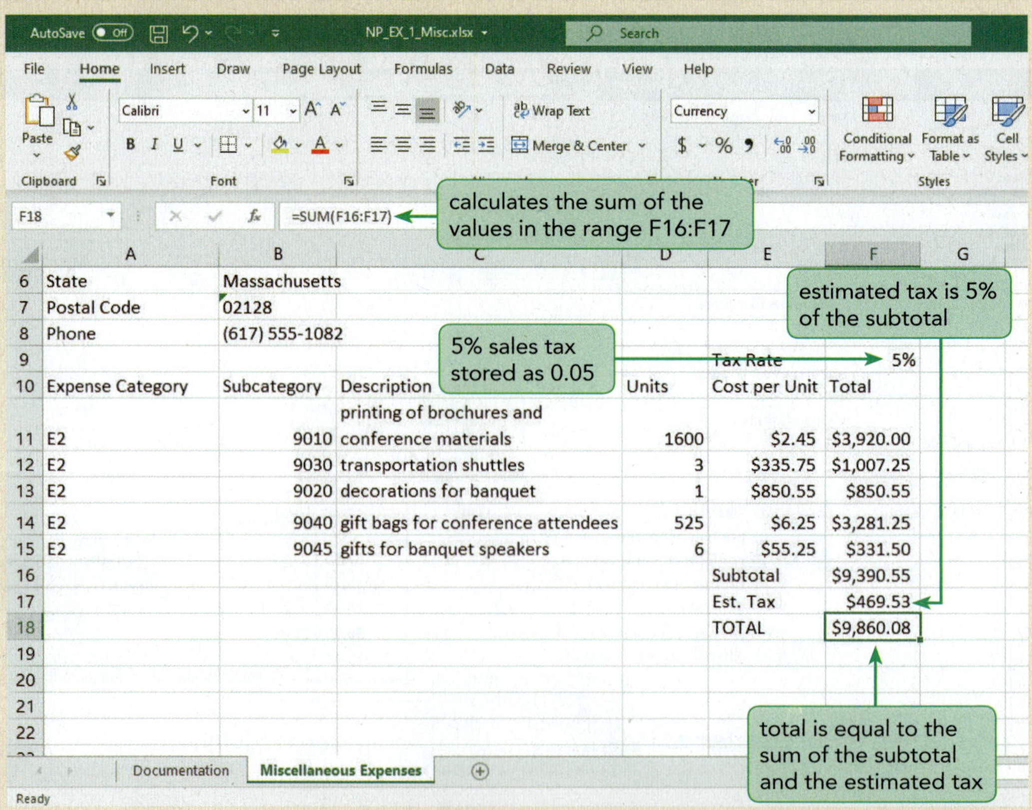

If you want to add all of the numbers in a column or row, you need to reference the entire column or row in the SUM function. For example, SUM(E:E) will return the sum of all numeric values in column E and SUM(5:5) will return the sum of all numeric values in row 5.

Proskills

Problem Solving: Writing Effective Formulas

You can use formulas to quickly perform calculations and solve problems. First, identify the problem you need to solve. Then, gather the data needed to solve the problem. Finally, create accurate and effective formulas that use the data to answer or resolve the problem. To write effective and useful formulas, consider these guidelines:

- **Keep your formulas simple.** Use functions in place of long, complex formulas whenever possible. For example, use the SUM function instead of entering a formula that adds individual cells, which makes it easier to confirm that the formula is making an accurate calculation as it provides answers needed to evaluate the problem.
- **Do not hide data values within formulas.** The worksheet displays formula results, not the actual formula. For example, to calculate a 5% interest rate on a currency value in cell A5, you could enter the formula =0.05*A5. However, this doesn't show how the value is calculated. A better approach places the 5% value in a cell accompanied by a descriptive label and uses the cell reference in the formula. Your worksheet will then display the interest rate as well as the resulting interest, making it clear to others what calculation is being performed.
- **Break up long formulas to show intermediate results.** Long formulas can be difficult to interpret and are prone to error. For example, the formula =SUM(A1:A10)/SUM(B1:B10) calculates the ratio of two sums but hides the two sum values. Instead of one long formula, consider calculating each sum in a separate cell, such as cells A11 and B11, and use the formula =A11/B11 to calculate the ratio. The worksheet will then show both the sums and the calculation of the ratio, making the workbook easier to interpret and manage.
- **Test complicated formulas with simple values.** Use values you can calculate in your head to confirm that your formula works as intended. For example, using 1s or 10s as the input values makes it easier to verify that your formula is working as intended.

Finding a solution to a problem requires accurate data and analysis. With workbooks, this means using formulas that are easy to understand, clearly showing the data being used in the calculations and demonstrating how the results are calculated. Only then can you be confident that you are choosing the best problem resolution.

Modifying a Worksheet

As you develop a worksheet, you will often need to modify its content and structure to create a cleaner and more readable document. You might need to move cells and ranges of cells or you may want to delete rows and columns from the worksheet. You can modify the worksheet's layout without affecting any data or calculations.

Moving and Copying a Cell or Range

One way to move a cell or range is to select it, position the pointer over the bottom border of the selection, drag the selection to a new location, and then release the mouse button. This technique is called **drag and drop** because you are dragging the range and dropping it in a new location. If the drop location is not visible, drag the selection to the edge of the workbook window to scroll the worksheet, and then drop the selection.

You can also use the drag-and-drop technique to copy cells by pressing CTRL as you drag the selected range to its new location. A copy of the original range is placed in the new location without removing the original range from the worksheet.

Reference

Moving or Copying a Cell Range

- Select the cell range to move or copy.
- Move the pointer over the border of the selection until the pointer changes shape.
- To move the range, click the border and drag the selection to a new location. To copy the range, hold down CTRL and drag the selection to a new location.

or

- Select the cell range to move or copy.
- On the Home tab, in the Clipboard group, click the Cut or Copy button; or right-click the selection, and then click Cut or Copy on the shortcut menu; or press CTRL+X or CTRL+C.
- Select the cell or the upper-left cell of the range where you want to paste the copied content.
- In the Clipboard group, click the Paste button; or right-click the selection and then click Paste on the shortcut menu; or press CTRL+V.

Carmen wants the labels and value in the range E16:F18 moved down one row to the range E17:F19 to set those calculations off from the list of miscellaneous expenses. You will use the drag-and-drop method to move the range.

To drag and drop the range E16:F18:

1. Select the range **E16:F18**. This is the range you want to move.
2. Point to the **bottom border** of the selected range so that the pointer changes to the move pointer.
3. Press and hold the mouse button to change the pointer to the arrow pointer, and then drag the selection down one row. Do not release the mouse button. A ScreenTip appears, indicating that the new range of the selected cells will be E17:F19. A dark green border also appears around the new range. See Figure 1–28.

Figure 1–28 Range being dragged

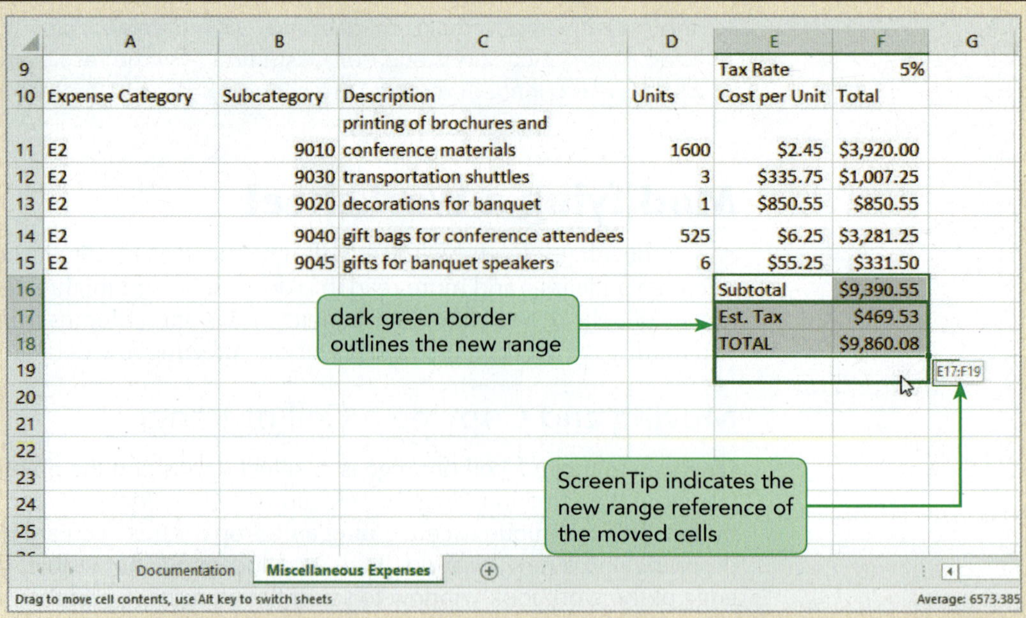

4. Make sure the ScreenTip displays the range E17:F19, and then release the mouse button. The selected cells move to their new location.

Some people find dragging and dropping a range difficult and awkward, particularly if the selected range is large or needs to move a long distance in the worksheet. In those situations, it is often more efficient to cut or copy and paste the cell contents. Cutting moves the selected content. Copying duplicates the selected content in the new location.

Carmen wants the worksheet to include a summary of the miscellaneous expenses at the top of the worksheet. To free up space for this summary, you'll cut the contents of the range A3:F19 and paste them into the range A7:F23.

To cut and paste the range A3:F19:

1. Click the Name box to the left of the formula bar, type **A3:F19** as the range to select, and then press **ENTER**. The range A3:F19 is selected.
2. On the Home tab, in the Clipboard group, click the **Cut** button (or press **CTRL+X**). The range is surrounded by a moving border, indicating that it has been cut.
3. Click cell **A7** to select it. This is the upper-left corner of the range where you want to paste the range that you cut.
4. In the Clipboard group, click the **Paste** button (or press **CTRL+V**). The range A3:F19 is pasted into the range A7:F23. Note that the cell references in the formulas were automatically updated to reflect the new location of those cells in the worksheet.

Using the COUNT Function

Many financial workbooks need to report the number of entries, such as the number of products in an order or the number of items in an expense or revenue category. To calculate the total number of items, you can use the COUNT function. The COUNT function has the syntax

```
COUNT(value1,[value2],[value3],…)
```

where ***value1*** is the range of numeric values to count and *value2*, *value3*, and so forth specify other ranges.

The COUNT function counts only numeric values. Any cells containing text are not included in the tally. To include cells containing non-numeric data such as text strings, you need to use the COUNTA function. The COUNTA function has the syntax

```
COUNTA(value1,[value2],[value3],…)
```

where ***value1*** is the range containing numeric or non-numeric values and *value2*, *value3*, and so forth specify other ranges to be included in the tally.

Next, you will enter a summary of the miscellaneous expenses by displaying the number of miscellaneous expense categories and the total cost of all the expenses. Because you are interested only in numeric values, you will use the COUNT function to count the number of miscellaneous expense values in the worksheet.

To use the COUNT and SUM functions to create an expense summary:

1. Scroll up the worksheet, click cell **A3** to make it the active cell, type **Summary** as the label, and then press **ENTER** to make cell A4 the active cell.
2. In cell A4, type **Expense Categories** as the label, and then press **TAB** to make cell B4 the active cell.
3. In cell B4, type **=COUNT(** to begin the COUNT function.
4. Select the range **F15:F19**. The range reference F15:F19 is entered into the COUNT function.
5. Type **)** to complete the function, and then press **ENTER** to make cell A5 the active cell. Cell B4 displays 5, indicating that the report includes five types of miscellaneous expenses.
6. In cell A5, type **Total Expenses** as the label, and then press **TAB** to make cell B5 the active cell.
7. In cell B5, type **=F23** as the formula, and then press **ENTER**. This formula displays contents of cell F23, which is the cell where you added the subtotal and taxes. See Figure 1–29.

Tip

To count all the values in a column, include only the column letter in the range reference; such as =COUNT(F:F) to count all values in column F.

Figure 1–29 Miscellaneous expenses summary

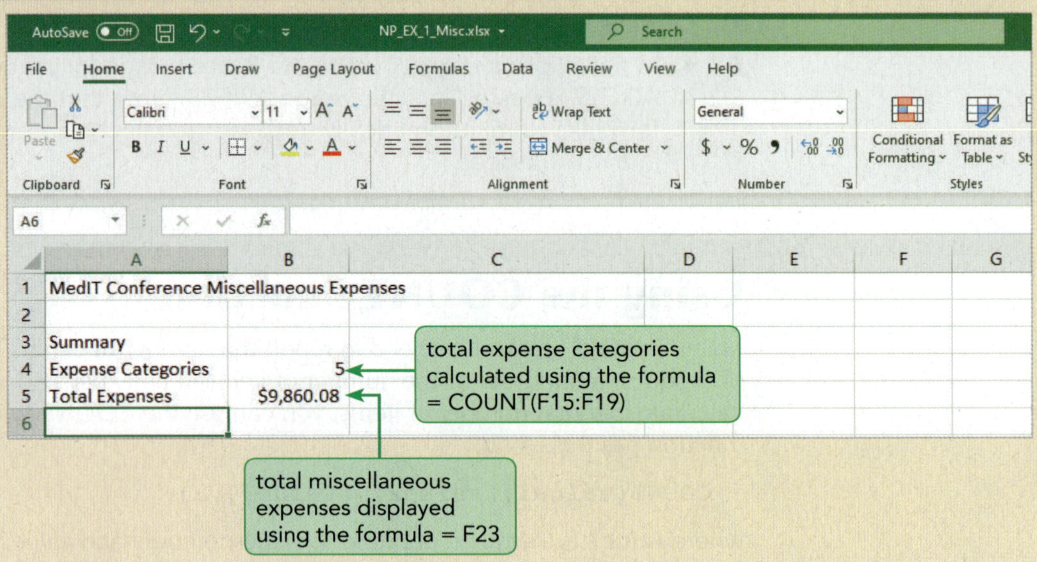

The formula in cell B5 that displays the sum of miscellaneous expenses calculated in cell F23 illustrates an important practice: Don't repeat the same calculation multiple times. Instead, use a formula that references the cell containing the formula results you wish to repeat. This way, if you must later change the formula, you need to edit only that one cell.

Modifying Rows and Columns

Another way to modify the structure of a workbook is by inserting or removing whole rows and columns from a worksheet.

Inserting Rows and Columns

When you insert a new column, the existing columns are shifted to the right, and the new column has the same width as the column directly to its left. When you insert a new row, the existing rows are shifted down, and the new row has the same height as the row above it. Because inserting a new row or column moves the location of the other cells in the worksheet, any cell references in a formula or function are updated to reflect the new layout.

Reference

Inserting and Deleting Rows or Columns

To insert rows and columns into a worksheet:
- Select the row or column headings where you want to insert new content.
- On the Home tab, in the Cells group, click the Insert button; or right-click the selected headings and click Insert on the shortcut menu; or press CTRL+SHIFT+=.

To delete rows or columns:
- Select the row or column headings for the content you want to delete.
- On the Home tab, in the Cells group, click the Delete button; or right-click the selecting headings, and then click Delete on the shortcut menu; or press CTRL+-.

MedIT is providing the flower arrangements for the tables at the closing banquet of the conference. Carmen asks you to add that expense category to the worksheet. You will insert a new row and enter that expense.

To insert the flower expense category:

1. Scroll down and click the **row 18** heading to select the entire row. You want to add the new expense category as row 18.
2. On the Home tab, in the Cells group, click the **Insert** button (or press **CTRL+SHIFT+=**). A new row 18 is inserted in the worksheet, and all the rows below the new row are shifted down.
3. Enter **E2** in cell A18, enter **9025** in cell B18, enter **flowers for the banquet tables** in cell C18, enter **20** in cell D18, and enter **$12.50** in cell E18.
4. Copy the formula from cell **F17** and paste it into cell **F18**. The formula =D18*E18 entered in cell F18, displaying $250.00 as the category expense total. The formula calculating the overall total of miscellaneous expenses in cell F22 is updated to include the new row. The subtotal, estimated taxes, and grand total are recalculated to include the new category. Cell F24 displays the grand total as ######## because the column is too narrow to display the entire value.
5. Increase the width of column F to **12** characters using whatever method you choose.
6. Click cell **F22**. See Figure 1-30.

Figure 1–30 New row inserted into the worksheet

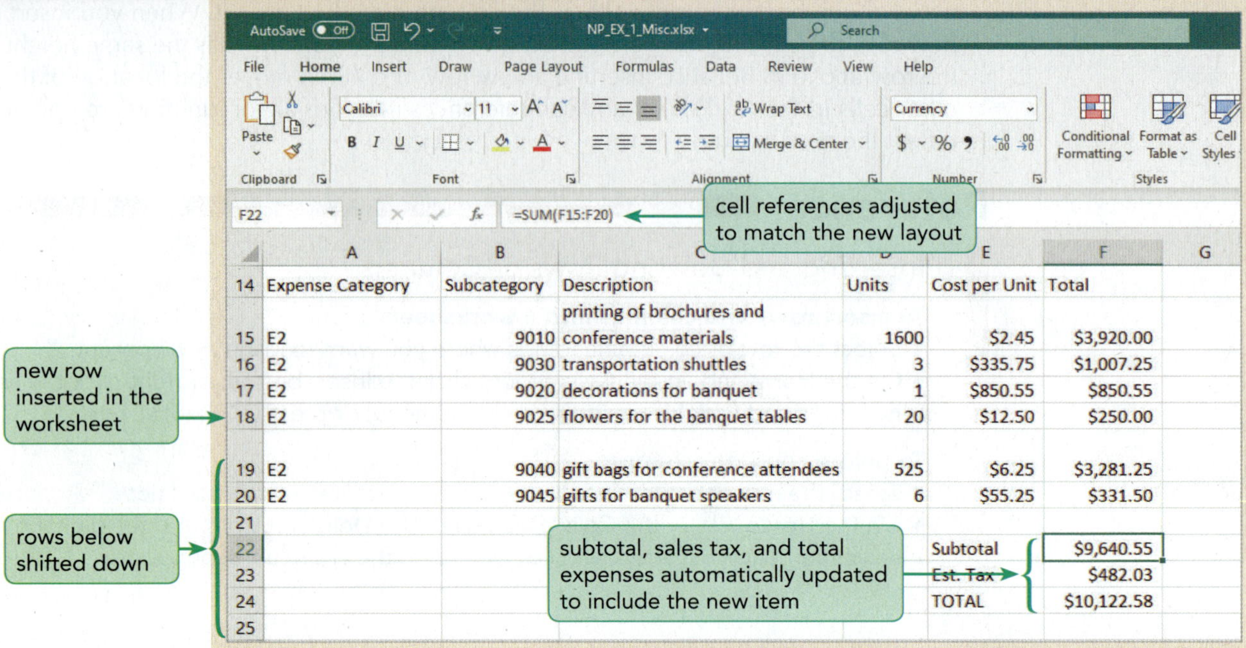

Notice that the formula in cell F22 is now =SUM(F15:F20). The range reference was updated to reflect the inserted row. The tax amount increased to $482.03 based on the new subtotal value of $9,640.55, and the total charge increased to $10,122.58 because of the added item. Also, the result of the COUNT function in cell B4 increased to 6 to reflect the added expense.

Deleting Rows and Columns

There are two ways of removing content from a worksheet: deleting and clearing. **Deleting** removes both the data and the selected cells from the worksheet. The rows below the deleted row shift up to fill the vacated space. Likewise, the columns to the right of the deleted column shift left to fill the vacated space. Also, all cell references in worksheet formulas are adjusted to reflect the change that removing the row or column makes to the worksheet structure. You click the Delete button in the Cells group on the Home tab to delete selected rows or columns.

Clearing removes the data from the selected cells, leaving those cells blank but preserving the current worksheet structure. You clear data from the selected cells by pressing DELETE.

The Boston conference isn't intended to make money for MedIT, but the company doesn't want to lose money either. Carmen needs to watch expenses and keep the total miscellaneous costs under $9,000. Carmen negotiated with the hotel to provide the transportation shuttles for free and asks you to remove that expense from the worksheet.

To delete the transportation shuttles row from the worksheet:

1. Click the **row 16** heading to select the entire row.
2. On the Home tab, in the Cells group, click the **Delete** button (or press **CTRL+–**). Row 16 is deleted, and the rows below it shift up to fill the space.

All the cell references from the formulas in the worksheet are again updated automatically to reflect the impact of deleting row 16. The subtotal value in cell F21 is now $8,633.30, which is the sum of the range F15:F19. The estimated tax in F22 decreases to $431.67. The total miscellaneous expenses are now $9,064.97, which is closer to the budget that Carmen must meet. Also, the result of the COUNT function in cell B4 returns to 5, reflecting the deleted expense category. As you can see, one of the great advantages of using Excel is that it modifies cell references within the formulas to reflect the additions and deletions made in the worksheet.

Inserting and Deleting a Range

You can also insert or delete cell ranges within a worksheet. When you use the Insert button to insert a range of cells, the existing cells shift down when the selected range is wider than it is long, and they shift right when the selected range is longer than it is wide, as shown in Figure 1–31. When you use the Insert Cells command, you specify whether the existing cells shift right or down, or whether to insert an entire row or column into the new range.

Figure 1–31 **Cells inserted into a worksheet**

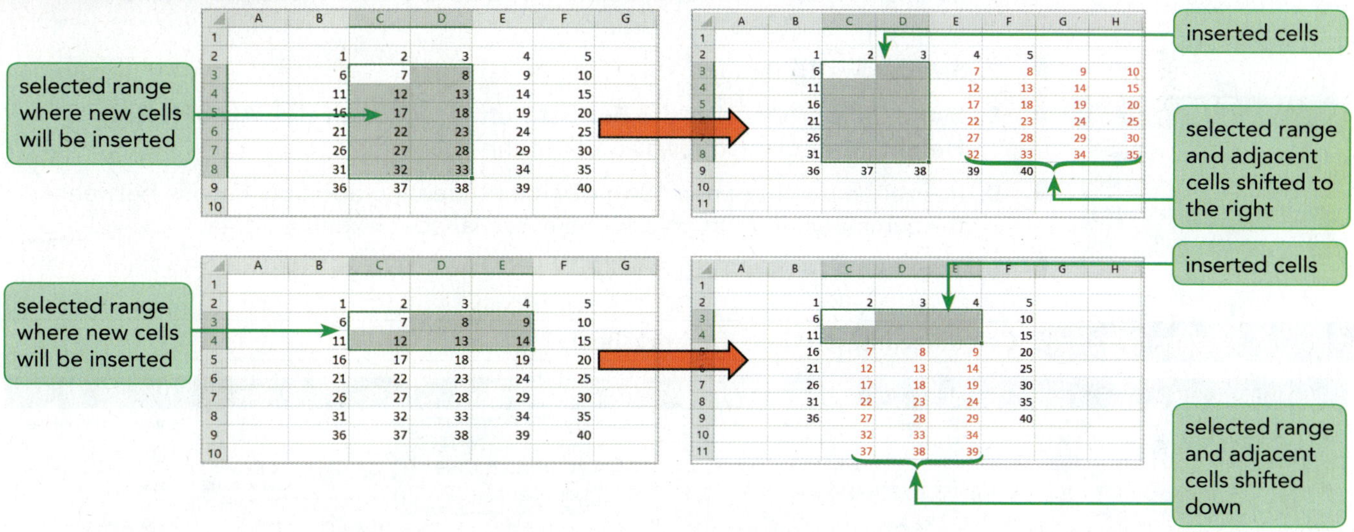

The process works in reverse when you delete a range. As with deleting a row or column, the cells adjacent to the deleted range either move up or left to fill in the space vacated by the deleted cells. The Delete Cells command lets you specify whether you want to shift the adjacent cells left or up or whether you want to delete the entire column or row.

When you insert or delete a range, cells that shift to a new location adopt the width of the columns they move into. As a result, you might need to resize columns and rows in the worksheet.

Reference

Inserting and Deleting a Range

- Select a range that matches the area you want to insert or delete.
- On the Home tab, in the Cells group, click the Insert button or the Delete button.

or

- Select the range that matches the range you want to insert or delete.
- On the Home tab, in the Cells group, click the Insert arrow and then click Insert Cells or click the Delete arrow and then click Delete Cells; or right-click the selected range, and then click Insert or Delete on the shortcut menu.
- Click the option button for the direction to shift the cells, columns, or rows.
- Click OK.

MedIT assigns an account ID for each type of revenue and expense item. Carmen asks you to insert this information into the worksheet. You will insert these new cells into the range A13:A23, shifting the adjacent cells to the right.

To insert a range to enter the account IDs:

1. Select the range **A13:A23** using any method you choose.
2. On the Home tab, in the Cells group, click the **Insert arrow**. A menu of insert options appears.
3. Click **Insert Cells**. The Insert dialog box opens.
4. Verify that the **Shift cells right** option button is selected.
5. Click **OK**. New cells are inserted into the selected range, and the adjacent cells move to the right. The shifted content does not fit well in the adjacent columns. You'll resize the columns and rows to fit their data.
6. Change the width of column B to **18** characters, the width of column C to **12** characters, the width of column D to **36** characters, and the widths of columns F and G to **14** characters.
7. Select rows **15** through **19**.
8. In the Cells group, click the **Format** button, and then click **AutoFit Row Height**. The selected rows autofit to their contents.
9. Resize the height of row 13 to **42** points, creating additional space between the summary information and the miscellaneous expenses data.
10. Click cell **A14**. See Figure 1–32.

Tip

You can also autofit rows by double-clicking the bottom border of the selected rows.

Figure 1–32 Cell range inserted into the worksheet

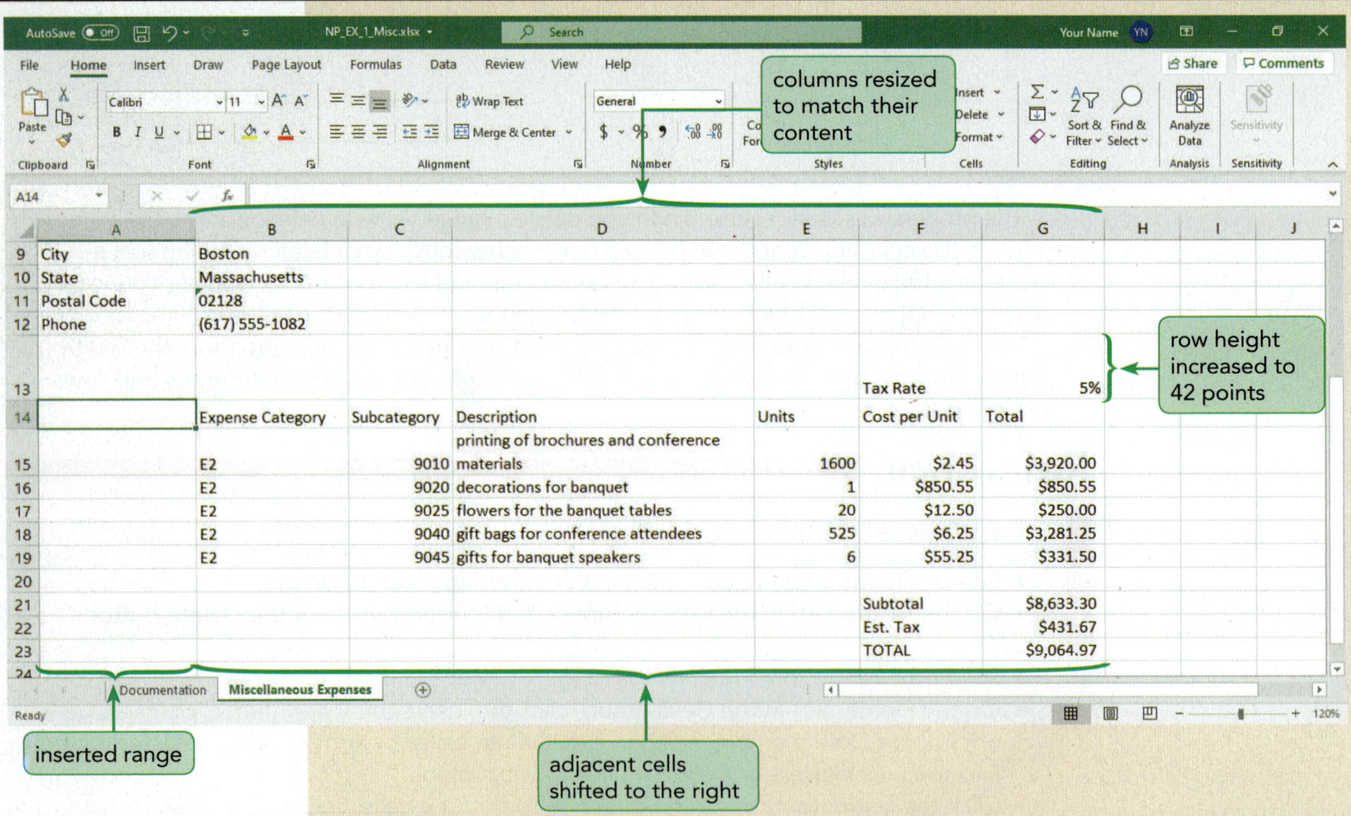

Notice that even though the account IDs will be entered in the range A14:A19, you inserted new cells into the A13:A23 range to retain the layout of the worksheet contents. Selecting the additional rows ensures that the tax rate and summary values still line up with the Cost per Unit and Total columns. Whenever you insert a new range, be sure to consider its impact on the layout of the entire worksheet.

Insight

Hiding and Unhiding Rows, Columns, and Worksheets

Workbooks can become long and complicated, filled with formulas and data that are important for performing calculations but are of little interest to readers. In those situations, you can simplify these workbooks by hiding rows, columns, and even worksheets. Although the contents of hidden cells cannot be seen, the data in those cells is still available for use in formulas and functions throughout the workbook.

Hiding removes a row or column from view while keeping it part of the worksheet. To hide a row or column, select the row or column heading, click the Format button in the Cells group on the Home tab, point to Hide & Unhide on the menu that appears, and then click Hide Rows or Hide Columns. The border of the row or column heading is doubled to mark the location of hidden rows or columns.

A worksheet often is hidden when the entire worksheet contains data that is not of interest to the reader and is better summarized elsewhere in the document. To hide a worksheet, make that worksheet active, click the Format button in the Cells group on the Home tab, point to Hide & Unhide, and then click Hide Sheet.

Unhiding redisplays the hidden content in the workbook. To unhide a row or column, click in a cell below the hidden row or to the right of the hidden column, click the Format button, point to Hide & Unhide, and then click Unhide Rows or Unhide Columns. To unhide a worksheet, click the Format button, point to Hide & Unhide, and then click Unhide Sheet. The Unhide dialog box opens. Click the sheet you want to unhide, and then click OK. The hidden content is redisplayed in the workbook.

Although hiding data can make a worksheet and workbook easier to read, be sure never to hide information that is important to the reader.

You will complete the miscellaneous expenses table by adding the account IDs for each expense. You can use Flash Fill to automatically create the account IDs.

Using Flash Fill

Flash Fill enters text based on patterns it finds in the data. As shown in Figure 1–33, Flash Fill generates names from the first and last names stored in the adjacent columns in the worksheet. To enter the rest of the names, press ENTER; to continue typing the names yourself, press ESC.

Figure 1–33 **Text automatically entered with Flash Fill**

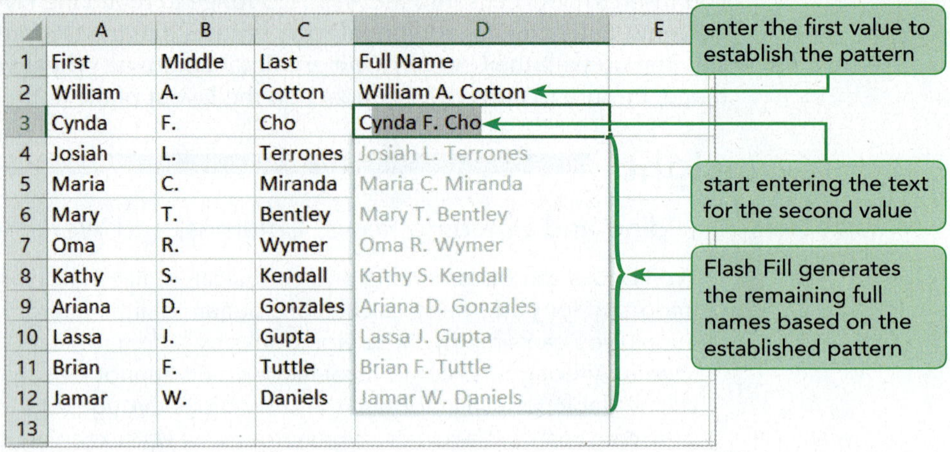

	A	B	C	D	E
1	First	Middle	Last	Full Name	
2	William	A.	Cotton	William A. Cotton	
3	Cynda	F.	Cho	Cynda F. Cho	
4	Josiah	L.	Terrones	Josiah L. Terrones	
5	Maria	C.	Miranda	Maria C. Miranda	
6	Mary	T.	Bentley	Mary T. Bentley	
7	Oma	R.	Wymer	Oma R. Wymer	
8	Kathy	S.	Kendall	Kathy S. Kendall	
9	Ariana	D.	Gonzales	Ariana D. Gonzales	
10	Lassa	J.	Gupta	Lassa J. Gupta	
11	Brian	F.	Tuttle	Brian F. Tuttle	
12	Jamar	W.	Daniels	Jamar W. Daniels	
13					

Flash Fill works best when the pattern is clearly recognized from the values in the data. Be sure to enter the data pattern in the column or row right next to the related data. The data used to generate the pattern must be in a rectangular grid and cannot have blank columns or rows.

MedIT account IDs combine the expense category and subcategory values. For example, an expense from the E2 expense category with a 9010 subcategory has the account ID of E2-9010. Rather than typing this information for every expense item, you will use Flash Fill to complete the data entry.

To enter the account IDs using Flash Fill:

1. Type **Account ID** in cell A14, and then press **ENTER**. The label is entered in cell A14, and cell A15 is the active cell.
2. Type **E2-9010** in cell A15, and then press **ENTER**. The first account ID is entered in cell A15, and cell A16 is the active cell.
3. Type **E2-9020** in cell A16. As soon as you complete those characters, Flash Fill generates the remaining entries in the column based on the pattern you entered. See Figure 1–34.

Figure 1–34 **Account IDs generated by Flash Fill**

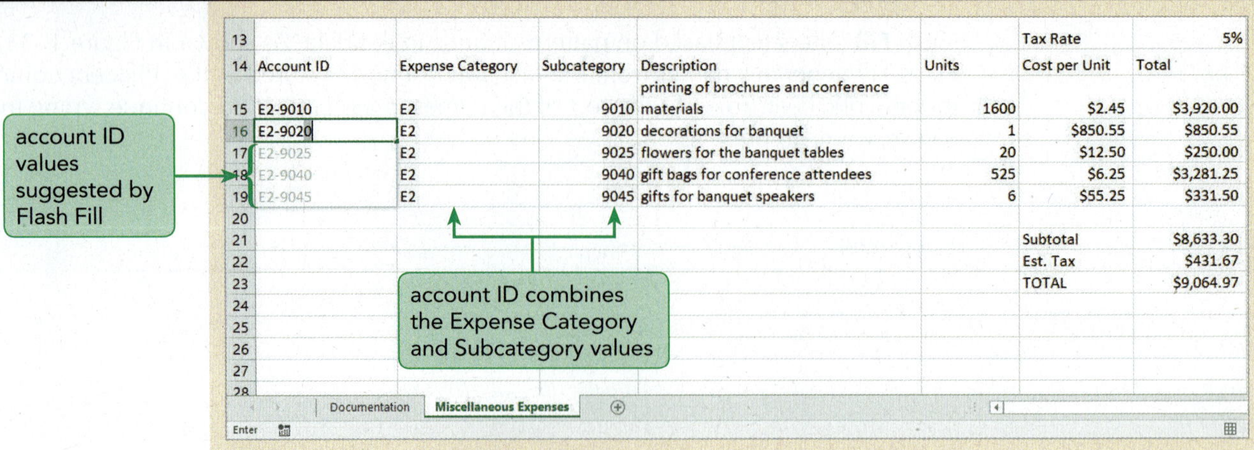

13						Tax Rate	5%
14	Account ID	Expense Category	Subcategory	Description	Units	Cost per Unit	Total
15	E2-9010	E2	9010	printing of brochures and conference materials	1600	$2.45	$3,920.00
16	E2-9020	E2	9020	decorations for banquet	1	$850.55	$850.55
17	E2-9025	E2	9025	flowers for the banquet tables	20	$12.50	$250.00
18	E2-9040	E2	9040	gift bags for conference attendees	525	$6.25	$3,281.25
19	E2-9045	E2	9045	gifts for banquet speakers	6	$55.25	$331.50
20							
21						Subtotal	$8,633.30
22						Est. Tax	$431.67
23						TOTAL	$9,064.97

Trouble? If you pause for an extended time between entering text to establish the pattern, Flash Fill might not extend the pattern for you.

4. Press **ENTER** to accept the suggested entries.

Note that Flash Fill generates text, not formulas. If you edit or replace the entry originally used to create the Flash Fill pattern, the other entries generated by Flash Fill in the column will not be updated.

Formatting a Worksheet

Formatting enhances the appearance of the worksheet data by changing its font, size, color, or alignment. Two common formatting changes are adding cell borders and changing the font size of text.

Adding Cell Borders

You can make spreadsheet content easier to read by adding borders around the worksheet cells. Borders can be added to the left, top, right, or bottom edge of any cell or range. You can set the color, thickness of and the number of lines in each border. Borders are especially useful when you print a worksheet because the gridlines that surround the cells in the workbook window are not printed by default. They appear on the worksheet only as a guide.

Carmen wants you to add borders around the cells that detail the miscellaneous expenses for the Boston conference to make that content easier to read when it's printed.

To add borders around the worksheet cells:

1. Select the range **F13:G13**. You'll add borders to these cells.
2. On the Home tab, in the Font group, click the **Borders arrow**, and then click **All Borders**. Borders are added around each cell in the selected range. The Borders button changes to reflect the last selected border option, which in this case is All Borders. The name of the selected border option appears in the button's ScreenTip.
3. Select the nonadjacent range **A14:G19,F21:G23**.
4. On the Home tab, in the Font group, click the **All Borders** button. Borders appear around all the cells in this range as well.
5. Click cell **A24** to deselect the range. See Figure 1–35.

Figure 1–35 Borders added to cells

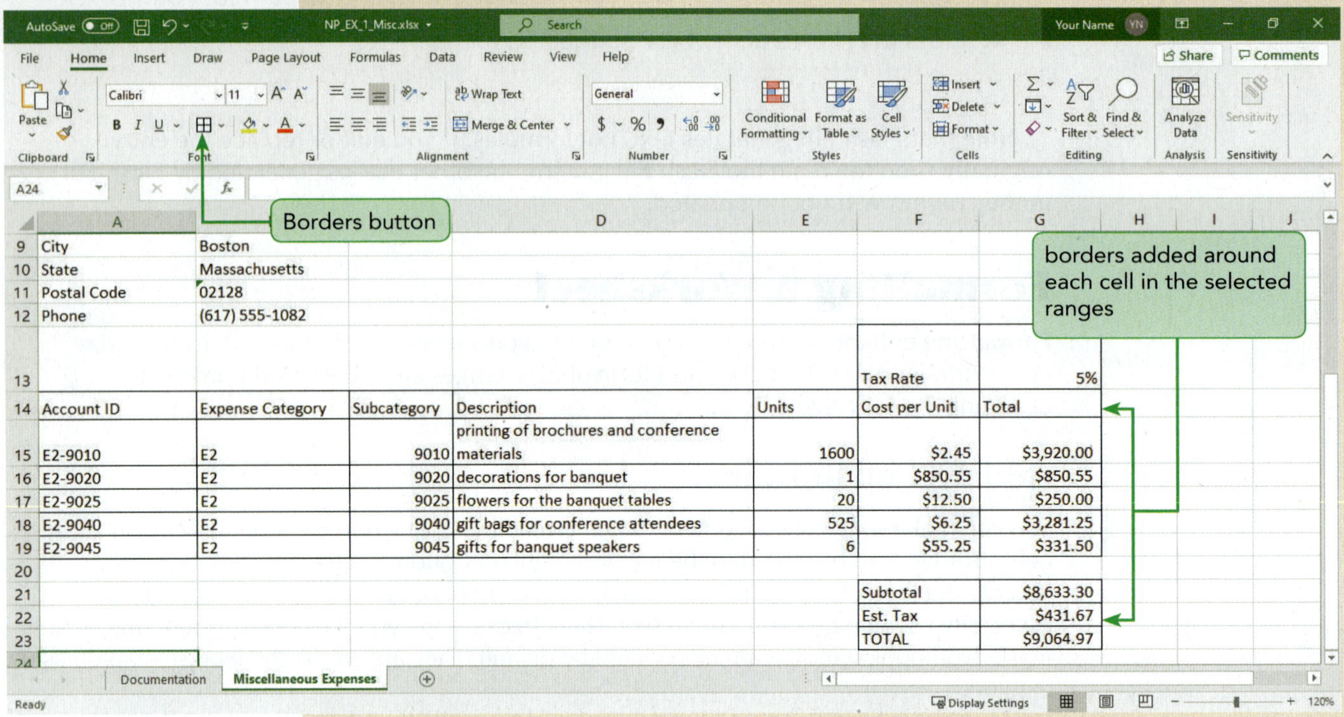

Changing the Font Size

Changing the size of text in a sheet provides a way to identify different parts of a worksheet, such as distinguishing a title or section heading from data. The size of the text is referred to as the font size and is measured in points. The default font size for worksheets is 11 points, but it can be made larger or smaller as needed. You can resize text in selected cells using the Font Size button in the Font group on the Home tab. You can also use the Increase Font Size and Decrease Font Size buttons to resize cell content to the next higher or lower standard font size.

Carmen wants you to increase the size of the worksheet title to 24 points to make it more visible and stand out from the rest of the worksheet content.

To change the font size of the worksheet title:

1. Scroll up the worksheet and click cell **A1** to select the worksheet title.
2. On the Home tab, in the Font group, click the **Font Size arrow** [11] to display a list of font sizes, and then click **24**. The worksheet title changes to 24 points. See Figure 1–36.

Figure 1–36 Font size increased in cell A1

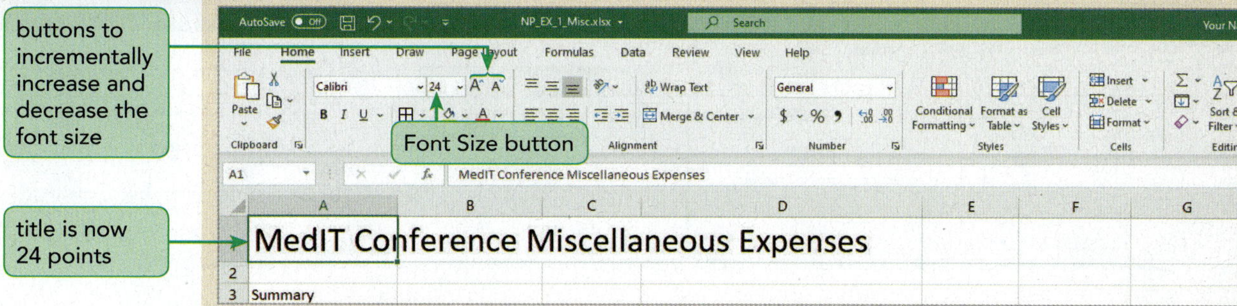

3. Press **CTRL+S** to save the workbook.

Now that the worksheet content and formatting are final, you can print the worksheet.

Printing a Workbook

Excel has many tools to control the print layout and appearance of a workbook. Before printing a worksheet, you will want to preview the printout to make sure that it will print correctly.

Changing Worksheet Views

You can view a worksheet in three ways. Normal view, which you have been using throughout this module, shows the contents of the worksheet. Page Layout view shows how the worksheet will appear when printed. Page Break Preview displays the location of the different page breaks within the worksheet. This is useful when a worksheet will span several printed pages, and you need to control what content appears on each page.

Carmen wants you to preview the print version of the Miscellaneous Expenses worksheet. You will do this by switching between views.

To switch the Miscellaneous Expenses worksheet between views:

1. Click the **Page Layout** button on the status bar. The page layout of the worksheet appears in the workbook window.
2. On the Zoom slider at the lower-right corner of the workbook window, click the **Zoom Out** button until the percentage is **60%**. The reduced magnification makes it clear that the worksheet will spread over two pages when printed. See Figure 1–37.

Figure 1–37 Worksheet in Page Layout view

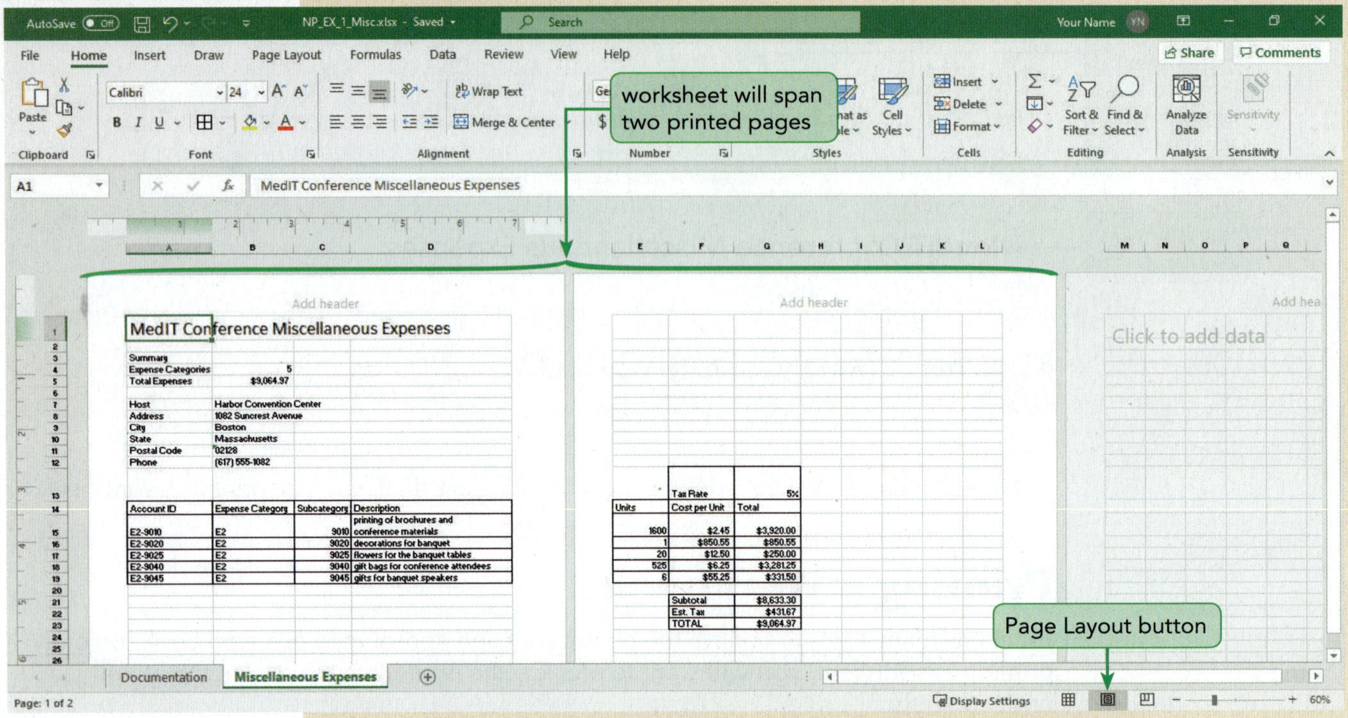

> **Tip**
>
> You can relocate a page break by dragging the dotted blue border in the Page Break Preview window.

3. Click the **Page Break Preview** button on the status bar. The view switches to Page Break Preview, which shows only those parts of the current worksheet that will print. A dotted blue border separates one page from another.
4. On the Zoom slider, drag the slider button to the right until the percentage is **80%**. You can now more easily read the contents of the worksheet. See Figure 1–38.

Figure 1–38 Worksheet in Page Break Preview view

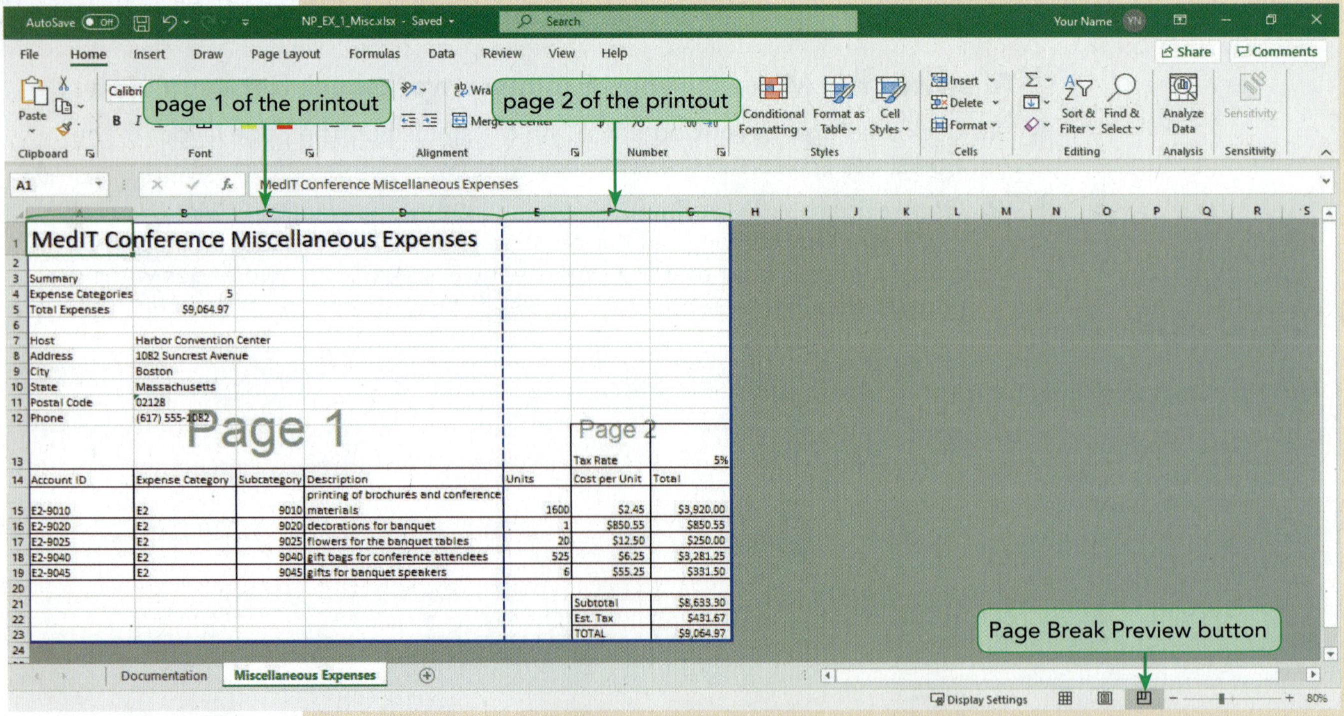

5. Click the **Normal** button on the status bar. The worksheet returns to Normal view. Notice that after viewing the worksheet in Page Layout or Page Break Preview, a dotted black line appears between columns D and E in Normal view to show where the page breaks occur.

Changing the Page Orientation

Page orientation specifies in which direction content is printed on the page. In **portrait orientation**, the page is taller than it is wide. In **landscape orientation**, the page is wider than it is tall. By default, Excel displays pages in portrait orientation. Changing the page orientation affects only the active sheet in the workbook and not the other, unselected, sheets.

As you saw in Page Layout view and Page Break Preview, the Miscellaneous Expenses worksheet will print on two pages—columns A through D will print on the first page, and columns E through G will print on the second page. Keep in mind that the columns that print on each page may differ slightly depending on the printer. Carmen wants the entire worksheet to print on a single page, so you'll change the page orientation from portrait to landscape.

To change the page orientation of the worksheet:

1. On the ribbon, click the **Page Layout** tab. The tab includes options for changing how the worksheet is arranged.
2. In the Page Setup group, click the **Orientation** button, and then click **Landscape**. The worksheet switches to landscape orientation, though you cannot see this change in Normal view.
3. Click the **Page Layout** button on the status bar to switch to Page Layout view. The worksheet will still print on two pages.

Even with the landscape orientation the contents of the worksheet will still not fit on one page. You can correct this by scaling the page.

Setting the Scaling Options

Scaling resizes the worksheet to fit within a single page or set of pages. There are several options for scaling a printout of a worksheet. You can scale the width or the height of the printout so that all the columns or all of the rows fit on a single page. You can also scale the printout to fit the entire worksheet (both columns and rows) on a single page. If the worksheet is too large to fit on one page, you can scale the print to fit on the number of pages you select. You can also scale the worksheet to a percentage of its size. For example, scaling a worksheet to 50% reduces the size of the sheet by half when it is sent to the printer. When scaling a printout, make sure that the worksheet is still readable after it is resized. Scaling affects only the active worksheet, so you can scale each worksheet separately to best fit its contents.

Carmen asks you to scale the printout so that the Miscellaneous Expenses worksheet fits on one page in landscape orientation.

To scale the printout of the worksheet:

1. On the Page Layout tab, in the Scale to Fit group, click the **Width arrow**, and then click **1 page** on the menu that appears. All the columns in the worksheet now fit on one page.

   If more rows are added to the worksheet, Carmen wants to ensure that they still fit within a single sheet.

2. In the Scale to Fit group, click the **Height** arrow, and then click **1 page**. All the rows in the worksheet will now always fit on one page. See Figure 1–39.

Figure 1–39 Printout scaled to fit on one page

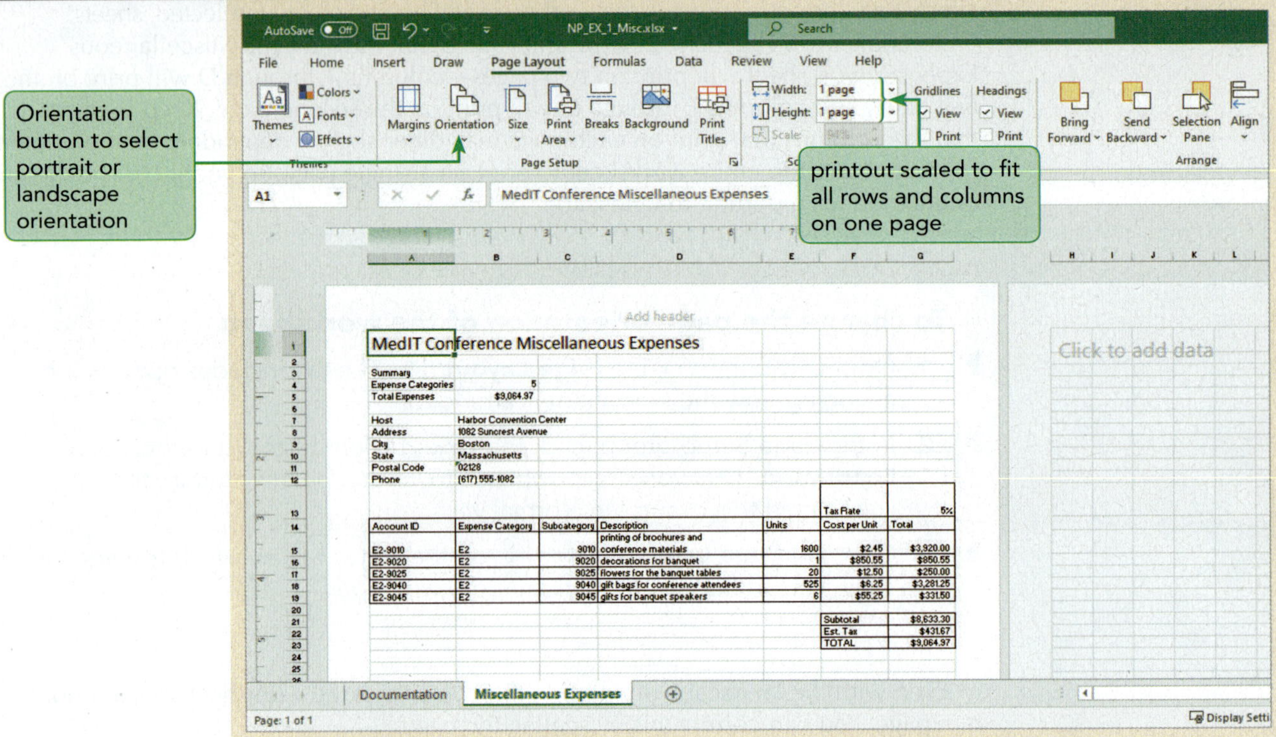

Setting the Print Options

Tip

To print the gridlines or the column and row headings, click the corresponding Print check box in the Sheet Options group on the Page Layout tab.

You can print the contents of a workbook by using the Print screen in Backstage view. The Print screen provides options for choosing where to print, what to print, and how to print. For example, you can specify the number of copies to print, which printer to use, and what to print. You can choose to print only the selected cells, only the active sheets, or all the worksheets in the workbook that contain data. The printout will include only the data in the worksheet. The other elements in the worksheet, such as the row and column headings and the gridlines around the worksheet cells, will not print by default. The preview shows you exactly how the printed pages will look with the current settings. You should always preview before printing to ensure that the printout looks exactly as you intended and avoid unnecessary reprinting.

Carmen asks you to preview and print the workbook containing the estimates of miscellaneous expenses for the conference.

To preview and print the workbook:

1. On the ribbon, click the **File** tab to display Backstage view.
2. Click **Print** in the navigation bar. The Print screen appears with the print options and a preview of the printout of the Miscellaneous Expenses worksheet. See Figure 1–40.

Figure 1–40 Print screen in Backstage view

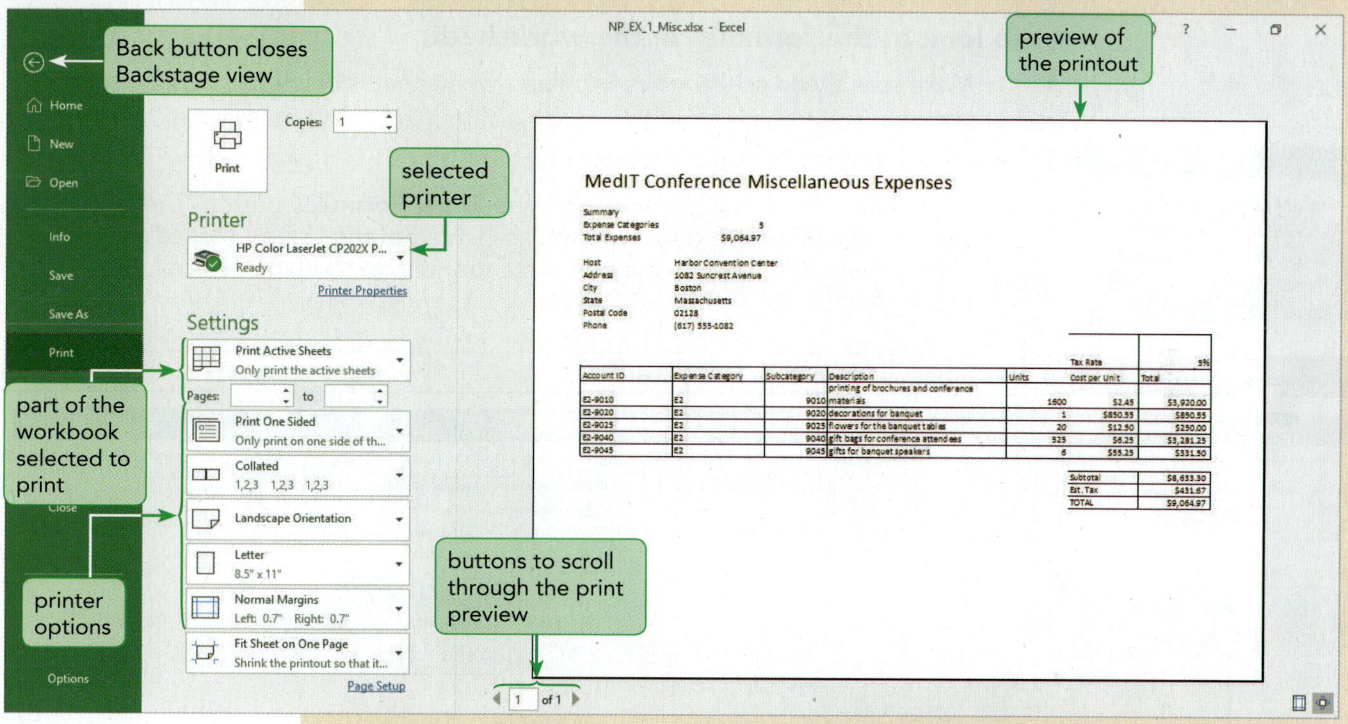

3. Click the **Printer** button, and then click the printer you want to print to, if it is not already selected. By default, Excel will print only the active sheet.
4. In the Settings options, click the top button, and then click **Print Entire Workbook** to print all of the sheets in the workbook—in this case, both the Documentation and the Miscellaneous Expenses worksheets. The preview shows the first sheet in the workbook—the Documentation worksheet. Note that this sheet is still in portrait orientation.
5. Below the preview, click the **Next Page** button ▶ to view the print preview for the Miscellaneous Expenses worksheet, which will print on a single page in landscape orientation.
6. If you are instructed to print, click the **Print** button to send the contents of the workbook to the specified printer. If you are not instructed to print, click the **Back** button ⊖ in the navigation bar to exit Backstage view.

Viewing Worksheet Formulas

Most of the time, you will be interested in only the final results of a worksheet, not the formulas used to calculate those results. However, in some cases, you might want to view the formulas used to develop the workbook. This is particularly useful when you encounter unexpected results and want to examine the underlying formulas, or you want to discuss the formulas with a colleague. You can display the formulas instead of the resulting values in cells.

If you print the worksheet while the formulas are displayed, the printout shows the formulas instead of the values. To make the printout easier to read, you should print the worksheet gridlines as well as the row and column headings so that cell references in the formulas are easy to find in the printed version of the worksheet.

You'll look at the formulas in the Miscellaneous Expenses worksheet.

To look at the formulas in the worksheet:

1. Make sure the Miscellaneous Expenses worksheet is displayed in Page Layout view.
2. On the ribbon, click the **Formulas** tab.
3. In the Formula Auditing group, click the **Show Formulas** button. The worksheet changes to display formulas instead of the values. Notice that the columns widen to display the complete formula text within each cell. See Figure 1–41.

Tip

You can also switch to the formula view by pressing CTRL+` (the grave accent symbol ` is usually located above TAB).

Figure 1–41 Worksheet with formulas displayed

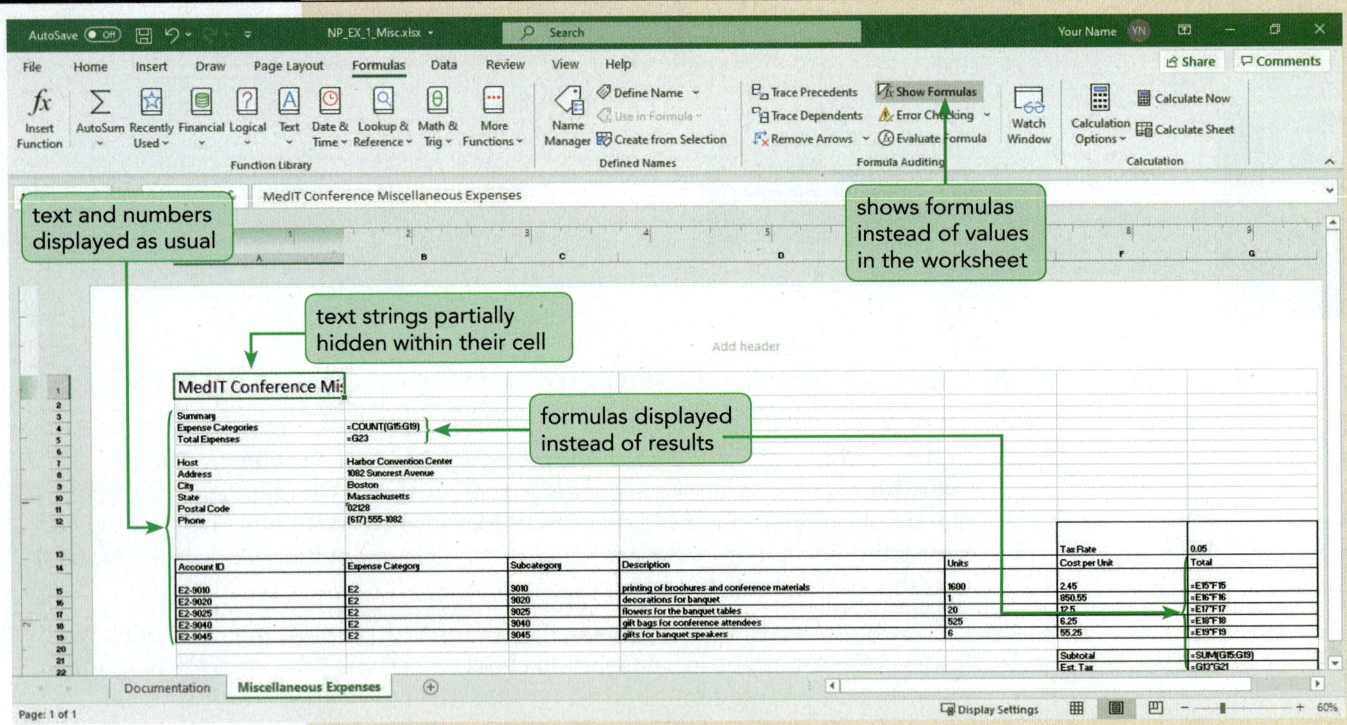

4. When you are done reviewing the formulas, click the **Show Formulas** button again to hide the formulas and display the resulting values.
5. Click the **Normal** button on the status bar to return the workbook to Normal view.
6. On the Zoom slider, drag the slider button to the right until the percentage is **120%** (or the magnification you want to use).
7. sam Save the workbook, and then close it.

Carmen is pleased with the workbook you created and will use your estimates in the workbook she is using to track all of the cost estimates for the Boston conference. Carmen will continue to adjust the revenue and expense projections as the conference data approaches and will get back to you she needs to you to do additional analysis.

Review

Session 1.2 Quick Check

1. What is the formula to add values in cells A1, B1, and C1? What function will achieve the same result?
2. What is the formula to count the number of numeric values in the range A1:A30?
3. If you insert cells into the range C1:D10, shifting the cells to the right, what is the new location of the data that was previously in cell F4?
4. Cell E11 contains the formula =SUM(E1:E10). How is the formula adjusted when a new row is inserted above row 5?
5. In the following function, which arguments are required and which arguments are optional:

   `AVERAGE(`***`number1`***`,[`*`number2`*`],[`*`number3`*`],...)`

6. What is the formula to sum all the numeric values in column C.
7. Describe the four ways of viewing worksheet contents in Excel.
8. How are page breaks indicated in Page Break Preview?

Practice

Review Assignments

There are no Data Files needed for the Review Assignments.

Carmen needs to estimate the total costs for supplying computers, audio/video equipment, and Internet access to the participants at the Boston conference. She has some documentation on the cost of different expense items. Carmen asks you to enter that information into a workbook and calculate the total cost of items in this expense category. Complete the following:

1. Create a new, blank workbook, and then save it as **NP_EX1_Equipment** in the location specified by your instructor.
2. Rename the Sheet1 worksheet using **Documentation** as the new name.
3. Enter the data shown in Figure 1–42 in the specified cells.

Figure 1–42 Documentation sheet data

Cell	Text
A1	MedIT
A3	Author
A4	Date
A5	Purpose
B3	*your name*
B4	*current date*
B5	To estimate the cost of renting computers, audio/video equipment, Internet access, and hiring technical support at the MedIT conference in Boston

4. Set the font size of the title text in cell A1 to 24 points.
5. Set the width of column B to 32 characters, and then wrap the contents of cell B5 within the cell.
6. Add borders around all of the cells in the range A3:B5.
7. Add a new worksheet after the Documentation sheet, and then rename the worksheet using **Equipment Expenses** as the new name.
8. In cell A1, enter **MedIT Conference Equipment Expenses** as the worksheet title. Set the font size of the title text in cell A1 to 20 points.
9. Enter the data summarizing the conference in the specified cells as shown in Figure 1–43. Make sure that the postal code value is treated as text rather than a number.

Figure 1–43 Conference Summary data

Cell	Text	Cell	Text
A4	Equipment Categories	A12	Phone
A5	Total Expenses	B7	Conference Connections
A7	Vendor	B8	480 Technology Lane
A8	Street Address	B9	Boston
A9	City	B10	Massachusetts
A10	State	B11	02155
A11	Postal Code	B12	(617) 555-7814

10. Enter the column titles and expenses for various equipment that will be used at the conference in the range A14:E20 as shown in Figure 1–44.

Figure 1–44 Equipment expenses

Expense Category	Subcategory	Description	Units	Cost per Unit
E2	5010	computer workstation rental	25	$105.00
E2	5020	audio/video rental	10	$85.00
E2	5030	screen projector rentals	10	$75.00
E2	5040	high-speed Internet access	1	$450.00
E2	5050	onsite wiring	1	$500.00
E2	5060	web hosting	1	$700.00

11. In cell F14, enter **Total** as the label. In the range F15:F20, calculate the total cost of each equipment item by entering formulas that return the value of the number of units ordered multiplied by the cost per unit.
12. In cell E22, enter **Subtotal** as the label, and then in cell F22, use the SUM function to calculate the sum of the values in the range F15:F20.
13. In cell E13, enter **Tax Rate** as the label, and then in cell F13, enter **3%** as the value.
14. In cell E23, enter **Est. Tax** as the label, and then in cell F23, calculate the estimated tax by entering a formula that multiplies the subtotal value in cell F22 by the tax rate in cell F13.
15. In cell E24, enter **TOTAL** as the label, and then in cell F24, use the SUM function to calculate the sum of the subtotal value in cell F22 and the estimated tax in cell F23.
16. Insert new cells in the range A13:A24, shifting the other cells to the right.
17. In cell A14, enter **Account ID** as the label. In cell A15, enter **E2-5010** as the first ID. In cell A16, enter **E2-5020** as the second ID, and allow Flash Fill to enter the remaining IDs.
18. Add borders around all of the cells in the range F13:G13,A14:G20,F22:G24.
19. Set the width of columns A and B to 22 characters. Set the width of columns C, E, F, and G to 13 characters. Set the width of column D to 24 characters. Set the height of row 13 to 30 points.
20. Wrap the text in the range D15:D20 so all of the content is visible.
21. In cell B4, use the COUNT function to count the number of numeric values in the range E15:E20. In cell B5, display the value of the total expenses that was calculated in cell G24.
22. Carmen wants to keep the equipment budget under $6,000. If the total cost of the equipment is less than $6,000, enter **within budget** in cell B3, otherwise enter **over budget** in the cell.
23. Change the page orientation of the Equipment Expenses worksheet to landscape orientation, and then scale the width and height of the Equipment Expenses worksheet to print on a single page.
24. Save the workbook. If you are instructed to print, then print the entire workbook.
25. Display the formulas in the Equipment Expenses worksheet. If you are instructed to print, then print the worksheet. Remove the worksheet from formula view.
26. Save the workbook, and then close it.

Apply

Case Problem 1

Data File needed for this Case Problem: NP_EX_1-2.xlsx

Cross State Trucking Brian Eagleton is a dispatch manager at Cross State Trucking, a major freight hauler based in Chicago, Illinois. Brian needs to develop a workbook that will summarize the driving log of Cross State drivers. Brian has a month of travel data from one of the company's drivers and wants you to create a workbook that he can use to analyze this data. Complete the following:

1. Open the **NP_EX_1-2.xlsx** workbook located in the Excel1 > Case1 folder included with your Data Files. Save the workbook as **NP_EX_1_Trucking** in the location specified by your instructor.
2. Change the name of the Sheet1 worksheet using **Travel Log** as the name, and then move it to the end of the workbook. Rename the Sheet2 worksheet using **Documentation** as the name.
3. In the Documentation sheet, enter your name in cell B3 and the current date in cell B4.
4. Go to the Travel Log worksheet. Resize the columns so that all the data is visible in the cells.
5. Between the Odometer Ending column and the Hours column, insert a new column. Enter **Miles** as the column label in cell I4.
6. In the Miles column, in the range I5:I25, enter formulas to calculate the number of miles driven each day by subtracting the odometer beginning value from the odometer ending value.
7. Between the Price per Gallon column and the Seller column, insert a new column. Enter **Total Fuel Purchase** as the label in cell N4.
8. In the Total Fuel Purchase column, in the range N5:N25, enter formulas to calculate the total amount spent on fuel each day by multiplying the gallons value by the price per gallon value.
9. In cell B5, use the COUNT function to calculate the total number of driving days using the values in the Date column in the range D5:D25.
10. In cell B6, use the SUM function to calculate the total number of driving hours using the values in the Hours column in the range J5:J25.
11. In cell B7, enter a formula that divides the hours of driving value (cell B6) by the days of driving value (cell B5) to calculate the average hours of driving per day.
12. In cell B9, use the SUM function to calculate the driver's total expenses for the month for fuel, tolls, and miscellaneous expenditures using the nonadjacent range N5:N25,P5:Q25.
13. In cell B10, use the SUM function to calculate the total amount the driver spent on fuel using the range N5:N25. In cell B11, use the SUM function to calculate the total amount spent on tolls and miscellaneous expenses using the range P5:Q25.
14. In cell B13, use the SUM function to calculate the total gallons of gas the driver used during the month using the range L5:L25. In cell B14, use the SUM function to calculate the total number of miles driven that month using the range I5:I25.
15. In cell B15, enter a formula that divides the total miles (cell B14) by the total gallons (cell B13) to calculate the miles per gallon. In cell B16, enter a formula that divides the total expenses (cell B9) by the total miles driven (cell B14) to calculate the cost per mile.
16. Cross State Trucking wants to keep the cost of driving and delivering goods to less than 65 cents per mile. If the cost per mile is greater than 65 cents, enter **over budget** in cell B4, otherwise enter **on budget** in cell B4.
17. In cell A1, increase the font size of the text to 28 points. In cell D3 and cell L3, increase the font size of the Mileage Table and Expense Table labels to 18 points.
18. Change the worksheet to landscape orientation. Scale the printout so that the worksheet is scaled to 1 page wide by 1 page tall. If you are instructed to print, print the entire workbook.
19. Save the workbook, and then close it.

Create

Case Problem 2

Data File needed for this Case Problem: NP_EX_1-3.xlsx

Meucci Digital, Inc. Travon Lee is a manager in the human resources department of Meucci Digital, a company that specializes in digital communications hardware and software. Travon wants to use a workbook to summarize employee data. The report will include the average employee's base salary, bonus salary, sick days, performance review, and the average number of years of employment at the company. You will add formulas and functions to the workbook to analyze the data. Because Travon may be adding data on other employees to the worksheet, all the calculations should be applied to entire columns of data rather than specified ranges within those columns. Complete the following:

1. Open the **NP_EX_1-3.xlsx** workbook located in the Excel1 > Case2 folder included with your Data Files. Save the workbook as **NP_EX_1_HRDepartment** in the location specified by your instructor.
2. In the Documentation sheet, enter your name in cell B3 and the current date in cell B4.
3. Add borders around the range A3:B5.
4. Go to the Sheet2 worksheet and rename it using **Employees** as the sheet name.
5. In cell I5 of the Employees worksheet, calculate the number of days that Clay Aaron has worked for the company by subtracting the hire date in cell H5 from the report date in cell G5. Copy the formula and then paste it to the range I6:I582.
6. Insert a new column between columns E and F. In the new cell F4, enter **Full Name** as the label. In cell F5, enter **Clay Aaron** as the first name, and in cell F6, enter **Angel Abarca** as the second name. Allow Flash Fill to enter the remaining full names of employees in the column.
7. In cell A1, enter **Meucci Digital, Inc.** as the title. In cell A2, enter **Employee Summary** as the label. Increase the font size of cell A1 to 22 points and increase the font size of cell A2 to 16 points.
8. Enter the labels shown in Figure 1–45 in the specified cells in preparation for adding a summary of the employee data.

Figure 1–45 Labels for employee information

Cell	Text
A4	Number of Employees
A6	Average Days of Employment
A7	Average Years of Employment
A9	Total Base Salary
A10	Average Base Salary
A11	Total Bonuses
A12	Average Bonuses
A13	Total Compensation
A14	Average Compensation
A16	Total Sick Days
A17	Average Sick Days
A19	Average Performance Rating

9. Resize the worksheet columns as necessary so that all of the cell content is visible.

Explore 10. Add the following calculations to the worksheet:

a. In cell B4, use the COUNT function to calculate the number of employees by counting the hiring dates in column I. (*Hint*: The column reference is I:I.)

b. In cell B6, calculate the average number of days of employment using the SUM function with the cells in column J (the column reference is J:J), and then dividing that sum by the number of employees reported in cell B4.
c. In cell B7, calculate the average years of employment by dividing the value in cell B6 by 365.25 (the number of days in a year).
d. In cell B9, calculate the total the company paid in base salaries by using the SUM function to sum the values in column K. In cell B10, calculate the average base salary by dividing the total value in cell B9 by the number of employees in cell B4.
e. In cell B11, calculate the total amount paid out in bonuses by summing the values in column L. In cell B12, calculate the average bonus per employee by dividing the total amount in bonuses by the total number of employees in cell B4.
f. In cell B13, calculate the total compensation the company paid by adding the values in cells B9 and B11. In cell B14, calculate the average compensation per employee by dividing cell B13 by cell B4.
g. In cell B16, sum the total number of sick days taken by employees of Meucci Digital. In cell B17, calculate the average number of sick days per employee.
h. In cell B19, calculate the average performance rating for the Meucci Digital employees.

Explore 11. Insert a new row directly below row 432 (between the entry for Pamela Randazzo and George Raymond) containing the employee information shown in Figure 1–46. Have Excel automatically calculate the days of employment value when it inserts the formula directly into cell J431.

Figure 1–46 New employee data for Meucci Digital

Information	Value
First	Aditya
Last	Rao
Full Name	Aditya Rao
Department	Sales
Report Date	7/31/2025
Hire Date	7/1/2025
Base Salary	$32,200
Bonus	$0
Sick Days	0
Performance Rating	3

12. Verify that the summary statistics in column B automatically update to reflect the addition of the new employee and that the total number of employees in the report is 579.
13. Make sure the Employees worksheet is set to portrait orientation, and then scale its width to 1 page but leave the height set to automatic.
14. If you are instructed to print, print only the first page of the Employees worksheet.
15. Save the workbook, and then close it.

Module 2

Formatting Workbook Text and Data

Creating a Sales Report

Objectives

Session 2.1

- Change fonts, font style, and font color
- Add fill colors and a background image
- Create formulas to calculate sales data
- Format numbers as currency and percentages
- Format dates and times
- Align, indent, and rotate cell contents
- Merge a group of cells

Session 2.2

- Use the AVERAGE function
- Apply cell styles
- Copy and paste formats with the Format Painter
- Find and replace text and formatting
- Change workbook themes
- Highlight cells with conditional formats
- Format a worksheet for printing

Case | **Bristol Bay**

Stefan Novak is a sales manager for the Northwest region of the Bristol Bay department store chain. Stefan needs to create a report on sales data in the Home Furnishing department of 20 Bristol Bay stores in Washington, Oregon, and Idaho. The report will include summaries of the Home Furnishing department's gross revenue and net income over the current fiscal year compared to the same sales data from the previous year. The report will also track the sales data by store and month so that Stefan can view monthly sales trends and identify those stores that exceed expectations or are falling short of sales goals. Stefan asks you to enter the formulas needed to summarize the data and to format the report to make it easier to read and analyze the data.

Starting Data Files

Excel2 →

Module
NP_EX_2-1.xlsx
Support_EX_2_Background.jpg

Review
NP_EX_2-2.xslx
Support_EX_2_Texture.jpg

Case1
NP_EX_2-3.xlsx

Case2
NP_EX_2-4.xlsx

Session 2.1 Visual Overview:

The Font group has buttons for setting the font, font size, font color, and **font style**, which indicates how characters are emphasized, such as **bold**, *italic*, or underline.

You can format text strings within a cell in Edit mode.

The Accounting format places the currency symbol on the left edge of the cell, adds a thousands separator, shows values to two decimals places, and displays negative values in parentheses.

A **font** defines the appearance and shape of letters, numbers, and special characters.

You can **merge**, or combine, several cells into one cell. This content is centered in the merged range A13:A21.

You can rotate content in the cell.

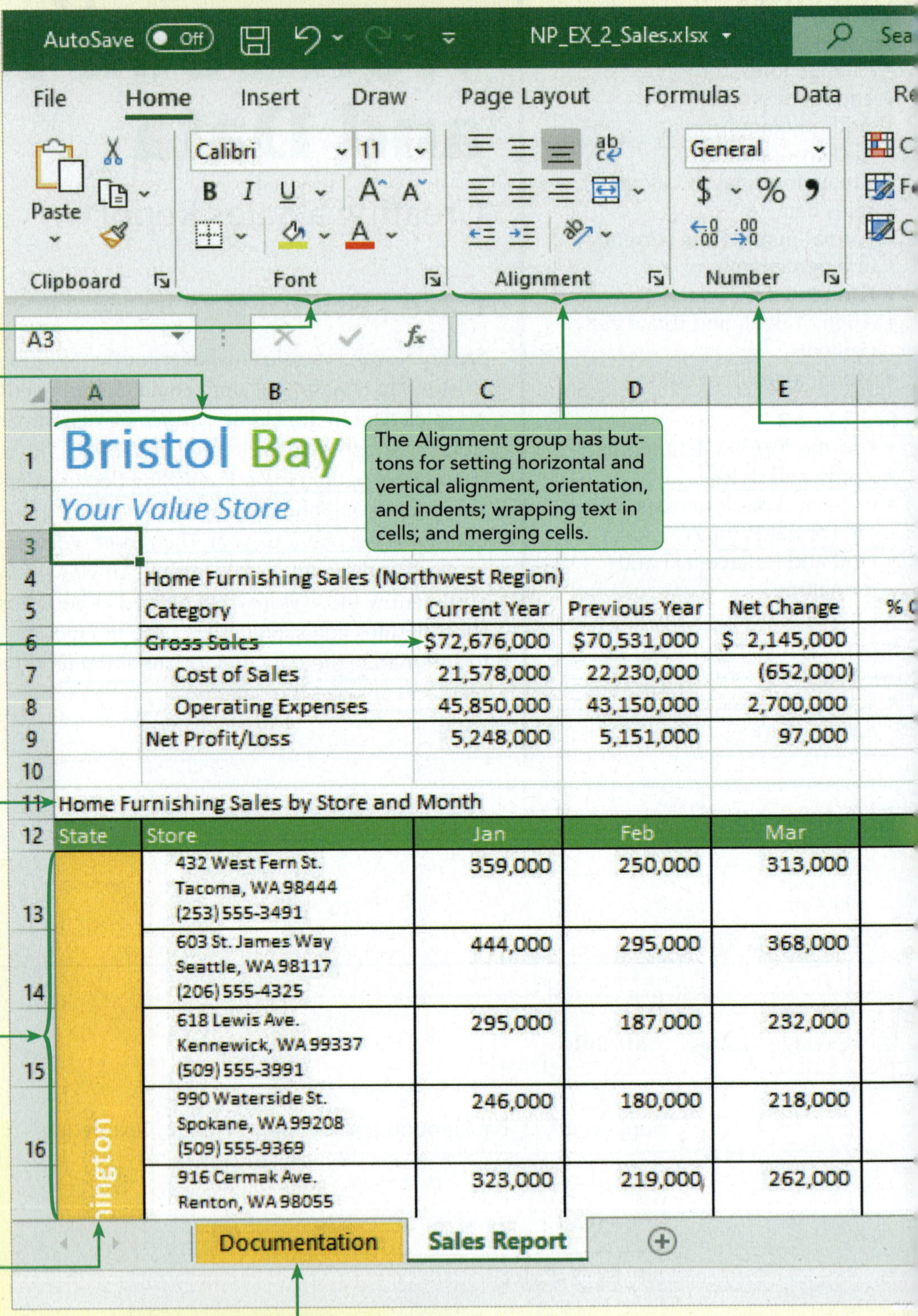

The Alignment group has buttons for setting horizontal and vertical alignment, orientation, and indents; wrapping text in cells; and merging cells.

You can change the fill color of a sheet tab to help organize your workbook.

Formatting a Worksheet

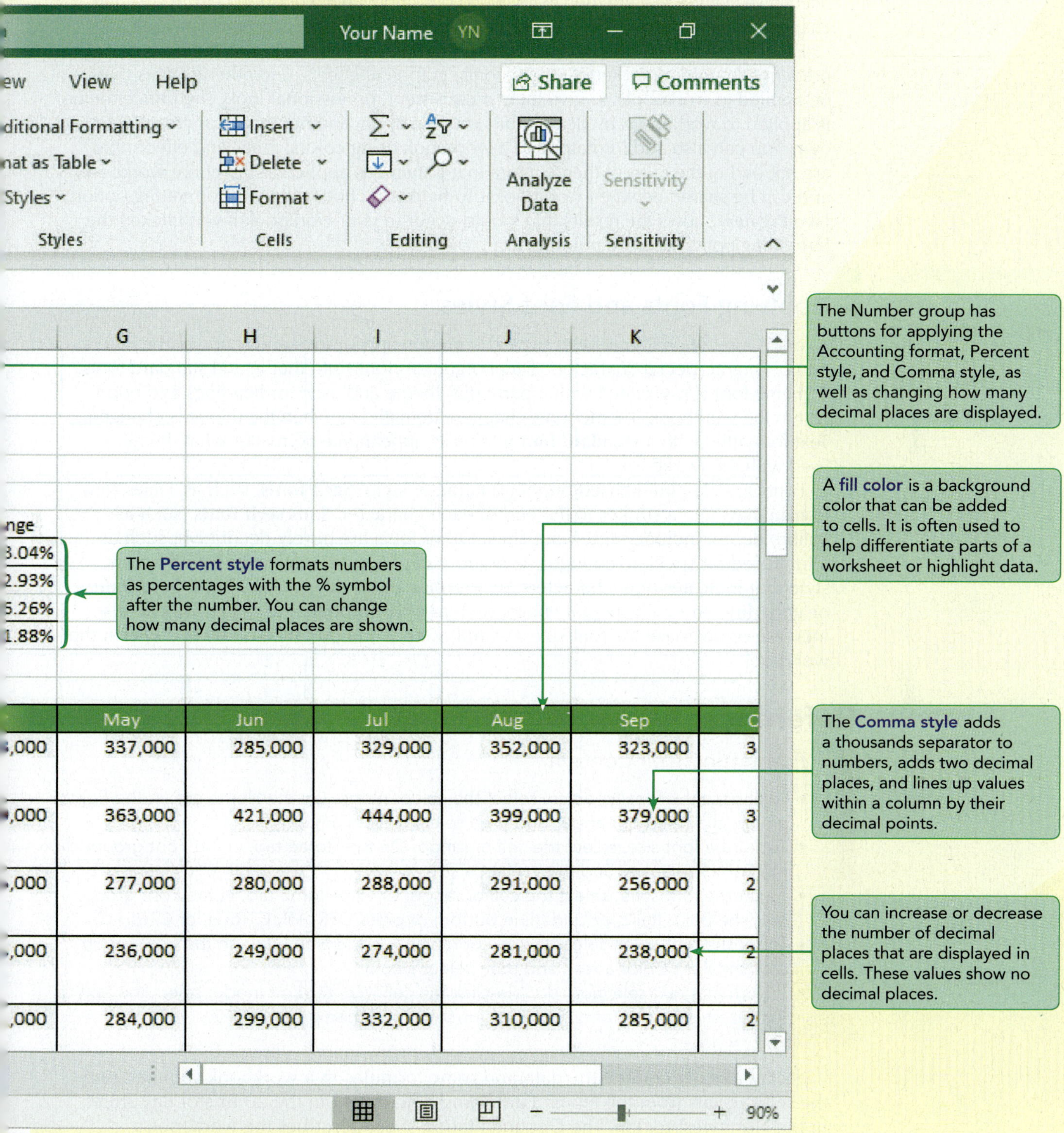

Formatting Cell Text

You can improve the readability of your workbooks by choosing the fonts, styles, colors, and decorative features that are used in the workbook and within worksheet cells. Formatting changes only the appearance of the workbook data—it does not affect the data itself.

Excel organizes complementary formatting options into themes. A **theme** is a predefined coordinated set of colors, fonts, graphical effects, and other formats that can be applied to workbooks to give them a consistent, professional look. The Office theme is applied to workbooks by default, but you can apply another theme or create your own. You can also add formatting to a workbook using colors, fonts, and effects that are not part of the current theme. Note that a theme is applied to the entire workbook and can be shared between workbooks. To help you choose the best formatting option, **Live Preview** shows the results that would occur in your workbook if you clicked the formatting option you are pointing to.

Applying Fonts and Font Styles

A font is a set of characters that share a common appearance and shape of the letters, numbers, and special characters. Excel organizes fonts into theme and standard fonts. A **theme font** is associated with a particular theme and used for headings and body text in the workbook. Theme fonts change automatically when the theme is changed. Text formatted with a **standard font** retains its appearance no matter what theme is used with the workbook.

Fonts are classified based on their character style. **Serif fonts**, such as Times New Roman, have extra strokes at the end of each character. **Sans serif fonts**, such as Calibri, do not include these flourishes. Other fonts are purely decorative, such as a font used for specialized logos. Every font can be further formatted with a font style that indicates how characters are emphasized, such as *italic*, **bold**, ***bold italic***, or <u>underline</u> and with special effects such as ~~strikethrough~~ and color. You can also increase or decrease the font size to emphasize the importance of the text within the workbook.

Reference

Formatting Cell Content

- To choose the font typeface, select the cell or range. On the Home tab, in the Font group, click the Font arrow, and then select a font name.
- To set the font size, select the cell or range. On the Home tab, in the Font group, click the Font Size arrow, and then select a size.
- To set the font style, select the cell or range. On the Home tab, in the Font group, click the Bold, Italic, or Underline button; or press CTRL+B, CTRL+I, or CTRL+U.
- To set the font color, select the cell or range. On the Home tab, in the Font group, click the Font Color arrow, and then select a color.
- To format a text selection, double-click the cell to enter Edit mode, select the text to format, change the font, size, style, or color, and then press ENTER.

Stefan already entered the data and some formulas in a workbook summarizing the sales results from the Home Furnishing department in the 20 Bristol Bay stores in the Northwest region. The Documentation sheet describes the workbook's purpose and content. The company name is at the top of the sheet. Stefan wants you to format the name in large, bold letters using the default heading font from the Office theme.

To format the company name:

1. sam Open the **NP_EX_2-1.xlsx** workbook located in the **Excel2 > Module** folder included with your Data Files, and then save the workbook as **NP_EX_2_Sales** in the location specified by your instructor.
2. In the Documentation sheet, enter your name in cell B4 and the date in cell B5.
3. Click cell **A1** to make it the active cell.
4. On the Home tab, in the Font group, click the **Font arrow** to display a gallery of fonts available on your computer. Each name is displayed in its font typeface. The first two fonts listed are the theme fonts for headings and body text—Calibri Light and Calibri.
5. Scroll down the Fonts gallery until you see Arial Black in the All Fonts list, and then point to **Arial Black** (or a similar font). Live Preview shows the effect of the Arial Black font on the text in cell A1. See Figure 2–1.

Figure 2–1 Font gallery

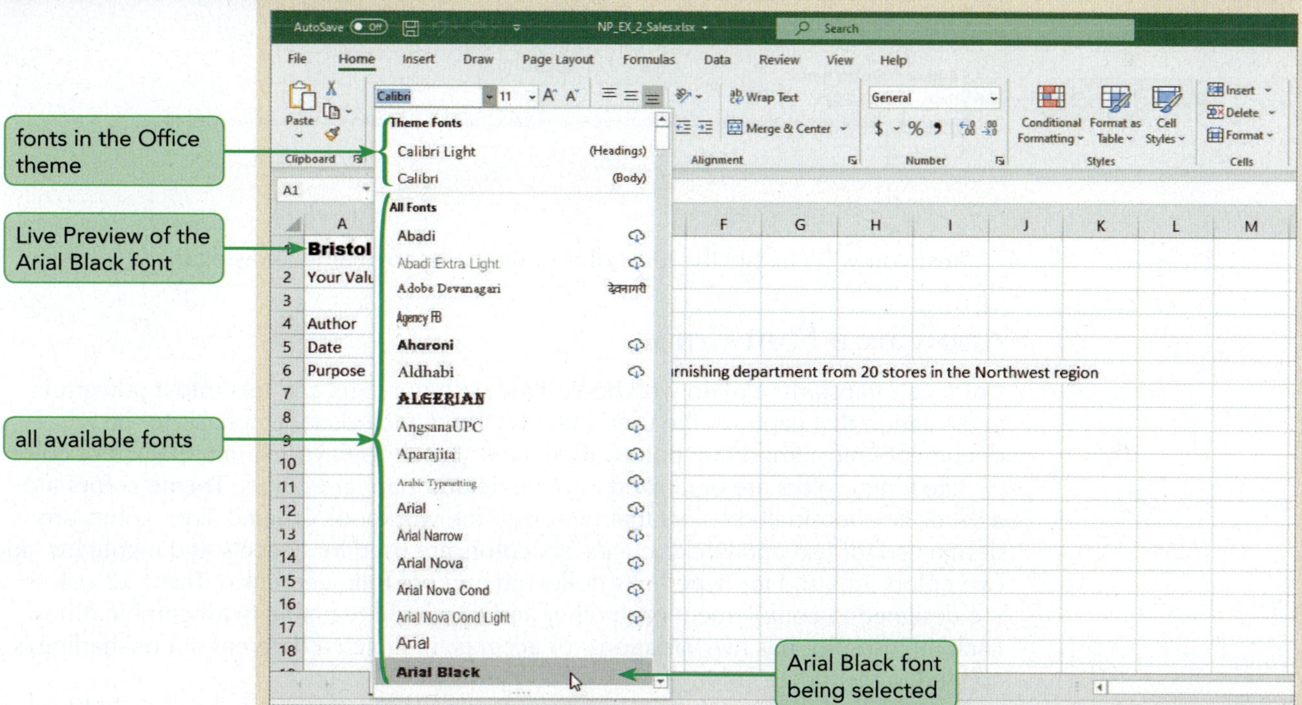

6. Point to three other fonts in the list to see the Live Preview of how the text in cell A1 appears in other fonts.
7. Click **Calibri Light** in the Theme Fonts list. The company name in cell A1 changes to the Calibri Light font, the default headings font in the current theme.
8. In the Font group, click the **Font Size arrow** [11] to display a list of font sizes, point to **28** to preview the text in that font size, and then click **28**. The font size of the company name is now 28 points.
9. In the Font group, click the **Bold** button [B] (or press **CTRL+B**). The text changes to a bold font.
10. Click cell **A2** to make it the active cell. The cell with the company slogan ("Your Value Store") is selected.
11. In the Font group, click the **Font Size arrow** [11], and then click **16**. The company slogan changes to 16 points.

12. In the Font group, click the **Italic** button *I* (or press **CTRL+I**). The company slogan is italicized.
13. Select the range **A4:A6**, and then press **CTRL+B**. The text in the selected range changes to bold.
14. Click cell **A7** to deselect the range. See Figure 2–2.

Figure 2–2 Formatted text in the Documentation sheet

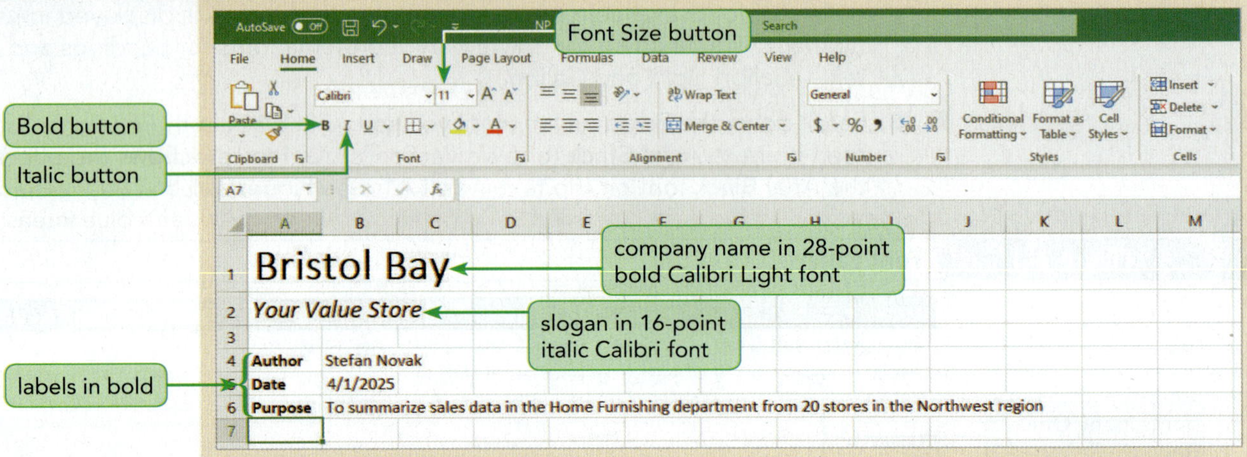

Next you will change the text color of the company name and slogan.

Applying a Font Color

Color can transform a plain workbook filled with numbers and text into a powerful presentation that captures the user's attention and adds visual emphasis to the document's most important points. By default, Excel displays text in a black font color.

Like fonts, colors are organized into theme and standard colors. **Theme colors** are a set of 12 coordinated colors that belong to the workbook's theme. Four colors are designated for text and backgrounds, six colors are used for accents and highlights, and two colors are used for hyperlinks (followed and not followed links). These 12 colors are designed to complement each other and to remain readable in all combinations. Each theme color has five variations, or accents, in which a different tint or shading is applied to the theme color.

Ten **standard colors**—dark red, red, orange, yellow, light green, green, light blue, blue, dark blue, and purple—are always available regardless of the workbook's theme. Beyond these easily accessible 10 standard colors, you can open an extended palette of 134 standard colors. You can also create a custom color by specifying a mixture of red, blue, and green color values, making available 16.7 million custom color combinations, which are more colors than the human eye can distinguish. Some dialog boxes have an automatic color option that uses your Windows default text and background colors, usually black text on a white background.

Insight

Creating Custom Colors

Custom colors let you add subtle and striking colors to a formatted workbook. To create custom colors, you use the **RGB Color model** in which each color is expressed with varying intensities of red, green, and blue. RGB color values are often represented as a set of numbers in the format

`(red, green, blue)`

where *red* is an intensity value assigned to red light, *green* is an intensity value assigned to green light, and *blue* is an intensity value assigned to blue light. The intensities are measured on a scale of 0 to 255—0 indicates no intensity (or the absence of the color) and 255 indicates the highest intensity. So, the RGB color value (255, 255, 0) represents a mixture of high-intensity red (255) and high-intensity green (255) with the absence of blue (0), creating the color yellow.

To create colors in Excel using the RGB model, click the More Colors option located in a color menu or dialog box to open the Colors dialog box. In the Colors dialog box, click the Custom tab, and then enter the red, green, and blue intensity values. A preview box shows the resulting RGB color.

Stefan wants the company name and slogan in the Documentation sheet to stand out by changing the font color in cells A1 and A2 to light blue.

To change the font color of the company name and slogan:

1. Select the range **A1:A2** containing the company name and slogan.
2. On the Home tab, in the Font group, click the **Font Color arrow** to display the gallery of theme and standard colors.
3. In the Standard Colors section, point to the **Light Blue** color (the seventh color). The color name appears in a ScreenTip, and Live Preview shows the text with the light blue font color. See Figure 2–3.

Figure 2–3 Font Color gallery

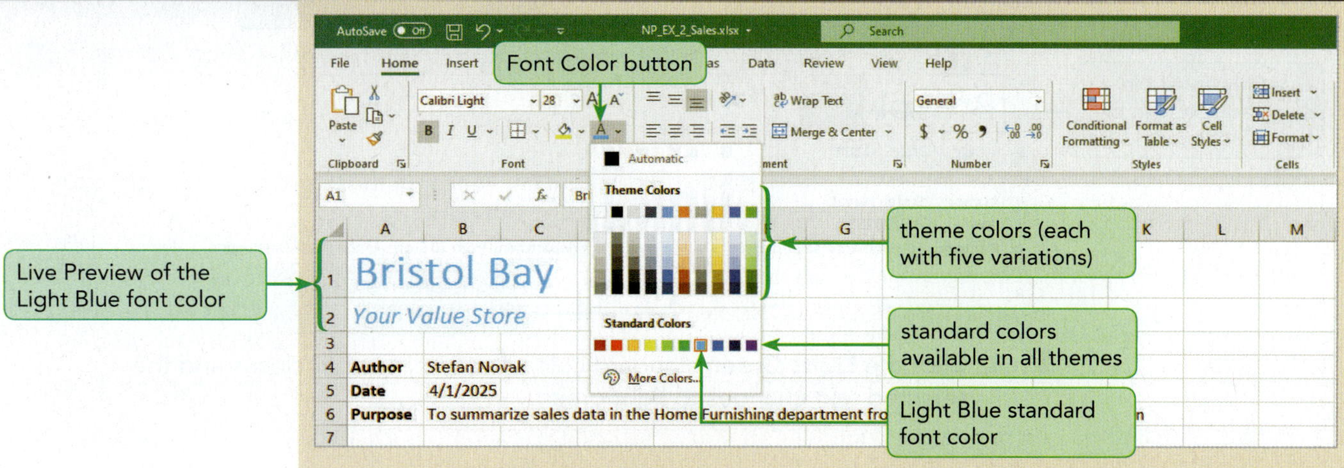

4. Click the **Light Blue** color. The company name and slogan change to that color.

Not all of the text within a cell has to have the same color. You can also format text strings within a cell.

Formatting Text Selections Within a Cell

In Edit mode, you can select and format selections of text within a cell. You can make these changes to selected text from the ribbon or from the Mini toolbar. The **Mini toolbar** is a small toolbar that appears next to selected content, containing the most frequently used formatting commands for that content.

Stefan asks you to format the company name in cell A1 so that the text "Bay" appears in light green.

To format part of the company name in light green:

1. Double-click cell **A1** to select the cell and enter Edit mode (or click cell **A1** and press **F2**). The status bar shows "Edit" to indicate that you are working with the cell in Edit mode. The pointer changes to the I-beam pointer over the cell that is in Edit mode.
2. Drag the pointer over the word **Bay** to select it. A Mini toolbar appears above the selected text with buttons to change the font, size, style, and color of the selected text in the cell. In this instance, you want to change the font color.
3. On the Mini toolbar, click the **Font Color arrow**, and then point to the **Light Green** color (the fifth color) in the Standard Colors section. Live Preview shows the color of the selected text as light green. See Figure 2–4.

Figure 2–4 Mini toolbar in Edit mode

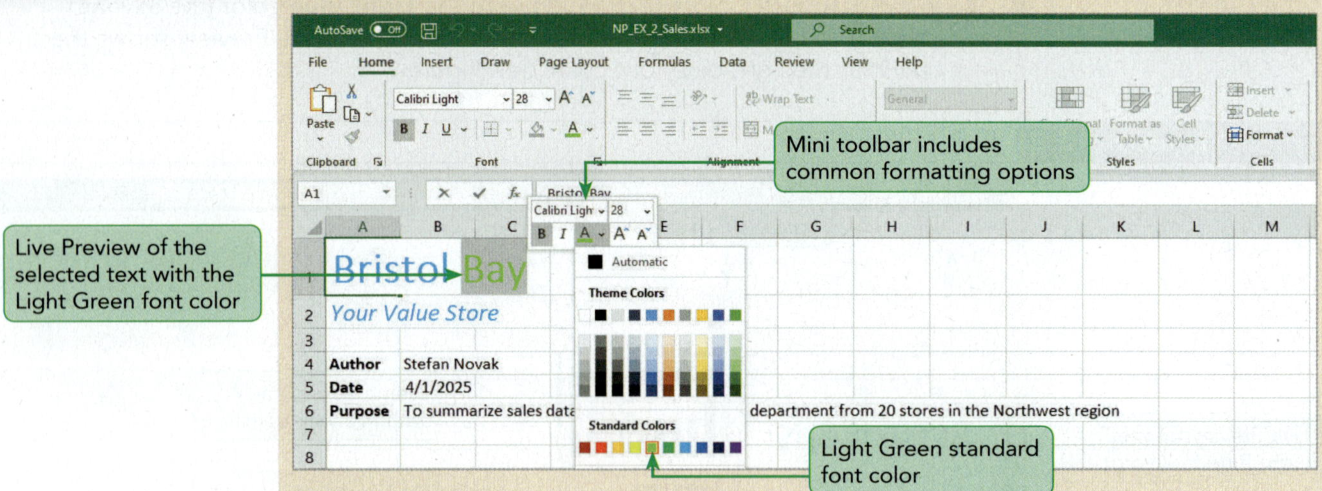

4. Click the **Light Green** standard color. The Mini toolbar closes and the selected text changes to light green.

In addition to font colors, you can also change the colors within cells.

Working with Fill Colors and Backgrounds

Another way to distinguish sections of a worksheet is by formatting the cell backgrounds. You can fill the cell background with color or with an image.

Changing a Fill Color

By default, worksheet cells do not include any background color. But filling a cell's background with color, also known as a fill color, can be helpful for highlighting data, differentiating parts of a worksheet, or adding visual interest to a report. The same selection of colors used to change the color of cell text can be used to change the cell background.

Insight

Using Color to Enhance a Workbook

When used wisely, color can enhance any workbook. However, when used improperly, color can distract the user, making the workbook more difficult to read. As you format a workbook, keep in mind the following tips:

- Use colors from the same theme to maintain a consistent look and feel across the worksheets. If the built-in themes do not fit your needs, you can create a custom theme.
- Use colors to differentiate types of cell content and to direct users where to enter data. For example, format a worksheet so that formula results appear in cells without a fill color and users enter data in cells with a light gray fill color.
- Avoid color combinations that are difficult to read.
- Print the workbook on both color and black-and-white printers to ensure that the printed copy is readable in both versions.
- Understand your printer's limitations and features. Colors that look good on your monitor might not look as good when printed.

Be sensitive to your audience. About 8% of all men and 0.5% of all women have some type of color vision deficiency and might not be able to see the text when certain color combinations are used. Red-green color vision deficiency is the most common, so avoid using red text on a green background or green text on a red background.

Stefan wants you to change the background color of the range A4:A6 in the Documentation sheet to light blue and the font color to white.

To change the font and fill colors in the Documentation sheet:

1. Select the range **A4:A6**.
2. On the Home tab, in the Font group, click the **Fill Color arrow**, and then click the **Light Blue** color (the seventh color) in the Standard Colors section.
3. In the Font group, click the **Font Color arrow**, and then click the **White, Background 1** color (the first color in the first row) in the Theme Colors section. The labels are formatted as white text on a light blue background.
4. Select the range **B4:B6**, and then format the cells with the **Light Blue** standard font color and the **White, Background 1** theme fill color.

5. Increase the width of column B to **30** characters, and then wrap the text in the selected range.
6. Select the range **A4:B6**, and then add all borders around each of the selected cells.
7. Click cell **A7** to deselect the range. See Figure 2–5.

Figure 2–5 Font and fill colors added to the Documentation sheet

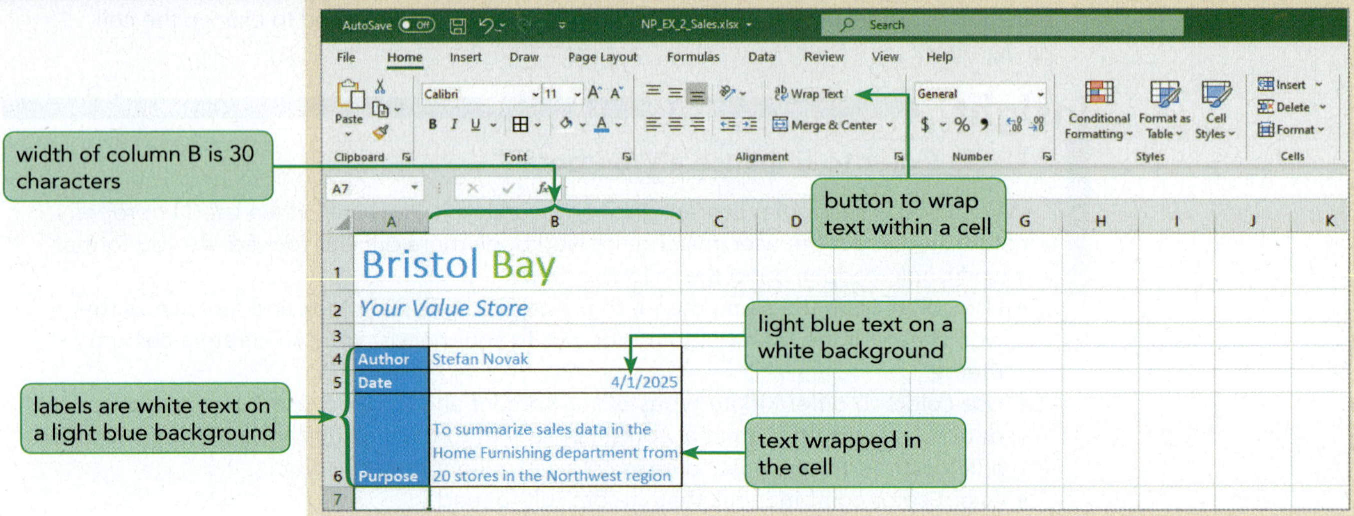

Setting the Worksheet Tab Color

Fill colors can also be used with the sheet tabs. You can add the same tab color to sheets that share a common purpose to create a visual structure in the workbook. Stefan wants you to change the tab color of the Documentation sheet to gold.

To change the tab color of the Documentation sheet:

1. Right-click the **Documentation** sheet tab. A shortcut menu appears with options related to the sheet tab.
2. On the shortcut menu, point to **Tab Color** to display the palette of theme and standard colors.
3. In the Theme Colors section, click **Gold, Accent 4** (the eighth color in the first row). The Documentation sheet tab now has a gold fill. Because the Documentation sheet is the active sheet, its sheet tab shows a gold highlight.
4. Click the **Sales Report** tab to make it the active sheet. Now you can see the solid gold sheet tab color for the inactive Documentation sheet.
5. Click the **Documentation** sheet tab to make Documentation the active sheet.

Although you can change the sheet tab fill color, you cannot change its text color or text style.

Adding a Background Image

Tip

Background images are usually visible only on the screen; by default, they do not print.

Another way to add visual interest to worksheets is with a background image. Many background images are based on textures such as granite, wood, or fibered paper. The image does not need to match the size of the worksheet. Instead, a smaller image can be repeated until it fills the entire sheet. Background images do not affect any cell's format or content. Fill colors added to cells appear on top of the image, covering that portion of the image.

Stefan provided the image that he wants you to use as the background of the Documentation sheet.

To add a background image to the Documentation sheet:

1. On the ribbon, click the **Page Layout** tab to display the page layout options.
2. In the Page Setup group, click the **Background** button. The Insert Pictures dialog box opens with options to search for an image from a file on your computer, from the Bing Image server, or on your OneDrive account.
3. Click the **From a file** option. The Sheet Background dialog box opens.
4. In the Sheet Background dialog box, navigate to the **Excel2 > Module** folder included with your Data Files, click the **Support_EX_2_Background.jpg** image file, and then click **Insert**. The image is added to the background of the Documentation sheet. See Figure 2–6.

Figure 2–6 **Background image added to the Documentation sheet**

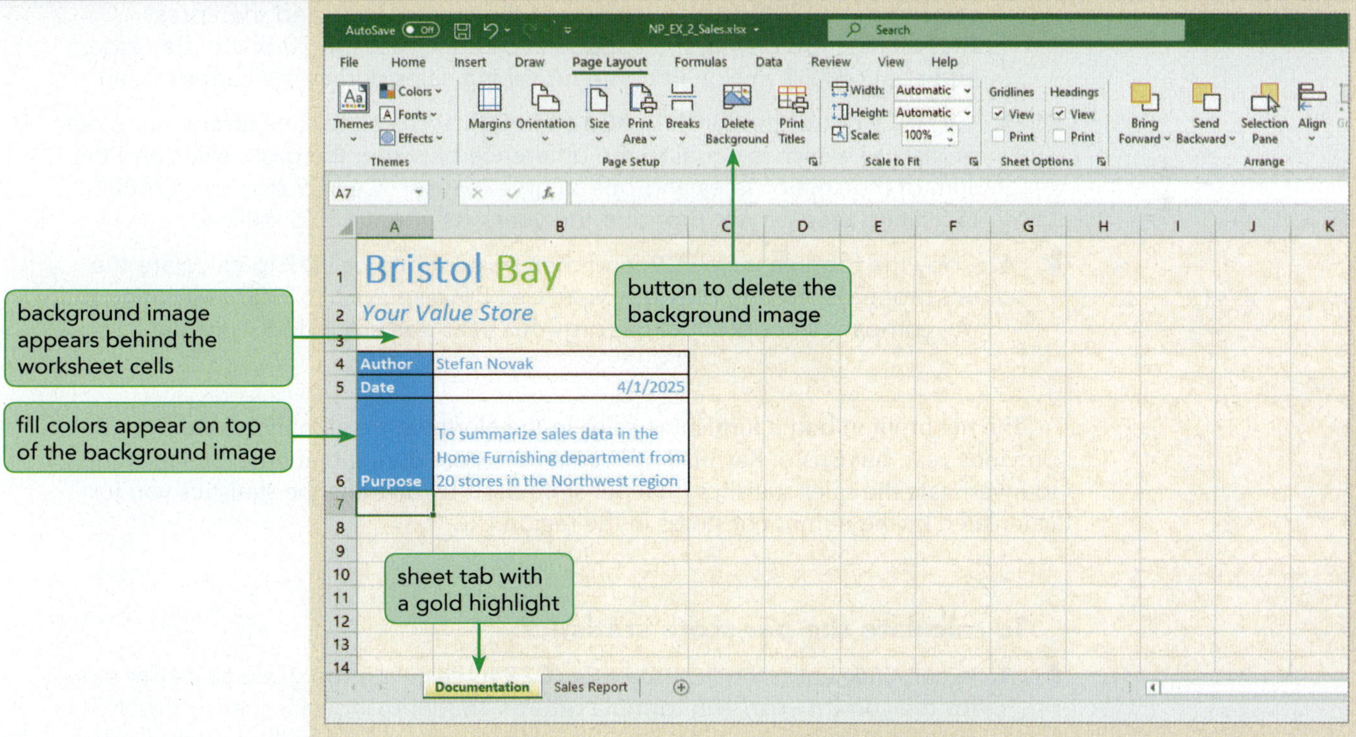

If you want to remove a background image from a worksheet, click the Delete Background button in the Page Setup group on the Page Layout tab.

You've completed the formatting the Documentation sheet. Next, you'll work on the Sales Report worksheet.

Using Functions and Formulas with Sales Data

In the Sales Report worksheet, you will format the data on the gross sales from each of Bristol Bay's 20 stores in the Northwest region. The worksheet is divided into two areas. The table at the bottom of the worksheet displays gross sales in the Home Furnishing department for the current year broken down by month and store. The section at the top of the worksheet compares sales from the current and previous year. Stefan has compiled the following sales data:

- **Gross Sales**—the total amount of sales incomes in the Home Furnishing department from the 20 stores in the Northwest region
- **Cost of Sales**—the cost to Bristol Bay for supplying the sales items in those 20 stores
- **Operating Expenses**—the cost of running the Home Furnishing department in those 20 stores
- **Net Profit/Loss**—the difference between the income from the gross sales and the total cost of sales and operating expenses
- **Items Sold**—the total number of home furnishing items sold by the 20 Bristol Bay stores

Stefan wants you to calculate these sales statistics for the 20 Bristol Bay stores in the Northwest region. First, you will calculate the gross sales from current year and the overall net profit and loss.

To calculate Bristol Bay's sales and profit/loss:

1. Click the **Sales Report** sheet tab to make the Sales Report worksheet active.
2. Click cell **C6**, type the formula **=SUM(C26:N45)** to calculate the total gross sales from the 20 Bristol Bay stores in the current year, and then press **ENTER**. Cell C6 displays 72676000, indicating that the 20 Bristol Bay stores had about $72.7 million in home furnishing sales during the current year.
3. In cell **C9**, enter the formula **=C6-(C7+C8)** to calculate the current year's net profit/loss, which is equal to the difference between the gross sales and the sum of the cost of sales and operating expenses. Cell C9 displays 5248000, indicating that the net profit for the year was about $5.25 million.
4. Copy the formula in cell **C9**, and then paste it into cell **D9** to calculate the net profit/loss for the previous year. Cell D9 displays 5151000, indicating that the company's net profit in the previous year was around $5.1 million.

The net profit in home furnishing sales in the Northwest region increased from the previous year, but Bristol Bay also opened a new store during that time. Stefan wants to investigate the sales statistics on a per-store basis by dividing the statistics you just calculated by the number of stores in the region.

To calculate the per-store statistics:

1. In cell **C15**, enter the formula **=C6/C22** to calculate the gross sales per store for the current year. The formula returns 3633800, indicating each Bristol Bay store in Northwest region had, on average, about $3.6 million in gross sales during the year.
2. In cell **C16**, enter the formula **=C7/C22** to calculate the cost of sales per store for the year. The formula returns the value 1078900, indicating each Bristol Bay store had a little more than $1 million in home furnishing sales cost.

3. In cell **C17**, enter the formula **=C8/C22** to calculate the operating expenses per store for the year. The formula returns the value 2292500, indicating that annual operating expense of a typical store was about $2.3 million.
4. In cell **C18**, enter the formula **=C9/C22** to calculate the net profit/loss per store for the year. The formula returns the value 262400, indicating that the net profit/loss in the Home Furnishing department of a typical Bristol Bay stores was $262,400.
5. In cell **C20**, enter the formula **=C11/C22** to calculate the units sold per store for the year. The formula returns the value 70040, indicating that a typical store sold more than 70,000 units.
6. Copy the formulas in the range **C15:C20** and paste them into the range **D15:D20**. The cell references in the formulas change to calculate the sales data for the previous year.
7. Click cell **B4** to deselect the range. See Figure 2–7.

Figure 2–7 Overall and per-store sales

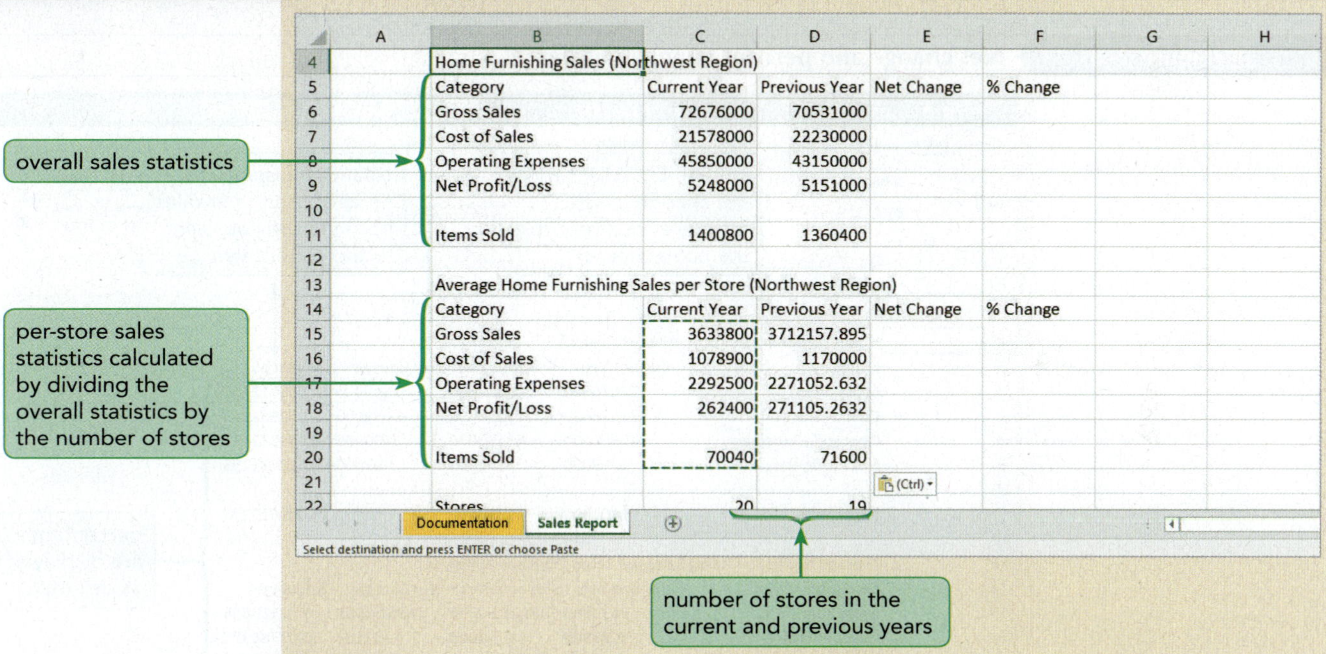

Stefan also wants to report how the company's sales and expenses have changed from the previous year to the current year. To do this, you will calculate the net change in the sales statistics as well as the percent change. The percent change is calculated using the following formula:

$$\text{percent change} = \frac{\text{current year value} - \text{previous year value}}{\text{previous year value}}$$

You will calculate the net change and percentage for all of the statistics in the Sales Report worksheet.

Be sure to include the parentheses as shown to calculate the percent change correctly.

To calculate the net and percent changes:

1. In cell **E6**, enter the formula **=C6-D6** to calculate the difference in gross sales between the previous year and the current year. The formula returns 2145000, indicating that gross sales increased by about $2.15 million.
2. In cell F6, enter the formula =(C6-D6)/D6 to calculate the percent change in gross sales from the previous year to the current year. The formula returns 0.030412159, indicating an increase in gross sales of about 3.04%.

   Next, you'll copy and paste the formulas in cells E6 and F6 to the rest of the sales data to calculate the net change and percent change from the previous year to the current year.
3. Select the range **E6:F6**, and then copy the selected range. The two formulas are copied to the Clipboard.
4. Select the nonadjacent range **E7:F9,E11:F11,E15:F18,E20:F20**, and then paste the formulas from the Clipboard into the selected range. The net and percent changes are calculated for the remaining sales data.
5. Click cell **A4** to deselect the range. See Figure 2–8.

Figure 2–8 Net change and percent change in sales

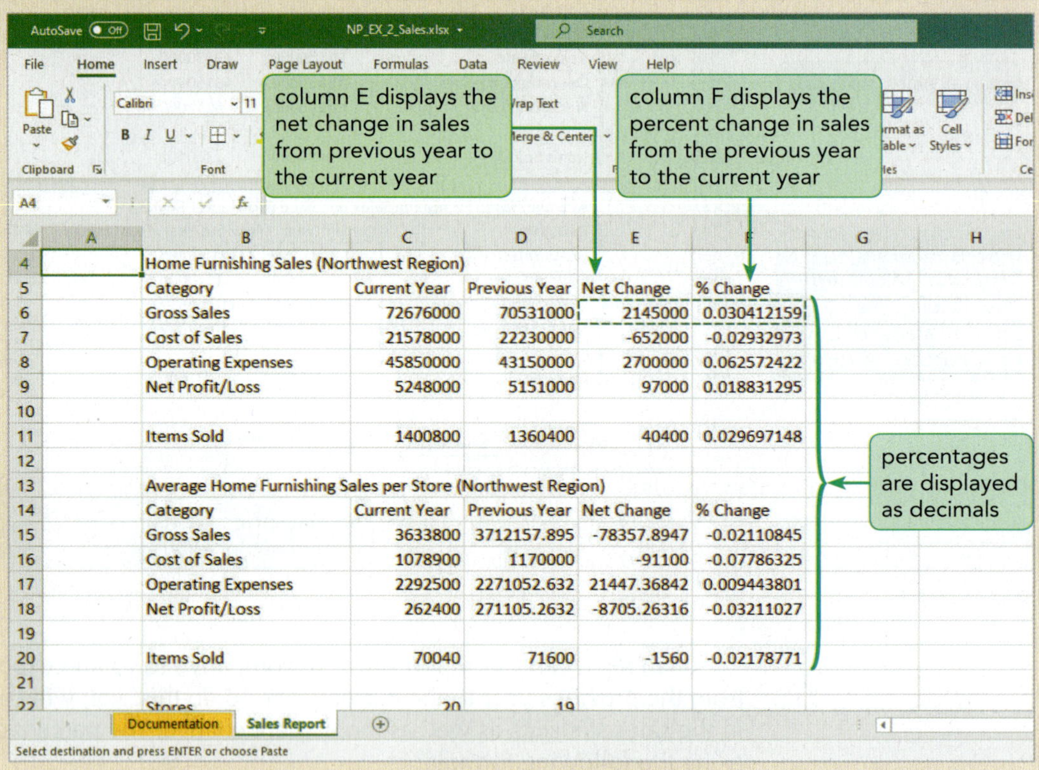

The bottom of the worksheet contains the home furnishing sales from each store during each month of the current year. You will use the SUM function to calculate the total gross sales for each store during the entire year, the total monthly sales of all 20 stores, and the total gross sales of all stores and months.

To calculate different subtotals of the gross sales:

1. Scroll down and to the right, click cell **P25**, type **Yearly Totals** as the label, and then press **ENTER**. Cell P26 is the active cell.
2. In cell **P26**, enter the formula **=SUM(C26:N26)** to calculate the total gross sales for the store located in Tacoma, Washington. Excel returns the value 3942000 indicating that the Tacoma store had total gross sales of $3.942 million in its Home Furnishing department during the current fiscal year.
3. Copy the formula in cell **P26** to the range **P27:P45** to calculate the gross sales for all 20 Bristol Bay stores in the Northwest region.

   Next, you will calculate the monthly gross sales across all stores.
4. Click cell **B46**, enter **Monthly Totals** as the label, and then press **TAB**. Cell C46 is the active cell.
5. Select the range **C46:N46**.
6. On the Home tab, in the Editing group, click the **AutoSum** button to calculate the sum of the gross sales for each month. For example, the formula in cell N46 returns the value 7879000, indicating that across the 20 Northwest region stores, Bristol Bay had $7.879 million in gross sales from its Home Furnishing department in the month of December.
7. Click cell **P46**, and then click the **AutoSum** button to insert the formula =SUM(P26:P45), and then press **ENTER**. This formula returns the value 72676000, the total gross sales for all Northwest stores for the entire year, matching the value shown earlier in cell C6.
8. Click cell **P47** to deselect the range. See Figure 2–9.

Figure 2–9 Gross sales by store and month

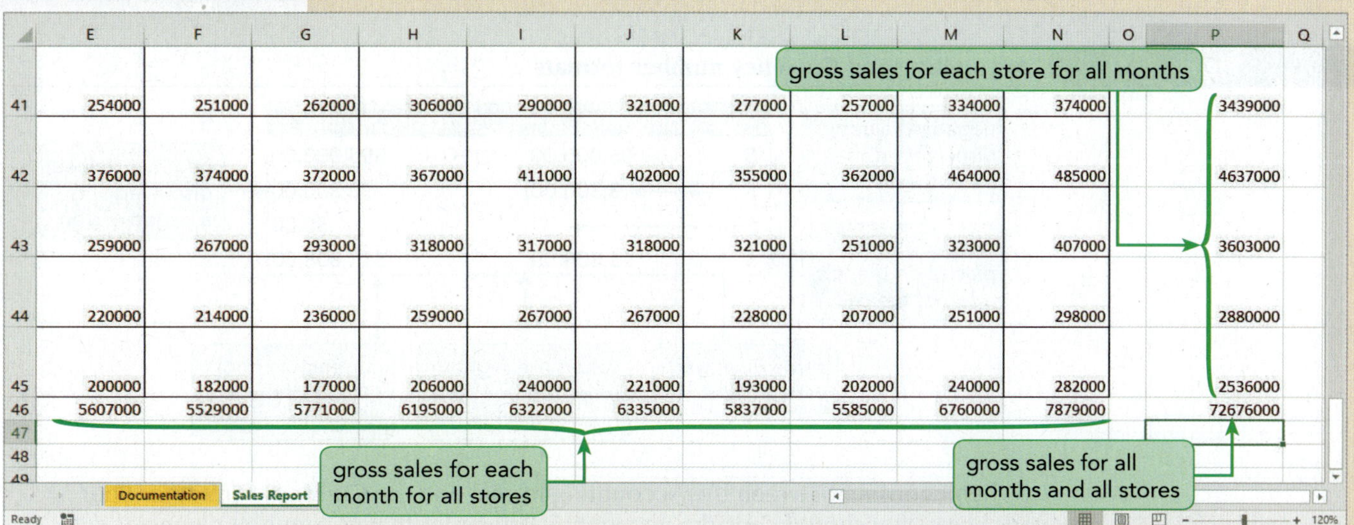

	E	F	G	H	I	J	K	L	M	N	O	P	Q
41	254000	251000	262000	306000	290000	321000	277000	257000	334000	374000		3439000	
42	376000	374000	372000	367000	411000	402000	355000	362000	464000	485000		4637000	
43	259000	267000	293000	318000	317000	318000	321000	251000	323000	407000		3603000	
44	220000	214000	236000	259000	267000	267000	228000	207000	251000	298000		2880000	
45	200000	182000	177000	206000	240000	221000	193000	202000	240000	282000		2536000	
46	5607000	5529000	5771000	6195000	6322000	6335000	5837000	5585000	6760000	7879000		72676000	
47													
48													

The Sales Report worksheet financial totals that are difficult to read in their current form. You can improve the readability of the data by adding number formats.

Formatting Numbers

You can make the financial figures in your workbooks easier to read by using commas to separate the thousands values. Other formatting options include setting the number of decimal places and using currency and percent symbols. Changing the number format does not affect the stored value, only how that value is displayed in the cell.

Applying Number Formats

Cells start out formatted with the **General format**, which, for the most part, displays numbers exactly as they are typed. If a value is calculated from a formula or function, the General format displays as many digits after the decimal point as will fit in the cell and rounds the last digit.

The General format is fine for small numbers, but some values require additional formatting to make the numbers easier to interpret. For example, you might want to:

- Change the number of digits displayed to the right of the decimal point
- Add commas to separate thousands in large numbers
- Include currency symbols to numbers to identify the monetary unit being used
- Identify percentages using the % symbol

Tip

To apply the Currency format, click the Number Format arrow and click Currency, or press CTRL+SHIFT+$.

Excel supports two monetary formats—Accounting and Currency. Both formats add thousands separators to the monetary values and display two digits to the right of the decimal point. The **Accounting format** places the currency symbol at the left edge of the column and displays negative numbers within parentheses and zero values with a dash. It also slightly indents the values from the right edge of the cell to allow room for parentheses around negative values. The **Currency format** places the currency symbol directly to the left of the first digit of the monetary value and displays negative numbers with a negative sign. Figure 2–10 compares the two formats.

Figure 2–10 **Accounting and Currency number formats**

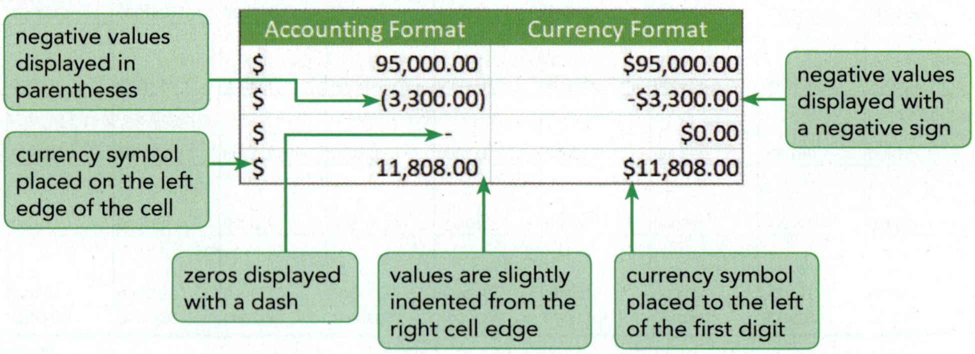

When choosing between the Accounting format and the Currency format for your worksheets, you should consider accounting principles that govern how financial data should be formatted and displayed.

Proskills

Written Communication: Formatting Monetary Values

Spreadsheets commonly include monetary values. To make these values simpler to read and comprehend, keep in mind the following guidelines when formatting the currency data in a worksheet:

- **Format for your audience.** For general financial reports, round values to the nearest hundred, thousand, or million. Investors are generally more interested in the big picture than in exact values. However, for accounting reports, accuracy is important and often legally required. So, for those reports, be sure to display the exact monetary value.
- **Use thousands separators.** Large strings of numbers can be challenging to read. For monetary values, use the thousands separator to make the amounts easier to comprehend.
- **Apply the Accounting format to columns of monetary values.** The Accounting format makes columns of numbers easier to read than the Currency format. Use the Currency format for individual cells that are not part of long columns of numbers.
- **Use only two currency symbols in a column of monetary values.** Standard accounting format displays one currency symbol with the first monetary value in the column and optionally displays a second currency symbol with the last value in that column. Use the Accounting format to fix the currency symbols, lining them up within the column.

Following these standard accounting principles will make your financial data easier to read both on the screen and in printouts.

Stefan wants you to format the gross sales values in the Accounting format so that they are easier to read.

To format the gross sales in the Accounting format:

1. Select the range **C6:E6** containing the gross sales for the current and previous year and the net change between the years.
2. On the Home tab, in the Number group, click the **Accounting Number Format** button $. The numbers are formatted in the Accounting format. You cannot see the format because the cells display ##########.

Tip

To choose a different currency symbol, click the Accounting Number Format arrow in the Number group on the Home tab and click a symbol.

The selected cells display ########## because the formatted numbers don't fit into the columns. One reason for this is that monetary values, by default, show both dollars and cents in the cell. However, you can increase or decrease the number of decimal places displayed in a cell. If you remove the cents value, the displayed values will be rounded to the nearest dollar so that a value such as 11.7 will be displayed as $12. Changing the number of decimal places displayed in a cell does not change the value stored in the cell.

Stefan suggests that you to hide the cents values in the report by decreasing the number of decimal places to zero.

To decrease the number of decimal places in the report:

1. Make sure the range **C6:E6** is still selected.
2. On the Home tab, in the Number group, click the **Decrease Decimal button** .00→.0 twice. The cents are hidden for gross sales and the net change in sales.
3. Click cell **A3** to deselect the range. See Figure 2–11.

Figure 2–11 Formatted gross sales values

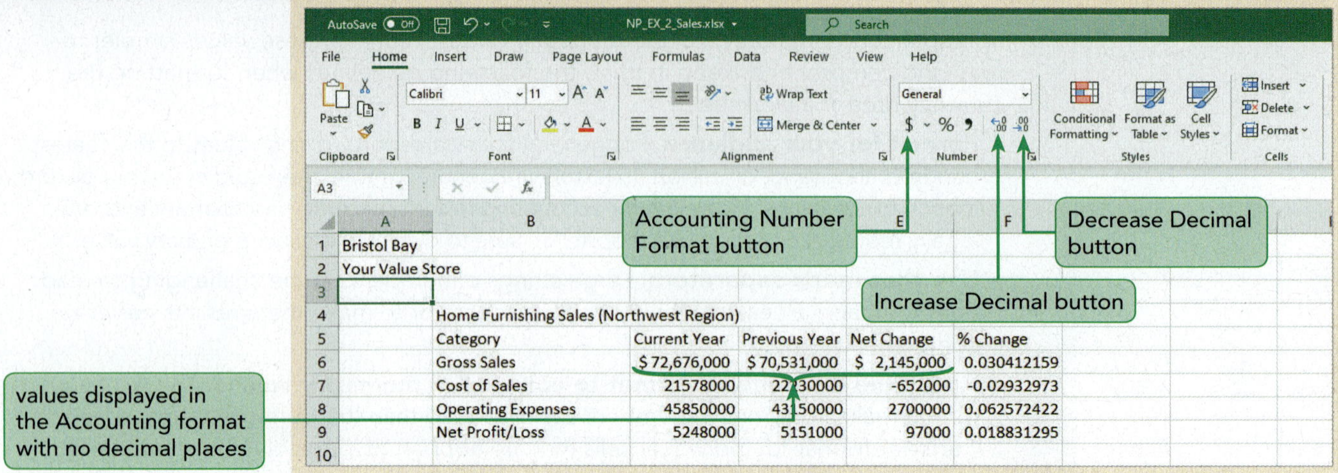

The Comma style is identical to the Accounting format except that it does not place a currency symbol on the left edge of the cell. The advantage of using the Comma style and the Accounting format together is that the numbers will be aligned in the column.

Stefan asks you to apply the Comma style to the remaining sales statistics.

To apply the Comma style to a range of values:

1. Select the nonadjacent range **C7:E9,C11:E11** containing the sales figures for all stores in the current and previous year.
2. On the Home tab, in the Number group, click the **Comma Style** button. For some of the selected cells, the number is now too large to be displayed in the cell.
3. In the Number group, click the **Decrease Decimal** button twice to remove two decimal places. Digits to the right of the decimal point are hidden for all selected cells, and all of the numbers are now visible.
4. Click cell **A3** to deselect the range. See Figure 2–12.

Figure 2–12 Formatted sales values

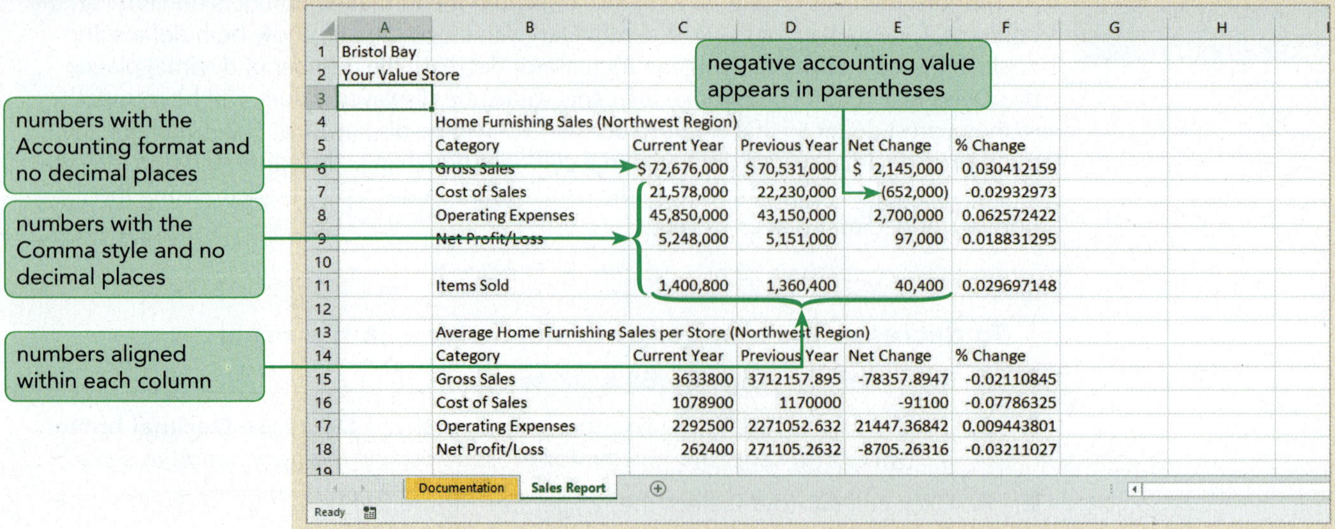

Notice that the net change value in cell E7 is displayed as (652,000) with the parentheses indicating a negative net change so that the cost of sales decreased from the previous year into the current year.

Displaying Percentages

The Percent style formats numbers as percentages with no decimal places so that a number such as 0.124 appears as 12%. You can always change how many decimal places are displayed in the cell if that is important to show with your data.

Stefan wants you to display the percent change in sales and expenses between the previous year and the current year using the % symbol.

To format the percent change values as percentages:

1. Select the nonadjacent range **F6:F9,F11** containing the percent change values.
2. On the Home tab, in the Number group, click the **Percent Style** button [%] (or press **CTRL+SHIFT+%**). The values are displayed as percentages with no decimal places.
3. In the Number group, click the **Increase Decimal** button twice. The displayed number includes two decimal places.
4. Click cell **A3** to deselect the range. See Figure 2–13.

Figure 2–13 Formatted percent change values

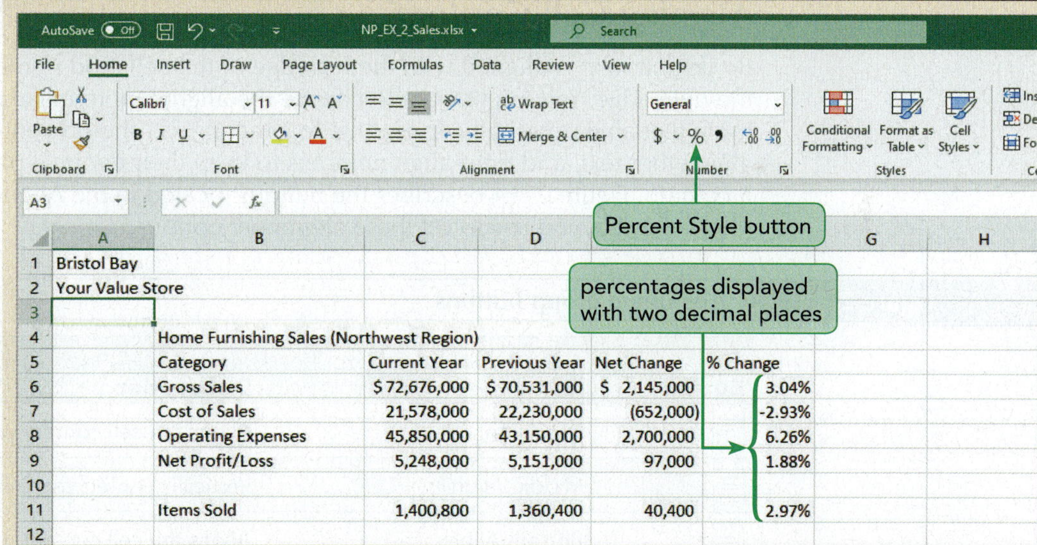

With the data reformatted, the worksheet clearly shows that the gross sales in home furnishing for the 20 Bristol Bay stores increased from the previous year to the current year by 3.04%, but the net profit on those sales increased by only 1.88% due to the large increase of 6.26% in operating expenses. This type of information is very important to the company executives planning for the upcoming year.

Formatting Dates and Times

Because Excel stores dates and times as numbers and not as text, you can apply different date formats without affecting the underlying date and time value. The abbreviated format, *mm/dd/yyyy*, entered in the Documentation sheet is referred to as the **Short Date format**. The **Long Date format** displays the day of the week and the full month name in addition to the day of the month and the year. Other built-in formats include formats for displaying time values in 12- or 24-hour time format.

Stefan asks you to change the date in the Documentation sheet to the Long Date format.

To format the date in the Long Date format:

1. Go to the **Documentation** sheet, and then select cell **B5**.
2. On the Home tab, in the Number group, click the **Number Format arrow** to display a list of number formats, and then click **Long Date**. The date is displayed with the weekday name, month name, day, and year.

Tip

To view the underlying date and time value, apply the General format or display the formulas.

Notice that the date in the formula bar did not change because you changed only the display format, not the date value. Next, you will learn about other options for formatting cell content.

Formatting Worksheet Cells

You can format the appearance of individual cells by modifying the alignment of text within the cell, indenting cell text, or adding borders of different styles and colors.

Aligning Cell Content

By default, text is aligned with the left edge of the cell, and numbers are aligned with the right edge. You might want to change the alignment to make the text and numbers more readable or visually appealing. In general, you should center column titles, left-align other text, and right-align numbers to keep their decimal places lined up within a column. Figure 2–14 describes the buttons located in the Alignment group on the Home tab that you use to set these alignment options.

Figure 2–14 **Alignment group buttons**

Button	Name	Description
	Top Align	Aligns the cell content with the cell's top edge
	Middle Align	Vertically centers the cell content within the cell
	Bottom Align	Aligns the cell content with the cell's bottom edge
	Align Left	Aligns the cell content with the cell's left edge
	Align Center	Horizontally centers the cell content within the cell
	Align Right	Aligns the cell content with the cell's right edge
	Decrease Indent	Decreases the size of the indentation used in the cell
	Increase Indent	Increases the size of the indentation used in the cell
	Orientation	Rotates the cell content to any angle within the cell
	Wrap Text	Forces the cell text to wrap within the cell borders
	Merge & Center	Merges the selected cells into a single cell

The date in the Documentation sheet is right-aligned in cell B5 because Excel treats dates and times as numbers. Stefan wants you to left-align the date from the Documentation sheet and center the column titles in the Sales Report worksheet.

To left-align the date and center the column titles:

1. In the Documentation sheet, make sure cell **B5** is still selected.
2. On the Home tab, in the Alignment group, click the **Align Left** button. The date shifts to the left edge of the cell.
3. Go to the **Sales Report** worksheet.
4. Select the range **C5:F5** containing the column titles.
5. In the Alignment group, click the **Center** button. The column titles are centered in the cells.

Indenting Cell Content

Sometimes you want a cell's content moved a few spaces from the cell's left edge. This is particularly useful to create subsections in a worksheet or to set off some entries from others. You can increase the indent to shift the contents of a cell away from the left edge of the cell, or you can decrease the indent to shift a cell's contents closer to the left edge of the cell.

Stefan wants you to indent the Cost of Sales and Operating Expenses labels in the sales statistics table from the other labels because they represent expenses to the company.

To indent the expense categories:

1. Select the range **B7:B8** containing the expense categories.
2. On the Home tab, in the Alignment group, click the **Increase Indent** button twice. Each label indents two spaces in its cell.

Another way to make financial data easier to read and interpret is with borders.

Adding Borders to Cells

Common accounting practices provide guidelines on when to add borders to cells. In general, a single black border should appear above a subtotal, a single bottom border should be added below a calculated number, and a double black bottom border should appear below the total.

Stefan wants you to follow common accounting practices in the Sales Report worksheet. You will add borders below the column titles and below the gross sales values. You will add a top border to the net profit/loss values and a top and bottom border to the Items Sold row.

To add borders to the sales statistics data:

1. Select the range **B5:F5** containing the table headings.
2. On the Home tab, in the Font group, click the **Borders arrow**, and then click **Bottom Border**. A border is added below the column titles.

3. Select the range **B6:F6** containing the gross sales amounts.
4. In the Font group, click the **Bottom Border** button. A border is added below the selected gross sales amounts.
5. Select the range **B9:F9**, click the **Borders arrow**, and then click **Top Border**. A border is added above the net profit/loss amounts.

   The Items Sold row does not contain monetary values as the other rows do. You will distinguish this row by adding a top and bottom border.
6. Select the range **B11:F11**, click the **Borders arrow**, and then click **Top and Bottom Border**.
7. Click cell **A3** to deselect the range. See Figure 2–15.

Figure 2–15 **Borders, indents, and alignment added to cells**

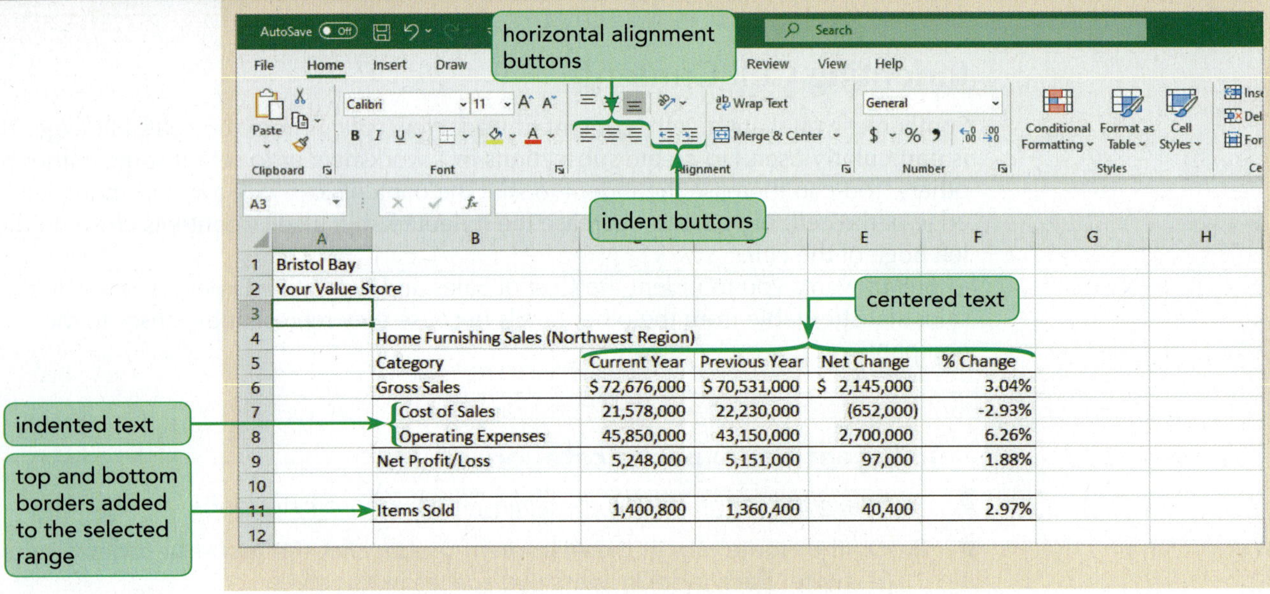

You can apply multiple formats to the same cell to create the look that best fits the data. For example, one cell might be formatted with a number format, alignments, borders, indents, fonts, font sizes, and so on. The monthly sales data needs to be formatted with number styles, alignments, indents, and borders. You'll add these formats now.

To format the monthly sales data:

1. Select the range **C26:P46** containing the monthly gross sales by store.
2. On the Home tab, in the Number group, click the **Comma Style** button to add the thousands separator to the values.
3. In the Number group, click the **Decrease Decimal** button twice to hide the cents from the sales results.
4. In the Alignment group, click the **Top Align** button to align the sales numbers with the top of each cell.
5. Select the nonadjacent range **C25:N25,P25** containing the labels for the month abbreviations and the Yearly Totals column.
6. In the Alignment group, click the **Center** button to center the column labels.

7. Select the range **B26:B45** containing the store addresses.
8. Reduce the font size of the store addresses to **9** points.
9. In the Alignment group, click the **Increase Indent** button twice to indent the store addresses.
10. Select the range **B46:N46** containing the monthly totals.
11. In the Font group, click the **Borders arrow**, and then click **All Borders** to add borders around each monthly totals cell.
12. Select the range **P25:P46** containing the annual totals for each restaurant, and then click the **All Borders** button to add borders around each store total.
13. Click cell **A23** to deselect the range. See Figure 2–16.

Figure 2–16 Formatted monthly gross sales

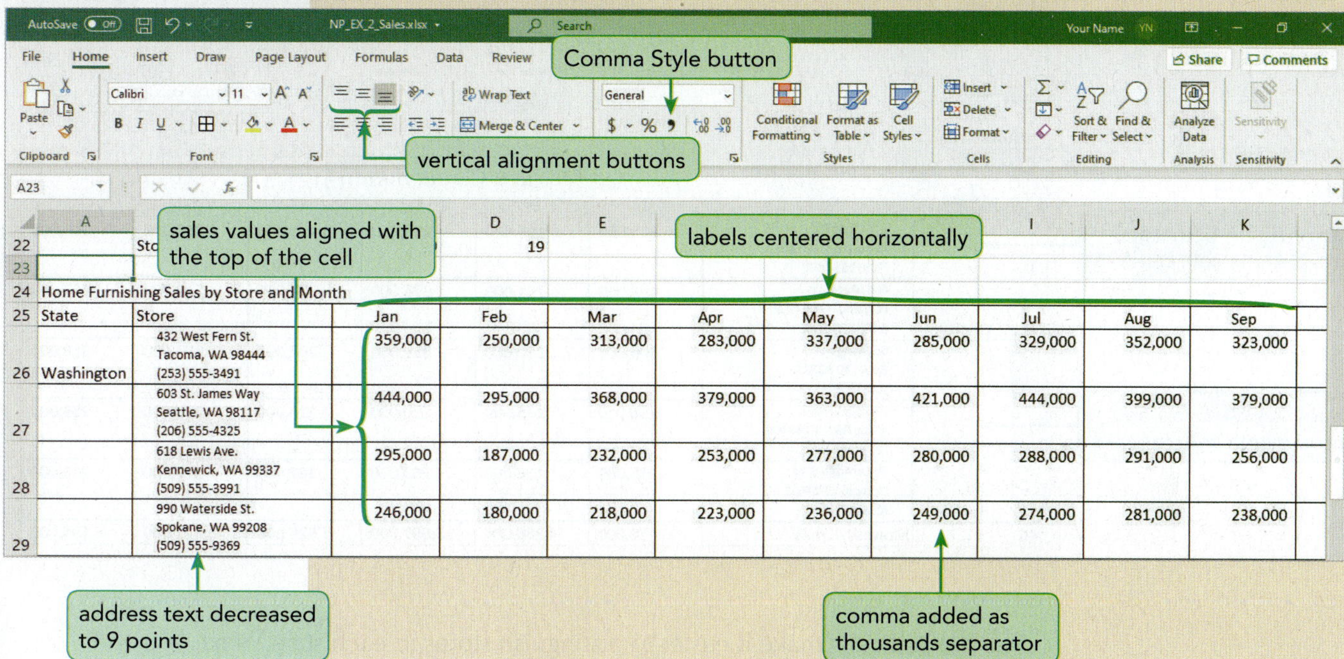

Merging Cells

You can merge, or combine, several cells into one cell. A merged cell contains two or more cells with a single cell reference. When you merge cells, only the content from the upper-left cell in the range is retained. The cell reference for the merged cell is the upper-left cell reference. So, if you merge cells A1 and A2, the merged cell reference is cell A1. After you merge cells, you can align the content within the merged cell. The Merge & Center button in the Alignment group on the Home tab includes the following options:

- **Merge & Center**—merges the range into one cell and horizontally centers the content
- **Merge Across**—merges each row in the selected range across the columns in the range
- **Merge Cells**—merges the range into a single cell but does not horizontally center the cell content
- **Unmerge Cells**—reverses a merge, returning the merged cell to a range of individual cells

Column A of the monthly sales data lists the states in Bristol Bay's Northwest region. You'll merge the cells for each state name into a single cell.

To merge the state name cells:

1. Select the range **A26:A34** containing the cells for the Washington stores. You will merge these cells into a single cell.
2. On the Home tab, in the Alignment group, click the **Merge & Center** button. The range A26:A34 merges into one cell with the cell reference A26, and the text is centered and bottom-aligned within the cell.
3. Select the range **A35:A42**, and then click the **Merge & Center** button. The cells for stores in the state of Oregon are merged and centered.
4. Select the range **A43:A45**, and then merge and center the cells for the Idaho stores. See Figure 2–17.

Figure 2–17 Merged cells

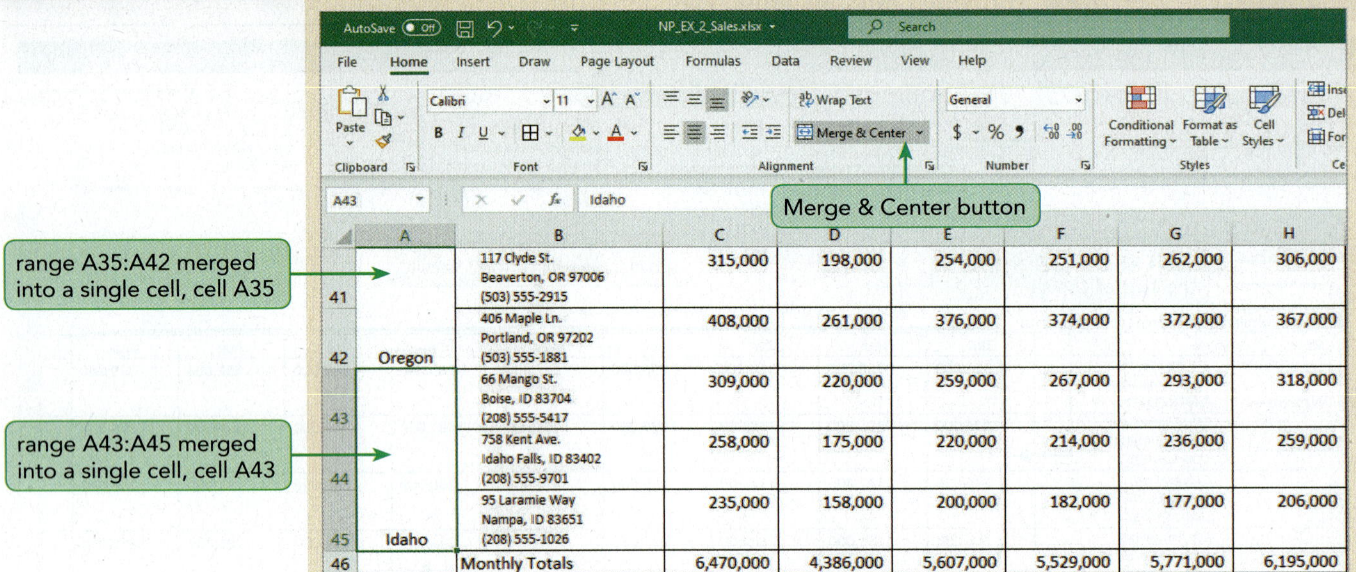

The merged cells make it easier to distinguish stores in each state. Next, you will rotate the cells so that the state names are displayed vertically in the merged cells.

Rotating Cell Contents

Text and numbers are displayed horizontally within cells. However, you can rotate cell text to any angle to save space or to provide visual interest to a worksheet. The state names at the bottom of the merged cells would look better and take up less room if they were rotated vertically within their cells. Stefan asks you to rotate the state names.

To rotate the state names:

1. Select the merged cell **A26**.
2. On the Home tab, in the Alignment group, click the **Orientation** button to display a list of rotation options, and then click **Rotate Text Up**. The state name rotates 90 degrees counterclockwise.

3. In the Alignment group, click the **Middle Align** button to vertically center the rotated text in the merged cell.
4. Repeat Steps 2 and 3 for the merged contents in cells A35 and A43.
5. Reduce the width of column A to **7** characters because the rotated state names take up less horizontal space.
6. Select cell **A46**. See Figure 2–18.

Figure 2–18 Rotated cell content

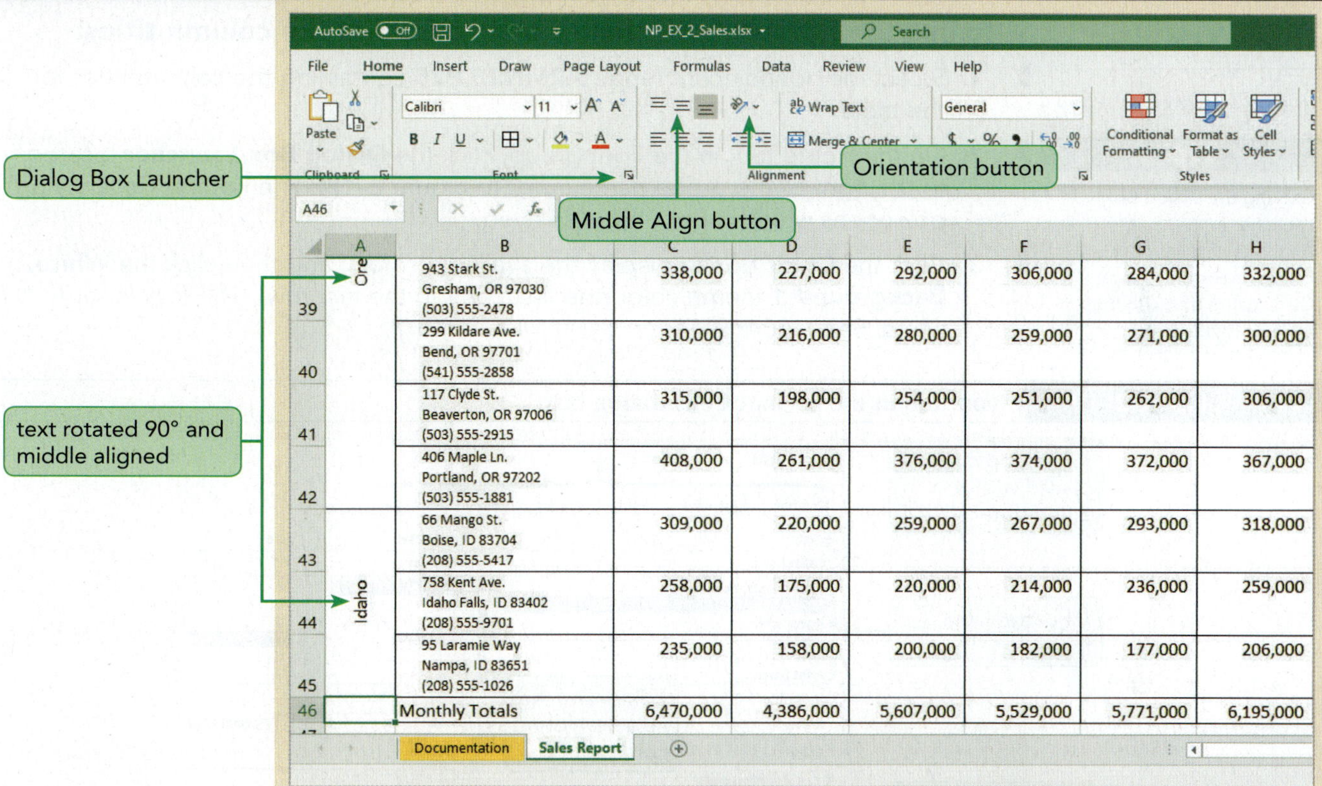

In addition to using the ribbon to apply formatting to a worksheet, you can also use the Format Cells dialog box to apply formatting.

Exploring the Format Cells Dialog Box

The buttons on the Home tab provide quick access to the most commonly used formatting choices. For more options, you can use the Format Cells dialog box. You can apply the formats in this dialog box to the selected worksheet cells. The Format Cells dialog box has six tabs, each focusing on a different set of formatting options, as described below:

- **Number**—options for formatting the appearance of numbers, including dates and numbers treated as text such as telephone or Social Security numbers
- **Alignment**—options for how data is aligned within a cell
- **Font**—options for selecting font types, sizes, styles, and other formatting attributes such as underlining and font colors

- **Border**—options for adding and removing cell borders as well as selecting a line style and color
- **Fill**—options for creating and applying background colors and patterns to cells
- **Protection**—options for locking or hiding cells to prevent other users from modifying their contents

Although you have applied many of these formats from the Home tab, the Format Cells dialog box presents them in a different way and provides more choices. You will use the Font and Fill tabs to format the column titles with a white font on a green background.

To use the Format Cells dialog box to format the column titles:

1. Select the nonadjacent range **A25:N25,P25** containing the column titles for the table.
2. On the Home tab, in the Font group, click the **Dialog Box Launcher** located to the right of the group name (refer to Figure 2–18). The Format Cells dialog box opens with the Font tab displayed.
3. Click the **Color** box to display the available colors, and then click the **White, Background 1** theme color (the first color in the first row). The font is set to white. See Figure 2–19.

Tip

Clicking the Dialog Box Launcher in the Font, Alignment, or Number group opens the Format Cells dialog box with that tab displayed.

Figure 2–19 Font tab in the Format Cells dialog box

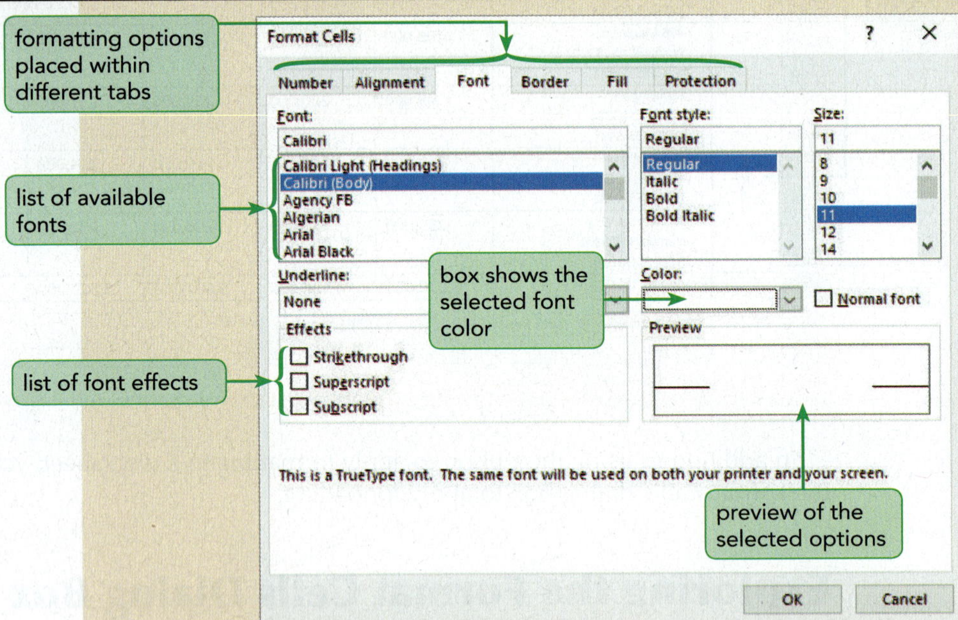

4. Click the **Fill** tab to display background options.
5. In the Background Color section, click the **Green, Accent 6** theme color (the last color in the first row). The background is set to green, as previewed in the Sample box.
6. Click **OK**. The dialog box closes, and the font and fill options you selected are applied to the selected cells.

You will also use the Format Cells dialog box to change the appearance of the row titles. You'll format them to be displayed in a larger white font on a gold background.

To format the row titles:

1. Select the range **A26:A45** containing the rotated state names.
2. Right-click the selected range, and then click **Format Cells** on the shortcut menu. The Format Cells dialog box opens with the last tab used displayed—in this case, the Fill tab.
3. In the Background Color section, click the **Gold, Accent 4** theme color (the eighth color in the first row). Its preview is shown in the Sample box.
4. Click the **Font** tab to display the font formatting options.
5. Click the **Color** box, and then click the **White, Background 1** theme color to set the font color to white.
6. In the Size box, click **16** to set the font size to 16 points.
7. In the Font style box, click **Bold** to change the font to boldface.
8. Click **OK**. The dialog box closes, and the font and fill formats are applied to the state names.
9. Scroll up and click cell **A23** to deselect the range. See Figure 2–20.

Figure 2–20 Formatted row and column titles

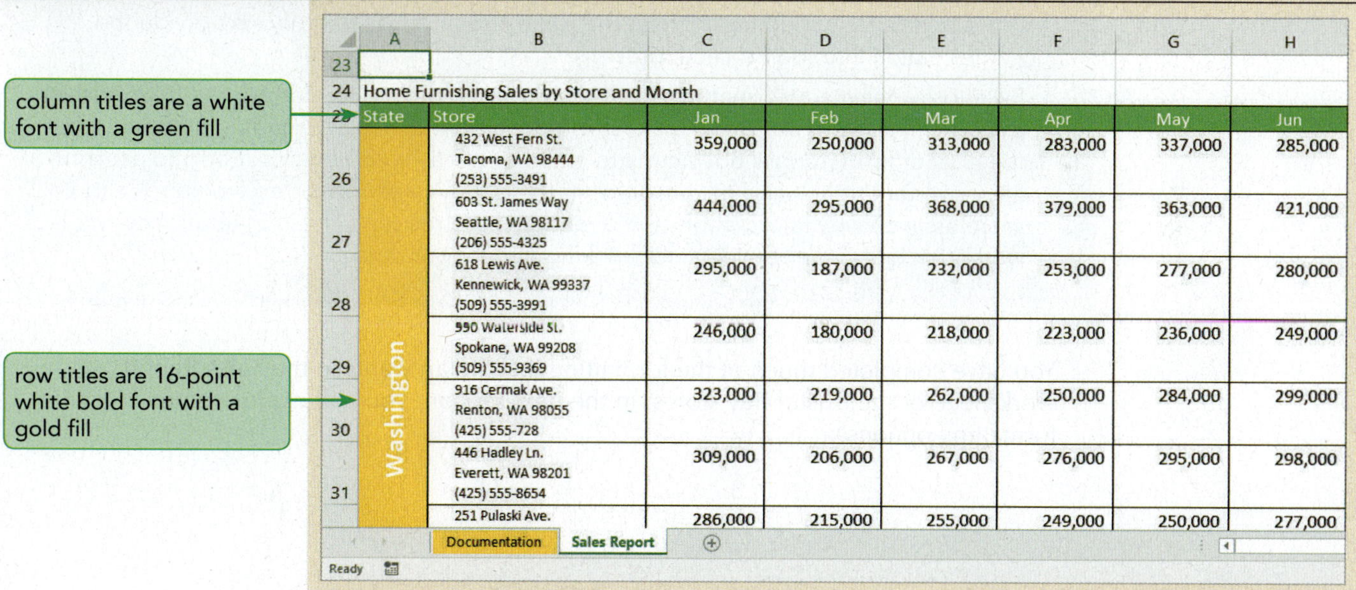

10. Save the workbook.

With the formats you have added to the Sales Report worksheet, readers will be able to more easily read and interpret the large table of store sales.

Proskills

Written Communication: Formatting Workbooks for Readability and Appeal

Designing a workbook requires the same care as designing any written document or report. A well-formatted workbook is easy to read and establishes a sense of professionalism with readers. You can improve the readability of your worksheets with the following guidelines:

- **Clearly identify each worksheet's purpose.** Include column or row titles and a descriptive sheet name.
- **Include only one or two topics on each worksheet.** Don't crowd individual worksheets with too much information. Place extra topics on separate sheets. Readers should be able to interpret each worksheet with a minimal amount of horizontal and vertical scrolling.
- **Put worksheets with the most important information first in the workbook.** Place worksheets summarizing your findings near the front of the workbook. Place worksheets with detailed and involved analysis near the end as an appendix.
- **Use consistent formatting throughout the workbook.** If negative values appear in red on one worksheet, format them in the same way on all sheets. Also, be consistent in the use of thousands separators, decimal places, and percentages.
- **Pay attention to the format of the printed workbook.** Make sure your printouts are legible with informative headers and footers. Check that the content of the printout is scaled correctly to the page size and that page breaks divide the information into logical sections.

Excel provides many formatting tools. However, too much formatting can be intrusive, overwhelming your data, and making the document difficult to read. Remember that the goal of formatting is not simply to make a "pretty workbook" but also to accentuate important trends and relationships in the data. A well-formatted workbook should seamlessly convey information to the reader. If the reader is thinking about how your workbook looks, the reader is not thinking about your data.

You have completed much of the formatting that Stefan wants in the Sales Report worksheet for the Bristol Bay stores. In the next session, you will explore other formatting options.

Review

Session 2.1 Quick Check

1. What is the difference between a serif font and a sans serif font?
2. What is the difference between theme colors and standard colors?
3. A cell containing a number displays #######. Why does this occur, and what can you do to fix it?
4. How do you change the color of a worksheet tab?
5. What is the General format?
6. Describe the differences between the Accounting format and the Currency format.
7. The range B3:B13 is merged into a single cell. What is its cell reference?
8. How do you format text so that it is set vertically within the cell?

Session 2.2 Visual Overview:

The Page Layout tab has options for setting how the worksheet will print.

The **Format Painter** copies and pastes formatting from one cell or range to another without duplicating any data.

Print titles are rows and/or columns that are included on every page of the printout. In this case, the text in rows 1 and 2 will print on every page.

A **manual page break**, identified by a solid blue line, is a page break you set to indicate where a new page of the printout starts.

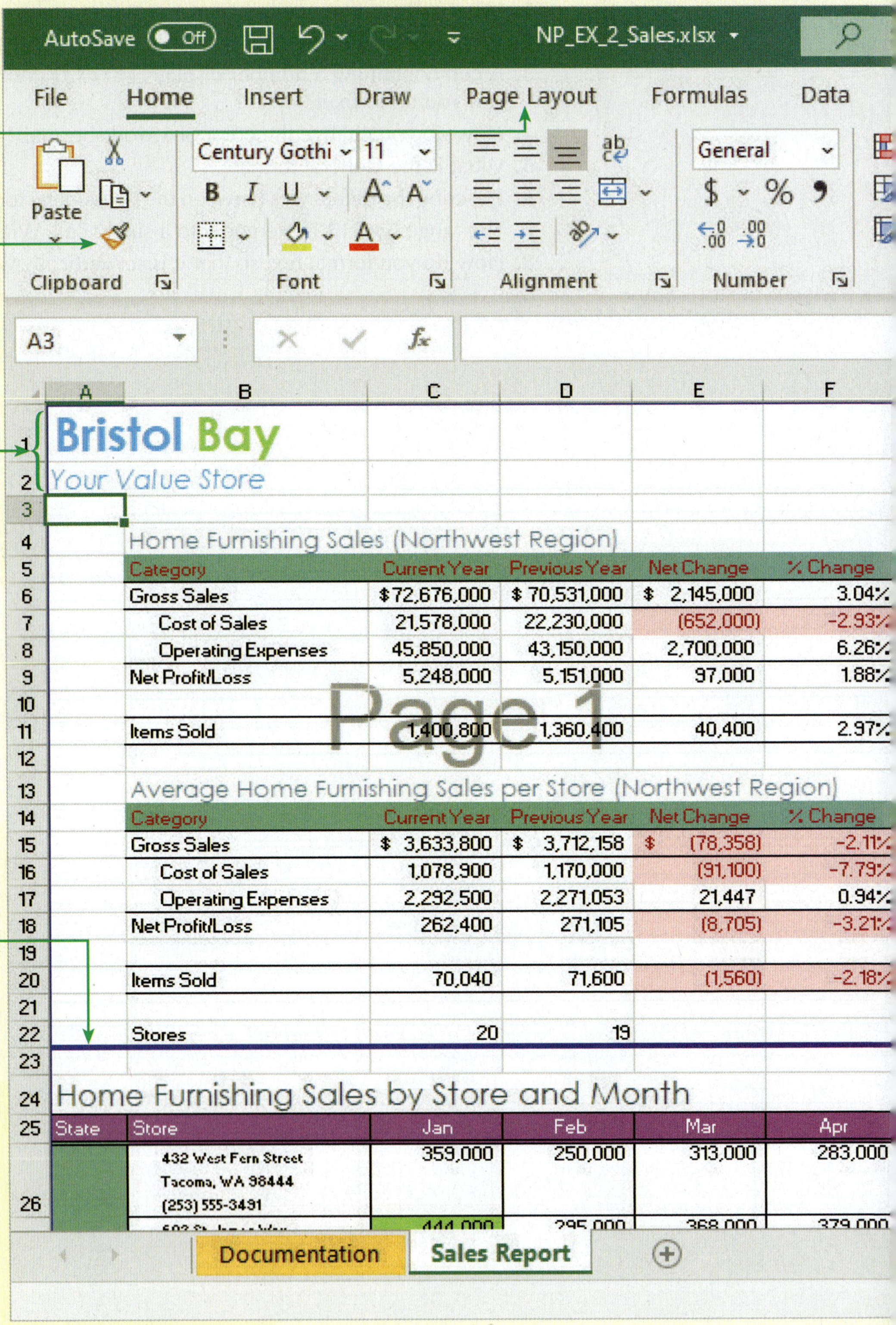

Designing a Printout

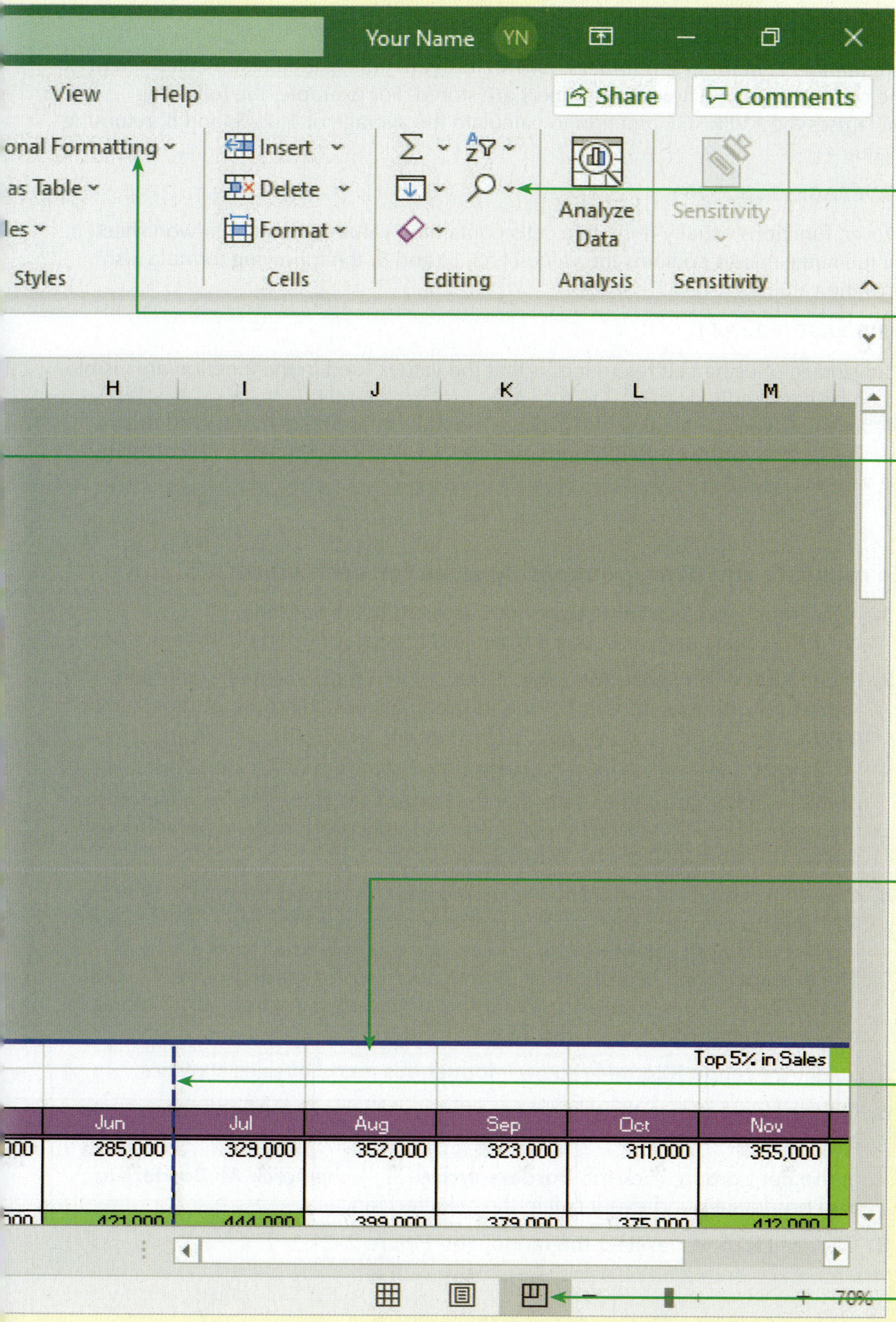

The Find and Replace commands, which are available from the Find & Select button, are used to quickly make content and format changes throughout a workbook.

Conditional formatting applies a format to a cell when its value meets a specified condition.

A **cell style** is a predesigned combination of font, font size, and font color that you can apply to a cell.

The **print area** is the range or ranges in a worksheet that you specify to be printed. In Page Break Preview, the print area is not grayed out.

An **automatic page break**, identified by a dotted blue line, is a page break that Excel sets when a page of the printout is full.

Page Break Preview shows the location of the print area and all page breaks.

Calculating Averages

The **AVERAGE function** calculates the average value from a collection of numbers. It has the syntax

```
AVERAGE(number1,[number2],[number3],...)
```

where ***number1***, *number2*, *number3*, and so forth are either numbers or cell references to the cells or a range where the numbers are stored. For example, the following formula uses the AVERAGE function to calculate the average of 1, 2, 5, and 8, returning the value 4:

```
=AVERAGE(1,2,5,8)
```

However, functions usually reference cells containing values entered in a worksheet. So, if the range A1:A4 contains the values 1, 2, 5, and 8, the following formula also returns the value 4:

```
=AVERAGE(A1:A4)
```

The advantage of using cell references is that the values used in the function are visible and can be easily edited.

Stefan wants you to calculate the average monthly sales for each of the 20 Bristol Bay stores in the Northwest Region. You will use the AVERAGE function to calculate these values.

To calculate the average monthly sales for each store:

1. If you took a break after the previous session, make sure the NP_EX_2_Sales.xslx workbook is open and the Sales Report worksheet is active.
2. In cell **R25**, enter **Store Average** as the column title. The cell is automatically formatted with a white font color and green fill, matching the other column titles.
3. In cell **R26**, enter the formula **=AVERAGE(C26:N26)** to calculate the average of the monthly gross sales values in the range C26:N26. The formula returns the value 328,500, which is the average monthly gross sales in home furnishing for the store in Tacoma, Washington.
4. Copy the formula in cell **R26**, and then paste the copied formula in the range **R27:R46** to calculate the average monthly gross sales for each of the remaining Bristol Bay stores as well as the average monthly sales from all stores. The average monthly gross sales for individual stores range from $211,333 to $397,417. The monthly gross sales in home furnishing from all 20 stores in the Northwest region is $6,056,333.
5. Select the range **R26:R46**. You will format this range of sales statistics.
6. On the Home tab, in the Alignment group, click the **Top Align** button to align each average value with the top edge of its cell.
7. In the Font group, click the **Borders arrow**, then click **All Borders** to add borders around every cell in the selected range.
8. Click cell **R26** to deselect the range. See Figure 2–21.

Figure 2–21 Average sales results

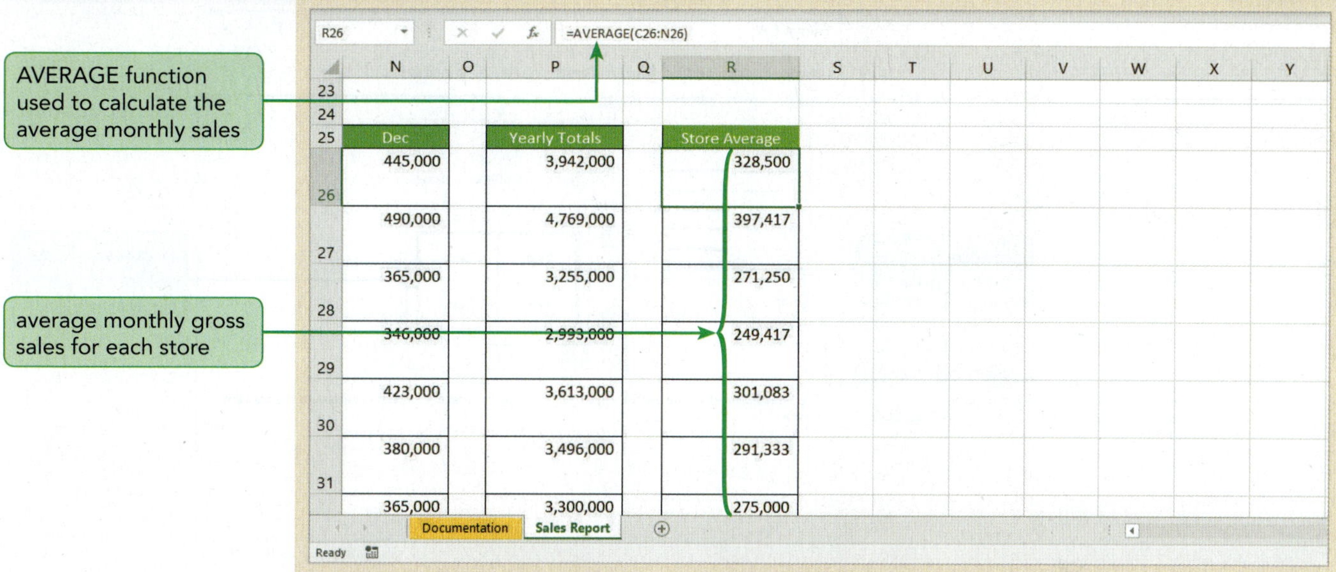

With so many values in the data, Stefan wants you to insert double borders around the sales values for each state. The Border tab in the Format Cells dialog box provides options for changing the border style and color and placement.

To add a double border to the state results:

1. Select the range **A26:N34** containing the Washington monthly gross sales totals.
2. Right-click the selection, click **Format Cells** on the shortcut menu to open the Format Cells dialog box, and then click the **Border** tab.
3. In the Line section, click the **double line** in the lower-right corner of the Style box.
4. In the Presets section, click the **Outline** option. The double border appears around the selected cells in the Border preview. See Figure 2–22.

Figure 2–22 **Border tab in the Format Cells dialog box**

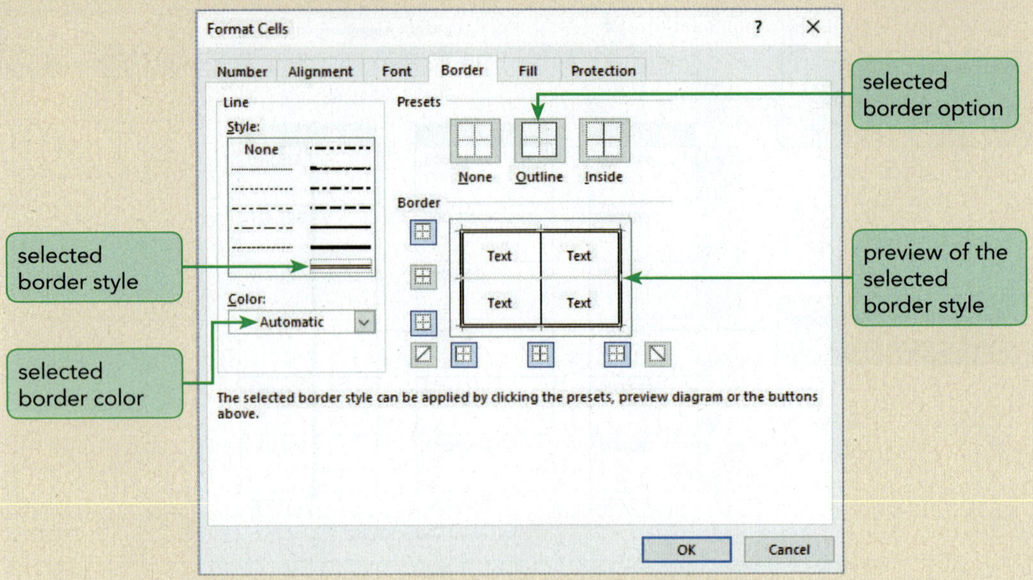

5. Click **OK**. The selected border is applied to the Washington monthly sales.
6. Repeat Steps 1 through 5 to apply double borders to the ranges **A35:N42** and **A43:N45**.
7. Click cell **A48** to deselect the range. See Figure 2–23.

Figure 2–23 **Worksheet with font, fill, and border formatting**

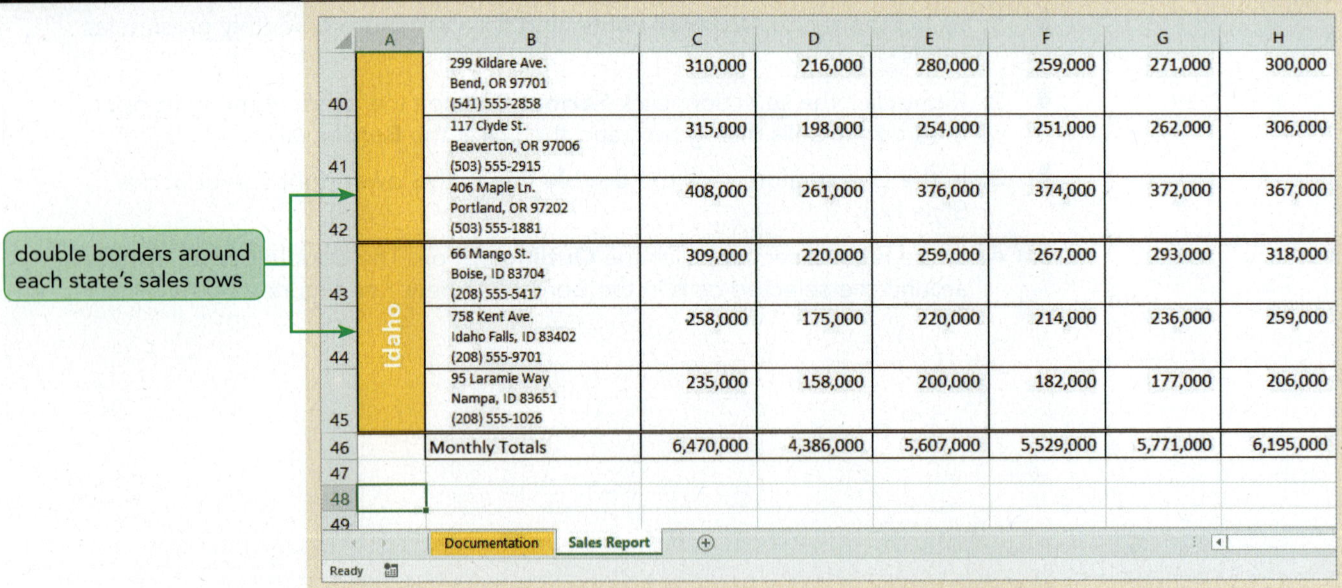

Applying Cell Styles

Cells throughout a workbook often store the same type of data. For example, a cell displaying the sheet title might appear on each worksheet, or cells containing totals and averages might appear several times within a range of financial data. It is good design practice to apply the same formatting to cells that contain the same type of data.

One way to ensure that similar data is displayed consistently is with cell styles. A **cell style** is a collection of formatting options—such as a specified font, font size, font styles, font color, fill color, and borders—that you can apply to cells. You can use the cell styles that come with Excel to format your workbooks. For example, you can use the built-in Heading 1 cell style to display sheet titles in a bold, blue-gray, 15-point Calibri font with no fill color and a blue bottom border. You can also create your own styles for each workbook.

All cell styles are listed in the Cell Styles gallery, which you access on the Home tab in the Styles group. The Cell Styles gallery also includes Accounting, Comma, and Percent number format styles that you already applied to the Sales Report worksheet using buttons in the Number group on the Home tab.

Reference

Applying a Cell Style

- Select the cell or range to which you want to apply a cell style.
- On the Home tab, in the Styles group, click the Cell Styles button.
- Point to each cell style in the Cell Styles gallery to see a Live Preview of that cell style on the selected cell or range.
- Click the cell style you want to apply to the selected cell or range.

Stefan wants you to add more color and visual interest to the Sales Report worksheet using cell styles in the Cell Styles gallery.

To apply cell styles to the Sales Report worksheet:

1. Scroll up and click cell **B4** containing the text "Home Furnishing Sales (Northwest Region)."
2. On the Home tab, in the Styles group, click the **Cell Styles** button. The Cell Styles gallery opens.
3. Point to the **Heading 1** cell style in the Titles and Headings section. Live Preview shows cell B4 in a 15-point, bold font with a solid blue bottom border. See Figure 2–24.

Figure 2–24 Cell Styles gallery

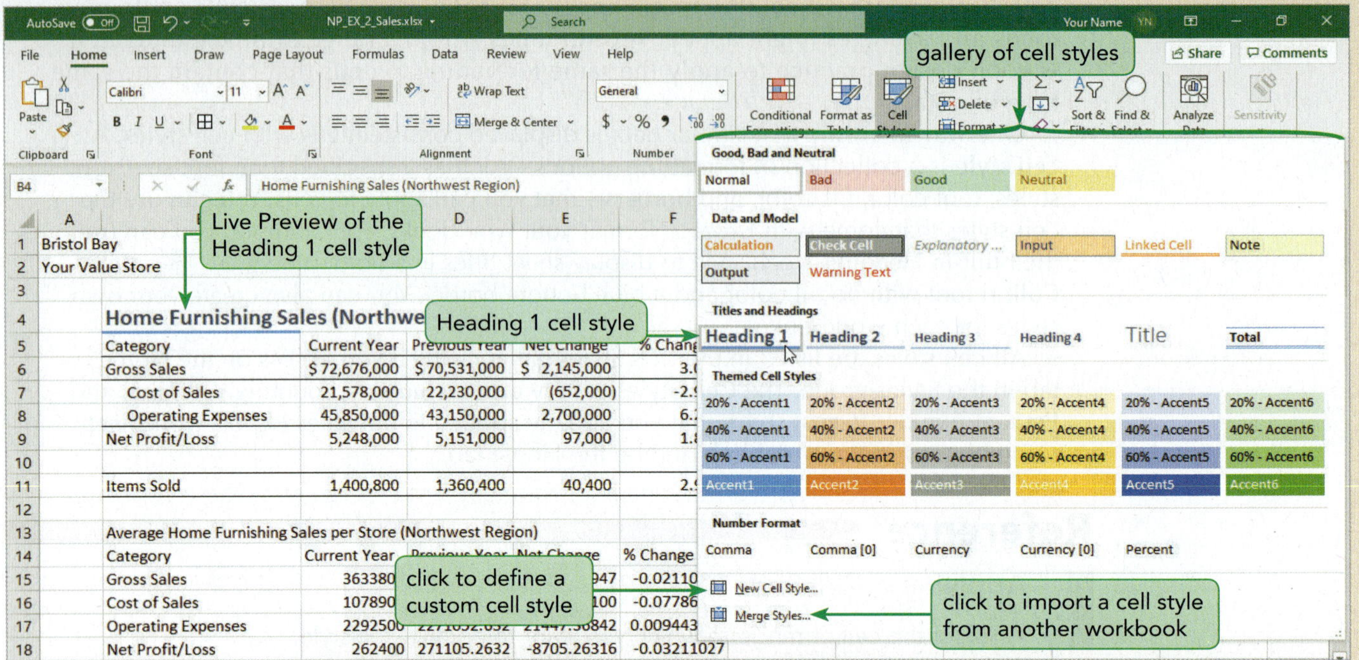

4. Move the pointer over different styles in the Cell Styles gallery to see cell B4 with a Live Preview of each cell style.
5. Click the **Title** cell style. The Title cell style—18-point, Blue-Gray, Text 2 Calibri Light font—is applied to cell B4.
6. Select the range **B5:F5** containing the column titles for the Sales Statistics data.
7. In the Styles group, click the **Cell Styles** button, and then click the **Accent4** cell style in the Themed Cell Styles section of the Cell Styles gallery.
8. Click cell **A24** containing the text "Home Furnishing Sales by Store and Month," and then apply the **Title** cell style to the cell.
9. Click cell **A3**. See Figure 2–25.

Figure 2–25 Cell styles applied to the worksheet

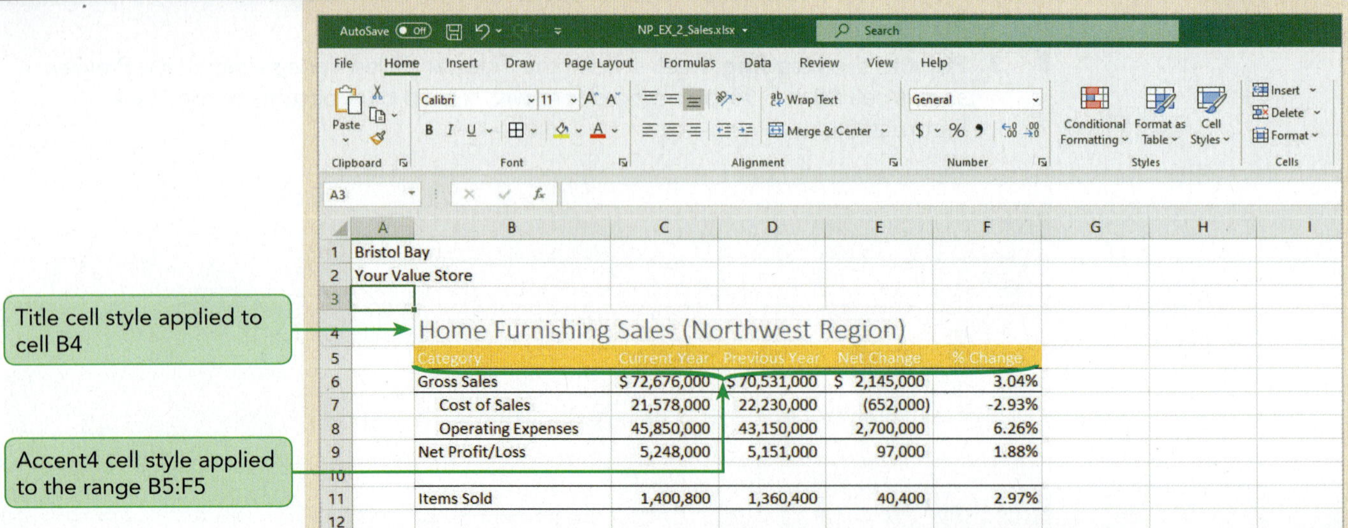

To remove all styles and formats, apply the Normal cell style to a selected cell or cell range.

Creating a Custom Cell Style

When you create a custom cell style, you select the font, font size, font styles, alignment, number format, borders, and fill you want to include in that cell style. You can base a new cell style on an existing cell style or on formatting that you applied to a cell. The custom cell style will then appear in the Cell Style gallery so you can apply it to any cell in your worksheet.

Stefan suggests that you create a custom cell style named "Bristol Bay Title" based on the Title cell style applied to cell B4. He wants you to reduce the font size and change the font color for the custom cell style.

To create the Bristol Bay Title custom cell style:

1. Click cell **B4** to select it. The Title cell style is applied to this cell.
2. Change the font size to **14** points and the font color to the **Blue, Accent 5** theme color (the ninth color in the first row).
3. On the Home tab, in the Styles group, click the **Cell Styles** button to display the Cell Styles gallery.
4. At the bottom of the Cell Styles gallery, click **New Cell Style** to open the Style dialog box.
5. In the Style name box, type **Bristol Bay Title** as name of the custom cell style. See Figure 2–26.

Tip

To apply only certain formatting options, click the check boxes of the format categories you want.

Figure 2–26 Style dialog box

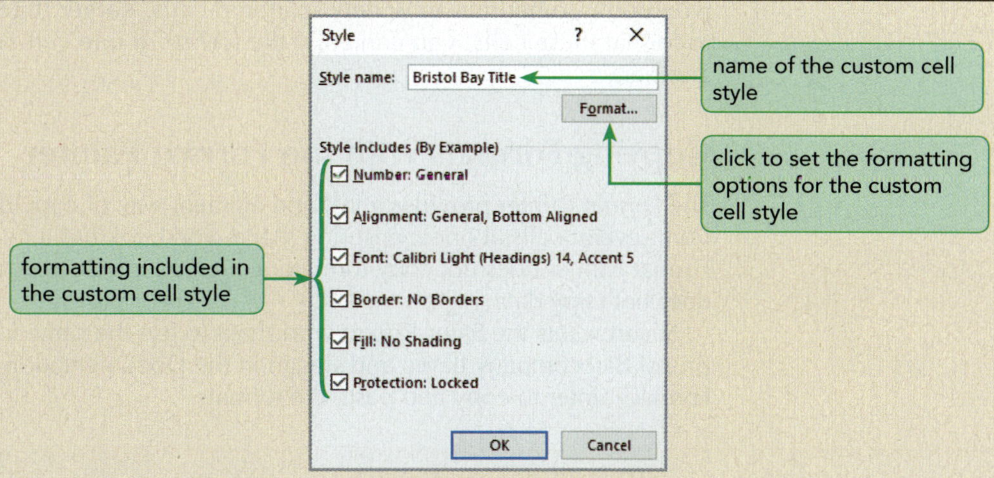

6. Click **OK**. The cell style applied to cell B4 is saved as the Bristol Bay Title custom cell style.
7. Click the **Cell Styles** button to open the Cell Styles gallery, and verify that the Bristol Bay Title custom cell style has been added to the Custom section at the top of the gallery.
8. Press **ESC** to close the Cell Styles gallery.

If you want to change the formatting included in a custom cell style, right-click the name of the custom cell style in the Cell Styles gallery and then click Modify on the shortcut menu. You can then change the formatting options specified in the Style dialog box.

Merging Custom Cell Styles

Custom cell styles are created in the current workbook. However, you can copy custom cell styles from one workbook to another so that you can use the same cell styles in multiple workbooks without recreating those cell styles. This is especially useful when a company or department wants to easily apply consistent formatting in all its workbooks.

Use the following steps to copy custom cell styles from one workbook to another:

1. Open the workbook containing the custom cell styles (the source workbook).
2. Open the workbook you want to copy the cell styles to (the destination workbook).
3. In the destination workbook, open the Cell Styles gallery, and then click Merge Styles at the bottom of the gallery.
4. Select the source workbook containing the custom cell styles, and then click OK.

All of the custom cell styles from the source workbook are copied into the destination workbook. Keep in mind that if you later modify a custom cell style in the source workbook, those changes will not appear in the destination workbook until you repeat the merge process.

Another way of repeating the same cell formats across a workbook is by copying and pasting.

Copying and Pasting Formats

Large workbooks often use the same formatting on similar data throughout the workbook, sometimes in widely scattered cells. Rather than repeating the same steps to format these cells, you can copy the format of one cell or range and paste it to another.

Copying Formats with the Format Painter

The Format Painter provides a fast and efficient way of copying and pasting formats from several cells at once, ensuring that a workbook has a consistent look and feel. The Format Painter does not copy formatting applied to selected text within a cell, and it does not copy data.

Stefan wants the Sales Report worksheet to use the same formats you applied to the Bristol Bay company name and slogan in the Documentation sheet. You will use the Format Painter to copy and paste the formats.

To use the Format Painter to copy and paste a format:

1. Go to the **Documentation** worksheet, and then select the range **A1:A2**.
2. On the Home tab, in the Clipboard group, click the **Format Painter** button. The formats from the selected cells are copied to the Clipboard, a flashing border appears around the selected range, and the pointer changes to the Format Painter pointer for cells.
3. Go to the **Sales Report** worksheet, and then click cell **A1**. The formatting from the range A1:A2 in the Documentation worksheet is applied to the range A1:A2 in the Sales Report worksheet.

Tip

To paste the same format multiple times, double-click the Format Painter button. Click the button again or press ESC to turn it off.

Notice that green font color you applied to the text selection "Bay" was not included in the pasted formats because the Format Painter does not work with formats applied to text strings within cells.

4. Double-click cell **A1** to enter Edit mode, select **Bay**, and then change the font color to the **Light Green** standard color. The format for the company title now matches the company title in the Documentation sheet.
5. Press **ENTER** to exit Edit mode and select cell A2.

You can use the Format Painter to copy all formats within a selected range and then apply those formats to another range that has the same size and shape by clicking the upper-left cell of the range. Stefan wants you to copy all the formats that you applied to the Sales Statistics data to the sales statistics per store data.

Tip

If you paste formats in a bigger range than the range you copied, Format Painter will repeat the copied formats to fill the pasted range.

To copy and paste multiple formats in the sales statistics data:

1. Select the range **B4:F11** in the Sales Report worksheet.
2. On the Home tab, in the Clipboard group, click the **Format Painter** button.
3. Click cell **B13**. The number formats, cell borders, fonts, and fill colors are pasted in the range B13:F20.
4. Click cell **A21**. See Figure 2–27.

Figure 2–27 Formats copied and pasted between ranges

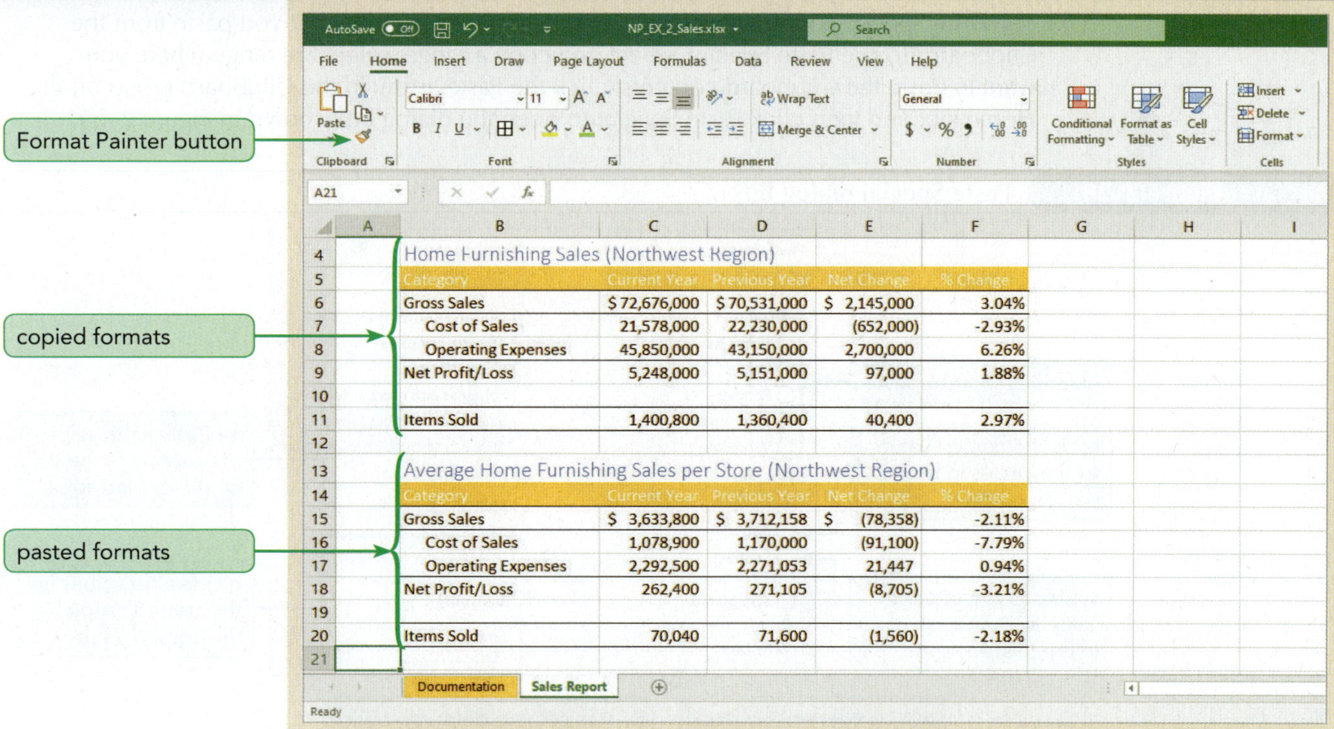

Copying Formats with the Paste Options Button

Another way to copy and paste formats is with the Paste Options button (Ctrl), which provides options for pasting only values, only formats, or some combination of values and formats. Each time you paste, the Paste Options button appears in the lower-right corner of the pasted cell or range. You click the Paste Options button to open a list of pasting options, shown in Figure 2–28, such as pasting only the values or only the formatting.

Figure 2–28 Paste Options button

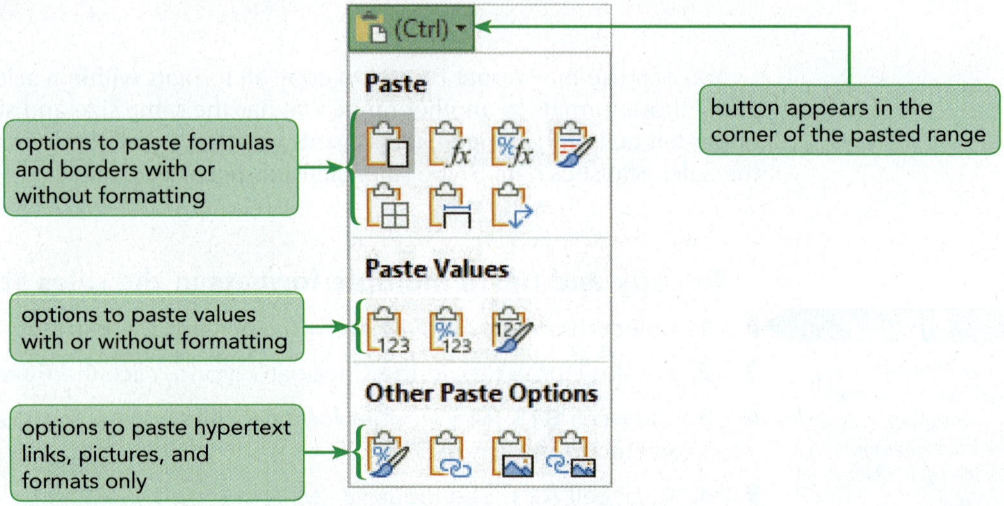

Copying Formats with Paste Special

The Paste Special command provides another way to control what you paste from the Clipboard. To use Paste Special, select and copy a range, select the range where you want to paste the Clipboard contents, click the Paste arrow in the Clipboard group on the Home tab, and then click Paste Special to open the dialog box shown in Figure 2–29.

Figure 2–29 Paste Special dialog box

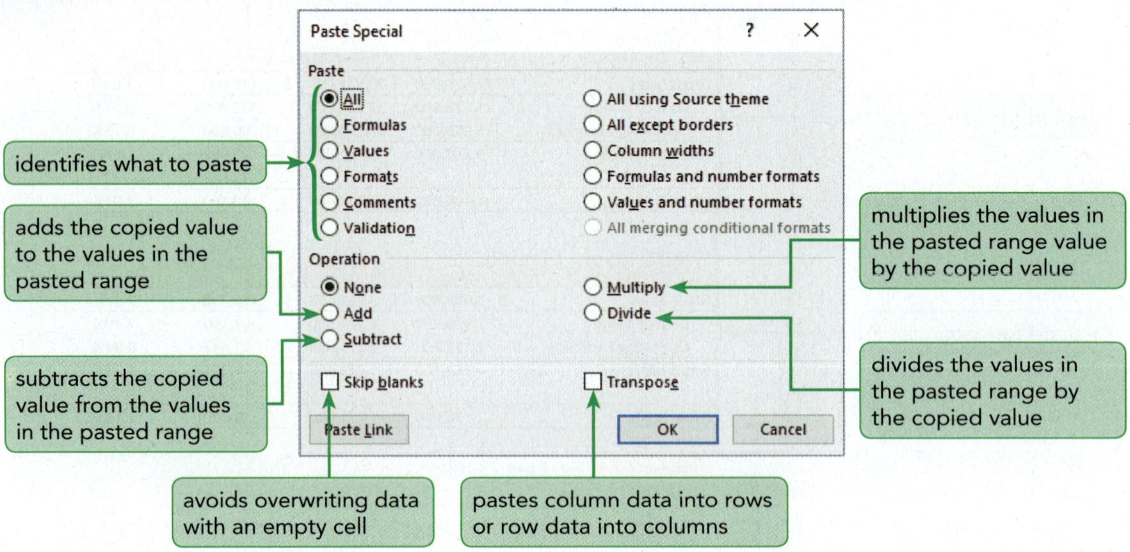

From the Paste Special dialog box, you can control exactly how to paste the copied range.

Insight

Performing Special Tasks with Paste Special

Excel has many options for copying and pasting data in different formats and layouts. The Paste Special dialog box provides access to these many different options. From the Paste Special dialog box, you can accomplish the following tasks in which you copy content from a selected source range and paste that content into a destination range:

- **Paste values only.** Rather than pasting both the cell values and formatting, you can paste only the values of selected cells by selecting the Values option in the Paste Special dialog box. Any formatting already applied to the cells in the destination range is unchanged when the values are pasted into the cells.
- **Paste column widths.** You can copy and paste column widths from one range to another. First, copy a range whose column widths you want to duplicate. Then, select the range whose columns you want to change. In the Paste Special dialog box, select the Column widths. No cell values are pasted.
- **Paste with no borders.** You can copy all formats applied to a cell *except* the cell borders by selecting the All except borders option in the Paste Special dialog box.
- **Skip blanks.** The source range may have empty or blank cells. If you want to copy only cells that contain content, use the Skip Blanks option in the Paste Special dialog box. This option prevents pasting over data in the destination range with blanks.
- **Perform a mathematical operation.** Rather than pasting a value, you can use the copied value in a mathematical operation that adds, subtracts, multiplies, or divides the values in the destination range by the copied value. For example, if you copy the number 2 from a cell and then choose the Multiply option in the Operation section of the Paste Special dialog box, all of the values in the destination range will be doubled in value.
- **Paste a link.** Rather than pasting a value, you can paste the cell references to the cells in the source range with the Paste Link button in the Paste Special dialog box. For example, copying cell A1 and then pasting a link in cell B4 enters the formula `=A1` rather than the value in cell B4.

These paste special features help you work more efficiently as you develop large and complex worksheets.

Transposing Data

Data values are usually arranged in a rectangular grid. However, sometimes you might want to change the orientation of that rectangle, switching the rows and columns. You can easily do this with the Transpose option. Figure 2–30 shows a range of sales data that was copied and then pasted so that the rows and columns are transposed. As you can see, the store data switched from the rows to the columns and the month data switched from columns to rows. Both the cell values and cell formats are transposed in the pasted content.

Figure 2–30 **Transposed pasted range**

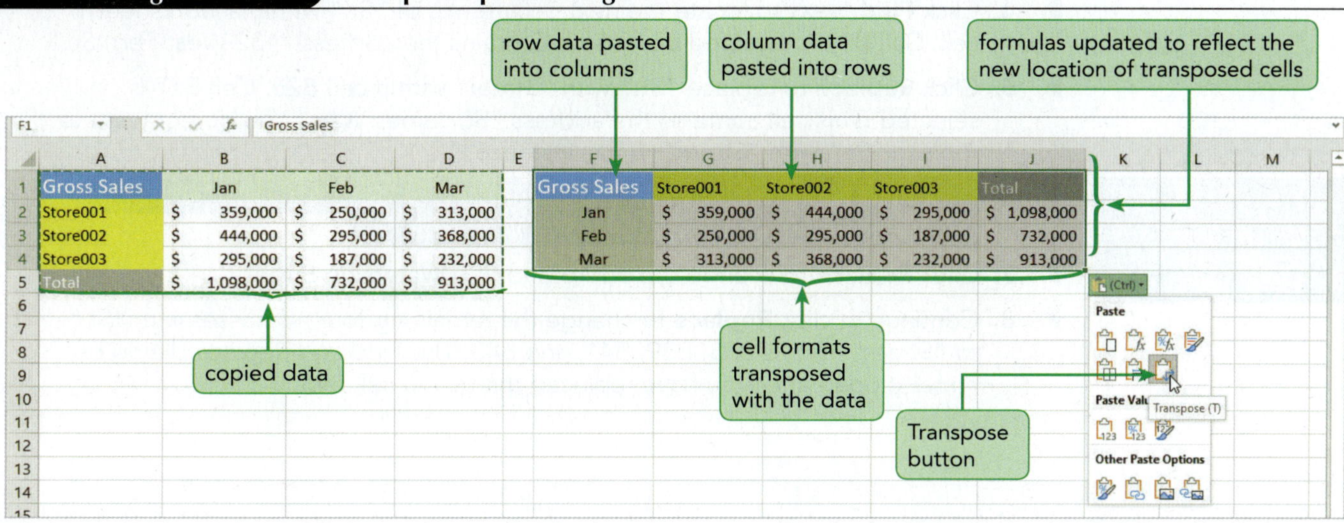

When you paste and transpose cells containing formulas, the cell references in those formulas are automatically updated to reflect the new layout of the data.

Finding and Replacing Text and Formats

The Find and Replace commands let you make content and design changes to a worksheet or the entire workbook quickly. The Find command searches through the current worksheet or workbook for the content or formatting you want to locate, and the Replace command then substitutes it with the new content or formatting you specify.

The Find and Replace commands are versatile. You can find each occurrence of the search text one at a time and decide whether to replace it. You can highlight all occurrences of the search text in the worksheet. Or, you can replace all occurrences at once without reviewing them.

Stefan wants you to replace all the street title abbreviations (such as St. and Ave.) in the Sales Report with their full names (such as Street and Avenue). You will use Find and Replace to make these changes.

To find and replace the street abbreviations:

1. On the Home tab, in the Editing group, click the **Find & Select** button, and then click **Replace** (or press **CTRL+H**). The Find and Replace dialog box opens.
2. Type **St.** in the Find what box.
3. Press **TAB** to move the insertion point to the Replace with box, and then type **Street** in the box. See Figure 2–31.

Figure 2–31 Find and Replace dialog box

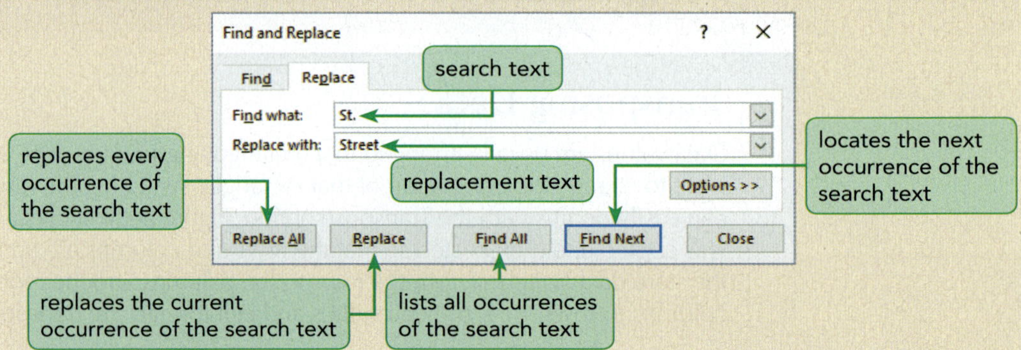

4. Click **Find Next** to locate the next occurrence of "St." within a worksheet cell. Cell B26 is selected because it contains the address "432 West Fern St."
5. Click **Replace** to replace "St." with "Street" within cell B26. Cell B27 is selected. This cell contains the address "St. James Way." You do not want to replace "St." with "Street" in this instance.
6. Click **Find Next** to go to the next occurrence of "St." in a cell. Cell B29 is selected containing the address "990 Waterside St."
7. Click **Replace** to change the address to 990 Waterside Street.
8. Continue to click **Replace** to change the remaining four addresses with "St." to "Street" in cells B35, B39, B41, and B43. The Find and Replace dialog box remains open after you have replaced the text in cell B43.

Always check the matched text so that you do not inadvertently replace text that should not be replaced.

Rather than reviewing each possible replacement, you can use the Replace All button in the Find and Replace dialog box to make all the replacements at once. You should do this only if you are sure there is no chance for a replacement error. You'll use the Replace All button to change all instances of "Ave." in the store addresses with "Avenue" and all instances of "Ln." with "Lane."

To replace all occurrences of "Ave." and "Ln.":

1. In the Find and Replace dialog box, type **Ave.** in the Find what box, and then type **Avenue** in the Replace with box.
2. Click **Replace All**. A dialog box appears, indicating Excel made seven replacements in the worksheet.
3. Click **OK** to return to the Find and Replace dialog box.
4. Type **Ln.** in the Find what box, and then type **Lane** in the Replace with box.
5. Click **Replace All**. A dialog box appears, indicating that Excel replaced Ln. with Lane five times in the worksheet.
6. Click **OK** to return to the Find and Replace dialog box.

Tip

All searches are case-insensitive. To include upper- and lowercase characters in the search, click the Options button and select the Match Case check box.

The Find and Replace dialog box can also be used with cell formatting, replacing both the content and the format of cells within the worksheet. Stefan wants you to replace all occurrences of the white text on a gold fill in the Sales Report worksheet with blue text on a gold fill. You'll do this using the Find and Replace dialog box.

To replace content based on formatting:

1. In the Find and Replace dialog box, click **Options** to expand the list of formatting options.
2. Delete the search text from the Find what and Replace with boxes, leaving those two boxes empty. By not specifying a text string to find and replace, the dialog box will search through all cells regardless of their content.
3. Click **Format** in the Find what row to open the Find Format dialog box, which is similar to the Format Cells dialog box you used earlier to format a range.
4. Click the **Font** tab to make it active, click the **Color** box, and then click the **White, Background 1** theme color.
5. Click the **Fill** tab, and then in the Background Color section, click the **gold** theme color (the eighth color in the first row).
6. Click **OK** to close the Find Format dialog box and return to the Find and Replace dialog box.
7. Click **Format** in the Replace with row to open the Replace Format dialog box.
8. On the Fill tab, click the **gold** theme color (the eighth color in the first row).
9. Click the **Font** tab, click the **Color** box, and then click the **Blue Accent 1** theme color (the fifth color in the first row).
10. Click **OK** to return to the Find and Replace dialog box. See Figure 2–32.

Tip

To search the entire workbook, select Workbook in the Within box.

Figure 2–32 **Expanded Find and Replace dialog box**

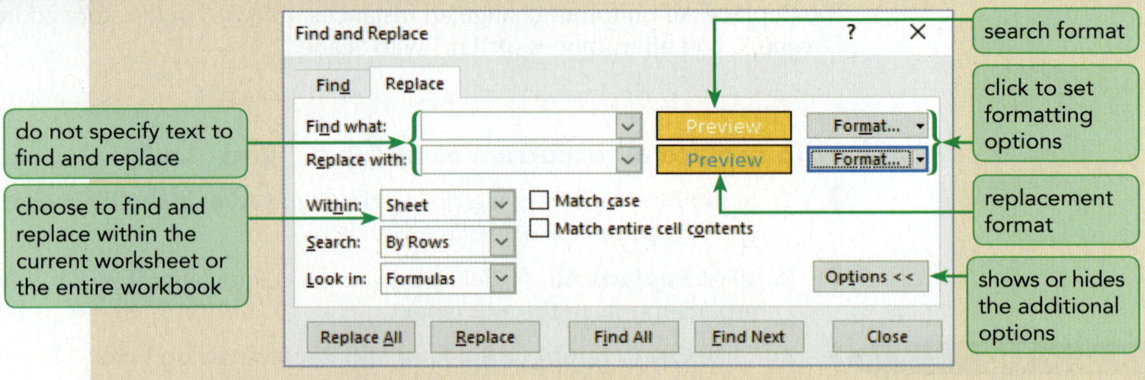

11. Click **Replace All** to replace all occurrences of white text on a gold fill in the Sales Report worksheet with blue text on a gold fill. A dialog box opens, reporting that Excel made 13 replacements.
12. Click **OK** to return to the Find and Replace dialog box.

It is a good idea to clear the find and replace formats after you are done so they won't affect any future searches and replacements. Stefan asks you to remove the formats from the Find and Replace dialog box.

To clear the options from the Find and Replace dialog box:

1. In the Find and Replace dialog box, click the **Format arrow** in the Find what row, and then click **Clear Find Format**. The search format is removed.
2. Click the **Format arrow** in the Replace with row, and then click **Clear Replace Format**. The replacement format is removed.
3. Click **Close**. The Find and Replace dialog box closes.

The font color for cells in the range B5:F5,B14:F14,A26:A45 all changed to blue because of the cell format you found and replaced.

Working with Themes

Another way to make multiple changes to the formats used in your workbook is through themes. Recall that a theme is a predefined, coordinated set of colors, fonts, graphical effects, and other formats that are applied throughout a workbook to give them a consistent, professional look.

Applying a Theme

The Office theme is the default theme applied to workbooks. When you switch to a different theme, the theme-related fonts, colors, and effects change throughout the workbook to reflect the new theme. The appearances of standard fonts, colors, and effects remain unchanged no matter which theme is applied to the workbook.

Most of the formatting used in the Sales Report workbook is based on the Office theme. Stefan wants you to change the theme to see how it affects the workbook's appearance.

To change the workbook's theme:

1. Scroll up the worksheet and click cell **A1**.
2. On the ribbon, click the **Page Layout** tab.
3. In the Themes group, click the **Themes** button. The Themes gallery opens. Office—the current theme—is the default.
4. Point to different themes in the Themes gallery using Live Preview to preview the impact of each theme on the fonts and colors used in the worksheet.
5. Point to the **Ion** theme to see a Live Preview of that theme to the workbook. See Figure 2–33.

Figure 2–33 **Live Preview of the Ion theme**

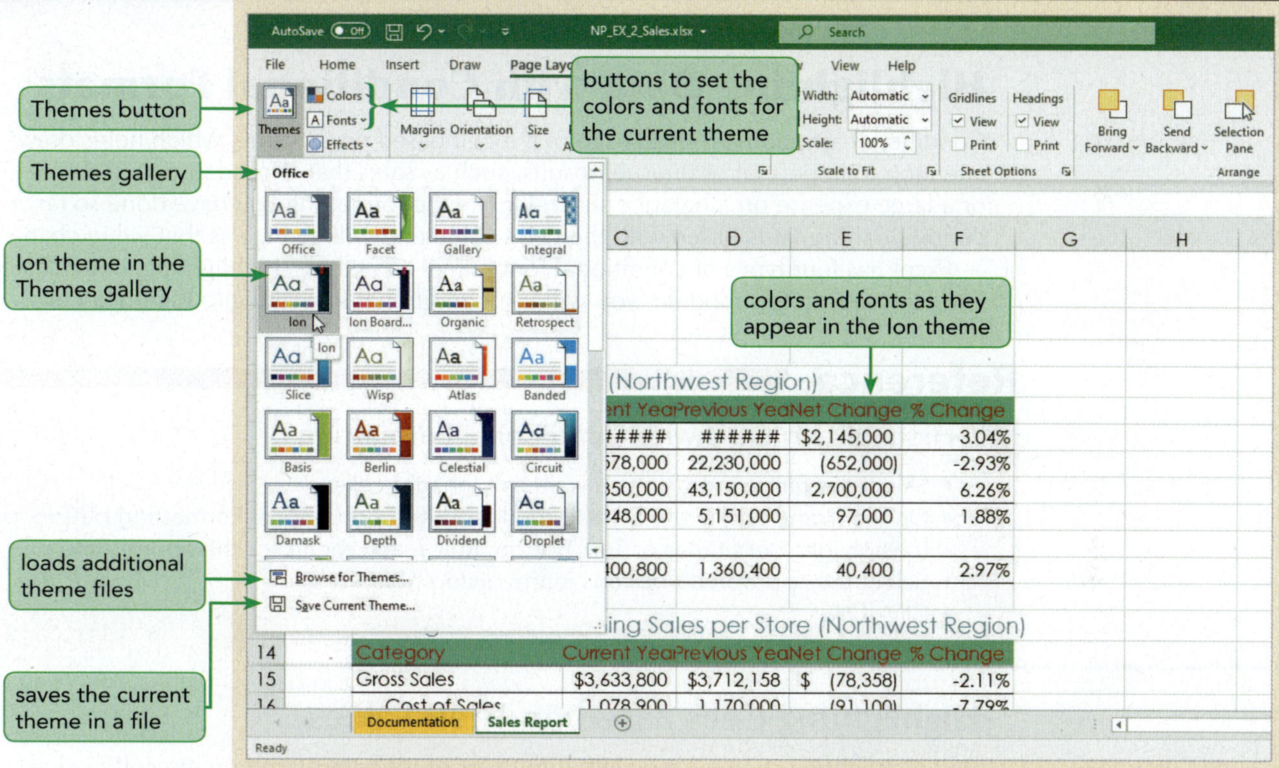

6. Click the **Ion** theme. The theme is applied to the workbook.

Changing the theme made a significant difference in the worksheet's appearance. The most obvious changes to the worksheet are the fill colors and the fonts. Only formatting options directly tied to a theme change when you select a different theme. Any formatting options you selected that are not theme-based remain unaffected by the change. For example, a standard color or font is not affected by the theme. That is why the standard colors used in cells A1 and A2 do not change when you change the theme.

Setting Theme Colors and Fonts

Businesses often use custom themes that match their company's logo colors and fonts. To change the theme colors, click the Colors button in the Themes group on the Page Layout tab, and then select one of the color palettes. To create your own color palette, click Customize Colors to open the Create New Theme Colors dialog box. In this dialog box, you can select colors for the text and background and the six accent colors used by that theme and save the custom colors with a name of your choosing.

To change the theme fonts, click the Fonts button in the Themes group on the Page Layout tab, and then select one of the font themes for heading and body text. To create your own theme fonts, click Customize Fonts to open the Create New Theme Fonts dialog box. From this dialog box, select the fonts for heading and body text and save the custom fonts under a new name.

Saving a Theme

Once you've changed a theme's colors or fonts, you can save the custom theme in its own theme file. You do this by clicking the Themes button in the Themes group on the Page Layout tab, and then clicking Save Current Theme. Theme files are stored in the Office Theme folder on your computer and are available to all Office applications, including Excel, Word, and PowerPoint.

Highlighting Data with Conditional Formats

Conditional formatting is used to format a cell based on its value, which helps draw attention to important or unusual results, such as sales that exceed a specified goal or a large expense on a balance sheet. Unlike the formatting you have done so far, a conditional format is based with the cell's value and will change as that value changes.

Excel has four types of conditional formatting—data bars, highlighting, color scales, and icon sets. In this module, you will use conditional formatting to highlight cells.

Reference

Highlighting Cells with Conditional Formatting

- Select the range in which you want to highlight cells.
- On the Home tab, in the Styles group, click the Conditional Formatting button, point to Highlight Cells Rules or Top/Bottom Rules, and then click the appropriate rule.
- Select the appropriate options in the dialog box.
- Click OK.

Highlighting Cells Based on Their Values

Cell highlighting changes the cell's font color or fill color based on the cell's value. Figure 2–34 describes the seven rules supported by Excel for choosing the cell value.

Figure 2–34 **Highlight cells rules**

Rule	Highlights Cell Values
Greater Than	Greater than a specified number
Less Than	Less than a specified number
Between	Between two specified numbers
Equal To	Equal to a specified number
Text that Contains	That contain specified text
A Date Occurring	That contain a specified date
Duplicate Values	That contain duplicate or unique values

Stefan wants to highlight important trends and sales values in the Sales Report worksheet by highlighting sales statistics that show a negative trend from the previous year to the current year. You will use conditional formatting to highlight the negative net change and percent change values in red.

To highlight negative values in red:

1. In the Sales Report worksheet, select the range **E6:F20** containing the net and percent changes in sales from the previous year to the current year.
2. On the ribbon, click the **Home** tab.
3. In the Styles group, click the **Conditional Formatting** button, and then point to **Highlight Cells Rules** to display a menu of the available rules.
4. Click **Less Than**. The Less Than dialog box opens so you can select the value and format to highlight negative values.
5. Make sure the value in the first box is selected, and then type **0** so that cells in the selected range that contain values that are less than 0 are formatted with a light red fill and dark red text. Live Preview shows the conditional formatting applied to the cells with negative numbers. See Figure 2–35.

Figure 2–35 Live Preview of the Less Than conditional format

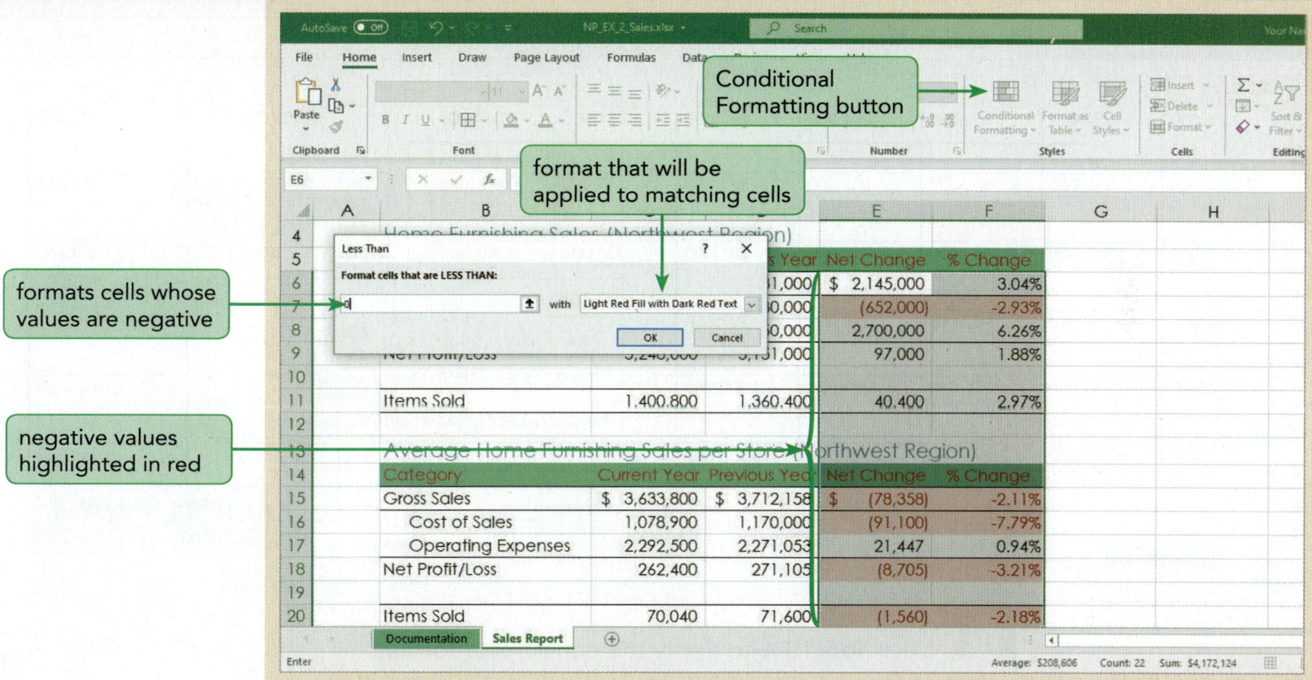

6. Click **OK** to apply the highlighting rule.

Conditional formatting highlights some very important sales facts for Stefan. While the net profit for Northwest region stores increased by 1.88% (cell F9), this is not true when the data is adjusted for the number of stores. The net profit per store has decreased by 3.21% (cell F16). While the number of items sold in the Northwest region increased by 2.97% (cell F11), the items sold per store decreased by 2.18% (cell F20).

The net decline in the per-store statistics might be due to the new store that opened in the Northwest region still not finding its market. It also might be due to an overall decline in sales at brick-and-mortar stores over the past year. Stefan will need to do further research to determine the cause of the decline in per-store sales and profits.

Highlighting Cells with a Top/Bottom Rule

Another way of applying conditional formatting is with the Quick Analysis tool. The **Quick Analysis tool**, which appears whenever you select a range of cells, provides access to the most common tools for data analysis and formatting of the selected range. The Formatting category includes buttons for the Greater Than and Top 10% conditional formatting rules. You can highlight cells based on their values in comparison to other cells. For example, you can highlight cells with the 10 highest or lowest values in a selected range, or you can highlight the cells with above-average values in a range.

Stefan wants to know which stores and months rank in highest in sales. You will highlight the top 10% in monthly sales from all stores using the Quick Analysis tool.

To highlight the lowest-performing stores:

1. Select the range **C26:N45** containing the monthly sales from each of the 20 Bristol Bay stores in the Northwest region.
2. Click the **Quick Analysis** button, and then point to **Top 10%**. Live Preview formats the cells in the top 10% with red font and a red fill. See Figure 2–36.

Figure 2–36 Quick Analysis tool applying a conditional format

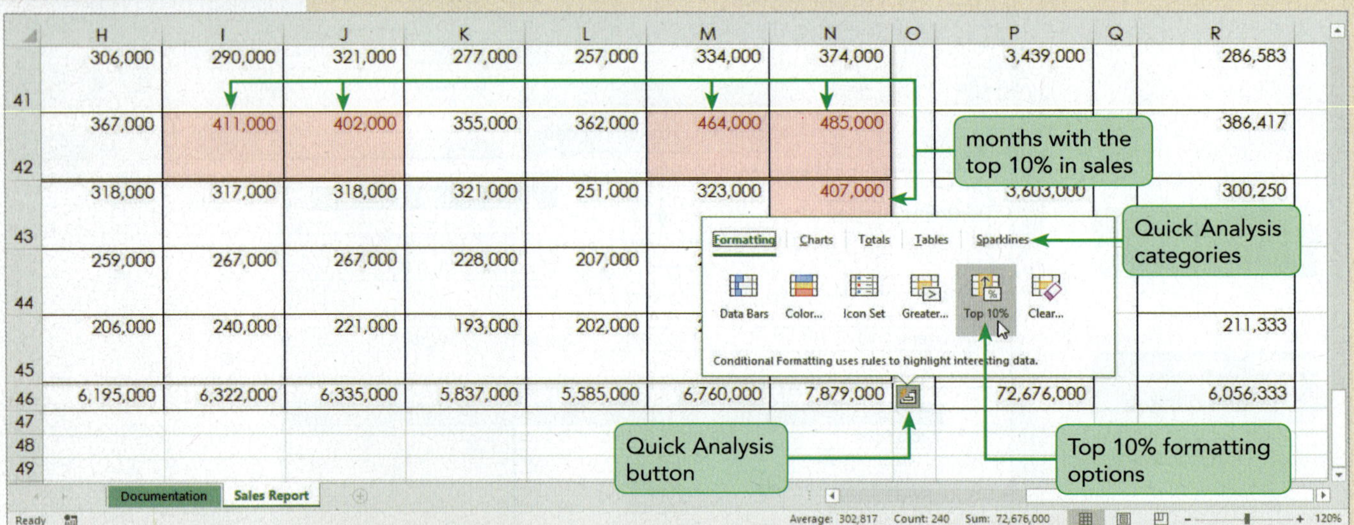

3. Click **Top 10%** to apply the conditional format.
4. Click cell **O46** to deselect the range.

A total of 24 cells are highlighted from the stores with the greatest monthly sales.

Editing a Conditional Formatting Rule

You can modify any conditional formatting rule to change what is being formatted, as well as change what formatting is applied. Stefan wants you to revise the conditional formatting rule you created with the Quick Analysis tool so that only the top 5% of monthly sales are highlighted and that the fill color is green rather than red. You will use the Manage Rules command to make this change.

To edit the Top 10% conditional formatting rule:

1. On the Home tab, in the Styles group, click the **Conditional Formatting** button and then click **Manage Rules**. The Conditional Formatting Rules Manager dialog box opens.
2. Click the **Show formatting rules for arrow**, and then click **This Worksheet** to list all conditional formatting rules in the current worksheet. See Figure 2–37.

Figure 2–37 **Conditional Formatting Rules Manager**

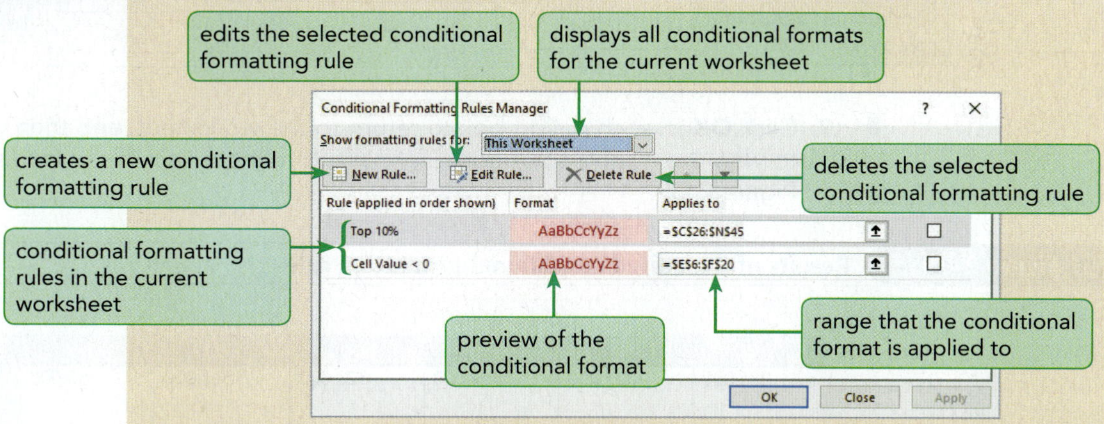

3. Make sure the **Top 10%** rule is highlighted, and then click **Edit Rule**. The Edit Formatting Rule dialog box opens.
4. In the Edit the Rule Description section, change the value in the box from 10 to **5**. This changes the rule to highlight only the top 5% of sales values.
5. Click **Format** to open the Format Cells dialog box.
6. On the Font tab in the dialog box, change the font color to the **Black, Text 1** theme color (the second color in the first row).
7. Click the **Fill** tab, change the background color to the **Light Green** standard color (the fifth standard color).
8. Click **OK** to return to the Edit Formatting Rule dialog box. See Figure 2–38.

Figure 2–38 **Edit Formatting Rule dialog box**

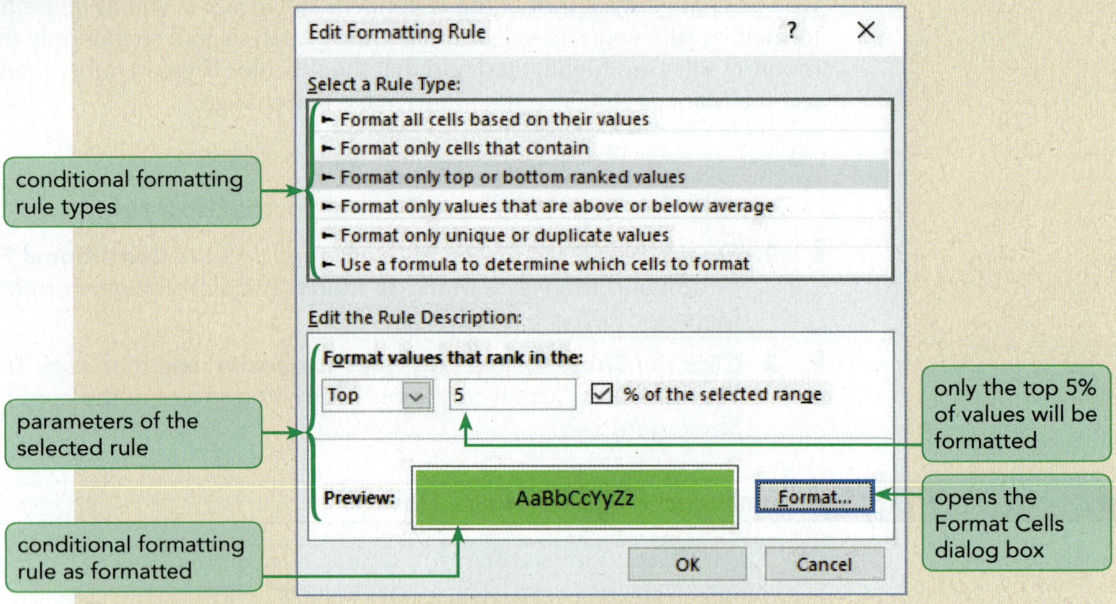

9. Click **OK** in each dialog box to return to the worksheet, and then scroll up to view the edited conditional formatting rule applied to the worksheet. See Figure 2–39.

Figure 2–39 **Results of the edited conditional formatting rule**

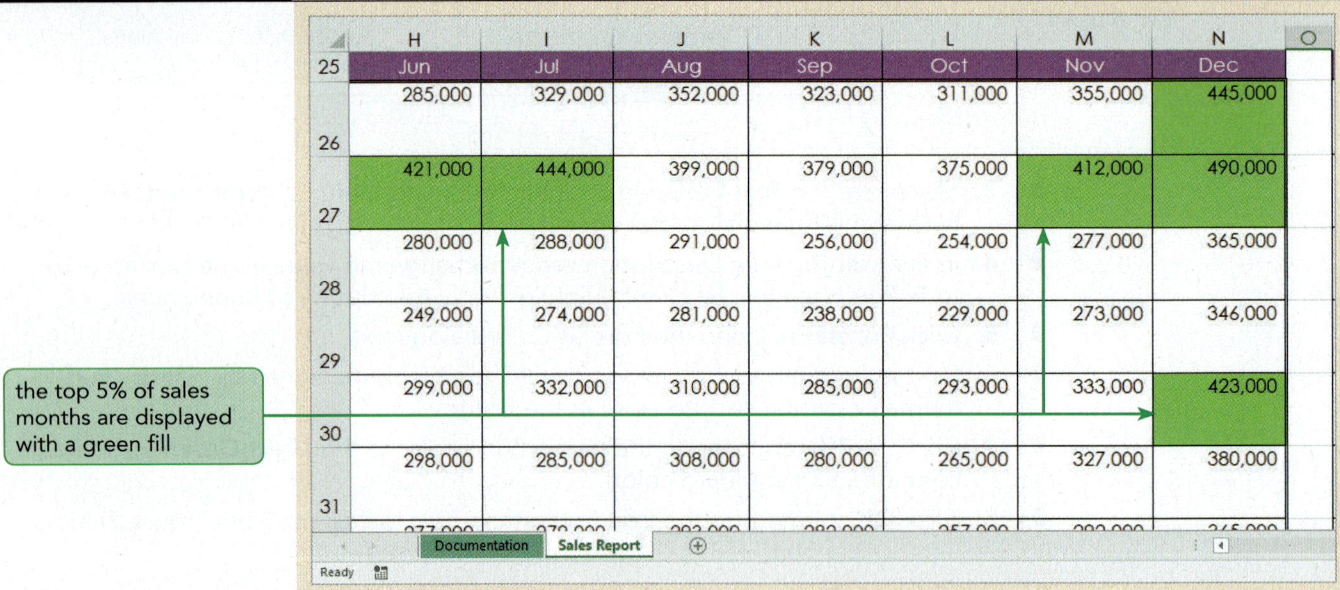

Stefan is not surprised that 7 of the 12 highlighted cells are in December when sales are always high because of the holiday season. However, Stefan is interested that the Seattle store accounts for five of the top-selling months, with large sales in January, June, July, November, and December. In fact, the June sales at the Seattle store exceed the December sales at 14 other stores.

Clearing Conditional Formatting Rules

You can remove a conditional format at any time without affecting the underlying data. Just select the range containing the conditional format, click the Conditional Formatting button in the Styles group on the Home tab, and then click the Clear Rules command. A menu opens, providing options to clear the conditional formatting rules from the selected cells or the entire worksheet. You can also click the Quick Analysis button that appears in the lower-right corner of the selected range, and then click the Clear Format button in the Formatting category. Note that you might see only "Clear..." as the button name.

Insight

Dynamic Conditional Formatting

Conditional formats can be static so that a specific value triggers the conditional format, such as highlighting monthly sales that exceed $400,000. Conditional formats can also be dynamic so that the conditional format is based on the value in a specified cell.

To create dynamic conditional formats that are based on a cell value, you enter a cell reference rather than a constant value in the dialog box when you create the conditional formatting rule. For example, you can highlight all cells whose value is greater than the value in cell B10 by entering the formula =$B$10 in the dialog box. Note that the $ character keeps the cell reference from changing if that formula moves to another cell. This lets you quickly change what is highlighted without having to continually edit the rule, making it easier to see different aspects of your data.

Documenting Conditional Formats

When you use conditional formatting to highlight cells in a worksheet, the purpose of the formatting is not always immediately apparent. To ensure that everyone knows why certain cells are highlighted, you should document the meaning of the format.

Stefan wants you to add text to the Sales Report worksheet to indicate that the green cells in the sales table represent the stores and months in the top 5% of all sales.

To document the top 5% conditional formatting rule:

1. In cell **M23**, enter **Top 5% in Sales** as the label, and then select cell **M23** again.
2. On the Home tab, in the Alignment group, click the **Align Right** button to right-align the contents of the selected cell. The cell entry now overlaps the blank cell L23.
3. In cell **N23**, type **green** to identify the conditional formatting color you used to highlight the values in the top 5%, and then select cell **N23** again.
4. In the Alignment group, click the **Center** button to center the contents of the cell.

   You will use a highlighting rule to format cell N23 using black text on a green fill.
5. On the Home tab, in the Styles group, click the **Conditional Formatting** button, point to **Highlight Cells Rules**, and then click **Text that Contains**. The Text That Contains dialog box opens. The text string "green" from the selected cell is already entered into the left input box.

6. In the right box, click the **arrow** button, and then click **Custom Format** to open the Format Cells dialog box.
7. Click the **Fill** tab, and then change the background fill color to the **Light Green** standard color.
8. Click the **Font** tab, and then change the font color to the **Black, Text 1** theme color to match the formatting used for sales in the top 5%.
9. Click **OK** in each dialog box to apply the conditional formatting to cell N23. See Figure 2–40.

Figure 2–40 Conditional formatting documented in worksheet

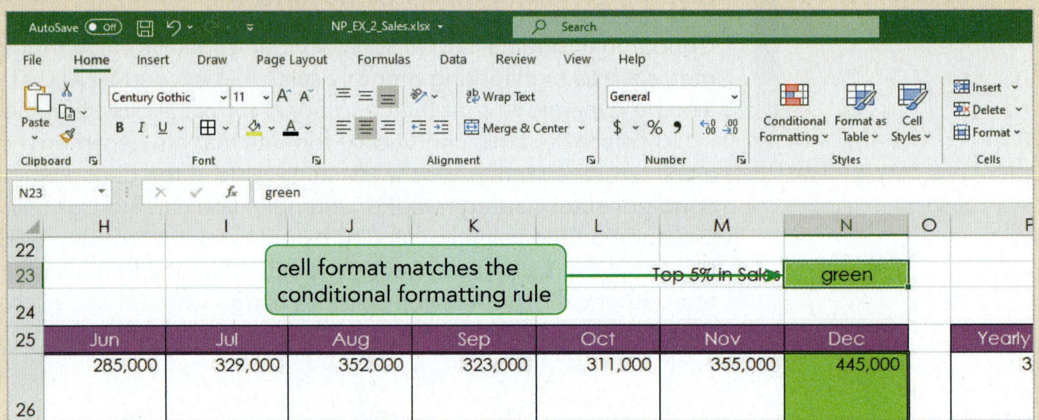

You've completed formatting the appearance of the workbook for the computer screen. Next, you will explore how to format the workbook for the printer.

Proskills

Written Communication: Using Conditional Formatting Effectively

Conditional formatting is an excellent way to highlight important trends and data values to clients and colleagues. However, be sure to use it judiciously. Overusing conditional formatting might obscure the very data you want to emphasize. Keep in mind the following tips as you make decisions about what to highlight and how it should be highlighted:

- **Document the conditional formats you use.** If a bold, green font means that a sales number is in the top 10% of all sales, document that information in the worksheet.
- **Don't clutter data with too much highlighting.** Limit highlighting rules to one or two per data set. Highlights are designed to draw attention to points of interest. If you use too many, you will end up highlighting everything—and, therefore, nothing.
- **Consider alternatives to conditional formats.** If you want to highlight the top 10 sales regions, it might be more effective to simply sort the data with the best-selling regions at the top of the list.

Remember that the goal of highlighting is to provide a strong visual clue to important data or results. Careful use of conditional formatting helps readers to focus on the important points you want to make rather than distracting them with secondary issues and facts.

Formatting a Worksheet for Printing

You should format any worksheets you plan to print so that they are easy to read and understand. You can do this using the print settings, which enable you to set the page orientation, the print area, page breaks, print titles, and headers and footers. Print settings can be applied to an entire workbook or to individual sheets. Because other people will likely see your printed worksheets, you should format the printed output as carefully as you format the electronic version.

Stefan wants you to format the printed version of the Sales Report worksheet to be distributed to the sales team at Bristol Bay.

Using Page Break Preview

Page Break Preview shows only those parts of the active sheet that will print and how the content will be split across pages. A dotted blue border indicates a page break, which separates one page from another. As you format the worksheet for printing, you can use this view to control what content appears on each page.

Stefan wants to know how the Sales Report worksheet would print in portrait orientation and how many pages would be required. You will look at the worksheet in Page Break Preview to find these answers.

To view the Sales Report worksheet in Page Break Preview:

1. Scroll up the worksheet and click cell **A1**.
2. Click the **Page Break Preview** button on the status bar. The worksheet switches to Page Break Preview.
3. Change the zoom level of the worksheet to **25%** so you can view the entire contents of this large worksheet. See Figure 2–41.

Figure 2–41 Sales Report worksheet in Page Break Preview

Trouble? If you see a different page layout or the worksheet is split onto a different number of pages, don't worry. Each printer is different, so the layout and pages might differ from what is shown in Figure 2–41.

Page Break Preview shows that a printout of the Sales Report worksheet requires six pages in portrait orientation and that pages 3 and 5 would be mostly blank. Note that each printer is different, so your Page Break Preview might show a different number of pages. With this layout, each page would be difficult to interpret because the data is separated from the descriptive labels. Stefan wants you to fix the layout so that the contents are easier to read and understand.

Defining the Print Area

By default, all cells in a worksheet containing text, formulas, or values are printed. If you want to print only part of a worksheet, you can set a print area, which is the region of the worksheet that is sent to the printer. Each worksheet has its own print area. Although you can set the print area in any view, Page Break Preview shades the areas of the worksheet that are not included in the print area, making it simple to confirm what will print.

Stefan doesn't want the blank cells in the range G1:R22 to be included in the printout, so you will set the print area to exclude those cells.

To set the print area of the Sales Report worksheet:

1. Change the zoom level of the worksheet to **80%** to make it easier to select cells and ranges.
2. Select the range **A1:F22**, hold down **CTRL**, select the range **A23:R46**, and then release **CTRL**. The nonadjacent range is selected.
3. On the ribbon, click the **Page Layout** tab.
4. In the Page Setup group, click the **Print Area** button, and then click **Set Print Area**. The print area changes to cover only the nonadjacent range A1:F22,A23:R46. The rest of the worksheet content is shaded to indicate that it will not be part of the printout.
5. Click cell **A1** to deselect the range.
6. Change the zoom level to **50%** so you can view more of the worksheet. See Figure 2–42.

Figure 2–42 Print area set for the Sales Report worksheet

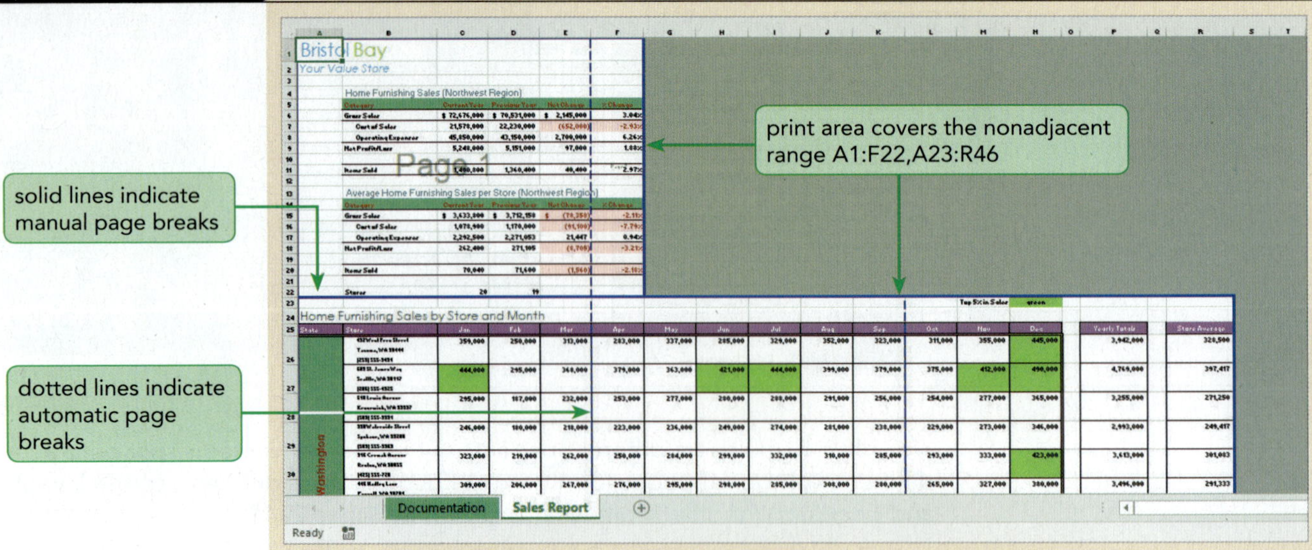

Inserting Page Breaks

Often, the contents of a worksheet will not fit onto a single printed page. When this happens, Excel prints as much of the content that fits on a single page without resizing, and then inserts automatic page breaks to continue printing the remaining worksheet content on successive pages. The resulting printouts might split worksheet content in awkward places, such as in the middle of a table of data.

Tip

When you remove a page break, Excel rescales the printout to fit into the allotted pages.

To split the printout into logical segments, you can insert manual page breaks. Page Break Preview identifies manual page breaks with a solid blue line and automatic page breaks with a dotted blue line. When you specify a print area for a nonadjacent range, as you did for the Sales Report worksheet, manual page breaks are inserted around the adjacent ranges and appear in the print area you defined (refer again to Figure 2–42). You can remove a page break in Page Break Preview by dragging it out of the print area.

Reference

Inserting and Removing Page Breaks

To insert a page break:
- Click the first cell below the row where you want to insert a page break, click a column heading, or click a row heading.
- On the Page Layout tab, in the Page Setup group, click the Breaks button, and then click Insert Page Break.

To remove a page break:
- Select any cell below or to the right of the page break you want to remove.
- On the Page Layout tab, in the Page Setup group, click the Breaks button, and then click Remove Page Break.

or

- In Page Break Preview, drag the page break line out of the print area.

The Sales Report worksheet has automatic page breaks along columns F and L. Stefan wants you to remove these automatic page breaks from the Sales Report worksheet.

To remove the automatic page breaks and insert manual page breaks:

1. Point to the **dotted blue page break** directly to the left of column L in Home Furnishing Sales by Store and Month table until the pointer changes to the double-headed horizontal pointer ↔.

   Trouble? If the dotted blue page break appears to the left of a different column, don't worry. Depending on your printer, the page breaks might be in a different column of the worksheet. Just point to the dotted blue page break that is closest to column L.

2. Drag the page break to the right and out of the print area. The page break is removed from the worksheet.

3. Point to the page break located in column F so that the pointer changes to the double-headed horizontal pointer ↔, and then drag the page break between column H and column I so that the first 6 months of sales are on one page and the last 6 months of sales data are on the next page.

   Trouble? If the dotted blue page break appears to the right of a different column, don't worry. Depending on your printer, the page breaks might be in a different column of the worksheet. Just drag the dotted blue page break that is closest to column F.

You will add a manual page break between columns N and O to place the total annual sales and store averages on their own pages.

4. Click cell **O23**.

5. On the Page Layout tab, in the Page Setup group, click the **Breaks** button, and then click **Insert Page Break**. A manual page break is added between columns N and O, forcing the total annual sales and average sales onto a fourth page. See Figure 2–43.

Figure 2–43 Manual page breaks in the print area

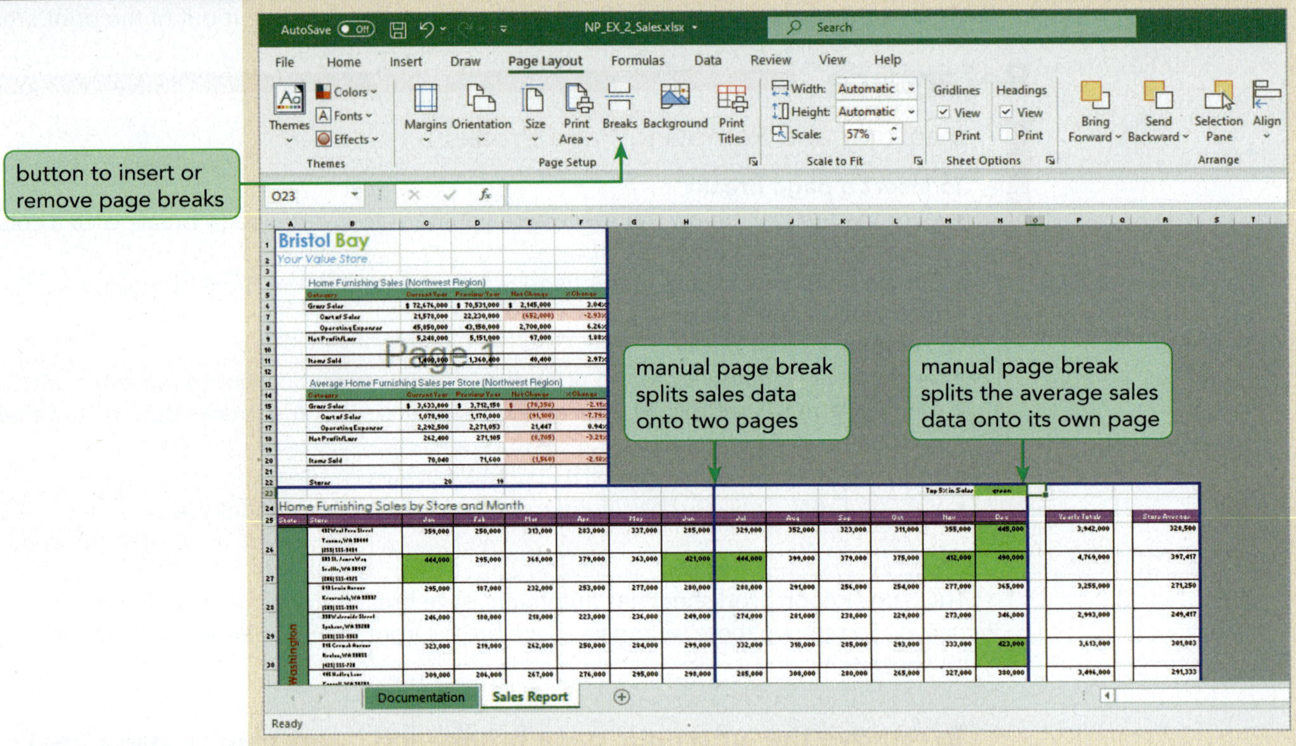

Adding Print Titles

It is a good practice to include descriptive information such as the company name, logo, and worksheet title on each page of a printout in case a page becomes separated from the other pages. You can repeat information, such as the company name, by specifying which rows or columns in the worksheet act as print titles. If a worksheet contains a large table, you can print the table's column headings and row headings on every page of the printout by designating those columns and rows as print titles.

In the Sales Report worksheet, the company name appears on the first page of the printout but does not appear on subsequent pages. Also, the descriptive row titles for the monthly sales table in column A do not appear on the third page of the printout. You will add print titles to fix these issues.

Tip

You can also open the Page Setup dialog box by clicking the Dialog Box Launcher in the Page Setup group on the Page Layout tab.

To set the print titles:

1. On the Page Layout tab, in the Page Setup group, click the **Print Titles** button. The Page Setup dialog box opens with the Sheet tab displayed.
2. In the Print titles section, click the **Rows to repeat at top** box, move the pointer over the worksheet, and then select rows **1** and **2**. A flashing border appears around the first two rows of the worksheet to indicate that the contents of the first two rows will be repeated on each page of the printout. The row reference $1:$2 appears in the Rows to repeat at top box.
3. Click the **Columns to repeat at left** box, move the pointer over the worksheet, and then select columns **A** and **B**. The column reference $A:$B appears in the Columns to repeat at left box. See Figure 2–44.

Figure 2–44 Sheet tab in the Page Setup dialog box

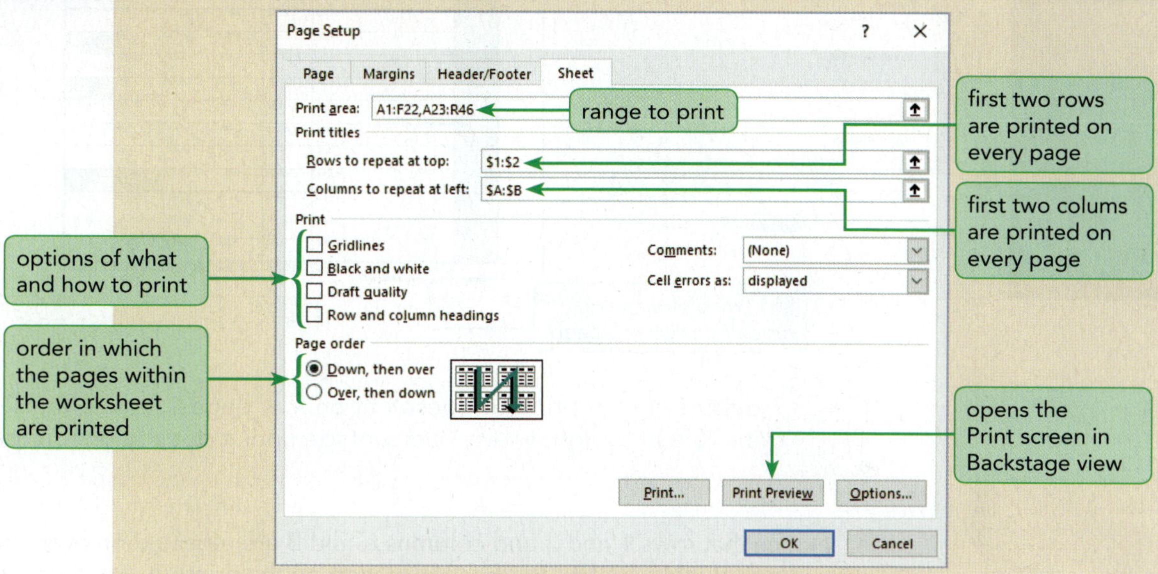

You will rescale the worksheet so that the cell values are easily readable in the printout.

To rescale the printout:

1. In the Page Setup dialog box, click the **Page** tab.
2. In the Scaling section, change the Adjust to amount to **70%** normal size.
3. Click the **Print Preview** button to preview the four pages of printed material on the Print screen in Backstage view.
4. Use the arrow buttons to scroll through the four pages of the report. Figure 2–45 shows a preview of the page three printout, containing the monthly sales from July to December of the current year.

Figure 2–45 **Print preview of page 3**

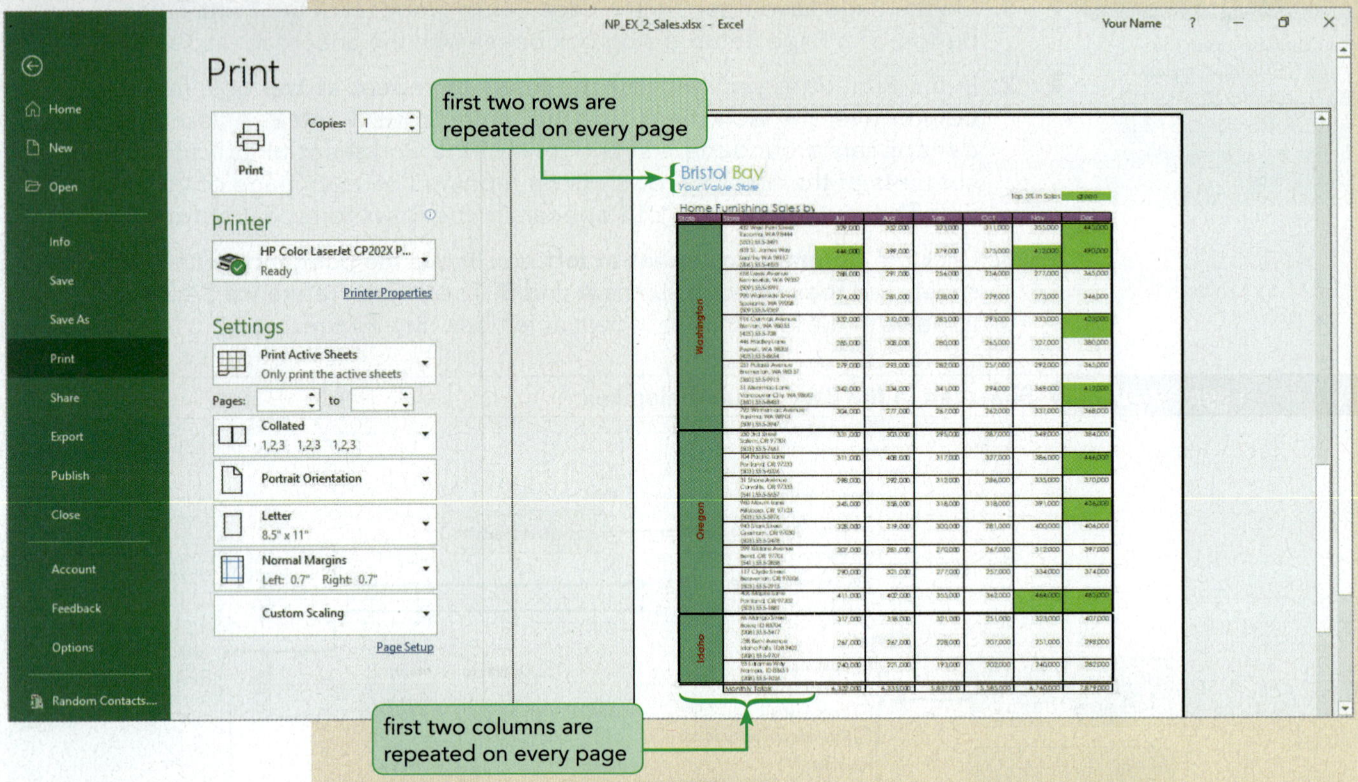

Trouble? If your printout doesn't fit on four pages, reduce the scaling factor from 70% to a slightly lower percentage until it does fit on four pages.

Notice that rows 1 and 2 and columns A and B are repeated on every page, providing valuable context for the information on the printout. Another way of repeating information on every page is with headers and footers.

Designing Headers and Footers

Headers and footers provide descriptive information on the printout. A **header** is information that appears at the top of each printed page, and a **footer** is the information that appears on the bottom of every page. Headers and footers are usually reserved for information that does not appear within the document. For example, the header might include the name of the document author and the date on which the document was printed. If the printout spans several pages, the page number and total number of pages might be displayed in the footer.

Headers and footers are divided into a left section, a center section, and a right section. In each section, you can insert elements with information about the workbook, worksheet, or general document properties, such as the worksheet name or the current date and time. These header and footer elements are dynamic; if you rename the worksheet, for example, the name is automatically updated in the header or footer. You can also type specific text that you want to appear in each section. The text you type doesn't change unless you edit the text in that section.

You can create multiple headers and/or footers in the printout. For example, you can create one header and footer for even pages and another for odd pages. You can also create one header and footer for the first page in the printout and a different header and footer for subsequent pages.

Stefan wants the printout to display the workbook's file name in the header's left section, and the current date in the header's right section. The center footer should display the page number and the total number of pages in the printout and the right footer should display your name as the workbook's author.

To set up the page header:

1. Near the bottom of the Print screen, click the **Page Setup** link. The Page Setup dialog box opens.
2. Click the **Header/Footer** tab to display the header and footer options.
3. Click the **Different first page** check box to select it. This creates one set of headers and footers for the first page, and one set for the rest of the pages.
4. Click the **Custom Header** button. The Header dialog box opens. Because you selected the Different first page option, the dialog box contains two tabs named Header and First Page Header.
5. Click the **First Page Header** tab.
6. On the Header tab, in the Left section box, type **File name:** and press **SPACEBAR**, and then click the **Insert File Name** button. The code `&[File]`, which displays the file name of the current workbook, is added to the left section of the header.
7. Press **TAB** twice to move to the right section of the header, and then click the **Insert Date** button. The code `&[Date]` is added to the right section of the header. See Figure 2–46.

Tip

You can create or edit headers and footers in Page Layout view by clicking in the Header & Footer section and using the tools on the Design tab.

Figure 2–46 Header dialog box

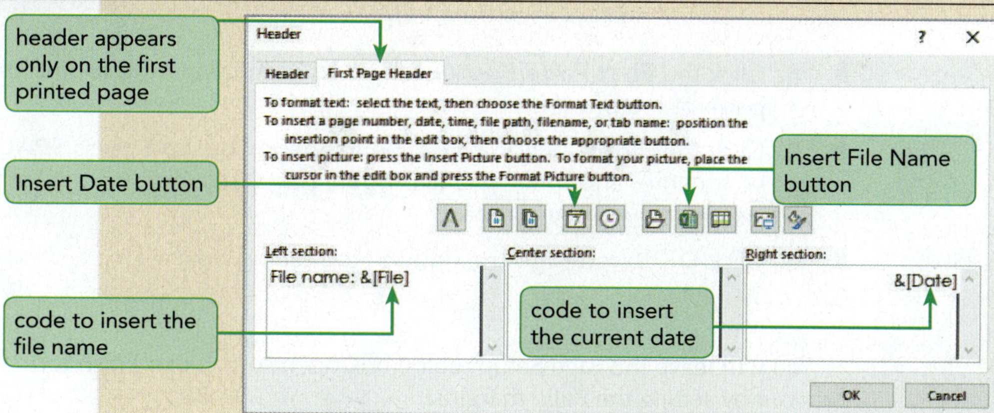

8. Click **OK** to return to the Header/Footer tab in the Page Setup dialog box.

The header text you just created will appear only on the first page of the printout; subsequent pages will not display that header information. Stefan wants a footer to appear on all pages of the printout. Because you selected different headers and footers for the first page, you will create one footer for the first page and another footer for subsequent pages.

To create the page footer:

1. On the Header/Footer tab of the Page Setup dialog box, click the **Custom Footer** button. The Footer dialog box opens.
2. On the Footer tab, click the **Center** section box, type **Page** and press **SPACEBAR**, and then click the **Insert Page Number** button. The code `&[Page]`, which inserts the current page number, appears after the label "Page."
3. Press **SPACEBAR**, type **of** and press **SPACEBAR**, and then click the **Insert Number of Pages** button. The code `&[Pages]`, which inserts the total number of pages in the printout, is added to the Center section box. See Figure 2–47.

Figure 2–47 Footer dialog box

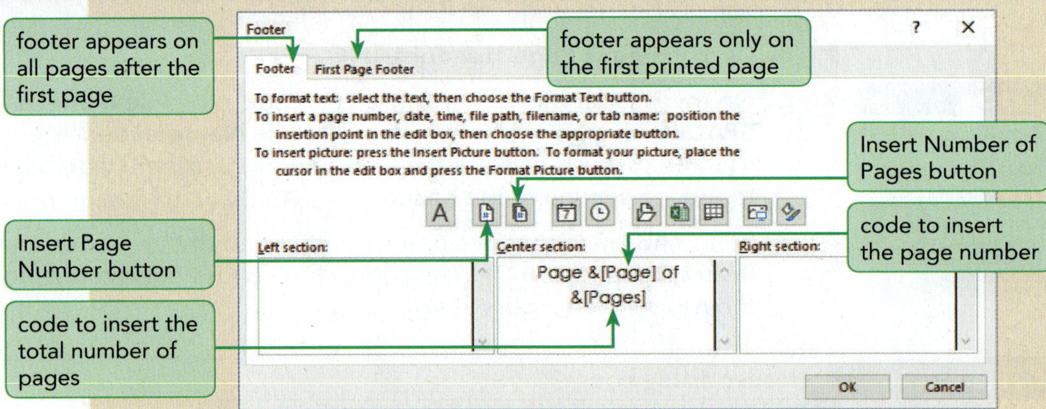

4. Click the **First Page Footer** tab so you can create the footer for the first page of the printout.
5. Click the **Right** section box, type **Prepared by:** and press **SPACEBAR**, type your name, and then type **(&[Pages] pages)** to indicate the total number of pages in the printed report.
6. Click **OK** to return to the Page Setup dialog box.

You will leave the Page Setup dialog box open so you can finish formatting the printout by setting the page margins.

Setting the Page Margins

A **margin** is the space between the page content and the edges of the page. By default, Excel sets the page margins to 0.7 inch on the left and right sides, and 0.75 inch on the top and bottom; and it allows for 0.3-inch margins around the header and footer. You can reduce or increase these margins as needed by selecting predefined margin sizes or setting your own.

Stefan's reports need a wider margin along the left side of the page to accommodate a binder, so you will increase the left margin for the printout from 0.7 inch to 1 inch.

Tip

To select preset margins, click the Margins button in the Page Setup group on the Page Layout tab.

To set the left margin:

1. Click the **Margins** tab in the Page Setup dialog box to display options for changing the page margins.
2. Double-click the **Left** box to select the setting, and then type **1** to increase the size of the left margin to 1 inch. See Figure 2–48.

Figure 2–48 Margins tab in the Page Setup dialog box

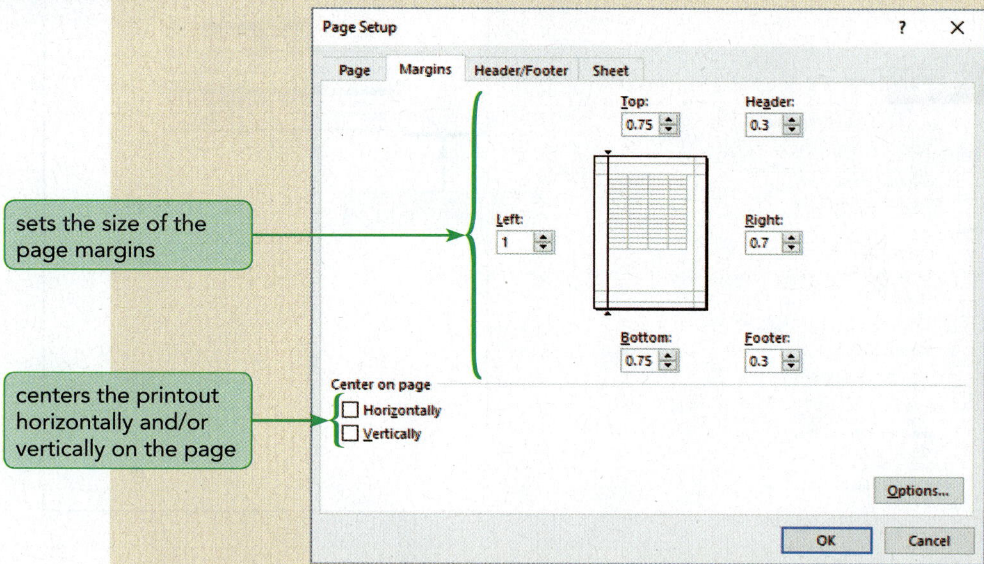

3. Click **OK** to close the Page Setup dialog box. In the preview, the left margin shifts to reflect the new margin setting.

You can also center the worksheet contents both horizontally and vertically within the margins by selecting the Horizontally and Vertically check boxes on the Margins tab in the Page Setup dialog box.

Now that you have formatted the printout, you can print the final version of the worksheet.

To preview, print, and save the workbook:

1. On the Print screen in Backstage view, preview the final version of the printed report. Figure 2–49 shows a preview of page 1 of the printout.

Figure 2–49 **Preview of the completed first page**

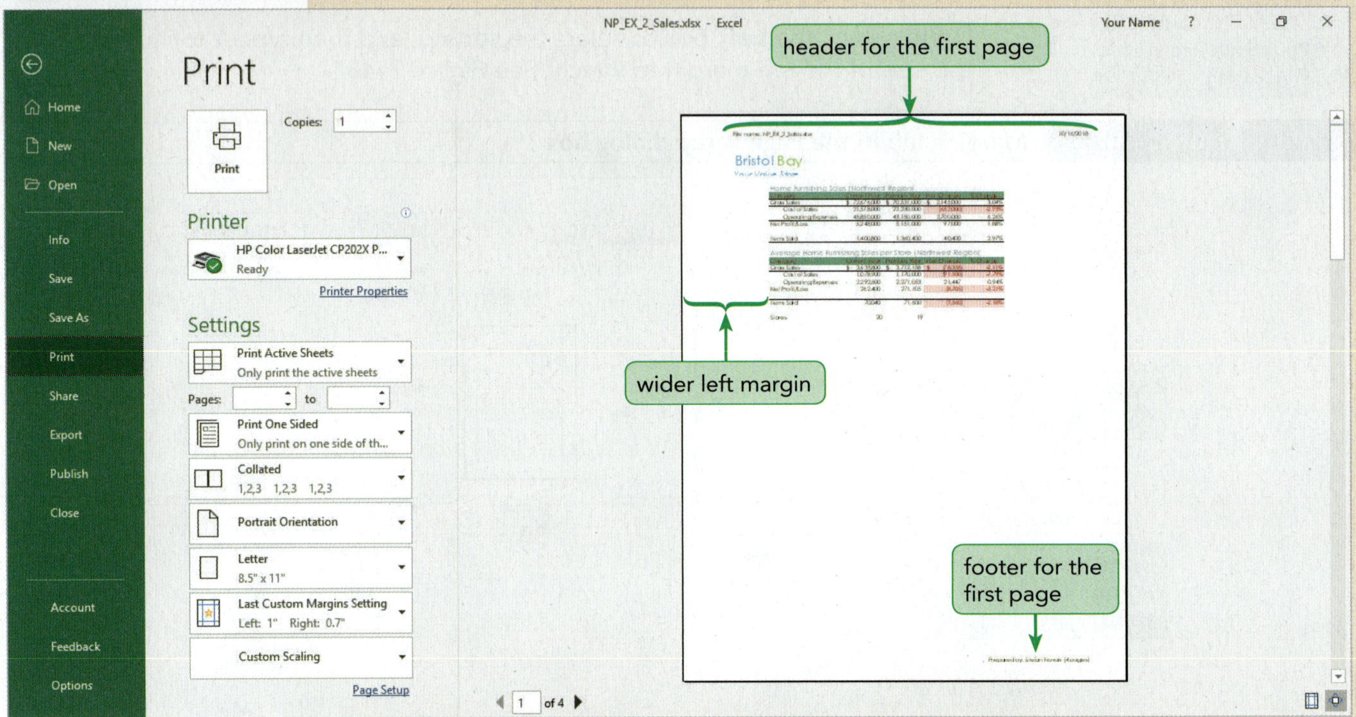

2. On the Print screen, in the Settings section, click the first box, and then click **Print Entire Workbook**. The printout will include five pages—one page for the Documentation sheet and four pages for the Sales Report sheet.
3. If you are instructed to print, click the **Print** button to print the entire workbook. If you are not instructed to print, click the **Back** button on the Backstage view navigation bar to return to the workbook window.
4. Click the **Normal** button on the status bar to return the view of the workbook to normal.
5. Increase the zoom level to **120%** (or whatever zoom level you have been using).
6. sam Save the workbook, and then close it.

Stefan is pleased that your work on formatting the workbook has made the sales report easier to read and interpret. Stefan will get have future projects for you to complete using what you've learned about formatting data in Excel.

Review

Session 2.2 Quick Check

1. Describe two methods of applying the same format to different ranges.
2. Red is a standard color. What happens to red text when you change the workbook's theme?
3. What is a conditional format?
4. How would you highlight the top 10% values in the range A1:C20?
5. How do you insert a manual page break in a worksheet?
6. What is a print area?
7. What are print titles?
8. Describe how to add the workbook file name to the center section of the footer on every page of the printout.

Practice

Review Assignments

Data Files needed for the Review Assignments: NP_EX_2-2.xlsx, Support_EX_2_Texture.jpg

Stefan has another workbook for you to work on. This report will also deal with home furnishing sales in the Northwest region; but rather than breaking down the sales figures by store, Stefan wants to analyze the data by product to determine whether specific product categories have seen an increase or decrease in sales from the previous year. Stefan already compiled the data in a workbook but needs you to develop a finished report that will be distributed among the sales team. Complete the following:

1. Open the **NP_EX_2-2.xlsx** workbook located in the Excel2 > Review folder included with your Data Files, and then save the workbook as **NP_EX_2_Products** in the location specified by your instructor.
2. In the Documentation sheet, enter your name in cell B4 and the date in cell B5. Format the date in cell B5 with the Long Date cell format and left-align the date in the cell.
3. Set the background of the Documentation sheet to the **Support_EX_2_Texture.jpg** image file located in the Excel2 > Review folder included with your Data Files, and then change the fill color of the range B4:B6 to white.
4. In the Product Sales worksheet, enter formulas to make the following calculations:
   a. In cell B6, use the SUM function to calculate the total of the Decorative sales for the current year using the values in the range C31:N35.
   b. In cell B7, use the SUM function to calculate the sum of the Living sales using the values in the range C36:N40.
   c. In cell B8, calculate the sum of the Utility sales using the values in the range C41:N44.
   d. In cell B9, calculate the total sales from all three categories in the current year by adding the values in the range B6:B8.
   e. In cell C9, add the total sales from all three categories in the previous year.
   f. In the range D6:D9, calculate the net change in sales by subtracting the previous year values in column C from the current year values in column B for all three product categories and overall.
   g. In the range E6:E9, calculate the percent change in sales for the three categories and total sales by dividing the net change values in column D by the previous year's sales values in column C.
5. Apply the following formats to the data:
   a. Format the range B6:D9 with Accounting style and no decimal places.
   b. Format the range E6:E9 in Percent style showing two decimal places.
   c. Format cell A4 with the Title cell style.
   d. Format the range A5:E5 with the Heading 3 cell style.
   e. Format the range A9:E9 with the Total cell style.
6. Complete the following calculations for the Sales by Product Type data using the monthly sales data for each product:
   a. In cell B13, use the SUM function to calculate the total sales for Home Decorations from the range C31:N31, and then copy that formula into the range B14:B26.
   b. In cell B27, use the SUM function to calculate the sum of the values in the range B13:B26. Copy your formula and paste it into cell C27. Verify that the values in the range B27:C27 equal the values in the range B9:C9.
   c. In cell D13, calculate the difference between the value in cell B13 and cell C13. Copy the formula to the range D14:D27.
   d. In cell E13, divide the value in cell D13 by the value in cell C13. Copy the formula to the range E14:E27.
7. Use Format Painter to do the following:
   a. Copy the formatting from cell A4 to cell A11.
   b. Copy the formatting from the range A5:E5 to the range A12:E12.
   c. Copy the formatting from the range A6:E6 to the range A13:E26.
   d. Copy the formatting from the range A9:E9 to the range A27:E27.

8. Add conditional formatting that displays negative values in the nonadjacent range D6:E9,D13:E27 in a dark red font on a light red background to highlight sales categories and product types that show a decrease in sales from the previous year.
9. In the range C45:N45, use the SUM function to calculate the sum of monthly sales across all product types.
10. In the range O31:O45, use the SUM function to calculate the sum of sales for each product category and across all product types. Verify that the value in cell O45 equals the value in cells B9 and B27.
11. Format the monthly sales data as follows:
    a. In the range C31:N44, format the sales data in Comma style with no decimal places.
    b. In the nonadjacent range C45:N45,O31:O45, format the calculated values in Accounting format with no decimal places.
    c. Format cell A29 with the Title cell style.
    d. Format the range A30:O30 with the 60% - Accent6 cell style.
    e. Format the range A31:A45 with the 60% - Accent3 cell style.
    f. Format the range B31:B45 with the 40% - Accent3 cell style.
    g. Format B45:O45 using the Total cell style.
12. Add a left border to the monthly totals in the range O31:O45.
13. Merge and center the cells in the range A31:A35. In the merged cell, rotate the text up, and then middle-align the text in the cell. Bold the text within the merged cell. Repeat for the ranges A36:A40 and A41:A44. Reduce the width of column A to 16 characters.
14. Add thick outside borders around the ranges A31:O35, A36:O40, and A41:O44.
15. Do the following to highlight the top-selling product types in the report:
    a. In the range O31:O44, use conditional formatting to highlight the top three selling product types in dark green text on a green fill.
    b. In cell O29, enter the text **Top 3 Sellers** and use the Text That Contains conditional format to change the format of this cell to a dark green text on a green fill to match the conditional formatting you added to the top three product types.
16. Change the theme of the workbook to Wisp.
17. Change the tab color of the Documentation sheet tab to the Brown, Accent 3 theme color. Change the tab color of the Product Sales sheet tab to the Olive Green, Accent 5 theme color.
18. Make the following format changes to the printed version of the Product Sales worksheet:
    a. Set the print area to the nonadjacent range A1:E28,A29:O45.
    b. Insert page breaks below rows 9 and 28 and to the right of columns H and N. Remove any automatic page breaks that were added to the sheet.
    c. Set the print titles to repeat rows 1 and 2 and columns A and B on every page.
    d. Set the size of the left margin to 1 inch.
    e. Scale the printout to 60% of its normal size.
    f. Add a different first page for headers and footers. On the first page header, display your name in the left section, display the file name in center, and display the date in the right section.
    g. For the first page footer and subsequent page footers, enter the code **Page &[Page] of &[Pages]** in the center section.
19. Preview the workbook. The printout should have only five pages. If you are instructed to print, print the entire workbook.
20. Save the workbook, and then close it.

Apply

Case Problem 1

Data File needed for this Case Problem: NP_EX_2-3.xlsx

Vestis Wholesale Suppliers Jacinta Safar is an inventory manager at Vestis Wholesale Suppliers, a major clothing supplier for stores and vendors across the United States. Every week Jacinta compiles an inventory report for different warehouses, detailing the contents in the warehouse, the value of those contents, and the anticipated time until those contents need to be restocked. Jacinta wants you to make workbook containing the weekly report for the Akron, Ohio, warehouse easier to read and understand. Complete the following:

1. Open the **NP_EX_2-3.xlsx** workbook located in the Excel2 > Case1 folder included with your Data Files, and then save the workbook as **NP_EX_2_Inventory** in the location specified by your instructor.
2. In the Documentation sheet, enter your name in cell B4 and the date in cell B5.
3. Change the theme of the workbook to View.
4. In the Documentation sheet, make the following formatting changes:
   a. In cell A1, change the font to Impact, increase the font size to 20 points, and change the font color to Brown, Accent 6.
   b. Change cell A2 to a 14-point bold font.
   c. Add borders around the cells in the range A4:B6.
   d. In the range A4:A6, change the fill color to Brown, Accent 6, Lighter 60% and top-align the cell contents.
5. Use the Format Painter to copy the formatting from the range A1:A2 in the Documentation sheet to the range A1:A2 in the Inventory worksheet.
6. In the Inventory worksheet, add borders around the cells in the range A4:B7 and change the fill color of the range A4:A7 to Brown, Accent 6, Lighter 60%.
7. Enter formulas to add the following calculations to the Inventory worksheet:
   a. In the range G10:G391, calculate the value of each item in the warehouse inventory by multiplying the item's unit price by the quantity in stock.
   b. In the range I10:I391, calculate the difference between the Quantity in Stock values in column F and the Reorder at Quantity values in column H to determine whether items have dropped below the automatic reorder level.
   c. In cell B5, use the COUNT function to count the values in column F to calculate the total number of items in the warehouse. Use the range reference F:F to reference the entire column.
   d. In cell B6, use the SUM function to sum the values in column G to calculate the total inventory value.
   e. In cell B7, use the AVERAGE function to average the values in column J to determine the average days to reorder new items.
8. Add the following formats to the worksheet:
   a. Format cell B6 with the Currency style.
   b. Format cell B7 to show one decimal place.
   c. Format the nonadjacent range E10:E391,G10:G391 in Currency style.
   d. Format the range A9:J9 with the Accent3 cell style.
9. Display the inventory table with banded rows of alternating colors by setting the fill color of the range A10:J10 to Olive Green, Accent 3 - Lighter 80%, and then using the Format Painter to copy the formatting in the range A10:J11 to the range A12:J391.
10. Use conditional formatting to highlight all of the values in the range I10:I391 that are less than 0 in a light red fill and dark red text to make inventory items that must be immediately reordered stand out.
11. Format the Inventory worksheet for printing as follows:
    a. Set the print area to the range A9:J391 so only the inventory table will print.
    b. Remove the column page breaks that would divide the inventory table into separate pages.

c. Set the print titles so that rows 1 through 9 of the worksheet print on every page.
d. Set the header of the first page to display the file name in the left section and your name and the date on separate lines in the right section.
e. For the first page and all subsequent pages, display a center footer that shows **Page** followed the page number followed by **of** followed by the number of pages in the printout.

12. Preview the workbook. If you are instructed to print, print the entire workbook.
13. Save the workbook, and then close it.

Create

Case Problem 2

Data File needed for this Case Problem: NP_EX_2-4.xlsx

TechMasters Javon Lee is the customer service manager at TechMasters, an electronics and computer firm located in Scottsdale, Arizona. Javon is analyzing the records for technical support calls to TechMasters to determine which times are understaffed, resulting in unacceptable wait times. Javon has compiled several months of data and calculated the average wait times in one-hour intervals for each day of the week. You will format Javon's workbook to make it easier to determine when TechMasters should hire more staff to assist with customer support requests. Complete the following:

1. Open the **NP_EX_2-4.xlsx** workbook located in the Excel2 > Case2 folder included with your Data Files, and then save the workbook as **NP_EX_2_Support** in the location specified by your instructor.
2. In the Documentation sheet, enter your name in cell B3 and the current date in cell B4.
3. Apply the Vapor Trail theme to the workbook.
4. Apply the following formats to the Documentation sheet:
   a. Format the title in cell A1 using a 36-point Impact font with the Bright Green, Accent 5 font color.
   b. Format the range A3:A5 with the Accent5 cell style.
   c. Add a border around the cells in the range A3:B5. Wrap the text within each cell, and top-align the cell text.

Explore 5. Click cell A1, and then save the format you applied to that cell as a new cell style using **TechMasters Title** as the cell style name.

6. Go to the Wait Times worksheet and apply the TechMasters Title cell style to cell A1.

Explore 7. Change the font color in cell A2 to Bright Green, Accent 5 and increase the font size to 12 points. Save the format used in this cell as a new cell style using **TechMasters Subtitle** as the cell style name.

8. Format the average customer wait time values in the range A14:H39 as follows:
   a. Merge and center the range A14:H14, and then apply the Heading 2 cell style to the merged contents.
   b. Format the data in the range B16:H39 to show one decimal place.
   c. Format the column and row labels in the nonadjacent range A15:H15,A16:A39 with the Light Yellow, 60% - Accent3 cell style.
   d. Center the column headings in the range B15:H15.
9. In cell B5, enter **22** as an excellent wait time. In cell B6, enter **28** as a good wait time. In cell B7, enter **47** as an acceptable wait time. In cell B8, enter **69** as a poor wait time. In cell B9, enter **84** as a very poor wait time. In cell B10, enter **90** as an unacceptable wait time.
10. Merge and center the range A4:C4 and apply the Heading 2 cell style to the merged cell. Add borders around all of the cells in the range A5:C10.
11. Do the following to create a table summarizing the wait time data that has been collected:
    a. In cell E4, enter **Average Wait Time (All Days)** as the label. In cell E7, enter **Average Wait Time (Weekdays)** as the label. In cell E10, enter **Average Wait Time (Weekends)** as the label.
    b. In cell H4, enter a formula to calculate the average of the wait times in the range B16:H39. In cell H7, calculate the average weekday wait times in the range C16:G39. In cell H10, calculate the average weekend rate times in the nonadjacent range B16:B39,H16:H39.

12. Apply the following formats to the data in the range E4:H12:
    a. Merge and center the range E4:G6, wrap the text in the merged cell, center the cell content both horizontally and vertically, and then apply the Light Yellow, 60% - Accent3 cell style to the merged cell.
    b. Merge and center the range H4:H6, and then center the averaged value in the merged cell H4 both horizontally and vertically.
    c. Add borders around the cells in the range E4:H6.
    d. Copy the formatting in the range E4:H6 and apply them to the range E7:H12.
13. Apply the following formats to the wait time categories in the range A5:C10 to color code the different wait times:
    a. Change the fill color of the range A5:C5 to the standard green color and the font color to white.
    b. Change the fill color of the range A6:C6 to the standard light green color.
    c. Change the fill color of the range A7:C7 to the standard yellow color.
    d. Change the fill color of the range A8:C8 to the standard orange color.
    e. Change the fill color of the range A9:C9 to the standard red color and the font color to white.
    f. Change the fill color of the range A10:C10 to black and the font color to white.
14. Apply the following conditional formats in the specified order to the nonadjacent range H4:H12,B16:H39:
    a. Highlight values less than 22 with a standard green fill and white font. (*Hint:* When applying the conditional format, use the Custom Format option and choose the fill and font colors from the Format Cells dialog box.)
    b. Highlight values greater than 90 with black fill and white font.
    c. Highlight values between 22 and 34 with a standard light green fill.
    d. Highlight values between 34 and 60 with a standard yellow fill.
    e. Highlight values between 60 and 78 with a standard orange fill.
    f. Highlight values between 78 and 90 with a standard red fill and white font.
15. Create a cell to record wait time results as follows:
    a. In cell A41, enter **Notes** as the label, and then format it with the TechMasters Subtitle cell style.
    b. Merge the range A42:H50. Top- and left-align the contents of the merged cell, turn on text wrapping, and then add a thick outside border in the Blue, Accent 6 color to the merged cell.
16. In cell A42, summarize your conclusions about the wait times. Answer whether the wait times are within acceptable limits on average for the entire week, on weekdays, and on weekends. Also indicate whether there are times during the week that customers experience very poor to unacceptable delays.
17. Indent your comments in the merged cell to the right twice to provide additional space between your comment text and the border.
18. Change the tab color of the Documentation sheet tab to Bright Green, Accent 5. Change the tab color of the Wait Times sheet tab to Gold, Accent 3.
19. Format the printed version of the Wait Times worksheet as follows:
    a. Scale the sheet so that it fits on a single page in portrait orientation.
    b. Center the sheet on the page horizontally and vertically.
    c. In the right section of the header, type **Prepared by** followed by your name and the date on a separate line.
    d. In the left section of the footer, insert the file name. In the right section of the footer, insert the worksheet name.
20. Preview the workbook. If you are instructed to print, print the entire workbook.
21. Save the workbook, and then close it.

Module 3

Performing Calculations with Formulas and Functions

Staffing a Call Center

Objectives

Session 3.1
- Translate an equation into a function
- Do calculations with dates and times
- Extend data and formulas with AutoFill
- Use the Function Library
- Calculate statistics

Session 3.2
- Using the Quick Analysis tool
- Use absolute and relative cell references
- Use a logical function
- Retrieve data with lookup tables
- Do what-if analysis with Goal Seek

Case | **Evergreen Fidelity Insurance**

Kiara Patel is the manager of the call center for Evergreen Fidelity Insurance. The call center, which handles customer queries and new applications, is open Monday through Friday from 8 a.m. to 6 p.m., Central Time. Part of Kiara's responsibility is to hire operators to answer the calls that come into the center and maintain quality customer support. Good customer support includes handling calls promptly with a minimum of time spent on hold waiting for the next available operator. To do this, Kiara needs enough operators to handle the call volume. But with a fixed budget, the call center has a limited number of operators it can hire.

You will work with Kiara to develop an Excel worksheet that will analyze the call center's current response times and make recommendations on the correct number of operators for the company to hire to handle the work.

Starting Data Files

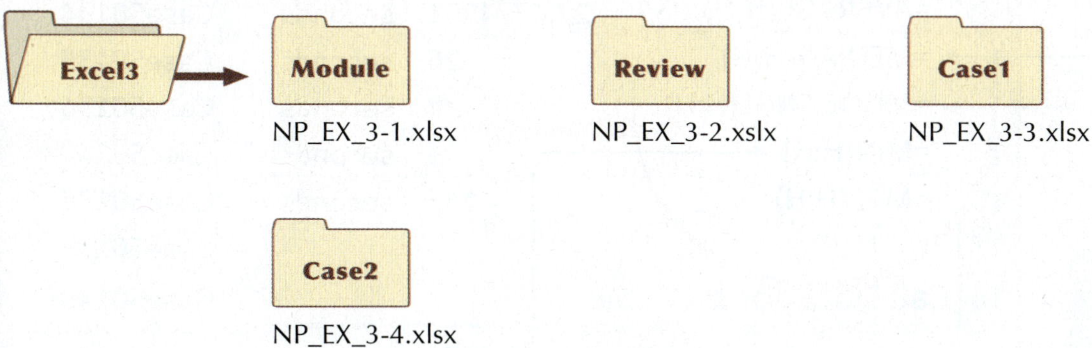

Session 3.1 Visual Overview:

Functions are organized by category in the Function Library group. When you select a function, the Function Arguments dialog box opens.

The Insert Function button opens the Insert Function dialog box from which you can select a function.

The **AVERAGE function** returns the average of values in the range.

The **MEDIAN function** returns the middle value in the range.

The **MODE.SNGL function** returns the single value that is repeated most often in the range.

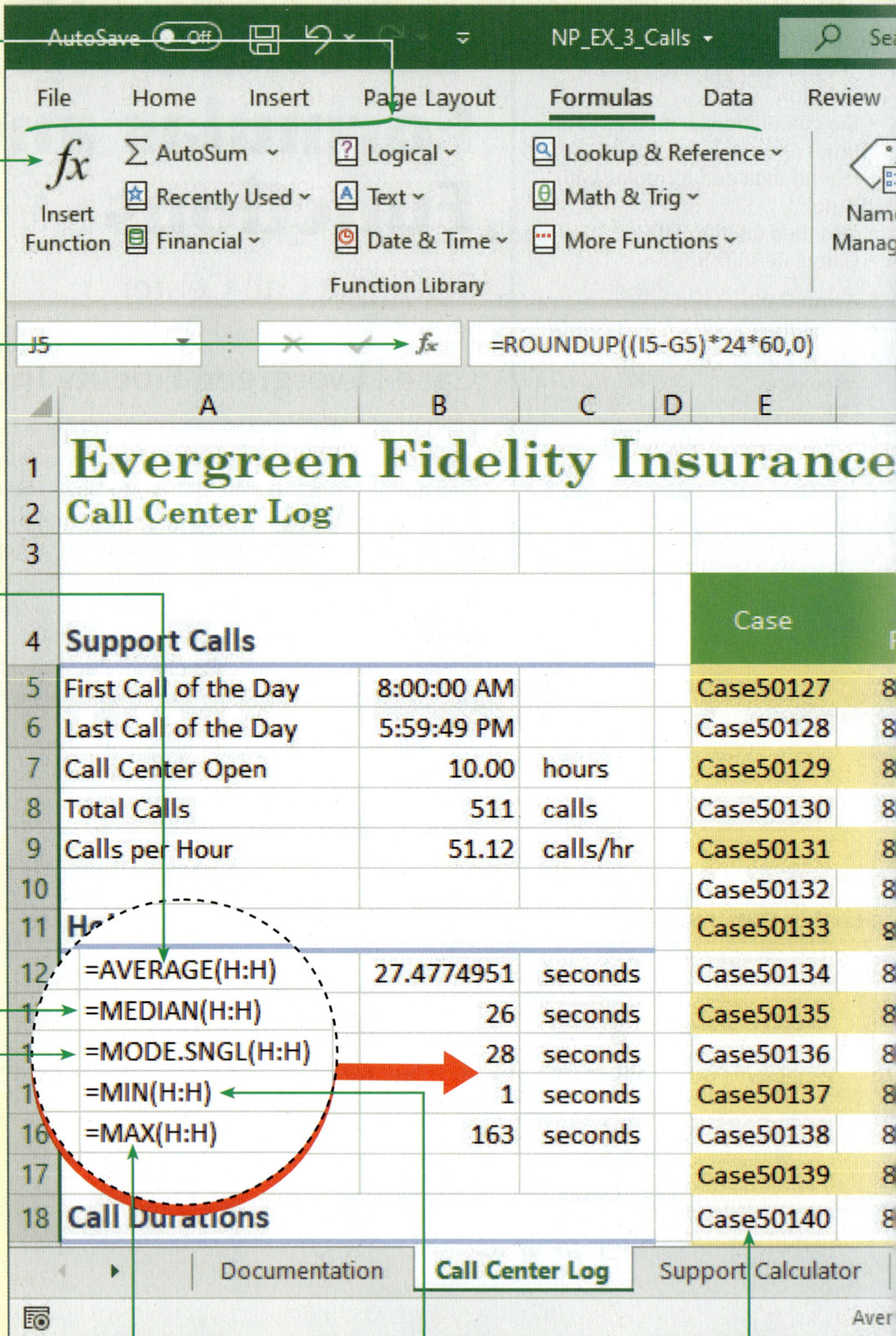

The **MAX function** returns the highest (maximum) value in the range.

The **MIN function** returns the lowest (minimum) value in the range.

AutoFill extends patterns of data.

Formulas and Functions

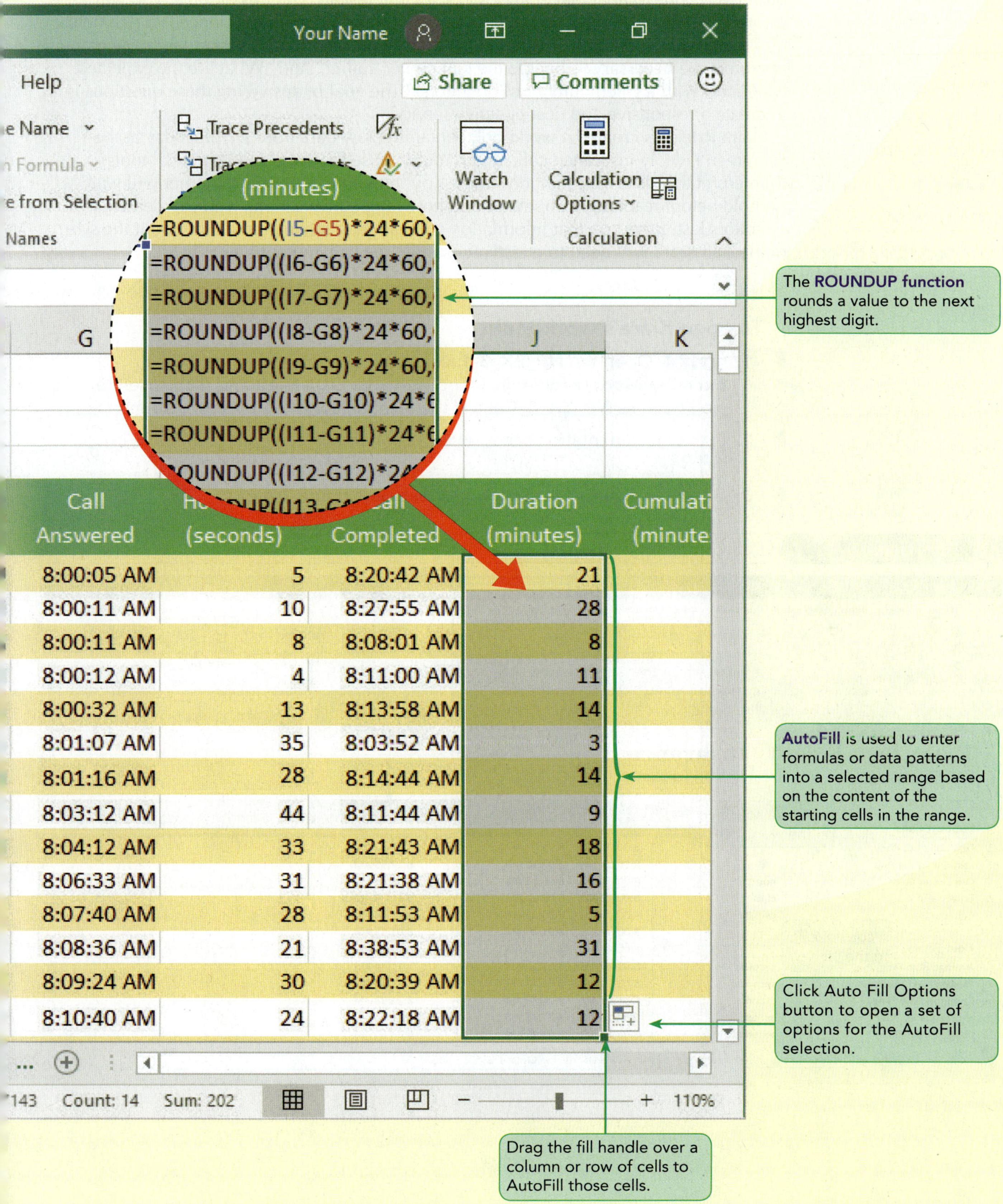

Designing a Workbook for Calculations

Excel is a powerful application for interpreting data with a wide variety of uses from business reports to financial analyses to scientific research. In this module, you will create a workbook to analyze data from a call center. Call center science is a rich field of research that uses many mathematical tools to answer questions such as "How many operators are necessary to handle the call center traffic?" and "What are the expected wait times with a given number of operators?" The goal of answering these questions is to create a responsive and cost-effective service.

Kiara Patel has created a workbook containing raw data from a typical day at the Evergreen Fidelity Insurance call center. You will use the Excel mathematical tools to interpret this data. This includes finding out how long a typical customer will wait on hold before reaching an operator and how long conversations with call center operators last. Based on that information you can then make predictions about the size of the staff Kiara will need to effectively handle the call center traffic.

To open Kiara's workbook:

1. sam Open the **NP_EX_3-1.xlsx** workbook located in the **Excel3 > Module** folder included with your Data Files, and then save the workbook as **NP_EX_3_Calls** in the location specified by your instructor.
2. In the Documentation sheet, enter your name in cell B3 and the date in cell B4.
3. Go to the **Call Center Log** worksheet. See Figure 3–1.

Figure 3–1 Call Center Log worksheet

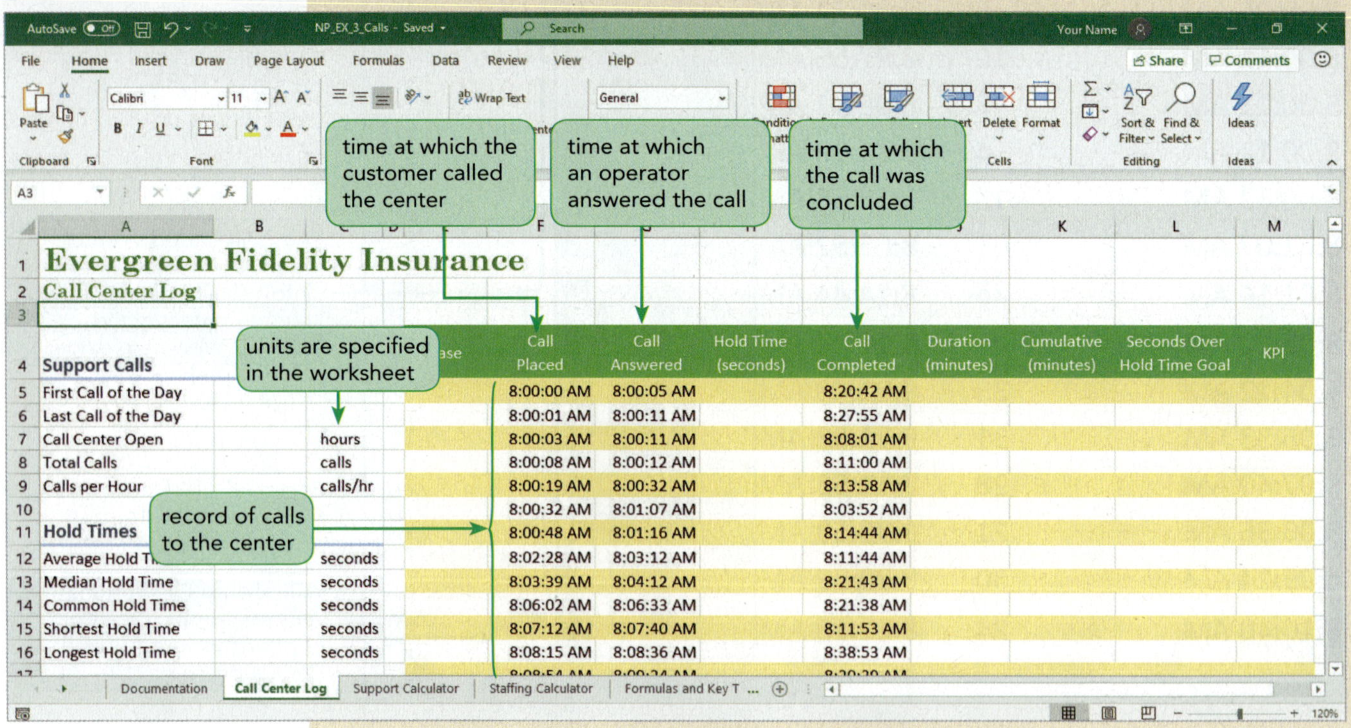

The Call Center Log worksheet contains the call records from a typical workday. Kiara has entered the time each call was received, the time an operator answered the call, and the time the call with the operator ended. Other information, such as how long the customer was on hold and the length of each conversation with the operator, are not included in the call log and need to be calculated.

Documenting Calculations

A workbook with many calculations can be challenging for the author to write and for others to use. To help everyone, it is important to list the formulas used in the workbook and to explain the assumptions behind those formulas. The workbook documentation should also include the definitions of key terms to make it clear what is being calculated and why.

Kiara included a worksheet containing explanations of the equations and key terms used in this workbook. Before you start creating the formulas, you will review this worksheet.

To review the workbook's formulas and key terms:

1. Go to the **Formulas and Key Terms** worksheet.
2. Review the worksheet contents, paying attention to the equations and key terms that you will be using in this workbook.
3. Go to the **Call Center Log** worksheet.

Constants and Units

One skill you need when working with Excel is the ability to translate an equation into an Excel formula. Some equations use **constants**, which are terms in an equation whose values don't change. For example, the following equation converts a duration value measured in days to a duration value measured in seconds by multiplying the *day* value by three constants—24, 60, and 60, because there are 24 hours in a day, 60 minutes in each hour, and 60 seconds in each minute:

$$seconds = day \times 24 \times 60 \times 60$$

It is good practice in worksheets to include the units in any calculation. In some situations, the unit is obvious, such as when a currency value is formatted with the appropriate currency symbol. In other situations, such as reporting time intervals, the unit is unknown unless you include it (hours, minutes, or seconds) as text in the worksheet.

Insight

Deciding Where to Place a Constant

Constants can be placed in an Excel formula or in a worksheet cell that is referenced by the formula. Which approach is better?

The answer depends on the constant being used, the purpose of the workbook, and the intended audience. Placing constants in separate cells that you reference in the formulas can help users better understand the worksheet because no values are hidden within the formulas. Also, when a constant is entered in a cell, you can add explanatory text next to each constant to document how it is being used in the formula. On the other hand, you don't want a user to inadvertently change the value of a constant and alter the formula result. You will need to evaluate how important it is for other people to immediately see the constant and whether the constant requires any explanation for other people to understand the formula.

In general, if the constant is a common one, such as the constant 60 used to multiply an hour value into a minute value, you can place the constant directly in a formula. However, if the constant is less well-known, it is better to place the constant in its own cell, making it more visible. If you decide to place a constant in a cell, you can lock that cell value, to prevent users from changing the constant without permission. This ensures that the constant value remains unchanged.

You will use constants to calculate each customer's hold time during their calls to center.

Calculating with Dates and Times

Excel stores dates and times as the number of days since January 0, 1900. Full days are a whole number and partial days are a fraction such as 0.5 for a half day or 12 hours. Storing dates and times as numbers makes it easier to calculate time and date intervals.

Kiara wants you to calculate the amount of time the first customer in the call log spent on hold and the length of the conversation with the Evergreen Fidelity Insurance operator.

To calculate the first customer's hold time and call duration:

1. In cell **H5**, enter the formula **=G5-F5** to calculate the hold time of the first call, which is equal to difference between the time when the call was placed and when the call was answered. The time value 12:00:05 AM appears in cell H5.
2. In cell **J5**, enter the formula **=I5-G5** to calculate the length of time of the first conversation, which is equal to the difference between the time the call was answered and the time the conversation was concluded. The time value 12:20:37 AM appears in cell J5.

The results of the two formulas are not what you might have expected. The issue is that the Excel applies the same number format to a formula result as was used in the cells referenced by the formula. In this case, cells H5 and J5 are formatted to appear as time values.

Kiara wants these time differences formatted as seconds and minutes. You'll remove the date/time format applied to cells H5 and J5 to view their underlying numeric values, and change the formulas to convert those time differences as seconds and minutes.

To convert the first customer's hold time and call duration to seconds and minutes:

1. Click cell **H5** containing the calculated hold time for the first customer.
2. Change the formula to **=(G5-F5)*24*60*60** to multiply the hold time by the number of seconds in one day and then press **ENTER**.
3. Click cell **J5** containing the call duration for the first customer.
4. Change the formula to **=(I5-G5)*24*60** to multiply the call duration by the number of minutes in one day and then press **ENTER**.
5. Select the nonadjacent range **H5,J5** and on the Home tab, in the Number group, click the **Number Format arrow**, and then click **General**.

   The values 5 and 20.6166667 appear in the cells, indicating that the first customer was on hold for 5 seconds with a call length of 20 minutes plus a fraction of a minute.

6. Click cell **K5**. See Figure 3-2.

Figure 3-2 First hold time and call length calculations

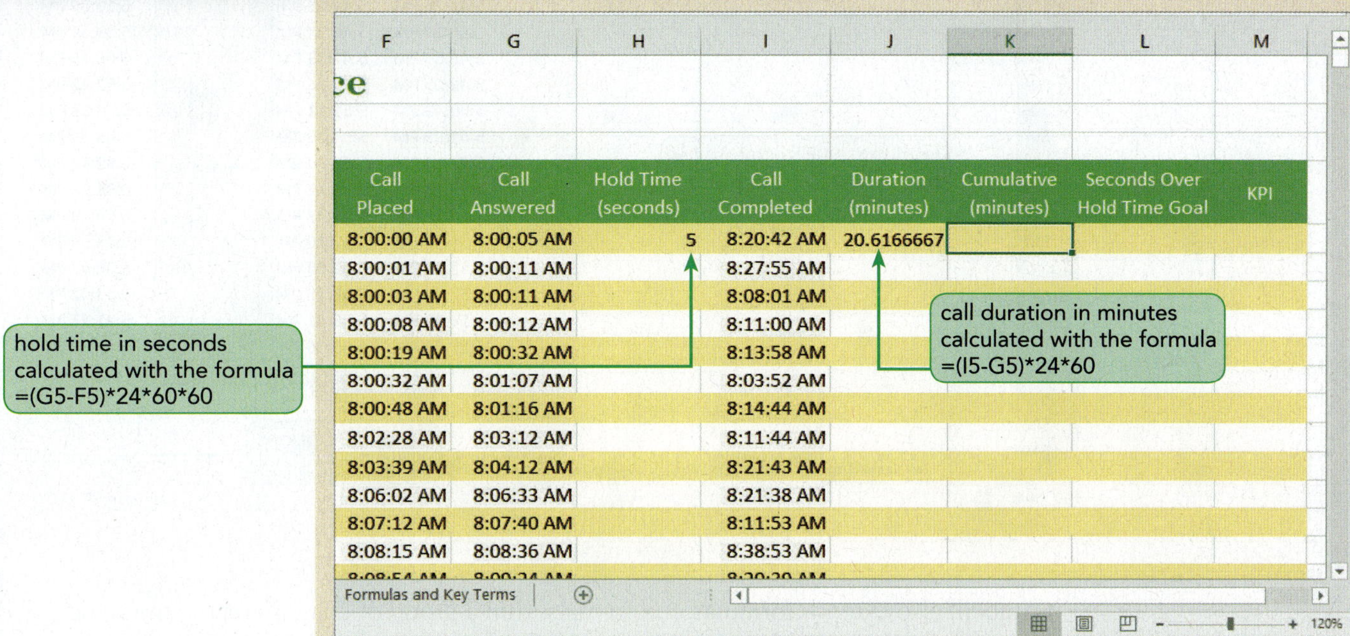

Now that you have calculated the hold time and call duration for the first customer, you will apply these formulas to the remaining entries in the call log.

AutoFilling Formulas and Data Patterns

One way to efficiently enter long columns or rows of formulas and data values is with AutoFill. AutoFill extends a formula or a pattern of data values into a selected range and is often faster than copying and pasting, which requires two distinct actions on the part of the user.

AutoFilling a Formula

Tip

You can also select a range, click the Fill button in the Editing group on the Home tab, and then select the direction to fill.

To extend a formula into range with AutoFill, you select the cell containing the formula to be extended. When the cell is selected, the **fill handle** appears as a green square in the lower-right corner of the cell. Dragging the fill handle down or across extends the formula and the cell formats into a new range.

You will use AutoFill to extend the formula in cell H5 over the entire call log in the range H5:H515.

To use AutoFill to extend the formula in cell H5:

1. Click cell **H5** to select it. The fill handle, the small green square, appears in the lower-right corner of the selected cell.
2. Drag the **fill handle** over the range **H5:H515**. The worksheet window will scroll as you drag the fill handle down to cell H515. See Figure 3–3.

Figure 3–3 Formula extended with AutoFill

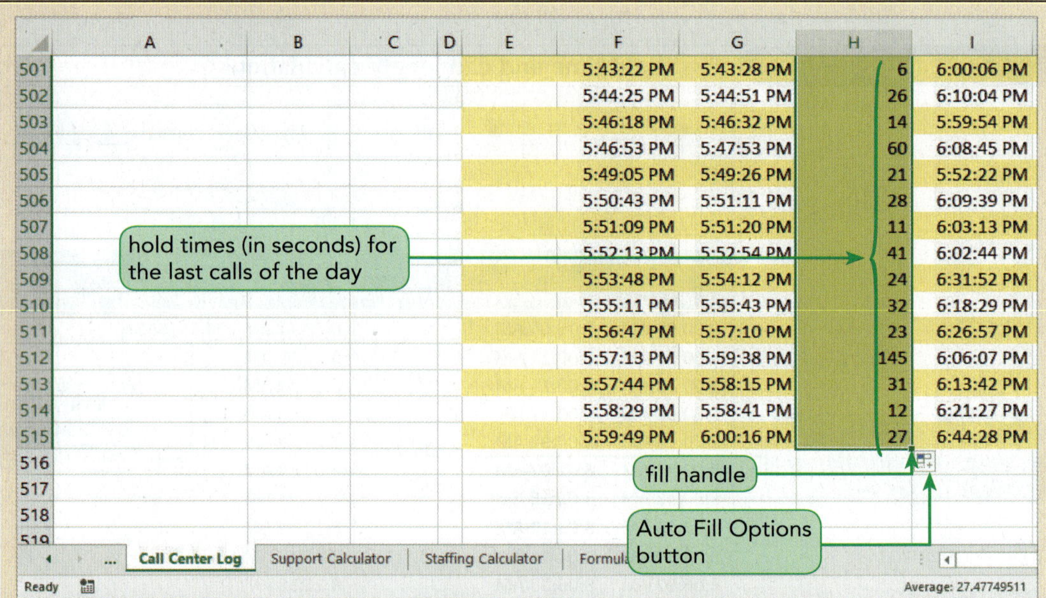

AutoFill also extends formulas and formats from a group of cells. To repeat the same group of formulas and formats, select the cell range with the formulas and formats you want to extend, and then drag the fill handle over the range that you want to fill.

Exploring Auto Fill Options

By default, AutoFill extends both the formulas and the formatting of the initial cell or cells. However, you might want to extend only the formulas or only the formatting. The Auto Fill Options button that appears after you release the mouse button lets you specify what part of the initial cells should be extended. Figure 3–4 shows the menu of AutoFill options.

Figure 3–4 **Auto Fill Options menu**

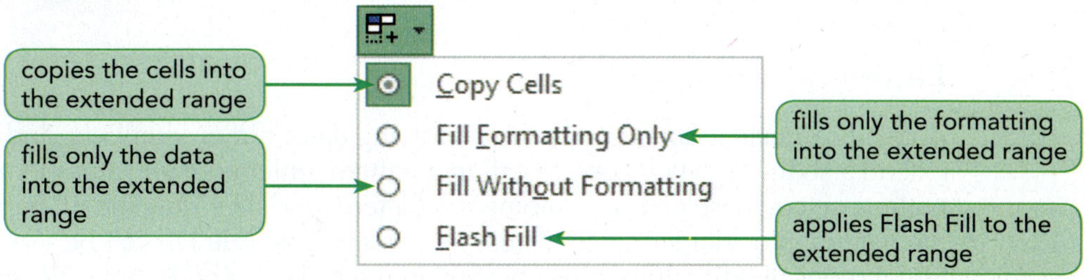

Kiara used banded rows to make the call log easier to read. By extending cell H5 into the range H5:H515, you copied cell H5's format as well as its formula, removing the banded row effect for the entries in column H. You'll use the Auto Fill Options button to restore the banded row effect to the table.

To use the Auto Fill Options button to copy only formulas:

1. Click the **Auto Fill Options** button. A menu of AutoFill options appears.
2. Click the **Fill Without Formatting** option button. The original formatting of the range is restored without affecting the copied formulas.
3. Click cell **J5** to select it.
4. Drag the **fill handle** down over the range **J5:J515**. Both the formulas and formatting are copied.
5. Click the **Auto Fill Options** button, and then click the **Fill Without Formatting** option button to restore the original formatting.
6. Scroll up the worksheet and click cell **D3** to deselect the range. Figure 3–5 shows the hold time and call duration for the first several customers in the call log.

Figure 3–5 **Hold time and call duration formulas extended**

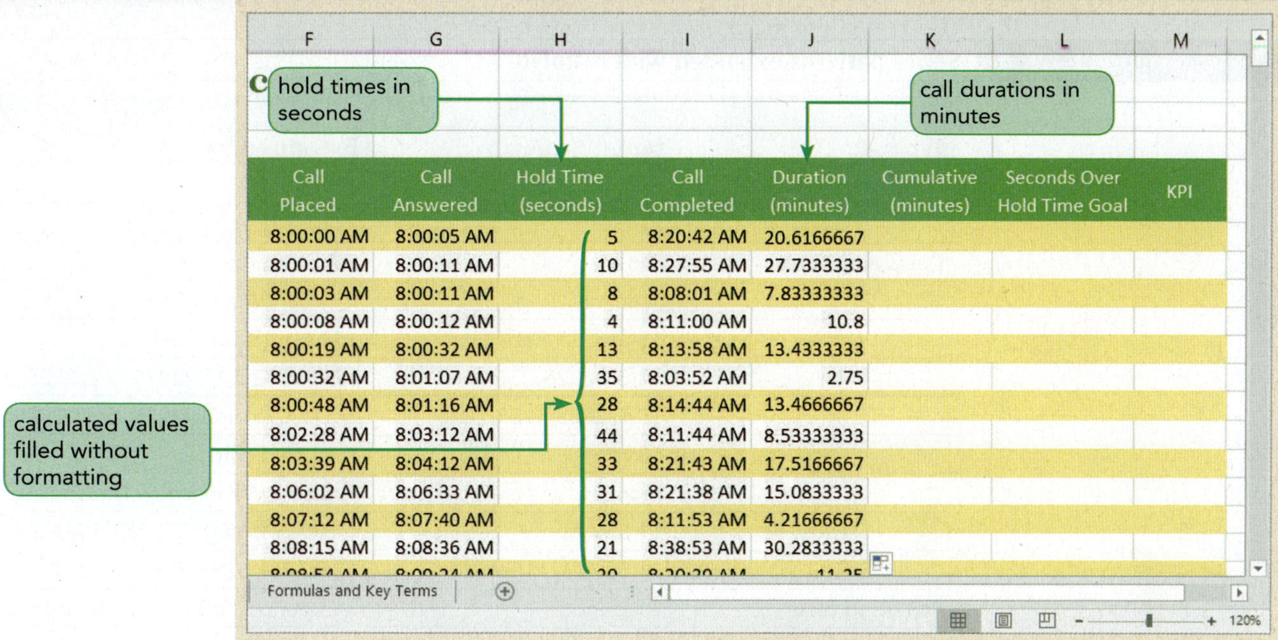

The call log should display the case number for each call. You can also enter this information with AutoFill.

Filling a Series

AutoFill can extend any data pattern involving dates, times, numbers, and text. To extend a series of data values based on a pattern, enter enough values to establish the pattern, select those cells containing the pattern, and then drag the fill handle extending the pattern into a larger range. Figure 3–6 shows how AutoFill can be used to extend an initial series of odd numbers established in the cells A2 and A3 into the range A2:A9.

Figure 3–6 AutoFill used to extend a series

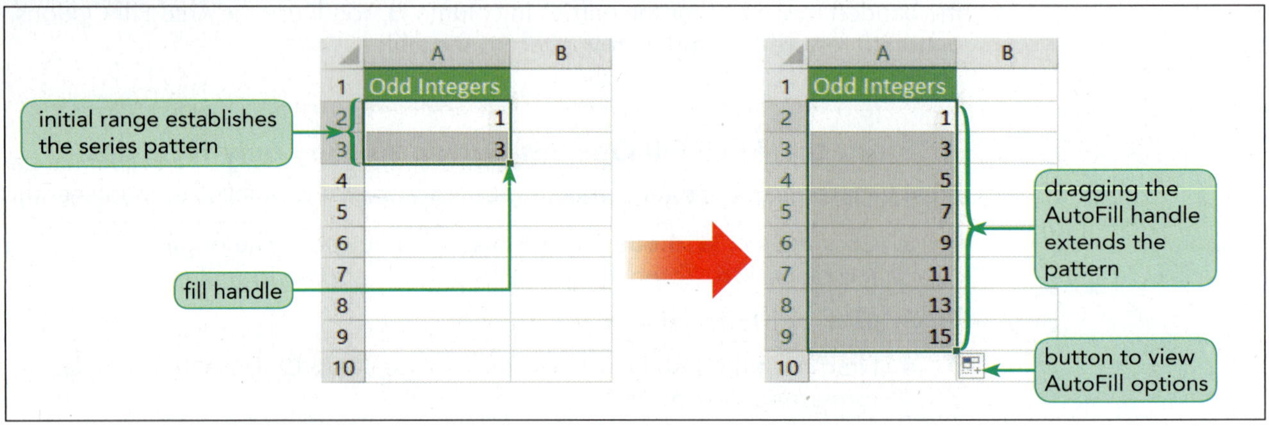

Figure 3–7 shows other extended patterns created with AutoFill. In each case, you must provide enough information for AutoFill to identify the pattern. AutoFill recognizes some patterns from only a single entry—such as Jan or January to create a series of month abbreviations or names, and Mon or Monday to create a series of the days of the week. A text pattern that includes text and a number such as Region 1, Region 2, and so on can also be automatically extended using AutoFill. You can start the series at any point, such as Weds, June, or Region 10, and AutoFill will continue with the next days, months, or text.

Figure 3–7 Series patterns extended with AutoFill

Type	Initial Value(s)	Extended Values
Numbers	1, 2, 3	4, 5, 6, ...
	2, 4, 6	8, 10, 12, ...
Dates and Times	Jan	Feb, Mar, Apr, ...
	January	February, March, April, ...
	15-Jan, 15-Feb	15-Mar, 15-Apr, 15-May, ...
	12/30/2025	12/31/2025, 1/1/2025, 1/2/2025, ...
	1/31/2025, 2/28/2025	3/31/2025, 4/30/2025, 5/31/2025, ...
	Mon	Tue, Wed, Thu, ...
	Monday	Tuesday, Wednesday, Thursday, ...
	11:00 AM	12:00 PM, 1:00 PM, 2:00 PM, ...
	11:58 AM, 11:59 AM	12:00 PM, 12:01 PM, 12:02 PM, ...
Patterned Text	1st period	2nd period, 3rd period, 4th period, ...
	Region 1	Region 2, Region 3, Region 4, ...
	Quarter 3	Quarter 4, Quarter 1, Quarter 2, ...
	Qtr3	Qtr4, Qtr1, Qtr2, ...

AutoFill can extend patterns either horizontally across columns within a single row or vertically across rows within a single column.

Reference

Extending a Series with AutoFill

- Enter the first few values of the series into a range.
- Select the range, and then drag the fill handle over the cells you want to fill.
- To copy only the formats or only the formulas, click the Auto Fill Options button and select the appropriate option.

or

- Enter the first few values of the series into a range.
- Select the entire range into which you want to extend the series.
- On the Home tab, in the Editing group, click the Fill button, and then click Down, Right, Up, Left, Series, or Justify.

At Evergreen Fidelity Insurance, calls are automatically assigned a sequential case number following the general pattern Case*number*, where *number* is an integer that increases by 1 with each new call. In this call log, the first case number assigned on this day is Case50127, the case number for the second call is Case50128, and so forth. You will use AutoFill to insert of all the case numbers in column E of the call log.

To extend the case number series in the call log:

1. In cell **E5**, enter the text **Case50127** as the first case number for the day.
2. Click cell **E5** again to select the cell, and then drag the fill handle down over the range **E5:E515**. Case numbers are entered sequentially into the extended range, ending with Case50637 in cell E515.
3. Click the **Auto Fill Options** button, and then click the **Fill Without Formatting** option button to retain the banded rows design used in the table.

Another way of defining a series is with the Series dialog box shown in Figure 3–8. To access the Series dialog box, select the range in which you want to place a series of values, click the Fill button in the Editing group on the Home tab, and then select Series. You can specify a linear or growth series for numbers; a date series for dates that increase by day, weekday, month, or year; or an AutoFill series for patterned text. With numbers, you can also specify the step value (how much each number increases over the previous entry) and a stop value (the endpoint for the entire series).

Figure 3-8 **Series dialog box**

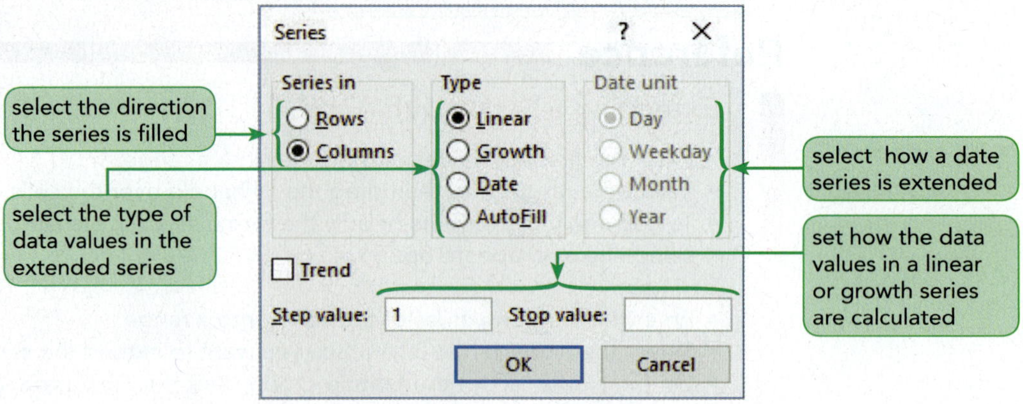

You have finished with using AutoFill to enter formulas and data patterns. Next, you will analyze the call data using Excel functions.

Applying Excel Functions

Excel supports several hundred functions covering a wide range of topics, including finance, statistics, and engineering. With so many functions, it can be challenging to find the function you need to accomplish a specific task. To make it easier to find a specific function, Excel organizes the functions into a function library with the 13 categories described in Figure 3–9.

Figure 3-9 **Function library categories**

Category	Description
Compatibility	Functions from Excel 2010 or earlier, still supported to provide backward compatibility
Cube	Retrieve data from multidimensional databases involving online analytical processing (OLAP)
Database	Retrieve and analyze data stored in databases
Date & Time	Analyze or create date and time values and time intervals
Engineering	Analyze engineering problems
Financial	Analyze information for business and finance
Information	Return information about the format, location, or contents of worksheet cells
Logical	Return logical (true-false) values
Lookup & Reference	Look up and return data matching a set of specified conditions from a range
Math & Trig	Perform math and trigonometry calculations
Statistical	Provide statistical analyses of data sets
Text	Return text values or evaluate text
Web	Provide information on web-based connections

You can access the function library from the Function Library group on the Formulas tab or from the Insert Function dialog box. The Insert Function dialog box includes a search tool to find a function based on a general description. It also displays the function syntax, making it easier to enter a function without syntax errors. You'll use the library to find a function to round the call duration values to whole minutes.

Rounding Data Values

Excel supports three rounding functions: ROUND, ROUNDDOWN, and ROUNDUP. The **ROUND function** rounds a value to the nearest digit, the **ROUNDDOWN function** rounds the value to the next lowest digit, and the **ROUNDUP function** rounds the value to the next highest digit. These functions use the same arguments in their syntax

```
ROUND(number, Num_digits)
ROUNDDOWN(number, Num_digits)
ROUNDUP(number, Num_digits)
```

where ***number*** is the number to be rounded and ***Num_digits*** is the digit to round the number to—0 rounds the number to the nearest integer, 1 rounds the number to the nearest tenth, 2 rounds the number to the nearest hundredth and so forth. For example, the following expression returns a value of 132.44:

```
ROUND(132.438, 2)
```

But when you change the *Num_digits* value from 2 to 1, as in the following expression, the returned value is 132.4:

```
ROUND(132.438, 1)
```

A negative *Num_digits* value rounds the number to a power of 10. For example, the *Num_digits* value of -1 rounds the number to the nearest power of ten. So, the expression

```
ROUND(132.438, -1)
```

returns the value 130.

Reference

Using Functions to Round Values

- To round a number to the nearest digit, use

  ```
  ROUND(number, Num_digits)
  ```

  where ***number*** is the numeric value and ***Num_digits*** is the number of digits to which the numeric value is rounded.
- To round a number down to the next lowest digit, use

  ```
  ROUNDDOWN(number, Num_digits)
  ```
- To round a number to the next highest digit, use

  ```
  ROUNDUP(number, Num_digits)
  ```
- To round a number to nearest integer, use

  ```
  INT(number)
  ```
- To round a number to nearest multiple of a value, use

  ```
  MROUND(number, multiple)
  ```

  where ***multiple*** is a multiple to be rounded to.

Kiara wants the call durations in column J displayed as whole minutes with any fraction of a minute rounded up to the next minute. For example, a call duration of 2.3 minutes should be rounded up to 3 minutes. You will use the Insert Function dialog box to locate and apply the ROUNDUP function to the call duration data.

To use the Insert Function dialog box with the ROUNDUP function:

1. Click cell **J5**, and then press **DELETE** to remove the formula stored in the cell.
2. On the ribbon, click the **Formulas** tab to access the Function Library.
3. In the Function Library group, click the **Insert Function** button. The Insert Function dialog box opens.
4. In the Search for a function box, type **round** to describe the function you want to find, and then click **Go**. Functions that deal with rounding appear in the search results. See Figure 3–10.

Figure 3–10 Insert Function dialog box

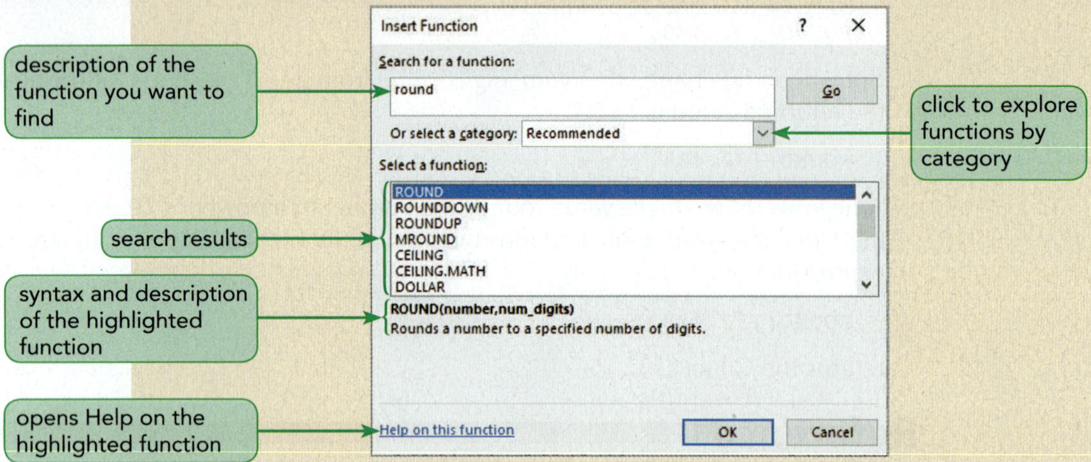

5. In the Select a function box, click **ROUNDUP** from the search results, and then click **OK**. The Function Arguments dialog box opens, describing the arguments used by the function.
6. In the Number box, type the formula **(I5-G5)*24*60** to calculate the duration of the first call in minutes. The value 20.61666667, which is the unrounded value of this calculation, appears next to the Number box.
7. Press **TAB**, and then type **0** in the Num_digits box to round up the calculated value to the next highest integer. In this case, the formula result 20.61666667 will be rounded up to 21. See Figure 3–11.

Figure 3–11 Function Arguments dialog box

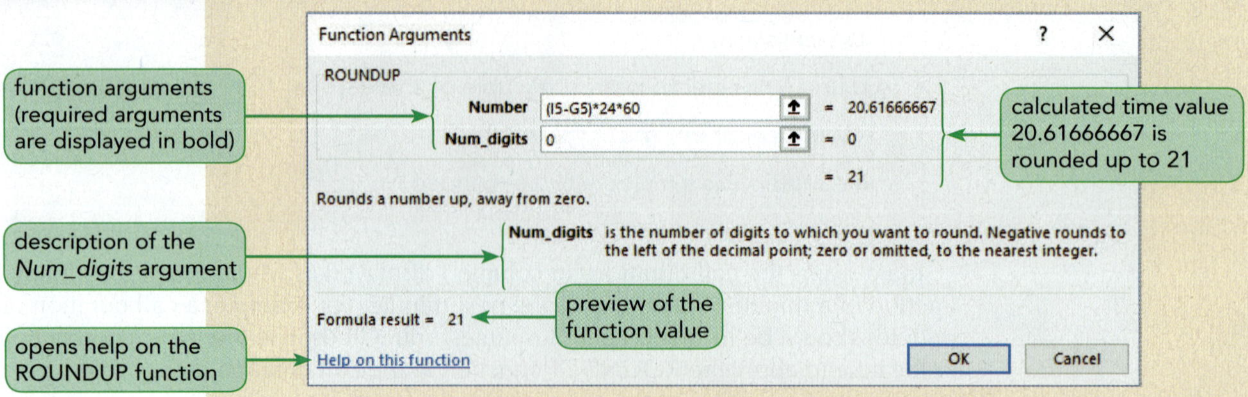

8. Click **OK** to close the dialog box and insert the formula. The value 21 appears in cell J5, indicating that the first call required about 21 minutes of the operator's time.
9. Drag the **fill handle** down over the range **J5:J515** to extend the formula to the rest of the entries in the call log.
10. Click the **Auto Fill Options** button, and then click the **Fill Without Formatting** option button to retain the banded rows.
11. Scroll up the worksheet and click cell **J5** to deselect the range. See Figure 3–12.

Figure 3–12 **Rounded up call duration values**

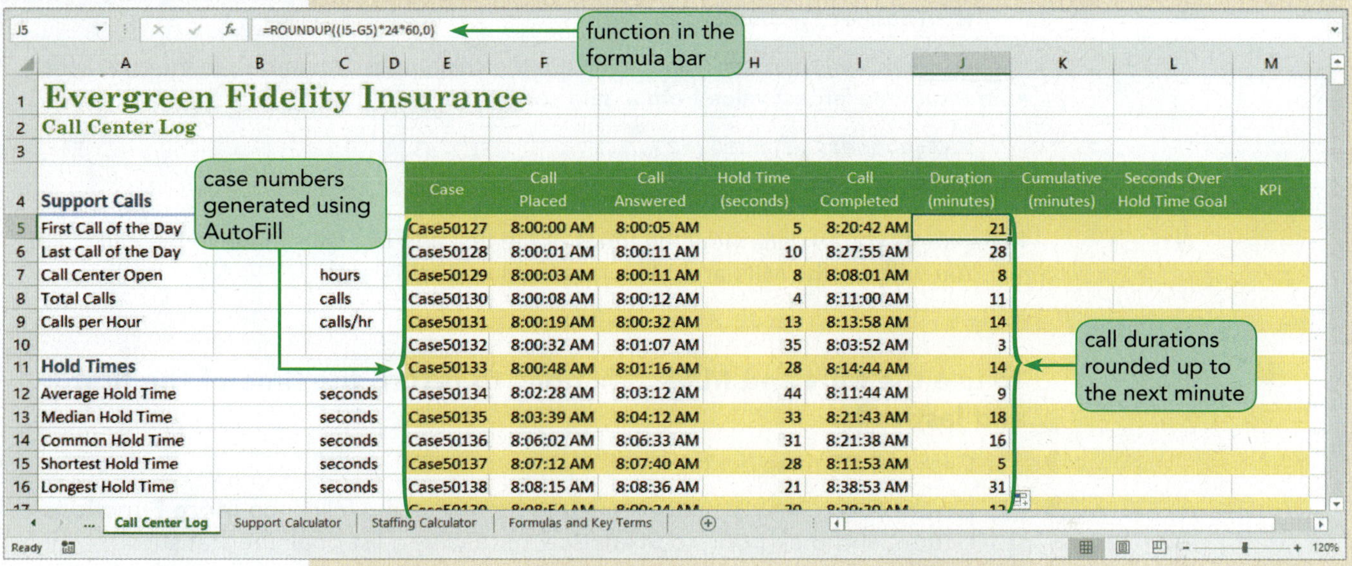

The ROUND, ROUNDDOWN, and ROUNDUP functions all round values to the nearest power of 10 such as 1/100, 1/10, 1, 10, 100, and so forth. To round values to powers other than 10, use the following **MROUND function**

```
MROUND(number, multiple)
```

where ***number*** is the number to be rounded and ***multiple*** is a multiple of a value to be rounded to. For example, the following function rounds 5241 to the nearest multiple of 25, returning 5250 :

```
MROUND(5241, 25)
```

To always rounds a value down to the next lowest integer, use the **INT function**:

```
INT(number)
```

For example, the following expression returns a value of 52:

```
INT(52.817)
```

You can learn more about the rounding functions available in Excel using Excel Help.

Calculating Minimums and Maximums

The MIN and MAX functions return the smallest and largest values from a specified set of numbers:

```
MIN(number1, [number2], …)
MAX(number1, [number2], …)
```

where *number1*, *number2*, and so on are the numbers or cell ranges from which to find the smallest or largest value.

Reference

Using Functions to Find Minimums and Maximums

- To return the smallest value from a data series, use

  ```
  MIN(number1, [number2], …)
  ```

  where **number1**, *number2*, and so on are the cell ranges or numbers in the data series.
- To return the largest value from a data series, use

  ```
  MAX(number1, [number2], …)
  ```

Kiara wants you to determine the times of the first and last calls made to the call center. You will use the MIN and MAX functions to do this.

To use the MIN and MAX functions to return the time of the first and last calls:

1. Click cell **B5** to select it.
2. On the Formulas tab, in the Function Library group, click the **More Functions** button, and then point to **Statistical** to display a list of all the statistical functions.
3. Scroll down the list, and then click **MIN**. The Function Arguments dialog box for the MIN function opens.
4. In the Number1 box, type **F:F** to find the smallest value from all of the time values in column F. You won't enter anything in the Number2 box because you want to search only this range of cells.
5. Click **OK**. The function returns 0.3333333, which is the numeric value of the minimum time value in column F.
6. On the ribbon, click the **Home** tab. In the Number group, click the **Number Format arrow**, and then click **Time**. The value displayed in cell B5 changes to 8:00:00 AM (the time of the first call).
7. Click cell **B6**, and then repeat Steps 2 through 6, clicking the **MAX** function in Step 3 to return the time of the last call of the day. Cell B6 displays 5:59:49 PM, indicating that the last call was placed just before the call center closed.

The Call Center Log worksheet should also display the total hours the call center was open, the number of calls received during that time and the number of calls per hour. You'll add these calculations to the worksheet.

To calculate the total call center hours, calls, and calls per hour:

1. In cell **B7**, enter the formula **=(B6-B5)*24** to calculate the difference between the last call and first call.
2. Click cell **B7** to select it, and then on the Home tab, in the Number group, click the **Number Format arrow**, and then click **Number**. A time interval of 10 hours is displayed in the cell.
3. In cell **B8**, enter the formula **=COUNT(F:F)** to count all of the cells in column F containing numeric values. Cell B8 displays 511, indicating that 511 calls were placed during the day.
4. In cell **B9**, enter the formula **=B8/B7** to calculate the number of calls per hour.
5. Click cell **B9** to select it, and then in the Number group, click the **Number Format arrow**, and then click **Number** to display the value to two decimal places. Cell B9 displays 51.12, indicating that the call center received more than 51 calls every hour. See Figure 3–13.

Figure 3–13 Completed support calls data

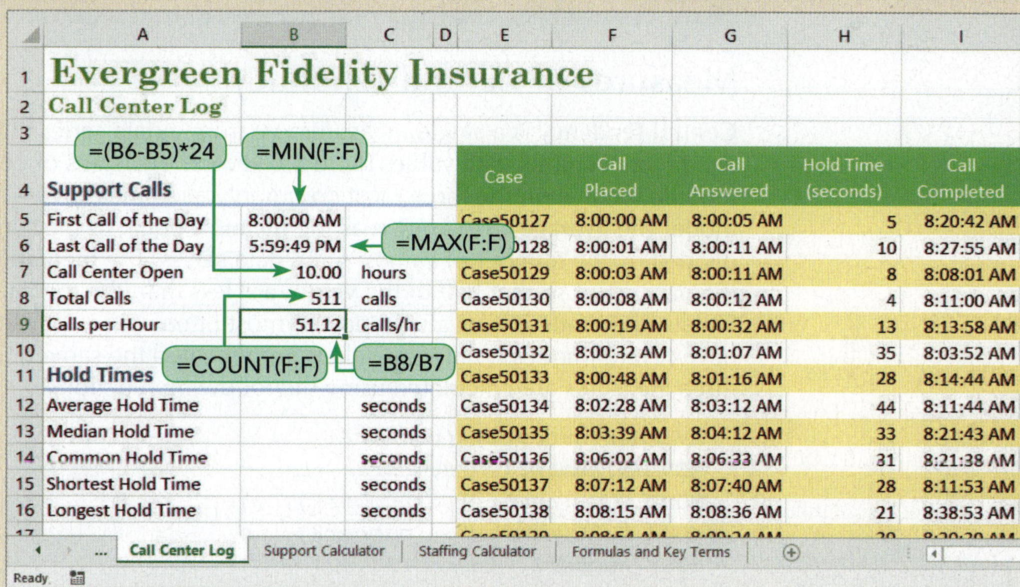

Kiara now has a better picture of the level of traffic at the call center. Next, you will calculate how long a typical caller waits before reaching an operator.

Proskills

Written Communication: Displaying Significant Digits

Excel stores numbers with a precision up to 15 digits and displays as many digits as will fit into the cell. So even the result of a simple formula such as =10/3 will display 3.33333333333333 if the cell is wide enough.

A number with 15-digit accuracy is difficult to read, and calculations rarely need that level of precision. Many scientific disciplines, such as chemistry or physics, have rules specifying exactly how many digits should be displayed with any calculation. These digits are called **significant digits** because they indicate the accuracy of the measured and calculated values. For example, the value 19.32 has four significant digits.

The rules for determining the number of significant digits reported in a calculation vary between disciplines. Generally, a calculated value should display no more digits than are found in any of the values used in the calculation. For example, because the input value 19.32 has four significant digits, any calculated value based on that input should have no more than four significant digits. Showing more digits would be misleading because it implies a level of accuracy beyond what was measured.

Because Excel displays calculated values with as many digits as can fit into a cell, you need to know the standards that your profession uses for reporting significant digits and format the results accordingly.

Measures of Central Tendency

Central tendency is a single measurement from a data series that returns the most typical or "central" data value. There are several measures of central tendency. This module focuses on the three most commonly used measures—average, median, and mode. The **average**, also known as the **mean**, is equal to the sum of the data values divided by the number of values in the data series. The **median** is the central value of the data series so that half of the values are less than the median and half are greater. Finally, the **mode** is the value repeated most often in the data series. A data series can have several modes if different values are repeated the same number of times. These three measures are calculated using the following functions:

```
AVERAGE(number1, [number2], …)
MEDIAN(number1, [number2], …)
MODE.SNGL(number1, [number2], …)
MODE.MULT(number1, [number2], …)
MODE(number1, [number2], …)
```

Tip

If there are several possible modes, both the MODE.SNGL and MODE functions return the first mode value listed in the data series.

where ***number1***, ***number2***, and so on are the values from a data series. Notice that Excel includes three different mode functions. The MODE.SNGL function returns a single value representing the mode from the data series. The **MODE.MULT function** returns either a single value or a list of values if more than one value is repeated the same number of times. The MODE function is the older version of the function for calculating modes and is equivalent to the MODE.SNGL function.

The average, while the most commonly used measure of central tendency, can be adversely effected by extreme values. Consider an exam in which every student receives a 90 except one student who receives a zero. That single zero value will cause the class average to drop, making it appear that students did worse on the exam than all but one actually did. On the other hand, the median and mode will both be 90, providing a more accurate assessment of a typical student's performance. However, the median and mode are also limited because they obscure information that might be useful. The instructor might want to know that one student did extremely poorly on the exam, which only the average indicates. For these reasons, it's often best to compare the results of all three measures.

Reference

Calculating Measures of Central Tendency

- To calculate the average from a data series, use

  `AVERAGE(number1, [number2], …)`

- To calculate the median or midpoint from a data series, use

  `MEDIAN(number1, [number2], …)`

- To return a single value that is repeated most often in a data series, use

  `MODE.SNGL(number1, [number2], …)`

- To return the value or list of values that is repeated most often in a data series, use

  `MODE.MULT(number1, [number2], …)`

Kiara wants to know the typical hold time that customers will experience at the call center based on the average, median, and mode measures of the hold-time data. Kiara also wants to know the shortest and longest hold times that customers experienced during the day. You'll calculate these measures using the AVERAGE, MEDIAN, MODE.SNGL, MIN, and MAX functions.

To calculate the average, median, and mode hold times:

1. Click cell **B12**, and then click the **Formulas** tab on the ribbon.
2. In the Function Library group, click the **More Functions** button, and then point to **Statistical** in the list of function categories. A list of statistical functions appears.
3. In the Statistical functions list, click **AVERAGE** to open the Function Arguments dialog box.
4. In the Number1 box, type **H:H** as the range reference, and then click **OK**. The cell displays 27.477495, indicating that the average time spent on hold was about 27 and a half seconds.
5. Click cell **B13**, and then repeat Steps 2 through 4, selecting **MEDIAN** as the statistical function in Step 3. The cell displays a median value of 26.
6. Click cell **B14**, and then repeat Steps 2 through 4, selecting **MODE.SNGL** as the statistical function in Step 3. The cell displays a mode value of 28.
7. In cell **B15**, enter the formula **= MIN(H:H)** to calculate the minimum hold-time value in column H. The shortest hold time was 1 second.
8. In cell **B16**, enter the formula **=MAX(H:H)** to calculate the maximum hold-time value in column H. The longest hold time was 163 seconds. See Figure 3–14.

Figure 3–14 Completed customer hold-times data

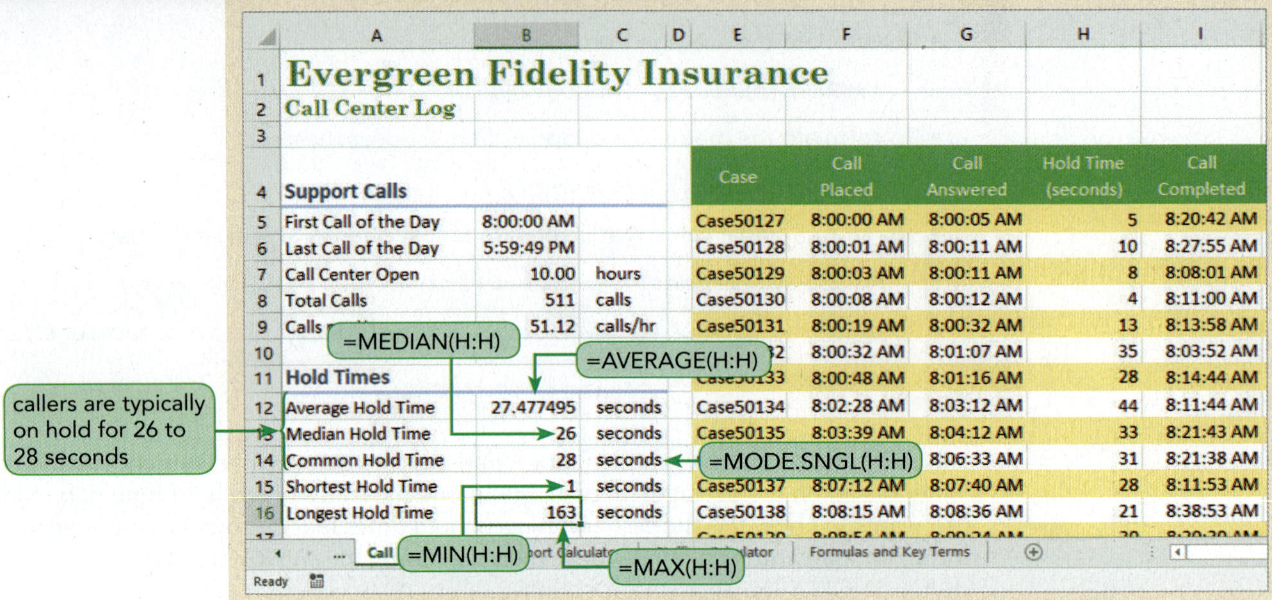

The average, median, and mode values all indicate that the typical caller waits on hold for about 26 to 28 seconds. Kiara wants you to do a similar analysis for the length of each customer conversation with an operator.

To calculate the typical length of the support conversations:

1. In cell **B19**, enter the formula **=AVERAGE(J:J)** using whatever method you prefer. The average conversation is 16.154599 minutes.
2. In cell **B20**, enter the formula **=MEDIAN(J:J)** to calculate the middle value. The median conversation is 13 minutes.
3. In cell **B21**, enter the formula **=MODE.SNGL(J:J)** to calculate the most common value. The most common conversation lasts 6 minutes.
4. In cell **B22**, enter the formula **=MIN(J:J)** to calculate the smallest value. The shortest conversation lasted 1 minute.
5. In cell **B23**, enter the formula **=MAX(J:J)** to calculate the largest value. The longest conversation was 73 minutes. See Figure 3–15.

Figure 3–15 Completed call duration data

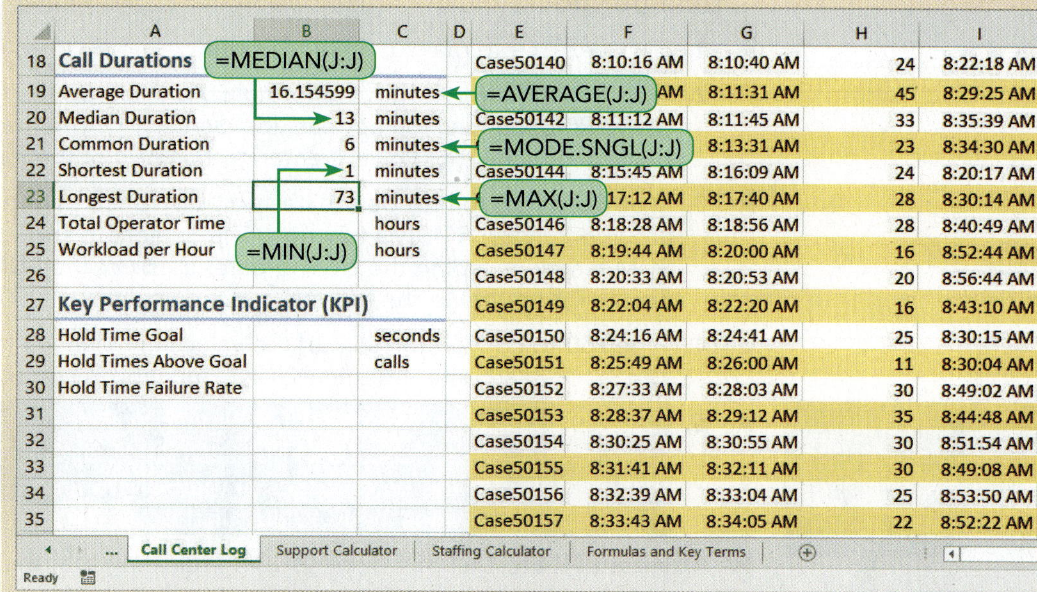

The three measures of central tendency for the length of the conversations show distinctly different values. The average conversation with the operator lasts a little over 16 minutes, but the most common length, as indicated by the mode, is 6 minutes with a median of 13 minutes. It would seem that many calls could be dealt with in a short time, although some longer calls (up to 73 minutes) require more operator time, bringing up the average. This information tells Kiara that the call center might handle calls more efficiently by sending more difficult, time-consuming calls to the most experienced operators and having all other calls handled by the rest of the operators.

Nesting Functions

Functions can be placed inside, or **nested**, within other functions. When functions are nested, Excel evaluates the innermost function first and then moves outward to evaluate the remaining functions with the inner function acting as an argument for the next outer function. For example, the following expression nests the AVERAGE function within the ROUND function. In this expression, the average of the values in the range A1:A100 is calculated first, and then that average is rounded to the nearest integer:

```
ROUND(AVERAGE(A1:A100),0)
```

Formulas that involve several layers of nested functions can be challenging to read. The more nested functions there are, the more difficult it becomes to associate each set of arguments with its corresponding function. To help interpret nested functions, Excel displays the opening and closing parentheses of each function level in a different color. If a syntax error occurs, Excel offers suggestions for rewriting the formula.

The last part of the Call Durations section in the Call Center Log worksheet calculates the total amount of time operators spent on the phone throughout the day. Knowing how long operators are actively engaged with customers is important to determining the call center's staffing needs. Kiara wants the total support time rounded to the nearest hour. To do that, you will use both the SUM function and the ROUND function nested in a single formula. Kiara also wants to know the total operator time per hour, rounded to the nearest tenth of an hour. You'll calculate this value by dividing the total operator time by the total number of hours the call center was open.

To calculate and round the total operator time and the operator time per hour:

1. Click cell **B24** to make it the active cell.
2. Type **=ROUND(** to begin the formula. As you type the formula, the syntax of the ROUND function appears in a ScreenTip. The number argument is in bold to indicate that you are entering this part of the function.
3. Type **SUM(J:J)** to include the nested SUM function as part of the number argument in the ROUND function. The ScreenTip shows the syntax of the SUM function. Typing the closing parenthesis of the SUM function returns the ScreenTip returns to the ROUND function syntax.
4. Type **/60** to convert the sum of the values in column J from minutes to hours. The number argument of the ROUND function is complete.
5. Type **, 0)** to enter the number of decimal places to include in the results. The formula with nested functions =ROUND(SUM(J:J)/60, 0) is complete. Notice that the color for the parentheses of the SUM function differs from the color of the parentheses for the ROUND function.

Make sure the formula contains two sets of parentheses—one for the SUM function and the other for the ROUND function.

6. Press **ENTER**. Cell B24 displays 138, indicating that the call center operators spend around 138 hours on the phone with customers during the day.
7. In cell **B25**, type the formula **=ROUND(B24/B7, 1)** to divide the total operator time in cell B24 by the total number of hours the call center was open in cell B7 and round the total to the nearest tenth of an hour, and then press **ENTER**. Cell B25 displays 13.8, which is the workload per hour rounded to tenths. See Figure 3–16.

Figure 3–16 Using nested functions to calculate operator time

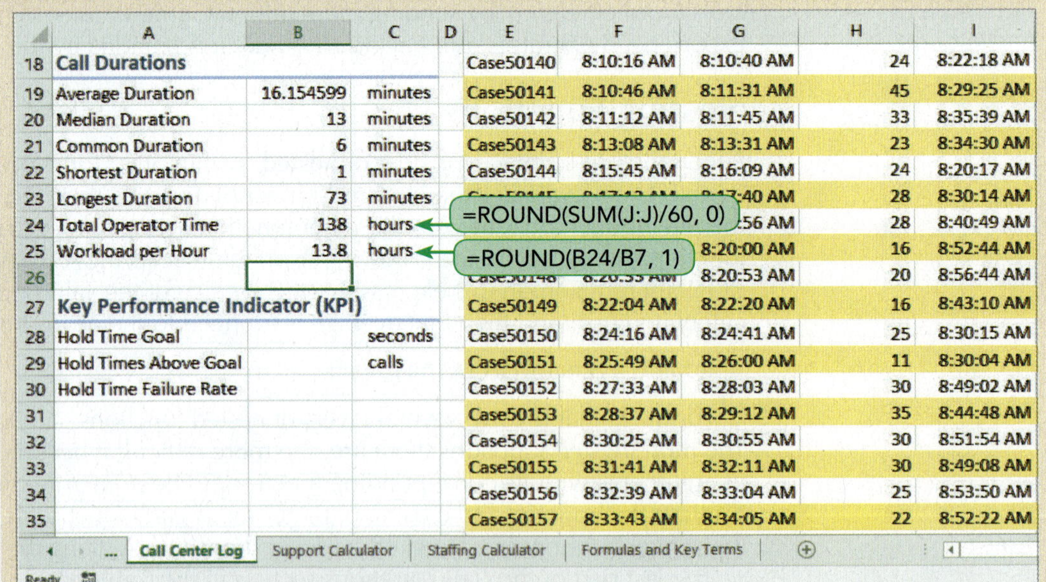

The value in cell B25 shows that each hour the call center is open requires 13.8 hours of operator time. In other words, the call center needs about 14 operators every hour to keep up with the traffic. Fewer than 14 operators will result in a backlog that will only get worse as the day progresses.

The Role of Blanks and Zeroes

The functions you've entered were applied to whole columns of data even though those columns contained empty cells and cells with text strings. Mathematical and statistical functions like SUM, COUNT, AVERAGE, and MEDIAN include only numeric data in their calculations, ignoring empty cells and text entries. A blank cell is considered a text entry and is not treated as the number zero. Figure 3–17 shows how the results differ when a blank replaces a zero in a data series.

Figure 3–17 **Calculations with blank cells and zeroes**

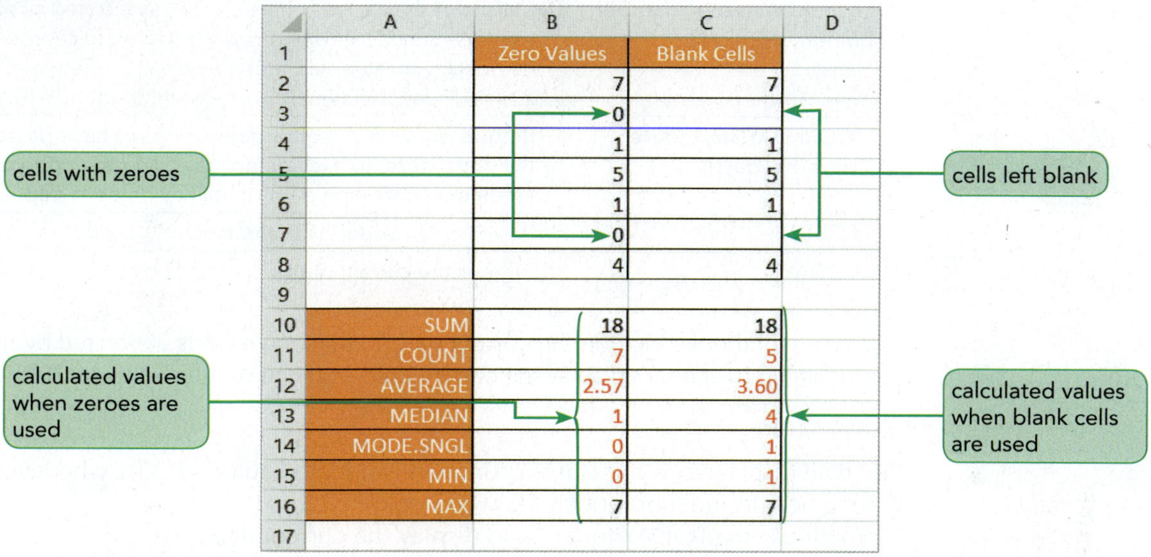

Whether you use a blank cell or a zero in a data series depends on what you are trying to measure. For example, to calculate the average number of hours per day that the call center is open, Kiara could enter 0 for holidays in which the call center is closed or leave the cell blank. Using a zero returns the average hours worked across all calendar days and gives a good overall summary of the company's annual staffing needs. Using a blank cell would summarize staffing needs only for the days that the call center is open. Both approaches have their uses. So consider the ultimate goal of any calculation and choose the approach that best achieves your goal.

Date and Time Functions

Excel supports a large collection of date and time functions. Figure 3–18 summarizes some of the most useful ones.

Figure 3-18 Date and time functions

Function	Description
DATE(***year***,***month***,***day***)	Creates a date value for the date represented by the ***year***, ***month***, and ***day*** arguments
DAY(***serial_number***)	Extracts the day of the month from a date value stored as ***serial_number***
MONTH(***serial_number***)	Extracts the month number from a date value stored as ***serial_number***, where 1=January, 2=February, and so on
YEAR(***serial_number***)	Extracts the 4-digit year value from a date value stored as ***serial_number***
NETWORKDAYS(***start_date***, ***end_date***,[*holidays*])	Calculates the number of whole working days between ***start_date*** and ***end_date***; to exclude holidays, add the optional holidays argument containing a list of holiday dates to skip
WEEKDAY(***serial_number***, [*return_type*])	Calculates the weekday from a date value stored as ***serial_number***, where 1=Sunday, 2=Monday, and so forth; to choose a different numbering scheme, set *return_type* to 1 (1=Sunday, 2=Monday, ...), 2 (1=Monday, 2=Tuesday, ...), or 3 (0=Monday, 1=Tuesday, ...)
WORKDAY(***start_date***, ***days***,[*holidays*])	Returns the workday after ***days*** workdays have passed since the ***start_date***; to exclude holidays, add the optional holidays argument containing a list of holiday dates to skip
NOW( )	Returns the current date and time
TODAY( )	Returns the current date

Many workbooks include the current date so that any reports generated by the workbook are identified by date. To display the current date, you can use the following **TODAY function**:

```
TODAY()
```

The date displayed by the TODAY function is updated automatically whenever you enter a new formula or reopen the workbook.

You'll use the TODAY function to display the current date.

To display the current date:

1. Go to the **Documentation** sheet.
2. In cell **B4**, enter the formula **=TODAY()** to display the current date in the cell. The date displayed in cell B4 will be updated every time you reopen the workbook.

To display the current date and the current time, use the NOW function. The NOW function, like the TODAY function, is automatically updated whenever you add a new calculation to the workbook or reopen the workbook.

Insight

Date Calculations with Working Days

Businesses are often more interested in workdays rather than calendar days. For example, to estimate a delivery date in which packages are not shipped or delivered on weekends, it is more useful to know the date of the next weekday rather than the date of the next day.

To display the date of a working day that is a specified number of workdays past a start date, use the **WORKDAY function**

```
WORKDAY(start_date, days, [holidays])
```

where ***start_date*** is the starting date, ***days*** is the number of workdays after that starting date, and *holidays* is an optional list of holiday dates to skip. For example, if cell A1 contains the date 12/23/2025, a Tuesday, the following formula displays the date 1/5/2026, a Monday that is nine working days later:

```
WORKDAY(A1,9)
```

The optional *holidays* argument references a series of dates that the WORKDAY function will skip in performing its calculations. So, if both 12/25/2025 and 1/1/2026 are entered in the range B1:B2 as holidays, the following function will return the date 1/7/2026, a Thursday that is nine working days, excluding the holidays, after 12/23/2025:

```
WORKDAY(A1,9,B1:B2)
```

To reverse the process and calculate the number of working days between two dates, use the following **NETWORKDAYS function**

```
NETWORKDAYS(start_date, end_date, [holidays])
```

where ***start_date*** is the starting date, ***end_date*** is the ending date, and *holidays* is an optional list of holiday dates to skip. So, if cell A1 contains the date 12/23/2025 and cell A2 contains the date 1/3/2026, the following function returns the value 6, indicating that there are six working days between the start and ending date, excluding the holidays specified in the range B1:B2:

```
NETWORKDAYS(A1,A2,B1:B2)
```

For international applications, which might have a different definition of working day, Excel supports the WORKDAY.INTL function. See Excel Help for more information.

Interpreting Error Values

It's easy to mistype a formula. When you make a mistake writing a formula, Excel returns an **error value** indicating that some part of a formula was entered incorrectly. Figure 3–19 lists the common error values you might see in place of calculated values from formulas and functions. For example, the error value #VALUE! indicates that the wrong type of value is used as an argument for an Excel function or formula.

Figure 3-19 Common error values

Error Value	Description
#DIV/0!	The formula or function contains a number divided by 0.
#NAME?	Excel doesn't recognize text in the formula or function, such as when the function name is misspelled.
#N/A	A value is not available to a function or formula, which can occur when a workbook is initially set up prior to entering actual data values.
#NULL!	A formula or function requires two cell ranges to intersect, but they don't.
#NUM!	Invalid numbers are used in a formula or function, such as text entered in a function that requires a number.
#REF!	A cell reference used in a formula or function is no longer valid, which can occur when the cell used by the function was deleted from the worksheet.
#VALUE!	The wrong type of argument is used in a function or formula. This can occur when you reference a text value for an argument that should be strictly numeric.

Error values by themselves might not be particularly descriptive or helpful. To help you locate the error, an error indicator appears in the upper-left corner of the cell with the error value. When you point to the error indicator, a ScreenTip appears with more information about the error. Although the ScreenTips provide hints as to the reason for the error, you will usually need to examine the formulas in the cells with error values to determine exactly what went wrong.

Kiara wants you to test the workbook to verify that it will catch common arithmetic errors. You will change the value of cell B7 from its current calculated value of 10 hours to a blank cell to see its impact on other cells in the worksheet.

To create an error value:

1. Go to the **Call Center Log** sheet in the workbook.
2. Click cell **B7**, and then press **DELETE** to remove the formula from the cell. Cell B7 is now blank.
3. Verify that both cells B9 and B25 show the error value #DIV/0! indicating that the formulas in those cells contain expressions in which a value is divided by zero.
4. Click cell **B9**, and then point to the **Error** button that appears to the left of the cell. A ScreenTip appears, providing information about the cause of the error value. In this case, the ScreenTip "The formula or function used is dividing by zero or empty cells." appears. See Figure 3–20.

Figure 3–20 Error value in the worksheet

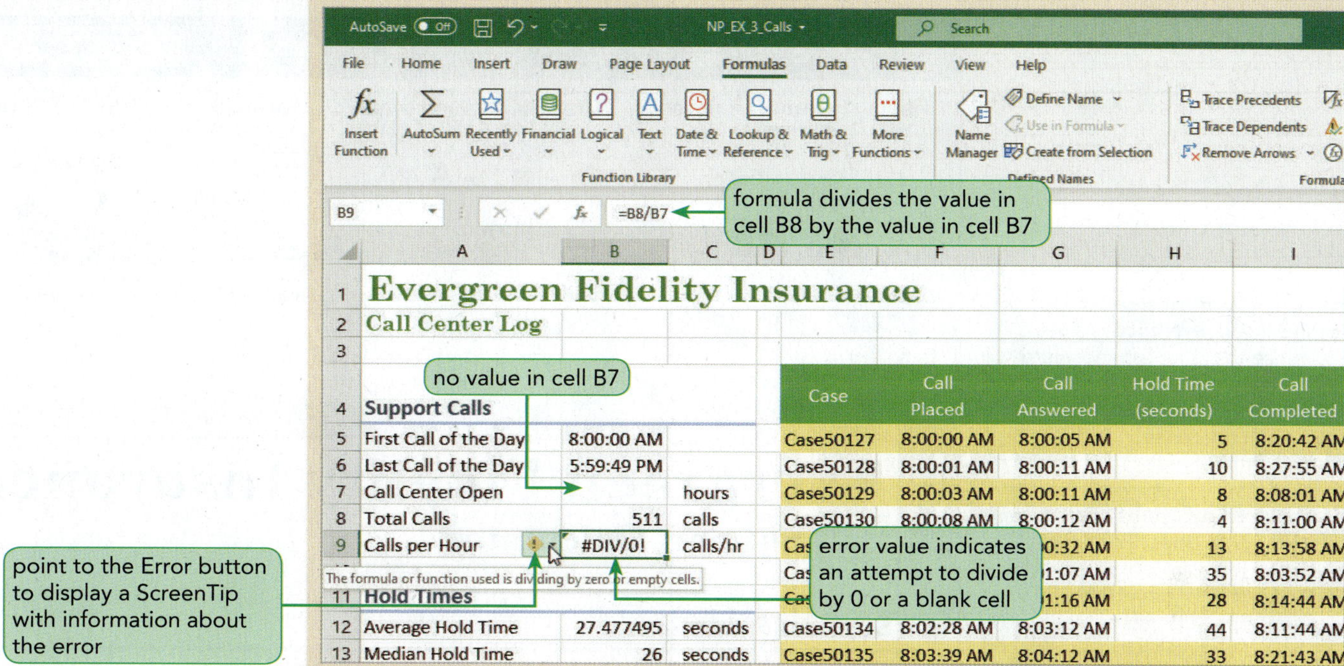

5. On the Quick Access Toolbar, click the **Undo** button to restore the original formula in cell B7. The cell again displays 10 hours as the formula result.
6. Verify that no error values appear in the worksheet, and then save the workbook.

You've completed your initial work in using Excel formulas and functions to analyze the call center data that Kiara compiled. In the next session, you will continue your analysis and use it to determine the optimal number of operators required to provide fast and efficient service for Evergreen Fidelity Insurance customers.

Review

Session 3.1 Quick Check

1. Write a formula to convert the number of days entered in cell B10 to seconds.
2. If 4/30/2025 and 5/31/2025 are the initial values in a range, list the next two values that AutoFill will insert.
3. Write a formula to round the value in cell A5 to the nearest multiple of 1000.
4. Write a formula to return the single value that is repeated the most times in the range Y1:Y100.
5. The range of values is defined as the maximum value minus the minimum value. Write a nested formula that calculates the range of values in the range Y1:Y100 and then rounds that value to the nearest integer.
6. Houses in a neighborhood usually sell for between $250,000 and $350,000 except for a large mansion that sold for $1,200,000. Which best expresses the typical home sales price: Average or median? Why?
7. Stephen is entering hundreds of temperature values into a worksheet for a climate research project, and wants to speed up data entry by leaving freezing point values as blanks rather than typing zeroes. Explain why this will cause complications in the calculation of the average temperature.
8. Cell B2 contains the formula =SUME(A1:A100) with the name of the SUM function misspelled as SUME. What error value will appear in the cell?

Session 3.2 Visual Overview:

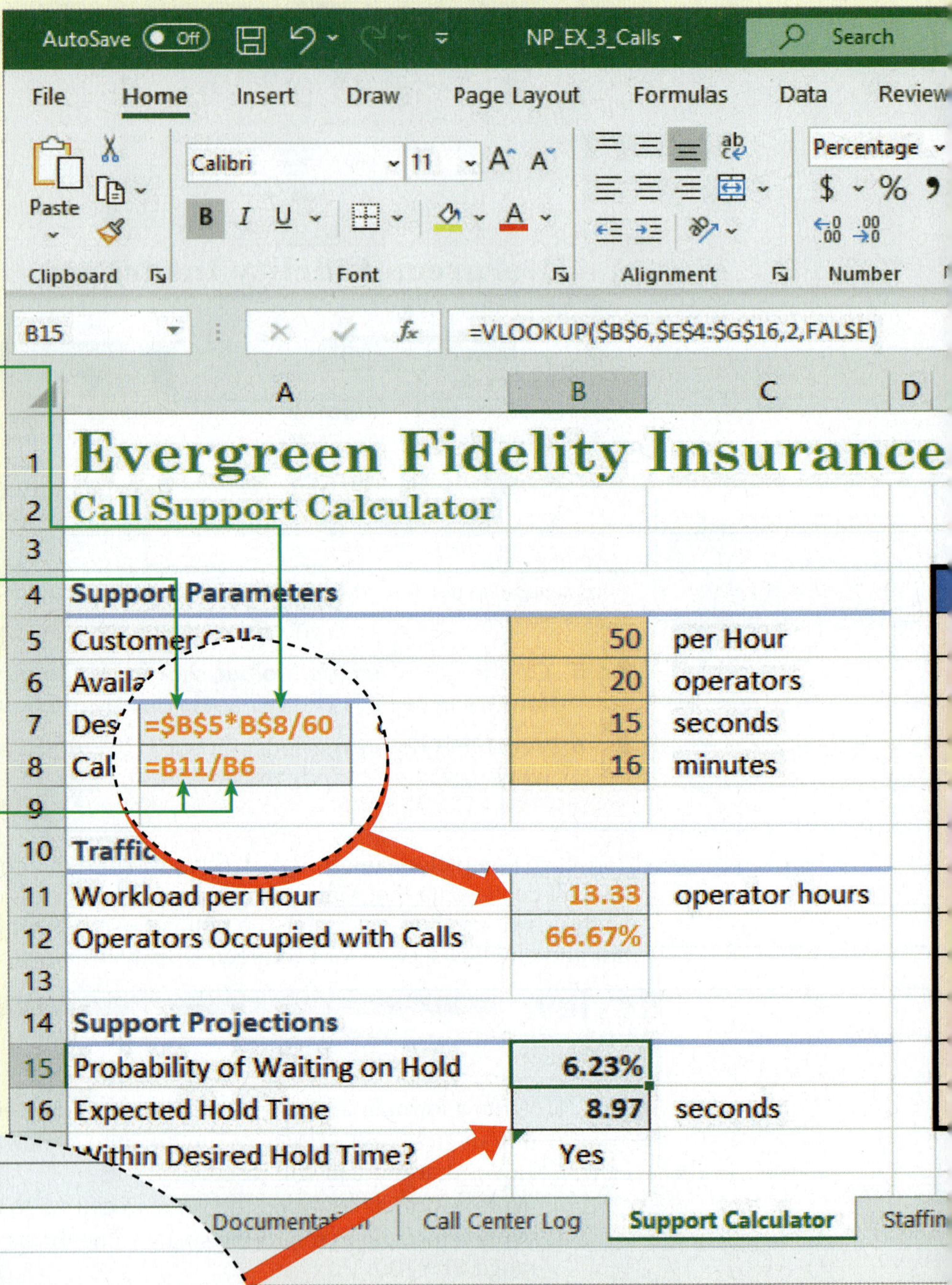

A **mixed cell reference** is a cell reference that has both absolute and relative components in the reference. For example, B$8 is a mixed cell reference.

An **absolute cell reference** is a cell reference that does not change when the formula containing that reference is moved to a new location. Absolute references have "$" before the row and column components. For example, $B$5 is an absolute cell reference.

A **relative cell reference** is a cell reference that changes when the formula containing that reference is moved to a new location. For example, B11 and B6 are both relative cell references.

The **VLOOKUP function** returns values from a vertical lookup table by specifying the value to be matched, the location of the lookup table, and the column containing the return values.

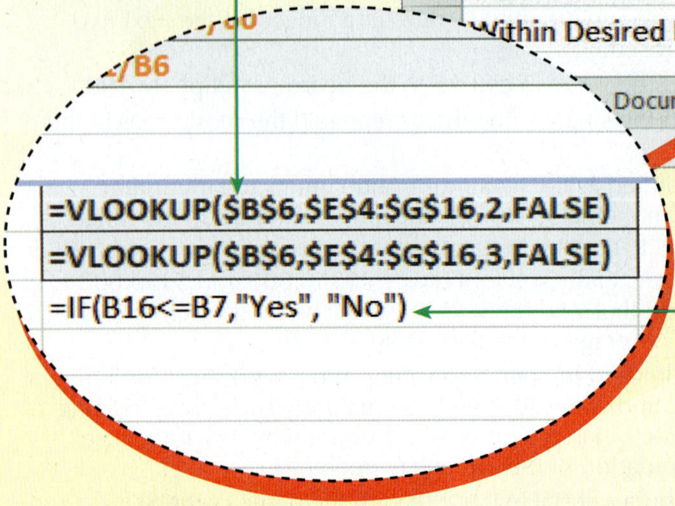

The **IF function** is a logical function that tests a condition and then returns one value if the condition is true and another value if the condition is false.

Lookup Tables and Logical Functions

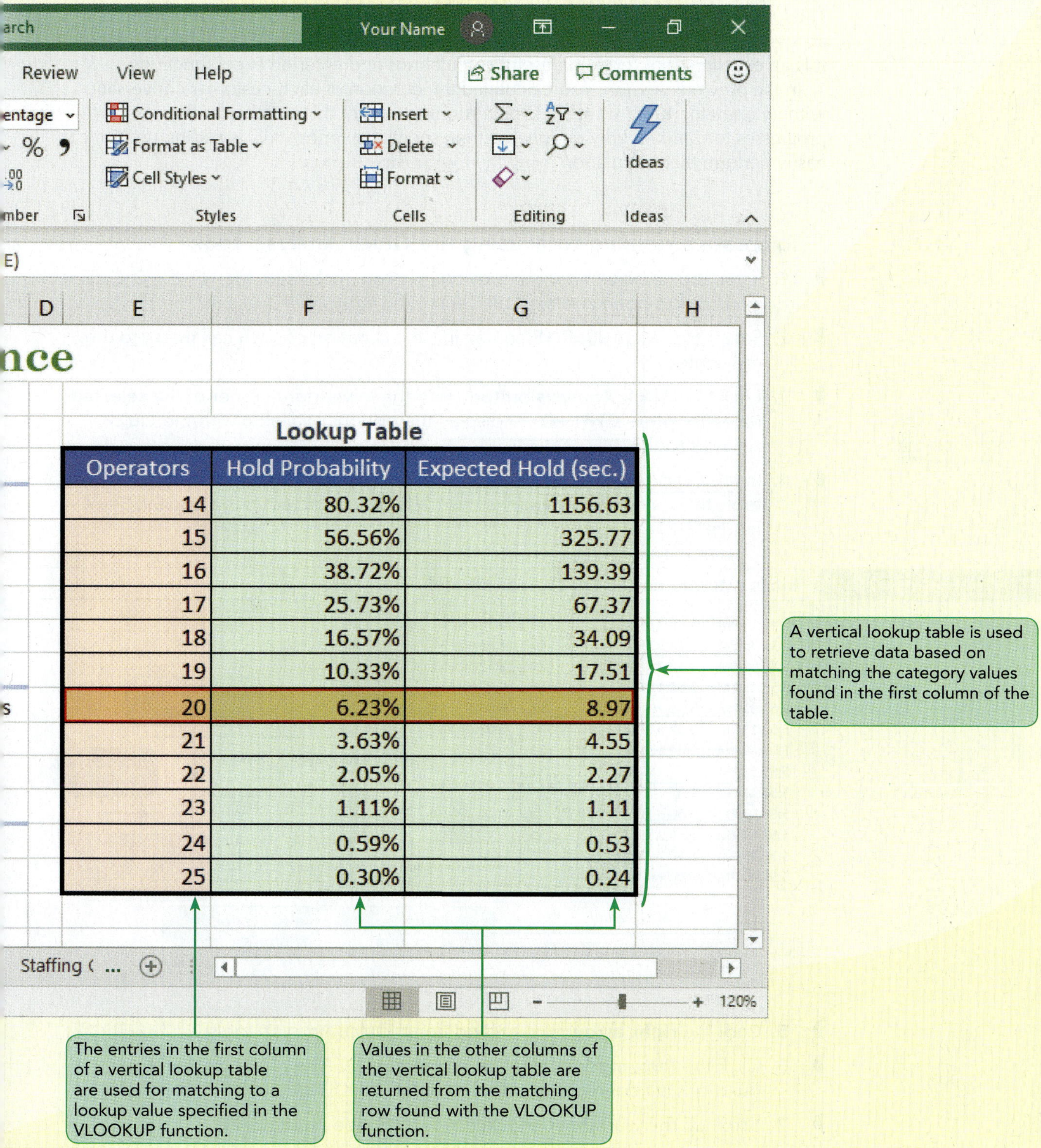

Lookup Table

Operators	Hold Probability	Expected Hold (sec.)
14	80.32%	1156.63
15	56.56%	325.77
16	38.72%	139.39
17	25.73%	67.37
18	16.57%	34.09
19	10.33%	17.51
20	6.23%	8.97
21	3.63%	4.55
22	2.05%	2.27
23	1.11%	1.11
24	0.59%	0.53
25	0.30%	0.24

Calculating Running Totals with the Quick Analysis Tool

The Quick Analysis tool appears whenever you select a range of cells, providing easy access to the most common tools for data analysis, chart creation, and data formatting. It is an excellent tool for doing useful calculations and entering Excel functions.

In the previous session, you calculated the duration of each customer conversation with an operator. Kiara wants to keep a running total of that number as the day progresses to evaluate how rapidly the time spent answering calls is adding up. You can easily perform this calculation using the Quick Analysis tool.

To create a running total using the Quick Analysis tool:

1. If you took a break after the previous session, make sure the NP_EX_3_Calls.xlsx workbook is open and the Call Center Log worksheet is active.
2. Select the range **J5:J515** containing the duration of each call made to the call center.
3. Click the **Quick Analysis** button in the lower-right corner of the selected range (or press **CTRL+Q**) to display the options available with the Quick Analysis tool.
4. In the Quick Analysis tool categories, click **Totals**. The Quick Analysis tools that calculate summary statistics for the selected range appear. See Figure 3–21.

Figure 3–21 Totals category on the Quick Analysis tool

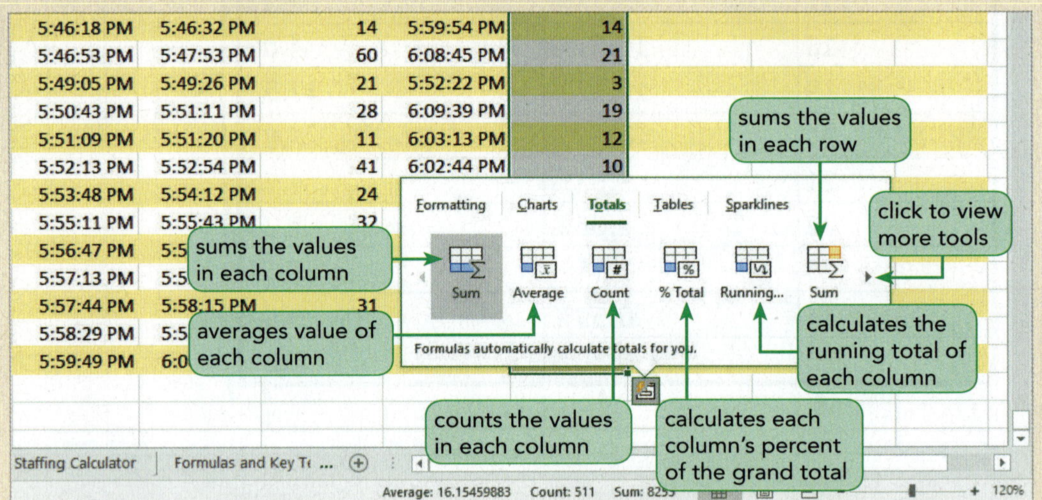

5. Click the **right arrow** to view additional Quick Analysis tools.
6. Click the **Running** tool (the last icon in the list). The running total of call durations is added to the adjacent range K5:K515.
7. Scroll up the worksheet and select cell **K5**. See Figure 3–22.

Figure 3–22 Running total of the call durations

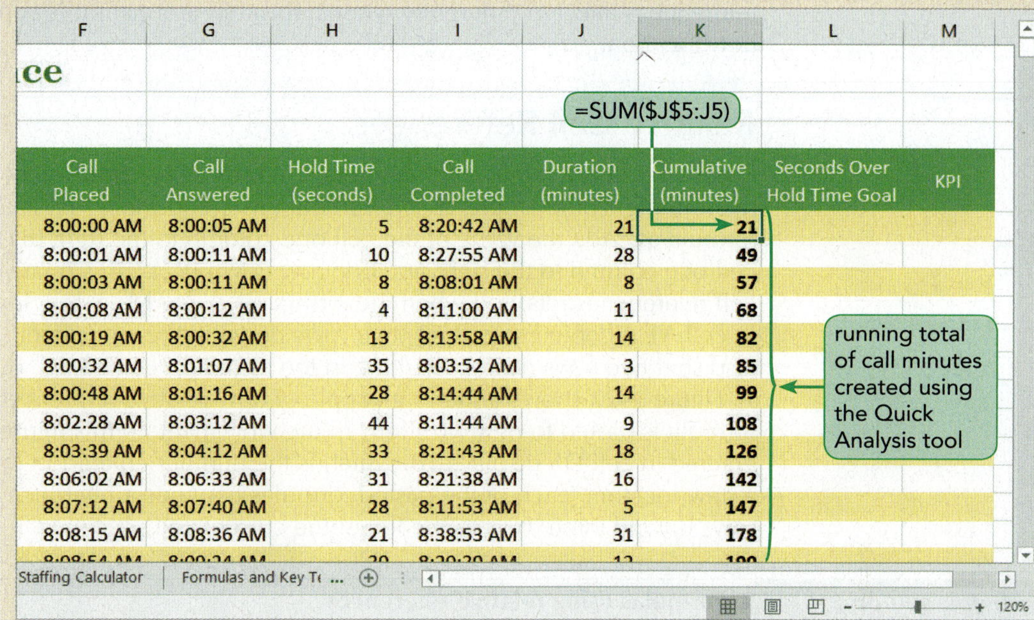

Column K now shows the running total of call duration in minutes. The first two calls required a combined 49 minutes of operator time. The first three calls required a combined 57 minutes—nearly an hour—of operator time. With each call added to the previous sum, Kiara can track how total operator time grows throughout the day. For example by 9 AM, operators have logged 980 minutes of customer support time (cell K56) or the equivalent of more than 16 hours of support within the first hour that call center was open.

By default, Quick Analysis summary statistics are displayed in bold. You'll remove the bold formatting so that the values in column K have same formatting as column J.

To remove the bold formatting from the running total:

1. Select the range **K5:K515**.
2. On the ribbon, click **Home** tab, and then in the Font group, click the **Bold** button **B** to remove bold formatting from the selected text.
3. Click cell **K5** to deselect the range K5:K515.

To create the running totals in column K, the Quick Analysis tool first adds the following formula to cell K5:

```
=SUM($J$5:J5)
```

When that formula is extended down the column, the formula changes in cell K6 to

```
=SUM($J$5:J6)
```

and the formula changes in cell K7 to

```
=SUM($J$5:J7)
```

As the formula is extended through the range K5:K515, the SUM function covers a longer and longer range of cells. By cell K515, the formula is =SUM($J$5:J515). To make those changes to the argument of the SUM function, the Quick Analysis tool used a mixture of relative and absolute cell references.

Exploring Cell References

Excel has three types of cell references: relative, absolute, and mixed. Each type of cell reference is affected differently when a formula or function is copied and pasted to a new location.

Relative Cell References

Excel interprets a relative cell reference relative to the position of the cell containing the formula. For example, if cell A1 contains the formula =B1+B2, Excel interprets that formula as "Add the value of the cell one column to the right (B1) to the value of the cell one column to the right and one row down (B2)." This relative interpretation of the cell reference is retained when the formula is copied to a new location. If the formula in cell A1 is copied to cell A3 (two rows down in the worksheet), the relative references also shift two rows down, resulting in the formula =B3+B4.

Figure 3–23 shows another example of how relative references change when a formula is pasted to new locations in the worksheet. In this figure, the formula =A3 entered in cell D6 displays 10, which is the number entered in cell A3. When pasted to a new location, each of the pasted formulas contains a reference to a cell that is three rows up and three rows to the left of the current cell's location.

Figure 3–23 Formulas using relative references

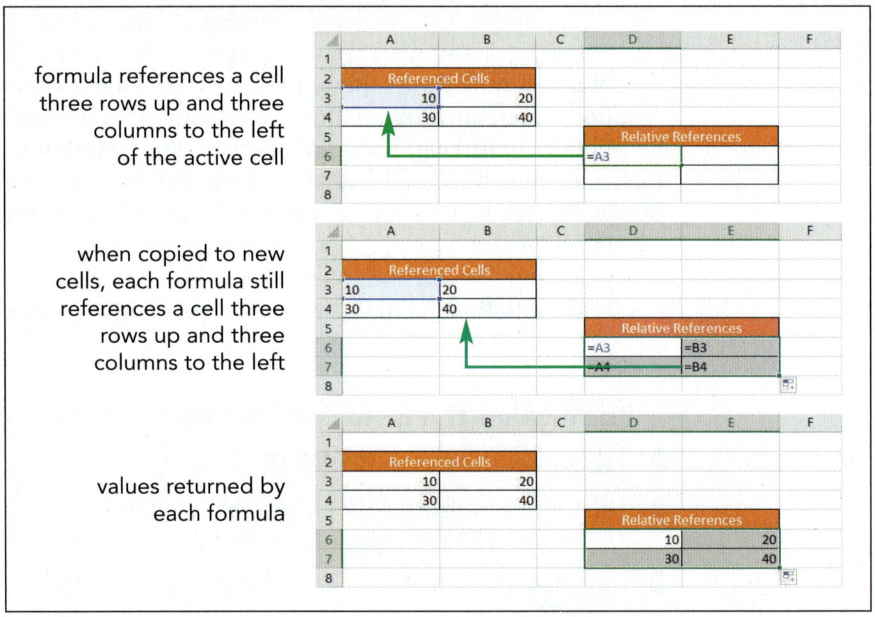

Relative references are why you can copy the same formula down a column or across a row. As long as the relative location of the referenced cells remains the same, the formula can be applied anywhere in the worksheet.

Absolute Cell References

An absolute cell reference remains fixed even when a formula or function is copied to a new location. Absolute references include $ (a dollar sign) before each column and row designation. For example, B8 is a relative reference to cell B8, while $B$8 is an absolute reference to that cell.

Figure 3–24 shows how copying a formula with an absolute reference results in the same cell reference being pasted in different cells regardless of their position compared to the location of the original copied cell. In this example, the formula =$A$3 will always reference cell A3 no matter where the formula is copied to.

Figure 3–24 **Formulas using absolute references**

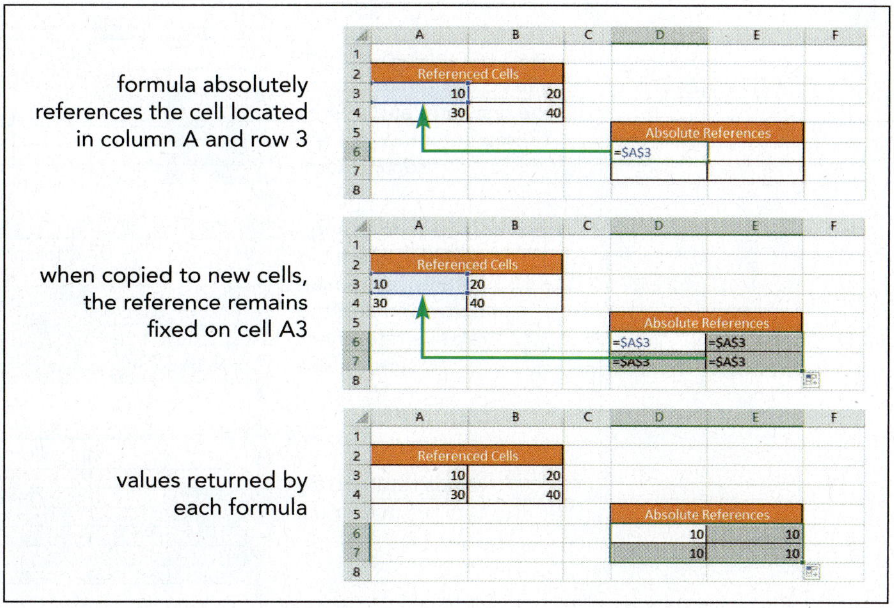

The running total formula, =SUM($J$5:J5) from cell K5 in the Call Center Log worksheet uses the absolute cell reference $J$5 so that the first cell in the SUM function always points to cell J5, no matter where the formula is copied to. However, the relative portion of that formula, J5, will move down as the location of the formula moves down so that when the formula is copied to cell K6, it then becomes =SUM($J$5:J6) expanding to =SUM($J$5:J515) for cell K515.

Mixed Cell References

A mixed cell reference contains both relative and absolute components. For example, a mixed cell reference for cell A2 can be either $A2 where the column is the absolute component and the row is the relative component, or it can be entered as A$2 with a relative column component and a fixed row component. A mixed cell reference "locks" only one part of the cell reference. When copied to a new location, the absolute portion of the cell reference remains fixed but the relative portion shifts.

Figure 3–25 shows mixed cell references used to complete a multiplication table. The first cell in the table, cell B3, contains the formula =$A3*B$2, which multiplies the first column entry (cell A3) by the first-row entry (cell B2), returning 1. When this formula is copied to another cell, the absolute portions of the cell references remain unchanged, and the relative portions of the references change. For example, if the formula is copied to cell E6, the first mixed cell reference changes to $A6 because the column reference is absolute and the row reference is relative, and the second cell reference changes to E$2 because the row reference is absolute and the column reference is relative. The result is that cell E6 contains the formula =$A6*E$2 and returns a value of 16. Other cells in the multiplication table are similarly modified so that each entry returns the multiplication of the intersection of the row and column headings.

Figure 3-25 **Formulas using mixed references**

mixed cell references with a fixed column reference for the first term and a fixed row reference for the second term

when copied to the range B3:F7, the fixed references remain unchanged and the relative references are shifted

values returned by each formula

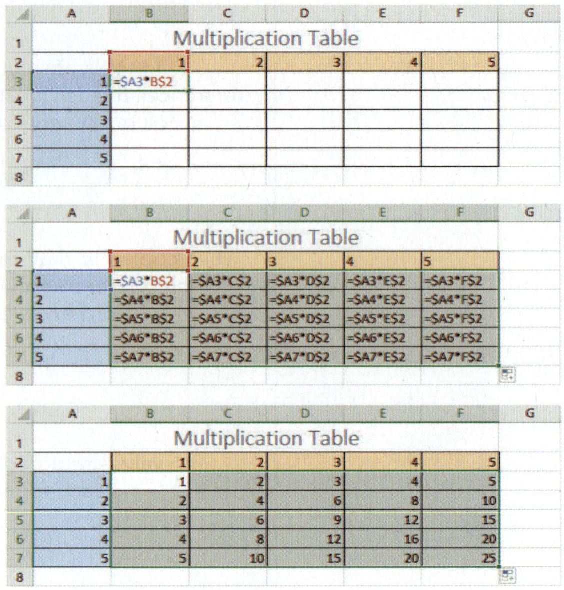

You will use relative and absolute references when you enter a formula in the Call Center Log worksheet.

Proskills

Problem Solving: When to Use Relative, Absolute, and Mixed Cell References

Part of effective workbook design is knowing when to use relative, absolute, and mixed cell references. Use relative references when you want to apply the same formula with input cells that share a common layout or pattern. Relative references are commonly used when copying a formula that calculates summary statistics across columns or rows of data values. Use absolute references when you want your copied formulas to always refer to the same cell. This usually occurs when a cell contains a constant value, such as a tax rate, that will be referenced in formulas throughout the worksheet. Mixed references are seldom used other than when creating tables of calculated values such as a multiplication table in which the values of the formula or function can be found at the intersection of the rows and columns of the table.

Entering an Absolute Cell Reference

Kiara's goal for the call center is to have every call answered within 15 seconds. To analyze how well the call center is meeting this goal, you will determine by how much each call meets or exceeds the 15-second goal.

To calculate the difference between the hold times and the 15-second goal:

1. In cell **B28**, enter **15** as the hold-time goal.
2. Scroll up the worksheet and in cell **L5**, enter the formula **=H5-$B$28** to subtract 15 seconds from the hold time, and then press **ENTER**. The cell

displays −10, indicating that the customer was on hold for 10 seconds less than the 15-second goal.

3. Drag the **fill handle** over the range **L5:L515** to extend the formula through the rest of the call log. The final call has a value of 12, indicating that the caller was on hold for 12 seconds more than the hold-time goal that Kiera established.

4. Click the **Auto Fill Options** button, and then click the **Fill Without Formatting** option button to retain the banded rows.

5. Scroll up the worksheet, and then click cell **L5** to deselect the range. See Figure 3–26.

Figure 3–26 Formulas with absolute references

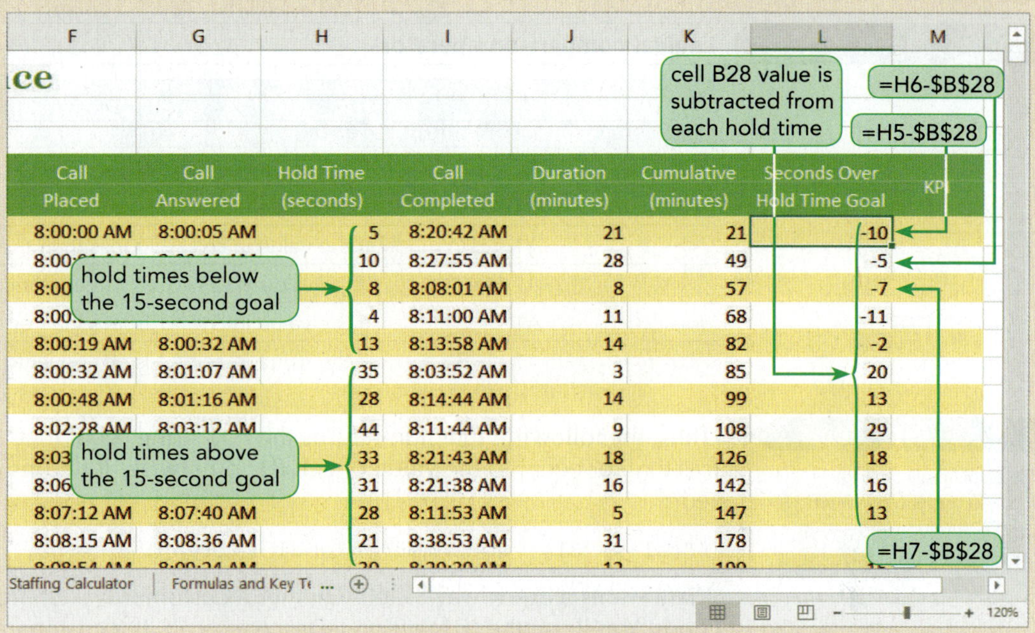

Because the formula uses an absolute reference to cell B28, it will always point to cell B28 even as it's extended through the range L5:L515. Thus, the formula in cell L6 is =H6-$B$28, the formula in L7 is =H7-$B$28, and so forth.

You can easily cycle between relative, absolute, and mixed cell references in formulas by selecting the cell reference in the formula and pressing F4 while in Edit mode. For example, if you type the formula =A4 and then press F4, the formula changes to =$A$4. Pressing F4 again changes the formula to =A$4. Pressing F4 a third time changes the formula to =$A4. Pressing F4 a fourth time returns the formula to =A4 where the cycle begins again.

Kiara wants to know how many calls were on hold for longer than 15 seconds. One way of answering this question is with a logical function.

Working with the IF Logical Function

A **logical function** is a function that returns one of two possible values depending on whether a given condition is true or false. The condition is entered as an expression, such as A5=3. If cell A5 is equal to 3, the condition is true; if cell A5 is not equal to 3, the condition is false.

You use conditional expressions in logical functions like the IF function

```
IF(logical_test, value_if_true, [value_if_false])
```

Tip

If no *value_if_false* argument is provided, the IF function returns the value FALSE if the condition is false.

where ***logical_test*** is a condition that is either true or false, ***value_if_true*** is the value returned by the function if the condition is true, and *value_if_false* is an optional argument containing the value if the condition is false. For example, the following function returns a value of 100 if A1=B1, otherwise it returns a value of 50:

```
IF(A1=B1, 100, 50)
```

The *value_if_true* and the *value_if_false* in the IF function can also be cell references. For example, the following function returns the value of cell C1 if the condition is true, otherwise it returns the value of cell D1:

```
IF(A1=B1, C1, D1)
```

The = symbol in IF function is a **comparison operator**, which is an operator expressing the relationship between two values. Figure 3–27 describes other comparison operators that can be used with logical functions.

Figure 3–27 **Logical comparison operators**

Operator	Expression	Tests
=	A1 = B1	If value in cell A1 is equal to the value in cell B1
>	A1 > B1	If the value in cell A1 is greater than the value in cell B1
<	A1 < B1	If the value in cell A1 is less than the value in cell B1
>=	A1 >= B1	If the value in cell A1 is greater than or equal to the value in cell B1
<=	A1 <= B1	If the value in cell A1 is less than or equal to the value in cell B1
<>	A1 <> B1	If the value in cell A1 is not equal to the value in cell B1

Tip

To apply multiple logical conditions, you can nest one IF function within another.

Thus, the following function returns the text string "goal met" if the value in cell A1 is less than or equal to the value of cell B1; otherwise, it returns the text string "goal failed":

```
IF(A1 <= B1, "goal met", "goal failed")
```

Kiara wants a quick way to tell whether a customer was on hold longer than 15 seconds. You'll use the IF function to test each call. If a customer's hold time is greater than zero, the IF function will return a value of 1 (a long hold time); otherwise, it will return a value of 0 (a short hold time).

To use the IF function to indicate if a call exceeds the hold-time goal:

1. Click cell **M5** to select it.
2. On the ribbon, click the **Formulas** tab, and then in the Function Library group, click the **Logical** button to display a list of all of the logical functions.
3. Click **IF** to open the Function Arguments dialog box for the IF function.
4. In the Logical_test box, type the expression **L5>0** to test whether the value in cell L5 is greater than 0.
5. Type **1** in the Value_if_true box, and then type **0** in the Value_if_false box.
6. Click **OK** to enter the formula **=IF(L5>0, 1, 0)** into cell M5. The value 0 appears in cell M5, indicating that this first call was within the 15-second hold-time goal.
7. Drag the **fill handle** over the range **M5:M515** to extend the formula through the rest of the call log.

8. Click the **Auto Fill Options** button, and then click the **Fill Without Formatting** option button to retain the banded rows.
9. Scroll up the worksheet and click cell **M5** to deselect the range. See Figure 3–28.

Figure 3–28 **IF function that evaluates customer hold time**

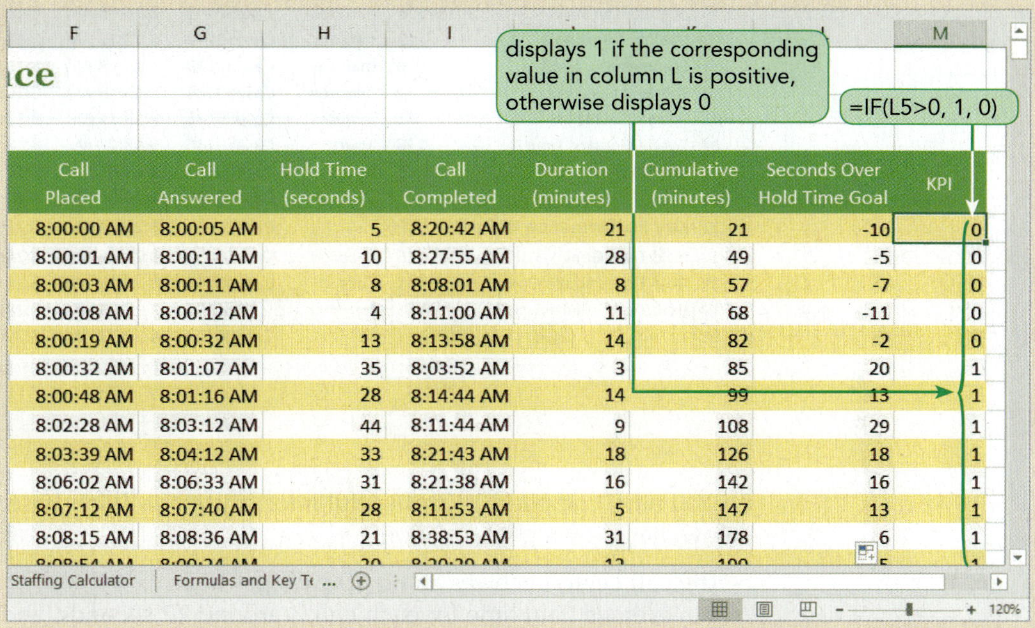

Businesses often report success in terms of a **key performance indicator** (**KPI**), which measures the achievement of a specific goal. The percentage of customers experiencing long hold times is one KPI that Kiara uses to measure the success of the call center. A high percentage would indicate that the call center needs to improve its service.

You can count the number of calls that exceeded the 15-second goal by summing up the values in column M, because every call is graded as either a 0 (success) or 1 (failure). You'll use the SUM function to determine how many calls placed to the call center get a failing grade.

To sum the number of failed calls:

1. Scroll the worksheet down and in cell **B29**, enter the formula **=SUM(M:M)** to add all the values in column M. Cell B29 displays 441, indicating that 441 customers had hold times longer than 15 seconds.
2. In cell **B30**, enter the formula **=B29/B8** to calculate the percentage of calls with long hold times by dividing the number of failed calls by the total number of calls.
3. Click cell **B30**, and then on the Home tab, in the Number group, click the **Percent Style** button % (or press **CTRL+SHIFT+%**) to display the value as a percentage. The cell shows that 86% of the calls failed the 15-second hold-time goal. See Figure 3–29.

Figure 3–29 **Calls that fail the hold-time goal**

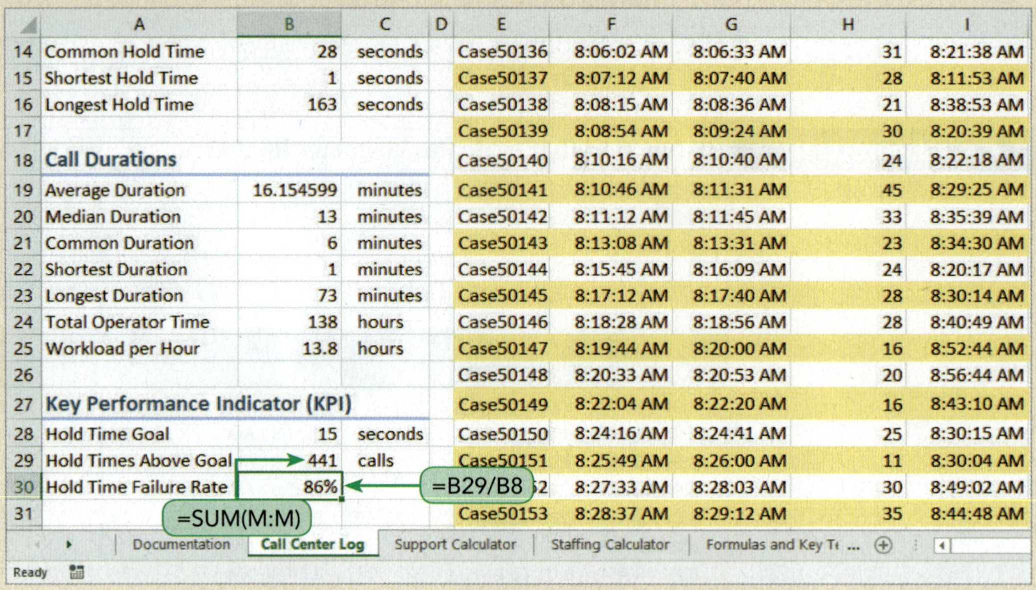

You have compiled a lot of useful information for Kiara. Based on your analysis, you know the following information:

- The call center receives about 50 calls per hour.
- The average hold time for each call is around 27 seconds, and 86% of calls are not answered within Kiara's 15-second goal.
- Conversations last around 6 minutes, but can sometimes take over an hour. The average conversation lasts around 16 minutes.
- It takes about 14 hours of operator time every hour to handle the call center traffic.

Kiara wants to know whether customer support can be improved by increasing the number of available operators. And, if so, how many operators are needed to provide effective and efficient service? You will answer those questions next.

Insight

Using the IFERROR Function to Catch Error Values

An error value does not mean that your formula is wrong. Some errors appear simply because you have not yet entered any data into the workbook. For example, if you apply the AVERAGE function to range that does not yet contain any data values, the #DIV/0! error value appears because Excel cannot calculate averages without data. However, as soon as you enter your data, the #DIV/0! error value disappears, replaced with the calculated average.

Error values of this type can make your workbook confusing and difficult to read. One way to hide them is with the following **IFERROR function**

```
IFERROR (Value, Value_if_error)
```

where ***Value*** is the value to be calculated and ***Value_if_error*** is the value returned by Excel if any error is encountered in the function. For example, the following IFERROR function returns the average of the values in column F, but if no values have yet been entered in that column, it returns a blank text string (""):

```
IFERROR(AVERAGE(F:F),"")
```

Using this logical function results in a cleaner workbook that is easier to read and use without distracting error values.

Formatting Input, Calculated, and Output Values

It's important in your worksheets to identify which cells contain input values for formulas and functions, which cells contain calculations, and which cells contain primary output values. Formatting cells based on their purpose helps others correctly use and interpret your worksheet. The Cell Styles gallery includes cell styles to format cells containing input, calculation, and output values.

You will use these styles in the Support Calculator worksheet in which you will estimate the number of operators that the call center needs to provide good customer service. Before entering any values or formulas in the Support Calculator worksheet, you'll format the purpose of each cell using built-in cell styles in the Cell Styles gallery.

To apply cell styles to input, calculated, and output values:

1. Go to the **Support Calculator** worksheet.
2. Select the range **B6:B9**. You will format this range as input cells.
3. On the Home tab, in the Styles group, click the **Cell Styles** button to open the Cell Styles gallery.
4. In the Data and Model section, click the **Input** cell style. The selected cells are formatted with light blue font on a light orange background, identifying these cells as containing input values for the Support Calculator.
5. Select the nonadjacent range **B10,B13:B15**. These cells will contain calculations that will be entered later.
6. Format the selected cells with the **Calculation** cell style located in the Data and Model section of the Cell Styles gallery. The cells with the calculated values are formatted with a bold orange font on a light gray background.
7. Select the range **B18:B21**. These cells will contain the primary output measures used to predict the efficiency of the call center.
8. Format the selected range with the **Output** cell style located in the Data and Model section of the Cell Styles gallery. The cells with the calculated values are formatted with a bold dark gray font on a light gray background.

Now that the different types of cells in the Support Calculator worksheet are formatted distinctly, it is easier to enter the data about the call center in the correct cells. You'll enter the input and calculated values.

To enter the input values and calculated values:

1. In cell **B6**, enter the input value **50** as the anticipated calls per hour to the center.
2. In cell **B7**, enter the input value **14** as number of operators available to answer calls.
3. In cell **B8**, enter the input value **15** as the desired hold time in seconds.
4. In cell **B9**, enter the input value **16** as the average call duration in minutes.

5. In cell **B10**, enter the formula **=B9/60** to calculate the average call duration in hours. The formula returns the value 0.27 hours.
6. In cell **B13**, enter the formula **=B6*B10** to calculate the number of operator hours required each hour to handle the call traffic. The formula returns 13.33 operator hours.
7. In cell **B14**, enter the formula **=B13/B7** to calculate the anticipated percentage of operators who will be occupied with calls at any one time. At the current workload, 95.24% of the operators will be occupied.
8. In cell **B15**, enter the formula **=1-B14** to display the percentage of operators who will be free at any one time. In this case, 4.76% of the operators will be free. See Figure 3–30.

Figure 3–30 Formatted input and calculated values

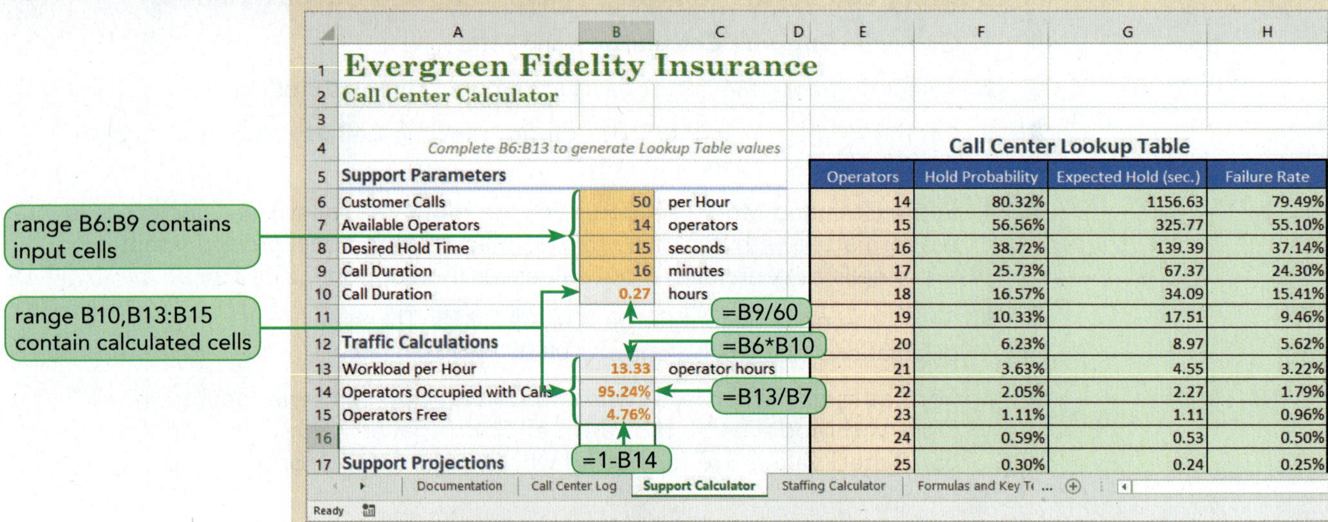

With the input and calculated values entered into the worksheet, you will next determine the optimal number of operators to handle the call volume. To do that analysis, you will use a lookup function.

Looking Up Data

A **lookup function** retrieves a value matching a specified condition from a table of data. For example, a lookup function can be used to retrieved a tax rate from a tax table for a given annual income or to retrieve a shipping rate for a specified delivery date.

The table storing the data to be retrieved is called a **lookup table**. The first row or column of the table contains the **lookup values**, which are the values that are being looked up. If the lookup values are in the first row, the table is a horizontal lookup table; if the values are in the first column, the table is a vertical lookup table. The remaining rows or columns contain the data values retrieved by the lookup function, known as **return values**.

Figure 3–31 displays a vertical lookup table for retrieving data about Evergreen Fidelity Insurance employees. The first column contains the lookup value (Employee ID) and the other columns contain return values (First Name, Last Name,

Department). In this example, the Employee ID "E54-0-2138" corresponds to the entry in the fifth row of the table and the employee's last name found in the third column is returned.

Figure 3–31 Exact match returned from a lookup table

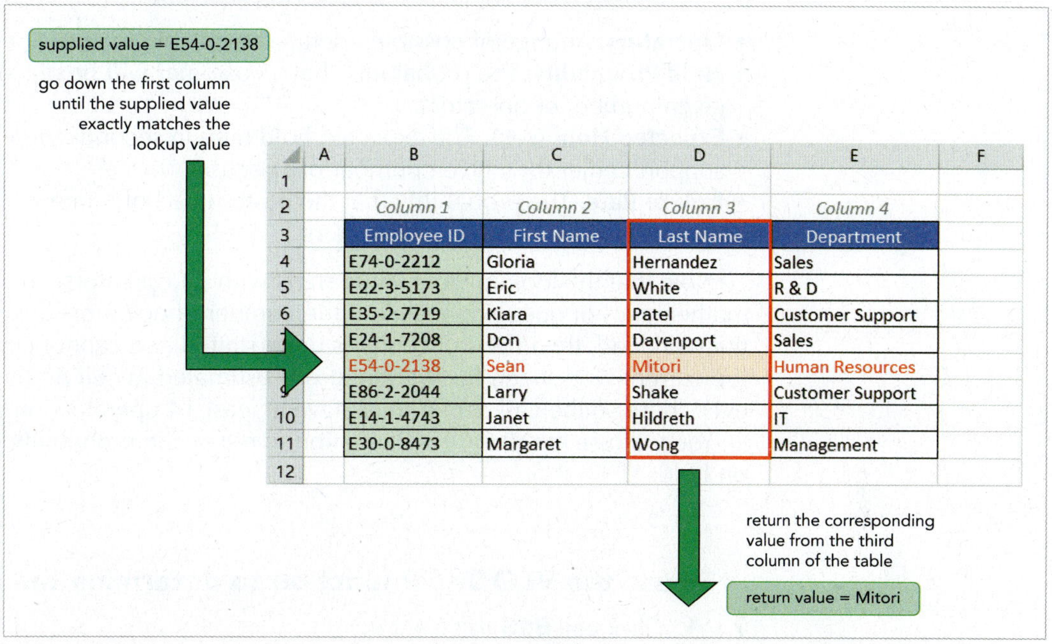

Lookup tables can be constructed for exact match or approximate match lookups. In an **exact match lookup**, like the one shown in Figure 3–31, the lookup value must exactly match one of the values from the table's first column (or first row for a horizontal lookup table). An **approximate match lookup** is used when the lookup value falls within a range of values in the first column or row. You will work only with exact match lookups in this module.

Finding an Exact Match with the VLOOKUP Function

To retrieve a return value from a vertical lookup table, you use the VLOOKUP function

```
VLOOKUP(lookup_value,table_array,col_index_num,[range_lookup=TRUE])
```

where ***lookup_value*** is the lookup value to find in the first column of the lookup table, ***table_array*** is the reference to the lookup table, and ***col_index_num*** is the number of the column in the lookup table that contains the return value. Keep in mind that ***col_index_num*** refers to the number of the column within the lookup table, not the worksheet column. So, a ***col_index_num*** of 2 refers to the lookup table's second column no matter where the lookup table is located within the worksheet.

Tip

If the VLOOKUP function cannot find a match in the lookup table, it returns the #N/A error value.

Finally, *range_lookup* is an optional argument that specifies whether the lookup should be done as an exact match or an approximate match. The default value of *range_lookup* is TRUE, creating an approximate match. To create an exact match, enter a value of FALSE for the *range_lookup* argument.

The following VLOOKUP function performs the exact match lookup shown in Figure 3–31 with "E54-0-2138" as the lookup value, returning the value from the third column of the table:

```
VLOOKUP("E54-0-2128", B3:E11, 3, FALSE)
```

Kiara included a lookup table in the range E5:H55 of the Support Calculator worksheet. The table was generated by Evergreen Fidelity Insurance statisticians using a branch of mathematics called "queuing theory" to predict call center performance assuming a given number of operators. A study of queueing theory is beyond the scope of this module, but you can use the results shown from the lookup table in your report.

The lookup table contains the following columns:

- **Operators.** A range of possible operators available to answer calls.
- **Hold Probability.** The probability that a customer will be placed on hold assuming a given number of operators.
- **Expected Hold (sec).** The expected hold time in seconds for a customer calling the support center for a given number of operators.
- **Failure Rate.** The probability that the customer's hold time will exceed the hold-time goal for a given number of operators.

Note that the lookup table value starts with 14 operators. This is due to the mathematics of queueing theory. If the number of operators answering calls is less than the workload, then the call center is understaffed and cannot keep up with demand. In the current worksheet, the workload was estimated in cell B13 as 13.33 operator hours every hour so the call center must have at least 14 operators on hand at all times.

You will use the VLOOKUP function to return the probability of a customer waiting on hold.

To use the VLOOKUP function to determine the hold probability:

1. Click cell **B18** to select it.
2. On the ribbon, click the **Formulas** tab, and then in the Formula Library group, click the **Insert Function** button. The Insert Function dialog box opens.
3. Click the **Or select a category** box, and then click **Lookup & References** in the list of function categories.
4. Scroll down the Select a function box, and then double-click **VLOOKUP**. The Function Arguments dialog box opens.
5. In the Lookup_value box, type **$B$7** to reference the number of operators entered in cell B7.
6. In the Table_array box, type **$E$5:$H$32** to reference the vertical lookup table containing the queueing theory predictions.
7. In the Col_index_num box, type **2** to return a matching value from the lookup table's second column.
8. In the Range_lookup box, type **FALSE** to do an exact match lookup. You have entered all of the arguments for the VLOOKUP function. See Figure 3–32.

Be sure to use FALSE to do an exact match lookup.

Figure 3–32 Function Arguments dialog box for the VLOOKUP function

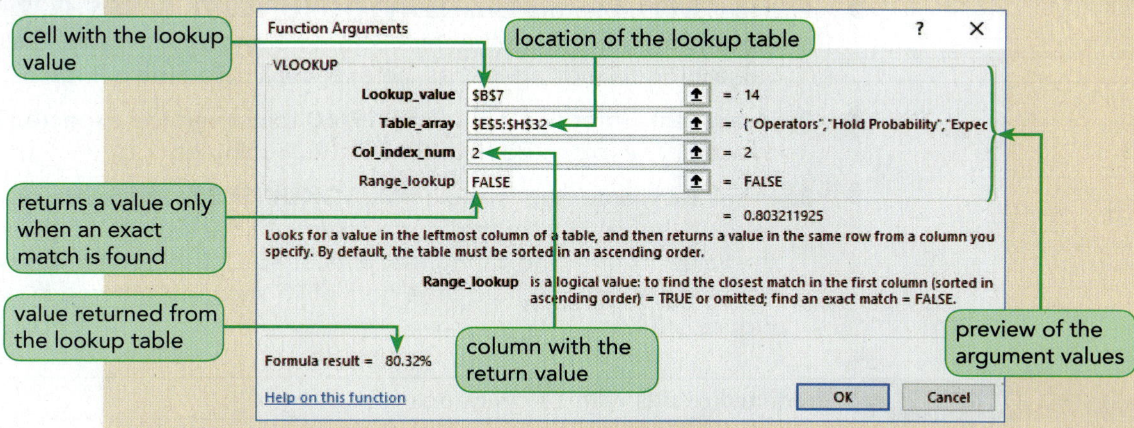

9. Click **OK**. The formula `=VLOOKUP($B$7, $E$5:$H$32, 2, FALSE)` is entered into cell B18, returning a value of 80.32%. See Figure 3–33.

Figure 3–33 VLOOKUP function results

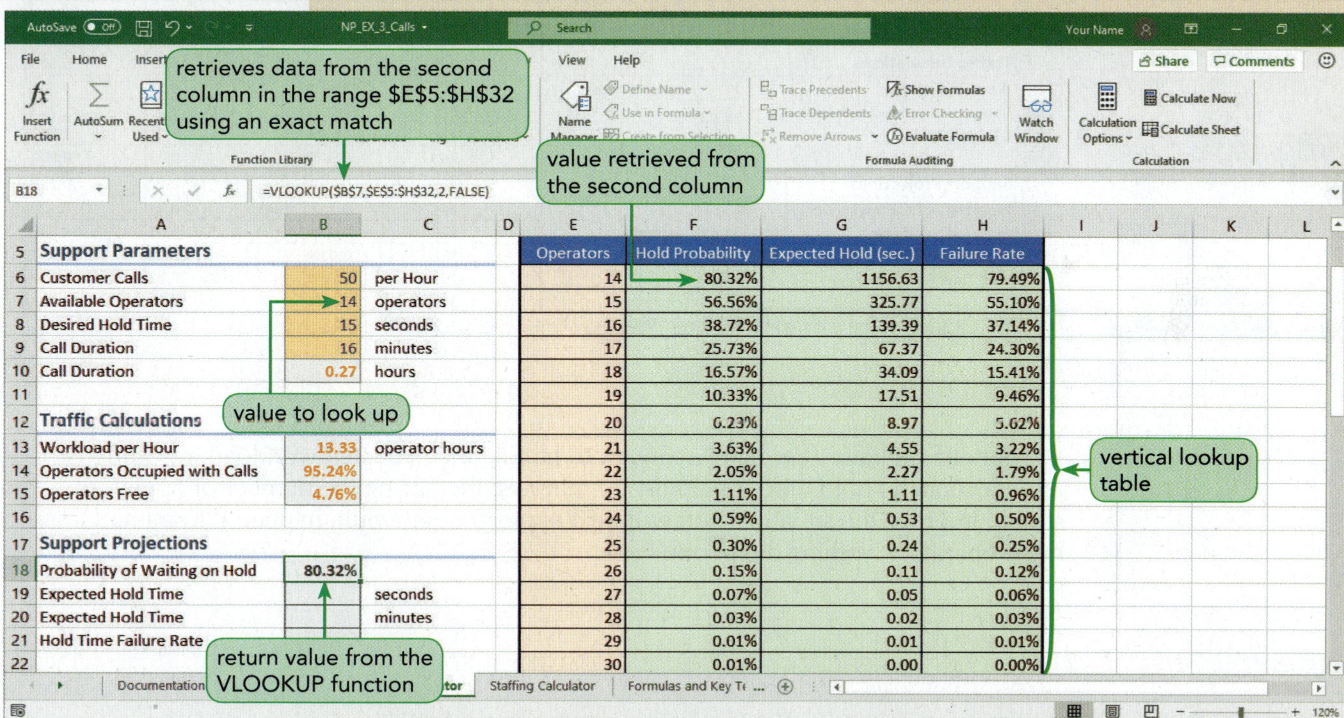

Trouble? If you cannot select or view the formulas in the lookup table, don't worry. The cells in the range E5:H55 have been locked and protected to prevent users from inadvertently changing their contents.

Based on the result of the VLOOKUP function, queueing theory estimates that 80.32% of the customers will have to wait on hold if only 14 operators are working the call center. You'll use the VLOOKUP function again to retrieve other call center predictions assuming only 14 available operators.

To use the VLOOKUP function for the other output cells:

1. In cell **B19**, enter the formula **=VLOOKUP($B$7, $E$5:$H$32, 3, FALSE)** to retrieve the value from the third column of the lookup table. Excel returns the value 1156.63 indicating that the expected hold time is 1156.63 seconds.
2. In cell **B20**, enter the formula **=B19/60** to convert the expected hold time to minutes. The expected hold time is 19.28 minutes.
3. In cell **B21**, enter the formula **=VLOOKUP($B$7, $E$5:$H$32, 4, FALSE)** to retrieve the value from the fourth column of the lookup table. Excel returns the value 79.49%, indicating that almost 80% of the customers will be on hold longer than the hold-time goal of 15 seconds, entered in cell B8. See Figure 3–34.

Figure 3–34 **Predicted results with 14 operators**

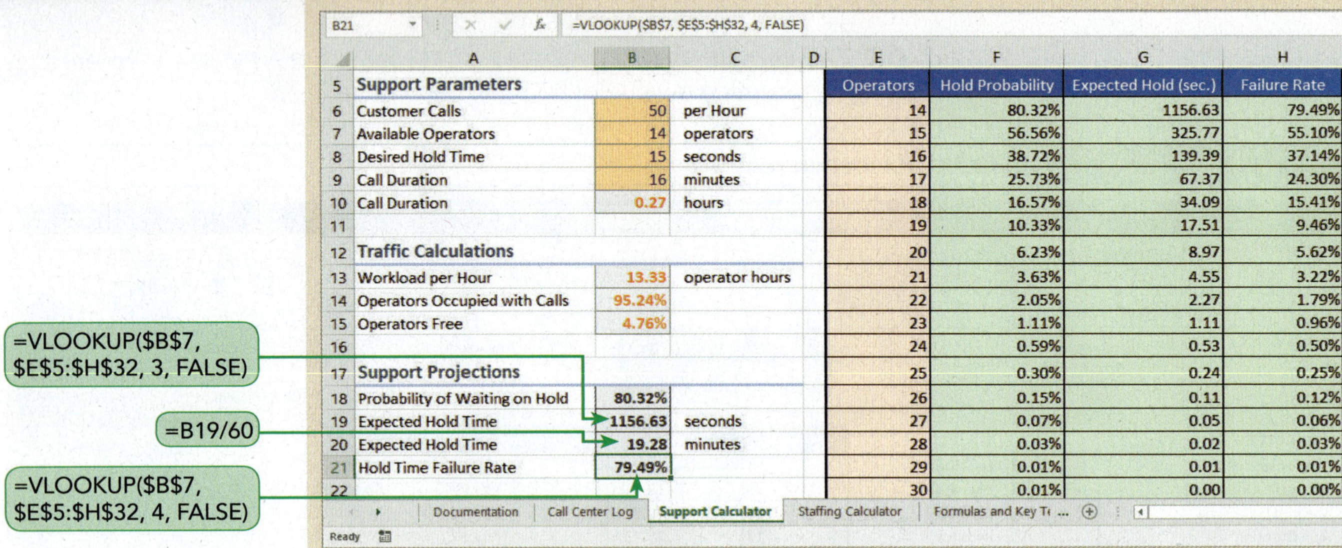

Fourteen operators are barely enough to handle the expected workload, resulting in unacceptable hold times of almost 20 minutes. Increasing the number of operators should improve the situation. You will next explore what would happen if Kiara had more operators working the phone lines.

Insight

Generating Random Data

For some projects you will want to simulate scenarios using randomly generated data. Excel provides the following RAND( ) function to create a random decimal between 0 and 1:

```
RAND()
```

To convert this random number to any decimal within a given range, apply the formula:

```
(top-bottom)*RAND()+bottom
```

where *bottom* is the bottom of the range and *top* is the top of the range. For example, the following expression generates a random decimal number between 10 and 50:

```
(50-10)*RAND()+10
```

To limit the random numbers to integers, apply the following RANDBETWEEN function:

```
RANDBETWEEN(bottom, top)
```

For example, to generate a random integer between 10 and 50, use the formula:

```
RANDBETWEEN(10, 50)
```

Random number functions are **volatile functions** in that they will automatically recalculate their values every time Excel does any calculation in the workbook. This means you will see a different set of random numbers with every new calculation in the workbook.

Performing What-If Analyses with Formulas and Functions

A **what-if analysis** explores the impact that changing input values has on calculated values and output values. By exploring a wide range of different input values, you will achieve a better understanding of your data and its implications.

Using Trial and Error

One way to perform a what-if analysis is by **trial and error** where you change one or more of the input values to see how they affect other cells in the workbook. Trial and error requires some guesswork as you estimate which values to change and by how much. You'll use trial and error to investigate how changing values such as the average call duration or number of operators impacts the call center operation.

To investigate call center scenarios using trial and error:

1. In cell **B9**, enter **11** to change the average call duration from 16 minutes to 11 minutes. With a shorter average call duration, the probability of waiting on hold drops to 10.06% (cell B18) and the expected hold time drops to 13.74 seconds (cell B19). Handling calls more efficiently will greatly improve the customer experience with the call center.
2. In cell **B9**, restore the value to **16** minutes because Kiara believes that the operators cannot successfully wrap up calls faster than the 16-minute average.
3. In cell **B7**, enter **18** to increase the number of operators at the call center. With 18 operators and average call durations of 16 minutes, the probability of callers waiting for an operator is 16.57% with an expected hold time

of 34.09 seconds. Kiara thinks this might still be too long, but additional operators would improve the situation markedly.

4. In cell **B7**, enter **25** to further increase the number of operators. With even more operators, the probability of customers being put on hold drops to 0.30% with expected hold time of 0.24 seconds. In other words, with 25 operators calls to support center will be almost always answered immediately. See Figure 3–35.

Figure 3–35 **Increased number of operators**

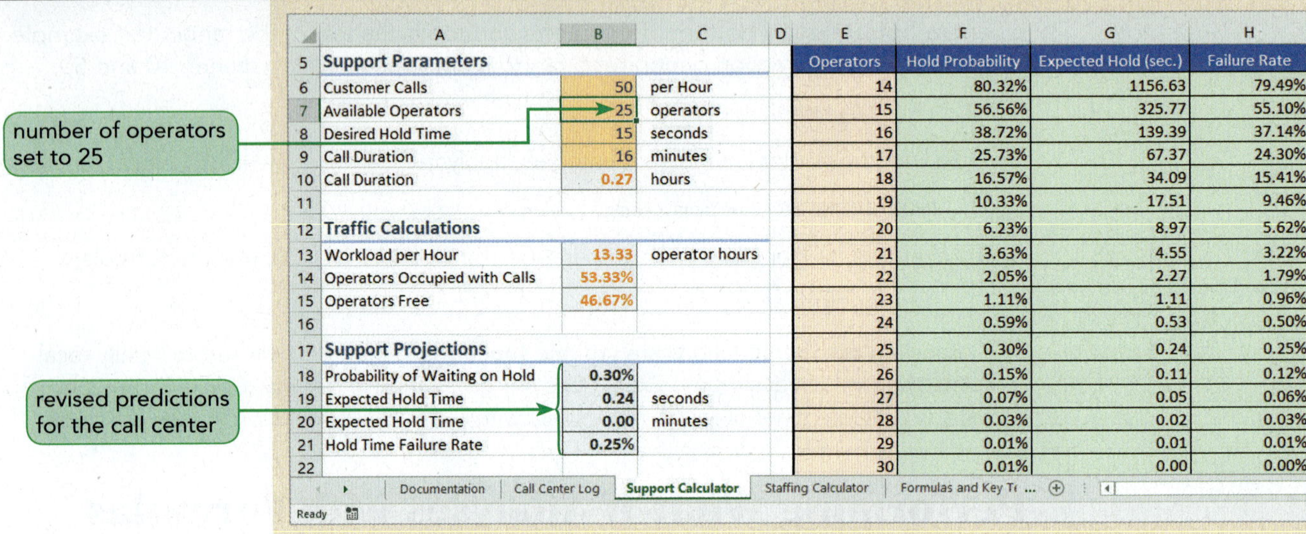

At some point, increasing the number of operators will no longer be cost effective as more operators will be idle waiting for the next call. Kiara believes having 25 operators on call at all hours provides the right balance of customer support and busy operators. Kiara wants to determine how many staff members are needed to ensure that 25 operators are available for every shift.

Staff size is affected by what is known in business as "shrinkage" in which the number of available employees to perform a task is reduced due to illness, vacations, and competing duties like staff meetings. For example, if half of the company's operators are absent due to shrinkage, to get 25 operators working the phones Kiara would have to hire a staff of 50. The general formula to calculate the size of the staff for a given level of shrinkage is

$$\text{staff size} = \frac{\text{required employees}}{1 - \%\text{absent}}$$

where *required employees* is the number of employees needed at any one time and *%absent* is the percentage of available employees that will be absent due to shrinkage. To determine the value of *%absent*, you calculate the total hours in which a typical employee is absent divided by the total hours of work that need to be covered.

Kiara created a Staffing Calculator worksheet to calculate the shrinkage factor for the operator staff and determine the staff size needed to compensate for shrinkage. First, you'll calculate the total hours that a typical operator works during the year and the number of working hours that operator will spend not answering customer support calls.

To calculate the total hours a typical operator works:

1. Go to the **Staffing Calculator** worksheet.
2. In cell **B9**, enter the formula **=B5*B6-B7** to calculate the total working days per year less days in which the call center is closed for holidays. The formula returns 253.5, indicating the call center is open 253 and half days per year.
3. In cell **B10**, enter the formula **=B9*B8** to multiply the number of days in which the call center is open by the number of hours per working day. The formula returns 2028, indicating that the call center is open 2028 hours per year.
4. In cell **B15**, enter the formula **=(B13+B14)*B8** to multiply the number of days allotted for vacation and sick leave by the number of hours per working day. The formula returns 160 hours, indicating that 160 working hours will be lost to vacation and sick leave.
5. In cell **B20**, enter the formula **=B9*(B18+B19)** to multiply the number of days in which the center is open by the number of hours spent on breaks and staff meetings. The formula returns 570.375 hours, indicating that 570.375 hours will be lost per year to duties that do not involve answering customer calls. See Figure 3–36.

Figure 3–36 **Total operator hours**

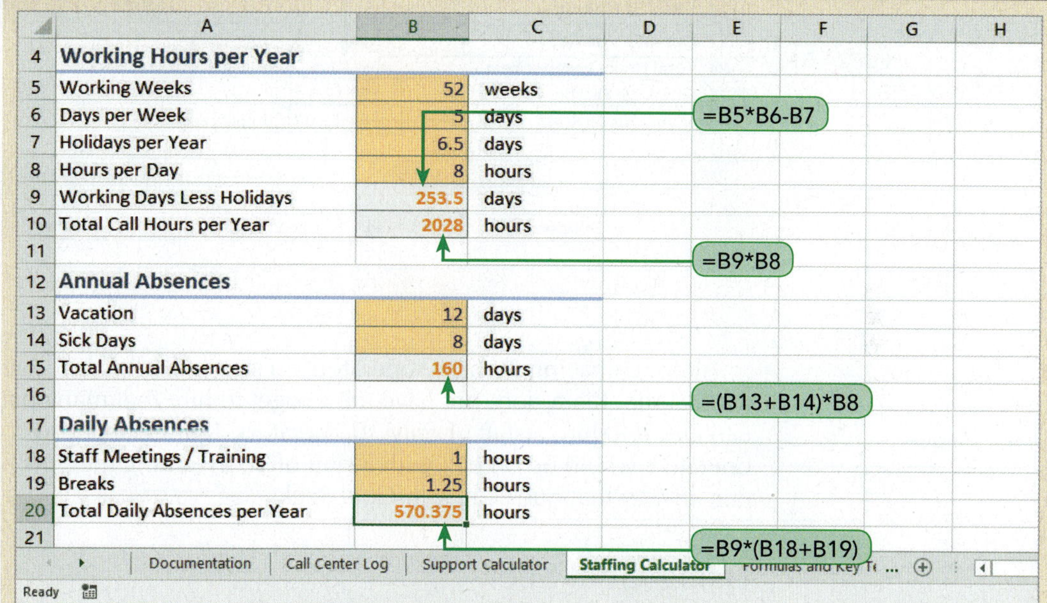

Next, you will calculate the shrinkage factor for staffing call center operators.

To calculate the shrinkage factor:

1. In cell **B23**, enter **25** as the number of operators Kiara wants available to answer calls.
2. In cell **B24**, enter the formula **=B15+B20** to add the total hours lost each year to absences to the total hours lost to daily tasks. The formula returns 730.375 hours, indicating that 730.375 hours will be lost each year to things not involved with answering customer calls.

3. In cell **B25**, enter the formula **=B24/B10** to divide the total hours lost by the total hours the call center will be open. The formula returns 36%, indicating that 36% of the available hours will not be spent on answering customer calls.
4. In cell **B26**, enter the formula **=B23/(1-B25)** to calculate the total staff required for shrinkage factor. The formula returns 39.07, indicating that Kiara would need a staff of 39 or 40 employees to cover the call center at the desired level of efficiency. See Figure 3–37.

Figure 3–37 Staff shrinkage calculations

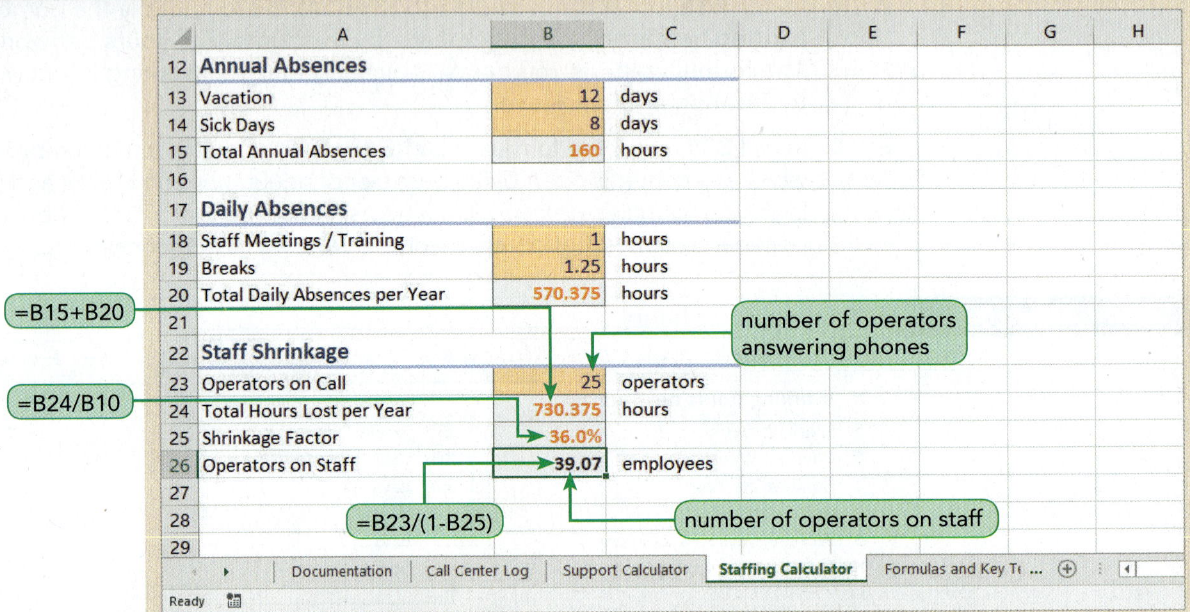

Although having 39 or 40 operators on staff will allow 25 operators to handle calls at any time, Kiara does not have the budget to hire that many people. The company can afford to hire a staff of only 30 operators. Kiara wants you to determine how many operators would be on call with a staff of 30 assuming the 36% shrinkage factor. You can answer that question with Goal Seek.

Using Goal Seek

Tip

Goal Seek can be used only with calculated numbers, not with text.

Goal Seek reverses the trial-and-error process by specifying an output value and working backward to find the input value needed to reach that goal. The output is always a calculated value and the input is always a constant that can be changed using the Goal Seek tool.

Reference

Performing What-If Analysis and Goal Seek

To perform a what-if analysis by trial and error:
- Change the value of a worksheet cell (the input cell).
- Observe its impact on one or more calculated cells (the result cells).
- Repeat until the desired results are achieved.

To perform a what-if analysis using Goal Seek:
- On the Data tab, in the Forecast group, click the What-If Analysis button, and then click Goal Seek.
- Select the result cell in the Set cell box, and then specify its value (goal) in the To value box.
- In the By changing cell box, specify the input cell.
- Click OK. The value of the input cell changes to set the value of the result cell.

In this situation, the output value is cell B26, which calculates the total staff size for the given shrinkage factor. The input value is the number of operators available at any one time to answer calls. You'll use Goal Seek to determine how many operators will be on call if the staff size is limited to 30 employees.

To use Goal Seek to set the staff size to 30 employees:

1. On the ribbon, click the **Data** tab.
2. In the Forecast group, click the **What-If Analysis** button, and then click **Goal Seek**. The Goal Seek dialog box opens.
3. In the Set cell box, type **B26** to specify the output cell whose value you will set using Goal Seek.
4. In the To value box, type **30** to set the value of cell B26 to 30.
5. In the By changing cell box, type **B23** to specify in the cell containing the input value that will be changed in order to reach your goal. See Figure 3–38.

Figure 3–38 Goal Seek dialog box

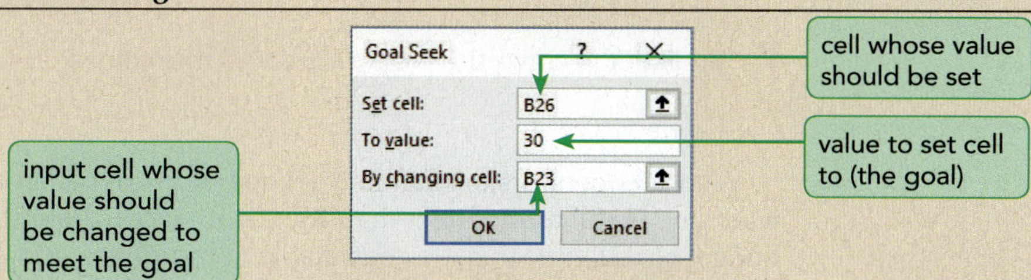

6. Click **OK**. The Goal Seek dialog box closes and the Goal Seek Status dialog box opens, indicating that Goal Seek has found a solution.
7. Click **OK**. The value in cell B23 changes to 19.1956361 and the value in cell B26 changes to goal value, 30. See Figure 3–39.

Figure 3–39 Staff shrinkage calculated by Goal Seek

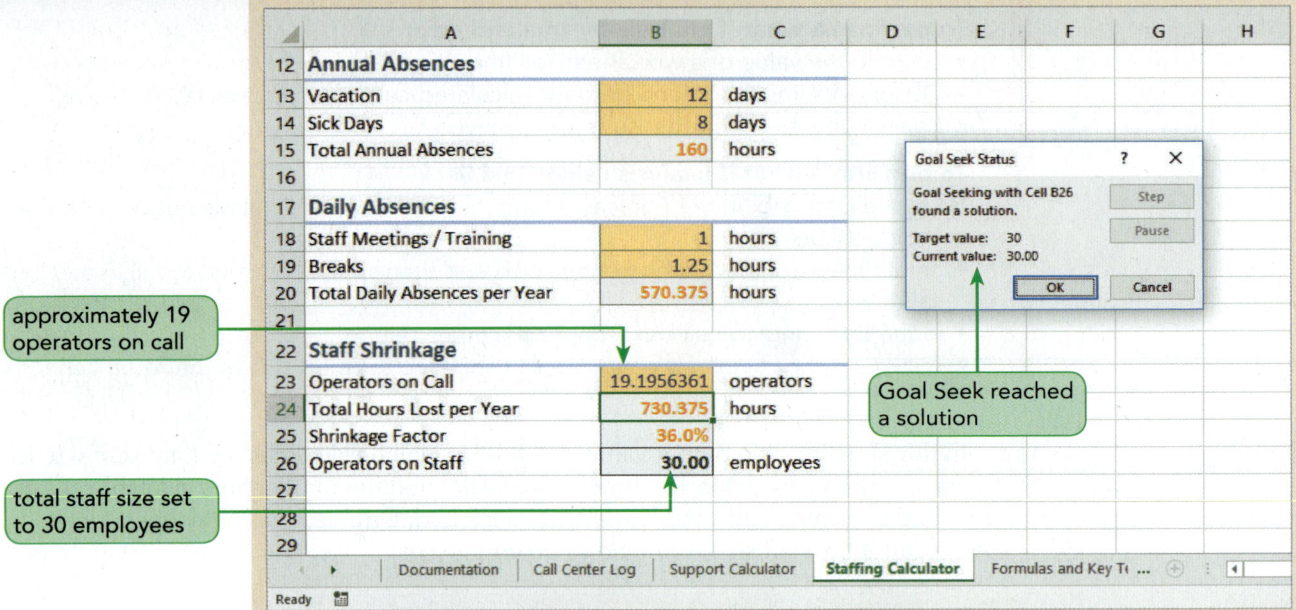

This analysis shows that with a staff of 30, Kiara will have approximately 19 operators available to answer calls at any time. Kiara wants to know whether 19 operators will be enough. To complete this analysis, you'll return to the Support Calculator worksheet and rerun the numbers to find the impact of limiting the call center to 19 available operators.

To calculate the performance of 19 operators:

1. Go to the **Support Calculator** worksheet.
2. In cell **B7**, enter **19** to set the number of call center operators. The results show that 10.33% of the customers will probably wait on hold (cell B18) for 17.51 seconds.
3. **sam** Save the workbook, and then close it.

With 30 operators on staff and 19 operators on call at any time, a 17- to 18-second wait time is still a bit longer than Kiara's 15-second wait-time goal. But given the budget constraints, this is a reasonable compromise. Kiara will review your analysis and consider other ways of improving the call center's performance while staying within budget.

Review

Session 3.2 Quick Check

1. Explain how to use the Quick Analysis tool to calculate a running total of the values in the range D1:D10.
2. You need to reference cell Q57 in a formula. What is its relative reference? What is its absolute reference? What are the two mixed references?
3. If cell R10 contains the formula =R1+R2 that is then copied to cell S20, what formula is entered in cell S20?
4. If cell R10 contains the formula =$R1+R$2 that is then copied to cell S20, what formula is entered in cell S20?
5. If cell Q3 is greater than cell Q4, you want to display the text "OK"; otherwise, display the text "RETRY". Write the formula that accomplishes this.
6. Write the formula to perform an exact match lookup with the lookup value from cell G5 using a vertical lookup table located in the range A1:F50. Return the value from the third column of the table.
7. What is the difference between a what-if analysis by trial and error and by Goal Seek?

Practice

Review Assignments

Data File needed for the Review Assignments: NP_EX_3-2.xlsx

Kiara has been asked to manage staffing for the claims center. The claims center manages requests from across the country, so its daily call volume is quite large. Kiara wants to determine the optimal number of agents to staff the claims center. You will examine sample data on the number of calls made to the claims center, the duration of each call, and the length of time customers will be put on hold before speaking to an agent. Complete the following:

1. Open the **NP_EX_3-2.xlsx** workbook located in the Excel3 > Review folder included with your Data Files. Save the workbook as **NP_EX_3_Claims** in the location specified by your instructor.
2. In the Documentation sheet, enter your name in cell B3 and the date in cell B4.
3. In cell B4, use the TODAY function to display the current date.
4. Claims are labeled sequentially according to the pattern Claim*number* where *number* is an integer that increases by 1 for each new claim. In the Claims Center Log worksheet, in cell E5, enter **Claim22515** and then use AutoFill to fill in the rest of the claim numbers. Fill in the values without formatting.
5. Enter the following calculations in the claims log (retaining the banded rows effect when you AutoFill formulas over rows):
   a. In column H, display the hold time in seconds for each call made to the claims center by calculating the difference between the column G and column F values and multiplying that difference by 24*60*60. Check your formula by verifying that the first hold time is 29 seconds.
   b. In column I, use the IF function to return the value **1** if the hold time from column H is greater than the hold-time goal in cell B10; otherwise, return the value **0**.
   c. In column K, calculate the length of the call with the agent in minutes by subtracting the values in column J from the values of column G, and then multiplying the difference by 24*60. Use the ROUNDUP function to round the value to the next highest integer. Check your formula by verifying that the first call duration is 21 minutes.
   d. In column L, use the Quick Analysis tool to calculate the running total of the call duration values in minutes. Remove the boldface font from the values. Check your work by verifying that the value in cell L1287 is 32597.
6. Enter formulas to calculate the following summary statistics:
   a. In cell B6, calculate the total number of calls to the claims center by using the COUNT function to count the values in column F. (Use the column reference F:F in the function.)
   b. In cell B7, divide the value in B6 by the value in B5 to calculate the calls per hour.
   c. In the range B11:B13, use the AVERAGE, MEDIAN, and MODE.SNGL functions to calculate the average, median, and mode of the hold times in column H.
   d. In cells B14 and B15, apply the MIN and MAX function to the values in column H to display the minimum and maximum hold times in seconds.
   e. In the range B18:B20, use the AVERAGE, MEDIAN, and MODE.SNGL functions to calculate the average, median, and mode of the call durations in column K.
   f. In cells B21 and B22, use the MIN and MAX functions to display the shortest and longest calls in minutes in column K.
   g. In cell B25, use the SUM function to calculate the total amount of agent time on the phone in column K, and then divide that value by 60 to express the total as hours. Use the ROUND function to round the total to the nearest whole hour.
   h. In cell B26, divide the value in B25 by the value in B5 to calculate the number of agent hours per hour. Use the ROUND function to round this calculation to the nearest tenth.
   i. In cell B27, determine the hold time failure rate by using the SUM function to total the values in column I and then dividing that sum by the total number of calls overall in cell B6.

7. Format the Claims Center Log worksheet as follows:
   a. Apply the Input cell style to cells B5 and B10.
   b. Apply the Calculation cell style to the nonadjacent range B6:B7,B11:B15,B18:B22.
   c. Apply the Output cell style to the range B25:B27.
8. In the Staffing Calculator worksheet, use Goal Seek to determine how many agents will be on call (cell B23) if the staff size is set to 92 agents (cell B26).
9. In the Claims Conclusion worksheet, enter the following constant values as integers (you do not have to use formulas):
   a. In cell B5, enter the expected calls per hour based on the calculated value in cell B7 on the Claims Center Log worksheet rounded up to the next highest integer.
   b. In cell B6, enter the number of available agents based on the calculation in cell B23 on the Staffing Calculator worksheet.
   c. In cell B7, enter **20** as the hold-time goal in seconds.
   d. In cell B8, enter the expected duration of the calls using the average value calculated in cell B18 of the Claims Center Log worksheet rounded up to the next highest integer.
10. In the Claims Conclusion worksheet, enter the following calculations to evaluate whether the number of agents on call will be sufficient to provide good customer service:
    a. In cell B9, divide the value in cell B8 by 60 to calculate the expected call duration in hours.
    b. In cell B12, calculate the Workload per Hour by multiplying the value in cell B5 by the value in cell B9.
    c. In cell B13, divide cell B12 by cell B6 to calculate the percent of agents occupied with calls.
11. Use the lookup table to the display the expected results from the claims center calls based on the number of operators and the call traffic:
    a. In cell B16, use the VLOOKUP function with cell B6 as the lookup value, the range E5:H32 as the reference to the lookup table, 2 as the column index, and FALSE as range_lookup type to return the hold probability for the given number of agents on call.
    b. In cell B17, enter the same VLOOKUP function but return the third column from the lookup table to show the expected hold time in seconds for the given number of agents on call (cell B6).
    c. In cell B18, divide the value in cell B17 by 60 to display the expected hold time in minutes.
    d. In cell B19, enter the same VLOOKUP function but return the fourth column from the lookup table to show the expected failure rate for the given number of agents.
12. In cell B22, write a short summary of your conclusions, answering the question: Is the number of agents that will be available on call sufficient to meet the demands of the claims center without sacrificing customer support performance?
13. Save the workbook, and then close it.

Apply

Case Problem 1

Data File needed for this Case Problem: NP_EX_3-3.xlsx

Multex Digital Liana Bonnet is a production quality control engineer for Multex Digital, a manufacturer of computer components. Part of Liana's job is to analyze batches of semiconductor wafers to ensure that the wafers are within design specifications. Wafers have to have a thickness of around 625 microns but that thickness will vary due to the inherit inaccuracy of the machines creating the wafers. Liana needs to ensure that machines are operating correctly because a machine that is constantly creating wafers that are too thin or too thick will have to be removed from the assembly line and retuned.

Liana will suspect a machine is out-of-alignment when the average wafer size of batch of wafers taken from that machine that operates beyond quality control limits. Control limits are established according to the following two equations:

$$\text{Lower Control Limit (LCL)} = \text{Xbar} - A_2 \times \text{Rbar}$$

$$\text{Upper Control Limit (UCL)} = \text{Xbar} + A_2 \times \text{Rbar}$$

where *Xbar* is the average wafer thickness from all sample batches, *Rbar* is the average range of wafer thickness from all sample batches, and A_2 is a constant that depends on the batch sample size.

Liana has recorded data from 50 machine batches with the sample size of each batch varying from 3 to 10 wafers. Liana wants you to report which of the 50 machines are no longer operating within control limits. Complete the following:

1. Open the **NP_EX_3-3.xlsx** workbook located in the Excel3 > Case1 folder included with your Data Files, and then save the workbook as **NP_EX_3_Quality** in the location specified by your instructor.
2. In the Documentation sheet, enter your name in cell B3. Use an Excel function to display the current date in cell B4.
3. In the Control Data worksheet, in the range A6:A55, use AutoFill to enter the text strings **Batch-1** through **Batch-50**. In the range B5:K5, use AutoFill to enter the text strings **Wafer-1** through **Wafer-10**.
4. Enter the following summary statistics to the worksheet:
   a. In cell M6, use the COUNT function to the count of number of values in the range B6:K6.
   b. In cell N6, calculate the difference between the maximum value in the range B6:K6 (using the MAX function) and the minimum value in the range B6:K6 (using the MIN function).
   c. In cell O6, use the AVERAGE function to calculate the average wafer size in the range B6:K6.
   d. Use AutoFill to extend the formulas in the range M6:O6 through the range M6:O55.
5. Calculate the following quality control statistics:
   a. In cell V5, display the value of *Xbar* by using the AVERAGE function to calculate the average of the values in column O.
   b. In cell V6, display the value of *Rbar* by using the AVERAGE function to calculate the average of the values in column N.
6. Do the following to complete a lookup table that you will use to calculate the lower and upper control limits for batch samples sizes of 2 up to 25:
   a. In cell W10, calculate the lower control limit by returning the value of cell V5 minus the value of cell V10 times cell V6. Use absolute references for cells V5 and V6 and a relative reference for cell V10. Check your formula by verifying that cell W10 shows the value 598.45.
   b. In cell X10, calculate the upper control limit by returning the value of cell V5 plus the value of cell V10 times cell V6. Once again, use absolute references for cells V5 and V6 and a relative reference for cell V10. Check your formula by verify that cell X10 shows the value 651.61.
   c. Use AutoFill to extend the formulas in the range W10:X10 over the range W10:X33 to show the lower and upper control limits for batch sizes ranging from 2 up to 25.
7. In cell P6, use the VLOOKUP function to display the lower control limit for the first batch from the assembly line using cell M6 as the lookup value, the range $U$9:$X$33 as the lookup table, 3 as the column index number, and FALSE for the range_lookup value. Extend the formula in cell P6 over the range P6:P55.

8. Repeat Step 7 in cell Q6 using 4 as the column index number in the VLOOKUP function to retrieve the upper control limit for the first batch and then extend the formula over the range Q6:Q55.
9. Determine whether a batch is not in control because the batch average falls below the lower control limit. In cell R6, use an IF function to test whether the value of sample average in cell O6 is less than the value of lower control limit in cell P6. If the condition is true, display "Out of Control"; otherwise, display "In Control" in the cell. Extend the formula over the range R6:R55 to indicate which batches are falling below the lower control limit for the machinery.
10. Repeat Step 9 for cell S6 except test for the condition that sample average in cell O6 is greater than the value of the upper control limit in cell Q6. Extend the formula over the range S6:S55 to indicate which batches are operating above the upper control limit.
11. Add conditional formatting to the range R6:S55, displaying any cell containing the text "Out of Control" in a red font on a light red background.
12. In cell A58, write your conclusions indicating which of the 50 machines on the assembly line are not within the control parameters set by Liana and indicate in what ways those machines are failing.
13. Save the workbook, and then close it.

Challenge

Case Problem 2

Data File needed for this Case Problem: NP_EX_3-4.xlsx

Canvas Scribe Michael Feinbaum is a production manager for Canvas Scribe, a manufacturer of digital games. To produce and release a quality game requires a team of programmers, animators, writers, and testers. Typically a game will take a year to develop from its initial planning stages to final release. Michael wants to create a production schedule for a new game called *Escape from Dunkirk*, to be released in time for holiday sales. To create this production schedule, you will use the WORKDAY and NETWORKDAYS functions described in Figure 3–18 and in the InSight box, "Date Calculations with Working Days." Complete the following:

1. Open the **NP_EX_3-4.xlsx** workbook located in the Excel3 > Case2 folder included with your Data Files, and then save the workbook as **NP_EX_3_Schedule** in the location specified by your instructor.
2. In the Documentation sheet, enter your name in cell B3. Use a function to enter the current date in cell B4.
3. In the Production Schedule worksheet, in cell B4, enter **9/12/2025** as an initial proposed start date for the project.
4. In cell B10, enter the formula **=B4** to reference the start date you entered in cell B4.
5. **Explore** In cell C10, calculate the date on which the Idea Development phase ends using the WORKDAY function. Use cell B10 as the starting date, cell D10 as the number of workdays, and the range $H$10:$H$29 as the reference to the holiday dates.
6. Use AutoFill to extend the formula in cell C10 to the range C10:C28 but do not extend the formatting.
7. In cell B5, enter the formula **=B28** to display the date on which the game will be released.
8. **Explore** In cell B6, use the NETWORKDAYS function to calculate the total number of working days that will be devoted to creating the *Escape from Dunkirk* game. Use cell B4 as the start_date, cell B5 as the end_date, and the range $H$10:$H$29 as the holidays argument.

9. In cell B7, calculate the total number of calendar days devoted to the project by taking the difference between the release date and the start date.
10. The game must be released no later than 10/12/2026 to take advantage of holiday sales. Use Goal Seek to determine the starting date that will meet this goal by entering cell B5 in the Set cell box, the date 10/12/2026 in the To value box, and cell B4 in the By changing cell box.
11. In cell D4, write a summary of your findings in developing this production schedule.
12. Save the workbook, and then close it.

Module 4

Analyzing and Charting Financial Data

Preparing an Investment Report

Objectives

Session 4.1

- Create a pie chart
- Format chart elements
- Create a line chart
- Work with chart legends
- Create a combination chart

Session 4.2

- Create a scatter chart
- Edit a chart data source
- Create a data callout
- Insert shapes and icons into a worksheet
- Create and edit a data bar
- Create and edit a group of sparklines

Case | **Philbin Financial Group**

Hideki Eto is an analyst for the Philbin Financial Group, a financial investment firm located in Phoenix, Arizona. Hideki needs to prepare financial reports that the company's clients will receive at meetings with a Philbin Financial Group advisor. One of the funds handled by the company is the Sunrise Fund, a large growth/large risk investment fund. Hideki needs you to summarize the fund's financial holdings as well as document its recent and long-term performance. Hideki has already entered the financial data into a workbook but wants you to finish the report. Because many clients are overwhelmed by tables of numbers, you will summarize the data using Excel financial charts and graphics.

Starting Data Files

Excel4 →

Module
NP_EX_4-1.xlsx

Review
NP_EX_4-2.xlsx

Case1
NP_EX_4-3.xlsx

Case2
NP_EX_4-4.xlsx

Session 4.1 Visual Overview:

A **chart legend** identifies the data markers associated with each data series.

The **chart title** is a descriptive label or name for the chart.

A **pie chart** presents data in the shape of a circle divided into slices with each slice representing a single data category.

A **data label** is text associated with an individual data marker, such as the percentage value next to a pie slice.

A **line chart** displays data values using a connected line rather than columns or bars.

Chart **gridlines** extend the values of the major or minor tick marks across the plot area.

Chart Elements

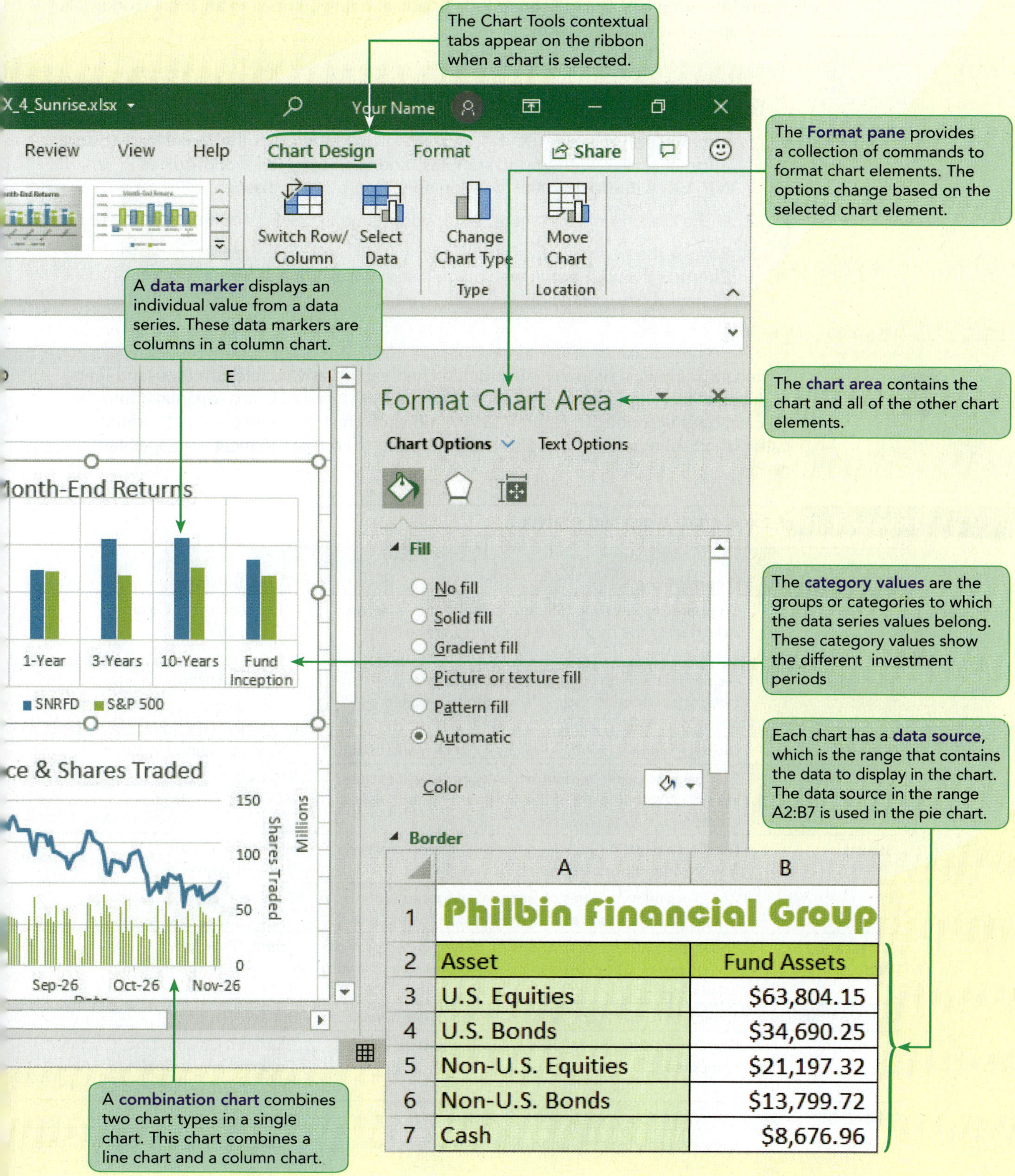

Getting Started with Excel Charts

In this module you will acquire the skills you need to analyze financial data using Excel **charts**, which are graphic elements that illustrate data. Hideki Eto from the Philbin Financial Group has already entered the financial data you need in an Excel workbook. You'll open that workbook now.

To open Hideki's workbook:

1. sam Open the **NP_EX_4-1.xlsx** workbook located in the **Excel4 > Module** folder included with your Data Files, and then save the workbook as **NP_EX_4_Sunrise** in the location specified by your instructor.
2. In the Documentation sheet, enter your name in cell B3 and the date in cell B4.
3. Review the financial data stored in the workbook and then return to the **Summary** worksheet in which you'll summarize data stored in the other sheets of the workbook.

In data analysis, a properly constructed chart can be as valuable as a thousand lines of financial facts and figures. Excel has more than 60 types of charts organized into the 10 categories described in Figure 4–1. Within each chart category are chart variations called chart subtypes. You can also design custom chart types to meet your specific needs.

Figure 4–1 Excel chart types and subtypes

Chart Category	Description	Chart Subtypes
Column or Bar	Compares values from different categories. Values are indicated by the height of the columns or the length of a bar.	2-D Column, 3-D Column, 2-D Bar, 3-D Bar
Hierarchy	Displays data that is organized into a hierarchy of categories where the size of the groups is based on a number.	Treemap, Sunburst
Waterfall or Stock	Displays financial cash flow values or stock market data.	Waterfall, Funnel, Stock
Line or Area	Compares values from different categories. Values are indicated by the height of the lines. Often used to show trends and changes over time.	2-D Line, 3-D Line, 2-D Area, 3-D Area
Statistic	Displays a chart summarizing the distribution of values from a sample population.	Histogram, Pareto, Box and Whisker
Pie	Compares relative values of different categories to the whole. Values are indicated by the areas of the pie slices.	2-D Pie, 3-D Pie, Doughnut
X Y (Scatter) or Bubble	Shows the patterns or relationship between two or more sets of values. Often used in scientific studies and statistical analyses.	Scatter, Bubble
Surface or Radar	Compares three sets of values in a three-dimensional chart.	Surface, Radar
Combo	Combines two or more chart types so the data can be compared.	Clustered Column-Line, Clustered Column-Line on Secondary Axis, Stacked Area-Clustered Column
Map	Compares data values across geographical regions.	Filled Map
PivotChart	Creates a chart summarizing data from a PivotTable.	PivotChart, PivotChart & PivotTable

Each chart type provides a different insight into your data. Figure 4–2 presents the same financial data displayed in pie chart, column chart, treemap chart, and a map chart. The chart you choose depends on what aspect of the data you are trying to highlight.

Figure 4–2 Data displayed with different Excel chart types

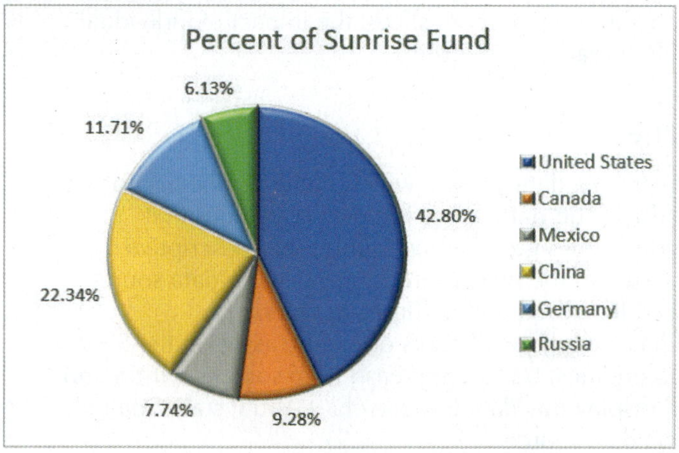

pie chart

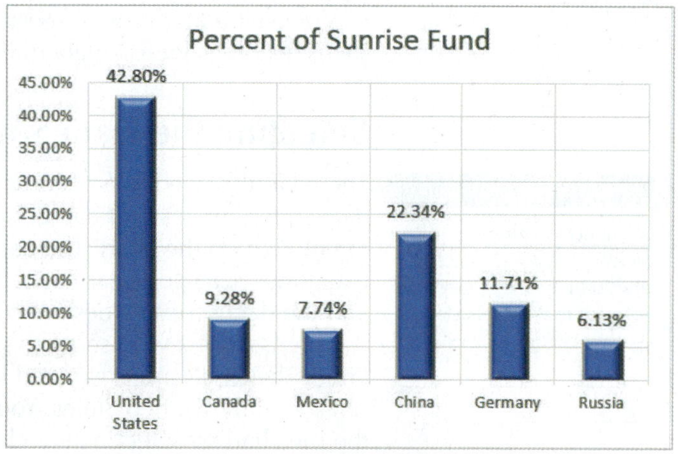

column chart

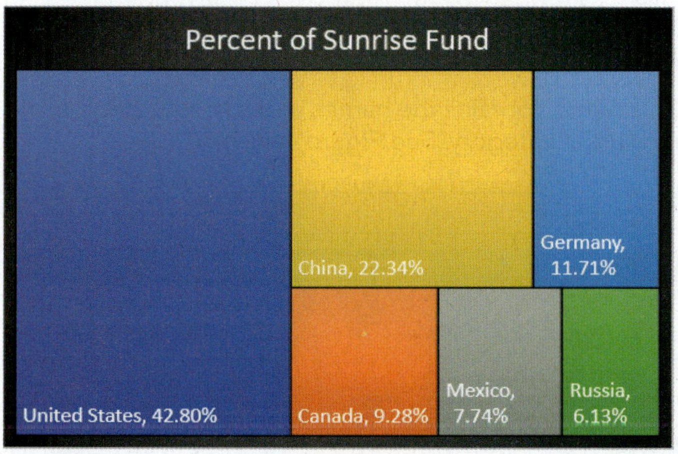

treemap chart

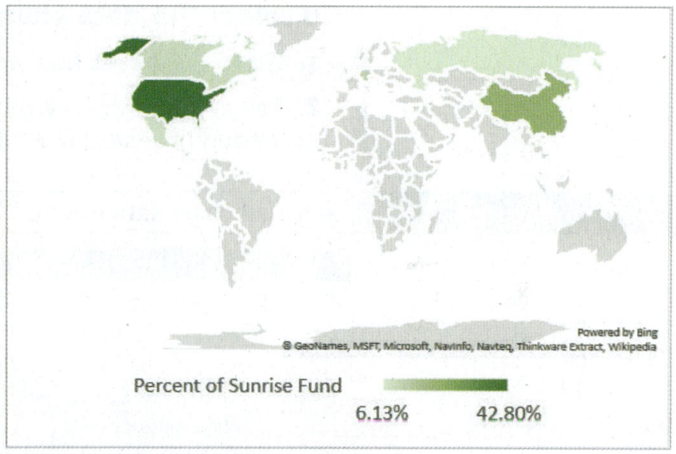

map chart

Creating a chart is a multistep process involving selecting the data to display, choosing the chart type best suited to that data, and finally formatting the chart's appearance to maximize the chart's impact. The first chart you will create for the Sunrise Fund report is a pie chart providing a visual breakdown of the fund's assets.

Reference

Creating a Chart

- Select the range containing the data you want to chart.
- On the Insert tab, in the Charts group, click the Recommended Charts button or a button representing the general chart type, and then click the chart you want to create; or click the Quick Analysis button, click the Charts category, and then click the chart you want to create.
- On the Chart Design tab, in the Location group, click the Move Chart button, select whether to embed the chart in a worksheet or place it in a chart sheet, and then click OK.
- Use the chart tools to format the appearance of individual chart elements.

Creating a Pie Chart

A pie chart presents data in a circle graph divided into slices with each slice representing a single data category. Categories whose data values take up larger percentages of the whole are represented with larger slices; categories that take up a smaller percentage of the whole are presented as smaller slices. Pie charts are most effective when the data can be divided into six or fewer categories. With more slices, the impact of individual slices becomes increasingly difficult to read and interpret.

Selecting the Data Source

Tip

Don't include row or column totals in the pie chart data because Excel will treat those totals as another category.

The data displayed in a chart come from a data source, which includes one or more data series and a set of category values. The **data series** is the actual values that are plotted on the chart. The category values groups those values into descriptive categories. Categories are usually listed in the first column or row of the data source and the data series values are placed in subsequent columns or rows.

The Asset Mix worksheet in Hideki's workbook breaks down the assets in the Sunrise Fund. The assets are organized into equities, bonds, and cash from sources within and outside of the United States. You'll display this data in a pie chart. You'll start creating the pie chart by selecting the chart's data source.

To select the data source for the pie chart:

1. Go to the **Asset Mix** worksheet.
2. Select the range **A4:B9**. This range contains the names of the assets and the amount invested within each asset category. See Figure 4–3.

Figure 4–3 Selected chart data source

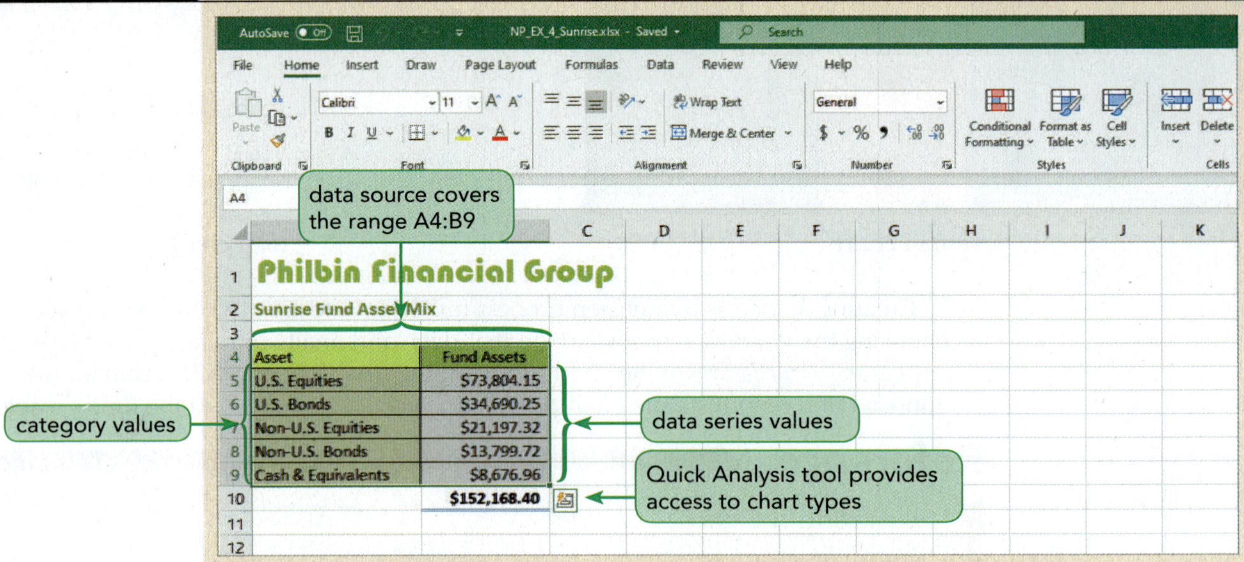

The selected data source covers two columns. The categories in the first column (Asset) will identify each pie slice and the data series in the second column (Fund Assets) will set the size of each slice.

Charting with the Quick Analysis Tool

After you select a data source, the Quick Analysis tool appears in the lower-right corner of the selection. The Charts category in the Quick Analysis tool displays chart types that are appropriate for the selected data source. For this data source, a pie chart provides a good way to compare the relative amount that the Sunrise Fund invests in five asset categories. You'll use the Quick Analysis tool to generate the pie chart for Hideki.

To create a pie chart with the Quick Analysis tool:

1. With the range A4:B9 still selected, click the **Quick Analysis** button in the lower-right corner of the selected range (or press **CTRL+Q**) to open the Quick Analysis tool.
2. Click the **Charts** category. The chart types you will most likely want to use with the selected data source are listed.
3. Point to each chart type to see a preview and a description of the data rendered as that chart. See Figure 4–4.

Figure 4–4 Charts category of the Quick Analysis tool

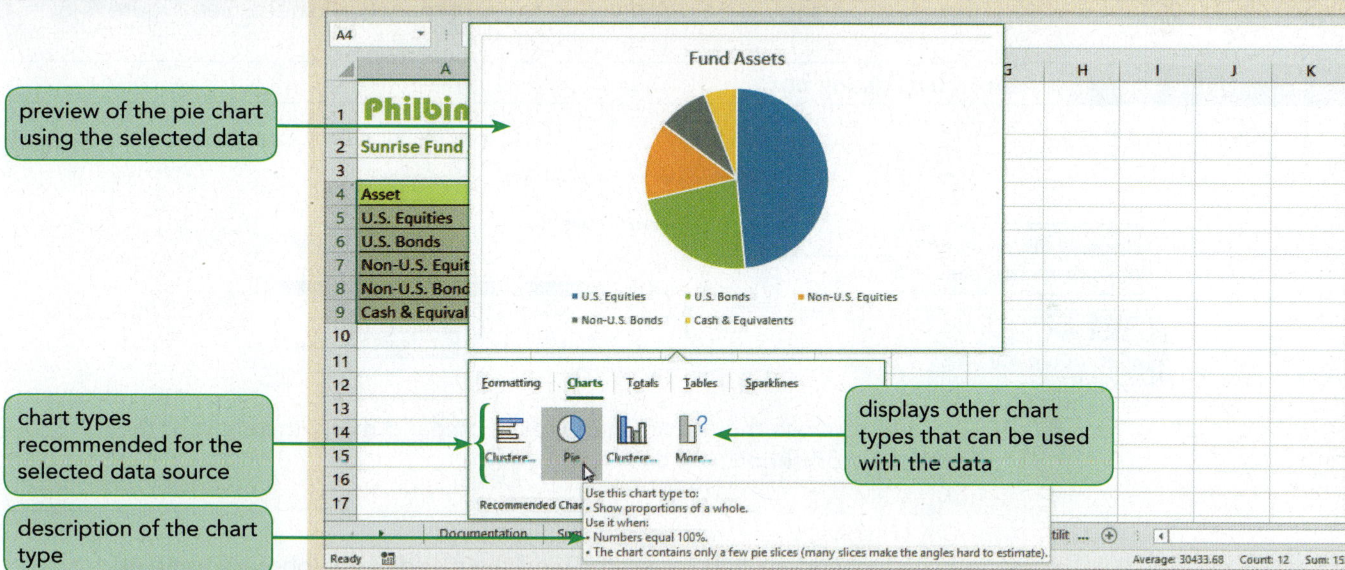

4. Click **Pie**. A pie chart appears in the Asset Mix worksheet.

Tip

You can also insert a chart by selecting a chart type in the Charts group on the Insert tab.

Excel automatically identifies the slice categories and the slice values from the data source. When the selected range is taller than it is wide, Excel assumes that the category values and data series are laid out in columns. Conversely, a data source that is wider than it is tall is assumed to have the category values and data series laid out in rows. The biggest slice in this pie chart represents the amount of the fund invested in U.S. equities, the smallest slice represents the amount invested in cash and equivalents. Slices start at the 12 o'clock position and are added clockwise around the pie.

Each new chart is given a reference name viewed in the Reference box. The default names are Chart 1, Chart 2, and so forth. When a chart is selected, two chart contextual tabs appear on the ribbon. The Chart Design tab is used to modify the chart's overall design and its data source, while the Format tab is used to format the individual parts of the chart, such as the chart's border or the slices from a pie chart. When the chart is not selected, the contextual tabs disappear.

Moving and Resizing a Chart

Tip

You can print an embedded chart with its worksheet, or you can print only the selected embedded chart without its worksheet.

A chart is placed either within its own chart sheet or embedded within a worksheet. The advantage of an embedded chart is that it can be displayed alongside relevant text and tables in the worksheet. Chart sheets are best used for charts that occupy a single page in a report or printout. In this report, all your charts will be embedded within the Summary worksheet. You'll move the pie chart you created in the Asset Mix worksheet to that sheet.

To move the embedded chart to the Summary worksheet:

1. Make sure the pie chart is selected, and then, on the ribbon, click the **Chart Design** tab, if necessary, to display it.
2. In the Location group, click the **Move Chart** button. The Move Chart dialog box opens.
3. Click the **Object in** arrow, and then click **Summary** in the list to indicate that the pie chart should be displayed in the Summary worksheet. See Figure 4–5.

Figure 4–5 Move Chart dialog box

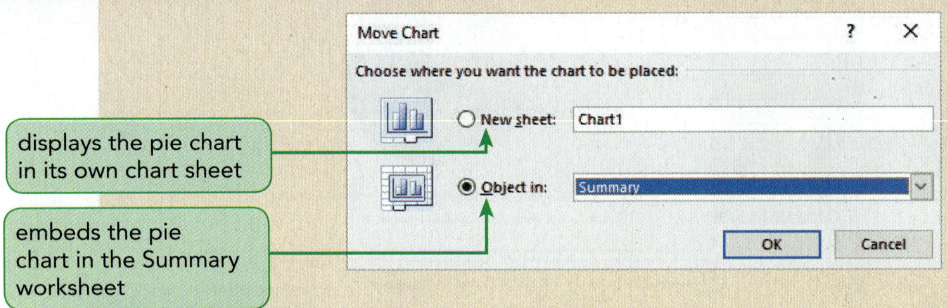

4. Click **OK** to close the Move Chart dialog box and move the chart to the Summary worksheet.

Because an embedded chart covers the worksheet grid, it can obscure some of the content. You can fix that problem by moving the chart to an empty location and resizing it. To move and resize a chart, the chart must be selected, which adds a selection box around the chart. The selection box has sizing handles to change the chart's width and height. As you move and resize a chart, holding down ALT snaps the chart to the worksheet grid. If you do not hold down ALT, you can move and resize the chart to any location on the grid.

Hideki wants the pie chart to cover the range G7:H14 in the Summary worksheet. You'll move and resize the chart to fit this space.

To move and resize the pie chart:

Make sure the ScreenTip shows "Chart Area" so the entire chart moves when you drag.

1. Move the pointer over an empty part of the chart so that the pointer changes to the Move pointer and the ScreenTip displays "Chart Area."
2. Hold down **ALT**, drag the chart to cell **G7** until its upper-left corner snaps to the upper-left corner of the cell, and then release the mouse button and **ALT**.

The upper-left corner of the chart now aligns with the upper-left corner of cell G7.

Trouble? If the pie chart resizes or does not move to the new location, you probably didn't drag the chart from an empty part of the chart area. Press CTRL+Z to undo your last action, and then repeat Steps 1 and 2, being sure to drag the pie chart from the chart area.

3. Point to the sizing handle in the lower-right corner of the selection box until the pointer changes to the Resizing pointer.
4. Hold down **ALT**, drag the sizing handle up to the lower-right corner of cell **H14**, and then release the mouse button and **ALT**, resizing the chart. The chart resizes to cover the range G7:H14 and remains selected. See Figure 4–6.

Figure 4–6 **Moved and resized pie chart**

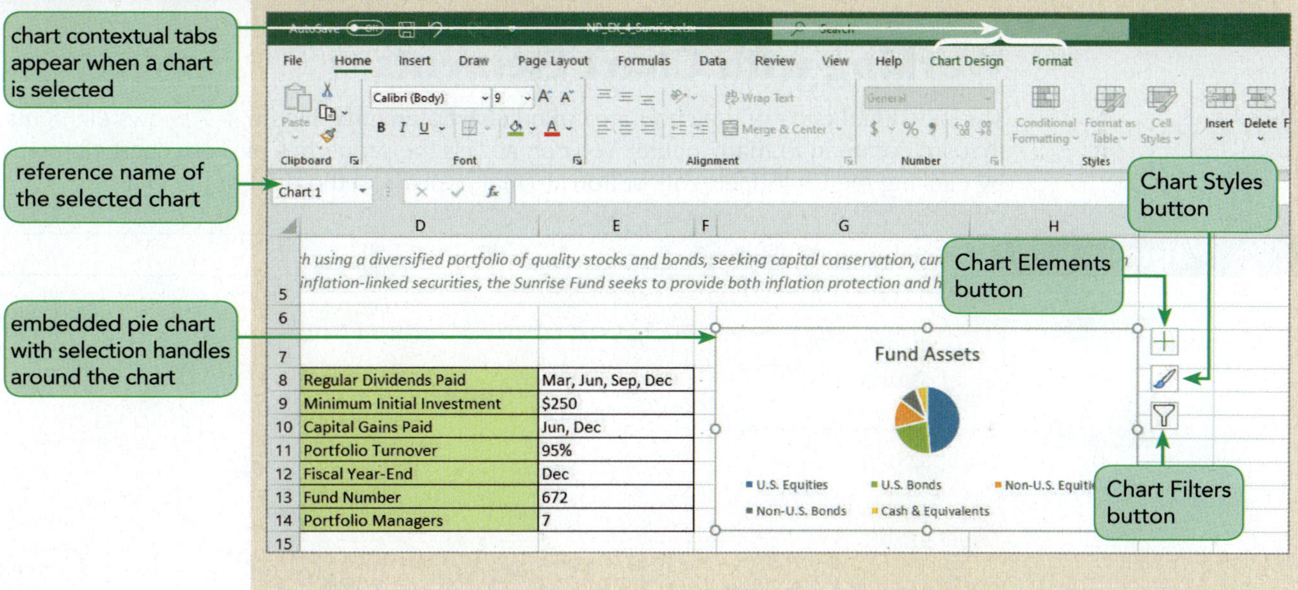

Another way of moving a chart is by cutting and pasting. Select the chart, click the Cut button in the Clipboard group on the Home tab, and then select the cell you want to place the chart. Click the Paste button to paste the chart at the new location.

Even though a chart is not part of the worksheet grid, it resizes with the grid. So if you change a column width or row height, the chart's width and height will also change. This ensures that an embedded chart always stays in the same relative location within the worksheet even as rows and columns are resized.

Insight

Exploding a Pie Chart

Pie slices do not need to be fixed within the pie. An **exploded pie chart** moves one slice away from the others as if someone were taking the piece away from the pie. Exploded pie charts are useful for emphasizing one category above the others. For example, to emphasize the fact that Sunrise Fund invests heavily in U.S. equities, you could explode that single slice, moving it away from the other slices.

To explode a pie slice, first click the pie to select it, and then click the single slice you want to move. Make sure that a selection box appears around only that slice. Drag the slice away from the pie, offsetting it from the others. You can explode multiple slices by selecting each slice in turn and dragging them away. To explode all the slices, select the entire pie and drag the pointer away from the pie's center. Although you can explode more than one slice, the resulting pie chart is rarely effective as a visual aid to the reader.

Working with Chart Elements

The individual parts of the chart are called **chart elements**. Figure 4–7 shows elements that are common to many charts. You can access the properties of these chart elements by clicking the Chart Elements button [+] that appears to the right of the chart.

Figure 4–7 Common chart elements

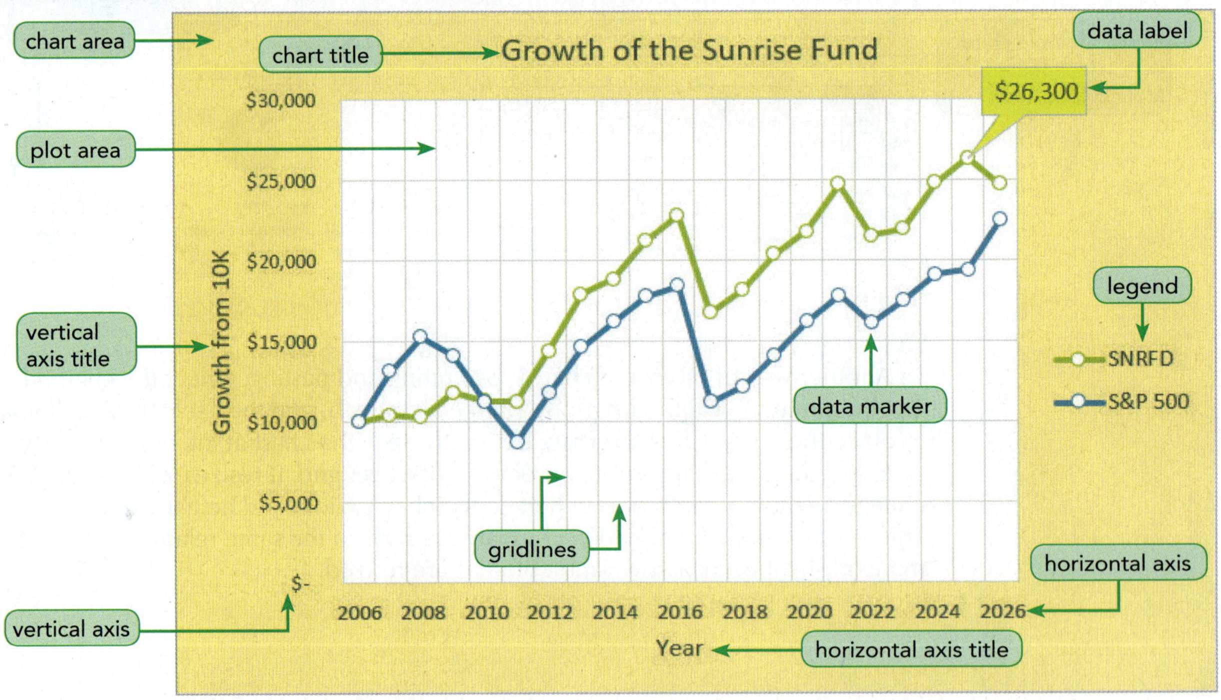

The pie chart you created does not contain any data labels. Hideki thinks showing the data values associated with each pie slice would make the chart easier to interpret. You will use the Chart Elements button [+] to add that element to the pie chart.

Tip

You can also add and remove chart elements with the Add Chart Element button in the Chart Layouts group on the Chart Design tab.

To add the data labels chart element to the pie chart:

1. With the pie chart still selected, click the **Chart Elements** button [+]. A menu of chart elements associated with the pie chart opens. As the checkmarks indicate, only the chart title and the chart legend are displayed in the pie chart.
2. Point to the **Data Labels** check box. Live Preview shows how the chart will look when the data labels show the dollar amount (in millions) invested within each category.
3. Click the **Data Labels** check box to select it. The data labels are added to the chart. See Figure 4–8.

Figure 4–8 Common chart elements

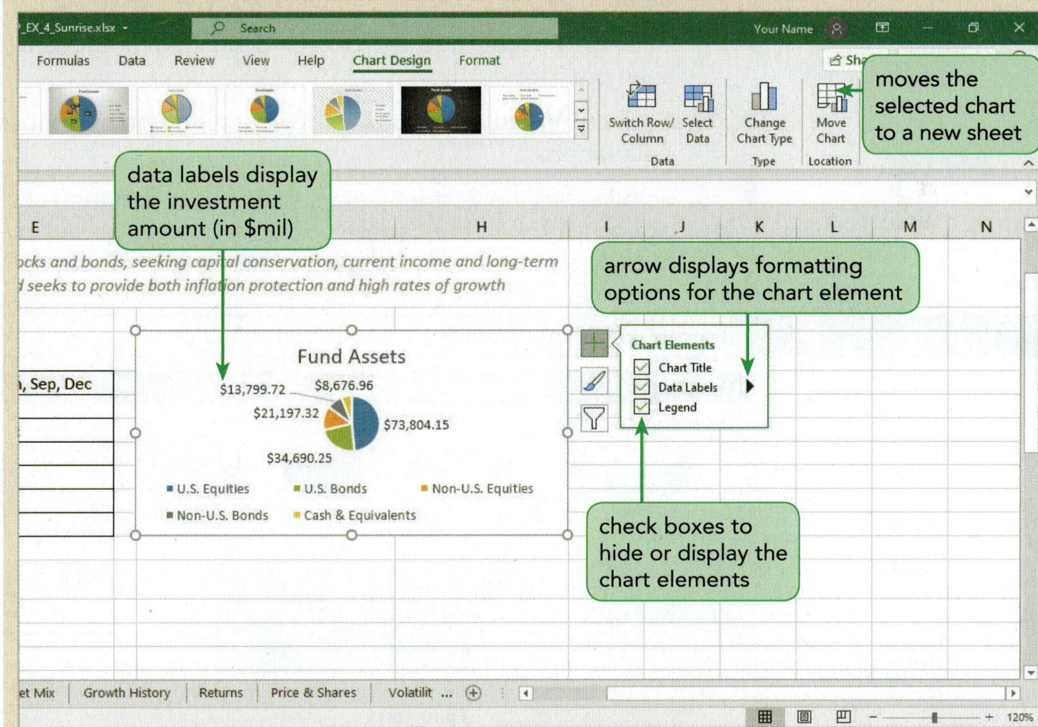

Hideki does not want the data labels to show the amount invested in each asset, but rather the percentage of the total invested in each asset. You can make that change by editing the properties of the Data Labels element.

Formatting a Chart Element

Each element listed in the Chart Elements button contains a submenu of common formatting choices, such as the placement of data labels relative to the position of the data marker or pie slice. From within that submenu, you can also open a formatting pane that has an extensive menu of formatting options. You'll explore the formatting choices available with the pie slice labels now.

To format a data label:

1. With the pie chart still selected, click the **Chart Elements** button [+] if necessary to display the submenu, point to **Data Labels**, and then click the **right arrow** icon [▶] to view the list of common formatting choices for data labels.
2. Point to each of the following options to get a Live Preview of data labels positioned at different locations around the pie chart: **Center**, **Inside End**, **Outside End**, **Best Fit**, and **Data Callout**.
3. Click **More Options** to view the extensive menu of formatting options for data labels in the Format Data Labels pane. The Format Data Labels pane is divided into different sections indicated by the icons near the top of the pane. The formatting options for the data labels [icon] is selected by default.
4. Click the **Percentage** check box to add percentages to the data labels for each pie slice.
5. Click the **Value** check box to deselect it, removing those data value from the data labels.
6. Scroll down the Format Data Labels pane, and then click the **Outside End** option button in the Label Position section to always place the data labels outside and at the end of each pie slice. See Figure 4–9.

Figure 4–9 Format Data Labels pane

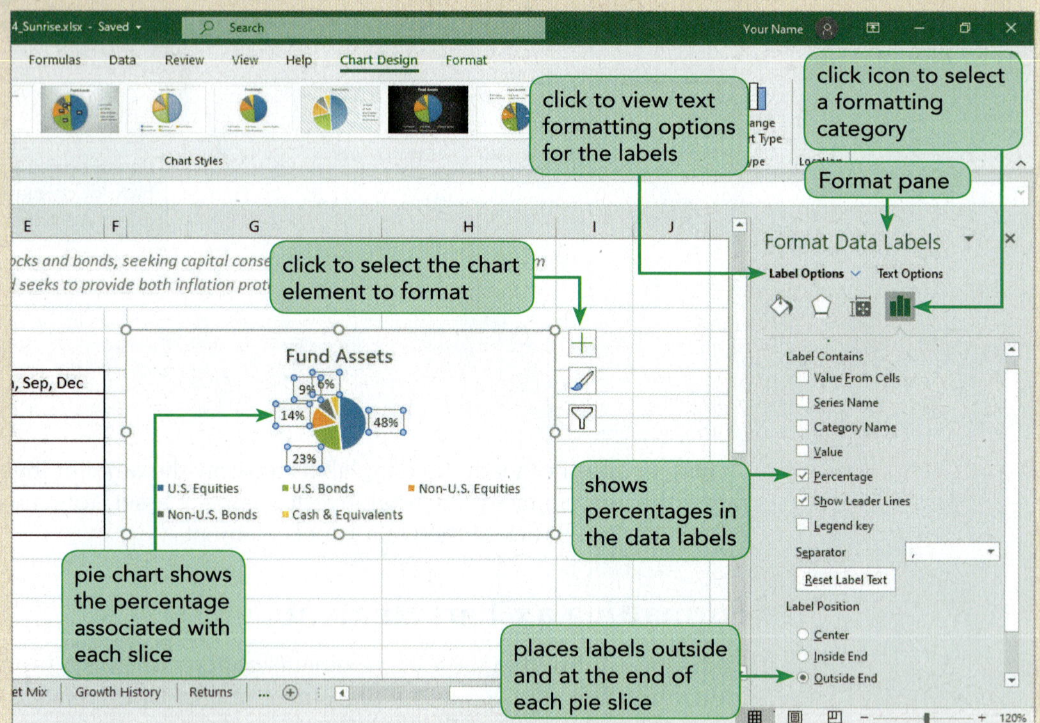

The Format pane is attached, or docked, to the right side of the workbook window. You can undock the pane so that it floats free above the worksheet grid by pointing to a blank area of the pane until the pointer changes to the Move pointer and then clicking and dragging the pane over the worksheet grid. To redock the pane, point to the floating pane until the pointer changes to the Move pointer and then drag to the right until the pane reattaches to the workbook window.

From the Format pane, you can format other chart elements. For example, Hideki thinks the pie chart would look better if the legend were aligned with the right edge of the chart area rather than its current position at the bottom. Hideki also wants the background of the legend to change to a light gold color. You'll use the Format pane to make those changes now.

Tip

You can also double-click any chart element to open its Format pane.

To move and format the pie chart legend:

1. In the Format Data Labels pane, click the **Label Options arrow** directly below the Format Data Labels title, and then click **Legend** in the list of chart elements. The name of the Format pane changes to Format Legend and options for formatting the pie chart legend appear in the pane.
2. In the Legend Options section, click the **Right** option button to place the pie chart legend on the right side of the chart area. See Figure 4–10.

Figure 4–10 Chart legend in chart area

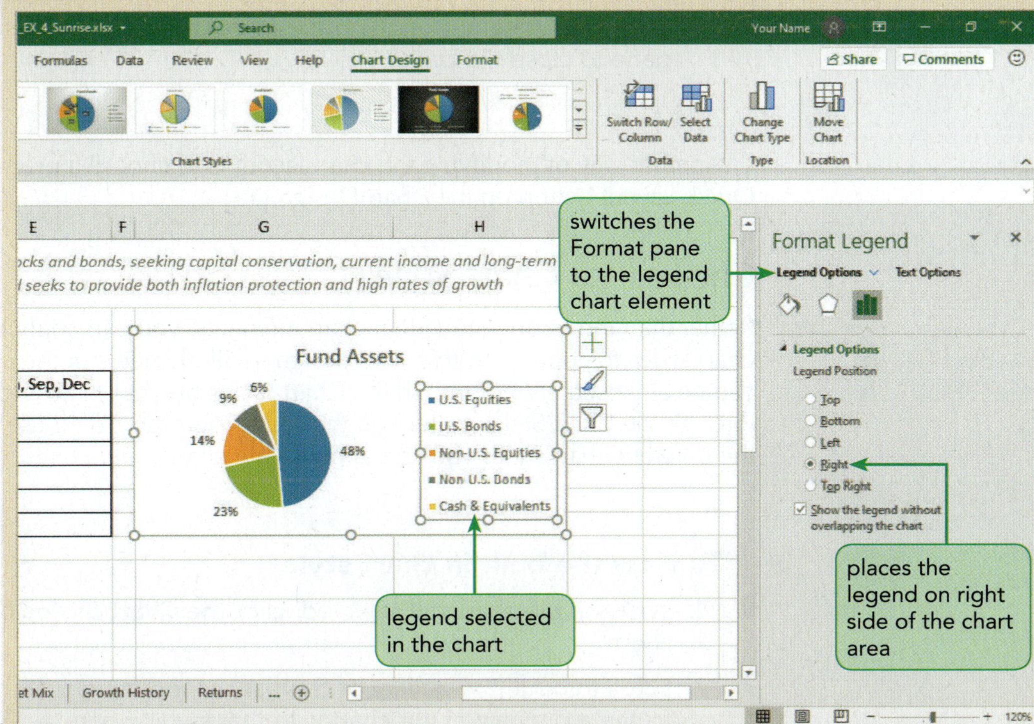

3. Click the **Fill & Line** icon, and then click the **Fill** heading to view the fill options for the legend.
4. Click the **Solid fill** option button, and then click the **Fill Color** button and select **Gold, Accent 5, Lighter 80%** (the ninth theme color in the second row) in the color palette. See Figure 4–11.

Figure 4–11 **Fill color for the chart legend**

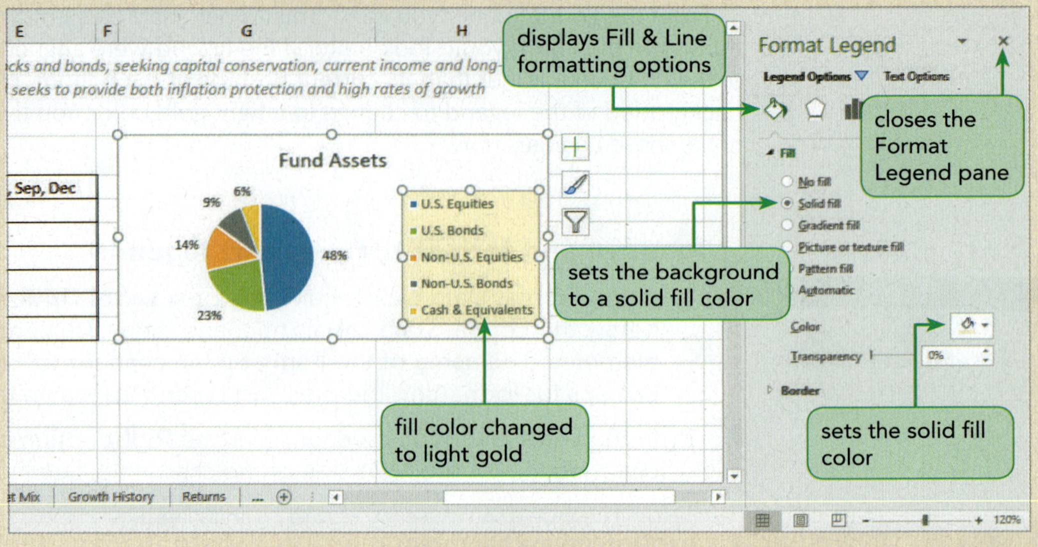

5. Click the **Close** button in the upper-right corner of the Format Legend pane to close the pane.

Another way of modifying the chart layout is to choose a predefined layout from the Quick Layout button on the Chart Design tab.

Choosing a Chart Style

Rather than formatting individual chart elements, you can apply one of the built-in chart styles to apply a professional design to all elements of the chart. Chart styles can be accessed either through the Chart Styles button next to a selected chart or through the Chart Styles gallery on the Chart Tools tab. You'll use Live Preview to view the different chart styles you can apply to pie charts.

To view the built-in chart styles:

1. With the pie chart still selected, click the **Chart Styles** button next to the chart.
2. Scroll through the gallery of chart styles, pointing to each entry in the gallery to see a preview of the chart with that style. Figure 4–12 shows a preview of design of the Style 6 chart style applied to the Asset Mix pie chart.

Figure 4–12 **Preview of a chart style**

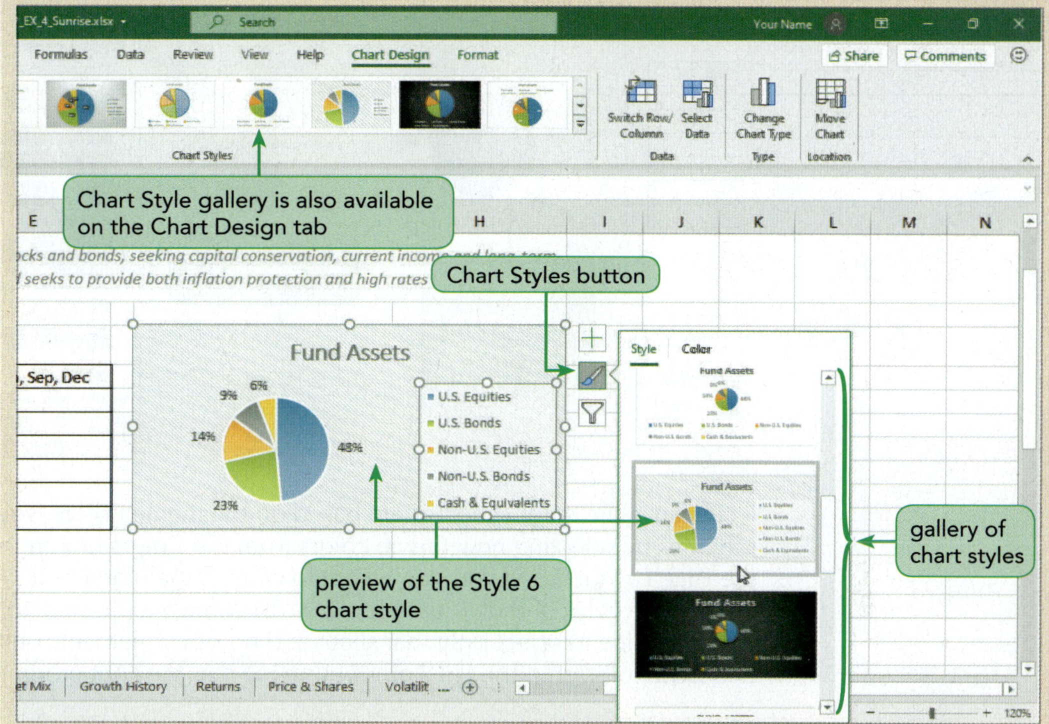

3. Press **ESC** to close the chart style gallery without changing the style of the Asset Mix pie chart.

Trouble? If you accidentally apply a chart style, click the Undo button on the Quick Access Toolbar to restore the chart to its previous style.

While Hideki doesn't want you to change the chart style of the Asset Mix pie chart, another concern is that the pie chart is difficult to interpret with its mix of colors. You can correct this problem by choosing a different color scheme.

Changing the Color Scheme

Each chart has a color scheme. By default, Excel applies the theme colors to the pie chart slices. You can select a different color scheme from the Chart Styles button in the Colors submenu. Hideki wants you to use colors in the same blue hue but with different levels of saturation so that the largest slice is displayed in dark blue and the smallest slice displayed in a light blue. You'll apply this color scheme to the Asset Mix pie chart.

Tip

You can also use the Change Colors button in the Chart Styles group on the Chart Design tab.

To change the pie slice colors:

1. Click the **Chart Styles** button to reopen the gallery of chart styles.
2. Click the **Color** tab to display a gallery of possible color schemes.
3. Select the blue monochromatic color scheme labeled **Monochromatic Palette 1**. See Figure 4–13.

Figure 4-13 Color schemes for the chart

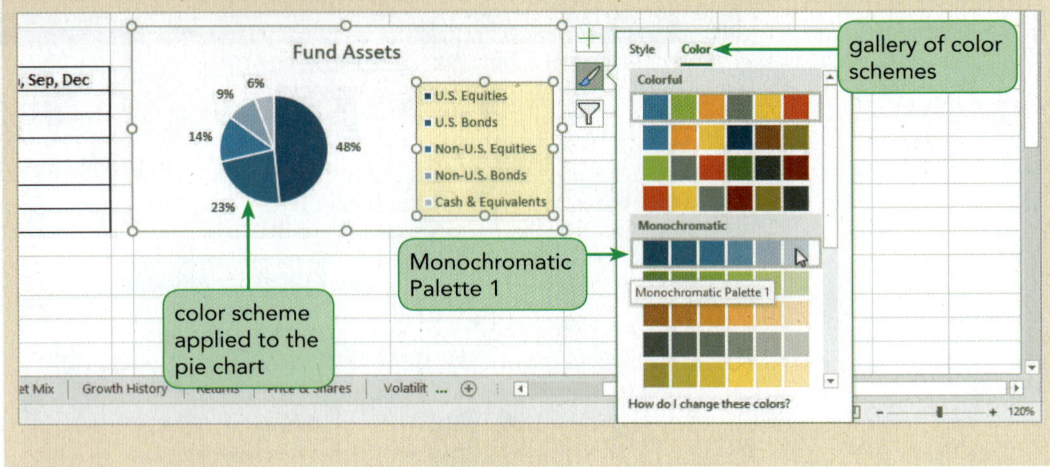

Because the color schemes are based on the theme colors, you can change the color schemes by selecting new theme colors from the Colors box in the Themes group on the Page Layout tab. If you don't want to change the workbook's color theme, you can change the color of individual pie slices. To change a pie slice to another color, double-click the slice to select only that slice (and no other elements on the chart) and then choose a color from the Fill Color button in the Font group on the Home tab.

Insight

Overlaying Chart Elements

An embedded chart takes up less space than a chart sheet. However, it can be challenging to fit all the chart elements into that smaller space. One solution is to overlay one element on top of another. The most commonly overlaid elements are the chart title and the chart legend. To overlay the chart title, click the Chart Title arrow in the Chart Elements list and select Centered Overlay as the position option. Excel will place the chart title on top of the plot area, freeing up more space for other chart elements. Chart legends can also be overlaid by opening the Format pane for the legend and deselecting the Show the legend without overlapping the chart check box in the Legend Options section. Other chart elements can be overlaid by dragging them to new locations in the chart area and then resizing the plot area to recover the empty space.

Don't overuse the technique of overlaying chart elements. Too much overlaying of chart elements can make a chart difficult to read.

Performing What-If Analyses with Charts

Because a chart is linked to its data source, any changes in the data source values will be reflected in the chart. This link between a chart and its data source provides a powerful tool for data exploration. For the Asset Mix pie chart, the chart title is linked to the text in cell B4 of the Asset Mix worksheet, the size of the pie slices is based on values in the range B5:B9 and the category names are linked to the category values in the range A4:A9.

Hideki notes that the value in cell B5 for the amount invested in U.S. Equities should be $63,804.15 instead of $73,804.15. You will change the value in the cell and change the category name in cell B9 from "Cash & Equivalents" to simply "Cash."

To modify the pie chart's data:

1. Go to the **Asset Mix** worksheet, and then in cell **B5**, change the value to **$63,804.15** to reflect the correct amount invested in U.S. Equities.
2. In cell **A9**, change the text to **Cash** to update the label.
3. Go to the **Summary** worksheet and confirm that the percent of assets invested in U.S. equities has decreased to 45% and that the last legend entry changed to "Cash."

If you want a chart to focus on fewer categories, you can filter the chart by removing one or more categories. Removing a category has no impact on the data source. To focus on U.S. investments, you'll filter the pie chart to show the breakdown of assets between U.S. equities and U.S. bonds.

To filter the pie chart:

1. Select the pie chart if it is not already selected and then click the **Filter** button next to the chart, opening a list of data categories.
2. Click the **Non-U.S. Equities**, **Non-U.S. Bonds**, and **Cash** check boxes to remove the checkmarks from those boxes.
3. Click **Apply** to apply the filters to the chart. The pie chart shows that 65% of the non-cash U.S. investments are in equities and 35% are in bonds. See Figure 4–14.

Tip

When you point to a category, Live Preview highlights the pie slice corresponding to that category.

Figure 4–14 Filtered pie chart

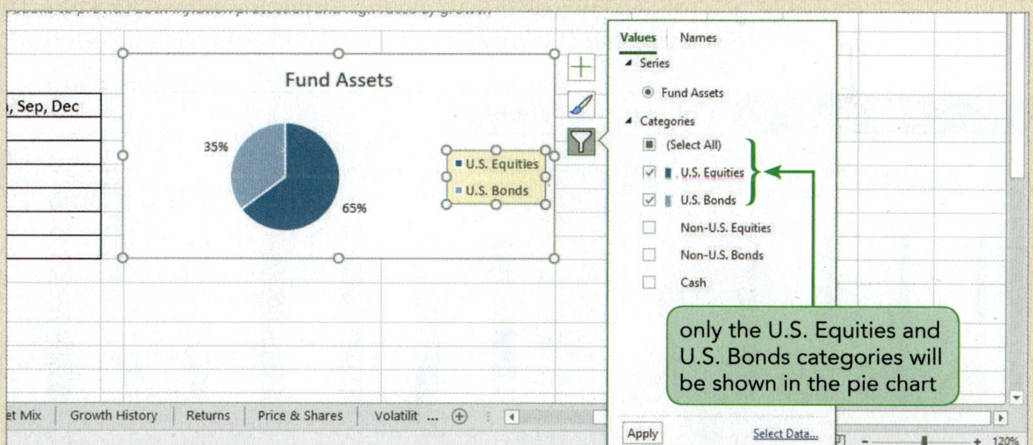

4. Double-click the **(Select All)** check box to select all chart categories, and then click **Apply** to return the pie chart to its former state.

The pie chart revealed some important information about the assets of the Sunrise Fund. Next, you will use a column chart to explore the level of returns that the fund has provided for investors over the past ten years.

Creating a Column Chart

A **column chart** displays data values as columns with the height of each column based on the data value. A column chart turned on its side is called a **bar chart**, with the length of the bar determined by the data value. It is better to use column and bar charts than pie charts when the number of categories is large, or when the data categories are close in value. Figure 4–15 displays the same data as a pie chart and a column chart. As you can see, it's difficult to determine which pie slice is biggest and by how much. It is much simpler to make those comparisons in a column or bar chart.

Figure 4–15 **Data displayed as different chart types**

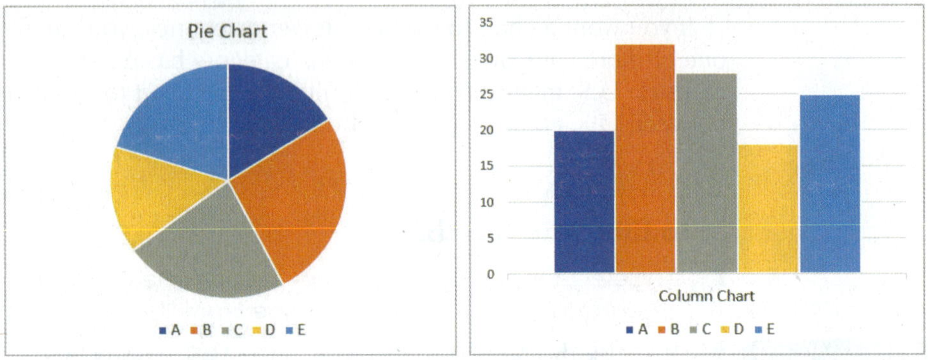

Comparing Column Chart Subtypes

Unlike pie charts, which can show only one data series, column and bar charts can display multiple data series. Figure 4–16 shows three examples of column charts in which five data series (U.S. Equities, U.S. Bonds, Non-U.S. Equities, Non-U.S. Bonds, and Cash) are plotted against one category series (Years). Column charts are plotted against a **value axis** displaying the values from the data series and a **category axis** displaying the category values associated with each data series.

Figure 4–16 **Column chart subtypes**

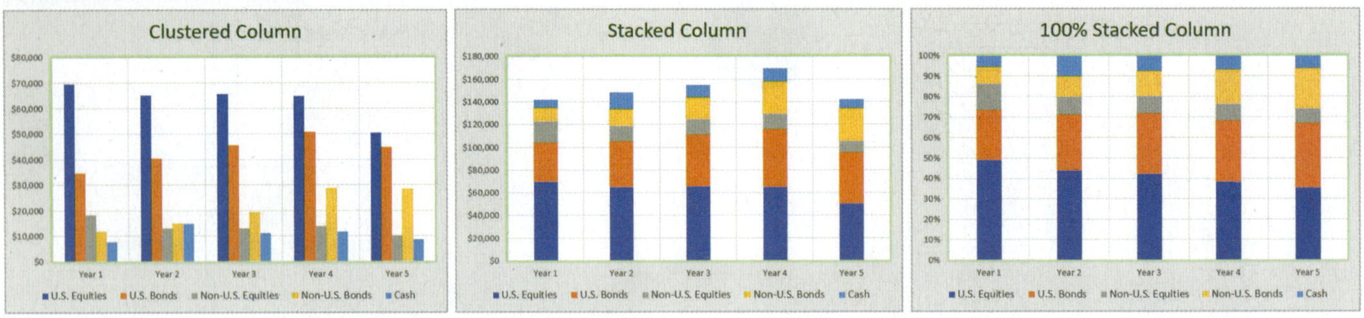

A **clustered column chart** displays the data series values in separate columns side by side so that you can compare the relative heights of values across categories. The clustered column chart in Figure 4–16 compares the amount invested in each category in year 1 through year 5. Note that the amount invested in U.S. equities steadily declines as the amount invested in U.S. bonds and non-U.S. bonds increases.

A **stacked column chart** combines the data series values within a single column to show how much of the total is contributed by each item. The stacked column chart in Figure 4–16 gives information on the total amount invested each year in the fund and how each year's investment is split among five investment categories. This chart makes it clear that the total investment in fund dropped between the fourth and fifth year.

Finally, a **100% stacked column chart** makes the same comparison as the stacked column chart except that the stacked sections are expressed as percentages of the whole. As you can see from the 100% stacked column chart in Figure 4–16, the investment in U.S. equities and bonds starts out at over 70% in the first year and steadily decreases to about 65% by the fifth year as more of the fund is invested in non-U.S. bonds. Each chart, while working with the same data source, reveals something different about the activity of the investment fund over the 5-year period.

Creating a Clustered Column Chart

The process for creating a column chart is the same as for creating a pie chart: Select the data source and then choose a chart type and subtype. After the chart is embedded in the worksheet, you can move and resize the chart as well as change the chart's design, layout, and format.

Hideki wants a column chart showing the returns of the Sunrise Fund adjusted over 1-year, 3-year, and 10-year periods, as well as year-to-date (YTD) and since the fund's inception. The column chart will include the returns from the Standard & Poor's 500 index (S&P 500) to indicate how the fund compares to an industry standard. You'll create that chart now.

To create a clustered column chart:

1. Go to the **Returns** worksheet containing the returns based on month-end values.
2. Select the range **A4:C9** containing the categories and values to chart.
3. On the ribbon, click the **Insert** tab, and then in the Charts group, click the **Recommended Charts** button. The Insert Chart dialog box opens to the Recommended Charts tab. From this tab, you can preview and select a chart best suited to the data source. See Figure 4–17.

Figure 4–17 **Recommended Charts tab in the Insert Chart dialog box**

4. Confirm that the **Clustered Column** chart is selected, and then click **OK**.
5. On the Chart Design tab, in the Location group, click the **Move Chart** button.
6. From the Object in box, click **Summary** and then click **OK** to move the column chart to the Summary worksheet.
7. In the Summary worksheet, hold down **ALT** as you move and resize the chart to cover the range **A17:B28**, and then release **ALT**. The chart snaps to the grid. See Figure 4–18.

Tip

To set an exact chart size, enter the height and width values in the Size group on the Format tab.

Figure 4–18 Column chart of return data

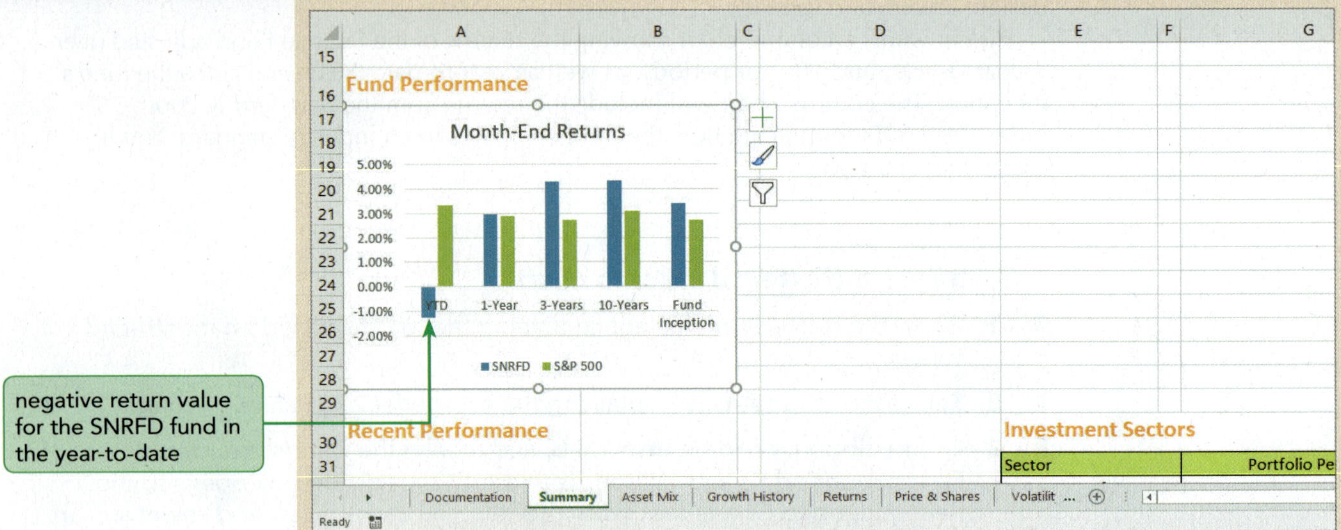

The column chart shows that the Sunrise Fund has generally outperformed the S&P 500 index for most of its life and especially during the previous 3-year and 10-year periods. However, in the current year-to-date, the fund is performing worse than the S&P 500 and, in fact, is showing a negative return in value.

Editing a Chart Title

When a chart has a single data series, the name of the data series is used for the chart title. When a chart has more than one data series, "Chart Title" is used as the temporary title of the chart. Hideki wants you to change the chart title to "Month-End Returns." You will edit the chart title now.

To change the title of the column chart:

1. At the top of the column chart, click **Chart Title** to select it.
2. Type **Month-End Returns** as the new title, and then press **ENTER**. The new title is inserted into the chart.

Tip

You can change the font size and style of the chart title by clicking the formatting buttons in the Font group on the Home tab.

Note that because the chart title is not linked to any worksheet cell, it will not be updated if changes are made to the data source.

Setting the Gap Width

Excel automatically sets the space between the data series in a column chart as well as the gap width between one category value and the next. If the column chart contains several data series, there might be too little room between the categories, making it difficult to know when one category ends and the next begins. You can modify the space between the data series and gap width using the Format pane.

Hideki wants you to reduce the space between the two data series and increase the interval width between the Year categories.

Tip

Use the up and down spin arrows in the Series Overlap and Gap Width boxes to change the values in 1% increments.

To set the column chart gap and interval widths:

1. Double-click any column in the column chart to display the Format Data Series pane with the Series Options section already selected.
2. Select the **Series Overlap** box, and then change the space between the data series to **-10%**.
3. Select the **Gap Width** box and increase the value of the gap between the category values to **300%**. See Figure 4–19.

Figure 4–19 Series overlap and gap width values

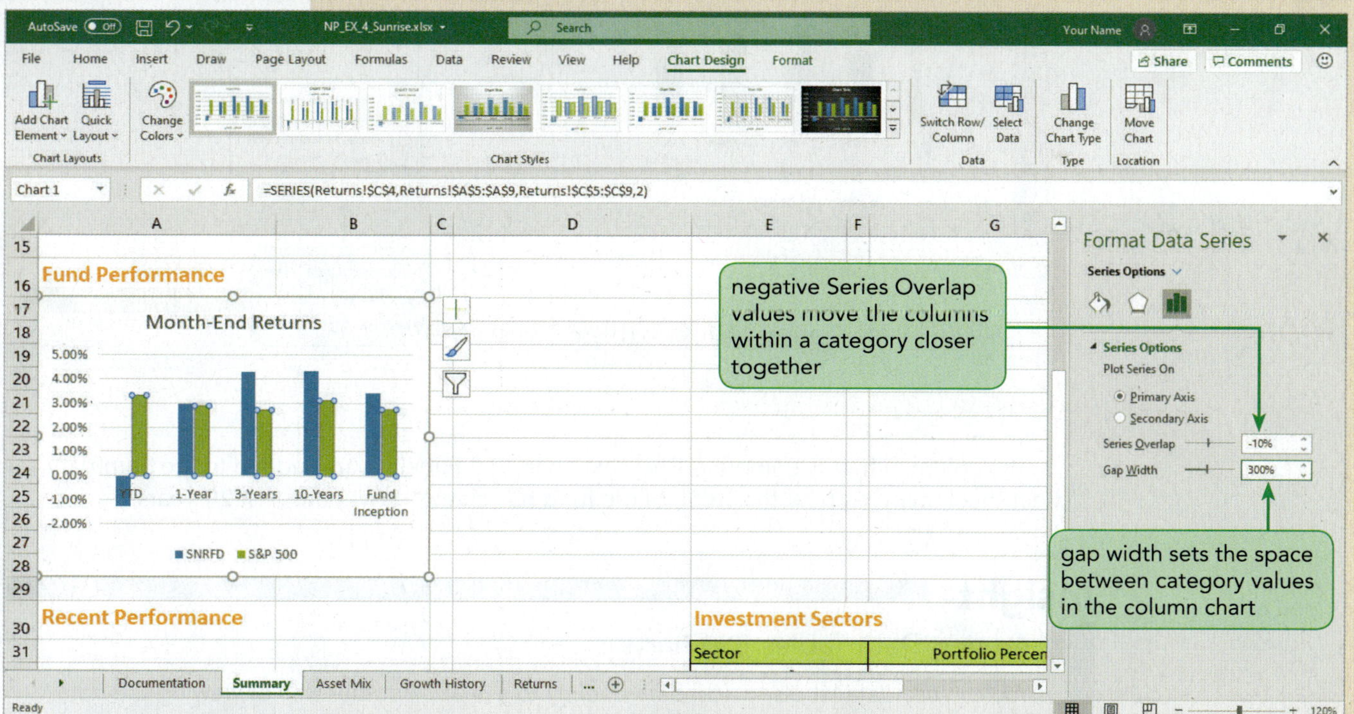

4. Close the Format Data Series pane.

Adding Gridlines to a Chart

Another way of distinguishing columns in separate categories is with gridlines. A gridline is a line that extends from the chart's horizontal and vertical axis into the plot area, making it easier to identify the values or categories associated with the chart's data markers. For example, the horizontal gridlines in Month-End Returns chart make it easier to see where the return from the Sunrise Fund exceeds 4% growth, as it did for the 3-year and 10-year time periods.

Hideki wants you to add vertical gridlines to provide an additional visual aid for separating the time intervals from each other.

To add vertical gridlines to the chart:

1. With the column chart still selected, click the **Chart Elements** button [+] to the right of chart to display the list of chart elements associated with column charts.
2. Click the **arrow** [▸] to the right of Gridlines, and then click **Primary Major Vertical** to add vertical gridlines to the chart. See Figure 4–20.

Figure 4–20 Gridlines added to the column chart

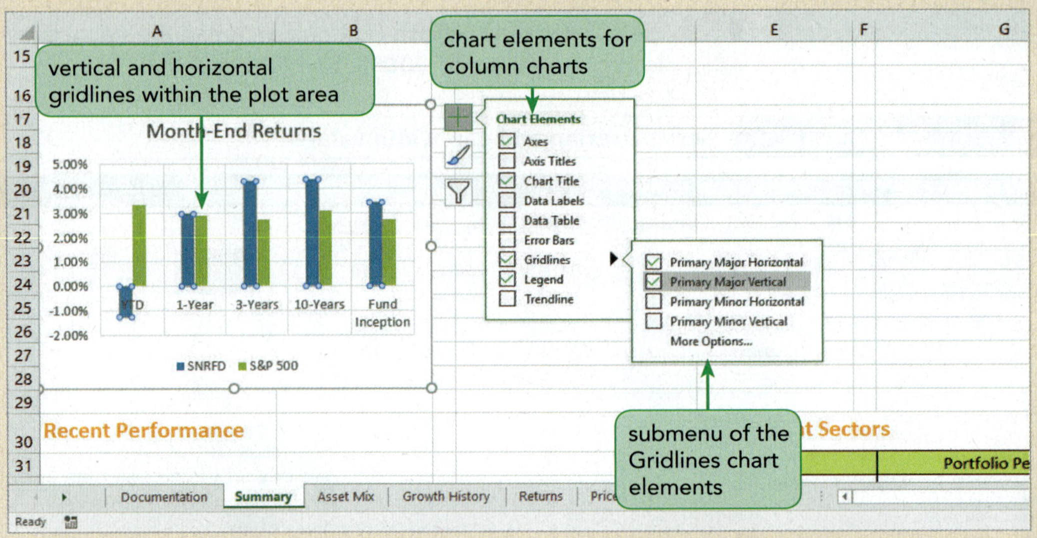

The column chart is complete. The next chart that Hideki wants added to the Summary worksheet analyzes how the value of the fund has changed over the past 20 years.

Insight

Adding Data Tables to Charts

You can use data labels to add data directly to a chart. Another way of viewing the data values associated with a chart is by adding a data table. The data table will be inserted within the chart area directly below the plot area. Each data series will appear as a separate row within the data table with category values placed in the first column of the table.

Creating a Line Chart

A line chart uses lines to plot one or more data series against a set of categories. The categories should follow a sequential order that is evenly spaced. For example, if the categories represent calendar months the space between one month and the next must be constant. Otherwise, the line chart will give an inaccurate depiction of change over time.

Hideki wants a line chart that compares the growth of an investment in the Sunrise Fund over the past 20 years to the same investment in the Standard & Poor's 500 index. You'll create this line chart using the data in the Growth History worksheet.

To create the growth history line chart:

1. Go to the **Growth History** worksheet, and then select the range **A4:C25** containing the growth of the Sunrise Fund and the S&P 500 index from a hypothetical $10,000 initial investment.
2. On the ribbon, click the **Insert** tab, and then in the Charts group, click the **Recommended Charts** button. The Insert Chart dialog box opens to the Recommended Charts tab.
3. Confirm that the **Line** chart type is selected, and then click **OK** to insert the line chart into the Growth History worksheet.
4. Move the chart to the Summary worksheet.
5. Move and resize the line chart so that it covers the range **D17:E28**, holding down **ALT** to snap the chart to the worksheet grid.
6. In the chart, click **Chart Title** to select it, type **Growth of 10K Investment** as the title, and then press **ENTER**. Figure 4–21 shows the appearance of the line chart.

Figure 4–21 Line chart of the fund value over time

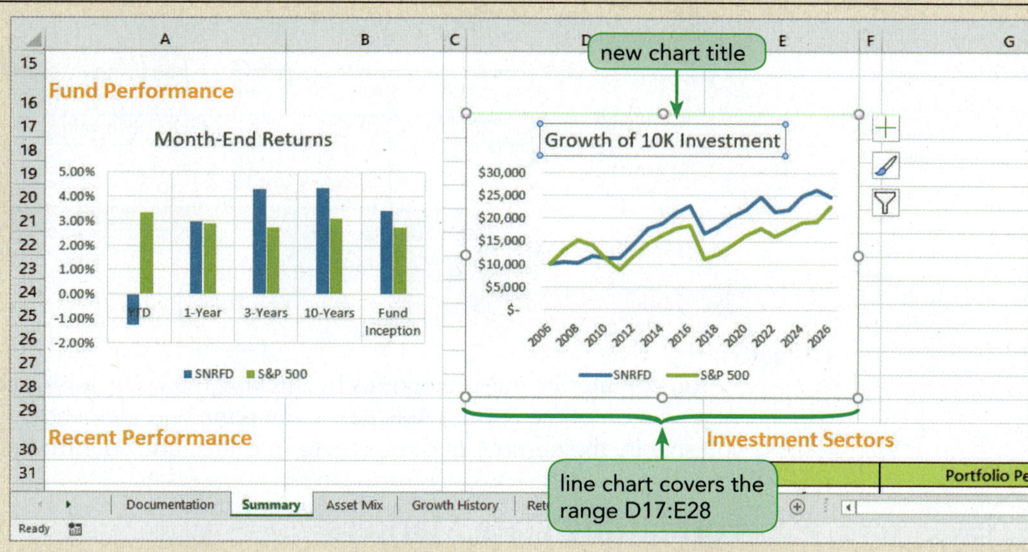

The line chart shows that the value of the Sunrise Fund exceeds the S&P 500 index for most of the past 20 years. Only in its early history did the fund fall below the S&P 500 in value. However, Hideki also notes that in the last year the Sunrise Fund has lost value, though it is still slightly above the value of the S&P 500 index.

Editing the Category Axis

You can modify the axis labels and tick marks to change which category values are displayed in the chart. Hideki doesn't like how crowded the year values are displayed in the horizontal axis. You'll revise the axis so that it lists years in 5-year increments.

To format the horizontal axis:

1. Double-click one of the years on the horizontal axis to open the Format Axis pane.
2. At the top of the Format pane, click the **Axis Options** button.
3. Scroll down and click **Tick Marks** to view options for modifying the tick marks on the category axis.
4. In the Interval between marks box, change the value to **5** so that the tick marks are laid out in 5-year intervals.
5. Click the **Major type** arrow, and then click **Cross** so that the tick marks are displayed as crosses.
6. Click **Labels** to expand that section, click the **Specify interval unit** option button, enter **5** in the box next to the option button to display the year labels at 5-year intervals, and then press **ENTER**. See Figure 4–22.

Figure 4–22 New category intervals for the horizontal axis

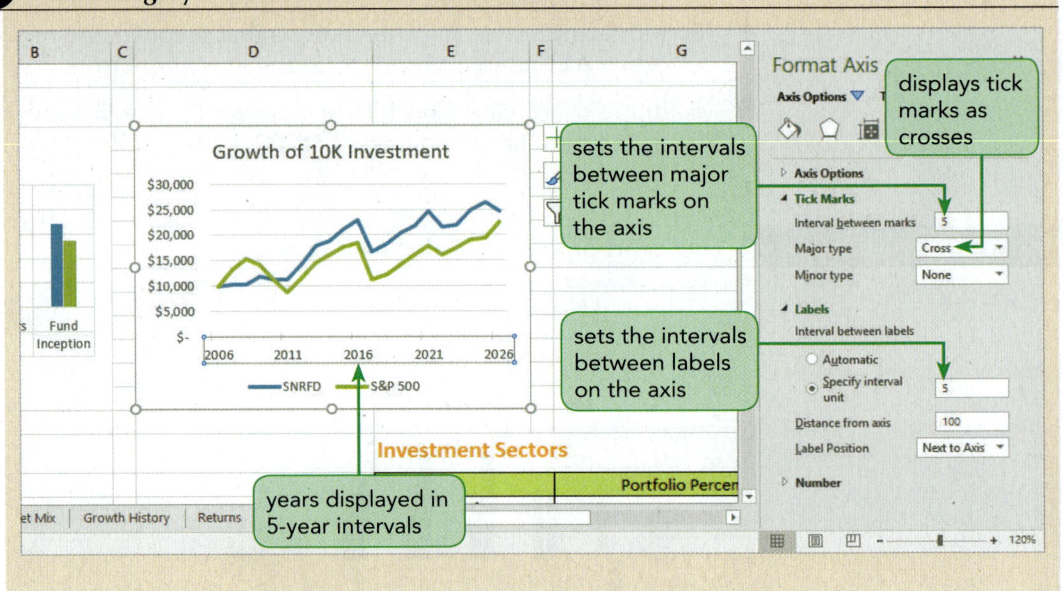

You can modify date categories by clicking the Date axis option button in the Axis Type section of the Format Axis pane. The pane will then show input box from which you specify the number of days, weeks, months, and so forth between date values.

Formatting Data Markers

Each value from a data series is represented by a data marker. In pie charts, the data markers are the individual pie slices. In column charts, the columns are the data markers. In a line chart, the data markers are the points connected by the line. Depending on the line chart style, these data marker points can be displayed or hidden.

In the line chart you created, the data marker points are hidden, and only the line connecting those markers is visible. Hideki wants you to display those data markers and change their fill color to white so that they stand out, making it easier to view the data values.

To display and format the line chart data markers:

1. Within the line chart, double-click the blue line for the Sunrise Fund (SNRFD) to display the Format Data Series pane.
2. At the top of the Format pane, click the **Fill & Line** button.
3. Scroll to the top of the pane, click **Marker**, and then click **Marker Options** to display options specific to data markers.
4. Click the **Automatic** option button to automatically display the markers along with the line for the Sunrise Fund data series. The data markers are now visible in the line chart, but they have a blue fill color. You will change this fill color to white.
5. In the Fill section, click the **Solid fill** option button, and then click the **Color** button and select the **White, Background 1** theme color. The fill color for the data markers for the Sunrise Fund line changes to white.
6. Repeat Steps 1 through 5 for the green line representing the S&P 500 index. See Figure 4–23.

Figure 4–23 Formatted data markers in a line chart

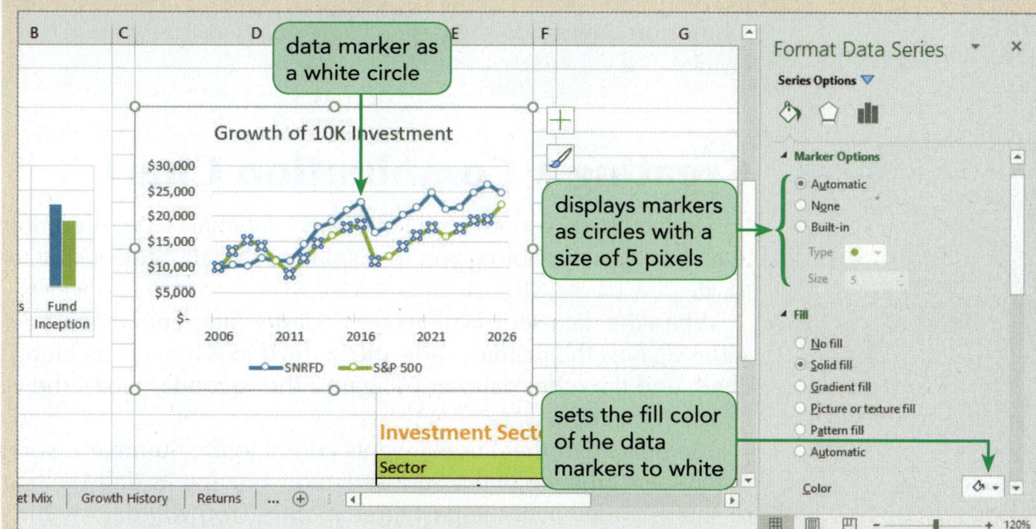

7. Close the Format Data Series pane.

By adding the data markers, you now have a better view of individual values in plotted in the line chart.

Proskills

Written Communication: Communicating Effectively with Charts

Studies show that people more easily interpret information when it is presented as a graphic rather than in a table. As a result, charts can help communicate the real story underlying the facts and figures you present to colleagues and clients. A well-designed chart can illuminate the bigger picture that might be hidden by viewing only the numbers. However, poorly designed charts can mislead readers and make it more difficult to interpret data.

To create effective and useful charts, keep in mind the following tips as you design your charts:

- **Keep it simple.** Do not clutter a chart with too many graphical elements. Focus attention on the data rather than on decorative elements that do not inform.
- **Focus on the message.** Design the chart to highlight the points you want to convey to readers.
- **Limit the number of data series.** Most charts should display no more than four or five data series. Pie charts should have no more than six slices.
- **Choose colors carefully.** Display different data series in contrasting colors to make it easier to distinguish one series from another. Modify the default colors as needed to make them distinct on the screen and in the printed copy.
- **Limit your chart to a few text styles.** Use a maximum of two or three different text styles in the same chart. Having too many text styles in one chart can distract attention from the data.

The goal of written communication is always to inform the reader in the simplest, most accurate, and most direct way possible. Everything in your workbook should be directed toward that end.

Creating a Combination Chart

So far, the charts you created have only one chart type. A combination chart combines two chart types enabling you to display each data series using the chart type best suited for it.

When the data series values cover vastly different ranges, you can plot one data series against the **primary axis**, the vertical axis appearing along the left edge of the chart, and the other data series against the **secondary axis**, the vertical axis on the chart's right edge.

The next chart that Hideki wants added to the Summary worksheet will display the recent performance of the Sunrise Fund, showing its daily selling price and the number of shares traded over the past three months. You will display the daily selling price in a line chart plotted against the primary axis and the number of shares traded in a column chart plotted against the secondary axis.

To create the combination chart:

1. Go to the **Price & Shares** worksheet and select the range **A4:C69**.
2. On the ribbon, click the **Insert** tab, and then in the Charts group, click the **Recommended Charts** button. The Insert Chart dialog box opens showing the recommended Line chart.
3. Click the **All Charts** tab to see previews of all Excel chart types.
4. In the list of chart types, click **Combo**.

5. Click the **Custom Combination** chart subtype (the last subtype listed for the Combo chart). At the bottom of the dialog box, the "Choose the chart type and axis for your data series" box lists two data series in the selected data. First you need to select the chart type to display the Price data.
6. In the "Choose the chart type and axis for your data series" box, click the **Price** Chart Type box arrow, and then click **Line**. Now you need to select the chart type for the Shares Traded data series.
7. Click the **Shares Traded** Chart type box arrow, and then click **Clustered Columns** from list of chart types.
8. In the Shares Traded row, click the **Secondary Axis** check box to plot the Shares Traded values on the secondary axis. See Figure 4–24.

Figure 4–24 **Combination chart preview**

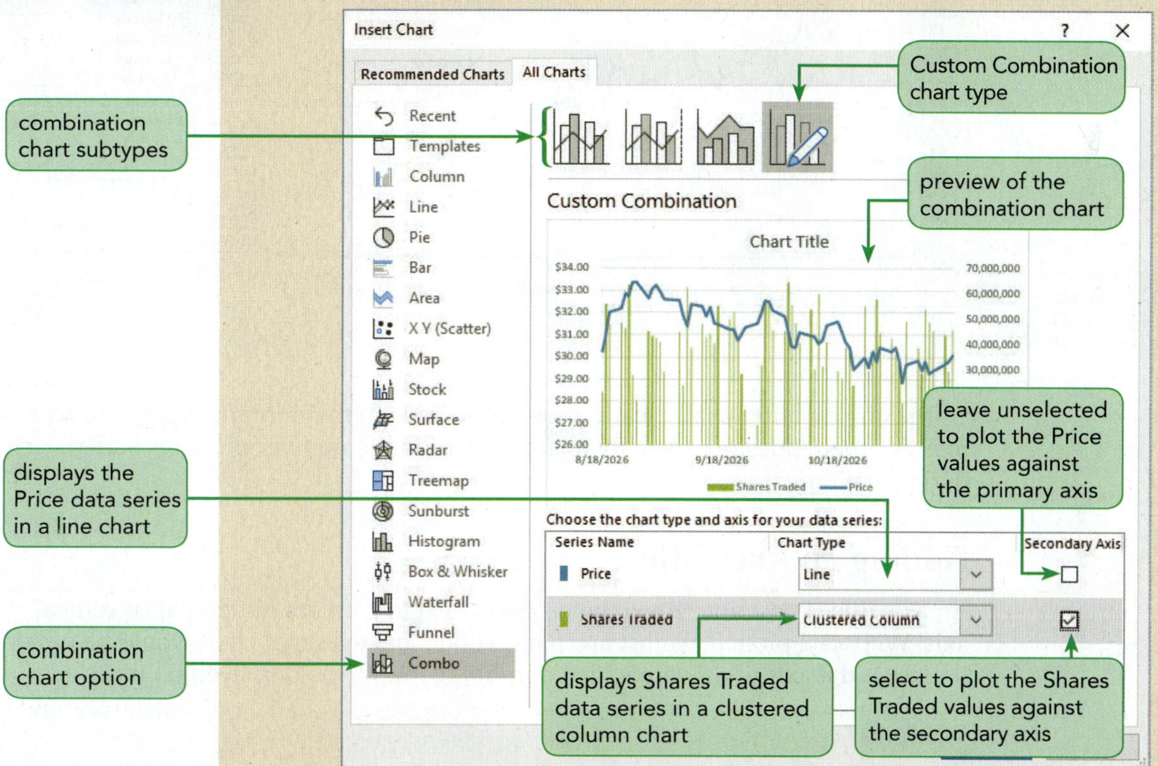

9. Click **OK** to embed the chart into the Price & Shares worksheet.

Next, you'll move the combination chart to the Summary worksheet and format it.

To move and format the combination chart:

Tip

To retain the chart's proportions as it is resized, hold down SHIFT as you drag the resizing handle.

1. Move the combination chart to the Summary worksheet, and then move and resize the chart to cover the range **A31:D43**, holding down the **ALT** key to snap the worksheet to the grid. You may have to scroll through the worksheet to find the chart.
2. Click **Chart Title** in the combination chart to select it, type **Price & Shares Traded** as the new title, and then press **ENTER** to insert the new chart title.

3. Click the **Chart Elements** button ⊞ and then click the **arrow** ▶ next to the Legend entry in the list of chart elements to display a submenu of formatting choices for the chart legend.

4. Click **Right** to move the legend to the right of the chart area. See Figure 4–25.

Figure 4–25 Combination chart of Price and Shares traded

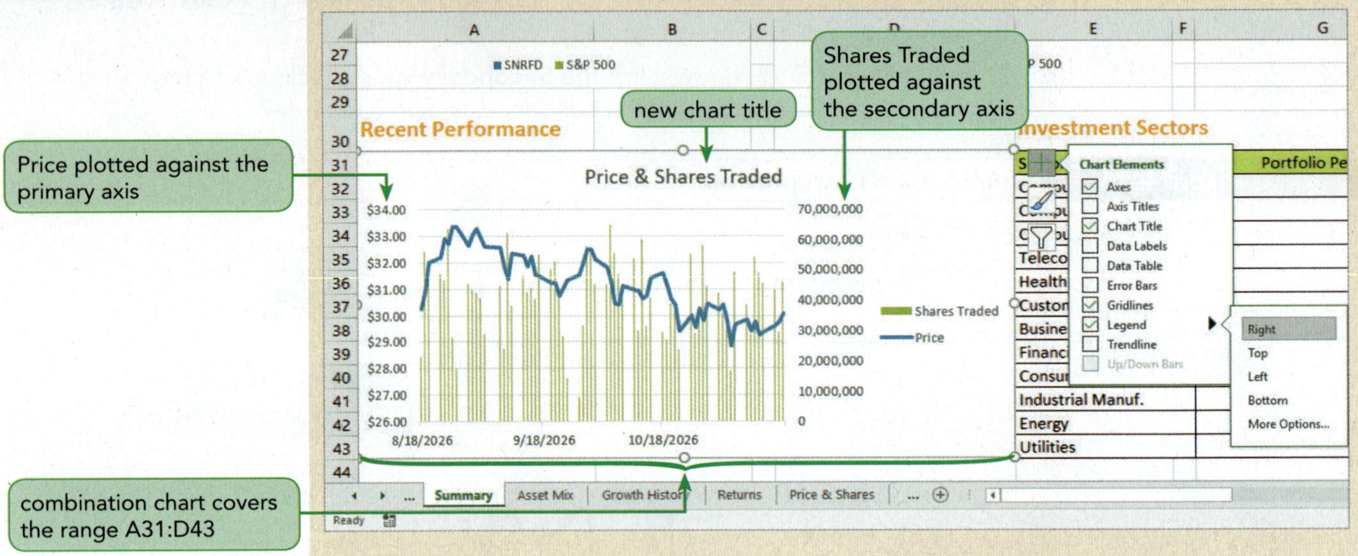

The combination chart clearly shows a downward trend in prices over the past three months. There does not seem to be any pattern in the number of shares traded each day during that time.

Adding an Axis Title

An **axis title** is descriptive text that appears next to a chart's horizontal or vertical axis. With data plotted against two axes, Hideki believes that chart would be easier to understand if axis titles were added describing the values displayed on those axes.

To add axis titles to the chart:

1. With the combination chart still selected, click the **Chart Elements** button ⊞ and then click the **Axis Titles** check box to select it. Titles are added to all three axes.
2. Click **Axis Title** next to the primary axis (on the left side of the chart), type **Price** as the axis title, and then press **ENTER**. The primary axis title is changed.
3. Click **Axis Title** along the category (bottom) axis, type **Date** as the axis title, and then press **ENTER**. The horizontal axis title is changed.
4. Click **Axis Title** next to the secondary axis (on the right side of the chart), type **Shares Traded** as the axis title, and then press **ENTER**. The secondary axis title is changed.

5. With the Shares Traded title still selected, click the **Home** tab on the ribbon, and then in the Alignment group, click the **Orientation** button and click **Rotate Text Down**. The axis title is rotated for better visibility. See Figure 4–26.

Figure 4–26 **Axis titles added to a chart**

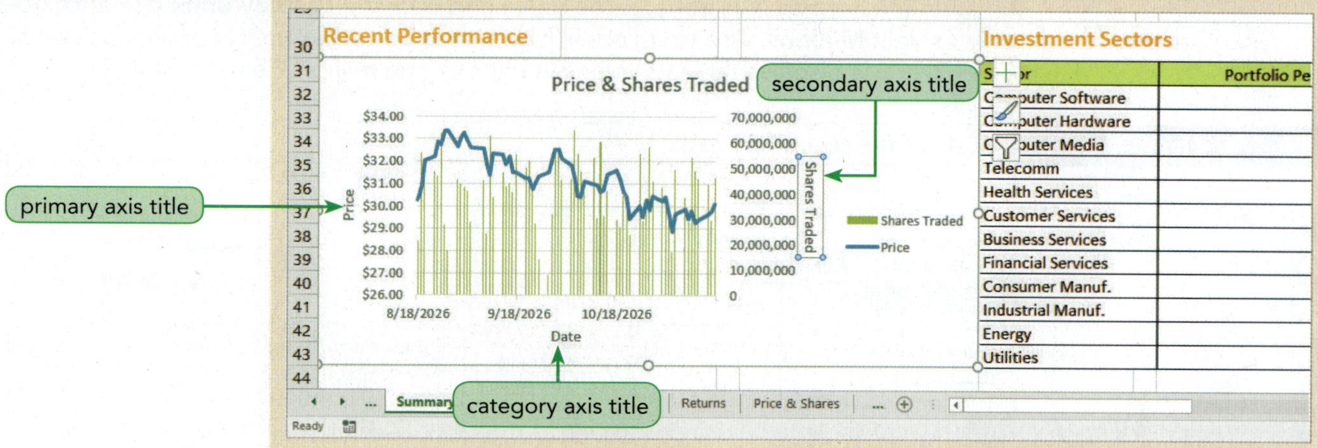

Editing a Value Axis Scale

Excel automatically chooses the range of values, or **scale**, used on the value primary and secondary axes. For the Price data series, the scale ranges from $26 to $34 and for the Shares Traded data series, the scale ranges from 0 to 70,000,000.

Excel automatically divides the scale into regular intervals, marked on the axis with tick marks and labels. **Major tick marks** identify the main units on the chart axis while **minor tick marks** identify the smaller intervals between the major tick marks. The major tick marks for the Price series are placed at intervals of $1 and the major tick marks for the Shares Traded Series are placed at intervals of 10,000,000 shares. There are no minor tick marks in combination chart. Tick marks placed so close together so that the tick mark labels overlap can make the chart difficult to read. On the other hand, increasing the gap between tick marks could make the chart less informative.

You'll use the Format Axis pane to specify a different scale for the secondary axis, changing the size of the scale used with the Shares Traded data. Hideki also wants you to expand the scale of the secondary axis so that the data markers for the column chart don't overlap the contents of the line chart.

To set the scale of the secondary axis:

1. Double-click the secondary axis values to open the Format Axis pane.
2. Click the **Axis Options** button if necessary, and then click the **Axis Options** label.
3. In the Bounds section at the top of the list of Axis Options, click the **Maximum** box and enter **1.6E08** (representing 160,000,000 in exponential notation) as the top-end of the scale for the secondary axis.
4. Press **TAB** to enter the new scale value. The scale of the secondary axis expands so that the column chart is displayed below the line chart.

When the range of the axis covers values of a large magnitude, you can simplify the axis labels by including the units as part of the scale. Hideki thinks the secondary axis numbers will look better without all the zeros in the axis values. You will display the secondary axis values in units of one million.

To set the display units for the secondary axis:

1. In the Format Axis pane, scroll down and click the **Display units** box and select **Millions**. The Unit Label "Millions" is added to the secondary axis and the axis displays the axis values in units of one million. See Figure 4–27.

Figure 4–27 Scale of the secondary axis

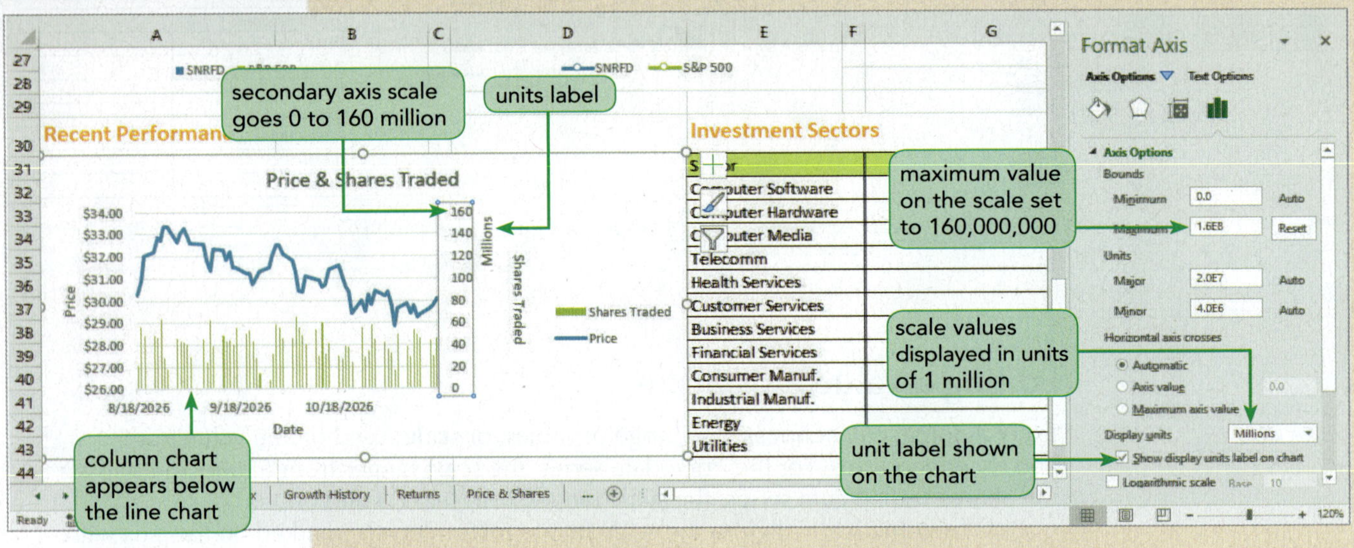

2. Close the Format Axis pane, and then save the workbook.

The combination chart comparing the yearly value of the Sunrise Fund to the S&P 500 index is complete. In the next session, you will create other charts and graphics that reveal valuable information about the Sunrise Fund.

Review

Session 4.1 Quick Check

1. In a chart's data source, where does Excel assume that category values are placed?
2. What three chart elements are included in a pie chart?
3. A data series contains values grouped into 12 categories. Would this data be better displayed as a pie chart or a column chart? Explain why.
4. A research firm wants to display the population of a state organized into five geographic locations. Which chart should it use? Explain why.
5. If the firm wants to display the total population growth of a state over a 10-year period organized by those five geographic locations, which chart type best displays this information? Explain why.
6. If the firm wants to display how the population of the geographic locations within the state changes over time as a percentage of the whole population, which chart type should it use? Explain why.
7. If the firm wants to display both the average annual income and the total population of the state over the 10-year period, what chart should it use and why?
8. What are major tick marks and minor tick marks?

Session 4.2 Visual Overview:

Icons from the Icon gallery on the Insert menu can be inserted in cells.

Data callouts are data labels that appear as callout bubbles pointing to data markers.

A **scatter chart** plots two data series of numeric values against each other.

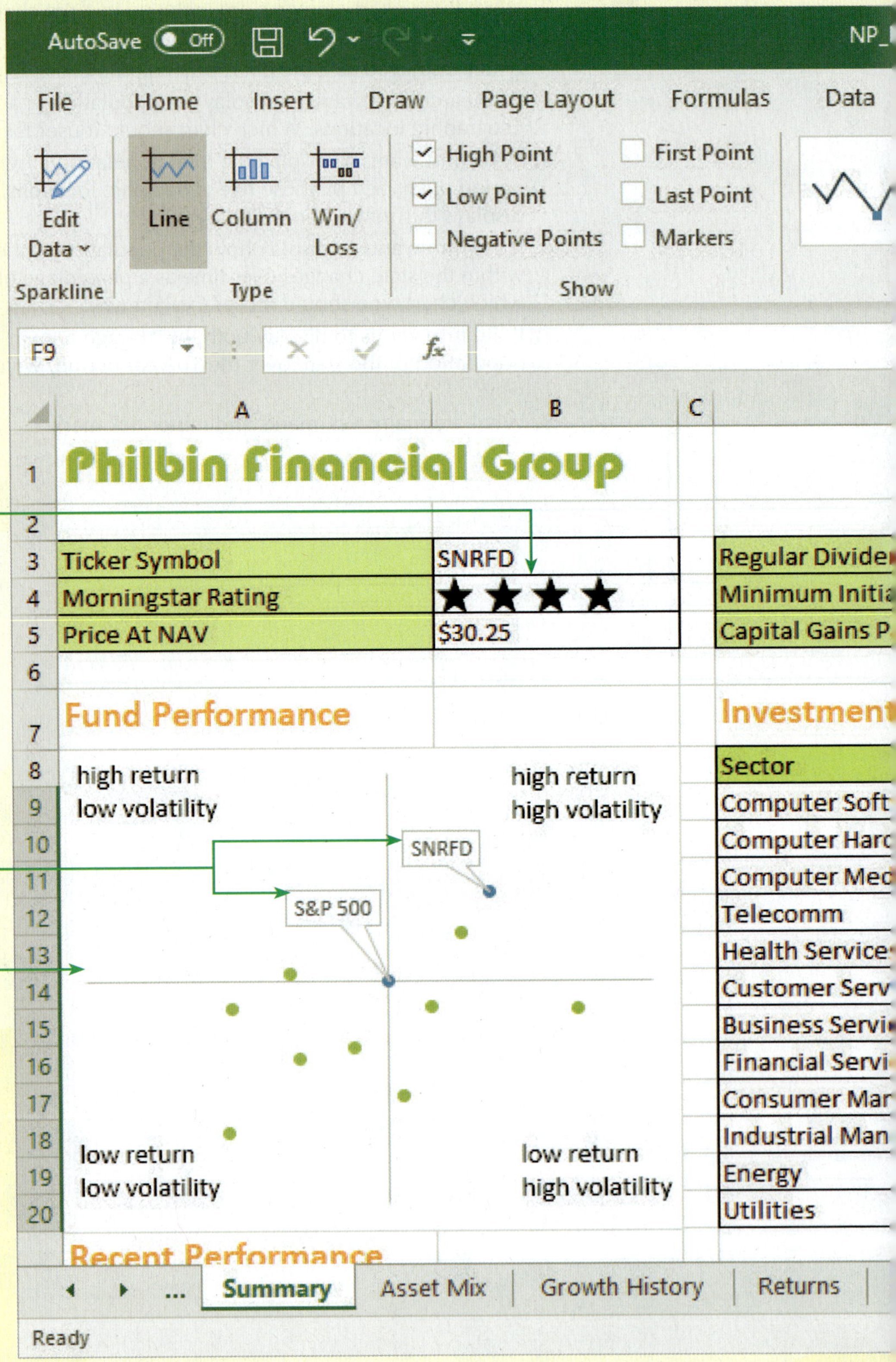

Scatter Charts, Data Bars, and Sparklines

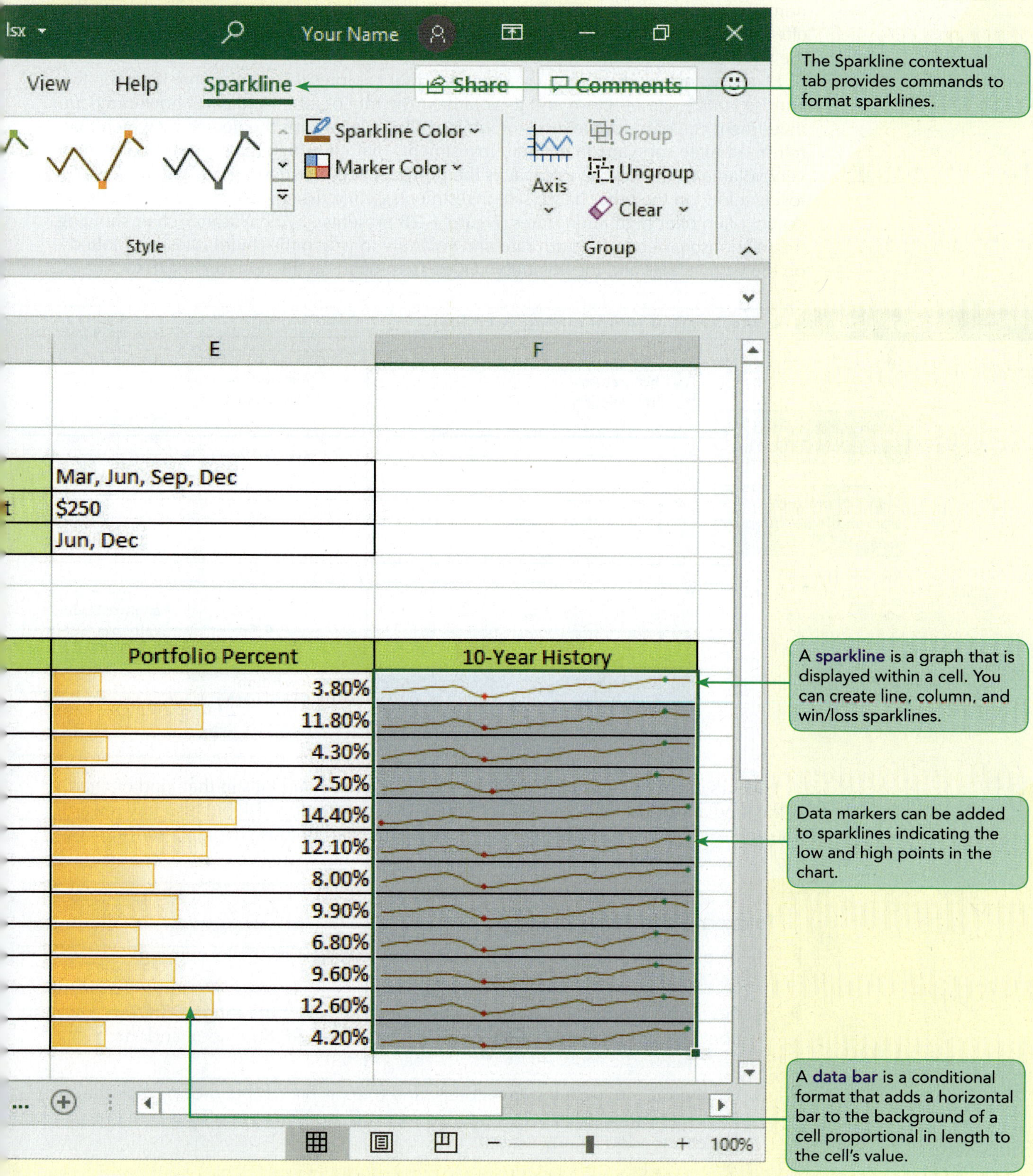

Creating a Scatter Chart

The charts you created in the previous session all involve plotting numeric data against categorical data. Another important type of chart is the scatter chart, which plots two data series of numeric values against each other. Scatter charts are widely used in science and engineering applications when investigators want to discover how two numeric variables are related. For example, an economist might want to investigate the effect of high tax rates on tax revenue or the effect of increasing the minimum wage on the unemployment rate.

Hideki wants you to create a scatter chart that explores the relationship between the Sunrise Fund's rate of return and its volatility. The rate of return indicates how much an investment can earn for the investor while volatility measures the degree by which that return estimate can vary. In general, investments that have high rates of return are often very volatile so that the investor faces the prospect of either making a lot of money or losing a lot. On the other hand, safe investments, while usually not very volatile, also do not often offer high return rates. Figure 4–28 presents a typical scatter chart showing the relationship between return rate and volatility in which the return rates are plotted on the vertical axis and the volatility values are plotted on the horizontal axis.

Figure 4–28 Scatter chart of return rate vs. volatility

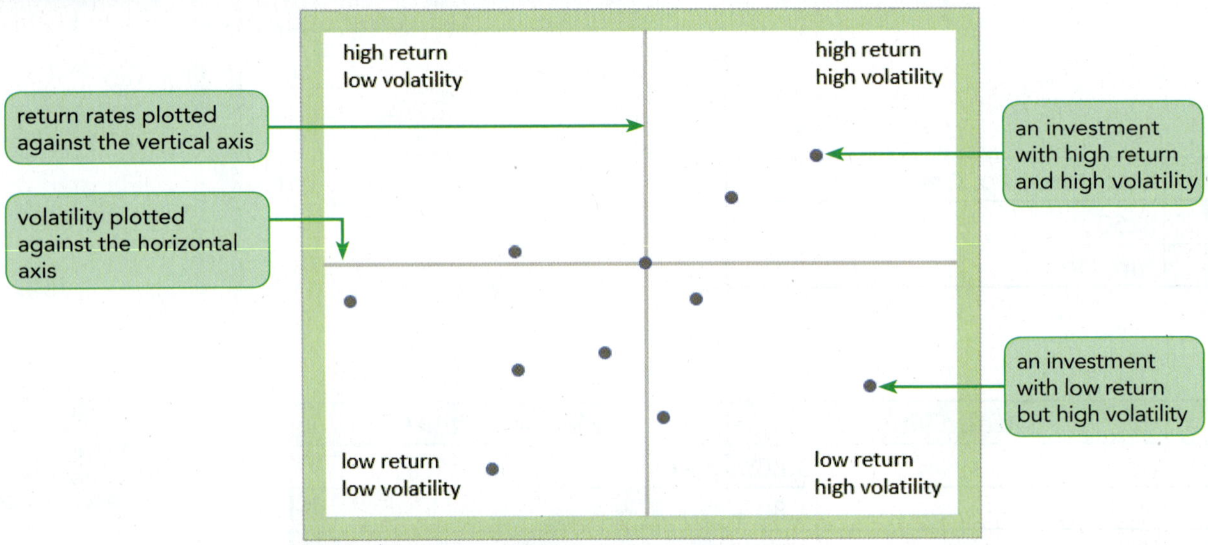

Hideki's clients will want to know where the Sunrise Fund falls in that kind of chart. Is the fund a high risk/high reward venture or does it offer low risk but also low reward? You will explore this question by creating a scatter chart of those two data series.

To create a scatter chart:

1. If you took a break at the end of the previous session, make sure the NP_EX_4_Sunrise workbook is open.
2. Go to the **Volatility & Return** worksheet and select the range **B5:C7** containing the volatility and return rates for the S&P 500 index and the Sunrise Fund calculated over a 10-year interval.
3. On the ribbon, click the **Insert** tab, and then in the Charts group, click the **Recommended Charts** button. The Insert Chart dialog box opens to the Recommended Charts tab.

4. In the gallery of recommended chart types, select **Scatter**. See Figure 4–29.

Figure 4–29 Scatter chart preview

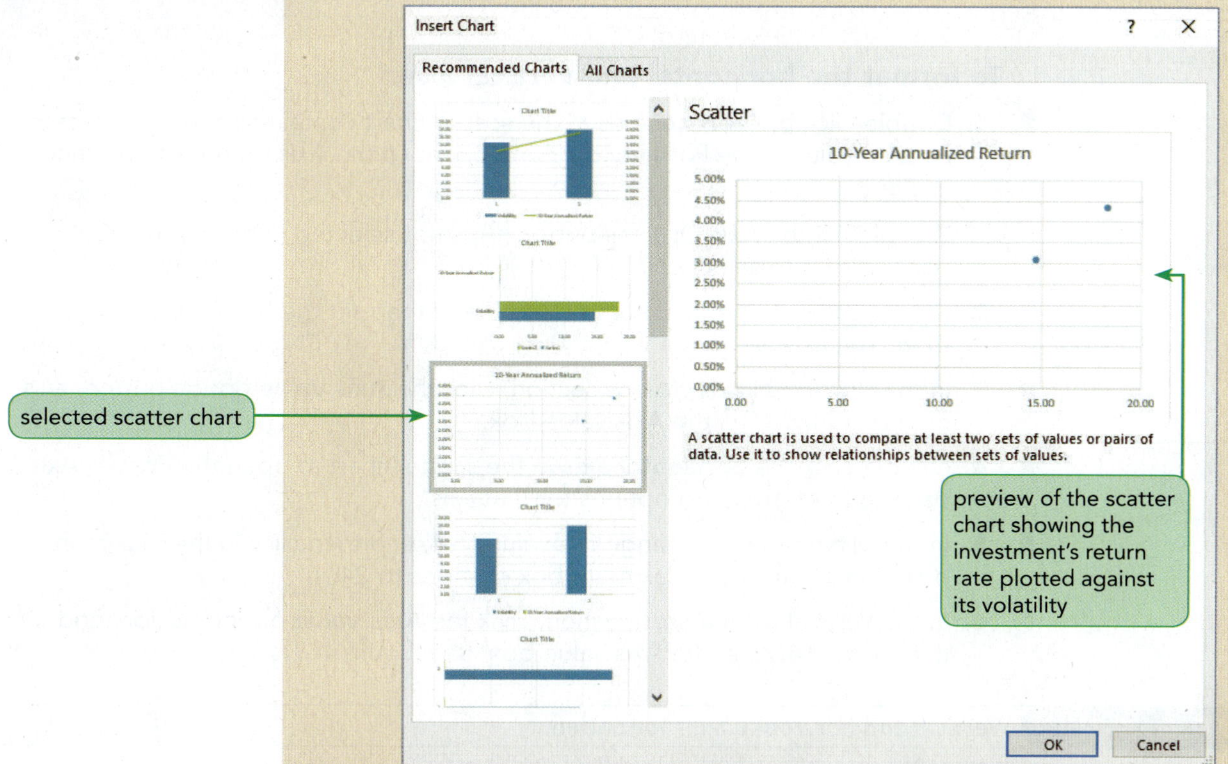

5. Click **OK** to insert the scatter chart.
6. Click the **Move Chart** button, select **Summary** from the Object in box, and then click **OK** to move the scatter chart to the Summary worksheet.
7. Move and resize the scatter chart to cover the range **G17:H28**, holding down the **ALT** key to snap the chart to the worksheet grid. See Figure 4–30.

Figure 4–30 Scatter chart

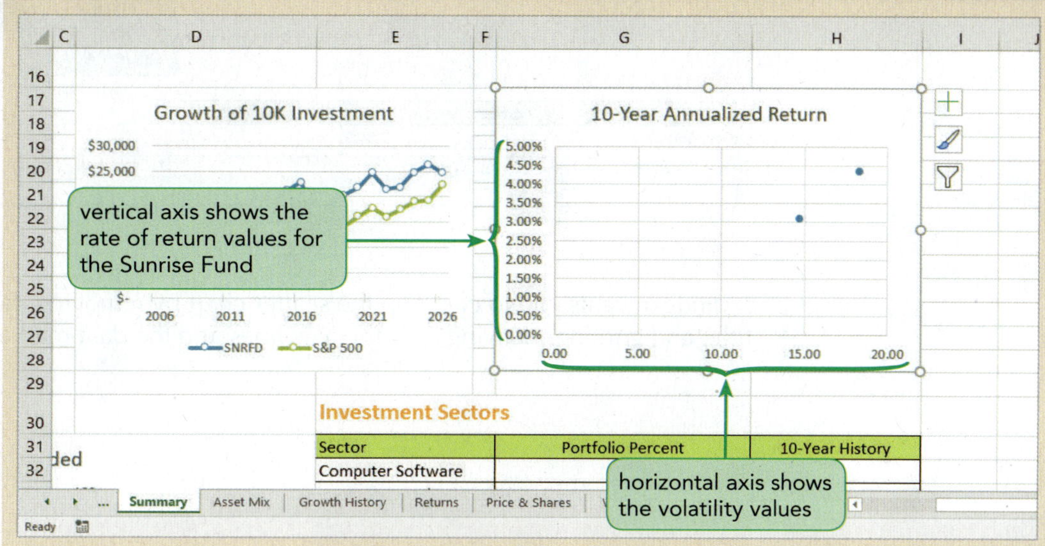

Scatter charts comparing rates to volatility are usually centered at a point representing a balance between the two. In most cases, this is an investment standard such as the S&P 500 index. To center the chart at that point you will modify the properties of both the vertical and horizontal axis so that those axes cross at the chart coordinates (0.031, 14.71), which is the return rate and volatility of the S&P 500 index. You'll format these axes now.

To format the horizontal and vertical axes:

1. Double-click the **vertical axis** in the scatter chart containing the rate of return percent values. The Format Axis pane opens to the Axis Options formatting choices.

   Trouble? If the Axis Options button is not selected in the Format Axis pane, click it to select it.

2. Set the value of the Minimum box to **0** and then set the Maximum box to **0.06**. The axis will range from 0.00% to 6.00%.
3. In the Horizontal axis crosses section, click the **Axis value** option button, and then enter **0.031** in the Axis value box.
4. Double-click the **horizontal axis** in the scatter chart to open the Format Axis pane to the formatting options for that axis.
5. In the Minimum box, change the value to **4**, and then click in the Maximum box. The value in the Maximum box changes to 24.
6. In the Vertical axis crosses section, click the **Axis value** option button, and then enter **14.71** in the Axis value box. See Figure 4–31.

Figure 4–31 Vertical and horizontal axes formatted

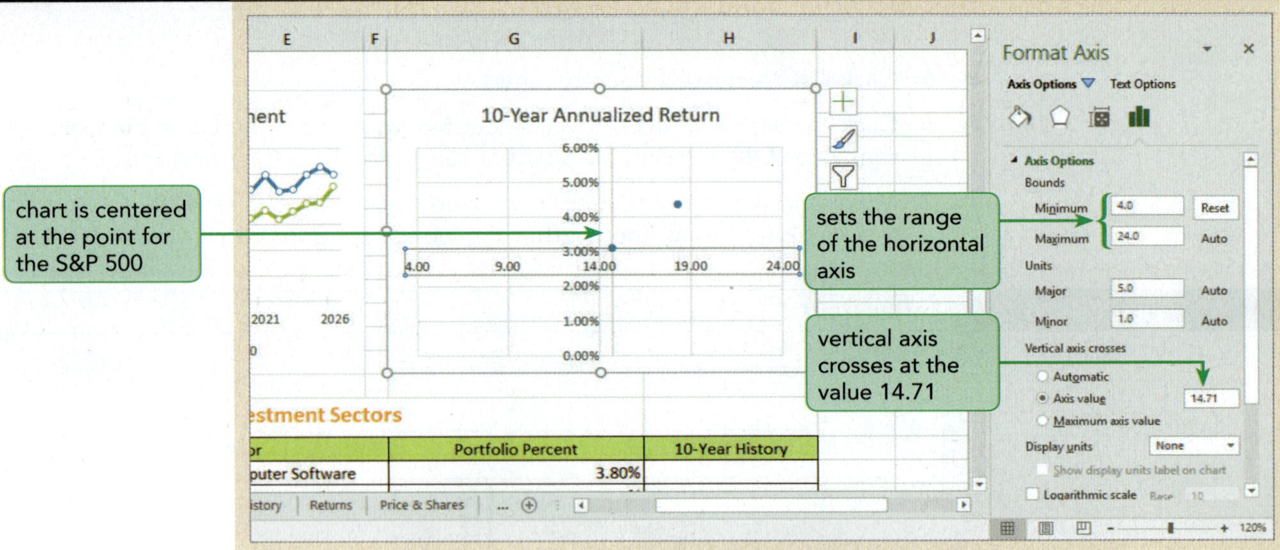

Hideki wants you to clean up the scatter chart by removing the axis labels, chart title, and gridlines, leaving only the axis lines and the data markers.

To remove elements from the scatter chart:

1. Scroll down the Format Axis pane for the horizontal axis, click the **Labels** section head, and then in the Label Position box, select **None** to remove the axis labels from the chart.
2. Double-click the labels for the vertical axis to display the Format Axis pane for the vertical axis.
3. Scroll down to the Labels section for that axis, and then select **None** from the Label Position box to remove the vertical axis labels.
4. On the Chart Design tab, in the Chart Layouts group, click the **Add Chart Element** button, point to **Chart Title**, and then click **None** to remove the chart title.
5. Click the **Add Chart Element** button, point to **Gridlines**, and then click **Primary Major Horizontal** and **Primary Major Vertical** to deselect those two options, removing them from the scatter chart.
6. Close the Format pane.

The scatter chart now contains only the two data points and the two axes lines. But with only two data markers in the chart, there's not a lot of basis for comparison with other investments. Hideki asks you to add data markers representing other funds to the scatter chart.

Insight

Copying and Pasting Chart Formats

You will often want to repeat the same design for the charts in your worksheet. Rather than rerun the same commands, you can copy the formatting from one chart to another. To copy a chart format, first select the chart with the existing design that you want to replicate, and then click the Copy button in the Clipboard group on the Home tab (or press CTRL+C). Next, select the chart that you want to format, click the Paste arrow in the Clipboard group, and then click Paste Special to open the Paste Special dialog box. In the Paste Special dialog box, select the Formats option button, and then click OK. All the copied formats from the original chart—including fill colors, font styles, axis scales, and chart types—are then pasted into the new chart. Be aware that the pasted formats will overwrite any formats previously used in the new chart.

Editing the Chart Data Source

Excel automates most of the process of assigning a data source to the chart. However, sometimes the completed chart is not what you want, and you need to edit the chart's data source. At any time, you can modify the chart's data source to add more data series or change the current data series in the chart.

Reference

Modifying a Chart's Data Source

- Select the chart to make it active.
- On the Chart Design tab, in the Data group, click the Select Data button.
- In the Legend Entries (Series) section of the Select Data Source dialog box, click the Add button to add another data series to the chart or click the Remove button to remove a data series from the chart.
- Click the Edit button in the Horizontal (Category) Axis Labels section to select the category values for the chart.
- Click OK.

Hideki wants you to add a data series containing information from other funds to the scatter chart of returns vs. volatility. You'll edit the chart's data source definition to make that change.

To edit the chart's data source:

1. With the scatter chart still selected, on the Chart Design tab, in the Data group, click the **Select Data** button. The Select Data Source dialog box opens. See Figure 4–32.

Figure 4–32 Select Data Source dialog box

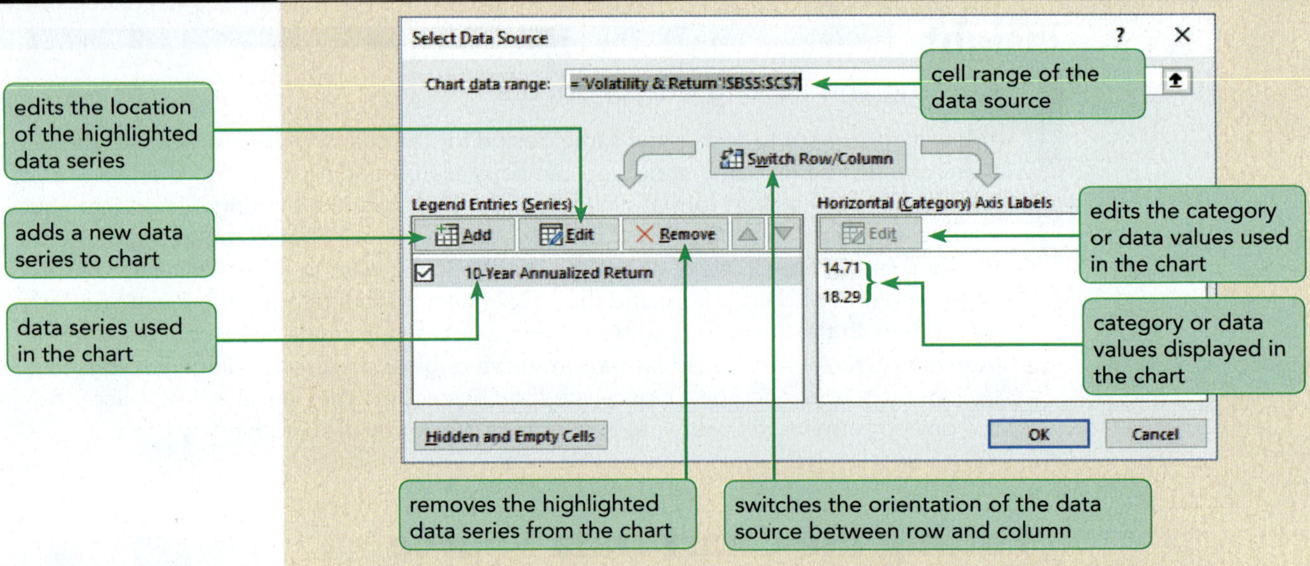

Tip

To organize a chart's data source by rows rather than columns (or vice-versa), click the Switch Row/Column button in the Select Data Source dialog box.

2. Click **Add** to open the Edit Series dialog box. You can add another data series to the chart from here.
3. With the insertion point in the Series name box, click the **Volatility & Return** sheet tab, and then click cell **G5** in that worksheet. The expression `='Volatility & Return'!$G$5` is entered into the Series name box.
4. Click the **Series X values** box, click the **Volatility & Return** sheet tab if necessary, and then select the range **F6:F14** to enter the expression `='Volatility & Return'!$F$6:$F$14`.
5. Click the **Series Y values** box, delete any expression in that box, and then select the range **G6:G14** in the Volatility & Return worksheet, inserting the expression `='Volatility & Return!'$G$6:$G$14` into the box. See Figure 4–33.

Values or expressions might already be entered into the Edit Series dialog box, so you must delete any expressions before inserting a new reference.

Figure 4–33 Edit Series dialog box

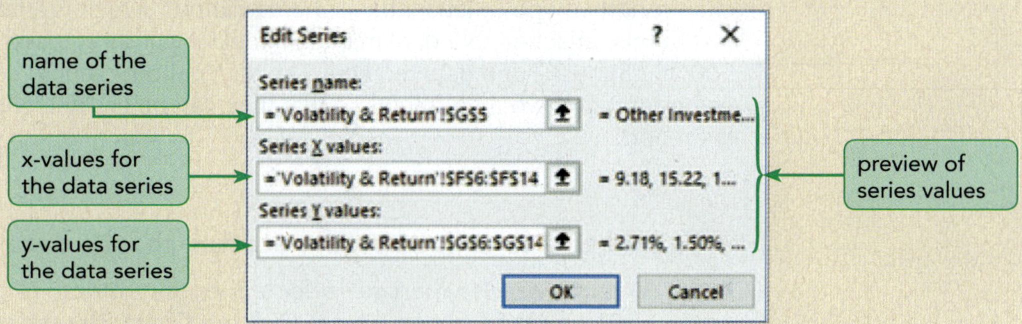

6. Click **OK** to return to Select Data Source dialog box. Note that the data series "Other Investment Fund Returns" has been added to the list of data series.
7. Click **OK** to return to the Summary worksheet. Data markers for the second data series are added to the scatter chart.

You've simplified the scatter chart by removing elements that Hideki feels will not be of interest to the company's investors (such as the exact values of the stock's volatility). However, the chart still needs some descriptive information to aid in its interpretation. You'll add this additional text and graphics to the chart and worksheet next.

Insight

Adding Trendlines to Charts

Scatter charts are often used in statistical analysis and scientific studies in which the researcher attempts to find a relationship between one variable and another. For that purpose, Excel includes several statistical tools to augment scatter charts. One of these tools is a **trendline**, which is a line representing the general direction in a data series. Excel supports several different kinds of trendlines, include linear (or straight) lines, exponential curves, power curves, and logarithmic curves. Excel draws the trendline to best fit the data in the scatter chart.

You can add a trendline to any scatter chart by right-clicking the data series in the chart, and then clicking Add Trendline on the shortcut menu to open the Format Trendline pane. From the Format Trendline pane, you can select the trendline type. If the scatter chart plots a data series against a time variable, you can also extend the trendline to project future values, as might be done if a company wanted to project future earnings based on the trend of current earnings. Excel also provides summary statistics indicating how well the trendline fits the data.

Adding Graphic Objects to a Workbook

Another way of enhancing your workbooks is with graphic art. Excel supports a large gallery of clip art and icons to supplement your charts and worksheet data. One graphic feature you can add to charts is a data callout.

Adding a Data Callout to a Chart

In the previous session, you used a data label to display percentage values in a pie chart. Another type of data label is a **data callout**, which is a label that appears as a text bubble attached to a data marker. Hideki suggests you add data callouts to S&P 500 and Sunrise Fund data markers. The data callouts should contain the abbreviated names of those two investments so that they can be easily identified by clients viewing the report.

To add a data callout to the scatter chart's data markers:

1. With the scatter chart still selected, on the ribbon, click the **Format** tab. In the Current Selection group, click the **Chart Elements arrow**, and then click **Series "10-Year Annualized Return"** to select the two data makers for that data series.
2. Click the **Chart Design** tab. In the Chart Layouts group, click the **Add Chart Element** button, point to **Data Labels**, and then click **Data Callout** to add callouts to the two data makers in the series. Excel inserts the volatility and return values into the two data callouts. You will change those values, so they reference the abbreviated names of the two investments.
3. Right-click either of the two data labels, and then click **Format Data Labels** on the shortcut menu. The Format Data Labels pane opens.
4. Click the **Value from Cells** check box. The Data Label Range dialog box opens.
5. Click the **Volatility & Return** sheet tab, and then select the range **A6:A7** to enter the expression `='Volatility & Return!'$A$6:$A7` into the Select Data Label Range box.
6. Click **OK**.
7. Click the **X Value** and **Y Value** check boxes to deselect them. See Figure 4–34.

Tip

You can change the shape of the callout by right-clicking the data callout, clicking Change Data Label Shapes, and choosing a callout shape.

Figure 4–34 Data callouts added to the scatter chart

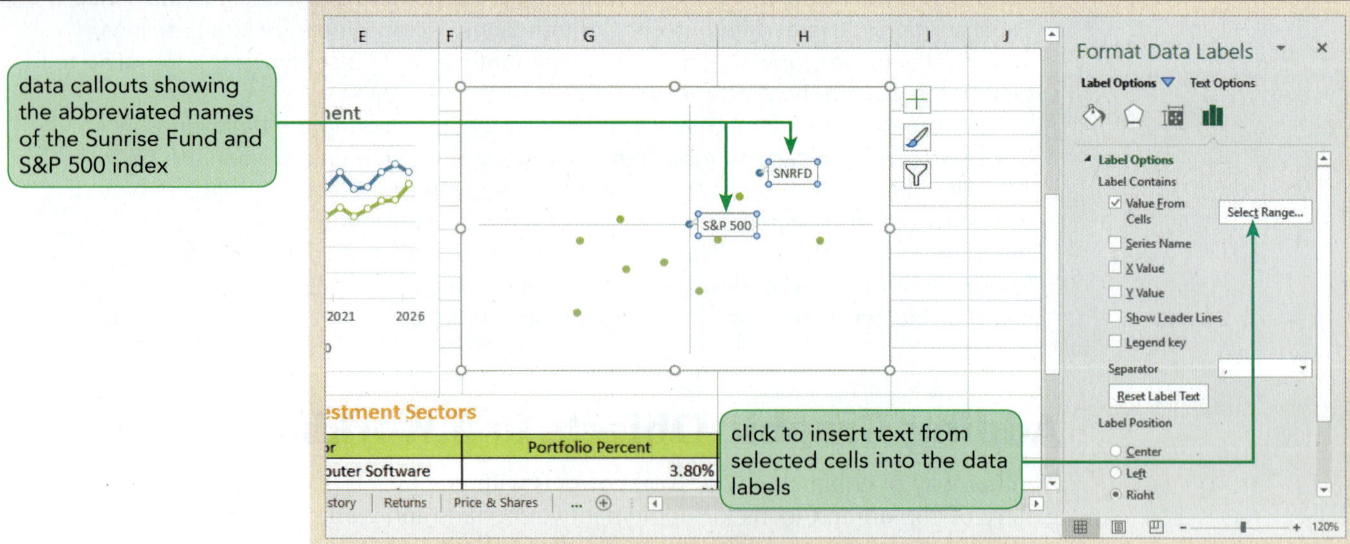

8. Close the Format Data Labels pane.

Inserting a Graphic Shape

Microsoft Office supports a gallery of over 160 shapes that can be added to any workbook or other Office document. The shape gallery includes rectangles, circles, arrows, stars, flow chart symbols, and text boxes. Each shape can be resized and formatted with a wide selection of colors, line styles, and special effects such as drop shadows and glowing borders. You can insert text strings, including numbered and bulleted lists, to any graphic shape.

Hideki asks you to complete the return rate/volatility scatter chart by inserting text boxes in the four corners of the chart, indicating which chart quadrant corresponds to high or low return rates and high or low volatility. You will insert the text box from the shape gallery.

To insert a text box:

1. With the scatter chart still selected, click the **Insert** tab on the ribbon.
2. In the Illustrations group, click the **Illustrations** button, and then click the **Shapes** button. The Shapes gallery opens, organized into the categories of Recently Used Shapes, Lines, Rectangles, Basic Shapes, Block Arrows, Equations Shapes, Flowchart, Stars and Banners, and Callouts.

   Trouble? Depending on your monitor and settings, you may not see the Illustrations button. In that case, click the Shapes button in the Illustrations group.
3. In the Basic Shapes group, click the **Text Box** shape.
4. Click near the upper-left corner of the scatter chart. A box opens in which the text box will be entered.
5. Type **high return** as the first line of text in the text box, press **ENTER**, and then type **low volatility** as the second line of text in the text box.
6. Click and drag the **sizing handles** around the selected text box as needed to reduce the text box to fit the text.
7. Point to the text box border so the pointer changes to the Move pointer, and then drag the text box so that it aligns with the upper-left corner of the scatter chart.
8. Repeat Steps 2 through 7 to insert a text box containing **high return** and **high volatility** (placing the return and volatility text strings on different lines) in the upper-right corner of the chart.
9. Repeat Steps 2 through 7 to insert a text box containing **low return** and **low volatility** on separate lines in the lower-left corner of the chart.
10. Repeat Steps 2 through 7 to insert a text box containing **low return** and **high volatility** on separate lines in the lower-right corner of the chart. See Figure 4–35, which shows the final design of the scatter chart of return rate versus volatility.

Figure 4–35 Text boxes added to a scatter chart

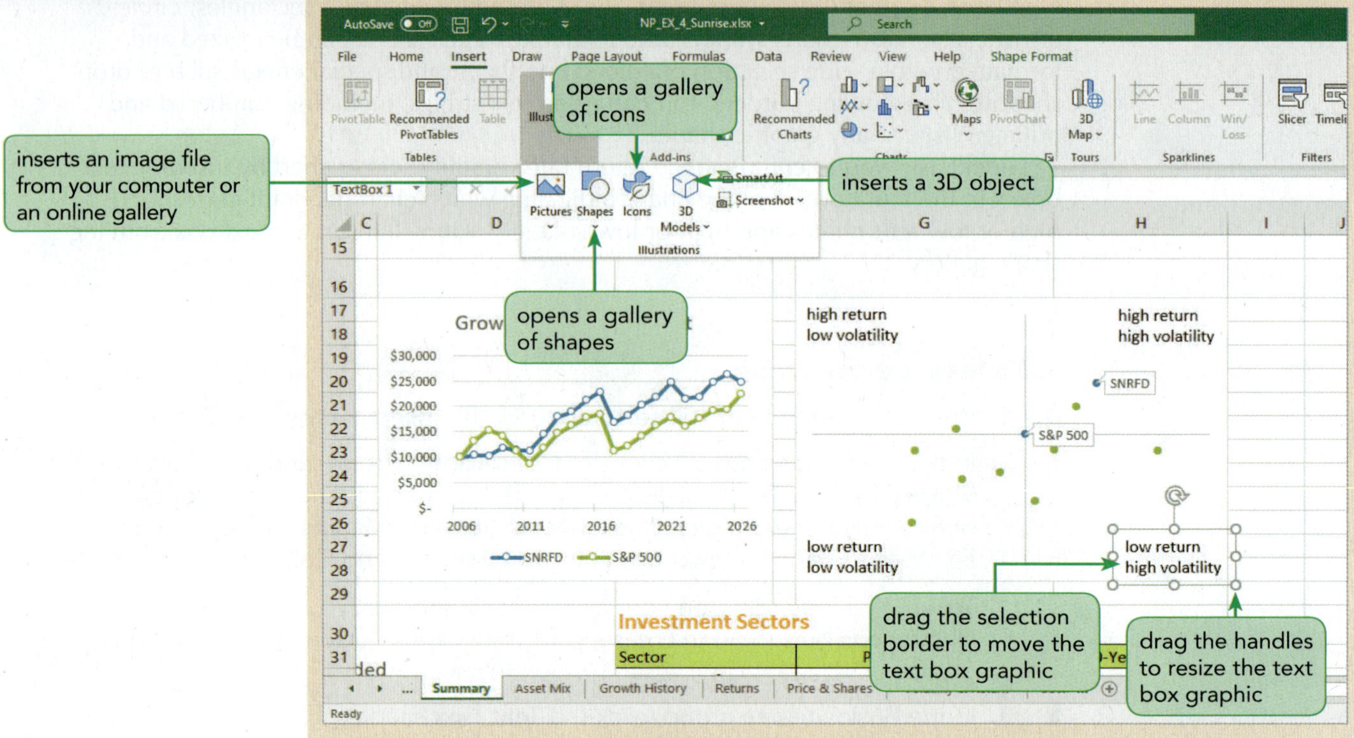

With the final version of the scatter chart, Hideki's clients can quickly identify the Sunrise Fund as a high return, high volatility investment, particularly when compared to the S&P 500 index and other sample investments.

Inserting Graphic Icons

Graphic icons, another type of graphic object supported by Microsoft Office, are common symbols often found in signs and posters. Like shapes, icons can be resized and reformatted to meet a variety of design needs. Office organizes icons in a wide range of categories from icons used for business to icons of animals to icons with a sports theme.

In cell B9 of the Summary worksheet, Hideki entered the rating of the Sunrise Fund given by Morningstar, an investment research firm that rates investments and funds. Ratings range from 1 star (poor) to 5 stars (the best). Morningstar has given the Sunrise Fund a 4-star rating. Hideki wants to replace the text "4 stars" with four star icons. You'll use the icon gallery to insert those images into cell B9.

Tip

You can also insert star images using the star shape from the Shapes gallery.

To insert the star icons from the icon gallery:

1. In the Summary worksheet, select cell **B9**, and then press **DELETE** to delete the contents of the cell.
2. On the Insert tab, in the Illustrations group, click the **Illustrations** button, and then click **Icons**. The Insert Icons dialog box opens.

   Trouble? Depending on your monitor and settings, you may not see the Illustrations button. In that case, click the Icons button in the Illustrations group.
3. Type **Celebration** in the Search box, press **ENTER**, and then click the **star** icon to select it. See Figure 4–36.

Figure 4–36 **Insert Icons dialog box**

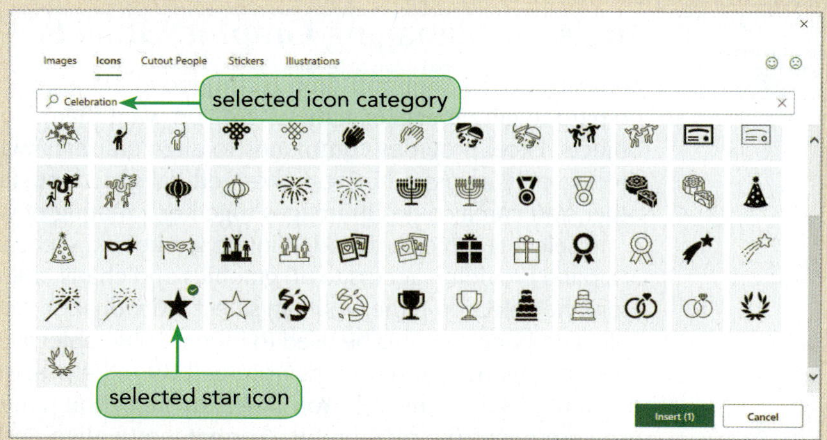

4. Click **Insert** to insert the icon into cell B9. Because the icon is selected, the Graphics Format tab appears on the ribbon.
5. On the Graphics Format tab, in the Size group, click the **Height** box, type **0.25**, and then press **ENTER**. Both the height and width change to 0.25 inches.
6. With the star icon still selected, press **CTRL+C** to copy the icon, and then press **CTRL+V** three times to paste three more star icons into the worksheet.
7. Click and drag each of the four icons so that they are aligned in cell B9. Don't worry about exactly arranging the icons within the cell. See Figure 4–37.

Figure 4–37 **Icons in the worksheet**

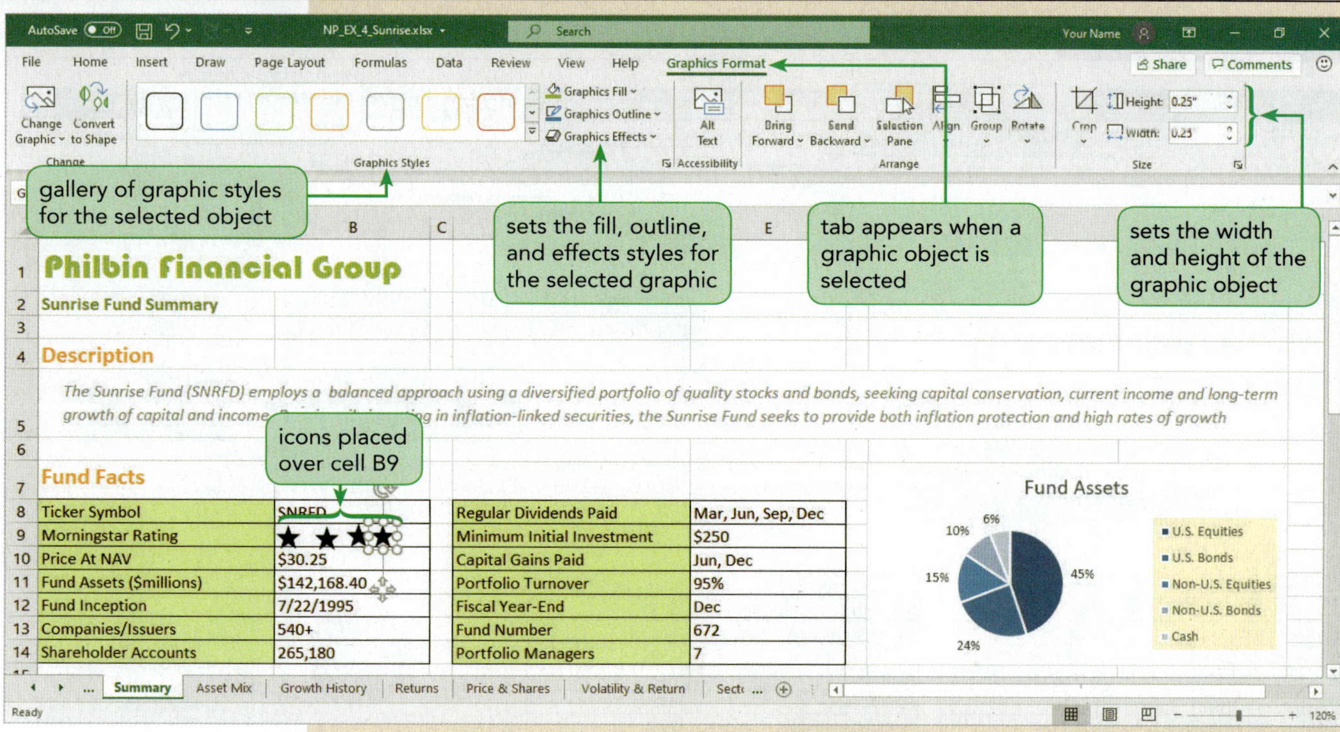

Tip

To align a graphic object with the edges of a cell, hold down ALT as you drag and drop the object image.

The star icons appear in cell B9 but note that they are not part of the cell's content. Like embedded charts, a graphic shape icon is placed on top of the worksheet grid.

Tools for Managing Graphic Objects

You can use the drag-and-drop technique to place your graphic objects, but it can be hard to get objects exactly where you want them. For more precise placement of objects, Excel provides commands to align graphics within a row or column, distribute them evenly across a horizontal or vertical space, or stack graphics on top of each other. You can also group images together, creating new classes of graphic objects.

To select graphics embedded in the workbook, you can open the Selection pane, which is a pane providing access to all graphics and charts embedded in the current workbook. From the Selection pane, you can select individual or groups of graphic objects. The Selection pane can also be used to hide graphic objects or reveal hidden graphics.

Hideki wants the star icons from cell B9 to be precisely aligned and evenly distributed across the cell. You'll use the Selection pane to select those icons and then use commands on the Graphics Format tab to align and distribute the icons.

To select and place icons within the worksheet:

1. On the Graphics Format tab, in the Arrange group, click the **Selection Pane** button. A list of graphics and charts in the current worksheet appears in the Selection pane.
2. Hold down **CTRL** and click the names of the four graphics listed in the Selection pane so that all four are selected in both the pane and the worksheet.
3. On the Graphics Format tab, in the Arrange group, click the **Align** button, and then click **Align Middle** so that the icons are aligned through their middles.
4. Click the **Align** button again, and then click **Distribute Horizontally** so that the icons are evenly distributed in the horizontal direction. See Figure 4–38.

Figure 4–38 **Graphics aligned in the worksheet**

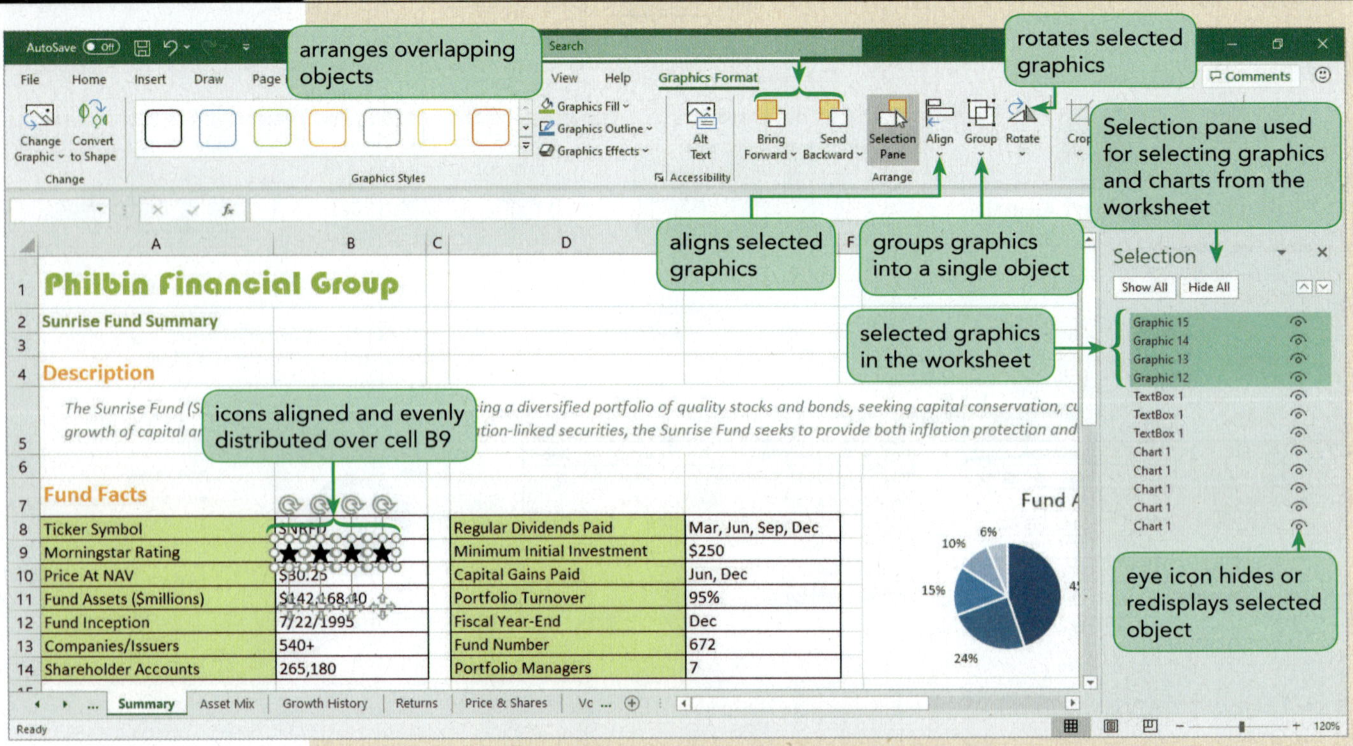

Trouble? Depending on how you created your graphics and charts, you might have different names assigned to the graphic and chart objects in the Selection pane.

5. Click the **Close** button in the upper-right corner of the Selection pane to close it.

You can also use your mouse to select graphic objects, but first you must switch to Select Object mode by clicking the Find & Select button in the Editing group on the Home tab and then clicking the Select Object command. The pointer will switch to a mode for selecting objects rather than worksheet cells. To turn off the Select Object mode so the mouse can select cells again, click the Select Object command on the Find & Select button, disabling Select Object mode.

Exploring Other Chart Types

At this point, you've used only a few of the many Excel chart types. Excel has other chart types that are useful for financial and scientific research, which you can access from the Charts group on the Insert tab. If you want to change the chart type of an existing chart, click the Change Chart Type button in the Type group on the Chart Design tab and then select the new chart type from the dialog box.

Hierarchy Charts

Hierarchy charts are like pie charts in that they show the relative contribution of groups to a whole. Unlike pie charts, a hierarchy chart also shows the organizational structure of the data with subcategories displayed within main categories. Excel supports two types of hierarchy charts: treemap charts and sunburst charts.

In a **treemap chart**, each category is placed within a rectangle, and subcategories are nested as rectangles within those rectangles. The rectangles are sized to show the relative proportions of the two groups based on values from a data series. The treemap chart in Figure 4–39 shows the investor sectors of the Sunrise Fund broken down by group and category. You can create a treemap chart by clicking the Recommended Charts button and then selecting Treemap from the list of chart types on the All Charts tab.

Figure 4–39 Treemap and Sunburst charts

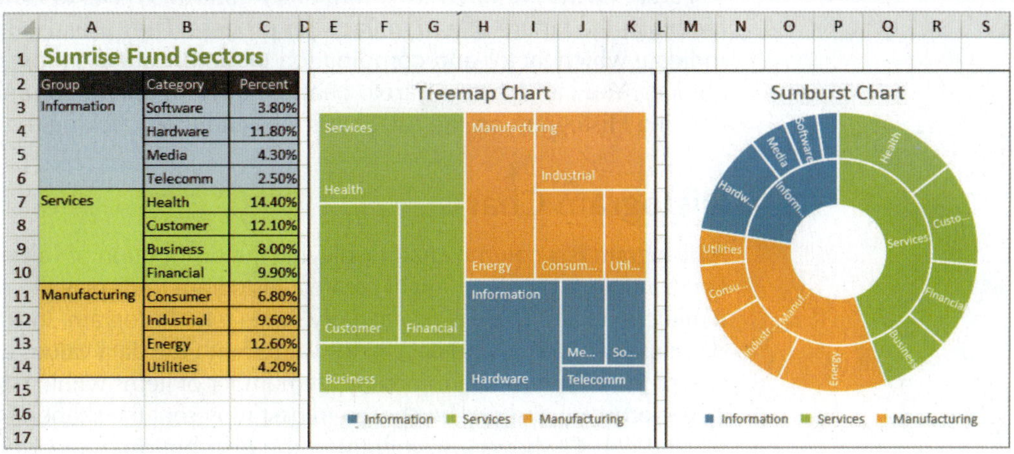

A **sunburst chart** organizes hierarchical data through a series of concentric rings with the innermost rings showing the highest category levels and the outer rings showing categories from lower levels. The size of the rings indicates the relative proportions of the different groups and categories within groups. See Figure 4–39. Sunburst charts are better than treemap charts at conveying information from multiple levels of nested groups. But treemaps are better at displaying the relative sizes of the categories within each group level. You can create a sunburst chart by clicking the Recommended Charts button and then selecting Sunburst from the list of chart types on the All Charts tab.

Pareto Charts

A special kind of combination chart is the **Pareto chart**, which combines a column chart and a line chart to indicate which factors are the largest contributors to the whole. Figure 4–40 shows a Pareto chart of investment categories. The categories are sorted in descending order of importance so that the largest investment category, Health, is listed first followed by Energy, Customer, Hardware, and so forth. The line chart provides a running total of the percentage that each category adds to the overall total. Roughly 50% of the Sunrise Fund is invested in the first four categories listed in the chart.

Figure 4–40 Pareto chart

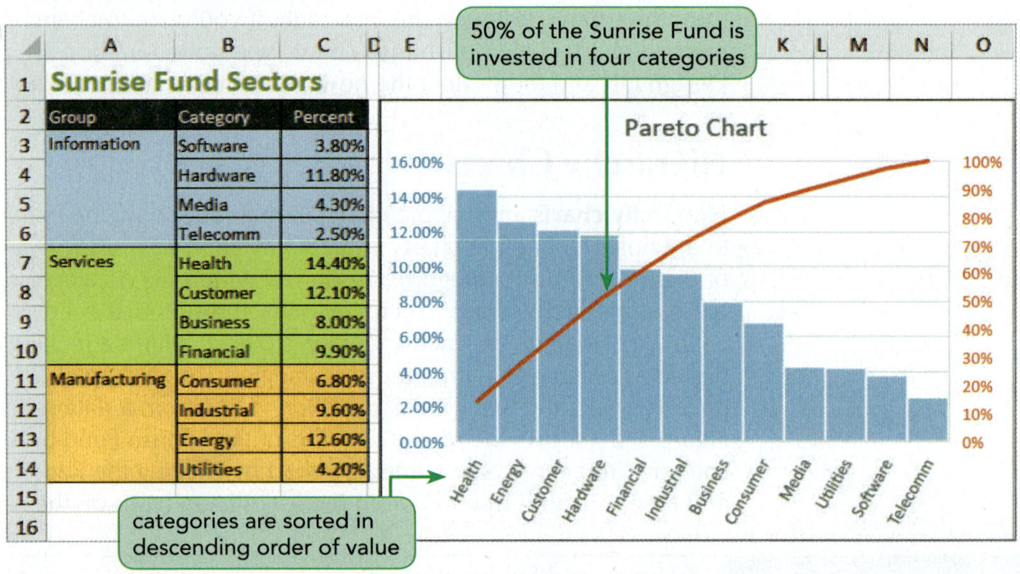

Pareto charts are often used in quality control studies to isolate the most significant factors in the failure of a manufacturer process. They are also in market research to indicate which factor and combination of factors are the most crucial in consumer choices. You can create a Pareto chart by clicking the Recommended Charts button, clicking Histogram on the All Charts tab, and then clicking the Pareto chart type.

Histogram Charts

A **histogram** is a column chart displaying the distribution of values from a single data series. For example, a professor might create a histogram to display the distribution of scores from a midterm exam. There is no category series for a histogram. Instead, the categories are determined based on the data series values with the data values allocated to **bins** and the size of the columns determined by the number of items within each bin. The number of bins is arbitrary and can be chosen to best represent the shape of the distribution.

Figure 4–41 shows a histogram of the distribution of the weekly price of the Sunrise Fund over a 15-month period. From the histogram it's clear that the price of the Sunrise Fund most often falls between $29 and $30 (the bin with the most values), but there are a few values as low as $23 to $24 and as high as $36 to $37. You can create a Histogram by clicking the Recommended Charts button, clicking Histogram on the All Charts tab, and then selecting the Histogram chart type.

Figure 4–41 **Histogram chart**

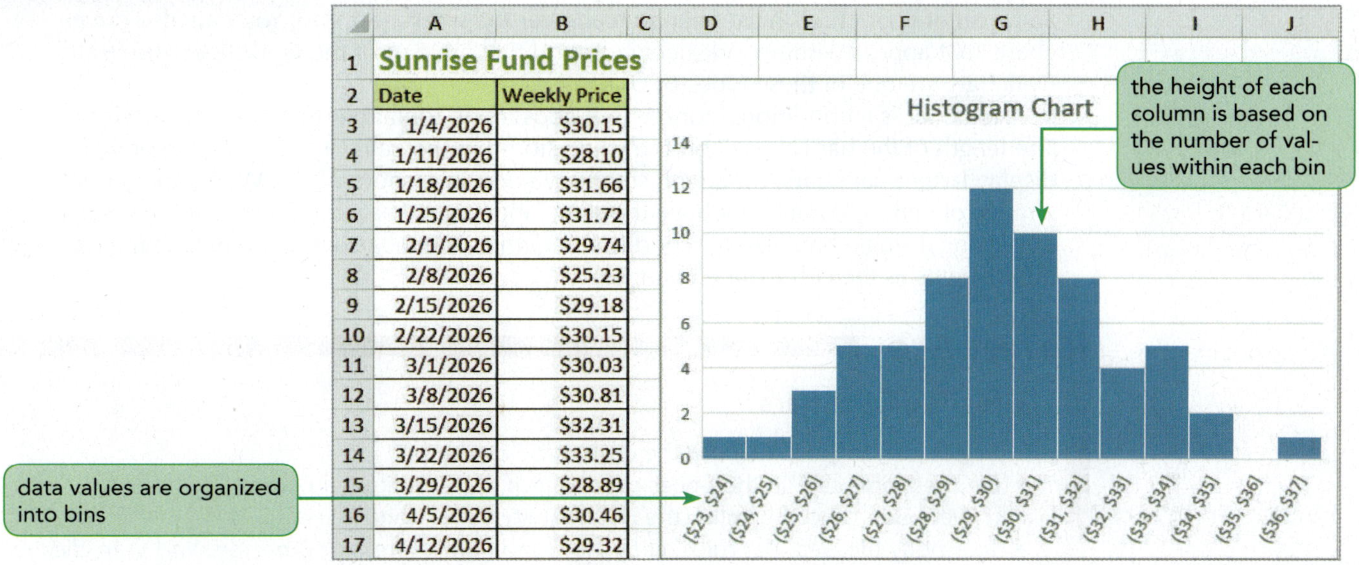

To modify the bins used in the histogram, double-click the horizontal axis to open the Format Axis pane and then set the bin size or the number of bins in the Bins section of the Axis Options section.

Waterfall Charts

A **waterfall chart** tracks the addition and subtraction of values within a sum. Figure 4–42 shows a waterfall chart of the value of an investment in the Sunrise Fund over five years. The initial and final value of the fund are shown in red. Positive changes in the fund's value are shown in green. Years in which the fund decreased in value are shown in dark gray. The waterfall chart is so named because the increasing and decreasing steps in the graph resemble a waterfall.

Figure 4–42 **Waterfall chart**

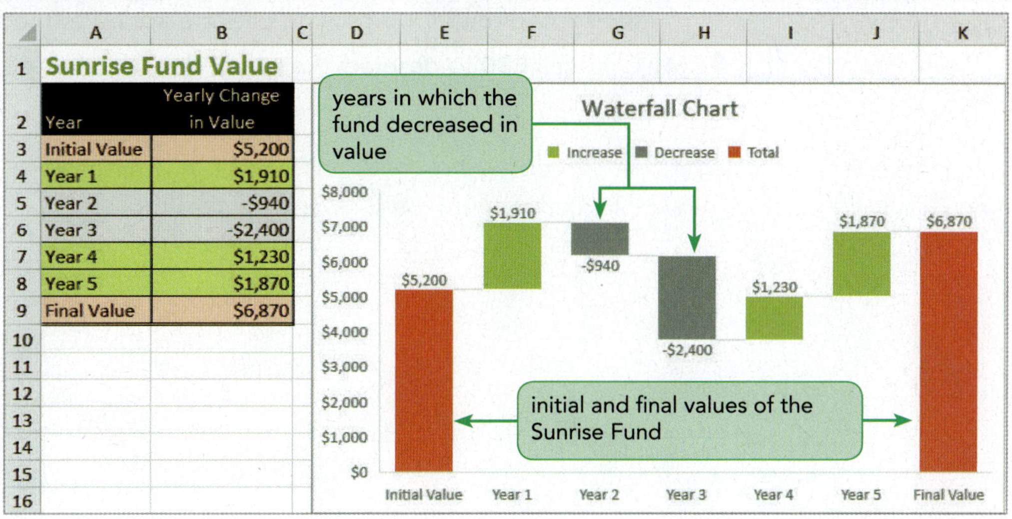

Waterfall charts are often used with Profit and Loss statements to track the impact of revenue and expenses on a company's net profit.

Creating Data Bars

So far all of your charts have been placed over the worksheet grid. You can also create charts that appear within worksheet cells and that are part of the worksheet grid itself. Data bars are one of these types of charts.

A data bar is a conditional format that adds a horizontal bar to a cell background. The length of the bar is based on the value stored in the cell. Cells storing larger values display longer data bars; cells with smaller values have shorter bars. When applied to a range of cells, the data bars have the same appearance as a bar chart, with each cell displaying a single bar. Like all conditional formats, data bars are dynamic, changing their lengths as the cell's value changes.

Reference

Creating Data Bars

- Select the range containing the data to be charted.
- On the Home tab, in the Styles group, click the Conditional Formatting button, point to Data Bars, and then click the data bar style you want to use.
- To modify the data bar rules, click the Conditional Formatting button, and then click Manage Rules.

Hideki inserted data on the economic sectors in which the Sunrise Fund invests in the range E31:G43 on the Summary worksheet. You'll display the percentage figures in the range G32:G43 with data bars.

To add data bars to the portfolio percentages in the worksheet:

1. On the Summary worksheet, select the range **G32:G43**.
2. On the ribbon, click the **Home** tab. In the Styles group, click the **Conditional Formatting** button, and then click **Data Bars**. A gallery of data bar styles opens.
3. In the Gradient Fill section, click the **Orange Data Bar** style (the first style in the second row). Orange data bars are added to the selected cells.
4. Click cell **E30** to deselect the range. See Figure 4–43.

Figure 4–43 Data bars added to the Summary worksheet

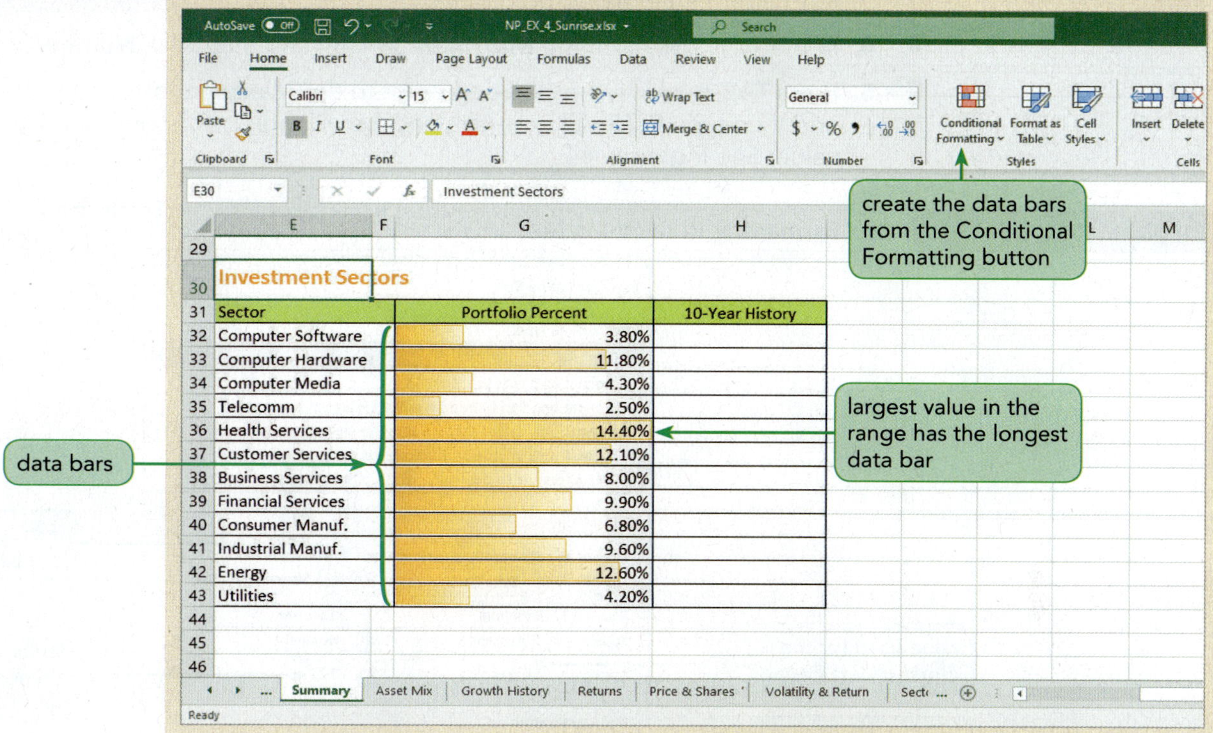

The data bars allow comparison of the relative size of the investment sectors for the Sunrise Fund. However, some of the data bars cover their cell value. Hideki wants you to shorten the length of the bars so that there is no overlap.

Modifying a Data Bar Rule

By default, the cell with the largest value in the range will have a data bar that stretches across the width of the cell. You can modify the length of the data bars by altering the rules of the conditional format.

The longest data bar is in cell G36, representing the amount of the fund invested in health services (14.40%). You'll modify the conditional format rule for the data bar, setting the maximum length to 0.25 so that the longest bar doesn't overlap the value in its cell.

Tip

When the range contains negative values, the data bars originate from the center of the cell—negative bars extend to the left, and positive bars extend to the right.

To modify the data bar conditional formatting rule:

1. On the Home tab, in the Styles group, click the **Conditional Formatting** button, and then click **Manage Rules**. The Conditional Formatting Rules Manager dialog box opens, displaying all the rules applied to any conditional format in the workbook.
2. In the Show formatting rules for box, select **This Worksheet** to show all the conditional formatting rules for the current sheet.

3. With the Data Bar rule selected, click the **Edit Rule** button. The Edit Formatting Rule dialog box opens.
4. In the Type row, click the **Maximum arrow**, and then click **Number**.
5. Press **TAB** to move the insertion point to the Maximum box in the Value row, and then type **0.25**. All data bar lengths will then be defined relative to this value. See Figure 4–44.

Figure 4–44 Edit Formatting Rule dialog box

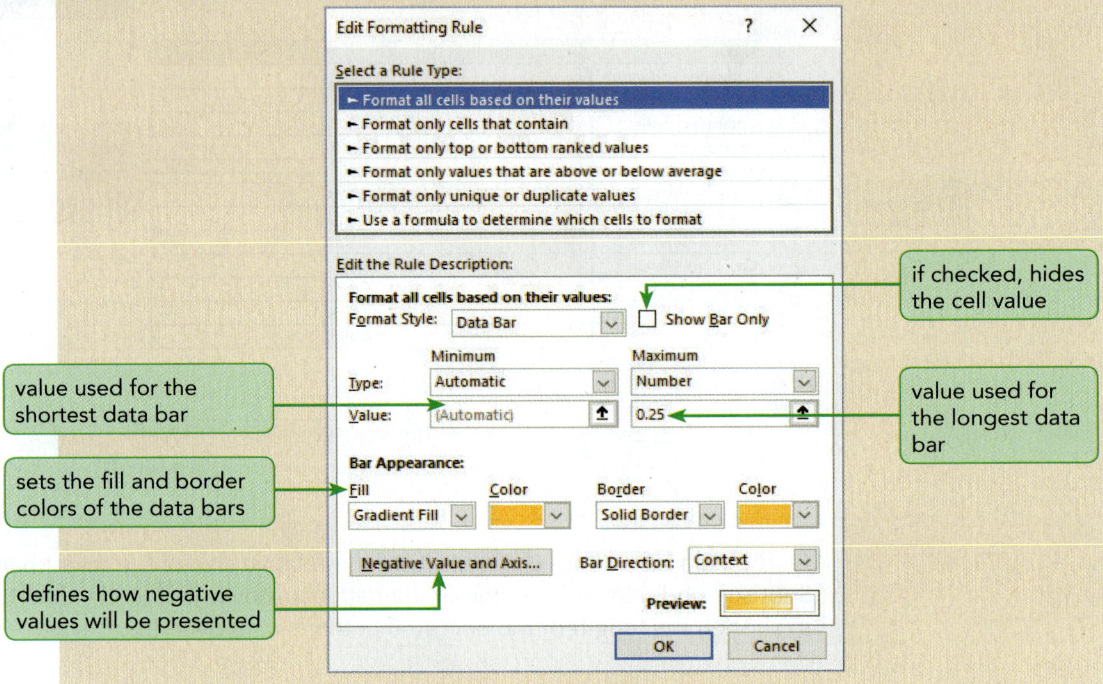

6. Click **OK** in each dialog box to return to the worksheet, and then verify that the data bars no longer span the width of the selected cells.

Creating Sparklines

Another way of adding a chart to a cell is with a sparkline, which is a small chart completely confined to the borders of a single cell. Because of their small size, sparklines don't include chart elements such as legends, titles, or gridlines. The goal of a sparkline is to display the maximum amount of information in the smallest amount of space. As a result, sparklines are useful when you only need to convey a general impression of the data without any distracting detail.

Excel supports three types of sparklines: line sparklines, column sparklines, and win/loss sparklines. Figure 4–45 shows an example of each type in which the price history, shares traded, and increases and declines of 10 investments are displayed within a worksheet.

Figure 4–45 **Sparklines types**

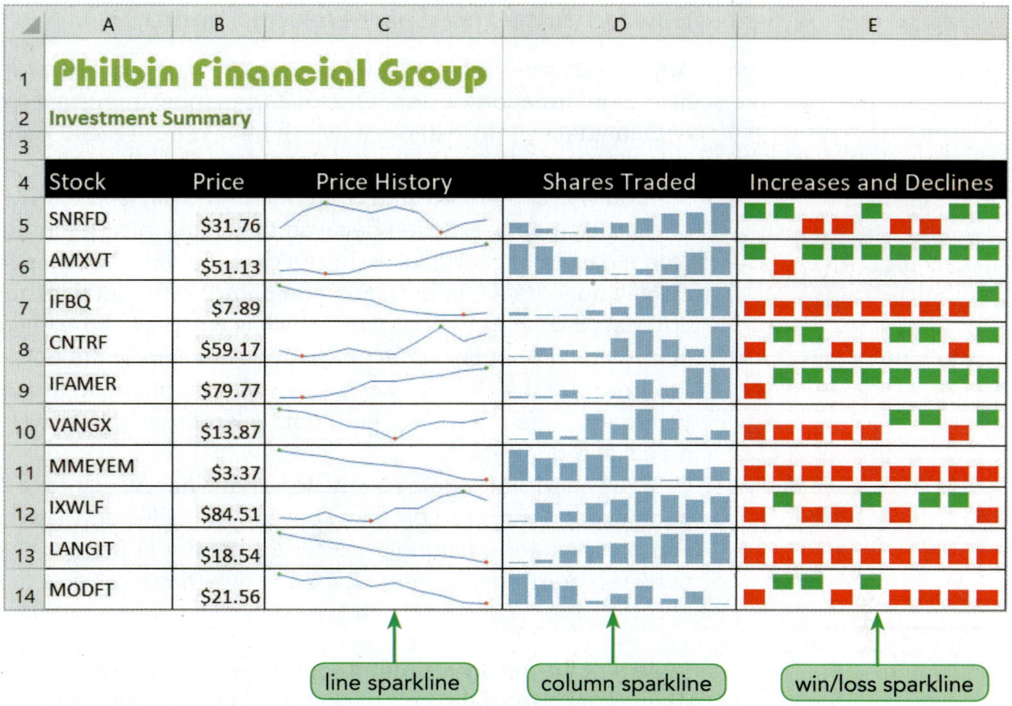

The line sparkline indicates the daily fluctuation in the selling price of each investment. While the sparkline does not provide specific prices, it's clear that the selling price of the Sunrise Fund (SNRFD) has seen an increase followed by a decline over its history, with prices rebounding in the last few days. Other investments such as the IFBQ stock (cell C7) have shown a steady decline in price while the IFAMER stock (cell C9) has shown a steady increase.

The column sparkline indicates the volume of shares traded. Once again, specific details are not provided, but an investor can see that the trading volume for the Sunrise Fund has generally increased over the last several days (cell D5).

Finally, the win/loss sparkline displays a green block for positive values on those days in which the investment's selling price increased and a red block for days in which the selling price declined. The selling price of an investment like MMEYEM (cell E11) is quickly seen to have declined every day, while the IFAMER investment (cell E9) showed an increase in its selling price every day except the first.

The range C5:E14 displays 30 different charts. Although these charts show only general trends, they give the investor a quick and easily interpreted snapshot of the 10 investments and their recent performance. More details can always be provided elsewhere with more informative Excel charts.

Insight

Edward Tufte and Chart Design Theory

Any serious study of charts will include the works of Edward Tufte, who pioneered the field of information design. One of Tufte's most important works is The Visual Display of Quantitative Information, in which he laid out several principles for the design of charts and graphics.

Tufte was concerned with what he termed as "chart junk," in which a proliferation of chart elements—chosen because they look "nice"—confuse and distract the reader. One measure of chart junk is Tufte's data-ink ratio, which is the amount of "ink" used to display quantitative information compared to the total ink required by the chart. Tufte advocated limiting nondata ink, which is any part of the chart that does not convey information about the data. One way of measuring the data-ink ratio is to determine how much of the chart you can erase without affecting the user's ability to interpret your data. Tufte argued for high data-ink ratios with a minimum of extraneous elements and graphics.

To this end, Tufte helped develop sparklines, which convey information with a high data-ink ratio within a compact space. Tufte believed that charts that can be viewed and comprehended at a glance have a greater impact on the reader than large and cluttered graphs, no matter how attractive they might be.

Note that the cells containing sparklines do not need to be blank because the sparklines are part of the cell background and do not replace any content.

Reference

Creating and Editing Sparklines

- On the Insert tab, in the Sparklines group, click the Line, Column, or Win/Loss button to open the Create Sparklines dialog box.
- In the Data Range box, enter the range for the data source of the sparkline.
- In the Location Range box, enter the range into which to place the sparkline.
- Click OK.
- On the Sparkline tab, in the Show group, click the appropriate check boxes to specify which markers to display on the sparkline.
- In the Group group, click the Axis button, and then click Show Axis to add an axis to the sparkline.

Hideki wants you to use line sparklines in the range H32:H43 of the Summary worksheet to display the general trend of the growth of the Sunrise Fund's investment into 12 economic sectors.

To create the line sparklines showing the sector history growth trends:

1. Select the range **H32:H43** in the Summary worksheet.
2. On the ribbon, click the **Insert** tab, and then in the Sparklines group, click the **Line** button. The Create Sparklines dialog box opens.
3. Make sure the insertion point is in the Data Range box, click the **Sector History** sheet tab, and then select the range **B6:M45** on the Sector History

worksheet. This range contains the growth of investments in 12 economic sectors given a hypothetical $10,000 initial investment.

4. Verify that the range **$H$32:$H$43** is entered in the Location Range box. See Figure 4–46.

Figure 4–46 Create Sparklines dialog box

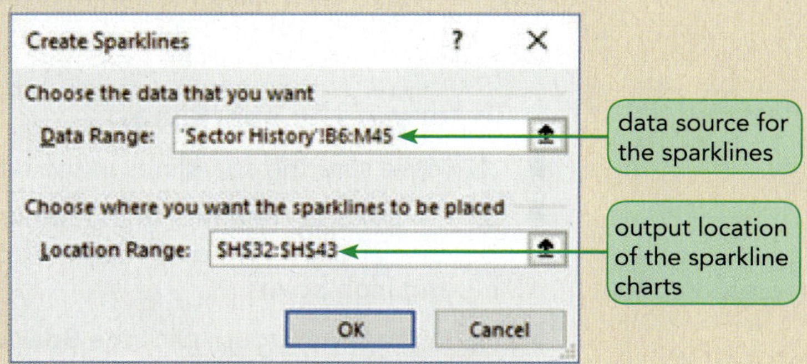

5. Click **OK** to insert the sparklines into the range H32:H43 of the Summary worksheet. See Figure 4–47.

Figure 4–47 Line sparklines in the Summary worksheet

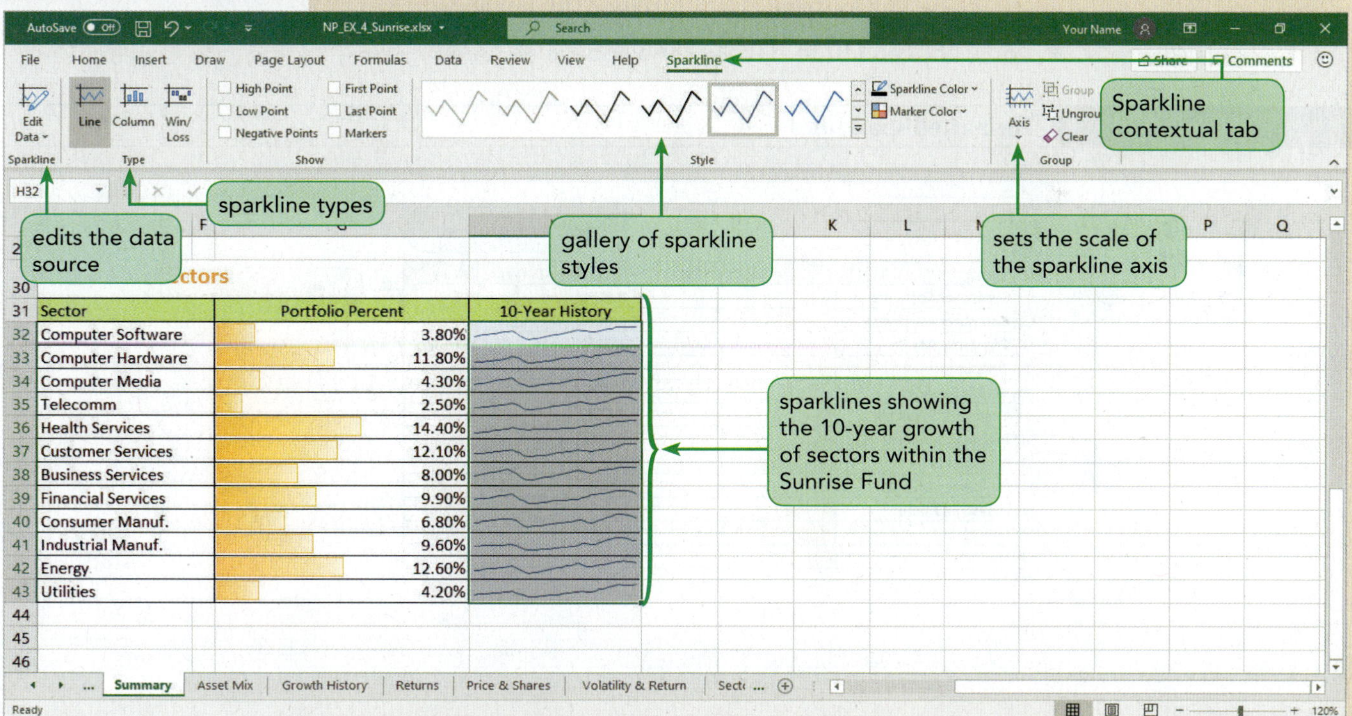

The Sparkline contextual tab appears on the ribbon when a sparkline is selected. From this tab, you can change the sparkline type, edit the sparkline's data source, and format the sparkline's appearance.

Formatting a Sparkline

Because of their compact size, sparklines have fewer formatting options than other Excel charts. You can add data markers to highlight low and high values, initial and ending values, and negative values. From the Style gallery on the Sparkline tab, you can apply built-in styles to the sparklines. From the Sparkline Color and Marker Color buttons in the Style group, you can set the color of the sparklines and their data markers.

Hideki wants you to add data markers identifying the low and high points within the time interval to each sparkline and to change the sparkline color to dark orange.

To format the sparklines:

1. Make sure the sparklines in the range H32:H43 are still selected.
2. On the Sparkline tab, in the Show group, click the **High Point** and **Low Point** check boxes. Two data markers appear on each sparkline identifying the low and high points.
3. In the Style group, click the **Sparkline Color** button, and then click the **Orange, Accent 3, Darker 25%** theme color (the seventh theme color in the fifth row) in the color palette. The sparkline colors change to orange.
4. In the Style group, click the **Marker Color** button, click **High Point**, and then click the **Green** standard color. The high point data marker color changes to green.
5. Click the **Marker Color** button, click **Low Point**, and then click the **Red** standard color. The low point data marker color changes to red.
6. Click cell **I30** to deselect the sparklines. See Figure 4–48.

Figure 4–48 Formatted sparklines

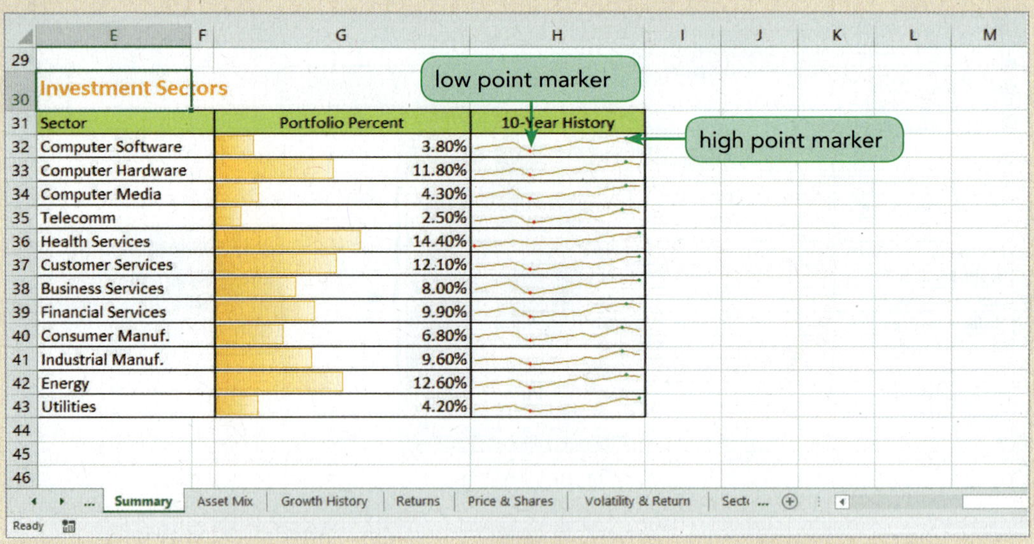

7. **sam** Save the workbook, and then close it.

The sparklines show that the 12 economic sectors experienced the same general growth trend over the previous 10 years with negative growth occurring around years 3 and 4 followed by steady growth thereafter. The lowest for all sectors seem to come around the fourth year.

Sparkline Groups and Sparkline Axes

Sparklines are grouped together by default so that the format choices are applied to every sparkline chart in the group. Grouping ensures that sparklines for related data series are formatted consistently. To format a single sparkline, click the cell containing the sparkline and then click the Ungroup button in the Group group on the Sparkline tab. The selected sparkline is split from the rest of the sparkline group. You can then apply a unique format to it. To regroup the sparklines, select all the cells containing the sparklines, and then click the Group button in the Group group.

Excel displays each sparkline on its own vertical axis ranging from the data series' low point and high point. That means comparing one sparkline to another can be misleading if they are all plotted on a different scale. You can modify the vertical axes by clicking the Axis button in the Group group on the Sparkline tab. To ensure that the vertical scale is the same for all charts in the sparkline group, click the Same for All Sparklines option for both the minimum and maximum scale values. To explicitly define the scale of the vertical axis, click the Custom Value option and specify the minimum and maximum values.

Proskills

Written Communication: Honesty in Charting

One of the great challenges in chart design is to not mislead your audience by misrepresenting the data. Here are a few of the ways in which a chart, created even with the best of intentions, can mislead the viewer:

- **Improper scaling.** This is a very common mistake in which the range of the data scale is set so narrow that even small changes seem large or so wide that all values appear to be the same. For example, a 1% change in a data value will appear large if the scale goes from 0% to 2% and it will appear insignificant if the scale goes from 0% to 100%.
- **Scaling data values differently.** If improper scaling can exaggerate or minimize differences, the problem can be compounded with combination charts in which two data series that should be plotted on the same scale are instead plotted against vastly different scales. For example, one data series might appear to show a significant trend while the other shows none and yet the only difference is the scale on which the values have been plotted.
- **Truncating the vertical axis.** You can make trends appear more significant than they are if you cut off what might appear to be irrelevant information. Is an increase in the interest rate from 4% to 4.05% a significant jump? If you set the scale of the vertical axis to cover the range from 0% to 4.1% it will not appear to be. However, if your chart only covers the range from 4% to 4.1% it will appear to be significant jump.
- **3-D distortions.** Displaying charts in 3D can be eye-catching, but the effect of perspective in which objects appear to recede into the distance can exaggerate or minimize important differences that would be more apparent with a 2D chart.

To be fair, one should not assume that a misleading chart was designed with malicious intent. Because Excel and other software packages include charting, they can lead to the kinds of mistakes discussed above. To avoid misleading the audience, check your assumptions and verify that you are not altering your chart to make it appear more dramatic or interesting. View your charts under different formatting options to confirm that it is truly the data that is telling the story.

You have finished creating charts and graphics to summarize the history and performance of the Sunrise Fund. Hideki is pleased that so much information fits on a single worksheet. Figure 4–49 shows a preview of the printed worksheet containing all the charts and graphics you have created for the report.

Figure 4–49 **Final Summary report**

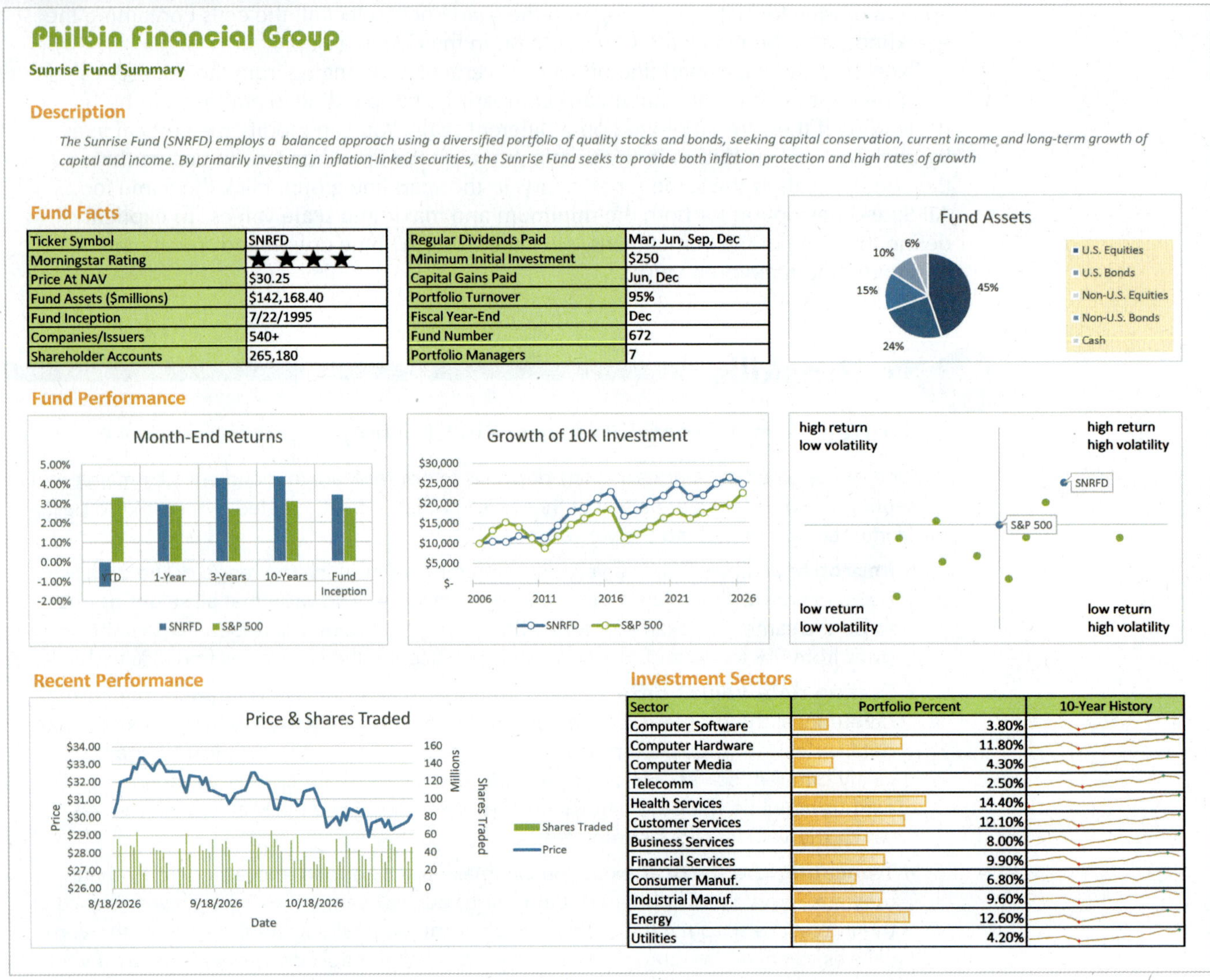
Philbin Financial Group

Sunrise Fund Summary

Description

The Sunrise Fund (SNRFD) employs a balanced approach using a diversified portfolio of quality stocks and bonds, seeking capital conservation, current income and long-term growth of capital and income. By primarily investing in inflation-linked securities, the Sunrise Fund seeks to provide both inflation protection and high rates of growth

Fund Facts

Ticker Symbol	SNRFD
Morningstar Rating	★★★★
Price At NAV	$30.25
Fund Assets ($millions)	$142,168.40
Fund Inception	7/22/1995
Companies/Issuers	540+
Shareholder Accounts	265,180

Regular Dividends Paid	Mar, Jun, Sep, Dec
Minimum Initial Investment	$250
Capital Gains Paid	Jun, Dec
Portfolio Turnover	95%
Fiscal Year-End	Dec
Fund Number	672
Portfolio Managers	7

Investment Sectors

Sector	Portfolio Percent	10-Year History
Computer Software	3.80%	
Computer Hardware	11.80%	
Computer Media	4.30%	
Telecomm	2.50%	
Health Services	14.40%	
Customer Services	12.10%	
Business Services	8.00%	
Financial Services	9.90%	
Consumer Manuf.	6.80%	
Industrial Manuf.	9.60%	
Energy	12.60%	
Utilities	4.20%	

Hideki will continue to study the workbook and get back to you with future reports for the Philbin Financial Group clients.

Review

Session 4.2 Quick Check

1. A researcher wants to plot weight vs. blood pressure. Should the researcher use a line chart or a scatter chart? Explain why.
2. How would you select multiple graphic objects within a worksheet?
3. When would you use a Pareto chart?
4. When would you use a histogram?
5. Describe the three types of sparklines.
6. Under what circumstances would you use sparklines in a report?
7. Why would you not use a sparkline?
8. What are data bars? How do data bars differ from sparklines?

Practice

Review Assignments

Data File needed for the Review Assignments: NP_EX_4-2.xlsx

Hideki wants you to develop another investment report for a Philbin Financial Group client on the Ortus Fund. As with the report you generated for the Sunrise Fund, this workbook will include a worksheet that uses Excel charts and graphics to summarize financial data about the fund. Complete the following:

1. Open the **NP_EX_4-2.xlsx** workbook located in the Excel4 > Review folder included with your Data Files, and then save the workbook as **NP_EX_4_Ortus** in the location specified by your instructor.
2. In the Documentation sheet, enter your name and the date in the range B3:B4.
3. Hideki wants a pie chart that breaks down the allocation of the assets in the Ortus Fund. Do the following:
   a. In the Allocation worksheet, create a pie chart from the data in the range A4:B8.
   b. Move the pie chart to the range D7:E14 in the Prospectus worksheet.
   c. Place the legend on the right side of the chart area.
   d. Change the color scheme to the Monochromatic Palette 5.
   e. Add data labels showing the percentage allocated to each category, positioning the label on the outside end of each pie slice.
4. Hideki wants the report to display a column chart of the month-end returns for the Ortus Fund and the S&P 500 over different time intervals. Do the following:
   a. In the Returns worksheet, create a clustered column chart from the data in the range A4:C9.
   b. Move the chart to the range F7:H14 of the Prospectus worksheet.
   c. Change the chart title to **Month-End Returns**.
   d. Place the legend on the right side of the chart area.
5. Hideki wants a line chart comparing the growth of a theoretical investment of $10,000 in the Ortus Fund and the S&P 500 over the past 10 years. Do the following:
   a. In the Growth worksheet, create a line chart of the data in the range A4:C25, showing the Year value on the horizontal axis.
   b. Move the chart to the range D15:E24 of the Prospectus worksheet.
   c. Change the chart title to **Growth of 10K Investment**.
   d. Add primary major vertical gridlines to the chart.
   e. Place the legend on the right side of the chart area.
   f. Change the interval between the major tick marks and between labels on the category axis to 5 units so that the years 2005, 2010, 2015, 2020, and 2025 appear on the horizontal axis.
6. Hideki wants the report to show the recent selling price and shares traded of the Ortus Fund in a combination chart. Do the following:
   a. In the Recent History worksheet, create a combination chart of the data in the range A4:C58. Display the price data as a line chart plotted on the primary axis and the shares traded data as a clustered column chart plotted on the secondary axis.
   b. Move the chart to the range A26:D38 of the Prospectus worksheet.
   c. Change the chart title to **Recent History**.
   d. Display axis titles on the chart. Change the primary vertical axis title to **Price**, the secondary vertical axis title to **Shares Traded**, and the category axis title to **Date**. Change the angle of rotation of the Shares Traded axis title to Rotate Text Down.
   e. Place the legend on the right side of the chart area.
   f. Change the scale of the secondary axis to go from 0 to 1.6E08 and display the scale in units of 1 million with the units label displayed on the chart.

7. Hideki needs to compare the return rate and volatility of the Ortus Fund to other investment vehicles. Do the following:
   a. In the Performance worksheet, create a scatter chart from the data in the range B5:C7 using the scatter chart from the list of recommended charts.
   b. Move the chart to the range F15:H24 of the Prospectus worksheet.
   c. Remove the chart title and the gridlines from the chart.
   d. Rescale the vertical axis to go from 0.0 to 0.06 with the horizontal axis crossing at 0.031. Rescale the horizontal axis to go from 4 to 24 with the vertical axis crossing at 14.71.
   e. Set the label position to none for both the vertical and horizontal axis labels.
   f. Add data callouts to the data markers in the data series showing only the text from the range A6:A7 in the Performance worksheet.
   g. Complete the scatter chart by adding a new data series to the chart with cell G5 in the Performance worksheet as the series name, the range F6:F15 in the Performance worksheet as the Series X values, and the range G6:G15 in the Performance worksheet as the Series Y values.
8. Add the four text boxes shown earlier in Figure 4–28 to the scatter chart, placing the return and volatility descriptions on separate lines. Resize and move the text boxes so that they align with the chart corners.
9. On the Prospectus worksheet, replace the text in cell B9 with three star icons from the Celebration group in the icon gallery. Set the height and width of each icon 0.20". Align and evenly distribute the icons within cell B9.
10. Add solid blue data bars to the values in the range G28:G38. Keep the data bars from overlapping the values in those cells by modifying the conditional formatting rule so that the maximum length of the data bar corresponds to a value of 0.30.
11. Add line sparklines to the range H28:H38 using the data values from the range B5:L44 of the Sectors worksheet. Add data markers for the high and low points of each sparkline using the Red standard color.
12. Save the workbook, and then close it.

Apply

Case Problem 1

Data File needed for this Case Problem: NP_EX_4-3.xlsx

Certus Car Rental John Tretow is an account manager for Certus Car Rental, an industry-leading car rental firm that serves customers across the United States and overseas. John is developing a market report for an upcoming sales conference and needs your assistance in summarizing market information into a collection of Excel charts and graphics. Complete the following.

1. Open the **NP_EX_4-3.xlsx** workbook located in the Excel4 > Case1 folder included with your Data Files. Save the workbook as **NP_EX_4_Certus** in the location specified by your instructor.
2. In the Documentation sheet, enter your name and the date in the range B3:B4.
3. John wants the report to include pie charts that break down the current year's revenue in terms of market (Airport vs. Off-Airport), car type (Leisure vs. Commercial), and location (Americas vs. International). In the Rentals by Type worksheet, do the following:
   a. Create a pie chart of the data in the range A6:B7. Move the chart cover the range D5:F9 in the Analysis worksheet.
   b. Remove the chart title from the pie chart.
   c. Add data labels to the outside end of the two slices showing the percentage of the Airport vs. Off-Airport sales.
4. Repeat Step 3 for the data in the range A11:B12 of the Rentals by Type worksheet, placing the pie chart comparing Leisure and Commercial sales in the range H5:H9 of the Analysis worksheet.

5. Repeat Step 3 for the data in the range A16:B17 of the Rentals by Type worksheet, placing the pie chart comparing revenue between the Americas and International sales in the range J5:J9 of the Analysis worksheet.
6. John wants to present the company revenue broken down by car type. In the Car Models worksheet, create a clustered bar chart of the data in the range A4:B9. Move the bar chart to the range B11:F21 of the Analysis worksheet. Remove the chart legend if it exists. Add data labels to the end of the data markers showing the revenue for each car model.
7. John also wants to track revenue for each car model over the years to determine whether certain car models have increased or decreased in popularity. In the Revenue by Year worksheet, create a line chart of the data in the range A4:F15. Move the chart to the range H11:J21 in the Analysis worksheet.
8. Apply the following formats to the line chart you created in Step 7:
   a. Remove the chart title.
   b. Add major gridlines for the primary vertical and horizontal axes.
   c. Move the chart legend to the right side of the chart area.
   d. Add axis titles to the chart. Set the vertical axis title to the text **Revenue ($bil)** and the horizontal axis title to **Year**.
   e. Set the interval between tick marks and between the labels on the category (horizontal) axis to 2 units so that the category labels are Y2015, Y2017, Y2019, Y2021, Y2023, and Y2025.
9. John wants to compare the Certus brand to competing car rental companies. In the range F25:F29, insert line sparklines showing the trend in market share percentages using the data from the range B19:F29 on the Market Share worksheet.
10. Add green data bars with a gradient fill to the data values in the range E25:E29.
11. In the range F32:F36, insert line sparklines showing the trend in revenue using the data from the range B5:F15 on the Market Share worksheet.
12. Add orange data bars with a gradient fill to the data values in the range E32:E36.
13. John wants to present a more detailed chart of the revenue values from the five competing rental car agencies over the past several years. In the Market Share worksheet, create a Stacked Column chart from the data in the range A4:F15. Move the chart over the range H24:J36 in the Analysis worksheet.
14. Apply the following formatting to the column chart you created in Step 13:
   a. Remove the chart title
   b. Add axis titles to the chart. Set the vertical axis title to the text **Revenue ($bil)** and the horizontal axis title to **Year**.
   c. Move the legend to the right side of the chart area.
   d. Set the interval between tick marks and between the labels on the category (horizontal) axis to 2 units to display the category values Y2015, Y2017, Y2019, Y2021, Y2023, and Y2025.
   e. Set the gap width between the bars in the chart to 30%.
15. The company revenue decreased in the past year. John wants you to highlight this fact by adding a down-arrow shape from the Shape gallery to the right side of the merged cell B5 on the Analysis worksheet. Set the height of the down arrow to 1" and the width to 0.5".
16. While the company revenue has decreased in the last year, its market share has increased. Add an up-arrow shape to the right side of the merged cell B25. Set the arrow to be 1" high and 0.5" wide.
17. Save the workbook, and then close it.

Challenge

Case Problem 2

Data File needed for this Case Problem: NP_EX_4-4.xlsx

Spirit Care Hospital & Clinic Dakota Kohana is the site coordinator for the Spirt Care Hospital & Clinic on the Pine Ridge reservation in South Dakota. As part of an annual report for the clinic's trustees, Dakota needs to document patient care at the clinic including inpatient and outpatient admissions, length of stay, and average waiting time. Dakota has asked your help in supplementing the report with informative charts and graphics. Complete the following.

1. Open the **NP_EX_4-4.xlsx** workbook located in the Excel4 > Case2 folder included with your Data Files. Save the workbook as **NP_EX_4_Spirit** in the location specified by your instructor.
2. In the Documentation sheet, enter your name in cell B3. Use an Excel function to enter the current date in cell B4.
3. In the Summary worksheet, in the range D5:D11, Dakota has broken down the number of inpatient admissions by department. Add solid green data bars to the range, setting to maximum length of the data bars to 8000.
4. Repeat Step 3 for the outpatient admissions in the range E5:E11, using solid blue data bars.
5. **Explore** In the Patients by Month worksheet, create a Sunburst chart of the data in the nonadjacent range A4:C4,A17:C17. Move the chart to the Summary worksheet covering the range G4:J11.
6. Apply the following formatting to the Sunburst chart you created in Step 5:
   a. Remove the chart title.
   b. Display the chart legend at the top of the chart.
   c. Change the data labels to show the values only and not the category names.
7. **Explore** Dakota also wants to view the admission data by month. In the Patients by Month worksheet, create a Stacked Area chart of the data in the range A4:C16. Move the chart to the Summary worksheet covering the range L4:P11.
8. Apply the following formats to the Stacked Area chart you created in Step 7.
   a. Remove the chart title.
   b. Add primary major vertical gridlines to the chart.
9. **Explore** The report will also include an analysis of the length of inpatient stays. Dakota has retrieved length of stay data for 300 randomly selected patients and wants you to display the distribution of those stays in a histogram chart. In the Length of Stay worksheet, create a histogram of the data in the range A4:A304. Move the chart to the range C13:E25 in the Summary worksheet. (Note: If the chart is placed at the bottom of the worksheet, you can quickly move the chart to the top by selecting the chart, and then cutting and pasting the chart to a cell near the top of the worksheet.)
10. Apply the following formatting options to the histogram chart you created in Step 9:
    a. Change the chart title to **Length of Stay (Days)**.
    b. Double-click the histogram categories along the horizontal axis to display the Format Axis pane. Change the Bin Width value to **1**. Change the Overflow Bin value to 10 so that length of stay values larger than 10 are pooled together in a single category.
11. When patients are admitted to the hospital and then discharged, they might be readmitted within 30 days. Dakota wants the report to include the inpatient admission totals and the 30-day readmission rates for each quarter of the past year. In the Readmission worksheet, create a combination chart of the data in the range A4:C8. Display the Inpatient Admissions data series as a clustered column chart. Display the Readmission Rate data series as a line chart on the secondary axis. Move the chart to the range G13:J25 of the Summary worksheet.
12. Apply the following formatting options to the combination chart you created in Step 11:
    a. Change the chart title to **Admissions and 30-Day Readmission Rate**.
    b. Add axis titles to the chart. Name the primary vertical axis **Inpatient Admissions**. Name the secondary vertical axis **Readmission Rate** and rotate the text down. Name the category axis **Quarter**.
    c. Change the scale of the secondary axis to go from 0.1 to 0.3.

Explore 13. Dakota's report needs to break down admissions by payer (Medicare, Medicaid, Private Insurance, or Uninsured). Dakota thinks this data would be best presented in a Pareto chart. In the Payer worksheet, create a Pareto chart of the data in the range A4:B8. Move the chart to range L13:P25 in the Summary worksheet and change the chart title to **Admissions by Payer**.

14. Monitoring the length of time that patients must wait before being treated is an important task for Dakota. On the Summary worksheet, add solid red data bars to range D29:D35 containing the wait times for different departments. Set the maximum length of the data bars to 40.
15. Dakota wants to track how wait times within each department have changed over the past year. Add line sparklines to the range E29:E35 using the data from the range B5:H16 of the Waiting Times worksheet. Mark the high and low point within each sparkline using the Red standard color.
16. Trustees want to track the nurse-to-patient ratio during both the day and the night shifts. Dakota included this information in the Summary worksheet and augmented it with graphic icons, but the alignment is off and wants you to fix it. Do the following:
    a. Open the Selection pane and select the Graphic 1 through Graphic 3 icons in cell I29 and align them along their middle positions.
    b. Use the Selection pane to select the Graphic 4 through Graphic 7 icons in cell I33 and distribute them evenly in the horizontal direction.
17. Save the workbook, and then close it.

MODULE 1

Creating a Database

Tracking Patient, Visit, and Billing Data

OBJECTIVES

Session 1.1

- Define basic database concepts and terms
- Start and exit Access
- Identify the Microsoft Access window and Backstage view
- Create a blank database
- Create and save a table in Datasheet view and Design view
- Add fields to a table in Datasheet view and Design view
- Set a table's primary key in Design view

Session 1.2

- Open an Access database
- Open a table using the Navigation Pane
- Copy and paste records from another Access database
- Navigate a table datasheet and enter records
- Create and navigate a simple query
- Create and navigate a simple form
- Create, preview, navigate, and print a simple report
- Use Help in Access
- Identify how to compact, back up, and restore a database

Case | *Lakewood Community Health Services*

Lakewood Community Health Services, a nonprofit health clinic located in the greater Atlanta, Georgia area, provides a range of medical services to patients of all ages. The clinic specializes in chronic disease management, cardiac care, and geriatrics. Donna Taylor, the office manager for Lakewood Community Health Services, oversees a small staff and is responsible for maintaining records for the clinic's patients.

In order to best manage the clinic, Donna and her staff rely on electronic medical records for patient information, billing, inventory control, purchasing, and accounts payable. Several months ago, the clinic upgraded to **Microsoft Access 2019** (or simply **Access**), a computer program used to enter, maintain, and retrieve related data in a format known as a database. Donna and her staff want to use Access to store information about patients, billing, vendors, and products. She asks for your help in creating the necessary Access database.

STARTING DATA FILES

Access1 →

Module: Support_AC_1_Donna.accdb

Review: Support_AC_1_Company.accdb

Case1: Support_AC_1_Records.accdb

Case2: Support_AC_1_Residents.accdb

Session 1.1 Visual Overview:

The **Quick Access Toolbar** provides one-click access to commonly used commands, such as Save.

The **Table Tools Fields tab** provides options for adding, removing, and formatting the fields in a table.

The **Shutter Bar Open/Close Button** allows you to close and open the Navigation Pane; you might want to close the pane so that you have more room on the screen to view the object's contents.

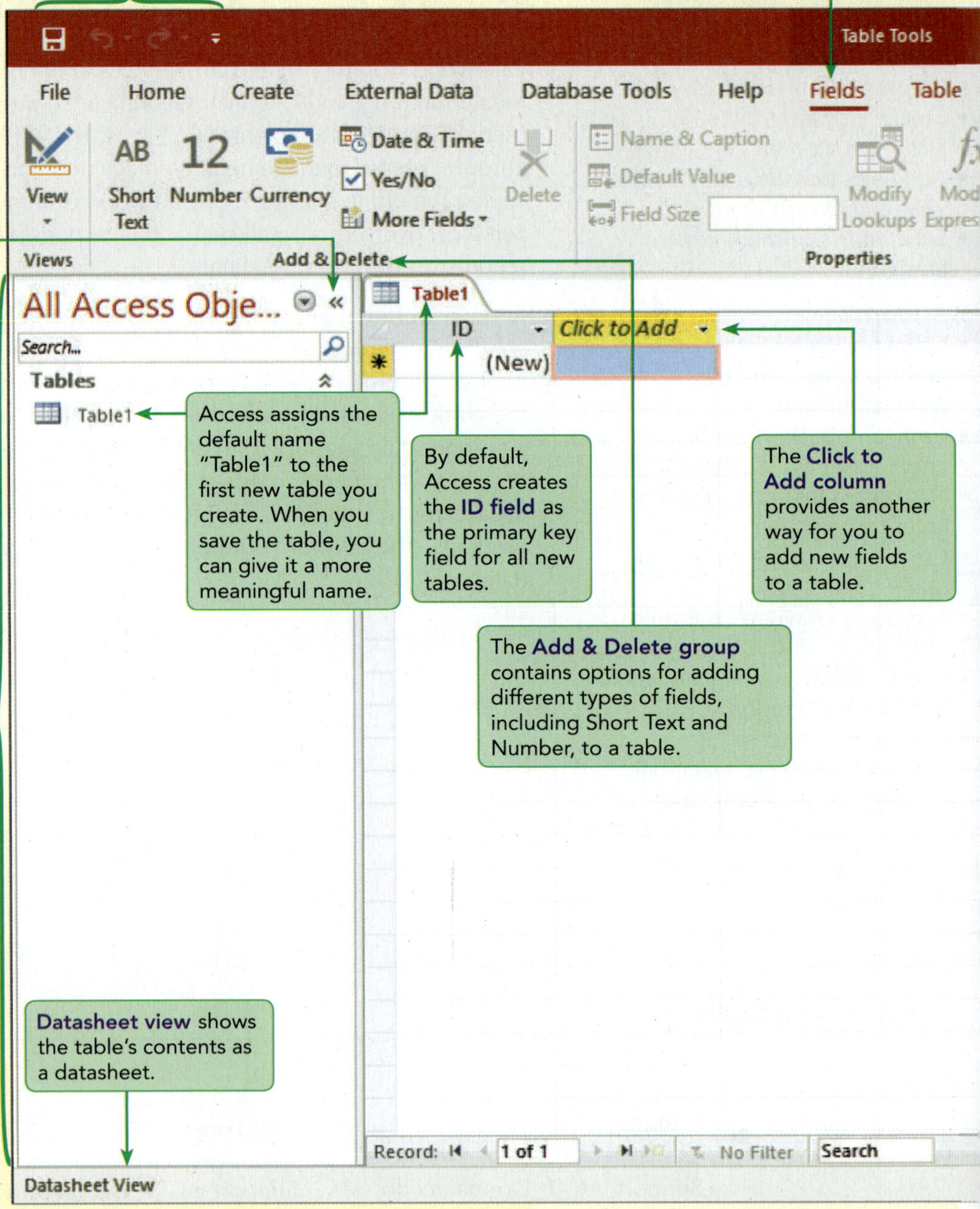

Access assigns the default name "Table1" to the first new table you create. When you save the table, you can give it a more meaningful name.

By default, Access creates the **ID field** as the primary key field for all new tables.

The **Click to Add column** provides another way for you to add new fields to a table.

The **Add & Delete group** contains options for adding different types of fields, including Short Text and Number, to a table.

The **Navigation Pane** lists all the objects (tables, reports, and so on) in the database; it is the main control center for opening and working with database objects.

Datasheet view shows the table's contents as a datasheet.

The Access Window

The **Access window** is the program window that appears when you create a new database or open an existing database.

You use the window buttons to minimize, maximize, and close the Access window.

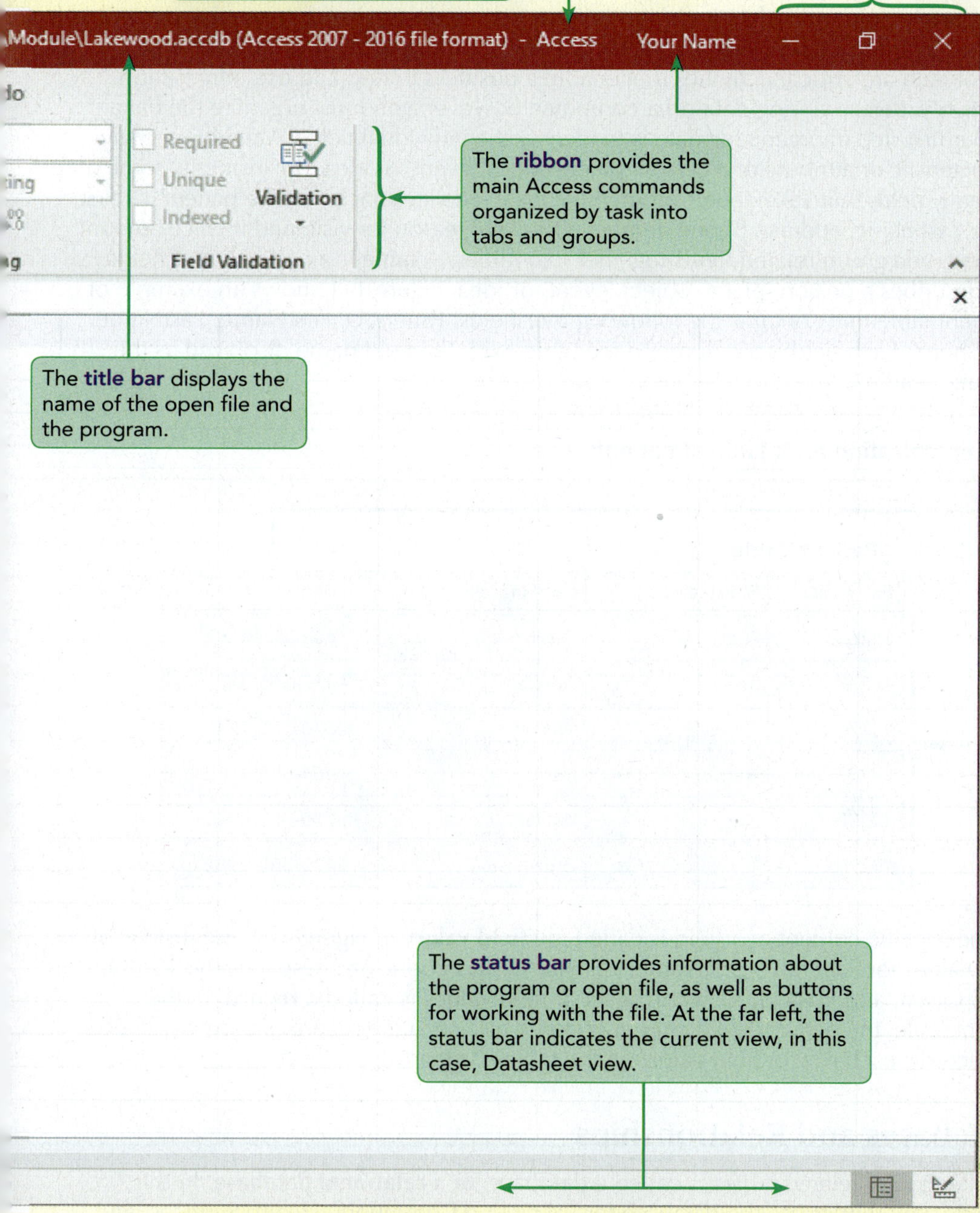

If you are signed into your Office account, your name appears here. If not are not signed in, the **Sign in link** will appear here, and you can click it to sign into your Office account.

The **ribbon** provides the main Access commands organized by task into tabs and groups.

The **title bar** displays the name of the open file and the program.

A **datasheet** displays the table's contents in rows and columns, similar to a table that you create in a Word document or an Excel worksheet. Each row will be a separate record in the table, an each column will contain the field values for one field in the table.

The **status bar** provides information about the program or open file, as well as buttons for working with the file. At the far left, the status bar indicates the current view, in this case, Datasheet view.

Introduction to Database Concepts

Before you begin using Access to create the database for Donna, you need to understand a few key terms and concepts associated with databases.

Organizing Data

Data is a valuable resource to any business. At Lakewood Community Health Services, for example, important data includes the patients' names and addresses, visit dates, and billing information. Organizing, storing, maintaining, retrieving, and sorting this type of data are critical activities that enable a business to find and use information effectively. Before storing data on a computer, however, you must organize the data.

Your first step in organizing data is to identify the individual fields. A **field** is a single characteristic or attribute of a person, place, object, event, or idea. For example, some of the many fields that Lakewood Community Health Services tracks are the patient ID, first name, last name, address, phone number, visit date, reason for visit, and invoice amount.

Next, you group related fields together into tables. A **table** is a collection of fields that describes a person, place, object, event, or idea. Figure 1–1 shows an example of a Patient table that contains the following four fields: PatientID, FirstName, LastName, and Phone. Each field is a column in the table, with the field name displayed as the column heading.

Figure 1–1 **Data organization for a table of patients**

fields

Patient Table

PatientID	FirstName	LastName	Phone
13264	Alex	Olsen	404-555-9132
13273	Sofia	Garcia	470-555-3126
13276	Claire	Wilson	678-555-1247
13283	Harper	Rowe	404-555-1712
13290	Jim	Williams	770-555-4910
13299	Terry	Cruz	470-555-9982

records

The specific content of a field is called the **field value**. In Figure 1–1, the first set of field values for PatientID, FirstName, LastName, and Phone are, respectively: 13264, Alex, Olsen, and 404-555-9132. This set of field values is called a **record**. In the Patient table, the data for each patient is stored as a separate record. Figure 1–1 shows six records; each row of field values in the table is a record.

Databases and Relationships

A collection of related tables is called a **database**, or a **relational database**. In this module, you will create the database for Lakewood Community Health Services, and within that database, you'll create a table named Visit to store data about patient visits. Later on, you'll create two more tables, named Patient and Billing, to store related information about patients and their invoices.

As Donna and her staff use the database that you will create, they will need to access information about patients and their visits. To obtain this information, you must have a way to connect records in the Patient table to records in the Visit table. You connect the records in the separate tables through a **common field** that appears in both tables.

In the sample database shown in Figure 1–2, each record in the Patient table has a field named PatientID, which is also a field in the Visit table. For example, Jim Williams is the fifth patient in the Patient table and has a PatientID field value of 13290. This same PatientID field value, 13290, appears in two records in the Visit table. Therefore, Jim Williams is the patient that was seen at these two visits.

Figure 1–2 Database relationship between tables for patients and visits

primary keys

common field

foreign key

two visits for Jim Williams

Patient table

PatientID	FirstName	LastName	Phone
13264	Alex	Olsen	404-555-9132
13273	Sofia	Garcia	470-555-3126
13276	Claire	Wilson	678-555-1247
13283	Harper	Rowe	404-555-1712
13290	Jim	Williams	770-555-4910
13299	Terry	Cruz	470-555-9982

Visit table

VisitID	PatientID	VisitDate	Reason
1459	13276	11/3/2020	Asthma
1483	13264	12/1/2020	Influenza
1509	13273	1/7/2021	Annual wellness visit
1565	13290	2/24/2021	Laceration of right calf
1567	13283	2/26/2021	Annual wellness visit
1575	13290	3/10/2021	Laceration follow-up
1596	13299	3/24/2021	Pneumonia

Each ID value in the Patient table must be unique so that you can distinguish one patient from another. These unique PatientID values also identify each patient's specific visits in the Visit table. The PatientID field is referred to as the primary key of the Patient table. A **primary key** is a field, or a collection of fields, whose values uniquely identify each record in a table. No two records can contain the same value for the primary key field. In the Visit table, the VisitID field is the primary key because Lakewood Community Health Services assigns each visit a unique identification number.

When you include the primary key from one table as a field in a second table to form a relationship between the two tables, it is called a **foreign key** in the second table, as shown in Figure 1–2. For example, PatientID is the primary key in the Patient table and a foreign key in the Visit table.

The PatientID field must have the same characteristics in both tables. Although the primary key PatientID contains unique values in the Patient table, the same field as a foreign key in the Visit table does not necessarily contain unique values. The PatientID value 13290, for example, appears two times in the Visit table because Jim Williams made two visits to the clinic.

Each foreign key value, however, must match one of the field values for the primary key in the other table. In the example shown in Figure 1–2, each PatientID value in the Visit table must match a PatientID value in the Patient table. The two tables are related, enabling users to connect the facts about patients with the facts about their visits to the clinic.

INSIGHT

Storing Data in Separate Tables

When you create a database, you must create separate tables that contain only fields that are directly related to each other. For example, in the Lakewood database, the patient and visit data should not be stored in the same table because doing so would make the data difficult to update and prone to errors. Consider Jim Williams and his visits to the clinic, and assume that he has many more than just two visits. If all the patient and visit data was stored in the same table, so that each record (row) contained all the information about each visit and the patient, the patient data would appear multiple times in the table. This causes problems when the data changes. For example, if the phone number for Jim Williams changed, you would have to update the multiple occurrences of the phone number throughout the table. Not only would this be time-consuming, it would increase the likelihood of errors or inconsistent data.

Relational Database Management Systems

To manage its databases, a company uses a database management system. A **database management system (DBMS)** is a software program that lets you create databases, and then manipulate the data they contain. Most of today's database management systems, including Access, are called relational database management systems. In a **relational database management system**, data is organized as a collection of tables. As stated earlier, a relationship between two tables in a relational DBMS is formed through a common field.

A relational DBMS controls the storage of databases and facilitates the creation, manipulation, and reporting of data, as illustrated in Figure 1–3.

Figure 1–3 **Relational database management system**

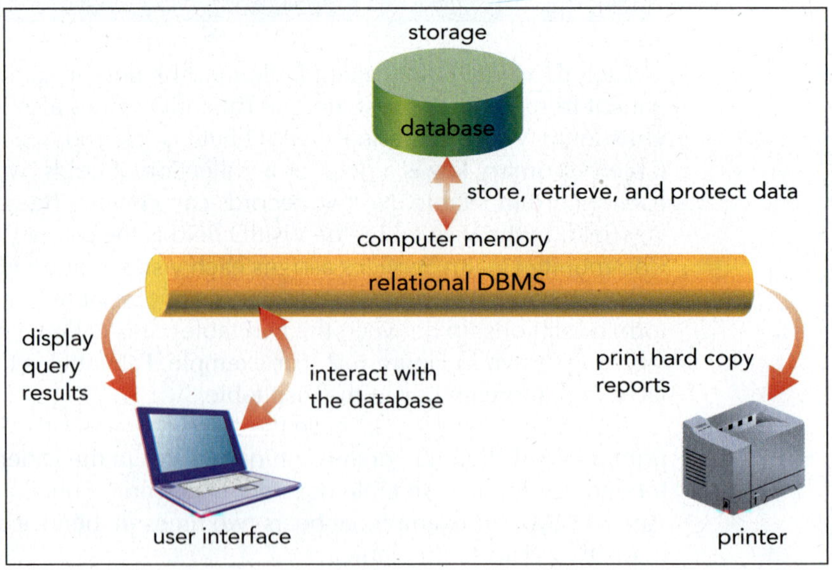

Specifically, a relational DBMS provides the following functions:

- It allows you to create database structures containing fields, tables, and table relationships.
- It lets you easily add new records, change field values in existing records, and delete records.
- It contains a built-in query language, which lets you obtain immediate answers to the questions (or queries) you ask about your data.
- It contains a built-in report generator, which lets you produce professional-looking, formatted reports from your data.
- It protects databases through security, control, and recovery facilities.

An organization such as Lakewood Community Health Services benefits from a relational DBMS because it allows users working in different groups to share the same data. More than one user can enter data into a database, and more than one user can retrieve and analyze data that other users have entered. For example, the database for Lakewood Community Health Services will contain only one copy of the Visit table, and all employees will use it to access visit information.

Finally, unlike other software programs, such as spreadsheet programs, a DBMS can handle massive amounts of data and allows relationships among multiple tables. Each Access database, for example, can be up to two gigabytes in size, can contain up to 32,768 objects (tables, reports, and so on), and can have up to 255 people using the database at the same time. For instructional purposes, the databases you will create and work with throughout this text contain a relatively small number of records compared to databases you would encounter outside the classroom, which would likely contain tables with very large numbers of records.

Starting Access and Creating a Database

Now that you've learned some database terms and concepts, you're ready to start Access and create the Lakewood database for Donna.

To start Access:

1. On the Windows taskbar, click the **Start** button. The Start menu opens.
2. On the Start menu, scroll down the list of apps, and then click **Access**. Access starts and displays the Recent screen in Backstage view. See Figure 1–4.

Figure 1–4 Recent screen in Backstage view

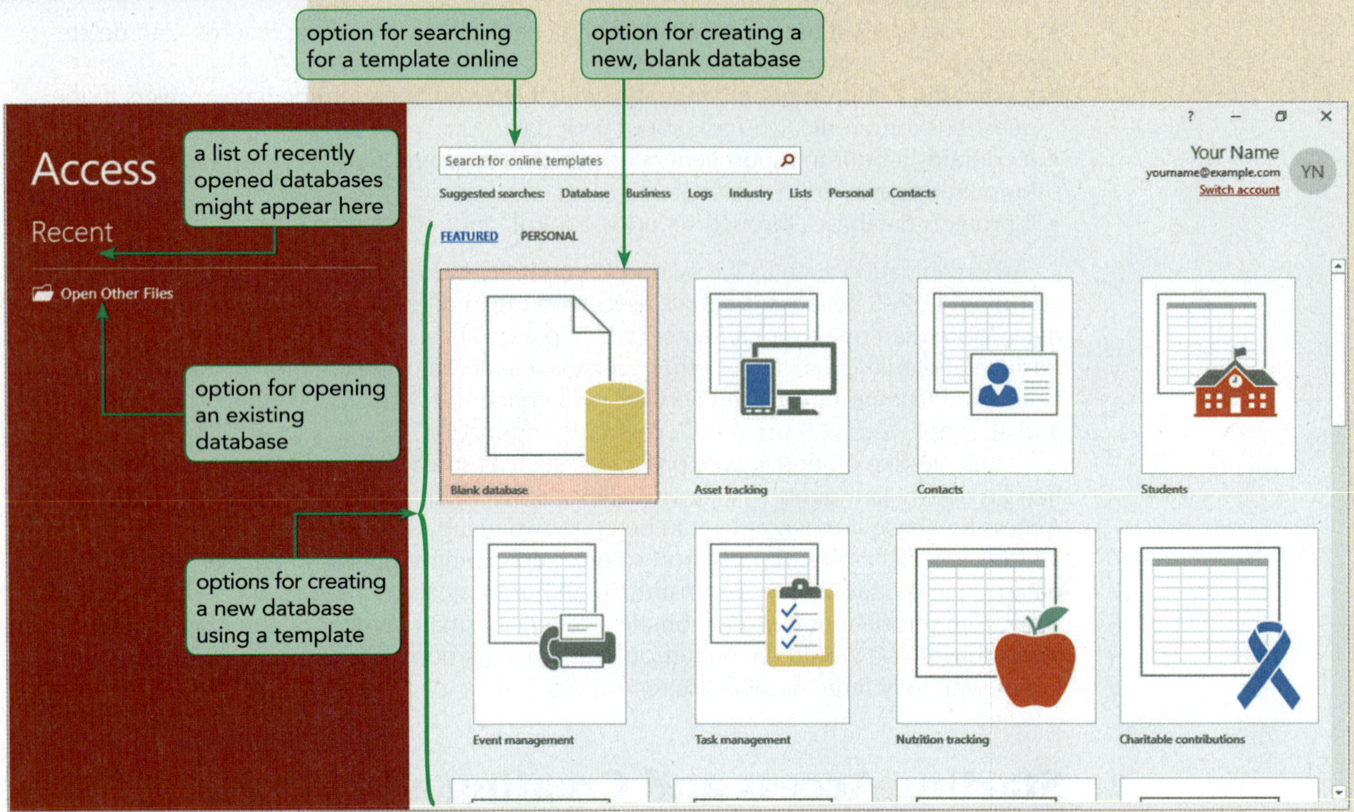

When you start Access, the first screen that appears is Backstage view, which is the starting place for your work in Access. **Backstage view** contains commands that allow you to manage Access files and options. The Recent screen in Backstage view provides options for you to create a new database or open an existing database. To create a new database that does not contain any data or objects, you use the Blank database option. If the database you need to create contains objects that match those found in common databases, such as databases that store data about contacts or tasks, you can use one of the templates provided with Access. A **template** is a predesigned database that includes professionally designed tables, reports, and other database objects that can make it quick and easy for you to create a database. You can also search for a template online using the Search for online templates box.

In this case, the templates provided do not match Donna's needs for the clinic's database, so you need to create a new, blank database from scratch.

To create the new Lakewood database:

1. sam Make sure you have the Access starting Data Files on your computer.

   Trouble? If you don't have the starting Data Files, you need to get them before you can proceed. Your instructor will either give you the Data Files or ask you to obtain them from a specified location (such as a network drive). If you have any questions about the Data Files, see your instructor or technical support person for assistance.

2. On the Recent screen, click **Blank database** (see Figure 1–4). The Blank database screen opens.

Be sure to type **Lakewood** or you'll create a database named Database1.

3. In the File Name box, type **Lakewood** to replace the selected database name provided by Access, Database1. Next you need to specify the location for the file.
4. Click the **Browse** button to the right of the File Name box. The File New Database dialog box opens.
5. Navigate to the drive and folder where you are storing your files, as specified by your instructor.
6. Make sure the Save as type box displays "Microsoft Access 2007–2016 Databases."

   Trouble? If your computer is set up to show file name extensions, you will see the Access file name extension ".accdb" in the File name box.

TIP

If you don't type the filename extension, Access adds it automatically.

7. Click **OK**. You return to the Blank database screen, and the File Name box now shows the name Lakewood.accdb. The filename extension ".accdb" identifies the file as an Access 2007–2016 database.
8. Click **Create**. Access creates the new database, saves it to the specified location, and then opens an empty table named Table1.

   Trouble? If you see only ribbon tab names and no buttons, click the Home tab to expand the ribbon, and then in the lower-right corner of the ribbon, click the Pin this pane button to pin the ribbon.

Refer back to the Session 1.1 Visual Overview and spend some time becoming familiar with the components of the Access window.

INSIGHT

Understanding the Database File Type

Access 2019 uses the .accdb file extension, which is the same file extension used for databases created with Microsoft Access 2007, 2010, 2013, and 2016. To ensure compatibility between these earlier versions and the Access 2019 software, new databases created using Access 2019 have the same file extension and file format as Access 2007, Access 2010, Access 2013, and Access 2016 databases.

Working in Touch Mode

TIP

On a touch device, you *tap* instead of *click*.

If you are working on a touch device, such as a tablet, you can switch to Touch Mode in Access to make it easier for you to tap buttons on the ribbon and perform other touch actions. Your screens will not match those shown in the book exactly, but this will not cause any problems.
Note: The following steps assume that you are using a mouse. If you are instead using a touch device, please read these steps but don't complete them, so that you remain working in Touch Mode.

To switch to Touch Mode:

1. On the Quick Access Toolbar, click the **Customize Quick Access Toolbar** button. A menu opens listing buttons you can add to the Quick Access Toolbar as well as other options for customizing the toolbar.

   Trouble? If the Touch/Mouse Mode command on the menu has a checkmark next to it, press ESC to close the menu, and then skip to Step 3.

2. Click **Touch/Mouse Mode**. The Quick Access Toolbar now contains the Touch/Mouse Mode button, which you can use to switch between Mouse Mode, the default display, and Touch Mode.

3. On the Quick Access Toolbar, click the **Touch/Mouse Mode** button. A menu opens with two commands: Mouse, which shows the ribbon in the standard display and is optimized for use with the mouse; and Touch, which provides more space between the buttons and commands on the ribbon and is optimized for use with touch devices. The icon next to Mouse is shaded to indicate that it is selected.

   Trouble? If the icon next to Touch is shaded red, press ESC to close the menu and skip to Step 5.

4. Click **Touch**. The display switches to Touch Mode with more space between the commands and buttons on the ribbon. See Figure 1–5.

Figure 1–5 **Ribbon displayed in Touch Mode**

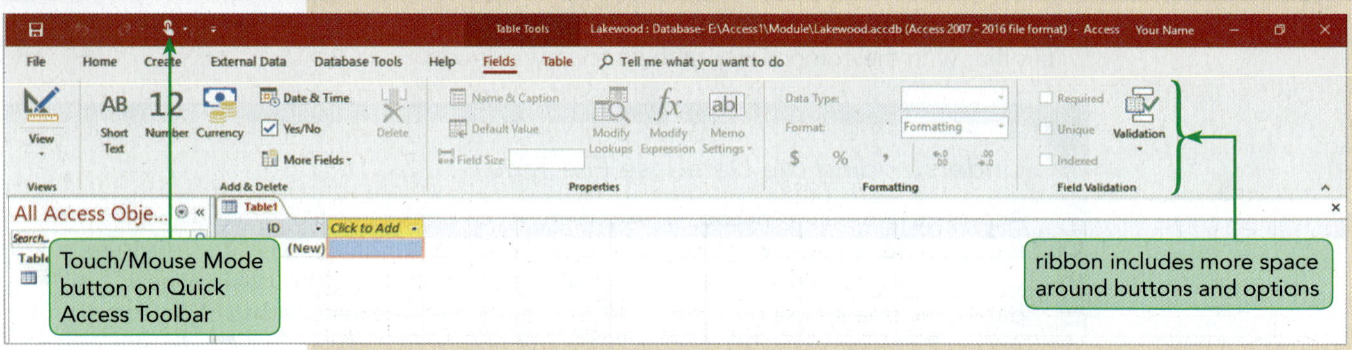

The figures in this text show the standard Mouse Mode display, and the instructions assume you are using a mouse to click and select options, so you'll switch back to Mouse Mode.

Trouble? If you are using a touch device and want to remain in Touch Mode, skip Steps 5 and 6.

5. On the Quick Access Toolbar, click the **Touch/Mouse Mode** button, and then click **Mouse**. The ribbon returns to the standard display, as shown in the Session 1.1 Visual Overview.

6. On the Quick Access Toolbar, click the **Customize Quick Access Toolbar** button, and then click **Touch/Mouse Mode** to deselect it. The Touch/Mouse Mode button is removed from the Quick Access Toolbar.

Creating a Table in Datasheet View

Tables contain all the data in a database and are the fundamental objects for your work in Access. You can create a table in Access in different ways, including entering the fields and records for the table directly in Datasheet view.

REFERENCE

Creating a Table in Datasheet View

- On the ribbon, click the Create tab.
- In the Tables group, click the Table button.
- Rename the default ID primary key field and change its data type, if necessary; or accept the default ID field with the AutoNumber data type.
- On the Fields tab in the Add & Delete group, click the button for the type of field you want to add to the table (for example, click the Short Text button), and then type the field name; or, in the table datasheet, click the Click to Add column heading, click the type of field you want to add from the list that opens, and then press TAB or ENTER to move to the next column in the datasheet. Repeat this step to add all the necessary fields to the table.
- In the first row below the field names, enter the value for each field in the first record, pressing TAB or ENTER to move from one field to the next.
- After entering the value for the last field in the first record, press TAB or ENTER to move to the next row, and then enter the values for the next record. Continue this process until you have entered all the records for the table.
- On the Quick Access Toolbar, click the Save button, enter a name for the table, and then click OK.

For Lakewood Community Health Services, Donna needs to track information about each patient visit at the clinic. She asks you to create the Visit table according to the plan shown in Figure 1–6.

Figure 1–6 Plan for the Visit table

Field	Purpose
VisitID	Unique number assigned to each visit; will serve as the table's primary key
PatientID	Unique number assigned to each patient; common field that will be a foreign key to connect to the Patient table
VisitDate	Date on which the patient visited the clinic
Reason	Reason/diagnosis for the patient visit
WalkIn	Whether the patient visit was a walk-in or scheduled appointment

As shown in Donna's plan, she wants to store data about visits in five fields, including fields to contain the date of each visit, the reason for the visit, and if the visit was a walk-in or scheduled appointment. These are the most important aspects of a visit and, therefore, must be tracked. Also, notice that the VisitID field will be the primary key for the table; each visit at Lakewood Community Health Services is assigned a unique number, so this field is the logical choice for the primary key. Finally, the PatientID field is needed in the Visit table as a foreign key to connect the information about visits to patients. The data about patients and their invoices will be stored in separate tables, which you will create later.

Notice the name of each field in Figure 1–6. You need to name each field, table, and object in an Access database.

PROSKILLS

Decision Making: Naming Fields in Access Tables

One of the most important tasks in creating a table is deciding what names to specify for the table's fields. Keep the following guidelines in mind when you assign field names:

- A field name can consist of up to 64 characters, including letters, numbers, spaces, and special characters, except for the period (.), exclamation mark (!), grave accent (`), and square brackets ([ ]).
- A field name cannot begin with a space.
- Capitalize the first letter of each word in a field name that combines multiple words, for example VisitDate.
- Use concise field names that are easy to remember and reference and that won't take up a lot of space in the table datasheet.
- Use standard abbreviations, such as Num for Number, Amt for Amount, and Qty for Quantity, and use them consistently throughout the database. For example, if you use Num for Number in one field name, do not use the number sign (#) for Number in another.
- Give fields descriptive names so that you can easily identify them when you view or edit records.
- Although Access supports the use of spaces in field names (and in other object names), experienced database developers avoid using spaces because they can cause errors when the objects are involved in programming tasks.

By spending time obtaining and analyzing information about the fields in a table, and understanding the rules for naming fields, you can create a well-designed table that will be easy for others to use.

Renaming the Default Primary Key Field

As noted earlier, Access provides the ID field as the default primary key for a new table you create in Datasheet view. Recall that a primary key is a field, or a collection of fields, whose values uniquely identify each record in a table. However, according to Donna's plan, the VisitID field should be the primary key for the Visit table. You'll begin by renaming the default ID field to create the VisitID field.

To rename the ID field to the VisitID field:

TIP

A shortcut menu opens when you right-click an object and provides options for working with that object.

1. Right-click the **ID** column heading to open the shortcut menu, and then click **Rename Field**. The column heading ID is selected, so that whatever text you type next will replace it.
2. Type **VisitID** and then click the row below the heading. The column heading changes to VisitID, and the insertion point moves to the row below the heading. The **insertion point** is a flashing cursor that shows where text you type will be inserted. In this case, it is hidden within the selected field value (New). See Figure 1–7.

   Trouble? If you make a mistake while typing the field name, use BACKSPACE to delete characters to the left of the insertion point or use DELETE to delete characters to the right of the insertion point. Then type the correct text. To correct a field name by replacing it entirely, press ESC, and then type the correct text.

Figure 1–7 **ID field renamed to VisitID**

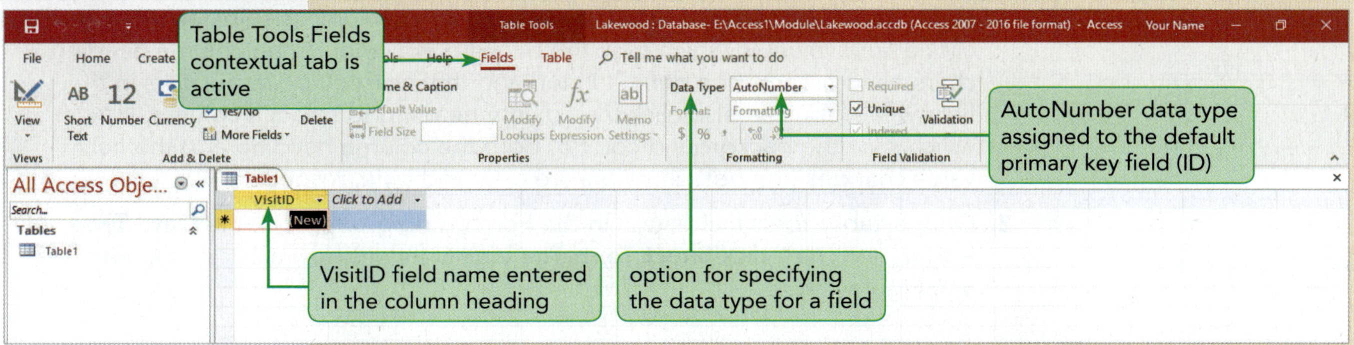

Notice that the Table Tools Fields tab is active on the ribbon. This is an example of a **contextual tab**, which is a tab that appears and provides options for working with a specific object that is selected—in this case, the table you are creating. As you work with other objects in the database, other contextual tabs will appear with commands and options related to each selected object.

INSIGHT

Buttons and Labels on the Ribbon

Depending on the size of the monitor you are using and your screen resolution settings, you might see more or fewer buttons on the ribbon, and you might not see labels next to certain buttons. The screenshots in these modules were created using a screen resolution setting of 1366 x 768 with the program window maximized. If you are using a smaller monitor or a lower screen resolution, some buttons will appear only as icons, with no labels next to them, because there is not enough room on the ribbon to display the labels.

You have renamed the default primary key field, ID, to VisitID. However, the VisitID field still retains the characteristics of the ID field, including its data type. Your next task is to change the data type of this field.

Changing the Data Type of the Default Primary Key Field

Notice the Formatting group on the Table Tools Fields tab. One of the options available in this group is the Data Type option (see Figure 1–7). Each field in an Access table must be assigned a data type. The **data type** determines what field values you can enter for the field. In this case, the AutoNumber data type is displayed. Access assigns the AutoNumber data type to the default ID primary key field because the **AutoNumber** data type automatically inserts a unique number in this field for every record, beginning with the number 1 for the first record, the number 2 for the second record, and so on. Therefore, a field using the AutoNumber data type can serve as the primary key for any table you create.

Visit numbers at Lakewood Community Health Services are specific, four-digit numbers, so the AutoNumber data type is not appropriate for the VisitID field, which is the primary key field in the table you are creating. A better choice is the **Short Text** data type, which allows field values containing letters, digits, and other characters, and which is appropriate for identifying numbers, such as visit numbers, that are never used in calculations. So, Donna asks you to change the data type for the VisitID field from AutoNumber to Short Text.

To change the data type for the VisitID field:

1. Make sure that the VisitID column is selected. A column is selected when you click a field value, in which case the background color of the column heading changes to orange (the default color) and the insertion point appears in the field value. You can also click the column heading to select a column, in which case the background color of both the column heading and the field value changes (the default colors are gray and blue, respectively).
2. On the Table Tools Fields tab, in the Formatting group, click the **Data Type arrow**, and then click **Short Text**. The VisitID field is now a Short Text field. See Figure 1–8.

Figure 1–8 Short Text data type assigned to the VisitID field

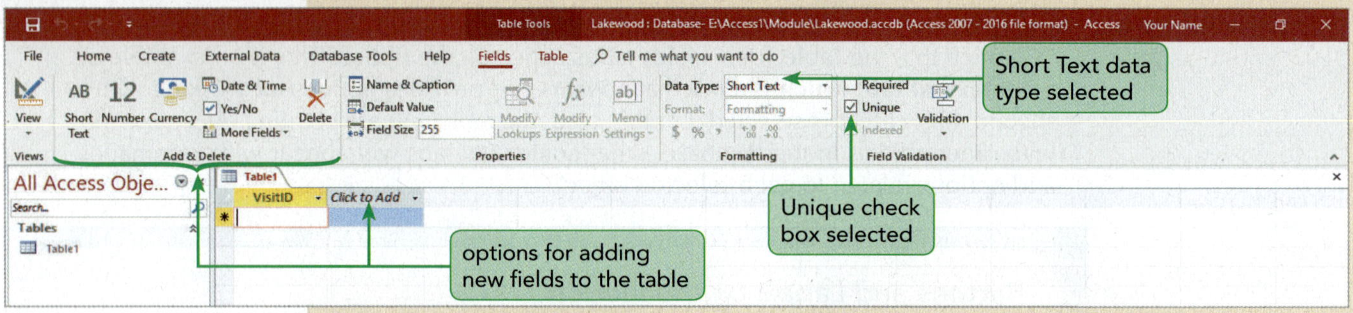

Note the Unique check box in the Field Validation group. This check box is selected because the VisitID field assumed the characteristics of the default primary key field, ID, including the fact that each value in the field must be unique. Because this check box is selected, no two records in the Visit table will be allowed to have the same value in the VisitID field.

With the VisitID field created and established as the primary key, you can now enter the rest of the fields in the Visit table.

Adding New Fields

When you create a table in Datasheet view, you can use the options in the Add & Delete group on the Table Tools Fields tab to add fields to your table. You can also use the Click to Add column in the table datasheet to add new fields. (See Figure 1–8.) You'll use both methods to add the four remaining fields to the Visit table. The next field you need to add is the PatientID field. Similar to the VisitID field, the PatientID field will contain numbers that will not be used in calculations, so it should be a Short Text field.

To add the rest of the fields to the Visit table:

1. On the Table Tools Fields tab, in the Add & Delete group, click the **Short Text** button. Access adds a new field named "Field1" to the right of the VisitID field. See Figure 1–9.

Figure 1–9 New Short Text field added to the table

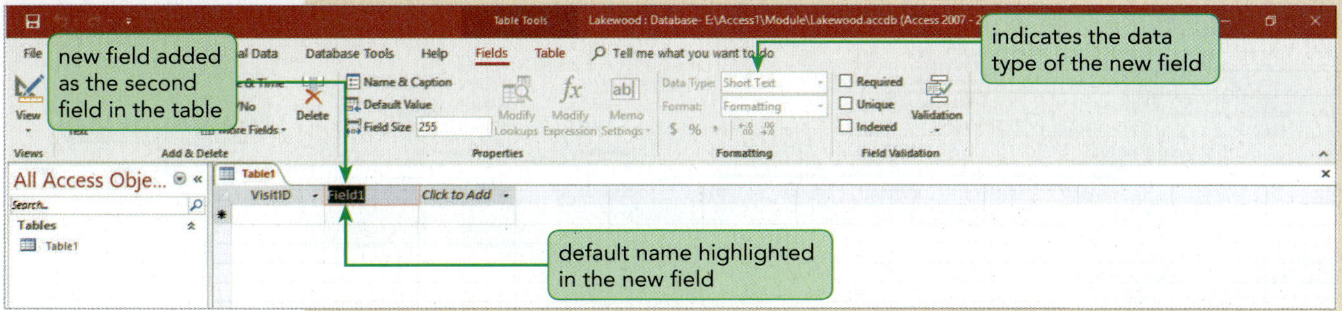

The text "Field1" is selected, so you can simply type the new field name to replace it.

2. Type **PatientID**. Access adds the second field to the table. Next, you'll add the VisitDate field. Because this field will contain date values, you'll add a field with the **Date/Time** data type, which allows field values in a variety of date and time formats.
3. In the Add & Delete group, click the **Date & Time** button. Access adds a third field to the table, this time with the Date/Time data type.
4. Type **VisitDate** to replace the selected name "Field1." The fourth field in the Visit table is the Reason field, which will contain brief descriptions of the reason for the visit to the clinic. You'll add another Short Text field—this time using the Click to Add column.
5. Click the **Click to Add** column heading. Access displays a list of available data types for the new field.
6. Click **Short Text** in the list. Access adds a fourth field to the table.
7. Type **Reason** to replace the highlighted name "Field1," and then press **ENTER**. The Click to Add column becomes active and displays the list of field data types.

   The fifth and final field in the Visit table is the WalkIn field, which will indicate whether the patient had a scheduled appointment. The **Yes/No** data type is suitable for this field because it defines fields that store values representing one of two options—true/false, yes/no, or on/off.

TIP

You can also type the first letter of a data type to select it and close the Click to Add list.

8. Click **Yes/No** in the list, and then type **WalkIn** to replace the highlighted name "Field1."

   Trouble? If you pressed TAB or ENTER after typing the WalkIn field name, press ESC to close the Click to Add list.

9. Click in the row below the VisitID column heading. You have entered all five fields for the Visit table. See Figure 1–10.

Figure 1–10 **Table with all fields entered**

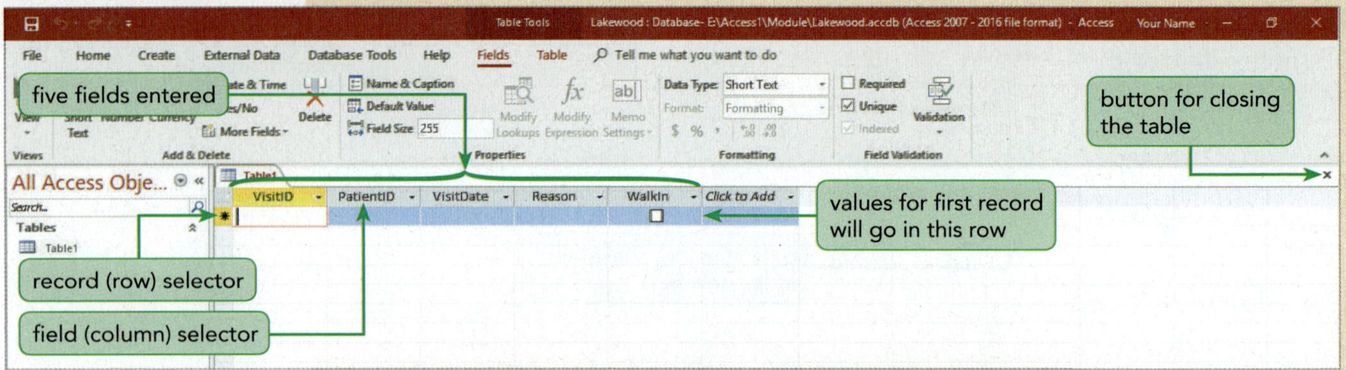

The table contains three Short Text fields (VisitID, PatientID, and Reason), one Date/Time field (VisitDate), and one Yes/No field (WalkIn). You'll learn more about field data types in the next module.

As noted earlier, Datasheet view shows a table's contents in rows (records) and columns (fields). Each column is headed by a field name inside a field selector, and each row has a record selector to its left (see Figure 1–10). Clicking a **field selector** or a **record selector** selects that entire column or row (respectively), which you then can manipulate. A field selector is also called a **column selector**, and a record selector is also called a **row selector**.

Saving the Visit Table Structure

As you find out later, the records you enter are immediately stored in the database as soon as you enter them; however, the table's design—the field names and characteristics of the fields themselves, plus any layout changes to the datasheet—are not saved until you save the table. When you save a new table for the first time, you should give it a name that best identifies the information it contains. Like a field name, a table name can contain up to 64 characters, including spaces.

REFERENCE

Saving a Table

- Make sure the table you want to save is open.
- On the Quick Access Toolbar, click the Save button. The Save As dialog box opens.
- In the Table Name box, type the name for the table.
- Click OK.

According to Donna's plan, you need to save the table with the name "Visit."

TIP

You can also use the Save command in Backstage view to save and name a new table.

To save, name, and close the Visit table:

1. On the Quick Access Toolbar, click the **Save** button. The Save As dialog box opens.

2. With the default name Table1 selected in the Table Name box, type **Visit** and then click **OK**. The tab for the table now displays the name "Visit," and the Visit table design is saved in the Lakewood database.

3. Click the **Close 'Visit'** button [X] on the object tab (see Figure 1–10 for the location of this button). The Visit table closes, and the main portion of the Access window is now blank because no database object is currently open. The Lakewood database file is still open, as indicated by the filename in the Access window title bar.

Creating a Table in Design View

The Lakewood database also needs a table that will hold all of the invoices generated by each office visit. Donna has decided to call this new table the Billing table. You created the structure for the Visit table in Datasheet view. An alternate method of creating the structure of a table is by using Design view. You will create the new Billing table using Design view.

Creating a table in Design view involves entering the field names and defining the properties for the fields, specifying a primary key for the table, and then saving the table structure. Donna began documenting the design for the new Billing table by listing each field's name, data type, and purpose, and will continue to refine the design. See Figure 1–11.

Figure 1–11 Initial design for the Billing table

Field Name	Data Type	Purpose
InvoiceNum	Short Text	Unique number assigned to each invoice; will serve as the table's primary key
VisitID	Short Text	Unique number assigned to each visit; common field that will be a foreign key to connect to the Visit table
InvoiceAmount	Currency	Dollar amount of each invoice
InvoiceDate	Date/Time	Date the invoice was generated
InvoicePaid	Yes/No	Whether the invoice has been paid or not

You'll use Donna's design as a guide for creating the Billing table in the Lakewood database.

To begin creating the Billing table:

1. If the Navigation Pane is open, click the **Shutter Bar Open/Close Button** [«] to close it.

2. On the ribbon, click the **Create** tab.

3. In the Tables group, click the **Table Design** button. A new table named Table1 opens in Design view.

Defining Fields

When you first create a table in Design view, the insertion point is located in the first row's Field Name box, ready for you to begin defining the first field in the table. You enter values for the Field Name, Data Type, and Description field properties (optional), and then select values for all other field properties in the Field Properties pane. These other properties will appear when you move to the first row's Data Type box.

REFERENCE

Defining a Field in Design View

- In the Field Name box, type the name for the field, and then press TAB.
- Accept the default Short Text data type, or click the arrow and select a different data type for the field. Press TAB.
- Enter an optional description for the field, if necessary.
- Use the Field Properties pane to type or select other field properties, as appropriate.

The first field you need to define is the InvoiceNum field. This field will be the primary key for the Billing table. Each invoice at Lakewood Community Health Services is assigned a specific five-digit number. Although the InvoiceNum field will contain these number values, the numbers will never be used in calculations; therefore, you'll assign the Short Text data type to this field. Any time a field contains number values that will not be used in calculations—such as phone numbers, postal codes, and so on—you should use the Short Text data type instead of the Number data type.

TIP

You can also press ENTER to move from one property to the next in the Table Design grid.

To define the InvoiceNum field:

1. Type **InvoiceNum** in the first row's Field Name box, and then press **TAB** to advance to the Data Type box. The default data type, Short Text, appears highlighted in the Data Type box, which now also contains an arrow, and the field properties for a Short Text field appear in the Field Properties pane. See Figure 1–12.

Figure 1–12 Table window after entering the first field name

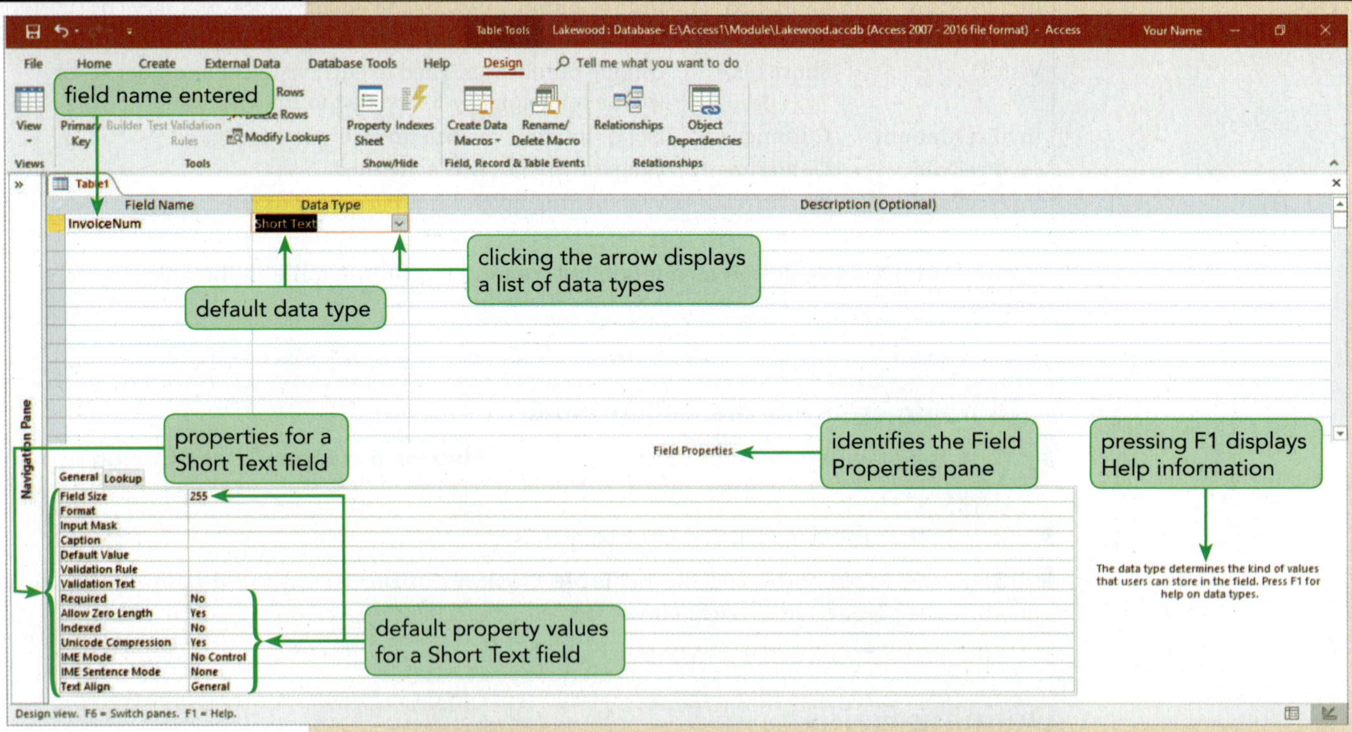

The right side of the Field Properties pane now provides an explanation for the current property, Data Type.

Trouble? If you make a typing error, you can correct it by clicking to position the insertion point, and then using either BACKSPACE to delete characters to the left of the insertion point or DELETE to delete characters to the right of the insertion point. Then type the correct text.

Because the InvoiceNum field values will not be used in calculations, you will accept the default Short Text data type for the field.

2. Press **TAB** to accept Short Text as the data type and to advance to the Description (Optional) box.

   Next you'll enter the Description property value as "Primary key." The value you enter for the Description property will appear on the status bar when you view the table datasheet. Note that specifying "Primary key" for the Description property does *not* establish the current field as the primary key; you use a button on the ribbon to specify the primary key in Design view, which you will do later in this session.

3. Type **Primary key** in the Description (Optional) box and press **ENTER**.

   At this point, you have entered the first field (InvoiceNum) into the table and are ready to enter the remaining fields into the table.

TIP

You can also use TAB to advance to the second row's Field Name box.

Figure 1–13 InvoiceNum field defined

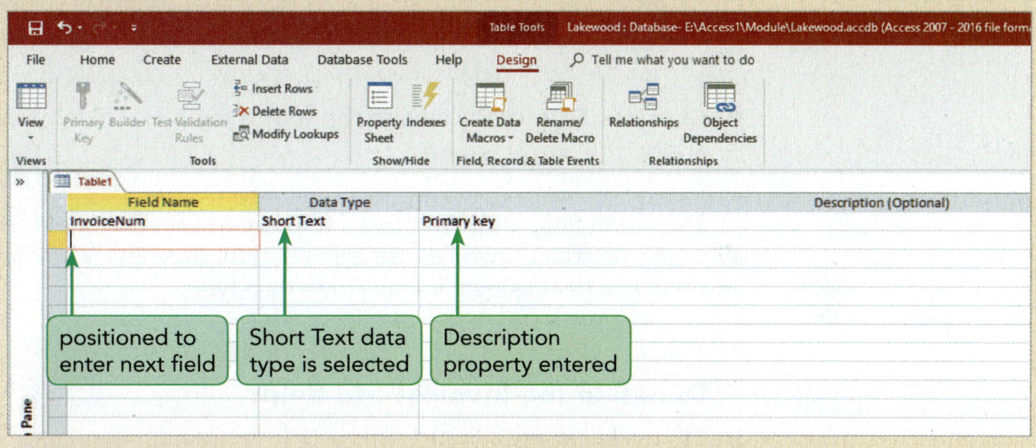

Donna's Billing table design (Figure 1–11) shows VisitID as the second field. Because Donna and other staff members need to relate information about invoices to the visit data in the Visit table, the Billing table must include the VisitID field, which is the Visit table's primary key. Recall that when you include the primary key from one table as a field in a second table to connect the two tables, the field is a foreign key in the second table.

To define the VisitID field:

1. If the insertion point is not already positioned in the second row's Field Name box, click the second row's Field Name box. Once properly positioned, type **VisitID** in the box, and then press **TAB** to advance to the Data Type box.

2. Press **TAB** to accept Short Text as the field's data type. Because the VisitID field is a foreign key to the Visit table, you'll enter "Foreign key" in the Description (Optional) box to help users of the database understand the purpose of this field.
3. Type **Foreign key** in the Description (Optional) box and press **ENTER**.

TIP

The quickest way to move back to the Table Design grid is to use the mouse.

The third field in the Billing table is the InvoiceAmt field, which will display the dollar amount of each invoice the clinic sends to the patients. The Currency data type is the appropriate choice for this field.

To define the InvoiceAmount field:

1. In the third row's Field Name box, type **InvoiceAmount** and then press **TAB** to advance to the Data Type box.
2. Click the **Data Type** arrow, click **Currency** in the list, and then press **TAB** to advance to the Description (Optional) box.

   The InvoiceAmount field is not a primary key, nor does it have a relationship with a field in another table, so you do not need to enter a description for this field. If you've assigned a descriptive field name and the field does not fulfill a special function (such as primary key), you usually do not enter a value for the optional Description property.
3. Press **TAB** to advance to the fourth row's Field Name box.

The fourth field in the Billing table is the InvoiceDate field. This field will contain the dates on which invoices are generated for the clinic's patients. You'll define the InvoiceDate field using the Date/Time data type.

To define the InvoiceDate field:

1. In the fourth row's Field Name box, type **InvoiceDate** and then press **TAB** to advance to the Data Type box.

   You can select a value from the Data Type list as you did for the InvoiceAmount field. Alternately, you can type the property value in the box or type just the first character of the property value.
2. Type **d**. The value in the fourth row's Data Type box changes to "date/Time," with the letters "ate/Time" highlighted. See Figure 1-14.

Figure 1–14 Selecting a value for the Data Type property

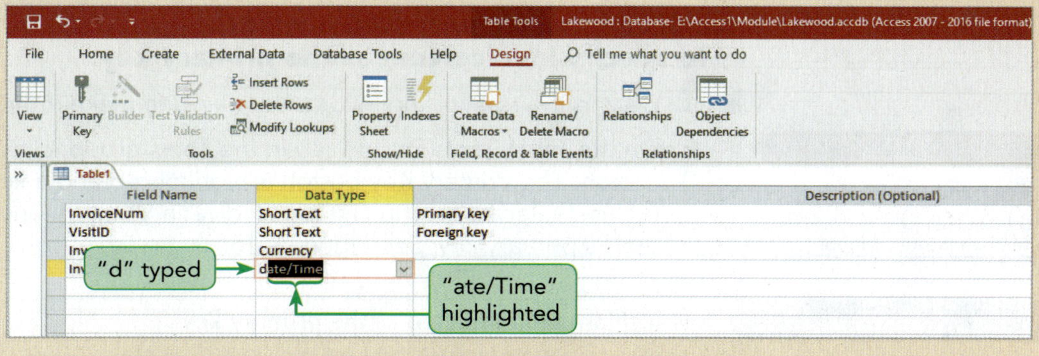

3. Press **TAB** to advance to the Description (Optional) box. Note that Access changes the value for the Data Type property to "Date/Time."
4. Because the InvoiceDate field does not need a special description, press **TAB**.

The fifth, and final, field to be defined in the Billing table is InvoicePaid. This field will be a Yes/No field to indicate the payment status of each invoice record stored in the Billing table. Recall that the Yes/No data type defines fields that store true/false, yes/no, and on/off field values. When you create a Yes/No field in a table, the default Format property is set to Yes/No.

To define the InvoicePaid field:

1. In the fifth row's Field Name box, type **InvoicePaid** and then press **TAB** to advance to the Data Type box.
2. Type **y**. Access completes the data type as "yes/No." Press **TAB** to select the Yes/No data type and move to the Description (Optional) box.
3. Because the InvoicePaid field does not need a special description, press **TAB**.

You've finished defining the fields for the Billing table. Next, you need to specify the primary key for the table.

Specifying the Primary Key

As you learned previously, the primary key for a table uniquely identifies each record in the table.

REFERENCE

Specifying a Primary Key in Design View

- Display the table in Design view.
- Click in the row for the field you've chosen to be the primary key to make it the active field. If the primary key will consist of two or more fields, click the row selector for the first field, press and hold down CTRL, and then click the row selector for each additional primary key field.
- On the Table Tools Design tab in the Tools group, click the Primary Key button.

According to Donna's design, you need to specify InvoiceNum as the primary key for the Billing table. You can do so while the table is in Design view.

To specify InvoiceNum as the primary key:

1. Click in the row for the InvoiceNum field to make it the current field.
2. On the Table Tools Design tab in the Tools group, click the **Primary Key** button. The Primary Key button is highlighted and a key symbol appears in the row selector for the first row, indicating that the InvoiceNum field is the table's primary key. See Figure 1–15.

TIP

The Primary Key button is a toggle; you can click it to remove the key symbol.

Figure 1–15 InvoiceNum field selected as the primary key

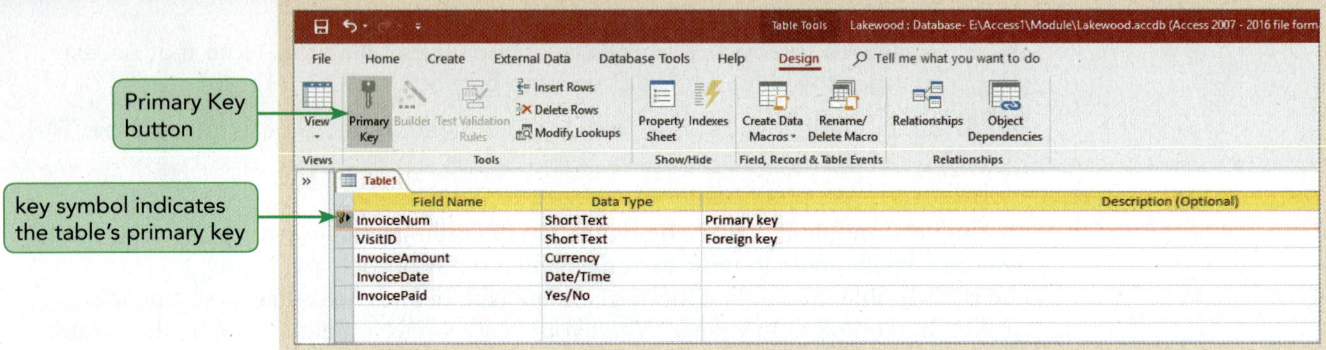

Renaming Fields in Design View

Donna has decided to rename the InvoiceAmount field in the Billing table to InvoiceAmt. Since Amt is an appropriate abbreviation for Amount, this new name will be just as readable, yet a little shorter.

To rename a field in Design view:

1. Click to position the insertion point to the right of the word "InvoiceAmount" in the third row's Field Name box, and then press **BACKSPACE** four times to delete the letters "ount." The name of the fourth field is now InvoiceAm. Now add the final letter by pressing the letter **t**. The name of the new field is now InvoiceAmt as Donna wants it to be. See Figure 1–16.
2. Click in the row for the InvoiceAmt field to make it the current field.

TIP

You can also select an entire field name and then type new text to replace it.

Figure 1–16 Billing table after renamed field

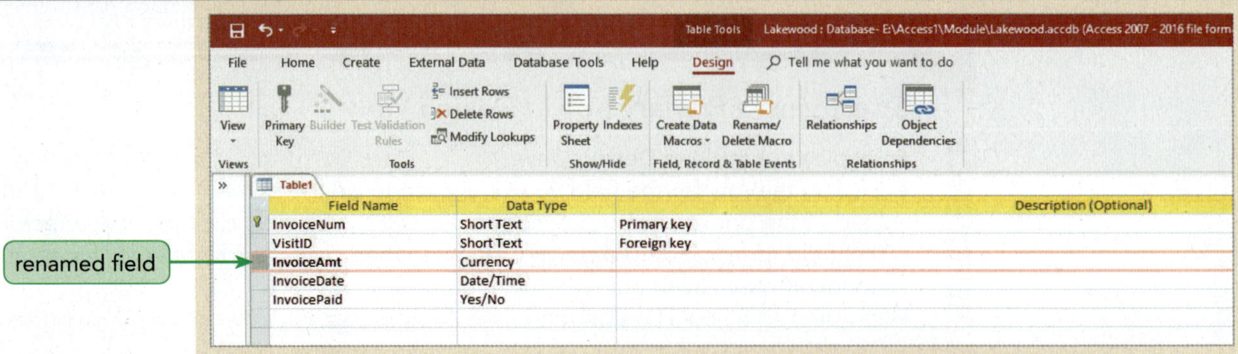

Saving the Billing Table Structure

As with the Visit table, the last step in creating a table is to name the table and save the table's structure. When you save a table structure, the table is stored in the database file (in this case, the Lakewood database file). After saving the table, you can enter data into it. According to Donna's plan, you need to save the table you've defined as "Billing."

To save, name, and close the Billing table:

1. On the Quick Access Toolbar, click the **Save** button. The Save As dialog box opens.
2. With the default name Table1 selected in the Table Name box, type **Billing**, and then click **OK**. The tab for the table now displays the name "Billing," and the Billing table design is saved in the Lakewood database.
3. Click the **Close 'Billing'** button on the object tab. The Billing table closes, and the main portion of the Access window is now blank because no database object is currently open. The Lakewood database file is still open, as indicated by the filename in the Access window title bar.

You have now successfully created and saved the structures for the Visit and Billing tables; however, you have not yet added any data to these tables. You can view and work with these objects in the Navigation Pane.

To view objects in the Lakewood database:

1. On the Navigation Pane, click the **Shutter Bar Open/Close Button** to open it. See Figure 1–17.

Figure 1–17 Visit and Billing tables (database objects) displayed in the Navigation Pane

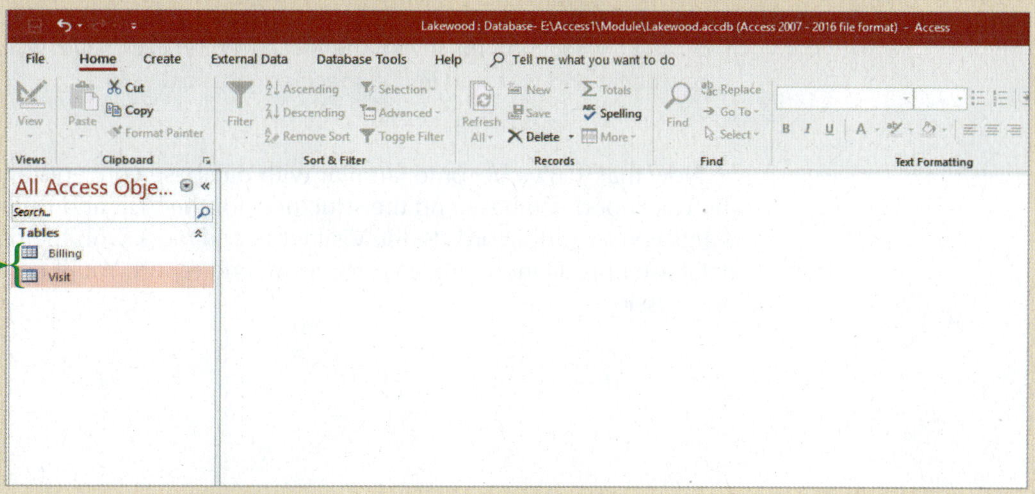

Closing a Table and Exiting Access

When you are finished working in an Access table, it's a good idea to close the table so that you do not make unintended changes to the table data. You can close a table by clicking its Close button on the object tab, as you did earlier. Or, if you want to close the Access program as well, you can click the program's Close button. When you do, any open tables are closed, the active database is closed, and you exit the Access program.

To close any opened tables and exit Access:

1. Click the **Close** button on the program window title bar. Any opened tables would close, along with the Lakewood database, and then the Access program closes.

TIP

To close a database without exiting Access, click the File tab to display Backstage view, and then click Close.

INSIGHT

Saving a Database

Unlike the Save buttons in other Office programs, the Save button on the Quick Access Toolbar in Access does not save the active document (database). Instead, you use the Save button to save the design of an Access object, such as a table (as you saw earlier), or to save datasheet format changes, such as resizing columns. Access does not have or need a button or option you can use to save the active database.

Access saves changes to the active database automatically when you change or add a record or close the database. If your database is stored on a removable storage device, such as a USB drive, you should never remove the device while the database file is open. If you do, Access will encounter problems when it tries to save the database, which might damage the database. Make sure you close the database first before removing the storage device.

It is possible to save a database with a different name. To do so, you would click the File tab to open Backstage view, and then click the Save As option. You save the database in the default database format unless you select a different format, so click the Save As button to open the Save As dialog box. Enter the new name for the database, choose the location for saving the file, and then click Save. The database is saved with a new name and is stored in the specified location.

Now that you've become familiar with database concepts and Access, and created the Lakewood database and the structures for the Visit and Billing tables, Donna wants you to add records to the Visit table and work with the data stored in it to create database objects including a query, form, and report. You'll complete these tasks in the next session.

REVIEW

Session 1.1 Quick Check

1. A(n) ________ is a single characteristic of a person, place, object, event, or idea.
2. You connect the records in two separate tables through a(n) ________ that appears in both tables.
3. The ________, whose values uniquely identify each record in a table, is called a(n) ________ when it is placed in a second table to form a relationship between the two tables.
4. The ________ is the area of the Access window that lists all the objects in a database, and it is the main control center for opening and working with database objects.
5. What is the name of the field that Access creates, by default, as the primary key field for a new table in Datasheet view?
6. Which group on the Table Tools Fields tab contains the options you use to add new fields to a table?
7. What are the two views you can use to create a table in Access?
8. Explain how the saving process in Access is different from saving in other Office programs.

Session 1.2 Visual Overview:

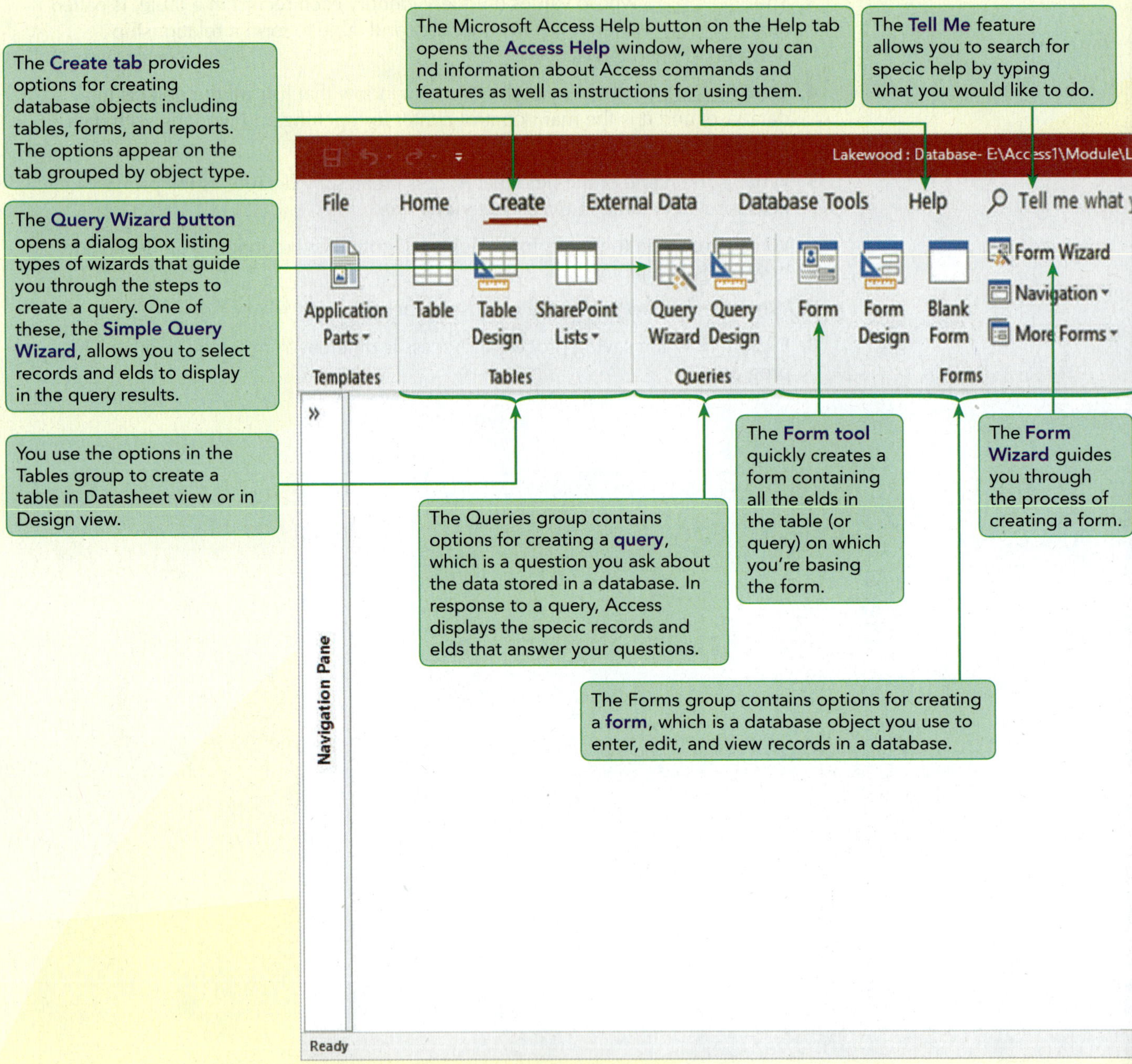

The Create Tab Options

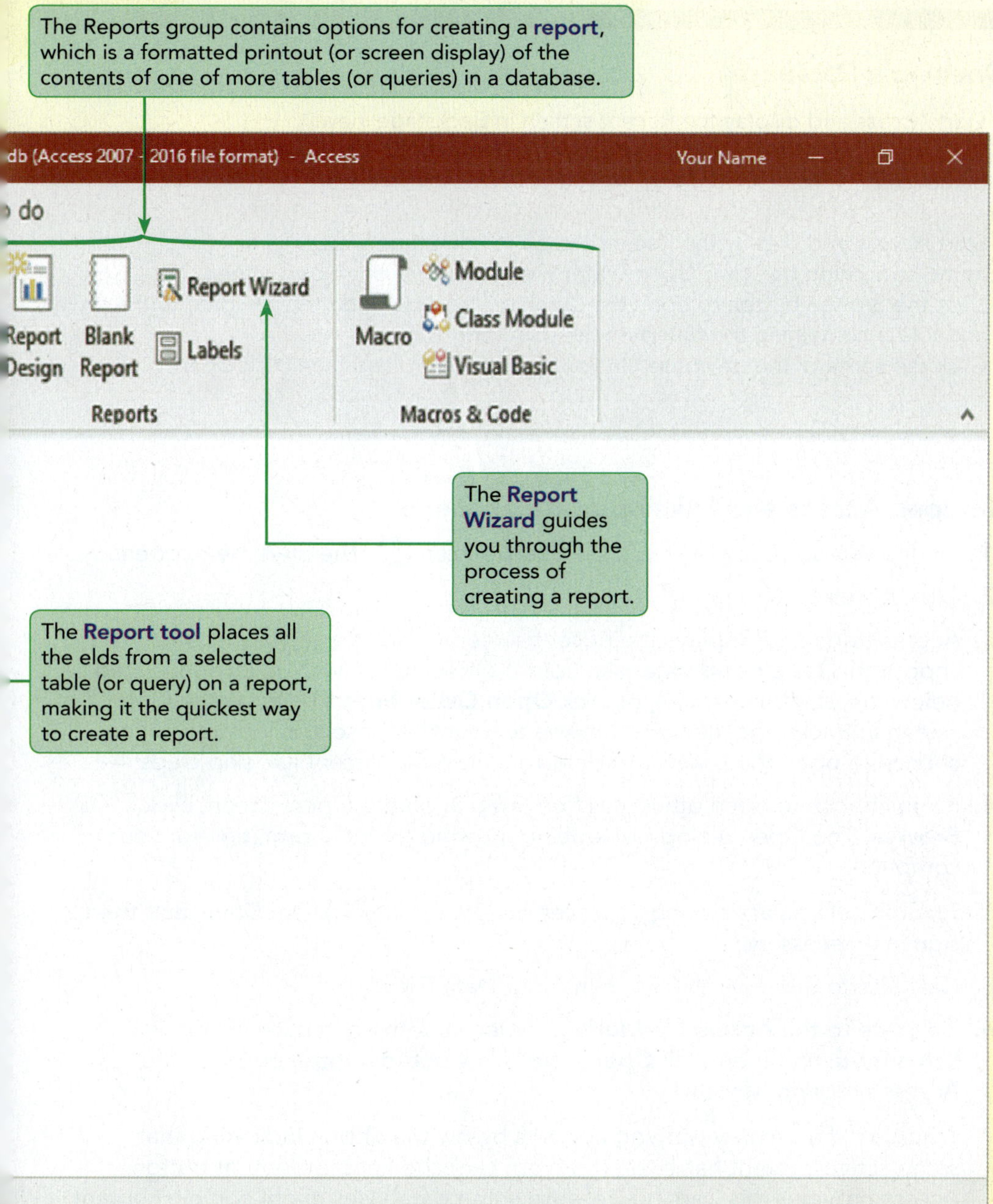

Entering Data into Tables

With the fields in place for the Visit table, you can now enter the field values for each record. However, if you closed Access, as instructed, after the previous session, you must first open Access and the Lakewood database to be able to work with the Visit table. If you did not close Access in the previous session and the Lakewood database is still open (see previous Figure 1–17), you may skip the steps below that open Access and the Lakewood database, and go directly to the steps to enter data into the Visit table.

REFERENCE

Opening a Database

- Start Access and display the Recent screen in Backstage view.
- Click the name of the database you want to open in the list of recently opened databases.

or

- Start Access and display the Recent screen in Backstage view.
- In the navigation bar, click Open Other Files to display the Open screen.
- Click the Browse button to open the Open dialog box, and then navigate to the drive and folder containing the database file you want to open.
- Click the name of the database file you want to open, and then click Open.

To open Access and Lakewood database:

1. On the Windows taskbar, click the **Start** button. The Start menu opens.
2. Click **Access**.
3. Access starts and displays the Recent screen in Backstage view. You may choose the **Lakewood** database from the Recent list (with its location listed below the database name), or click **Open Other Files** to display the Open screen in Backstage view and browse to your database and location. If you choose to open the Lakewood database from the Recent list, skip steps 4–6.
4. If you choose to open other files from step 3, on the Open screen, click **Browse**. The Open dialog box opens, showing folder information for your computer.

   Trouble? If you are storing your files on OneDrive, click OneDrive, and then sign in if necessary.
5. Navigate to the drive that contains your Data Files.
6. Navigate to the **Access1 > Module** folder, click the database file named **Lakewood**, and then click **Open**. The Lakewood database opens in the Access program window.

   Trouble? If a security warning appears below the ribbon indicating that some active content has been disabled, click the Enable Content button. Access provides this warning because some databases might contain content that could harm your computer. Because the Lakewood database does not contain objects that could be harmful, you can open it safely. If you are accessing the file over a network, you might also see a dialog box asking if you want to make the file a trusted document; click Yes.

Note that the Lakewood database contains two objects, the Billing and Visit tables you created at the end of the previous session (see Figure 1–17). The next step is for you to open the Visit table to begin adding records.

To open the Visit table:

1. In the Navigation Pane, double-click **Visit** to open the Visit table in Datasheet view.
2. On the Navigation Pane, click the **Shutter Bar Open/Close Button** « to close the pane.
3. Click the first row value for the VisitID field. See Figure 1–18.

Figure 1–18 Visit table opened and ready to enter data

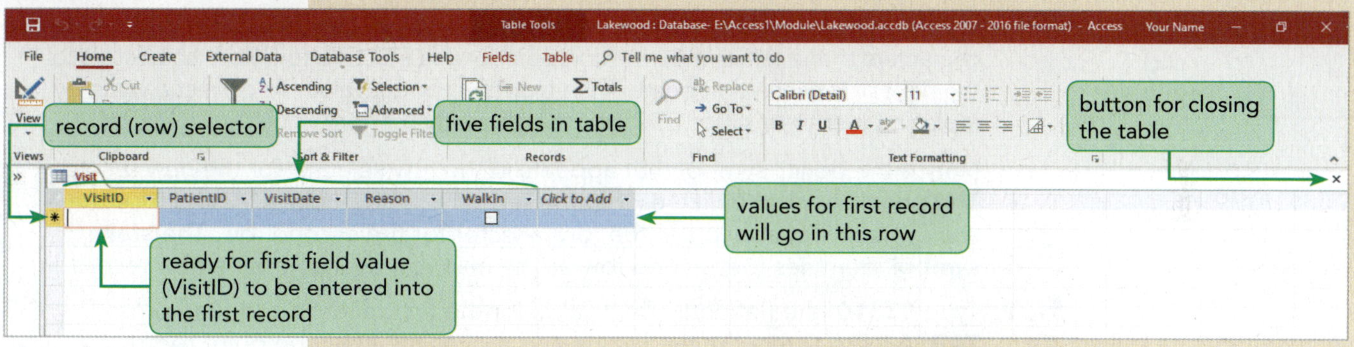

You are now ready to begin adding records and are positioned in the first field (VisitID) of the first record. Donna requests that you enter eight records into the Visit table, as show in Figure 1–19.

Figure 1–19 Visit table records

VisitID	PatientID	VisitDate	Reason	WalkIn
1495	13310	12/23/2020	Rhinitis	Yes
1450	13272	10/26/2020	Influenza	Yes
1461	13250	11/3/2020	Dermatitis	Yes
1615	13308	4/1/2021	COPD management visit	No
1596	13299	3/24/2021	Pneumonia	Yes
1567	13283	2/26/2021	Annual wellness visit	No
1499	13264	12/28/2020	Hypotension	No
1475	13261	11/19/2020	Annual wellness visit	No

To enter the first record for the Visit table:

1. In the first row for the VisitID field, type **1495** (the VisitID field value for the first record), and then press **TAB**. Access adds the field value and moves the insertion point to the right, into the PatientID column. See Figure 1–20.

Be sure to type the numbers "0" and "1" and not the letters "O" and "I" when entering numeric values, even though the field is of the Short Text data type.

Figure 1–20 First field value entered

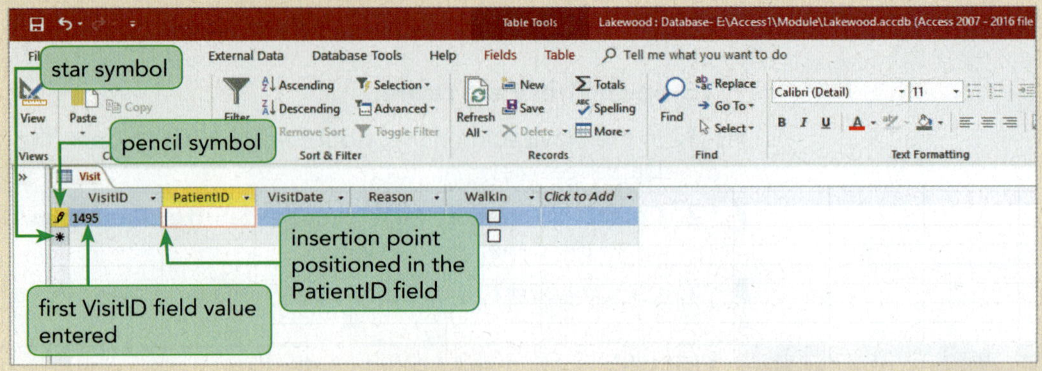

Trouble? If you make a mistake when typing a value, use BACKSPACE to delete characters to the left of the insertion point or use DELETE to delete characters to the right of the insertion point. Then type the correct value. To correct a value by replacing it entirely, press ESC, and then type the correct value.

Notice the pencil symbol that appears in the row selector for the new record. The **pencil symbol** indicates that the record is being edited. Also notice the star symbol that appears in the row selector for the second row. The **star symbol** identifies the second row as the next row available for a new record.

2. Type **13310** (the PatientID field value for the first record), and then press **TAB**. Access enters the field value and moves the insertion point to the VisitDate column.
3. Type **12/23/20** (the VisitDate field value for the first record), and then press **TAB**. Access displays the year as "2020" even though you entered only the final two digits of the year. This is because the VisitDate field has the Date/Time data type, which automatically formats dates with four-digit years.
4. Type **Rhinitis** (the Reason field value for the first record), and then press **TAB** to move to the WalkIn column.

   Recall that the WalkIn field is a Yes/No field. Notice the check box displayed in the WalkIn column. By default, the value for any Yes/No field is "No"; therefore, the check box is initially empty. For Yes/No fields with check boxes, you press TAB to leave the check box unchecked, or you press SPACEBAR to insert a checkmark in the check box. The record you are entering in the table is for a walk-in visit, so you need to insert a checkmark in the check box to indicate "Yes."

TIP

You can also click a check box in a Yes/No field to insert or remove a checkmark.

5. Press **SPACEBAR** to insert a checkmark, and then press **TAB**. The first record is entered into the table, and the insertion point is positioned in the VisitID field for the second record. The pencil symbol is removed from the first row because the record in that row is no longer being edited. The table is now ready for you to enter the second record. See Figure 1–21.

Figure 1–21 **Datasheet with first record entered**

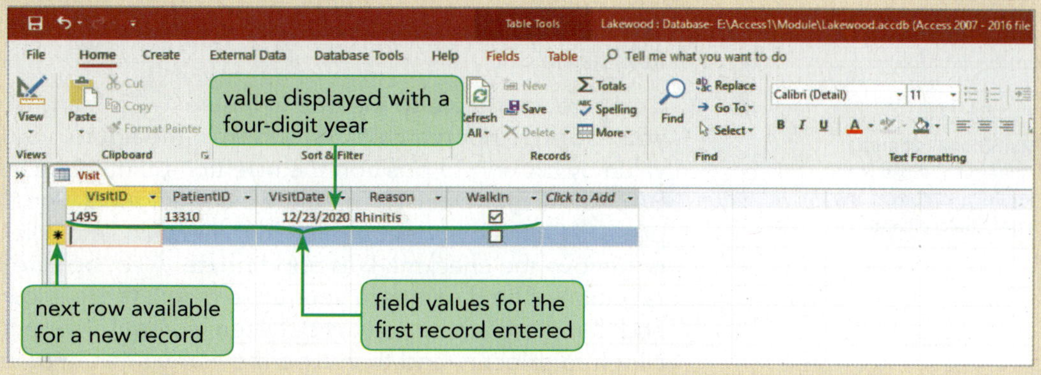

Now you can enter the remaining seven records in the Visit table.

TIP

You can also press ENTER instead of TAB to move from one field to another and to the next row.

To enter the remaining records in the Visit table:

1. Referring to Figure 1–19, enter the values for records 2 through 8, pressing **TAB** to move from field to field and to the next row for a new record. Keep in mind that you do not have to type all four digits of the year in the VisitDate field values; you can enter only the final two digits, and Access will display all four. Also, for any WalkIn field values of "No," be sure to press TAB to leave the check box empty.

   Trouble? If you enter a value in the wrong field by mistake, such as entering a Reason field value in the VisitDate field, a menu might open with options for addressing the problem. If this happens, click the "Enter new value" option in the menu. You'll return to the field with the incorrect value selected, which you can then replace by typing the correct value.

   Notice that not all of the Reason field values are fully displayed. To see more of the table datasheet and the full field values, you'll resize the Reason column.

2. Place the pointer on the vertical line to the right of the Reason field name until the pointer changes to the column resizing pointer ✛, and then double-click the vertical line. All the Reason field values are now fully displayed. See Figure 1–22.

Figure 1–22 **Datasheet with eight records entered**

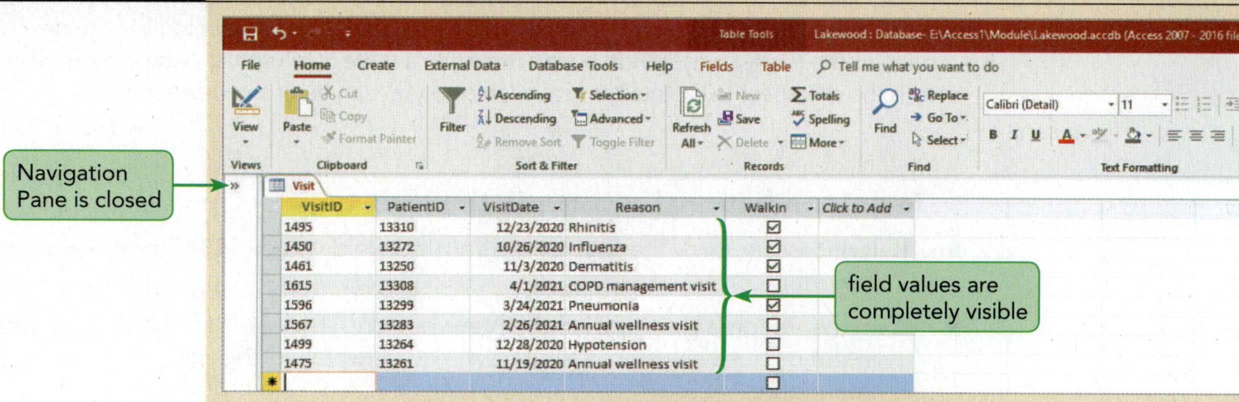

When you resize a datasheet column by double-clicking the column dividing line, you are sizing the column to its **best fit**—that is, so the column is just wide enough to display the longest visible value in the column, including the field name.

Carefully compare your VisitID and PatientID values with those in the figure, and correct any errors before continuing.

3. Compare your table to the one in Figure 1–22. If any of the field values in your table do not match those shown in the figure, you can correct a field value by clicking to position the insertion point in the value, and then using BACKSPACE or DELETE to delete incorrect text. Type the correct text and press ENTER. To correct a value in the WalkIn field, click the check box to add or remove the checkmark as appropriate. Also, be sure the spelling and capitalization of field names in your table match those shown in the figure exactly and that there are no spaces between words. To correct a field name, double-click it to select it, and then type the correct name; or use the Rename Field option on the shortcut menu to rename a field with the correct name.

Remember that Access automatically saves the data stored in a table; however, you must save any new or modified structure to a table. Even though you have not clicked the Save button, your data has already been saved. To ensure this is the case, you can close the table and then reopen it.

To close and reopen Visit table:

1. Click the **Close 'Visit'** button ✕ on the object tab for the Visit table. When asked if you would like to save the changes to the layout of the Visit table, click **Yes**. The Visit table closes.
2. On the Navigation Pane, click the **Shutter Bar Open/Close Button** » to open it.
3. In the Navigation Pane, double-click **Visit** to open the Visit table in Datasheet view.

Notice that after you closed and reopened the Visit table, Access sorted and displayed the records in order by the values in the VisitID field because it is the primary key. If you compare your screen to Figure 1–22, which shows the records in the order you entered them, you'll see that the current screen shows the records in order by the VisitID field values.

Donna asks you to add two more records to the Visit table. When you add a record to an existing table, you must enter the new record in the next row available for a new record; you cannot insert a row between existing records for the new record. In a table with just a few records, such as the Visit table, the next available row is visible on the screen. However, in a table with hundreds of records, you would need to scroll the datasheet to see the next row available. The easiest way to add a new record to a table is to use the New button, which scrolls the datasheet to the next row available so you can enter the new record.

To enter additional records in the Visit table:

1. If necessary, click the first record's VisitID field value (**1450**) to make it the current record.
2. In the Records group, click the **New** button. The insertion point is positioned in the next row available for a new record, which in this case is row 9. See Figure 1–23.

Figure 1–23 **Entering a new record**

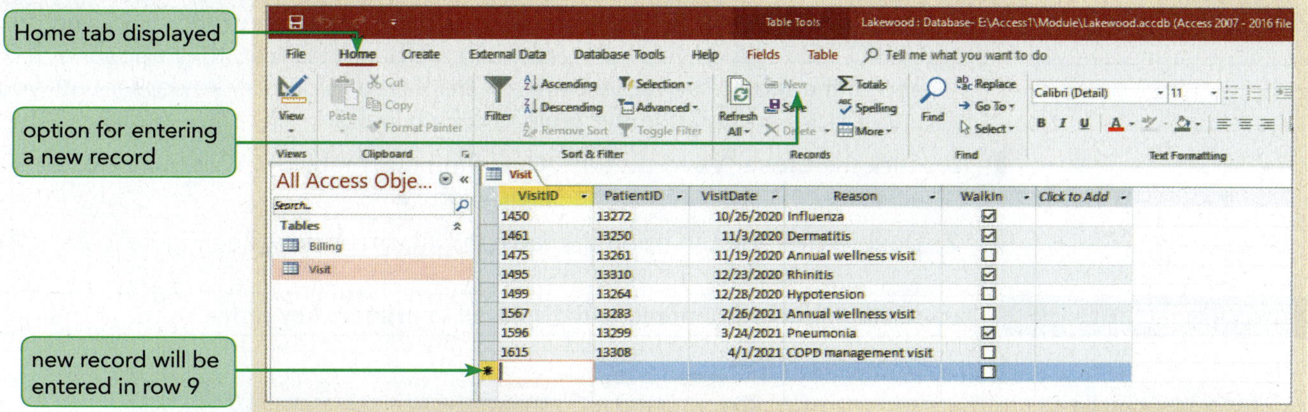

3. With the insertion point in the VisitID field for the new record, type **1548** and then press **TAB**.
4. Complete the entry of this record by entering each value shown below, pressing **TAB** to move from field to field:

   PatientID = **13301**

   VisitDate = **2/10/2021**

   Reason = **Hypothyroidism**

   WalkIn = **No (unchecked)**
5. Enter the values for the next new record, as follows, and then press **TAB** after entering the WalkIn field value:

   VisitID = **1588**

   PatientID = **13268**

   VisitDate = **3/19/2021**

   Reason = **Cyst removal**

   WalkIn = **Yes (checked)**

   Your datasheet should look like the one shown in Figure 1–24.

Figure 1–24 **Datasheet with additional records entered**

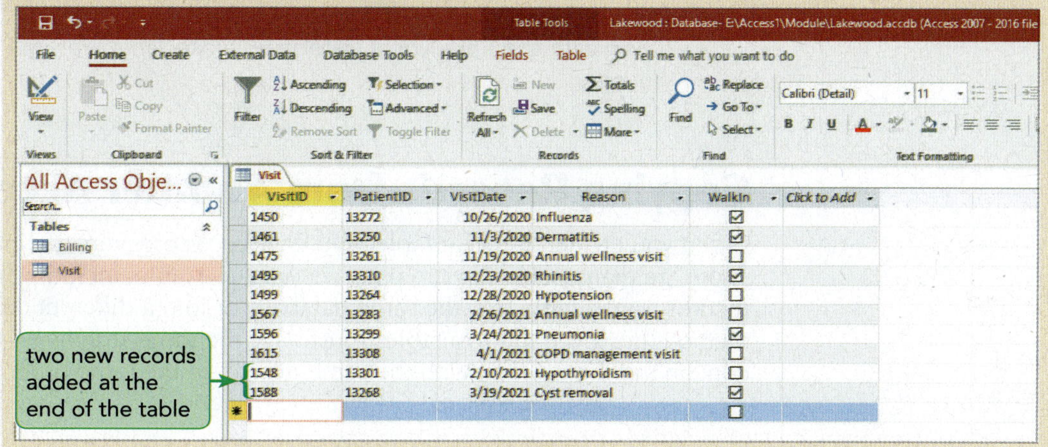

The new records you added appear at the end of the table, and are not sorted in order by the primary key field values. For example, VisitID 1548 should be the sixth record in the table, placed between VisitID 1499 and VisitID 1567. When you add records to a table datasheet, they appear at the end of the table. The records are not displayed in primary key order until you either close and reopen the table or switch views.

6. Click the **Close 'Visit'** button on the object tab. The Visit table closes; however, it is still listed in the Navigation Pane.
7. Double-click **Visit** to open the table in Datasheet view. See Figure 1–25.

Figure 1–25 **Table with 10 records entered and displayed in primary key order**

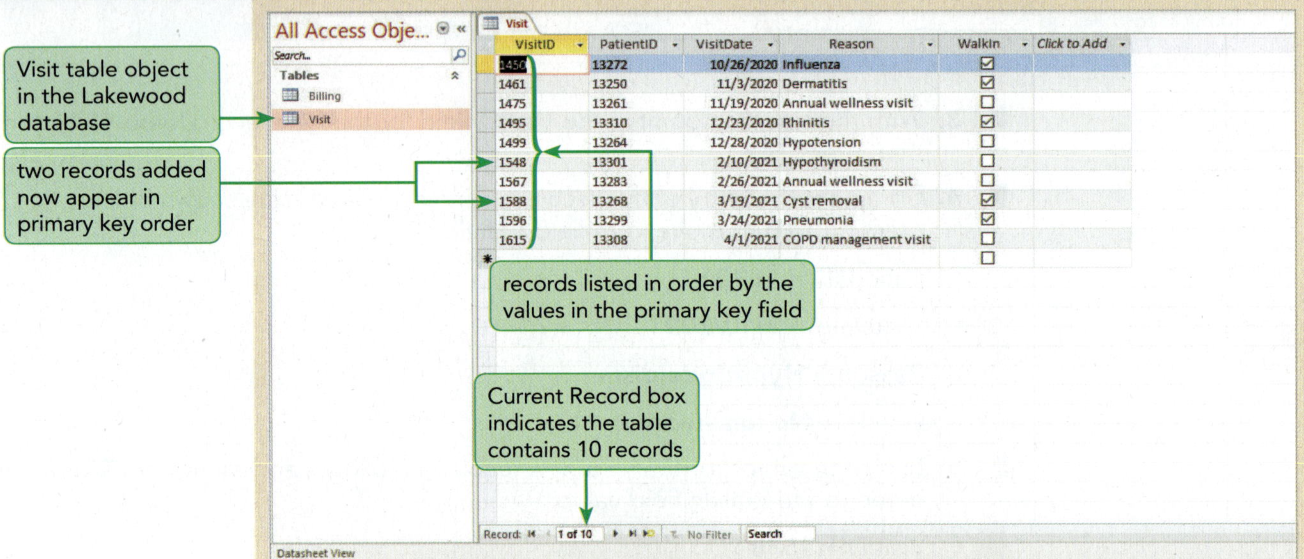

The two records you added, with VisitID field values of 1548 and 1588, now appear in the correct primary key order. The table contains a total of 10 records, as indicated by the **Current Record box** at the bottom of the datasheet. The Current Record box displays the number of the current record as well as the total number of records in the table.

Each record contains a unique VisitID value because this field is the primary key. Other fields, however, can contain the same value in multiple records; for example, the Reason field has two values of "Annual wellness visit."

8. Click the **Close** button on the program window title bar. The Visit table, along with the Lakewood database, close, and then the Access program closes.

Copying Records from Another Access Database

When you created the Visit table, you entered records directly into the table datasheet. There are many other ways to enter records in a table, including copying and pasting records from a table into the same database or into a different database. To use this method, however, the two tables must have the same structure—that is, the tables must contain the same fields, with the same design, in the same order.

Donna has already created a table named Appointment that contains additional records with visit data. The Appointment table is contained in a database named Support_AC_1_Donna.accdb located in the Access1 > Module folder included with your Data Files. The Appointment table has the same table structure as the Visit table you created.

Your next task is to copy the records from the Appointment table and paste them into your Visit table. To do so, you need to open the Support_AC_1_Donna.accdb database.

To copy the records from the Appointment table:

1. On the Windows taskbar, click the **Start** button. The Start menu opens.
2. Click **Access**.
3. Click **Open Other Files** to display the Open screen in Backstage view.
4. On the Open screen, click **Browse**. The Open dialog box opens, showing folder information for your computer.

   Trouble? If you are storing your files on OneDrive, click OneDrive, and then log in if necessary.
5. Navigate to the drive that contains your Data Files.
6. Navigate to the **Access1 > Module** folder, click the database file **Support_AC_1_Donna.accdb**, and then click **Open**. The Support_AC_1_Donna database opens in the Access program window. Note that the database contains only one object, the Appointment table.

   Trouble? If a security warning appears below the ribbon indicating that some active content has been disabled, click the Enable Content button. Access provides this warning because some databases might contain content that could harm your computer. Because the Support_AC_1_Donna.accdb database does not contain objects that could be harmful, you can open it safely. If you are accessing the file over a network, you might also see a dialog box asking if you want to make the file a trusted document; click Yes.
7. In the Navigation Pane, double-click **Appointment** to open the Appointment table in Datasheet view. The table contains 76 records and the same five fields, with the same characteristics, as the fields in the Visit table. See Figure 1–26.

Figure 1–26 Appointment table in the Support_AC_1_Donna database

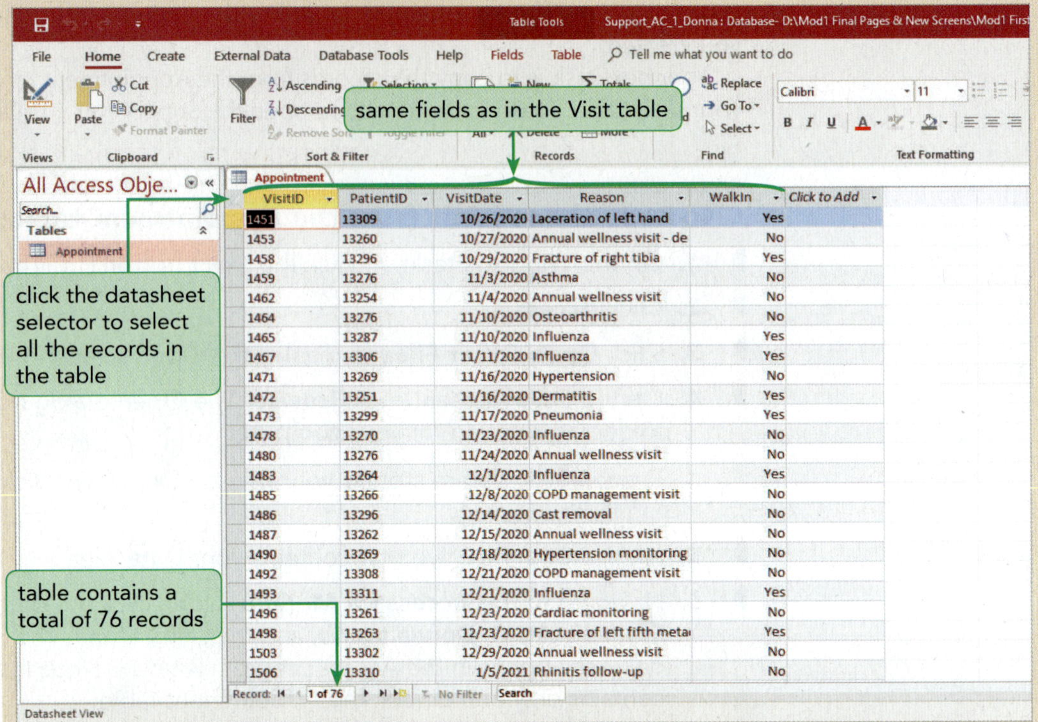

Donna wants you to copy all the records in the Appointment table. You can select all the records by clicking the **datasheet selector**, which is the box to the left of the first field name in the table datasheet, as shown in Figure 1–26.

8. Click the **datasheet selector** to the left of the VisitID field. All the records in the table are selected.
9. In the Clipboard group, click the **Copy** button to copy all the records to the Clipboard.
10. Click the **Close 'Appointment'** button on the object tab. A dialog box may open asking if you want to save the data you copied to the Clipboard. This dialog box opens only when you copy a large amount of data to the Clipboard. If asked, click **Yes**. If opened, the dialog box closes, and then the Appointment table closes.

With the records copied to the Clipboard, you can now paste them into the Visit table. First you need to close the Support_AC_1_Donna.accdb database while keeping the Access program open, and then open the Lakewood database.

To close the Support_AC_1_Donna.accdb database and then paste the records into the Visit table:

1. Click the **File** tab to open Backstage view, and then click **Close** in the navigation bar to close the Support_AC_1_Donna.accdb database. You return to a blank Access program window, and the Home tab is the active tab on the ribbon.
2. Click the **File** tab to return to Backstage view, and then click **Open** in the navigation bar. Recent is selected on the Open screen, and the recently opened database files are listed. This list should include the Lakewood database.

3. Click **Lakewood** to open the Lakewood database file.

   Trouble? If the Lakewood database file is not in the list of recent files, click Browse. In the Open dialog box, navigate to the drive and folder where you are storing your files, and then open the Lakewood database file.

   Trouble? If the security warning appears below the ribbon, click the Enable Content button, and then, if necessary, click Yes to identify the file as a trusted document.

4. In the Navigation Pane, double-click **Visit** to open the Visit table in Datasheet view.
5. On the Navigation Pane, click the **Shutter Bar Open/Close Button** « to close the pane.
6. Position the pointer on the star symbol in the row selector for row 11 (the next row available for a new record) until the pointer changes to a right-pointing arrow ➡, and then click to select the row.
7. In the Clipboard group, click the **Paste** button. The pasted records are added to the table, and a dialog box opens asking you to confirm that you want to paste all the records (76 total).

   Trouble? If the Paste button isn't active, click the row selection ➡ pointer on the row selector for row 11, making sure the entire row is selected, and then repeat Step 7.

8. Click **Yes**. The dialog box closes, and the pasted records are selected. See Figure 1–27. Notice that the table now contains a total of 86 records—10 records that you entered previously and 76 records that you copied and pasted.

Figure 1–27 Visit table after copying and pasting records

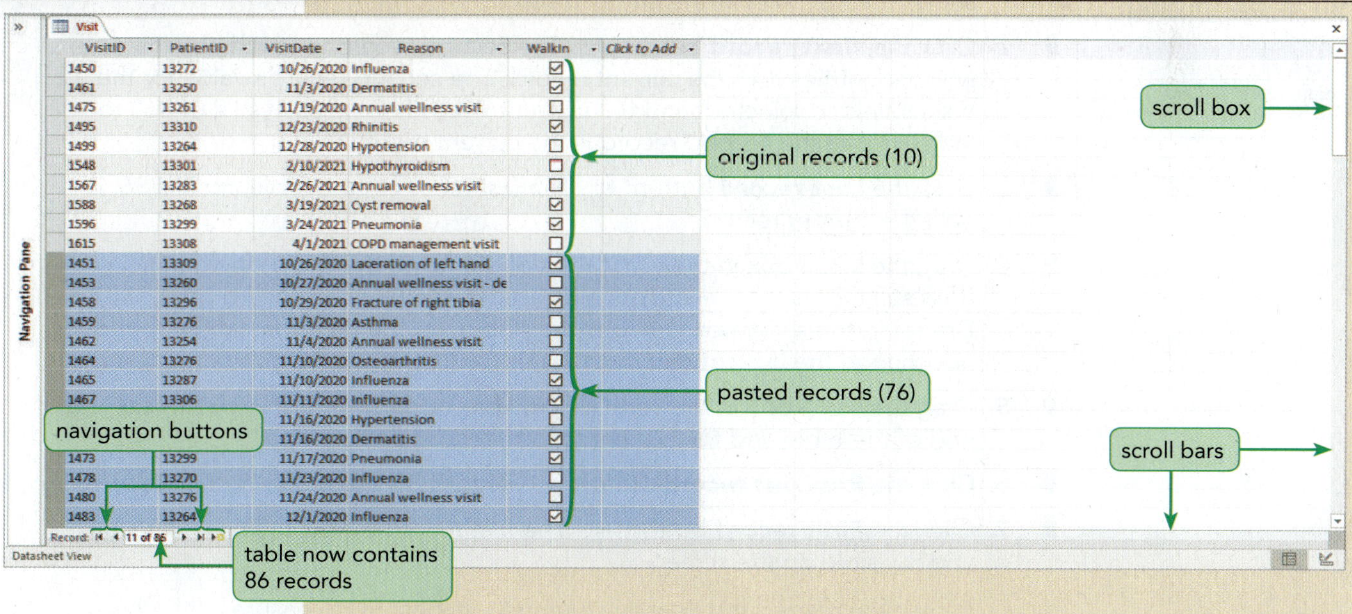

Not all the Reason field values are completely visible, so you need to resize this column to its best fit.

9. Place the pointer on the column dividing line to the right of the Reason field name until the pointer changes to the column resizing pointer ✛, and then double-click the column dividing line. The Reason field values are now fully displayed.

Navigating a Datasheet

The Visit table now contains 86 records, but only some of the records are visible on the screen. To view fields or records not currently visible on the screen, you can use the horizontal and vertical scroll bars to navigate the data. The **navigation buttons**, shown in Figure 1–27 and also described in Figure 1–28, provide another way to move vertically through the records. The Current Record box appears between the two sets of navigation buttons and displays the number of the current record as well as the total number of records in the table. Figure 1–28 shows which record becomes the current record when you click each navigation button. The New (blank) record button works the same way as the New button on the Home tab, which you used earlier to enter a new record in the table.

Figure 1–28 Navigation buttons

Navigation Button	Record Selected	Navigation Button	Record Selected
	First record		Last record
	Previous record		New (blank) record
	Next record		

Donna suggests that you use the various navigation techniques to move through the Visit table and become familiar with its contents.

TIP

You can make a field the current field by clicking anywhere within the column for that field.

To navigate the Visit datasheet:

1. Click the first record's VisitID field value (**1450**). The Current Record box shows that record 1 is the current record.
2. Click the **Next record** button. The second record is now highlighted, which identifies it as the current record. The second record's value for the VisitID field is selected, and the Current Record box displays "2 of 86" to indicate that the second record is the current record.
3. Click the **Last record** button. The last record in the table, record 86, is now the current record.
4. Drag the scroll box in the vertical scroll bar up to the top of the bar. Record 86 is still the current record, as indicated in the Current Record box. Dragging the scroll box changes the display of the table datasheet, but does not change the current record.
5. Drag the scroll box in the vertical scroll bar back down until you can see the end of the table and the current record (record 86).
6. Click the **Previous record** button. Record 85 is now the current record.
7. Click the **First record** button. The first record is now the current record and is visible on the screen.

   Earlier you resized the Reason column to its best fit, to ensure all the field values were visible. However, when you resize a column to its best fit, the column expands to fully display only the field values that are visible on the screen at that time. If you move through the complete datasheet and notice that not all of the field values are fully displayed after resizing the column, you need to resize the column again.

8. Scroll down through the records and observe if the field values for the Reason field are fully displayed. The Reason field values for visit 1595 and visit 1606 are not fully displayed. With these records displayed, place the pointer on the column dividing line to the right of the Reason field name until the pointer changes to the column resizing pointer ✛, and then double-click the column dividing line. The field values are now fully displayed.

The Visit table now contains all the data about patient visits for Lakewood Community Health Services. To better understand how to work with this data, Donna asks you to create simple objects for the other main types of database objects—queries, forms, and reports.

Creating a Simple Query

A query is a question you ask about the data stored in a database. When you create a query, you tell Access which fields you need and what criteria it should use to select the records that will answer your question. Then Access displays only the information you want, so you don't have to navigate through the entire database for the information. In the Visit table, for example, Donna might create a query to display only those records for visits that occurred in a specific month. Even though a query can display table information in a different way, the information still exists in the table as it was originally entered.

Donna wants to see a list of all the visit dates and reasons for visits in the Visit table. She doesn't want the list to include all the fields in the table, such as PatientID and WalkIn. To produce this list for Donna, you'll use the Simple Query Wizard to create a query based on the Visit table.

To start the Simple Query Wizard:

1. On the ribbon, click the **Create** tab.
2. In the Queries group, click the **Query Wizard** button. The New Query dialog box opens.
3. Make sure **Simple Query Wizard** is selected, and then click **OK**. The first Simple Query Wizard dialog box opens. See Figure 1–29.

Figure 1–29 First Simple Query Wizard dialog box

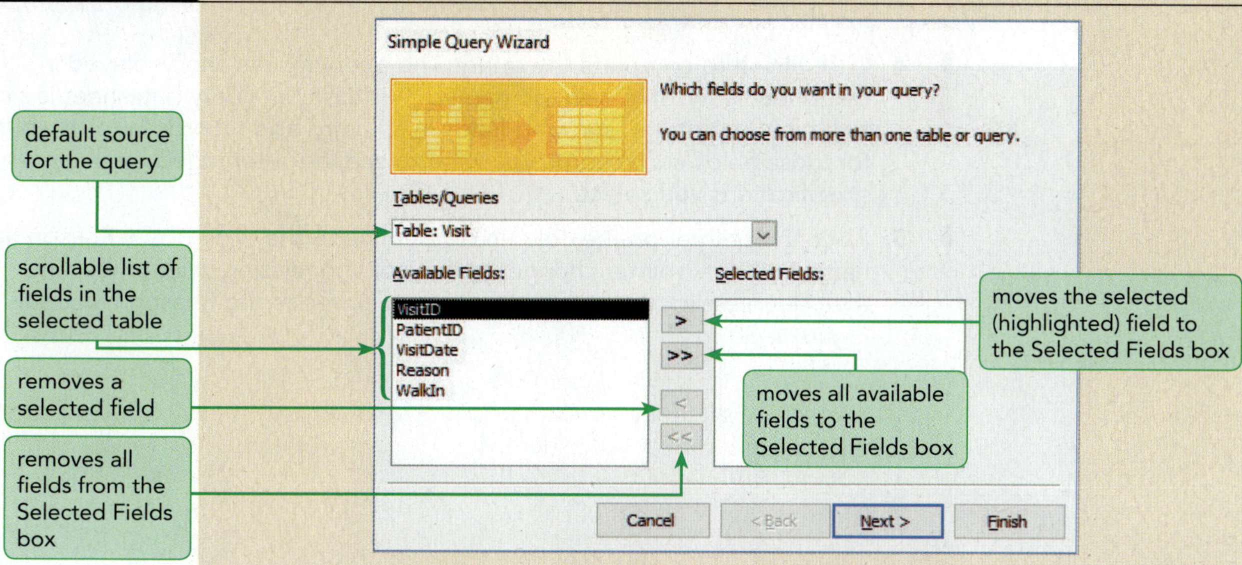

Because the Visit table is open in the Lakewood database, it is listed in the Tables/Queries box by default. If the database contained more objects, you could click the Tables/Queries arrow and choose another table or a query as the basis for the new query you are creating. In this case you could choose the Billing table; however, the Visit table contains the fields you need. The Available Fields box lists all the fields in the Visit table.

Trouble? If the Visit table is not the default source for the query, click the Tables/Queries arrow to choose the Visit table (Table: Visit) from the list.

You need to select fields from the Available Fields box to include them in the query. To select fields one at a time, click a field and then click the Select Single Field [>] button. The selected field moves from the Available Fields box on the left to the Selected Fields box on the right. To select all the fields, click the Select All Fields [>>] button. If you change your mind or make a mistake, you can remove a field by clicking it in the Selected Fields box and then clicking the Remove Single Field [<] button. To remove all fields from the Selected Fields box, click the Remove All Fields [<<] button.

Each Simple Query Wizard dialog box contains buttons that allow you to move to the previous dialog box (Back button), move to the next dialog box (Next button), or cancel the creation process (Cancel button). You can also finish creating the object (Finish button) and accept the wizard's defaults for the remaining options.

Donna wants her query results list to include data from only the following fields: VisitID, VisitDate, and Reason. You need to select these fields to include them in the query.

To create the query using the Simple Query Wizard:

TIP

You can also double-click a field to move it from the Available Fields box to the Selected Fields box.

1. Click **VisitID** in the Available Fields box to select the field (if necessary), and then click the Select Single Field [>] button. The VisitID field moves to the Selected Fields box.
2. Repeat Step 1 for the fields **VisitDate** and **Reason**, and then click **Next**. The second, and final, Simple Query Wizard dialog box opens and asks you to choose a name (title) for your query. The suggested name is "Visit Query" because the query you are creating is based on the Visit table. You'll change the suggested name to "VisitList."
3. Click at the end of the suggested name, use **BACKSPACE** to delete the word "Query" and the space, and then type **List**. Now you can view the query results.
4. Click **Finish** to complete the query. The query results are displayed in Datasheet view, on a new tab named "VisitList." A query datasheet is similar to a table datasheet, showing fields in columns and records in rows—but only for those fields and records you want to see, as determined by the query specifications you select.
5. Place the pointer on the column divider line to the right of the Reason field name until the pointer changes to the column resizing pointer ↔, and then double-click the column divider line to resize the Reason field. See Figure 1-30.

Figure 1–30 Query results

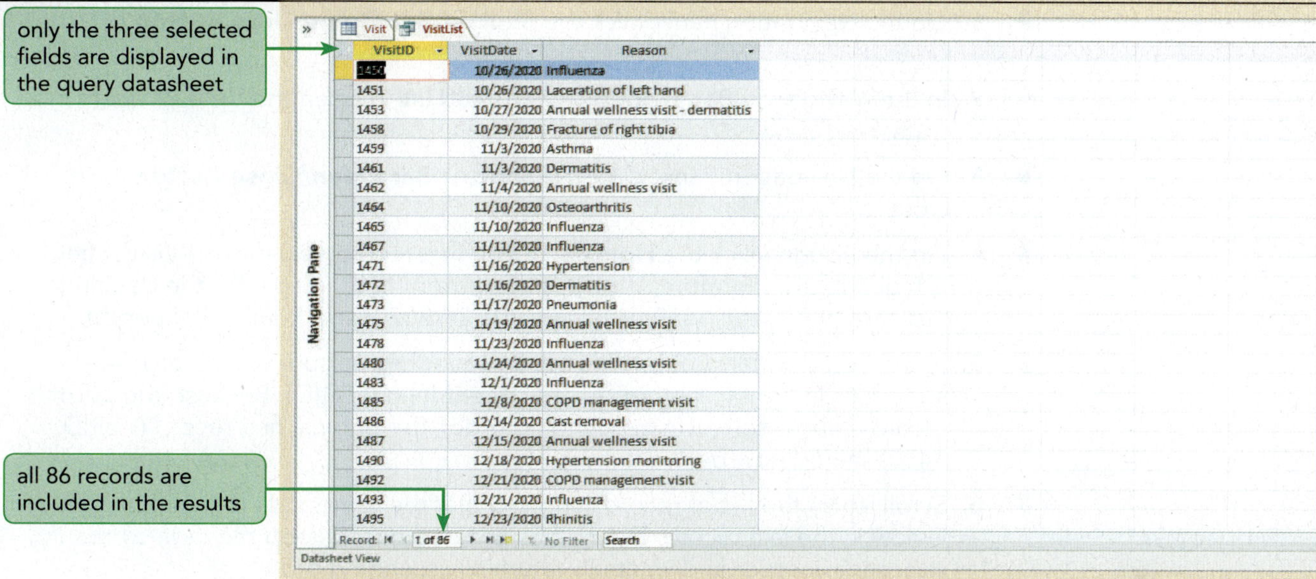

The VisitList query datasheet displays the three fields in the order you selected them in the Simple Query Wizard, from left to right. The records are listed in order by the primary key field, VisitID. Even though the query datasheet displays only the three fields you chose for the query, the Visit table still includes all the fields for all records.

Navigation buttons are located at the bottom of the window. You navigate a query datasheet in the same way that you navigate a table datasheet.

6. Click the **Last record** button ▶|. The last record in the query datasheet is now the current record.
7. Click the **Previous record** button ◀. Record 85 in the query datasheet is now the current record.
8. Click the **First record** button |◀. The first record is now the current record.
9. Click the **Close 'VisitList'** button ✕ on the object tab. A dialog box opens asking if you want to save the changes to the layout of the query. This dialog box opens because you resized the Reason column.
10. Click **Yes** to save the query layout changes and close the query.

The query results are not stored in the database; however, the query design is stored as part of the database with the name you specified. You can re-create the query results at any time by opening the query again. When you open the query later, the results displayed will reflect up-to-date information to include any new records entered in the Visit table.

Donna asks you to display the query results again; however, this time she would like to list the records in descending order showing the most current VisitID first. The records are currently displayed in ascending order by VisitID, which is the primary key for the Visit table. In order to display the records in descending order, you can sort the records in Query Datasheet view.

To sort records in a query datasheet:

1. On the Navigation Pane, click the **Shutter Bar Open/Close Button** » to open it.
2. In the Navigation Pane, double-click **VisitList** to open the VisitList query in Datasheet view.
3. On the Navigation Pane, click the **Shutter Bar Open/Close Button** « to close it.
4. On the ribbon, click the **Home** tab. The first record value in the VisitID field is highlighted; therefore, VisitID is the current field. Also note the data in the first record (VisitID: 1450; VisitDate: 10/26/2020; and Reason: Influenza).
5. In the Sort & Filter group, click the **Descending** button. The records are sorted in descending order by the current field (VisitID). Because the list of records is now sorted in descending order, the original first record (VisitID 1450) should now be the last record.
6. Scroll down the list of records and see that the same data for VisitID 1450 is now in the last record. Donna has decided not to keep the data sorted in descending order and wants to return to ascending order.
7. In the Sort & Filter group, click the **Remove Sort** button. The data returns to its original state in ascending order with VisitID 1450 (and its corresponding data) listed in the first record.
8. Click the **Close 'VisitList'** button ✕ on the object tab for the VisitList query. When asked if you would like to save the changes to the design of the VisitList query, click **No**. The VisitList query closes.

Next, Donna asks you to create a form for the Visit table so the staff at Lakewood Community Health Services can use the form to enter and work with data in the table easily.

Creating a Simple Form

As noted earlier, you use a form to enter, edit, and view records in a database. Although you can perform these same functions with tables and queries, forms can present data in many customized and useful ways.

Donna wants a form for the Visit table that shows all the fields for one record at a time, with fields listed one below another in a column. This type of form will make it easier for her staff to focus on all the data for a particular visit. You'll use the Form Wizard to create this form quickly and easily.

To create the form using the Form Wizard

1. Make sure the Visit table is still open in Datasheet view.

   Trouble? If the Visit table is not open, click the Shutter Bar Open/Close Button » to open the Navigation Pane. Double-click Visit to open the Visit table in Datasheet view. Click the Shutter Bar Open/Close Button « to close the pane.
2. On the ribbon, click the **Create** tab if necessary.

3. In the Forms group, click the **Form Wizard** button. The first Form Wizard dialog box opens. Make sure the Visit table is the default data source for the form.

   Trouble? If the Visit table is not the default source for the form, click the Tables/Queries arrow to choose the Visit table (Table: Visit) from the list.

   The first Form Wizard dialog box is very similar to the first Simple Query Wizard dialog box you used in creating a query.

4. Click the **Select All Fields** button >> to move all the fields to the Selected Fields box.

5. Click **Next** to display the second Form Wizard dialog box, in which you select a layout for the form. See Figure 1–31.

Figure 1–31 Choosing a layout for the form

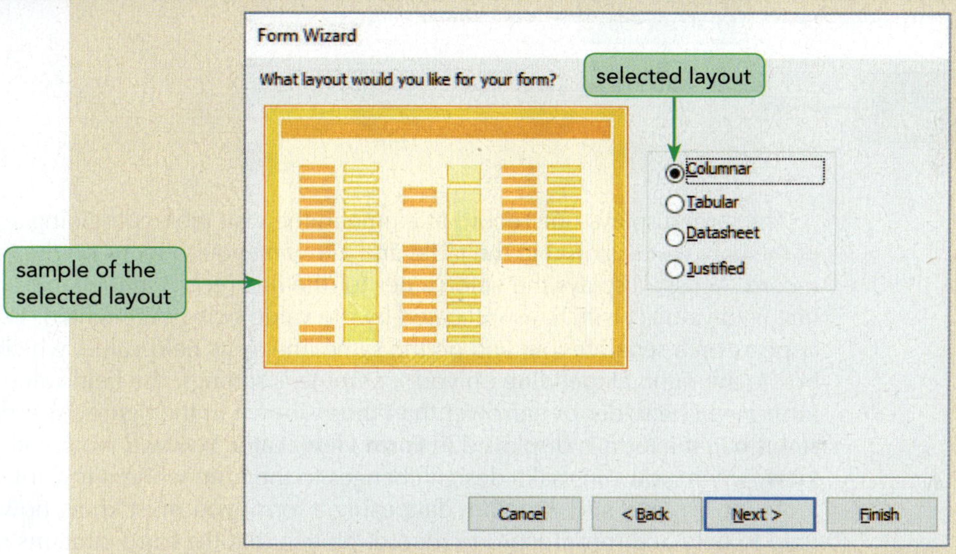

The layout choices are Columnar, Tabular, Datasheet, and Justified. A sample of the selected layout appears on the left side of the dialog box.

6. Click each option button and review the corresponding sample layout.

7. Because Donna wants to arrange the form data in a column with each field listed one below another, click the **Columnar** option button (if necessary), and then click **Next**.

   The third and final Form Wizard dialog box shows the Visit table's name as the default name for the form name. "Visit" is also the default title that will appear on the tab for the form.

   You'll use "VisitData" as the form name, and because you don't need to change the form's design at this point, you'll display the form.

8. Click to position the insertion point to the right of 'Visit' in the box, type **Data**, and then click the **Finish** button.

   The completed form opens in Form view, displaying the values for the first record in the Visit table. The Columnar layout places the field captions in labels on the left and the corresponding field values in boxes to the right, which vary in width depending on the size of the field. See Figure 1–32.

Figure 1–32 VisitData form in Form view

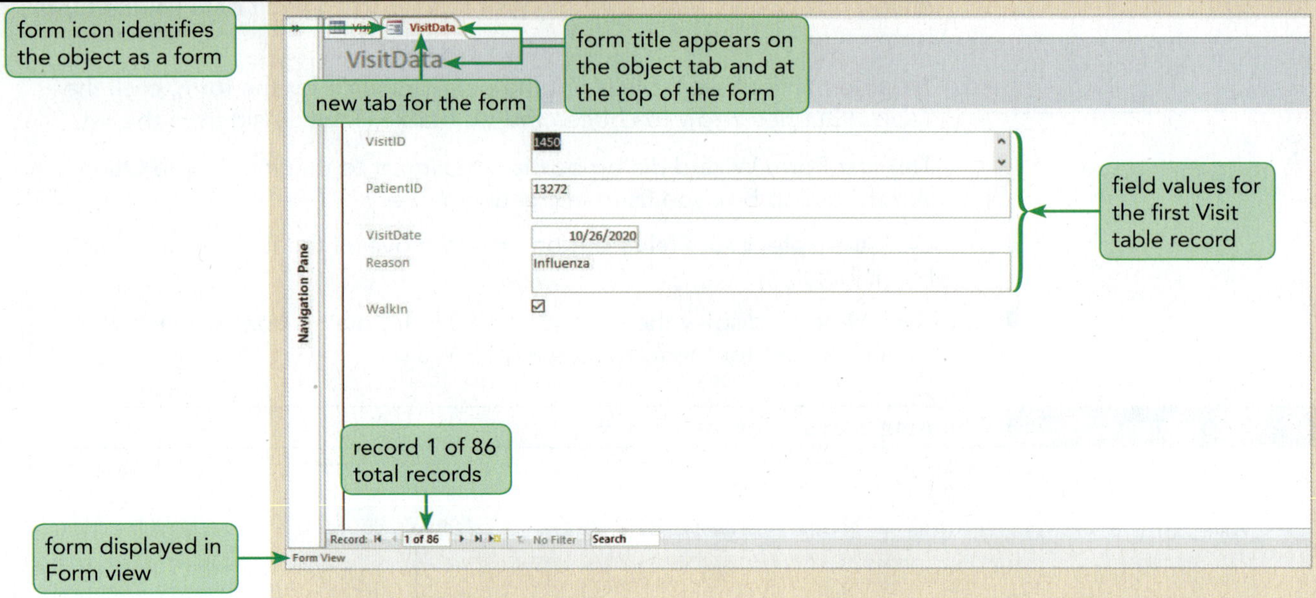

The form displays one record at a time in the Visit table, providing another view of the data that is stored in the table and allowing you to focus on the values for one record. Access displays the field values for the first record in the table and selects the first field value (VisitID), as indicated by the value being highlighted. Each field name appears on a separate line and on the same line as its field value, which appears in a box to the right. Depending on your computer's settings, the field value boxes in your form might be wider or narrower than those shown in the figure. As indicated in the status bar, the form is displayed in **Form view**. Later, you will work with a form in **Layout view**, where you can make design changes to the form while it is displaying data.

To view, enter, and maintain data using a form, you must know how to move from field to field and from record to record. Notice that the form contains navigation buttons, similar to those available in Datasheet view, which you can use to display different records in the form. You'll use these now to navigate the form; then you'll save and close the form.

To navigate, save, and close the form:

1. Click the **Next record** button ▶. The form now displays the values for the second record in the Visit table.
2. Click the **Last record** button ▶| to move to the last record in the table. The form displays the information for VisitID 1623.
3. Click the **Previous record** button ◀ to move to record 85.
4. Click the **First record** button |◀ to return to the first record in the Visit table.
5. Click the **Close 'VisitData'** button ✕ on the object tab to close the form.

INSIGHT

Saving Database Objects

In general, it is best to save a database object—query, form, or report—only if you anticipate using the object frequently or if it is time-consuming to create, because all objects use storage space and increase the size of the database file. For example, you most likely would not save a form you created with the Form tool because you can re-create it easily with one click. (However, for the purposes of this text, you usually need to save the objects you create.)

Donna would like to see the information in the Visit table presented in a more readable and professional format. You'll help Donna by creating a report.

Creating a Simple Report

A report is a formatted printout (or screen display) of the contents of one or more tables or queries. You'll use the Report Wizard to guide you through producing a report based on the Visit table for Donna. The Report Wizard creates a report based on the selected table or query.

To create the report using the Report Wizard:

1. On the ribbon, click the **Create** tab.
2. In the Reports group, click the **Report Wizard** button. The first Report Wizard dialog box opens. Make sure the Visit table is the default data source for the report.

   Trouble? If the Visit table is not the default source for the report, click the Tables/Queries arrow to choose the Visit table (Table: Visit) from the list.

   The first Report Wizard dialog box is very similar to the first Simple Query Wizard dialog box you used in creating a query, and to the first Form Wizard dialog box you used in creating a form.

   You select fields in the order you want them to appear on the report. Donna wants to include only the VisitID, PatientID, and Reason fields (in that order) on the report.
3. Click **VisitID** in the Available Fields box (if necessary), and then click the **Select Single Field** button [>] to move the field to the Selected Fields box.
4. Repeat step 3 to add the **PatientID** and **Reason** fields to the Selected Fields box. The VisitID, PatientID, and Reason fields (in that order) are listed in the Selected Fields box to add to the report. See Figure 1–33.

Figure 1–33 **First Report Wizard dialog box**

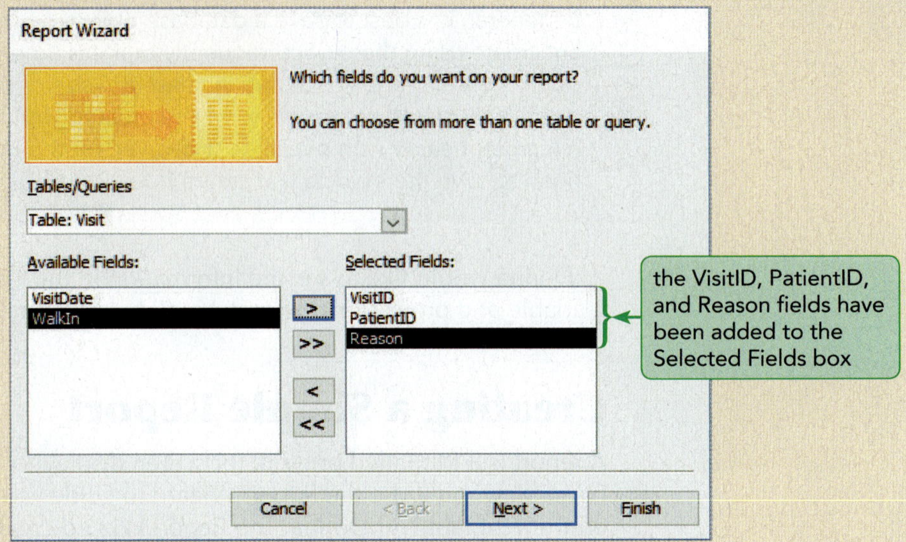

5. Click **Next** to open the second Report Wizard dialog box, which asks whether you want to add grouping levels to your report. This concept will be discussed later; Donna's report does not have any grouping levels.
6. Click **Next** to proceed to the third Report Wizard dialog box, which asks whether to sort records in a certain order by a particular field on the report. Donna wants to list the records by the VisitID field in ascending order. Access allows up to four levels of sorting, although Donna wants only one.
7. Click the arrow in the first sort option box, and then click **VisitID**. See Figure 1-34. The default option for sorting on the VisitID field is ascending.

Figure 1–34 **Third Report Wizard dialog box**

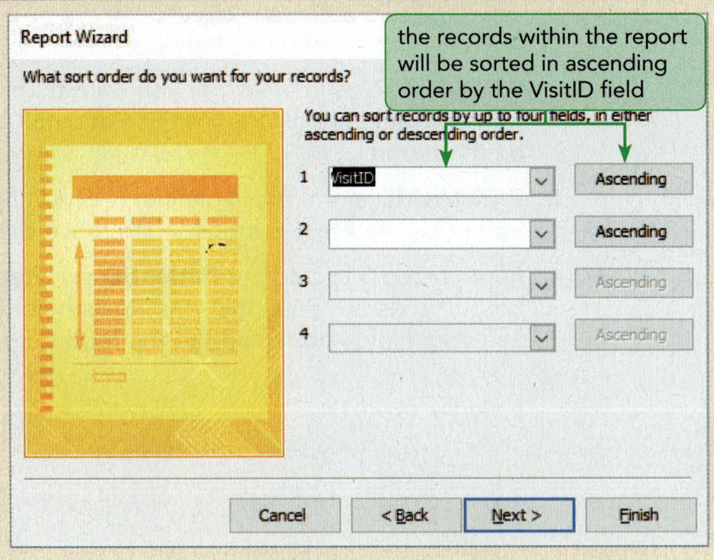

8. Click **Next** to proceed to the fourth Report Wizard dialog box, which asks you to select the layout for the report. You can click a Layout option to display an example of the layout.
9. Click the **Tabular** option button (if necessary). Later you can select other options for a report; however, this report uses the current default options.

10. Click **Next** to proceed to the final Report Wizard dialog box, in which you name the report. Donna wants to name the report "VisitDetails."
11. Click to position the insertion point to the right of 'Visit' in the box, and then type **Details**. Click **Finish** to preview the report. See Figure 1–35.

Figure 1–35 **Report in Print Preview**

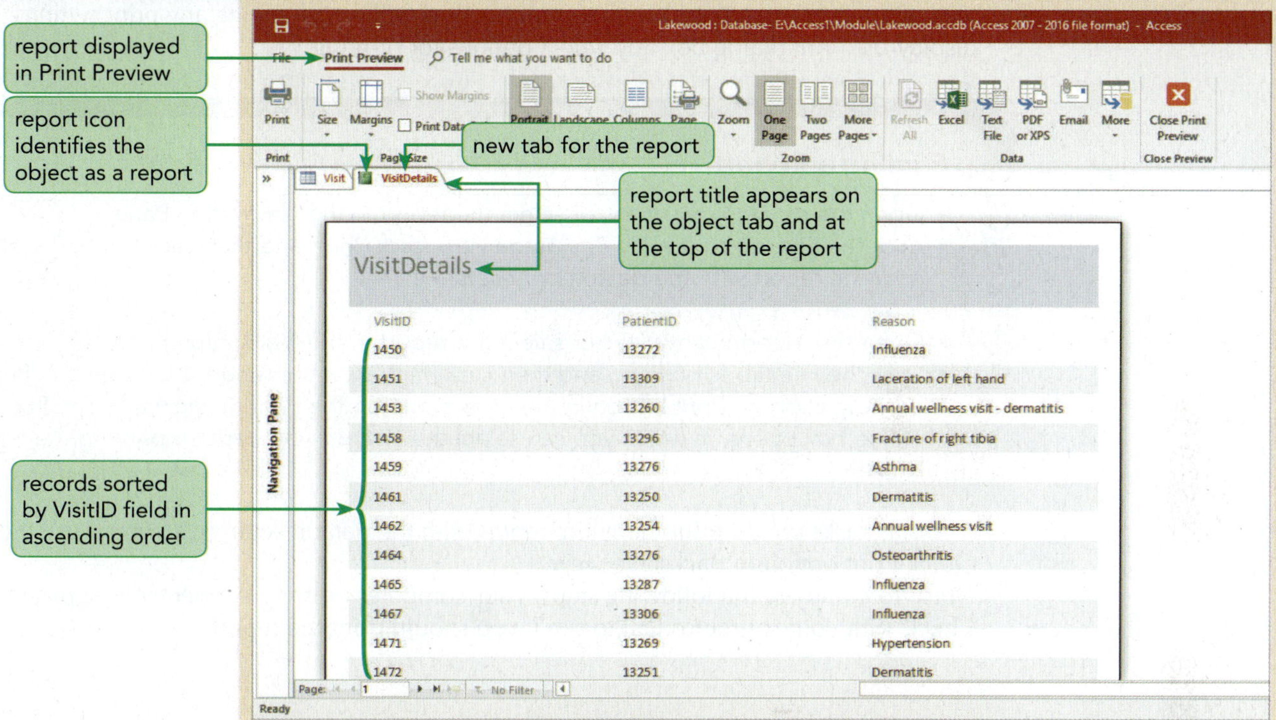

The report shows each field in a column, with the field values for each record in a row, similar to a table or query datasheet. However, a report offers a more visually appealing format for the data. The report is currently shown in Print Preview. **Print Preview** shows exactly how the report will look when printed. Print Preview also provides page navigation buttons at the bottom of the window, similar to the navigation buttons you've used to move through records in a table, query, and form.

To navigate the report in Print Preview:

1. Click the **Next Page** button ▶. The second page of the report is displayed in Print Preview.
2. Click the **Last Page** button ▶| to move to the last page of the report.
3. Drag the scroll box in the vertical scroll bar down until the bottom of the report page is displayed. The current date is displayed at the bottom left of the page. The notation "Page 3 of 3" appears at the bottom right of the page, indicating that you are on page 3 out of a total of 3 pages in the report.

   Trouble? Depending on the printer you are using, your report might have more or fewer pages, and some of the pages might be blank. If so, don't worry. Different printers format reports in different ways, sometimes affecting the total number of pages and the number of records printed per page.

4. Click the **First Page** button to return to the first page of the report, and then drag the scroll box in the vertical scroll bar up to display the top of the report.

Printing a Report

After creating a report, you might need to print it to distribute it to others who need to view the report's contents. You can print a report without changing any print settings, or display the Print dialog box and select options for printing.

REFERENCE

Printing a Report

- Open the report in any view, or select the report in the Navigation Pane.
- Click the File tab to display Backstage view, click Print, and then click Quick Print to print the report with the default print settings.

or

- Open the report in any view, or select the report in the Navigation Pane.
- Click the File tab, click Print, and then click Print; or, if the report is displayed in Print Preview, click the Print button in the Print group on the Print Preview tab. The Print dialog box opens, in which you can select the options you want for printing the report.

Donna asks you to print the entire report with the default settings, so you'll use the Quick Print option in Backstage view.
Note: To complete the following steps, your computer must be connected to a printer. Check with your instructor first to see if you should print the report.

To print the report and then close it:

1. On the ribbon, click the **File** tab to open Backstage view.
2. In the navigation bar, click **Print** to display the Print screen, and then click **Quick Print**. The report prints with the default print settings, and you return to the report in Print Preview.

   Trouble? If your report did not print, make sure that your computer is connected to a printer, and that the printer is turned on and ready to print. Then repeat Steps 1 and 2.
3. Click the **Close 'VisitDetails'** button on the object tab to close the report.
4. Click the **Close 'Visit'** button on the object tab to close the Visit table.

   Trouble? If you are asked to save changes to the layout of the table, click Yes.

You can also use the Print dialog box to print other database objects, such as table and query datasheets. Most often, these objects are used for viewing and entering data, and reports are used for printing the data in a database.

Viewing Objects in the Navigation Pane

The Lakewood database now contains five objects—the Billing table, the Visit table, the VisitList query, the VisitData form, and the VisitDetails report. When you work with the database file—such as closing it, opening it, or distributing it to others—the file includes all the objects you created and saved in the database. You can view and work with these objects in the Navigation Pane.

To view the objects in the Lakewood database:

1. On the Navigation Pane, click the **Shutter Bar Open/Close Button** » to open the pane. See Figure 1-36.

Figure 1-36 Lakewood database objects displayed in the Navigation Pane

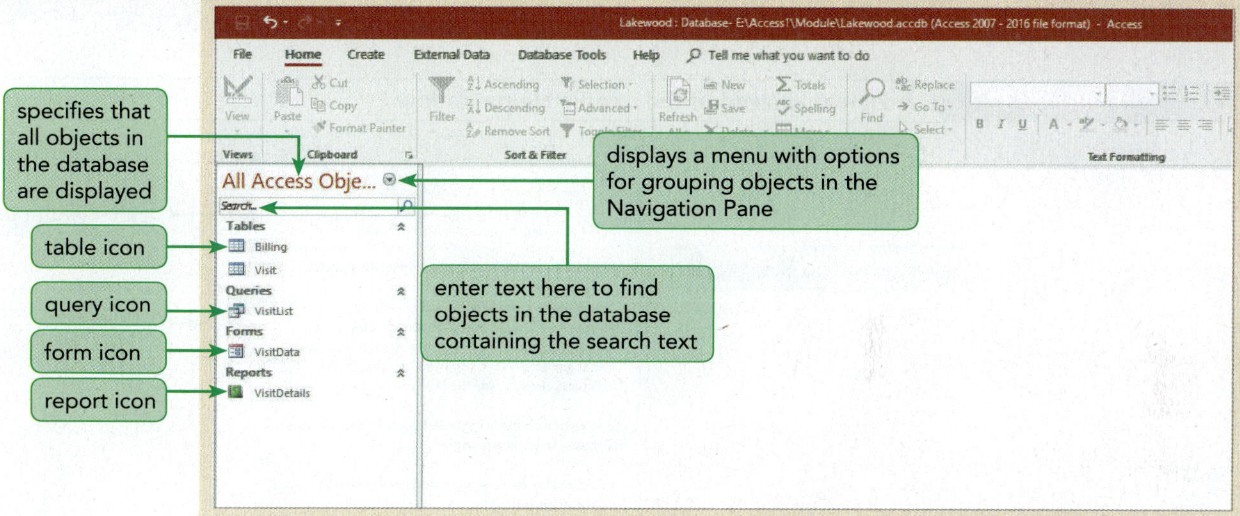

The Navigation Pane currently displays the default category, **All Access Objects**, which lists all the database objects in the pane. Each object type (Tables, Queries, Forms, and Reports) appears in its own group. Each database object (the Billing table, the Visit table, the VisitList query, the VisitData form, and the VisitDetails report) has a unique icon to its left to indicate the type of object. This makes it easy for you to identify the objects and choose which one you want to open and work with.

The arrow on the All Access Objects bar displays a menu with options for various ways to group and display objects in the Navigation Pane. The Search box enables you to enter text for Access to find; for example, you could search for all objects that contain the word "Visit" in their names. Note that Access searches for objects only in the categories and groups currently displayed in the Navigation Pane.

As you continue to build the Lakewood database and add more objects to it in later modules, you'll use the options in the Navigation Pane to manage those objects.

Using Microsoft Access Help

Access includes a Help system you can use to search for information about specific program features. You start Help by clicking the Microsoft Access Help tab on the ribbon, or by pressing F1.

You'll use Help now to learn more about the Navigation Pane.

To search for information about the Navigation Pane in Help:

TIP

You can also get help by typing keywords in the Tell Me box on the ribbon to access information about topics related to those words in the Access Help window.

1. On the ribbon, click the **Help** tab. Multiple buttons are displayed, with the first being the Help button. Click the **Help** button. The Access Help window opens.
2. Click in the **Search** box (if necessary), type **Navigation Pane**, and then press **ENTER**. The Access Help window displays a list of topics related to the Navigation Pane.
3. Click the topic **Show or hide the Navigation Pane in Access**. The Access Help window displays the article you selected. See Figure 1-37.

Figure 1-37 **Article displayed in the Access Help window**

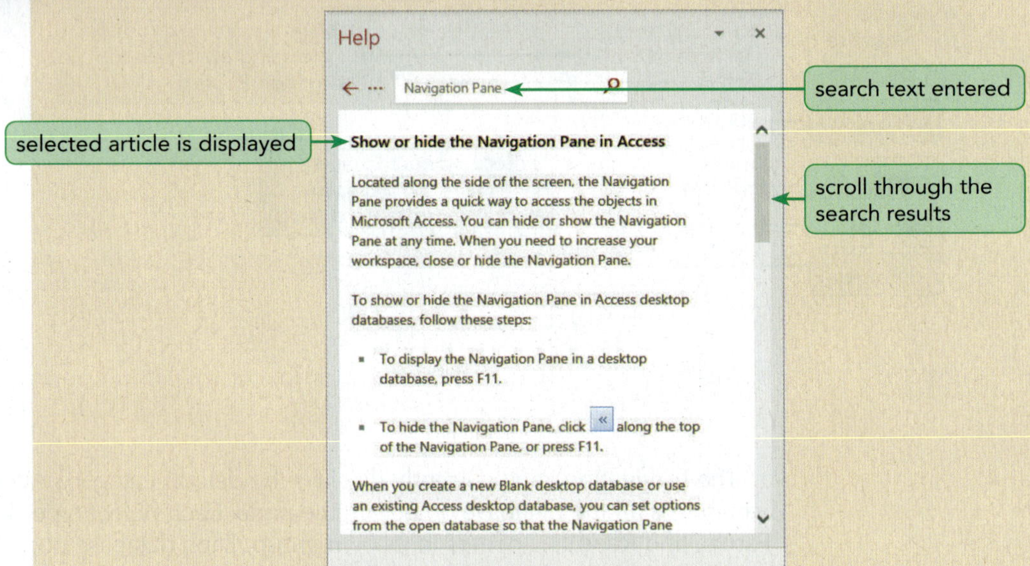

Trouble? If the article on managing database objects is not listed in your Help window, choose another article related to the Navigation Pane to read. Your Help window may also look different from the figure.

4. Scroll through the article to read detailed information about working with the Navigation Pane.
5. When finished, click the **Close** button ✕ on the Access Help window to close it.

The Access Help system is an important reference tool for you to use if you need additional information about databases in general, details about specific Access features, or support with problems you might encounter.

Managing a Database

One of the main tasks involved in working with database software is managing your databases and the data they contain. Some of the activities involved in database management include compacting and repairing a database and backing up and restoring a database. By managing your databases, you can ensure that they operate in the most efficient way, that the data they contain is secure, and that you can work with the data effectively.

Compacting and Repairing a Database

Whenever you open an Access database and work in it, the size of the database increases. Further, when you delete records or when you delete or replace database objects—such as queries, forms, and reports—the storage space that had been occupied by the deleted or replaced records or objects does not automatically become available for other records or objects. To make the space available, and to increase the speed of data retrieval, you must compact the database. **Compacting** a database rearranges the data and objects in a database to decrease its file size, thereby making more storage space available and enhancing the performance of the database. Figure 1-38 illustrates the compacting process.

Figure 1-38 Compacting a database

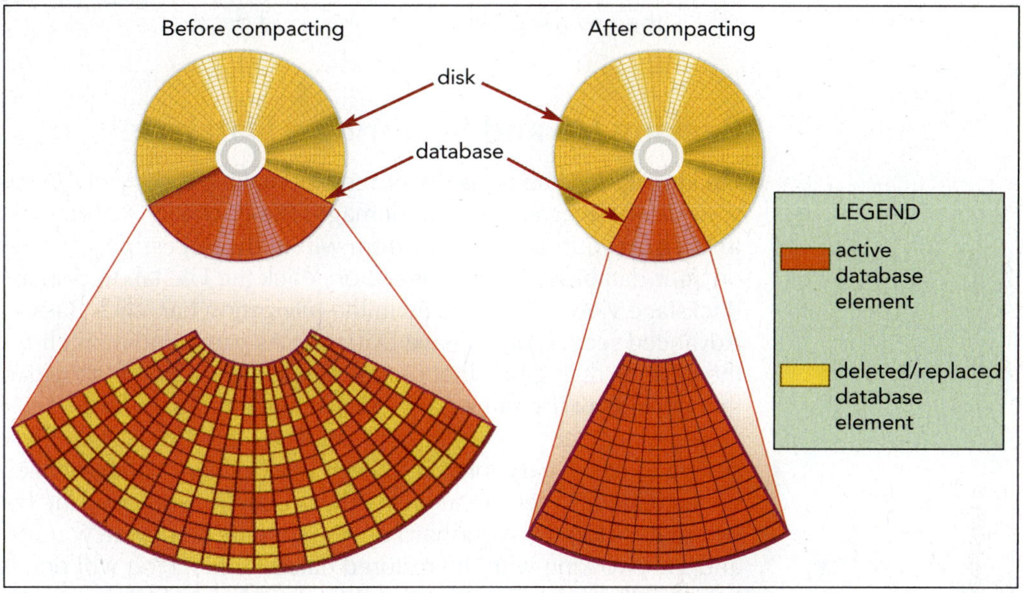

When you compact a database, Access repairs the database at the same time, if necessary. In some cases, Access detects that a database is damaged when you try to open it and gives you the option to compact and repair it at that time. For example, the data in your database might become damaged, or corrupted, if you exit the Access program suddenly by turning off your computer. If you think your database might be damaged because it is behaving unpredictably, you can use the Compact & Repair Database option to fix it.

REFERENCE

Compacting and Repairing a Database

- Make sure the database file you want to compact and repair is open.
- Click the File tab to display the Info screen in Backstage view.
- Click the Compact & Repair Database button.

Access also allows you to set an option to compact and repair a database file automatically every time you close it. The Compact on Close option is available in the Current Database section of the Access Options dialog box, which you open from Backstage view by clicking the Options command in the navigation bar. By default, the Compact on Close option is turned off.

Next, you'll compact the Lakewood database manually using the Compact & Repair Database option. This will make the database smaller and allow you to work with it more efficiently. After compacting the database, you'll close it.

To compact and repair the Lakewood database:

1. On the ribbon, click the **File** tab to open the Info screen in Backstage view.
2. Click the **Compact & Repair Database** button. Although nothing changes on the screen, Access compacts the Lakewood database, making it smaller, and repairs it at the same time. The Home tab is again the active tab on the ribbon.
3. **sam** Click the **File** tab to return to Backstage view, and then click **Close** in the navigation bar. The Lakewood database closes.

Backing Up and Restoring a Database

Backing up a database is the process of making a copy of the database file to protect your database against loss or damage. The Back Up Database command enables you to back up your database file from within the Access program while you are working on your database. To use this option, click the File tab to display the Info screen in Backstage view, click Save As in the navigation bar, click Back Up Database in the Advanced section of the Save Database As pane, and then click the Save As button. In the Save As dialog box that opens, a default filename is provided for the backup copy that consists of the same filename as the database you are backing up (for example, "Lakewood"), and an underscore character, plus the current date. This file naming system makes it easy for you to keep track of your database backups and when they were created. To restore a backup database file, you copy the backup from the location where it is stored to your hard drive, or whatever device you use to work in Access, and start working with the restored database file. (You will not actually back up the Lakewood database in this module unless directed by your instructor to do so.)

INSIGHT

Planning and Performing Database Backups

Experienced database users make it a habit to back up a database before they work with it for the first time, keeping the original data intact. They also make frequent backups while continuing to work with a database; these backups are generally on flash drives, recordable CDs or DVDs, external or network hard drives, or cloud-based storage (such as OneDrive). Also, it is recommended to store the backup copy in a different location from the original. For example, if the original database is stored on a flash drive, you should not store the backup copy on the same flash drive. If you lose the drive or the drive is damaged, you would lose both the original database and its backup copy.

If the original database file and the backup copy have the same name, restoring the backup copy might replace the original. If you want to save the original file, rename it before you restore the backup copy. To ensure that the restored database has the most current data, you should update the restored database with any changes made to the original between the time you created the backup copy and the time the original database became damaged or lost.

By properly planning for and performing backups, you can avoid losing data and prevent the time-consuming effort required to rebuild a lost or damaged database.

PROSKILLS

Decision Making: When to Use Access vs. Excel

Using a spreadsheet application like Microsoft Excel to manage lists or tables of information works well when the data is simple, such as a list of contacts or tasks. As soon as the data becomes complex enough to separate into tables that need to be related, you see the limitations of using a spreadsheet application. The strength of a database application such as Access is in its ability to easily relate one table of information to another. Consider a table of contacts that includes home addresses, with a separate row for each person living at the same address. When an address changes, it's too easy to make a mistake and not update the home address for each person who lives there. To ensure you have the most accurate data at all times, it's important to have only one instance of each piece of data. By creating separate tables that are related and keeping only one instance of each piece of data, you ensure the integrity of the data. Trying to accomplish this in Excel is complex, whereas Access is specifically designed for this functionality.

Another limitation of using Excel instead of Access to manage data has to do with the volume of data. Although a spreadsheet can hold thousands of records, a database can hold millions. A spreadsheet containing thousands of pieces of information is cumbersome to use. Think of large-scale commercial applications such as enrollment at a college or tracking customers for a large company. It's hard to imagine managing such information in an Excel spreadsheet. Instead, you'd use a database. Finally, with an Access database, multiple users can access the information it contains at the same time. Although an Excel spreadsheet can be shared, there can be problems when users try to open and edit the same spreadsheet at the same time.

When you're trying to decide whether to use Excel or Access, ask yourself the following questions.

1. Do you need to store data in separate tables that are related to each other?
2. Do you have a very large amount of data to store?
3. Will more than one person need to access the data at the same time?

If you answer "yes" to any of these questions, an Access database is most likely the appropriate application to use.

In the following modules, you'll help Donna complete and maintain the Lakewood database, and you'll use it to meet the specific information needs of the employees of the clinic.

REVIEW

Session 1.2 Quick Check

1. To copy the records from a table in one database to another table in a different database, the two tables must have the same ________.
2. A(n) ____________ is a question you ask about the data stored in a database.
3. The quickest way to create a form is to use the ________.
4. Which view enables you to see the total number of pages in a report and navigate through the report pages?
5. In the Navigation Pane, each database object has a unique ________ to its left that identifies the object's type.
6. ________ a database rearranges the data and objects in a database to decrease its file size and enhance the speed and performance of the database.
7. ________ a database is the process of making a copy of the database file to protect the database against loss or damage.

PRACTICE

Review Assignments

Data File needed for the Review Assignments: Support_AC_1_Company.accdb

For Lakewood Community Health Services, Donna asks you to create a new database to contain information about the vendors that the clinic works with to obtain medical supplies and equipment, and the vendors who service and maintain the equipment. Complete the following steps:

1. Create a new, blank database named **Vendor** and save it in the folder where you are storing your files, as specified by your instructor.
2. In Datasheet view, begin creating a table. Rename the default ID primary key field to **SupplierID**. Change the data type of the SupplierID field to Short Text.
3. Add the following 10 fields to the new table in the order shown; all of them are Short Text fields *except* InitialContact, which is a Date/Time field: **Company**, **Category**, **Address**, **City**, **State**, **Zip**, **Phone**, **ContactFirst**, **ContactLast**, and **InitialContact**. Resize the columns as necessary so that the complete field names are displayed.
4. Save the table as **Supplier** and close the table.
5. In Design view, begin creating a second table containing the following three Short Text fields in the order shown: **ProductID**, **SupplierID**, and **ProductName**.
6. Make ProductID the primary key and use **Primary key** as its description. Use **Foreign key** as the description for the SupplierID field.
7. Add a field called **Price** to the table, which is of the Currency data type.
8. Add the following two fields to the table in the order shown: **TempControl** and **Sterile**. Both are of the Yes/No data type.
9. Add the final field called **Units** to the table, which is of the Number data type.
10. Save the table as **Product** and close the table.
11. Use the Navigation Pane to open the Supplier table.
12. Enter the records shown in Figure 1–39 into the Supplier table. For the first record, enter your first name in the ContactFirst field and your last name in the ContactLast field.
    Note: When entering field values that are shown on multiple lines in the figure, do not try to enter the values on multiple lines. The values are shown on multiple lines in the figure for page spacing purposes only.

Figure 1–39 **Supplier table records**

SupplierID	Company	Category	Address	City	State	Zip	Phone	Contact First	Contact Last	Initial Contact
ABC123	ABC Pharmaceuticals	Supplies	123 Hopson Ave	Manchester	NH	03102	603-555-8125	*Student First*	*Student Last*	9/22/2020
HAR912	Harper Surgical, LLC	Supplies	912 Huntington Pl	Knoxville	TN	37909	865-555-4239	Betty	Harper	10/26/2020
DUR725	Durham Medical Equipment	Equipment	725 Pike Dr	Durham	NC	27705	919-555-4226	Katherine	Wayles	12/14/2020
TEN247	Tenneka Labs, LLC	Service	247 Asland Dr	Norcross	GA	30071	678-555-5392	Thomas	Tenneka	11/30/2020
BAZ412	Bazarrack Enterprises	Supplies	412 Harper Dr	Alpharetta	GA	30004	678-555-2201	Adrian	Bazarrack	9/3/2020

13. Donna created a database named Support_AC_1_Company.accdb that contains a Business table with supplier data. The Supplier table you created has the same design as the Business table. Copy all the records from the **Business** table in the **Support_AC_1_Company.accdb** database (located in the Access1 > Review folder provided with your Data Files) and then paste them at the end of the Supplier table in the Vendor database.
14. Resize all datasheet columns to their best fit, and then save the Supplier table.
15. Close the Supplier table, and then use the Navigation Pane to reopen it. Note that the records are displayed in primary key order by the values in the SupplierID field.
16. Use the Simple Query Wizard to create a query that includes the Company, Category, ContactFirst, ContactLast, and Phone fields (in that order) from the Supplier table. Name the query **SupplierList**, and then close the query.
17. Use the Form Wizard to create a form for the Supplier table. Include all fields from the Supplier table on the form and use the Columnar layout. Save the form as **SupplierInfo**, and then close it.
18. Use the Report Wizard to create a report based on the Supplier table. Include the SupplierID, Company, and Phone fields on the report (in that order), and sort the report by the SupplierID field in ascending order. Use a Tabular layout, save the report as **SupplierDetails**, and then close it.
19. Close the Supplier table, and then compact and repair the Vendor database.
20. Close the Vendor database.

APPLY

Case Problem 1

Data File needed for this Case Problem: Support_AC_1_Records.accdb

Great Giraffe Jeremiah Garver is the operations manager at Great Giraffe, a career school in Denver, Colorado. Great Giraffe offers part-time and full-time courses in areas of study that are in high demand by industries in the area, including data science, digital marketing, and bookkeeping. Jeremiah wants to use Access to maintain information about the courses offered by Great Giraffe, the students who enroll at the school, and the payment information for students. He needs your help in creating this database. Complete the following steps:

1. Create a new, blank database named **Career** and save it in the folder where you are storing your files, as specified by your instructor.
2. In Datasheet view, begin creating a table. Rename the default ID primary key field to **StudentID**. Change the data type of the StudentID field to Short Text.
3. Add the following eight fields to the new table in the order shown; all of them are Short Text fields: **FirstName**, **LastName**, **Address**, **City**, **State**, **Zip**, **Phone**, and **Email**. Resize the columns as necessary so that the complete field names are displayed.
4. Add a field called **BirthDate** to the table, which is of the Date/Time data type.
5. Add a final field called **Assessment** to the table, which is of the Yes/No data type.
6. Save the table as **Student** and close the table.
7. In Design view, begin creating a second table containing the following three Short Text fields in the following order: **SignupID**, **StudentID**, and **InstanceID**.
8. Make SignupID the primary key and use **Primary key** as its description. Use **Foreign key** as the descriptions for the StudentID and InstanceID fields.
9. Add the following two fields to the table in the following order: **TotalCost** and **BalanceDue**. Both are of the Currency data type.
10. Add the final field called **PaymentPlan** to the table. It is of the Yes/No data type.
11. Save the table as **Registration** and close the table.
12. Use the Navigation Pane to open the Student table.
13. Enter the records shown in Figure 1–40 into the Student table.

Figure 1–40 **Student table records**

StudentID	First Name	LastName	Address	City	State	Zip	Phone	Email	BirthDate	Assessment
ALB7426	*Student First*	*Student Last*	378 North River Avenue	Denver	CO	80227	(303) 555-8364	student @example. com	3/28/1980	Yes
MAR4120	Jennifer	Marshall	185 St Clair Way	Denver	CO	80223	(303) 555-1434	j.marshall75 @example. com	4/7/1967	Yes
WAL5737	Michael	Walker	367 Lawler Avenue	Englewood	CO	80110	(303) 555-6369	m.walker61 @example. com	1/17/1971	No
PER4083	Richard	Perry	923 Charles Avenue	Denver	CO	80211	(303) 555-8773	r.perry15 @example. com	2/14/1987	Yes
DRE9559	Angelina	Dressler	370 Dower Street	Denver	CO	80233	(303) 555-7491	a.dressler80 @example. com	8/6/2000	No

14. Jeremiah created a database named Support_AC_1_Records.accdb that contains a MoreStudents table with additional student data. The Student table you created has the same design as the MoreStudents table. Copy all the records from the **MoreStudents** table in the **Support_AC_1_Records.accdb** database (located in the Access1 > Case1 folder provided with your Data Files), and then paste them at the end of the Student table in the Career database.
15. Resize all datasheet columns to their best fit, and then save the Student table.
16. Close the Student table, and then use the Navigation Pane to reopen it. Note that the records are displayed in primary key order by the values in the StudentID field.
17. Use the Simple Query Wizard to create a query that includes the StudentID, FirstName, LastName, and Email fields (in that order) from the Student table. Save the query as **StudentData**, and then close the query.
18. Use the Form Wizard to create a form for the Student table. Include only the StudentID, FirstName, LastName, Phone, and Email fields (in that order) from the Student table on the form and use the Columnar layout. Save the form as **StudentInfo**, and then close it.
19. Use the Report Wizard to create a report based on the Student table. Include the StudentID, FirstName, and Email fields on the report (in that order), and sort the report by the StudentID field in ascending order. Use a Tabular layout, save the report as **StudentList**, and then close it.
20. Close the Student table, and then compact and repair the Career database.
21. Close the Career database.

CHALLENGE

Case Problem 2

Data File needed for this Case Problem: Support_AC_1_Residents.accdb

Drain Adopter Tandrea Austin manages the Drain Adopter program for the Department of Water and Power in Bellingham, Washington. The program recruits volunteers to regularly monitor and clear storm drains near their homes to ensure the drains are clear and unobstructed when large rainstorms are predicted. The program has been a hit with residents, and has increased the capacity of department staff to deal with other issues that arise during major storms. Tandrea wants to use Access to maintain information about the residents who have signed up for the program, the locations of selected storm drains throughout the city, and the inventory of supplies given to program participants, such as safety vests and gloves. She needs your help in creating this database. Complete the following steps:

1. Create a new, blank database named **DrainAdopter** and save it in the folder where you are storing your files, as specified by your instructor.
2. In Datasheet view, begin creating a table. Rename the default ID primary key field to **VolunteerID**. Change the data type of the VolunteerID field to Short Text.
3. Add the following eight fields to the new table in the order shown; all of them are Short Text fields: **FirstName**, **LastName**, **Street**, **City**, **State**, **Zip**, **Phone**, and **Email**. Resize the columns as necessary so that the complete field names are displayed.
4. Add a field called **SignupDate** to the table, which is of the Date/Time data type.
5. Add a final field called **Trained** to the table, which is of the Yes/No data type.
6. Save the table as **Volunteer** and close the table.
7. In Design view, begin creating a second table containing the following five Short Text fields in the following order: **DrainID**, **MainStreet**, **CrossStreet**, **Direction**, and **VolunteerID**.
8. Make DrainID the primary key and use **Primary key** as its description. Use **Foreign key** as the description for the VolunteerID field.
9. Add the final field called **MaintReq** to the table. It is of the Yes/No data type.
10. Save the table as **Drain** and close the table.
11. Use the Navigation Pane to open the Volunteer table.
12. Enter the records shown in Figure 1–41 into the Volunteer table.

Figure 1–41 **Volunteer table records**

VolunteerID	First Name	Last Name	Street	City	State	Zip	Phone	Email	SignupDate	Trained
ABE2300	*Student First*	*Student Last*	734 Abbott Street	Bellingham	WA	98225	360-555-6202	student @example.com	3/12/2021	Yes
MUR1125	Tiffany	Murphy	308 Pollock Street	Bellingham	WA	98225	360-555-9025	t.murphy18 @example.com	11/16/2021	Yes
WIL2190	John	Wills	947 Quincy Street	Bellingham	WA	98225	360-555-9396	j.wills81 @example. com	3/9/2021	No
SER8504	Joyce	Serrano	857 Kenta Avenue	Bellingham	WA	98229	360-555-2965	j.serrano28 @example. com	7/13/2022	Yes
HAR6150	Mario	Harris	915 Oriole Street	Bellingham	WA	98226	360-555-8705	m.harris41 @example. com	12/31/2022	No

13. Tandrea created a database named Support_AC_1_Residents.accdb that contains a MoreVolunteers table with additional volunteer data. The Volunteer table you created has the same design as the MoreVolunteers table. Copy all the records from the **MoreVolunteers** table in the **Support_AC_1_Residents.accdb** database (located in the Access1 > Case2 folder provided with your Data Files), and then paste them at the end of the Volunteer table in the DrainAdopter database.
14. Resize all datasheet columns to their best fit, and then save the Volunteer table.
15. Close the Volunteer table, and then use the Navigation Pane to reopen it. Note that the records are displayed in primary key order by the values in the VolunteerID field.
16. Use the Simple Query Wizard to create a query that includes the VolunteerID, FirstName, LastName, SignupDate, Email, and Trained fields (in that order) from the Volunteer table. Choose the Detail option. Save the query as **VolunteerData**, and then close the query.

Explore 17. The results of the VolunteerData query are displayed in order by the VolunteerID value. Sort the query results so that they are displayed in ascending order by the SignupDate. Close the query and save the query changes.

Explore 18. Use the Form Wizard to create a form using the VolunteerData query results as the data source, not the Volunteer table. The fields to include on the report are the VolunteerID, FirstName, SignupDate, and Email (in that order). Use the Columnar layout and save the form as **VolunteerInfo**, and then close it.

Explore 19. Use the Report Wizard to create a report based on the VolunteerData query. Include the VolunteerID, Email, and FirstName fields (in that order) on the report, and sort the report by the VolunteerID field in ascending order. The results of the VolunteerData query are sorted by the SignupDate field; however, when you sort the report by the VolunteerID field, the results will also be in order by the VolunteerID field (the primary key for the Volunteer table). Use a Tabular layout, save the report as **VolunteerList**, print the report, and then close it.

20. Close the Volunteer table, and then compact and repair the DrainAdopter database.

21. Close the DrainAdopter database.

MODULE 2

Building a Database and Defining Table Relationships

Creating the Billing and Patient Tables

OBJECTIVES

Session 2.1

- Identify the guidelines for designing databases and setting field properties
- Define fields and set field properties
- Modify the structure of a table
- Change the order of fields in Design view
- Add new fields in Design view
- Change the Format property for a field in Datasheet view
- Modify field properties in Design view

Session 2.2

- Import data from Excel
- Import an existing table structure
- Add fields to a table with the Data Type gallery
- Delete fields
- Change the data type for a field in Design view
- Set the Default Value property for a field
- Import a text file
- Define a relationship between two tables

Case | ***Lakewood Community Health Services***

The Lakewood database currently contains one table with data, the Visit table, and the basic structure of an additional table, the Billing table. Donna would like to further refine the structure of the Billing table, which will be used to track information about the invoices sent to patients. In addition, Donna would like to track information about each patient the clinic serves, including their name and contact information.

In this module, you'll modify the existing Billing table and create a new table in the Lakewood database—named Patient—to contain the additional data Donna wants to track. After adding records to the tables, you will define the necessary relationships between the tables in the Lakewood database to relate the tables, enabling Donna and her staff to work with the data more efficiently.

STARTING DATA FILES

Access1 →

Module

Lakewood.accdb (cont.)
Support_AC_2_Invoices.xlsx
Support_AC_2_Patient.txt
Support_AC_2_Taylor.accdb

Review

Vendor.accdb (cont.)
Support_AC_2_Products.xlsx

Case1

Career.accdb (cont.)
Support_AC_2_Course.txt
Support_AC_2_Registration.xlsx

Case2

DrainAdopter.accdb (cont.)
Support_AC_2_Drain.xlsx
Support_AC_2_Supplies.xlsx

Session 2.1 Visual Overview:

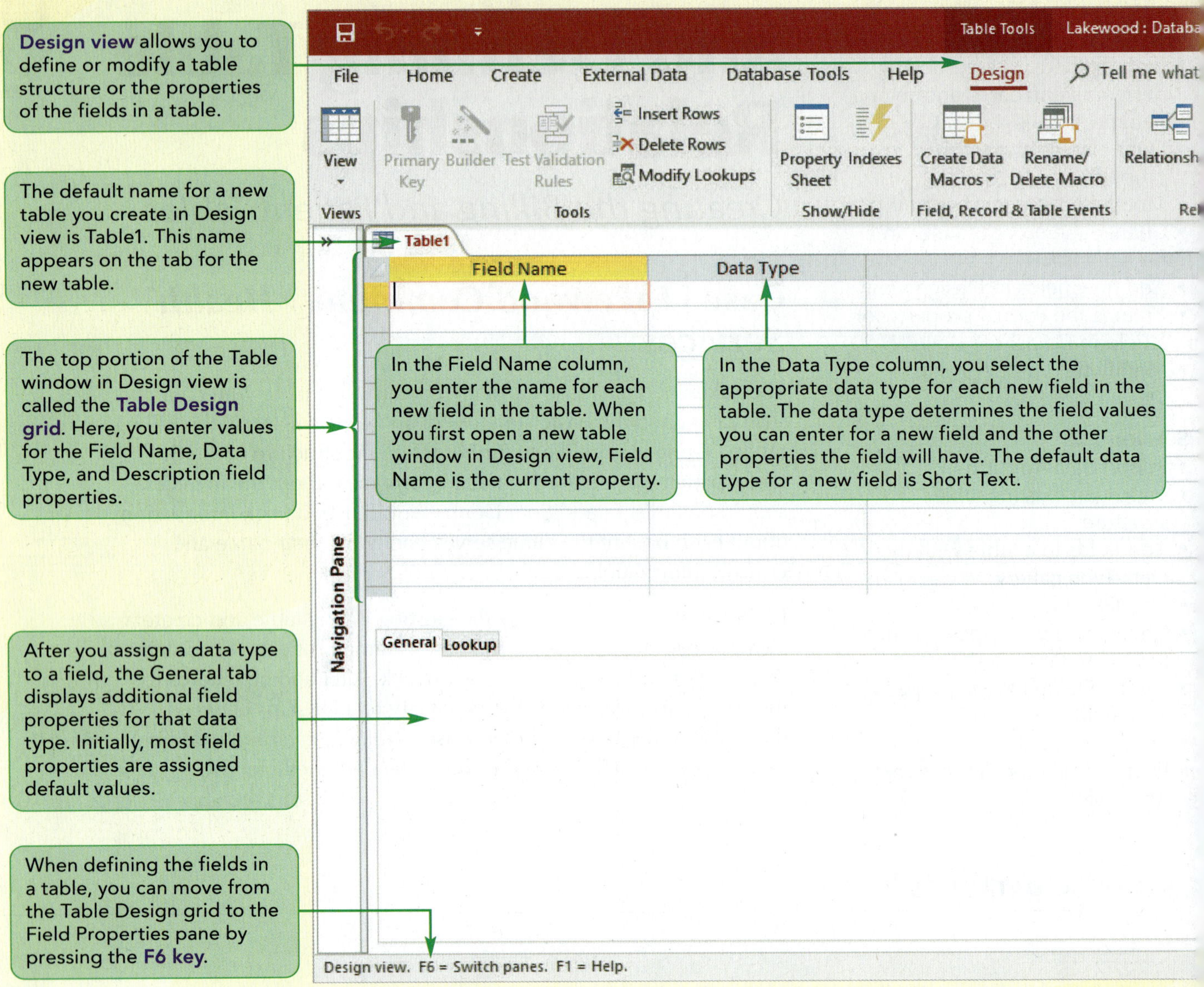

Table Window in Design View

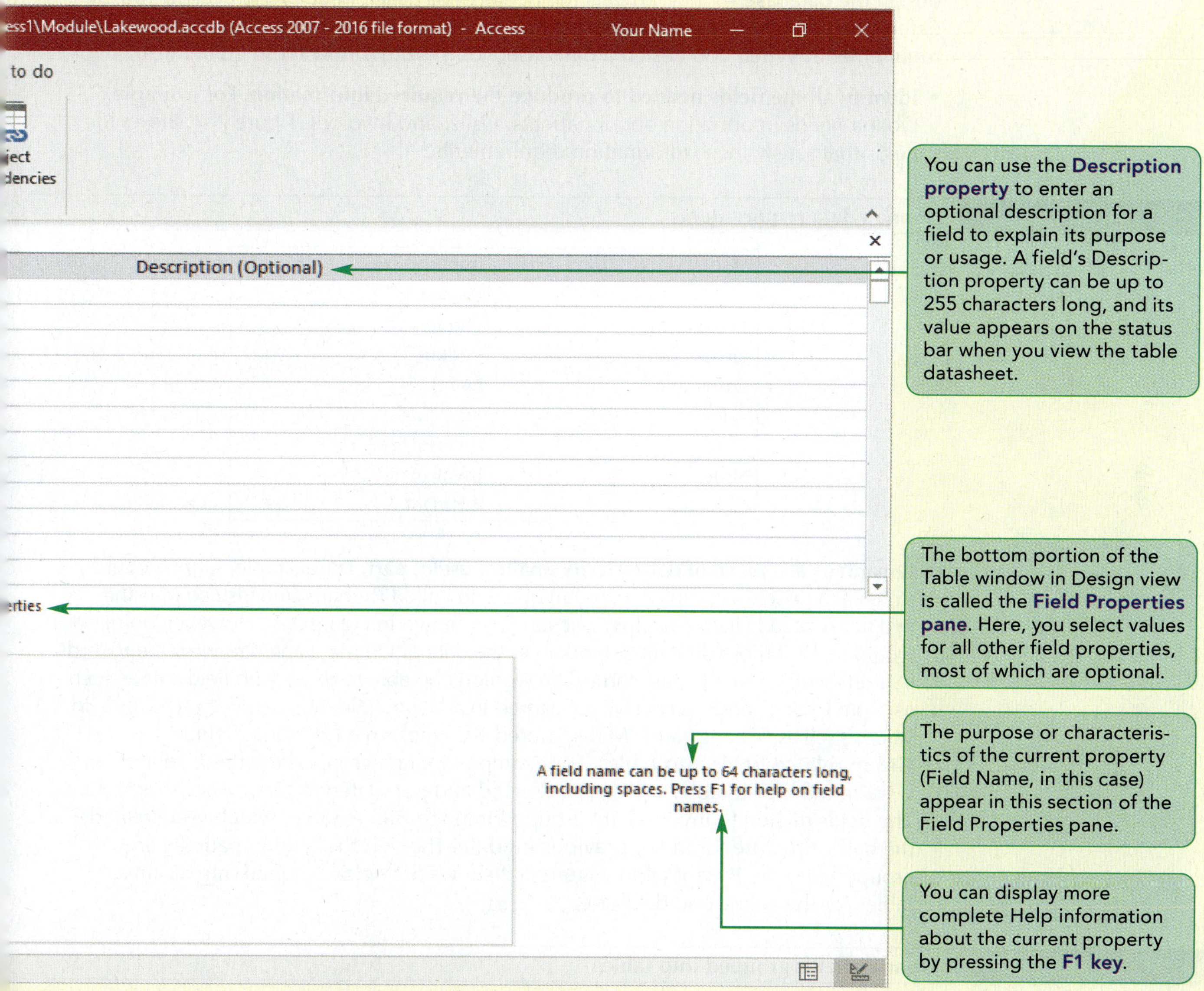

Guidelines for Designing Databases

A database management system can be a useful tool, but only if you first carefully design the database so that it meets the needs of its users. In database design, you determine the fields, tables, and relationships needed to satisfy the data and processing requirements. When you design a database, you should follow these guidelines:

- **Identify all the fields needed to produce the required information.** For example, Donna needs information about patients, visits, and invoices. Figure 2–1 shows the fields that satisfy these information requirements.

Figure 2–1 **Donna's data requirements**

VisitID	InvoiceDate
PatientID	Reason
InvoiceAmt	Phone
FirstName	WalkIn
LastName	Email
Address	VisitDate
City	InvoiceNum
State	InvoicePaid
Zip	BirthDate

- **Organize each piece of data into its smallest useful part.** For example, Donna could store each patient's complete name in one field called PatientName instead of using two fields called FirstName and LastName, as shown in Figure 2–1. However, doing so would make it more difficult to work with the data. If Donna wanted to view the records in alphabetical order by last name, she wouldn't be able to do so with field values such as "Tom Chang" and "Keisha Miller" stored in a Name field. She could do so with field values such as "Chang" and "Miller" stored separately in a LastName field.
- **Group related fields into tables.** For example, Donna grouped the fields related to visits into the Visit table, which you created and populated in the previous module. The fields related to invoices are grouped into the Billing table, which you created the basic structure for in the previous module. The fields related to patients are grouped into the Patient table. Figure 2–2 shows the fields grouped into all three tables for the Lakewood database.

Figure 2–2 **Donna's fields grouped into tables**

Visit table	Billing table	Patient table
VisitID	InvoiceNum	PatientID
PatientID	VisitID	LastName
VisitDate	InvoiceDate	FirstName
Reason	InvoiceAmt	BirthDate
WalkIn	InvoicePaid	Phone
		Address
		City
		State
		Zip
		Email

- **Determine each table's primary key.** Recall that a primary key uniquely identifies each record in a table. For some tables, one of the fields, such as a credit card number, naturally serves as a primary key. For other tables, two or more fields might be needed to function as the primary key. In these cases, the primary key is called a

composite key. For example, a school grade table might use a combination of student number, term, and course code to serve as the primary key. For a third category of tables, no single field or combination of fields can uniquely identify a record in a table. In these cases, you need to add a field whose sole purpose is to serve as the table's primary key. For Donna's tables, VisitID is the primary key for the Visit table, InvoiceNum is the primary key for the Billing table, and PatientID is the primary key for the Patient table.

- **Include a common field in related tables.** You use the common field to connect one table logically with another table. In the Lakewood database, the Visit and Patient tables include the PatientID field as a common field. Recall that when you include the primary key from one table as a field in a second table to form a relationship, the field in the second table is called a foreign key; therefore, the PatientID field is a foreign key in the Visit table. With this common field, Donna can find all visits to the clinic made by a particular patient; she can use the PatientID value for a patient and search the Visit table for all records with that PatientID value. Likewise, she can determine which patient made a particular visit by searching the Patient table to find the one record with the same PatientID value as the corresponding value in the Visit table. Similarly, the VisitID field is a common field, serving as the primary key in the Visit table and a foreign key in the Billing table.
- **Avoid data redundancy.** When you store the same data in more than one place, **data redundancy** occurs. With the exception of common fields to connect tables, you should avoid data redundancy because it wastes storage space and can cause inconsistencies. Data would be inconsistent, for example, if you type a field value one way in one table and a different way in the same table or in a second table. Figure 2–3, which contains portions of potential data stored in the Patient and Visit tables, shows an example of incorrect database design that has data redundancy in the Visit table. In Figure 2–3, the LastName field in the Visit table is redundant, and one value for this field was entered incorrectly, in three different ways.

Figure 2–3 **Incorrect database design with data redundancy**

PatientID	LastName	FirstName	Address
13254	Brown	Gayle	452 Canipe St
13270	Li	Chen	85 Peach St
13283	Rowe	Harper	14 Long Ave
13291	Taylor	Bailey	847 Grace Ave
13300	Miller	Marjorie	90 Baxter Dr

data redundancy

VisitID	PatientID	LastName	VisitDate	WalkIn
1462	13254	Brown	11/4/2020	No
1478	13270	Lee	11/23/2020	No
1517	13283	Rowe	1/11/2021	Yes
1529	13270	Le	1/25/2021	Yes
1533	13291	Taylor	1/26/2021	Yes
1544	13300	Miller	2/4/2021	Yes
1546	13270	Leigh	2/8/2021	No

Inconsistent data

- **Determine the properties of each field.** You need to identify the **properties**, or characteristics, of each field so that the database knows how to store, display, and process the field values. These properties include the field's name, data type, maximum number of characters or digits, description, valid values, and other field characteristics. You will learn more about field properties later in this module.

The Billing table you need to modify, and the Patient table you need to create, will contain the fields shown in Figure 2–2. Before modifying and creating these new tables in the Lakewood database, you first need to learn some guidelines for setting field properties.

Guidelines for Setting Field Properties

As just noted, the last step of database design is to determine which values to assign to the properties, such as the name and data type, of each field. When you select or enter a value for a property, you **set** the property. Access has rules for naming fields and objects, assigning data types, and setting other field properties.

Naming Fields and Objects

You must name each field, table, and other object in an Access database. Access stores these items in the database, using the names you supply. Choose a field or object name that describes the purpose or contents of the field or object so that later you can easily remember what the name represents. For example, the three tables in the Lakewood database are named Visit, Billing, and Patient because these names suggest their contents. A table or query name must be unique within a database. A field name must be unique within a table, but it can be used again in another table.

Assigning Field Data Types

Each field must have a data type, which is either assigned automatically by Access or specifically by the table designer. The data type determines what field values you can enter for the field and what other properties the field will have. For example, the Patient table will include a BirthDate field, which will store date values, so you will assign the Date/Time data type to this field. Then Access will allow you to enter and manipulate only dates or times as values in the BirthDate field.

Figure 2–4 lists the most commonly used data types in Access, describes the field values allowed for each data type, explains when you should use each data type, and indicates the field size of each data type. You can find more complete information about all available data types in Access Help.

Figure 2–4 **Common data types**

Data Type	Description	Field Size
Short Text	Allows field values containing letters, digits, spaces, and special characters. Use for names, addresses, descriptions, and fields containing digits that are *not used in calculations.*	0 to 255 characters; default is 255
Long Text	Allows field values containing letters, digits, spaces, and special characters. Use for long comments and explanations.	1 to 65,535 characters; exact size is determined by entry
Number	Allows positive and negative numbers as field values. A number can contain digits, a decimal point, commas, a plus sign, and a minus sign. Use for fields that will be used in calculations, except those involving money.	1 to 15 digits
Date/Time	Allows field values containing valid dates and times from January 1, 100 to December 31, 9999. Dates can be entered in month/day/year format, several other date formats, or a variety of time formats, such as 10:35 PM. You can perform calculations on dates and times, and you can sort them. For example, you can determine the number of days between two dates.	8 bytes
Currency	Allows field values similar to those for the Number data type, but is used for storing monetary values. Unlike calculations with Number data type decimal values, calculations performed with the Currency data type are not subject to round-off error.	Accurate to 15 digits on the left side of the decimal point and to 4 digits on the right side
AutoNumber	Consists of integer values created automatically by Access each time you create a new record. You can specify sequential numbering or random numbering, which guarantees a unique field value, so that such a field can serve as a table's primary key.	9 digits
Yes/No	Limits field values to yes and no, on and off, or true and false. Use for fields that indicate the presence or absence of a condition, such as whether an order has been filled or whether an invoice has been paid.	1 character
Hyperlink	Consists of text used as a hyperlink address, which can have up to four parts: the text that appears in a field or control; the path to a file or page; a location within the file or page; and text displayed as a ScreenTip.	Up to 65,535 characters total for the four parts of the hyperlink

Setting Field Sizes

The **Field Size property** defines a field value's maximum storage size for Short Text, Number, and AutoNumber fields only. The other data types have no Field Size property because their storage size is either a fixed, predetermined amount or is determined automatically by the field value itself, as shown in Figure 2–4. A Short Text field has a default field size of 255 characters; you can also set its field size by entering a number from 0 to 255. For example, the FirstName and LastName fields in the Patient table will be Short Text fields with sizes of 20 characters and 25 characters, respectively. These field sizes will accommodate the values that will be entered in each of these fields.

PROSKILLS

Decision Making: Specifying the Field Size Property for Number Fields

When you use the Number data type to define a field, you need to decide what the Field Size setting should be for the field. You should set the Field Size property based on the largest value that you expect to store in that field. Access processes smaller data sizes faster, using less memory, so you can optimize your database's performance and its storage space by selecting the correct field size for each field. Field Size property settings for Number fields are as follows:

- **Byte**: Stores whole numbers (numbers with no fractions) from 0 to 255 in 1 byte
- **Integer**: Stores whole numbers from –32,768 to 32,767 in 2 bytes
- **Long Integer** (default): Stores whole numbers from –2,147,483,648 to 2,147,483,647 in 4 bytes
- **Single**: Stores positive and negative numbers to precisely 7 decimal places in 4 bytes
- **Double**: Stores positive and negative numbers to precisely 15 decimal places in 8 bytes
- **Replication ID**: Establishes a unique identifier for replication of tables, records, and other objects in databases created using Access 2003 and earlier versions in 16 bytes
- **Decimal**: Stores positive and negative numbers to precisely 28 decimal places in 12 bytes

Choosing an appropriate field size is important to optimize efficiency. For example, it would be wasteful to use the Long Integer field size for a Number field that will store only whole numbers ranging from 0 to 255 because the Long Integer field size uses 4 bytes of storage space. A better choice would be the Byte field size, which uses 1 byte of storage space to store the same values. By first gathering and analyzing information about the number values that will be stored in a Number field, you can make the best decision for the field's Field Size property and ensure the most efficient user experience for the database.

Setting the Caption Property for Fields

The **Caption property** for a field specifies how the field name is displayed in database objects, including table and query datasheets, forms, and reports. If you don't set the Caption property, Access displays the field name as the column heading or label for a field. However, field names such as InvoiceAmt and InvoiceDate in the Billing table can be difficult to read. Setting the Caption property for these fields to "Invoice Amt" and "Invoice Date" makes it easier for users to read the field names and work with the database.

INSIGHT

Setting the Caption Property vs. Naming Fields

Although Access allows you to include spaces in field names, this practice is not recommended because the spaces cause problems when you try to perform more complex tasks with the data in your database. Setting the Caption property allows you to follow best practices for naming fields, such as not including spaces in field names, while still providing users with more readable field names in datasheets, forms, and reports.

In the previous module, you created the Lakewood database file and, within that file, you created the Visit table working in Datasheet view. In addition, you created the Billing table working in Design view. Donna would like to further refine the design for the Billing table. So next, you'll modify the design for the Billing table for Donna in Design view.

Modifying a Table in Design View

In the previous module, you created the basic structure for the Billing table in Design view. To review, creating a basic table in Design view involves entering the field names, entering the data types for each field, entering an optional description for the fields, specifying a primary key for the table, and then saving the table structure. Creating a table in Design view can also involve defining properties for each field, which Donna would like you to do now. She has further refined the design for the Billing table by listing each field's name, data type, size, description (if applicable), and any other properties to set for each field. See Figure 2–5.

Figure 2–5 **Design for the Billing table**

Field Name	Data Type	Field Size	Description	Other
InvoiceNum	Short Text	5	Primary key	Caption = Invoice Num
VisitID	Short Text	4	Foreign key	Caption = Visit ID
InvoiceAmt	Currency			Format = Currency
				Decimal Places = 2
				Caption = Invoice Amt
InvoiceDate	Date/Time			Format = mm/dd/yyyy
				Caption = Invoice Date
InvoicePaid	Yes/No			Caption = Invoice Paid

You'll use Donna's design as a guide for modifying the Billing table in the Lakewood database.

Start Access and open the Billing table in Design view:

1. sam Start Access and open the **Lakewood** database you created in the previous module.

   Trouble? If the security warning is displayed below the ribbon, click the Enable Content button.

2. In the Navigation Pane, right-click the **Billing** table object and then click **Design View** on the shortcut menu.
3. Click the **Shutter Bar Open/Close Button** « to close the Navigation Pane.
4. Position the pointer in the row selector for row 1 (the InvoiceNum field) until the pointer changes to a right-pointing arrow ➡. Placing it over the key symbol is fine.
5. Click the **row selector** to select the entire InvoiceNum row. See Figure 2–6.

Figure 2–6 **Billing table in Design view**

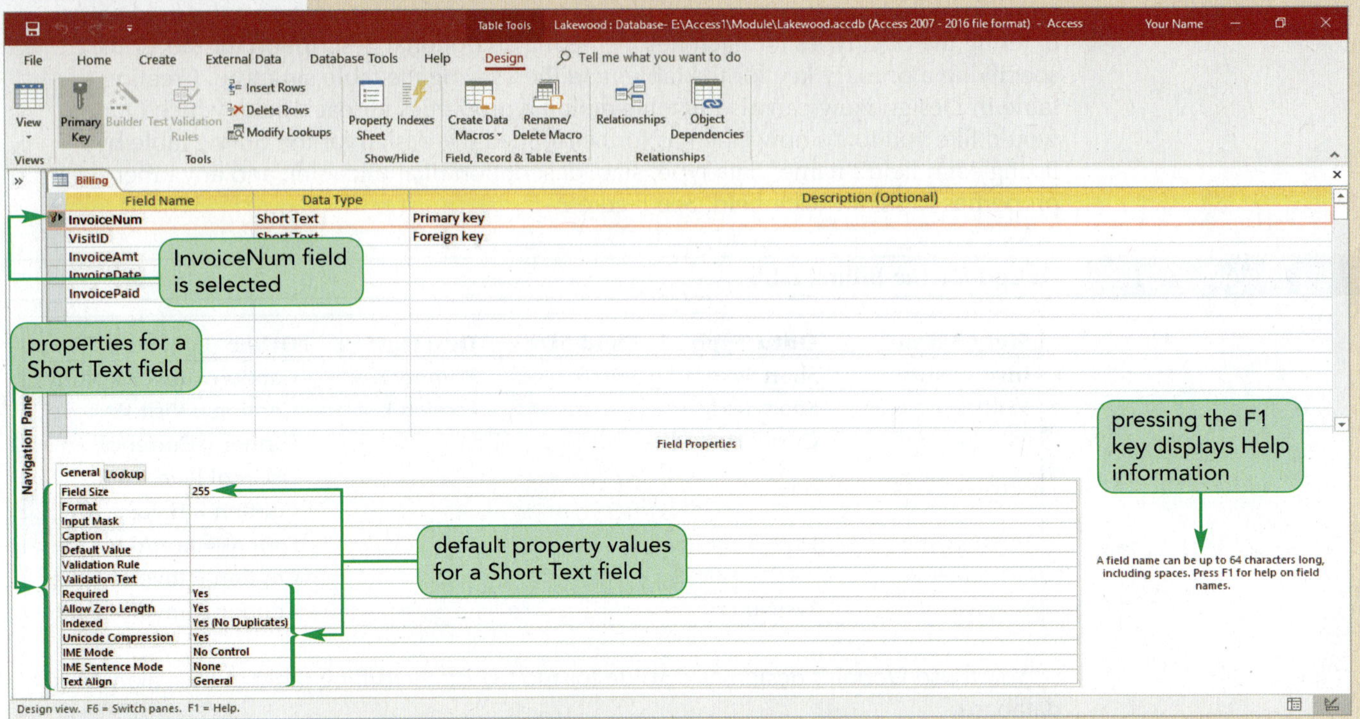

The Billing table contains the same fields as when you created it in the previous module. Donna wants you to continue to modify the fields in the table as listed in Figure 2–5. The first step is to add properties to the InvoiceNum field.

Because you have already defined the Field Name, Data Type, and Description properties for the InvoiceNum field, you will use the Field Properties Pane to set the additional properties Donna wants. When you created the InvoiceNum field, you gave it a data type of Short Text. Figure 2–6 shows that the default number of characters for a field of the Short Text data type is 255. In addition, a Short Text field by default has no Caption property, which specifies how the name appears. Updating the Caption property will make the field name more readable. Donna wants you to update the Field Size and Caption properties.

To add properties to the InvoiceNum field:

1. Double-click the number **255** in the Field Size property box to select it, and then type **5**.

   You also need to set the Caption property for the field so that its name appears with a space, as "Invoice Num."

2. Click the **Caption** property box, and then type **Invoice Num** (be sure to include a space between the two words). You have set properties for the InvoiceNum field. See Figure 2–7.

Figure 2–7 InvoiceNum field properties updated

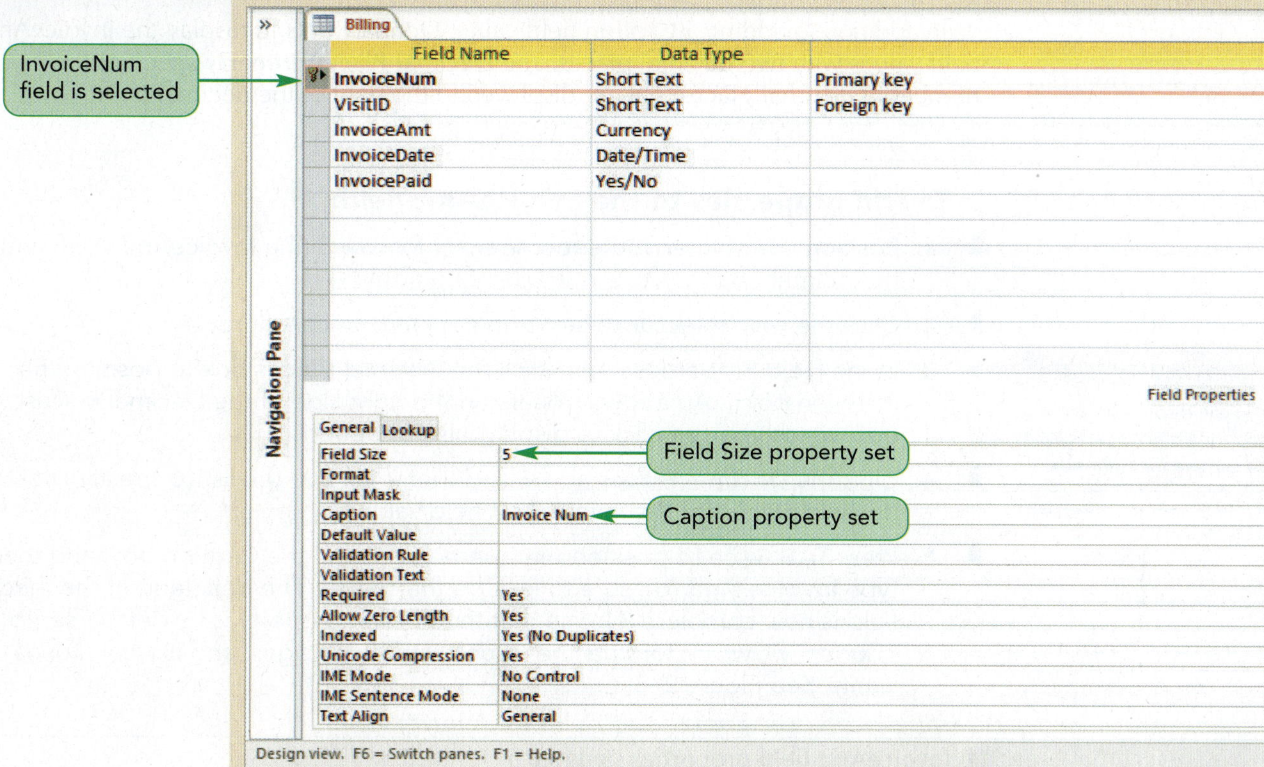

Next, you will add the properties Donna wants to the VisitID field. As with the InvoiceNum field, you will update the Field Size and Caption properties. Donna wants the field size of the VisitID field to be 4.

Recall that when you include the primary key from one table as a field in a second table to connect the two tables, the field is a foreign key in the second table. The field must be defined in the same way in both tables—that is, the field properties, including field size and data type, must match exactly. Later in this session, you'll change the Field Size property for the VisitID field in the Visit table to 4 so that the field definition is the same in both tables.

To add properties to the VisitID field:

1. Position the pointer in the row selector for row 2 (the VisitID field) until the pointer changes to a right-pointing arrow ➡.
2. Click the **row selector** to select the entire VisitID row.
3. Press **F6** to move to the Field Properties pane. The current entry for the Field Size property, 255, is selected.
4. Type **4** to set the Field Size property. Next, you need to set the Caption property for this field.
5. Press **TAB** three times to position the insertion point in the Caption box, and then type **Visit ID** (be sure to include a space between the two words). You have finished modifying the VisitID field.

The third field in the Billing table is the InvoiceAmt field, which has the Currency data type. Donna wants you to make a few modifications to the properties of this field.

In addition to adding a Caption field value, Donna wants to display the InvoiceAmt field values with two decimal places. The **Decimal Places property** specifies the number of decimal places that are displayed to the right of the decimal point.

To add properties to the InvoiceAmt field:

1. Position the pointer in the row selector for row 3 (the InvoiceAmt field) until the pointer changes to a right-pointing arrow ➡.
2. Click the **row selector** to select the entire InvoiceAmt row.
3. In the Field Properties pane, click the **Decimal Places** box to position the insertion point. An arrow appears on the right side of the Decimal Places box, which you can click to display a list of options.
4. Click the **Decimal Places** arrow, and then click **2** in the list to specify two decimal places for the InvoiceAmt field values.
5. Press **TAB** twice to position the insertion point in the Caption box, and then type **Invoice Amt** (be sure to include the space). The definition of the third field is now complete. Notice that the Format property is by default set to "Currency," which formats the values with dollar signs, and is what Donna wants. See Figure 2–8.

TIP

You can display the arrow and the list simultaneously by clicking the right side of a box.

Figure 2–8 InvoiceAmt field properties updated

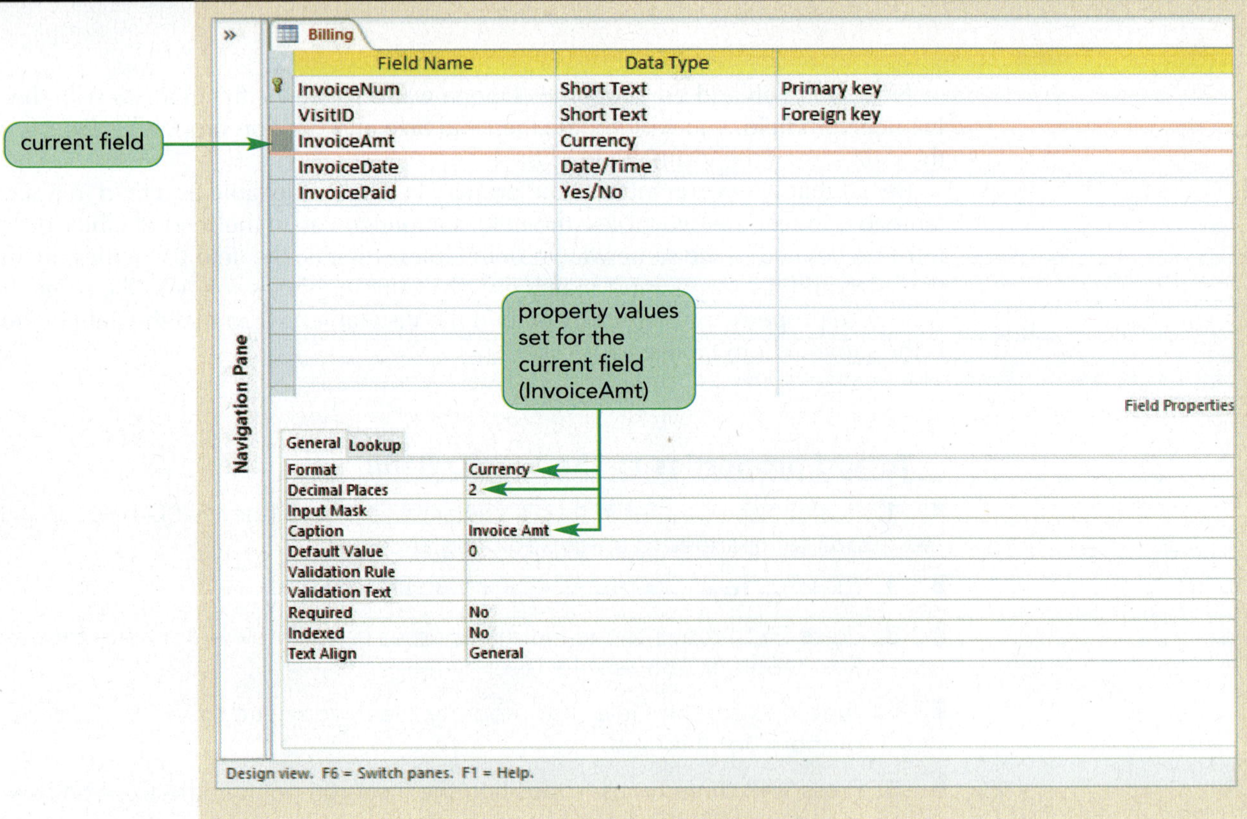

In these steps, you set the Decimal Places property for the InvoiceAmt field in Design view; however, it is also possible to change the number of decimal places for a field in Datasheet view. For fields of the Currency and Number data types, you can change the number of decimal places in either view. To change the number of decimal places in Datasheet view, you would first click a field to make it the active field. On the Table Tools Fields tab, in the Formatting group, use the Increase Decimals and Decrease Decimals buttons to add or remove decimal places in the field. When you do, Access makes the change in the corresponding Decimal Places property in Design view.

The fourth field in the Billing table is the InvoiceDate field. According to Donna's design (Figure 2–5), the date values should be displayed in the format mm/dd/yyyy, which is a two-digit month, a two-digit day, and a four-digit year. In addition, she wants you to update the Caption property.

To add properties to the InvoiceDate field:

1. Position the pointer in the row selector for row 4 (the InvoiceDate field) until the pointer changes to a right-pointing arrow ➡.
2. Click the **row selector** to select the entire InvoiceDate row.

   Donna wants to display the values in the InvoiceDate field in a format showing the month, the day, and a four-digit year, as in the following example: 05/24/2021. You use the Format property to control the display of a field value.
3. In the Field Properties pane, click the right side of the **Format** box to display the list of predefined formats for Date/Time fields. See Figure 2–9.

Figure 2–9 Displaying available formats for Date/Time fields

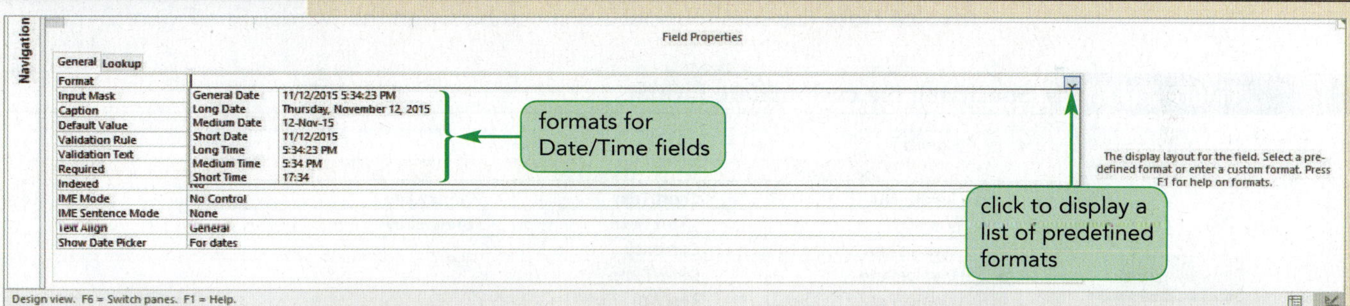

Trouble? If you see an arrow instead of a list of predefined formats, click the arrow to display the list.

As noted in the right side of the Field Properties pane, you can choose a predefined format or enter a custom format. Even though the Short Date format seems to match the format Donna wants, it displays only one digit for January to September. For example, it would display the month of May with only the digit "5"—as in 5/24/2021—instead of displaying the month with two digits, as in 05/24/2021.

Because none of the predefined formats matches the exact layout Donna wants for the InvoiceDate values, you need to create a custom date format. Figure 2–10 shows some of the symbols available for custom date and time formats.

Figure 2–10 Symbols for some custom date formats

Symbol	Description
/	date separator
d	day of the month in one or two numeric digits, as needed (1 to 31)
dd	day of the month in two numeric digits (01 to 31)
ddd	first three letters of the weekday (Sun to Sat)
dddd	full name of the weekday (Sunday to Saturday)
w	day of the week (1 to 7)
ww	week of the year (1 to 53)
m	month of the year in one or two numeric digits, as needed (1 to 12)
mm	month of the year in two numeric digits (01 to 12)
mmm	first three letters of the month (Jan to Dec)
mmmm	full name of the month (January to December)
yy	last two digits of the year (01 to 99)
yyyy	full year (0100 to 9999)

Donna wants to display the dates with a two-digit month (mm), a two-digit day (dd), and a four-digit year (yyyy).

4. Click the **Format** arrow to close the list of predefined formats, and then type **mm/dd/yyyy** in the Format box.
5. Press **TAB** twice to position the insertion point in the Caption box, and then type **Invoice Date** (be sure to include a space between the words). See Figure 2–11.

Figure 2–11 Specifying the custom date format

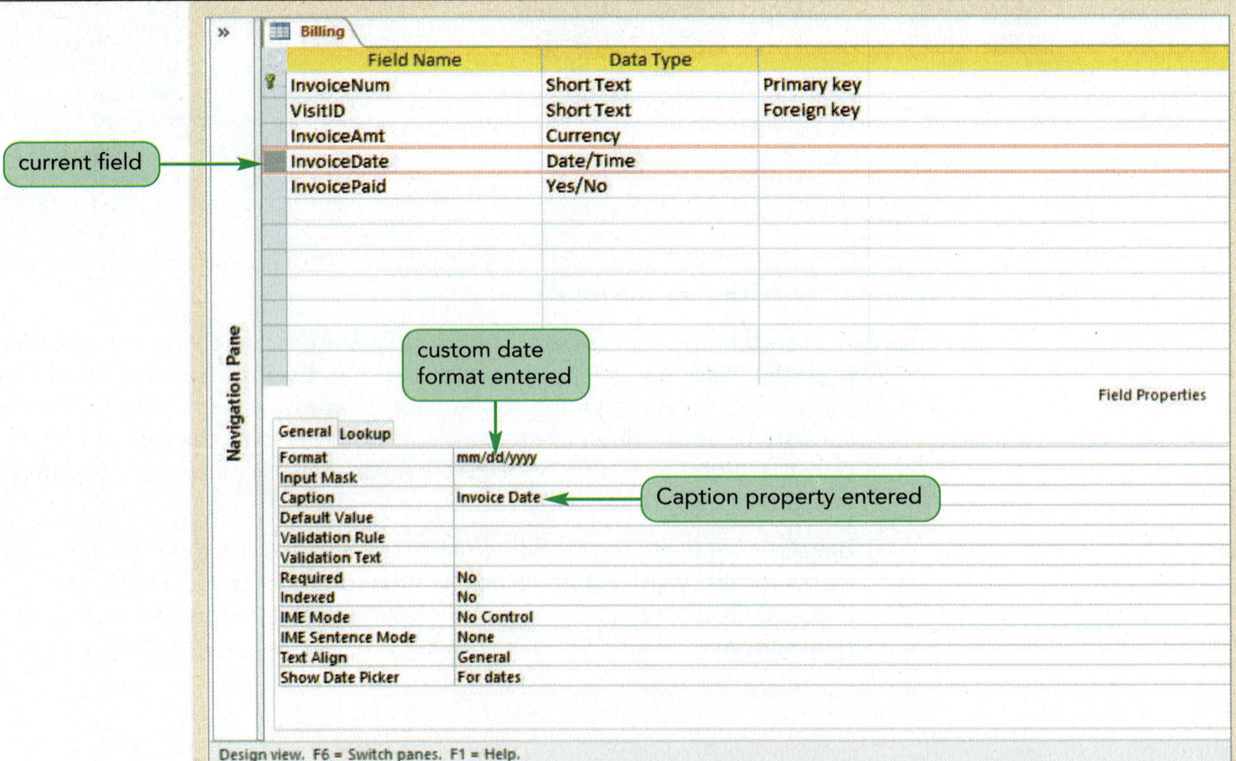

The fifth and final field to modify in the Billing table is the InvoicePaid field. The only property Donna wants to update for the InvoicePaid field is the Caption property.

To add property to the InvoicePaid field:

1. Position the pointer in the row selector for row 5 (the InvoicePaid field) until the pointer changes to a right-pointing arrow ➡.
2. Click the **row selector** to select the entire InvoicePaid row.
3. In the Field Properties pane, click the **Caption** box, and then type **Invoice Paid** (once again, be sure to include a space between the words).

You've finished adding properties to the fields for the Billing table. Normally after entering the fields and properties for a table in Design view, you would specify the primary key for the table; however, in the previous module you specified the primary key for the Billing table to be the InvoiceNum field.

INSIGHT

Understanding the Importance of the Primary Key

Although Access does not require a table to have a primary key, including a primary key offers several advantages:

- A primary key uniquely identifies each record in a table.
- Access does not allow duplicate values in the primary key field. For example, if the Visit table already has a record with a VisitID value of 1549, Access prevents you from adding another record with this same value in the VisitID field. Preventing duplicate values ensures the uniqueness of the primary key field.
- When a primary key has been specified, Access forces you to enter a value for the primary key field in every record in the table. This is known as **entity integrity**. If you do not enter a value for a field, you have actually given the field a **null value**. You cannot give a null value to the primary key field because entity integrity prevents Access from accepting and processing that record.
- You can enter records in any order, but Access displays them by default in order of the primary key's field values. If you enter records in no specific order, you will later be able to work with them in a more meaningful, primary key sequence.
- Access responds faster to your requests for specific records based on the primary key.

Saving the Table Structure

You have already given the table a name, Billing; however, because you added many property values, you should save the changes you made to the table structure.

To save the Billing table changes:

1. On the Quick Access Toolbar, click the **Save** button 💾.

   Unlike the first time you saved the Billing table, you are not prompted for a name for the table. Because the name has already been assigned, Access updates the structure of the table using the same name.

Modifying the Structure of an Access Table

Even a well-designed table might need to be modified. Some changes that you can make to a table's structure in Design view include changing the order of fields and adding new fields.

After meeting with her assistant, Taylor Bailey, and reviewing the structure of the Billing table, Donna asks you to make changes to the table. First, she wants to move the InvoiceAmt field so that it appears right before the InvoicePaid field. Then, she wants you to add a new Short Text field named InvoiceItem to include information about what the invoice is for, such as office visits, lab work, and so on. Donna would like to insert the InvoiceItem field between the InvoiceAmt and InvoicePaid fields.

Moving a Field in Design View

To move a field, you use the mouse to drag it to a new location in the Table Design grid. Although you can move a field in Datasheet view by dragging its column heading to a new location, doing so rearranges only the *display* of the table's fields; the table structure is not changed. To move a field permanently, you must move the field in Design view.

Next, you'll move the InvoiceAmt field so that it appears before the InvoicePaid field in the Billing table.

To move the InvoiceAmt field:

1. Position the pointer on the row selector for the InvoiceAmt field until the pointer changes to a right-pointing arrow ➡.
2. Click the **row selector** to select the entire InvoiceAmt row.
3. Place the pointer on the row selector for the InvoiceAmt field until the pointer changes to a selection pointer, press and hold the mouse button, and then drag to the row selector for the InvoicePaid field. As you drag, the pointer changes to a move pointer. See Figure 2–12.

Figure 2–12 **Moving the InvoiceAmt field in the table structure**

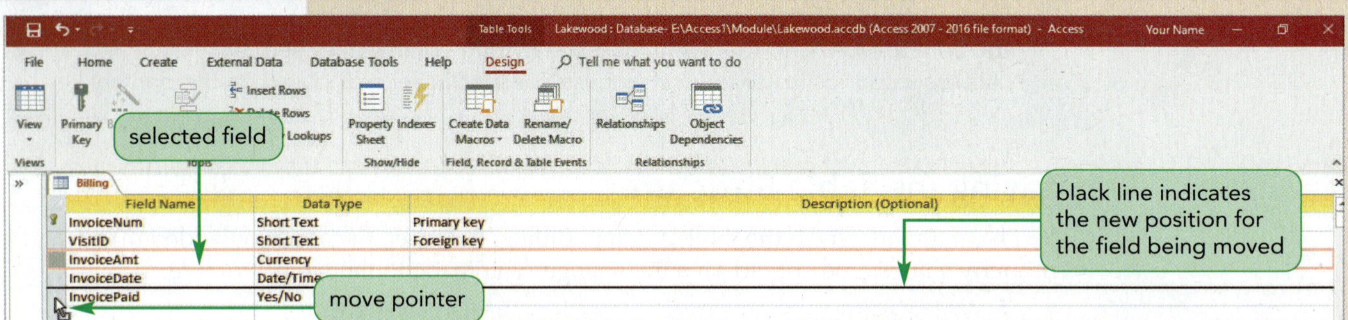

4. Release the mouse button. The InvoiceAmt field now appears between the InvoiceDate and InvoicePaid fields in the table structure.

   Trouble? If the InvoiceAmt field did not move, repeat Steps 1 through 4, making sure you hold down the mouse button while dragging.

Adding a Field in Design View

To add a new field between existing fields, you must insert a row. You begin by selecting the row below where you want to insert the new field.

REFERENCE

Adding a Field Between Two Existing Fields

- In the Table window in Design view, select the row below where you want to insert the new field.
- In the Tools group on the Table Tools Design tab, click the Insert Rows button.
- Define the new field by entering the field name, data type, optional description, and any property specifications.

Next, you need to add the InvoiceItem field to the Billing table structure between the InvoiceAmt and InvoicePaid fields.

To add the InvoiceItem field to the Billing table:

1. Click the **InvoicePaid** Field Name box. You need to establish this field as the current field to insert the row for the new field above this field.
2. On the Table Tools Design tab, in the Tools group, click **Insert Rows**. A new, blank row is added between the InvoiceAmt and InvoicePaid fields. The insertion point is positioned in the Field Name box for the new row, ready for you to type the name for the new field. See Figure 2–13.

Figure 2–13 Table structure after inserting a row

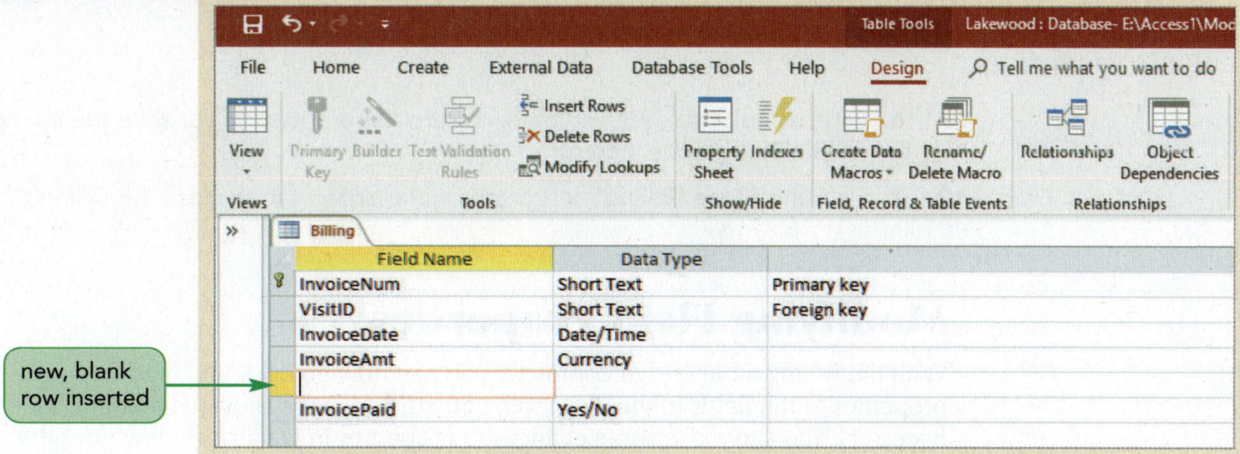

Trouble? If you selected the InvoicePaid field's row selector and then inserted the new row, you need to click the new row's Field Name box to position the insertion point in it.

You'll define the InvoiceItem field in the new row of the Billing table. This field will be a Short Text field with a field size of 40. You also need to set the Caption property to include a space between the words in the field name.

3. Type **InvoiceItem**, press **TAB** to move to the Data Type property, and then press **TAB** again to accept the default Short Text data type.

4. Press **F6** to select the default field size in the Field Size box, and then type **40**.
5. Press **TAB** three times to position the insertion point in the Caption box, and then type **Invoice Item**. The definition of the new field is complete. See Figure 2–14.

Figure 2–14 **InvoiceItem field added to the Billing table**

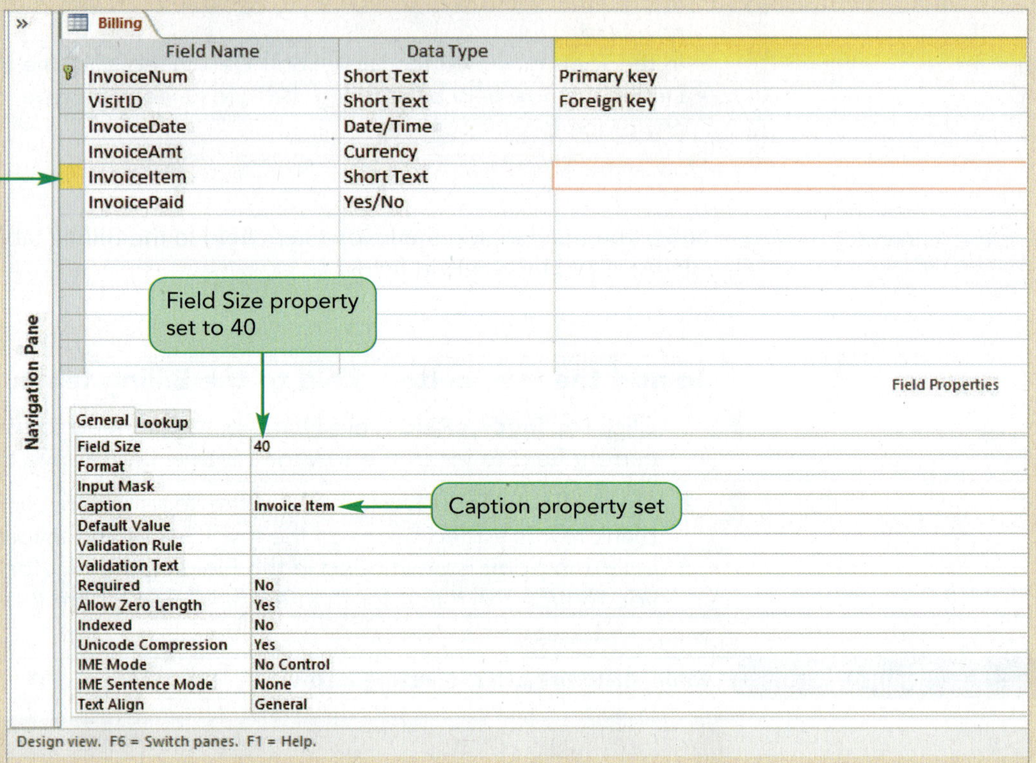

6. On the Quick Access Toolbar, click the **Save** button to save the changes to the Billing table structure.
7. Click the **Close 'Billing'** button on the object tab to close the Billing table.

Modifying Field Properties

With the Billing table design complete, you can now go back and modify the properties of the fields in the Visit table you created in the previous module, as necessary. You can make some changes to properties in Datasheet view; for others, you'll work in Design view.

Changing the Format Property in Datasheet View

The Formatting group on the Table Tools Fields tab in Datasheet view allows you to modify some formatting properties for certain field types. When you format a field, you change the way data is displayed, but not the actual values stored in the table.

Next, you'll check the properties of the VisitDate field in the Visit table to see if any changes would improve the display of the date values.

To modify the VisitDate field's Format property:

1. In the Navigation Pane, click the **Shutter Bar Open/Close Button** » to open the pane. Notice that the Billing table is listed above the Visit table in the Tables section. By default, objects are listed in alphabetical order in the Navigation Pane.
2. Double-click **Visit** to open the Visit table in Datasheet view.
3. In the Navigation Pane, click the **Shutter Bar Open/Close Button** « to close the pane.
4. Position the pointer in the row selector for the first record (VisitID 1450) until the pointer changes to a right-pointing arrow ➡.
5. Click the **row selector** to select the entire first record. See Figure 2–15.

Figure 2–15 Visit table datasheet

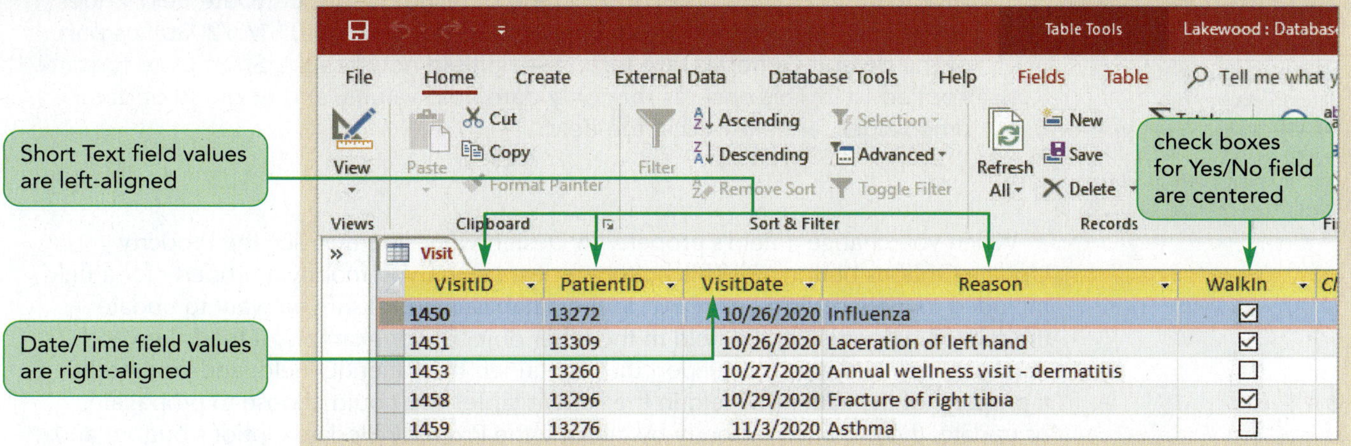

The values in the three Short Text fields—VisitID, PatientID, and Reason—appear left-aligned within their boxes, and the values in the Date/Time field (VisitDate) appear right-aligned. In Access, values for Short Text fields are left-aligned, and values for Number, Date/Time, and Currency fields are right-aligned. The WalkIn field is a Yes/No field, so its values appear in check boxes that are centered within the column.

6. On the ribbon, click the **Table Tools Fields** tab.
7. Click the **first field value** in the VisitDate column. The Data Type option shows that this field is a Date/Time field.

   By default, Access assigns the General Date format to Date/Time fields. Note the Format box in the Formatting group, which you use to set the Format property (similar to how you set the Format property in the Field Properties pane in Design view). Even though the Format box is empty, the VisitDate field has the General Date format applied to it. The General Date format includes settings for date or time values, or a combination of date and time values. However, Donna wants to display *only date values* in the VisitDate field, so she asks you to specify the Short Date format for the field.
8. In the Formatting group, click the **Format** arrow, and then click **Short Date**. See Figure 2–16.

Figure 2–16 **VisitDate field after modifying the format**

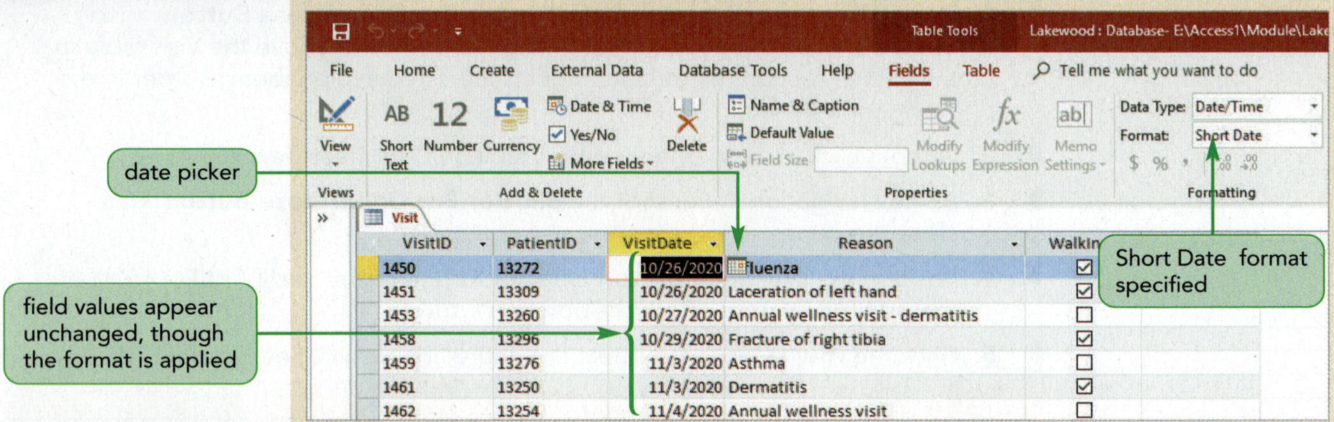

Although no change is apparent in the datasheet—the VisitDate field values already appear with the Short Date setting (for example, 11/3/2020), as part of the default General Date format—the field now has the Short Date format applied to it. This ensures that only date field values, and not time or date/time values, are allowed in the field.

TIP

When working with date values, you can type dates directly or click the date picker shown in Figure 2–16 to select a date from an interactive calendar.

When you change a field's property in Design view, you may see the Property Update Options button. This button appears when you modify a property for a field included in a query, form, or report in the database and asks if you want to update the related properties of the field in the other objects. For example, if the Lakewood database included a form or report that contained the PatientID field, and you modified a property of the PatientID field in the Patient table, you could choose to propagate, or update, the modified property by clicking the Property Update Options button, and then choosing the option to make the update everywhere the field is used. You are not required to update the related objects; however, in most cases, it is a good idea to perform the update.

Changing Properties in Design View

Recall that each of the Short Text fields in the Visit table—VisitID, PatientID, and Reason—still has the default field size of 255, which is too large for the data contained in these fields. Also, the VisitID and PatientID fields need descriptions to identify them as the primary and foreign keys, respectively, in the table. Finally, each of these fields needs a caption to include a space between the words in the field name or to make the name more descriptive. You can make all of these property changes more easily in Design view.

To modify the Field Size, Description, and Caption field properties:

TIP

You can also click the Design View button on the far right end of the status bar to switch to Design view.

1. On the Table Tools Fields tab, in the Views group, click the **View** button. The table is displayed in Design view with the VisitID field selected. You need to enter a Description property value for this field, the primary key in the table, and change its Field Size property to 4 because each visit number at Lakewood Community Health Services consists of four digits.

Trouble? If you clicked the arrow on the View button, a menu appears. Choose Design View from the menu.

2. Press **TAB** twice to position the insertion point in the Description (Optional) box, and then type **Primary key**.
3. Press **F6** to move to and select the default setting of 255 in the Field Size box in the Field Properties pane, and then type **4**. Next, you need to set the Caption property for this field.
4. Press **TAB** three times to position the insertion point in the Caption box, and then type **Visit ID**.
5. Click the **PatientID** Field Name box, press **TAB** twice to position the insertion point in the Description (Optional) box, and then type **Foreign key**.
6. Press **F6** to move to and select the default setting of 255 in the Field Size box in the Field Properties pane, and then type **5**.
7. Press **TAB** three times to position the insertion point in the Caption box, and then type **Patient ID**.
8. Click the **VisitDate** Field Name box, click the **Caption** box, and then type **Date of Visit**.

   For the Reason field, you will set the Field Size property to 60. This size can accommodate the longer values in the Reason field. You'll also set this field's Caption property to provide a more descriptive name.

9. Click the **Reason** Field Name box, press **F6**, type **60**, press **TAB** three times to position the insertion point in the Caption box, and then type **Reason/Diagnosis**.

   Finally, you'll set the Caption property for the WalkIn field.

10. Click the **WalkIn** Field Name box, click the **Caption** box, and then type **Walk-in?**. See Figure 2–17.

Figure 2–17 **Visit table after modifying field properties**

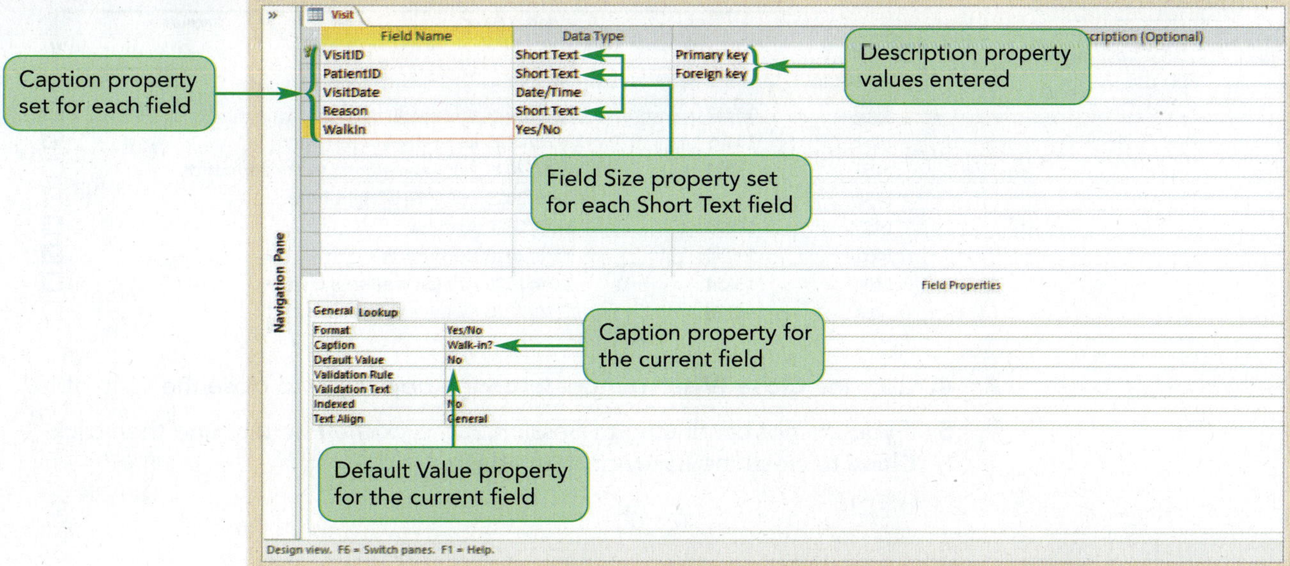

The WalkIn field's Default Value property is automatically set to "No," which means the check box for this field will be empty for each new record. This is the default for this property for any Yes/No field. You can set the Default Value property for other types of fields to make data entry easier. You'll learn more about setting this property in the next session.

The changes to the Visit table's properties are now complete, so you can save the table and view the results of your changes in Datasheet view.

To save and view the modified Visit table:

1. On the Quick Access Toolbar, click the **Save** button to save the modified table. A dialog box opens informing you that some data may be lost because you decreased the field sizes. Because all of the values in the VisitID, PatientID, and Reason fields contain the same number of or fewer characters than the new Field Size properties you set for each field, you can ignore this message.
2. Click the **Yes** button.
3. On the Table Tools Design tab, in the Views group, click the **View** button to display the Visit table in Datasheet view. Each column (field) heading now displays the text you specified in the Caption property for that field. See Figure 2–18.

Figure 2–18 Modified Visit table in Datasheet view

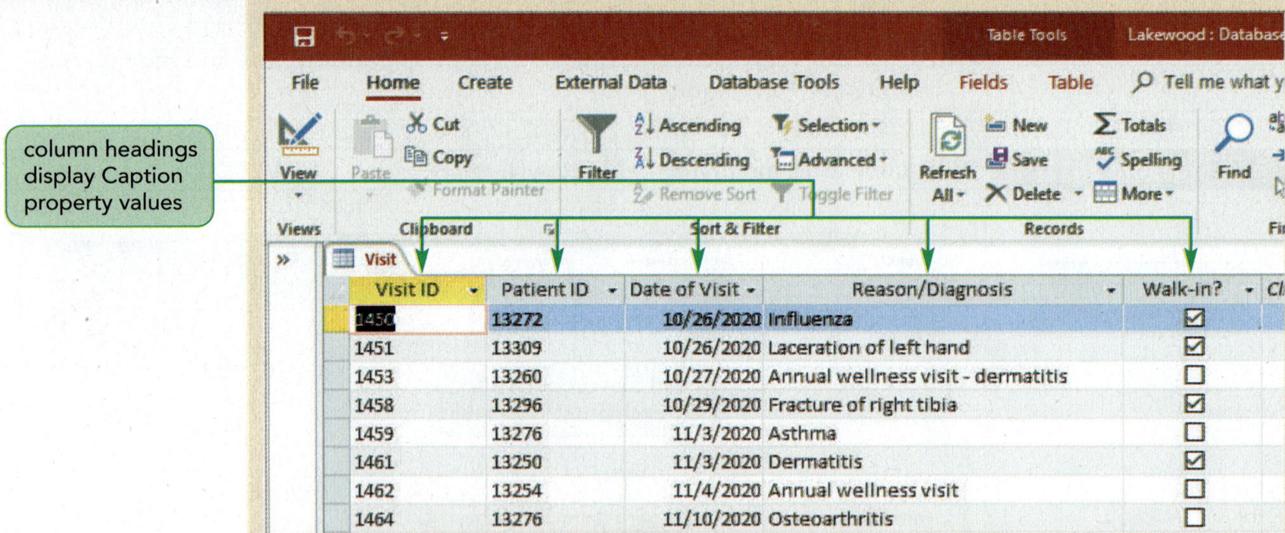

4. Click the **Close 'Visit'** button on the object tab to close the Visit table.
5. If you are not continuing to Session 2.2, click the **File** tab, and then click **Close** to close the Lakewood database.

You have modified the design of the Billing table. In the next session, you'll add records to the Billing table and create the Patient table in the Lakewood database.

REVIEW

Session 2.1 Quick Check

1. What guidelines should you follow when designing a database?
2. What is the purpose of the Data Type property for a field?
3. The ________ property specifies how a field's name is displayed in database objects, including table and query datasheets, forms, and reports.
4. For which three types of fields can you assign a field size?
5. The default Field Size property setting for a Short Text field is ________.
6. In Design view, which key do you press to move from the Table Design grid to the Field Properties pane?
7. List three reasons you should specify a primary key for an Access table.

Session 2.2 Visual Overview:

Click the Close button to close the Relationships window.

You click the **Show Table button** to open the Show Table dialog box. From there, you can choose a table to add to the Relationships window

The **Relationships window** illustrates the relationships among database tables. Using this window, you can view or change existing relationships, define new relationships between tables, and rearrange the layout of the tables in the window.

The key symbol next to a field name indicates that the field is the table's primary key. For example, PatientID is the primary key for the Patient table.

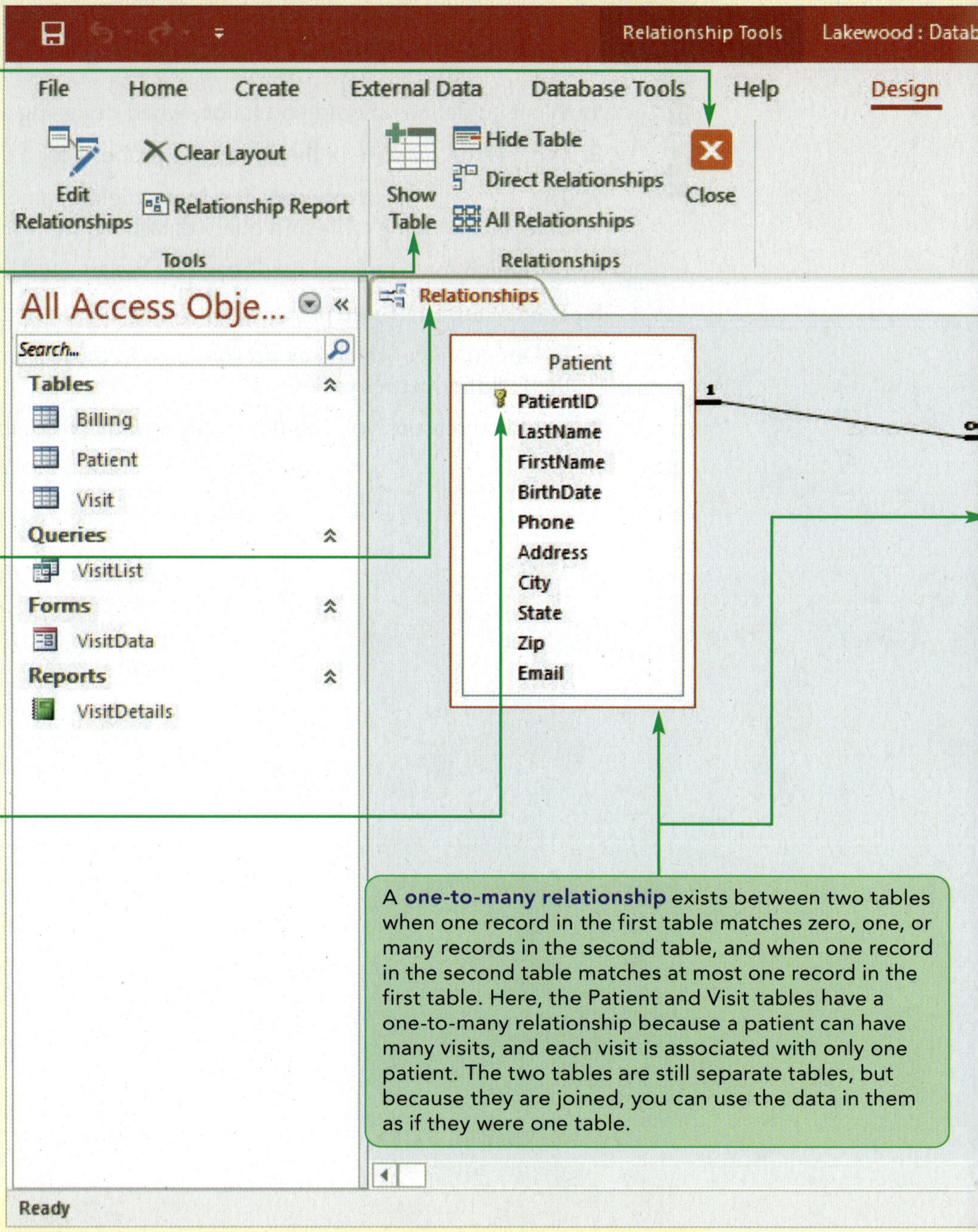

A **one-to-many relationship** exists between two tables when one record in the first table matches zero, one, or many records in the second table, and when one record in the second table matches at most one record in the first table. Here, the Patient and Visit tables have a one-to-many relationship because a patient can have many visits, and each visit is associated with only one patient. The two tables are still separate tables, but because they are joined, you can use the data in them as if they were one table.

Understanding Table Relationships

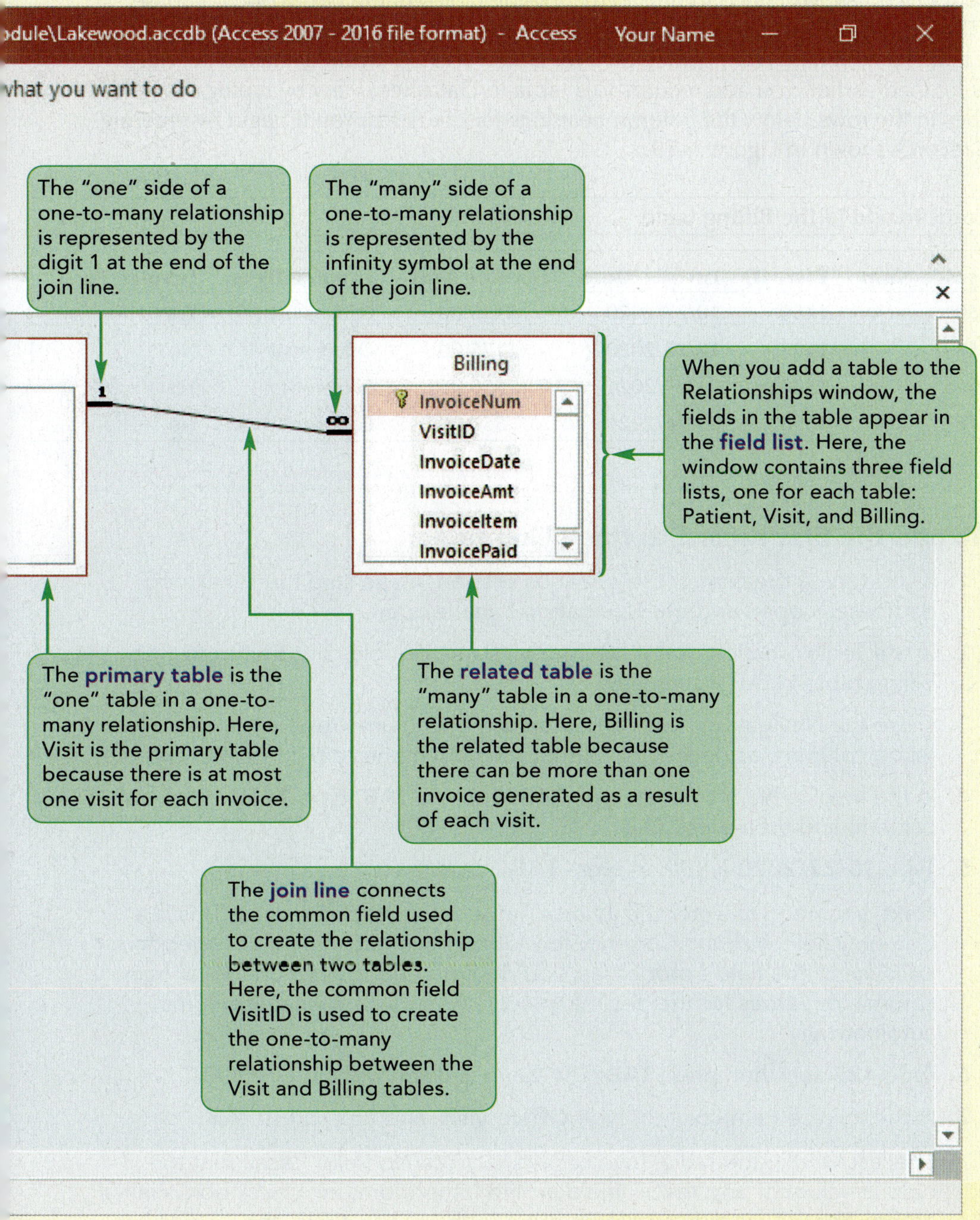

Adding Records to a New Table

Before you can begin to define the table relationships illustrated in the Session 2.2 Visual Overview, you need to finish creating the tables in the Lakewood database.

The Billing table design is complete. Now, Donna would like you to add records to the table so it contains the invoice data for Lakewood Community Health Services. As you learned earlier, you add records to a table in Datasheet view by typing the field values in the rows below the column headings for the fields. You'll begin by entering the records shown in Figure 2–19.

Figure 2–19 **Records to add to the Billing table**

Invoice Num	Visit ID	Invoice Date	Invoice Amt	Invoice Item	Invoice Paid
26501	1450	10/27/2020	$125.00	Office visit	Yes
26589	1495	12/28/2020	$125.00	Office visit	No
26655	1530	01/27/2021	$50.00	Lab work	Yes
26767	1598	03/26/2021	$50.00	Lab work	No

To add the first record to the Billing table:

1. If you took a break after the previous session, make sure the Lakewood database is open and the Navigation Pane is open.
2. In the Tables section of the Navigation Pane, double-click **Billing** to open the Billing table in Datasheet view.
3. Close the Navigation Pane, and then use the column resizing pointer ✛ to resize columns, as necessary, so that the field names are completely visible.

Be sure to type the numbers "0" and "1" and *not* the letters "O" and "I" in the field values.

4. In the Invoice Num column, type **26501**, press **TAB**, type **1450** in the Visit ID column, and then press **TAB**.
5. Type **10/27/2020** and then press **TAB**.

   Next, you need to enter the invoice amount for the first record. This is a Currency field with the Currency format and two decimal places specified. Because of the field's properties, you do not need to type the dollar sign, comma, or zeroes for the decimal places; Access displays these items automatically.

6. Type **125** and then press **TAB**. The value is displayed as "$125.00."
7. In the Invoice Item column, type **Office visit**, and then press **TAB**.

   The last field in the table, InvoicePaid, is a Yes/No field. Recall that the default value for any Yes/No field is "No"; therefore, the check box is initially empty. For the record you are entering in the Billing table, the invoice has been paid, so you need to insert a checkmark in the check box in the Invoice Paid column.

8. Press **SPACEBAR** to insert a checkmark, and then press **TAB**. The values for the first record are entered. See Figure 2–20.

Figure 2–20 First record entered in the Billing table

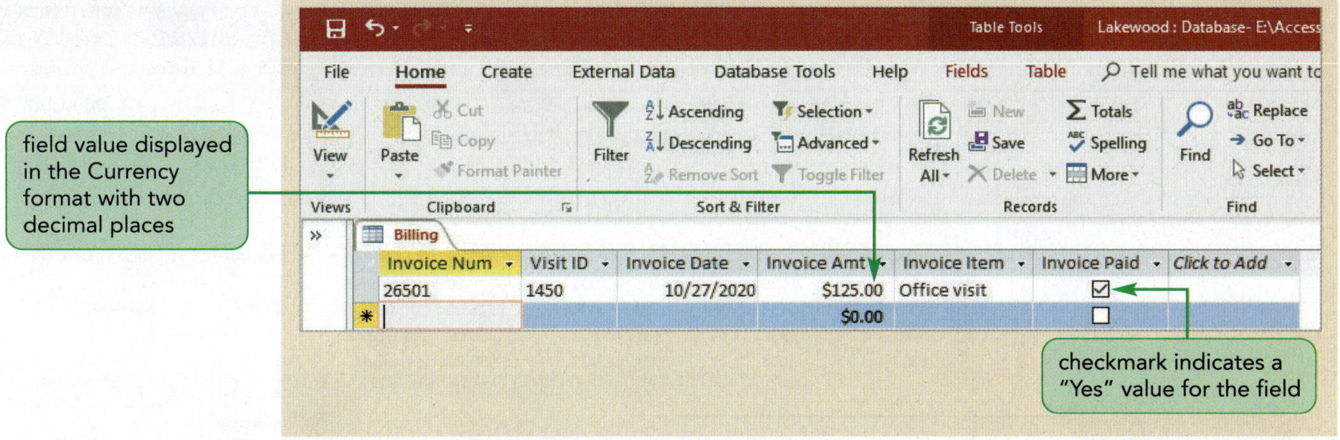

Now you can add the remaining three records. As you do, you'll learn a keyboard shortcut for inserting the value from the same field in the previous record. A **keyboard shortcut** is a key or combination of keys you press to complete an action more efficiently.

To add the next three records to the Billing table:

1. Refer to Figure 2–19 and enter the values in the second record's Invoice Num, Visit ID, and Invoice Date columns.

   Notice that the value in the second record's Invoice Amt column is $125.00. This value is the exact same value as in the first record. You can quickly insert the value from the same column in the previous record using the CTRL+' (apostrophe) keyboard shortcut. To use this shortcut, you press and hold CTRL, press the ' key once, and then release both keys. (The plus sign in the keyboard shortcut indicates you are pressing two keys at once; you do not press the + key.)
2. With the insertion point in the Invoice Amt column, press **CTRL+'**. The value "$125.00" is inserted in the Invoice Amt column for the second record.
3. Press **TAB** to move to the Invoice Item column. Again, the value you need to enter in this column—Office visit—is the same as the value for this column in the previous record. So, you can use the keyboard shortcut again.
4. With the insertion point in the Invoice Item column, press **CTRL+'**. Access inserts the value "Office visit" in the Invoice Item column for the second record.
5. Press **TAB** to move to the Invoice Paid column, and then press **TAB** to leave the Invoice Paid check box unchecked to indicate the invoice has not been paid. The second record is entered in the Billing table.
6. Refer to Figure 2–19 to enter the values for the third and fourth records, using CTRL+' to enter the value in the fourth record's Invoice Amt and Invoice Item columns. Your table should look like the one in Figure 2–21.

Figure 2–21 **Billing table with four records entered**

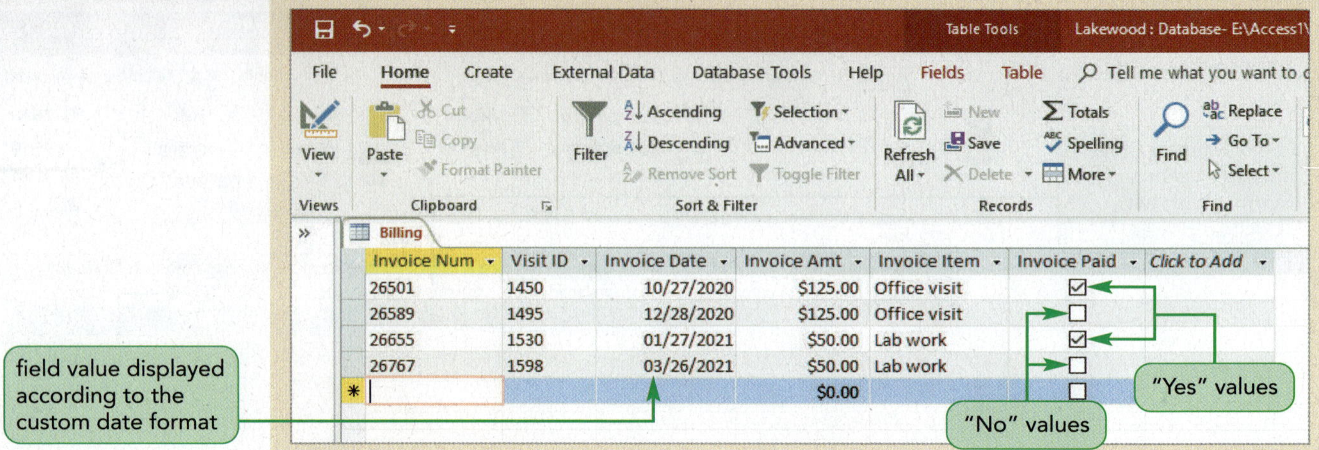

To finish entering records in the Billing table, you'll use a method that allows you to import the data.

Importing Data from an Excel Worksheet

Often, the data you want to add to an Access table is stored in another file, such as a Word document or an Excel workbook. You can add the data from other files to Access in different ways. For example, you can copy and paste the data from an open file, or you can **import** the data, which is a process that allows you to copy the data from a source without having to open the source file.

INSIGHT

Caption Property Values and the Import Process

When you import data from an Excel worksheet into an Access table, the import process does not consider any Caption property values set for the fields in the table. For example, the Access table could have fields such as InvoiceDate and InvoiceAmt with Caption property values of Invoice Date and Invoice Amt, respectively. If the Excel worksheet you are importing has the column headings Invoice Date and Invoice Amt, you might think that the data matches and you can proceed with the import. However, if the underlying field names in the Access table do not match the Excel worksheet column headings exactly, the import process will fail. It is a good idea to double-check to make sure that the actual Access field names—and not just the column headings displayed in a table datasheet (as specified by the Caption property)—match the Excel worksheet column headings. If there are differences, you can change the column headings in the Excel worksheet to match the Access table field names before you import the date, ensuring that the process will work correctly.

Donna had been using Excel to track invoice data for Lakewood Community Health Services and already created a workbook, named Support_AC_2_Invoices.xlsx, containing this data. You'll import the Billing worksheet from this Excel workbook into your Billing table to complete the entry of data in the table. To use the import method, the columns in the Excel worksheet must match the names and data types of the fields in the Access table.

The Billing worksheet contains the following columns: InvoiceNum, VisitID, InvoiceDate, InvoiceAmt, InvoiceItem, and InvoicePaid. These column headings match the field names in the Billing table exactly, so you can import the data. Before you import data into a table, you need to close the table.

To import the Excel data into the Billing table:

1. Click the **Close 'Billing'** button [X] on the object tab to close the Billing table, and then click the **Yes** button in the dialog box asking if you want to save the changes to the table layout. This dialog box opens because you resized the table columns.
2. On the ribbon, click the **External Data** tab.
3. In the Import & Link group, click the **New Data Source** button.
4. In the New Data Source list, click the **From File** option. You may also point to the option.
5. In the From File list, click **Excel**. The Get External Data - Excel Spreadsheet dialog box opens. See Figure 2–22.

Figure 2–22 Get External Data – Excel Spreadsheet dialog box

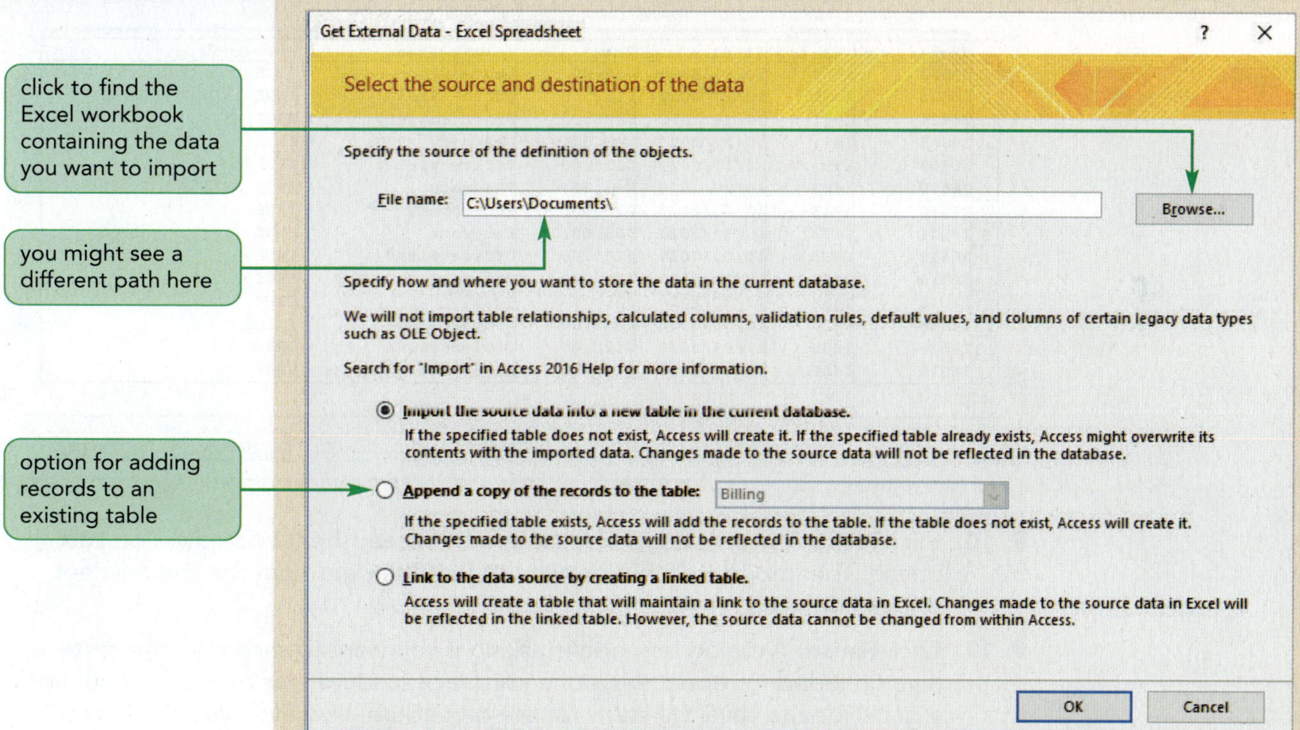

The dialog box provides options for importing the entire worksheet as a new table in the current database, adding the data from the worksheet to an existing table, or linking the data in the worksheet to the table. You need to add, or append, the worksheet data to the Billing table.

6. Click the **Browse** button. The File Open dialog box opens. The Excel workbook file is named "Support_AC_2_Invoices.xlsx" and is located in the Access1 > Module folder provided with your Data Files.

7. Navigate to the **Access1 > Module** folder, where your Data Files are stored, and then double-click the **Support_AC_2_Invoices.xlsx** Excel file. You return to the dialog box.
8. Click the **Append a copy of the records to the table** option button. The box to the right of this option becomes active and displays the Billing table name because it is the first table listed in the Navigation Pane.
9. Click **OK**. The first Import Spreadsheet Wizard dialog box opens. The dialog box confirms that the first row of the worksheet you are importing contains column headings. The bottom section of the dialog box displays some of the data contained in the worksheet. See Figure 2–23.

Figure 2–23 **First Import Spreadsheet Wizard dialog box**

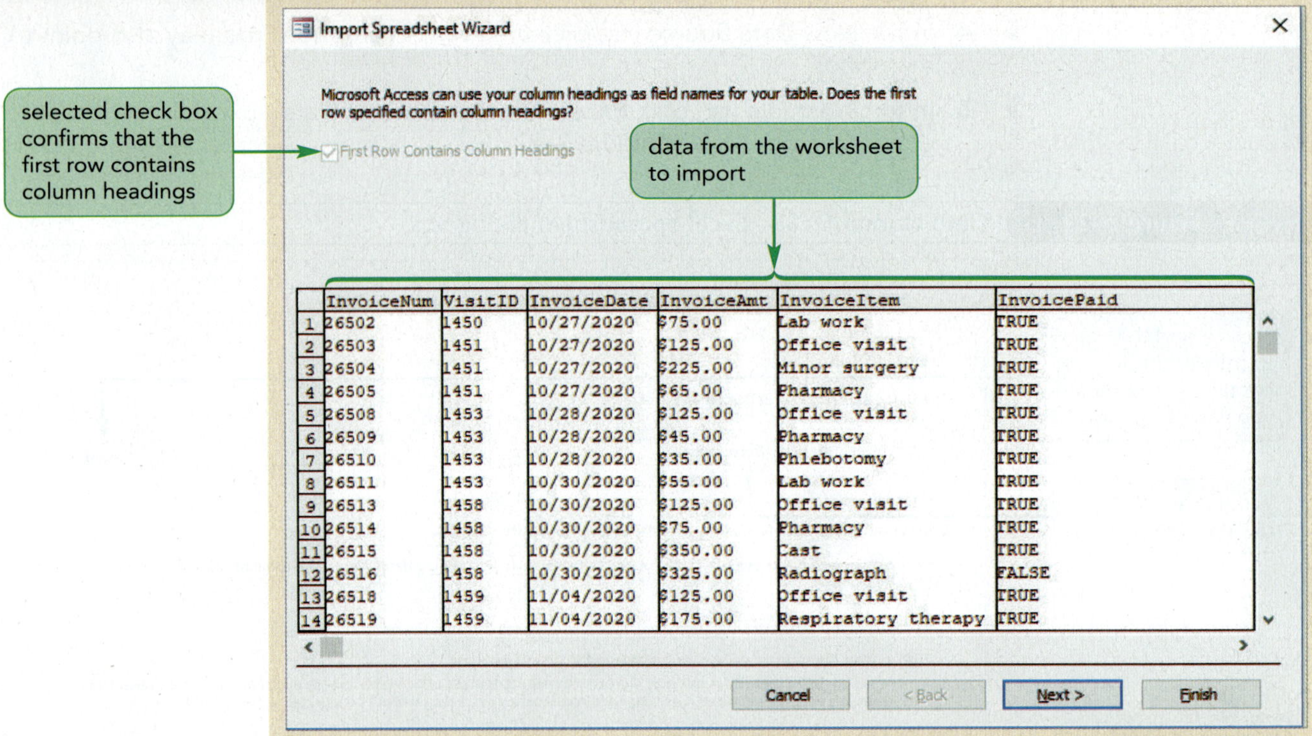

10. Click **Next**. The second, and final, Import Spreadsheet Wizard dialog box opens. The Import to Table box shows that the data from the spreadsheet will be imported into the Billing table.
11. Click **Finish**. A dialog box opens asking if you want to save the import steps. If you needed to repeat this same import procedure many times, it would be a good idea to save the steps for the procedure. However, you don't need to save these steps because you are importing the data only one time. After the data is in the Billing table, Donna will no longer use Excel to track invoice data.
12. Click **Close** in the dialog box to close it without saving the steps.

The data from the Billing worksheet in the Support_AC_2_Invoices.xlsx workbook has been added to the Billing table. Next, you'll open the table to view the new records.

To open the Billing table and view the imported data:

1. Open the Navigation Pane, and then double-click **Billing** in the Tables section to open the table in Datasheet view.
2. Resize the Invoice Item column to its best fit, scrolling the worksheet and resizing, as necessary.
3. Press **CTRL+HOME** to scroll to the top of the datasheet. The table now contains a total of 205 records—the four records you entered plus 201 records imported from the Invoices worksheet. The records are displayed in primary key order by the values in the Invoice Num column. See Figure 2–24.

Figure 2–24 Billing table after importing data from Excel

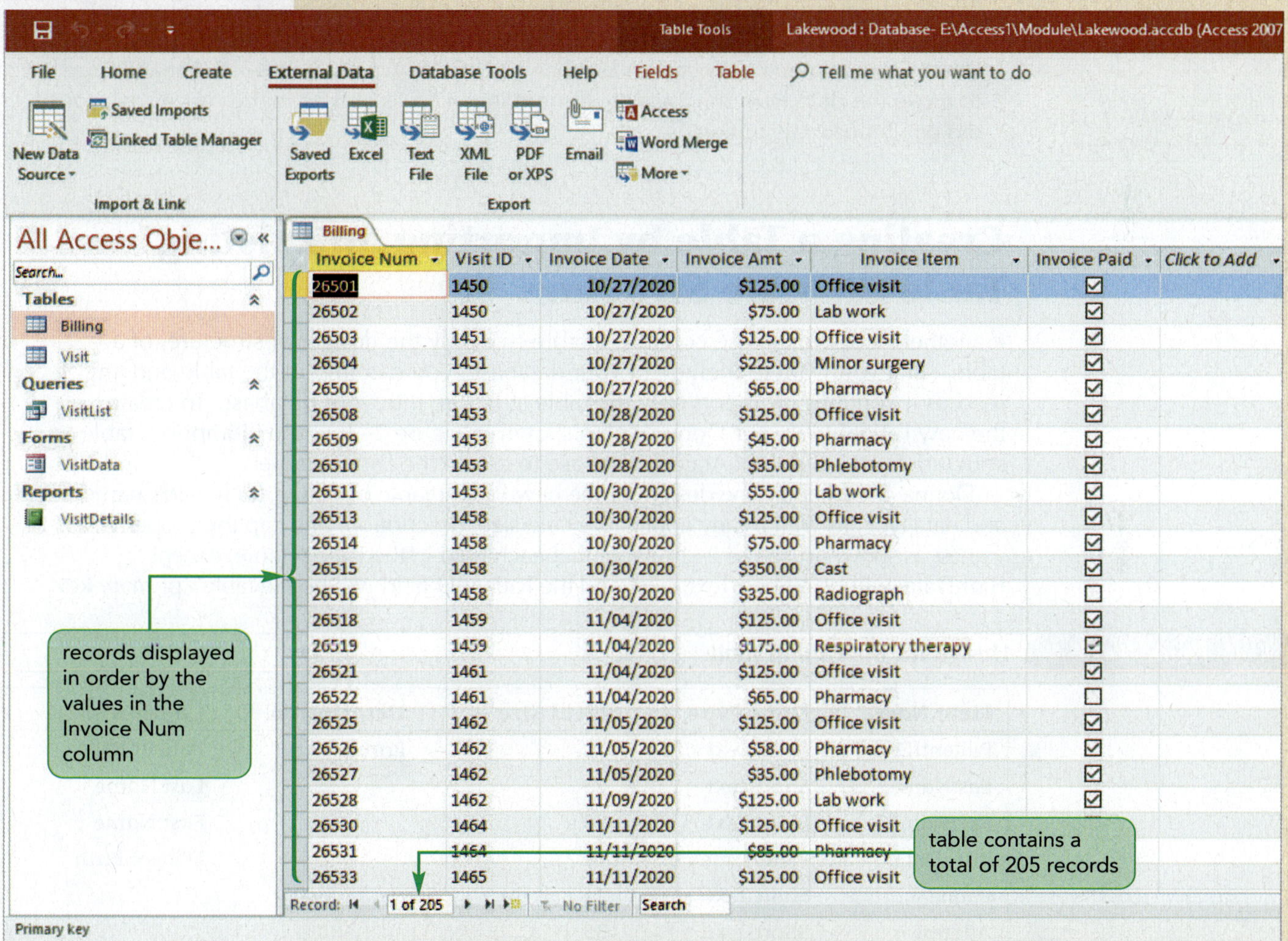

Invoice Num	Visit ID	Invoice Date	Invoice Amt	Invoice Item	Invoice Paid	Click to Add
26501	1450	10/27/2020	$125.00	Office visit	☑	
26502	1450	10/27/2020	$75.00	Lab work	☑	
26503	1451	10/27/2020	$125.00	Office visit	☑	
26504	1451	10/27/2020	$225.00	Minor surgery	☑	
26505	1451	10/27/2020	$65.00	Pharmacy	☑	
26508	1453	10/28/2020	$125.00	Office visit	☑	
26509	1453	10/28/2020	$45.00	Pharmacy	☑	
26510	1453	10/28/2020	$35.00	Phlebotomy	☑	
26511	1453	10/30/2020	$55.00	Lab work	☑	
26513	1458	10/30/2020	$125.00	Office visit	☑	
26514	1458	10/30/2020	$75.00	Pharmacy	☑	
26515	1458	10/30/2020	$350.00	Cast	☑	
26516	1458	10/30/2020	$325.00	Radiograph	☐	
26518	1459	11/04/2020	$125.00	Office visit	☑	
26519	1459	11/04/2020	$175.00	Respiratory therapy	☑	
26521	1461	11/04/2020	$125.00	Office visit	☑	
26522	1461	11/04/2020	$65.00	Pharmacy	☐	
26525	1462	11/05/2020	$125.00	Office visit	☑	
26526	1462	11/05/2020	$58.00	Pharmacy	☑	
26527	1462	11/05/2020	$35.00	Phlebotomy	☑	
26528	1462	11/09/2020	$125.00	Lab work	☑	
26530	1464	11/11/2020	$125.00	Office visit		
26531	1464	11/11/2020	$85.00	Pharmacy		
26533	1465	11/11/2020	$125.00	Office visit		

4. Save and close the Billing table, and then close the Navigation Pane.

Two of the tables—Visit and Billing—are now complete. According to Donna's plan for the Lakewood database, you still need to create the Patient table. You'll use a different method to create this table.

INSIGHT

Options for Importing Data from a Spreadsheet

Because you already created and added the initial four records to the Billing table, you chose the option to append the additional records from the Invoices worksheet to the Billing table. The Get External Data – Excel Spreadsheet dialog box also has two other options (see Figure 2–22).

The first option is to import the source data into a new table in the current database. If the Invoices worksheet contained all the records to add to the Billing table, you could have chosen this option to import all the records. If the specified table does not exist, Access creates it. If the specified table already exists, Access might overwrite its contents with the imported data. Changes made to the source data would not be reflected in the database.

The second option is to link to the data source by creating a linked table. With this option, Access creates a table that maintains a link to the source data in Excel. Changes made to the source data in Excel will be reflected in the linked table. However, the source data cannot be changed within Access. Because Donna wanted to move the data from the Excel worksheet into Access and no longer use Excel, you did not choose this option.

Creating a Table by Importing an Existing Table or Table Structure

If another Access database contains a table—or only the design, or structure, of a table—that you want to include in your database, you can import the table and any records it contains or import only the table structure into your database. To create the new Patient table per Donna's plan shown in Figure 2–2, you will import a table structure from a different Access database to create the Patient table.

Donna documented the design for the new Patient table by listing each field's name and data type, as well as any applicable field size, description, and caption property values, as shown in Figure 2–25. Note that each field in the Patient table, except BirthDate, will be a Short Text field, and the PatientID field will be the table's primary key.

Figure 2–25 **Design for the Patient table**

Field Name	Data Type	Field Size	Description	Caption
PatientID	Short Text	5	Primary key	Patient ID
LastName	Short Text	25		Last Name
FirstName	Short Text	20		First Name
BirthDate	Date/Time			Date of Birth
Phone	Short Text	14		
Address	Short Text	35		
City	Short Text	25		
State	Short Text	2		
Zip	Short Text	10		
Email	Short Text	50		

Donna's assistant Taylor already created an Access database containing a Patient table design; however, she hasn't entered any records into the table. After reviewing the table design, both Taylor and Donna agree that it contains some of the fields they want, but that some changes are needed. You will import the table structure in Taylor's database to create the Patient table in the Lakewood database, and later in this session, you will modify the imported table to produce the final table structure according to Donna's design.

To create the Patient table by importing the structure of another table:

1. Make sure the External Data tab is the active tab on the ribbon.
2. In the Import & Link group, click the **New Data Source** button.
3. In the New Data Source list, click the **From Database** option. You may also point to the option.
4. In the From Database list, click **Access**. The Get External Data – Access Database dialog box opens. This dialog box is similar to the one you used earlier when importing the Excel spreadsheet.
5. Click the **Browse** button. The File Open dialog box opens. The Access database file from which you need to import the table structure is named "Support_AC_2_Taylor.accdb" and is located in the Access1 > Module folder provided with your Data Files.
6. Navigate to the **Access1 > Module** folder, where your Data Files are stored, and then double-click the **Support_AC_2_Taylor.accdb** database file. You return to the dialog box.
7. Make sure the **Import tables, queries, forms, reports, macros, and modules into the current database** option button is selected, and then click **OK**. The Import Objects dialog box opens. The dialog box contains tabs for importing all types of Access database objects—tables, queries, forms, and so on. The Tables tab is the current tab.
8. Click the **Options** button in the dialog box to see all the options for importing tables. See Figure 2–26.

Figure 2–26 Import Objects dialog box

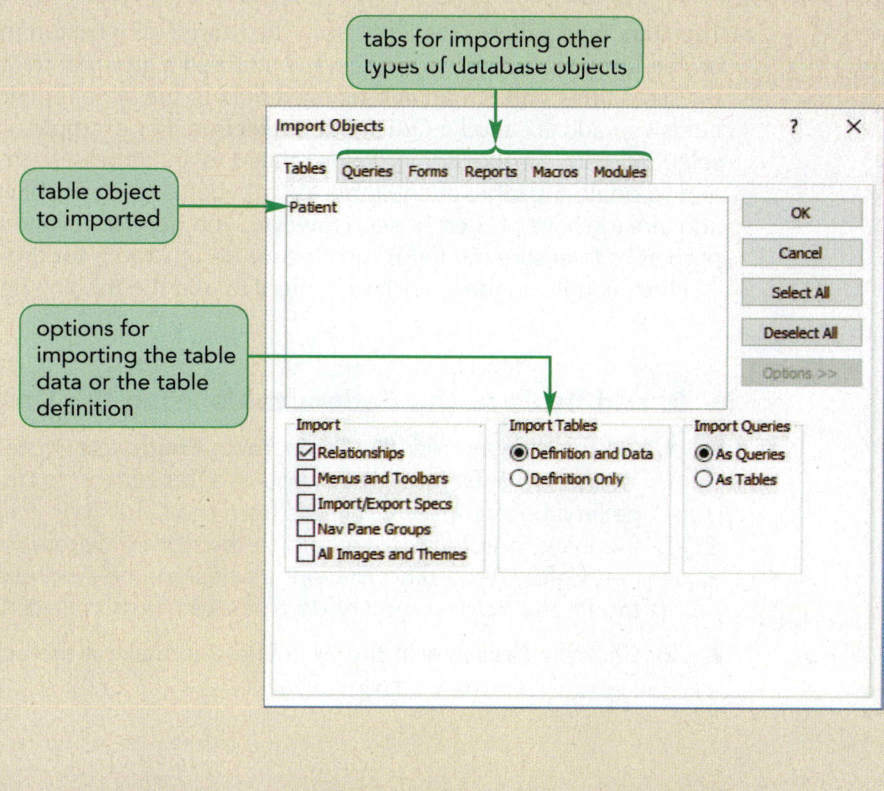

9. On the Tables tab, click **Patient** to select this table.
10. In the Import Tables section of the dialog box, click the **Definition Only** option button, and then click **OK**. Access creates the Patient table in the Lakewood database using the structure of the Patient table in the Support_AC_2_Taylor.accdb database, and opens a dialog box asking if you want to save the import steps.
11. Click **Close** to close the dialog box without saving the import steps.
12. Open the Navigation Pane, double-click **Patient** in the Tables section to open the table, and then close the Navigation Pane. The Patient table opens in Datasheet view. The table contains no records. See Figure 2–27.

Figure 2–27 **Imported Patient table in Datasheet view**

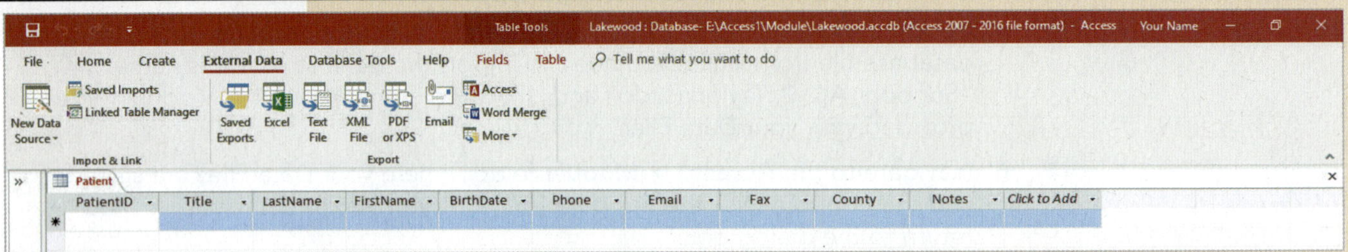

The table structure you imported contains some of the fields Donna wants, but not all (see Figure 2–25); it also contains some fields Donna does not want in the Patient table. You can add the missing fields using the Data Type gallery.

Adding Fields to a Table Using the Data Type Gallery

The **Data Type gallery**, available from the More Fields button in the Add & Delete group on the Table Tools Fields tab, allows you to add a group of related fields to a table at the same time, rather than adding each field to the table individually. The group of fields you add is called a **Quick Start selection**. For example, the **Address Quick Start selection** adds a collection of fields related to an address, such as Address, City, State, and so on, to the table at one time. When you use a Quick Start selection, the fields you add already have properties set. However, you need to review and possibly modify the properties to ensure the fields match your design needs for the database.

Next, you'll use the Data Type gallery to add the missing fields to the Patient table.

To add fields to the Patient table using the Data Type gallery:

1. On the ribbon, click the **Table Tools Fields** tab. Note the More Fields button in the Add & Delete group; you use this button to display the Data Type gallery. Before inserting fields from the Data Type gallery, you need to place the insertion point in the field to the right of where you want to insert the new fields. According to Donna's design, the Address field should come after the Phone field, so you need to make the next field, Email, the active field.

Make sure the correct field is active before adding new fields.

2. Click the **first row** in the Email field to make it the active field.

3. In the Add & Delete group, click the **More Fields** button. The Data Type gallery opens and displays options for types of fields you can add to your table.
4. Scroll down the gallery until the Quick Start section is visible. See Figure 2–28.

Figure 2–28 Patient table with the Data Type gallery displayed

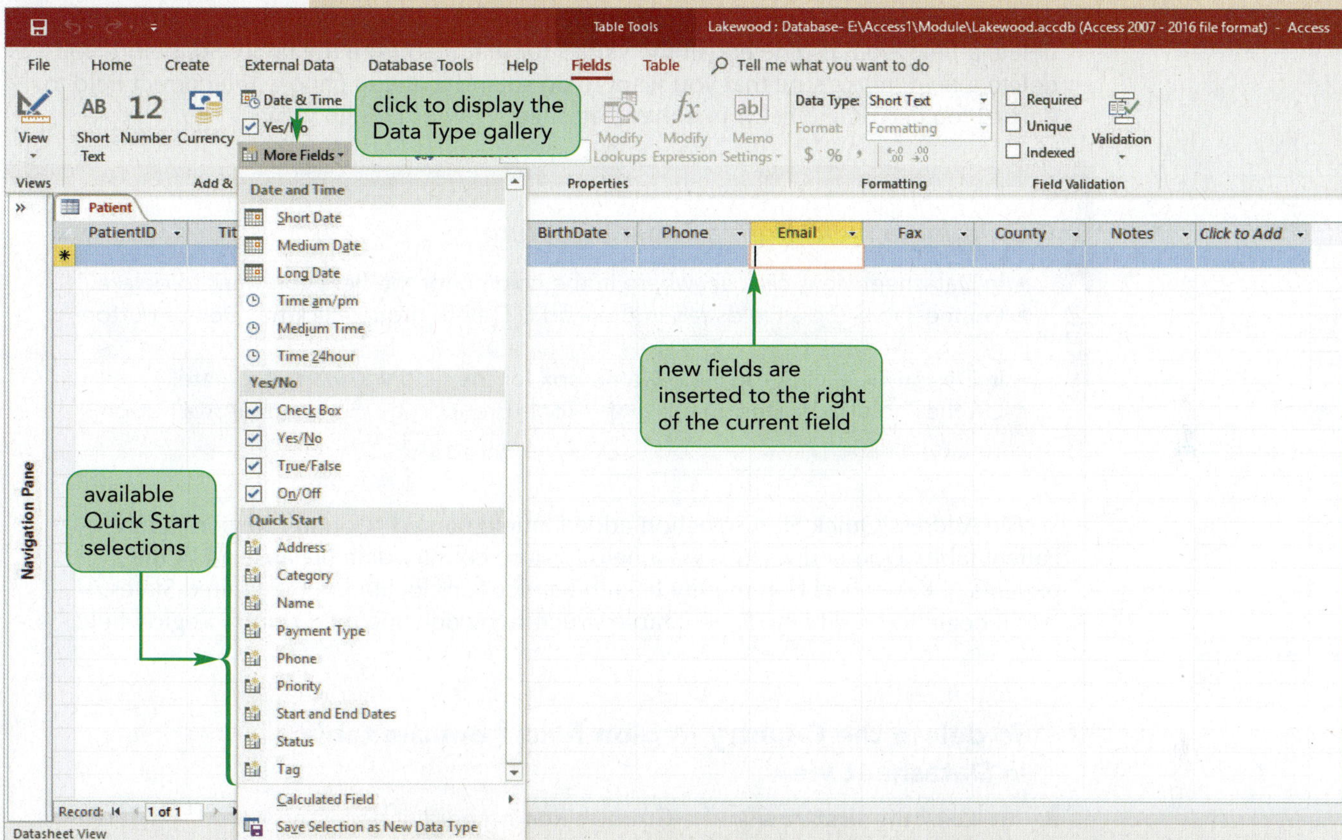

The Quick Start section provides options that add related fields to the table at one time. The new fields will be inserted to the right of the current field.

5. In the Quick Start section, click **Address**. Five fields are added to the table: Address, City, State Province, ZIP Postal, and Country Region. See Figure 2–29.

Figure 2–29 Patient table after adding fields from the Data Type gallery

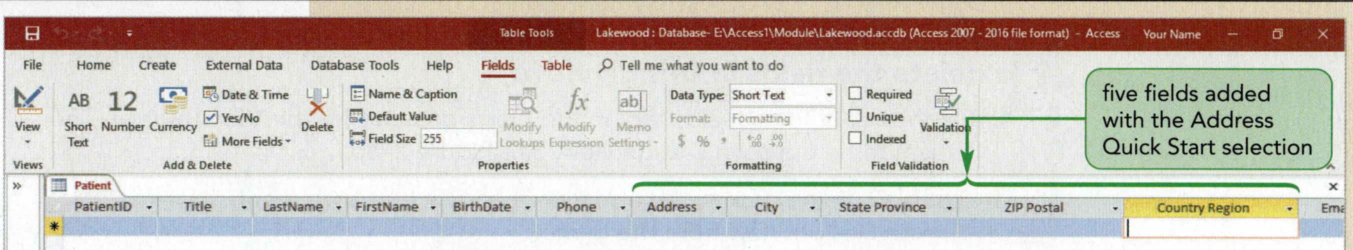

Modifying the Structure of an Imported Table

Refer back to Donna's design for the Patient table (Figure 2–25). To finalize the table design, you need to modify the imported table by deleting fields, renaming fields, and changing field data types. You'll begin by deleting fields.

Deleting Fields from a Table Structure

After you've created a table, you might need to delete one or more fields. When you delete a field, you also delete all the values for that field from the table. So, before you delete a field, make sure that you want to do so and that you choose the correct field to delete. You can delete fields in either Datasheet view or Design view.

REFERENCE

Deleting a Field from a Table Structure

- In Datasheet view, click anywhere in the column for the field you want to delete.
- On the Table Tools Fields tab in the Add & Delete group, click the Delete button.

or

- In Design view, click the Field Name box for the field you want to delete.
- On the Table Tools Design tab in the Tools group, click the Delete Rows button.

The Address Quick Start selection added a field named "Country Region" to the Patient table. Donna doesn't need a field to store country data because all of the patients of Lakewood Community Health Services are located in the United States. You'll begin to modify the Patient table structure by deleting the Country Region field.

To delete the Country Region field from the table in Datasheet view:

1. Click the **first row** in the Country Region field (if necessary).
2. On the Table Tools Fields tab, in the Add & Delete group, click the **Delete** button. The Country Region field is removed and the first field, PatientID, is now the active field.

You can also delete fields from a table structure in Design view. You'll switch to Design view to delete the other unnecessary fields.

To delete the fields in Design view:

1. On the Table Tools Fields tab, in the Views group, click the **View** button. The Patient table opens in Design view. See Figure 2–30.

   Trouble? If you clicked the arrow on the View button, a menu appears. Choose Design View from the menu.

Figure 2–30 Patient table in Design view

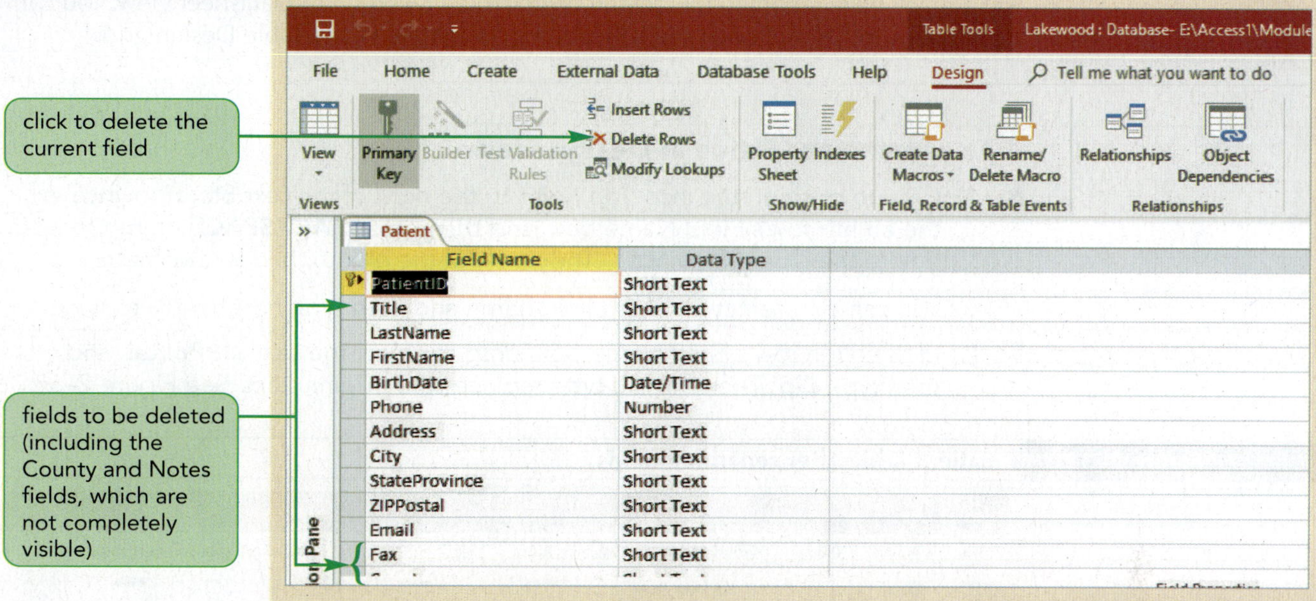

2. Click the **Title** Field Name box to make it the current field.
3. On the Table Tools Design tab, in the Tools group, click the **Delete Rows** button. The Title field is removed from the Patient table structure. You'll delete the Fax, County, and Notes fields next. Instead of deleting these fields individually, you'll select and delete them at the same time.
4. On the row selector for the **Fax** field, press and hold the mouse button and then drag the mouse to select the **County** and **Notes** fields.
5. Release the mouse button. The rows for the three fields are outlined in red, indicating all three fields are selected.

   You may not be able to see the Notes field; however, you can scroll down to view the selection.
6. In the Tools group, click the **Delete Rows** button. See Figure 2–31.

Figure 2–31 Patient table after deleting fields

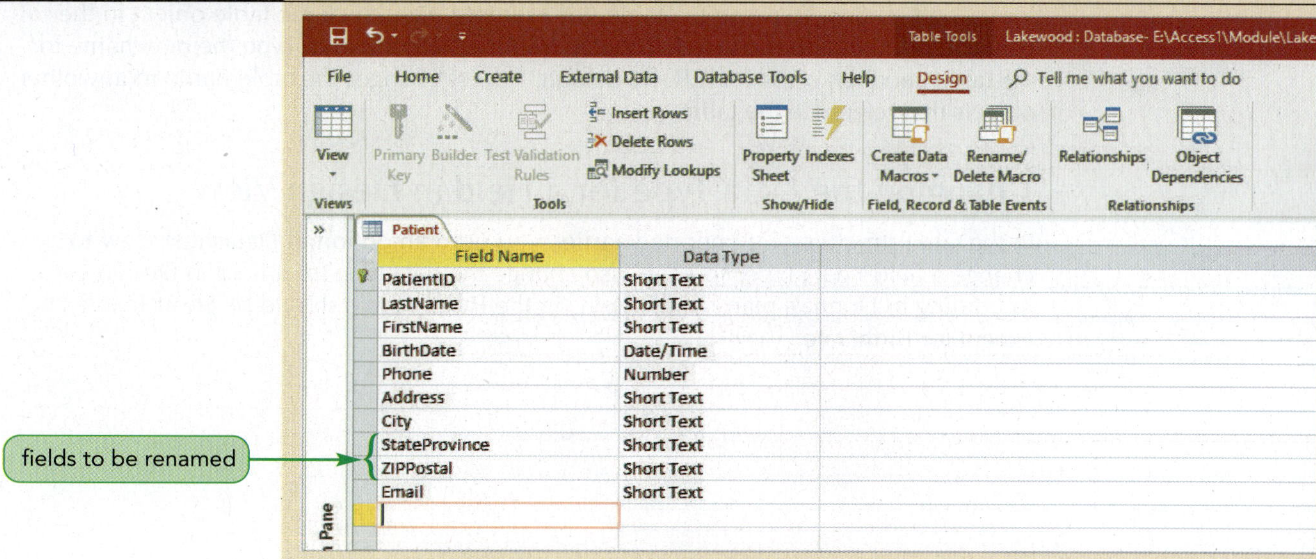

Renaming Fields in Design View

To match Donna's design for the Patient table, you need to rename some of the fields. You already have renamed the default primary key field (ID) in Datasheet view. You can also rename fields in Design view by editing the names in the Table Design grid.

To rename the fields in Design view:

1. Click to position the insertion point to the right of the text StateProvince in the eighth row's Field Name box, and then press **BACKSPACE** eight times to delete the word "Province." The name of the eighth field is now State.

   You can also select an entire field name and then type new text to replace it.

2. In the ninth row's Field Name box, drag to select the text **ZIPPostal**, and then type **Zip**. The text you type replaces the original text. See Figure 2–32.

Figure 2–32 Patient table after renaming fields

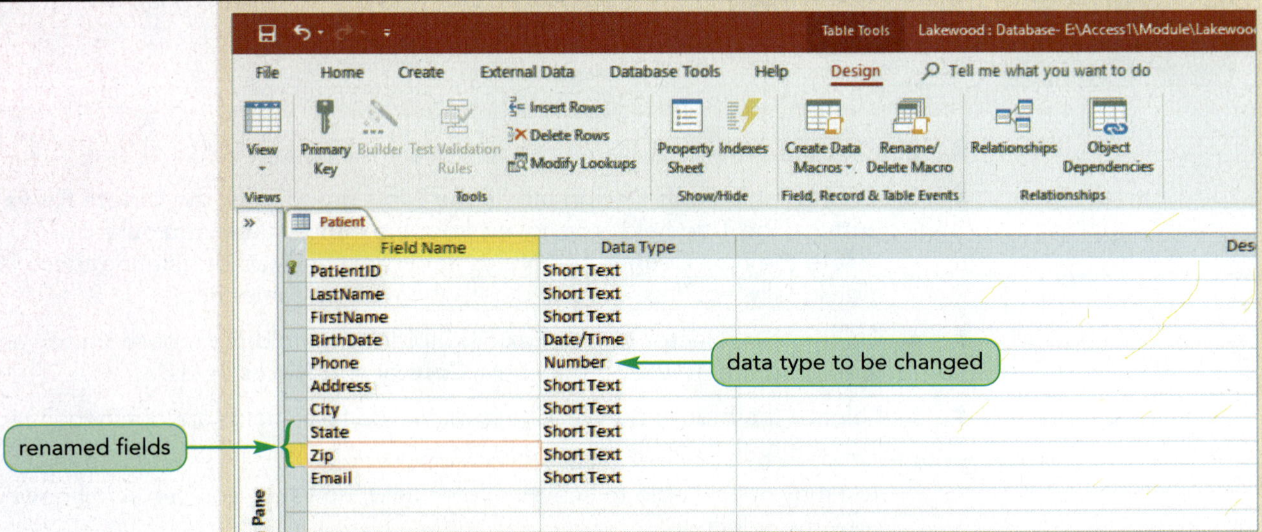

Besides renaming fields, you can rename Access objects such as tables, queries, forms, and reports. To rename a table, for example, right-click the table object in the Navigation Pane, and then click Rename on the shortcut menu. Type the new name for the table and then press ENTER. By default, Access changes the table name in any other objects that reference the table.

Changing the Data Type for a Field in Design View

In the table structure you imported earlier, you used an option in Datasheet view to change a field's data type. You can also change the data type for a field in Design view. According to Donna's plan, all the fields in the Patient table should be Short Text fields, except for BirthDate.

To change the data type of the Phone field in Design view:

1. Click the right side of the Data Type box for the Phone field to display the list of data types.
2. Click **Short Text** in the list. The Phone field is now a Short Text field. By default, the Field Size property is set to 255. According to Donna's plan, the Phone field should have a Field Size property of 14. You'll make this change next.
3. Press **F6** to move to and select the default Field Size property, and then type **14**.

Each of the remaining fields you added using the Address Quick Start selection—Address, City, State, and Zip—also has the default field size of 255. You need to change the Field Size property for these fields to match Donna's design. You'll also delete any Caption property values for these fields because the field names match how Donna wants them displayed, so captions are unnecessary.

To change the Field Size and Caption properties for the fields:

1. Click the **Address** Field Name box to make it the current field.
2. Press **F6** to move to and select the default Field Size property, and then type **35**. Because the Caption property setting for this field is the same as the field name, the field doesn't need a caption, so you can delete this value.
3. Press **TAB** three times to select Address in the Caption box, and then press **Delete**. The Caption property value is removed.
4. Repeat Steps 1 through 3 for the City field to change the Field Size property to **25** and delete its Caption property value.
5. Change the Field Size property for the State field to **2**, and then delete its Caption property value.
6. Change the Field Size property for the Zip field to **10**, and then delete its Caption property value.
7. On the Quick Access Toolbar, click the **Save** button to save your changes to the Patient table.

Finally, Donna would like you to set the Description property for the PatientID field and the Caption property for the PatientID, LastName, and FirstName fields. You'll make these changes now.

To enter the Description and Caption property values:

1. Click the **Description (Optional)** box for the PatientID field, and then type **Primary key**.
2. In the Field Properties pane, click the **Caption** box.
3. In the Caption box for the PatientID field, type **Patient ID**.
4. Click the **LastName** Field Name box to make it the current field, click the **Caption** box, and then type **Last Name**.

5. Click the **FirstName** Field Name box to make it the current field, click the **Caption** box, and then type **First Name**.
6. Click the **BirthDate** Field Name box to make it the current field, click the **Caption** box, and then type **Date of Birth**. See Figure 2–33.

Figure 2–33 **Patient table after entering descriptions and captions**

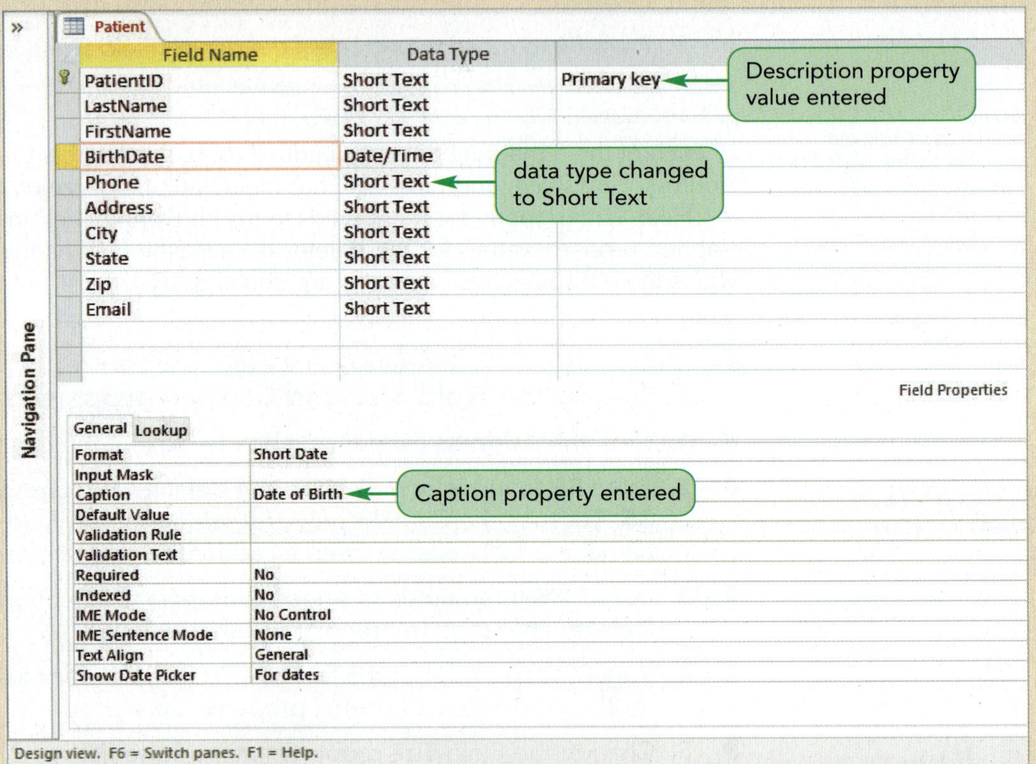

7. On the Quick Access Toolbar, click the **Save** button to save your changes to the Patient table.
8. On the Table Tools Design tab, in the Views group, click the **View** button to display the table in Datasheet view.
9. Resize each column to its best fit, and then click in the first row for the **Patient ID** column. See Figure 2–34.

Figure 2–34 **Modified Patient table in Datasheet view**

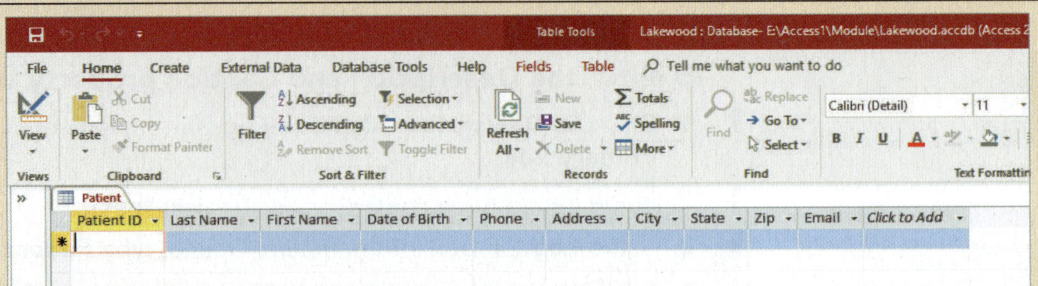

Donna mentions that data entry would be easier if the State field had the value of "GA" for each new record added to the table, because all of the patients live in Georgia. You can accomplish this by setting the Default Value property for the field.

Setting the Default Value Property for a Field

The **Default Value property** for a field specifies what value will appear, by default, for the field in each new record you add to a table.

Because all the patients at Lakewood Community Health Services live in Georgia, you'll specify a default value of "GA" for the State field in the Patient table. With this setting, each new record in the Patient table will have the correct State field value entered automatically.

To set the Default Value property for the State field:

1. In the Views group, click the **View** button to display the Patient table in Design view.
2. Click the **State** Field Name box to make it the current field.
3. In the Field Properties pane, click the **Default Value** box, type **GA**, and then press **TAB**. See Figure 2–35.

Figure 2–35 Specifying the Default Value property for the State field

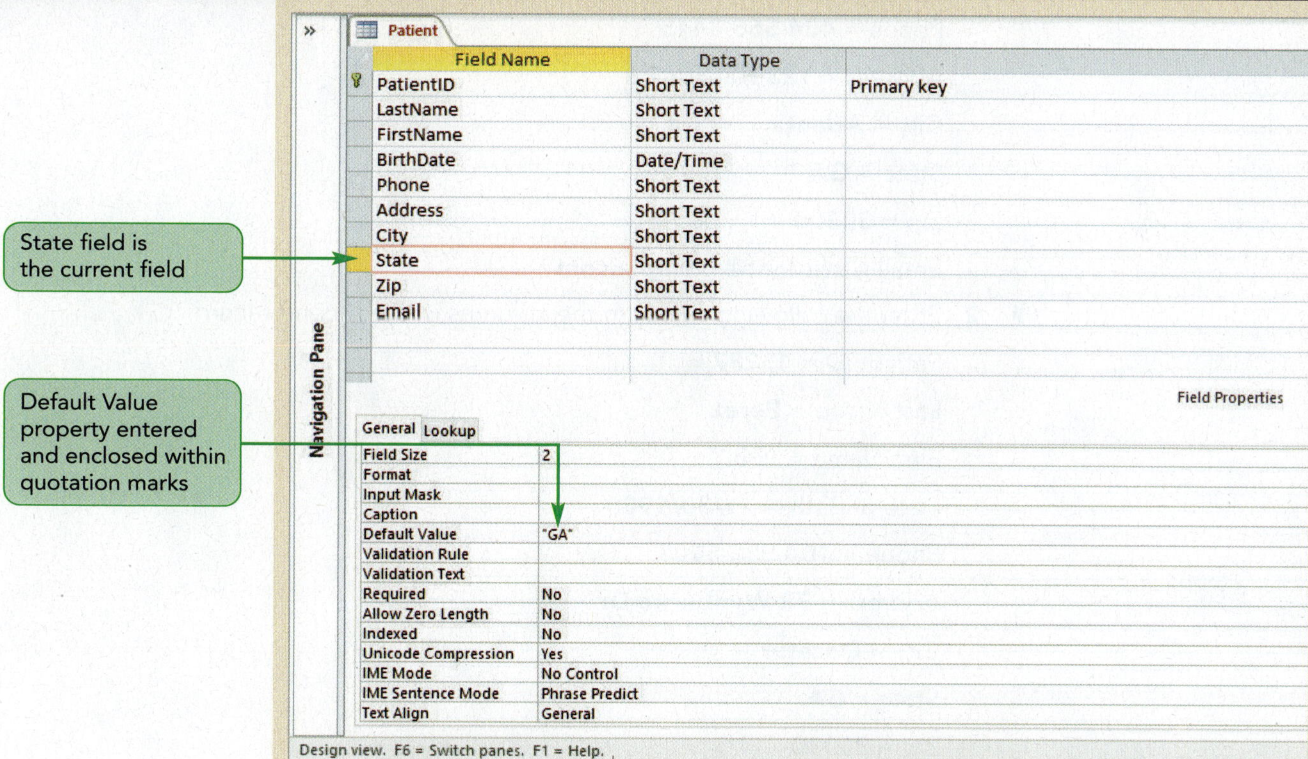

Note that a text entry in the Default Value property must be enclosed within quotation marks. If you do not type the quotation marks, Access adds them for you. However, for some entries, such as those that include punctuation, you would receive an error message indicating invalid syntax if you omitted the quotation marks. In such cases, you have to enter the quotation marks yourself.

4. On the Quick Access Toolbar, click the **Save** button to save your changes to the Patient table.

5. Display the table in Datasheet view. Note that the State field for the first row now displays the default value "GA" as specified by the Default Value property. Each new record entered in the table will automatically have this State field value entered.

TIP

You can change the value in a record from the default value to another value, if necessary.

With the Patient table design set, you can now enter records in it. You'll begin by entering two records in the datasheet, and then use a different method to add the remaining records.

To add two records to the Patient table:

Be sure to enter your last name and first name where indicated.

1. Enter the following values in the columns in the first record; press **TAB** to move past the default State field value:

   Patient ID = **13250**

   Last Name = **[student's last name]**

   First Name = **[student's first name]**

   Date of Birth = **4/9/1995**

   Phone = **404-555-8445**

   Address = **123 Harbor Rd**

   City = **Atlanta**

   State = **GA**

   Zip = **30303**

   Email = **student@example.com**

2. Enter the following values in the columns in the second record:

   Patient ID = **13287**

   Last Name = **Perez**

   First Name = **Luis**

   Date of Birth = **11/30/1988**

   Phone = **404-555-5903**

   Address = **78 Wynborne Dr**

   City = **Decatur**

   State = **GA**

   Zip = **30030**

   Email = **l.perez12@example.com**

3. Resize columns to their best fit, as necessary, and then save and close the Patient table.

Before Donna decided to store data using Access, Taylor managed the patient data for the clinic in a different system. She exported that data into a text file and now asks you to import it into the new Patient table. You can import the data contained in this text file to add the remaining records to the Patient table.

Adding Data to a Table by Importing a Text File

So far, you've learned how to add data to an Access table by importing an Excel spreadsheet, and you've created a new table by importing the structure of an existing table. You can also import data contained in text files.

To finish entering records in the Patient table, you'll import the data contained in Taylor's text file. The file is named "Support_AC_2_Patient.txt" and is located in the Access1 > Module folder provided with your Data Files.

To import the data contained in the Patient text file:

1. On the ribbon, click the **External Data** tab.
2. In the Import & Link group, click the **New Data Source** button.
3. In the New Data Source list, click the **From File** option. You may also point to the option.
4. In the From File list, click **Text File**. The Get External Data – Text File dialog box opens. This dialog box is similar to the one you used earlier when importing the Excel spreadsheet.
5. Click the **Browse** button. The File Open dialog box opens.
6. Navigate to the **Access1 > Module** folder, where your Data Files are stored, and then double-click the **Support_AC_2_Patient.txt** file. You return to the Get External Data – Text File dialog box.
7. Click the **Append a copy of the records to the table** option button. The box to the right of this option becomes active. Next, you need to select the table to which you want to add the data.
8. Click the arrow in the box, and then click **Patient**.
9. Click **OK**. The first Import Text Wizard dialog box opens. The dialog box indicates that the data to import is in a delimited format. In a **delimited text file**, fields of data are separated by a character such as a comma or a tab. In this case, the dialog box shows that data is separated by the comma character in the text file.
10. Make sure the **Delimited** option button is selected in the dialog box, and then click **Next**. The second Import Text Wizard dialog box opens. See Figure 2–36.

Figure 2–36 **Second Import Text Wizard dialog box**

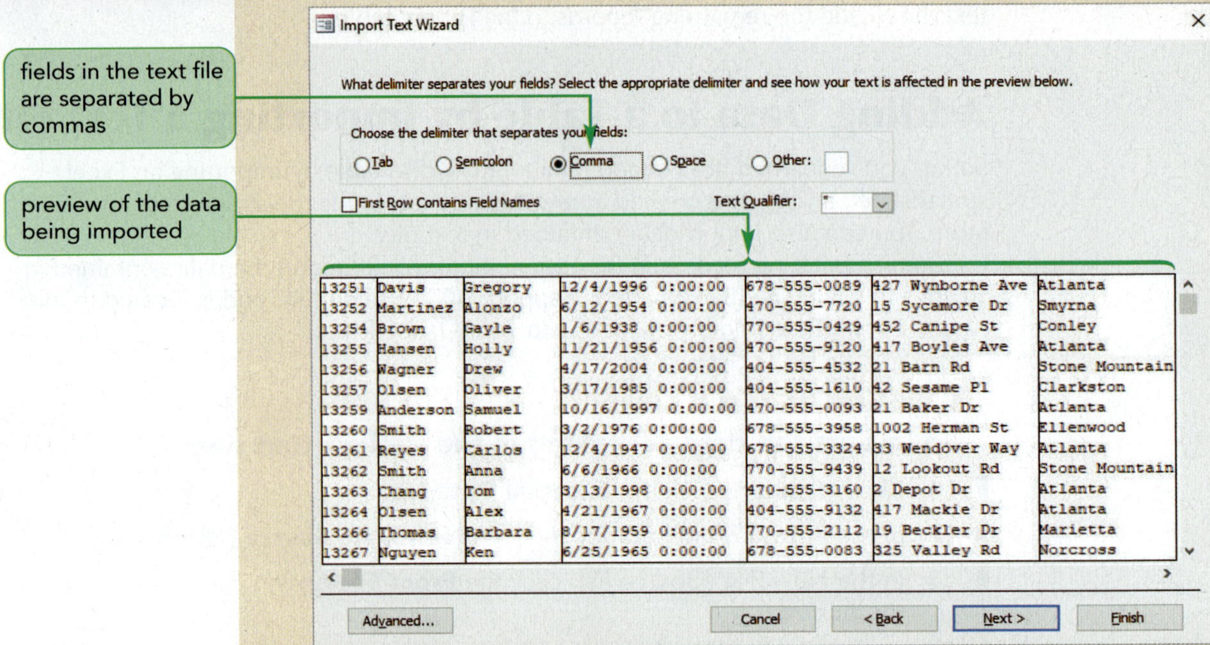

This dialog box asks you to confirm the delimiter character that separates the fields in the text file you're importing. Access detects that the comma character is used in the Patient text file and selects this option. The bottom area of the dialog box provides a preview of the data you're importing.

11. Make sure the **Comma** option button is selected, and then click **Next**. The third and final Import Text Wizard dialog box opens. The Import to Table box shows that the data will be imported into the Patient table.

12. Click **Finish**, and then click **Close** in the dialog box that opens to close it without saving the import steps.

Donna asks you to open the Patient table in Datasheet view so she can see the results of importing the text file.

To view the Patient table datasheet:

1. Open the Navigation Pane (if necessary), and then double-click **Patient** to open the Patient table in Datasheet view. The Patient table contains a total of 51 records.

2. Close the Navigation Pane, and then resize columns to their best fit, scrolling the table datasheet as necessary, so that all field values are displayed. Scroll back to display the first fields in the table, and then click the first row's **Patient ID** field, if necessary. See Figure 2–37.

Figure 2–37 **Patient table after importing data from the text file**

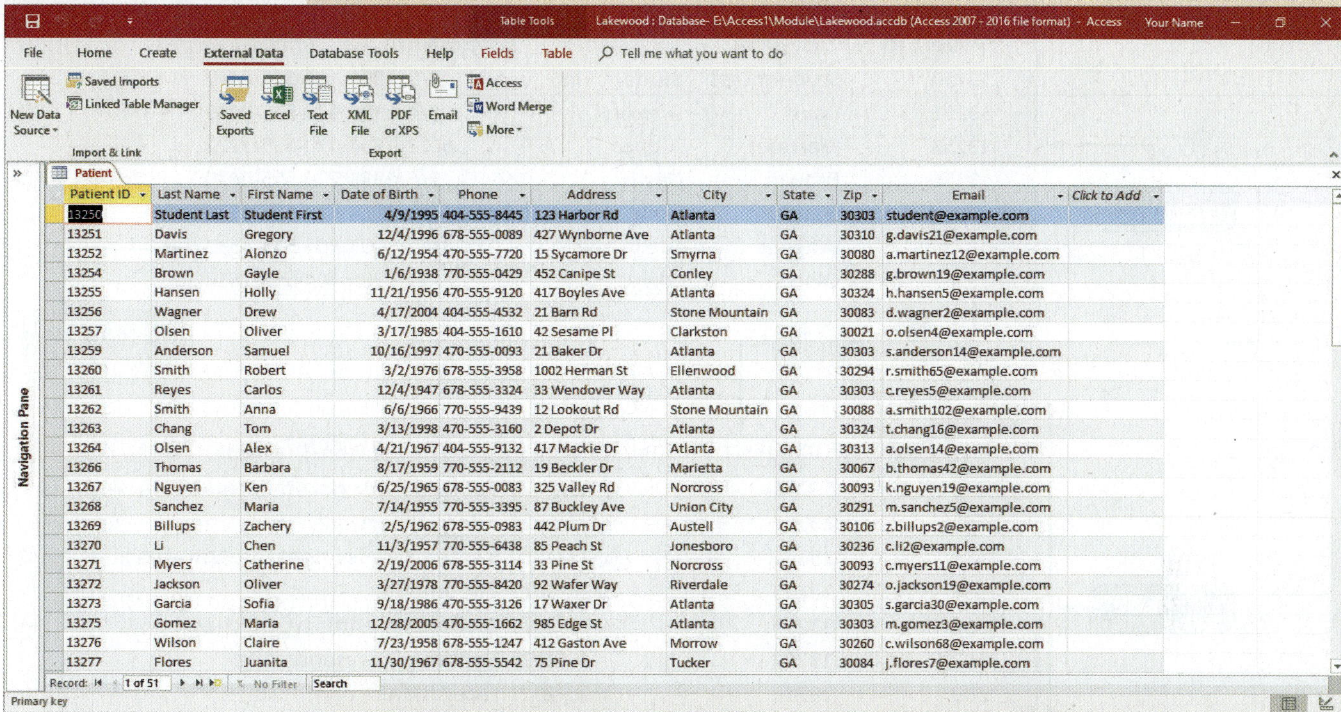

3. Save and close the Patient table, and then open the Navigation Pane.

The Lakewood database now contains three tables—Billing, Patient, and Visit—and the tables contain all the necessary records. Your final task is to complete the database design by defining the necessary relationship between its tables.

Defining Table Relationships

One of the most powerful features of a relational database management system is its ability to define relationships between tables. You use a common field to relate one table to another. The process of relating tables is often called performing a **join**. When you join tables that have a common field, you can extract data from them as if they were one larger table. For example, you can join the Patient and Visit tables by using the PatientID field in both tables as the common field. Then you can use a query, form, or report to extract selected data from each table, even though the data is contained in two separate tables, as shown in Figure 2–38. The PatientVisits query shown in Figure 2–38 includes the PatientID, LastName, and FirstName fields from the Patient table, and the VisitDate and Reason fields from the Visit table. The joining of records is based on the common field of PatientID. The Patient and Visit tables have a type of relationship called a one-to-many relationship.

Figure 2–38 One-to-many relationship and sample query

primary table

Patient

Patient ID	Last Name	First Name	Date of Birth	Phone
13250	Student Last	Student First	4/9/1995	404-555-8445
13251	Davis	Gregory	12/4/1996	678-555-0089
13252	Martinez	Alonzo	6/12/1954	470-555-7720
13254	Brown	Gayle	1/6/1938	770-555-0429
13255	Hansen	Holly	11/21/1956	470-555-9120
13256	Wagner	Drew	4/17/2004	404-555-4532
13257	Olsen	Oliver	3/17/1985	404-555-1610

common field

two visits for patient 13256

related table

Visit

Visit ID	Patient ID	Date of Visit	Reason/Diagnosis
1590	13256	3/19/2021	Spotted fever rickettsiosis
1593	13259	3/22/2021	Allergic reaction
1595	13275	3/24/2021	Wound care for right forearm abrasion
1596	13299	3/24/2021	Pneumonia
1598	13257	3/25/2021	Diabetes mellitis type 2 checkup
1602	13307	3/26/2021	Hypotension monitoring
1603	13286	3/26/2021	Laceration of right foot
1605	13268	3/26/2021	Cyst removal follow-up
1606	13256	3/26/2021	Spotted fever rickettsiosis follow-up
1608	13293	3/29/2021	Irritable bowel syndrome

query that joins fields from the Patient and Visit tables

fields from Patient table

fields from Visit table

PatientVisits

Patient ID	Last Name	First Name	Date of Visit	Reason/Diagnosis
13250	Student Last	Student First	11/3/2020	Dermatitis
13251	Davis	Gregory	11/16/2020	Dermatitis
13252	Martinez	Alonzo	3/17/2021	Annual wellness visit
13254	Brown	Gayle	11/4/2020	Annual wellness visit
13255	Hansen	Holly	1/8/2021	Annual wellness visit
13256	Wagner	Drew	3/19/2021	Spotted fever rickettsiosis
13256	Wagner	Drew	3/26/2021	Spotted fever rickettsiosis follow-up
13257	Olsen	Oliver	1/26/2021	Diabetes mellitis type 2 checkup

One-to-Many Relationships

As shown in the Session 2.2 Visual Overview, two tables have a one-to-many relationship when one record in the first table matches zero, one, or many records in the second table, and when one record in the second table matches at most one record in the first table. For example, as shown in Figure 2–38, patient 13256 has two visits in the Visit table. Other patients have one or more visits. Every visit has a single matching patient.

In Access, the two tables that form a relationship are referred to as the primary table and the related table. The primary table is the "one" table in a one-to-many relationship; in Figure 2–38, the Patient table is the primary table because there is only one patient for each visit. The related table is the "many" table; in Figure 2–38, the Visit table is the related table because a patient can have zero, one, or many visits.

Because related data is stored in two tables, inconsistencies between the tables can occur. Referring to Figure 2–38, consider the following three scenarios:

- Donna adds a record to the Visit table for a new patient, Edgar Faust, using Patient ID 13500. She did not first add the new patient's information to the Patient table, so this visit does not have a matching record in the Patient table. The data is inconsistent, and the visit record is considered to be an **orphaned record**.
- In another situation, Donna changes the PatientID in the Patient table for Drew Wagner from 13256 to 13510. Because the Patient table no longer has a patient with the PatientID 13256, this change creates two orphaned records in the Visit table, and the database is inconsistent.
- In a third scenario, Donna deletes the record for Drew Wagner, Patient 13256, from the Patient table because this patient has moved and no longer receives care from Lakewood. The database is again inconsistent; two records for Patient 13256 in the Visit table have no matching record in the Patient table.

You can avoid these types of problems and avoid having inconsistent data in your database by specifying referential integrity between tables when you define their relationships.

Referential Integrity

Referential integrity is a set of rules that Access enforces to maintain consistency between related tables when you update data in a database. Specifically, the referential integrity rules are as follows:

- When you add a record to a related table, a matching record must already exist in the primary table, thereby preventing the possibility of orphaned records.
- If you attempt to change the value of the primary key in the primary table, Access prevents this change if matching records exist in a related table. However, if you choose the **Cascade Update Related Fields option**, Access permits the change in value to the primary key and changes the appropriate foreign key values in the related table, thereby eliminating the possibility of inconsistent data.
- When you attempt to delete a record in the primary table, Access prevents the deletion if matching records exist in a related table. However, if you choose the **Cascade Delete Related Records option**, Access deletes the record in the primary table and also deletes all records in related tables that have matching foreign key values.

INSIGHT

Understanding the Cascade Delete Related Records Option

Although using the Cascade Delete Related Records option has some advantages for enforcing referential integrity, it presents risks as well. You should rarely select the Cascade Delete Related Records option because doing so might cause you to inadvertently delete records you did not intend to delete. It is best to use other methods that give you more control over deleting records.

Defining a Relationship Between Two Tables

When two tables have a common field, you can define a relationship between them in the Relationships window, as shown in the Session 2.2 Visual Overview. Next, you'll define a one-to-many relationship between the Patient and Visit tables, with Patient as the primary table and Visit as the related table, and with PatientID as the common field (the primary key in the Patient table and the foreign key in the Visit table). You'll also define a one-to-many relationship between the Visit and Billing tables, with Visit being the primary table and Billing being the related table, and with VisitID as the common field (the primary key in the Visit table and a foreign key in the Billing table).

To define the one-to-many relationship between the Patient and Visit tables:

1. On the ribbon, click the **Database Tools** tab.
2. In the Relationships group, click the **Relationships** button to display the Relationships window and then click the **Show Table** button to open the Show Table dialog box. See Figure 2–39.

Figure 2–39 Show Table dialog box

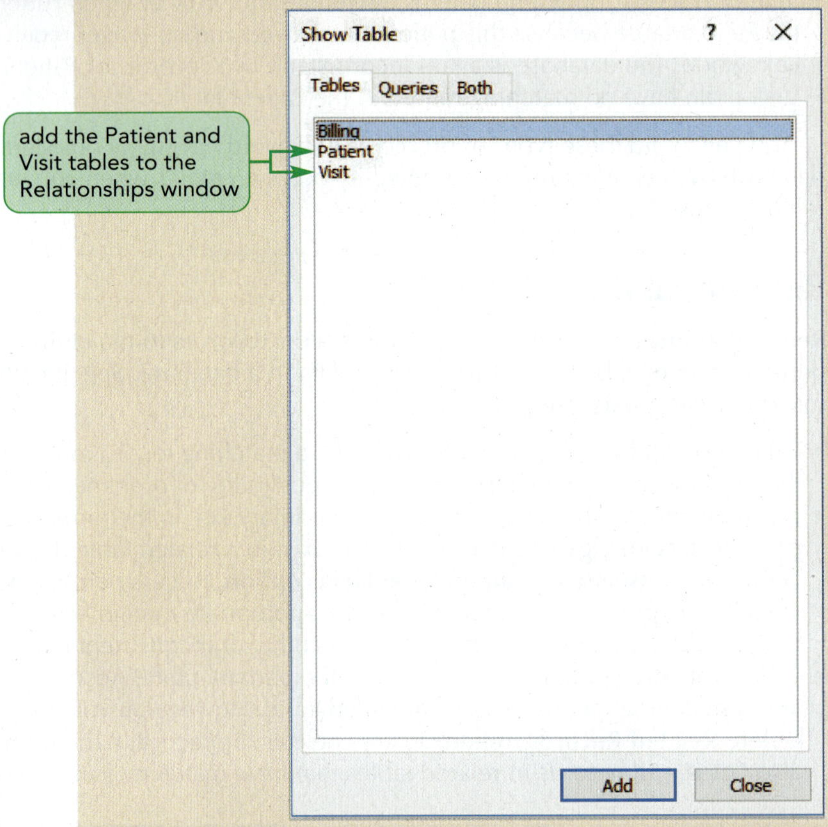

You must add each table participating in a relationship to the Relationships window. Because the Patient table is the primary table in the relationship, you'll add it first.

TIP

You can also double-click a table in the Show Table dialog box to add it to the Relationships window.

3. Click **Patient**, and then click the **Add** button. The Patient table's field list is added to the Relationships window.
4. Click **Visit**, and then click the **Add** button. The Visit table's field list is added to the Relationships window.
5. Click the **Close** button in the Show Table dialog box to close it.

   So that you can view all the fields and complete field names, you'll resize the Patient table field list.

6. Position the pointer on the bottom border of the Patient table field list until it changes to a two-headed arrow ↕, and then drag the bottom of the Patient table field list to lengthen it until the vertical scroll bar disappears and all the fields are visible.

   To form the relationship between the two tables, you drag the common PatientID field from the primary table to the related table. Access opens the Edit Relationships dialog box, in which you select the relationship options for the two tables.

7. Click **PatientID** in the Patient field list, and then drag it to **PatientID** in the Visit field list. When you release the mouse button, the Edit Relationships dialog box opens. See Figure 2–40.

Figure 2–40 **Edit Relationships dialog box**

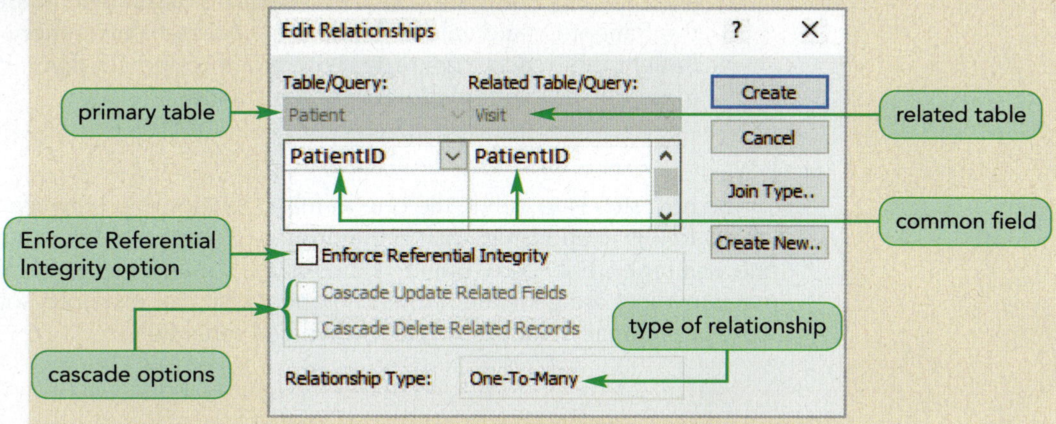

The primary table, related table, common field, and relationship type (One-To-Many) appear in the dialog box. Access correctly identifies the "One" side of the relationship and places the primary table Patient in the Table/Query section of the dialog box; similarly, Access correctly identifies the "Many" side of the relationship and places the related table Visit in the Related Table/Query section of the dialog box.

8. Click the **Enforce Referential Integrity** check box. The two cascade options become available. If you select the Cascade Update Related Fields option, Access will update the appropriate foreign key values in the related table when you change a primary key value in the primary table. You will *not* select the Cascade Delete Related Records option because doing so could cause you to delete records that you do not want to delete; this option is rarely selected.

9. Click the **Cascade Update Related Fields** check box.

10. Click the **Create** button to define the one-to-many relationship between the two tables and to close the dialog box. The completed relationship appears in the Relationships window, with the join line connecting the common field of PatientID in each table. See Figure 2–41.

Figure 2–41 **Defined relationship in the Relationships window**

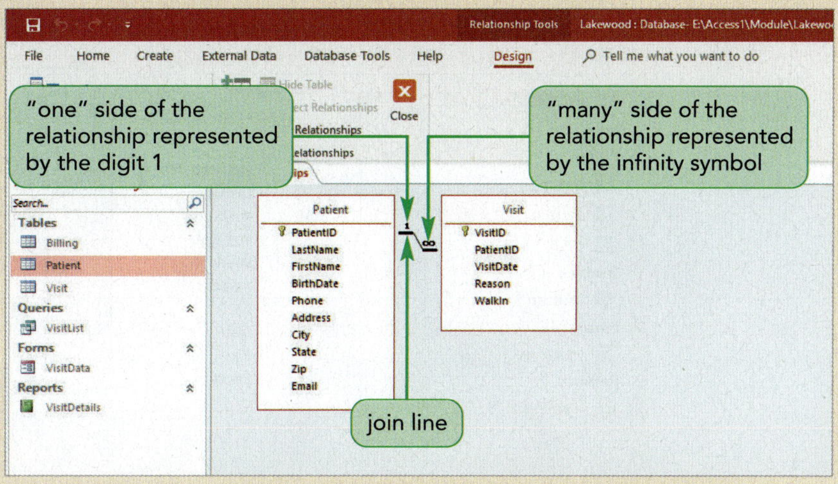

Trouble? If a dialog box opens indicating a problem that prevents you from creating the relationship, you most likely made a typing error when entering the two records in the Patient table. If so, click OK in the dialog box and then click Cancel in the Edit Relationships dialog box. Refer back to the earlier steps instructing you to enter the two records in the Patient table and carefully compare your entries with those shown in the text, especially the PatientID field values. Make any necessary corrections to the data in the Patient table, and then repeat Steps 7 through 10. If you still receive an error message, ask your instructor for assistance.

The next step is to define the one-to-many relationship between the Visit and Billing tables. In this relationship, Visit is the primary ("one") table because there is at most one visit for each invoice. Billing is the related ("many") table because zero, one, or many invoices are generated for each patient visit. For example, some visits require lab work or pharmacy charges, which is invoiced separately.

To define the relationship between the Visit and Billing tables:

1. On the Relationship Tools Design tab, in the Relationships group, click the **Show Table** button to open the Show Table dialog box.
2. Click **Billing** on the Tables tab, click the **Add** button, and then click the **Close** button to close the Show Table dialog box. The Billing table's field list appears in the Relationships window to the right of the Visit table's field list.
3. Click and drag the **VisitID** field in the Visit field list to the **VisitID** field in the Billing field list. The Edit Relationships dialog box opens.
4. In the Edit Relationships dialog box, click the **Enforce Referential Integrity** check box, click the **Cascade Update Related Fields** check box, and then click the **Create** button to define the one-to-many relationship between the two tables and to close the dialog box. The completed relationships for the Lakewood database appear in the Relationships window. See Figure 2–42.

TIP

You can also use the mouse to drag a table from the Navigation Pane to add it to the Relationships window.

Figure 2–42 Two relationships defined

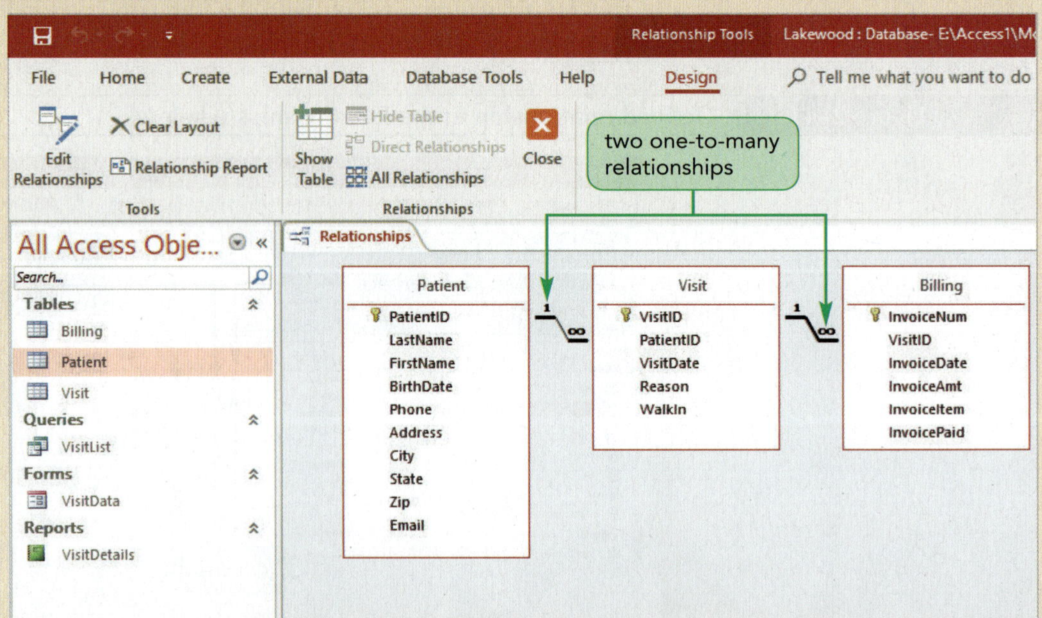

5. On the Quick Access Toolbar, click the **Save** button to save the layout in the Relationships window.
6. On the Relationship Tools Design tab, in the Relationships group, click the **Close** button to close the Relationships window.
7. sam Compact and repair the Lakewood database, and then close the database.

PROSKILLS

Problem Solving: Creating a Larger Database

The Lakewood database is a relatively small database containing only a few tables, and the data and the reports you will generate from it are fairly simple. A larger database would most likely have many more tables and different types of relationships that can be quite complex. When creating a large database, follow this standard process:

- Consult people who will be using the data to gain an understanding of how it will be used. Gather sample reports and representative data if possible.
- Plan the tables, fields, data types, other properties, and the relationships between the tables.
- Create the tables and define the relationships between them.
- Populate the tables with sample data.
- Design some queries, forms, and reports that will be needed, and then test them.
- Modify the database structure, if necessary, based on the results of your tests.
- Enter the actual data into the database tables.

Testing is critical at every stage of creating a database. Once the database is finalized and implemented, it's not actually finished. The design of a database evolves as new functionality is required and as the data that is gathered changes.

REVIEW

Session 2.2 Quick Check

1. What is the keyboard shortcut for inserting the value from the same field in the previous record into the current record?
2. _________ data is a process that allows you to copy the data from a source without having to open the source file.
3. The _________ gallery allows you to add a group of related fields to a table at the same time, rather than adding each field to the table individually.
4. What is the effect of deleting a field from a table structure?
5. A(n) _________ text file is one in which fields of data are separated by a character such as a comma or a tab.
6. The _________ is the "one" table in a one-to-many relationship, and the _________ is the "many" table in the relationship.
7. _________ is a set of rules that Access enforces to maintain consistency between related tables when you update data in a database.

PRACTICE

Review Assignments

Data File needed for the Review Assignments: Vendor.accdb (*cont. from Module 1*) and Support_AC_2_Products.xlsx

In addition to tracking information about the vendors Lakewood Community Health Services works with, Donna also wants to track information about their products and services. First, Donna asks you to modify the necessary properties in the Supplier table in the Vendor database. Afterwards, Donna wants you to modify the structure and properties of the Product table in the Vendor database. Finally, Donna would like you to create the relationship between the tables. Complete the following:

1. Open the **Vendor** database you created in the previous module.
2. Open the **Supplier** table in Design view, and set the field properties shown in Figure 2–43.

Figure 2–43 Field properties for the Supplier table

Field Name	Data Type	Description	Field Size	Other
SupplierID	Short Text	Primary key	6	Caption = Supplier ID
Company	Short Text		50	
Category	Short Text		15	
Address	Short Text		35	
City	Short Text		25	
State	Short Text		2	
Zip	Short Text		10	
Phone	Short Text		14	Caption = Contact Phone
ContactFirst	Short Text		20	Caption = Contact First Name
ContactLast	Short Text		25	Caption = Contact Last Name
InitialContact	Date/Time			Format = Short Date
				Caption = Initial Contact

3. Save the Supplier table. Click the **Yes** button when a message appears, indicating some data might be lost. Switch to Datasheet view and resize columns, as necessary, to their best fit. Then save and close the Supplier table.
4. Open the **Product** table in Design view, and then set the field properties as shown in Figure 2–44.

Figure 2–44 Design for the Product table

Field Name	Data Type	Description	Field Size	Other
ProductID	Short Text	Primary key	5	Caption = Product ID
SupplierID	Short Text	Foreign key	6	Caption = Supplier ID
ProductName	Short Text		75	Caption = Product Name
Price	Currency			Format = Standard
				Decimal Places = 2
TempControl	Yes/No			Caption = Temp Controlled?
Sterile	Yes/No			Caption = Sterile?
Units	Number		Integer	Decimal Places = 0
				Caption = Units/Case
				Default Value = [no entry]

5. Modify the Product table structure by adding a new field between the Price and TempControl fields. Name the new field **Weight** (data type: **Number**; field size: **Single**; Decimal Places: **2**; Caption: **Weight in Lbs**; Default Value: [no entry]). Move the **Units** field between the Price and Weight fields.
6. In Datasheet view, resize the columns so all column headings are completely visible and then save the changes to the Product table.
7. Enter the records shown in Figure 2–45 in the Product table. Resize all datasheet columns to their best fit again. When finished, save and close the Product table.

Figure 2–45 **Records for the Product table**

Product ID	Supplier ID	Product Name	Price	Units/Case	Weight in Lbs	Temp Controlled?	Sterile?
TH930	GON470	Digital thermometer	35.00	1	1	Yes	No
EG397	TUR005	Non-latex exam gloves	5.50	100	2	No	No

8. Use the Import Spreadsheet Wizard to add data to the Product table. The data you need to import is contained in the Support_AC_2_Products.xlsx workbook, which is an Excel file located in the Access1 > Review folder provided with your Data Files.
   a. Specify the Support_AC_2_Products.xlsx workbook as the source of the data.
   b. Select the option for appending the data.
   c. Select Product as the table.
   d. In the Import Spreadsheet Wizard dialog boxes, make sure Access confirms that the first row contains column headings, and import to the Product table. Do not save the import steps.
9. Open the **Product** table in Datasheet view, and resize columns to their best fit, as necessary. Then save and close the Product table.
10. Define a one-to-many relationship between the primary Supplier table and the related Product table. Resize the table field lists so that all field names are visible. Select the referential integrity option and the cascade updates option for the relationship.
11. Save the changes to the Relationships window and close it, compact and repair the Vendor database, and then close the database.

APPLY

Case Problem 1

Data Files needed for this Case Problem: Career.accdb *(cont. from Module 1)*, **Support_AC_2_Course.txt, and Support_AC_2_Registration.xlsx**

Great Giraffe Jeremiah wants you to further refine the design of the existing tables (Student and Registration) in the Career database by modifying the field properties. Jeremiah would also like you to populate the Course and Registration tables. Complete the following:

1. Open the **Career** database you created in the previous module.
2. Open the **Student** table in Design view, and set the field properties shown in Figure 2–46.

Figure 2–46 **Field properties for the Student table**

Field Name	Data Type	Description	Field Size	Other
StudentID	Short Text	Primary key	7	Caption = Student ID
FirstName	Short Text		20	Caption = First Name
LastName	Short Text		25	Caption = Last Name
Address	Short Text		35	
City	Short Text		25	
State	Short Text		2	
Zip	Short Text		10	
Phone	Short Text		14	
Email	Short Text		50	
BirthDate	Date/Time			Format = Short Date Caption = Birth Date
Assessment	Yes/No			Default Value = No

3. Save the Student table. Click the **Yes** button when a message appears, indicating some data might be lost. Switch to Datasheet view and resize columns, as necessary, to their best fit. Then save and close the Student table.
4. Open the **Registration** table in Design view, and set the field properties as shown in the Figure 2–47.

Figure 2–47 **Field properties for the Registration table**

Field Name	Data Type	Description	Field Size	Other
SignupID	Short Text	Primary key	10	Caption = Signup ID
StudentID	Short Text	Foreign key	7	Caption = Student ID
InstanceID	Short Text	Foreign key	10	Caption = Instance ID
TotalCost	Currency			Format = Currency Decimal Places = 2 Caption = Total Cost Default Value = 0
BalanceDue	Currency			Format = Currency Decimal Places = 2 Caption = Balance Due Default Value = 0
PaymentPlan	Yes/No			Caption = Payment Plan Default Value = No

5. Switch to Datasheet view and resize columns, as necessary, to their best fit. Then save and close the Registration table.
6. Use the Import Spreadsheet Wizard to add data to the Registration table. The data you need to import is contained in the Support_AC_2_Registration.xlsx workbook, which is an Excel file located in the Access1 > Case1 folder provided with your Data Files.
   a. Specify the Support_AC_2_Registration.xlsx workbook as the source of the data.
   b. Select the option for appending the data.
   c. Select Registration as the table.
   d. In the Import Spreadsheet Wizard dialog boxes, make sure Access confirms that the first row contains column headings, and import to the Registration table. Do not save the import steps.

7. Open the **Registration** table in Datasheet view and resize columns to their best fit, as necessary. Then save and close the Registration table.
8. Create a new table in Design view, using the table design shown in Figure 2–48.

Figure 2–48 Field properties for the Course table

Field Name	Data Type	Description	Field Size	Other
InstanceID	Short Text	Primary key	10	Caption = Instance ID
StartDate	Date/Time	Date course begins		Format = Short Date Caption = Start Date
EndDate	Date/Time	Date course ends		Format = Short Date Caption = End Date
HoursPerWeek	Number		Integer	Decimal Places = 0 Caption = Hours Per Week Default Value = 40
Cost	Currency			Format = Currency Decimal Places = 0

9. Specify **InstanceID** as the primary key, and then save the table as **Course**.
10. Insert a new field named **Title** between the InstanceID and StartDate fields. The Title field is of the **Short Text** data type and has a field size of **25**. Save the changes to the Course table and close the table.
11. Use the Import Text File Wizard to add data to the Course table. The data you need to import is contained in the Support_AC_2_Course.txt text file, which is located in the Access1 > Case1 folder provided with your Data Files.
    a. Specify the Support_AC_2_Course.txt text file as the source of the data.
    b. Select the option for appending the data.
    c. Select Course as the table.
    d. In the Import Text File Wizard dialog boxes, choose the options to import delimited data, to use a comma delimiter, and to import the data into the Course table. Do not save the import steps.
12. Open the **Course** table in Datasheet view and resize columns to their best fit, as necessary. Then save and close the Course table.
13. Define a one-to-many relationship between the primary Student table and the related Registration table. Resize the Student table field list so that all field names are visible. Select the referential integrity option and the cascade updates option for this relationship.
14. Define a one-to-many relationship between the primary Course table and the related Registration table. Select the referential integrity option and the cascade updates option for this relationship. (*Hint*: The Registration table is positioned between the Student and Courses tables in the Relationships window.)
15. Save the changes to the Relationships window and close it, compact and repair the Career database, and then close the database.

CHALLENGE

Case Problem 2

Data Files needed for this Case Problem: DrainAdopter.accdb *(cont. from Module 1)*, **Support_AC_2_Drain.xlsx, and Support_AC_2_Supplies.xlsx**

Drain Adopter Tandrea wants you to further refine the design of the existing tables (Drain and Volunteer) in the DrainAdopter database by modifying the existing properties. Tandrea asks you to populate the Drain table. Finally, Tandrea would like you to create and populate a new table that will contain information on supplies needed for projects. Complete the following:

1. Open the **DrainAdopter** database you created in the previous module.
2. Open the **Volunteer** table in Design view, and set the field properties as shown in Figure 2–49.

Figure 2–49 **Field properties for the Volunteer table**

Field Name	Data Type	Description	Field Size	Other
VolunteerID	Short Text	Primary key	7	Caption = Volunteer ID
FirstName	Short Text		20	Caption = First Name
LastName	Short Text		25	Caption = Last Name
Street	Short Text		35	
City	Short Text		25	
State	Short Text		2	
Zip	Short Text		10	
Phone	Short Text		14	
Email	Short Text		50	
SignupDate	Date/Time			Format = Short Date Caption = Signup Date
Trained	Yes/No			Default Value = No

3. Save and close the Volunteer table. Click the Yes button when a message appears, indicating some data might be lost.
4. Open the **Drain** table in Design view, and set the field properties shown in Figure 2–50.

Figure 2–50 **Field properties for the Drain table**

Field Name	Data Type	Description	Field Size	Other
DrainID	Short Text	Primary key	7	Caption = Drain ID
MainStreet	Short Text		25	Caption = Main Street
CrossStreet	Short Text		20	Caption = Cross Street
Direction	Short Text		2	
VolunteerID	Short Text	Foreign key	7	Caption = Volunteer ID
MaintReq	Yes/No			Caption = Maint Req Default Value = No

5. Switch to Datasheet view and resize columns, as necessary, to their best fit. Then save and close the Drain table.

6. Use the Import Spreadsheet Wizard to add data to the Drain table. The data you need to import is contained in the Support_AC_2_Drain.xlsx workbook, which is an Excel file located in the Access1 > Case2 folder provided with your Data Files.
   a. Specify the Support_AC_2_Drain.xslx workbook as the source of the data.
   b. Select the option for appending the data.
   c. Select Drain as the table.
   d. In the Import Spreadsheet Wizard dialog boxes, make sure Access confirms that the first row contains column headings, and import to the Drain table. Do not save the import steps.
7. Open the **Drain** table in Datasheet view and resize columns to their best fit, as necessary. Then save and close the Drain table.

Explore 8. Use the Import Spreadsheet Wizard to create a new table in the DrainAdopter database. As the source of the data, specify the Support_AC_2_Supplies.xlsx workbook, which is located in the Access1 > Case2 folder provided with your Data Files. Select the option to import the source data into a new table in the database.

Explore 9. Complete the Import Spreadsheet Wizard dialog boxes as follows:
   a. Select Support_AC_2_Supplies.xlsx as the worksheet you want to import.
   b. Specify that the first row contains column headings.
   c. Accept the field options suggested by the wizard, and do not skip any fields.
   d. Choose SupplyID as your primary key.
   e. Import the data to a table named Supply, and do not save the import steps.

10. Open the **Supply** table in Design view, and then modify the table so it matches the design shown in Figure 2–51, including changes to data types and field properties. For the Short Text fields, delete any formats specified in the Format property boxes.

Figure 2–51 **Field properties for the Supply table**

Field Name	Data Type	Description	Field Size	Other
SupplyID	Short Text	Primary key	12	Caption = Supply ID
Description	Short Text		30	
Cost	Currency			Format = Currency
				Decimal Places = 2
NumberOnHand	Number		Double	Caption = Number On Hand
				Format = Standard
				Decimal Places = 2
				Default Value = 0
LastOrderDate	Date/Time			Format = Short Date
				Caption = Last Order Date

11. Save your changes to the Supply table design, click Yes for the message about lost data, and then switch to Datasheet view.
12. Resize the columns in the Supply datasheet to their best fit. Then save the Supply table.

Explore 13. Tandrea realizes that the values in the NumberOnHand column would never need two decimal places. Make this field the current field in the datasheet. Then, on the Table Tools Fields tab, in the Formatting group, use the Decrease Decimals button to remove the two decimal places and the period from these values. Switch back to Design view, and note that the Decimal Places property for the NumberOnHand field is now set to 0.

14. Save and close the Supply table.
15. Define a one-to-many relationship between the primary Volunteer table and the related Drain table. Select the referential integrity option and the cascade updates option for this relationship.
16. Save the changes to the Relationships window and close it, compact and repair the DrainAdopter database, and then close the database.

MODULE 3

Maintaining and Querying a Database

Updating and Retrieving Information About Patients, Visits, and Invoices

OBJECTIVES

Session 3.1

- Find, modify, and delete records in a table
- Hide and unhide fields in a datasheet
- Work in the Query window in Design view
- Create, run, and save queries
- Update data using a query datasheet
- Create a query based on multiple tables
- Sort data in a query
- Filter data in a query

Session 3.2

- Specify an exact match condition in a query
- Use a comparison operator in a query to match a range of values
- Use the And and Or logical operators in queries
- Change the font size and alternate row color in a datasheet
- Create and format a calculated field in a query
- Perform calculations in a query using aggregate functions and record group calculations
- Change the display of database objects in the Navigation Pane

Case | *Lakewood Community Health Services*

At a recent meeting, Donna Taylor and her staff discussed the importance of maintaining accurate information about the clinic's patients, visits, and invoices, and regularly monitoring the business activities of Lakewood Community Health Services. For example, Taylor Bailey, Donna's assistant, needs to make sure she has up-to-date contact information, such as phone numbers and email addresses, for all the clinic's patients. The office staff also must monitor billing activity to ensure that invoices are paid on time and in full. In addition, the staff handles marketing efforts for the clinic and tracks services provided to develop new strategies for promoting these services. Donna is also interested in analyzing other aspects of the business related to patient visits and finances. You can satisfy all these informational needs for Lakewood Community Health Services by updating data in the Lakewood database and by creating and using queries that retrieve information from the database.

STARTING DATA FILES

Access1 →

Module
Lakewood.accdb (cont.)

Review
Vendor.accdb (cont.)

Case1
Career.accdb (cont.)

Case2
DrainAdopter.accdb (cont.)

Session 3.1 Visual Overview:

When you are constructing a query, you can see the results at any time by clicking the View button or the Run button. In response, Access displays the query datasheet, which contains the set of fields and records that results from answering, or **running**, the query.

The top portion of the Query window in Design view contains the field list (or lists) for the table(s) used in the query.

The default query name, Query1, is displayed on the tab for the query. You change the default query name to a more meaningful one when you save the query.

The bottom portion of the Query window in Design view contains the design grid. In the **design grid**, you include the fields and record selection criteria for the information you want to see.

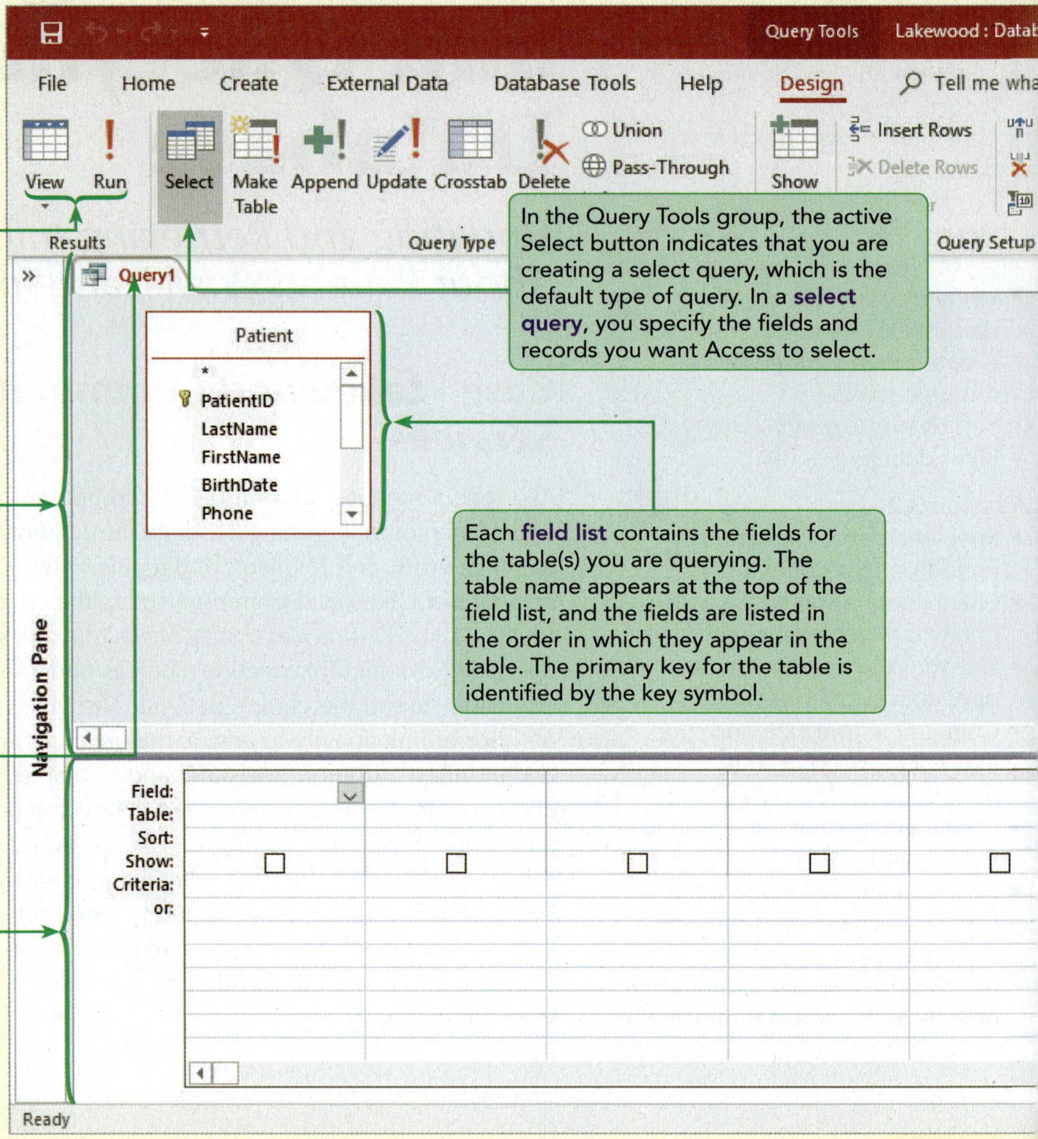

In the Query Tools group, the active Select button indicates that you are creating a select query, which is the default type of query. In a **select query**, you specify the fields and records you want Access to select.

Each **field list** contains the fields for the table(s) you are querying. The table name appears at the top of the field list, and the fields are listed in the order in which they appear in the table. The primary key for the table is identified by the key symbol.

Query Window in Design View

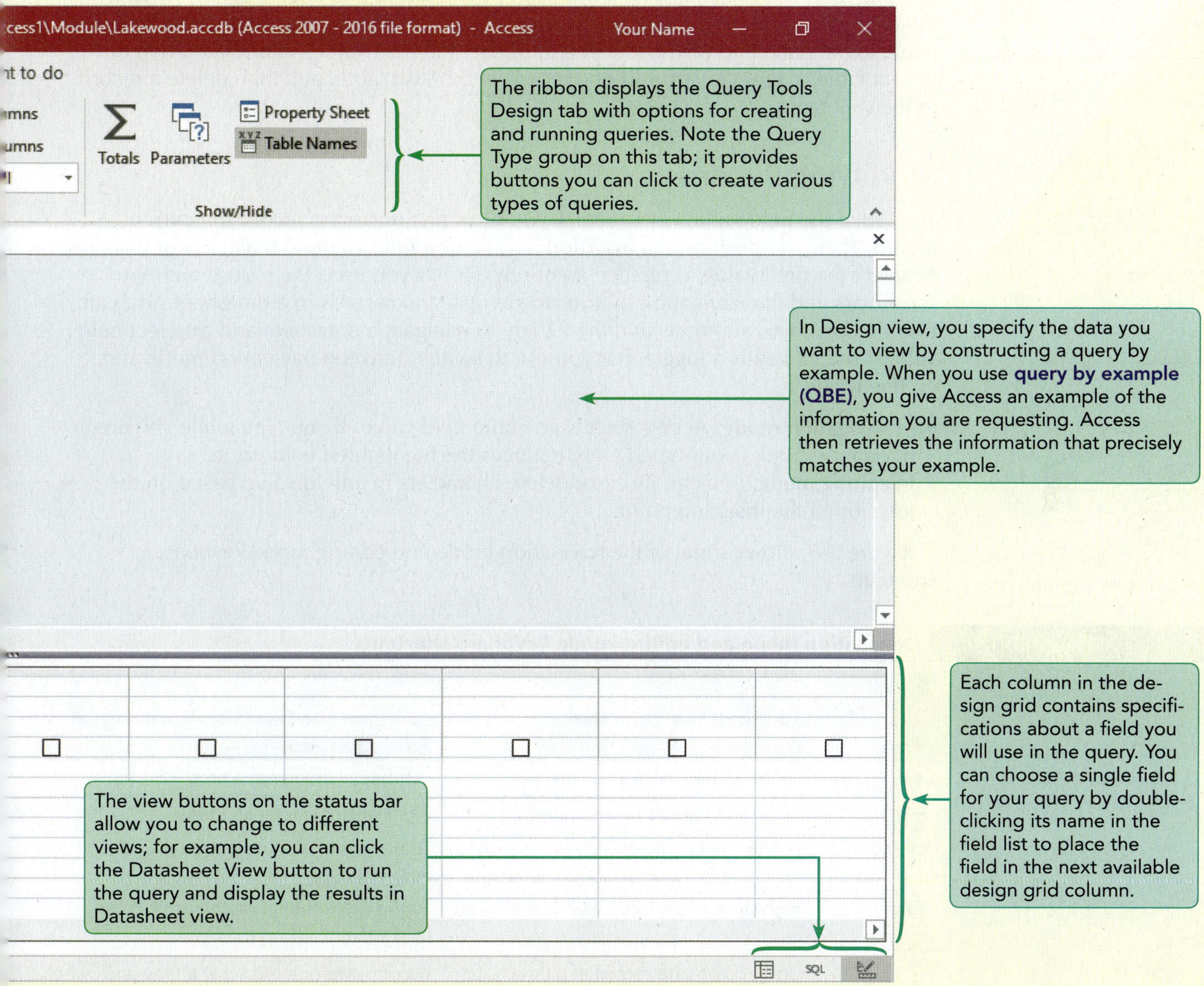

Updating a Database

Updating, or **maintaining**, a database is the process of adding, modifying, and deleting records in database tables to keep them current and accurate. After reviewing the data in the Lakewood database, Taylor identified some changes that need to be made to the data. She would like you to update the field values in one record in the Patient table, correct an error in one record in the Visit table, and then delete a record in the Visit table.

Modifying Records

To modify the field values in a record, you must first make the record the current record. Then you position the insertion point in the field value to make minor changes or select the field value to replace it entirely. Earlier you used the mouse with the scroll bars and the navigation buttons to navigate the records in a datasheet. You can also use keyboard shortcuts and the F2 key to navigate a datasheet and to select field values. The **F2 key** is a toggle that you use to switch between navigation mode and editing mode.

- In **navigation mode**, Access selects an entire field value. If you type while you are in navigation mode, your typed entry replaces the highlighted field value.
- In **editing mode**, you can insert or delete characters in a field value based on the location of the insertion point.

Figure 3–1 shows some of the navigation mode and editing mode keyboard shortcuts.

Figure 3–1 **Navigation mode and editing mode keyboard shortcuts**

Press	To Move the Selection in Navigation Mode	To Move the Insertion Point in Editing Mode
←	Left one field value at a time	Left one character at a time
→	Right one field value at a time	Right one character at a time
Home	Left to the first field value in the record	To the left of the first character in the field value
End	Right to the last field value in the record	To the right of the last character in the field value
↑ or ↓	Up or down one record at a time	Up or down one record at a time and switch to navigation mode
Tab or Enter	Right one field value at a time	Right one field value at a time and switch to navigation mode
Ctrl + Home	To the first field value in the first record	To the left of the first character in the field value
Ctrl + End	To the last field value in the last record	To the right of the last character in the field value

The Patient table record Taylor wants you to change is for 13309. This patient recently moved to another location in Atlanta and his zip code also changed, so you need to update the Patient table record with the new street address and zip code.

To open the Patient table in the Lakewood database:

1. **sam** Start Access and open the Lakewood database you created and worked with earlier.

   Trouble? If the security warning is displayed below the ribbon, click the Enable Content button.

2. Open the **Patient** table in Datasheet view.

The Patient table contains many fields. Sometimes, when updating data in a table, it can be helpful to remove the display of some fields on the screen.

Hiding and Unhiding Fields

TIP

Hiding a field removes it from the datasheet display only; the field and its contents are still part of the table.

When you are viewing a table or query datasheet in Datasheet view, you might want to temporarily remove certain fields from the displayed datasheet, making it easier to focus on the data you're interested in viewing. The **Hide Fields** command allows you to remove the display of one or more fields, and the **Unhide Fields** command allows you to redisplay any hidden fields.

To make it easier to modify the patient record, you'll first hide a couple of fields in the Patient table.

To hide fields in the Patient table and modify the patient record:

1. Right-click the **Date of Birth** field name to display the shortcut menu, and then click **Hide Fields**. The Date of Birth column is removed from the datasheet display.
2. Right-click the **Phone** field name, and then click **Hide Fields** on the shortcut menu. The Phone column is removed from the datasheet display.

   With the fields hidden, you can now update the patient record. The record you need to modify is near the end of the table and has a PatientID field value of 13309.

3. Scroll the datasheet until you see the last record in the table.
4. Click the PatientID field value **13309**, for Jose Rodriguez. The insertion point appears within the field value, indicating you are in editing mode.
5. Press **TAB** to move to the Last Name field value, Rodriguez. The field value is selected, indicating you are in navigation mode.
6. Press **TAB** two times to move to the Address field and select its field value, type **42 Ridge Rd**, and then press **TAB** three times to move to the Zip field.
7. Type **30305**, and then press **TAB** twice to move to the PatientID field of the next record. The changes to the record are complete. See Figure 3–2.

Figure 3–2 Table after changing field values in a record

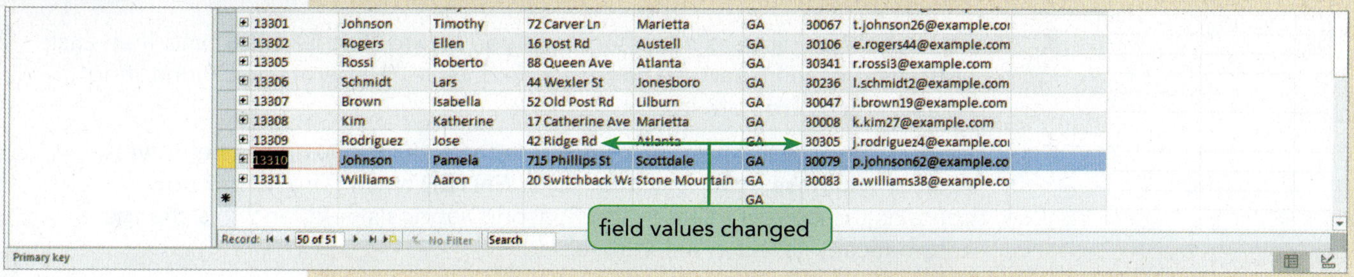

Access saves changes to field values when you move to a new field or another record, or when you close the table. You don't have to click the Save button to save changes to field values or records.

8. Press **CTRL+HOME** to move to the first field value in the first record. With the changes to the record complete, you can unhide the hidden fields.
9. Right-click any field name to display the shortcut menu, and then click **Unhide Fields**. The Unhide Columns dialog box opens. See Figure 3–3.

Figure 3–3 Unhide Columns dialog box

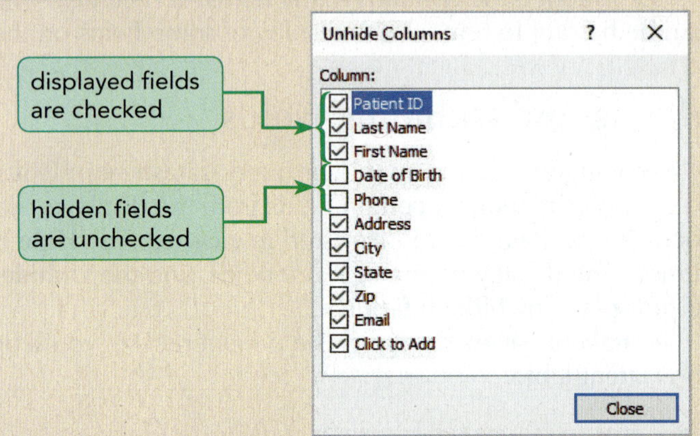

All currently displayed fields are checked in this dialog box, and all hidden fields are unchecked. To redisplay them, you click their check boxes to select them.

10. In the Unhide Columns dialog box, click the **Date of Birth** check box to select it, click the **Phone** check box to select it, and then click **Close** to close the dialog box. The two hidden fields are now displayed in the datasheet.
11. Close the Patient table, and then click **No** in the dialog box that opens, asking if you want to save changes to the layout of the Patient table. This dialog box appears because you hid fields and redisplayed them.

In this case, you can click either the Yes button or the No button, because no changes were actually made to the table layout or design.

Next you need to correct an error in the Visit table for a visit made by Mariana Salinas, Patient ID 13285. A staff member incorrectly entered "Hypertension monitoring" as the reason for the visit, when the patient actually came to the clinic that day for an annual wellness visit. Ensuring the accuracy of the data in a database is an important maintenance task.

To correct the record in the Visit table:

1. Open the **Visit** table in Datasheet view. The record containing the error is for Visit ID 1528.
2. Scroll the Visit table as necessary until you locate Visit ID **1528**, and then click at the end of the **Reason/Diagnosis** field value "Hypertension monitoring" for this record. You are in editing mode.
3. Delete **Hypertension monitoring** from the Reason/Diagnosis field, type **Annual wellness visit**, and then press **ENTER** twice. The record now contains the correct value in the Reason/Diagnosis field, and this change is automatically saved in the Visit table.

The next update Taylor asks you to make is to delete a record in the Visit table. One of the clinic's patients, Carlos Reyes, recently notified Taylor that he received an invoice for an annual wellness visit, but that he had canceled this scheduled appointment. Because this visit did not take place, the record for this visit needs to be deleted from the Visit table. Rather than scrolling through the table to locate the record to delete, you can use the Find command.

Finding Data in a Table

Access provides options you can use to locate specific field values in a table. Instead of scrolling the Visit table datasheet to find the visit that you need to delete—the record for Visit ID 1475—you can use the Find command to find the record. The **Find command** allows you to search a table or query datasheet, or a form, to locate a specific field value or part of a field value. This feature is particularly useful when searching a table that contains a large number of records.

TIP

You can click any value in the column containing the field you want to search to make the field current.

To search for the record in the Visit table:

1. Make sure the VisitID field value 1529 is still selected, and the Home tab is selected on the ribbon. You need to search the VisitID field to find the record containing the value 1475, so the insertion point is already correctly positioned in the field you want to search.
2. In the Find group, click **Find**. The Find and Replace dialog box opens. See Figure 3–4.

Figure 3–4 Find and Replace dialog box

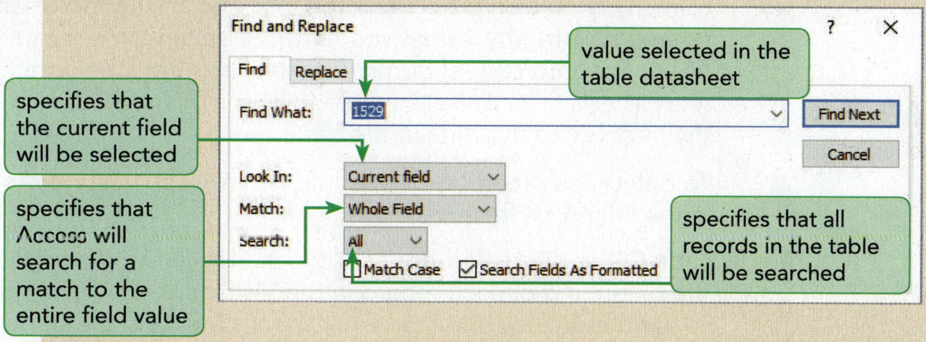

The field value 1529 appears in the Find What box because this value is selected in the table datasheet. You also can choose to search for only part of a field value, such as when you need to find all Visit IDs that start with a certain value. The Search box indicates that all the records in the table will be searched for the value you want to find. You also can choose to search up or down from the currently selected record.

Trouble? Some of the settings in your dialog box might be different from those shown in Figure 3–4 depending on the last search performed on the computer you're using. If so, change the settings so that they match those in the figure.

3. Make sure the value 1529 is selected in the Find What box, type **1475** to replace the selected value, and then click **Find Next**. Record 14 appears with the field value you specified selected.
4. Click **Cancel** to close the Find and Replace dialog box.

Deleting Records

To delete a record, you need to select the record in Datasheet view and then delete it using the Delete button in the Records group on the Home tab, or the Delete Record option on the shortcut menu.

REFERENCE

Deleting a Record

- With the table open in Datasheet view, click the row selector for the record you want to delete.
- In the Records group on the Home tab, click the Delete button; or right-click the row selector for the record, and then click Delete Record on the shortcut menu.
- In the dialog box asking you to confirm the deletion, click the Yes button.

Now that you have found the record with Visit ID 1475, you can delete it. To delete a record, you must first select the entire row for the record.

To delete the record:

1. Click the **row selector** ➡ for the record containing the VisitID field value **1475**, which should still be highlighted. The entire row is selected.
2. On the Home tab, in the Records group, click **Delete**. A dialog box opens indicating that you cannot delete the record because the Billing table contains records that related to VisitID 1475. Recall that you defined a one-to-many relationship between the Visit and Billing tables and you enforced referential integrity. When you try to delete a record in the primary table (Visit), the enforced referential integrity prevents the deletion if matching records exist in the related table (Billing). This protection helps to maintain the integrity of the data in the database.

   To delete the record in the Visit table, you first must delete the related record in the Billing table.
3. Click **OK** in the dialog box to close it. Notice the plus sign that appears at the beginning of each record in the Visit table. The plus sign, also called the **expand indicator**, indicates that the Visit table is the primary table related to another table—in this case, the Billing table. Clicking the expand indicator displays related records from other tables in the database in a **subdatasheet.**
4. Scroll down the datasheet until the selected record is near the top of the datasheet, so that you have room to view the related records for the visit record.
5. Click the **expand indicator** ⊞ next to VisitID 1475. One related record from the Billing table for this visit is displayed in the subdatasheet. See Figure 3–5.

Figure 3–5 **Related records from the Billing table in the subdatasheet**

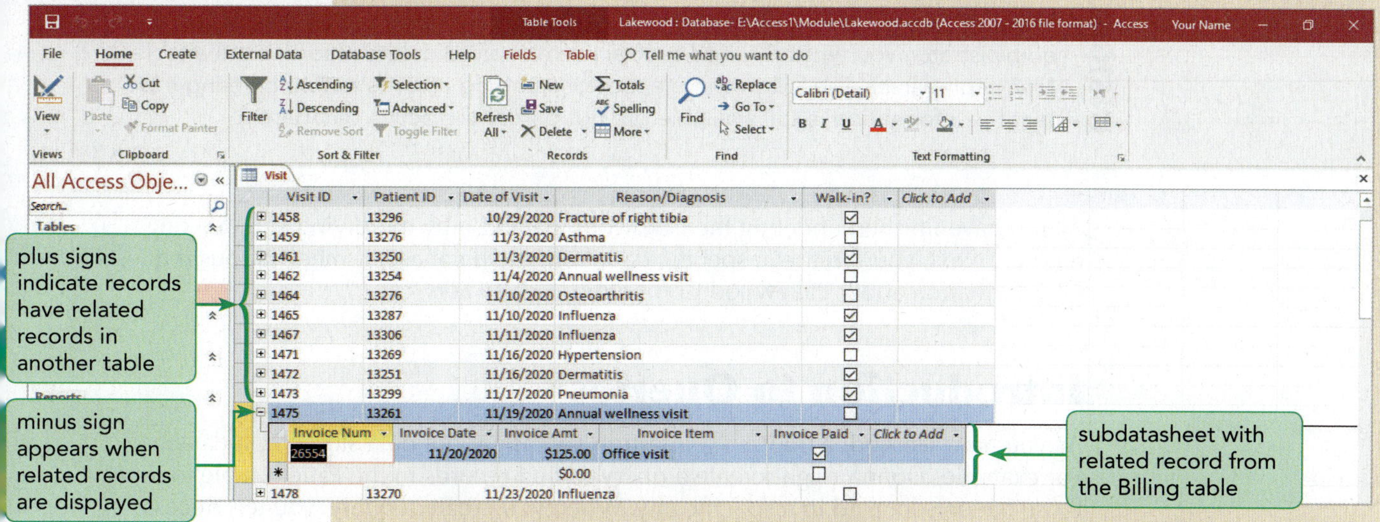

When the subdatasheet is open, you can navigate and update it, just as you can using a table datasheet. The expand indicator for an open subdatasheet is replaced by a minus sign. Clicking the minus sign, or **collapse indicator**, hides the subdatasheet.

You need to delete the record in the Billing table that is related to Visit ID 1475 before you can delete this visit record. The record is for the invoice that was mistakenly sent to the patient, Carlos Reyes, who had canceled his annual wellness visit to the clinic. You could open the Billing table and find the related record. However, an easier way is to delete the record right in the subdatasheet. The record will be deleted from the Billing table automatically.

6. In the Billing table subdatasheet, click the **row selector** ➡ for invoice number **26554**. The entire row is selected.
7. On the Home tab, in the Records group, click **Delete**. Because the deletion of a record is permanent and cannot be undone, a dialog box opens asking you to confirm the deletion of the record.
8. Click **Yes** to confirm the deletion and close the dialog box. The record is removed from the Billing table, and the subdatasheet is now empty.
9. Click the **collapse indicator** ⊟ next to Visit ID 1475 to close the subdatasheet.

Now that you have deleted the related record in the Billing table, you can delete the record for Visit ID 1475. You'll use the shortcut menu to do so.

Be sure to select the correct record before deleting it.

10. Right-click the row selector ➡ for the record for Visit ID **1475** to select the record and open the shortcut menu.
11. Click **Delete Record** on the shortcut menu, and then click **Yes** in the dialog box to confirm the deletion. The record is deleted from the Visit table.
12. Close the Visit table.

INSIGHT

Process for Deleting Records

When working with more complex databases that are managed by a database administrator, you typically need special permission to delete records from a table. Many companies also follow the practice of archiving records before deleting them so that the information is still available but not part of the active database.

You have finished updating the Lakewood database by modifying and deleting records. Next, you'll retrieve specific data from the database to meet various requests for information about Lakewood Community Health Services.

Introduction to Queries

As you have learned, a query is a question you ask about data stored in a database. For example, Donna might create a query to find records in the Patient table for only those patients located in a specific city. When you create a query, you tell Access which fields you need and what criteria Access should use to select the records. Access provides powerful query capabilities that allow you to do the following:

- Display selected fields and records from a table
- Sort records
- Perform calculations
- Generate data for forms, reports, and other queries
- Update data in the tables in a database
- Find and display data from two or more tables

Most questions about data are generalized queries in which you specify the fields and records you want Access to select. These common requests for information, such as "Which patients are located in Atlanta?" or "How many invoices have been paid?" are select queries. The answer to a select query is returned in the form of a datasheet. The result of a query is also referred to as a **recordset** because the query produces a set of records that answers your question.

INSIGHT

Designing Queries vs. Using a Query Wizard

More specialized, technical queries, such as finding duplicate records in a table, are best formulated using a Query Wizard. A **Query Wizard** prompts you for information by asking a series of questions and then creates the appropriate query based on your answers. For example, earlier you used the Simple Query Wizard to display only some of the fields in the Visit table; Access provides other Query Wizards for more complex queries. For common, informational queries, designing your own query is more efficient than using a Query Wizard.

Taylor wants you to create a query to display the patient ID, last name, first name, city, and email address for each record in the Patient table. She needs this information to complete an email campaign advertising special services and screenings being offered to patients of Lakewood Community Health Services. You'll open the Query window in Design view to create the query for Taylor.

To open the Query window in Design view:

1. Close the Navigation Pane, and then, on the ribbon, click the **Create** tab.
2. In the Queries group, click the **Query Design** button to display the Query window in Design view, with the Show Table dialog box open and the Tables tab selected. See Figure 3–6.

Figure 3–6 **Show Table dialog box**

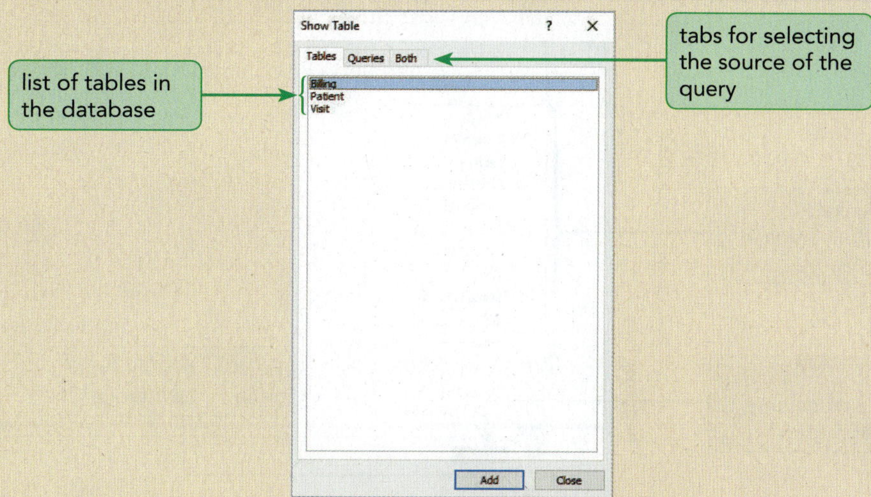

The Show Table dialog box lists all the tables in the Lakewood database. You can choose to base a query on one or more tables, on other queries, or on a combination of tables and queries. The query you are creating will retrieve data from the Patient table, so you need to add this table to the Query window.

3. In the Tables list, click **Patient**, click **Add**, and then click **Close** to close the Show Table dialog box. The Patient table's field list appears in the Query window. Refer to the Session 3.1 Visual Overview to familiarize yourself with the Query window in Design view.

   Trouble? If you add the wrong table to the Query window, right-click the bar at the top of the field list containing the table name, and then click Remove Table on the shortcut menu. To add the correct table to the Query window, repeat Steps 2 and 3.

Now you'll create and run the query to display selected fields from the Patient table.

Creating and Running a Query

The default table datasheet displays all the fields in the table in the same order as they appear in the table. In contrast, a query datasheet can display selected fields from a table, and the order of the fields can be different from that of the table, enabling those viewing the query results to see only the information they need and in the order they want.

You need the PatientID, LastName, FirstName, City, and Email fields from the Patient table to appear in the query results. You'll add each of these fields to the design grid. First you'll resize the Patient table field list to display all of the fields.

To select the fields for the query, and then run the query:

1. Drag the bottom border of the Patient field list to resize the field list so that all the fields in the Patient table are visible.
2. In the Patient field list, double-click **PatientID** to place the field in the design grid's first column Field box. See Figure 3–7.

Figure 3–7 Field added to the design grid

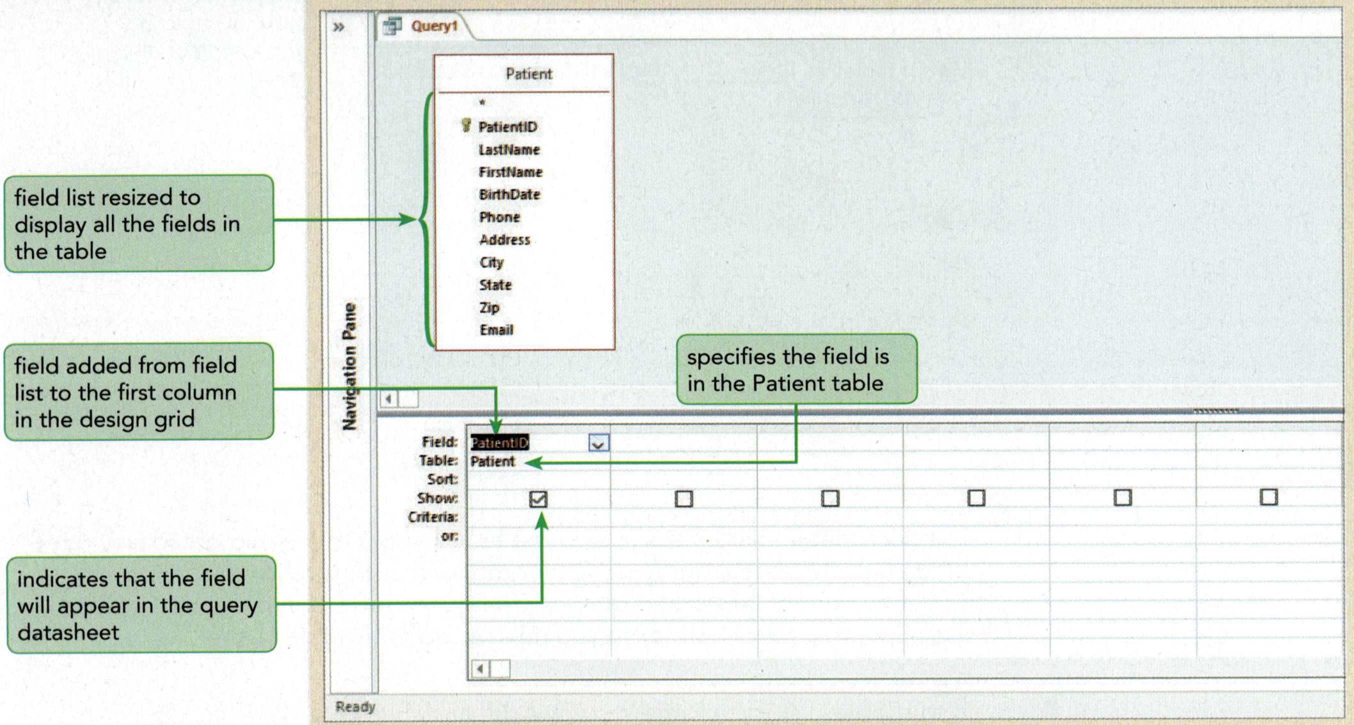

In the design grid's first column, the field name PatientID appears in the Field box, the table name Patient appears in the Table box, and the checkmark in the Show check box indicates that the field will be displayed in the datasheet when you run the query. Sometimes you might not want to display a field and its values in the query results. For example, if you are creating a query to list all patients located in Atlanta, and you assign the name "AtlantaPatients" to the query, you do not need to include the City field value for each record in the query results—the query design lists only patients with the City field value of "Atlanta." Even if you choose not to display a field in the query results, you can still use the field as part of the query to select specific records or to specify a particular sequence for the records in the datasheet. You can also add a field to the design grid using the arrow on the Field box; this arrow appears when you click the Field box, and if you click the arrow or the right side of an empty Field box, a menu of available fields opens.

TIP

You can also use the mouse to drag a field from the field list to a column in the design grid.

3. In the design grid, click the right side of the second column's Field box to display a menu listing all the fields in the Patient table, and then click **LastName** to add this field to the second column in the design grid.
4. Add the **FirstName**, **City**, and **Email** fields to the design grid in that order.

Trouble? If you accidentally add the wrong field to the design grid, select the field's column by clicking the selection pointer ⬇ on the field selector, which is the thin bar above the Field box, for the field you want to delete, and then press DELETE (or in the Query Setup group on the Query Tools Design tab, click the Delete Columns button).

Now that the five fields for the query have been selected, you can run the query.

5. On the Query Tools Design tab, in the Results group, click the **Run** button. Access runs the query and displays the results in Datasheet view. See Figure 3–8.

Figure 3–8 **Datasheet displayed after running the query**

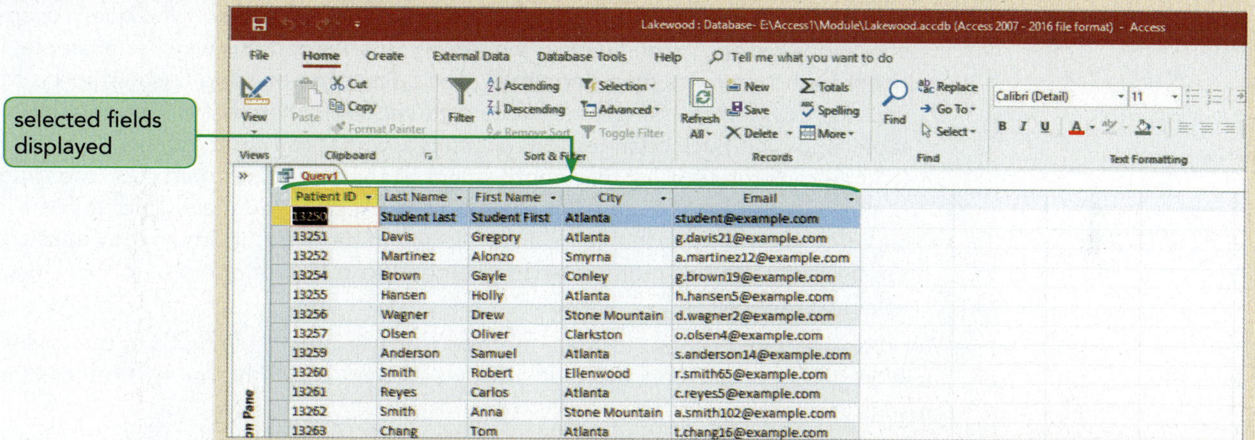

The five fields you added to the design grid appear in the datasheet in the same order as they appear in the design grid. The records are displayed in primary key sequence by PatientID. The query selected all 51 records from the Patient table for display in the query datasheet. You will save the query as "PatientEmail" so that you can easily retrieve the same data again.

6. On the Quick Access Toolbar, click the **Save** button. The Save As dialog box opens.

7. In the Query Name box, type **PatientEmail** and then press **ENTER**. The query is saved with the specified name in the Lakewood database, and its name appears on the tab for the query.

PROSKILLS

Decision Making: Comparing Methods for Adding All Fields to the Design Grid

If the query you are creating includes every field from the specified table, you can use one of the following three methods to transfer all the fields from the field list to the design grid:

- Double-click (or click and drag) each field individually from the field list to the design grid. Use this method if you want the fields in your query to appear in an order that is different from the order in the field list.
- Double-click the asterisk at the top of the field list. The table name, followed by a period and an asterisk (as in "Patient.*"), appears in the Field box of the first column in the design grid, which signifies that the order of the fields is the same in the query as it is in the field list. Use this method if you don't need to sort the query or specify conditions based on the fields in the table you added in this way (for example, in a query based on more than one table). The advantage of using this method is that you do not need to change the query if you add or delete fields from the underlying table structure. Such changes are reflected automatically in the query.
- Double-click the field list title bar to select all the fields, and then click and drag one of the selected fields to the first column in the design grid. Each field appears in a separate column, and the fields are arranged in the order in which they appear in the field list. Use this method when you need to sort your query or include record selection criteria.

By choosing the most appropriate method to add all the table fields to the query design grid, you can work more efficiently and ensure that the query produces the results you want.

The record for one of the patients in the query results contains information that is not up to date. This patient, Drew Wagner, had informed the clinic that he now prefers to go by the name Andrew; he also provided a new email address. You need to update the record with the new first name and email address for this patient.

Updating Data Using a Query

A query datasheet is temporary, and its contents are based on the criteria in the query design grid; however, you can still update the data in a table using a query datasheet. In this case, you want to make changes to a record in the Patient table. Instead of making the changes in the table datasheet, you can make them in the PatientEmail query datasheet because the query is based on the Patient table. The underlying Patient table will be updated with the changes you make.

To update data using the PatientEmail query datasheet:

1. Locate the record with PatientID 13256, Drew Wagner (record 6 in the query datasheet).
2. In the First Name column for this record, double-click **Drew** to select the name, and then type **Andrew**.
3. Press **TAB** twice to move to the Email column, type **a.wagner6@example.com**, and then press **TAB**.

4. Close the PatientEmail query, and then open the Navigation Pane. Note that the PatientEmail query is listed in the Queries section of the Navigation Pane. Now you'll check the Patient table to verify that the changes you made in the query datasheet are reflected in the Patient table.
5. Open the **Patient** table in Datasheet view, and then close the Navigation Pane.
6. Locate the record for PatientID 13256 (record 6). Notice that the changes you made in the query datasheet to the First Name and Email field values were made to the record in the Patient table.
7. Close the Patient table.

Taylor also wants to view specific information in the Lakewood database. She would like to review the visit data for patients while also viewing certain contact information about them. So, she needs to see data from both the Patient table and the Visit table at the same time.

Creating a Multitable Query

A multitable query is a query based on more than one table. If you want to create a query that retrieves data from multiple tables, the tables must have a common field. Earlier, you established a relationship between the Patient (primary) and Visit (related) tables based on the common PatientID field that exists in both tables, so you can now create a query to display data from both tables at the same time. Specifically, Taylor wants to view the values in the City, FirstName, and LastName fields from the Patient table and the VisitDate and Reason fields from the Visit table.

To create the query using the Patient and Visit tables:

1. On the ribbon, click the **Create** tab.
2. In the Queries group, click the **Query Design** button. The Show Table dialog box opens in the Query window. You need to add the Patient and Visit tables to the Query window.
3. Click **Patient** in the Tables list, click the **Add** button, click **Visit**, click the **Add** button, and then click the **Close** button to close the Show Table dialog box. The Patient and Visit field lists appear in the Query window.
4. Resize the Patient and Visit field lists if necessary so that all the fields in each list are displayed.

   The one-to-many relationship between the two tables is shown in the Query window in the same way that a relationship between two tables is shown in the Relationships window. Note that the join line is thick at both ends; this signifies that you selected the option to enforce referential integrity. If you had not selected this option, the join line would be thin at both ends, and neither the "1" nor the infinity symbol would appear, even though the tables have a one-to-many relationship.

   You need to place the City, FirstName, and LastName fields (in that order) from the Patient field list into the design grid and then place the VisitDate and Reason fields from the Visit field list into the design grid. This is the order in which Taylor wants to view the fields in the query results.
5. In the Patient field list, double-click **City** to place this field in the design grid's first column Field box.

6. Repeat Step 5 to add the **FirstName** and **LastName** fields from the Patient table to the second and third columns of the design grid.
7. Repeat Step 5 to add the **VisitDate** and **Reason** fields (in that order) from the Visit table to the fourth and fifth columns of the design grid. The query specifications are complete, so you can now run the query.
8. In the Results group on the Query Tools Design tab, click **Run**. After the query runs, the results are displayed in Datasheet view. See Figure 3–9.

Figure 3–9 **Datasheet for query based on the Patient and Visit tables**

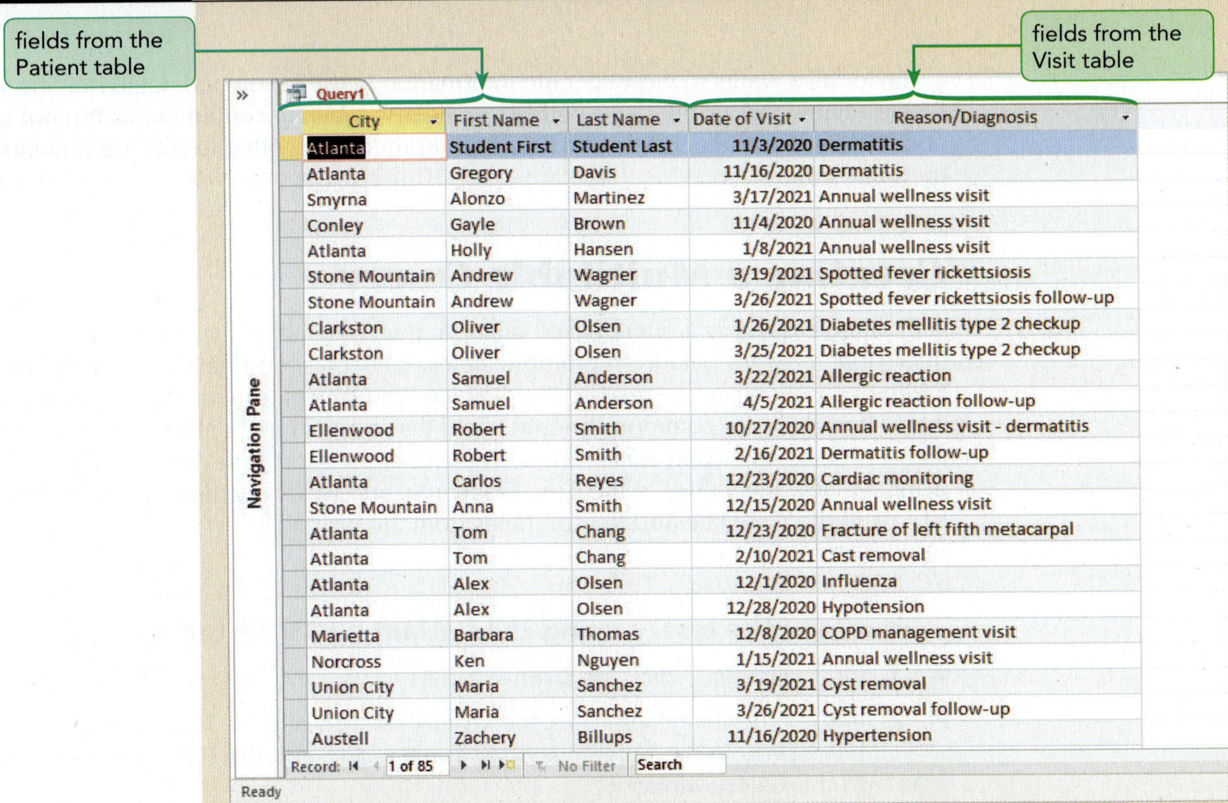

City	First Name	Last Name	Date of Visit	Reason/Diagnosis
Atlanta	Student First	Student Last	11/3/2020	Dermatitis
Atlanta	Gregory	Davis	11/16/2020	Dermatitis
Smyrna	Alonzo	Martinez	3/17/2021	Annual wellness visit
Conley	Gayle	Brown	11/4/2020	Annual wellness visit
Atlanta	Holly	Hansen	1/8/2021	Annual wellness visit
Stone Mountain	Andrew	Wagner	3/19/2021	Spotted fever rickettsiosis
Stone Mountain	Andrew	Wagner	3/26/2021	Spotted fever rickettsiosis follow-up
Clarkston	Oliver	Olsen	1/26/2021	Diabetes mellitis type 2 checkup
Clarkston	Oliver	Olsen	3/25/2021	Diabetes mellitis type 2 checkup
Atlanta	Samuel	Anderson	3/22/2021	Allergic reaction
Atlanta	Samuel	Anderson	4/5/2021	Allergic reaction follow-up
Ellenwood	Robert	Smith	10/27/2020	Annual wellness visit - dermatitis
Ellenwood	Robert	Smith	2/16/2021	Dermatitis follow-up
Atlanta	Carlos	Reyes	12/23/2020	Cardiac monitoring
Stone Mountain	Anna	Smith	12/15/2020	Annual wellness visit
Atlanta	Tom	Chang	12/23/2020	Fracture of left fifth metacarpal
Atlanta	Tom	Chang	2/10/2021	Cast removal
Atlanta	Alex	Olsen	12/1/2020	Influenza
Atlanta	Alex	Olsen	12/28/2020	Hypotension
Marietta	Barbara	Thomas	12/8/2020	COPD management visit
Norcross	Ken	Nguyen	1/15/2021	Annual wellness visit
Union City	Maria	Sanchez	3/19/2021	Cyst removal
Union City	Maria	Sanchez	3/26/2021	Cyst removal follow-up
Austell	Zachery	Billups	11/16/2020	Hypertension

Only the five selected fields from the Patient and Visit tables appear in the datasheet. The records are displayed in order according to the values in the PatientID field because it is the primary key field in the primary table, even though this field is not included in the query datasheet.

Taylor plans on frequently tracking the data retrieved by the query, so she asks you to save it as "PatientVisits."

9. On the Quick Access Toolbar, click the **Save** button. The Save As dialog box opens.
10. In the Query Name box, type **PatientVisits** and then press **ENTER**. The query is saved, and its name appears on the object tab.

Taylor decides she wants the records displayed in alphabetical order by city. Because the query displays data in order by the field values in the PatientID field, which is the primary key for the Patient table, you need to sort the records by the City field to display the data in the order Taylor wants.

Sorting Data in a Query

Sorting is the process of rearranging records in a specified order or sequence. Sometimes you might need to sort data before displaying or printing it to meet a specific request. For example, Taylor might want to review visit information arranged by the VisitDate field because she needs to know which months are the busiest for Lakewood Community Health Services in terms of patient visits. Donna might want to view billing information arranged by the InvoiceAmt field because she monitors the finances of the clinic.

When you sort data in a query, you do not change the sequence of the records in the underlying tables. Only the records in the query datasheet are rearranged according to your specifications.

To sort records, you must select the **sort field**, which is the field used to determine the order of records in the datasheet. In this case, Taylor wants the data sorted alphabetically by city, so you need to specify City as the sort field. Sort fields can be Short Text, Number, Date/Time, Currency, AutoNumber, or Yes/No fields, but not Long Text, Hyperlink, or Attachment fields. You sort records in either ascending (increasing) or descending (decreasing) order. Figure 3–10 shows the results of each type of sort for these data types.

Figure 3–10 **Sorting results for different data types**

Data Type	Ascending Sort Results	Descending Sort Results
Short Text	A to Z (alphabetical)	Z to A (reverse alphabetical)
Number	lowest to highest numeric value	highest to lowest numeric value
Date/Time	oldest to most recent date	most recent to oldest date
Currency	lowest to highest numeric value	highest to lowest numeric value
AutoNumber	lowest to highest numeric value	highest to lowest numeric value
Yes/No	yes (checkmark in check box) then no values	no then yes values

Access provides several methods for sorting data in a table or query datasheet and in a form. One of the easiest ways is to use the AutoFilter feature for a field.

Using an AutoFilter to Sort Data

TIP

You can also use the Ascending and Descending buttons in the Sort & Filter group on the Home tab to quickly sort records based on the currently selected field in a datasheet.

As you've probably noticed when working in Datasheet view for a table or query, each column heading has an arrow to the right of the field name. This arrow gives you access to the **AutoFilter** feature, which enables you to quickly sort and display field values in various ways. When you click this arrow, a menu opens with options for sorting and displaying field values. The first two options on the menu enable you to sort the values in the current field in ascending or descending order. Unless you save the datasheet or form after you've sorted the records, the rearrangement of records is temporary.

Next, you'll use an AutoFilter to sort the PatientVisits query results by the City field.

To sort the records using an AutoFilter:

1. Click the **arrow** on the City column heading to display the AutoFilter menu. See Figure 3-11.

Figure 3-11 Using AutoFilter to sort records in the datasheet

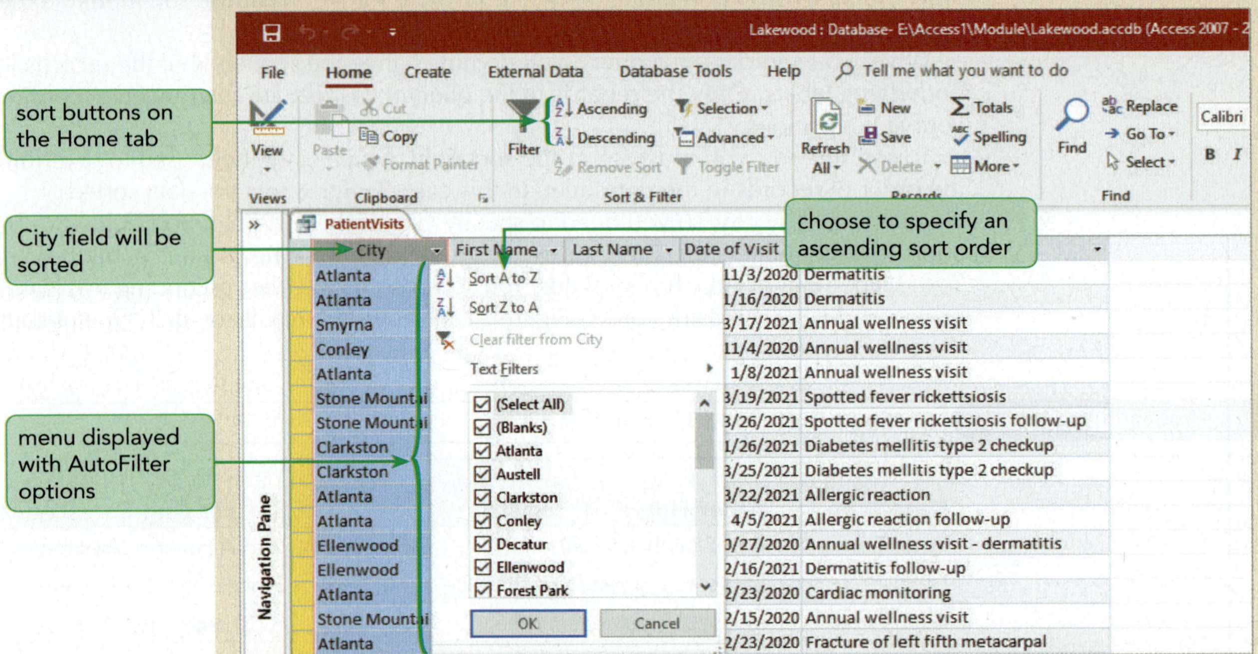

Taylor wants the data sorted in ascending (alphabetical) order by the values in the City field, so you need to select the first option in the menu.

2. Click **Sort A to Z**. The records are rearranged in ascending alphabetical order by city. A small, upward-pointing arrow appears on the right side of the City column heading. This arrow indicates that the values in the field have been sorted in ascending order. If you used the same method to sort the field values in descending order, a small downward-pointing arrow would appear there instead.

After viewing the query results, Taylor decides that she would also like to see the records arranged by the values in the VisitDate field, so that the data is presented in chronological order. She still wants the records to be arranged by the City field values as well. To produce the results Taylor wants, you need to sort using two fields.

Sorting on Multiple Fields in Design View

Sort fields can be unique or nonunique. A sort field is **unique** if the value in the sort field for each record is different. The PatientID field in the Patient table is an example of a unique sort field because each patient record has a different value in this primary key field. A sort field is **nonunique** if more than one record can have the same value for the sort field. For example, the City field in the Patient table is a nonunique sort field because more than one record can have the same City value.

TIP

The primary sort field is not the same as a table's primary key. A table has at most one primary key, which must be unique, whereas any field in a table can serve as a primary sort field.

When the sort field is nonunique, records with the same sort field value are grouped together, but they are not sorted in a specific order within the group. To arrange these grouped records in a specific order, you can specify a **secondary sort field**, which is a second field that determines the order of records that are already sorted by the **primary sort field** (the first sort field specified).

In Access, you can select up to 10 different sort fields. When you use the buttons on the ribbon to sort by more than one field, the sort fields must be in adjacent columns in the datasheet. (Note that you cannot use an AutoFilter to sort on more than one field. This method works for a single field only.) You can specify only one type of sort—either ascending or descending—for the selected columns in the datasheet. You select the adjacent columns, and Access sorts first by the first column and then by each remaining selected column in order from left to right.

Taylor wants the records sorted first by the City field values, as they currently are, and then by the VisitDate values. The two fields are in the correct left-to-right order in the query datasheet, but they are not adjacent, so you cannot use the Ascending and Descending buttons on the ribbon to sort them. You could move the City field to the left of the VisitDate field in the query datasheet, but both columns would have to be sorted with the same sort order. This is not what Taylor wants—she wants the City field values sorted in ascending order so that they are in the correct alphabetical order, for ease of reference; and she wants the VisitDate field values to be sorted in descending order, so that she can focus on the most recent patient visits first. To sort the City and VisitDate fields with different sort orders, you must specify the sort fields in Design view.

In the Query window in Design view, you must arrange the fields you want to sort from left to right in the design grid, with the primary sort field being the leftmost. In Design view, multiple sort fields do not have to be adjacent to each other, as they do in Datasheet view; however, they must be in the correct left-to-right order.

REFERENCE

Sorting a Query Datasheet

- In the query datasheet, click the arrow on the column heading for the field you want to sort.
- In the menu that opens, click Sort A to Z for an ascending sort, or click Sort Z to A for a descending sort.

or

- In the query datasheet, select the column or adjacent columns on which you want to sort.
- In the Sort & Filter group on the Home tab, click the Ascending button or the Descending button.

or

- In Design view, position the fields serving as sort fields from left to right.
- Click the right side of the Sort box for each field you want to sort, and then click Ascending or Descending for the sort order.

To achieve the results Taylor wants, you need to modify the query in Design view to specify the sort order for the two fields.

TIP

In Design view, the sort fields do not have to be adjacent, and fields that are not sorted can appear between the sort fields.

To select the two sort fields in Design view:

1. On the Home tab, in the Views group, click the **View** button to open the query in Design view. The fields are currently in the correct left-to-right order in the design grid, so you only need to specify the sort order for the two fields.

   First, you need to specify an ascending sort order for the City field. Even though the records are already sorted by the values in this field, you need to modify the query so that this sort order, and the sort order you will specify for the VisitDate field, are part of the query's design. Any time the query is run, the records will be sorted according to these specifications.

2. Click the right side of the **City Sort** box to display the arrow and the sort options, and then click **Ascending**. You've selected an ascending sort order for the City field, which will be the primary sort field. The City field is a Short Text field, and an ascending sort order will display the field values in alphabetical order.

3. Click the right side of the **VisitDate Sort** box, click **Descending**, and then click in one of the empty boxes below the VisitDate field to deselect the setting. You've selected a descending sort order for the VisitDate field, which will be the secondary sort field because it appears to the right of the primary sort field (City) in the design grid. The VisitDate field is a Date/Time field, and a descending sort order will display the field values with the most recent dates first. See Figure 3–12.

Figure 3–12 Selecting two sort fields in Design view

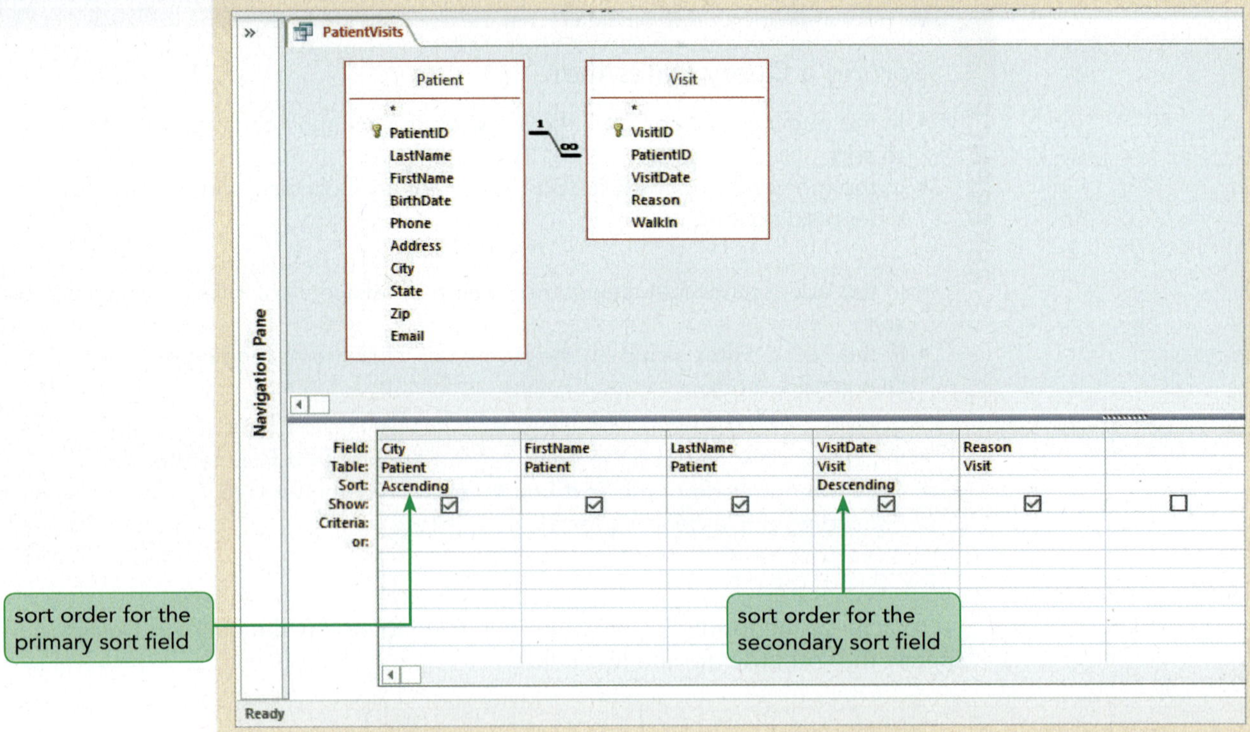

You have finished your query changes, so now you can run the query and then save the modified query with the same name.

4. On the Query Tools Design tab, in the Results group, click **Run**. After the query runs, the records appear in the query datasheet in ascending order based on the values in the City field. Within groups of records with the same City field value, the records appear in descending order by the values of the VisitDate field. See Figure 3–13.

Figure 3–13 Datasheet sorted on two fields

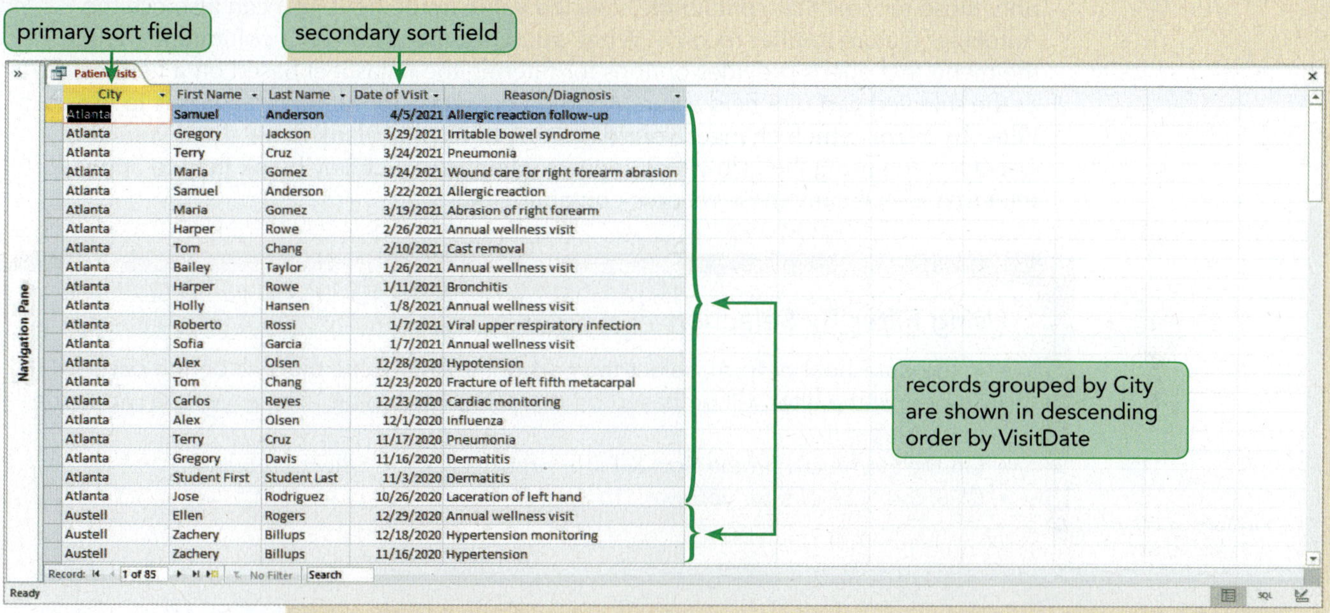

City	First Name	Last Name	Date of Visit	Reason/Diagnosis
Atlanta	Samuel	Anderson	4/5/2021	Allergic reaction follow-up
Atlanta	Gregory	Jackson	3/29/2021	Irritable bowel syndrome
Atlanta	Terry	Cruz	3/24/2021	Pneumonia
Atlanta	Maria	Gomez	3/24/2021	Wound care for right forearm abrasion
Atlanta	Samuel	Anderson	3/22/2021	Allergic reaction
Atlanta	Maria	Gomez	3/19/2021	Abrasion of right forearm
Atlanta	Harper	Rowe	2/26/2021	Annual wellness visit
Atlanta	Tom	Chang	2/10/2021	Cast removal
Atlanta	Bailey	Taylor	1/26/2021	Annual wellness visit
Atlanta	Harper	Rowe	1/11/2021	Bronchitis
Atlanta	Holly	Hansen	1/8/2021	Annual wellness visit
Atlanta	Roberto	Rossi	1/7/2021	Viral upper respiratory infection
Atlanta	Sofia	Garcia	1/7/2021	Annual wellness visit
Atlanta	Alex	Olsen	12/28/2020	Hypotension
Atlanta	Tom	Chang	12/23/2020	Fracture of left fifth metacarpal
Atlanta	Carlos	Reyes	12/23/2020	Cardiac monitoring
Atlanta	Alex	Olsen	12/1/2020	Influenza
Atlanta	Terry	Cruz	11/17/2020	Pneumonia
Atlanta	Gregory	Davis	11/16/2020	Dermatitis
Atlanta	Student First	Student Last	11/3/2020	Dermatitis
Atlanta	Jose	Rodriguez	10/26/2020	Laceration of left hand
Austell	Ellen	Rogers	12/29/2020	Annual wellness visit
Austell	Zachery	Billups	12/18/2020	Hypertension monitoring
Austell	Zachery	Billups	11/16/2020	Hypertension

When you save the query, all of your design changes—including the selection of the sort fields—are saved with the query. The next time Taylor runs the query, the records will appear sorted by the primary and secondary sort fields.

5. On the Quick Access Toolbar, click the **Save** button to save the revised PatientVisits query.

Taylor knows that Lakewood Community Health Services has seen an increase in the number of patients from Atlanta. She would like to focus briefly on the information for patients in that city only. Also, she is interested in knowing how many patients from Atlanta have had annual wellness visits. She is concerned that, although more patients are coming to the clinic from this city, not enough of them are scheduling wellness visits. Selecting only the records with a City field value of "Atlanta" and a Reason field value beginning with "Annual" is a temporary change that Taylor wants in the query datasheet, so you do not need to switch to Design view and change the query. Instead, you can apply a filter.

Filtering Data

A **filter** is a set of restrictions you place on the records in an open datasheet or form to *temporarily* isolate a subset of the records. A filter lets you view different subsets of displayed records so that you can focus on only the data you need. Unless you save a query or form with a filter applied, an applied filter is not available the next time you run the query or open the form.

The simplest technique for filtering records is Filter By Selection. **Filter By Selection** lets you select all or part of a field value in a datasheet or form and then display only those records that contain the selected value in the field. You can also use the AutoFilter feature to filter records. When you click the arrow on a column heading, the menu that opens provides options for filtering the datasheet based on a field value or the selected part of a field value. Another technique for filtering records is to use **Filter By Form**, which changes your datasheet to display blank fields. Then you can select a value using the arrow that appears when you click any blank field to apply a filter that selects only those records containing that value.

REFERENCE

Using Filter By Selection

- In the datasheet or form, select the part of the field value that will be the basis for the filter; or, if the filter will be based on the entire field value, click anywhere within the field value.
- On the Home tab, in the Sort & Filter group, click the Selection button.
- Click the type of filter you want to apply.

For Taylor's request, you need to select a City field value of Atlanta and then use Filter By Selection to display only those records with this value. Then you will filter the records further by selecting only those records with a Reason value that begins with "Annual" (for Annual wellness visit).

To display the records using Filter By Selection:

1. In the query datasheet, locate the first occurrence of a City field containing the value **Atlanta**, and then click anywhere within that field value.
2. On the Home tab, in the Sort & Filter group, click the **Selection** button. A menu opens with options for the type of filter to apply. See Figure 3–14.

Figure 3–14 Using Filter By Selection

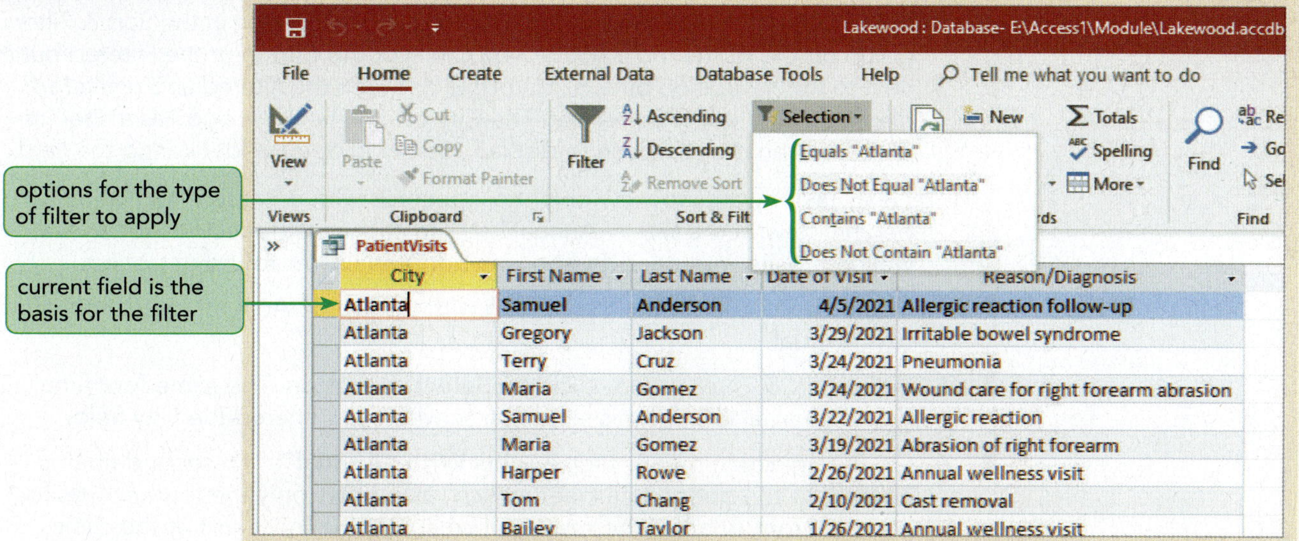

The menu provides options for displaying only those records with a City field value that equals the selected value (in this case, Atlanta); does not equal the value; contains the value somewhere within the field; or does not contain the value somewhere within the field. You want to display all the records whose City field value equals Atlanta.

3. In the Selection menu, click **Equals "Atlanta"**. Only the 21 records that have a City field value of Atlanta appear in the datasheet. See Figure 3–15.

Figure 3–15 Datasheet after applying filter

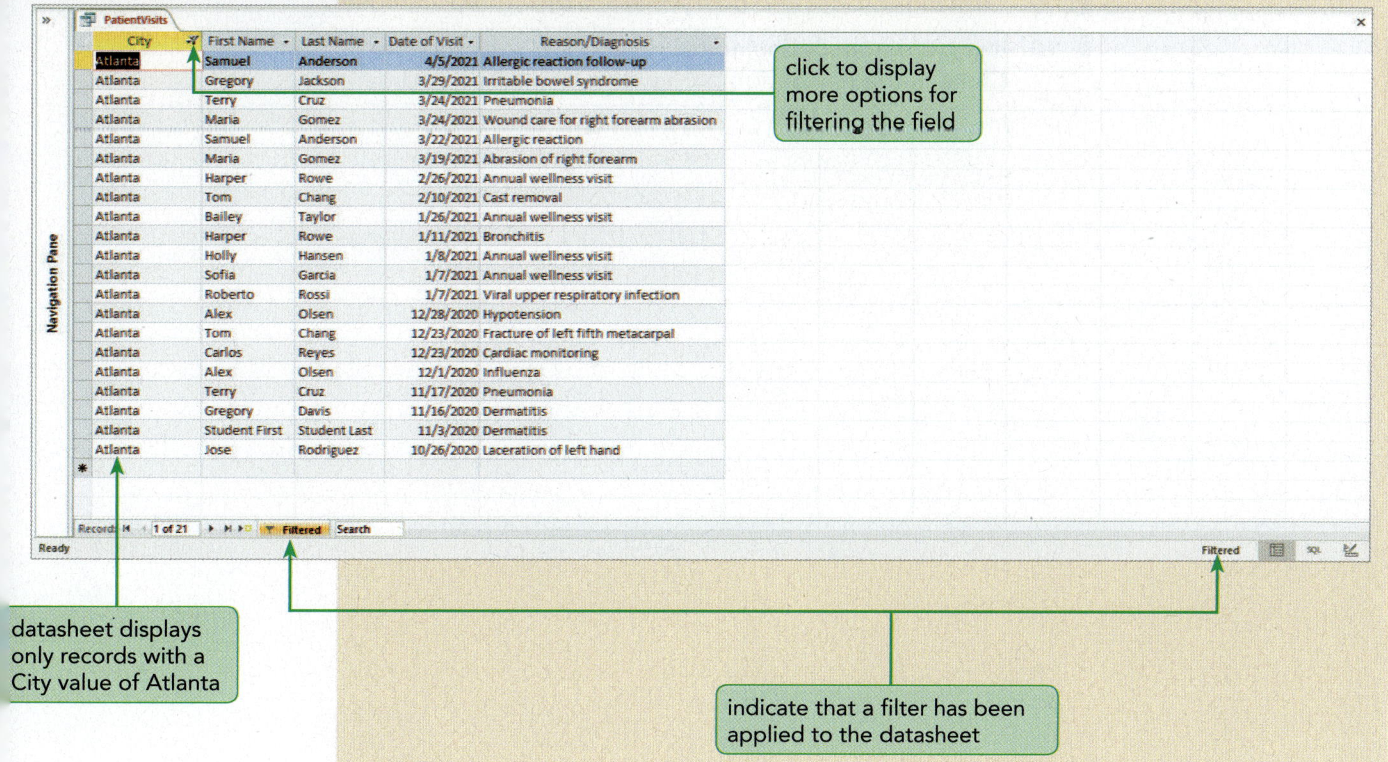

The button labeled "Filtered" to the right of the navigation buttons and the notation "Filtered" on the status bar both indicate a filter has been applied to the datasheet. Also, notice that the Toggle Filter button in the Sort & Filter group on the Home tab is active; you can click this button or the Filtered button next to the navigation buttons to toggle between the filtered and unfiltered displays of the query datasheet. The City column heading also has a filter icon on it; you can click this icon to display additional options for filtering the field.

Next, Taylor wants to view only those records with a Reason field value beginning with the word "Annual" so she can view the records for annual wellness visits. You need to apply an additional filter to the datasheet.

4. In any Reason field value beginning with the word "Annual", select only the text **Annual**.
5. In the Sort & Filter group, click the **Selection** button. The same four filter types are available for this selection as when you filtered the City field.
6. On the Selection menu, click **Begins With "Annual"**. The second filter is applied to the query datasheet, which now shows only the four records for patients from Atlanta who have had an annual wellness visit at the clinic.

Now you can redisplay all the query records by clicking the Toggle Filter button, which you use to switch between the filtered and unfiltered displays.

TIP

The ScreenTip for this button is Remove Filter.

7. In the Sort & Filter group, click the **Toggle Filter** button. The filter is removed, and all 85 records appear in the query datasheet.
8. Close the PatientVisits query. A dialog box opens, asking if you want to save your changes to the design of the query—in this case, the filtered display, which is still available through the Toggle Filter button. Taylor does not want the query saved with the filter because she doesn't need to view the filtered information on a regular basis.
9. Click **No** to close the query without saving the changes.
10. If you are not continuing to Session 3.2, click the **File** tab, and then click **Close** in the navigation bar to close the Lakewood database.

REVIEW

Session 3.1 Quick Check

1. In Datasheet view, what is the difference between navigation mode and editing mode?
2. What command can you use in Datasheet view to remove the display of one or more fields from the datasheet?
3. What is a select query?
4. Describe the field list and the design grid in the Query window in Design view.
5. How are a table datasheet and a query datasheet similar? How are they different?
6. For a Date/Time field, how do the records appear when sorted in ascending order?
7. When you define multiple sort fields in Design view, describe how the sort fields must be positioned in the design grid.
8. A(n) ____________ is a set of restrictions you place on the records in an open datasheet or form to isolate a subset of records temporarily.

Session 3.2 Visual Overview:

When creating queries in Design view, you can enter criteria so that Access will display only selected records in the query results.

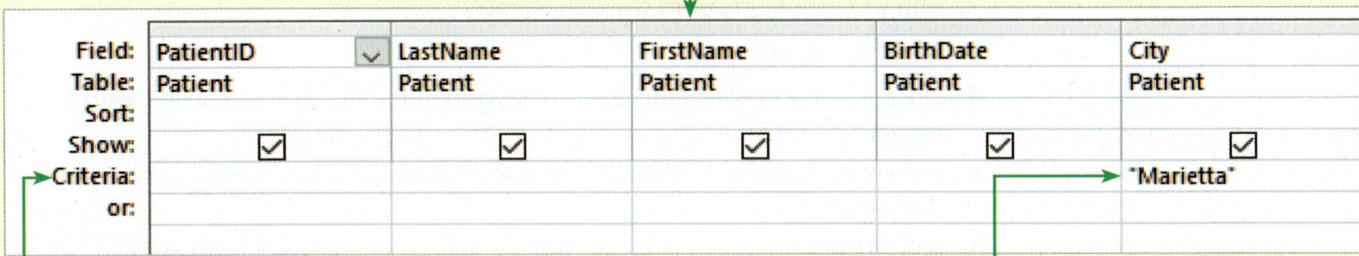

To define a condition for a field, you place the condition in the field's Criteria box in the design grid.

To tell Access which records you want to select, you must specify a condition as part of the query. A **condition** is a criterion, or rule, that determines which records are selected.

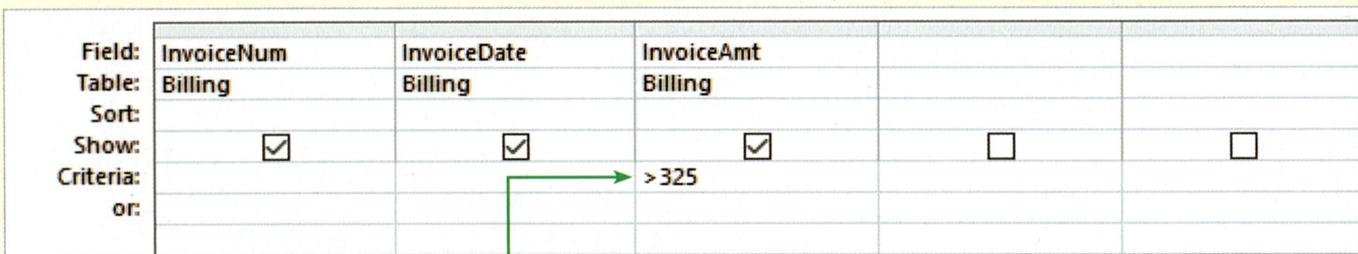

A condition usually consists of an operator, often a comparison operator, and a value. A **comparison operator** asks Access to compare the value to the condition value and to select all the records for which the condition is true.

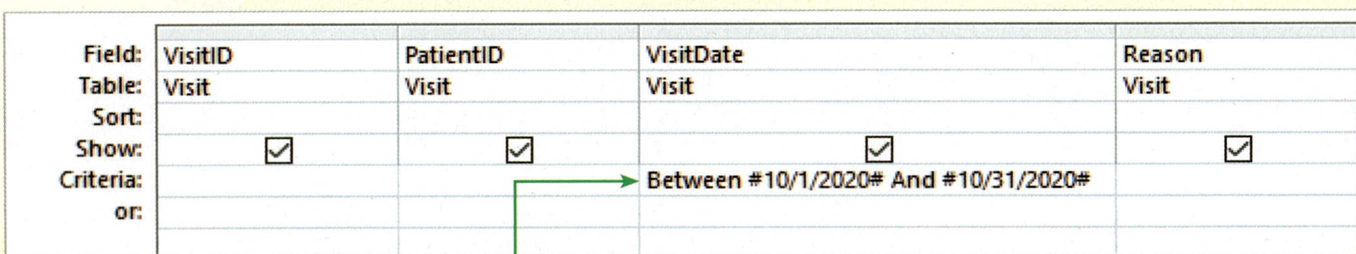

Most comparison operators (such as Between … And …) ask Access to select records that match a range of values for the condition—in this case, all records with dates that fall within the range shown.

Selection Criteria in Queries

The results of a query containing selection criteria include only the records that meet the specified criteria.

MariettaPatients

Patient ID	Last Name	First Name	Date of Birth	City
13266	Thomas	Barbara	8/17/1959	Marietta
13279	Michaels	Thomas	4/19/1982	Marietta
13301	Johnson	Timothy	10/6/1962	Marietta
13308	Kim	Katherine	12/17/1960	Marietta
*				

The results of this query show only patients from Marietta because the condition "Marietta" in the City field's Criteria box specifies that Access should select records only with City field values of Marietta. This type of condition is called an **exact match** because the value in the specified field must match the condition exactly in order for the record to be included in the query results.

LargeInvoiceAmts

Invoice Num	Invoice Date	Invoice Amt
26515	10/30/2020	$350.00
26600	12/28/2020	$350.00
*		$0.00

The results of this query show only those invoices with amounts greater than $325 because the condition >325, which uses the greater than comparison operator, specifies that Access should select records only with InvoiceAmt field values over $325.

OctoberVisits

Visit ID	Patient ID	Date of Visit	Reason/Diagnosis
1450	13272	10/26/2020	Influenza
1451	13309	10/26/2020	Laceration of left hand
1453	13260	10/27/2020	Annual wellness visit - dermatitis
1458	13296	10/29/2020	Fracture of right tibia
*			

The results of this query show only those patient visits that took place in October 2020 because the condition in the VisitDate's Criteria box specifies that Access should select only records with a visit date between 10/1/2020 and 10/31/2020.

Defining Record Selection Criteria for Queries

Donna wants to display patient and visit information for all patients who live in Stone Mountain. She is considering having the clinic hold a health fair in Stone Mountain, so she is interested in knowing more about patients from this city. For this request, you could create a query to select the correct fields and all records in the Patient and Visit tables, select a City field value of Stone Mountain in the query datasheet, and then click the Selection button and choose the appropriate filter option to display the information for only those patients in Stone Mountain. However, a faster way of displaying the data Donna needs is to create a query that displays the selected fields and only those records in the Patient and Visit tables that satisfy a condition.

Just as you can display selected fields from a database in a query datasheet, you can display selected records. To identify which records you want to select, you must specify a condition as part of the query, as illustrated in the Session 3.2 Visual Overview. A condition usually includes one of the comparison operators shown in Figure 3–16.

Figure 3–16 Access comparison operators

Operator	Meaning	Example
=	equal to (optional; default operator)	="Hall"
<>	not equal to	<>"Hall"
<	less than	<#1/1/99#
<=	less than or equal to	<=100
>	greater than	>"C400"
>=	greater than or equal to	>=18.75
Between … And …	between two values (inclusive)	Between 50 And 325
In ()	in a list of values	In ("Hall", "Seeger")
Like	matches a pattern that includes wildcards	Like "706*"

Specifying an Exact Match

For Donna's request, you need to first create a query that will display only those records in the Patient table with the value Stone Mountain in the City field. This type of condition is an exact match because the value in the specified field must match the condition exactly in order for the record to be included in the query results. You'll create the query in Design view.

To create the query in Design view:

1. If you took a break after the previous session, make sure that the Lakewood database is open and the Navigation Pane is closed, and then on the ribbon, click the **Create** tab.
2. In the Queries group, click the **Query Design** button. The Show Table dialog box opens. You need to add the Patient and Visit tables to the Query window.
3. Click **Patient** in the Tables list, click **Add**, click **Visit**, click **Add**, and then click the **Close** button. The field lists for the Patient and Visit tables appear in the top portion of the window, and join lines indicating one-to-many relationships connect the tables.

4. Resize both field lists so that all the fields are displayed.
5. Add the following fields from the Patient table to the design grid in this order: **LastName**, **FirstName**, **Phone**, **Address**, **City**, and **Email**.

   Donna also wants information from the Visit table included in the query results.
6. Add the following fields from the Visit table to the design grid in this order: **VisitID**, **VisitDate**, and **Reason**. See Figure 3–17.

Figure 3–17 Design grid after adding fields from both tables

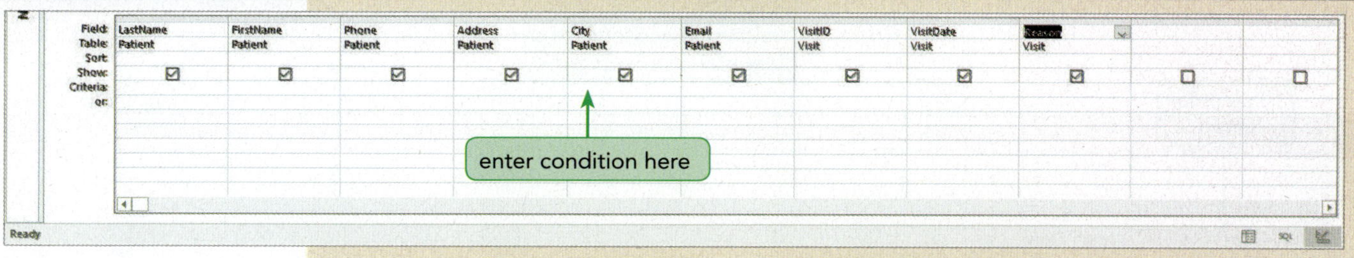

To display the information Donna wants, you need to enter the condition for the City field in its Criteria box, as shown in Figure 3–17. Donna wants to display only those records with a City field value of Stone Mountain.

To enter the exact match condition, and then save and run the query:

1. Click the **City Criteria** box, type **Stone Mountain**, and then press **ENTER**. The condition changes to "Stone Mountain".

   Access automatically enclosed the condition you typed in quotation marks. You must enclose text values in quotation marks when using them as selection criteria. If you omit the quotation marks, however, Access will include them automatically in most cases. Some words—including "in" and "select"—are special keywords in Access that are reserved for functions and commands. If you want to enter one of these keywords as the condition, you must type the quotation marks around the text or an error message will appear indicating the condition cannot be entered.
2. Save the query with the name **StoneMountainPatients**. The query is saved, and its name is displayed on the object tab.
3. Run the query. After the query runs, the selected field values for only those records with a City field value of Stone Mountain are shown. A total of 10 records is selected and displayed in the datasheet. See Figure 3–18.

Figure 3–18 **Datasheet displaying selected fields and records**

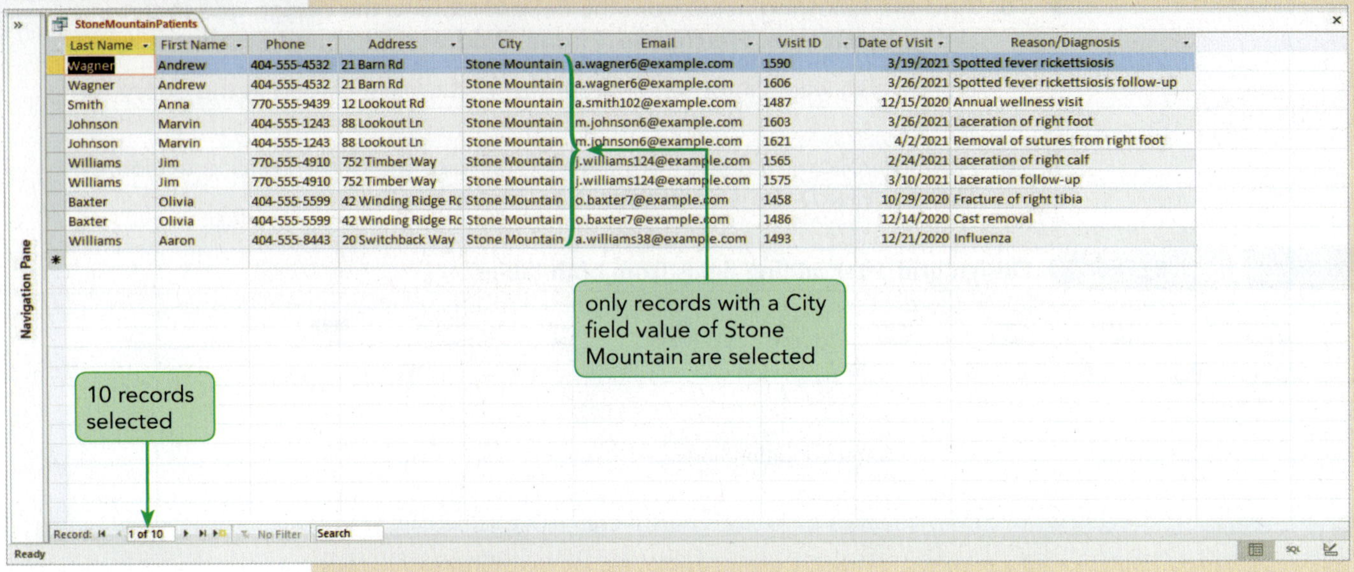

Donna realizes that it's not necessary to include the City field values in the query results. The name of the query, StoneMountainPatients, indicates that the query design includes all patients who live in Stone Mountain, so the City field values are unnecessary and repetitive in the query results. Also, she decides that she would prefer the query datasheet to show the fields from the Visit table first, followed by the Patient table fields. You need to modify the query to produce the results Donna wants.

Modifying a Query

After you create a query and view the results, you might need to make changes to the query if the results are not what you expected or require. First, Donna asks you to modify the StoneMountainPatients query so that it does not display the City field values in the query results.

To remove the display of the City field values:

1. On the Home tab, in the Views group, click the **View** button. The StoneMountainPatients query opens in Design view.

   You need to keep the City field as part of the query design because it contains the defined condition for the query. You only need to remove the display of the field's values from the query results.

2. Click the **City Show** check box to remove the checkmark. The query will still find only those records with the value Stone Mountain in the City field, but the query results will not display these field values.

Next, you need to change the order of the fields in the query so that the visit information is listed first.

To move the Visit table fields to precede the Patient table fields:

1. Position the pointer on the VisitID field selector until the selection pointer appears ⬇, and then click to select the field. See Figure 3–19.

Figure 3–19 Selected VisitID field

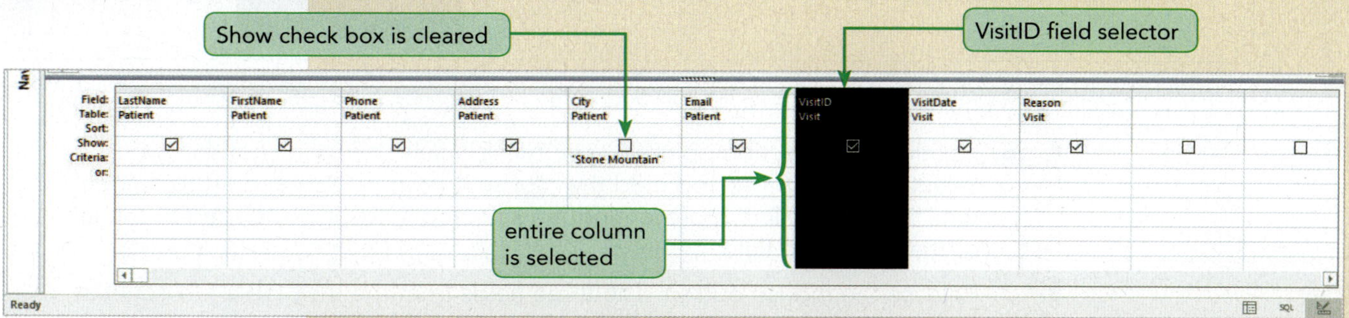

2. Position the pointer on the VisitID field selector, and then press and hold the mouse button; notice that the pointer changes to the move pointer, and a black vertical line appears to the left of the selected field. This line represents the selected field when you drag the mouse to move it.
3. Drag the pointer to the left until the vertical line representing the selected field is positioned to the left of the LastName field. See Figure 3–20.

Figure 3–20 Dragging the field in the design grid

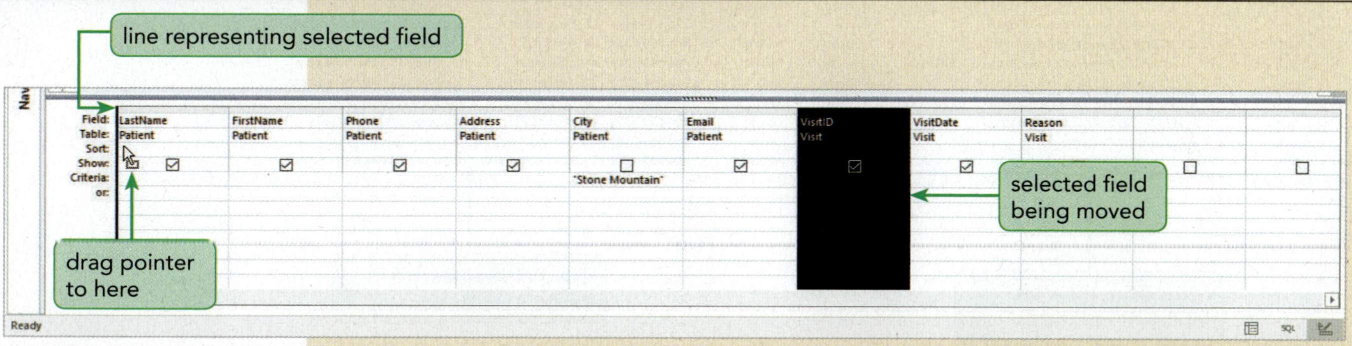

TIP

Instead of moving a field by dragging, you can also delete the field and then add it back to the design grid in the location you want.

4. Release the mouse button. The VisitID field moves to the left of the LastName field.

   You can also select and move multiple fields at once. You need to select and move the VisitDate and Reason fields so that they follow the VisitID field in the query design. To select multiple fields, you click and drag the mouse over the field selectors for the fields you want.
5. Click and hold the selection pointer ⬇ on the VisitDate field selector, drag the pointer to the right to select the Reason field, and then release the mouse button. Both fields are now selected. See Figure 3–21.

Figure 3–21 Multiple fields selected to be moved

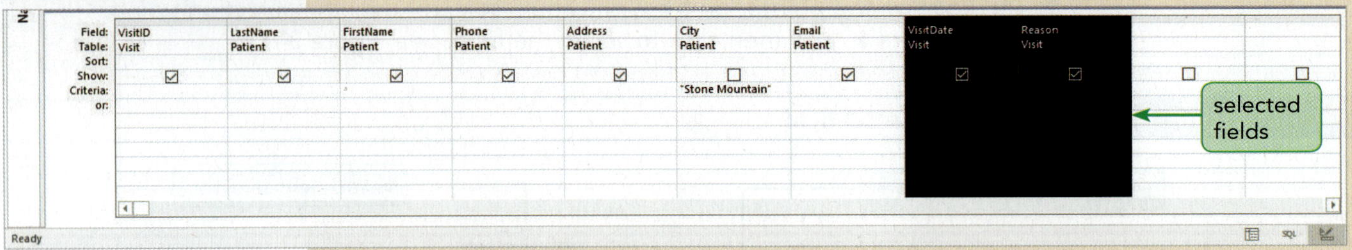

6. Position the selection pointer on the field selector for any of the two selected fields, press and hold the mouse button, and then drag to the left until the vertical line representing the selected fields is positioned to the left of the LastName field.

7. Release the mouse button. The three fields from the Visit table are now the first three fields in the query design.

   You have finished making the modifications to the query Donna requested, so you can now run the query.

8. Run the query. The results of the modified query are displayed. See Figure 3-22.

Figure 3–22 Results of the modified query

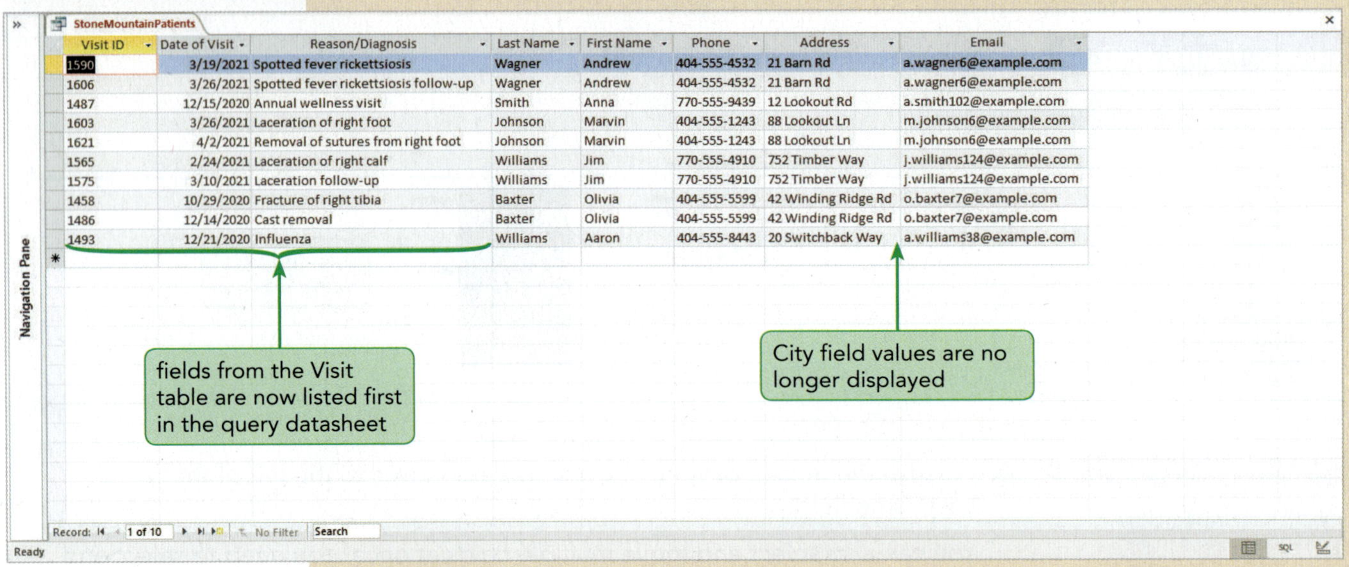

StoneMountainPatients

Visit ID	Date of Visit	Reason/Diagnosis	Last Name	First Name	Phone	Address	Email
1590	3/19/2021	Spotted fever rickettsiosis	Wagner	Andrew	404-555-4532	21 Barn Rd	a.wagner6@example.com
1606	3/26/2021	Spotted fever rickettsiosis follow-up	Wagner	Andrew	404-555-4532	21 Barn Rd	a.wagner6@example.com
1487	12/15/2020	Annual wellness visit	Smith	Anna	770-555-9439	12 Lookout Rd	a.smith102@example.com
1603	3/26/2021	Laceration of right foot	Johnson	Marvin	404-555-1243	88 Lookout Ln	m.johnson6@example.com
1621	4/2/2021	Removal of sutures from right foot	Johnson	Marvin	404-555-1243	88 Lookout Ln	m.johnson6@example.com
1565	2/24/2021	Laceration of right calf	Williams	Jim	770-555-4910	752 Timber Way	j.williams124@example.com
1575	3/10/2021	Laceration follow-up	Williams	Jim	770-555-4910	752 Timber Way	j.williams124@example.com
1458	10/29/2020	Fracture of right tibia	Baxter	Olivia	404-555-5599	42 Winding Ridge Rd	o.baxter7@example.com
1486	12/14/2020	Cast removal	Baxter	Olivia	404-555-5599	42 Winding Ridge Rd	o.baxter7@example.com
1493	12/21/2020	Influenza	Williams	Aaron	404-555-8443	20 Switchback Way	a.williams38@example.com

Note that the City field values are no longer displayed in the query results.

9. Save and close the StoneMountainPatients query.

After viewing the query results, Donna decides that she would like to see the same fields, but only for those records with a VisitDate field value before 1/1/2021. She is interested to know which patients of Lakewood Community Health Services in all cities have not been to the clinic recently, so that her staff can follow up with the patients by sending them reminder notes or emails. To create the query that will produce the results Donna wants, you need to use a comparison operator to match a range of values—in this case, any VisitDate value less than 1/1/2021. Because this new query will include information from several of the same fields as the StoneMountainPatients query, you can use that query as a starting point in designing this new query.

Using a Comparison Operator to Match a Range of Values

After you create and save a query, you can double-click the query name in the Navigation Pane to run the query again. You can then click the View button to change its design. You can also use an existing query as the basis for creating another query. Because the design of the query you need to create next is similar to the StoneMountainPatients query, you will copy, paste, and rename this query to create the new query. Using this approach keeps the StoneMountainPatients query intact.

To create the new query by copying the StoneMountainPatients query:

1. Open the Navigation Pane. Note that the StoneMountainPatients query is listed in the Queries section.

   You need to use the shortcut menu to copy the StoneMountainPatients query and paste it in the Navigation Pane; then you'll give the copied query a different name.

2. In the Queries section of the Navigation Pane, right-click **StoneMountainPatients** to select it and display the shortcut menu.
3. Click **Copy** on the shortcut menu.
4. Right-click the empty area near the bottom of the Navigation Pane, and then click **Paste** on the shortcut menu. The Paste As dialog box opens with the text "Copy Of StoneMountainPatients" in the Query Name box. Because Donna wants the new query to show data for patients that have not visited the clinic recently, you'll name the new query "EarlierVisits".
5. In the Query Name box, type **EarlierVisits** and then press **ENTER**. The new query appears in the Queries section of the Navigation Pane.
6. Double-click the **EarlierVisits** query to open, or run, the query. The design of this query is currently the same as the original StoneMountainPatients query.
7. Close the Navigation Pane.

Next, you need to open the query in Design view and modify its design to produce the results Donna wants—to display records for all patients and only those records with VisitDate field values that are earlier than, or less than, 1/1/2021.

To modify the design of the new query:

1. Display the query in Design view.
2. Click the **VisitDate Criteria** box, type **<1/1/2021** and then press **TAB**. Note that Access automatically encloses the date criteria with number signs. The condition specifies that a record will be selected only if its VisitDate field value is less than (earlier than) 1/1/2021. See Figure 3–23.

Figure 3–23 **Criteria entered for the VisitDate field**

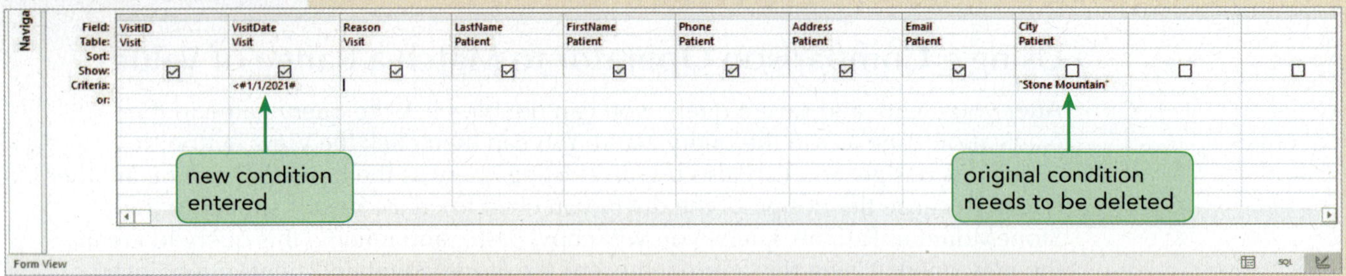

Note that Access automatically encloses the date criteria with number signs. The condition specifies that a record will be selected only if its VisitDate field value is less than (earlier than) 1/1/2021.

Before you run the query, you need to delete the condition for the City field. Recall that the City field is part of the query, but its values are not displayed in the query results. When you modified the query to remove the City field values from the query results, Access moved the field to the end of the design grid. You need to delete the City field's condition, specify that the City field values should be included in the query results, and then move the field back to its original position following the Address field.

3. Press **TAB** six times to select the condition for the City field, and then press **DELETE**. The condition for the City field is removed.
4. Click the **Show** check box for the City field to insert a checkmark so that the field values will be displayed in the query results.
5. Use the pointer to select the City field, drag the selected field to position it to the left of the Email field, and then click in an empty box to deselect the City field. See Figure 3–24.

Figure 3–24 **Design grid after moving the City field**

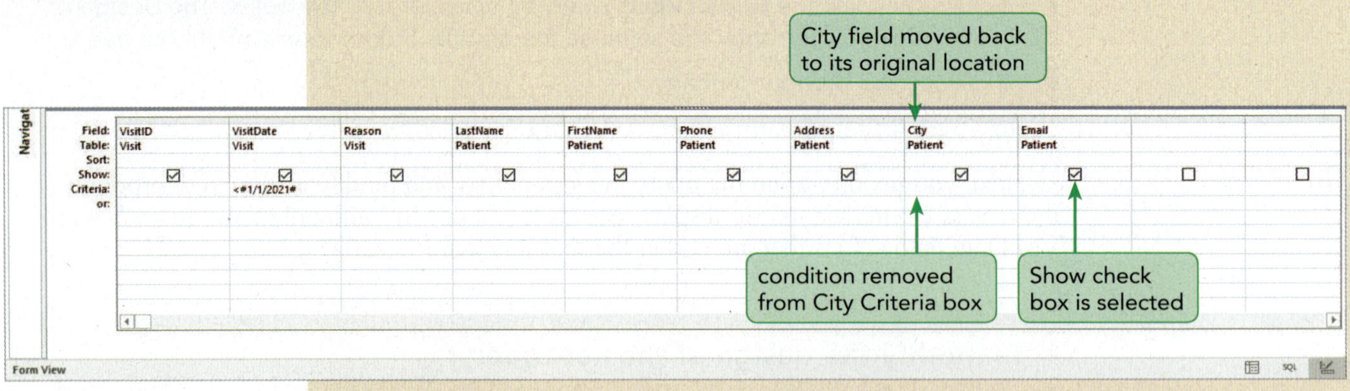

6. Run the query. The query datasheet displays the selected fields for only those records with a VisitDate field value less than 1/1/2021, a total of 27 records. See Figure 3–25.

Figure 3–25 **Running the modified query**

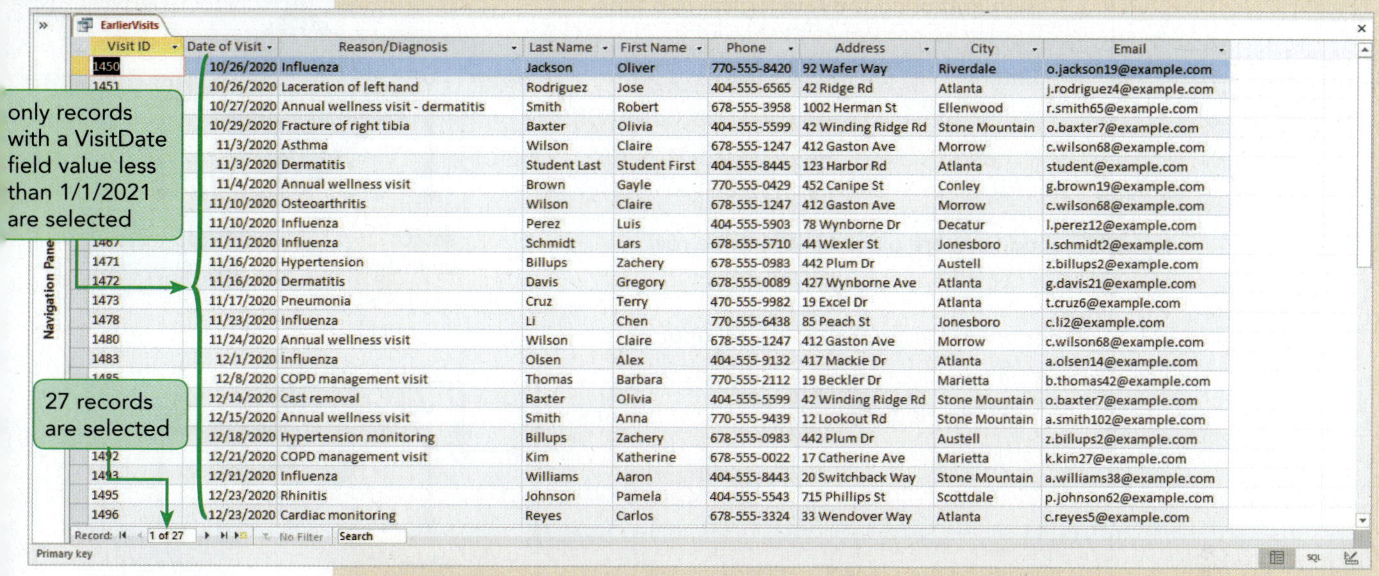

Visit ID	Date of Visit	Reason/Diagnosis	Last Name	First Name	Phone	Address	City	Email
1450	10/26/2020	Influenza	Jackson	Oliver	770-555-8420	92 Wafer Way	Riverdale	o.jackson19@example.com
1451	10/26/2020	Laceration of left hand	Rodriguez	Jose	404-555-6565	42 Ridge Rd	Atlanta	j.rodriguez4@example.com
	10/27/2020	Annual wellness visit - dermatitis	Smith	Robert	678-555-3958	1002 Herman St	Ellenwood	r.smith65@example.com
	10/29/2020	Fracture of right tibia	Baxter	Olivia	404-555-5599	42 Winding Ridge Rd	Stone Mountain	o.baxter7@example.com
	11/3/2020	Asthma	Wilson	Claire	678-555-1247	412 Gaston Ave	Morrow	c.wilson68@example.com
	11/3/2020	Dermatitis	Student Last	Student First	404-555-8445	123 Harbor Rd	Atlanta	student@example.com
	11/4/2020	Annual wellness visit	Brown	Gayle	770-555-0429	452 Canipe St	Conley	g.brown19@example.com
	11/10/2020	Osteoarthritis	Wilson	Claire	678-555-1247	412 Gaston Ave	Morrow	c.wilson68@example.com
	11/10/2020	Influenza	Perez	Luis	404-555-5903	78 Wynborne Dr	Decatur	l.perez12@example.com
	11/11/2020	Influenza	Schmidt	Lars	678-555-5710	44 Wexler St	Jonesboro	l.schmidt2@example.com
1471	11/16/2020	Hypertension	Billups	Zachery	678-555-0983	442 Plum Dr	Austell	z.billups2@example.com
1472	11/16/2020	Dermatitis	Davis	Gregory	678-555-0089	427 Wynborne Ave	Atlanta	g.davis21@example.com
1473	11/17/2020	Pneumonia	Cruz	Terry	470-555-9982	19 Excel Dr	Atlanta	t.cruz6@example.com
1478	11/23/2020	Influenza	Li	Chen	770-555-6438	85 Peach St	Jonesboro	c.li2@example.com
1480	11/24/2020	Annual wellness visit	Wilson	Claire	678-555-1247	412 Gaston Ave	Morrow	c.wilson68@example.com
1483	12/1/2020	Influenza	Olsen	Alex	404-555-9132	417 Mackie Dr	Atlanta	a.olsen14@example.com
	12/8/2020	COPD management visit	Thomas	Barbara	770-555-2112	19 Beckler Dr	Marietta	b.thomas42@example.com
	12/14/2020	Cast removal	Baxter	Olivia	404-555-5599	42 Winding Ridge Rd	Stone Mountain	o.baxter7@example.com
	12/15/2020	Annual wellness visit	Smith	Anna	770-555-9439	12 Lookout Rd	Stone Mountain	a.smith102@example.com
	12/18/2020	Hypertension monitoring	Billups	Zachery	678-555-0983	442 Plum Dr	Austell	z.billups2@example.com
1492	12/21/2020	COPD management visit	Kim	Katherine	678-555-0022	17 Catherine Ave	Marietta	k.kim27@example.com
1493	12/21/2020	Influenza	Williams	Aaron	404-555-8443	20 Switchback Way	Stone Mountain	a.williams38@example.com
1495	12/23/2020	Rhinitis	Johnson	Pamela	404-555-5543	715 Phillips St	Scottdale	p.johnson62@example.com
1496	12/23/2020	Cardiac monitoring	Reyes	Carlos	678-555-3324	33 Wendover Way	Atlanta	c.reyes5@example.com

7. Save and close the EarlierVisits query.

Donna continues to analyze patient visits to Lakewood Community Health Services. She is especially concerned about being proactive and reaching out to older patients well in advance of flu season. With this in mind, she would like to see a list of all patients who are age 50 or older and who have visited the clinic suffering from influenza. She wants to track these patients in particular so that her staff can contact them early for flu shots. To produce this list, you need to create a query containing two conditions—one for the patient's date of birth and another for the reason/diagnosis for each patient visit.

Defining Multiple Selection Criteria for Queries

Multiple conditions require you to use **logical operators** to combine two or more conditions. When you want a record selected only if two or more conditions are met, you need to use the **And logical operator**. In this case, Donna wants to see only those records with a BirthDate field value less than or equal to 12/31/1970 *and* a Reason field value of "Influenza." If you place conditions in separate fields in the *same* Criteria row of the design grid, all conditions in that row must be met in order for a record to be included in the query results. However, if you place conditions in *different* Criteria rows, a record will be selected if at least one of the conditions is met. If none of the conditions are met, Access does not select the record. When you place conditions in different Criteria rows, you are using the **Or logical operator**. Figure 3–26 illustrates the difference between the And and Or logical operators.

Figure 3–26 Logical operators And and Or for multiple selection criteria

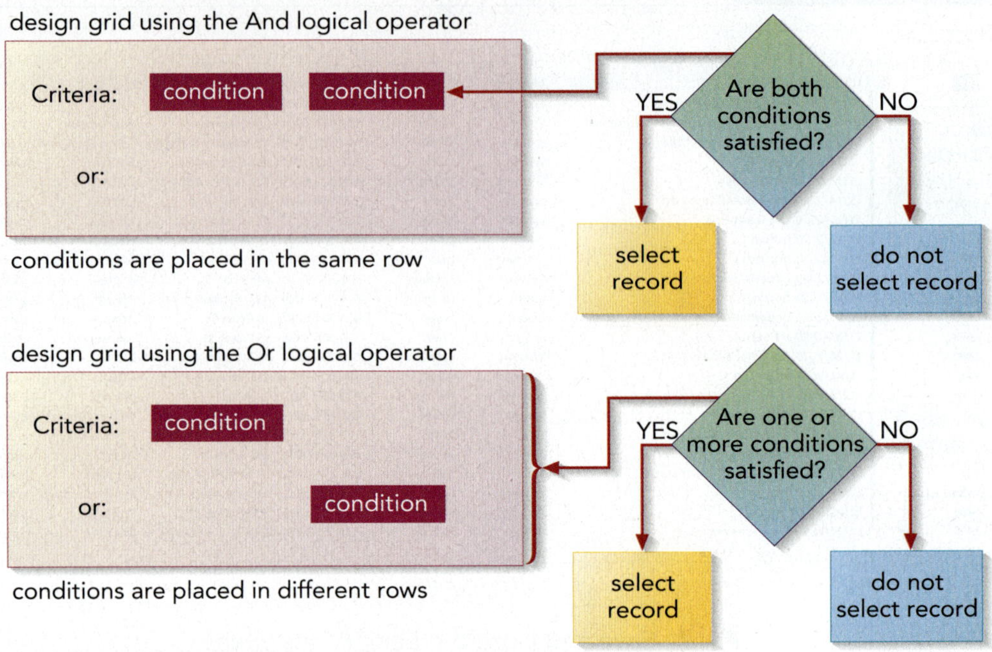

The And Logical Operator

To create the query for Donna, you need to use the And logical operator to show only the records for patients that were born on or after 12/31/1970 *and* who have visited the clinic because of influenza. You'll create a new query based on the Patient and Visit tables to produce the necessary results. In the query design, both conditions you specify will appear in the same Criteria row; therefore, the query will select records only if both conditions are met.

To create a new query using the And logical operator:

1. On the ribbon, click the **Create** tab.
2. In the Queries group, click the **Query Design** button.
3. Add the **Patient** and **Visit** tables to the Query window, and then close the Show Table dialog box. Resize both field lists to display all the field names.
4. Add the following fields from the Patient field list to the design grid in the order shown: **FirstName**, **LastName**, **BirthDate**, **Phone**, and **City**.
5. Add the **VisitDate** and **Reason** fields from the Visit table to the design grid. Now you need to enter the two conditions for the query.
6. Click the **BirthDate Criteria** box, and then type **<=12/31/1970**.
7. Press **TAB** four times to move to the **Reason Criteria** box, type **Influenza**, and then press **TAB**. See Figure 3–27.

Figure 3–27 Query to find older patients who have had influenza

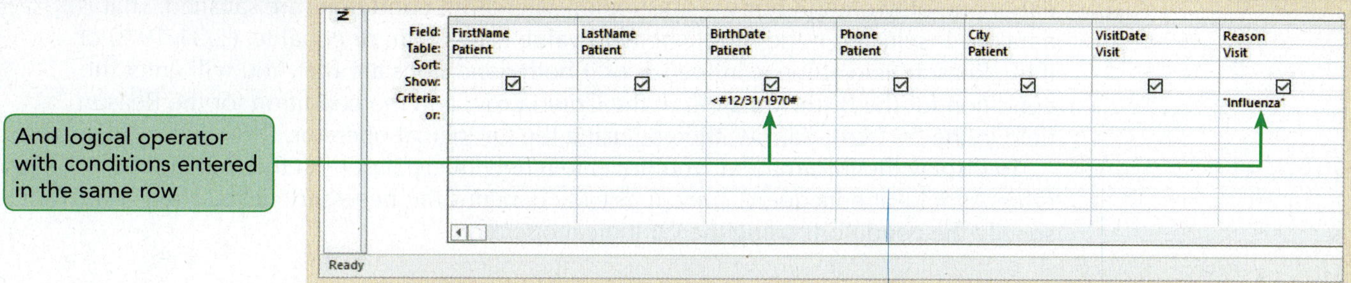

8. Run the query. The query displays only those records that meet both conditions: a BirthDate field value less than or equal to 12/31/1970 *and* a Reason field value of Influenza. Two records are displayed for two different patients. See Figure 3–28.

Figure 3–28 Results of query using the And logical operator

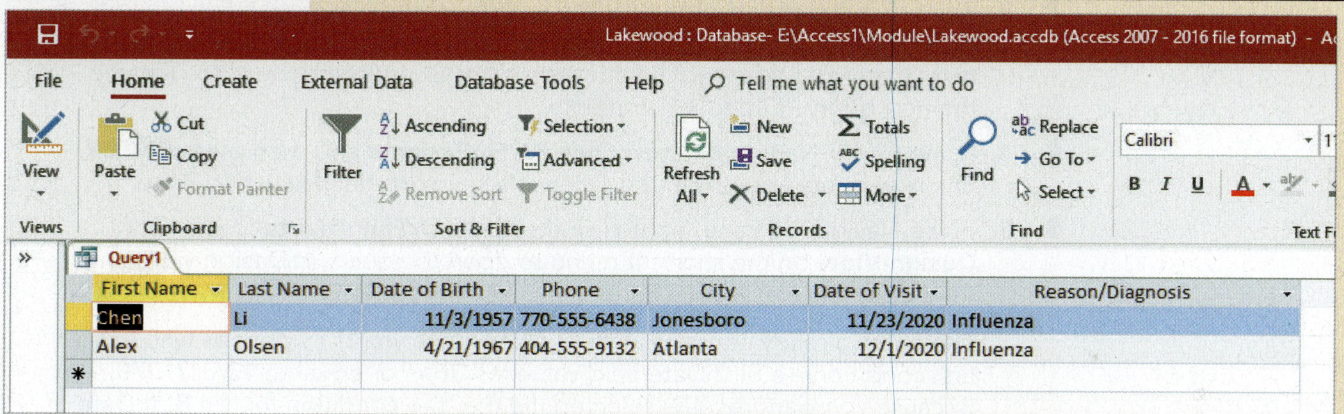

9. On the Quick Access Toolbar, click the **Save** button, and then save the query as **OlderAndFluPatients**.

10. Close the query.

Donna meets with staff members to discuss the issue of influenza and patients being informed about receiving flu shots at the clinic. After viewing the results of the OlderAndFluPatients query, the group agrees that the clinic should reach out to older patients regarding flu shots, because this segment of the population is particularly susceptible to the flu. In addition, the group feels the clinic should contact patients who have visited the clinic suffering from influenza to keep these patients informed about flu shots well in advance of flu season. To help with their planning, Donna asks you to produce a list of all patients that were born on or before 12/31/1970 or who visited the clinic because of influenza. To create this query, you need to use the Or logical operator.

The Or Logical Operator

To create the query that Donna requested, your query must select a record when either one of two conditions is satisfied or when both conditions are satisfied. That is, a record is selected if the BirthDate field value is less than or equal to 12/31/1970 *or* if the Reason field value is Influenza *or* if both conditions are met. You will enter the condition for the BirthDate field in the Criteria row and the condition for the Reason field in the "or" criteria row, thereby using the Or logical operator.

To display the information, you'll create a new query based on the existing OlderAndFluPatients query, since it already contains the necessary fields. Then you'll specify the conditions using the Or logical operator.

To create a new query using the Or logical operator:

1. Open the Navigation Pane. You'll use the shortcut menu to copy and paste the OlderAndFluPatients query to create the new query.
2. In the Queries section of the Navigation Pane, right-click **OlderAndFluPatients**, and then click **Copy** on the shortcut menu.
3. Right-click the empty area near the bottom of the Navigation Pane, and then click **Paste** on the shortcut menu. The Paste As dialog box opens with the text "Copy Of OlderAndFluPatients" in the Query Name box. You'll name the new query "OlderOrFluPatients".
4. In the Query Name box, type **OlderOrFluPatients** and then press **ENTER**. The new query appears in the Queries section of the Navigation Pane.
5. In the Navigation Pane, right-click the **OlderOrFluPatients** query, click **Design View** on the shortcut menu to open the query in Design view, and then close the Navigation Pane.

   The query already contains all the fields Donna wants to view, as well as the first condition—a BirthDate field value less than or equal to 12/31/1970. Because you want records selected if either the condition for the BirthDate field or the condition for the Reason field is satisfied, you must delete the existing condition for the Reason field in the Criteria row and then enter this same condition in the "or" row of the design grid for the Reason field.
6. In the design grid, delete **"Influenza"** in the Reason Criteria box.
7. Press **DOWN ARROW ↓** to move to the "or" row for the Reason field, type **Influenza**, and then press **TAB**. See Figure 3–29.

Figure 3–29 Query window with the Or logical operator

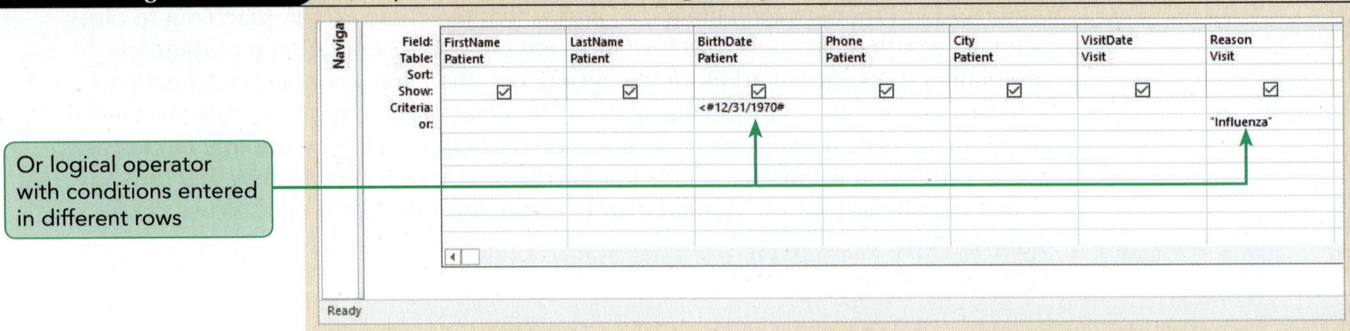

To better analyze the data, Donna wants the list displayed in descending order by BirthDate.

8. Click the right side of the **BirthDate Sort** box, and then click **Descending**.
9. Run the query. The query datasheet displays only those records that meet either condition: a BirthDate field value less than or equal to 12/31/1970 *or* a Reason field value of Influenza. The query also returns records that meet both conditions. The query displays a total of 43 records. The records in the query datasheet appear in descending order based on the values in the BirthDate field. See Figure 3–30.

Figure 3–30 Results of query using the Or logical operator

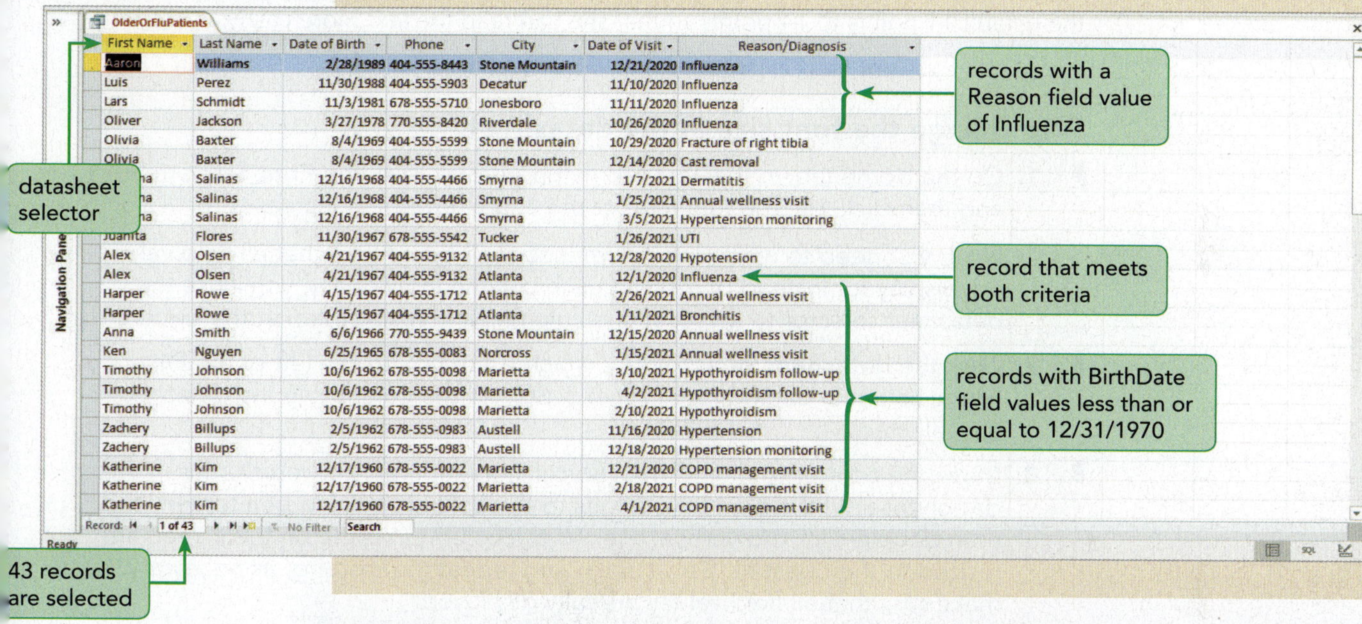

First Name	Last Name	Date of Birth	Phone	City	Date of Visit	Reason/Diagnosis
Aaron	Williams	2/28/1989	404-555-8443	Stone Mountain	12/21/2020	Influenza
Luis	Perez	11/30/1988	404-555-5903	Decatur	11/10/2020	Influenza
Lars	Schmidt	11/3/1981	678-555-5710	Jonesboro	11/11/2020	Influenza
Oliver	Jackson	3/27/1978	770-555-8420	Riverdale	10/26/2020	Influenza
Olivia	Baxter	8/4/1969	404-555-5599	Stone Mountain	10/29/2020	Fracture of right tibia
Olivia	Baxter	8/4/1969	404-555-5599	Stone Mountain	12/14/2020	Cast removal
[illegible]	Salinas	12/16/1968	404-555-4466	Smyrna	1/7/2021	Dermatitis
[illegible]	Salinas	12/16/1968	404-555-4466	Smyrna	1/25/2021	Annual wellness visit
[illegible]	Salinas	12/16/1968	404-555-4466	Smyrna	3/5/2021	Hypertension monitoring
Juanita	Flores	11/30/1967	678-555-5542	Tucker	1/26/2021	UTI
Alex	Olsen	4/21/1967	404-555-9132	Atlanta	12/28/2020	Hypotension
Alex	Olsen	4/21/1967	404-555-9132	Atlanta	12/1/2020	Influenza
Harper	Rowe	4/15/1967	404-555-1712	Atlanta	2/26/2021	Annual wellness visit
Harper	Rowe	4/15/1967	404-555-1712	Atlanta	1/11/2021	Bronchitis
Anna	Smith	6/6/1966	770-555-9439	Stone Mountain	12/15/2020	Annual wellness visit
Ken	Nguyen	6/25/1965	678-555-0083	Norcross	1/15/2021	Annual wellness visit
Timothy	Johnson	10/6/1962	678-555-0098	Marietta	3/10/2021	Hypothyroidism follow-up
Timothy	Johnson	10/6/1962	678-555-0098	Marietta	4/2/2021	Hypothyroidism follow-up
Timothy	Johnson	10/6/1962	678-555-0098	Marietta	2/10/2021	Hypothyroidism
Zachery	Billups	2/5/1962	678-555-0983	Austell	11/16/2020	Hypertension
Zachery	Billups	2/5/1962	678-555-0983	Austell	12/18/2020	Hypertension monitoring
Katherine	Kim	12/17/1960	678-555-0022	Marietta	12/21/2020	COPD management visit
Katherine	Kim	12/17/1960	678-555-0022	Marietta	2/18/2021	COPD management visit
Katherine	Kim	12/17/1960	678-555-0022	Marietta	4/1/2021	COPD management visit

INSIGHT

Understanding the Results of Using And vs. Or

When you use the And logical operator to define multiple selection criteria in a query, you *narrow* the results produced by the query because a record must meet more than one condition to be included in the results. For example, the OlderAndFluPatients query you created resulted in only 2 records. When you use the Or logical operator, you *broaden* the results produced by the query because a record must meet only one of the conditions to be included in the results. For example, the OlderOrFluPatients query you created resulted in 43 records. This is an important distinction to keep in mind when you include multiple selection criteria in queries, so that the queries you create will produce the results you want.

Donna would like to spend some time reviewing the results of the OlderOrFluPatients query. To make this task easier, she asks you to change how the datasheet is displayed.

Changing a Datasheet's Appearance

You can make many formatting changes to a datasheet to improve its appearance or readability. Many of these modifications are familiar types of changes you can also make in Word documents or Excel spreadsheets, such as modifying the font type, size, color, and the alignment of text. You can also remove gridlines to improve the appearance of the datasheet, and apply different colors to the rows and columns in a datasheet to make it easier to read.

Modifying the Font Size

Depending on the size of the monitor you are using or the screen resolution, you might need to increase or decrease the size of the font in a datasheet to view more or fewer columns of data. Donna asks you to change the font size in the query datasheet from the default 11 points to 14 points so that she can read the text more easily.

To change the font size in the datasheet:

1. On the Home tab, in the Text Formatting group, click the **Font Size** arrow, and then click **14**. The font size for the entire datasheet increases to 14 points.

   Next, you need to resize the columns to their best fit, so that all field values are displayed. Instead of resizing each column individually, you'll use the datasheet selector to select all the columns and resize them at the same time.

2. Click the **datasheet selector**, which is the box to the left of the First Name column heading (see Figure 3–30). All the columns in the datasheet are selected.
3. Move the pointer to one of the vertical lines separating two columns in the datasheet until the pointer changes to the column resizing pointer, and then double-click the vertical line. All the columns visible on the screen are resized to their best fit. Scroll down and repeat the resizing, as necessary, to make sure that all field values are fully displayed.

   Trouble? If all the columns are not visible on your screen, you need to scroll the datasheet to the right to make sure all field values for all columns are fully displayed. If you need to resize any columns, click a field value first to deselect the columns before resizing an individual column.

4. Click any value in the First Name column to make it the current field and to deselect the columns in the datasheet.

Changing the Alternate Row Color in a Datasheet

TIP

When choosing a row color, be sure not to select a color that is too dark because it might obscure the data rather than enhance it.

Access uses themes to format the objects in a database. A **theme** is a predefined set of formats including colors, fonts, and other effects that enhance an object's appearance and usability. When you create a database, Access applies the Office theme to objects as you create them. By default, the Office theme formats every other row in a datasheet with a gray background color to distinguish one row from another, making it easier to view and read the contents of a datasheet. The gray alternate row color provides a subtle difference compared to the rows that have the default white color. You can change the alternate row color in a datasheet to something more noticeable using the Alternate Row Color button in the Text Formatting group on the Home tab. Donna suggests that you change the alternate row color in the datasheet to see the effect of using this feature.

To change the alternate row color in the datasheet:

1. On the Home tab, in the Text Formatting group, click the **Alternate Row Color arrow** to display the gallery of color choices. See Figure 3-31.

Figure 3–31 Gallery of color choices for alternate row color

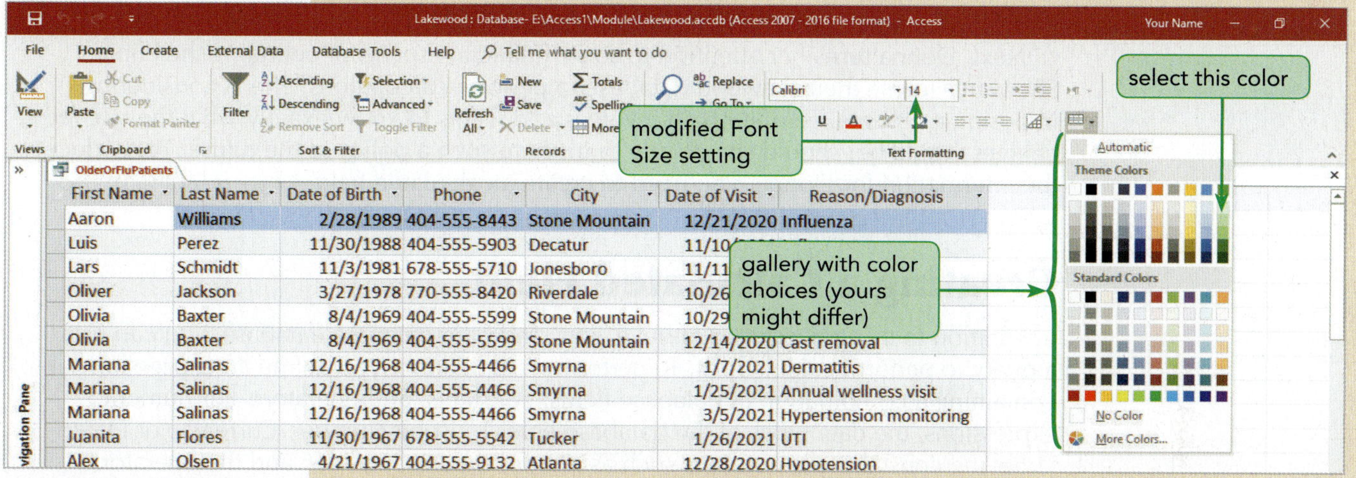

TIP

The name of the color appears in a ScreenTip when you point to a color in the gallery.

The Theme Colors section provides colors from the default Office theme, so that your datasheet's color scheme matches the one in use for the database. The Standard Colors section provides many standard color choices. You might also see a Recent Colors section, with colors that you have recently used in a datasheet. The No Color option, which appears at the bottom of the gallery, sets each row's background color to white. If you want to create a custom color, you can do so using the More Colors option. You'll use one of the theme colors.

2. In the Theme Colors section, click the **Green, Accent 6, Lighter 60%** color (third row, tenth color). The alternate row color is applied to the query datasheet. See Figure 3–32.

Figure 3–32 Datasheet formatted with alternate row color

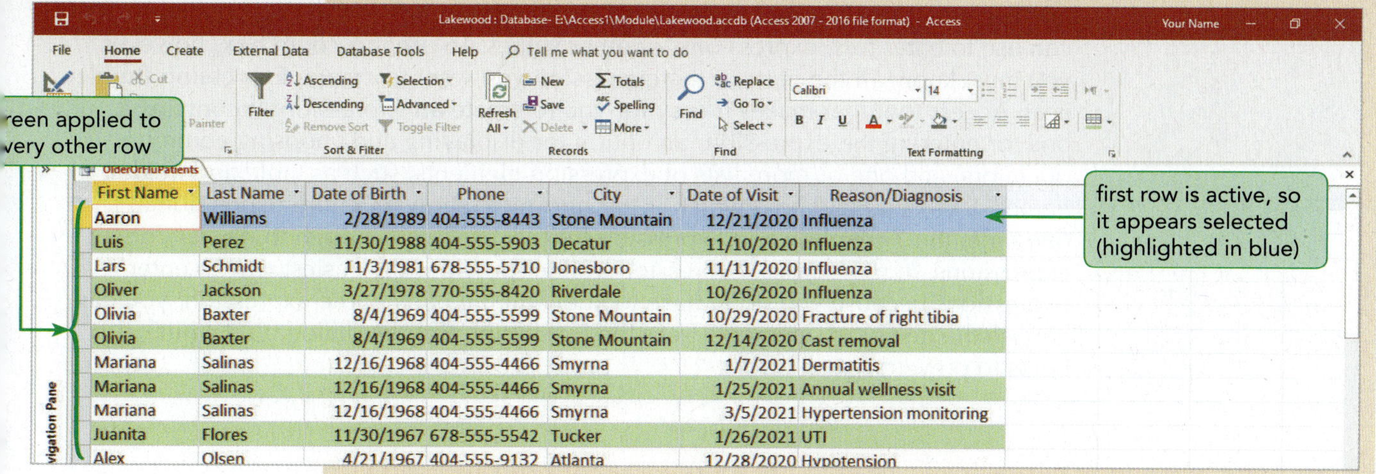

Every other row in the datasheet uses the selected theme color. Donna likes how the datasheet looks with this color scheme, so she asks you to save the query.

3. Save and close the OlderOrFluPatients query. The query is saved with both the increased font size and the green alternate row color.

Next, Donna turns her attention to some financial aspects of operating the clinic. She wants to use the Lakewood database to perform calculations. She is considering imposing a 2% late fee on unpaid invoices and wants to know exactly what the late fee charges would be, should she decide to institute such a policy in the future. To produce the information for Donna, you need to create a calculated field.

Creating a Calculated Field

In addition to using queries to retrieve, sort, and filter data in a database, you can use a query to perform calculations. To perform a calculation, you define an **expression** containing a combination of database fields, constants, and operators. For numeric expressions, the data types of the database fields must be Number, Currency, or Date/Time; the constants are numbers such as .02 (for the 2% late fee); and the operators can be arithmetic operators (+ – * /) or other specialized operators. In complex expressions, you can enclose calculations in parentheses to indicate which one should be performed first; any calculation within parentheses is completed before calculations outside the parentheses. In expressions without parentheses, Access performs basic calculations using the following order of precedence: multiplication and division before addition and subtraction. When operators have equal precedence, Access calculates them in order from left to right.

To perform a calculation in a query, you add a calculated field to the query. A **calculated field** is a field that displays the results of an expression. A calculated field that you create with an expression appears in a query datasheet or in a form or report; however, it does not exist in a database. When you run a query that contains a calculated field, Access evaluates the expression defined by the calculated field and displays the resulting value in the query datasheet, form, or report.

To enter an expression for a calculated field, you can type it directly in a Field box in the design grid. Alternately, you can open the Zoom box or Expression Builder and use either one to enter the expression. The **Zoom box** is a dialog box that you can use to enter text, expressions, or other values. To use the Zoom box, however, you must know all the parts of the expression you want to create. **Expression Builder** is an Access tool that makes it easy for you to create an expression; it contains a box for entering the expression, an option for displaying and choosing common operators, and one or more lists of expression elements, such as table and field names. Unlike a Field box, which is too narrow to show an entire expression at one time, the Zoom box and Expression Builder are large enough to display longer expressions. In most cases, Expression Builder provides the easiest way to enter expressions because you don't have to know all the parts of the expression; you can choose the necessary elements from the Expression Builder dialog box, which also helps to prevent typing errors.

REFERENCE

Creating a Calculated Field Using Expression Builder

- Create and save the query in which you want to include a calculated field.
- Open the query in Design view.
- In the design grid, click the Field box in which you want to create an expression.
- In the Query Setup group on the Query Tools Design tab, click the Builder button.
- Use the expression elements and common operators to build the expression, or type the expression directly in the expression box.
- Click the OK button.

To produce the information Donna wants, you need to create a new query based on the Billing and Visit tables and, in the query, create a calculated field that will multiply each InvoiceAmt field value by .02 to calculate the proposed 2% late fee.

To create the new query:

1. On the ribbon, click the **Create** tab.
2. In the Queries group, click the **Query Design** button. The Show Table dialog box opens.

   Donna wants to see data from both the Visit and Billing tables, so you need to add these two tables to the Query window.
3. Add the **Visit** and **Billing** tables to the Query window, and resize the field lists as necessary so that all the field names are visible. The field lists appear in the Query window, and the one-to-many relationship between the Visit (primary) and Billing (related) tables is displayed.
4. Add the following fields to the design grid in the order given: **VisitID**, **PatientID**, and **VisitDate** from the Visit table; and **InvoiceItem**, **InvoicePaid**, and **InvoiceAmt** from the Billing table.

   Donna is interested in viewing data only for unpaid invoices because a late fee would apply only to them, so you need to enter the necessary condition for the InvoicePaid field. Recall that InvoicePaid is a Yes/No field. The condition you need to enter is the word "No" in the Criteria box for this field, so that Access will retrieve the records for unpaid invoices only.
5. In the **InvoicePaid Criteria box**, type **No**. As soon as you type the letter "N," a menu appears with options for entering various functions for the criteria. You don't need to enter a function, so you can close this menu.
6. Press **ESC** to close the menu.

   You must close the menu or you'll enter a function, which will cause an error.
7. Press **TAB**. The query name you'll use will indicate that the data is for unpaid invoices, so you don't need to include the InvoicePaid values in the query results.
8. Click the **InvoicePaid Show** check box to remove the checkmark.
9. Save the query with the name **UnpaidInvoiceLateFee**.

Now you can use Expression Builder to create the calculated field for the InvoiceAmt field.

TIP

You must first save and name a query in order for its fields to be listed in the Expression Categories section.

To create the calculated field:

1. Click the blank Field box to the right of the InvoiceAmt field. This field will contain the expression.
2. On the Query Tools Design tab, in the Query Setup group, click the **Builder** button. The Expression Builder dialog box opens.

   The insertion point is positioned in the large box at the top of the dialog box, ready for you to enter the expression. The Expression Categories section of the dialog box lists the fields from the query so you can include them in the expression. The Expression Elements section contains options for including other elements in the expression, including functions, constants, and operators. If the expression you're entering is a simple one, you can type it in the box; if it's more complex, you can use the options in the Expression Elements section to help you build the expression.

   The expression for the calculated field will multiply the InvoiceAmt field values by the numeric constant .02 (which represents a 2% late fee).
3. In the Expression Categories section of the dialog box, double-click **InvoiceAmt**. The field name is added to the expression box, within brackets and with a space following it. In an expression, all field names must be enclosed in brackets.

   Next you need to enter the multiplication operator, which is the asterisk (*), followed by the constant.
4. Type * (an asterisk) and then type **.02**. You have finished entering the expression. See Figure 3–33.

Figure 3–33 Completed expression for the calculated field

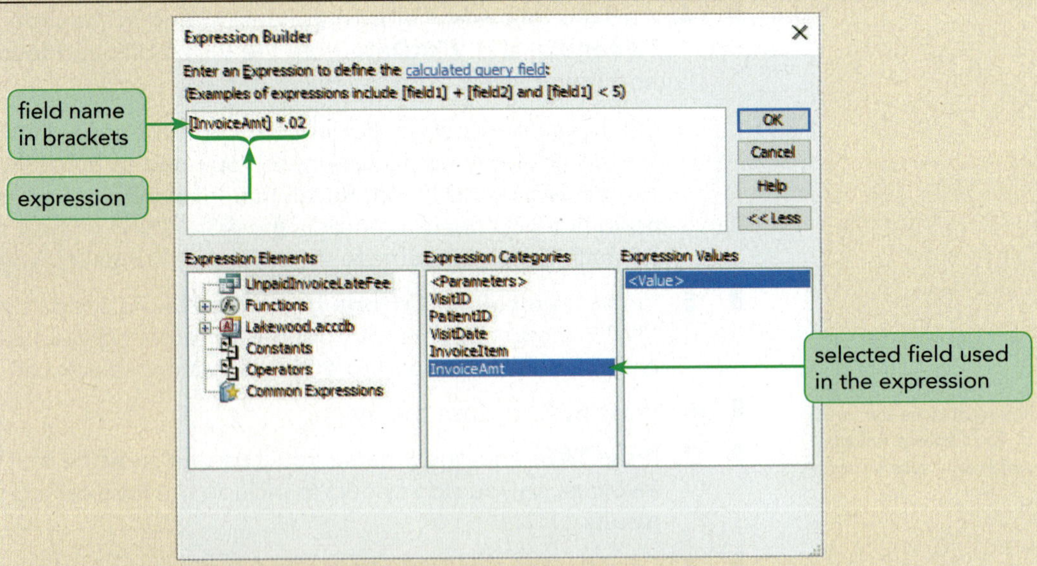

   If you're not sure which operator to use, you can click Operators in the Expression Elements section to display a list of available operators in the center section of the dialog box.
5. Click **OK**. The Expression Builder dialog box closes, and the expression is added to the design grid in the Field box for the calculated field. When you

create a calculated field, Access uses the default name "Expr1" for the field. You need to specify a more meaningful field name so it will appear in the query results. You'll enter the name "LateFee," which better describes the field's contents.

6. Click to the left of the text "Expr1:" at the beginning of the expression, and then press **DELETE** five times to delete the text **Expr1**. *Do not delete the colon*; it is needed to separate the calculated field name from the expression.
7. Type **LateFee**. Next, you'll set this field's Caption property so that the field name will appear as "Late Fee" in the query datasheet.
8. On the Query Tools Design tab, in the Show/Hide group, click the **Property Sheet** button. The Property Sheet for the current field, LateFee, opens on the right side of the window. See Figure 3–34.

Figure 3–34 **Property Sheet for the calculated field**

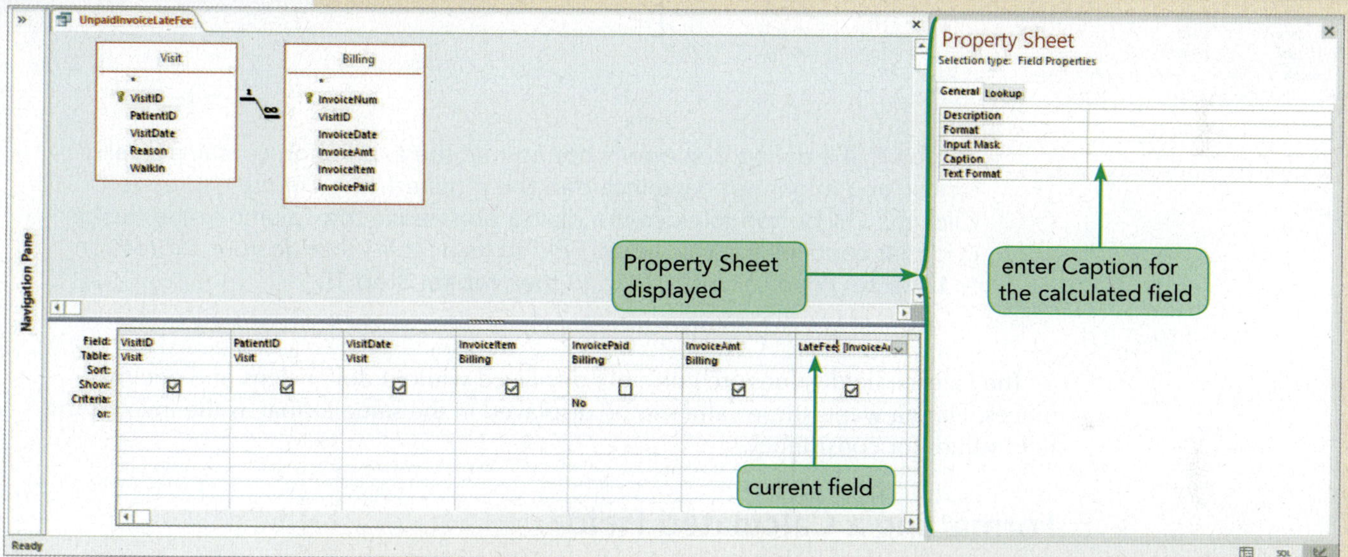

9. In the Property Sheet, click in the Caption box, type **Late Fee** and then close the Property Sheet.
10. Run the query. The query datasheet is displayed and contains the specified fields and the calculated field with the caption "Late Fee." See Figure 3–35.

Figure 3–35 Datasheet displaying the calculated field

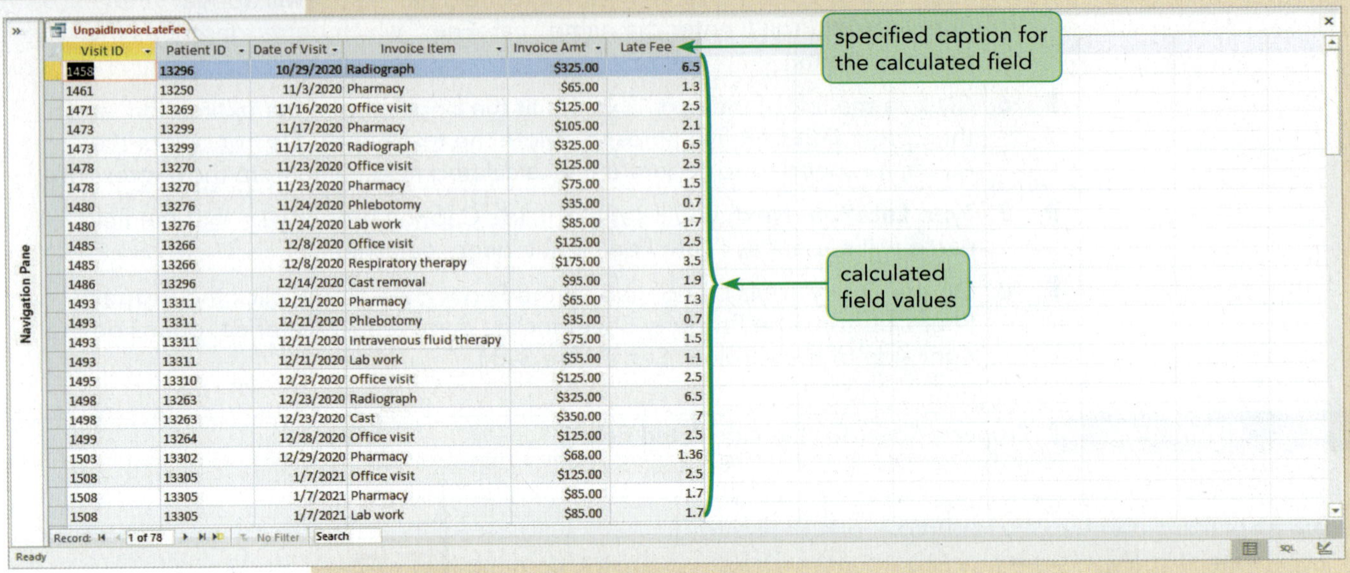

Visit ID	Patient ID	Date of Visit	Invoice Item	Invoice Amt	Late Fee
1458	13296	10/29/2020	Radiograph	$325.00	6.5
1461	13250	11/3/2020	Pharmacy	$65.00	1.3
1471	13269	11/16/2020	Office visit	$125.00	2.5
1473	13299	11/17/2020	Pharmacy	$105.00	2.1
1473	13299	11/17/2020	Radiograph	$325.00	6.5
1478	13270	11/23/2020	Office visit	$125.00	2.5
1478	13270	11/23/2020	Pharmacy	$75.00	1.5
1480	13276	11/24/2020	Phlebotomy	$35.00	0.7
1480	13276	11/24/2020	Lab work	$85.00	1.7
1485	13266	12/8/2020	Office visit	$125.00	2.5
1485	13266	12/8/2020	Respiratory therapy	$175.00	3.5
1486	13296	12/14/2020	Cast removal	$95.00	1.9
1493	13311	12/21/2020	Pharmacy	$65.00	1.3
1493	13311	12/21/2020	Phlebotomy	$35.00	0.7
1493	13311	12/21/2020	Intravenous fluid therapy	$75.00	1.5
1493	13311	12/21/2020	Lab work	$55.00	1.1
1495	13310	12/23/2020	Office visit	$125.00	2.5
1498	13263	12/23/2020	Radiograph	$325.00	6.5
1498	13263	12/23/2020	Cast	$350.00	7
1499	13264	12/28/2020	Office visit	$125.00	2.5
1503	13302	12/29/2020	Pharmacy	$68.00	1.36
1508	13305	1/7/2021	Office visit	$125.00	2.5
1508	13305	1/7/2021	Pharmacy	$85.00	1.7
1508	13305	1/7/2021	Lab work	$85.00	1.7

Trouble? If a dialog box opens noting that the expression contains invalid syntax, you might not have included the required colon in the expression. Click the OK button to close the dialog box, resize the column in the design grid that contains the calculated field to its best fit, change your expression to LateFee: [InvoiceAmt]*0.02 and then repeat Step 10.

The LateFee field values are currently displayed without dollar signs and decimal places. Donna wants these values to be displayed in the same format as the InvoiceAmt field values for consistency.

Formatting a Calculated Field

You can specify a particular format for a calculated field, just as you can for any field, by modifying its properties. Next, you'll change the format of the LateFee calculated field so that all values appear in the Currency format.

To format the calculated field:

1. Switch to Design view.
2. In the design grid, click in the **LateFee** calculated field to make it the current field, if necessary.
3. On the Query Tools Design tab, in the Show/Hide group, click the **Property Sheet** button to open the Property Sheet for the calculated field, if necessary.

   You need to change the Format property to Currency, which displays values with a dollar sign and two decimal places.
4. In the Property Sheet, click the right side of the **Format** box to display the list of formats, and then click **Currency**.
5. Close the Property Sheet, and then run the query. The amounts in the LateFee calculated field are now displayed with dollar signs and two decimal places.
6. Save and close the UnpaidInvoiceLateFee query.

PROSKILLS

Problem Solving: Creating a Calculated Field vs. Using the Calculated Field Data Type

You can also create a calculated field using the Calculated Field data type, which lets you store the result of an expression as a field in a table. However, database experts caution users against storing calculations in a table for several reasons. First, storing calculated data in a table consumes valuable space and increases the size of the database. The preferred approach is to use a calculated field in a query; with this approach, the result of the calculation is not stored in the database—it is produced only when you run the query—and it is always current. Second, the Calculated Field data type provides limited options for creating a calculation, whereas a calculated field in a query provides more functions and options for creating expressions. Third, including a field in a table using the Calculated Field data type limits your options if you need to upgrade the database at some point to a more robust DBMS, such as Oracle or SQL Server, that doesn't support this data type; you would need to redesign your database to eliminate this data type. Finally, most database experts agree that including a field in a table whose value is dependent on other fields in the table violates database design principles. To avoid such problems, it's best to create a query that includes a calculated field to perform the calculation you want, instead of creating a field in a table that uses the Calculated Field data type.

To better analyze costs at Lakewood Community Health Services, Donna wants to view more detailed information about invoices for patient care. Specifically, she would like to know the minimum, average, and maximum invoice amounts. She asks you to determine these statistics from data in the Billing table.

Using Aggregate Functions

You can calculate statistical information, such as totals and averages, on the records displayed in a table datasheet or selected by a query. To do this, you use the Access aggregate functions. **Aggregate functions** perform arithmetic operations on selected records in a database. Figure 3–36 lists the most frequently used aggregate functions.

Figure 3–36 **Frequently used aggregate functions**

Aggregate Function	Determines	Data Types Supported
Average	Average of the field values for the selected records	AutoNumber, Currency, Date/Time, Number
Count	Number of records selected	AutoNumber, Currency, Date/Time, Long Text, Number, OLE Object, Short Text, Yes/No
Maximum	Highest field value for the selected records	AutoNumber, Currency, Date/Time, Number, Short Text
Minimum	Lowest field value for the selected records	AutoNumber, Currency, Date/Time, Number, Short Text
Sum	Total of the field values for the selected records	AutoNumber, Currency, Date/Time, Number

Working with Aggregate Functions Using the Total Row

If you want to quickly perform a calculation using an aggregate function in a table or query datasheet, you can use the Totals button in the Records group on the Home tab. When you click this button, a row labeled "Total" appears at the bottom of the datasheet. You can then choose one of the aggregate functions for a field in the datasheet, and the results of the calculation will be displayed in the Total row for that field.

Donna wants to know the total amount of all invoices for the clinic. You can quickly display this amount using the Sum function in the Total row in the Billing table datasheet.

To display the total amount of all invoices in the Billing table:

1. Open the Navigation Pane, open the **Billing** table in Datasheet view, and then close the Navigation Pane.
2. Make sure the Home tab is displayed.
3. In the Records group, click the **Totals** button. A row with the label "Total" is added to the bottom of the datasheet.
4. Scroll to the bottom of the datasheet to view the Total row. You want to display the sum of all the values in the Invoice Amt column.
5. In the Total row, click the **Invoice Amt** field. An arrow appears on the left side of the field.
6. Click the **arrow** to display the menu of aggregate functions. The functions displayed depend on the data type of the current field; in this case, the menu provides functions for a Currency field. See Figure 3–37.

Figure 3–37 Using aggregate functions in the Total row

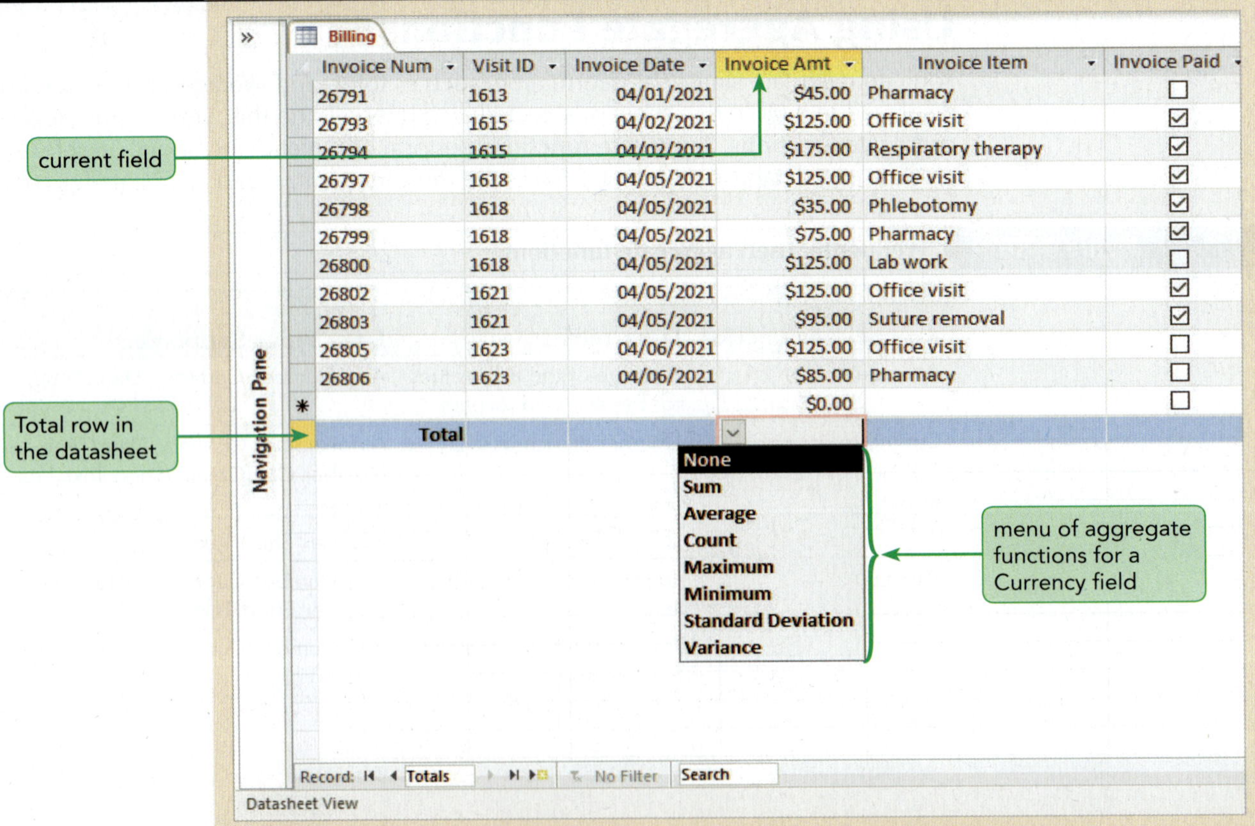

7. Click **Sum** on the menu. All the values in the Invoice Amt column are added, and the total $22,223.00 appears in the Total row for the column.

   Donna doesn't want to change the Billing table to always display this total. You can remove the Total row by clicking the Totals button again; this button works as a toggle to switch between the display of the Total row with the results of any calculations in the row, and the display of the datasheet without this row.

8. In the Records group, click the **Totals** button. The Total row is removed from the datasheet.
9. Close the Billing table without saving the changes.

Donna wants to know the minimum, average, and maximum invoice amounts for Lakewood Community Health Services. To produce this information for Donna, you need to use aggregate functions in a query.

Creating Queries with Aggregate Functions

Aggregate functions operate on the records that meet a query's selection criteria. You specify an aggregate function for a specific field, and the appropriate operation applies to that field's values for the selected records.

To display the minimum, average, and maximum of all the invoice amounts in the Billing table, you will use the Minimum, Average, and Maximum aggregate functions for the InvoiceAmt field.

To calculate the minimum of all invoice amounts:

1. Create a new query in Design view, add the **Billing** table to the Query window, and then resize the Billing field list to display all fields.

   To perform the three calculations on the InvoiceAmt field, you need to add the field to the design grid three times.

2. In the Billing field list, double-click **InvoiceAmt** three times to add three copies of the field to the design grid.

   You need to select an aggregate function for each InvoiceAmt field. When you click the Totals button in the Show/Hide group on the Design tab, a row labeled "Total" is added to the design grid. The Total row provides a list of the aggregate functions that you can select.

3. On the Query Tools Design tab, in the Show/Hide group, click the **Totals** button. A new row labeled "Total" appears between the Table and Sort rows in the design grid. The default entry for each field in the Total row is the Group By operator, which you will learn about later in this module. See Figure 3–38.

Figure 3–38 Total row inserted in the design grid

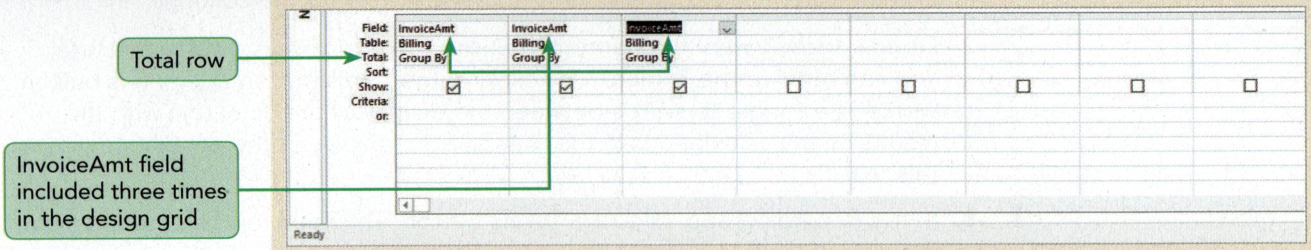

In the Total row, you specify the aggregate function you want to use for a field.

4. Click the right side of the first column's **Total** box, and then click **Min**. This field will calculate the minimum amount of all the InvoiceAmt field values.

   When you run the query, Access automatically will assign a datasheet column name of "MinOfInvoiceAmt" for this field. You can change the datasheet column name to a more descriptive or readable name by entering the name you want in the Field box. However, you must also keep the InvoiceAmt field name in the Field box because it identifies the field to use in the calculation. The Field box will contain the datasheet column name you specify followed by the field name (InvoiceAmt) with a colon separating the two names.

TIP

Be sure to type the colon following the name or the query will not work correctly.

5. In the first column's Field box, click to the left of InvoiceAmt, and then type **MinimumInvoiceAmt:** (including the colon).
6. Resize the column so that you can see the complete field name, MinimumInvoiceAmt:InvoiceAmt.

   Next, you need to set the Caption property for this field so that the field name appears with spaces between words in the query datasheet.

7. On the Query Tools Design tab, in the Show/Hide group, click the **Property Sheet** button to open the Property Sheet for the current field.
8. In the Caption box, type **Minimum Invoice Amt**, and then close the Property Sheet.

You'll follow the same process to complete the query by calculating the average and maximum invoice amounts.

To calculate the average and maximum of all invoice amounts:

1. Click the right side of the second column's **Total** box, and then click **Avg**. This field will calculate the average of all the InvoiceAmt field values.
2. In the second column's Field box, click to the left of InvoiceAmt, and then type **AverageInvoiceAmt**.
3. Resize the second column to fully display the field name, AverageInvoiceAmt:InvoiceAmt.
4. Open the Property Sheet for the current field, and then set its Caption property to **Average Invoice Amt**. Leave the Property Sheet open.
5. Click the right side of the third column's **Total** box, and then click **Max**. This field will calculate the maximum amount of all the InvoiceAmt field values.

6. In the third column's Field box, click to the left of InvoiceAmt, and then type **MaximumInvoiceAmt**.
7. Resize the third column to fully display the field name, MaximumInvoiceAmt:InvoiceAmt.
8. In the Property Sheet, set the Caption property to **Maximum Invoice Amt**, and then close the Property Sheet. See Figure 3–39.

Figure 3–39 Query with aggregate functions entered

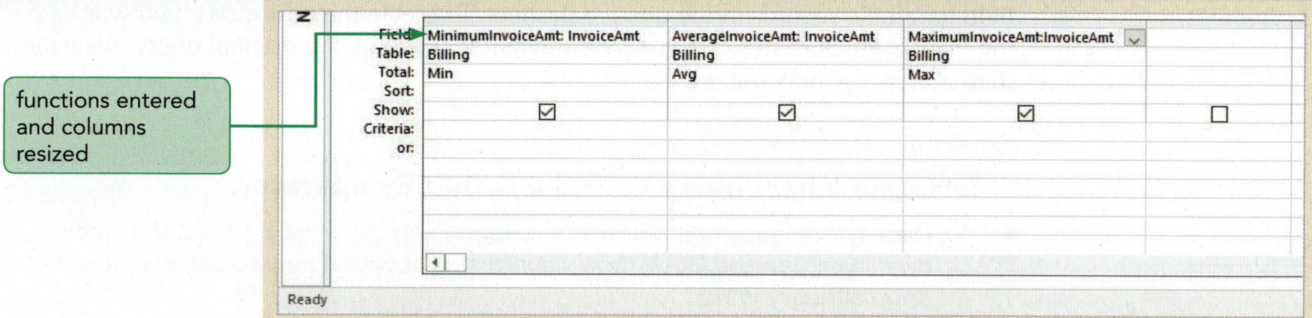

Trouble? Carefully compare your field names to those shown in the figure to make sure they match exactly; otherwise the query will not work correctly.

9. Run the query. One record is displayed containing the three aggregate function results. The single row of summary statistics represents calculations based on all the records selected for the query—in this case, all 204 records in the Billing table.
10. Resize all columns to their best fit so that the column names are fully displayed, and then click the field value in the first column to deselect the value and view the results. See Figure 3–40.

Figure 3–40 Result of the query using aggregate functions

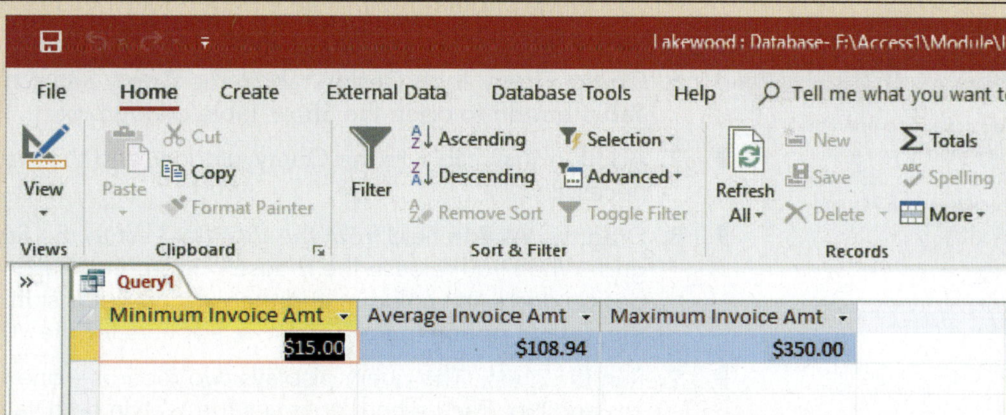

11. Save the query as **InvoiceAmtStatistics**.

Donna would like to view the same invoice amount statistics (minimum, average, and maximum) as they relate to both appointments at the clinic and walk-in visits.

Using Record Group Calculations

In addition to calculating statistical information on all or selected records in selected tables, you can calculate statistics for groups of records. The **Group By operator** divides the selected records into groups based on the values in the specified field. Those records with the same value for the field are grouped together, and the datasheet displays one record for each group. Aggregate functions, which appear in the other columns of the design grid, provide statistical information for each group.

To create a query for Donna's latest request, you will modify the current query by adding the WalkIn field and assigning the Group By operator to it. The Group By operator will display the statistical information grouped by the values of the WalkIn field for all the records in the query datasheet. To create the new query, you will save the InvoiceAmtStatistics query with a new name, keeping the original query intact, and then modify the new query.

To create a new query with the Group By operator:

1. Display the InvoiceAmtStatistics query in Design view. Because the query is open, you can use Backstage view to save it with a new name, keeping the original query intact.
2. Click the **File** tab to display Backstage view, and then click **Save As** in the navigation bar. The Save As screen opens.
3. In the File Types section on the left, click **Save Object As**. The right side of the screen changes to display options for saving the current database object as a new object.
4. Click **Save As**. The Save As dialog box opens, indicating that you are saving a copy of the InvoiceAmtStatistics query.
5. Type **InvoiceAmtStatisticsByWalkIn** to replace the selected name, and then press **ENTER**. The new query is saved with the name you specified and appears in Design view.

   You need to add the WalkIn field to the query. This field is in the Visit table. To include another table in an existing query, you open the Show Table dialog box.

TIP

You could also open the Navigation Pane and drag the Visit table from the pane to the Query window.

6. On the Query Tools Design tab, in the Query Setup group, click the **Show Table** button to open the Show Table dialog box.
7. Add the **Visit** table to the Query window, and then resize the Visit field list if necessary.
8. Drag the **WalkIn** field from the Visit field list to the first column in the design grid. When you release the mouse button, the WalkIn field appears in the design grid's first column, and the existing fields shift to the right. Group By, the default option in the Total row, appears for the WalkIn field.
9. Run the query. The query displays two records—one for each WalkIn group, Yes and No. Each record contains the WalkIn field value for the group and the three aggregate function values. The summary statistics represent calculations based on the 204 records in the Billing table. See Figure 3–41.

Figure 3–41 Aggregate functions grouped by WalkIn

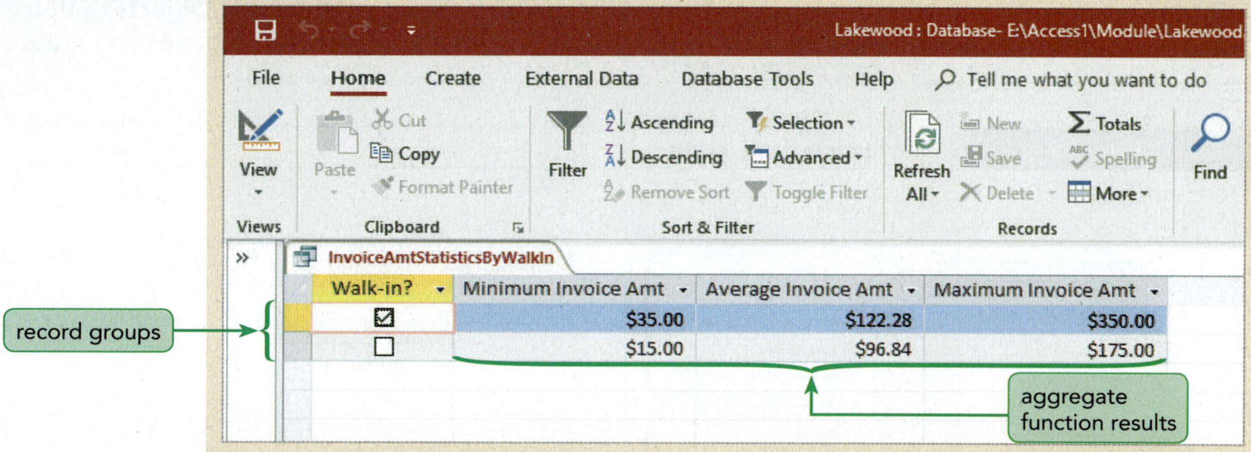

Donna notes that invoice amounts for walk-in visits are higher than those for scheduled appointments.

10. Save and close the query.
11. Open the Navigation Pane.

You have created and saved many queries in the Lakewood database. The Navigation Pane provides options for opening and managing the queries you've created, as well as the other objects in the database, such as tables, forms, and reports.

Working with the Navigation Pane

As noted earlier, the Navigation Pane is the main area for working with the objects in a database. As you continue to create objects in your database, you might want to display and work with them in different ways. The Navigation Pane provides options for grouping database objects in various ways to suit your needs. For example, you might want to view only the queries created for a certain table or all the query objects in the database.

INSIGHT

Hiding and Displaying Objects in the Navigation Pane

You can hide the display of a group's objects by clicking the button to the right of the group name; click the button again to expand the group and display its objects. You can also hide an object within a group, such as an individual query or report. To hide an object within a group, right-click the object and then click Hide in this Group. To display hidden objects without providing access to them, right-click the Navigation Pane menu and then click Navigation Options. In the Navigation Options dialog box, select the Show Hidden Objects check box, and then click OK. To fully enable the object, right-click the object, and then click Unhide in this Group.

As you know, the Navigation Pane divides database objects into categories. Each category contains groups, and each group contains one or more objects. The default category is **Object Type**, which arranges objects by type—tables, queries, forms, and reports. The default group is **All Access Objects**, which displays all objects in the database. You can also choose to display only one type of object, such as tables.

The default group name, All Access Objects, appears at the top of the Navigation Pane. Currently, each object type—Tables, Queries, Forms, and Reports—is displayed as a heading, and the objects related to each type are listed below the heading. To group objects differently, you can select another category by using the Navigation Pane menu. You'll try this next.

To group objects differently in the Navigation Pane:

1. At the top of the Navigation Pane, click the **All Access Objects** button. A menu opens with options for choosing different categories and groups. See Figure 3–42.

Figure 3–42 Navigation Pane menu

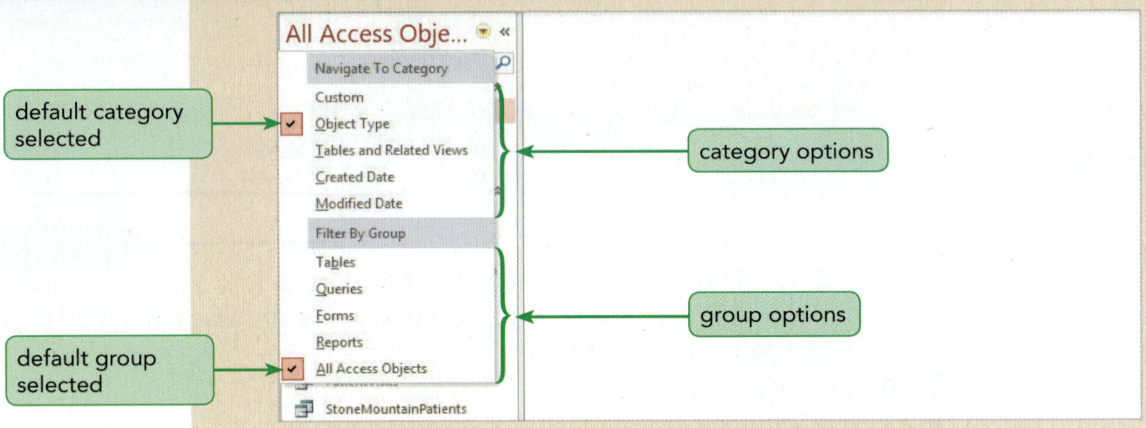

The top section of the menu provides the options for choosing a different category. The Object Type category has a checkmark next to it, signifying that it is the currently selected category. The lower section of the menu provides options for choosing a different group; these options might change depending on the selected category.

2. In the Navigate To Category section, click **Tables and Related Views**. The Navigation Pane is now grouped into categories of tables, and each table in the database—Visit, Billing, and Patient—is its own group. All database objects related to a table are listed below the table's name. Use the scroll bar to scroll to the bottom of the objects list. (Notice the Visit heading has scrolled out of the Navigation Pane.) See Figure 3–43.

Figure 3–43 Database objects grouped by table in the Navigation Pane

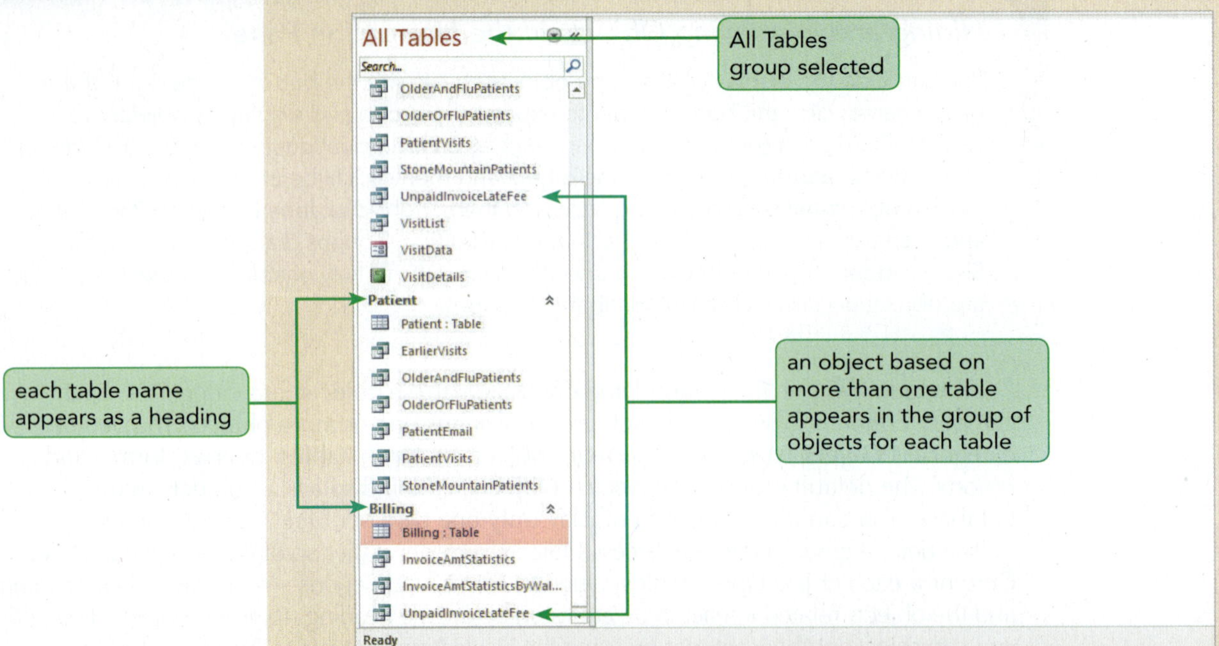

Some objects appear more than once. When an object is based on more than one table, that object appears in the group for each table. For example, the UnpaidInvoiceLateFee query is based on both the Visit and Billing tables, so it is listed in the group for both tables.

You can also choose to display the objects for only one table to better focus on that table.

3. At the top of the Navigation Pane, click the **All Tables** button to display the Navigation Pane menu, and then click **Patient**. The Navigation Pane now shows only the objects related to the Patient table—the table itself plus the six queries you created that include fields from the Patient table.
4. At the top of the Navigation Pane, click the **Patient** button, and then click **Object Type** to return to the default display of the Navigation Pane.
5. **sam** Compact and repair the Lakewood database, and then close the database.

   Trouble? If a dialog box opens and warns that this action will cause Microsoft Access to empty the Clipboard, click the Yes button to continue.

The default All Access Objects category is a predefined category. You can also create custom categories to group objects in the way that best suits how you want to manage your database objects. As you continue to build a database and the list of objects grows, creating a custom category can help you to work more efficiently with the objects in the database.

The queries you've created and saved will help Donna and her staff to monitor and analyze the business activity of Lakewood Community Health Services and its patients. Now any staff member can run the queries at any time, modify them as needed, or use them as the basis for designing new queries to meet additional information requirements.

REVIEW

Session 3.2 Quick Check

1. A(n) ____________ is a criterion, or rule, that determines which records are selected for a query datasheet.
2. In the design grid, where do you place the conditions for two different fields when you use the And logical operator, and where do you place them when you use the Or logical operator?
3. To perform a calculation in a query, you define a(n) ____________ containing a combination of database fields, constants, and operators.
4. Which Access tool do you use to create an expression for a calculated field in a query?
5. What is an aggregate function?
6. The ____________ operator divides selected records into groups based on the values in a field.
7. What is the default category for the display of objects in the Navigation Pane?

PRACTICE

Review Assignments

Data File needed for the Review Assignments: Vendor.accdb ***(cont. from Module 2)***

Donna asks you to update some information in the Vendor database and to retrieve specific information from the database. Complete the following:

1. Open the **Vendor** database you created and worked with in previous modules, and then click the Enable Content button next to the security warning, if necessary.
2. Open the **Supplier** table in Datasheet view, and then change the following field values for the record with the Supplier ID HAR912: Address to **912 Medical Dr**, Contact Phone to **865-555-1226**, Contact First Name to **Isabella**, and Contact Last Name to **Lopez**. Close the table.
3. Create a query based on the Supplier table. Include the following fields in the query, in the order shown: Company, Category, ContactFirst, ContactLast, Phone, and City. Sort the query in ascending order based on the Category field values. Save the query as **ContactList**, and then run the query.
4. Use the ContactList query datasheet to update the Supplier table by changing the Phone field value for Killington Medical to **762-555-9811**.
5. Change the size of the text in the ContactList query datasheet to use a 12-point font size. Resize columns, as necessary, so that all field values and column headings are visible.
6. Change the alternate row color in the ContactList query datasheet to the Theme Color named Blue, Accent 5, Lighter 60%, and then save and close the query.
7. Create a query based on the Supplier and Product tables. Select the Company, Category, and State fields from the Supplier table, and the ProductName, Price, Units, and Weight fields from the Product table. Sort the query results in descending order based on price. Select only those records with a Category field value of Supplies, but do not display the Category field values in the query results. Save the query as **SupplyProducts**, run the query, and then close it.
8. Create a query that lists all products that cost more than $50 and are temperature controlled. Display the following fields from the Product table in the query results: ProductID, ProductName, Price, Units, and Sterile. (*Hint*: The TempControl field is a Yes/No field that should not appear in the query results.) Save the query as **HighPriceAndTempControl**, run the query, and then close it.
9. Create a query that lists information about suppliers who sell equipment or sterile products. Include the Company, Category, ContactFirst, and ContactLast fields from the Supplier table; and the ProductName, Price, TempControl, and Sterile fields from the Product table. Save the query as **EquipmentOrSterile**, run the query, and then close it.
10. Create a query that lists all resale products, along with a 10% markup amount based on the price of the product. Include the Company field from the Supplier table and the following fields from the Product table in the query: ProductID, ProductName, and Price. Save the query as **ResaleProductsWithMarkup**. Display the markup amount in a calculated field named **Markup** that determines a 10% markup based on the Price field values. Set the Caption property to **MarkUp** for the calculated field. Display the query results in descending order by Price. Save and run the query.
11. Modify the format of the Markup field in the ResaleProductsWithMarkup query so that it uses the Standard format and two decimal places. Run the query, resize all columns in the datasheet to their best fit, and then save and close the query.
12. Create a query that calculates the lowest, highest, and average prices for all products using the field names **MinimumPrice**, **MaximumPrice**, and **AveragePrice**, respectively. Set the Caption property for each field to include a space between the two words in the field name. Run the query, resize all columns in the datasheet to their best fit, save the query as **PriceStatistics**, and then close it.

13. In the Navigation Pane, copy the PriceStatistics query, and then rename the copied query as **PriceStatisticsBySupplier**.
14. Modify the PriceStatisticsBySupplier query so that the records are grouped by the Company field in the Supplier table. The Company field should appear first in the query datasheet. Save and run the query, and then close it.
15. Compact and repair the Vendor database, and then close it.

APPLY

Case Problem 1

Data File needed for this Case Problem: Career.accdb *(cont. from Module 2)*

Great Giraffe Jeremiah needs to modify a few records in the Career database and analyze the data within the database. To help Jeremiah, you'll update the Career database and create queries to answer his questions. Complete the following:

1. Open the **Career** database you created and worked with in previous modules, and then click the Enable Content button next to the security warning, if necessary.
2. In the **Student** table, find the record for StudentID ART5210, and then change the Street value to **417 Barclay Avenue** and the Zip to **80202**.
3. In the **Student** table, find the record for StudentID ESP1734, and then delete the record. (*Hint*: Delete the related records in the Registration subdatasheet first.) Close the Student table.
4. Create a query that lists students who are on a payment plan for any of the courses offered by Great Giraffe. List only the StudentID, FirstName, and LastName fields for the students in your results, and sort the results in ascending order by the LastName field. Save the query as **AllPaymentPlanStudents**, run the query, and then close it.
5. In the Navigation Pane, copy the AllPaymentPlanStudents query, and then rename the copied query as **LittletonPaymentPlanStudents**.
6. Modify the LittletonPaymentPlanStudents query so that it only displays those students from the city of Littleton. (*Hint*: When you are entering the criteria for a Short Text field, Access usually places the quotation marks around the text; however, you may also type the quotation marks if you are having trouble entering the text properly.) The City field should not appear in the query datasheet. Save and run the query, and then close it.
7. Create a query that lists students who are taking one of the Computer Science courses offered. (*Hint*: Instead of looking at the individual sections, look at the Title of the courses.) In the query results, display only the StudentID, FirstName, LastName, and Phone of the students in the courses. Sort the results by StudentID in ascending order. Save the query as **CompSciStudents** and run the query.
8. Use the CompSciStudents query datasheet to update the Student table by using **(303) 555-0042** for the Phone value for Wendy Bradshaw.
9. Change the size of the text in the CompSciStudents query datasheet to use a 14-point font size. Resize columns, as necessary, so that all field values and column headings are visible.
10. Change the alternate row color in the CompSciStudents query datasheet to the Theme Color named Green, Accent 6, Lighter 80%, and then save and close the query.
11. Create a query that lists the InstanceID, Title, StartDate, HoursPerWeek, and Cost fields for courses that begin anytime in the first three months of 2021. Save the query as **FirstQuarterClassOptions**, run the query, and then close it.
12. Create a query that lists the total outstanding balances for students on a payment plan and for those students that are not on a payment plan. Show in the query results only the sum of the balance due, grouped by PaymentPlan. Name the summation column **Balances**. Run the query, resize all columns in the datasheet to their best fit, save the query as **TotalBalancesByPlan**, and then close it.
13. Compact and repair the Career database, and then close it.

CHALLENGE

Case Problem 2

Data File needed for this Case Problem: DrainAdopter.accdb *(cont. from Module 2)*

Drain Adopter Tandrea needs to modify some records in the Center database, and then she wants to find specific information about the program. Tandrea asks you to help her update the database and create queries to find the information she needs. Complete the following:

1. Open the **DrainAdopter** database you created and worked with in previous modules, and then click the Enable Content button next to the security warning, if necessary.
2. Create a query based on the Volunteer table that includes the VolunteerID, FirstName, LastName, and SignupDate fields, in that order. Display only those records whose SignupDate is in the first three months of the program, which began in January 2021. Save the query as **FirstVolunteers**, and then run it.
3. Modify the FirstVolunteers query design so that it sorts records in ascending order by SignupDate. Save and run the query.
4. Create a query to count the number of volunteers that have completed training, and those that did not complete training. Show in the query results only the count of each category, grouped by the Trained field. Name the summation column **Total**. Run the query, resize all columns in the datasheet to their best fit, save the query as **NumberTrainedAndNotTrained**.
5. Create a query to count the number of drains that need maintenance, and those that do not need maintenance. Show in the query results only the count of each category, grouped by the MaintReq field. Name the summation column **Total**. Run the query, resize all columns in the datasheet to their best fit, and save the query as **NumberMaintRequired**.
6. **Explore** Create a query that includes all the fields from the Supply table in the order they appear in the table and creates a calculated field called **Value** to determine the dollar amount of each supply item on hand. (*Hint*: Place brackets around each field in the calculation and multiply the Cost field by the NumberOnHand field.) Save the query as **InventoryCosts** and run the query.
7. Modify the InventoryCosts query to use the Currency format for the new Value field and to give the field a Caption property of **Inventory Value**. Run the query, and then resize the columns to display the complete field names and values. Save and close the query.
8. **Explore** Create a query to total the inventory amounts from the InventoryCosts query. (*Hint*: The data source for a query can be a table or another query. To choose a query, click the Queries tab in the Show Table dialog box.) Just as with any other aggregate function, sum the value of the calculated field (Value) from the InventoryCosts query. Name the summation column **Total Inventory** and display the total using a Currency format. Run the query, resize all columns in the datasheet to their best fit, save the query as **TotalInventoryValue**, and then close it.
9. **Explore** Format the datasheet of the FirstVolunteers query so that it does not display gridlines, uses an alternate row Standard Color of Maroon 2, and displays a font size of 12. (*Hint*: Use the Gridlines button in the Text Formatting group on the Home tab to select the appropriate gridlines option.) Resize the columns to display the complete field names and values, if necessary. Save and close the query.
10. **Explore** In the Volunteer table, each VolunteerID value has a plus sign (expand indicator) next to it indicating a relationship to another table. To view each corresponding relationship, you could scroll and click each expand indictor to show the relationship; however, since there are 150 volunteers, this would take a while. Instead, click the Datasheet Selector button to the left of the VolunteerID field, and then click one of the expand indicators to expand all of the records. You can now see all of the records expanded and scroll through them much more efficiently. To close all of the expanded records, click the Datasheet Selector button again, and then click one of the minus signs (collapse indicators). The records are now collapsed. To deselect the entire form, click a field value within the datasheet. Close the datasheet. Since there were no changes to the structure of the table, you will not be prompted about whether to save your changes.
11. Compact and repair the DrainAdopter database, and then close it.

MODULE 4

Creating Forms and Reports

Using Forms and Reports to Display Patient and Visit Data

OBJECTIVES

Session 4.1
- Create a form using the Form Wizard
- Apply a theme to a form
- Add a picture to a form
- Change the color of text on a form
- Find and maintain data using a form
- Preview and print selected form records
- Create a form with a main form and a subform

Session 4.2
- Create a report using the Report Wizard
- Apply a theme to a report
- Change the alignment of field values on a report
- Move and resize fields in a report
- Insert a picture in a report
- Change the color of text on a report
- Apply conditional formatting in a report
- Preview and print a report

Case | ***Lakewood Community Health Services***

Donna Taylor wants to continue enhancing the Lakewood database to make it easier for her staff to enter, locate, and maintain data. In particular, she wants the database to include a form based on the Patient table that staff can use to enter and change data about the clinic's patients. She also wants the database to include a form that shows data from both the Patient and Visit tables at the same time. This form will show the visit information for each patient along with the corresponding patient data, providing a complete picture of Lakewood Community Health Services patients and their visits to the clinic.

In addition, she would like the database to include a report of patient and visit data so that she and other staff members will have printed output when completing analyses and planning strategies for community outreach efforts. She wants the report to be formatted professionally and easy to use.

In this module, you will create the forms and reports in the Lakewood database for Donna and her staff.

STARTING DATA FILES

Access1 →

Module
Lakewood.accdb (cont.)
Support_AC_4_Medical.png

Review
Support_AC_4_Items.png
Support_AC_4_Supplies.png
Vendor.accdb (cont.)

Case1
Career.accdb (cont.)
Support_AC_4_Giraffe.png

Case2
Support_AC_4_Drain.png
DrainAdopter.accdb (cont.)

Session 4.1 Visual Overview:

The form object's name is displayed on the tab for the form.

The form title appears at the top of the form. By default, the form object name is used as the form title, but you can edit the title to display the text you want, as done here—a space was added between the two words for readability.

With the Columnar form layout, the field captions appear in a column on the left side of the form. If captions had not been specified for the fields, the field names would appear here instead.

The navigation buttons allow you to display the first, last, next, or previous record in the form, enter a specific record number and move to that record, and create a new record.

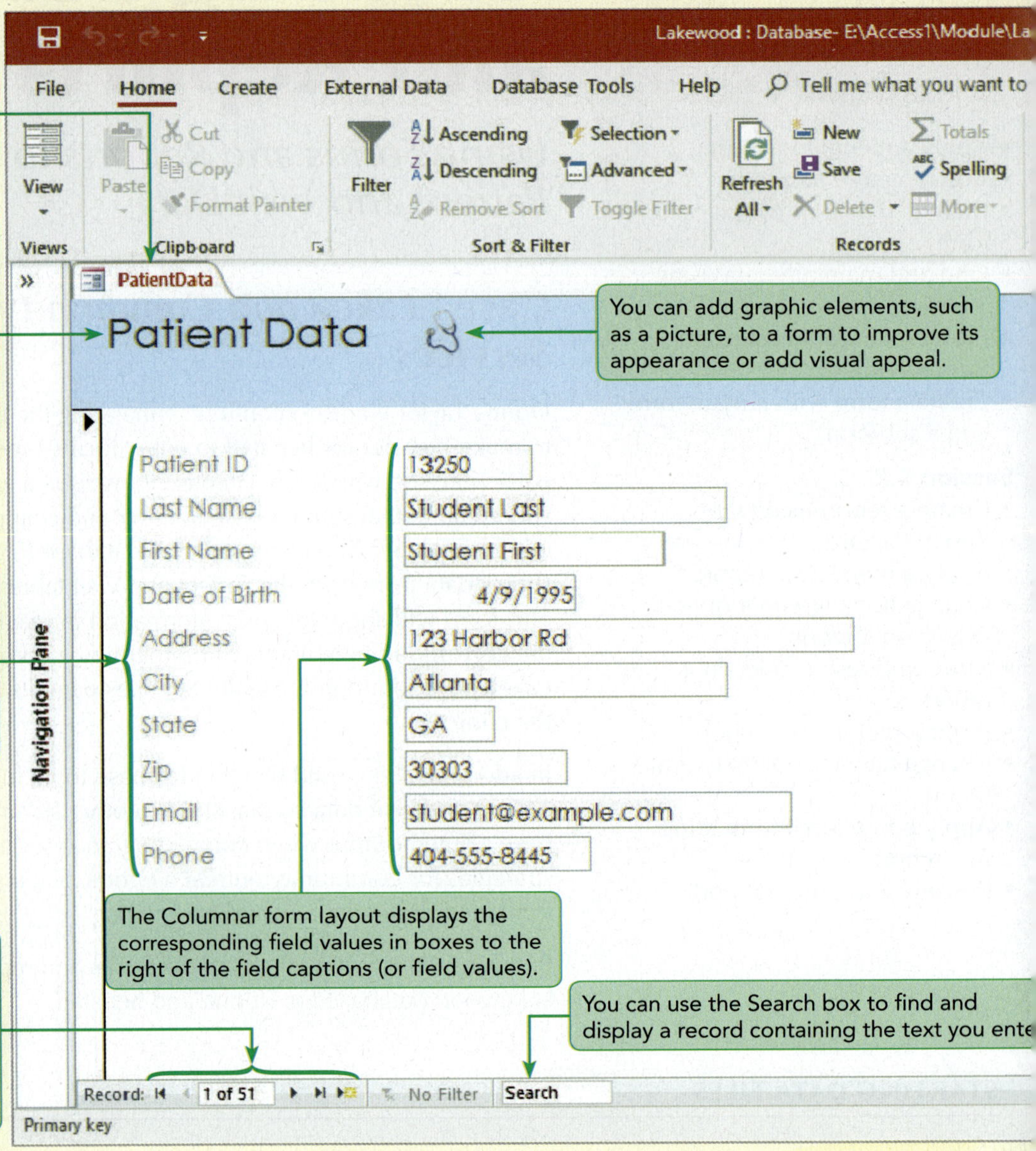

You can add graphic elements, such as a picture, to a form to improve its appearance or add visual appeal.

The Columnar form layout displays the corresponding field values in boxes to the right of the field captions (or field values).

You can use the Search box to find and display a record containing the text you ente

Form Displayed in Form View

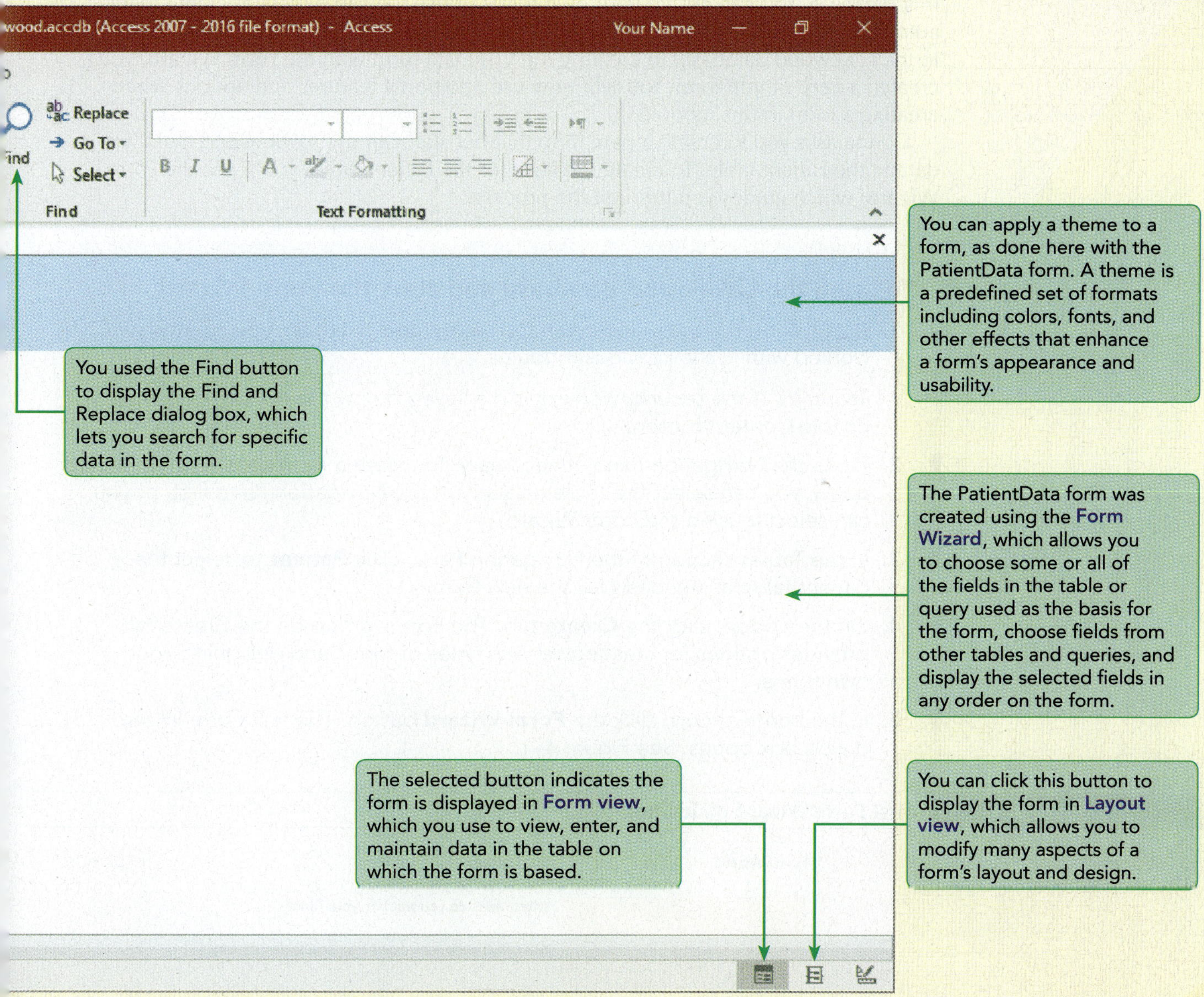

Creating a Form Using the Form Wizard

As you learned earlier, a form is an object you use to enter, edit, and view records in a database. You can design your own forms or use tools in Access to create them automatically. You have already used the Form Wizard to create the VisitData form in the Lakewood database. In creating the VisitData form with the Form Wizard, you created a very simple form. You will now use additional features and options when creating a form in this module.

Donna asks you to create a new form that her staff can use to view and maintain data in the Patient table. To create the form for the Patient table, you'll use the Form Wizard, which guides you through the process.

To open the Lakewood database and start the Form Wizard:

1. sam Start Access and open the **Lakewood** database you created and worked with in the previous modules.

   Trouble? If the security warning is displayed below the ribbon, click the Enable Content button.

2. Open the Navigation Pane, if necessary. To create a form based on a table or query, you can select the table or query in the Navigation Pane first, or you can select it using the Form Wizard.
3. In the Tables section of the Navigation Pane, click **Patient** to select the Patient table as the basis for the new form.
4. On the ribbon, click the **Create** tab. The Forms group on the Create tab provides options for creating various types of forms and designing your own forms.
5. In the Forms group, click the **Form Wizard** button. The first Form Wizard dialog box opens. See Figure 4–1.

Figure 4–1 First Form Wizard dialog box

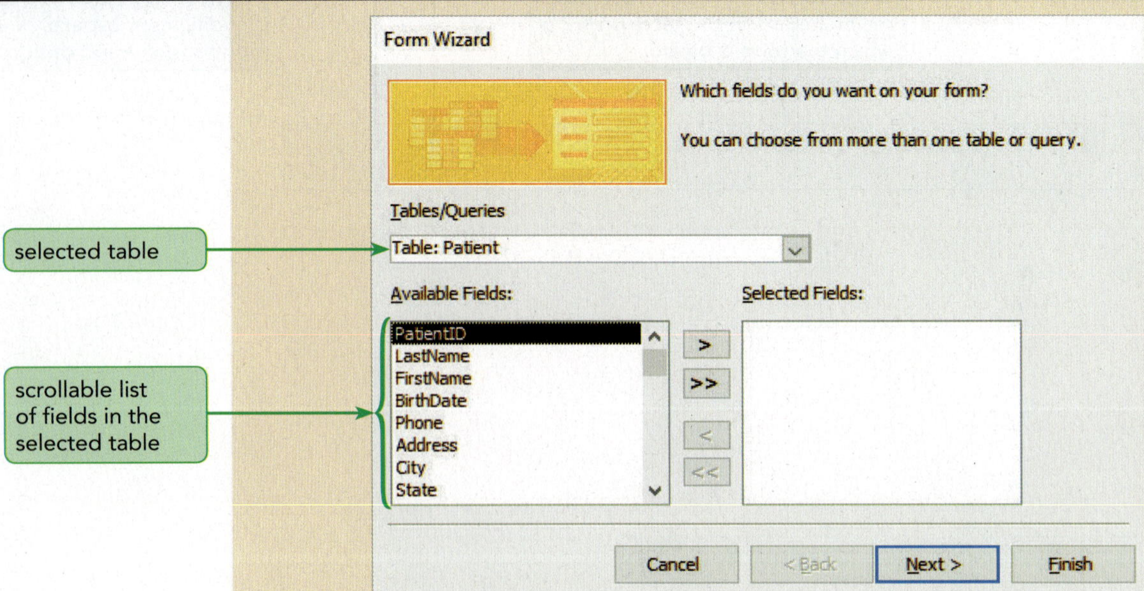

Because you selected the Patient table in the Navigation Pane before starting the Form Wizard, this table is selected in the Tables/Queries box, and the fields for the Patient table are listed in the Available Fields box.

Donna wants the form to display all the fields in the Patient table, but in a different order. She would like the Phone field to appear at the bottom of the form so that it stands out, making it easier for someone who needs to call patients to use the form to quickly locate the phone number for a patient.

To create the form using the Form Wizard:

1. Click the **Select All Fields** button >> to move all the fields to the Selected Fields box. Next, you need to position the Phone field so it will appear as the bottom-most field on the form. To accomplish this, you will first remove the Phone field and then add it back as the last selected field.
2. In the Selected Fields box, click the **Phone** field, and then click the **Remove Single Field** button < to move the field back to the Available Fields box.

   Because a new field is always added after the selected field in the Selected Fields box, you need to first select the last field in the list and then move the Phone field back to the Selected Fields box so it will be the last field on the form.
3. In the Selected Fields box, click the **Email** field.
4. With the Phone field selected in the Available Fields box, click the **Select Single Field** button > to move the Phone field to the end of the list in the Selected Fields box.
5. Click the **Next** button to display the second Form Wizard dialog box, in which you select a layout for the form. See Figure 4–2.

Figure 4–2 Choosing a layout for the form

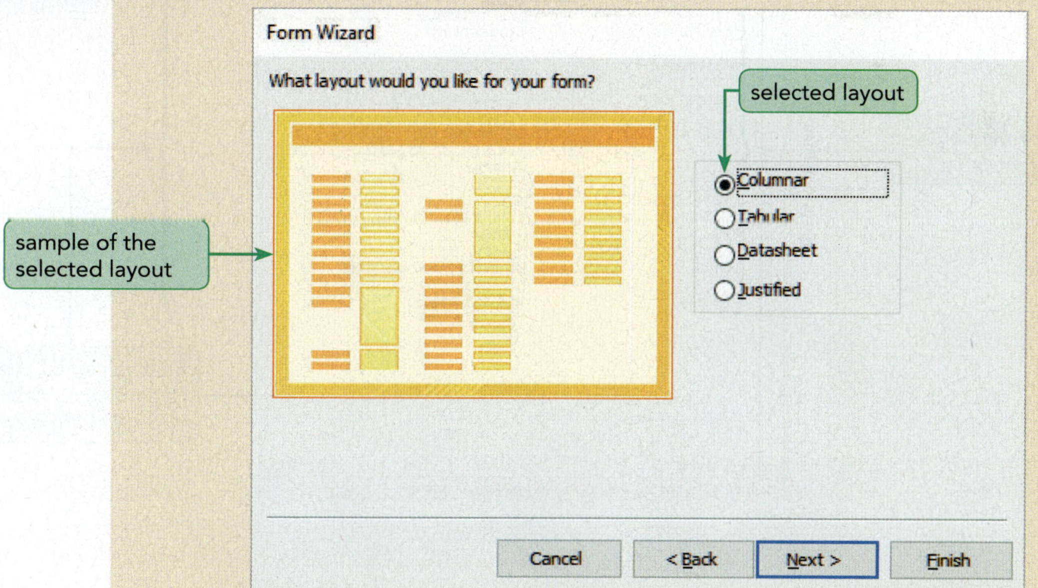

The layout choices are Columnar, Tabular, Datasheet, and Justified. A sample of the selected layout appears on the left side of the dialog box.

6. Click each of the option buttons and review the corresponding sample layout.

   The Tabular and Datasheet layouts display the fields from multiple records at one time, whereas the Columnar and Justified layouts display the fields from one record at a time. Donna thinks the Columnar layout is the appropriate arrangement for displaying and updating data in the table, so that anyone using the form can focus on just one patient record at a time.

7. Click the **Columnar** option button (if necessary), and then click the **Next** button.

   The third and final Form Wizard dialog box shows the Patient table's name as the default form name. "Patient" is also the default title that will appear on the tab for the form.

   You'll use "PatientData" as the form name, and, because you don't need to change the form's design at this point, you'll display the form.

8. Click to position the insertion point to the right of Patient in the box, type **Data**, and then click the **Finish** button.

   Close the Navigation Pane to display only the Form window. The completed form opens in Form view, displaying the values for the first record in the Patient table. The Columnar layout you selected places the field captions in labels on the left and the corresponding field values in boxes on the right, which vary in width depending on the size of the field. See Figure 4–3.

Figure 4–3 PatientData form in Form view

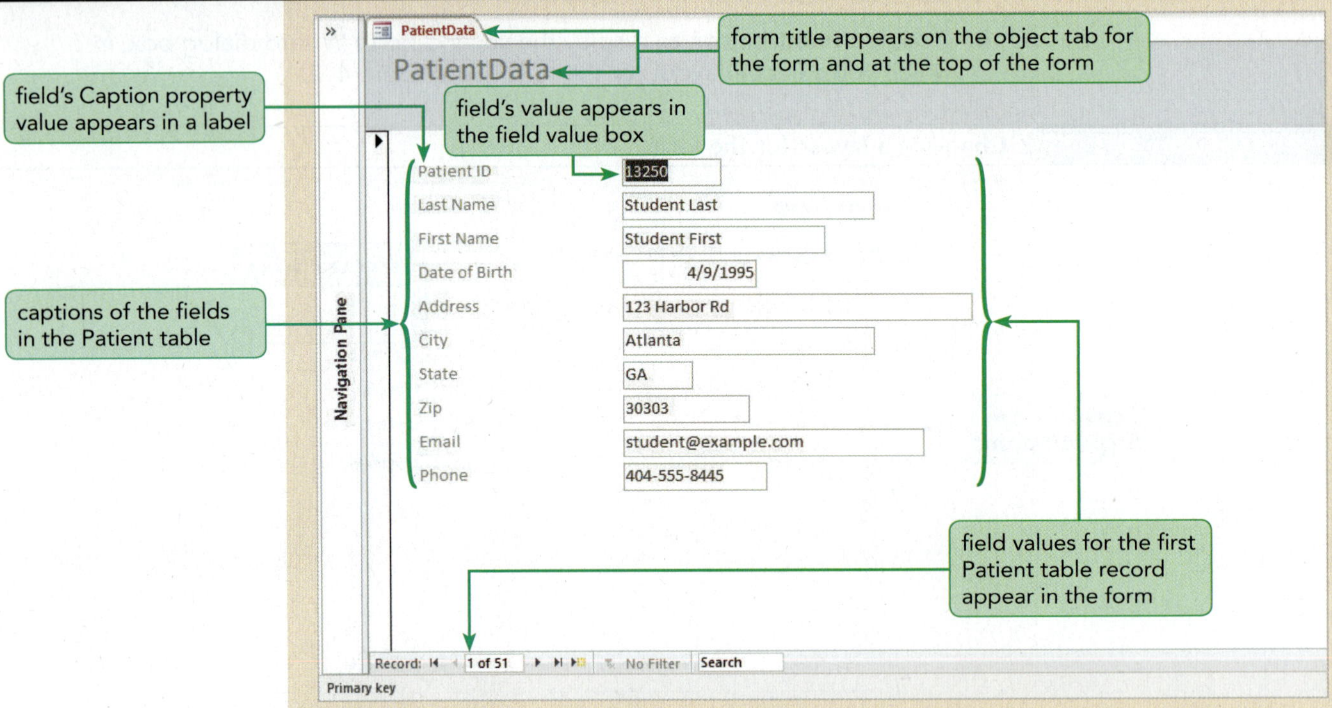

After viewing the form, Donna makes suggestions for improving the form's readability and appearance. The font used in the labels on the left is light in color and small, making them difficult to read. Also, she thinks inserting a graphic on the form would add visual interest, and modifying other form elements—such as the color of the title text—would improve the look of the form. You can make all of these changes working with the form in Layout view.

Modifying a Form's Design in Layout View

TIP

Some form design changes require you to switch to Design view, which gives you a more detailed view of the form's structure.

After you create a form, you might need to modify its design to improve its appearance or to make the form easier to use. You cannot make any design changes in Form view. However, Layout view displays the form as it appears in Form view while allowing you to modify the form's design. Because you can see the form and its data while you are modifying the form, Layout view makes it easy for you to see the results of any design changes you make.

The first modification you'll make to the PatientData form is to change its appearance by applying a theme.

Applying a Theme to a Database Object

By default, the objects you create in a database are formatted with the Office theme. A theme provides a design scheme for the colors and fonts used in the database objects. Access, like other Microsoft Office programs, provides many built-in themes, including the Office theme, making it easy for you to create objects with a unified look. You can also create a customized theme if none of the built-in themes suit your needs.

Sometimes a theme works well for one database object but is not as suitable for other objects in that database. Therefore, when applying a theme to an object, you can choose to apply the theme just to the open object, to objects of a particular type, or to all the existing objects in the database and set it as the default theme for any new objects that might be created.

To change a form's appearance, you can easily apply a new theme to it.

REFERENCE

Applying a Theme to Database Objects

- Display the object in Layout view.
- In the Themes group on the Form Layout Tools Design tab or Report Layout Tools Design tab, click the Themes button.
- In the Themes gallery, click the theme you want to apply to all objects; or, right-click the theme to display the shortcut menu, and then choose to apply the theme to the current object only or to all matching objects.

Donna would like to see if the PatientData form's appearance can be improved with a different theme. To apply a theme, you first need to switch to Layout view.

To apply a theme to the PatientData form:

1. On the ribbon, make sure the Home tab is displayed.
2. In the Views group, click **View**. The form is displayed in Layout view. See Figure 4–4.

Figure 4–4 Form displayed in Layout view

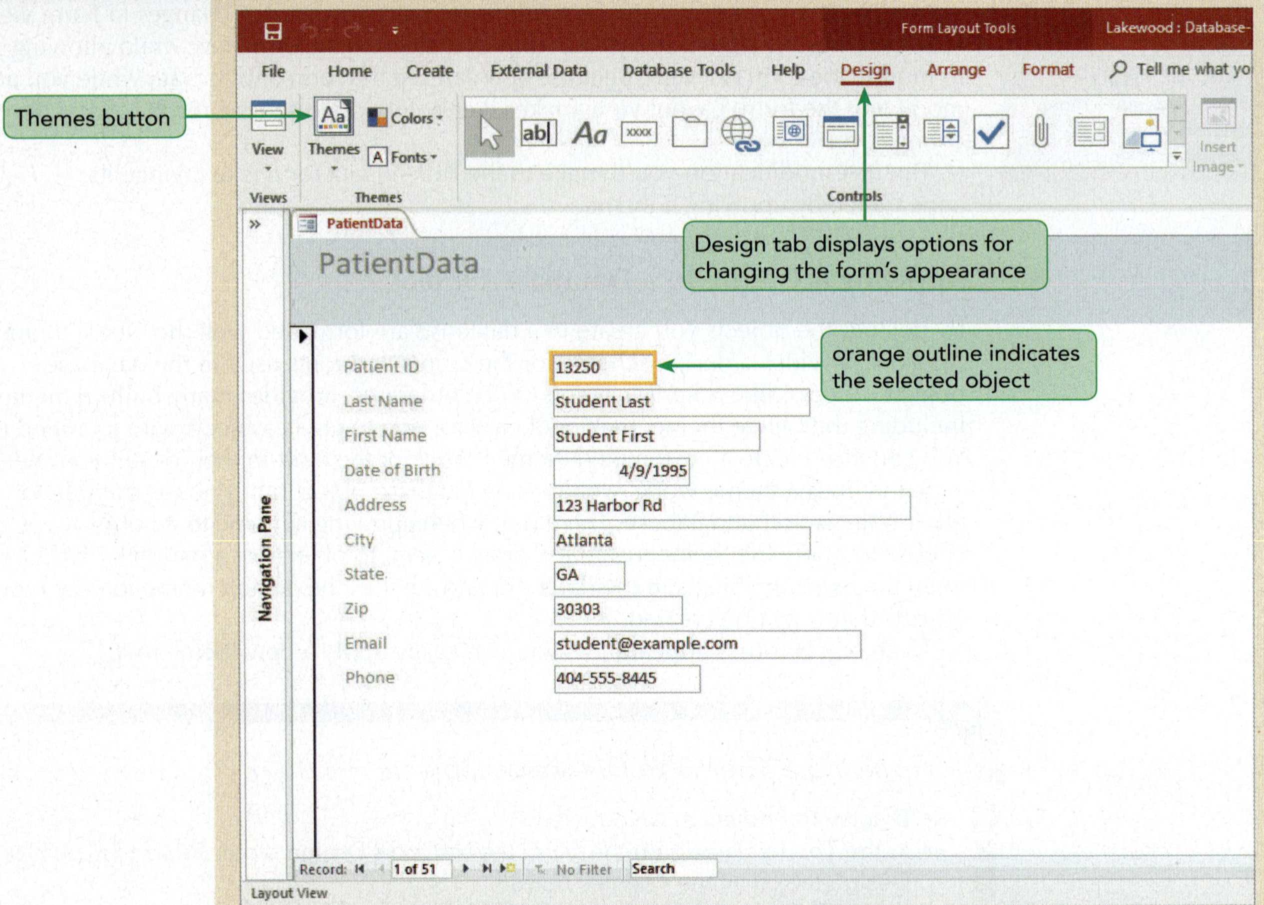

Trouble? If the Field List or Property Sheet opens on the right side of the program window, close it before continuing.

In Layout view, an orange border identifies the currently selected element on the form. In this case, the field value for the PatientID field, 13250, is selected. You need to apply a theme to the PatientData form.

3. On the Form Layout Tools Design tab, in the Themes group, click **Themes**. A gallery opens showing the available themes for the form. See Figure 4–5.

Figure 4–5 Themes gallery displayed

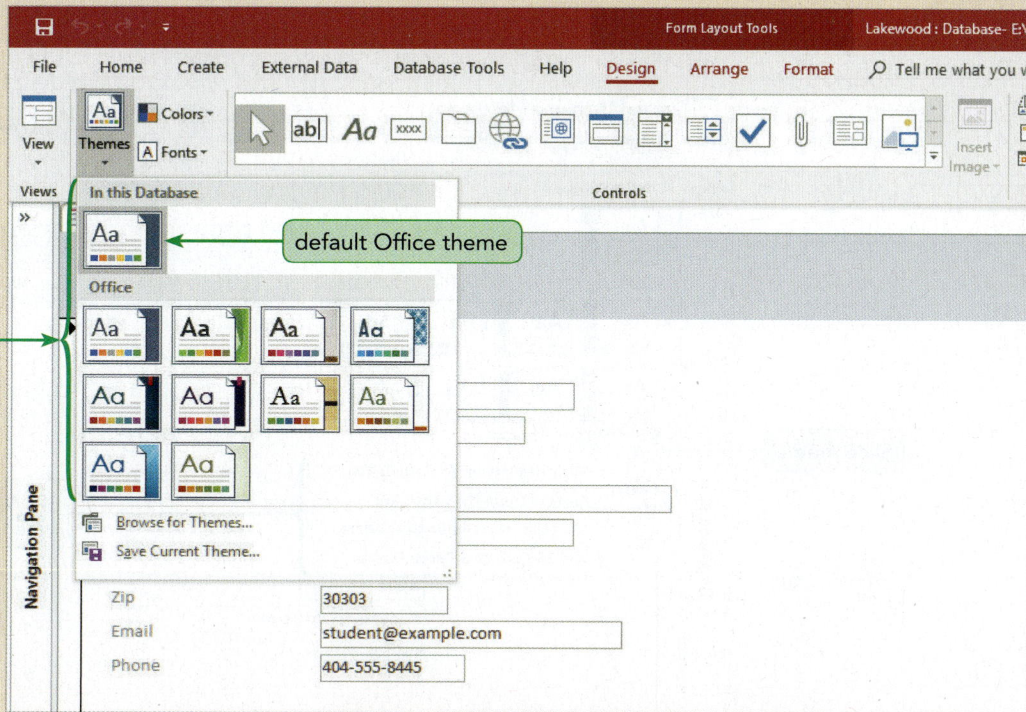

TIP

Themes other than the Office theme are listed in alphabetical order in the gallery.

The Office theme, the default theme currently applied in the database, is listed in the "In this Database" section and is also the first theme listed in the section containing other themes. You can point to each theme in the gallery to see its name in a ScreenTip. Also, when you point to a theme, the Live Preview feature shows the effect of applying the theme to the open object.

4. In the gallery, point to each of the themes to see how they would format the PatientData form. Notice the changes in color and font type of the text, for example.

Donna likes the Slice theme because of its bright blue color in the title area at the top and its larger font size, which makes the text in the form easier to read. She asks you to apply this theme to the form.

5. Right-click the **Slice** theme. A shortcut menu opens with options for applying the theme. See Figure 4–6.

Figure 4-6 **Shortcut menu for applying the theme**

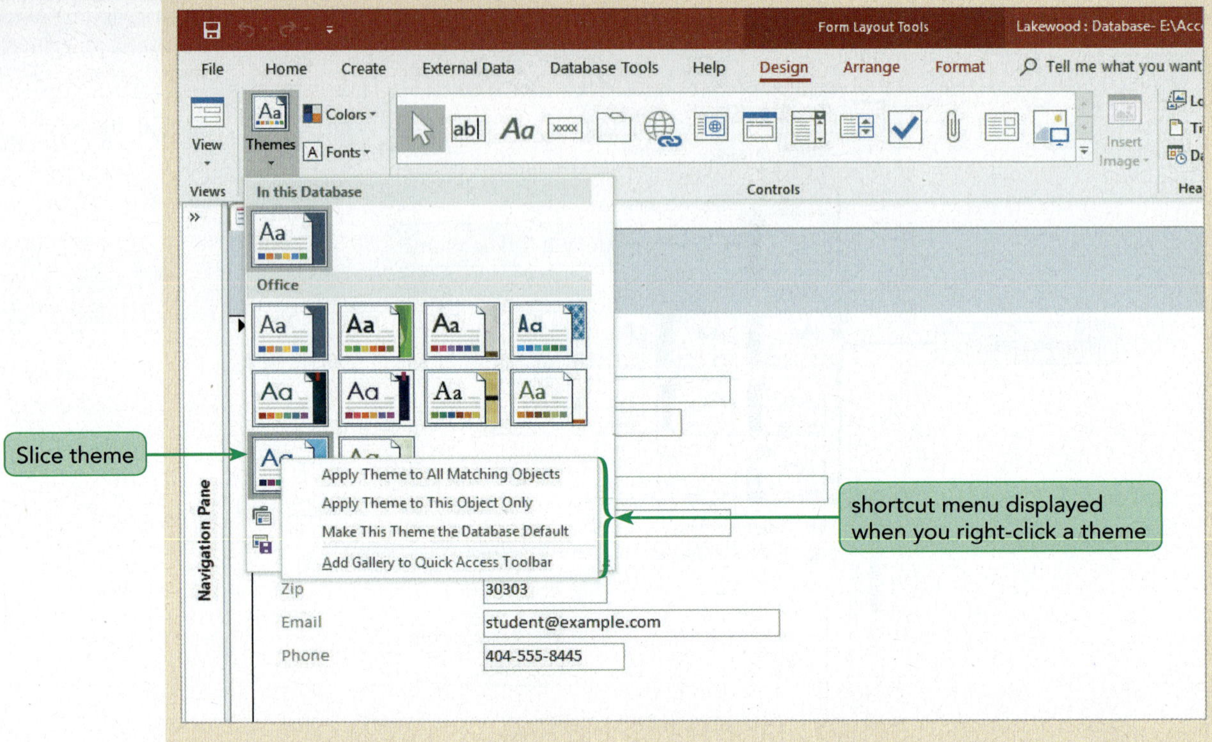

The menu provides options for applying the theme to all matching objects—for example, all the forms in the database—or to the current object only. You can also choose to make the theme the default theme in the database, which means any new objects you create will be formatted with the selected theme. Because Donna is not sure if all forms in the Lakewood database will look better with the Slice theme, she asks you to apply it only to the PatientData form.

Choose this option to avoid applying the theme to other forms in the database.

6. On the shortcut menu, click **Apply Theme to This Object Only**.

The gallery closes, and the Slice theme's colors and fonts are applied to the form.

Trouble? If you choose the wrong option by mistake, you might have applied the selected theme to other forms and reports in the database. Repeat Steps 3 through 6 to apply the Slice theme to the PatientData form. You can also follow the same process to reapply the default Office theme to the other forms and reports in the Lakewood database, as directed by your instructor.

INSIGHT

Working with Themes

Themes provide a quick and easy way for you to format the objects in a database with a consistent look, which is a good design principle to follow. In general, all objects of a type in a database—for example, all forms—should have a consistent design. However, keep in mind that when you select a theme in the Themes gallery and choose the option to apply the theme to all matching objects or to make the theme the default for the database, it might be applied to all the existing forms and reports in the database as well as to new forms and reports you create. Although this approach ensures a consistent design, it can cause problems. For example, if you have already created a form or report and its design is suitable, applying a theme that includes a larger font size could cause the text in labels and field value boxes to be cut off or to extend into other objects on the form or report. The colors applied by the theme could also interfere with elements on existing forms and reports. To handle these unintended results, you would have to spend time checking the existing forms and reports and fixing any problems introduced by applying the theme. A better approach is to select the option "Apply Theme to This Object Only," available on the shortcut menu for a theme in the Themes gallery, for each existing form and report. If the newly applied theme causes problems for any individual form or report, you can then reapply the original theme to return the object to its original design.

Next, you will add a picture to the form for visual interest. The picture, which is included on various flyers and other patient correspondence for Lakewood Community Health Services, is a small graphic of a stethoscope.

Adding a Picture to a Form

A picture is one of many controls you can add and modify on a form. A **control** is an item on a form, report, or other database object that you can manipulate to modify the object's appearance. The controls you can add and modify in Layout view for a form are available in the Controls group and the Header/Footer group on the Form Layout Tools Design tab. The picture you need to add is contained in a file named Support_AC_4_Medical.png, which is located in the Access1 > Module folder provided with your Data Files.

To add the picture to the form:

1. Make sure the form is still displayed in Layout view and that the Form Layout Tools Design tab is active.
2. In the Header/Footer group, click **Logo**. The Insert Picture dialog box opens.
3. Navigate to the **Access1 > Module** folder provided with your Data Files, click the **Support_AC_4_Medical.png** file, and then click **OK**. The picture appears on top of the form's title. See Figure 4–7.

Figure 4–7 Form with picture added

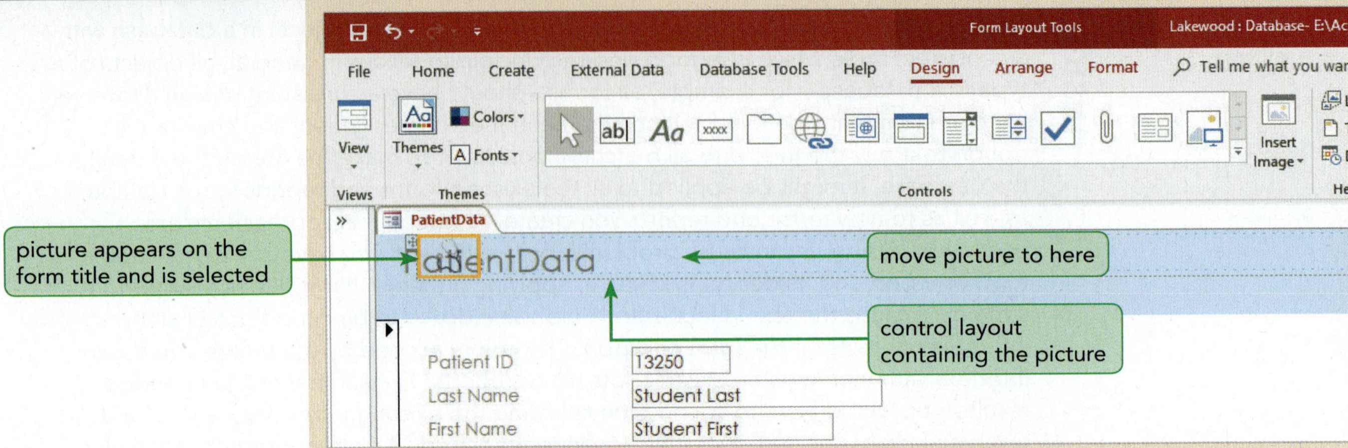

A solid orange border surrounds the picture, indicating it is selected. The picture is placed in a **control layout**, which is a set of controls grouped together in a form or report so that you can manipulate the set as a single control. The dotted blue outline indicates the control layout. The easiest way to move the picture off the form title is to first remove it from the control layout. Doing so allows you to move the picture independently.

4. Right-click the picture to open the shortcut menu, point to **Layout**, and then click **Remove Layout**. The dotted blue outline no longer appears, and the picture is removed from the control layout. Now you can move the picture to the right of the form title.
5. Position the pointer on the picture, and then drag to the right of the form title. Although the image may not be visible while dragging, you can use the position of the pointer as a guide to where the image will be placed.
6. When the pointer is roughly one-half inch to the right of the form's title, release the mouse button. The picture is positioned to the right of the form title.
7. Click in a blank area to the right of the field values in the form to deselect the picture. See Figure 4–8.

Trouble? Don't be concerned if the picture is not in the exact location as the one shown in Figure 4–8. Just make sure the picture is not blocking any part of the form title and that it appears to the right of the form title and within the gray shaded area at the top of the form.

TIP

You can resize a selected image by dragging a corner of the orange selection border.

Figure 4–8 Form with theme applied and picture repositioned

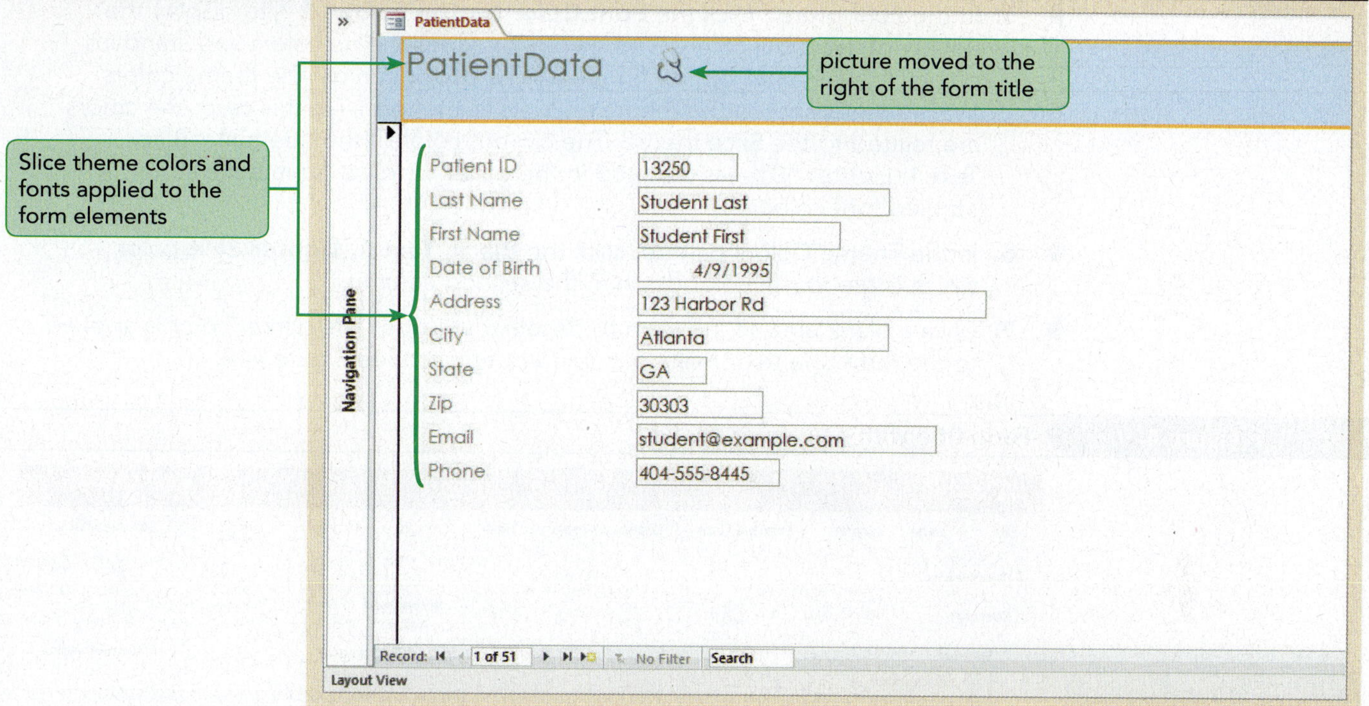

Next, Donna asks you to change the color of the form title to a darker color so that it will stand out more on the form.

Changing the Color of Text on a Form

The Font group on the Form Layout Tools Format tab provides many options you can use to change the appearance of text on a form. For example, you can bold, italicize, and underline text; change the font, font color, and font size; and change the alignment of text. Before you change the color of the "PatientData" title on the form, you'll change the title to two words so it is easier to read.

To change the form title's text and color:

1. Click the **PatientData** form title. An orange border surrounds the title, indicating it is selected.
2. Click between the letters "t" and "D" to position the insertion point, and press **SPACEBAR**. The title on the form is now "Patient Data," but the added space caused the words to appear on two lines. You can fix this by resizing the box containing the title.
3. Position the pointer on the right edge of the box containing the form title until the pointer changes to the width change pointer ↔, and then drag to the right until the word "Data" appears on the same line as the word "Patient."

   Trouble? You might need to repeat Step 3 until the title appears on one line. Also, you might have to move the picture farther to the right to make room for the title.

   Next you will change the title's font color.

TIP

Changing the form's title does not affect the form object name; it is still PatientData, as shown on the object tab.

4. On the ribbon, click the **Form Layout Tools Format** tab.
5. In the Font group, click the **Font Color button arrow** to display the gallery of available colors. The gallery provides theme colors and standard colors, as well as an option for creating a custom color. The theme colors available depend on the theme applied to the form—in this case, the colors are related to the Slice theme. The current color of the title text—Black, Text 1, Lighter 50%—is outlined in the gallery, indicating it is the currently applied font color.
6. In the Theme Colors palette, click the **Black, Text 1, Lighter 25%** color, which is the fourth color down in the second column.
7. Click a blank area of the form to deselect the title. The darker color is applied to the form title text, making it stand out more. See Figure 4–9.

Figure 4–9 **Form title with new color applied**

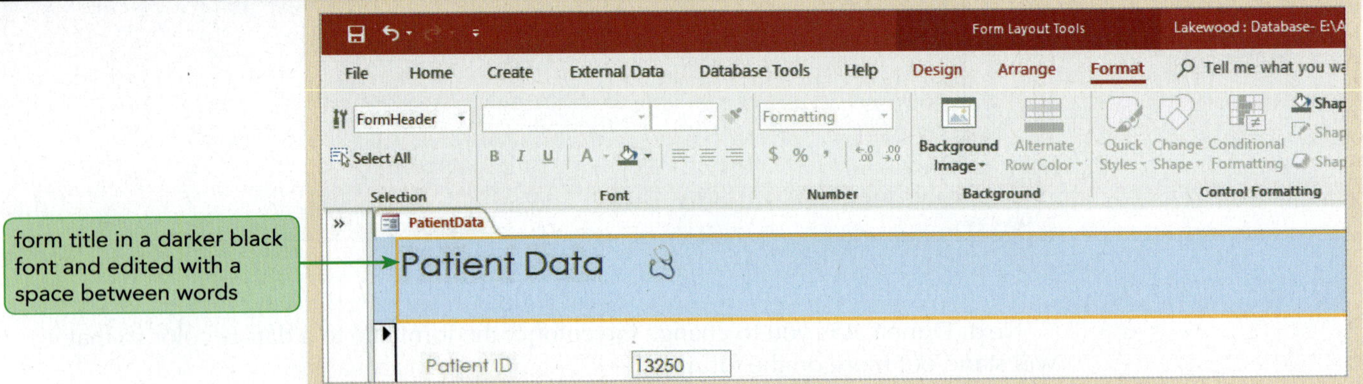

8. On the Quick Access Toolbar, click the **Save** button to save the modified form.
9. On the status bar, click the **Form View** button to display the form in Form view.

Donna is pleased with the modified appearance of the form.

PROSKILLS

Written Communication: Understanding the Importance of Form Design

Similar to any document, a form must convey written information clearly and effectively. When you create a form, it's important to consider how the form will be used, so that its design will accommodate the needs of people using the form to view, enter, and maintain data. For example, if a form in a database is meant to mimic a paper form that users will enter data from, the form in the database should have the same fields in the same order as on the paper form. This will enable users to easily tab from one field to the next in the database form to enter the necessary information from the paper form. Also, include a meaningful title on the form to identify its purpose and to enhance the appearance of the form. A form that is visually appealing makes working with the database more user-friendly and can improve the readability of the form, thereby helping to prevent errors in data entry. Also, be sure to use a consistent design for the forms in your database whenever possible. Users will expect to see similar elements—titles, pictures, fonts, and so on—in each form contained in a database. A mix of form styles and elements among the forms in a database could lead to problems when working with the forms. Finally, make sure the text on your form does not contain any spelling or grammatical errors. By producing a well-designed and well-written form, you can help to ensure that users will be able to work with the form in a productive and efficient manner.

Navigating a Form

To view, navigate, and change data using a form, you need to display the form in Form view. As you learned earlier, you navigate a form in the same way that you navigate a table datasheet. Also, the same navigation mode and editing mode keyboard shortcuts you have used working with datasheets can also be used when working with a form.

Donna wants to view data in the Patient table. Before using the PatientData form to display the specific information Donna wants to view, you will practice navigating between the fields in a record and navigating between records in the form. The PatientData form is already displayed in Form view, so you can use it to navigate through the fields and records of the Patient table.

To navigate the PatientData form:

1. If necessary, click in the **Patient ID** field value box to make it current.
2. Press **TAB** once to move to the Last Name field value box, and then press **END** to move to the Phone field value box.
3. Press **HOME** to move back to the Patient ID field value box. The first record in the Patient table still appears in the form.
4. Press **CTRL+END** to move to the Phone field value box for record 51, which is the last record in the table. The record number for the current record appears in the Current Record box between the navigation buttons at the bottom of the form.
5. Click the **Previous record** button ◂ to move to the Phone field value box in record 50.
6. Press ↑ twice to move to the Zip field value box in record 50.
7. Click to position the insertion point within the word "Phillips" in the Address field value to switch to editing mode, press **HOME** to move the insertion point to the beginning of the field value, and then press **END** to move the insertion point to the end of the field value.

8. Click the **First record** button [I◀] to move to the Address field value box in the first record. The entire field value is highlighted because you switched from editing mode to navigation mode.
9. Click the **Next record** button [▶] to move to the Address field value box in record 2, the next record.

Donna wants to find the record for a patient named Hansen. The paper form containing all the original contact information for this patient was damaged. Other than the patient's last name, Donna knows only the street the patient lives on. You will use the PatientData form to locate and view the complete record for this patient.

Finding Data Using a Form

As you learned earlier, the Find command lets you search for data in a datasheet so you can display only those records you want to view. You can also use the Find command to search for data in a form. You first choose a field to serve as the basis for the search by making that field the current field, and then you enter the value you want Access to match in the Find and Replace dialog box.

REFERENCE

Finding Data in a Form or Datasheet

- Open the form or datasheet, and then make the field you want to search the current field.
- On the Home tab, in the Find group, click the Find button to open the Find and Replace dialog box.
- In the Find What box, type the field value you want to find.
- Complete the remaining options, as necessary, to specify the type of search to conduct.
- Click the Find Next button to begin the search.
- Click the Find Next button to continue searching for the next match.
- Click the Cancel button to stop the search operation.

You need to find the record for the patient Donna wants to contact. The patient whose record she needs to find is named Hansen and lives on Boyles Ave. You'll search for this record using the Address field.

To find the record using the PatientData form:

1. Make sure the Address field value is still selected for the current record. This is the field you need to search.

   You can search for a record that contains part of the address anywhere in the Address field value. Performing a partial search such as this is often easier than matching the entire field value and is useful when you don't know or can't remember the entire field value.

2. On the Home tab, in the Find group, click the **Find** button. The Find and Replace dialog box opens. The Look In box indicates that the current field (in this case, Address) will be searched. You'll search for records that contain the word "boyles" in the address.

3. In the Find What box, type **boyles**. Note that you do not have to enter the word as "Boyles" with a capital letter "B" because the Match Case check box is not selected in the Find and Replace dialog box. The search will find any record containing the word "boyles" with any combination of uppercase and lowercase letters.
4. Click the **Match** arrow to display the list of matching options, and then click **Any Part of Field**. The search will find any record that contains the word "boyles" in any part of the Address field. See Figure 4–10.

Figure 4–10 **Completed Find and Replace dialog box**

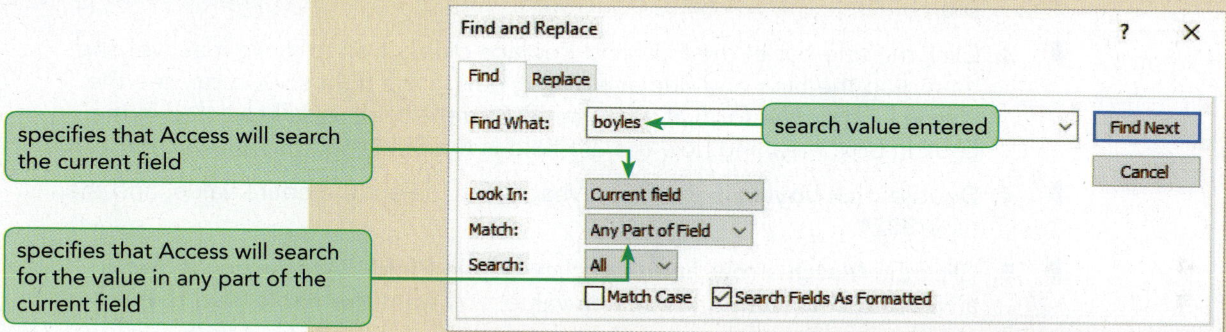

5. Click the **Find Next** button. The Find and Replace dialog box remains open, and the PatientData form now displays record 5, which is the record for Holly Hansen (PatientID 13255). The word "Boyles" is selected in the Address field value box because you searched for this word.

The search value you enter can be an exact value or it can include wildcard characters. A **wildcard character** is a placeholder you use when you know only part of a value or when you want to start or end with a specific character or match a certain pattern. Figure 4–11 shows the wildcard characters you can use when searching for data.

Figure 4–11 **Wildcard characters**

Wildcard Character	Purpose	Example
*	Match any number of characters it can be used as the first and/or last character in the character string	th* *finds* the, that, this, therefore, *and so on*
?	Match any single alphabetic character	a?t *finds* act, aft, ant, apt, *and* art
[]	Match any single character within the brackets	a[fr]t *finds* aft *and* art *but not* act, ant, *or* apt
!	Match any character not within brackets	a[!fr]t *finds* act, ant, *and* apt *but not* aft *or* art
-	Match any one of a range of characters the range must be in ascending order (a to z, not z to a)	a[d-p]t *finds* aft, ant, *and* apt *but not* act *or* art
#	Match any single numeric character	#72 *finds* 072, 172, 272, 372, *and so on*

Next, to see how a wildcard works, you'll view the records for any patients with zip codes that begin with 302. You could search for any record containing the digits 302 in any part of the Zip field, but this search may also find records with the digits 302 in any part of the zip code. To find only those records with the digits 302 at the beginning of the zip code, you'll use the * wildcard character.

To find the records using the * wildcard character:

1. Make sure the Find and Replace dialog box is still open.
2. Click anywhere in the PatientData form to make it active, and then press **TAB** until you reach the Zip field value box. This is the field you want to search.
3. Click the title bar of the Find and Replace dialog box to make it active, and then drag the Find and Replace dialog box to the right so you can see the Phone field on the form, if necessary. "Current field" is still selected in the Look In box, meaning now the Zip field is the field that will be searched.
4. Double-click **boyles** in the Find What box to select the entire value, and then type **302***.
5. Click the **Match** arrow, and then click **Whole Field**. Because you're using a wildcard character in the search value, you want the whole field to be searched.

   With the settings you've entered, the search will find records in which any field value in the Zip field begins with the value 302.
6. Click the **Find Next** button. Record 9 is displayed in the form, which is the first record found for a patient with a zip code that begins with 302. Notice that the search process started from the point of the previously displayed record in the form, which was record 5.
7. Click the **Find Next** button. Record 16 is displayed in the form, which is the next record found for a patient with a zip code that begins with 302.
8. Click the **Find Next** button to display record 18, and then click the **Find Next** button again. Record 20 is displayed, the fourth record found.
9. Click the **Find Next** button seven more times to display records 23, 26, 27, 33, 40, 42, and 46.
10. Click the **Find Next** button again. Record 4 is displayed. Notice that the search process cycles back through the beginning of the records in the underlying table.
11. Click the **Find Next** button. A dialog box opens, informing you that the search is finished.
12. Click the **OK** button to close the dialog box, and then click the **Cancel** button to close the Find and Replace dialog box.

Donna has identified some patient updates she wants you to make. You'll use the PatientData form to update the data in the Patient table.

Maintaining Table Data Using a Form

Maintaining data using a form is often easier than using a datasheet because you can focus on all the changes for a single record at one time. In Form view, you can edit the field values for a record, delete a record from the underlying table, or add a new record to the table.

Now you'll use the PatientData form to make the changes Donna wants to the Patient table. First, you'll update the record for patient Mariana Salinas, who recently moved from Smyrna to Marietta and provided a new mailing address. In addition to using the Find and Replace dialog box to locate a specific record, you can use the Search box to the right of the navigation buttons. You'll use the Search box to search for the patient's last name, Salinas, and display the patient record in the form.

To change the record using the PatientData form:

1. To the right of the navigation buttons, click the **Search** box and then type **Salinas**. As soon as you start to type, Access begins searching through all fields in the records to match your entry. Record 30 (Mariana Salinas) is now current.

   You will first update the address in this record.

TIP

The pencil symbol appears in the upper-left corner of the form when the form is in editing mode.

2. Select the current entry in the Address field value box, and then type **17 Wyndmere Rd** to replace it.
3. Press **TAB** to select the city in the City field value box, and then type **Marietta**.
4. Press **TAB** twice to move to and select the Zip field value, and then type **30067**. The updates to the record are complete. See Figure 4–12.

Figure 4–12 Patient record after changing field values

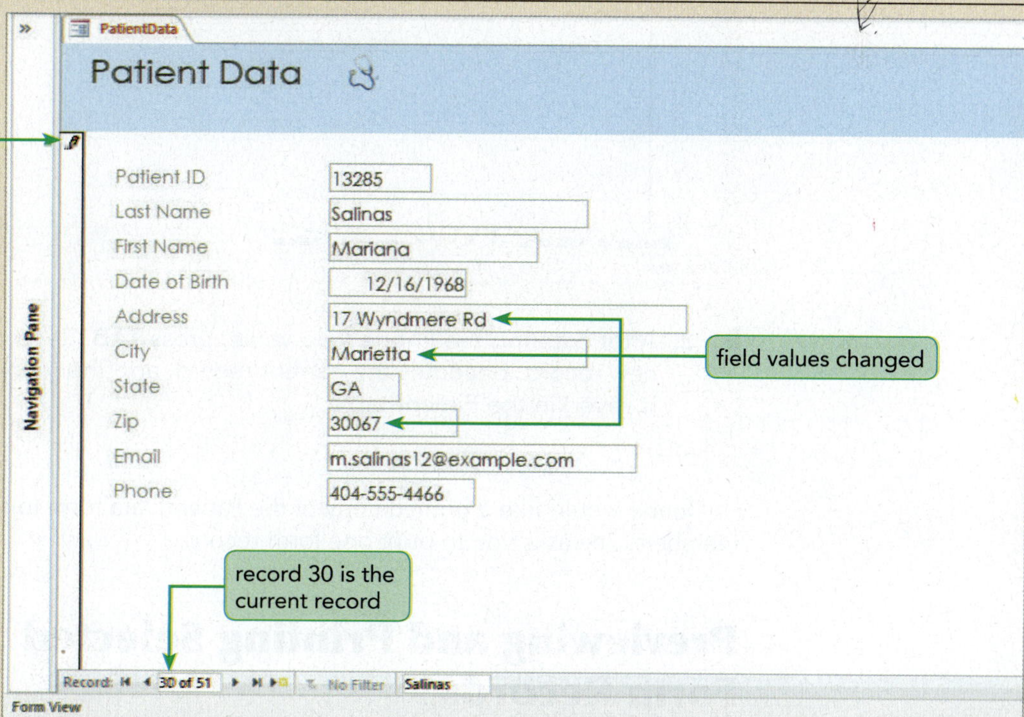

Next, Donna asks you to add a record for a new patient. This person signed up to be a patient of the clinic at a recent health fair held by Lakewood Community Health Services, but has not yet visited the clinic. You'll use the PatientData form to add the new record.

To add the new record using the PatientData form:

1. On the Home tab, in the Records group, click the **New** button. Record 52, the next available new record, becomes the current record. All field value boxes are empty (except the State field, which displays the default value of GA), and the insertion point is positioned in the Patient ID field value box.
2. Refer to Figure 4–13 and enter the value shown for each field, pressing **TAB** to move from field to field.

Figure 4–13 Completed form for the new record

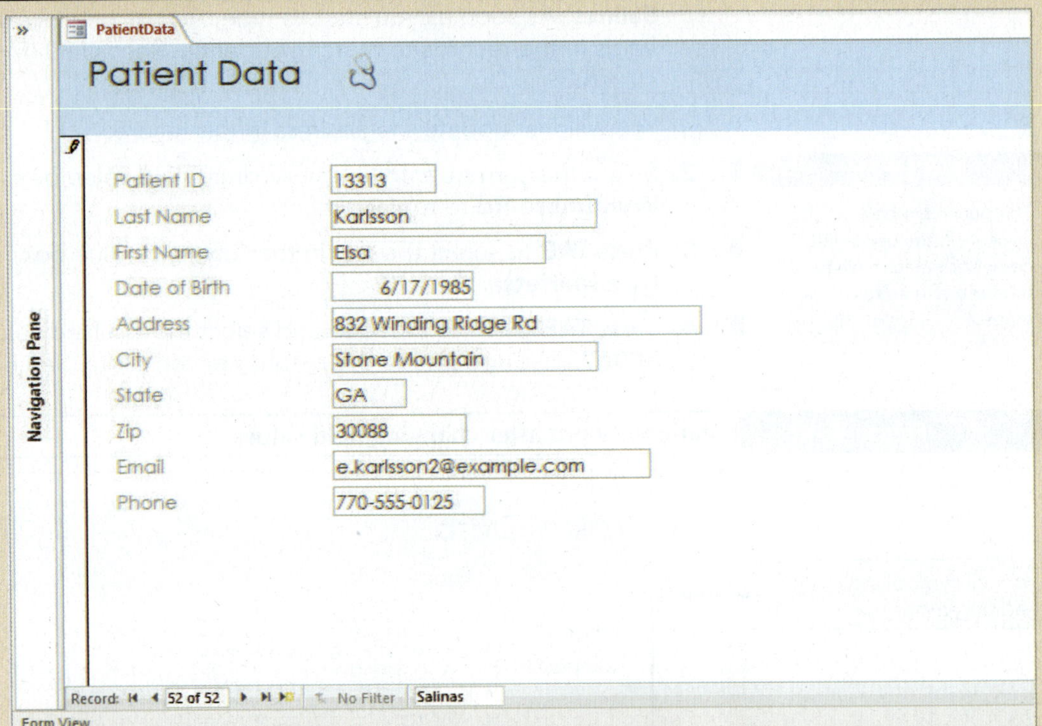

3. After entering the Phone field value, press **TAB**. Record 53, the next available new record, becomes the current record, and the record for PatientID 13313 is saved in the Patient table.

Donna would like a printed copy of the PatientData form to show to her staff members. She asks you to print one form record.

Previewing and Printing Selected Form Records

You can print as many form records as can fit on a printed page. If only part of a form record fits on the bottom of a page, the remainder of the record prints on the next page. You can print all pages or a range of pages. In addition, you can print just the currently selected form record.

Donna asks you to use the PatientData form to print the first record in the Patient table. Before you do, you'll preview the form record to see how it will look when printed.

To preview the form and print the data for record 1:

1. Click the **First record** button to display record 1 in the form. This is the record in which you have entered your first and last names.
2. Click the **File** tab to open Backstage view, click **Print** in the navigation bar, and then click **Print Preview**. The Print Preview window opens, showing the form records for the Patient table. Notice that each record appears in its own form and that shading is used to distinguish one record from another. See Figure 4–14.

Figure 4–14 **Form records displayed in Print Preview**

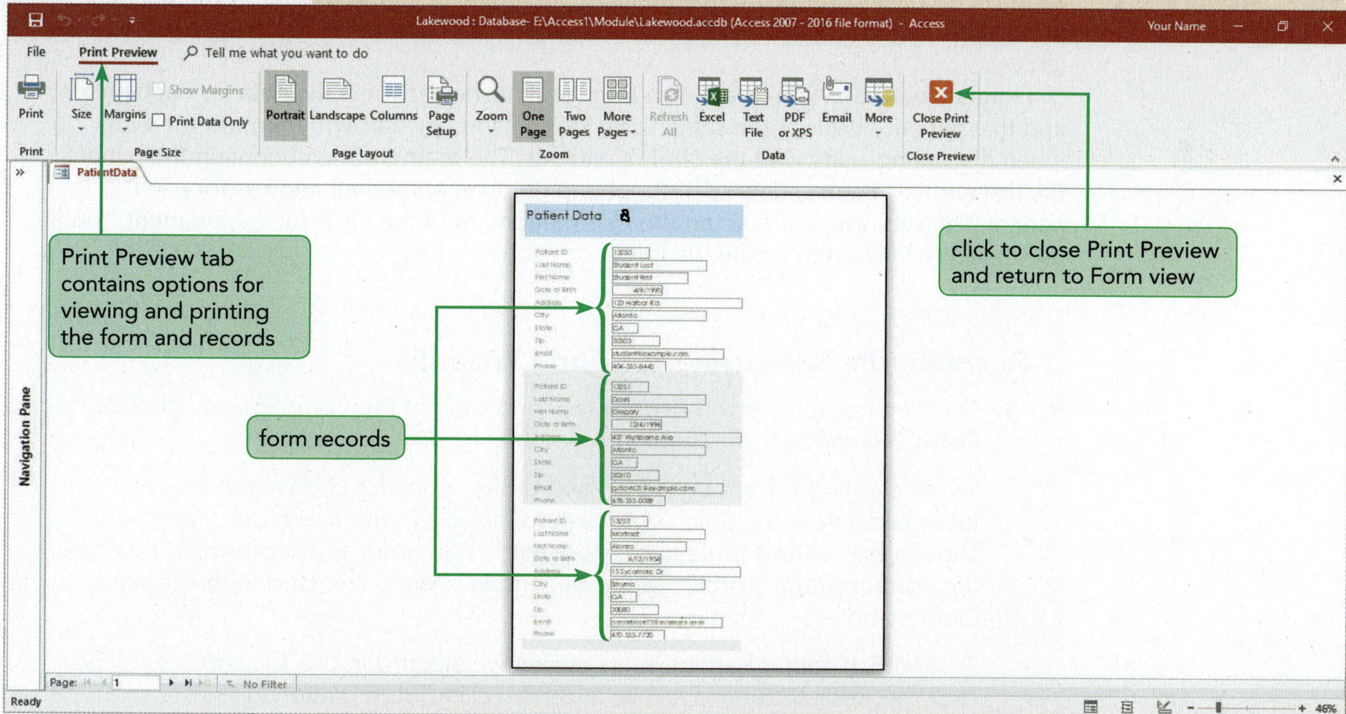

To print one selected record on a page by itself, you need to use the Print dialog box.

3. On the Print Preview tab, in the Close Preview group, click the **Close Print Preview** button. You return to Form view with the first record still displayed.
4. Click the **File** tab to open Backstage view again, click **Print** in the navigation bar, and then click **Print**. The **Print** dialog box opens.
5. Click the **Selected Record(s)** option button to print the current form record (record 1).

   Trouble? Check with your instructor to be sure you should print the form, then continue to the next step. If you should not print the form, click the Cancel button, and then skip to Step 7.
6. Click the **OK** button to close the dialog box and print the selected record.
7. Close the PatientData form.

After reviewing the printed PatientData form with her staff, Donna realizes that it would be helpful for staff members to also have a form showing information about both patients and their visits. Because this form will need to display information from two different tables, the type of form you need to create will include a main form and a subform.

Creating a Form with a Main Form and a Subform

To create a form based on two tables, you must first define a relationship between the two tables. Earlier, you defined a one-to-many relationship between the Patient (primary) and Visit (related) tables, so you can now create a form based on both tables.

When you create a form containing data from two tables that have a one-to-many relationship, you actually create a **main form** for data from the primary table and a **subform** for data from the related table. Access uses the defined relationship between the tables to join them automatically through the common field that exists in both tables.

Donna would like you to create a form so that she can view the data for each patient and that patient's visits at the same time. Donna and her staff will then use the form when discussing visits with the clinic's patients. The main form will contain the patient ID, first and last names, date of birth, phone number, and email address for each patient. The subform will contain the information about the visits for each patient. You'll use the Form Wizard to create the form.

To create the form using the Form Wizard:

1. On the ribbon, click the **Create** tab, and then in the Forms group, click the **Form Wizard** button. The first Form Wizard dialog box opens.

   When creating a form based on two tables, you first choose the primary table and select the fields you want to include in the main form; then you choose the related table and select fields from it for the subform. In this case, the correct primary table, Table: Patient, is already selected in the Tables/Queries box.

   Trouble? If Table: Patient is not currently selected in the Tables/Queries box, click the Tables/Queries arrow, and then click Table: Patient.

   The form needs to include only the PatientID, FirstName, LastName, BirthDate, Phone, and Email fields from the Patient table.

2. Click **PatientID** in the Available Fields box if necessary, and then click the **Select Single Field** button > to move the field to the Selected Fields box.
3. Repeat Step 2 for the **FirstName**, **LastName**, **BirthDate, Phone**, and **Email** fields, in that order.

   The subform needs to include all the fields from the Visit table, with the exception of the PatientID field, as that field has been added in the main form.

4. Click the **Tables/Queries** arrow, and then click **Table: Visit**. The fields from the Visit table appear in the Available Fields box. The quickest way to add the fields you want to include is to move all the fields to the Selected Fields box, and then remove the only field you don't want to include (PatientID).

TIP

The table name (Visit) is included in the PatientID field name to distinguish it from the same field in the Patient table.

5. Click the **Select All Fields** button [>>] to move all the fields in the Visit table to the Selected Fields box.
6. Click **Visit.PatientID** in the Selected Fields box, and then click the **Remove Single Field** button [<] to move the field back to the Available Fields box.
7. Click the **Next** button. The next Form Wizard dialog box opens. See Figure 4–15.

Figure 4–15 Choosing a format for the main form and subform

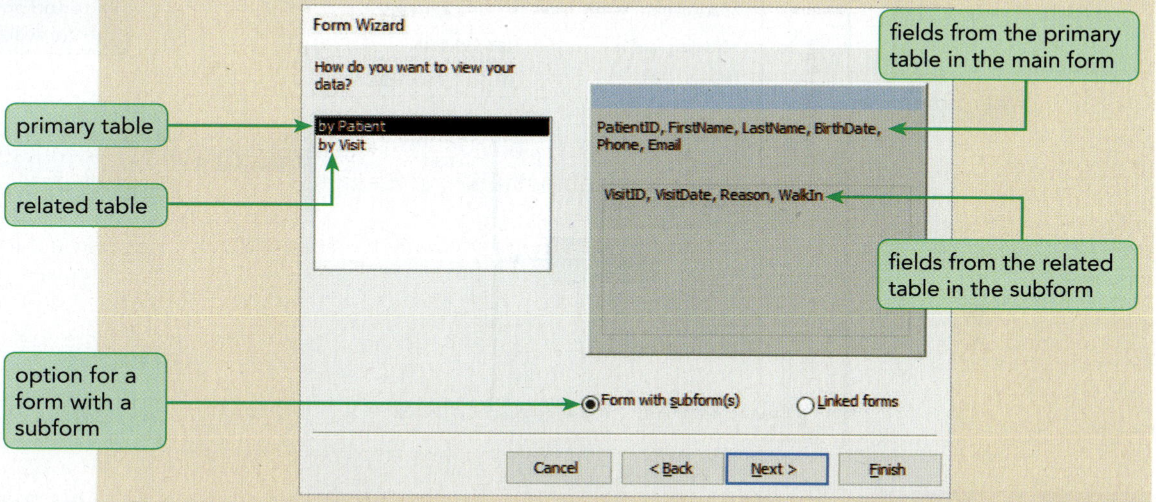

In this dialog box, the section on the left shows the order in which you will view the selected data: first by data from the primary Patient table, and then by data from the related Visit table. The form will be displayed as shown on the right side of the dialog box, with the fields from the Patient table at the top in the main form, and the fields from the Visit table at the bottom in the subform.

The default options shown in Figure 4–15 are correct for creating a form with Patient data in the main form and Visit data in the subform.

8. Click the **Next** button. The next Form Wizard dialog box opens, in which you choose the subform layout.

   The Tabular layout displays subform fields as a table, whereas the Datasheet layout displays subform fields as a table datasheet. The layout choice is a matter of personal preference. You'll use the Datasheet layout.

9. Click the **Datasheet** option button to select it if necessary, and then click the **Next** button. The next Form Wizard dialog box opens, in which you specify titles for the main form and the subform. You'll use the title "PatientVisits" for the main form and the title "VisitSubform" for the subform. These titles will also be the names for the form objects.
10. In the Form box, click to position the insertion point to the right of the last letter, and then type **Visits**. The main form name is now PatientVisits.
11. In the Subform box, delete the space between the two words so that the subform name appears as **VisitSubform**, and then click the **Finish** button. The completed form opens in Form view. See Figure 4–16.

Figure 4-16 Main form with subform in Form view

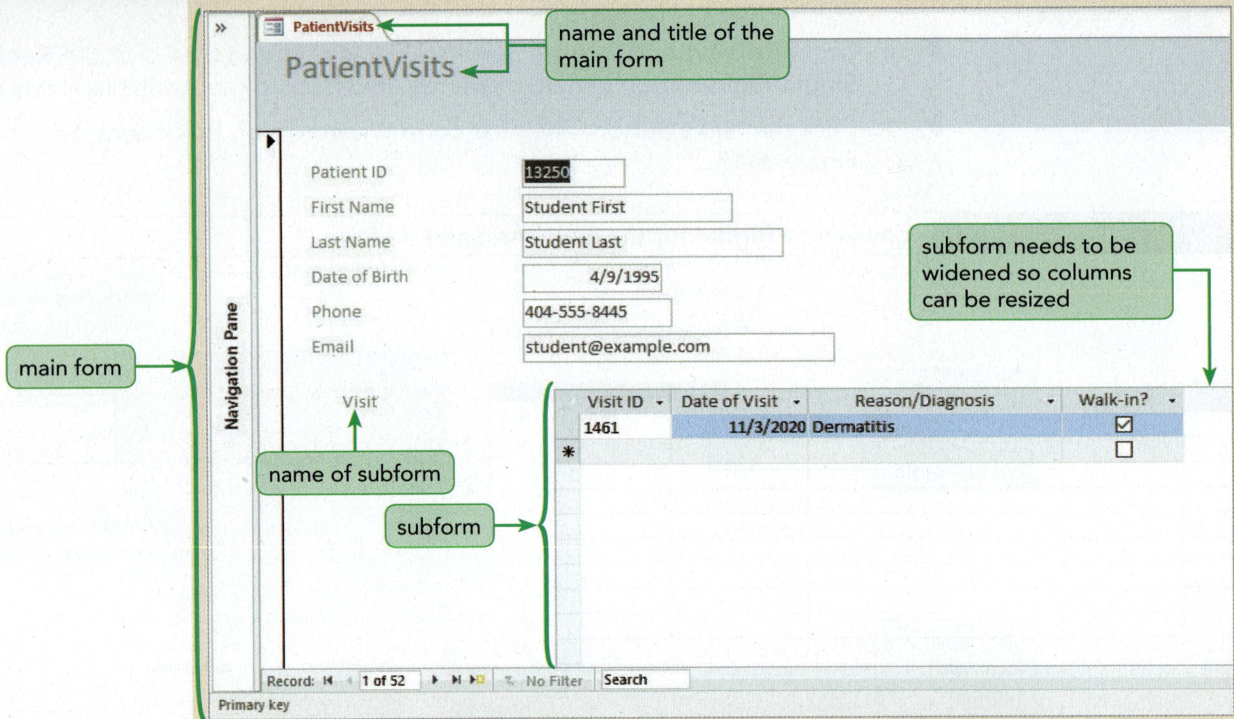

TIP

The PatientVisits form is formatted with the default Office theme because you applied the Slice theme only to the PatientData form.

The main form displays the fields from the first record in the Patient table in a columnar format. The records in the main form appear in primary key order by PatientID. PatientID 13250 has one related record in the Visit table; this record, for VisitID 1461, is shown in the subform, which uses the datasheet format. The main form name, "PatientVisits," appears on the object tab and as the form title. The name of the table "Visit" appears to the left of the subform indicating the underlying table for the subform. Note that only the word "Visit" and not the complete name "VisitSubform" appears on the form. Only the table name is displayed for the subform itself, but the complete name of the object, "VisitSubform," is displayed when you view and work with objects in the Navigation Pane. The subform designation is necessary in a list of database objects so that you can distinguish the Visit subform from other objects, such as the Visit table, but the subform designation is not needed in the PatientVisits form. Only the table name is required to identify the table containing the records in the subform.

Next, you need to make some changes to the form. First, you'll edit the form title to add a space between the words so that it appears as "Patient Visits." Then, you'll resize the subform so that it is wide enough to allow for all the columns to be fully displayed. To make these changes, you need to switch to Layout view.

To modify the PatientVisits form in Layout view:

1. Switch to Layout view.

   Trouble? If the Field List or Property Sheet opens on the right side of the program window, close it before continuing.

2. Click **PatientVisits** in the gray area at the top of the form. The form title is selected.

3. Click between the letters "t" and "V" to place the insertion point, and then press **SPACEBAR**. The title on the form is now "Patient Visits."
4. Click in a blank area of the form to the right of the field value boxes to deselect the title. Next, you'll increase the width of the subform.
5. Click the **subform**. An orange border surrounds the subform, indicating it is selected.
6. Position the pointer on the right border of the selected subform until the pointer changes to the width change pointer ↔, and then drag to the right approximately three inches. The wider subform makes all the columns visible, even when the Reason field contains a long entry. See Figure 4–17.

Figure 4–17 **Modified form in Layout view**

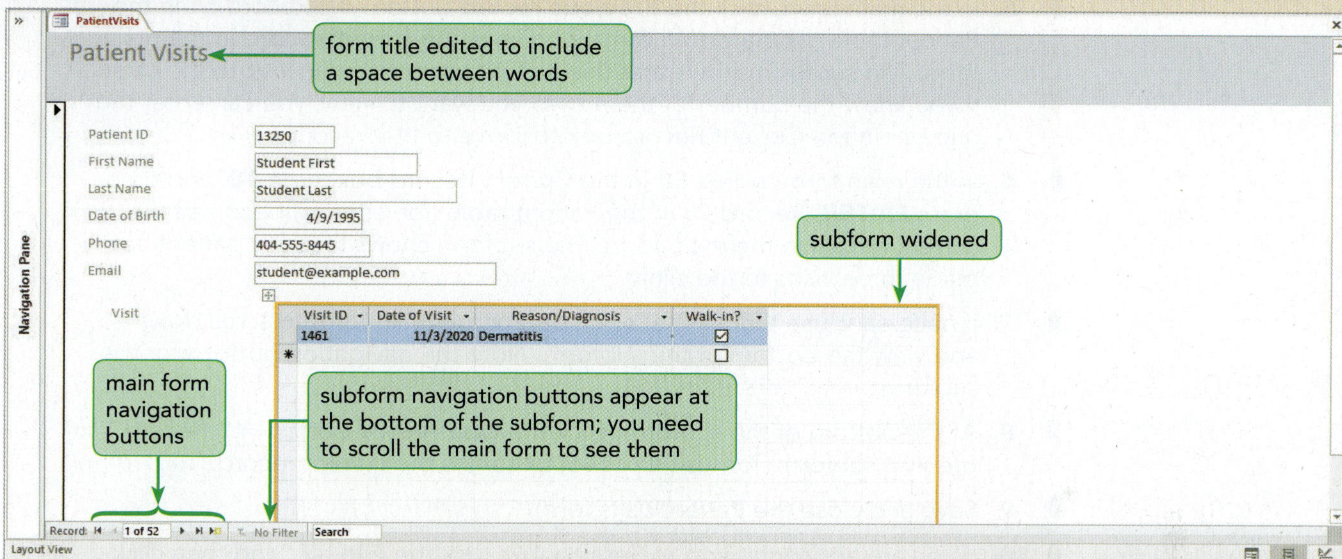

7. On the Quick Access Toolbar, click the **Save** button to save both the main form and the subform.
8. Switch to Form view, and then if necessary, scroll up to view all the fields in the main form.

The form includes two sets of navigation buttons. You use the set of navigation buttons at the bottom of the Form window to select records from the primary table in the main form (see Figure 4–17). The second set of navigation buttons is currently not visible; you need to scroll down the main form to see these buttons, which appear at the bottom of the subform. You use the subform navigation buttons to select records from the related table in the subform.

You'll use the navigation buttons to view different records.

To navigate to different main form and subform records:

1. In the main form, click the **Next record** button five times. Record 6 of 52 total records in the Patient table (for Andrew Wagner) becomes the current record in the main form. The subform shows that this patient made two visits to the clinic. Note that the field values in the Reason/Diagnosis columns are not fully displayed.

2. Double-click the column resizing pointer ✚ on the right column divider of the Reason/Diagnosis column in the subform to resize this field to its best fit and display the complete field values.
3. Use the main form navigation buttons to view each record, resizing any subform column to fully display any field values that are not completely visible.
4. In the main form, click the **Last record** button ▶|. Record 52 in the Patient table (for Elsa Karlsson) becomes the current record in the main form. The subform shows that this patient currently has made no visits to the clinic; recall that you just entered this record using the PatientData form. Donna could use the subform to enter the information on this patient's visits to the clinic, and that information will be updated in the Visit table.
5. In the main form, click the **Previous record** button ◀. Record 51 in the Patient table (for Aaron Williams) becomes the current record in the main form. The subform shows that this patient has made one visit to the clinic. If you know the number of the record you want to view, you can enter the number in the Current Record box to move to that record.
6. In the main form, select **51** in the Current Record box, type **18**, and then press **ENTER**. Record 18 in the Patient table (for Chen Li) becomes the current record in the main form. The subform shows that this patient has made three visits to the clinic.
7. If necessary, use the vertical scroll bar for the main form to scroll down and view the bottom of the subform. Note the navigation buttons for the subform.
8. At the bottom of the subform, click the **Last record** button ▶|. Record 3 in the Visit subform, for Visit ID 1546, becomes the current record.
9. Save and close the PatientVisits form.
10. If you are not continuing to Session 4.2, click the **File** tab, and then click **Close** in the navigation bar to close the Lakewood database.

Both the PatientData form and the PatientVisits form you created will enable Donna and her staff to view, enter, and maintain data easily in the Patient and Visit tables in the Lakewood database.

REVIEW

Session 4.1 Quick Check

1. Describe the difference between creating a form using the Form tool and creating a form using the Form Wizard.
2. What is a theme, and how do you apply one to an existing form?
3. A(n) ____________ is an item on a form, report, or other database object that you can manipulate to modify the object's appearance.
4. Which table record is displayed in a form when you press the CTRL+END keys while you are in navigation mode?
5. Which wildcard character matches any single alphabetic character?
6. To print only the current record displayed in a form, you need to select the ____________ option button in the Print dialog box.
7. In a form that contains a main form and a subform, what data is displayed in the main form and what data is displayed in the subform?

Session 4.2 Visual Overview:

The report object's name is displayed on the tab for the report.

The title appears at the top of the report. By default, the report object name is used as the report title, but you can edit the title to display the text you want, as done here, with spaces added between words for readability.

Fields from the primary Patient table appear first in the report.

Fields from the related Visit table appear below the fields from the primary table.

For a **grouped report**, the data from a record in the primary table (the Patient table in this report) appears as a group, followed on subsequent lines of the report by the joined records from the related table (the Visit table in this report.)

The navigation buttons allow you to display the first, last, next, or previous pages in the report, or to enter a specific page number and move to that page.

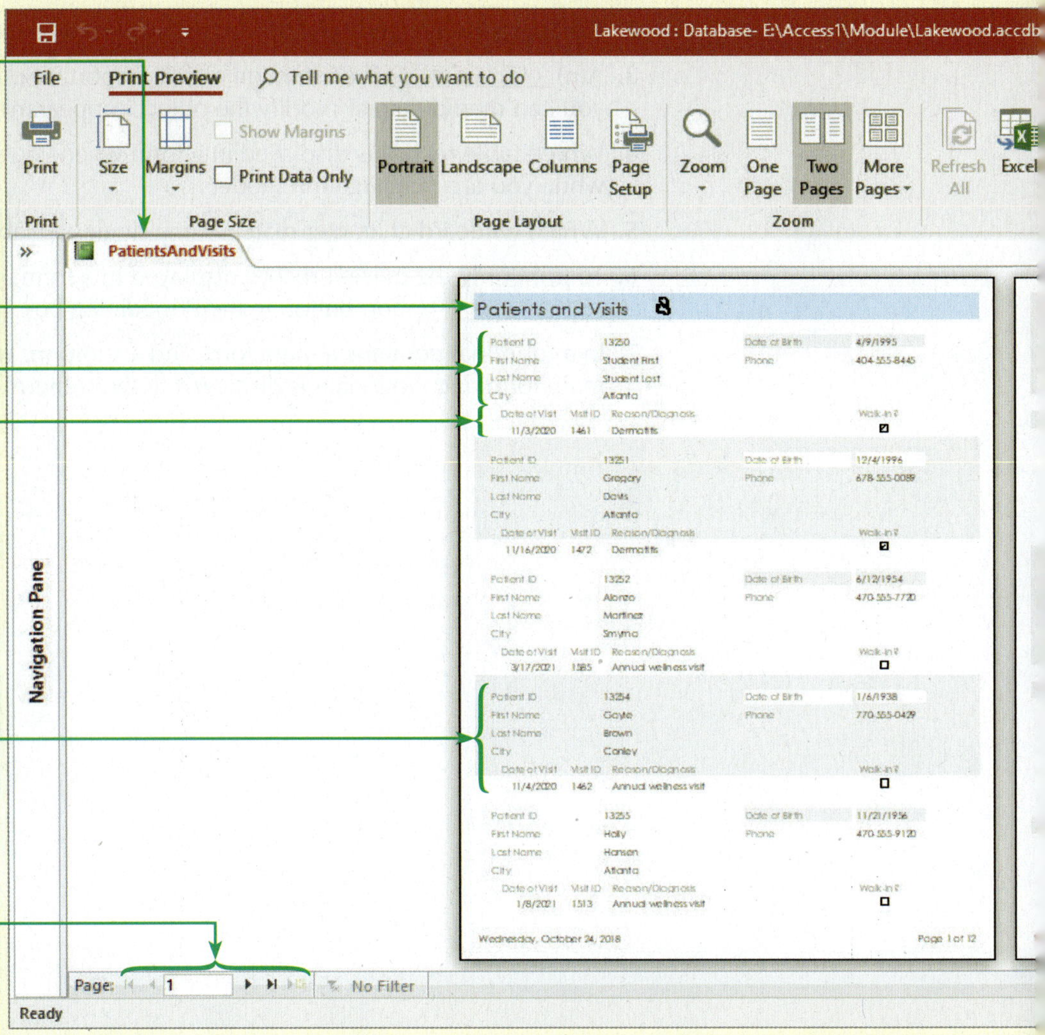

Report Displayed in Print Preview

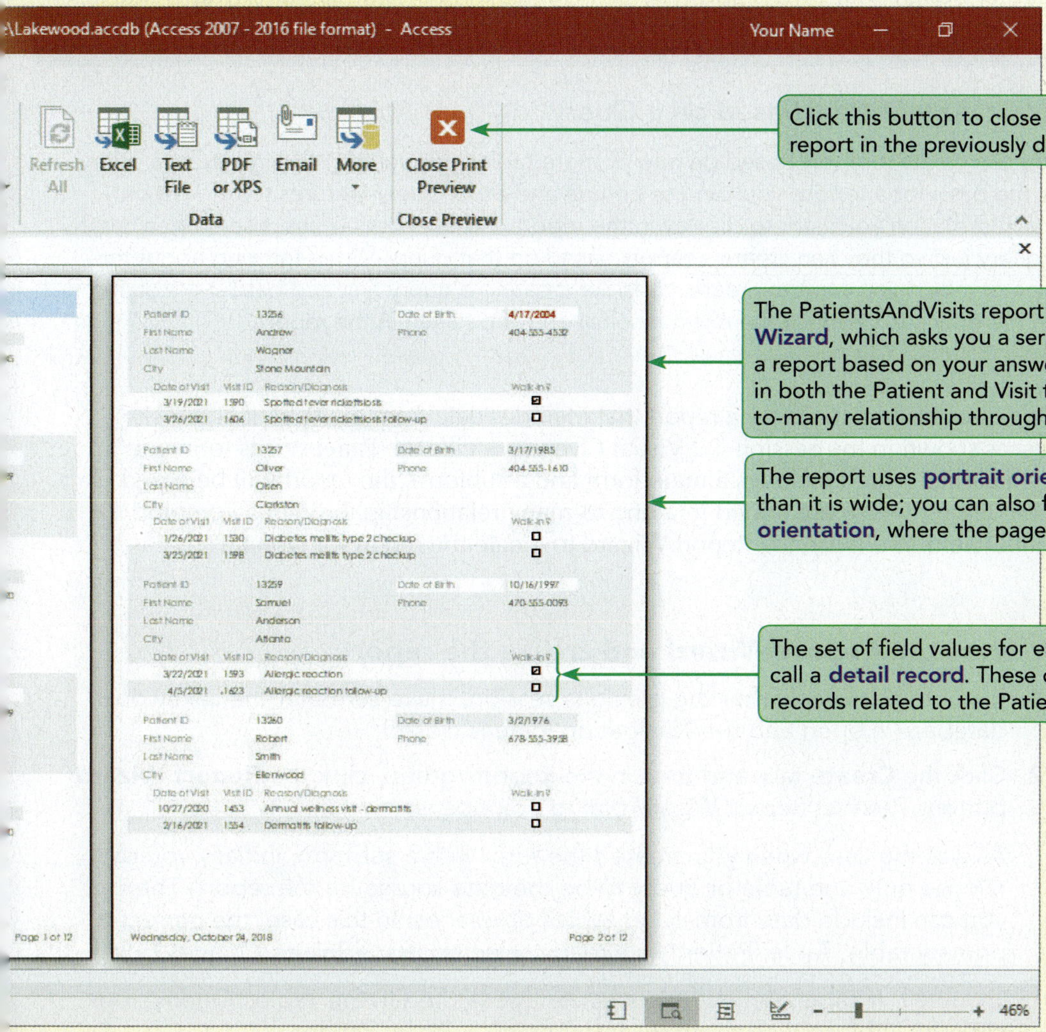

Click this button to close Print Preview and return to the report in the previously displayed view.

The PatientsAndVisits report was created using the **Report Wizard**, which asks you a series of questions and then creates a report based on your answers. This report is based on data in both the Patient and Visit tables, which are joined in a one-to-many relationship through the common PatientID field.

The report uses **portrait orientation**, where the page is taller than it is wide; you can also format a report in **landscape orientation**, where the page is wider than it is tall.

The set of field values for each record in the related table is call a **detail record**. These detail records are the Visit table records related to the Patient table records for this patient.

Creating a Report Using the Report Wizard

As you learned earlier, a report is a formatted printout or screen display of the contents of one or more tables or queries in a database. In Access, you can create your own reports or use the Report Wizard to create them for you. Whether you use the Report Wizard or design your own report, you can change a report's design after you create it.

INSIGHT

Creating a Report Based on a Query

You can create a report based on one or more tables or queries. When you use a query as the basis for a report, you can use criteria and other query features to retrieve only the information you want to display in the report. Experienced Access users often create a query just so they can create a report based on that query. When thinking about the type of report you want to create, consider creating a query first and basing the report on the query, to produce the exact results you want to see in the report.

Donna wants you to create a report that includes data from the Patient and Visit tables, as shown in the Session 4.2 Visual Overview. Like the PatientVisits form you created earlier, which includes a main form and a subform, the report will be based on both tables, which are joined in a one-to-many relationship through a common PatientID field. You'll use the Report Wizard to create the report for Donna.

To start the Report Wizard and create the report:

1. If you took a break after the previous session, make sure that the Lakewood database is open and the Navigation Pane is closed.
2. Click the **Create** tab, and then in the Reports group, click the **Report Wizard** button. The first Report Wizard dialog box opens.

   As was the case when you created the form with a subform, initially you can choose only one table or query to be the data source for the report. Then you can include data from other tables or queries. In this case, the correct primary table, Table: Patient, is already selected in the Tables/Queries box.

   Trouble? If Table: Patient is not currently selected in the Tables/Queries box, click the Tables/Queries arrow, and then click Table: Patient.

   You select fields in the order you want them to appear on the report. Donna wants the PatientID, FirstName, LastName, City, BirthDate, and Phone fields from the Patient table to appear on the report, in that order.
3. Click **PatientID** in the Available Fields box (if necessary), and then click the **Select Single Field** button [>]. The field moves to the Selected Fields box.
4. Repeat Step 3 to add the **FirstName**, **LastName**, **City**, **BirthDate**, and **Phone** fields to the report.
5. Click the **Tables/Queries** arrow, and then click **Table: Visit**. The fields from the Visit table appear in the Available Fields box.

   Donna wants all the fields from the Visit table to be included in the report.
6. Click the **Select All Fields** button [>>] to move all the fields from the Available Fields box to the Selected Fields box.
7. Click **Visit.PatientID** in the Selected Fields box, click the **Remove Single Field** button [<] to move the field back to the Available Fields box, and then click the **Next** button. The second Report Wizard dialog box opens. See Figure 4–18.

Figure 4–18 Choosing a grouped or ungrouped report

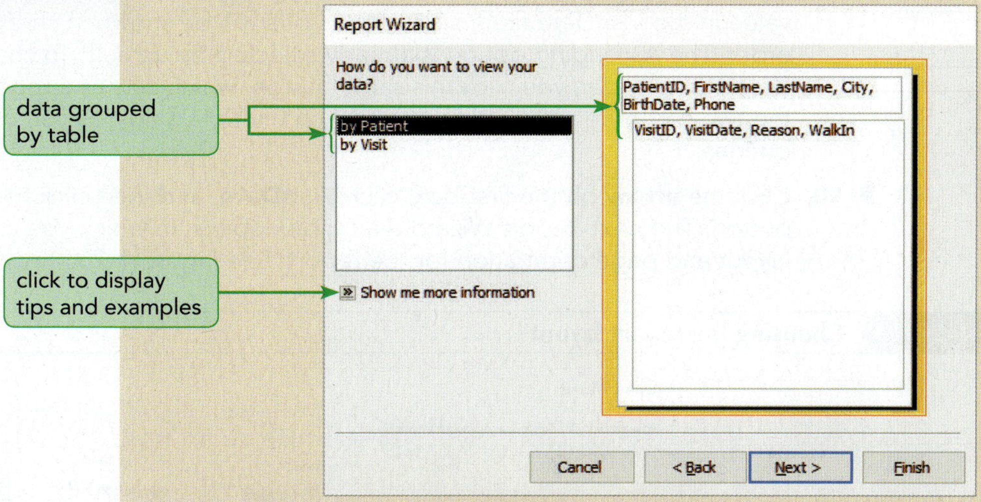

You can choose to arrange the selected data grouped by table, which is the default, or ungrouped. You're creating a grouped report; the data from each record in the Patient table will appear in a group, followed by the related records for that patient from the Visit table.

8. Click the **Next** button. The next Report Wizard dialog box opens, in which you choose additional grouping levels.

   Currently the report contains only one grouping level, which is for the patient's data. Grouping levels are useful for reports with multiple levels, such as those containing monthly, quarterly, and annual totals, or for those containing city and country groups. The report requires no further grouping levels, so you can accept the default options.

9. Click the **Next** button. The next Report Wizard dialog box opens, in which you choose the sort order for the detail records. See Figure 4–19.

Figure 4–19 Choosing the sort order for detail records

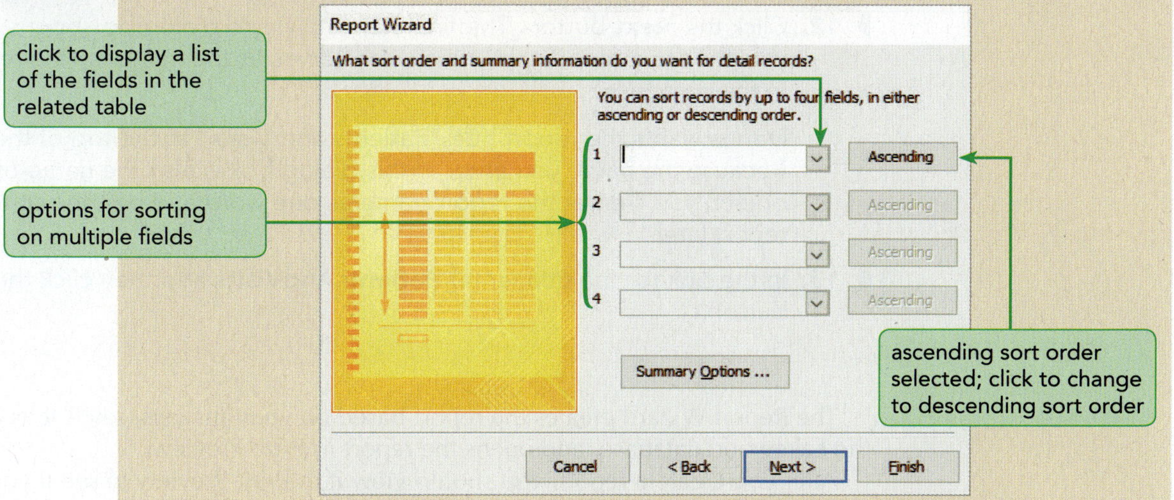

The records from the Visit table for a patient represent the detail records for Donna's report. She wants these records to appear in ascending order by the value in the VisitDate field, so that the visits will be shown in chronological order. The Ascending option is already selected by default. To change to descending order, you click this same button, which acts as a toggle between the two sort orders. Also, you can sort on multiple fields, as you can with queries.

10. Click the **arrow** on the first box, click **VisitDate**, and then click the **Next** button. The next Report Wizard dialog box opens, in which you choose a layout and page orientation for the report. See Figure 4–20.

Figure 4–20 Choosing the report layout

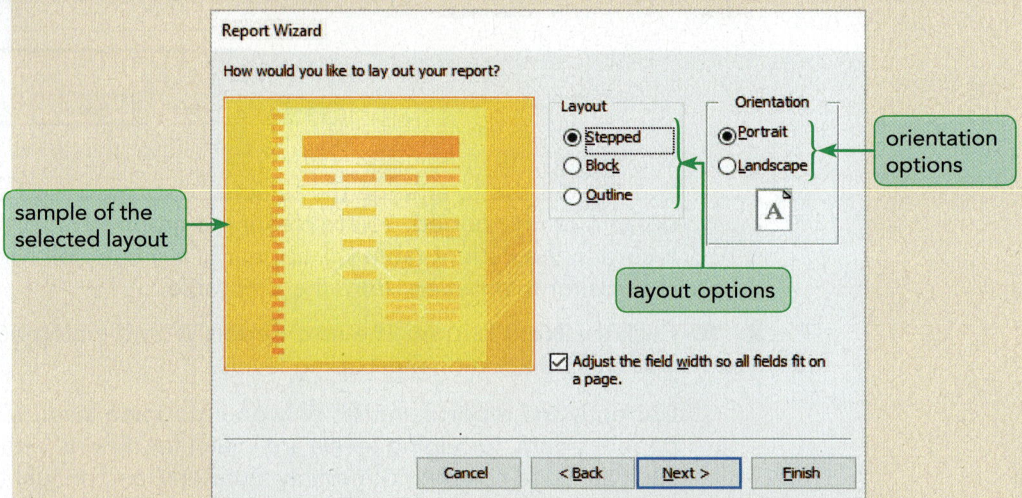

11. Click each layout option to view each sample that appears, and then click the **Outline** option button to select that layout for the report.

    Because most of the fields in both the Patient and Visit tables contain relatively short field values, the portrait page orientation should provide enough space across the page to display all the field values.

12. Click the **Next** button. The final Report Wizard dialog box opens, in which you choose a report title, which also serves as the name for the report object in the database.

    Donna wants the report title "Patients and Visits" at the top of the report. Because the name you enter in this dialog box is also the name of the report object, you'll enter the report name as one word and edit the title on the report later.

13. In the box for the title, enter **PatientsAndVisits** and then click the **Finish** button.

The Report Wizard creates the report based on your answers, saves it as an object in the Lakewood database, and opens the report in Print Preview.

After you create a report, you should view it in Print Preview to see if you need to make any formatting or design changes. To view the entire page, you need to change the Zoom setting.

To view the report in Print Preview:

1. On the Print Preview tab, in the Zoom group, click the **Zoom arrow**, and then click **Fit to Window**. The first page of the report is displayed in Print Preview.
2. At the bottom of the window, click the **Next Page** button to display the second page of the report.

   When a report is displayed in Print Preview, you can zoom in for a close-up view of a section of the report.
3. Move the pointer to the center of the report, and then click the **Zoom In** pointer at the center of the report. The display changes to show a close-up view of the report. See Figure 4–21.

Figure 4–21 Close-up view of the report

TIP

Clicking a report in Print Preview toggles between a full-page display and a close-up display of the report.

The detail records for the Visit table fields appear in ascending order based on the values in the VisitDate field. Because the VisitDate field is used as the basis for sorting records, it appears as the first field in this section, even though you selected the fields in the order in which they appear in the Visit table.

4. Scroll to the bottom of the second page, checking the text in the report as you scroll. Notice the current date and page number at the bottom of the page; the Report Wizard included these elements as part of the report's design.
5. Move the pointer onto the report, click the **Zoom Out** pointer to zoom back out, and then click the **Next Page** button to move to page 3 of the report.
6. Continue to move through the pages of the report, and then click the **First Page** button to return to the first page.

INSIGHT

Changing a Report's Page Orientation and Margins

When you display a report in Print Preview, you can easily change the report layout using options on the Print Preview tab (refer to the Session 4.2 Visual Overview). For example, sometimes fields with longer values cause the report content to overflow onto the next page. You can fix this problem by clicking the Landscape button in the Page Layout group on the Print Preview tab to switch the report orientation to landscape, where the page is wider than it is tall. Landscape orientation allows more space for content to fit across the width of the report page. You can also use the Margins button in the Page Size group to change the margins of the report, choosing from commonly used margin formats or creating your own custom margins. Click the Margins arrow to display the menu of available margin options and select the one that works best for your report.

When you created the PatientData form, you applied the Slice theme. Donna would like the PatientsAndVisits report to be formatted with the same theme. You need to switch to Layout view to make this change. You'll also make other modifications to improve the report's design.

Modifying a Report's Design in Layout View

Similar to Layout view for forms, Layout view for reports enables you to make modifications to the report's design. Many of the same options—such as those for applying a theme and changing the color of text—are provided in Layout view for reports.

Applying a Theme to a Report

The same themes available for forms are also available for reports. You can choose to apply a theme to the current report object only, or to all reports in the database. In this case, you'll apply the Slice theme only to the PatientsAndVisits report because Donna isn't certain if it is the appropriate theme for other reports in the Lakewood database.

To apply the Slice theme to the report and edit the report name:

1. On the status bar, click the **Layout View** button. The report is displayed in Layout view and the Report Layout Tools Design tab is the active tab on the ribbon.

   Trouble? If the Field List or Property Sheet opens on the right side of the program window, close it before continuing.

2. In the Themes group, click the **Themes** button. The "In this Database" section at the top of the gallery shows both the default Office theme and the Slice theme. The Slice theme is included here because you applied it earlier to the PatientData form.

3. At the top of the gallery, right-click the **Slice** theme to display the shortcut menu, and then click **Apply Theme to This Object Only**. The gallery closes and the theme is applied to the report.

   The larger font used by the Slice theme has caused the report title text to be cut off on the right. You'll fix this problem and edit the title text as well.

TIP

When you point to the Slice theme, a ScreenTip displays the names of the database objects that use the theme—in this case, the PatientData form.

4. Click the **PatientsAndVisits** title at the top of the report to select it.
5. Position the pointer on the right border of the title's selection box until it changes to the width change pointer ↔, and then drag to the right until the title is fully displayed.
6. Click between the letters "s" and "A" in the title, press **SPACEBAR**, change the capital letter "A" to **a**, place the insertion point between the letters "d" and "V," and then press **SPACEBAR**. The title is now "Patients and Visits."
7. Click to the right of the report title in the shaded area to deselect the title.

Donna views the report and notices some other formatting changes she would like you to make. First, she doesn't like how the VisitDate field values are aligned compared to the other field values from the Visit table. You'll fix this next.

Changing the Alignment of Field Values

The Report Layout Tools Format tab provides options for you to easily modify the format of various report objects. For example, you can change the alignment of the text in a field value. Recall that Date/Time fields, like VisitDate, automatically right-align their field values, whereas Short Text fields, like VisitID, automatically left-align their field values. Donna asks you to change the alignment of the BirthDate field so its values appear left-aligned, which will improve the format of the report.

To change the alignment of the VisitDate field values:

1. On the ribbon, click the **Report Layout Tools Format** tab. The ribbon changes to display options for formatting the report. The options for modifying the format of a report are the same as those available for forms.
2. In the report, click the **first BirthDate** field value box, which contains the date 4/9/1995. The field value box has an orange border, indicating it is selected. Note that the other BirthDate field value boxes have a lighter orange border, indicating they are selected as well. Any changes you make will be applied to all BirthDate field values throughout the report.
3. On the Report Layout Tools Format tab, in the Font group, click the **Align Left** button. The text in the BirthDate field value boxes is now left-aligned. See Figure 4–22.

Figure 4–22 Report after applying a theme and changing field alignment

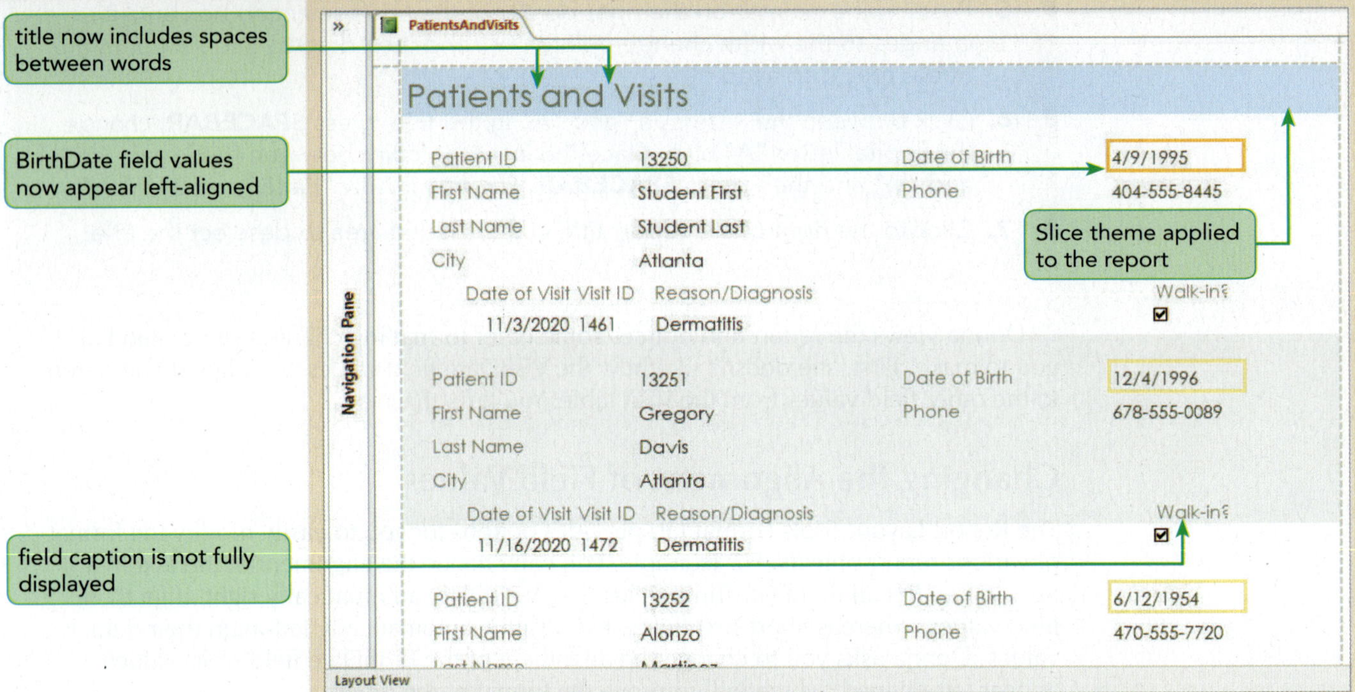

Moving and Resizing Fields on a Report

Working in Layout view, you can resize and reposition fields and field value boxes to improve the appearance and readability of a report. You resize field value boxes by dragging their borders to the desired size. You can also move field labels and field value boxes by selecting one or more of them and then dragging them to a new location; or, for more precise control over the move, you can use the keyboard arrow keys to move selected objects.

In the PatientsAndVisits report, you need to move and resize the WalkIn field label so that the complete caption, Walk-In?, is displayed. Donna also thinks the report would look better with more room between the VisitDate and VisitID fields, so you'll move the VisitDate field label and associated field value box to the left. First, you will move the WalkIn field label so it appears centered over its check box.

To move and resize the WalkIn field label:

1. In the report, click the first occurrence of the **WalkIn?** field label. All instances of the label are selected throughout the report.
2. Press ← repeatedly until the label is centered (roughly) over its check box.
3. Position the pointer on the right border of the field label's selection box until the pointer changes to the width change pointer ↔, and then drag to the right until the label text is fully displayed.

Next, you need to move the VisitDate field label (Date of Visit) and field value box to the left, to provide more space between the VisitDate field and the VisitID field in the report. You can select both objects and modify them at the same time.

To move the VisitDate field label and field value box:

1. In the report, click the first occurrence of the **Date of Visit** field label, press and hold **SHIFT**, click the first occurrence of the associated field value box, which contains the date 11/3/2020. Both the field label and its associated field value box are selected and can be moved. See Figure 4–23.

Figure 4–23 Report after selecting field label and field value box

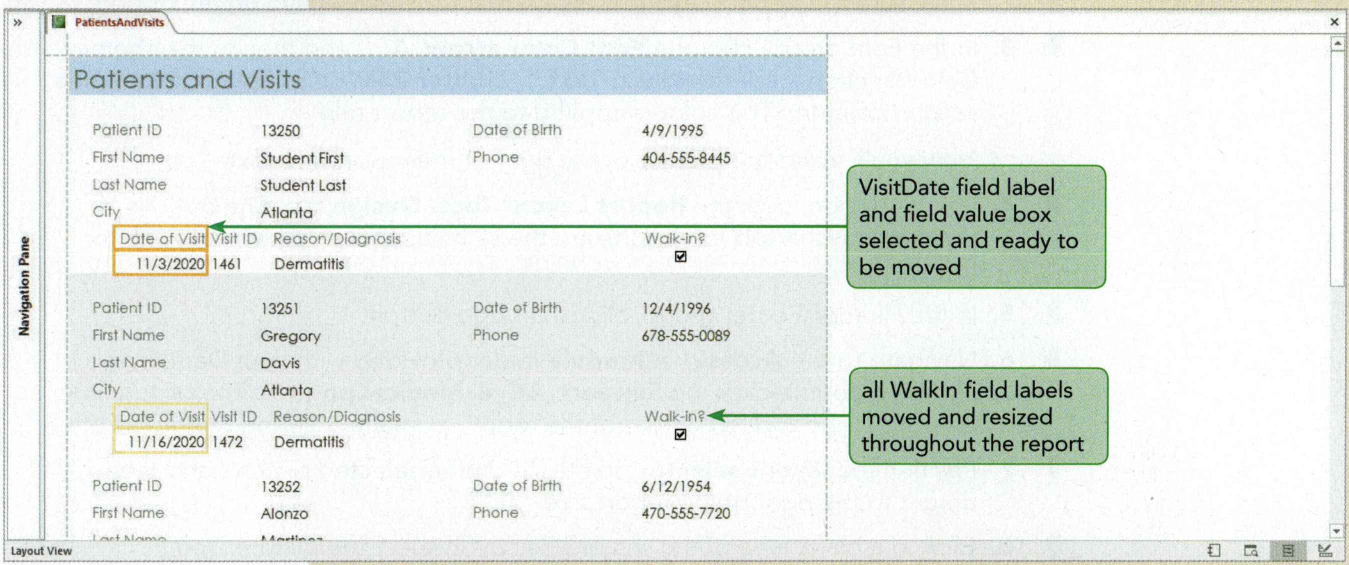

2. Press ← four times to move the field label and field value box to the left.

   Trouble? Once you press LEFT ARROW, the report might jump to display the end of the report. Just continue to press LEFT ARROW to move the labels and values. Then scroll the window back up to display the beginning of the report.

3. On the Quick Access Toolbar, click the **Save** button to save the modified report.
4. Click to the right of the report title in the shaded area to deselect the VisitDate field label and field value box.
5. Scroll through the report, checking the field labels and field values as you go to make sure all text is fully displayed. When finished, scroll back up to display the top of the report.

Next, Donna asks you to enhance the report's appearance to make it more consistent with the PatientData form.

Changing the Font Color and Inserting a Picture in a Report

You can change the color of text on a report to enhance its appearance. You can also add a picture to a report for visual interest or to identify a particular section of the report.

Before you print the report for Donna, she asks you to change the report title color to the darker black you applied earlier to the PatientData form and to include the Medical picture to the right of the report title.

To change the color of the report title and insert the picture:

Make sure the title is selected so the picture is inserted in the correct location.

1. At the top of the report, click the **Patients and Visits** title to select it.
2. Make sure the Report Layout Tools Format tab is still active on the ribbon.
3. In the Font group, click the **Font Color arrow**, and then in the Theme Colors section, click the **Black, Text 1, Lighter 25%** color (fourth color in the second column). The color is applied to the report title.

   Now you'll insert the picture to the right of the report title text.
4. On the ribbon, click the **Report Layout Tools Design** tab. The options provided on this tab for reports are the same as those you worked with for forms.
5. In the Header/Footer group, click the **Logo** button.
6. Navigate to the **Access1 > Module** folder provided with your Data Files, and then double-click the **Support_AC_4_Medical.png** file. The picture is inserted in the top-left corner of the report, partially covering the report title.
7. Position the **layout selector** pointer on the selected picture, and then drag it to the right of the report title.
8. Click in a blank area of the shaded bar to deselect the picture. See Figure 4–24.

Figure 4–24 Report after changing the title font color and inserting the picture

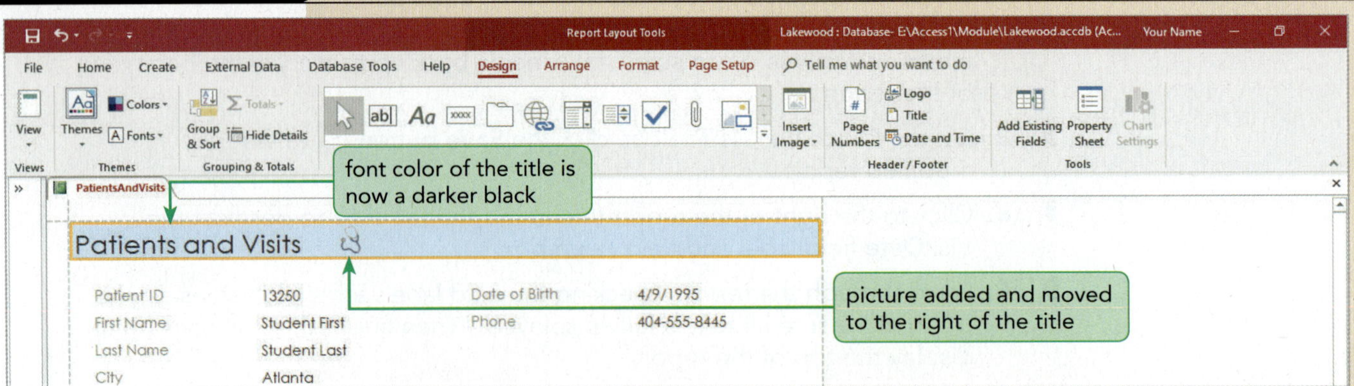

Trouble? Don't be concerned if the picture in your report is not in the exact same location as the one shown in the figure. Just make sure it is to the right of the title text and within the shaded area.

Donna approves of the report's contents and design, but has one final suggestion for the report. She'd like to draw attention to patient records for children and teenagers by formatting their birth date with a bold, red font. Lakewood Community Health Services is planning a special event specifically geared to children and teenagers regarding healthy diets, so this format will make it easier to find these patient records in the report. Because Donna does not want all the birth dates to appear in this font, you need to use conditional formatting.

Using Conditional Formatting in a Report

Conditional formatting in a report (or form) is special formatting applied to certain field values depending on one or more conditions—similar to criteria you establish for queries. If a field value meets the condition or conditions you specify, the formatting is applied to the value.

Donna would like the PatientsAndVisits report to show any birth date that is greater than 1/1/1999 in a bold, dark red font. This formatting will help to highlight the patient records for children and teenagers. Donna plans to review this report in a planning meeting for the upcoming special event.

To apply conditional formatting to the BirthDate field in the report:

1. Make sure the report is still displayed in Layout view, and then click the **Report Layout Tools Format** tab on the ribbon.

   To apply conditional formatting to a field, you must first make it the active field by clicking any field value in the field's column.

TIP

You must select a field value box, and not the field label, before applying a conditional format.

2. Click the first BirthDate field value, **4/9/1995**, for PatientID 13250 to select the BirthDate field values in the report. The conditional formatting you specify will affect all the values for the field.
3. In the Control Formatting group, click the **Conditional Formatting** button. The Conditional Formatting Rules Manager dialog box opens. Because you selected a BirthDate field value box, the name of this field is displayed in the "Show formatting rules for" box. Currently, there are no conditional formatting rules set for the selected field. You need to create a new rule.
4. Click the **New Rule** button. The New Formatting Rule dialog box opens. See Figure 4–25.

Figure 4–25 New Formatting Rule dialog box

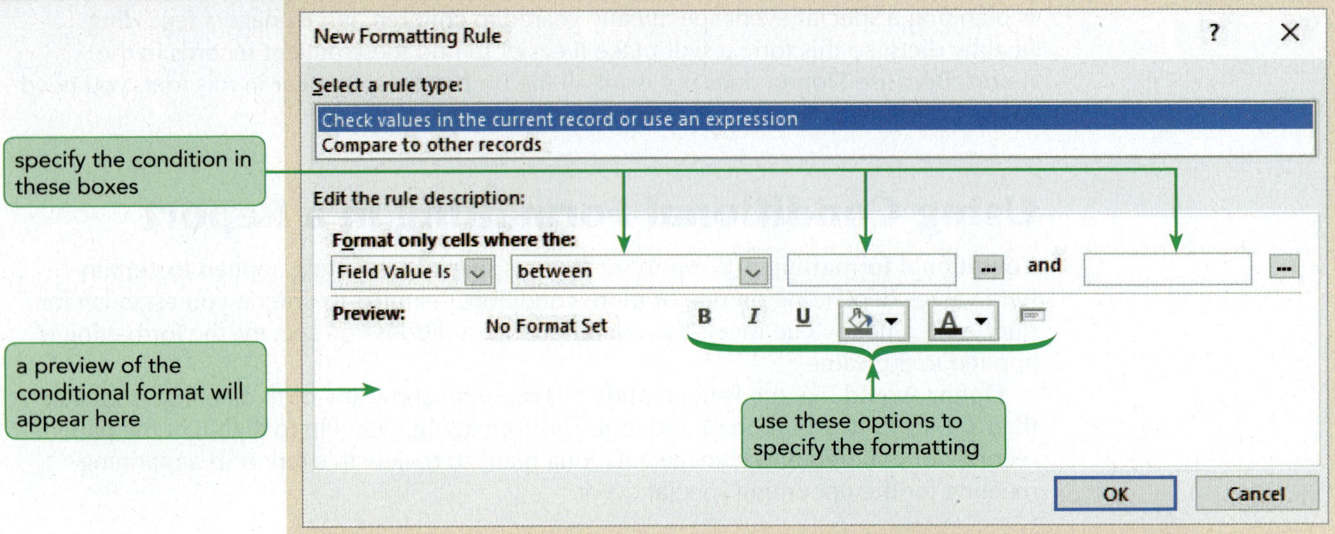

The default setting for "Select a rule type" specifies that Access will check field values and determine if they meet the condition. This is the setting you want. You need to enter the condition in the "Edit the rule description" section of the dialog box. The setting "Field Value Is" means that the conditional format you specify will be applied only when the value for the selected field, City, meets the condition.

5. Click the **arrow** for the box containing the word "between," and then click **greater than**. You want only the birth dates greater than 1/1/1999 to be formatted.
6. Click in the next box, and then type **1/1/1999**.
7. In the Preview section, click the **Font color arrow**, and then click the **Dark Red** color (first color in the last row in the Standard Colors section).
8. In the Preview section, click the **Bold** button. The specifications for the conditional formatting are complete. See Figure 4–26.

Figure 4–26 Conditional formatting set for the BirthDate field

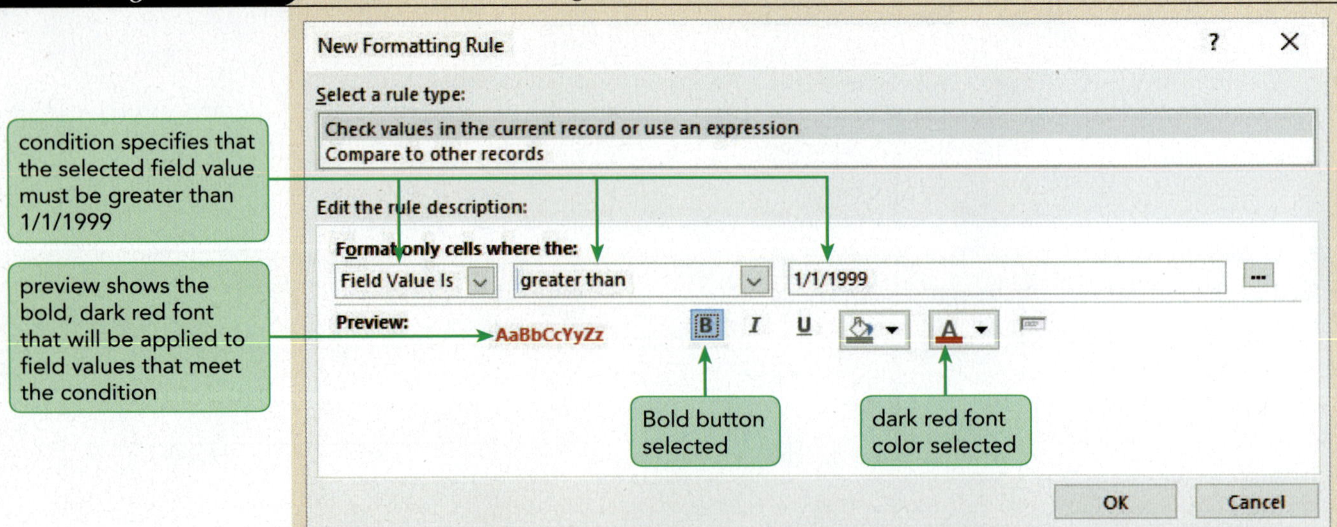

9. Click **OK**. The new rule you specified appears in the Rule section of the Conditional Formatting Rules Manager dialog box as Value > 1/1/1999; the Format section on the right shows the conditional formatting (dark red, bold font) that will be applied based on this rule.
10. Click **OK**. The conditional format is applied to the BirthDate field values. To get a better view of the report and the formatting, you'll switch to Print Preview.
11. On the status bar, click the **Print Preview** button.
12. Move to page 2 of the report. Notice that the conditional formatting is applied only to BirthDate field values greater than 1/1/1999. See Figure 4–27.

Figure 4–27 Viewing the finished report in Print Preview

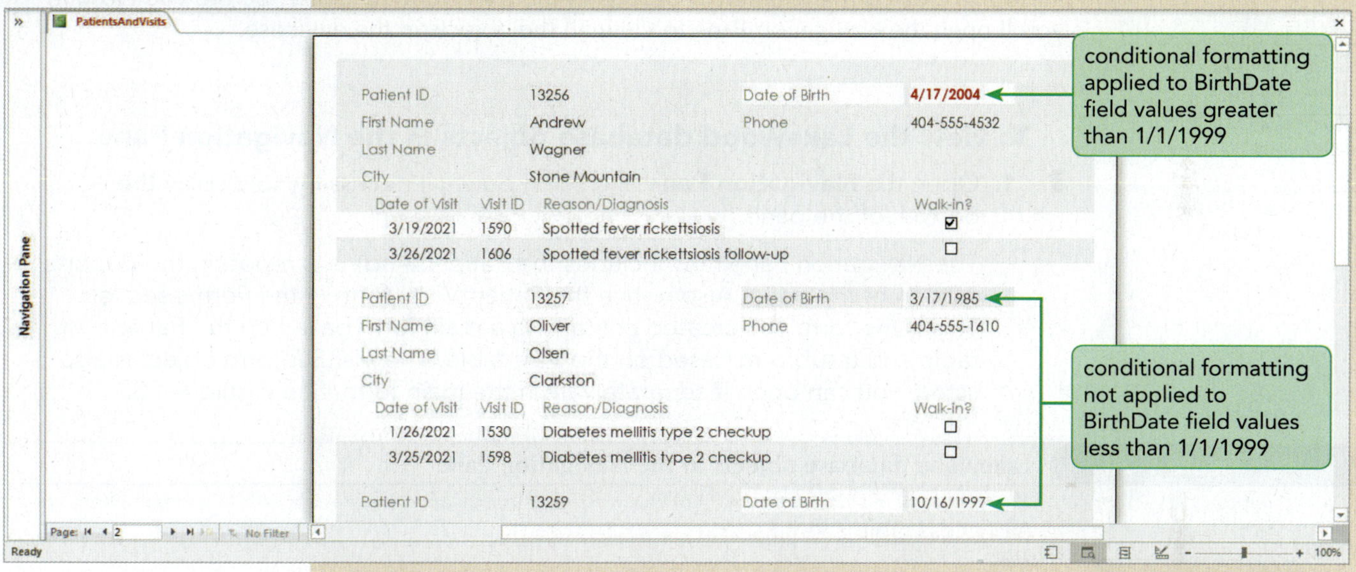

Problem Solving: Understanding the Importance of Previewing Reports

PROSKILLS

When you create a report, it is a good idea to display the report in Print Preview occasionally as you develop it. Doing so will give you a chance to identify any formatting problems or other issues so that you can make any necessary corrections before printing the report. It is particularly important to preview a report after you've made changes to its design to ensure that the changes you made have not created new problems with the report's format. Before printing any report, you should preview it so you can determine where the pages will break and make any necessary adjustments. Following this problem-solving approach not only will ensure that the final report looks exactly the way you want it to, but will also save you time and help to avoid wasting paper if you print the report.

The report is now complete. You'll print just the first page of the report so that Donna can view the final results and share the report design with other staff members before printing the entire report. (*Note*: Ask your instructor if you should complete the following printing steps.)

To print page 1 of the report:

1. On the Print Preview tab, in the Print group, click the **Print** button. The Print dialog box opens.
2. In the Print Range section, click the **Pages** option button. The insertion point now appears in the From box so that you can specify the range of pages to print.
3. Type **1** in the From box, press **TAB** to move to the To box, and then type **1**. These settings specify that only page 1 of the report will be printed.
4. Click **OK**. The Print dialog box closes, and the first page of the report is printed.
5. Save and close the PatientsAndVisits report.

You've created many different objects in the Lakewood database. Before you close it, you'll open the Navigation Pane to view all the objects in the database.

To view the Lakewood database objects in the Navigation Pane:

1. Open the **Navigation Pane** and scroll down, if necessary, to display the bottom of the pane.

   The Navigation Pane now includes the PatientsAndVisits report in the Reports section of the pane. Also notice the PatientVisits form in the Forms section. This is the form you created containing a main form based on the Patient table and a subform based on the Visit table. The VisitSubform object is also listed; you can open it separately from the main form. See Figure 4–28.

Figure 4–28 Lakewood database objects in the Navigation Pane

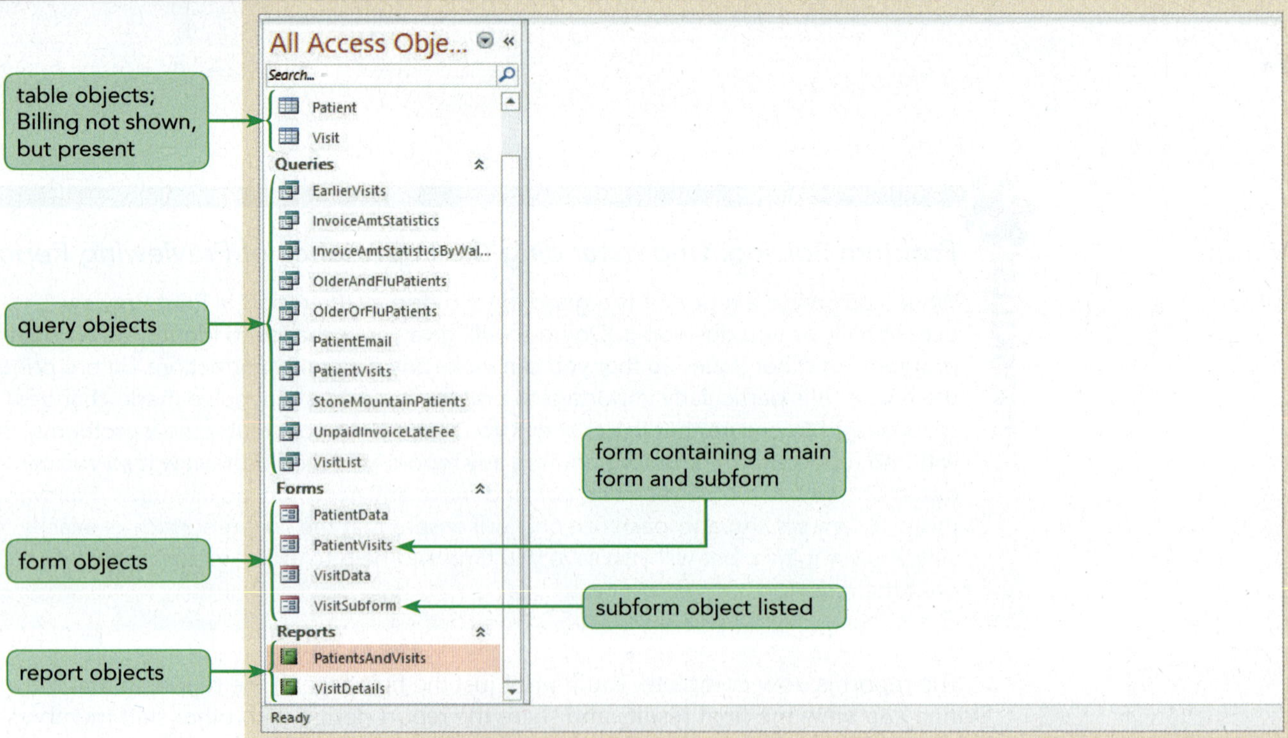

2. sam Compact and repair the Lakewood database, and then close the database.

Donna is satisfied that the forms you created—the PatientData form and the PatientVisits form—will make it easier to enter, view, and update data in the Lakewood database. The PatientsAndVisits report presents important information about the patients the clinic treats in an attractive and professional format, which will help Donna and other staff members in their work.

REVIEW

Session 4.2 Quick Check

1. In a(n) ________ report, the data from a record in the primary table appears together, followed on subsequent lines by the joined records from the related table.
2. When you create a report based on two tables that are joined in a one-to-many relationship, the field values for the records from the related table are called the ________ records.
3. Identify three types of modifications you can make to a report in Layout view.
4. Describe the process for moving a control to another location on a report in Layout view.
5. When working in Layout view for a report, which key do you press and hold down so that you can click to select multiple controls (field labels, field value boxes, and so on)?
6. ________ in a report (or form) is special formatting applied to certain field values depending on one or more conditions.

PRACTICE

Review Assignments

Data Files needed for the Review Assignments: Support_AC_4_Items.png, Support_AC_4_Supplies.png, and Vendor.accdb *(cont. from Module 3)*

Donna asks you to enhance the Vendor database with forms and reports. Complete the following steps:

1. Open the **Vendor** database you created and worked with in previous modules, and then click the Enable Content button next to the security warning, if necessary.
2. Use the Form Wizard to create a form based on the Product table. Select all fields for the form and the Columnar layout; specify the title **ProductData** for the form.
3. Apply the Integral theme to the ProductData form *only*.
4. Insert the **Support_AC_4_Supplies.png** picture, which is located in the Access1 > Review folder provided with your Data Files, in the ProductData form. Remove the picture from the control layout, and then move the picture to the right of the form title.
5. Edit the form title so that it appears as "Product Data" (two words), resize the title box as necessary so the title appears on a single line, and then change the font color of the form title to the Ice Blue, Background 2, Darker 50% theme color.
6. Resize the Weight in Lbs field value box so it is the same width (approximately) as the Units/Case field value box above it.
7. Change the alignment of the Price, Units/Case, and Weight in Lbs fields so that their values appear left-aligned in the field value boxes.
8. Save your changes to the form design.
9. Use the ProductData form to update the Product table as follows:
   a. Use the Find command to search for the word "penicillin" anywhere in the ProductName field, and then display the record for the Penicillin injections (ProductID PN284). Change the Price in this record to **262.00**.
   b. Add a new record with the following field values:
      Product ID: **GA606**
      Supplier ID: **CRO063**
      Product Name: **Gauze pads, 6x6"**
      Price: **124.00**
      Units/Case: **1000**
      Weight in Lbs: **19**
      Temp Controlled?: **no**
      Sterile?: **yes**
   c. Use the form to view each record with a ProductID value that starts with "XR".
   d. Save and close the form.
10. Use the Form Wizard to create a form containing a main form and a subform. Select all fields from the Supplier table for the main form, and select ProductID, ProductName, Price, TempControl, and Sterile—in that order—from the Product table for the subform. Use the Datasheet layout. Specify the title **SuppliersAndProducts** for the main form and **ProductSubform** for the subform.
11. Change the form title text to **Suppliers and Products**.
12. Resize the subform by widening it from its right side, increasing its width by approximately one inch, and then resize all columns in the subform to their best fit, working left to right. Navigate through each record in the main form to make sure all the field values in the subform are completely displayed, resizing subform columns and the subform itself, as necessary. Save and close the SuppliersAndProducts form.

13. Use the Report Wizard to create a report based on the primary Supplier table and the related Product table. Select the SupplierID, Company, City, Category, ContactFirst, ContactLast, and Phone fields—in that order—from the Supplier table, and the ProductID, ProductName, Price, and Units fields from the Product table. Do not specify any additional grouping levels, and sort the detail records in ascending order by ProductID. Choose the Outline layout and Portrait orientation. Specify the title **ProductsBySupplier** for the report.
14. Change the report title text to **Products by Supplier**.
15. Apply the Ion theme to the ProductsBySupplier report *only*.
16. Resize and reposition the following objects in the report in Layout view, and then scroll through the report to make sure all field labels and field values are fully displayed:
    a. Resize the report title so that the text of the title, Products by Supplier, is fully displayed.
    b. Move the ProductName field label and field value box to the right a bit (be sure not to move them too far so that the longest product name will still be completely visible).
    c. Resize the Product ID field label from its right side, increasing its width slightly so the label is fully displayed.
    d. Move the Units/Case field label and field value box to the right a bit; then resize the label on its left side, increasing its width slightly so the label is fully displayed.
17. Change the color of the report title text to the Light Gray, Background 2, Darker 75% theme color.
18. Insert the **Support_AC_4_Items.png** picture, which is located in the Access1 > Review folder provided with your Data Files, in the report. Move the picture to the right of the report title.
19. Apply conditional formatting so that the Category field values equal to **Supplies** appear as dark red and bold.
20. Preview each page of the report, verifying that all the fields fit on the page. If necessary, return to Layout view and make changes so the report prints within the margins of the page and so that all field names and values are completely displayed.
21. Save the report, print its first page (only if asked by your instructor to do so), and then close the report.
22. Compact and repair the Vendor database, and then close it.

APPLY

Case Problem 1

Data File needed for this Case Problem: Career.accdb *(cont. from Module 3)* and Support_AC_4_Giraffe.png

Great Giraffe Jeremiah uses the Career database to track and view information about the courses his business offers. He asks you to create the necessary forms and a report to help him work with this data more efficiently. Complete the following:

1. Open the **Career** database you created and worked with in previous modules, and then click the Enable Content button next to the security warning, if necessary.
2. Use the Form Wizard to create a form based on the Course table. Select all the fields for the form and the Columnar layout. Specify the title **CourseData** for the form.
3. Apply the Slice theme to the CourseData form *only*.
4. Edit the form title so that it appears as “Course Data” (two words); resize the title so that both words fit on the same line; and then change the font color of the form title to the Orange, Accent 5, Darker 25% theme color.

5. Use the CourseData form to add a new record to the Course table with the following field values:
   Instance ID: **DGTSCRF002**
   Title: **Digital Security**
   Start Date: **5/24/2021**
   End Date: **6/25/2021**
   Hours Per Week: **40**
   Cost: **24500**
6. Save and close the CourseData form.
7. Use the Form Wizard to create a form containing a main form and a subform. Select all the fields from the Course table for the main form, and select the StudentID, FirstName, LastName, and Phone fields from the Student table for the subform. Use the Datasheet layout. Specify the title **StudentsByCourse** for the main form and the title **StudentSubform** for the subform.
8. Change the form title text for the main form to **Students by Course**.
9. Resize all columns in the subform to their best fit, working from left to right; then move through all the records in the main form and check to make sure that all subform field values are fully displayed, resizing the columns as necessary.
10. Save and close the StudentsByCourse form.
11. Use the Report Wizard to create a report based on the primary Course table and the related Student table. Select all the fields from the Course table, and then select the StudentID, FirstName, LastName, Phone, and Email fields from the Student table. Do not select any additional grouping levels, and sort the detail records in ascending order by StudentID. Choose the Outline layout and Landscape orientation. Specify the title **CourseRosters** for the report.
12. Apply the Slice theme to the CourseRosters report *only*.
13. Resize the report title so that the text is fully displayed; edit the report title so that it appears as "Course Rosters" (two words); and change the font color of the title to the Orange, Accent 5, Darker 25% theme color.
14. Change the alignment of the Start Date and End Date fields so that their values appear left-aligned in the field value boxes.
15. Change the alignment of the Cost and Hours Per Week fields field so that their values appear left-aligned in the field value boxes.
16. Resize and reposition the following objects in the report in Layout view, and then scroll through the report to make sure all field labels and field values are fully displayed:
    a. Move the Email label and field value box to the right approximately 10 spaces.
    b. Move the Phone label and field value box to the right approximately 5 spaces.
    c. Move the LastName label and field value box to the right approximately 5 spaces.
    d. Move the FirstName label and field value box to the right approximately 5 spaces.
    e. Scroll to the bottom of the report; note that the page number might not be completely within the page border (the dotted vertical line). If necessary, select and move the box containing the text "Page 1 of 1" until the entire text is positioned to the left of the dotted vertical line marking the right page border by approximately 5 spaces.
17. Insert the **Support_AC_4_Giraffe.png** picture, which is located in the Access1 > Case1 folder provided with your Data Files, in the report. Move the picture to the right of the report title.
18. Apply conditional formatting so that any Hours Per Week field value equal to 40 appears as bold and with the Red color applied.
19. Preview the entire report to confirm that it is formatted correctly. If necessary, return to Layout view and make changes so that all field labels and field values are completely displayed.
20. Save the report, print its first page (only if asked by your instructor to do so), and then close the report.
21. Compact and repair the Career database, and then close it.

CHALLENGE

Case Problem 2

Data File needed for this Case Problem: DrainAdopter.accdb *(cont. from Module 2)* and Support_AC_4_Drain.png

Drain Adopter Tandrea uses the DrainAdopter database to track, maintain, and analyze data about the drains and volunteers. You'll help Tandrea by creating a form and a report based on this data. Complete the following:

1. Open the **DrainAdopter** database you created and worked with in previous modules, and then click the Enable Content button next to the security warning, if necessary.
2. Use the Form Wizard to create a form based on the Volunteer table. Select all the fields for the form and the Columnar layout. Specify the title **VolunteerMasterData** for the form.
3. Apply the Retrospect theme to the VolunteerMasterData form *only*.
4. Edit the form title so that it appears as "Volunteer Master Data" (three words) on one line, and change the font color of the form title to the Brown, Accent 3, Darker 25% theme color.
5. **Explore** Use the appropriate button in the Font group on the Form Layout Tools Format tab to italicize the form title. Save the form.
6. Use the VolunteerMasterData form to update the Volunteer table as follows:
   a. Use the Find command to search for the record that contains the value "BUC5101" for the VolunteerID field, and then change the Phone field value for this record to **360-555-8502**.
   b. Add a new record with the following values:
      Volunteer ID: **BAR1730**
      First Name: **Mikala**
      Last Name: **Barnes**
      Street: **342 Sycamore Court**
      City: **Bellingham**
      State: **WA**
      Zip: **98226**
      Phone: **360-555-0028**
      Email: **m.barnes19@example.com**
      Signup Date: **5/25/2021**
      Trained: **[leave blank]**
   c. **Explore** Find the record with VolunteerID MIT8951, and then delete the record. (*Hint*: After displaying the record in the form, you need to select it by clicking the right-pointing triangle in the bar to the left of the field labels. Then use the appropriate button on the Home tab in the Records group to delete the record. When asked to confirm the deletion, click the Yes button.) Close the form.
7. Use the Form Wizard to create a form containing a main form and a subform. Select all the fields from the Volunteer table for the main form, and select all fields except VolunteerID from the Drain table for the subform. Use the Datasheet layout. Specify the name **VolunteersAndDrains** for the main form and the title **DrainSubform** for the subform.
8. Make sure the default Office theme is applied to the VolunteersAndDrains form.
9. Edit the form title so that it appears as "Volunteers and Drains." Resize the form title so that the text fits on one line. Change the font color of the title to the Blue, Accent 5, Darker 25% theme color.
10. Insert the **Support_AC_4_Drain.png** picture, which is located in the Access1 > Case2 folder provided with your Data Files, in the VolunteersAndDrains form. Remove the picture from the control layout, and then move the picture to the right of the form title. Resize the picture so it is approximately double the original size.

Explore 11. Use the appropriate button in the Font group on the Form Layout Tools Format tab to apply the theme color Tan, Accent 5, Lighter 60% as a background color for all the field value boxes in the main form. Then use the appropriate button in the Control Formatting group to change the outline of all the main form field value boxes to have a line thickness of 1 pt. (*Hint*: Select all the field value boxes before making these changes.)

12. Resize the subform by extending it to the right, and then resize all columns in the subform to their best fit. Navigate through the records in the main form to make sure all the field values in the subform are completely displayed, resizing subform columns as necessary. Save and close the form.

13. Use the Report Wizard to create a report based on the primary Volunteer table and the related Drain table. Select all the fields from the Volunteer table, and select all fields except VolunteerID from the Drain table. Sort the detail records in *descending* order by DrainID. Choose the Outline layout and Landscape orientation. Specify the name **VolunteersAndDrains** for the report.

14. Apply the Retrospect theme to the VolunteersAndDrains report *only*.

15. Resize the report title so that the text is fully displayed; edit the report title so that it appears as "Volunteers and Drains"; and change the font color of the title to the Brown, Accent 3, Darker 25% theme color.

16. Move the Email field value box to the left approximately 10 spaces. Then resize the Email field value box on the right, expanding its size to the edge of the report. Left-justify the field value box for Signup Date. Save the report.

17. Insert the **Support_AC_4_Drain.png** picture, which is located in the Access1 > Case2 folder provided with your Data Files, in the VolunteersAndDrains report. Move the picture to the right of the report title.

18. Apply conditional formatting so that any Signup Date in the first three months of 2021 is formatted as bold and with the Brown 5 font color.

Explore 19. Preview the report so you can see two pages at once. (*Hint*: Use a button on the Print Preview tab.) Check the report to confirm that it is formatted correctly and all field labels and field values are fully displayed. Save the report, print its first page (only if asked by your instructor to do so), and then close the report.

20. Compact and repair the DrainAdopter database, and then close it.

Module 1

Creating a Presentation

Presenting Information About an Insurance Company

Objectives

Session 1.1
- Plan and create a new presentation
- Create a title slide and slides with lists
- Edit and format text
- Move and copy text
- Duplicate, rearrange, and delete slides
- Change the theme and theme variant
- Close a presentation

Session 1.2
- Open an existing presentation
- Insert and crop photos
- Resize and move objects
- Modify photo compression options
- Convert a list to a SmartArt diagram
- Create speaker notes
- Check the spelling
- Run a slide show
- Print slides, handouts, speaker notes, and the outline

Case | Southwest Insurance Company

Southwest Insurance Company is an insurance company with offices all over the American Southwest, including one in Houston, Texas. Anthony Scorsone, a sales manager in the Houston office, recently hired you as his assistant. Anthony frequently visits companies to try to convince them to offer insurance plans from Southwest Insurance Company to their employees. Many businesses have opened offices in the Houston area over the past several years. Anthony wants to use a PowerPoint presentation when he visits these businesses. He asks you to prepare a presentation to which he will later add data and cost information.

Microsoft PowerPoint (or simply **PowerPoint**) is a complete presentation app that lets you produce professional-looking presentation files and then deliver them to an audience. In this module, you'll use PowerPoint to create a file that includes text, graphics, and speaker notes. Anthony can use the presentation as a starting point for his more comprehensive sales pitch. Before you give the presentation to Anthony, you'll check the spelling, run the slide show to evaluate it, and print the file.

Starting Data Files

PowerPoint1 →

Module
NP_PPT_1-1.pptx
Support_PPT_1_Doctor.jpg
Support_PPT_1_Family.jpg
Support_PPT_1_Hands.jpg

Review
NP_PPT_1-2.pptx
Support_PPT_1_Anthony.jpg
Support_PPT_1_Meeting.jpg
Support_PPT_1_Standing.jpg
Support_PPT_1_Woman.jpg

Case1
NP_PPT_1-3.pptx
Support_PPT_1_Application.jpg
Support_PPT_1_Building.jpg
Support_PPT_1_Key.jpg
Support_PPT_1_Sophia.jpg

Case2
Support_PPT_1_Beach.jpg
Support_PPT_1_Black.jpg
Support_PPT_1_Blue.jpg
Support_PPT_1_Ensemble.jpg
Support_PPT_1_Pink.jpg

Session 1.1 Visual Overview:

The **Quick Access Toolbar** contains buttons for frequently used commands. You can click the Customize Quick Access Toolbar button (the small arrow on the right) to add and remove commands.

The ribbon is organized into tabs. Each **tab** contains buttons for performing related activities or tasks.

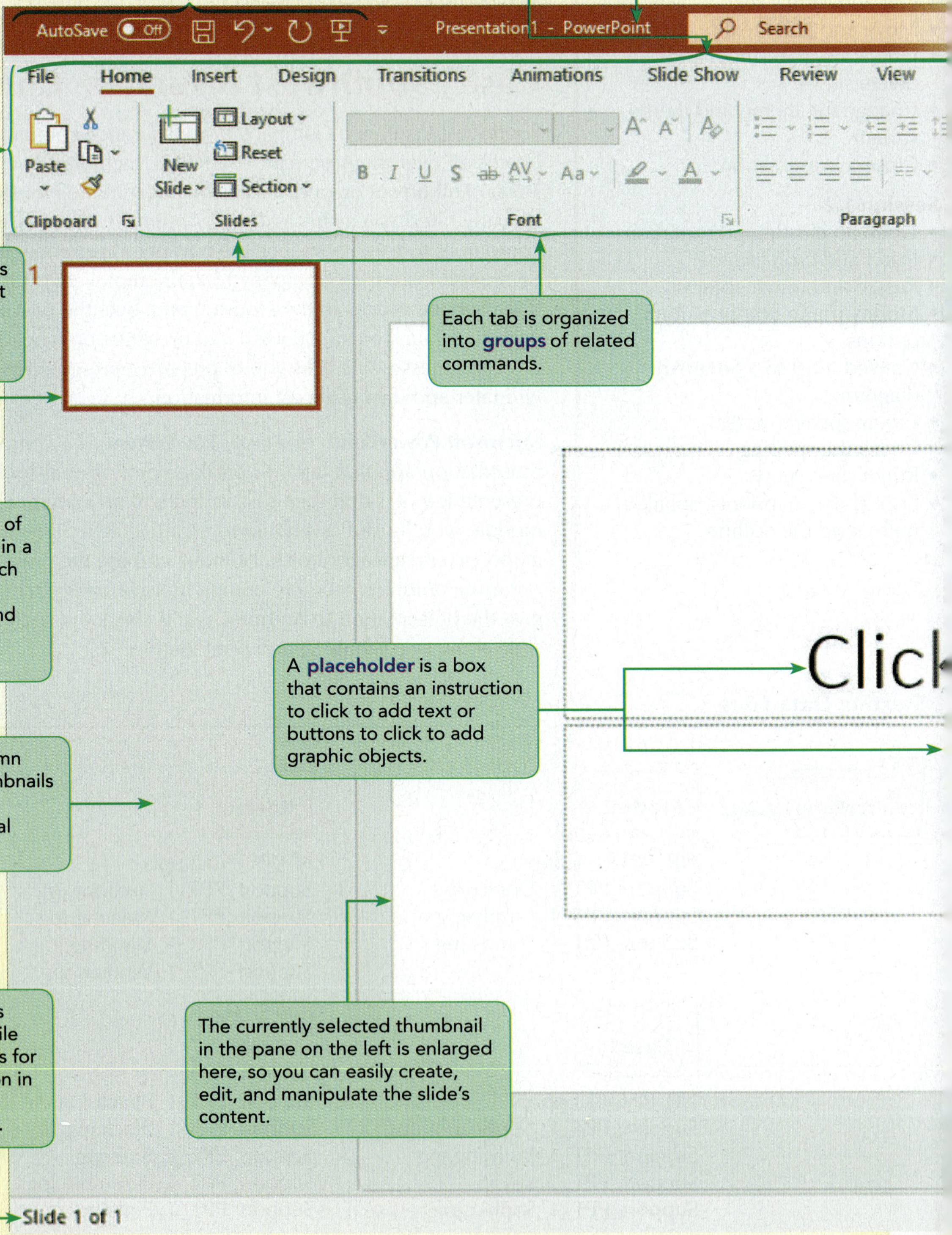

The **ribbon** contains tabs of grouped **buttons** that you click to execute commands you need to work with PowerPoint.

Each tab is organized into **groups** of related commands.

PowerPoint files consist of **slides**, which are pages in a presentation file on which you insert text, shapes, illustrations, pictures, and media objects such as videos.

A **placeholder** is a box that contains an instruction to click to add text or buttons to click to add graphic objects.

This pane shows a column of numbered slide thumbnails so you can see a visual representation of several slides at once.

The **status bar** provides information about the file and contains commands for viewing the presentation in different ways and for zooming in on the view.

The currently selected thumbnail in the pane on the left is enlarged here, so you can easily create, edit, and manipulate the slide's content.

The PowerPoint Window

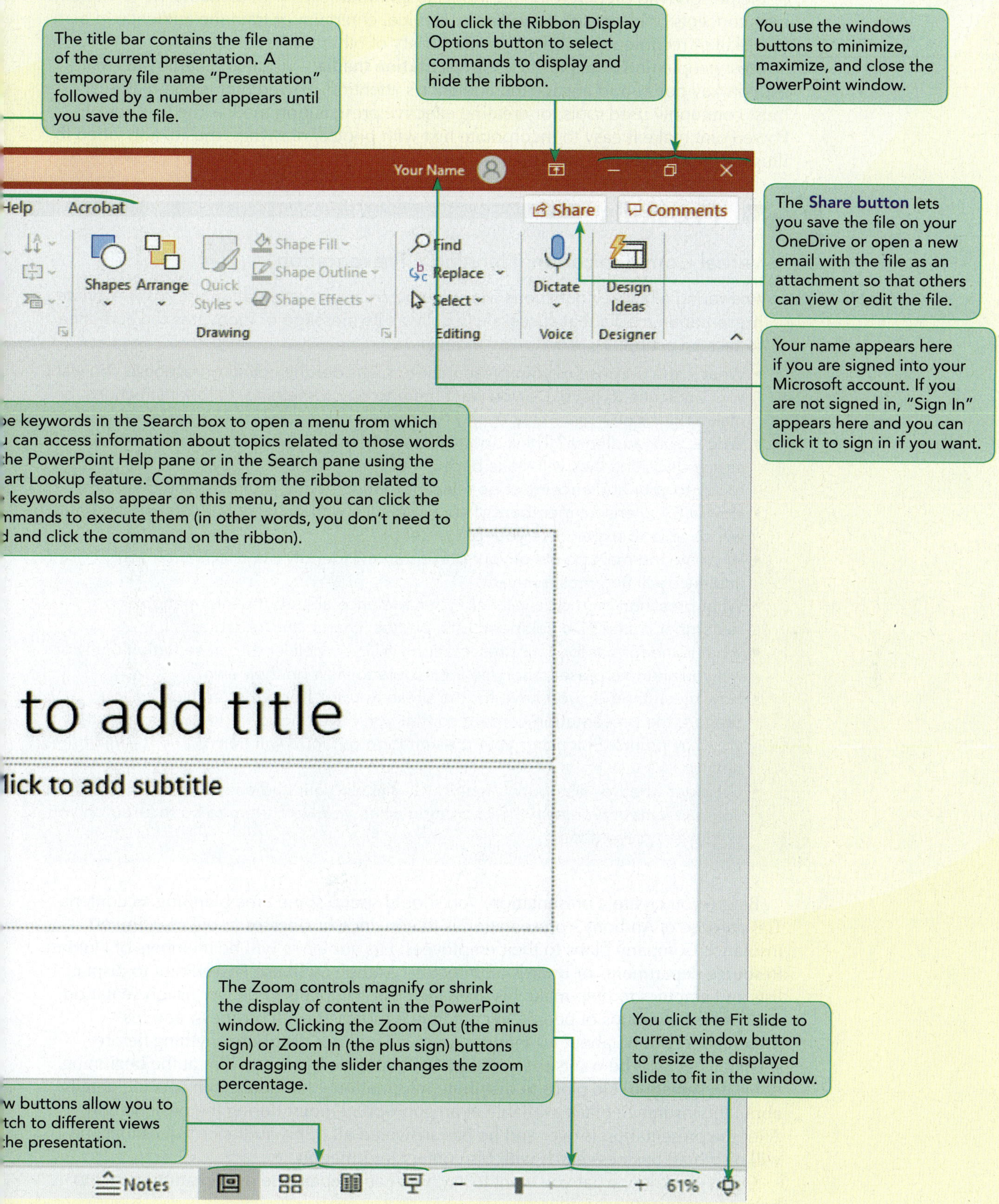

Planning a Presentation

A **presentation** is a talk, formal lecture, or prepared file in which the person speaking or the person who prepared the file wants to communicate with an audience to explain new concepts or ideas, sell a product or service, entertain, or train the audience in a new skill or technique, or any of a wide variety of other topics.

Most people find it helpful to use **presentation media**—visual and audio aids that support key points and engage the audience's attention. PowerPoint is one of the most commonly used tools for creating effective presentation media. The features of PowerPoint make it easy to incorporate text with photos, drawings, music, and video to illustrate key points of a presentation.

Proskills

Verbal Communication: Planning a Presentation

Answering a few key questions will help you create a presentation using appropriate presentation media that successfully delivers its message or motivates the audience to take an action.

- What is the purpose of your presentation? Consider the action or response you want your audience to have. Do you want them to buy something, follow instructions, or make a decision?
- Who is your audience? Think about the needs and interests of your audience as well as any decisions they will make because of what you have to say. What you choose to say to your audience must be relevant to their needs, interests, and decisions.
- How will you ensure members of your audience with visual or hearing impairments will be able to experience your presentation?
- What are the main points of your presentation? Identify the information your audience will find most relevant.
- What presentation media will help your audience absorb the information and remember it later? Do you need lists, photos, charts, and/or tables?
- What is the format for your presentation? Will you deliver the presentation orally or will you create a presentation file for people to view on their own?
- How much time do you have for the presentation? Keep that in mind as you prepare the presentation content so that you have enough time to present all of your key points. Practicing your presentation out loud will help you determine the timing.
- Consider whether distributing handouts will help your audience follow along with your presentation or steal their attention when you want them to be focused on you during the presentation.

Before you create a presentation, you should spend some time planning its content. The purpose of Anthony's presentation is to convince businesses to offer Southwest Insurance Company plans to their employees. His audience will be members of Human Resource departments or Boards of Directors. Anthony will use PowerPoint to display lists and graphics to help make his message clear. He plans to deliver his presentation orally to small groups of people in conference rooms at each business, and his presentation will be about 10 minutes long. He will not distribute anything before speaking because he wants the audience's full attention to be on him at the beginning of his presentation. He plans to distribute informational handouts with specific details about the insurance plans available at an appropriate point during the presentation. After the presentation is over and he has answered all of his audience's questions, he will distribute business cards with his contact information.

Once you know what you want to say, you can prepare the presentation media to help communicate your ideas.

Starting PowerPoint and Creating a New Presentation

PowerPoint is a tool you can use to create and display visual and audio aids on slides to help clarify the points you want to make in your presentation. You also can use PowerPoint to create a presentation that people view on their own without you.

When PowerPoint starts, Backstage view appears, showing the Home screen. **Backstage view** is the view that contains commands that allow you to manage the file and program settings. When you first start PowerPoint, the actions available to you in Backstage view are to create a new PowerPoint file, open an existing PowerPoint file, view your Account settings, submit feedback to Microsoft, and open the PowerPoint Options dialog box to change app settings.

You'll start PowerPoint now.

To start PowerPoint:

1. sam On the Windows taskbar, click the **Start** button. The Start menu opens.
2. On the Start menu, scroll the list of apps on the left, and then click **PowerPoint**. PowerPoint starts and displays the Home screen in Backstage view. Options for creating new presentations appear in a row at the top of the screen, and if you have recently viewed PowerPoint files, they appear below this row. See Figure 1–1.

Figure 1–1 Home screen in Backstage view

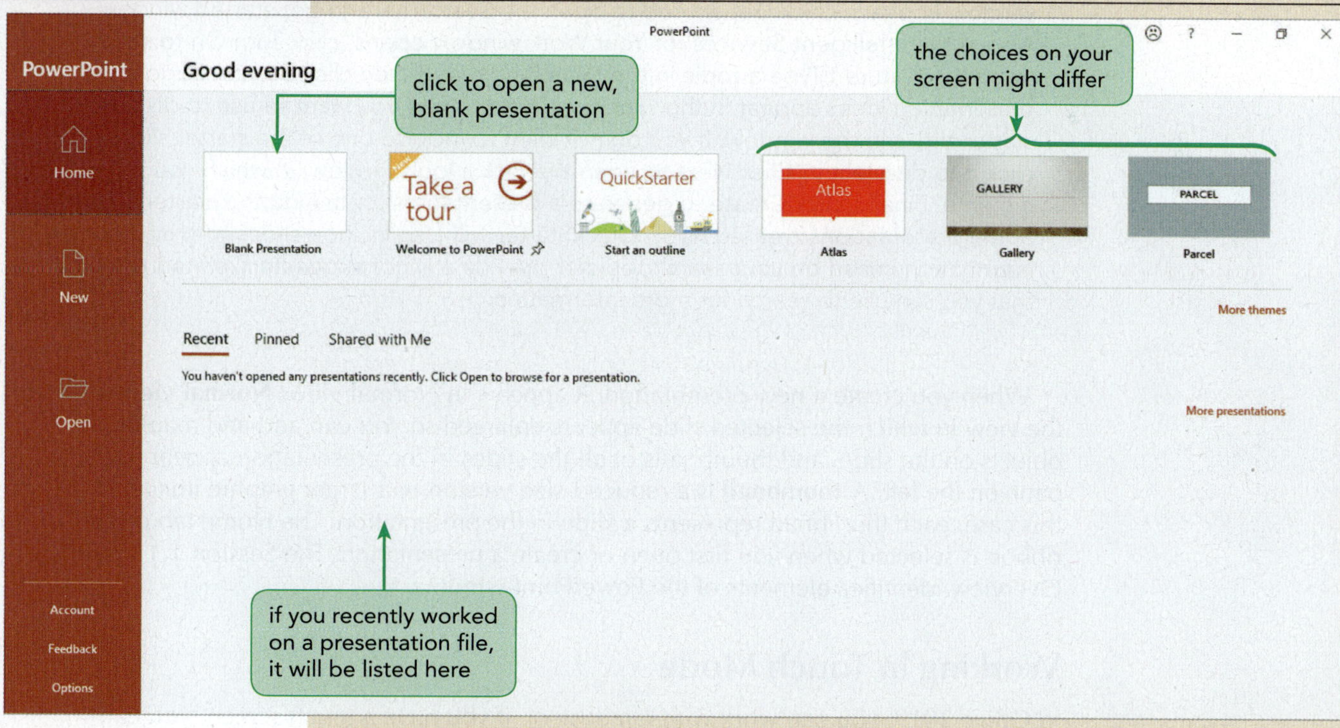

Tip

To create a new blank presentation when PowerPoint is already running, click the File tab on the ribbon, click New in the navigation pane, and then click Blank Presentation.

3. Click **Blank Presentation**. Backstage view closes and a new presentation window appears. The temporary filename "Presentation1" appears in the title bar. There is only one slide in the new presentation—Slide 1.

   Trouble? If you do not see the area on the ribbon that contains buttons and you see only the ribbon tab names, click the Home tab to expand the ribbon and display the commands, and then in the bottom-right corner of the ribbon, click the Pin the ribbon button.

   Trouble? If the window does not appear maximized, click the Maximize button in the upper-right corner.

Because you just started PowerPoint, you clicked Blank presentation on the Home screen. If PowerPoint was already running and you wanted to create a new, blank presentation, you would click the File tab, click New in the navigation pane, and then click Blank Presentation on the New screen in Backstage view.

Insight

Using QuickStarter

QuickStarter is a feature in PowerPoint that creates slide titles based on a topic you enter. To use QuickStarter when you first start PowerPoint, click QuickStarter on the Home screen. If you already are using PowerPoint, click the File tab, click New, and then click QuickStarter on the New screen. The Search here to get started window opens. (The first time you use this feature, the Welcome to PowerPoint QuickStarter window appears. Click Get started to open the Search here to get started window. Also, if the Intelligent Services for Your Work window opens, click Turn On to start using the feature.) Type a topic in the Search box, and then click Search. Suggested presentation ideas appear in the window. Click the one you want to use to display starter slides in the window. If you do not want to include one of the starter slides, click it to deselect it. Click Next to open the Pick a look window, in which you select a theme. Finally, click Create to generate a presentation containing the starter slides. Some presentations created using QuickStarter will also include slides with additional information based on your search topic or provide a list of suggested related topics that you can use to search for more information.

When you create a new presentation, it appears in Normal view. **Normal view** is the view in which the selected slide appears enlarged so you can add and manipulate objects on the slide, and thumbnails of all the slides in the presentation appear in the pane on the left. A **thumbnail** is a reduced-size version of a larger graphic image. In this case, each thumbnail represents a slide in the presentation. The Home tab on the ribbon is selected when you first open or create a presentation. The Session 1.1 Visual Overview identifies elements of the PowerPoint window.

Working in Touch Mode

In Office 2019, you can work with a mouse or, if you have a touch screen, you can work in Touch Mode. In **Touch Mode**, the ribbon increases in height, the buttons are larger, and more space appears around buttons so you can more easily use your finger or stylus to tap screen elements. Also, in the placeholders on the slide, "Double tap" replaces the instruction telling you to "Click." Note that the figures in this text show the screen with Mouse Mode on. You'll switch to Touch Mode and then back to Mouse Mode now.

Note: The following steps assume that you are using a mouse. If instead you are using a touch device, please read these steps, but don't complete them, to continue working in Touch Mode.

To switch between Touch Mode and Mouse Mode:

1. On the Quick Access Toolbar, click the **Customize Quick Access Toolbar** button. A menu opens. The Touch/Mouse Mode command near the bottom of the menu does not have a checkmark next to it.

   Trouble? If the Touch/Mouse Mode command has a checkmark next to it, press the Esc key to close the menu, and then skip Step 2.

2. On the menu, click **Touch/Mouse Mode**. The menu closes, and the Touch/Mouse Mode button appears on the Quick Access Toolbar.

3. On the Quick Access Toolbar, click the **Touch/Mouse Mode** button. A menu opens listing Mouse and Touch. The icon next to Mouse is shaded to indicate it is selected.

   Trouble? If the icon next to Touch is shaded, press ESC to close the menu and skip Step 4.

4. On the menu, click **Touch**. The menu closes, and the ribbon increases in height so that there is more space around each button on the ribbon. Notice that the instructions in the placeholders on the slide changed by replacing the instruction to "Click" with the instruction to "Double tap." See Figure 1–2. Now you'll change back to Mouse Mode.

Figure 1–2 PowerPoint window with Touch Mode active

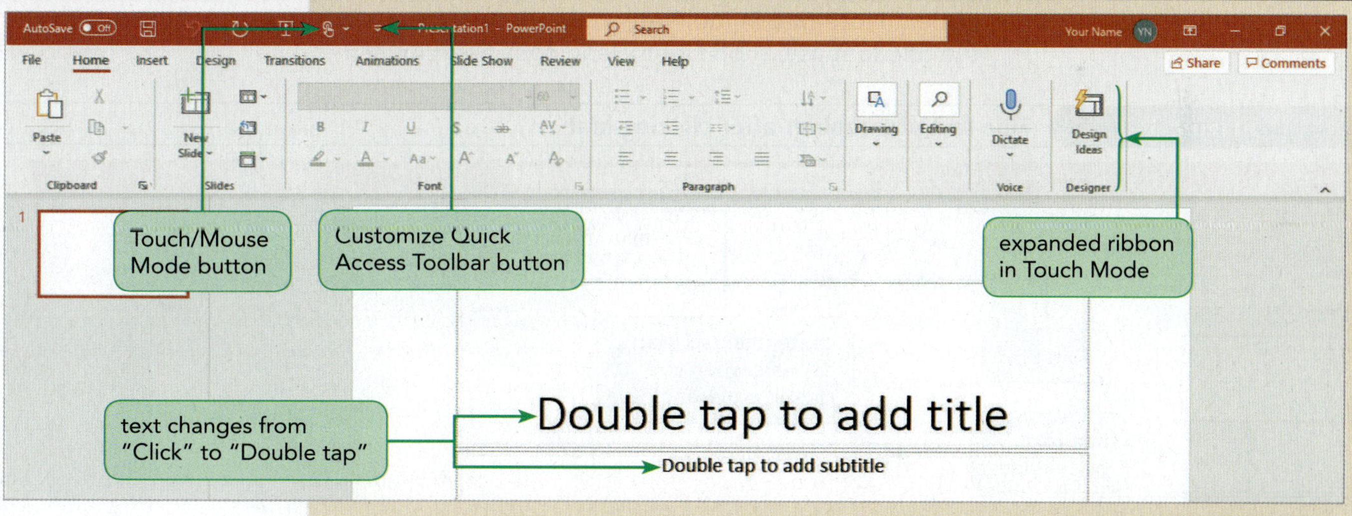

   Trouble? If you are working with a touch screen and want to use Touch Mode, skip Steps 5 and 6.

5. Click the **Touch/Mouse Mode** button, and then click **Mouse**. The ribbon and the instructions change back to Mouse Mode defaults, as shown in the Session 1.1 Visual Overview.

6. Click the **Customize Quick Access Toolbar** button, and then click **Touch/Mouse Mode** to deselect this option and remove the checkmark. The Touch/Mouse Mode button disappears from the Quick Access Toolbar.

Creating a Title Slide

The **title slide** is the first slide in a presentation. It usually contains the presentation title and other identifying information, such as a company name or logo, a company's slogan, or the presenter's name. The **font**—a set of letters, numbers, and symbols that all have the same style and appearance—used in the title and subtitle may be the same or may be different fonts that complement each other.

The title slide contains two objects called text placeholders. A **text placeholder** is a placeholder designed to contain text and that contains a prompt that instructs you to click to add text and might describe the purpose of the placeholder. The large placeholder on the title slide is for the presentation title. The small placeholder is for a subtitle. Once you enter text into a text placeholder, the instructional text disappears and it becomes an object called a text box. A **text box** is an object that contains text.

When you click in the placeholder, the insertion point appears. The **insertion point** is a blinking vertical line that indicates where new text will be inserted. Also, a new tab, the Shape Format tab, appears on the ribbon. This tab is a contextual tab. A **contextual tab** appears only in context—that is, when a particular type of object is selected or is active—and contains commands for modifying that object.

You'll add a title and subtitle for Anthony's presentation now. Anthony wants the title slide to contain the company name and slogan.

To add the company name and slogan to the title slide:

1. On **Slide 1**, move the pointer to position it in the title text placeholder (where it says "Click to add title") so that the pointer changes to the I-beam pointer, and then click. The insertion point replaces the placeholder text, and the Shape Format contextual tab appears as the rightmost tab on the ribbon. Note that in the Font group on the Home tab, the Font box identifies the title font as Calibri Light (Headings). See Figure 1–3.

Figure 1–3 Title text placeholder after clicking in it

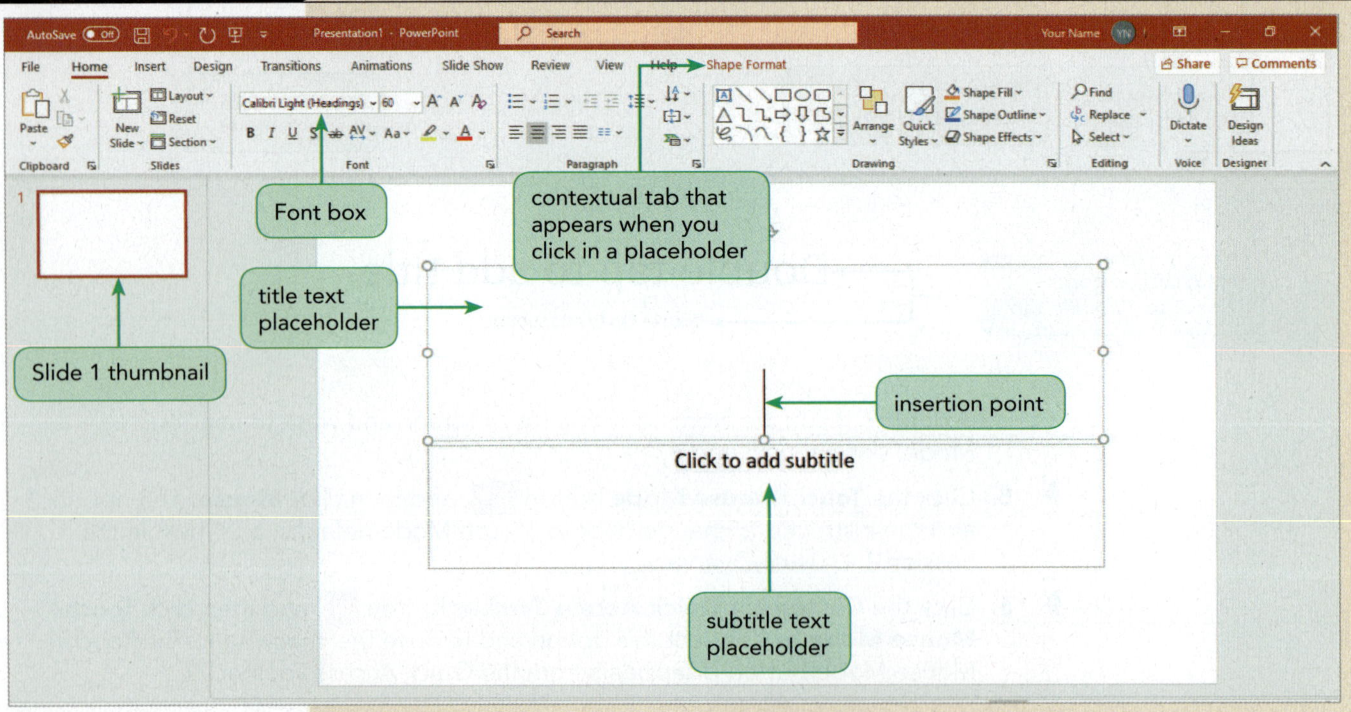

Tip

If your computer has a microphone, you can click the Dictate button in the Voice group on the Home tab, and then speak into your computer's microphone to dictate the text you want to add to the placeholder.

2. Type **Southwest Insurance Corp** in the placeholder. The placeholder is now a text box.
3. Click a blank area of the slide. The border of the text box disappears, and the Shape Format tab no longer appears on the ribbon.
4. Click in the subtitle text placeholder (where it says "Click to add subtitle"), and then type **Best in Health Care Since 1990** in the placeholder. Notice in the Font group that the subtitle font is Calibri (Body), a font that works well with the Calibri Light font used in the title text.
5. Click a blank area of the slide.

Saving and Editing a Presentation

Once you have created a presentation, you should name and save the presentation file. You can save the file on a hard drive or a network drive, on an external drive such as a USB drive, or to your account on OneDrive, Microsoft's free online storage area.

To save the presentation for the first time:

1. On the Quick Access Toolbar, point to the **Save** button. A box called a ScreenTip appears. A **ScreenTip** is a label that appears when you point to a button or object, which may include the name, purpose, or keyboard shortcut for the object, and may include a link to associated help topics.
2. Click the **Save** button. The Save this file dialog box opens, which you use to save a file on OneDrive. To save a new presentation on your hard drive or an external drive, you use the Save As screen.
3. Click the More options link. The Save As screen in Backstage view appears. See Figure 1–4. The navigation pane is the pane on the left that contains commands for working with the file and program options. Recently used folders on the selected drive appear in a list on the right.

Figure 1–4 Save As screen in Backstage view

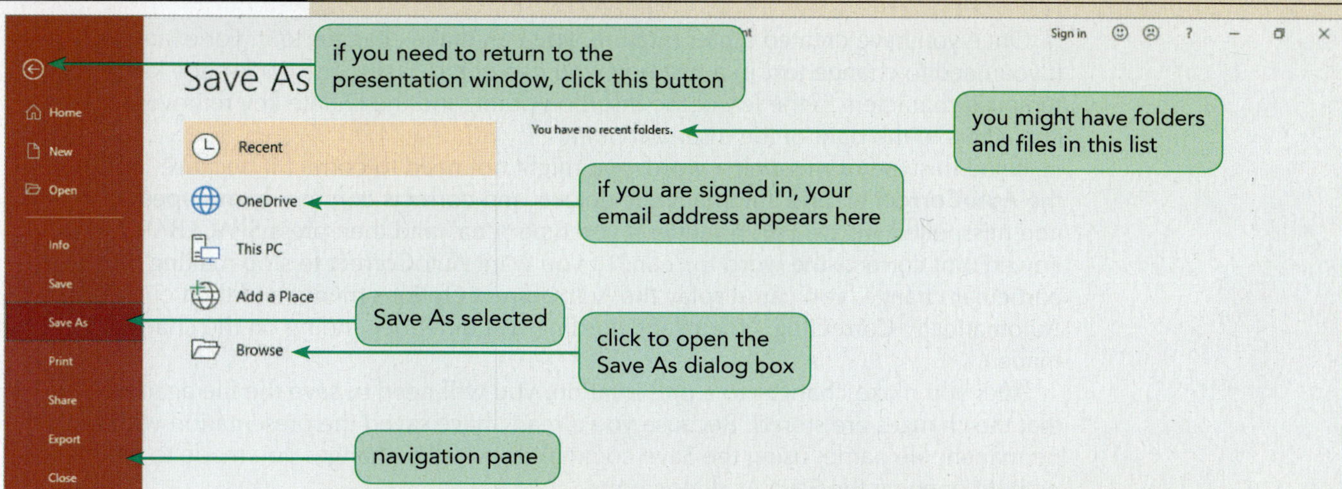

4. Click **Browse**. The Save As dialog box opens, similar to the one shown in Figure 1–5.

Figure 1–5 **Save As dialog box**

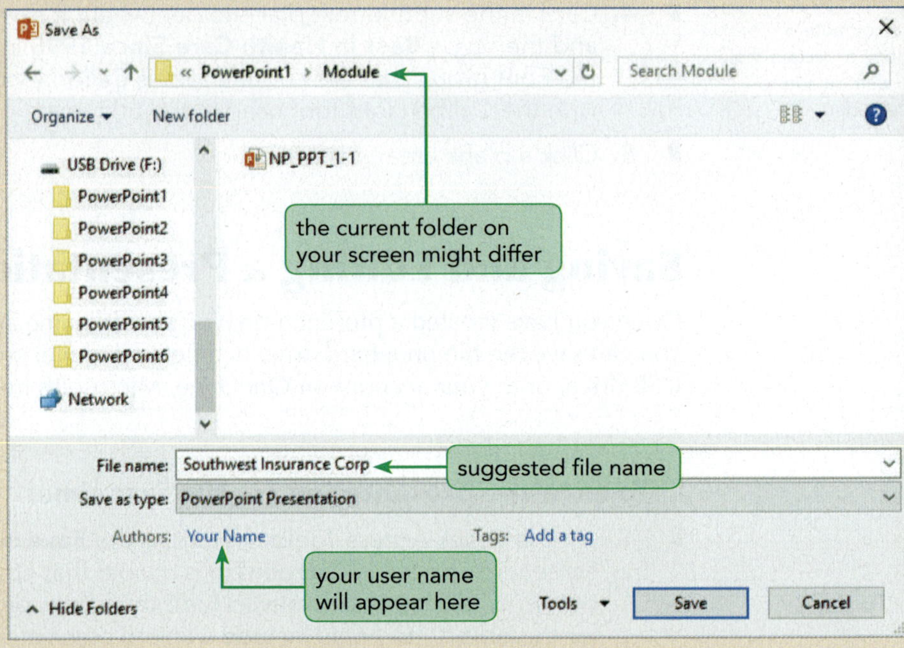

5. Navigate to the drive and folder where you are storing your Data Files, and then click in the **File name** box. The suggested file name, Southwest Insurance Corp, is selected.
6. Type **NP_PPT_1_NewBusiness** to replace the selected text in the File name box.
7. Click **Save**. The file is saved, the dialog box and Backstage view close, and the presentation window appears again with the new file name in the title bar.

Once you have created a presentation, you can make changes to it. For example, if you need to change text in a text box, you can edit it easily. The Backspace key removes characters to the left of the insertion point, and the Delete key removes characters to the right of the insertion point.

If you mistype or misspell a word, you might not need to correct it because the **AutoCorrect** feature automatically detects and corrects commonly mistyped and misspelled words. For instance, if you type "cna" and then press SPACEBAR, PowerPoint corrects the word to "can." If you want AutoCorrect to stop making a particular change, you can display the AutoCorrect Options menu, and then click Stop Automatically Correcting. (The exact wording will differ depending on the change made.)

After you make changes to a presentation, you will need to save the file again so that the changes are stored. Because you already have saved the presentation with a permanent file name, using the Save command saves the changes you made to the file without opening the Save As dialog box.

To edit the text on Slide 1 and save your changes:

1. On Slide 1, click the title, and then press **LEFT ARROW** or **RIGHT ARROW** as needed to position the insertion point to the right of the word "Corp."
2. Press **BACKSPACE** four times. The four characters "Corp" to the left of the insertion point are deleted.
3. Type **Company**. (Do not type the period.) "Southwest Insurance Company" now appears as the title.
4. In the subtitle text box, click to the left of the word "Best" to position the insertion point in front of that word, type **Teh**, and then press **SPACEBAR**. "Teh" is corrected to "The" after you press SPACEBAR. "The Best in Health Care Since 1990" now appears as the subtitle.
5. Move the pointer over the word "**The**." A small, faint rectangle appears below the first letter of the word. This rectangle indicates that an autocorrection was made.

   Trouble? If you can't see the rectangle, point to the letter "T," and then slowly move the pointer down until it is on top of the rectangle.

6. Move the pointer on top of the rectangle so that it changes to the AutoCorrect Options button, and then click the **AutoCorrect Options** button. A menu opens, as shown in Figure 1–6. You can change the word back to what you originally typed, instruct PowerPoint to stop making this type of correction in this file, or open the AutoCorrect dialog box.

Figure 1–6 AutoCorrect Options button menu

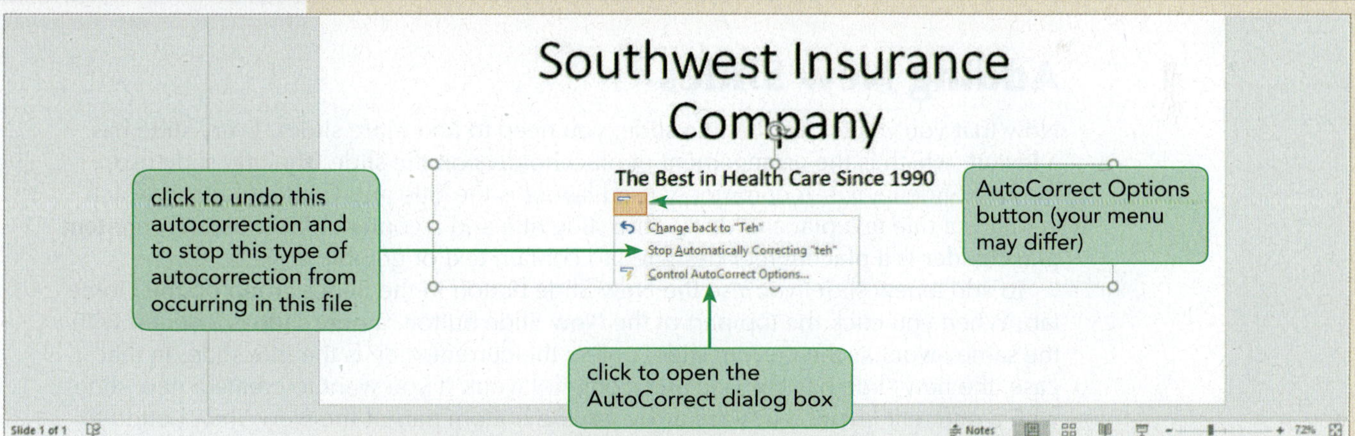

7. Click **Control AutoCorrect Options**. The AutoCorrect dialog box opens with the AutoCorrect tab selected. See Figure 1–7.

Figure 1–7 AutoCorrect tab in the AutoCorrect dialog box

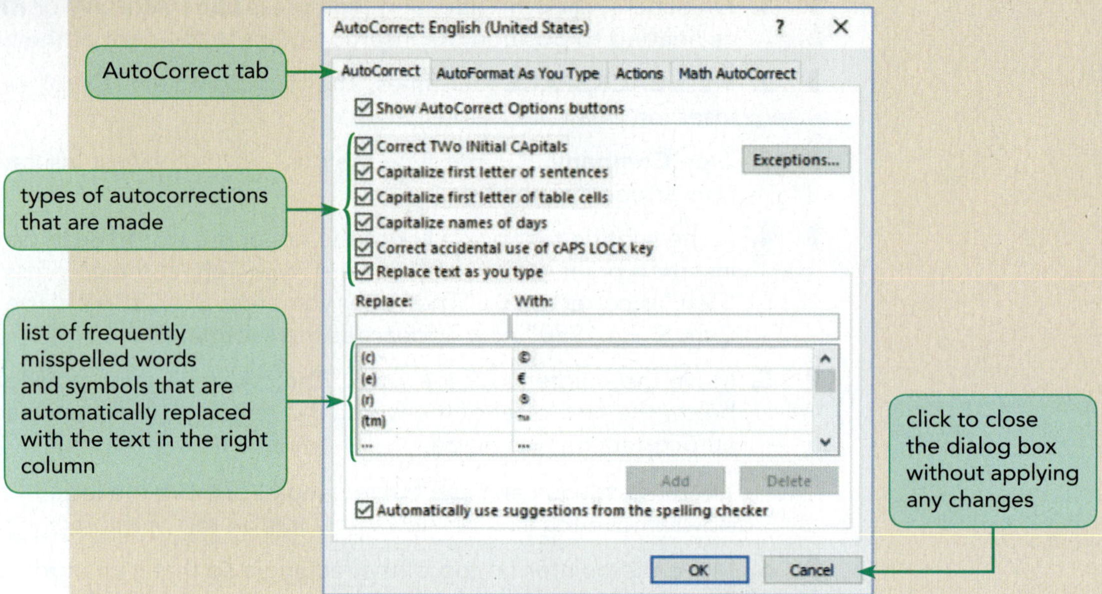

8. Examine the types of changes the AutoCorrect feature makes, and then click **Cancel**.
9. On the Quick Access Toolbar, click the **Save** button. The saved file now includes the new changes you made.

Trouble? If AutoSave is enabled, skip Step 9.

Adding New Slides

Now that you've created the title slide, you need to add more slides. Every slide has a **layout**, which is the arrangement of placeholders on the slide. The title slide uses the Title Slide layout. A commonly used layout is the Title and Content layout, which contains a title text placeholder for the slide title and a content placeholder. A **content placeholder** is a placeholder designed to contain text or graphic objects.

To add a new slide, you use the New Slide button in the Slides group on the Home tab. When you click the top part of the New Slide button, a new slide is inserted with the same layout as the current slide, unless the current slide is the title slide. In that case, the new slide has the Title and Content layout. If you want to create a new slide with a different layout, click the arrow on the bottom part of the New Slide button to open a gallery of layouts, and then click the layout you want to use.

You can change the layout of a slide at any time. To do this, click the Layout button in the Slides group to display the same gallery of layouts that appears in the New Slide gallery, and then click the slide layout you want to apply to the selected slide.

As you add slides, you can switch from one slide to another by clicking the slide thumbnails in the Slides pane. You need to add several new slides to the file.

To add new slides and apply different layouts:

1. Make sure the Home tab is displayed on the ribbon.
2. In the Slides group, click the top part of the **New Slide** button. A new slide appears, and its thumbnail appears in the pane on the left below the Slide 1 thumbnail. The new slide has the Title and Content layout applied. This layout contains a title text placeholder and a content placeholder. An orange

border appears around the new Slide 2 thumbnail, indicating that it is the current slide.

3. In the Slides group, click the **New Slide** button again. A new Slide 3 is added. Because Slide 2 had the Title and Content layout applied, Slide 3 also has that layout applied.

4. In the Slides group, click the **New Slide arrow** (the bottom part of the New Slide button). A gallery of the available layouts appears. See Figure 1–8.

Figure 1–8 **Gallery of layouts on the New Slide menu**

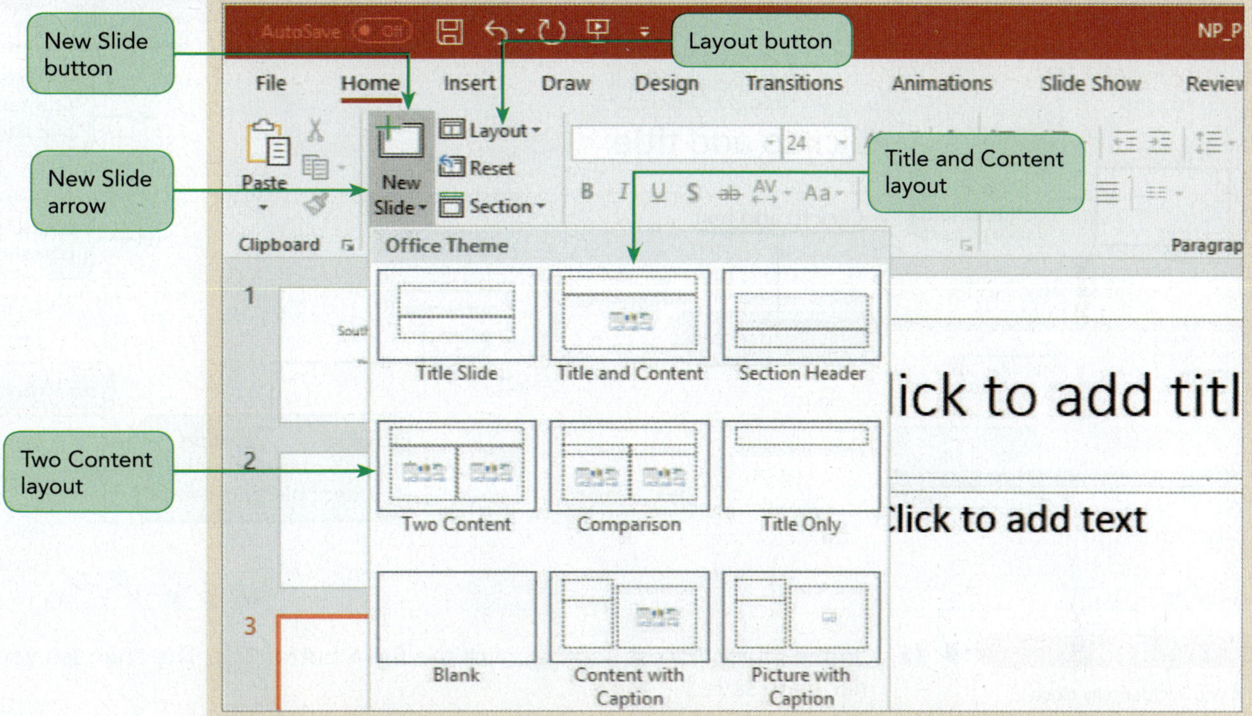

5. In the gallery, click the **Two Content** layout. The gallery closes, and a new Slide 4 is inserted with the Two Content layout applied. This layout includes three objects: a title text placeholder and two content placeholders.

6. In the Slides group, click the **New Slide** button twice. New Slides 5 and 6 are added to the presentation. Because Slide 4 had the Two Content layout applied, that layout is also applied to the new slides. You need to change the layout of Slide 6.

7. In the Slides group, click the **Layout** button. The same gallery of layouts that appeared when you clicked the New Slide arrow appears. The shading behind the Two Content layout indicates that it is applied to the current slide.

8. Click the **Title and Content** layout. The layout of Slide 6 changes to Title and Content.

Trouble? If the Design Ideas pane opens, click its Close button ☒.

9. In the Slides group, click the **New Slide** button to add Slide 7 with the Title and Content layout.

10. Add one more new slide with the Two Content layout. There are now eight slides in the presentation. In the pane that contains the slide thumbnails, some thumbnails have scrolled out of view, and vertical scroll bars appear along the right side of both panes in the program window.

11. In the pane that contains the slide thumbnails, drag the scroll box to the top of the vertical scroll bar, and then click the **Slide 2** thumbnail. Slide 2 appears in the program window and is selected in the pane that contains the slide thumbnails. See Figure 1–9.

Figure 1–9 Slide 2 with the Title and Content layout

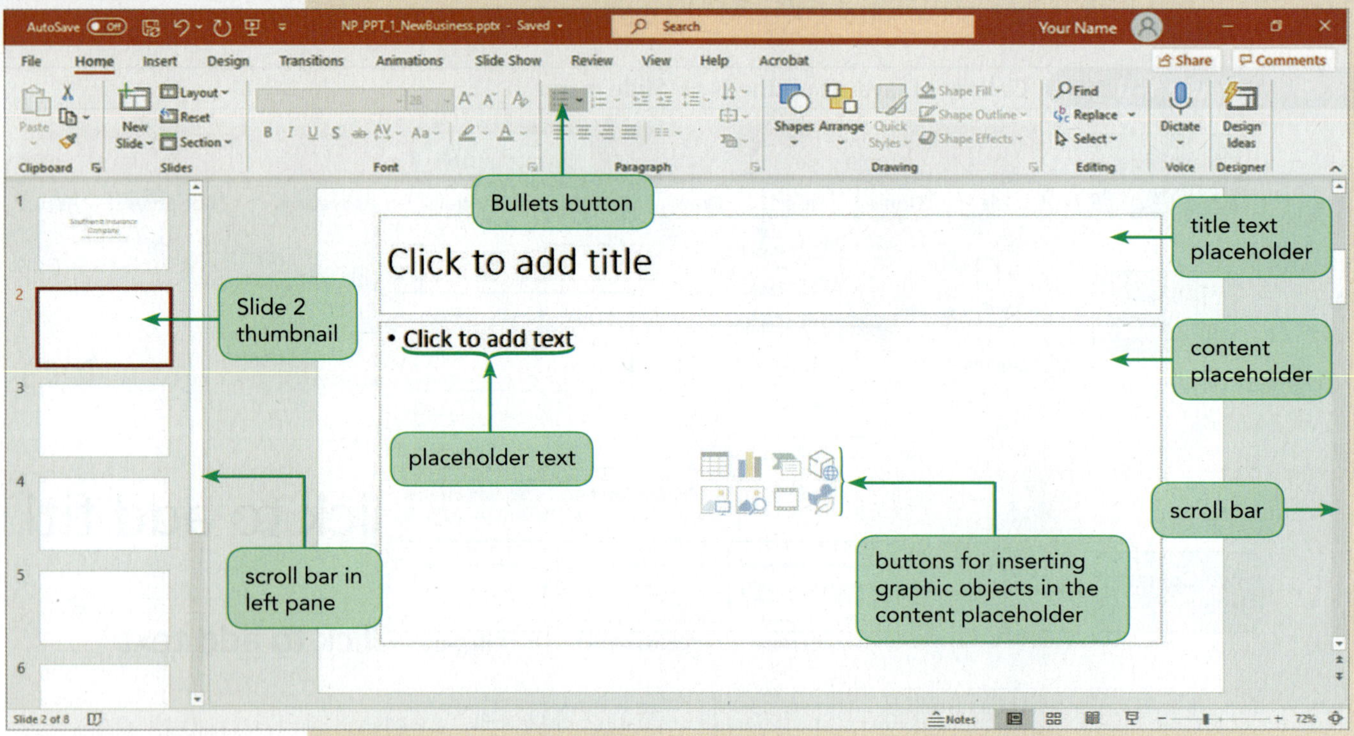

Tip

If you accidentally close a presentation without saving changes and need to recover it, click the File tab, click Open in the navigation bar, and then click the Recover Unsaved Presentations button.

12. On the Quick Access Toolbar, click the **Save** button. The changes you made are saved in the file.

Creating Lists

You can use a list to help explain a topic or concept. If you are preparing an oral presentation (one that you give in front of an audience), lists on your slides should enhance the oral presentation, not replace it. If you are preparing a self-running presentation (one that others will view on their own), list items might need to be longer and more descriptive.

Each item in a list is a paragraph. Items in a list can appear at different levels. A first-level item is a main item in a list. A second-level item is an item beneath and indented from a first-level item. A third-level item is an item beneath and indented from a second-level item, and so on. All items below the first level are subitems. A **subitem** is any item in a list that is beneath and indented from a higher-level item.

Usually, the size of the text in subitems on a slide is smaller than the size of the text in the level above. Text is measured in points. A **point** is the unit of measurement used for text size. One point is equal to 1/72 of an inch. Text in a book typically is printed in 10- or 12-point type. Text on a slide in a presentation that will be shown to an audience needs to be much larger so that the audience can easily read it.

Creating a Bulleted List

A **bulleted list** is a series of paragraphs, each beginning with a bullet character, such as a dot or checkmark. Subitems in a list often begin with a different or smaller bullet symbol. Use bulleted lists when the order of the items is not important.

You need to create a bulleted list that describes the types of insurance plans that Southwest Insurance Company offers and one that highlights why it would be the best insurance company for businesses to create a relationship with.

To create a bulleted list on Slides 2 and 3:

1. On Slide 2, click in the title text placeholder (with the placeholder text "Click to add title"), and then type **Types of Plans**. (Do not type the period.)
2. In the content placeholder, click any area where the pointer is the I-beam pointer (anywhere except on one of the buttons in the center of the placeholder). The placeholder text "Click to add text" disappears, the insertion point appears, and a light gray bullet symbol appears.
3. Type **Life** in the placeholder. As soon as you type the first character, the icons in the center of the content placeholder disappear, the bullet symbol darkens, and the content placeholder changes to a text box. On the Home tab, in the Paragraph group, the Bullets button is shaded to indicate that it is selected.
4. Press **ENTER**. The insertion point moves to a new line, and a light gray bullet appears on the new line.
5. Type **Health**, and then press **ENTER**. The bulleted list now consists of two first-level items, and the insertion point is next to a light gray bullet on the third line in the text box. On the Home tab, in the Font group, the point size in the Font Size box is 28 points.
6. Press **TAB**. The bullet symbol and the insertion point indent one-half inch to the right, the bullet symbol changes to a smaller size, and the number in the Font Size box changes to 24. See Figure 1–10.

Figure 1–10 **Subitem created on Slide 2**

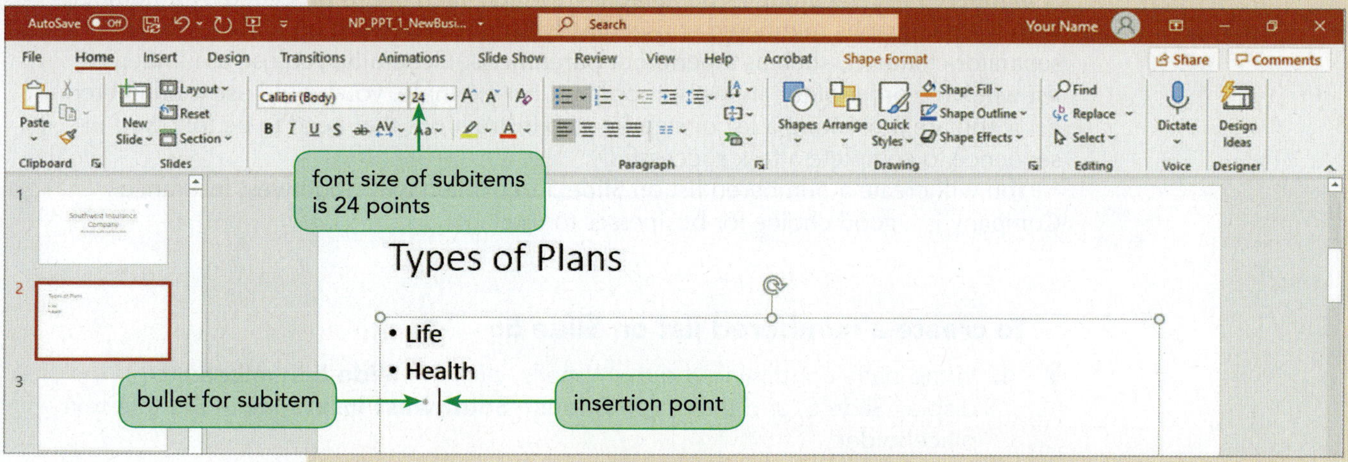

7. Type **HMO** and then press **ENTER**.
8. Type **PPO**, press **ENTER**, type **POS**, and then press **ENTER**. A fourth subitem is created. You will change it to a first-level item using a key combination. In this book, when you need to press two keys at the same time, the keys will be separated by a plus sign.

Tip

You don't need to press the keys at exactly the same time. Press and hold the first key, press the second key, and then release both keys.

9. Press **SHIFT+TAB**. The bullet symbol and the insertion point shift back to the left margin of the text box, the bullet symbol changes back to the larger size, and 28 again appears in the Font Size box because this line is now a first-level bulleted item.
10. Type **Disability**, and then press **ENTER**. A fourth first-level item is created. You need to enter subitems for the "Disability" first-level item.
11. On the Home tab, in the Paragraph group, click the **Increase List Level** button. Clicking the Increase List Level button is an alternative to pressing TAB to create a subitem.
12. Type **Long-term**, press **ENTER**, type **Short-term**, and then press **ENTER**. A third second-level item is created. You need to create a fourth first-level item.
13. In the Paragraph group, click the **Decrease List Level** button. Clicking the Decrease List Level button is an alternative to pressing SHIFT+TAB to change a lower-level item to a higher-level item.
14. Type **Stable**. The list now contains four first-level items.

If you add more text than will fit in the content placeholder, **AutoFit** adjusts the font size and line spacing to make the text fit. When AutoFit is active, the AutoFit Options button appears below the text box. You can click this button and then select from among several options, including turning off AutoFit for this text box and splitting the text between two slides. Although AutoFit can be helpful, be aware that it also enables you to crowd text on a slide, making the slide more difficult to read.

Creating a Numbered List

A **numbered list** is a group of paragraphs in which each one is preceded by a number, with the paragraphs numbered consecutively. The numbers can be followed by a separator character, such as a period or parenthesis. Generally, you use a numbered list when the order of the items is important. For example, you would use a numbered list if you are presenting a list of step-by-step instructions that need to be followed in sequence to complete a task successfully.

You will create a numbered list on Slide 5 to explain why Southwest Insurance Company is a good choice for businesses to use.

To create a numbered list on Slide 5:

1. In the pane containing the thumbnails, click the **Slide 5** thumbnail to display Slide 5, and then type **Choose Southwest Insurance** in the title text placeholder.
2. In the left content placeholder, click the placeholder text.
3. On the Home tab, in the Paragraph group, click the **Numbering** button. The Numbering button is selected, the Bullets button is deselected, and in the content placeholder, the number 1 followed by a period replaces the bullet symbol.

Trouble? If a menu containing a gallery of numbering styles appears, you clicked the Numbering arrow on the right side of the button. Click the Numbering arrow again to close the menu, and then click the left part of the Numbering button.

4. Type **Reliable**, and then press **ENTER**. As soon as you start typing, the number 1 darkens to black. After you press ENTER, the insertion point moves to the next line, next to the light gray number 2.
5. Type **Customer-focused**, and then press **ENTER**. The number 3 appears on the next line.
6. In the Paragraph group, click the **Increase List Level** button. The third line is an indented subitem under the second item, and the number 3 changes to a number 1 in a smaller font size than the first-level items.
7. Type **Dedicated customer service team**, press **ENTER**, type **24/7 support**, and then press **ENTER**.
8. In the Paragraph group, click the **Decrease List Level** button. The fifth line becomes a first-level item, and the number 3 appears next to it.
9. Type **Dependable**. The list now consists of three first-level numbered items and two subitems under number 2.
10. In the second item, click before the word "Customer," and then press **ENTER**. A blank line is inserted above the second item.
11. Press **UP ARROW**. A light-gray number 2 appears in the blank line. The item on the third line in the list is still numbered 2.
12. Type **Trustworthy**. As soon as you start typing, the new number 2 darkens in the second line, and the number of the third item in the list changes to 3. Compare your screen to Figure 1–11.

Tip

To change the style of a numbered list, click the Numbering arrow, and then click a new style on the menu.

Figure 1–11 Numbered list on Slide 5

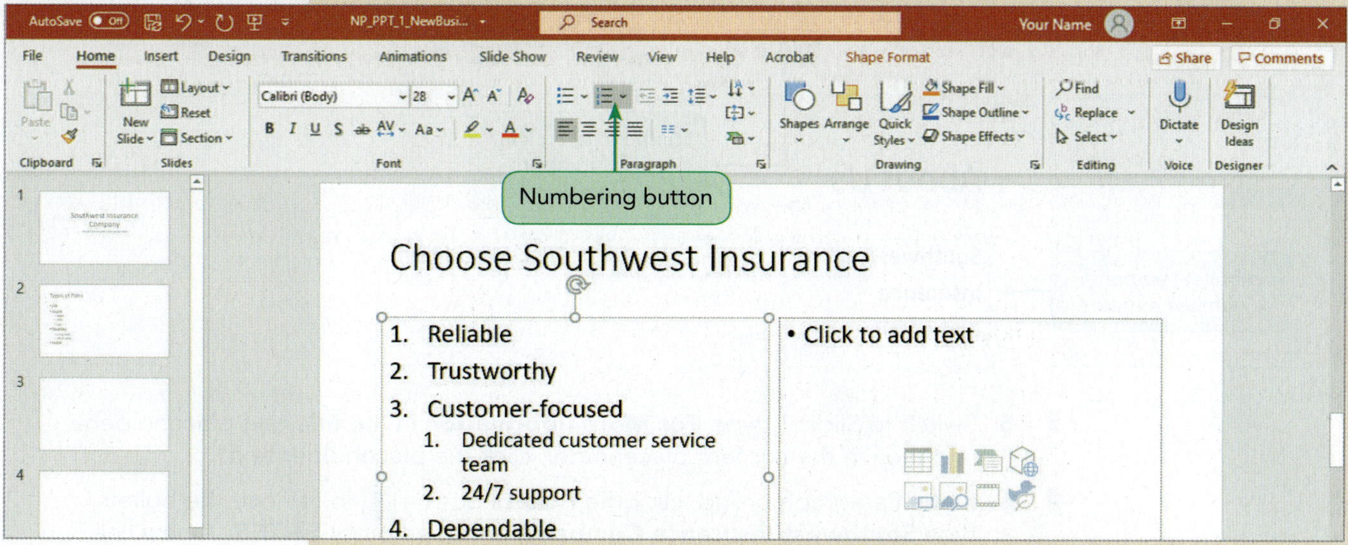

Creating an Unnumbered List

An **unnumbered list** is a list that does not have bullets or numbers preceding each item. Unnumbered lists are useful when you want to present information on multiple lines, but you do not want to start each item with a bullet or number.

Each item in lists is a paragraph. When you press ENTER to create a new item, you create a new paragraph with a little bit of extra space between the new item and the previous item. Sometimes, you don't want to create a new item, or you do not want extra space between lines. In that case, you can create a new line without creating a new paragraph by pressing SHIFT+ENTER. When you do this, the insertion point moves to the next line, but there is no extra space above it. If you do this in a bulleted or numbered list, the new line will not have a bullet or number next to it because it is not a new item.

You need to create a slide that highlights the company's name. Also, Anthony asks you to create a slide containing contact information.

To create unnumbered lists on Slides 4 and 7:

1. In the pane containing the thumbnails, click the **Slide 4** thumbnail to display Slide 4. Slide 4 has the Two Content layout applied.
2. Type **About Us** in the title text placeholder, and then in the left content placeholder, click the placeholder text.
3. On the Home tab, in the Paragraph group, click the **Bullets** button. The Bullets button is no longer selected, and the bullet symbol disappears from the content placeholder.
4. Type **Southwest**, press **ENTER**, type **Insurance**, press **ENTER**, and then type **Company**. (Do not type the period.) Compare your screen to Figure 1–12.

Figure 1–12 Unnumbered list on Slide 4

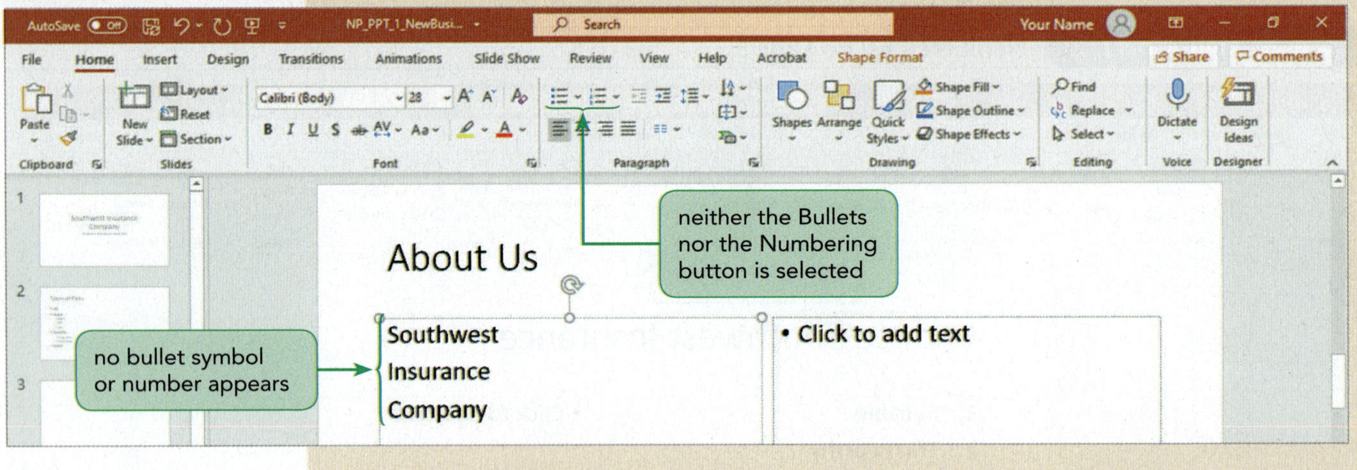

5. Switch to Slide 7, type **For More Information** in the title text placeholder, and then in the content placeholder, click the placeholder text.
6. In the Paragraph group, click the **Bullets** button to remove the bullets, type **Southwest Insurance Company**, and then press **ENTER**. A new line is created, but there is extra space above the insertion point. You want the address information to appear on multiple lines, but without the extra spacing between each line.
7. Press **BACKSPACE** to delete the new line and move the insertion point back to the end of the first line, and then press **SHIFT+ENTER**. The insertion

point moves to the next line. There is no extra space above the line, and the insertion point is aligned below the first character in the first line.

8. Type **9720 Birch Blvd.**, press **SHIFT+ENTER**, and then type **Houston, TX 77002**. (Do not type the period.) You need to insert the phone number on the next line, Anthony's email address on the line after that, and the website address on the last line. The extra space above these lines will set this information apart from the address and make it easier to read.
9. Press **ENTER** to create a new line with extra space above it, type **(281) 555-0187**, press **ENTER**, type **a.scorsone@sic.example.com**. (Do not type the period.)

   Trouble? If the first character in the email address changed to an uppercase letter "A," move the pointer on top of the "A" so that the AutoCorrect rectangle appears, move the pointer on top of the AutoCorrect rectangle so that the AutoCorrect Options button appears, click the AutoCorrect Options button, and then click Undo Automatic Capitalization.
10. Press **ENTER**. The insertion point moves to a new line with extra space above it, and the email address you typed changes color to blue and is underlined.

    When you type text that PowerPoint recognizes as an email or website address and then press SPACEBAR or ENTER, the text is automatically formatted as a link that can be clicked during a slide show. Formatted links generally appear in a different color and are underlined.
11. Type **www.sic.example.com**, and then press **SPACEBAR**. The text is formatted as a link. Anthony plans to click this link during his presentation to show the audience the website, so he wants it to stay formatted as a link. However, there is no need to have the email address formatted as a link.
12. Right-click **a.scorsone@sic.example.com**. A shortcut menu opens.
13. On the shortcut menu, click **Remove Link**. The email address is no longer formatted as a link. Compare your screen to Figure 1–13.

Figure 1–13 List on Slide 7

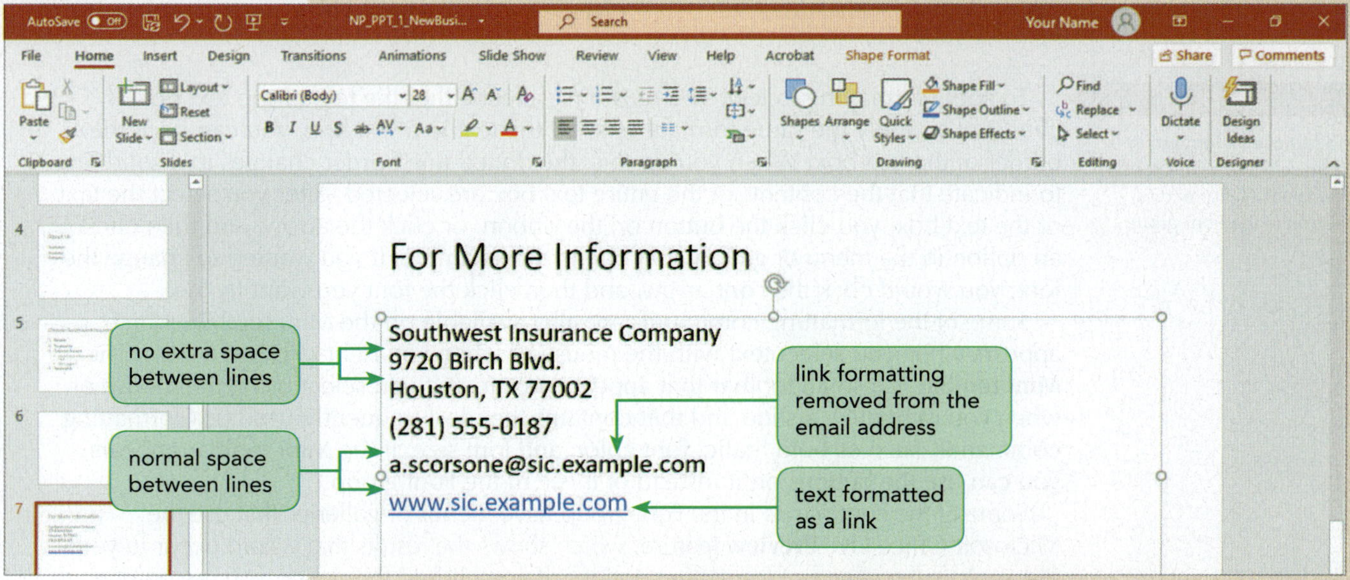

14. On the Quick Access Toolbar, click the **Save** button to save the changes.

Formatting Text

Slides in a presentation should have a consistent look and feel. For example, the slide titles and the text in content placeholders should be in complementary fonts. There are times, however, when you need to change the format of text. For instance, you might want to make specific words bold to make them stand out more.

The commands in the Font group on the Home tab are used to apply formatting to selected text. Figure 1–14 describes the buttons in this group.

Figure 1–14 **Formatting commands in the Font group on the Home tab**

Button	Name	Description
Calibri (Body)	Font	Change the font.
11	Font Size	Change the font size; click a size on the menu or type any value between 1 and 3600 in increments of 0.1 (for example, 42.4).
A	Increase Font Size	Increase the font size to the next size up listed on the Font Size menu.
A	Decrease Font Size	Decrease the font size to the next size down listed on the Font Size menu.
A	Clear All Formatting	Remove formatting of selected text.
B	Bold	Format text as bold.
I	Italic	Italicize text.
U	Underline	Underline text.
S	Text Shadow	Apply a shadow to text.
ab	Strikethrough	Add a line through text.
AV	Character Spacing	Change the spacing between characters.
Aa	Change Case	Change the case of selected text (for example, change to all uppercase).
	Text Highlight Color	Add a highlight color to selected text.
A	Font Color	Change the color of text.

Tip

To remove all formatting from selected text, click the Clear All Formatting button in the Font group.

To apply formatting to text, you must first select either the text or the text box. If you want to apply the same formatting to all the text in a text box, you can click the border of the text box. When you do this, the dotted line border changes to a solid line to indicate that the contents of the entire text box are selected. After you select the text or the text box, you click the button on the ribbon, or click the arrow, and then click an option in the menu or gallery that opens. For example, if you wanted to change the font, you would click the Font arrow, and then click the font you want to use.

Some of the formatting commands are also available on the Mini toolbar, which appears when you select text with the mouse or when you right-click on a slide. The **Mini toolbar** is a small toolbar that appears next to text you select using the mouse or when you right-click a slide and that contains the most frequently-used text formatting commands, such as bold, italic, font color, and font size. If the Mini toolbar appears, you can use the buttons on it instead of those in the Font group.

Some of the commands in the Font group have menus or galleries that use the Microsoft Office **Live Preview** feature, which shows the results that would occur in your file, such as the effects of formatting options, if you clicked the option you are pointing to.

Anthony wants the contact information on Slide 7 ("For More Information") to be larger. He also wants the first letter of each item in the unnumbered list on Slide 4 ("About Us") formatted so it is more prominent.

To format the text on Slides 7 and 4:

1. On Slide 7 ("For More Information"), position the pointer on the border of the text box containing the contact information so that it changes to the move pointer, and then click the border of the text box. The border changes to a solid line to indicate that the entire text box is selected.
2. On the Home tab, in the Font group, click the **Increase Font Size** button twice. All the text in the text box increases in size with each click and is now 36 points.
3. In the pane containing the thumbnails, click the **Slide 4** thumbnail to display that slide.
4. In the unnumbered list, click to the left of "Southwest," press and hold **SHIFT**, press **RIGHT ARROW**, and then release **SHIFT**. The letter "S" is selected. See Figure 1–15.

Figure 1–15 **Text selected to be formatted**

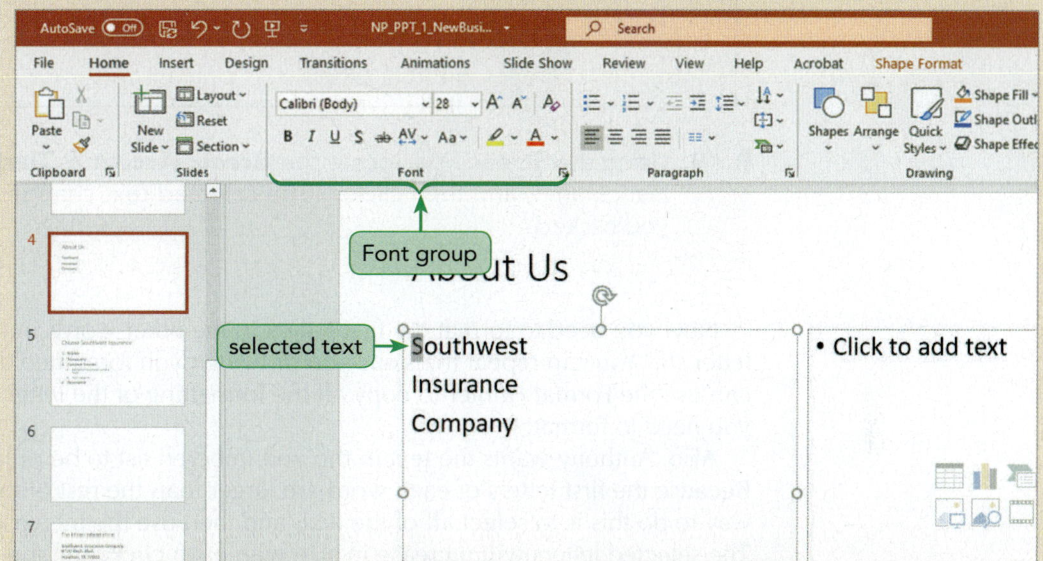

5. In the Font group, click the **Bold** button. The Bold button becomes selected, and the selected text is formatted as bold.
6. In the Font group, click the **Font Size arrow** to open the Font Size menu, and then click **48**. The selected text is now 48 points.
7. In the Font group, click the **Font Color arrow**. A menu containing color options opens.
8. Under Theme Colors, move the pointer over each color, noting the ScreenTips that appear and watching as Live Preview changes the color of the selected text as you point to each color. Figure 1–16 shows the pointer pointing to the Green, Accent 6, Darker 25% color.

Figure 1–16 **Font Color menu**

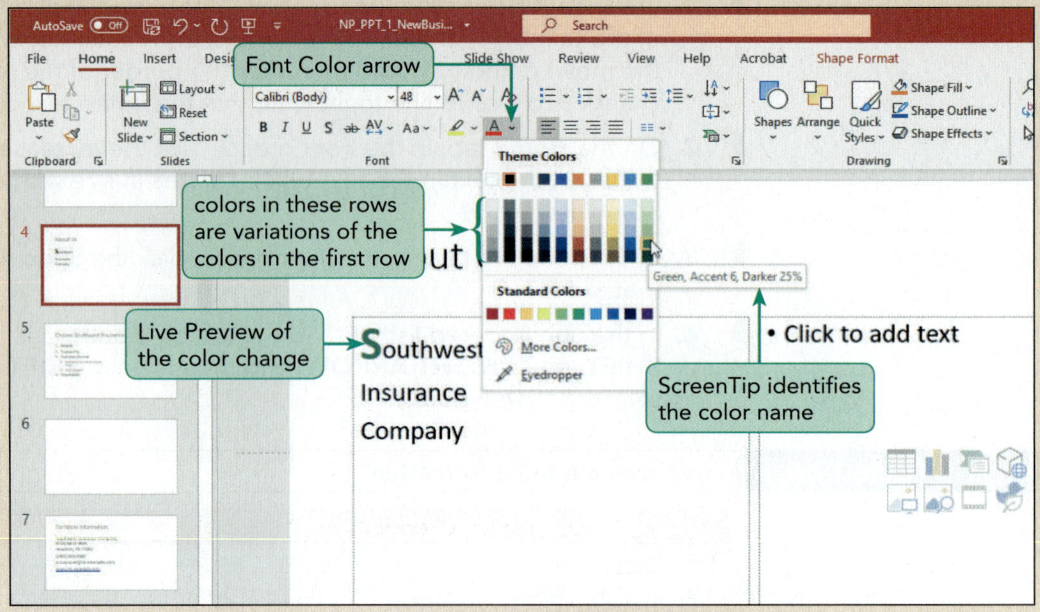

9. Using the ScreenTips, locate the **Green, Accent 6, Darker 25%** color in the last column, and then click it. The selected text changes to the green color you clicked.

Now you need to format the first letters in the other words in the list to match the letter "S." You can repeat the steps you did when you formatted the letter "S," or you can use the Format Painter to copy all the formatting of the letter "S" to the other letters you need to format.

Also, Anthony wants the text in the unnumbered list to be as large as possible. Because the first letters of each word are larger than the rest of the letters, the easiest way to do this is to select all of the text, and then use the Increase Font Size button. The selected letters will increase in size with each click, and the first letters will still be larger.

To use the Format Painter to copy and apply formatting on Slide 4:

1. Make sure the letter "S" is still selected.
2. On the Home tab, in the Clipboard group, click the **Format Painter** button, and then move the pointer on top of the slide. The button is selected, and the pointer changes to the Format Painter pointer for text.
3. Position the pointer before the letter "I" in "Insurance," press and hold the mouse button, drag over the letter **I**, and then release the mouse button. The formatting you applied to the letter "S" is copied to the letter "I," and the Mini toolbar appears. See Figure 1–17. The Mini toolbar appears whenever you drag over text to select it.

Figure 1–17 **Mini toolbar**

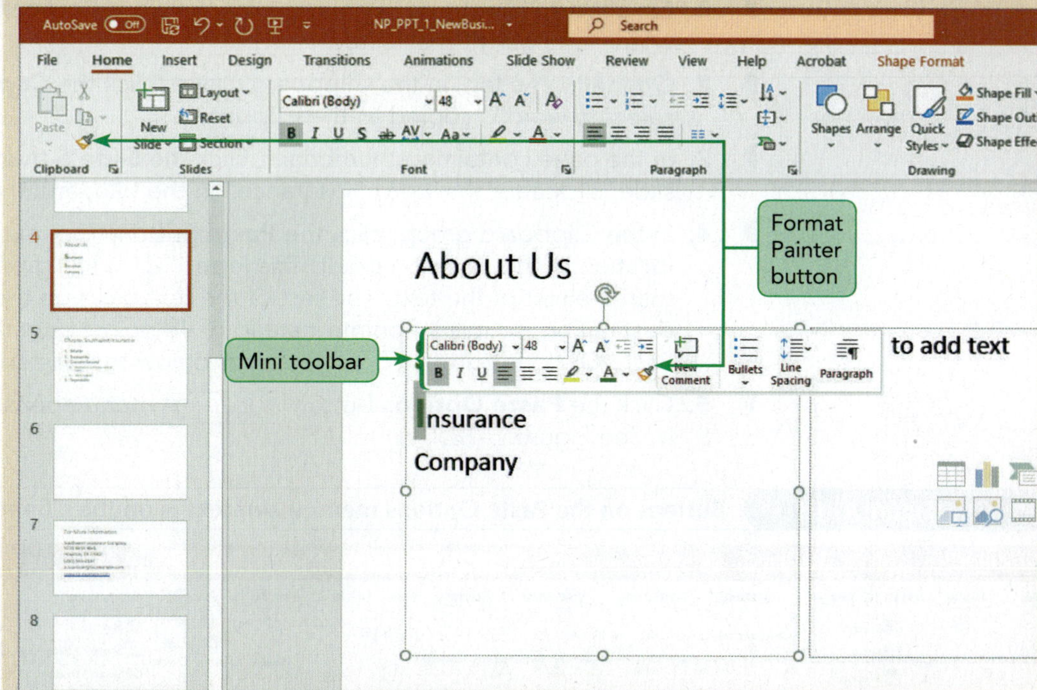

> **Tip**
>
> If you need to copy formatting to more than one location, double-click the Format Painter button to keep it selected until you deselect it by clicking it again.

4. On the Mini toolbar, click the **Format Painter** button, and then drag across the letter "C" in "Company."

5. Click the border of the text box to select the entire text box, and then in the Font group, click the **Increase Font Size** button five times. In the Font group, the Font Size button indicates that the text is 48+ points. This means that in the selected text box, the text that is the smallest is 48 points and there is some text that is larger.

6. On the Quick Access Toolbar, click the **Save** button to save the changes.

Moving and Copying

You can move and copy text and objects in a presentation using the Clipboard that is part of Windows. The **Clipboard** is a temporary Windows storage area that holds the selections you copy or cut so you can use them later. When you **cut** something, you remove the text or object from a file and place it on the Clipboard. You can also **copy** text or an object, which means you select it and place a duplicate of it on the Clipboard, leaving the text or object in its original location. You can then paste the text or object stored on the Clipboard anywhere in the presentation or in any file in any Windows program. To **paste** something means to place text or an object stored on the Clipboard in a location in a file.

The Clipboard holds only the most recently cut or copied item. As soon as you cut or copy another item, it replaces the previously cut or copied item on the Clipboard. You can paste an item on the Clipboard as many times and in as many locations as you like.

Note that cutting text or an object differs from deleting it. When you press DELETE or BACKSPACE to delete text or objects, they are not placed on the Clipboard and cannot be pasted.

Anthony wants a few changes made to Slides 5 and 2. You'll use the Clipboard as you make these edits.

To cut, copy, and paste text using the Clipboard:

1. On Slide 4 ("About Us"), double-click the word **Company** in the list. The word "Company" is selected.
2. On the Home tab, in the Clipboard group, click the **Copy** button. The selected word is copied to the Clipboard.
3. In the pane containing thumbnails, click the **Slide 5** thumbnail to display that slide, click after the word "Insurance" in the title, and then press **SPACEBAR**.
4. In the Clipboard group, click the **Paste** button. The text appears at the location of the insertion point. The letter "C" is still green and is larger than the rest of the text. The rest of the text picks up the formatting of its destination, so it is 44 points instead of 48 points as in the list on Slide 4. The Paste Options button (Ctrl) appears below the pasted text.
5. Click the **Paste Options** button (Ctrl). A menu opens with four buttons on it. See Figure 1–18.

Figure 1–18 **Buttons on the Paste Options menu when text is on the Clipboard**

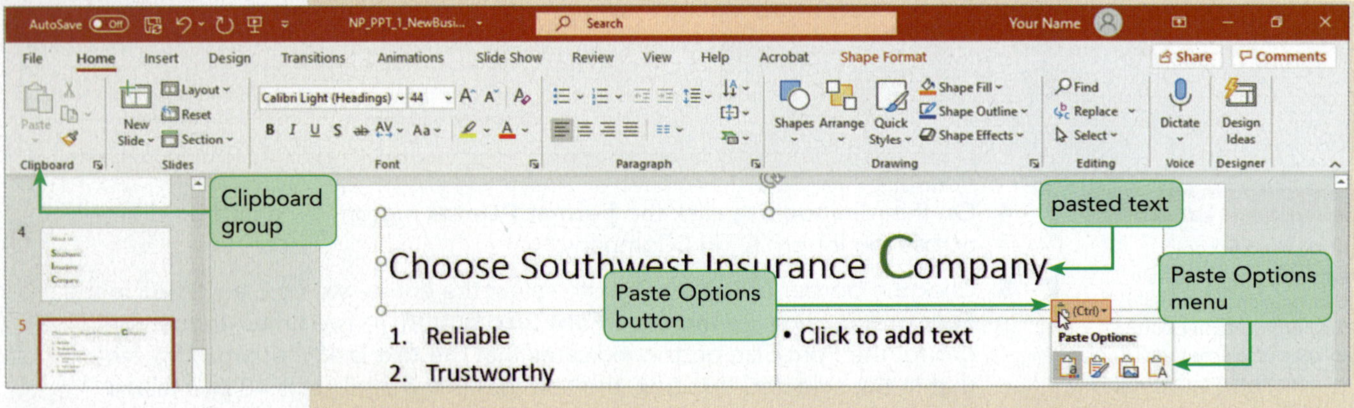

6. Point to each button on the menu, reading the ScreenTips and watching to see how the pasted text changes in appearance. The first button is the Use Destination Theme button, which is the default choice when you paste text.
7. On the Paste Options menu, click the **Keep Text Only** button. The pasted text changes so that its formatting matches the rest of the title text.
8. Display Slide 2 ("Types of Plans"). The last bulleted item ("Stable") belongs on Slide 5.
9. In the last bulleted item, position the pointer on top of the bullet symbol so that the pointer changes to the four-headed arrow pointer, and then click. The entire bulleted item is selected.
10. In the Clipboard group, click the **Cut** button. The last bulleted item is removed from the slide and is placed on the Clipboard.
11. Display Slide 5 ("Choose Southwest Insurance Company"), click after the last item ("Dependable"), and then press **ENTER** to create a fifth first-level item.
12. In the Clipboard group, click the **Paste** button. The bulleted item you cut becomes the fifth first-level item on Slide 5 using the default paste option of Use Destination Theme. The insertion point appears next to a sixth first-level item.
13. Press **BACKSPACE** twice to delete the extra line, and then on the Quick Access Toolbar, click the **Save** button to save the changes.

Tip

To cut text or an object, you can press CTRL+X. To copy text or an object, press CTRL+C. To paste the contents of the Clipboard, press CTRL+V.

Insight

Using the Office Clipboard

The **Office Clipboard** is a temporary storage area in the computer's memory that lets you collect text and objects from any Office document and then paste them into other Office documents. Once you activate the Office Clipboard, you can store up to 24 items on it and then select the item or items you want to paste. To activate the Office Clipboard, click the Home tab. In the Clipboard group, click the Dialog Box Launcher (the small square in the lower-right corner of the Clipboard group) to open the Clipboard pane to the left of the displayed slide.

Manipulating Slides

You can manipulate the slides in a presentation to suit your needs. For example, if you need to create a slide that is similar to another slide, you can duplicate the existing slide and then modify the copy. If you no longer want to include a slide in your presentation, you can delete it. You can also reorder slides as necessary.

To duplicate, rearrange, or delete slides, you select the slides in the pane containing the thumbnails in Normal view or switch to Slide Sorter view. In **Slide Sorter view** all the slides in the presentation are displayed as thumbnails in the window.

Anthony wants to display a slide that shows the name of the company at the end of the presentation. To create this slide, you will duplicate Slide 4 ("About Us").

To duplicate Slide 4:

1. Display Slide 4 ("About Us").
2. On the Home tab, in the Slides group, click the **New Slide arrow**, and then click **Duplicate Selected Slides**. A duplicate of Slide 4 appears as a new Slide 5 and is the current slide. If you had selected more than one slide, they would all be duplicated. The duplicate slide doesn't need the title; Anthony just wants to reinforce the company's name.
3. On Slide 5, click anywhere on the title **About Us**, click the text box border to select the text box, and then press **DELETE**. The title and the title text box are deleted, and the title text placeholder reappears.

You could delete the title text placeholder, but you do not need to. When you display a presentation to an audience as a slide show, any unused placeholders do not appear.

Next you need to rearrange the slides. You need to move the duplicate of the "About Us" slide so it becomes the last slide in the presentation because Anthony wants it to remain displayed after the presentation is over. He hopes this visual will reinforce the company's name for the audience. Anthony also wants Slide 6 ("Choose Southwest Insurance Company") moved before the "Types of Plans" slide (Slide 2), and he wants the original "About Us" slide (Slide 4) to be the second slide in the presentation.

To rearrange the slides in the presentation:

1. In the pane containing the thumbnails, scroll, if necessary, so that you can see Slides 2 and 6, and then click the **Slide 6** ("Choose Southwest Insurance Company") thumbnail. Slide 6 ("Choose Southwest Insurance Company") is the current slide.
2. Point to the **Slide 6** thumbnail, press and hold the mouse button, drag the Slide 6 thumbnail up above the Slide 2 ("Types of Plans") thumbnail, and then release the mouse button. As you drag, the Slide 6 thumbnail follows the pointer and the other slides move down to make room for the slide you are dragging. The "Choose Southwest Insurance Company" slide becomes Slide 2 and "Types of Plans" becomes Slide 3. You'll move the other two slides in Slide Sorter view.
3. On the status bar, click the **Slide Sorter** button [button icon]. The view switches to Slide Sorter view. Slide 2 appears with an orange border, indicating that it is selected.
4. On the status bar, click the **Zoom Out** button [button icon] as many times as necessary until you can see all nine slides in the presentation. See Figure 1–19.

Tip

You can also use the buttons in the Presentation Views group on the View tab to switch views.

Figure 1–19 Slide Sorter view

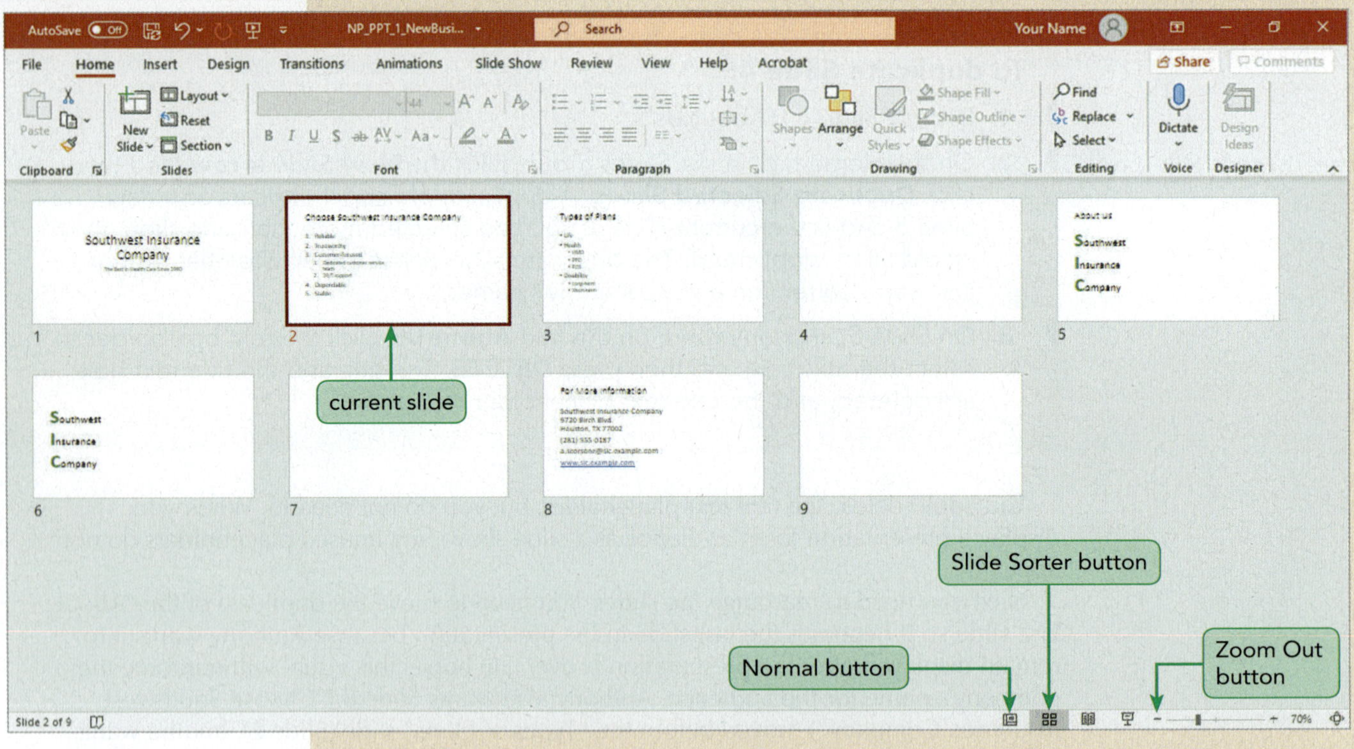

5. Drag the **Slide 5** ("About Us") thumbnail to between Slides 1 and 2. As you drag, the other slides move out of the way. The slides are renumbered so that the "About Us" slide is now Slide 2.
6. Drag the **Slide 6** thumbnail (the slide containing just the name of the company) after the last slide in the presentation (Slide 9).

Now you need to delete the blank slides. To delete a slide, you right-click its thumbnail to display a shortcut menu, and then click Delete Slide on that menu.

You already know that to select a single slide you click its thumbnail. You can also select more than one slide at a time. To select sequential slides, click the first slide, press and hold SHIFT, and then click the last slide you want to select. To select nonsequential slides, click the first slide, press and hold CTRL, and then click any other slides you want to select. When more than one slide is selected, you can delete or duplicate all of the selected slides with one command.

To delete the blank slides:

1. Click the **Slide 5** thumbnail (the first blank slide), press and hold **SHIFT**, click the **Slide 8** thumbnail (the last blank slide), and then release **SHIFT**. The two slides you clicked are selected, as well as the slides between them. Holding SHIFT when you click items selects the slides you click as well as the slides between the slides you click. You want to delete only the three blank slides. To select only the slides you click, you need to hold CTRL instead.
2. Click a blank area of the window to deselect the slides, click the **Slide 5** thumbnail, press and hold **CTRL**, click the **Slide 6** thumbnail, click the **Slide 8** thumbnail, and then release **CTRL**. Only the slides you clicked are selected.
3. Right-click any of the selected slides. A shortcut menu appears. See Figure 1–20.

Figure 1–20 Shortcut menu for selected slides

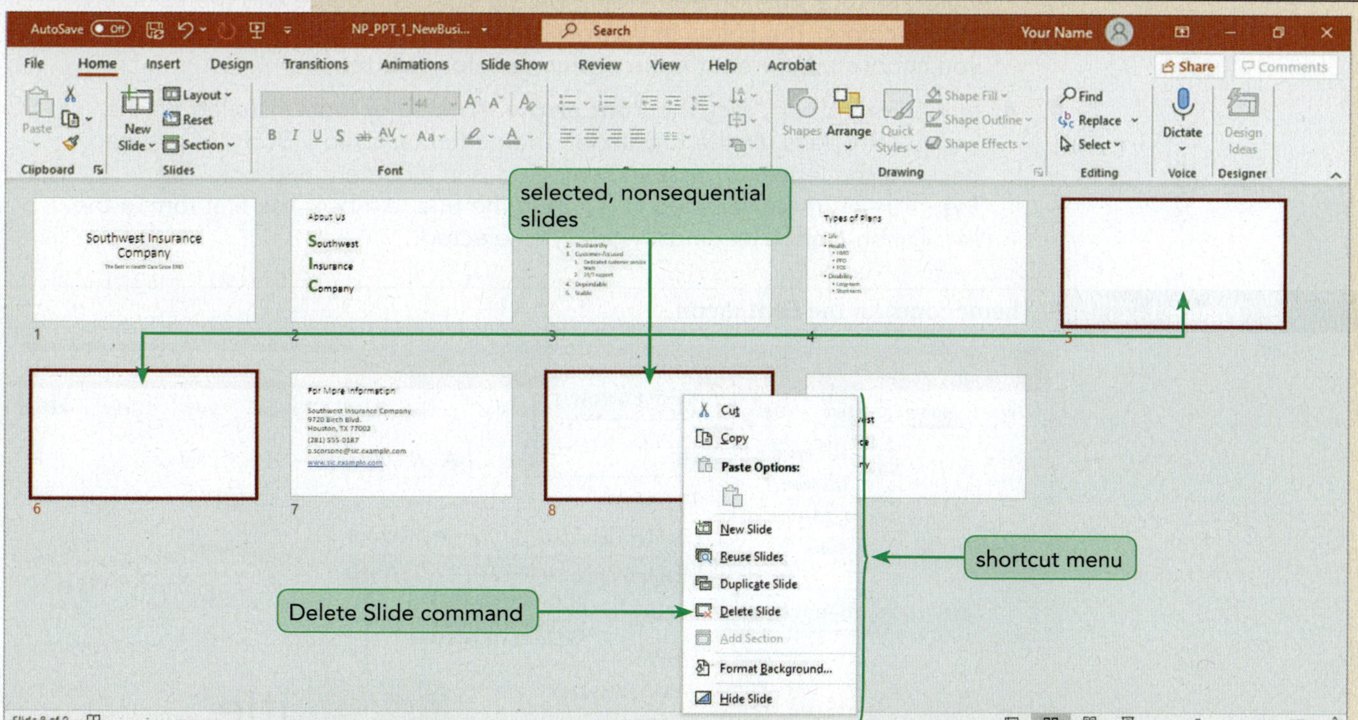

Tip

You can also double-click a slide thumbnail in Slide Sorter view to display that slide in the view the presentation was in prior to being in Slide Sorter view.

4. On the shortcut menu, click **Delete Slide**. The shortcut menu closes, and the three selected slides are deleted. The presentation now contains six slides.
5. On the status bar, click the **Normal** button. The presentation appears in Normal view.
6. On the Quick Access Toolbar, click the **Save** button to save the changes to the presentation.

Changing the Theme

A **theme** is a predefined, coordinated set of colors, fonts, graphical effects, and other formats that can be applied to a presentation. In PowerPoint, most themes have variants that have different coordinating colors and sometimes slightly different backgrounds. All presentations have a theme. If you don't choose one, the default Office theme is applied; that is the theme currently applied to the presentation you created.

Every theme has a palette of 12 coordinated colors. You saw the Office theme colors when you changed the color of the text on the "About Us" slide. If you don't like the color palette of the theme you chose, you can change to a different one.

Themes also have a font set. One font, called the Headings font, is used for slide titles. The other font, called the Body font, is used for the rest of the text on a slide. In the Office theme, the Headings font is Calibri Light, and the Body font is Calibri. In some themes, the Headings and Body font are the same font.

Anthony wants you to try changing the theme colors and fonts.

To examine the current theme and then change the theme color and theme fonts:

1. Display Slide 5 ("For More Information"). Notice that the link is blue.
2. Display Slide 6, and then, in the unnumbered list, select the green letter **S**.
3. On the Home tab, in the Font group, click the **Font Color arrow** A. Look at the colors under Theme Colors. The last column contains shades of green. In that column, the second to last color is selected. The colors in the Theme Colors section change depending on the selected theme and the selected theme colors. The colors in the row of Standard Colors do not change when you choose a different theme or theme color palette.
4. In the Font group, click the **Font arrow**. A menu of fonts installed on the computer opens. At the top under Theme Fonts, Calibri (Body) is selected because the letter "S" that you selected is in a content text box. See Figure 1–21. If the selected text was in the title text box, the first font in the list, Calibri Light (Headings) would be selected.

Figure 1–21 Theme fonts on the Font menu

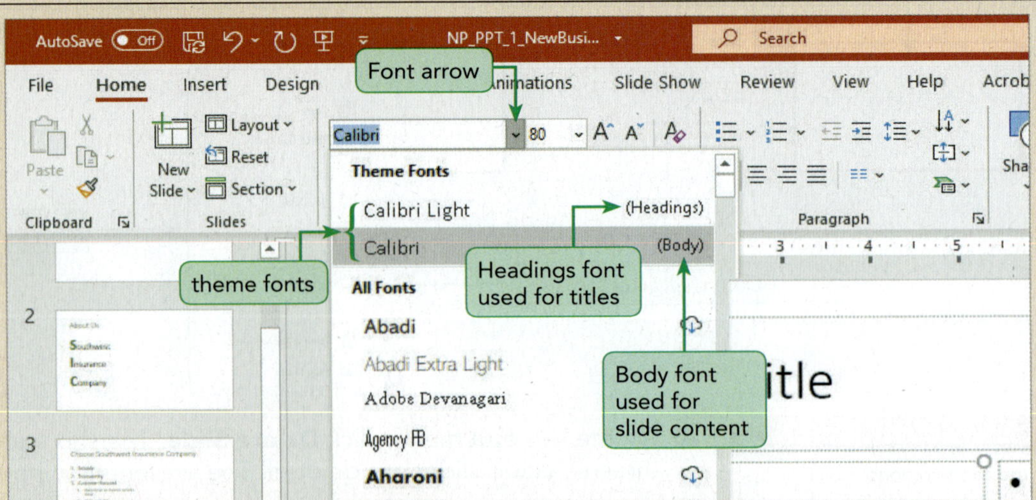

5. On the ribbon, click the **Design** tab. The Design tab is active. See Figure 1–22. In the Themes group, the first theme is the theme applied to the presentation. In this case, it is the Office theme. The second theme is also the Office theme and it is shaded to indicate that it is selected. In the Variants group, the first variant is shaded to indicate that it is selected.

Figure 1–22 Themes and variants on the Design tab

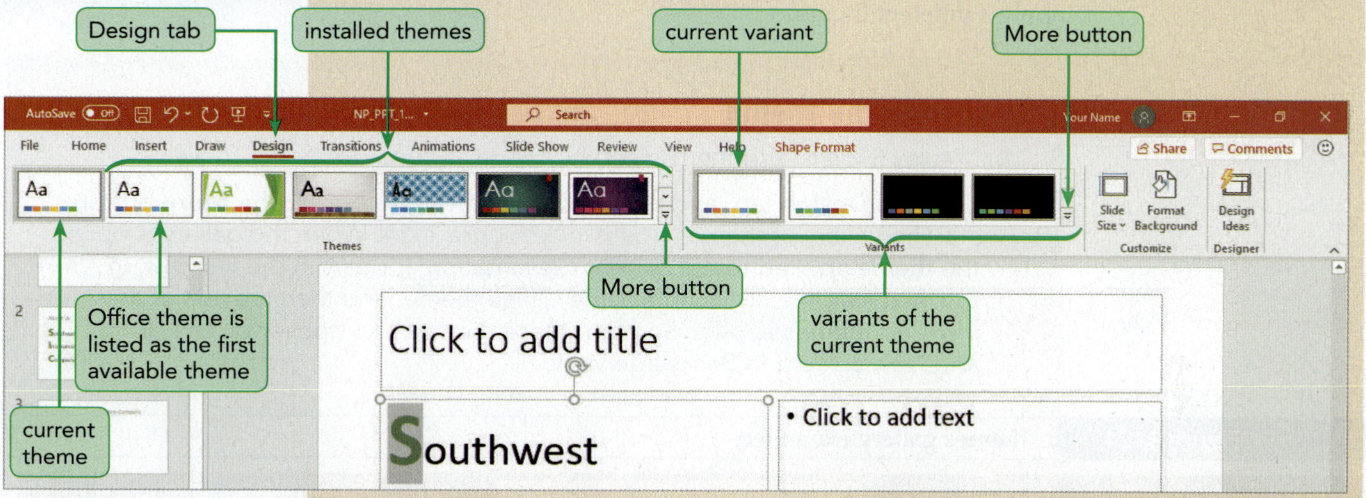

6. In the Variants group, click the **More** button. A menu opens containing commands for changing the theme colors and the theme fonts. See Figure 1–23.

Figure 1–23 More button menu in the Variants group

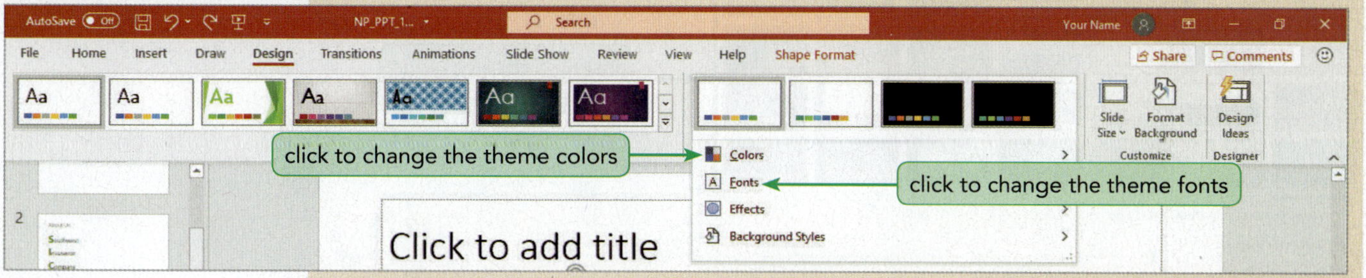

7. On the menu, point to **Colors** to open a submenu of color palettes, and then click the **Blue Warm** palette. The colored letters on Slide 6 change to a shade of grayish brown.

8. In the Variant group, click the **More** button, point to **Fonts**, scroll down, and then click **Tw Cen MT-Rockwell**. The font of the list and the title text placeholder on Slide 6 changes.

9. Click the **Home** tab, and then in the Font group, click the **Font Color arrow**. The second to last color in the last column is still selected, but now that column contains shades of grayish brown. The row of Standard Colors is the same as it was when the Office theme colors were applied.

10. In the Font group, click the **Font** arrow. The Headings and Body font have changed to the Tw Cen MT and the Rockwell fonts.

11. Display Slide 5. The link that was blue before you changed the theme colors is now purple.

PowerPoint comes with several installed themes, and many more themes are available online at Office.com. In addition, you can use a custom theme stored on your computer or network.

You can select a different installed theme when you create a new presentation by clicking one of the themes on the New or Home screen in Backstage view. If you want to change the theme of an open presentation, you can choose an installed theme on the Design tab, or you can apply a theme applied to another presentation or a theme stored on your computer or network.

Anthony still thinks the presentation could be more interesting, so he asks you to apply a different theme.

To change the theme

1. Display Slide 6, and then select the "S" in "Southwest."
2. Click the **Design** tab, and then in the Themes group, click the **More** button ▾. The gallery of themes opens. See Figure 1–24. When the gallery is open, the theme applied to the current presentation appears in the first row. In the next row, the first theme is the Office theme, and then the rest of the installed themes appear. Some of these themes also appear on the Home and New screens in Backstage view.

Figure 1–24 Themes gallery expanded

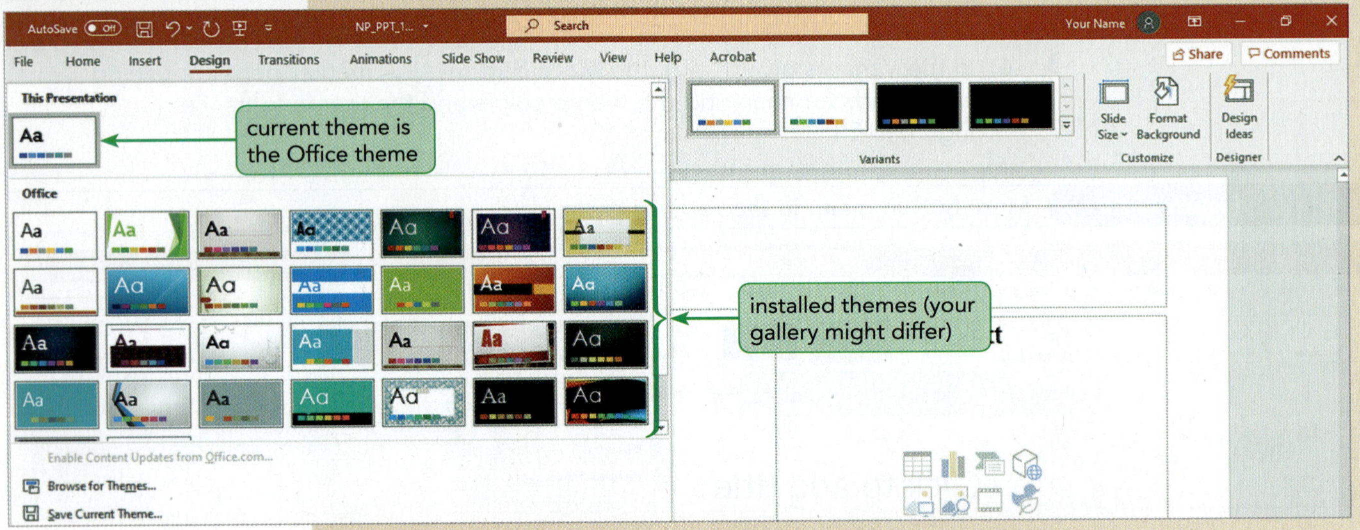

3. Point to several of the themes in the gallery to display their ScreenTips and to see a Live Preview of the theme applied to the current slide.
4. Click the **Wisp** theme. The gallery closes, and all the slides have the Wisp theme with the default variant (the first variant in the Variants group) applied. The background of the slides changes from white to tan, and the letters that you had colored green on Slide 6 change to a shade of grayish green. In the empty content placeholder on Slide 6, the bullet symbol changed from a circle to an arrow.
5. In the Variants group, point to the other three variants to see a Live Preview of each of them, and then click the third variant (the blue one). The letters on Slide 6 change to purple. You prefer the original colors. On the Quick Access Toolbar, click the **Undo** button.
6. Click the **Home** tab, and then in the Font group, click the **Font Color arrow** A ▾. The selected color is still the second to last color in the last column, but now the last column contains shades of purple. Again, the row of Standard Colors is the same as it was before you made changes.

7. In the Font group, click the **Font arrow**. You can see that the Theme Fonts are now Century Gothic for both Headings and the Body.
8. Press **ESC**. The Font menu closes.

After you apply a new theme, you should examine your slides to make sure that they look the way you expect them to. Slide 6 looks fine.

To examine the slides with the new theme and adjust font sizes:

1. Display Slides 5, 4, 3, and Slide 2. These slides look fine.
2. Display Slide 1 (the title slide). The title text is too large with the Wisp theme applied.
3. Click anywhere on the title text, and then click the text box border. The entire text box is selected.
4. In the Font group, click the **Decrease Font Size** button as many times as necessary until the font size of the title text decreases to 44 points.
5. On the Quick Access Toolbar, click **Save**. The changes to the presentation are saved.

Insight

Understanding the Difference Between Themes and Templates

As explained earlier, a theme is a coordinated set of colors, fonts, backgrounds, and effects. A **template** is a file that has a theme applied and contains text, graphics, and placeholders that direct you in creating content for a presentation. You can create and save your own custom templates or find everything from calendars to marketing templates among the thousands of templates available on Office.com. To find a template on Office.com, display the Home or New screen in Backstage view, type keywords in the "Search for online templates and themes" box, and then click the Search button in the box to display templates related to the search terms. To create a new presentation based on the template you find, click the template and then click Create.

If a template is stored on your computer, you can apply the theme used in the template to an existing presentation. If you want to apply the theme used in a template on Office.com to an existing presentation, you need to download the template to your computer first.

Closing a Presentation

When you are finished working with a presentation, you can close it and leave PowerPoint open. To do this, you click the File tab to open Backstage view, and then click the Close command. If you have only one presentation open, if you click the Close button ☒ in the upper-right corner of the PowerPoint window, you will not only close the presentation, you will exit PowerPoint as well.

You're finished working with the presentation for now, so you will close it. First you will add your name to the title slide.

To add your name to Slide 1 and close the presentation:

1. On Slide 1 (the title slide), click the subtitle, position the insertion point after "1990," press **ENTER**, and then type your full name.
2. Click the **File** tab. Backstage view appears with the Home screen displayed. See Figure 1–25.

Figure 1–25 Home screen in Backstage view

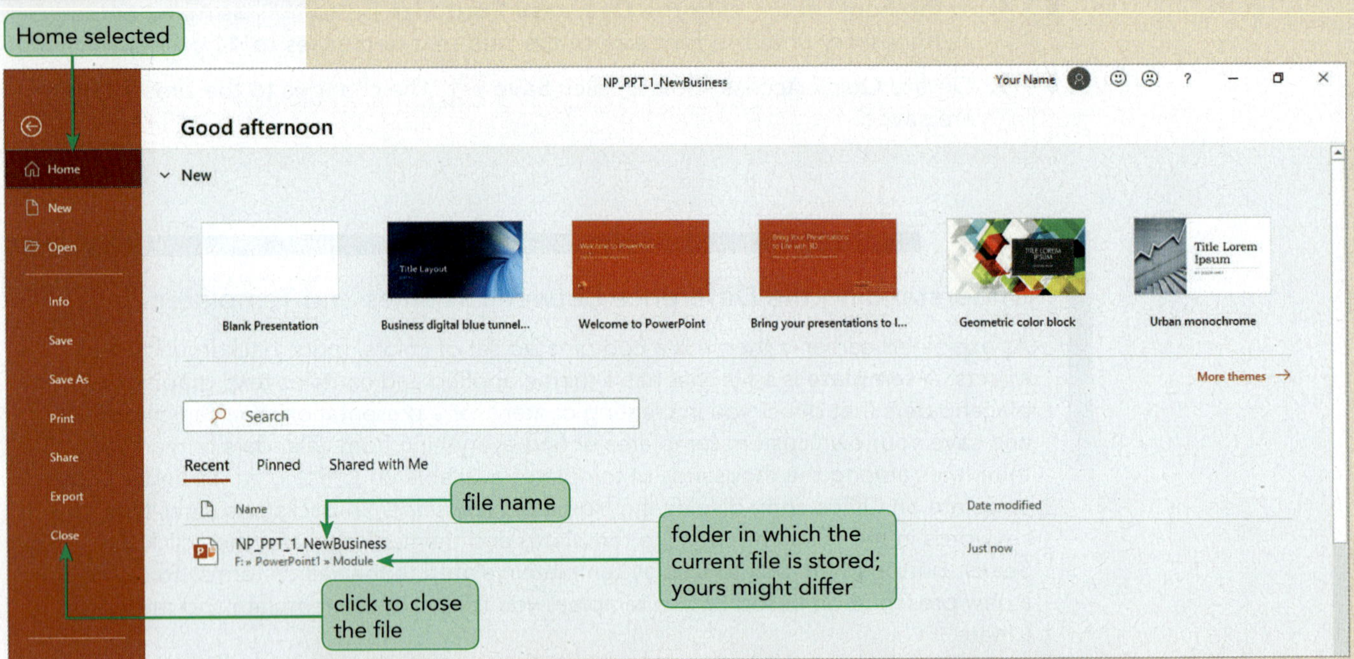

3. In the navigation pane, click **Close**. Backstage view closes, and a dialog box opens, asking if you want to save your changes.
4. In the dialog box, click **Save**. The dialog box and the presentation close, and the empty presentation window appears.

   Trouble? If you want to take a break, you can exit PowerPoint by clicking the Close button ☒ in the upper-right corner of the PowerPoint window.

You've created a presentation that includes slides to which you added bulleted, numbered, and unnumbered lists. You also formatted text, manipulated slides, and applied a theme. You are ready to give the presentation draft to Anthony to review.

Review

Session 1.1 Quick Check

1. Define "presentation."
2. How do you display Backstage view?
3. What is a slide layout?
4. In addition to a title text placeholder, what other type of placeholder do many layouts contain?
5. What is the term for an object that contains text?
6. What is the difference between the Clipboard and the Office Clipboard?
7. Explain what a theme is and what changes with each variant.

Session 1.2 Visual Overview:

In **Slide Show view**, each slide fills the screen, one after another.

The pointer is not visible in Slide Show view until you move it or right-click it. When you move the pointer, this faint row of buttons appears in the lower-left corner of the screen. All of these buttons are also available in Presenter view.

Click the Zoom into slide button to zoom into a portion of the slide during the slide show.

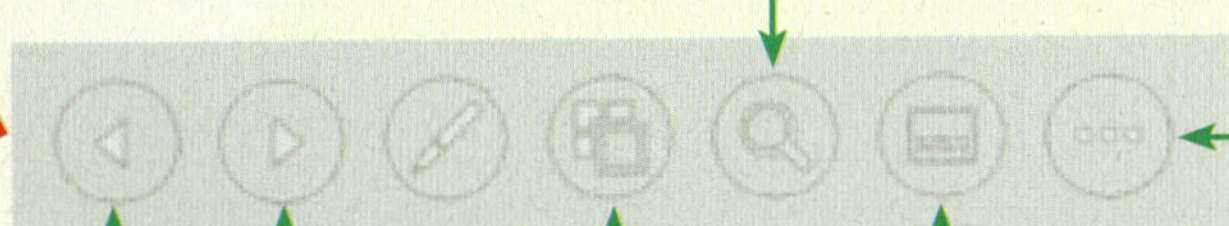

Click the More slide show options button to display additional commands.

Click the Return to the previous animation or slide and Advance to the next animation or slide buttons to move from slide to slide in Slide Show view.

Click the See all slides button to display all the slides, similar to Slide Sorter view.

Click the Subtitles button to have PowerPoint convert your speech into subtitles that appear on each slide.

Yuganov Konstantin/Shutterstock.com

Slide Show and Presenter Views

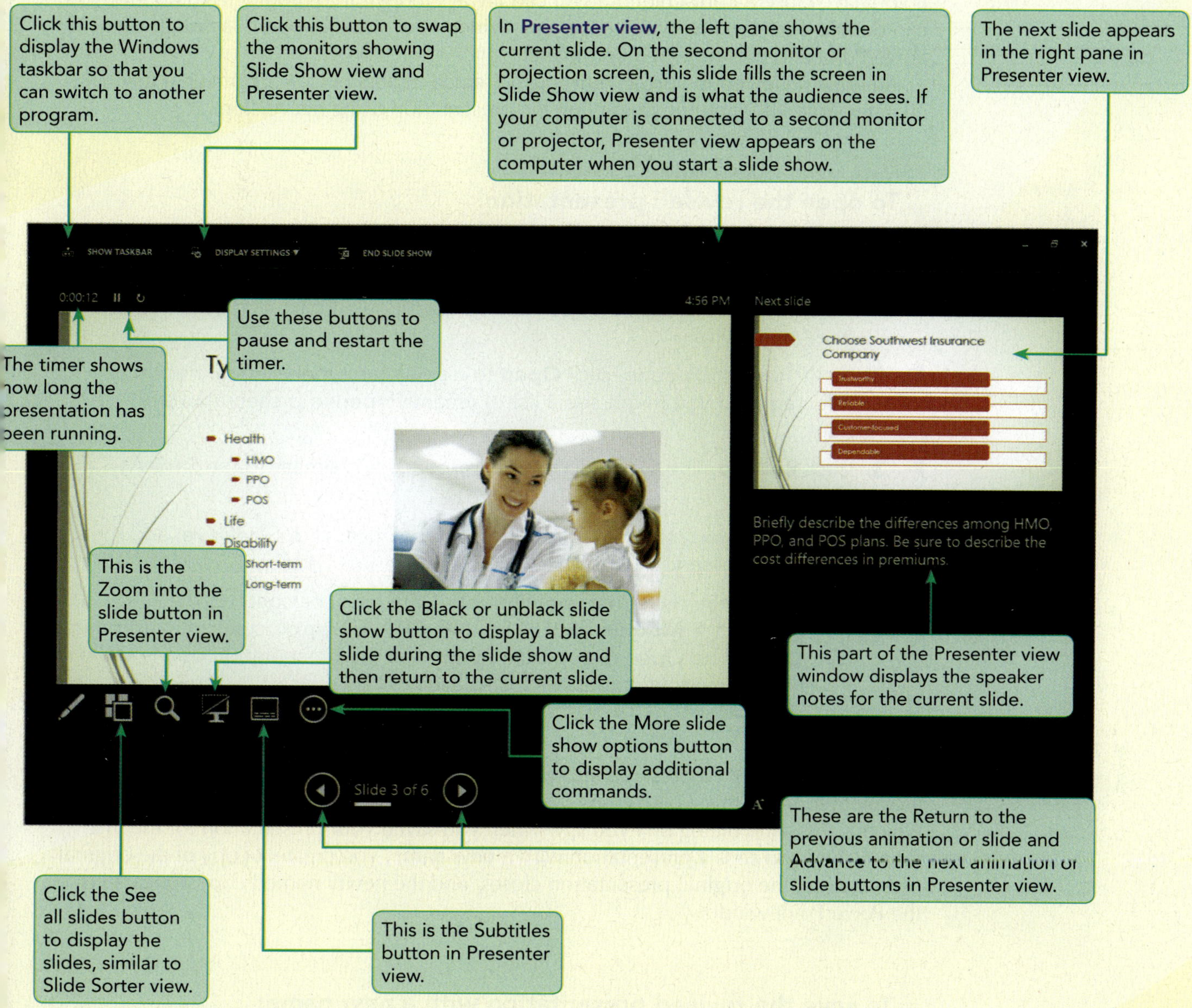

Yuganov Konstantin/Shutterstock.com

Opening a Presentation and Saving It with a New Name

If you have closed a presentation, you can always reopen it to modify it. To do this, you can double-click the file in a File Explorer window, or you can open Backstage view in PowerPoint and use the Open command.

Anthony reviewed the presentation you created in Session 1.1 and made a few changes. You will continue modifying the presentation using his version.

To open the revised presentation:

1. sam Click the **File** tab on the ribbon to display the Home screen in Backstage view.

   Trouble? If PowerPoint is not running, start PowerPoint, and then in the left pane, click Open.

2. In the navigation pane, click **Open** to display the Open screen. Recent is selected, and you might see a list of recently opened presentations on the right.
3. Click **Browse**. The Open dialog box appears. It is similar to the Save As dialog box.

   Trouble? If you store your files on your OneDrive, click OneDrive, and then log in if necessary.

4. Navigate to the drive that contains your Data Files, navigate to the **PowerPoint1 > Module** folder, click **NP_PPT_1-1.pptx** to select it, and then click **Open**. The Open dialog box closes, and the presentation opens in the PowerPoint window, with Slide 1 displayed.

If you want to edit a presentation without changing the original, you need to create a copy of it. To do this, you use the Save As command to open the Save As dialog box, which is the same dialog box you saw when you saved your presentation for the first time. When you save a presentation with a new name, you create a copy of the original presentation, the original presentation closes, and the newly named copy appears in the PowerPoint window.

To save the revised presentation with a new name:

1. Click the **File** tab, and then in the navigation pane, click **Save As**. The Save As screen in Backstage view appears.
2. Click **Browse** to open the Save As dialog box.
3. If necessary, navigate to the drive and folder where you are storing your Data Files.
4. In the File name box, change the filename to **NP_PPT_1_Revised**, and then click **Save**. The Save As dialog box closes, and a copy of the file is saved with the new name NP_PPT_1_Revised and appears in the PowerPoint window.

Inserting Pictures and Adding Alt Text

In many cases, graphics are more effective than words for communicating an important point or invoking an emotional reaction. For example, if a sales force has reached its sales goals for the year, including a photo in your presentation of a person reaching the top of a mountain can convey a sense of accomplishment to your audience. To add a graphic to a slide, you can use the buttons in a content placeholder or buttons on the Insert tab.

When you insert a graphic and when specific built-in layouts are applied to the slide, the Design Ideas pane opens containing suggestions for interesting layouts for the slide. You can click one of these layouts to apply it or close the Design Ideas pane without accepting any of the suggestions.

Anthony has a photo that he wants you to insert on Slide 2.

To insert a photo on Slide 2 and view the Design Ideas:

1. Display Slide 2 ("About Us"), and then in the content placeholder on the right, click the **Pictures** button. The Insert Picture dialog box opens. This dialog box is similar to the Open dialog box.
2. Navigate to the **PowerPoint1 > Module** folder included with your Data Files, click **Support_PPT_1_Family.jpg**, and then click **Insert**. The dialog box closes, and a picture of a family in front of medical professionals appears in the placeholder and is selected. Text that describes the picture might appear briefly at the bottom of the picture. Also, the Design Ideas pane might open listing suggestions for interesting layouts for this slide. On the ribbon, the contextual Picture Format tab appears and is the active tab. See Figure 1–26.

Figure 1–26 Picture inserted on Slide 2

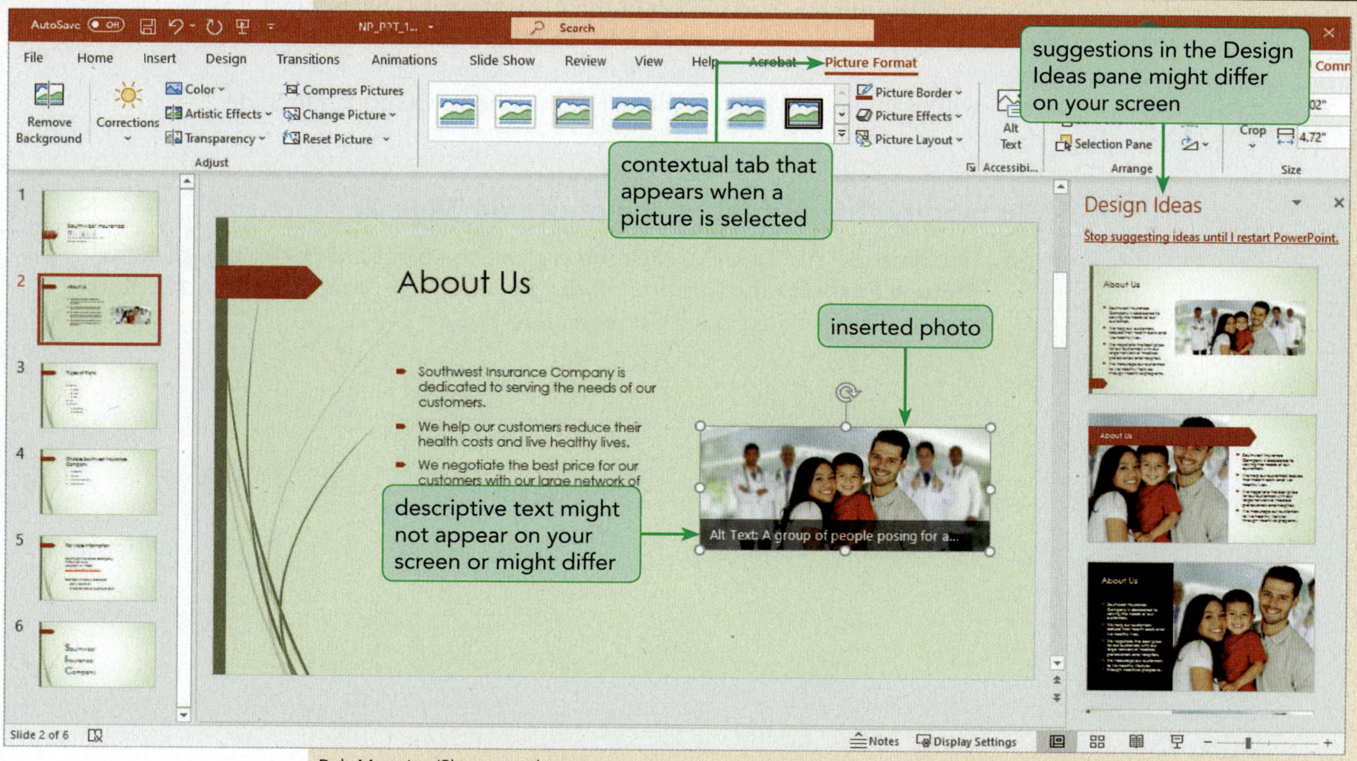

Rob Marmion/Shutterstock.com

Trouble? If the Design Ideas pane does not appear, click the Design tab, and then in the Designer group, click the Design Ideas button.

Trouble? If the descriptive text does not appear below the picture, do not be concerned. You will display it later.

3. In the Design Ideas pane, click each of the thumbnails to see the effect on the slide. Although Anthony likes some of the layouts suggested in the Design Ideas pane, he wants you to apply the Two Content layout again. First, you need to undo the change you made.
4. On the Quick Access Toolbar, click the **Undo arrow**. No matter how many thumbnails you clicked in the Design Ideas pane, only one "Apply Design Idea" action is listed in the Undo menu.
5. On the menu, click **Apply Design Idea**. The slide is reset to its original layout.
6. In the Design Ideas pane, in the top-right corner, click the **Close** button. The pane closes.

Tip

You can click the Redo button on the Quick Access Toolbar to redo an action.

The layout suggestions in the Design Ideas pane can help you create interesting slides. If you open the Design Ideas pane and it does not contain any suggestions, make sure you are using one of the themes that is included with PowerPoint, and change the slide layout to Title Slide or Title and Content.

Although graphics can make a slide more interesting, people with limited vision might not be able to see them clearly and people who are blind cannot see them at all. People with vision challenges might use a screen reader to view your presentation. A screen reader identifies objects on the screen and produces an audio of the text. Graphics cause problems for users of screen readers unless the graphics have alternative text. **Alternative text**, usually shortened to **alt text**, is descriptive text added to an object.

When you add a picture to a slide, alt text for the picture is automatically created and displayed at the bottom of the picture. The alt text on the picture disappears after a few moments, but you can view it in the Alt Text pane. The automatic alt text is not always correct, so you should check it to make sure that it accurately describes the image.

You will examine and edit the alt text of the photo you added to Slide 2.

To modify the alt text of the photo on Slide 2:

1. On Slide 2 ("About Us"), click the picture to select it if necessary, click the **Picture Format** tab, and then in the Accessibility group, click the **Alt Text** button. The Alt Text pane appears. See Figure 1–27.

Figure 1–27 Alt Text pane open showing automatically generated alt text

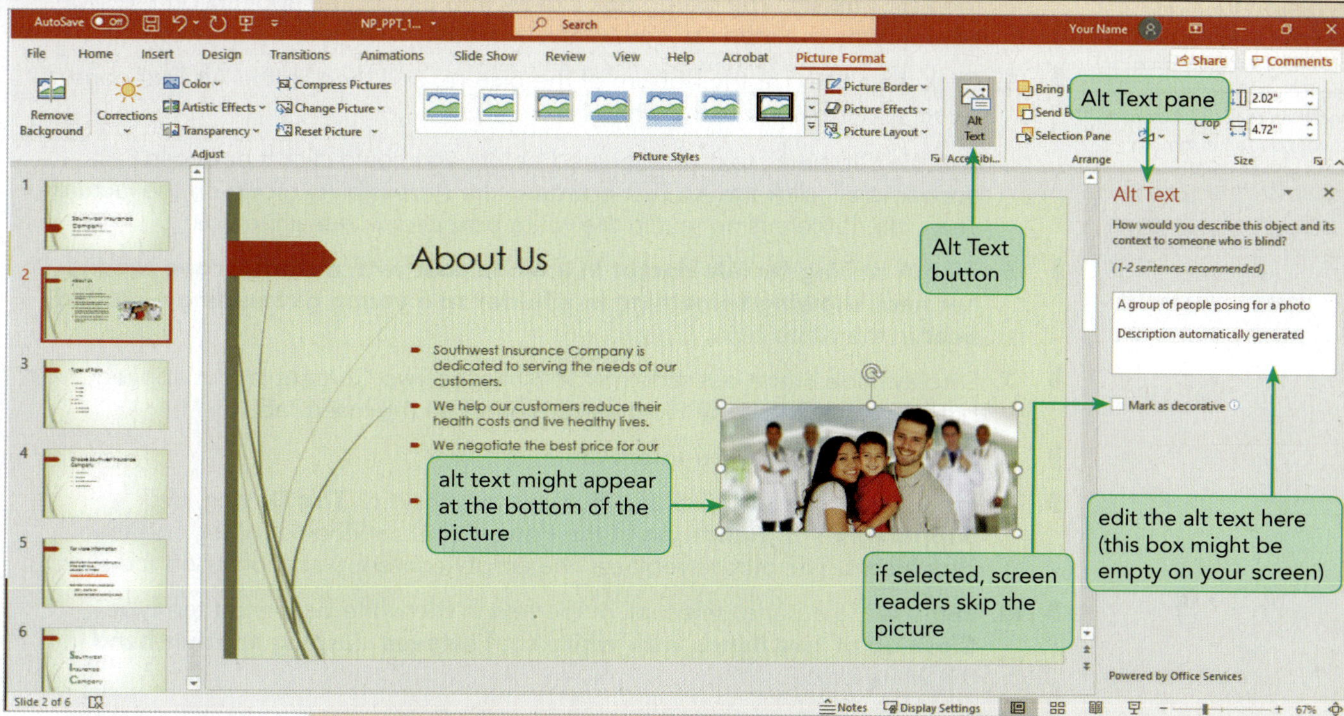

Rob Marmion/Shutterstock.com

Trouble? If alt text is not automatically generated, this feature might be turned off on your computer or your computer might not have been able to connect to the Microsoft server. Click in the white box in the Alt Text pane, and then skip Step 2.

Tip

Another way to open the Alt Text pane is to click the alt text when it appears on the bottom of the picture when the picture is first inserted.

2. In the Alt Text pane, in the white box, select all of the text, including the phrase "Description automatically generated."
3. Type **Happy mother, young son, and father standing in front of medical professionals** in the white box. The text you type replaces the selected text. The next time you select the picture, a new command—Generate a description for me—will appear. You could click that command to have the alt text generated again, replacing the text you typed.
4. In the Alt Text pane, in the top-right corner, click the **Close** button.

Anthony has two more photos that he wants you to add to the presentation. He asks you to add the photos to Slides 3 and 6.

To insert photos on Slides 3 and 6:

1. Display Slide 3 ("Types of Plans"). This slide has the Title and Content layout applied, so it does not have a second content placeholder. You can change the layout to include a second content placeholder, or you can use a command on the ribbon to insert a photo.
2. Click the **Insert** tab, and then in the Images group, click the **Pictures** button. The Insert Picture From gallery appears.
3. Click **This Device** to select a picture on your computer. The Insert Picture dialog box opens.

Tip

To convert pictures to SmartArt, select all the pictures on a slide, click the Picture Format tab, and then click the Picture Layout button in the Picture Styles group.

4. In the PowerPoint1 > Module folder, click **Support_PPT_1_Doctor.jpg**, and then click **Insert**. The dialog box closes, and the picture appears on the slide, covering the bulleted list. You will fix this later.
5. Click the alt text at the bottom of the picture, and then, in the Alt Text pane, select all of the text in the white box.

   Trouble? If the alt text disappeared before you could click it or doesn't appear at all, click the Alt Text button in the Accessibility group on the Picture Tools tab. If there is no text in the white box, click in the white box.
6. Type **A smiling female doctor in a white coat with a stethoscope around her neck showing something in a folder to a young girl holding a stuffed bear** in the white box.
7. Display Slide 6 (the last slide). Slide 6 has the Two Content layout applied, but you can still use the Pictures command on the Insert tab.
8. On the ribbon, click the **Insert** tab.
9. In the Images group, click the **Pictures** button, click **This Device**, click **Support_PPT_1_Hands.jpg** in the PowerPoint1 > Module folder, and then click **Insert**. The picture replaces the empty content placeholder on the slide.
10. In the Alt Text pane, select all of the text in the white box, and then type **Close-up of two hands with white coat sleeves clasping another hand** in the white box.
11. Close the Alt Text pane, and then close the Design Ideas pane, if necessary.

Proskills

Decision Making: Deciding Whether to Allow Alt Text to Be Generated

People are becoming much more aware of privacy concerns when posting information to the cloud or to social media. When you insert a picture on a slide, the picture is sent to Microsoft's servers in order to generate alt text. This means that you are sharing the picture in the cloud. If you are concerned about sharing your private pictures, you can turn this feature off. To do this, click the File tab, and then click Options to open the PowerPoint Options dialog box. On the left, click Ease of Access to display the options for making PowerPoint more accessible. In the Automatic Alt Text section, click the Automatically generate alt text for me check box to deselect it. If you change your mind and you want alt text generated for a specific picture, you can still click the command to generate new alt text in the Alt Text pane.

Cropping Pictures

Sometimes you want to display only part of a photo. For example, if you insert a photo of a party scene that includes a bouquet of colorful balloons, you might want to show only the balloons. To do this, you can crop the photo. To **crop** means to trim away part of a picture. In PowerPoint, you can crop a picture to any size you want, crop it to a preset ratio, or crop it to a shape.

It can be helpful to display rulers and gridlines in the window to help you crop photos to specific sizes. There are two rulers. One is horizontal and appears above the slide. The other is vertical and appears to the left of the slide. **Gridlines** are evenly spaced horizontal and vertical lines on the slide that help you align objects.

Anthony wants you to crop the photo on Slide 3 ("Types of Plans") to make the dimensions of the final photo smaller without making the images in the photo smaller.

To crop the photo on Slide 3:

1. Click the **View** tab, and then in the Show group, click the **Ruler** and the **Gridlines** check boxes. Rulers appear above and to the left of the displayed slide, and the gridlines appear on the slide.
2. Display Slide 3 ("Types of Plans"), click the photo to select it, and then click the **Picture Format** tab, if necessary.
3. In the Size group, click the **Crop** button. The Crop button is selected, and crop handles appear around the edges of the photo just inside the sizing handles. See Figure 1–28.

Figure 1–28 **Photo with crop handles**

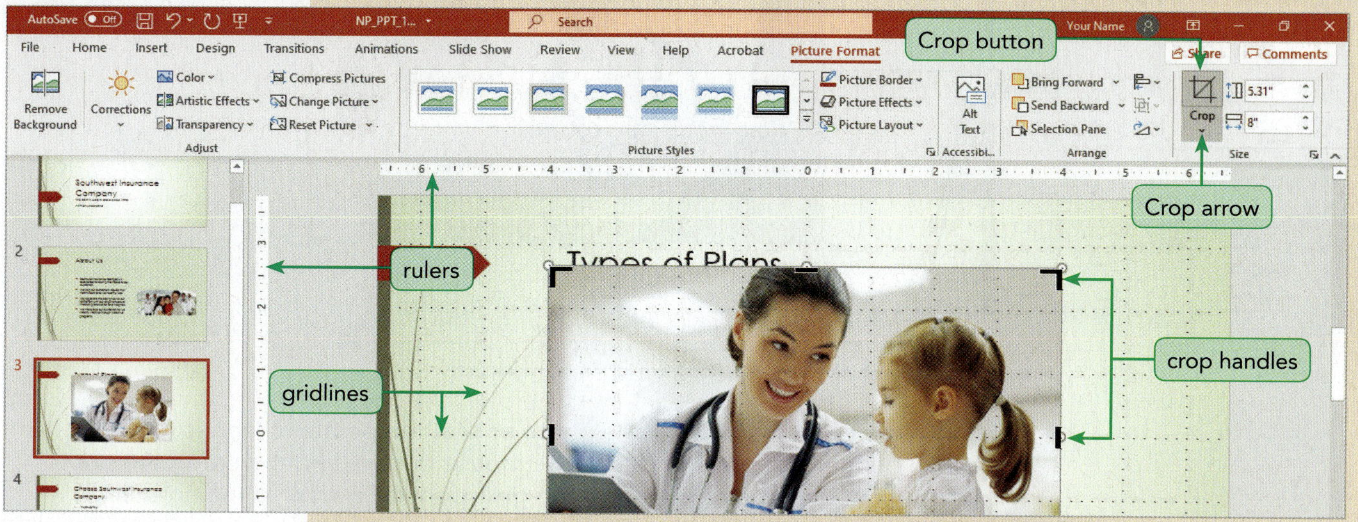

Yuganov Konstantin/Shutterstock.com; Rob Marmion/Shutterstock.com

4. Position the pointer directly on top of the middle crop handle on the left side of the picture so that it changes to the left-middle crop pointer ┫. On the rulers, a red dotted line shows the position of the pointer.
5. Press and hold the mouse button, drag the crop handle to the right until the left cropped edge is on the gridline that aligns with the negative 3-inch mark on the horizontal ruler, and then release the mouse button. The part of the photo that will be cropped off is shaded dark gray. See Figure 1–29.

Figure 1–29 Cropped photo

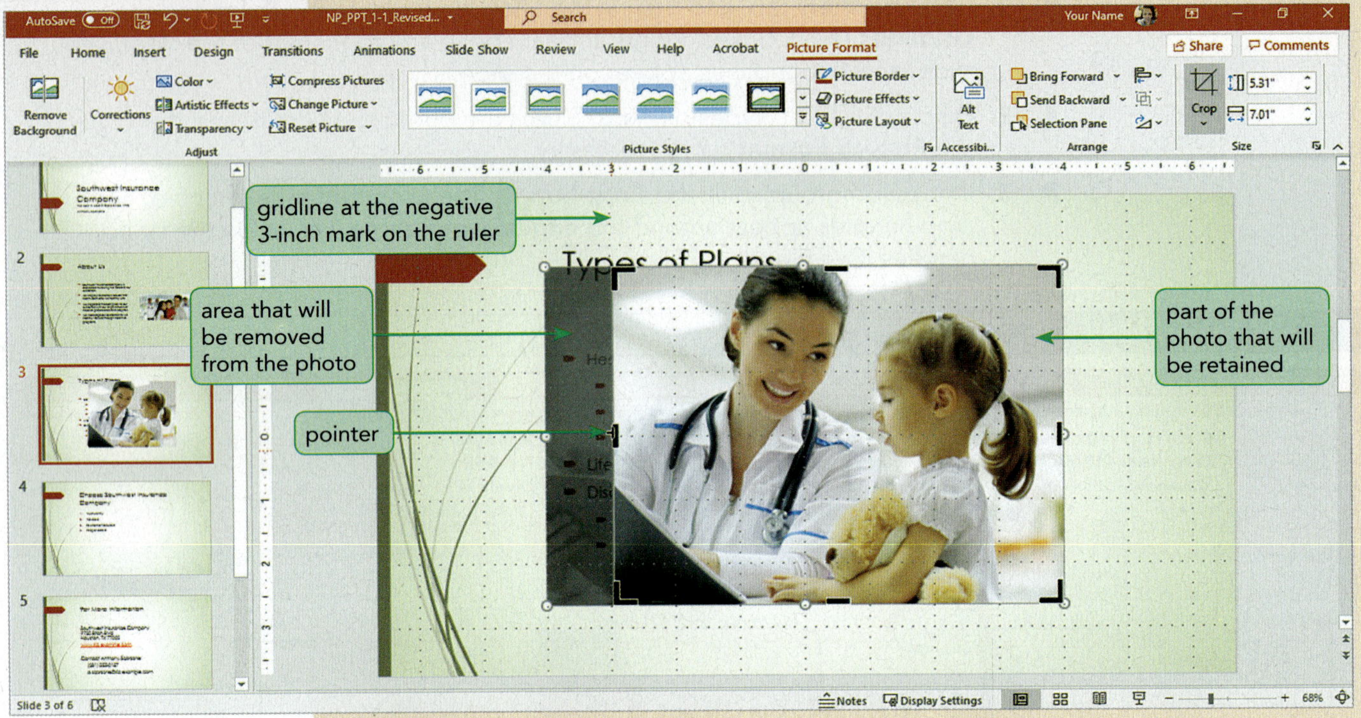

Yuganov Konstantin/Shutterstock.com; Rob Marmion/Shutterstock.com

6. Move the pointer on top of the photo so that the pointer changes to the move pointer, press and hold the mouse button, and then drag the photo to the right until the right side of the girl's ponytail is next to the right edge of the visible part of the photo. See Figure 1–30.

Figure 1–30 Photo moved inside cropped area

Yuganov Konstantin/Shutterstock.com; Rob Marmion/Shutterstock.com

7. Click the **Crop** button again. The Crop feature turns off, but the photo is still selected, and the Picture Format tab is still the active tab.

When you crop a picture to a shape, the picture fills the shape. Anthony wants you to crop the photo on Slide 6 (the last slide) so that it fills a cross shape.

To crop the photo on Slide 6 to a shape:

1. Display Slide 6 (the last slide), click the photo to select it, and then click the **Picture Format** tab, if necessary.
2. In the Size group, click the **Crop arrow**. The Crop menu opens. See Figure 1–31.

Figure 1–31 Crop button menu

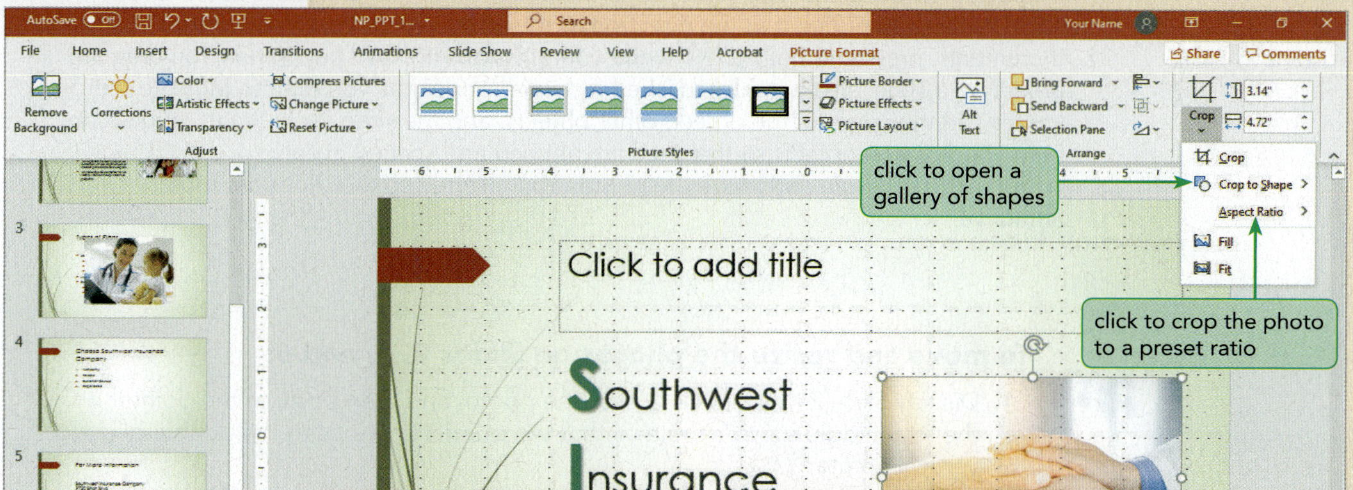

REDPIXEL.PL/Shutterstock.com; Yuganov Konstantin/Shutterstock.com; Rob Marmion/Shutterstock.com

Tip

Some SmartArt layouts include shapes with a Pictures button. You can click that button to insert a picture in the shape so that it fills the shape.

3. Point to **Crop to Shape** to open a gallery of shapes, and then in the second row under Basic Shapes, click the **Cross** shape. The photo is cropped to a cross shape. Notice that the rectangular selection border of the original photo is still showing.
4. In the Size group, click the **Crop** button. You can now see the cropped portions of the original, rectangle photo that are shaded gray.
5. Click a blank area of the slide. The picture is no longer selected, and the Home tab is the active tab on the ribbon.

If you want to change how a picture is cropped, you can adjust the crop by selecting the picture and clicking the Crop button again. The cropped portion of the picture will be visible, and you can move the picture inside the crop marks or drag the crop handles to change how the picture is cropped. To change the crop so that the entire picture appears in the shape at its original aspect ratio, click the Fit command on the Crop menu. To change it back so that the picture fills the shape again, click the Fill command on the Crop menu.

Resizing and Moving Objects

You can resize and move any object to best fit the space available on a slide. One way to resize an object is to drag a sizing handle. **Sizing handles** are small circles at the corners, and often the edges, of a selected object. When you use this method, you can adjust the size of the object so that it best fits the space visually. If you need to size an object to exact dimensions, you can modify the measurements in the Size group on the Format tab that appears when you select the object.

The **aspect ratio** of an object is the proportional relationship between an object's height and width. Pictures and other objects that cause the Picture Format tab to appear when you select them have their aspect ratios locked. This means that if you resize the object by dragging a corner sizing handle or by changing the measurement in either the Height or the Width box in the Size group on the Picture Format tab, both the height and the width of the object will change by the same proportions. However, if you drag one of the sizing handles on the side of the object, you will override the locked aspect ratio setting and resize the object only in the direction you drag. Generally, you do not want to do this with photos because the images will become distorted.

If you want to reposition an object on a slide, you drag it. If you need to move a selected object just a very small distance on the slide, you can press one of the ARROW keys to nudge it in the direction of the arrow. To move it in even smaller increments, press and hold CTRL while you press an ARROW key. When you drag an object on a slide, **smart guides**, dashed red lines, appear as you drag to indicate the center and the edges of the object, other objects, and the slide itself. Smart guides can help you position objects so that they are aligned and spaced evenly.

You need to resize and move the photos you inserted so the slides are more attractive.

To move and resize the photos on Slides 2, 3, and 6:

1. Display Slide 2 ("About Us"), click the photo, and then position the pointer on the top-middle sizing handle so that the pointer changes to the double-headed vertical pointer ↕.
2. Press and hold the mouse button so that the pointer changes to the thin cross pointer +, drag the top-middle sizing handle up approximately two inches, and then release the mouse button. The photo is two inches taller, but the image is distorted. You can undo the change you made.
3. On the Quick Access Toolbar, click the **Undo** button. The photo returns to its original size. You need to resize the photo by dragging a corner sizing handle to maintain the aspect ratio.
4. Click the **Picture Format** tab if necessary, and then note the measurements in the Height and Width boxes in the Size group. The photo is 2.02 inches high and 4.72 inches wide.
5. Position the pointer on the top-left corner sizing handle so that it changes to the double-headed diagonal pointer ⤡, press and hold the mouse button so that the pointer changes to the thin cross pointer +, and then drag the top-left sizing handle up. Even though you are dragging in only one direction, because you are dragging a corner sizing handle, both the width and height change proportionately to maintain the aspect ratio of the photo.
6. When the left edge of the photo is aligned with the gridline dots that are below the negative 0.5-inch mark on the horizontal ruler, release the mouse button. In the Height and Width boxes, the measurements changed to reflect the picture's new size.

Tip

To replace a picture with another picture at the same size and position, right-click the picture, and then click Change Picture.

7. If the measurement in the Shape Height box in the Size group is not 2.5, click in the Shape Height box to select the current measurement, type **2.5**, and then press **ENTER**.
8. Drag the photo so that the right edge of the photo aligns with the right edge of the slide, and the top of the photo is aligned with the top of the bulleted list, as shown in Figure 1–32.

Figure 1–32 Repositioning the photo on Slide 2 using smart guides and gridlines

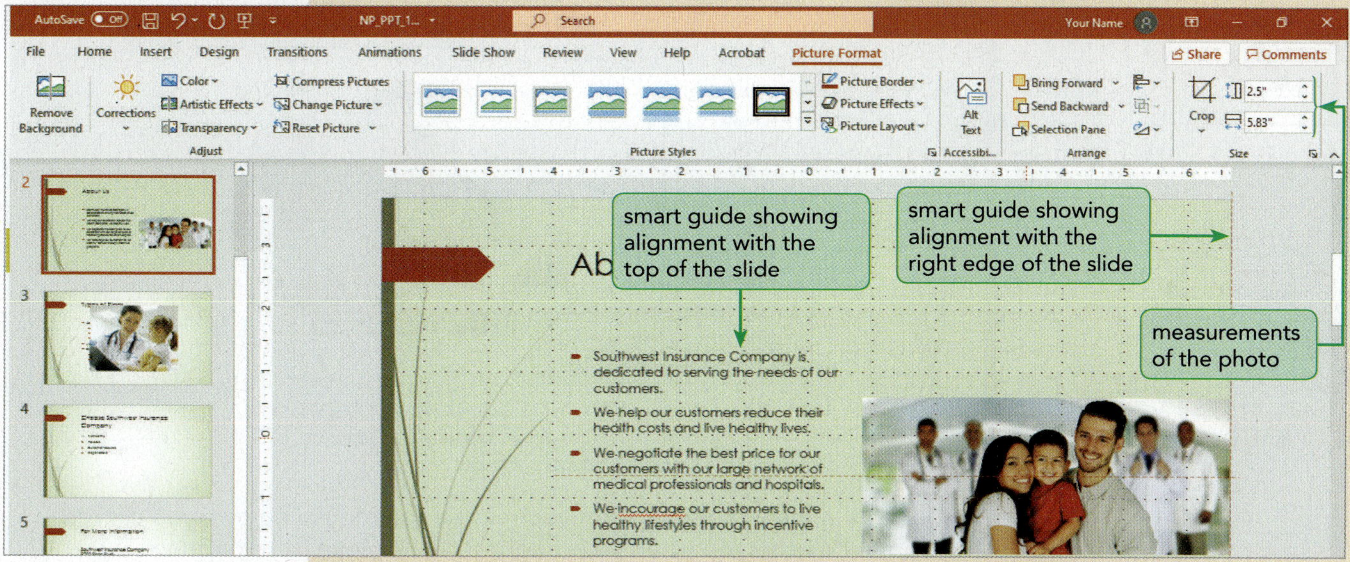

Rob Marmion/Shutterstock.com; Yuganov Konstantin/Shutterstock.com

Trouble? If the smart guides do not appear, click the View tab, and then in the Show group, click the Dialog Box Launcher to open the Grid and Guides dialog box. Click the "Display smart guides when shapes are aligned" check box to select it.

9. Release the mouse button. The photo is in its new location.
10. Display Slide 3 ("Types of Plans"), click the photo to select it, and then click the **Picture Format** tab if necessary.
11. In the Size group, click in the **Shape Height** box to select the current measurement, type **4**, and then press **ENTER**. The measurement in the Shape Width box in the Size group changes proportionately to maintain the aspect ratio, and the new measurements are applied to the photo.
12. Drag the photo down and to the right until a horizontal smart guide appears indicating that the top of the photo is about one-eighth of an inch above the top of the bulleted list and aligned with the gridline dots at the $1\frac{3}{8}$-inch mark on the vertical ruler, and a vertical smart guide appears showing that the left edge of the photo aligns with the center of the slide and with the gridline at the 0-inch mark on the horizontal ruler, as shown in Figure 1–33.

Figure 1–33 Moving the resized photo on Slide 3

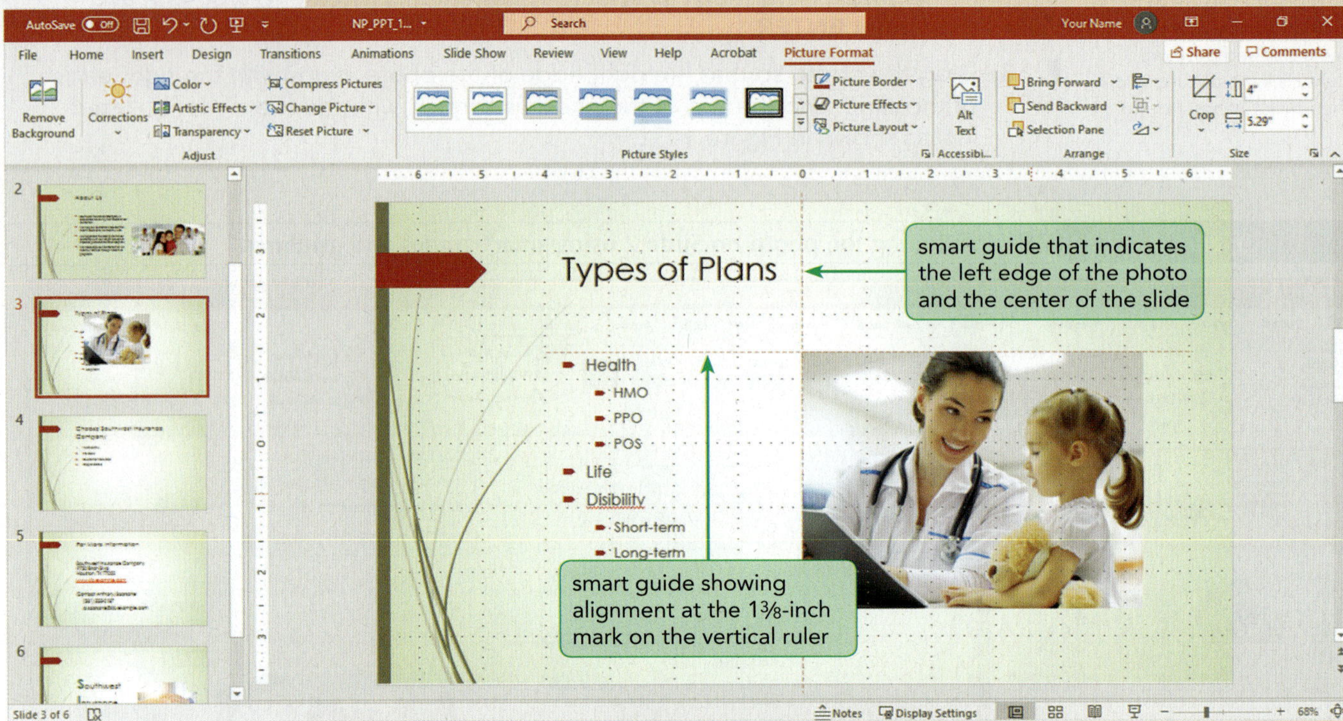

Rob Marmion/Shutterstock.com; Yuganov Konstantin/Shutterstock.com

Trouble? If a menu appears after you release the mouse button, you clicked the right mouse button when you dragged. Click Move Here on the menu, and then check to make sure the photo is positioned as described in Step 12.

13. When the photo is aligned as shown in Figure 1–33, release the mouse button.

14. Display Slide 6 (the last slide), and then position the photo so that the top of the photo aligns with the smart guide that indicates the middle of the title text box and the right edge aligns with the smart guide that indicates the right edge of the title text box.

Text boxes, like other objects that cause the Shape Format tab to appear when selected, do not have their aspect ratios locked. This means that when you resize a text box by dragging a corner sizing handle or changing one measurement in the Shape Height box or the Shape Width box in the Size group, the other dimension does not change.

Like any other object on a slide, you can reposition text boxes. To do this, you must position the pointer on the text box border, anywhere except on a sizing handle, to drag it to its new location.

To improve the appearance of Slide 6, you will resize the text box containing the unnumbered list so that it vertically fills the slide.

To resize the text box on Slide 6:

1. On Slide 6 (the last slide), click the unnumbered list to display the text box border.
2. Position the pointer on the top-middle sizing handle so that it changes to the double-headed vertical pointer, and then drag the sizing handle up until the top edge of the text box aligns with the top edge of the title text placeholder.
3. Drag the right-middle sizing handle to the left so that the right border of the text box is aligned with the negative 1.5-inch mark on the ruler. Next, you will shift the text box a little to the right.
4. Position the pointer on top of the border of the text box so that it changes to the move pointer, and then drag the text box to the right so that the right border of the text box aligns with the smart guide that indicates the center of the slide. Even though the title text placeholder will not appear during a slide show, you will delete it to see how the final slide will look.
5. Click the border of the title text placeholder, and then press **DELETE**. See Figure 1–34.

Tip

If you want to hide the smart guides while you are moving an object, press and hold ALT while you are dragging.

Figure 1–34 Slide 6 with resized text box

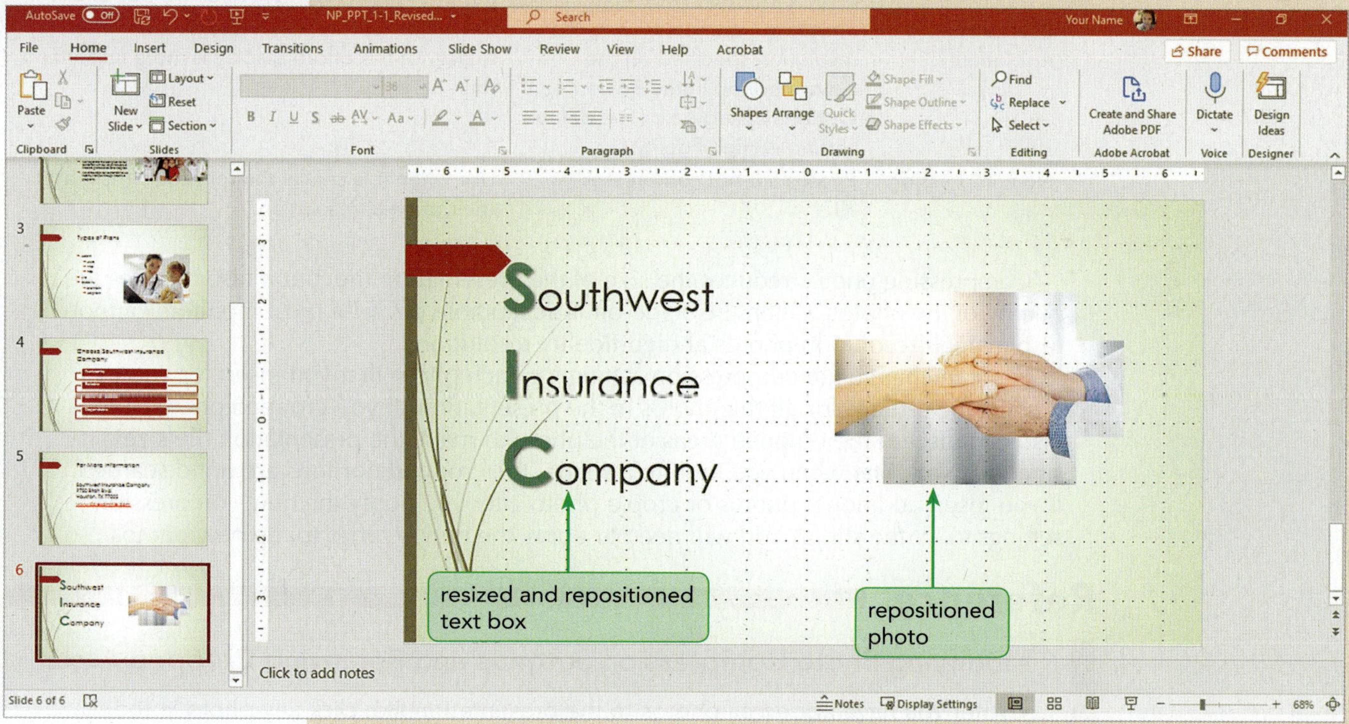

REDPIXEL.PL/Shutterstock.com; Yuganov Konstantin/Shutterstock.com; Rob Marmion/Shutterstock.com

6. Click the **View** tab, and then click the **Ruler** and **Gridlines** check boxes to deselect them. The ruler and the gridlines disappear.
7. Save the changes to the presentation.

Compressing Pictures

When you save a presentation that contains pictures, you can choose to compress the pictures to make the size of the PowerPoint file smaller. See Figure 1–35 for a description of the compression options available.

Figure 1–35 Photo compression settings

Compression Setting	Compression Value	When to Use
High fidelity	Photos are compressed very minimally, and only if they are larger than the slide.	Use when a presentation will be viewed on a high-definition (HD) display, when photograph quality is of the highest concern, and file size is not an issue. This is the default setting.
HD (330 ppi)	Photos are compressed to 330 pixels per inch.	Use when slides need to maintain the quality of the photograph when displayed on HD displays, but file size is of some concern.
Print (220 ppi)	Photos are compressed to 220 pixels per inch.	Use when slides need to maintain the quality of the photograph when printed.
Web (150 ppi)	Photos are compressed to 150 pixels per inch.	Use when the presentation will be viewed on a low-definition display.
E-mail (96 ppi)	Photos are compressed to 96 pixels per inch.	Use for presentations that need to be emailed or uploaded to a webpage or when it is important to keep the overall file size small.
Use default resolution	Photos are compressed to the resolution specified on the Advanced tab in the PowerPoint Options dialog box. (The default setting is High fidelity.)	Use when file size is not an issue, or when quality of the photo display is more important than file size.
No compression	Photos are not compressed at all.	Use when it is critical that photos remain at their original resolution.

Compressing photos reduces the size of the presentation file, but it also reduces the quality of the photos. Often this trade-off is acceptable because most monitors cannot display high-resolution photos at high-fidelity resolution.

You can change the compression setting for each photo that you insert, or you can change the settings for all the photos in the presentation. If you cropped photos, you also can discard the cropped areas of the photo to make the presentation file size smaller. (Note that when you crop to a shape, the cropped portions are not discarded.) If you insert additional photos or crop a photo after you apply the new compression settings to all the slides, you will need to apply the new settings to the new photos.

Reference

Modifying Photo Compression Settings and Removing Cropped Areas

- After you have added all photos to the presentation file, click any photo in the presentation to select it.
- Click the Picture Format tab. In the Adjust group, click the Compress Pictures button.
- In the Compress Pictures dialog box, click the option button next to the resolution you want to use.
- To apply the new compression settings to all the photos in the presentation, click the Apply only to this picture check box to deselect it.
- To keep cropped areas of photos, click the Delete cropped areas of pictures check box to deselect it.
- Click OK.

You will adjust the compression settings to make the file size of the presentation as small as possible so that Anthony can easily send it or post it for others without worrying about file size limitations on the receiving server.

To modify photo compression settings and remove cropped areas from photos:

1. On Slide 6 (the last slide), click the photo, and then click the **Picture Format** tab, if necessary.
2. In the Adjust group, click the **Compress Pictures** button. The Compress Pictures dialog box opens. See Figure 1–36. Under Resolution, the Use default resolution option button is selected. (If an option in this dialog box is gray and is not available for you to select, the photo is a lower resolution than that option.)

Figure 1–36 Compress Pictures dialog box

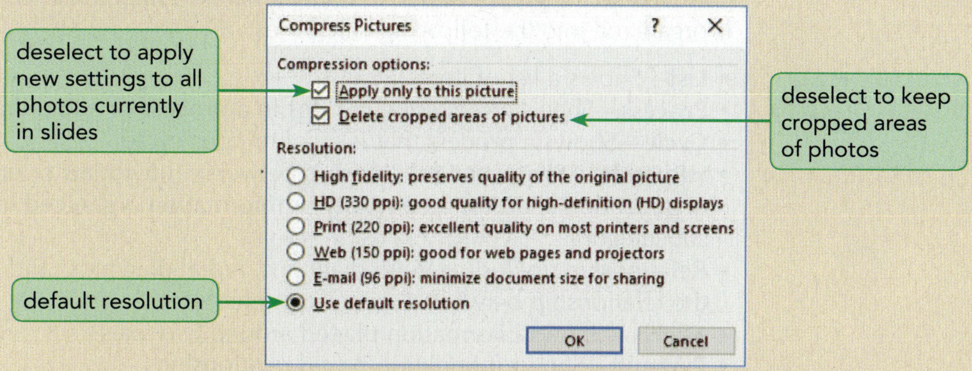

3. Click the **E-mail (96 ppi)** option button. This setting compresses the photos to the smallest size available. At the top of the dialog box under Compression options, the Apply only to this picture check box is selected. You want the settings applied to all the photos in the file.
4. Click the **Apply only to this picture** check box to deselect it. The Delete cropped areas of pictures check box is also selected. You want the presentation file size to be as small as possible, so you'll leave this option selected.

   Trouble? If the Delete cropped areas of pictures check box is not selected, click it.

Be sure you deselect the Apply only to this picture check box and be sure you are satisfied with the way you cropped the photo on Slide 3 before you click OK to close the dialog box.

5. Click **OK**.

   The dialog box closes and the compression settings are applied to all the photos in the presentation. You can confirm that the cropped areas of photos were removed by examining the photo on Slide 3. (The photo on Slide 6 was cropped to a shape, so the cropped areas on it were not removed, in case you later change to a different shape cropping.)
6. Display Slide 3 ("Types of Plans"), click the photo, and then click the **Picture Format** tab, if necessary.
7. In the Size group, click the **Crop** button. The Crop handles appear around the photo, but the portions of the photo that you cropped out no longer appear.
8. Click the **Crop** button again to deselect it, and then save the changes to the presentation.

Insight

Changing the Default Compression Settings for Pictures

In PowerPoint, the default compression setting for pictures is High fidelity. This means that High fidelity compression is automatically applied to pictures when the file is saved. You can change this setting if you want. To change the settings, click the File tab to open Backstage view, click Options in the navigation pane to open the PowerPoint Options dialog box, click Advanced in the navigation pane, and then locate the Image Size and Quality section. To choose a different compression setting, click the Default resolution arrow, and then select a setting in the list. To prevent pictures from being compressed at all, click the Do not compress images in file check box. Note that these changes affect only the current presentation.

Converting a List to a SmartArt Graphic

A **SmartArt graphic** is a diagram that shows information or ideas visually using a combination of shapes and text. Some SmartArt shapes also contain pictures. SmartArt is organized into the following categories:

- **List**—Shows a list of items
- **Process**—Shows a sequence of steps in a process or a timeline
- **Cycle**—Shows a process that is a continuous cycle
- **Hierarchy**—Shows the relationship between individuals or units, such as an organization chart for a company or information organized into categories and subcategories
- **Relationship** (including Venn diagrams, radial diagrams, and target diagrams)—Shows the relationship between two or more elements
- **Matrix**—Shows information placed around two axes
- **Pyramid**—Shows foundation-based relationships
- **Picture**—Provides a location for a picture or pictures that you insert

When you create a SmartArt graphic, you need to choose a SmartArt layout. In SmartArt, a **layout** is the shapes and arrangement of the shapes in the SmartArt graphic. Once you create a SmartArt graphic, you can easily change the layout to another one if you want.

A quick way to create a SmartArt graphic is to convert an existing list. There are two ways to do this. First, you can try displaying the Design Ideas pane. When the Design Ideas pane shows options for a slide that contains a list, some of the layouts include the list transformed into a SmartArt graphic. The other way you can create a SmartArt graphic from a list is to click the Convert to SmartArt Graphic button in the Paragraph group on the Home tab.

When you change a list to SmartArt, each first-level item in the list is converted to a shape in the SmartArt. If the list contains subitems, you might need to experiment with different layouts to find one that best suits the information in your list.

Reference

Converting a List into SmartArt

- Display the slide containing the list you want to convert to SmartArt.
- If the Design Ideas pane does not open, click the Design tab on the ribbon, and then in the Designer group, click the Design Ideas button.
- In the Design Ideas pane, select the SmartArt and slide layout that you want to use.

or

- Click anywhere in the list that you want to convert.
- In the Paragraph group on the Home tab, click the Convert to SmartArt button, and then click More SmartArt Graphics.
- In the Choose a SmartArt Graphic dialog box, select the desired SmartArt category in the list on the left.
- In the center pane, click the SmartArt you want to use.
- Click OK.

Anthony wants you to change the numbered list on Slide 4 into a SmartArt diagram.

To convert the list on Slide 4 into SmartArt:

1. Display Slide 4 ("Choose Southwest Insurance Company").
2. If the Design Ideas pane does not open, click the **Design** tab on the ribbon, and then, in the Designer group, click the **Design Ideas** button. The Design Ideas pane opens on the right. Your screen will look similar to the one shown in Figure 1–37.

Figure 1–37 Design Ideas pane with suggestions for the list on Slide 4

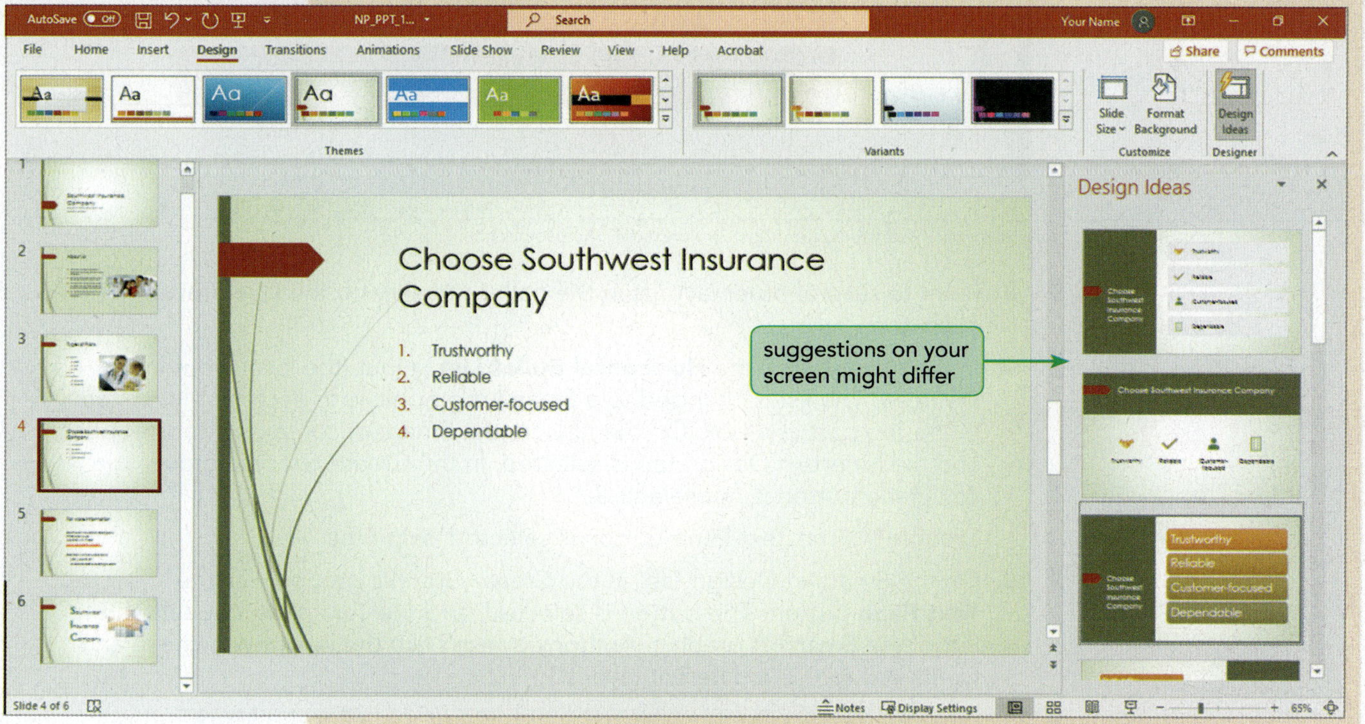

Rob Marmion/Shutterstock.com; Yuganov Konstantin/Shutterstock.com; REDPIXEL.PL/Shutterstock.com

3. In the Design Ideas pane, click several of the thumbnails to see the effect on the slide.

4. After you are finished exploring the layouts in the Design Ideas pane, click the **Undo** button on the Quick Access Toolbar. The slide resets to its original layout.
5. Close the Design Ideas pane, and then on the slide, click anywhere in the list.
6. On the ribbon, click the **Home** tab, and then in the Paragraph group, click the **Convert to SmartArt Graphic** button. A gallery opens listing SmartArt layouts.
7. Point to the first layout. The ScreenTip identifies this layout as the Vertical Bullet List layout, and Live Preview shows you what the list will look like with that layout applied. See Figure 1–38.

Figure 1–38 **Live Preview of the Vertical Bullet List SmartArt layout**

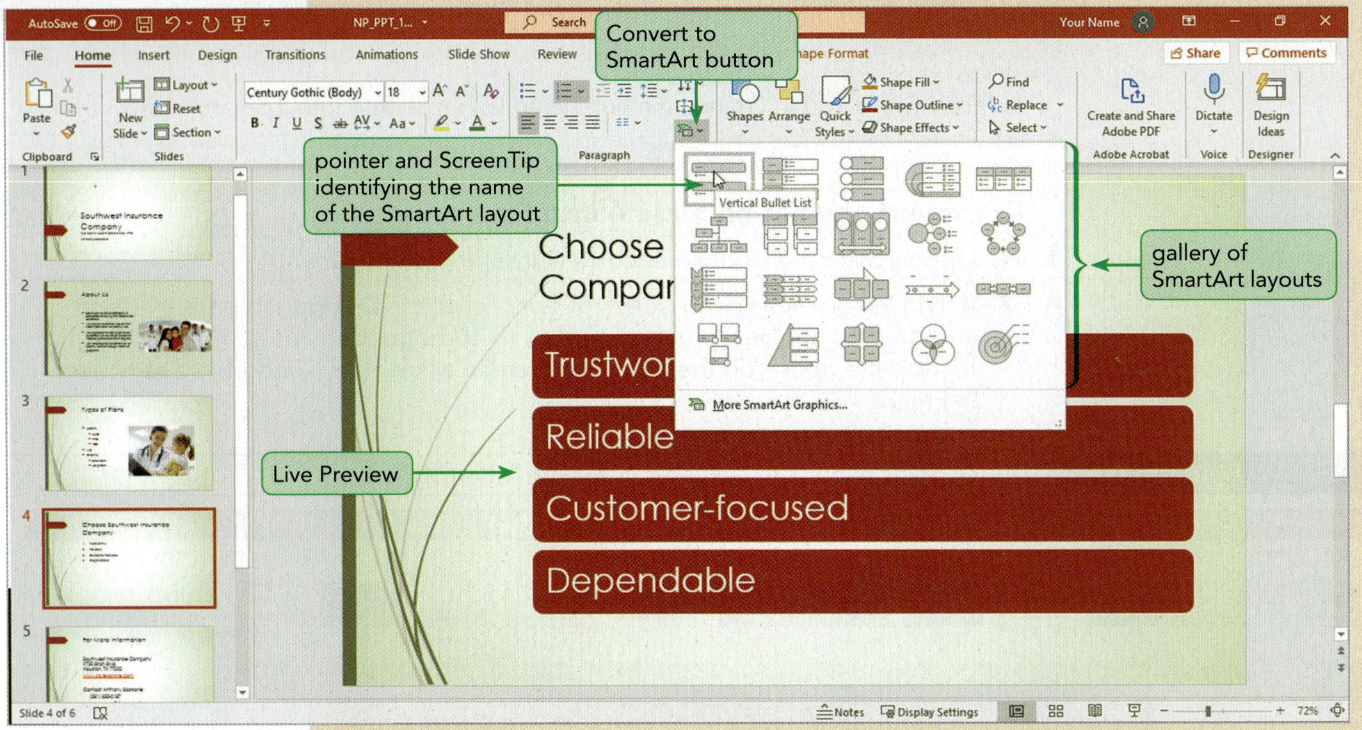

Rob Marmion/Shutterstock.com; Yuganov Konstantin/Shutterstock.com

8. Point to several other layouts in the gallery, observing the Live Preview of each one.
9. In the gallery, click the **Horizontal Bullet List** layout (the last layout in the first row). The list is changed to a SmartArt graphic with each first-level item in the top part of a box. On the ribbon, the SmartArt contextual tabs appear, and the SmartArt Design tab is selected. In the Create Graphic group, the Text Pane button is not selected.

   Trouble? If the Text Pane button is selected, skip Step 10.
10. On the SmartArt Design tab, in the Create Graphic group, click the **Text Pane** button. The button is selected, and the Text pane appears to the left of the SmartArt graphic. Anthony doesn't like the layout you chose and wants you to use a different layout.
11. On the SmartArt Design tab, in the Layouts group, click the **More** button. A gallery of SmartArt layouts appears.
12. At the bottom of the gallery, click **More Layouts**. The Choose a SmartArt Graphic dialog box opens. See Figure 1–39. You can click a category in the left pane to filter the middle pane to show only the layouts in that category.

Figure 1–39 Choose a SmartArt Graphic dialog box

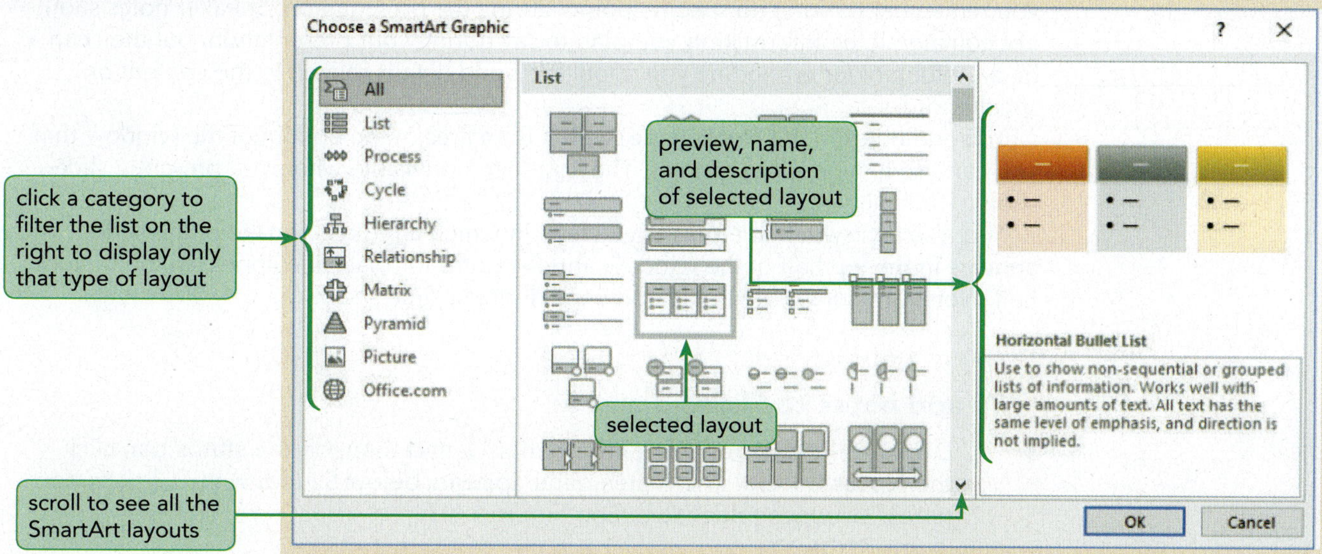

13. In the left pane, click **List**, and then in the middle pane, click the **Vertical Box List** layout, using the ScreenTips to identify it. The right pane changes to show a description of that layout.

14. Click **OK**. The dialog box closes, and each of the first-level items in the list appears in the colored shapes in the diagram. The items also appear as a bulleted list in the Text pane. See Figure 1–40.

Figure 1–40 SmartArt graphic with the Vertical Box List layout

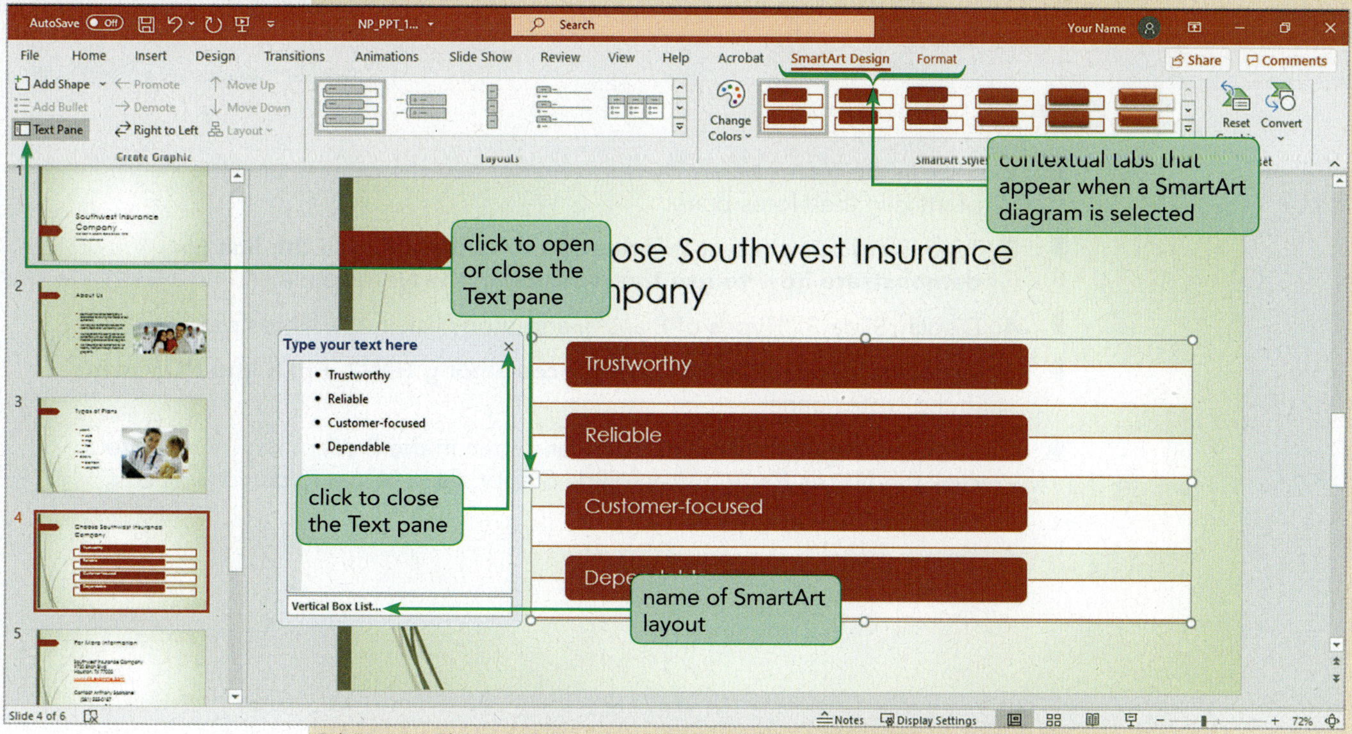

Rob Marmion/Shutterstock.com; Yuganov Konstantin/Shutterstock.com

15. To the right of the text pane, click the **Collapse text pane** button [>]. The text pane closes.

Adding Speaker Notes

Speaker notes, or simply **notes**, are information you add about slide content to help you remember to bring up specific points during the presentation. Speaker notes should not contain all the information you plan to say during your presentation, but they can be a useful tool for reminding you about facts and details related to the content on specific slides.

You add notes in the **Notes pane**, which is an area at the bottom of the window that you can use to type speaker notes. The notes are not visible when you present a slide show.

You also can switch to **Notes Page view**, in which a reduced image of the slide appears in the top half of the window and the notes for that slide appear in the bottom half. Notes are not visible to the audience during a slide show.

To add notes to Slides 3 and 5:

1. Display Slide 5 ("For More Information"), and then, on the status bar, click the **Notes** button. The Notes pane appears below Slide 5 with "Click to add notes" as placeholder text. See Figure 1–41.

Figure 1–41 Notes pane below Slide 5

REDPIXEL.PL/Shutterstock.com

2. Click in the Notes pane. The placeholder text disappears, and the insertion point is in the Notes pane.
3. Type **Hand out contact information to audience. Use the link to demonstrate how to use the website.** in the Notes pane.
4. Display Slide 3 ("Types of Plans"), and then click in the Notes pane.
5. Type **Briefly describe the differences among HMO, PPO, and POS plans.** in the Notes pane.
6. Click the **View** tab on the ribbon, and then in the Presentation Views group, click the **Notes Page** button. Slide 3 appears in Notes Page view. See Figure 1–42.

Figure 1–42 Slide 3 in Notes Page view

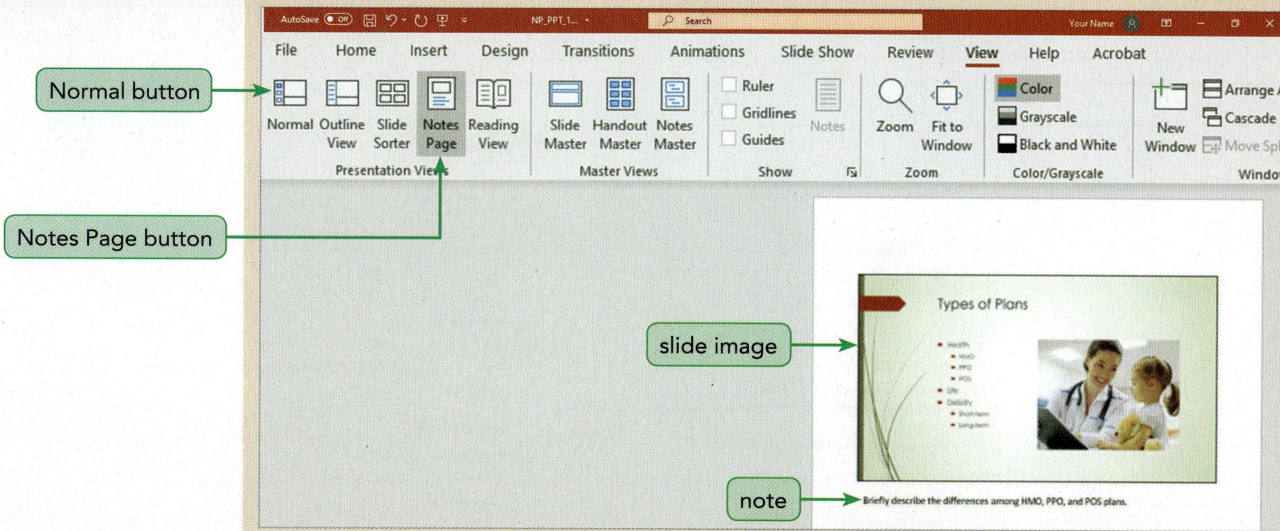

Yuganov Konstantin/Shutterstock.com

Tip

Use the Zoom in button on the status bar to magnify the text to make it easier to edit the note.

7. In the note, click after the period at the end of the sentence, press **SPACEBAR**, and then type **Be sure to describe the cost differences in premiums.** (including the period).
8. On the View tab, in the Presentation Views group, click the **Normal** button to return to Normal view. The Notes pane stays open until you close it again.
9. On the status bar, click the **Notes** button to close the Notes pane, and then save the changes to the presentation.

Editing Common File Properties

File **properties** are identifying information—characteristics—about a file that is saved along with the file that help others understand, identify, and locate the file. Common properties are the title, the author's name, and the date the file was created. You can use file properties to organize presentations or to search for files that have specific properties. To view or modify properties, you need to display the Info screen in Backstage view.

Anthony wants you to modify the Author property by adding yourself as an author and he wants you to add the Company property.

To add common file properties:

1. On the ribbon, click the **File** tab, and then click **Info** in the navigation pane. The Info screen in Backstage view appears. The document properties appear on the right side of the screen. See Figure 1–43. Because Anthony created the original document, his name is listed as the Author property. Because you saved the file after making changes, your name (or the user name on your computer) appears in the Last Modified By box. You'll add yourself as an author.

Figure 1–43 File properties on the Info screen in Backstage view

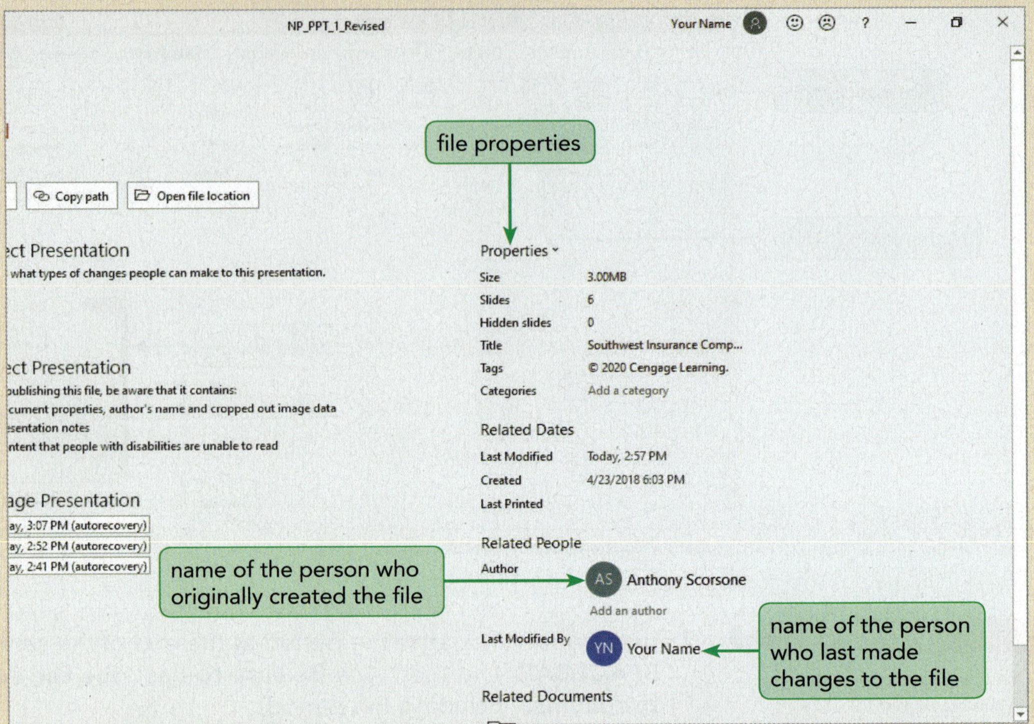

2. In the Related People section, click **Add an author**, type your name in the box that appears, and then click a blank area of the window. You and Anthony are now both listed as the Author property. Next, you need to add the Company property. The Company property does not appear in the list.
3. Scroll down, and then at the bottom of the Properties list, click **Show All Properties**. The Properties list expands to include all of the common document properties, including the Company property.
4. Next to Company, click **Specify the company**, type **Southwest Insurance Company**, and then click a blank area of the screen. You are finished adding properties to the file.
5. Scroll up if necessary, and at the top of the navigation pane, click the **Back** button to return to Slide 3 in Normal view.

Checking Spelling

Tip

You can click the Thesaurus button in the Proofing group on the Review tab to look up synonyms of a selected word, or you can click the Smart Lookup button in the Insights group to open the Search pane listing search results from the web.

You should always check the spelling and grammar in your presentation before you finalize it. To make this task easier, you can use PowerPoint's spelling checker. You can quickly tell if there are words on slides that are not in the built-in dictionary by looking at the Spelling button at the left end of the status bar. If there are no words flagged as possibly misspelled, the button is ; if words are flagged, the button changes to . To indicate that a word might be misspelled, a wavy red line appears under it.

To correct misspelled words, you can right-click a flagged word to see a list of suggested spellings on the shortcut menu, or you can check the entire presentation to locate possible misspellings. To check the spelling of all the words in the presentation, you click the Spelling button in the Proofing group on the Review tab. This opens the Spelling pane to the right of the displayed slide and starts the spell check from the current slide. When a possible misspelled word is found, suggestions for the correct spelling appear. If you want to accept one of the suggested spellings, you can change only the selected instance of the word or all of the instances of the word in the presentation. If the word is spelled correctly, you can ignore this instance of that word or all the instances of that word in the presentation. The pane also lists synonyms for the selected correct spelling.

To check the spelling in the presentation:

1. Display Slide 2 ("About Us"), and then right-click the misspelled word **incourage** in the fourth bulleted item. A shortcut menu opens listing spelling options. See Figure 1–44.

Figure 1–44 **Shortcut menu for a misspelled word**

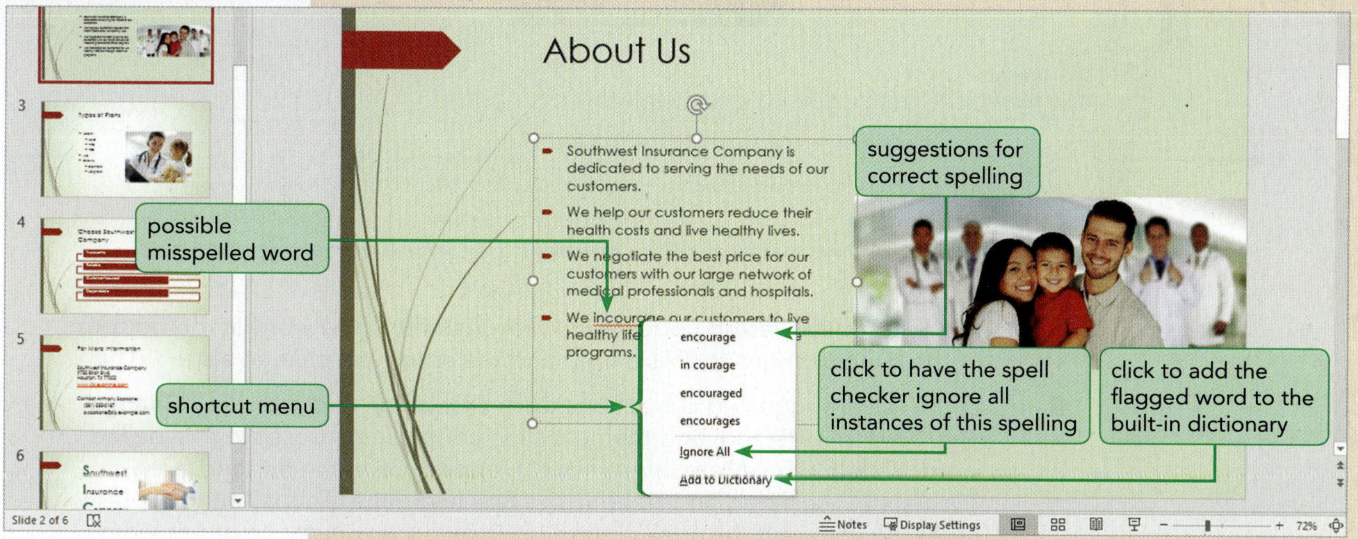

Rob Marmion/Shutterstock.com; Yuganov Konstantin/Shutterstock.com

Trouble? If the word "incourage" does not have a wavy red line under it, click the Review tab, and then in the Proofing group, click the Spelling button. The wavy red line should now appear. Right-click "incourage," continue with Step 2, and then do not do Step 3.

2. On the shortcut menu, click **encourage**. The menu closes, and the spelling is corrected.
3. Click the **Review** tab, and then in the Proofing group, click the **Spelling** button. The Spelling pane opens to the right of the displayed slide, and the next possible misspelled word, "Disibility" on Slide 3 ("Types of Plans"), is selected on the slide and in the Spelling pane. See Figure 1–45. In the Spelling pane, the first suggested correct spelling is selected. The selected correct spelling also appears at the bottom of the pane, with synonyms for the word listed below it and a speaker icon next to it.

Tip

If words are flagged with blue underlines, right-click the underlined words to see suggestions for fixing the possible grammatical error.

Figure 1–45 Spelling pane displaying a misspelled word

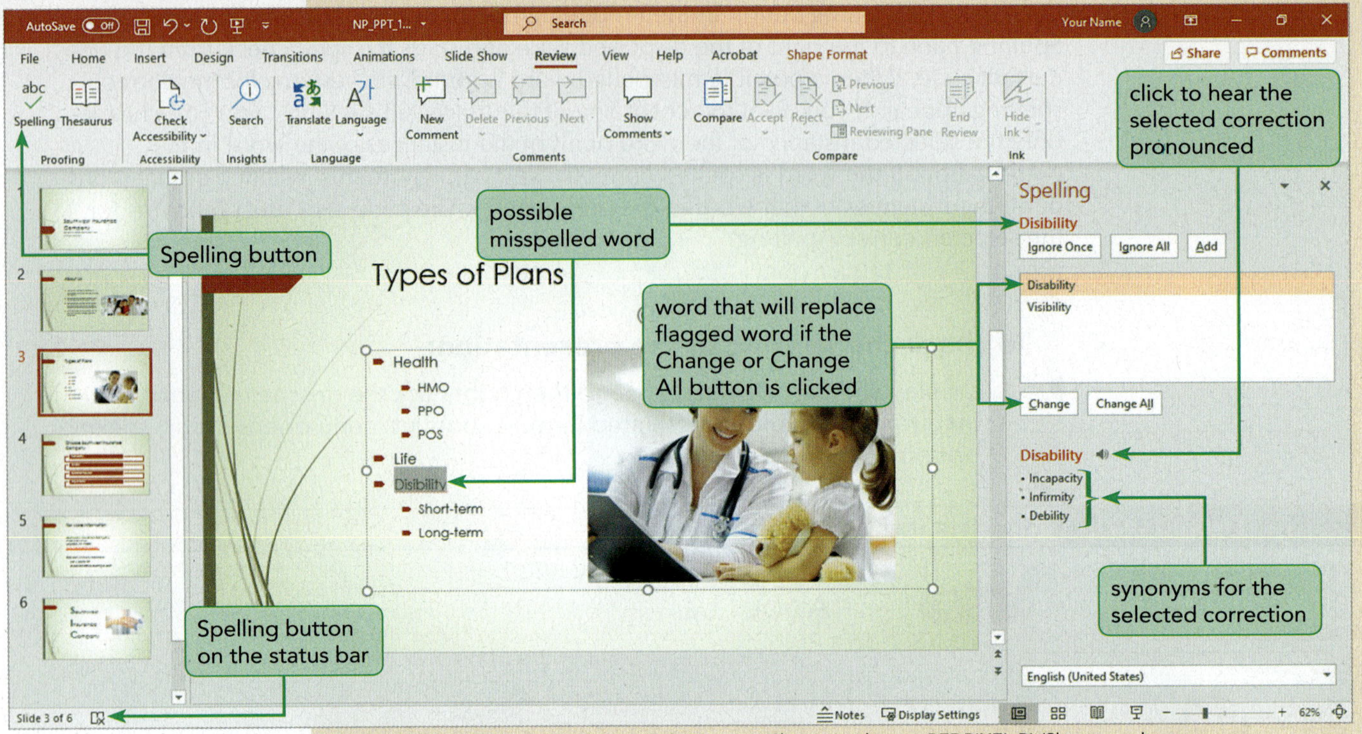

Yuganov Konstantin/Shutterstock.com; Rob Marmion/Shutterstock.com; REDPIXEL.PL/Shutterstock.com

4. In the Spelling pane, click the **speaker** icon 🔊. A voice says the word "Disability."
5. In the list of suggested corrections, click **Visibility**. The word at the bottom of the pane changes to "Visibility," and the synonyms change also.
6. In the list of suggested corrections, click **Disability**, and then click **Change**. The word is corrected, and the next slide containing a possible misspelled word, Slide 5 ("For More Information"), appears with the flagged word, "Scorsone," selected and listed in the Spelling pane. This is Anthony's last name, so you want the spell checker to ignore every instance of this word, not just this instance.
7. In the pane, click **Ignore All**. Because that was the last flagged word in the presentation, the Spelling pane closes, and a dialog box opens telling you that the spell check is complete.

   Trouble? If the spell checker finds any other misspelled words, correct them.
8. Click **OK**. The dialog box closes.
9. Display Slide 1 (the title slide). Anthony's last name no longer has a wavy red line under it because you clicked Ignore All when it was flagged as a possible misspelled word on Slide 5.
10. Save the changes to the presentation.

Running a Slide Show

After you have created and proofed your presentation, you should view it as a slide show to see how it will appear to your audience. You can do this in Slide Show view or in Presenter view.

You can use Slide Show view if your computer has only one monitor and you don't have access to a screen projector. If you have connected your computer to a second monitor or a screen projector, Slide Show view is the way an audience will see your slides. Refer to the Session 1.2 Visual Overview for more information about Slide Show and Presenter views.

In Slide Show and Presenter views, you can move from one slide to another in several ways. Figure 1–46 describes the methods you can use to move from one slide to another during a slide show.

Figure 1–46 **Methods of moving from one slide to another during a slide show**

Desired Result	Method
To display the next slide	• Press SPACEBAR. • Press ENTER. • Press RIGHT ARROW. • Press DOWN ARROW. • Press PGDN. • Press N. • Click the slide. • In Slide Show view, move the pointer to display the buttons in the lower-left corner of the slide, and then click the Advance to the next animation or slide button. • In Presenter view, click the Advance to the next animation or slide button. • Right-click the slide, and then on the shortcut menu, click Next.
To display the previous slide	• Press BACKSPACE. • Press LEFT ARROW. • Press UP ARROW. • Press PGUP. • Press P. • In Slide Show view, move the pointer to display the buttons in the lower-left corner of the slide, and then click the Return to the previous animation or slide button. • In Presenter view, click the Return to the previous animation or slide button • Right-click the slide, and then on the shortcut menu, click Previous.
To display a specific slide	• In Slide Show view, move the pointer to display the buttons in the lower-left corner of the slide, click the See all slides button, and then click the thumbnail of the slide you want to display. • In Presenter view, click the See all slides button, and then click the thumbnail of the slide you want to display. • Type the number of the slide you want to display, and then press ENTER. • Right-click the slide, and then on the shortcut menu, click See all slides.
To display the first slide	Press HOME.
To display the last slide	Press END.
To end the slide show	Press ESC. Right-click the slide, and then on the shortcut menu, click End Show.

Anthony asks you to review the slide show in Slide Show view to make sure the slides look professional.

Tip

To start the slide show from the current slide, click the Slide Show button on the status bar.

To use Slide Show view to view the final presentation:

1. On the Quick Access Toolbar, click the **Start From Beginning** button. Slide 1 appears on the screen in Slide Show view. Now you need to advance the slide show.
2. Press **SPACEBAR**. Slide 2 ("About Us") appears on the screen.
3. Click the mouse button. The next slide, Slide 3 ("Types of Plans"), appears on the screen.
4. Press **BACKSPACE**. The previous slide, Slide 2, appears again.
5. Move the mouse to display the buttons in the lower-left corner of the slide, and then click the **See all slides** button. All of the slides in the file are displayed as thumbnails on the screen, similar to Slide Sorter view.
6. Click the **Slide 5** thumbnail. Slide 5 ("For More Information") appears on the screen.
7. Move the mouse to display the pointer, and then position the pointer on the website address **www.sic.example.com**. The pointer changes to the pointing finger pointer to indicate that this is a link, and the ScreenTip that appears shows the full website address including "http://". If this were a real website, you could click the link to open your web browser and display the website to your audience. Because you moved the pointer, the faint row of buttons appears in the lower-left corner. See Figure 1–47.

Figure 1–47 Link and row of buttons in Slide Show view

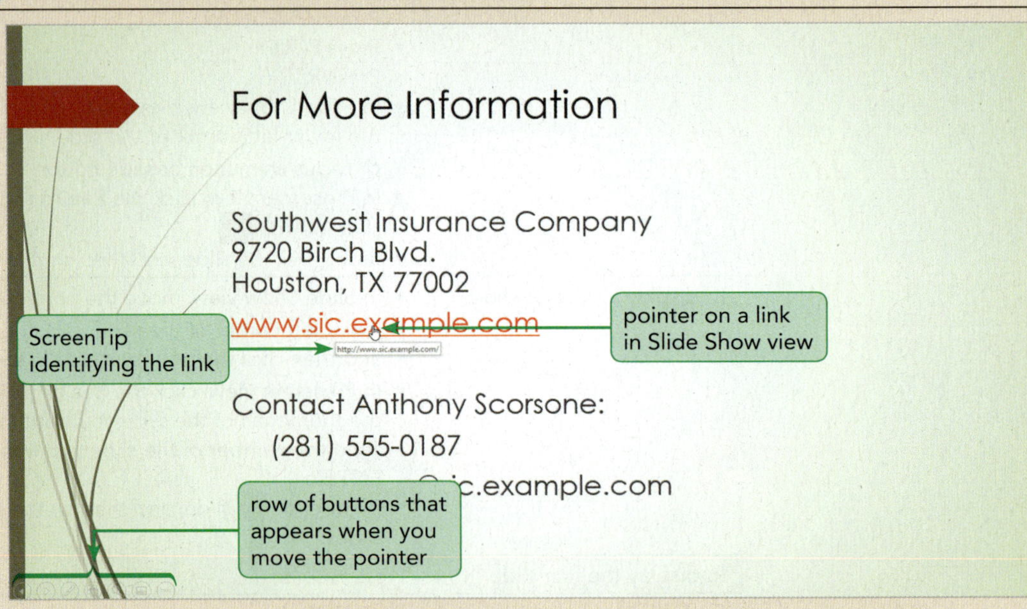

8. Move the pointer again, if necessary, to display the buttons that appear in the lower-left corner of the screen, and then click the **Return to the previous animation or slide** button twice to redisplay Slide 3 ("Types of Plans").

Trouble? If you can't see the buttons at the bottom of the screen, move the pointer to the lower-left corner so it is on top of the first button to darken that button, and then move the pointer to the right to see the rest of the buttons.

9. Display the buttons at the bottom of the screen again, and then click the **Zoom into the slide** button. The pointer changes to the zoom in pointer, and three-quarters of the slide is darkened. See Figure 1–48.

Figure 1–48 Zoom feature activated in Slide Show view

Yuganov Konstantin/Shutterstock.com

10. Move the pointer on top of the picture so that the top part of the picture does not appear darkened, and then click the picture. The slide zooms in so that the part of the slide inside the bright rectangle fills the screen, and the pointer changes to the hand pointer.
11. Press and hold the mouse button to change the pointer to the closed fist pointer, and then drag to the right to pull another part of the zoomed in slide into view.
12. Press **ESC** to zoom back out to see the whole slide.

Presenter view provides additional tools for running a slide show. In addition to seeing the current slide, you can also see the next slide, speaker notes, and a timer showing you how long the slide show has been running. Refer to the Session 1.2 Visual Overview for more information about Presenter view. Because of the additional tools available in Presenter view, you should consider using it if your computer is connected to a second monitor or projector.

If your computer is connected to a projector or second monitor, and you start a slide show in Slide Show view, Presenter view starts on the computer and Slide Show view appears on the second monitor or projection screen. If, for some reason, you don't want to use Presenter view in that circumstance, you can switch to Slide Show view. If you want to practice using Presenter view when your computer is not connected to a second monitor or projector, you can switch to Presenter view from Slide Show view.

Anthony wants you to switch to Presenter view and familiarize yourself with the tools available there.

Tip

To display the slide show in Reading view, click the Reading view button on the status bar. To advance through the slide show in Reading view, use the same commands as in Slide Show or Presenter view or click the Next and Previous buttons on the status bar.

To use Presenter view to review the slide show:

1. Move the pointer to display the buttons in the lower-left corner of the screen, click the **More slide show options** button to open a menu of commands, and then click **Show Presenter View**. The screen changes to show the presentation in Presenter view.
2. Below the current slide, click the **See all slides** button. The screen changes to show thumbnails of all the slides in the presentation, similar to Slide Sorter view.
3. Click the **Slide 4** thumbnail. Presenter view reappears, displaying Slide 4 ("Choose Southwest Insurance Company") as the current slide.
4. Click anywhere on Slide 4. The slide show advances to display Slide 5 ("For More Information").
5. At the bottom of the screen, click the **Advance to the next animation or slide** button. Slide 6 (the last slide) appears.
6. Click the **More slide show options** button, and then click **Hide Presenter View**. Slide 6 appears in Slide Show view.
7. Press **SPACEBAR**. A black slide appears displaying the text "End of slide show, click to exit."
8. Press **SPACEBAR** again. Presenter view closes, and you return to Normal view.

Proskills

Decision Making: Displaying a Blank Slide During a Presentation

Sometimes during a presentation, the audience has questions about the material and you want to pause the slide show to respond. Or you might want the audience to focus its attention on you instead of on the visuals on the screen. In these cases, you can display a black or white blank slide. Some presenters plan to use blank slides and insert them at specific points during their slide shows. Planning to use a blank slide can help you keep your presentation focused. It can also remind you that the purpose of the PowerPoint slides is to provide visual aids to enhance your presentation; the slides themselves are not the presentation.

If you did not create blank slides in your presentation file, but during your presentation you feel you need to display a blank slide, you can easily do this in Slide Show or Presenter view. To display a blank black slide, press B. To display a blank white slide, press W. You can also click the More slide show options button in Slide Show view, click Screen, and then Black Screen or White Screen. In Presenter view, you can click the More slide show options button, point to Screen, and then click Black Screen or White Screen. Or you can right-click the screen, point to Screen on the menu, and then click Black Screen or White Screen. To remove the black or white slide and redisplay the slide that had been on the screen before you displayed the blank slide, press any key on the keyboard or click anywhere on the screen. In Presenter view, you can also click the Black or unblack slide show button to toggle a blank slide on or off.

Printing a Presentation

Before you deliver your presentation, you might want to print it. PowerPoint provides several printing options. For example, you can print the slides in color, grayscale (white and shades of gray), or pure black and white, and you can print one, some, or all of the slides in several formats.

You use the Print screen in Backstage view to set print options such as specifying a printer and color options. First, you will add your name to the title slide.

To add your name to the title slide and choose a printer and color options:

1. Display Slide 1, click after "Scorsone" in the subtitle, press **ENTER**, and then type your name.
2. Click the **File** tab to display Backstage view, and then click **Print** in the navigation pane. Backstage view changes to display the Print screen. The Print screen contains options for printing your presentation, and a preview of the first slide as it will print with the current options. See Figure 1–49.

Figure 1–49 **Print screen in Backstage view**

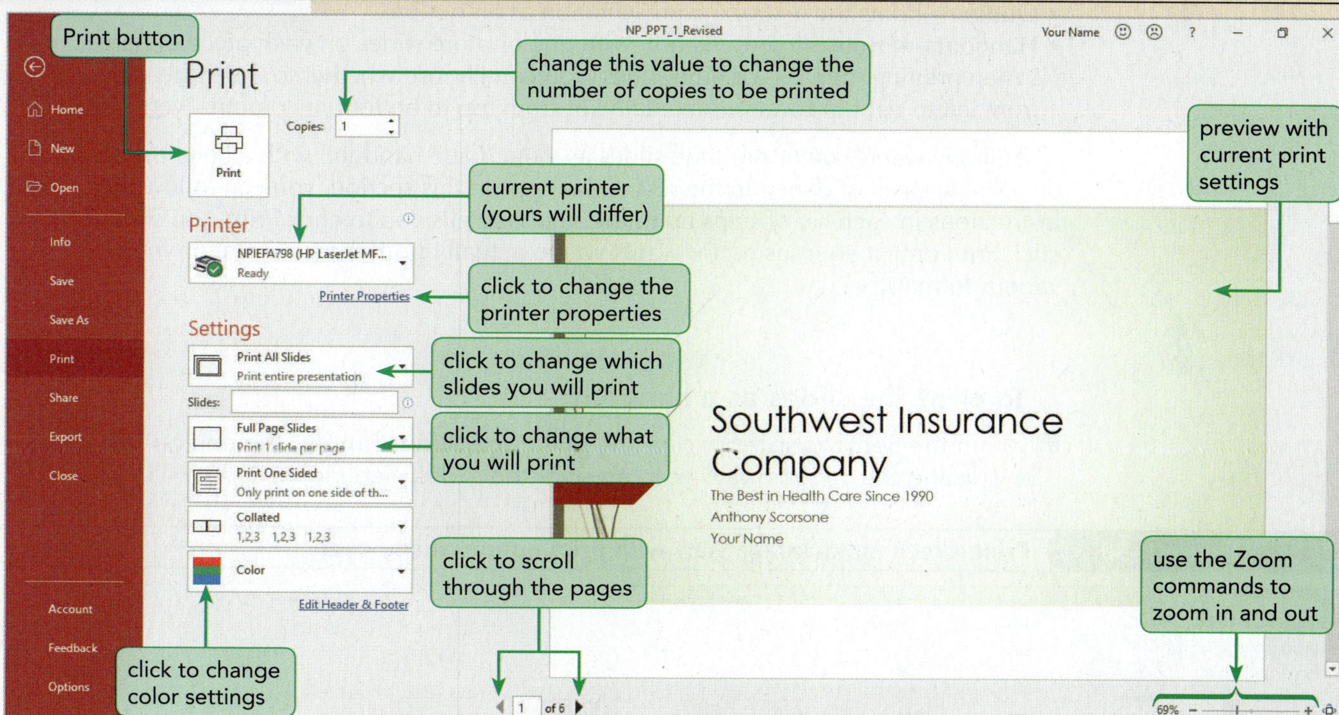

Trouble? If your screen does not match Figure 1–49, click the first button below Settings, click Print All Slides, click the second button below Settings, and then click Full Page Slides.

3. If you are connected to a network or to more than one printer, make sure the printer listed in the Printer box is the one you want to use; if it is not, click the **Printer** button, and then click the correct printer in the list.
4. Click the **Printer Properties** link to open the Properties dialog box for your printer. Usually, the default options are correct, but you can change any printer settings, such as print quality or the paper source, in this dialog box.

5. Click **Cancel** to close the Properties dialog box. Now you can choose whether to print the presentation in color, black and white, or grayscale. If you plan to print in black and white or grayscale, you should change this setting so that you can see what your slides will look like without color and to make sure they are legible.
6. Click the **Color** button, and then click **Grayscale**. The preview changes to grayscale.
7. At the bottom of the preview pane, click the **Next Page** button twice to display Slide 3 ("Types of Plans"). The slides are legible in grayscale.
8. If you will be printing in color, click the **Grayscale** button, and then click **Color**.

Tip

To view the presentation in black and white or grayscale in Normal view, click the View tab, and then click the Grayscale button or the Black and White button in the Color/Grayscale group.

In the Settings section on the Print screen, you can click the Full Page Slides button to choose from among several choices for printing the presentation, as described below:

- **Full Page Slides**—Prints each slide full size on a separate piece of paper.
- **Notes Pages**—Prints each slide as a notes page.
- **Outline**—Prints the text of the presentation as an outline.
- **Handouts**—Prints the presentation with one or more slides on each piece of paper. When printing four, six, or nine slides, you can choose whether to order the slides from left to right in rows (horizontally) or from top to bottom in columns (vertically).

Anthony wants you to print the slides as a one-page handout, with all eight slides on a single sheet of paper. In the rest of the steps in this section, you can follow the instructions in each set of steps up to the step that tells you to click Print. You should click Print only if your instructor wants you to actually print the presentation in the various formats.

To print the slides as a handout:

1. In the Settings section, click the **Full Page Slides** button. A menu opens listing the various ways you can print the slides. See Figure 1–50.

Figure 1–50 **Print screen in Backstage view with print options menu open**

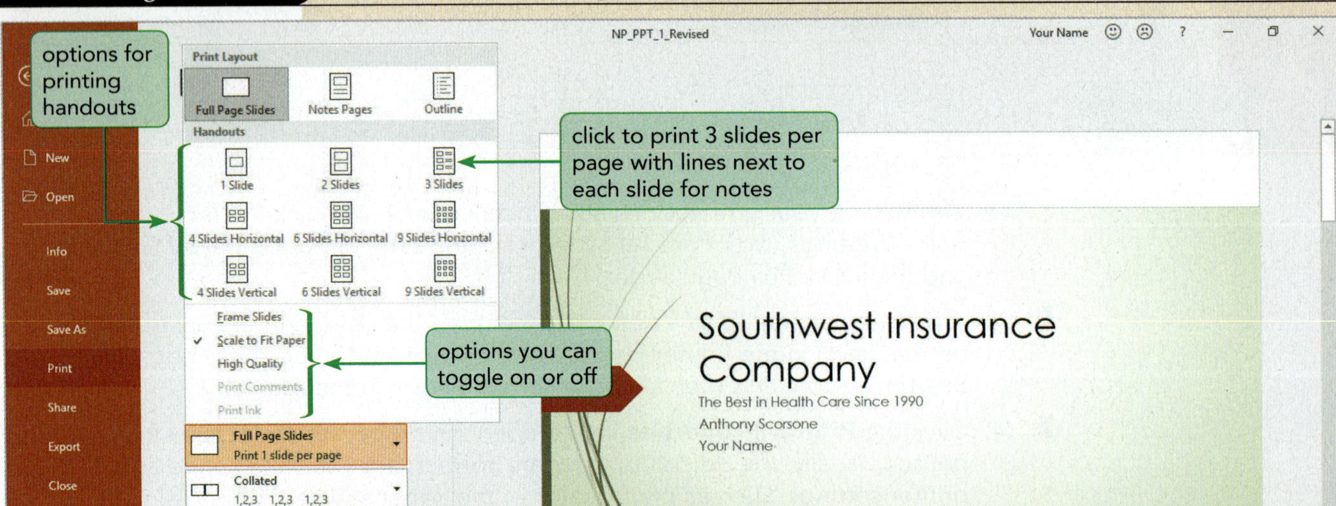

2. In the Handouts section, click **6 Slides Horizontal**. The preview changes to show all six slides in the preview pane, arranged in order horizontally in three rows from left to right. The current date appears in the top-right corner, and a page number appears in the bottom-right corner.
3. At the top of the Print section, click **Print**. Backstage view closes and the handout prints.

Next, Anthony wants you to print the title slide as a full-page slide so that he can use it as a cover page for his handouts.

To print the title slide as a full-page slide:

1. Click the **File** tab, and then click **Print** in the navigation pane. The Print screen appears in Backstage view. The preview still shows all six slides on one page. "6 Slides Horizontal" appears on the second button in the Settings section because that was the last printing option you chose.
2. In the Settings section, click **6 Slides Horizontal**, and then click **Full Page Slides**. Slide 1 (the title slide) appears as the preview. Below the preview of Slide 1, it indicates that you are viewing Slide 1 of six slides to print.
3. In the Settings section, click the **Print All Slides** button. Note on the menu that opens that you can print all the slides, selected slides, the current slide, or a custom range. You want to print just the title slide as a full-page slide.
4. Click **Print Current Slide**. Slide 1 appears in the preview pane, and at the bottom, it now indicates that you will print only one slide.
5. Click the **Print** button. Backstage view closes and Slide 1 prints.

Recall that you created speaker notes on Slides 3 and 5. Anthony would like you to print these slides as notes pages.

To print the nonsequential slides containing speaker notes:

1. Open the Print screen in Backstage view again, and then click the **Full Page Slides** button. The menu opens.
2. In the Print Layout section of the menu, click **Notes Pages**. The menu closes, and the preview displays Slide 1 as a Notes Page.
3. In the Settings section, click in the **Slides** box, type **3,5** and then click a blank area of the Print screen.
4. Scroll through the preview to confirm that Slides 3 ("Types of Plans") and 5 ("For More Information") will print, and then click **Print**. Backstage view closes, and Slides 3 and 5 print as notes pages.

Finally, Anthony would like you to print the outline of the presentation. Remember, Slide 6 is designed to be a visual that Anthony can leave displayed at the end of the presentation, so you don't need to include it in the outline.

To print Slides 1 through 5 as an outline:

1. Open the Print screen in Backstage view, click the **Notes Pages** button, and then in the Print Layout section, click **Outline**. The text on Slides 3 and 6 appears as an outline in the preview pane.
2. Click in the **Slides** box, type **1-5**, and then click a blank area of the Print screen. See Figure 1–51.

Figure 1–51 Print screen in Backstage view with Slides 1–5 previewed as an outline

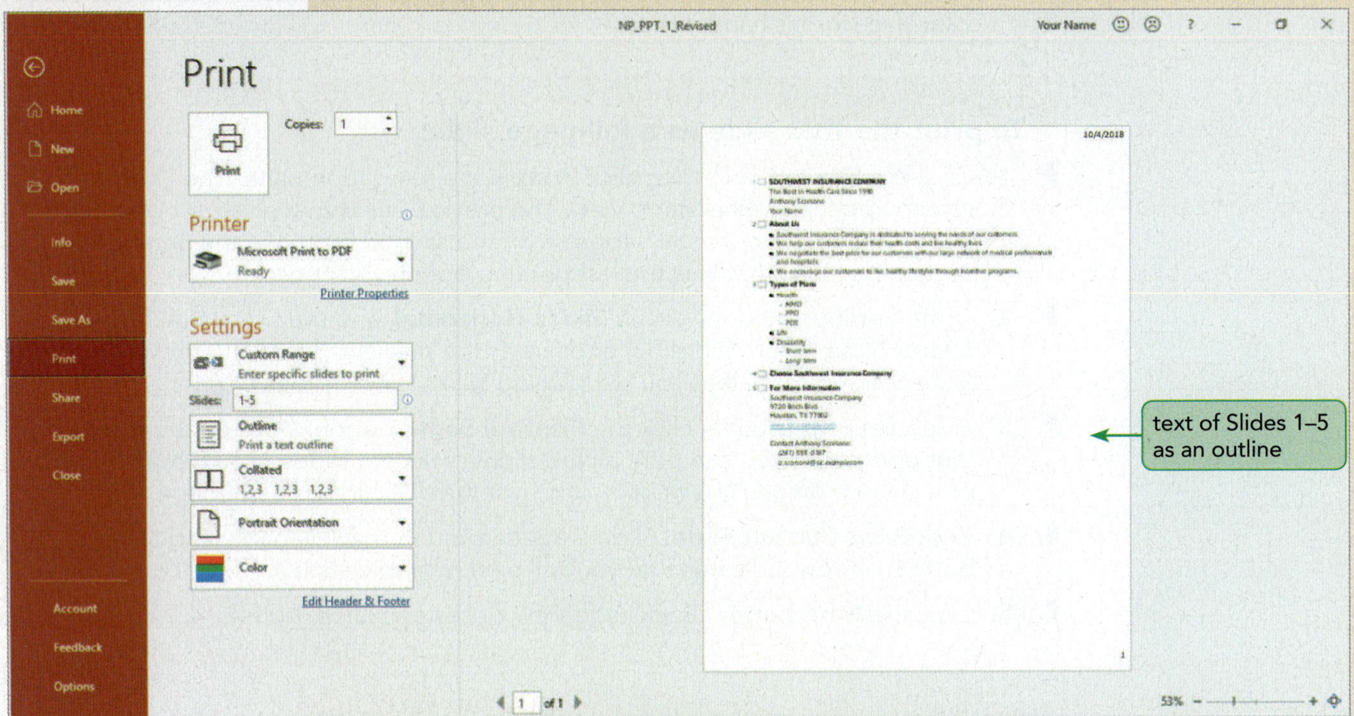

3. At the top of the Print section, click the **Print** button. Backstage view closes, and the text of Slides 1–5 prints.

Closing PowerPoint

When you are finished working with your presentation, you can close PowerPoint. If you only have one presentation open, you click the Close button in the upper-right corner of the program window. If you have more than one presentation open, clicking this button will close only the current presentation; to close PowerPoint, you need to click the Close button in each of the open presentation's windows.

To close PowerPoint:

1. In the upper-right corner of the program window, click the **Close** button. A dialog box opens, asking if you want to save your changes. This is because you did not save the file after you added your name to the title slide.
2. sam In the dialog box, click **Save**. The dialog box closes, the changes are saved, and PowerPoint closes.

   Trouble? If any other PowerPoint presentations are still open, click the Close button on each open presentation's program window until no more presentations are open to exit PowerPoint.

In this session, you opened an existing presentation and saved it with a new name, changed the theme, added and cropped photos and adjusted the photo compression, and resized and moved objects. You have also added speaker notes and checked the spelling. Finally, you printed the presentation in several forms and exited PowerPoint. Your work will help Anthony give an effective presentation to potential customers of Southwest Insurance Company.

Review

Session 1.2 Quick Check

1. What is alt text?
2. Explain what happens when you crop photos.
3. Describe sizing handles.
4. How do you use smart guides?
5. Why is it important to maintain the aspect ratio of photos?
6. How do you convert a list to a SmartArt diagram without using the Design Ideas pane?
7. What is the difference between Slide Show view and Presenter view?
8. List the four formats for printing a presentation.

Practice

Review Assignments

Data Files needed for the Review Assignments: NP_PPT_1-2.pptx, Support_PPT_1_Anthony.jpg, Support_PPT_1_Meeting.jpg, Support_PPT_1_Standing.jpg, Support_PPT_1_Woman.jpg

Anthony Scorsone, a sales manager in the Houston office of Southwest Insurance Company, is preparing a presentation for the upcoming summer sales meeting. Because his team has sold so many new policies, he has been asked to give a presentation to the branch managers. He will focus on how they can create new business from their current customers by actively selling the new policy types the company sells. He asks you to begin creating the presentation. Complete the following steps:

1. Start PowerPoint and create a new, blank presentation. On the title slide, type **New Sales Leads** as the title, and then type your name as the subtitle. Save the presentation as **NP_PPT_1_Leads** to the drive and folder where you are storing your files.
2. Edit the slide title by typing **Developing** before "New" so that the title is now "Developing New Sales Leads."
3. Add a new Slide 2 with the Title and Content layout, type **Contact Your Existing Clients** as the slide title, and then in the content placeholder type the following:
   - **Offer new plans**
     - **Auto**
     - **Boat**
     - **Worker's Comp**
   - **Offer competitive package pricing**
   - **Emphasize your personal connection and service**
   - **Contact Anthony Scorsone**
4. Create a new Slide 3 with the Two Content layout, then create a new Slide 4 with the Two Content layout. On Slide 4, add **Recipe for Success** as the slide title, and then type the following as a numbered list in the left content placeholder:
   1. **Offer new products to existing clients**
   2. **Present to local organizations**
      1. **Chamber of Commerce**
      2. **Service organizations**
      3. **Professional organizations**
   3. **Reach out to self-insured with customized packages**
5. Create a new Slide 5 using the Title and Content layout, and then create a new Slide 6 with the Title and Content layout. On Slide 6, add **For More Information** as the slide title.
6. Use the Cut and Paste commands to move the last bulleted item on Slide 2 ("Contact Anthony Scorsone") to Slide 6 as the first bulleted item in the content placeholder.
7. On Slide 6, remove the bullet symbol from the text you pasted, and then add the following as the next two items in the unnumbered list:

   Email: a.scorsone@sic.example.com

   Cell: (281) 555-0187
8. Click after "Scorsone" in the first item in the list, and then create a new line below it without creating a new item in the list so that there is no extra space above the new line. Type **Sales Manager, Houston Office** on the new line.
9. Remove the link formatting from the email address.
10. Duplicate Slide 2 ("Contact Your Existing Clients"). On the new Slide 3, do the following:
    - Edit the title so it is **Introduce New Products**
    - Edit the first bulleted item so it is **New Products**
    - Delete the second and third first-level bulleted items

11. Delete the blank Slides 4 and 6.
12. Move Slide 3 ("Introduce New Products") so it becomes Slide 2.
13. Change the theme to Banded and choose the second variant.
14. Save your changes, and then close the presentation.
15. Open the file **NP_PPT_1-2.pptx**, located in the PowerPoint1 > Review folder included with your Data Files, add your name as the subtitle on the title slide, and then save it as **NP_PPT_1_Updated** to the drive and folder where you are storing your files.
16. Change the theme colors to Orange Red. Change the theme fonts to Cambria.
17. Change the layout of Slide 3 ("Contact Your Existing Clients") to Two Content.
18. On Slide 3, insert the picture **Support_PPT_1_Woman.jpg**, located in the PowerPoint1 > Review folder. Add **Woman on the phone at a desk in an office.** as the alt text for this picture.
19. Open the Design Ideas pane if necessary, and then click several of the suggested layouts. When you are finished, close the pane, and then on the Quick Access Toolbar, click the Undo button to reset the slide, and then close the Design Ideas pane.
20. Resize the picture on Slide 3 while maintaining the aspect ratio so that the picture height is 4 inches. Reposition the picture so that its right edge aligns with the right edge of the slide and its top edge aligns with the top edge of the text box containing the list.
21. Change the layout of Slide 4 ("Create Custom Packages for Self-Employed") to Title and Content.
22. On Slide 4, insert the photo **Support_PPT_1_Standing.jpg**, located in the PowerPoint1 > Review folder. Add **Business people standing and chatting in a group, holding glasses of water, in an office setting.** as the alt text for this picture.
23. Resize the picture on Slide 4 while maintaining the aspect ratio so that the picture height is 4 inches. Reposition the picture so that its right edge aligns with the right edge of the slide and its bottom edge aligns with the bottom of the slide.
24. On Slide 5, insert the photo **Support_PPT_1_Meeting.jpg**, located in the PowerPoint1 > Review folder. Add **People in business casual attire at a conference table in an office setting listening to a man speak.** as the alt text for this picture.
25. Resize the picture on Slide 5 while maintaining the aspect ratio so that the picture height is 5 inches.
26. Display the rulers and the gridlines, and then crop 1 inch off the bottom of the picture on Slide 5. Resize the cropped part of the picture so that the head of the man standing is about one-eighth of an inch from the top of the picture. Then crop one-half inch off the right side of the picture.
27. Reposition the picture on Slide 5 so that its right edge aligns with the right edge of the slide, its top edge aligns with the gridline at the 1-inch mark on the vertical ruler, and its bottom edge aligns with the gridline at the negative 3-inch mark on the vertical ruler.
28. On Slide 5, change the width of the text box containing the bulleted list by dragging the sizing handle in the middle of the right border of the text box so that the right border aligns with the gridline at the negative 1-inch mark on the horizontal ruler. Then change the height of the text box by dragging the sizing handle in the middle of the top border down so that the top of the text box aligns with the top of the picture.
29. On Slide 6 ("Recipe for Success"), open the Design Ideas pane and click several of the suggested layouts. Then, on the Quick Access Toolbar, click the Undo button and close the Design Ideas pane.
30. On Slide 6, convert the numbered list to SmartArt using the Vertical Block List layout on the Convert to SmartArt menu.
31. On Slide 6, change the SmartArt layout to the Segmented Process layout.
32. On Slide 6, display the Notes pane, and then type **Some local organizations to consider are the Chamber of Commerce, service organizations, and professional organizations.** as a speaker note. When you are finished, close the Notes pane.
33. On Slide 7 ("For More Information"), increase the size of the text in the unnumbered list to 24 points. Then, in the first bulleted item, select the text "Anthony Scorsone." and format it as bold and 28 points.
34. On Slide 7, insert the picture **Support_PPT_1_Anthony.jpg**, and then **Portrait of Anthony Scorsone** as the alt text for this picture.

35. Crop the photo to the Oval shape. Click the Crop button, and then drag the bottom-middle crop handle up one inch. Reposition the picture so that the top of the picture aligns with the horizontal gridline at the 1-inch mark on the vertical ruler if necessary.
36. Hide the rulers and gridlines.
37. Compress all the photos in the slides to E-mail (96 ppi) and delete cropped areas of pictures.
38. Add your name as an author property, and add **Southwest Insurance Company** as the Company property.
39. Check the spelling in the presentation. Correct the spelling error on Slide 2 by selecting "Liability" as the correct spelling, and the error on Slide 3 by selecting "Emphasize" as the correct spelling. Ignore all instances of Anthony's last name. If you made any additional spelling errors, correct them as well. If your name on Slide 1 is flagged as misspelled, ignore this error. Save the changes to the presentation.
40. Review the slide show in Slide Show and Presenter views.
41. View the slides in grayscale, and then print the following in color or in grayscale depending on your printer: the title slide as a full-page-sized slide; Slides 2 through 7 as a handout on a single piece of paper with the slides in order horizontally; Slide 6 as a notes page; and Slides 2 through 5 and Slide 7 as an outline. Save and close the presentation and PowerPoint when you are finished.

Apply

Case Problem 1

Data Files needed for this Case Problem: NP_PPT_1-3.pptx, Support_PPT_1_Application.jpg, Support_PPT_1_Building.jpg, Support_PPT_1_Key.jpg, Support_PPT_1_Sophia.jpg

Upper Coast Bank Upper Coast Bank has branches all over the United States. Sophia Baker, the Vice President of Residential Lending at the Hartford, Connecticut branch, hired you as her executive assistant. Sophia wants to create a simple presentation that will help her explain some of the details about applying for a mortgage to first-time home buyers. She asks you to help complete the slides. Complete the following steps:

1. Open the presentation named **NP_PPT_1-3.pptx**, located in the PowerPoint1 > Case1 folder included with your Data Files, and then save it as **NP_PPT_1_Mortgage** to the drive and folder where you are storing your files.
2. Insert a new slide with the Title Slide layout. Add **Mortgage Essentials** as the presentation title on the title slide. In the subtitle text placeholder, type your name. Move this slide so it is the first slide in the presentation.
3. Apply the Frame theme, and then apply the third theme variant.
4. Change the theme fonts to Garamond-TrebuchetMs.
5. On Slide 1 (the title slide), change the font size of the title text to 36 points. Then resize the title text box so it is 2.25 inches wide. If necessary, reposition the title text box so that the left edge of the text box is aligned with the left edge of the subtitle text box and so that there is the same amount of space between the top of the text box and the top slide edge as there is between the bottom of the subtitle text box and the bottom of the slide. Resize the subtitle text box so it is 3.3 inches wide, and then align its left edge with the left edge of the title text box.
6. On Slide 1, insert the picture **Support_PPT_1_Application.jpg**, located in the PowerPoint1 > Case1 folder. Add **Picture of a mortgage application form with a red "Approved" stamp on it and the wooden stamp next to it.** as the alt text.
7. On Slide 1, resize the photo, maintaining the aspect ratio, so that it is 5.84 inches high. Position the photo so that its middle aligns with the middle of the tan rectangle and its right edge aligns with the right edge of the slide.
8. On Slides 2 through 6, increase the size of the text in the bulleted list so the first-level items are 24 points and any second-level items are 20 points.
9. On Slide 4 ("What Are Closing Costs?"), cut the last bulleted item ("$200,000 loan"), and then paste it in on Slide 3 ("What Are Points?") as the third bulleted item. If a blank line is added below the pasted text, delete it.

10. On Slide 3, add the following as second-level items below "$200,000 loan", adjusting the font size to 20 points if necessary:
    2 points (2%) = $4,000
    3 points (3%) = $6,000
11. On Slide 2 ("Steps"), convert the bulleted list to SmartArt using the Step Down Process layout. (*Hint*: You need to click More SmartArt Graphics to open the Choose a SmartArt Graphic dialog box.)
12. On Slide 5 ("Documents Needed"), change the layout to Two Content, then insert the picture **Support_PPT_1_Key.jpg**, located in the PowerPoint1 > Case1 folder. Add **Drawing of a hand passing an approved mortgage towards another person's hand holding a key on a key chain shaped like a house.** as the alt text.
13. On Slide 5, resize the picture, maintaining the aspect ratio, so that it is 4.5 inches square, and then position it so that its middle aligns with the middle of the text box containing the bulleted list and its right edge aligns with the left edge of the gray rectangle on the right side of the slide. (*Hint*: Position the picture as close as possible to the edge of the gray rectangle. Then with the picture selected, press RIGHT ARROW or LEFT ARROW to nudge it into the correct position.)
14. On Slide 5, in the last bulleted item, format "and" with italics. Enter **Make sure applicants understand that they need two forms of ID.** as a speaker note, and then close the Notes pane.
15. On Slide 6 ("Contact Information"), remove the link formatting from both the email address and the Internet address of the Mortgages page for the bank.
16. On Slide 6, click before the word "Contact" in the slide title, and then press ENTER three times. Insert the photo **Support_PPT_1_Sophia.jpg**, located in the PowerPoint1 > Case1 folder. Add **Portrait of smiling Sophia Baker.** as the alt text.
17. On Slide 6, crop 1.5 inches off the bottom of the picture, then crop the photo to the Rectangle: Rounded Corners shape.
18. On Slide 6, resize the photo so it is 2.8 inches high, maintaining the aspect ratio. Reposition the photo in the tan rectangle above the title so that the vertical smart guide that appears shows that the photo aligns with the center of the tan rectangle, and the bottom of the photo aligns with the middle of the slide.
19. Add a new Slide 7 with the Content with Caption layout. In the title text placeholder, type **Upper**, and then create a new line without creating a new paragraph. Type **Coast** on the new line, create another new line, and then type **Bank**. In the text placeholder below the title, type **The Friendly Bank**.
20. On Slide 7, change the size of the title text to 48 points and bold, and change its color to Brown, Accent 1, Darker 50%. Change the size of the text below the title to 24 points and make it italic.
21. On Slide 7, add the picture **Support_PPT_1_Building.jpg**, located in the PowerPoint1 > Case1 folder. Add **Photo of Upper Coast Bank building.** as the alt text.
22. Compress all the photos in the presentation to E-mail (96 ppi) and delete cropped portions of photos.
23. Add your name as an author property and add **Upper Coast Bank** as the Company property.
24. Check the spelling in the presentation and correct all misspelled words.
25. Save the changes to the presentation, view the slide show in Presenter view, and then print Slides 1–6 as a handout using the 6 Slides Horizontal arrangement, and print Slide 5 as a notes page.
26. Close the presentation and PowerPoint.

Create

Case Problem 2

Data Files needed for this Case Problem: Support_PPT_1_Beach.jpg, Support_PPT_1_Black.jpg, Support_PPT_1_Blue.jpg, Support_PPT_1_Ensemble.jpg, Support_PPT_1_Pink.jpg

Jumpstart Advertising Joaquin Castillo is an associate account executive at Jumpstart Advertising, an advertising agency in New York City. A national department store recently hired Jumpstart to promote a new line of women's clothing with a vintage look. A new design house named Retro Again designed the clothing line. Joaquin has started a presentation to introduce the design house to his team so that they can create an effective ad campaign. He asks you to finish the presentation. The completed presentation is shown in Figure 1–52. Refer to Figure 1–52 as you complete the following steps:

Figure 1–52 **Advertising presentation**

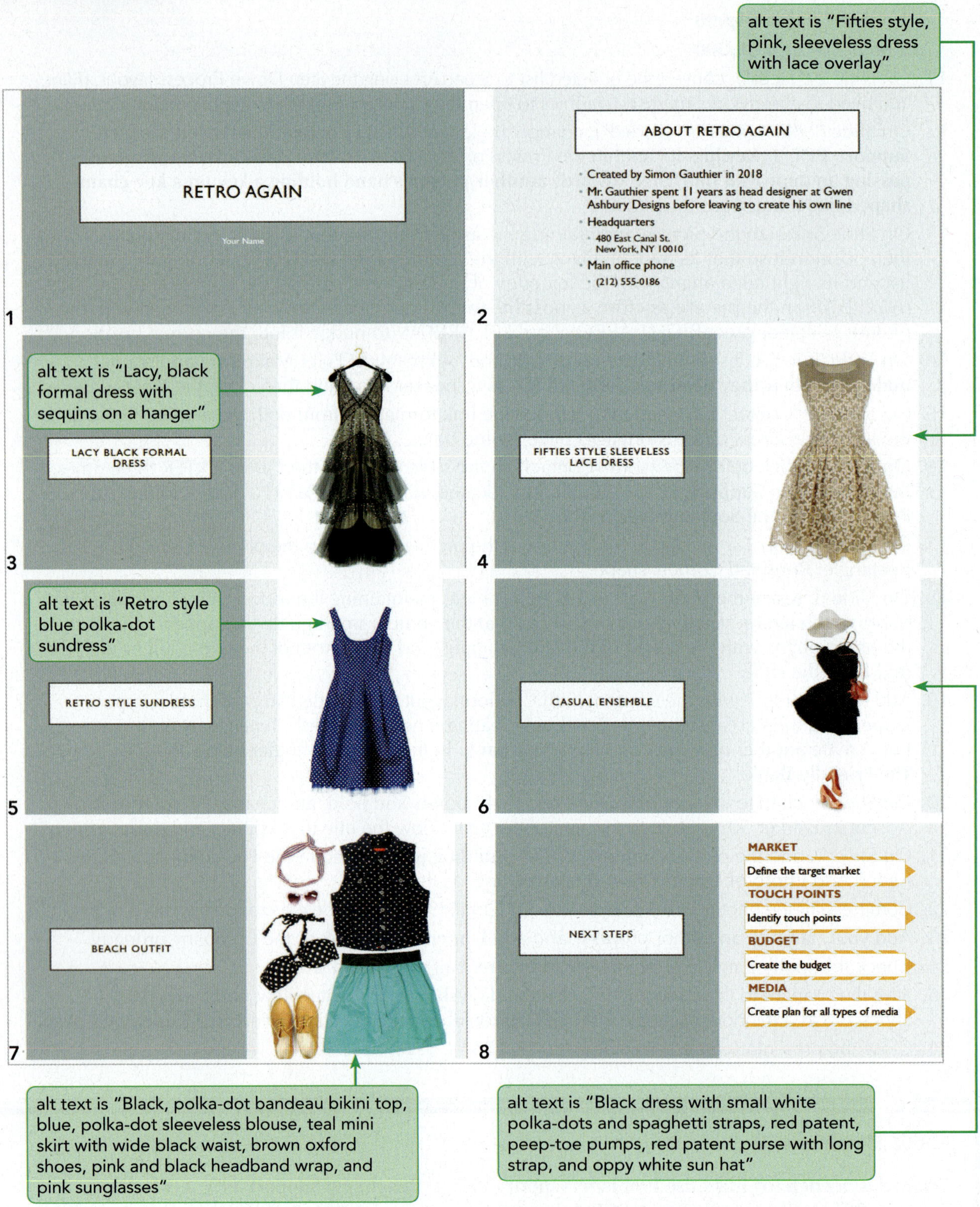

ladyfortune/Shutterstock.com; Maffi/Shutterstock.com; Tarzhanova/Shutterstock.com; urfin/Shutterstock.com; Africa Studio/Shutterstock.com

1. Create a new, blank PowerPoint presentation. Save it as **NP_PPT_1_Retro** to the drive and folder where you are storing your files. Add your name as the subtitle on Slide 1.
2. The theme is the Parcel theme with the first variant.
3. Slide 2 has the Title and Content layout applied. Slides 3 through 8 have the Content with Caption layout applied.
4. On Slides 3 through 8, the text placeholders below the title text are deleted. The title text boxes on Slides 3 through 8 are repositioned so that their middles are aligned with the horizontal gridlines at the 0-inch mark on the vertical ruler and so their left edges are aligned with the vertical gridline at the negative 6-inch mark on the horizontal ruler.
5. On Slide 2, the text box containing the bulleted list is resized so that the bottom of the text box aligns with the gridlines at the negative 3-inch mark on the vertical ruler and the top aligns with the gridline at the 1-inch mark on the vertical ruler. The first-level items are 26 points, and the second-level items are 22 points.
6. The pictures on Slides 3 through 7 are all located in the PowerPoint1 > Case2 folder included with your Data Files. Each photo is resized so that it is 7.5 inches high. Add the alt text as shown in Figure 1–52.
7. The left edges of the pictures on Slides 3 through 6 are aligned with the gridline at the 1-inch mark on the horizontal ruler. The left edge of the picture on Slide 7 is aligned with the 0.25-inch mark on the horizontal ruler.
8. Compress all the photos in the presentation to E-mail (96 ppi).
9. On Slide 8 ("NEXT STEPS"), type the text in the SmartArt as a bulleted list. Each uppercase word is a first-level item, and each sentence is a second-level item. The SmartArt layout is Vertical Accent List. All the text is 24 points. The first-level items (the words in all uppercase) are bold and Orange, Accent 3, Darker 25%. (*Hint*: Change the color of the text in the first-level items after you convert the list to a SmartArt graphic.)
10. Save the changes to the presentation, and then view the presentation in Slide Show view.
11. Close the presentation and PowerPoint.

Module 2

Adding Media and Special Effects

Using Media in a Presentation for a Veterinary Hospital

POWERPOINT

Objectives

Session 2.1
- Apply a theme used in another presentation
- Insert shapes
- Format shapes and pictures
- Duplicate objects
- Rotate and flip objects
- Create a table
- Modify and format a table
- Insert symbols
- Add footers and headers

Session 2.2
- Apply and modify transitions
- Animate objects and lists
- Change how an animation starts
- Use the Morph transition
- Add video and modify playback options
- Trim video and set a poster frame
- Understand animation effects applied to videos
- Compress media

Case | Windsor Veterinary Hospital

Teréza Gonçalves is the client service coordinator at Windsor Veterinary Hospital in Windsor, Ontario. One of her responsibilities is to recruit new clients by promoting hospital services. Because Windsor is on the border of Canada and the United States, Teréza is putting together a presentation to advertise the hospital to potential customers in the United States. Teréza prepared the text of a PowerPoint presentation, and she wants you to add photos and other features to make the presentation more interesting and compelling.

In this module, you will modify a presentation that highlights the state of the art services and competitive costs of the hospital. You will add formatting and special effects to photos and shapes; create a table; insert symbols; add footer and header information to slides, notes, and handouts; add transitions and animations to slides; and add and modify video.

Starting Data Files

PowerPoint2 →

Module
NP_PPT_2-1.pptx
Support_PPT_2_Chip.jpg
Support_PPT_2_MRI.jpg
Support_PPT_2_OR.jpg
Support_PPT_2_Running.mov
Support_PPT_2_Teeth.jpg
Support_PPT_2_Theme.pptx
Support_PPT_2_VetDog.jpg

Review
NP_PPT_2-2.pptx
Support_PPT_2_Bath.jpg
Support_PPT_2_NewTheme.pptx
Support_PPT_2_Plate.jpg
Support_PPT_2_Sign.jpg
Support_PPT_2_Writing.mov

Case1
NP_PPT_2-3.pptx
Support_PPT_2_Calendar.jpg
Support_PPT_2_Cornucopia.jpg
Support_PPT_2_Fourth.jpg
Support_PPT_2_Labor.png
Support_PPT_2_Logo.pptx
Support_PPT_2_Memorial.jpg
Support_PPT_2_NewYear.jpg
Support_PPT_2_Sayings.mp4
Support_PPT_2_Sixty.png

Case2
NP_PPT_2-4.pptx
Support_PPT_2_Corporate.jpg
Support_PPT_2_Hospital.jpg
Support_PPT_2_Residential.jpg
Support_PPT_2_School.jpg

Session 2.1 Visual Overview:

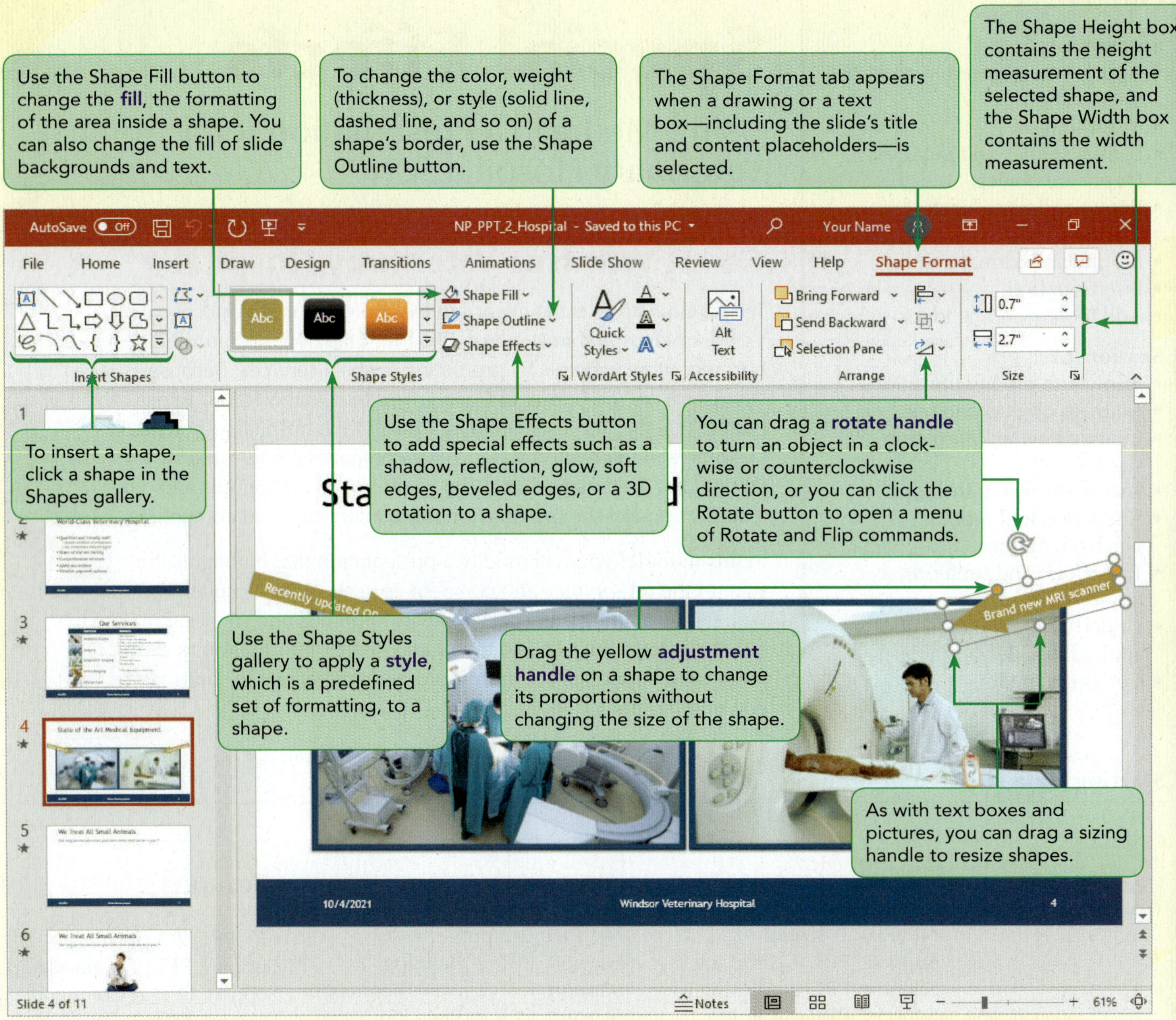

nimon/Shutterstock.com; Javier Brosch/Shutterstock.com; JPC-PROD/Shutterstock.com; Ivonne Wierink/Shutterstock.com; Africa Studio/Shutterstock.com; Veronica Louro/Shutterstock.com; santypan/Shutterstock.com; Rommel Canlas/Shutterstock.com; Ilike/Shutterstock.com

Formatting Graphics

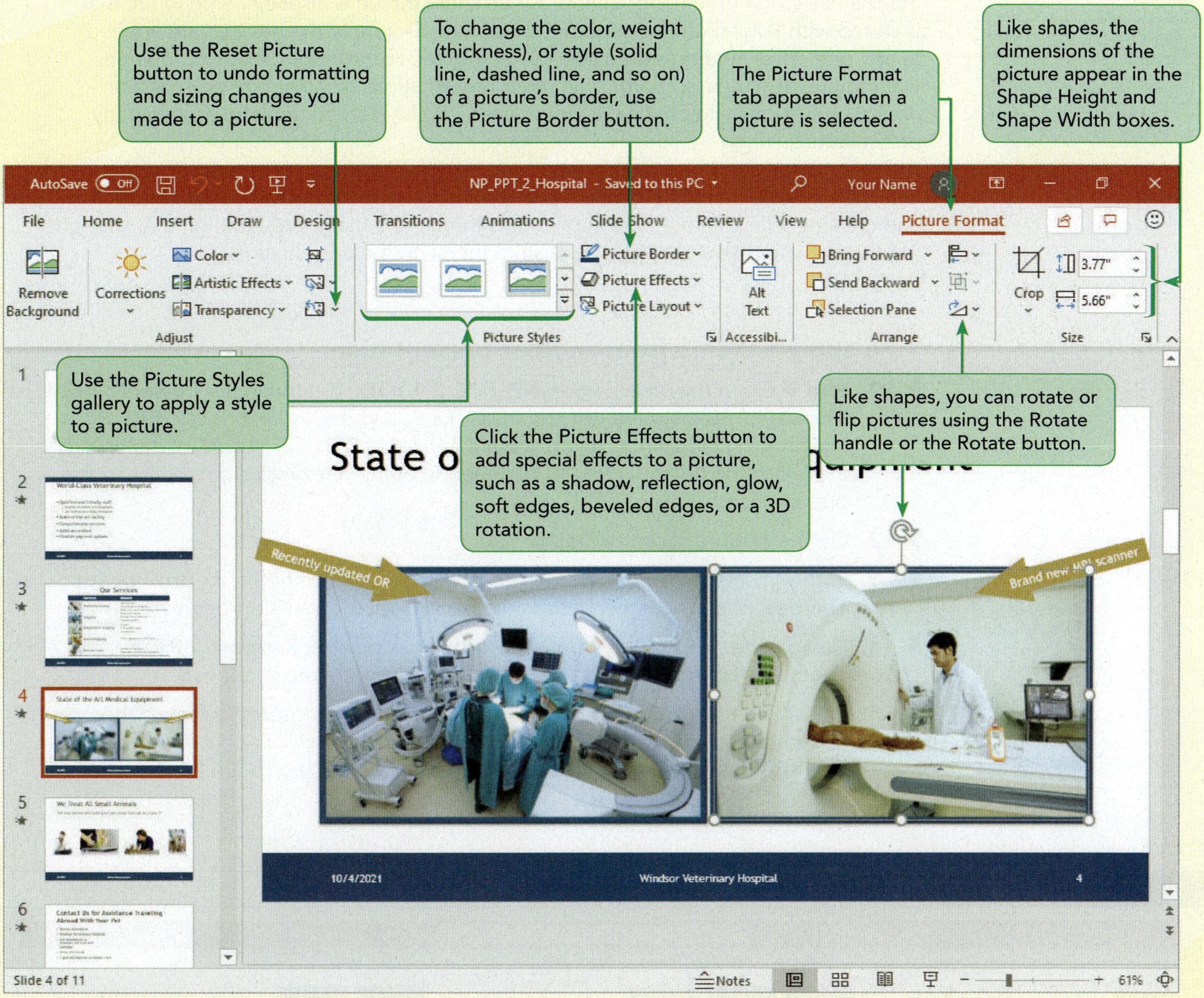

nimon/Shutterstock.com; Javier Brosch/Shutterstock.com; JPC-PROD/Shutterstock.com; Ivonne Wierink/Shutterstock.com; Africa Studio/Shutterstock.com; Veronica Louro/Shutterstock.com; santypan/Shutterstock.com; Rommel Canlas/Shutterstock.com; Ilike/Shutterstock.com

Applying a Theme Used in Another Presentation

As you learned earlier, you can apply an installed theme by clicking an option in the Themes group on the Design tab. An installed theme is a special type of file that is stored with PowerPoint program files. You can also apply themes that are applied to any other presentation stored on your computer. For example, many companies want to promote their brand through their presentations, so they hire presentation design professionals to create custom themes employees can apply to all company presentations.

Teréza created a presentation describing Windsor Veterinary Hospital. She also created a custom theme by changing the theme fonts and colors, modifying layouts, and creating a new layout. She applied this theme to a blank presentation that she sent to you. She wants you to apply the custom theme to the presentation.

To apply a theme from another presentation:

1. sam Open the presentation **NP_PPT_2-1.pptx**, located in the **PowerPoint2 > Module** folder included with your Data Files, and then save it as **NP_PPT_2_Hospital** in the location where you are saving your files. This presentation has the Office theme applied to it. You need to apply Teréza's custom theme to the presentation.
2. On the ribbon, click the **Design** tab.
3. In the Themes group, click the **More** button, and then click **Browse for Themes**. The Choose Theme or Themed Document dialog box opens.
4. Navigate to the **PowerPoint2 > Module** folder, click **Support_PPT_2_Theme.pptx**, and then click **Apply**. The custom theme is applied.
5. In the Themes group, point to the first theme in the gallery, which is the current theme. Its ScreenTip identifies it as Support_PPT_2_Theme. See Figure 2–1. The options that appear in the Variants group are the Office theme variants. If you click a variant, you will reapply the Office theme with the variant you selected.

Figure 2–1 Custom theme applied

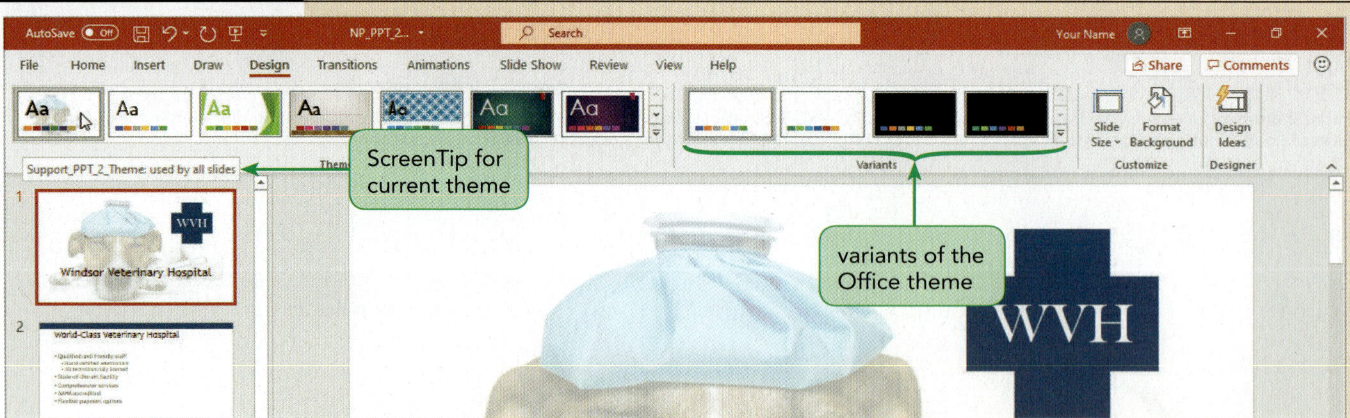

Javier Brosch/Shutterstock.com

After you apply a custom theme, you might need to adjust some of the slides in the presentation. You will check the slides now.

6. Click the **Home** tab, and then on Slide 1 (the title slide), click **Windsor Veterinary Hospital**, the title text.
7. In the Font group, click the **Font arrow**. Notice that Trebuchet MS is the theme font for both the headings and the body text. This is different from the Office theme, which uses Calibri for the body text and Calibri Light for the headings.
8. In the Slides group, click the **Layout button**. The Layout gallery appears. The custom layouts that Teréza created are listed in the gallery, as shown in Figure 2–2.

Figure 2–2 **Custom layouts in the custom theme**

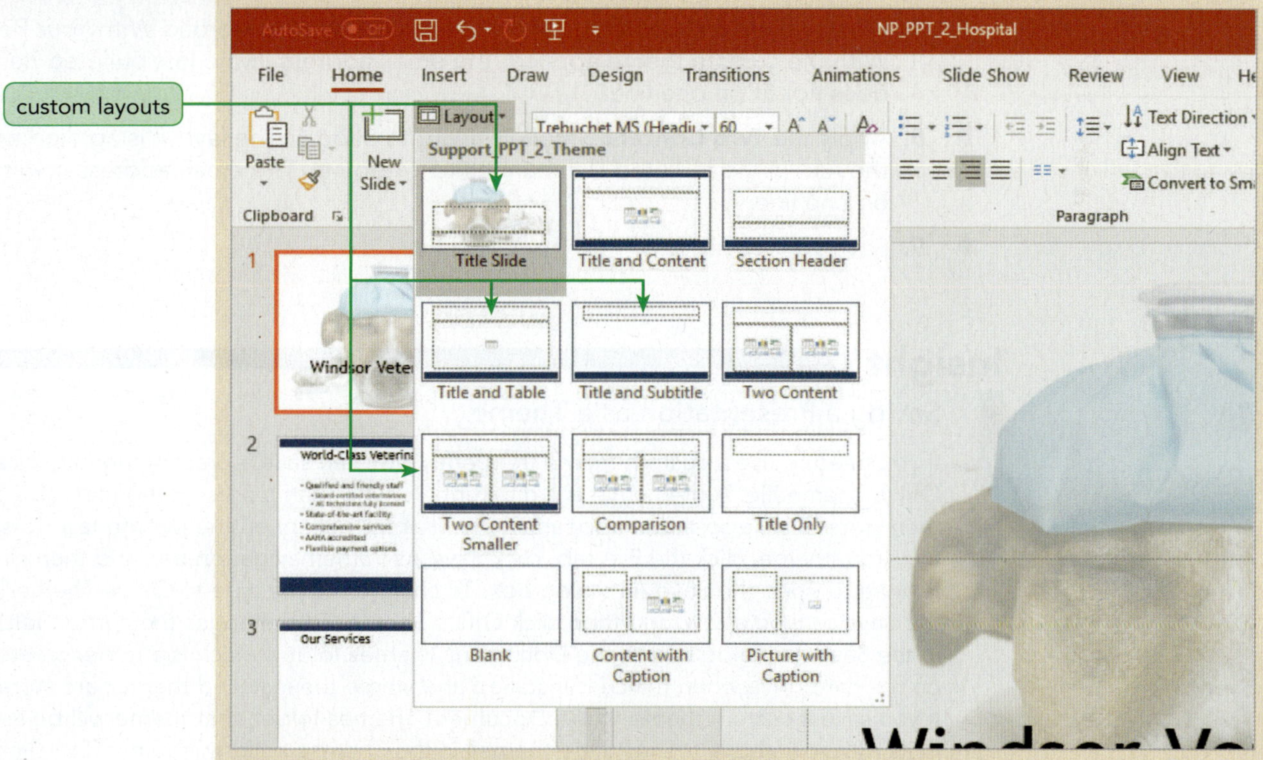

Javier Brosch/Shutterstock.com

9. Press **ESC** to close the Layout gallery.

When you applied the custom theme, the title slide and the slides with the Title and Content and Two Content layouts were changed to use the customized versions of these layouts. Teréza wants you to change the layout of Slide 3 to the custom Title and Table layout, change the layout of Slide 5 to the custom Title and Subtitle layout, and then add the hospital's slogan on Slide 5. You will also examine the other slides to make sure they are formatted correctly with the custom theme applied.

To examine the slides and apply custom layouts to Slides 3, 5, and 6:

1. Display Slide 2 ("World-Class Veterinary Hospital"). Slide 2 looks fine.
2. Display Slide 3 ("Our Services"). You need to apply a custom layout to this slide.
3. In the Slides group, click the **Layout** button, and then click the **Title and Table** layout. The custom layout is applied to Slide 3.
4. Display Slide 4 ("State of the Art Medical Equipment"). This slide looks fine.
5. Display Slide 5 ("We Treat All Small Animals"), and then apply the **Title and Subtitle** layout to it.
6. On Slide 5, click in the subtitle text placeholder, and then type **The only person who loves your pets more than we do is you.** (including the period).
7. Display Slide 6 ("Contact Us for Assistance Traveling Abroad With Your Pet"). With the custom theme applied, the email address in the last bulleted item does not fit on one line.
8. Apply the **Two Content Smaller** layout to Slide 6. The layout is applied and the text in the bulleted list changes to 24 points. The email address now fits on one line.
9. Save your changes.

Insight

Saving a Presentation as a Theme

If you need to use a custom theme frequently, you can save a presentation file as an Office Theme file. A theme file is a different file type than a presentation file. You can then store this file so that it appears in the Themes gallery on the Design tab. To save a custom theme, click the File tab, click Save As in the navigation bar, and then click Browse to open the Save As dialog box. To change the file type to Office Theme, click the Save as type arrow, and then click Office Theme. This changes the current folder in the Save As dialog box to the Document Themes folder, which is a folder created on the hard drive when Office is installed and where the installed themes are stored. If you save a custom theme to the Document Themes folder, that theme will be listed in its own row above the installed themes in the Themes gallery. (You need to click the More button in the Themes gallery to see this row.) You can also change the folder location and save the custom theme to any location on your computer or network or to a folder on your OneDrive. If you do this, the theme will not appear in the Themes gallery, but you can still access it using the Browse for Themes command on the Themes gallery menu.

Inserting Shapes

You can add many shapes to a slide, including lines, rectangles, stars, and more. To draw a shape, click the Shapes button in the Illustrations group on the Insert tab, click a shape in the gallery, and then click on the slide to draw a shape at the default size of about one-inch wide, or click and drag to draw the shape the size you want. Like any object, you can resize a shape after you insert it.

You've already had a little experience with one shape—a text box, which is a shape specifically designed to contain text. You can add additional text boxes to slides using the Text Box shape. You can also add text to any shape you place on a slide.

Teréza wants you to add a label describing one of the photos on Slide 4. You will do this with an arrow shape.

To insert an arrow shape on Slide 4 and add text to it:

1. Display Slide 4 ("State of the Art Medical Equipment").
2. Click the **Insert** tab, and then in the Illustrations group, click the **Shapes** button. The Shapes gallery opens. See Figure 2–3. In addition to the Recently Used Shapes group at the top, the gallery is organized into nine categories of shapes.

Figure 2–3 Shapes gallery

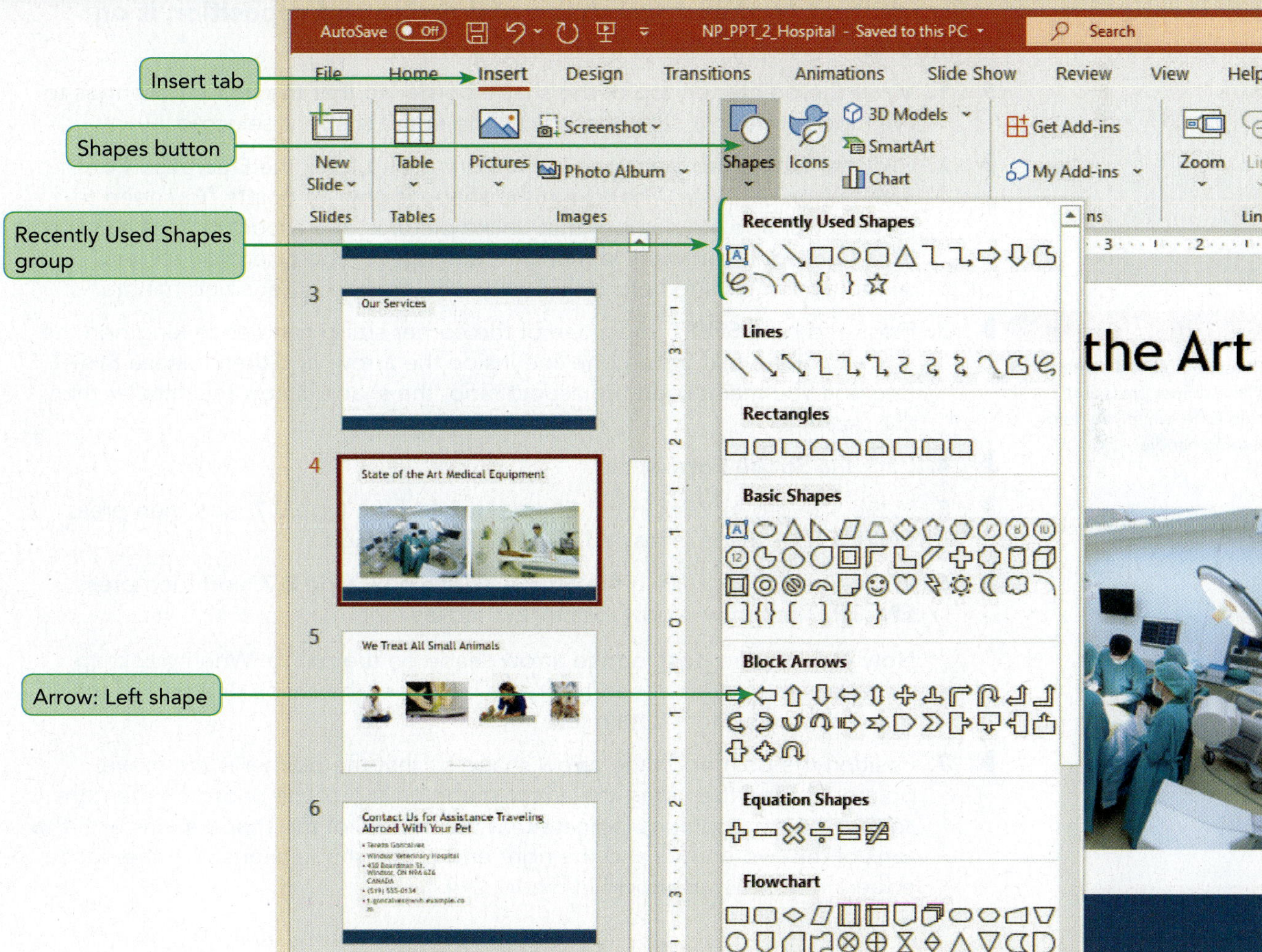

nimon/Shutterstock.com; Veronica Louro/Shutterstock.com; santypan/Shutterstock.com; Rommel Canlas/Shutterstock.com; Ilike/Shutterstock.com

Tip

You can also insert a shape using the Shapes gallery in the Drawing group on the Home tab.

3. Under Block Arrows, click the **Arrow: Left** shape. The gallery closes and the pointer changes to the thin cross pointer +.
4. On the slide, click above the photo on the right and below the word "Equipment" in the title. An orange, left-pointing arrow, approximately one-inch long, appears. (Don't worry about the exact placement of the arrow; you will move it later.) The Shape Format tab is the active tab on the ribbon.
5. With the shape selected, type **Brand new MRI scanner** in the arrow. The text you type appears in the arrow, but it does not all fit.

Next you need to resize the shape to fit the text. Then you will move the arrow to a new position on the slide.

To add text to the arrow shape and resize and reposition it on Slide 4:

1. Move the pointer on top of the shape border so that the pointer changes to the move pointer, and then click. The entire shape is selected.
2. Click the **Home** tab, and then in the Font group, click the **Decrease Font Size** button twice. The text in the shape is now 14 points. You need to resize the shape. Remember that unlike pictures, the aspect ratio of a shape is not locked. If you want to maintain the aspect ratio when you resize a shape, you press and hold SHIFT while you drag a corner sizing handle.
3. Press and hold **SHIFT**, drag one of the corner sizing handles to lengthen the arrow until the text fits on one line inside the arrow, and then release **SHIFT**. Because you maintained the aspect ratio, the shape is now much taller than the text in it.

Tip

To resize from the center of the shape, press and hold CTRL while you drag a sizing handle.

4. Click the **Shape Format** tab.
5. In the Size group, click in the **Shape Height** box, type **0.7**, and then press **ENTER**. The shape is resized so it is 0.7 inches high.
6. In the Size group, click in the **Shape Width** box, type **2.7**, and then press **ENTER**. The arrow is now exactly 2.7 inches long.

   Now you need to position the arrow shape on the photo. When you drag a shape with text, you need to drag a border of the shape or a part of the shape that does not contain text.

7. Position the pointer on the arrow shape so that the pointer is the move pointer, and then drag the arrow shape on top of the photo on the right so that the smart guides indicate that the middle of the shape aligns with the tops of the two photos and the right end of the shape aligns with the right edge of the slide, as shown in Figure 2–4.

Figure 2–4 Arrow shape with text resized and positioned on Slide 4

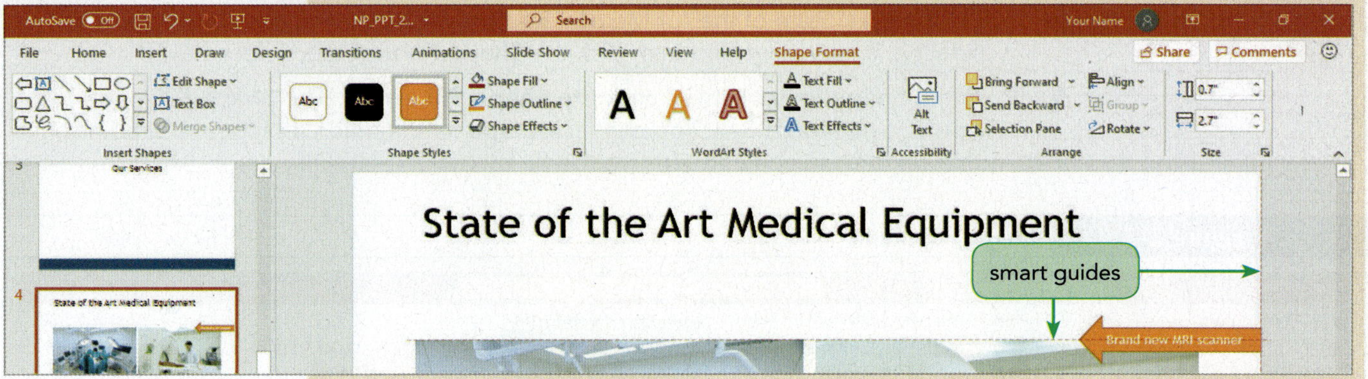

nimon/Shutterstock.com

8. Save your changes to the presentation.

Insight

Using the Draw Tab

The Draw tab on the ribbon contains commands that let you draw on a slide. If you have a device with a touchscreen, you can use your finger or a stylus to draw. If you do not have a touchscreen, you can use the mouse. To draw on a slide, click the Draw button, and then choose different colored pens, a pencil, a highlighter, or a pen style called Galaxy, which draws using a glitter effect. You can adjust any of the drawing tools to create a wider or more narrow line. You can click buttons in the convert group to convert your drawings to text, shapes, or mathematical equations. If you want to draw straight lines or align your drawings, you can use the Ruler button on the Draw tab to display a ruler across the slide that you can rotate to whatever position you want. The drawings are also recorded as a video. After you have finished drawing, you can "replay" the drawing action and watch the characters and shapes you drew get redrawn on the slide. The Draw tab appears on the ribbon automatically if you are using a touchscreen device. If the Draw tab does not appear, you can right-click a tab name on the ribbon, click Customize the Ribbon, and then in the Customize the Ribbon list, click the Draw check box to select it.

Formatting Objects

When you select a shape, including a text box, the Shape Format contextual tab appears. When you select a picture on a slide, the Picture Format contextual tab appears. These tabs contain tools for formatting shapes or pictures. For both shapes and pictures, you can apply borders or outlines and add special effects such as shadows, reflections, a glow effect, soft edges, bevels, and 3-D effects. Some formatting tools are available only for one or the other type of object. For example, the Remove Background tool is available only for pictures, and the Fill command is available only for shapes. Refer to the Session 2.1 Visual Overview for more information about the commands on the Format contextual tabs.

You can apply a style to both shapes and pictures. For example, a picture style can add both a border and a shadow effect to a picture. A shape style could apply a fill color, an outline color, and a shadow effect to a shape.

Formatting Shapes

You can modify the fill of a shape by filling it with a color, a gradient (shading in which one color blends into another or varies from one shade to another), a textured pattern, or a picture. When you add a shape to a slide, the shape is filled with the Accent 1 color from the set of theme colors, and the outline is a darker shade of that color.

Teréza wants you to change the color of the arrow shape on Slide 4.

To change the fill, outline, and style of the arrow shapes:

1. On Slide 4 ("State of the Art Medical Equipment"), click the arrow shape to select it, if necessary, and then click the **Shape Format** tab, if necessary.
2. In the Shape Styles group, click the **Shape Fill arrow**. The Shape Fill menu opens. See Figure 2–5. You can fill a shape with a color, a picture, a gradient, or a texture, or you can remove the fill by clicking No Fill.

Figure 2–5 **Shape Fill menu**

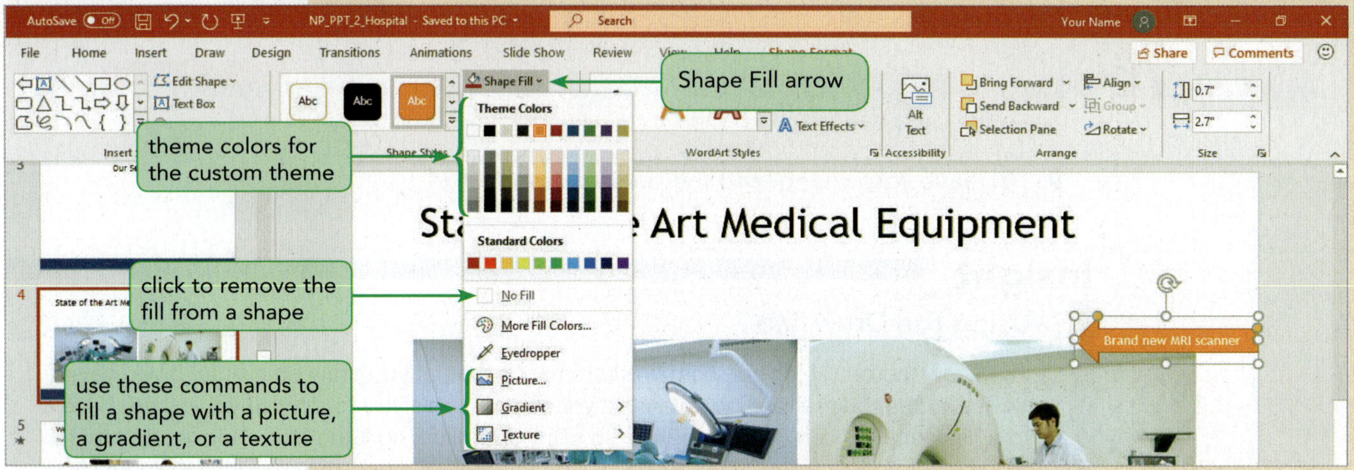

nimon/Shutterstock.com

Tip

You can fill a shape with a picture instead of a color. On the Shape Fill menu, click Picture to open the Insert Pictures dialog box, and then click the location of the picture (From a File, Online Pictures, or From Icons).

3. In the Theme Colors section, click the **Tan, Accent 6** square. The fill of the selected arrow changes to tan.
4. Click the **Shape Fill arrow**, point to **Gradient**, and then in the Dark Variations section click the **Linear Right** gradient (in the first column, second row in the Dark Variations section). The shape is filled with a gradient of tan that is darker on the left side of the shape and fades to a lighter shade on the right side of the shape.
5. In the Shape Styles group, click the **Shape Outline arrow**. The Shape Outline menu appears. See Figure 2–6. You can change the color of a shape outline, the width (by clicking Weight), or the style (by clicking Dashes).

Figure 2–6 **Shape Outline menu**

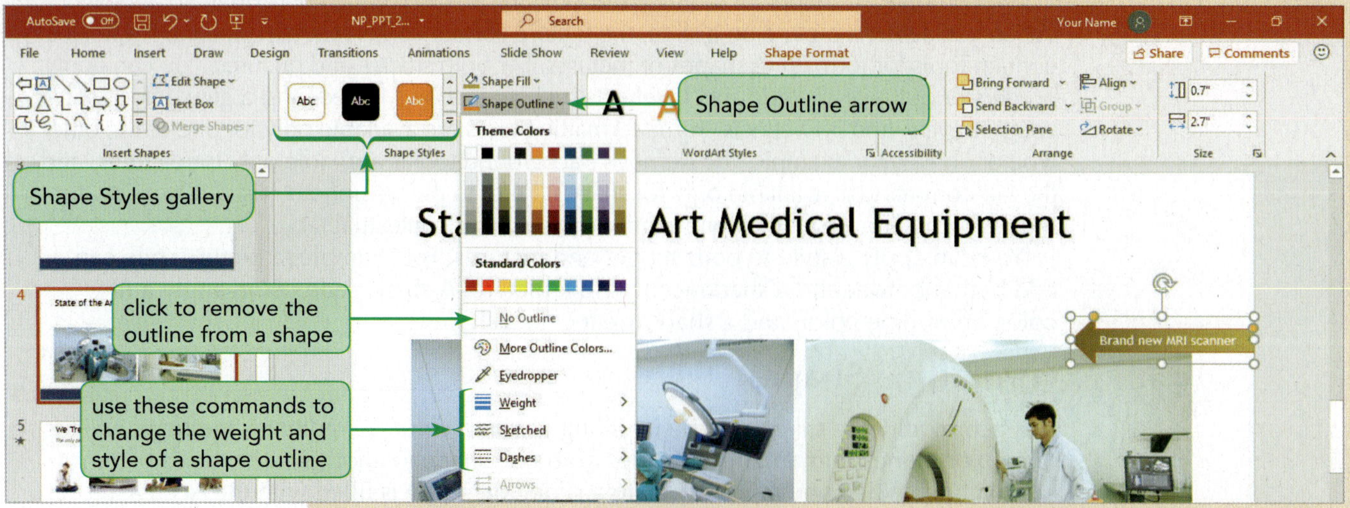

nimon/Shutterstock.com

6. On the menu, point to **Weight**, and then click **6 pt**. The width of the outline increases to six points. Teréza doesn't like this look, so she asks you to apply a style instead.
7. In the Shape Styles group, click the **More** button. The Shape Styles gallery opens.
8. Scroll down, and then in the Presets section, click the **Colored Fill – Tan, Accent 6, No Outline** style. The style, which fills the shape with tan and removes the outline, is applied to the shape.

Tip

To make other adjustments to shapes, in the Insert Shapes group on the Shape Format tab, click the Edit Points button, and then drag the points that appear on the shape. To replace a shape with a different one, click the Edit Shape button, point to Change Shape, and then click the shape you want.

On some shapes, you can drag the yellow adjustment handle to change the shape's proportions. For instance, if you drag one of the adjustment handles on the arrow shape, you would change the size of the arrowhead relative to the size of the arrow.

Teréza wants you to change the shape of the arrow by making the arrowhead larger relative to the size of the arrow shape.

To adjust the arrow shape:

1. Click the arrow shape, if necessary, to select it. There are two yellow adjustment handles on the arrow shape. One adjustment handle is at the right end of the arrow. The other adjustment handle is at the base of the arrowhead on the top border of the shape.
2. Drag the adjustment handle at the base of the arrowhead to the right so that the bottom edge of the arrowhead is approximately between the letters "a" and "n" in "Brand." Compare your screen to Figure 2–7.

Figure 2–7 Arrow shape after using the adjustment handle

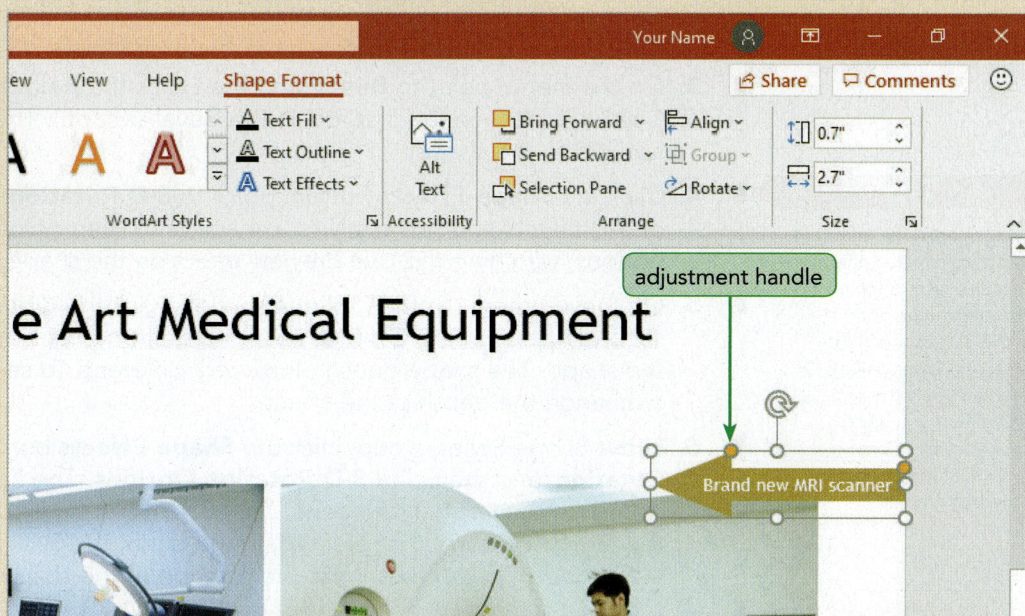

nimon/Shutterstock.com

Another way you can format a shape is to apply effects to it, such as a shadow, reflection, glow, soft edges, bevel, and 3-D rotation effect. Teréza placed a cross shape containing the hospital's initials on Slide 1. She wants you to make the cross shape look three-dimensional.

To apply 3-D effects to the shape on Slide 1:

1. Display Slide 1 (the title slide), click the cross shape, and then click the **Shape Format** tab.
2. In the Shape Styles group, click the **Shape Effects** button. The Shape Effects menu opens. The menu contains a list of the types of effects you can apply. See Figure 2–8.

Figure 2–8 Shape Effects menu

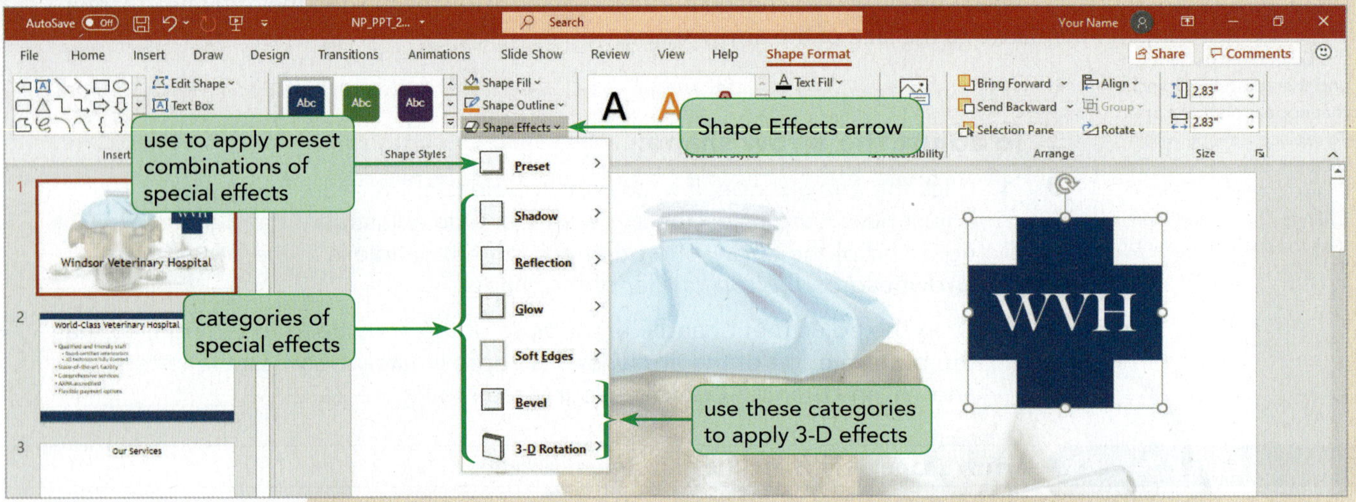

Javier Brosch/Shutterstock.com

3. On the menu, point to **Bevel**, and then click the **Relaxed Inset** button (second button in the first row in the Bevel section). The bevel effect is applied to the shape.
4. Click the **Shape Effects** button, point to **3-D Rotation** to open a submenu of 3-D effects you can apply to a shape, and then point to several of the options, watching the Live Preview effect on the shape.
5. On the submenu, in the Oblique section, click the **Oblique: Top Right** (the second option in the Oblique section) rotation effect. The effect is applied to the shape. The shape doesn't look very different. To see the effect, you need to change the depth of the effect.
6. In the Shape Styles group, click the **Shape Effects** button, point to **3-D Rotation**, and then click **3-D Rotation Options**. The Format Shape pane opens on the right. In the pane, Shape Options is selected at the top, and the Effects button is selected. In the pane, the 3-D Rotation section is expanded. You can customize the rotation of the shape in this section.
7. In the Format Shape pane, click **3-D Format**. The 3-D Format section expands. In this section of the pane, you can customize the bevel, the depth of the shape, the contour color, and the look of the shape by changing the material and lighting settings.

   Trouble? If the 3-D Format section is not expanded, it was already expanded before you clicked it. Click 3-D Format in the pane again.

Tip

You can apply an effect that mimics a 3-D effect to a SmartArt graphic by selecting an option in the 3D section in the SmartArt Styles gallery. Or you can apply the same 3-D effects you apply to shapes by selecting individual shapes in the SmartArt graphic.

8. In the 3-D Format section, in the Depth section, click in the **Size** box, and then edit the number so it is **120 pt**. The shape changes so that the depth is increased to 120 points. The cross now looks three-dimensional.

9. In the Depth section, click the **Color** button, and then click **Dark Blue, Accent 3, Darker 50%**. The color of the depth shading changes to dark blue. Compare your screen to Figure 2–9.

Figure 2–9 Cross shape formatted to look three-dimensional

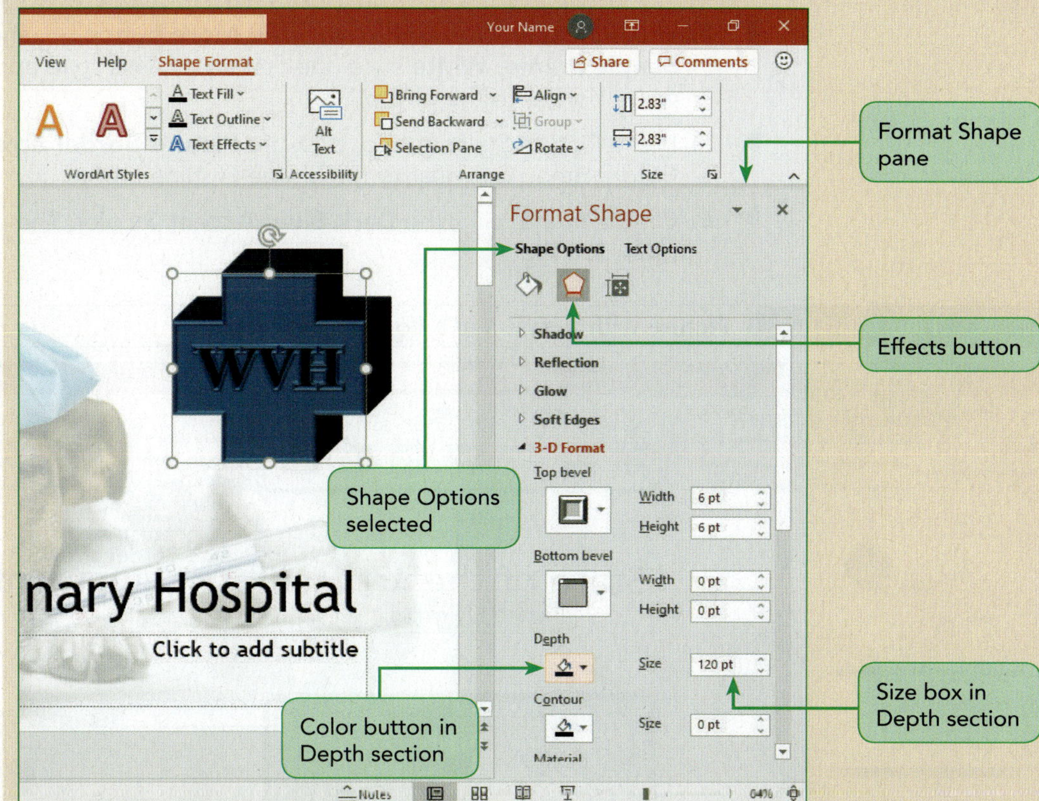

Javier Brosch/Shutterstock.com

10. In the upper-right corner of the Format Shape pane, click the **Close** button.

Formatting Pictures

You can format pictures as well as shapes. To format pictures, you use the tools on the Picture Format tab.

Teréza wants you to format the pictures on Slide 4 by adding colored borders. To create a border, you could apply a thick outline, or you can apply one of the styles that includes a border and then modify it.

To format the photos on Slide 4:

1. Display Slide 4 ("State of the Art Medical Equipment"), click the photo on the left, and then click the **Picture Format** tab.
2. In the Picture Styles group, click the **More** button, and then click the **Metal Oval** style (the last style in the last row). The style is applied to the picture. Teréza doesn't like that style.
3. In the Adjust group, click the **Reset Picture** button. The style is removed from the picture, and the picture is reset to its original condition.
4. In the Picture Styles group, click the **More** button, and then click the **Simple Frame, White** style (the first style). This style applies a 7-point white border to the photo.
5. In the Picture Styles group, click the **Picture Border arrow**. The Picture Border menu is similar to the Shape Outline menu.
6. On the menu, click the **Dark Blue, Accent 3** color. The picture border is now blue. See Figure 2–10.

Figure 2–10 Picture with a style and a border color applied

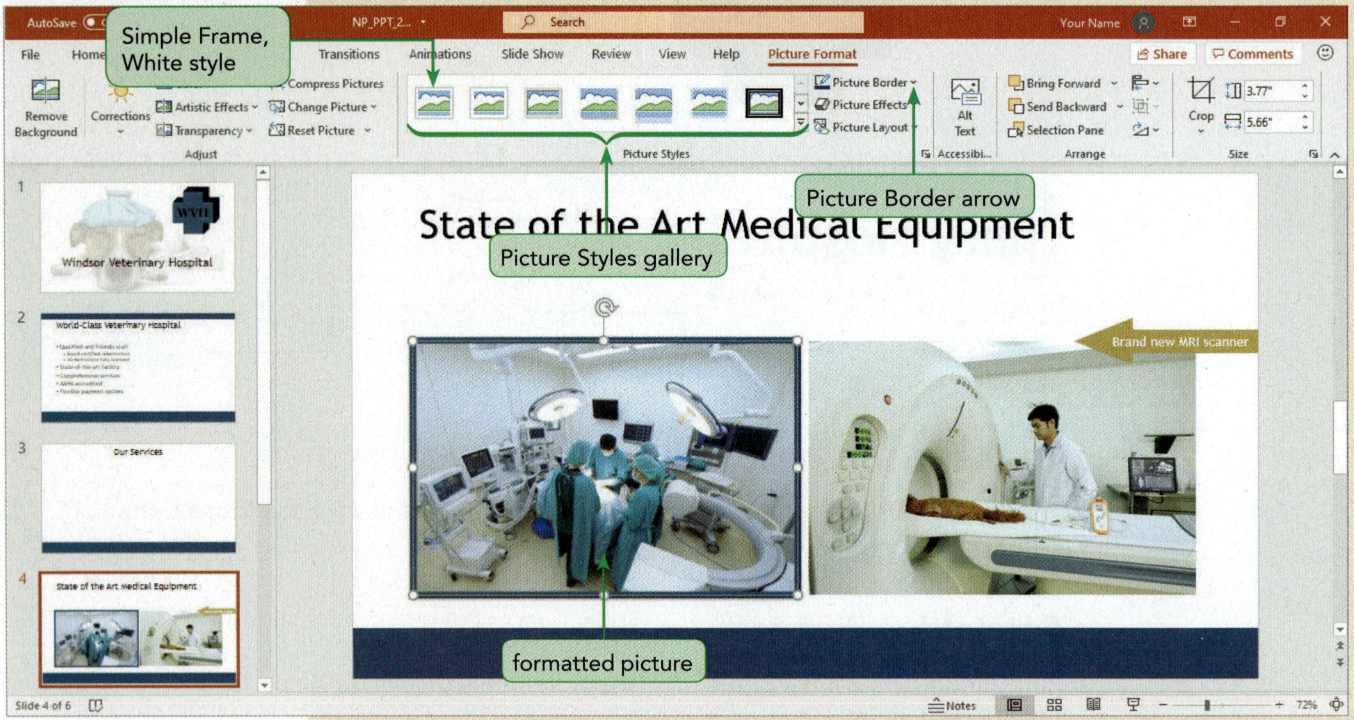

nimon/Shutterstock.com; Javier Brosch/Shutterstock.com

You need to apply the same formatting to the photo on the right on Slide 4. You can repeat the same formatting steps, or you can copy the formatting.

7. With the left photo on Slide 4 still selected, click the **Home** tab.
8. In the Clipboard group, click the **Format Painter** button, and then move the pointer to the slide. The pointer changes to the Format Painter pointer for objects.
9. Click the photo on the right. The style and border color of the photo on the left is copied and applied to the photo on the right.
10. Save your changes.

Tip

You can also use the Format Painter to copy the formatting of shapes and text.

Duplicating Objects

Teréza decides she wants you to add an arrow pointing to the picture of the operating room on the left of Slide 4. You could draw another arrow, but instead, you'll duplicate the arrow you just drew so that they have the same style and size. When you duplicate an object, you create a copy of the object, but nothing is placed on the Clipboard. You can only use the Duplicate command to duplicate objects, including text boxes. You cannot use the Duplicate command to duplicate selected text.

To duplicate the arrow on Slide 4 and edit the text in the shape:

1. On Slide 4 ("State of the Art Medical Equipment"), click the arrow shape to select it.
2. On the Home tab, in the Clipboard group, click the **Copy arrow**. A menu opens.
3. On the menu, click **Duplicate**. A duplicate of the arrow appears on the slide.
4. Move the pointer on top of the duplicate shape so that the pointer changes to the I-beam pointer, and then click before the first word "Brand." The insertion point appears in the shape before "Brand."

   Trouble? If the insertion point is not before "Brand," press LEFT ARROW or RIGHT ARROW as needed to move it to the correct position.

Tip

You can also press and hold SHIFT then press an arrow key to select adjacent text.

5. Press and hold **SHIFT**, click after the last word, "scanner," and then release **SHIFT**. All of the text between the locations where you clicked is selected.
6. Type **Recently updated OR** in the duplicate arrow. The text you type replaces the selected text.
7. Drag the duplicate arrow to the left so that the smart guides indicate that the left edge of the duplicate arrow shape aligns with the left edge of the slide and the duplicate arrow shape aligns with the original arrow shape as shown in Figure 2–11.

Figure 2–11 Duplicate arrow repositioned on Slide 4

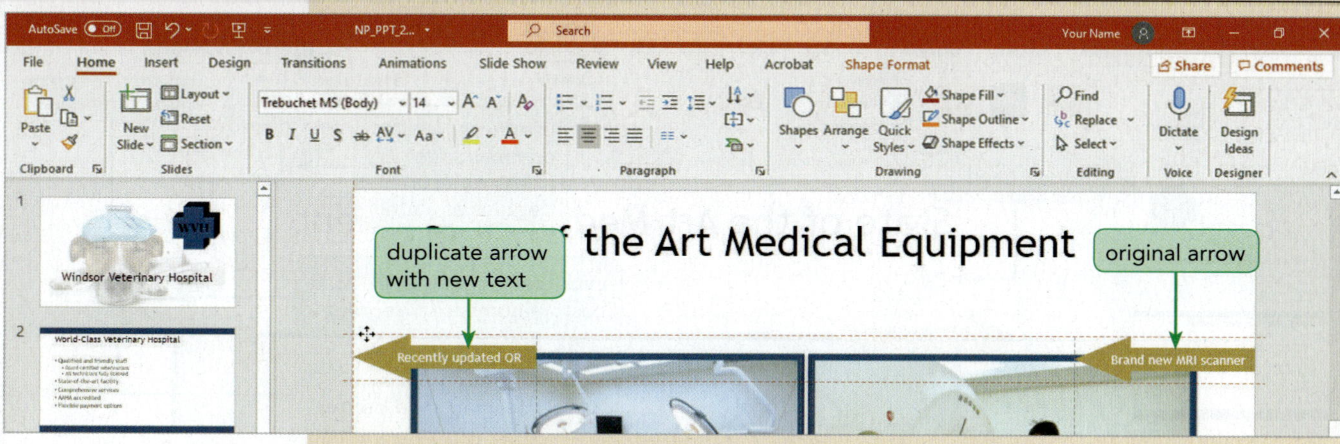

nimon/Shutterstock.com; Javier Brosch/Shutterstock.com

8. Save your changes.

Rotating and Flipping Objects

Tip

You can also click the Arrange button in the Drawing group on the Home tab to access the Rotate and Flip commands.

You can rotate and flip any object on a slide. To flip an object, you click the Rotate button in the Arrange group on the Shape Format tab or on the Picture Format tab to access the Flip commands on the Rotate menu. To rotate an object, you can use the Rotate commands on the Rotate menu to rotate objects in 90-degree increments. You can also drag the rotate handle that appears above the top-middle sizing handle to rotate a selected object to any position that you want.

Teréza wants you to rotate the arrows on Slide 4 so that they are slanted. Also, the "Recently updated OR" arrow on Slide 4 needs to point to the right. To make that change, you need to flip the arrow.

To flip the duplicate arrow shape on Slide 4:

1. On Slide 4 ("State of the Art Medical Equipment"), click the Brand new MRI scanner arrow to select it. The shape border appears with the Rotate handle above the shape. The right end of the arrow is touching the right side of the slide.
2. Position the pointer on the **rotate handle** so that the pointer changes to the rotate pointer, and then drag the **rotate handle** counter-clockwise to the left until only the bottom corner of the arrow shape is still touching the right side of the slide.
3. Click the **Recently updated OR** arrow, and then drag the rotate handle 180 degrees to the right so that the arrow is pointing to the right. Now the arrow is pointing in the correct direction, but the text in the arrow is now upside down.
4. On the Quick Access Toolbar, click the **Undo** button, and then click the **Shape Format** tab, if necessary.
5. In the Arrange group, click the **Rotate** button. The Rotate menu opens. See Figure 2–12.

Figure 2–12 Rotate menu

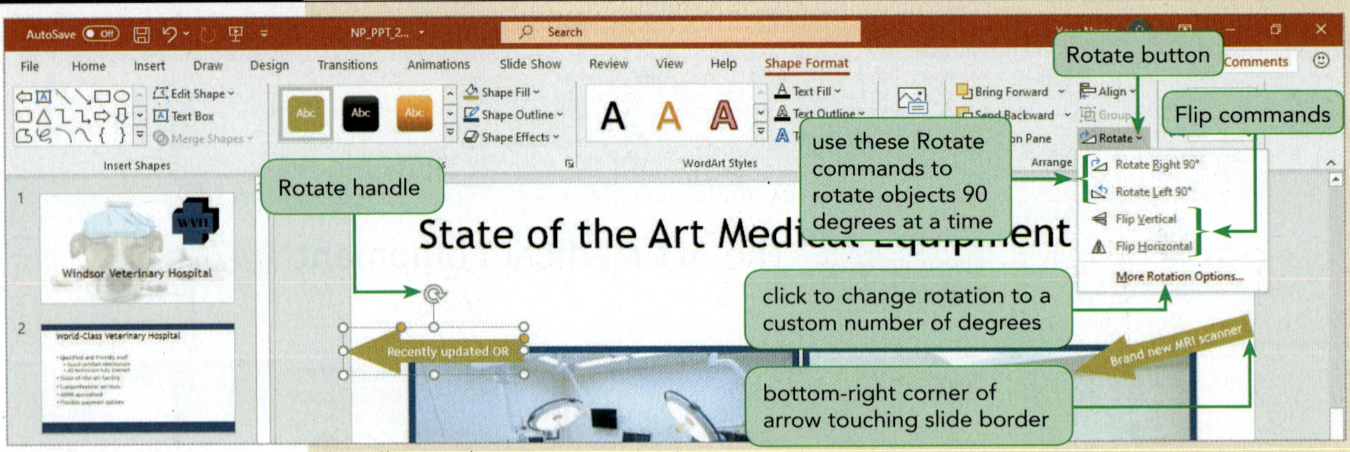

nimon/Shutterstock.com

6. Click **Flip Horizontal**. The arrow flips horizontally and is now pointing right. Unlike when you rotated the arrow, the text is still right-side up.
7. Drag the **rotate handle** clockwise to the right until only the bottom corner of the arrow shape is still touching the left side of the slide. Usually, using the rotate handle is fine, but you can also rotate objects by a precise number of degrees.

8. In the Arrange group, click the **Rotate** button, and then click **More Rotation Options**. The Format Shape pane opens with the Shape Options tab selected and the Size & Properties button selected. The Size section is expanded. The value in the Rotation box indicates the number of degrees the object was rotated in a clockwise direction from its original position.
9. If the value in the Rotation box is not 15°, click in the **Rotation** box, edit the value so it is **15°**, and then press **ENTER**.
10. Click the **Brand new MRI scanner** arrow shape. The value in the Rotation box will be a value between 270° and 360°. This is because no matter which way you dragged the rotate handle, the final value in the Rotation box is the number of degrees the object is rotated in a clockwise direction.
11. If the value in the Rotation box is not 345°, click in the **Rotation** box, and then edit the value so it is **345°**, and then press **ENTER**.
12. Close the Format Shape pane, and then save your changes.

Creating and Formatting a Table

A **table** is a grid of rows and columns that can contain text and graphics. A **cell** is the box where a row and column intersect. Each cell contains one piece of information. **Gridlines** in a table are the nonprinting lines that show cell boundaries. Gridlines create a table's structure.

Creating a Table and Adding Data to It

Teréza wants you to add a table to Slide 3 that describes some of the services the hospital offers. This table will have three columns—one to list the services, one to give examples of the services, and one to list notes.

Reference

Inserting a Table

- On the ribbon, click the Insert tab, and then in the Tables group, click the Table button.
- Click a box in the grid to create a table of that size.

or

- In a content placeholder, click the Insert Table button; or, click the Insert tab on the ribbon, click the Table button in the Tables group, and then click Insert Table.
- Specify the numbers of columns and rows, and then click the OK button.

Teréza hasn't decided how many services to include in the table, so she asks you to start by creating a table with four rows.

To add a table to Slide 3:

1. Display Slide 3 ("Our Services"). You can click the Table button in the content placeholder or you can use the Table command on the Insert tab.
2. Click the **Insert** tab, and then in the Tables group, click the **Table** button. A menu opens with a grid of squares above three commands.

3. Point to the grid, and without clicking the mouse button, move the pointer over the grid. The label above the grid indicates how large the table will be, and a preview of the table appears on the slide. See Figure 2–13.

Figure 2–13 **Inserting a 3×4 table on Slide 3**

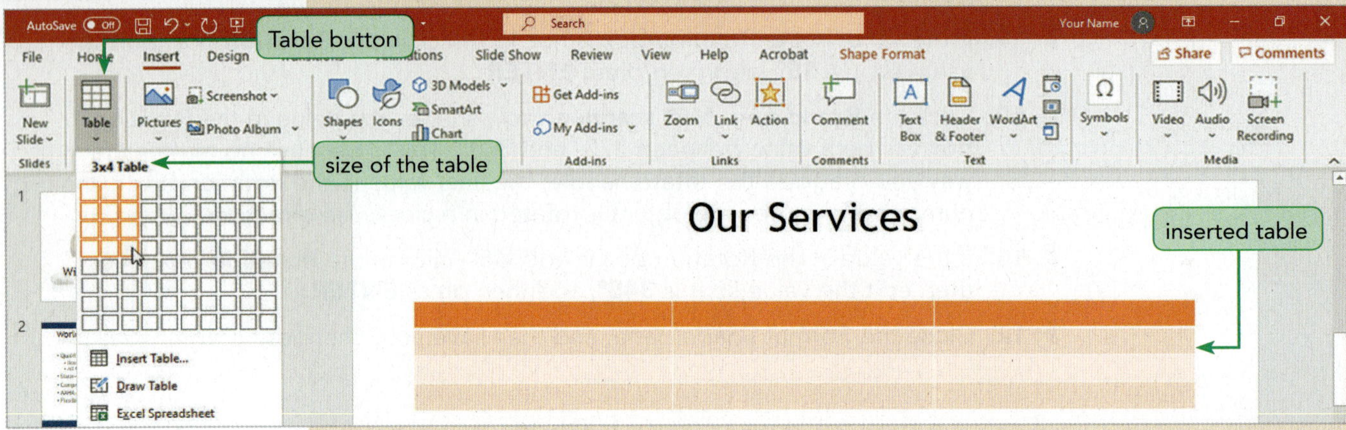

4. When the label above the grid indicates 3×4 Table, click to insert a table with three columns and four rows. A selection border appears around the table, and the insertion point is in the first cell in the first row. On the ribbon, two table contextual tabs appear.

Now you're ready to fill the blank cells with the information about the services. To enter data in a table, you click in the cells in which you want to enter data and then start typing. You can also use the Tab and arrow keys to move from one cell to another.

To add data to the table:

1. In the first cell in the first row, type **Service**. The text you typed appears in the first cell.
2. Press **TAB**. The insertion point moves to the second cell in the first row.
3. Type **Details**, press **TAB**, type **Notes**, and then press **TAB**. The insertion point is in the first cell in the second row.
4. In the first cell in the second row, type **Wellness Exams**, press **TAB**, and then type **Vaccinations** in the second cell. You need to add two more lines in the second cell in the second row.
5. Press **ENTER**, type **Nutritional counseling**, press **ENTER**, and then type **Flea, tick, and heartworm prevention**. The height of the second row increased to fit the extra lines of text in this cell.
6. Click in the first cell in the third row, type **Surgery**, and then press **TAB**.
7. In the second cell in the third row, type **Spay and neuter**, press **ENTER**, type **Foreign body removal**, press **ENTER**, and then type **Trauma repair**.
8. Click in the first cell in the last row, type **Diagnostic Imaging**, and then press **TAB**.
9. In the second cell in the last row, type **X-rays**, press **ENTER**, type **CT and MRI scans**, press **ENTER**, and then type **Ultrasounds**.

Inserting and Deleting Rows and Columns

You can modify the table by adding or deleting rows and columns. You need to add more rows to the table for additional services.

To insert rows and a column in the table:

1. Make sure the insertion point is in the last row in the table.
2. Click the **Layout** tab, and then in the Rows & Columns group, click the **Insert Below** button. A new row is inserted below the current row. See Figure 2–14.

Figure 2–14 Table with row inserted

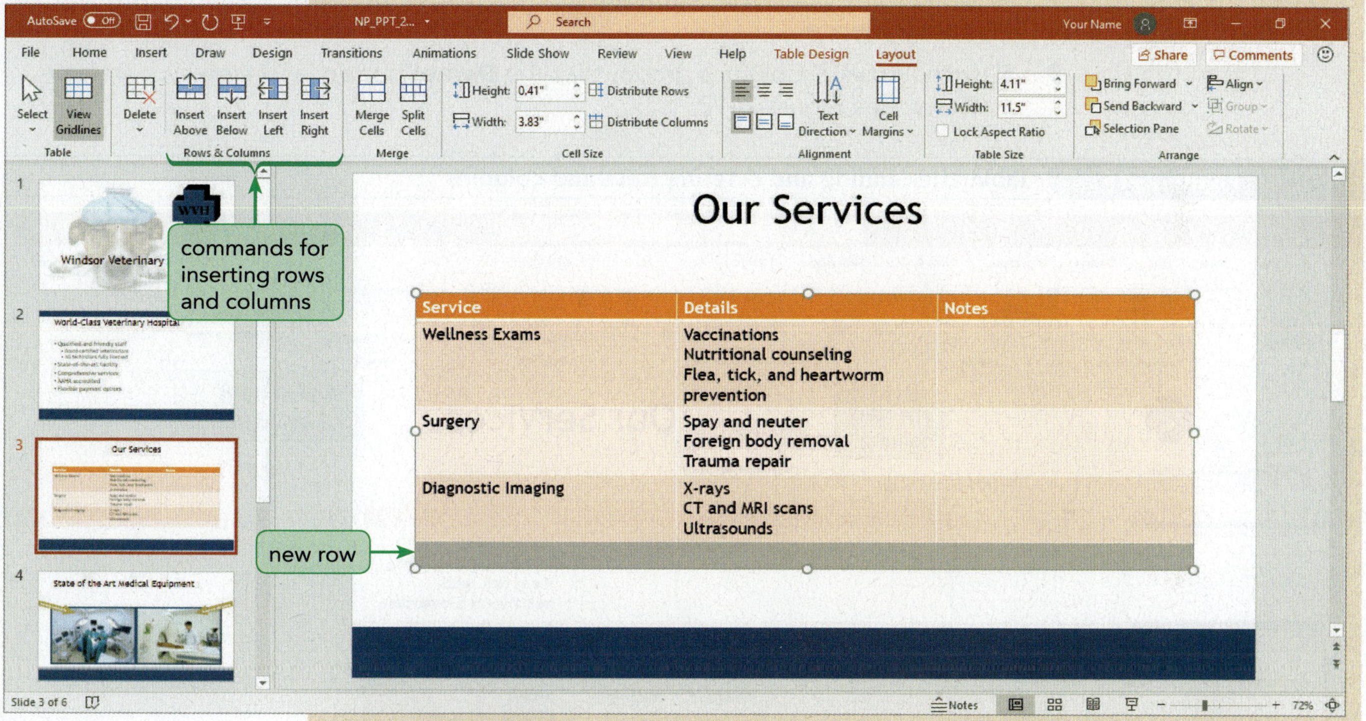

Javier Brosch/Shutterstock.com; nimon/Shutterstock.com

3. Click in the first cell in the new last row, type **Microchipping**, and then press **TAB**.
4. Type **Chip frequency is 134.2 kHz**, and then press **TAB**. The insertion point is in the last cell in the last row.
5. Press **TAB**. A new row is created, and the insertion point is in the first cell in the new row.
6. Type **Dental Care**, press **TAB**, type **Preventative care**, press **ENTER**, and then type **Treatment of all oral problems**. You need to insert a row above the last row.
7. In the Rows & Columns group, click the **Insert Above** button. A new row is inserted above the current row, and all of the cells in the new row are selected. You also need to insert a column to the left of the first column.
8. Click any cell in the first column, and then in the Rows & Columns group, click the **Insert Left** button. A new first column is inserted.

Teréza decided she doesn't want to add notes to the table, so you'll delete the last column. She also decided that she doesn't need the new row you added as the second to last row in the table, so you'll delete that row.

To delete a column and a row in the table:

1. Click in any cell in the last column in the table. This is the column you will delete.
2. On the Layout tab, in the Rows & Columns group, click the **Delete** button. The Delete button menu opens.
3. Click **Delete Columns**. The current column is deleted, and the entire table is selected.
4. Click in any cell in the second to last row (the empty row). This is the row you want to delete.
5. In the Rows & Columns group, click the **Delete** button, and then click **Delete Rows**. See Figure 2–15.

Figure 2–15 Table after adding and deleting rows and columns

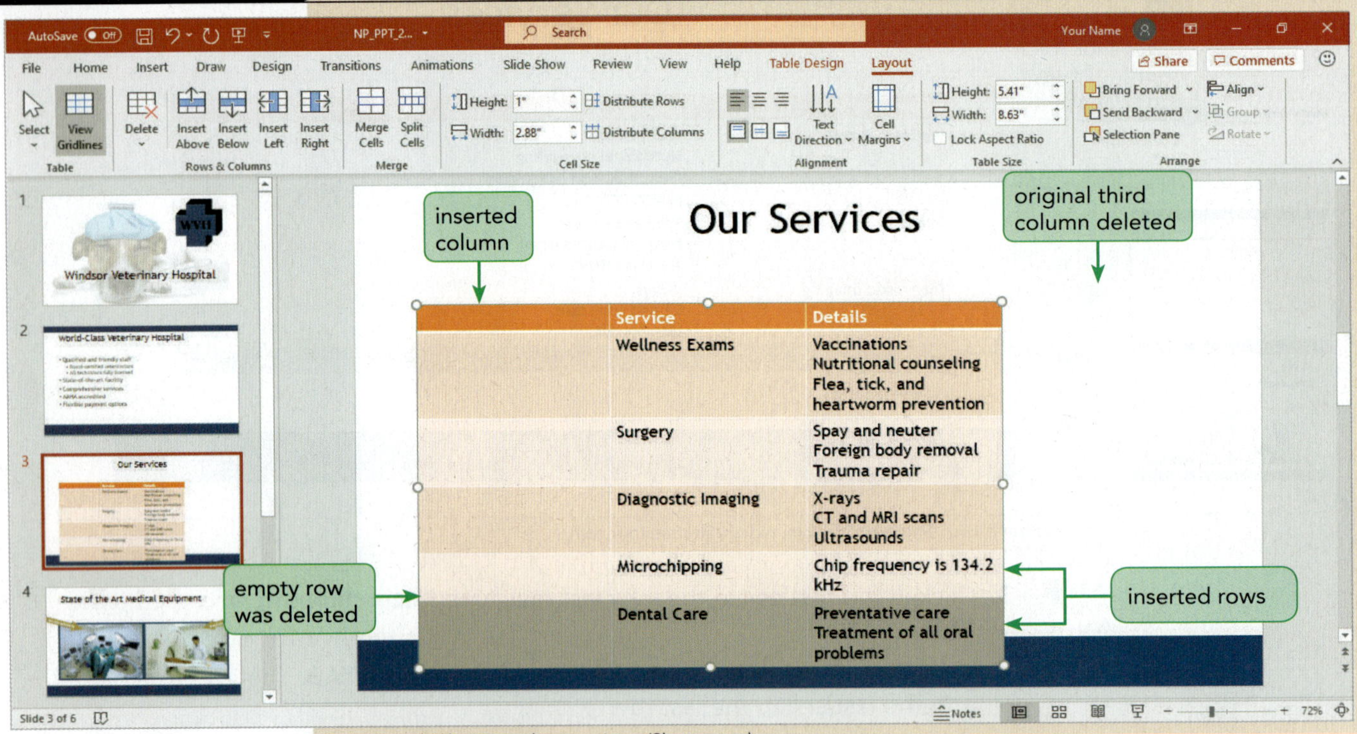

Javier Brosch/Shutterstock.com; nimon/Shutterstock.com

Formatting a Table

After you insert data into a table, you need to think about how the table looks and whether the table will be readable for the audience. As with any text, you can change the font, size, or color, and as with shapes and pictures, you can apply a style to a table. You can also change how the text fits in the table cells by changing the height of rows and the width of columns. You can also customize the formatting of the table by changing the border and fill of table cells.

You need to change the font size of the text in the table.

To change the font size of text in the table:

1. Move the pointer on top of the left edge of the cell containing "Service" so that the pointer changes to the cell selection pointer ↗, and then click. The entire cell is selected, and the Mini toolbar appears. You want to change the size of all the text in the table, so you will select the entire table. Notice that a selection border appears around the table. This border appears any time the insertion point is in a table cell or part of the table is selected.
2. Click the **Layout** tab, if necessary, and then in the Table group, click the **Select** button. The Select menu opens with options to select the entire table, the current column, or the current row.
3. Click **Select Table**. The entire table is selected. Because the selection border appears any time the insertion point is in the table, the only visual cues you have that the entire table is now selected are that no cells in the table are selected, the insertion point is not blinking in any cell in the table, and the Select button is gray and unavailable. See Figure 2–16.

Figure 2–16 Table selected on Slide 3

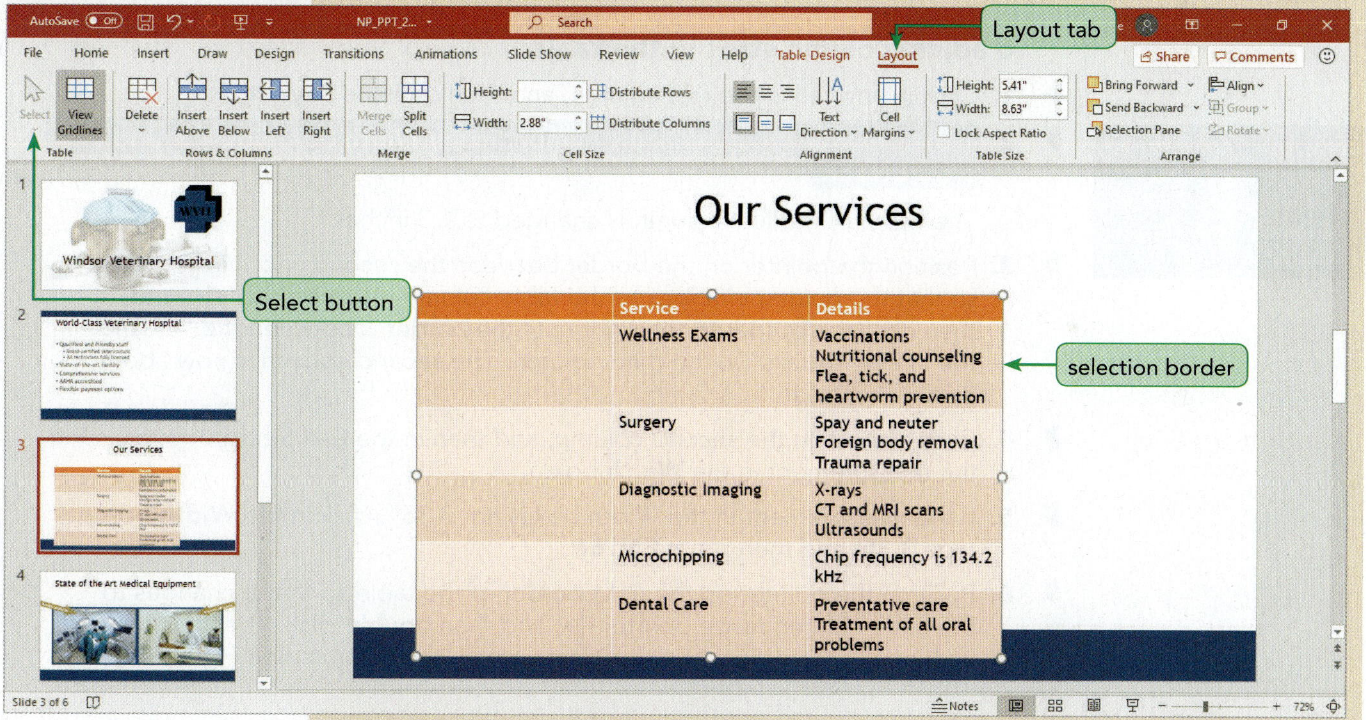

Javier Brosch/Shutterstock.com; nimon/Shutterstock.com

4. On the ribbon, click the **Home** tab.
5. In the Font group, click the **Font Size arrow**, and then click **24**. Because the entire table is selected, the size of all the text in the table changes to 24 points. The height of all the rows in the table increases to fit the larger text size.
6. Move the pointer on top of the top border of the table so that the pointer changes to the move pointer ✥, and then drag the table up until the top of the table aligns with the top of the slide and so that you can see the last row in the table. The table will be on top of the title.
7. Click any cell in the third column, and then click the **Layout** tab.

8. In the Table group, click the **Select** button, and then click **Select Column**. All of the cells in the third column are selected. You want to change the font size of only the text in the cells below the heading row.
9. Click in the second cell in the third column, press and hold **SHIFT**, and then click in the last cell in the third column. All of the cells in the third column except the first cell are selected.
10. On the ribbon, click the **Home** tab.
11. In the Font group, click the **Font Size arrow**, and then click **18**. The text in the selected cells changes to 18 points and the height of those rows decreases.

Next, you will adjust the column widths to better fit the data. To adjust column widths, you can drag a column border or type a number in the Width box in the Cell Size group on the Layout tab. You can also automatically adjust a column to fit its widest entry by double-clicking its right border.

To adjust column sizes in the table:

1. Click in any cell in the first column, and then click the **Layout** tab.
2. In the Cell Size group, click the number in the **Width** box, type **1.3**, and then press **ENTER**.

   The width of the first column is changed to 1.3 inches.

Make sure you change the value in the Width box in the Cell Size group and not the value in the Width box in the Table Size group.

3. Position the pointer on the border between the second and third columns so that the pointer changes to the table column resize pointer +||+, and then drag the border to the right until the border is between the "e" and the "t" in "Details" in the third column. The second column is now about 3.35 inches wide.
4. Click any cell in the second column, and then in the Cell Size group, examine the measurement in the **Width** box.
5. If the measurement in the Width box is not 3.35", click in the **Width** box, type **3.35**, and then press **ENTER**.
6. Position the pointer on the right border of the table so that it changes to the table column resize pointer +||+, and then double-click. The third column widens to accommodate the widest entry in the column. See Figure 2–17.

Figure 2–17 **Table column widths adjusted**

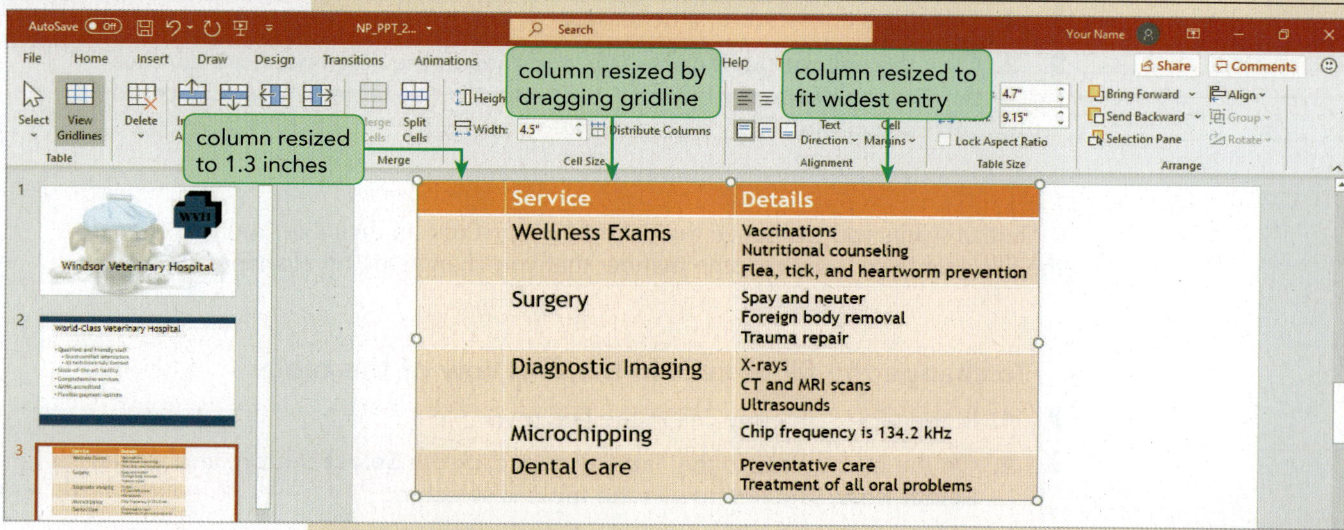

Javier Brosch/Shutterstock.com

Trouble? If you have trouble making the pointer change to the table column resize pointer, move the pointer a little to the left of the right border. If you still can't do it, click the Layout tab, click in the Width box in the Cell Size group, type 4.5, and then press ENTER.

7. Move the pointer on top of the top, bottom, or one of the side borders of the table so that the pointer changes to the move pointer, and then drag the table down so that the smart guides indicated that the table is centered horizontally and vertically on the slide.

On the Layout tab, in the Alignment group, you can change the alignment of text in cells. Figure 2–18 describes the buttons in the Alignment group that you can use to align text in table cells.

Figure 2–18 **Alignment commands on the Layout tab**

Button	Name	Description
	Align Left	Horizontally align the text along the left edge of the cell.
	Center	Horizontally align the text between the left and right edges of the cell.
	Align Right	Horizontally align the text along the right edge of the cell.
	Align Top	Vertically align the text along the top edge of the cell.
	Center Vertically	Vertically align the text between the top and bottom edges of the cell.
	Align Bottom	Vertically align the text along the bottom edge of the cell.

The text in all cells in the table is horizontally left-aligned and vertically aligned at the top of the cells. The table would look better if the text was vertically aligned in the center of the cells.

To adjust the alignment of text in cells:

1. Select the entire table, if necessary.
2. Click the **Layout** tab if necessary, and then in the Alignment group, click the **Center Vertically** button. The text in the table cells is now centered vertically in the cells.

Teréza wants you to change the color of the first row in the table. You can change the fill of table cells in the same manner that you change the fill of shapes.

To change the fill of cells in the first row of the table:

1. In the table, click any cell in the first row.
2. On the Layout tab, in the Table group, click the **Select** button, and then click **Select Row**. The first row in the table is selected.
3. Click the **Table Design** tab.
4. In the Table Styles group, click the **Shading arrow**. The Shading menu is similar to the Shape Fill menu you worked with earlier. The menu also includes the Table Background command that you can use to fill the table background with a color or a picture.
5. Click the **Tan, Background 2** color (in the third column), and then click any cell in the table to deselect the row. The menu closes and the cells in the first row are shaded with light tan. The white text is hard to read on the light background.
6. Move the pointer to the left of the first row so that it changes to the row selection pointer ➡, and then click. The first row is selected.
7. On the Table Design tab, in the WordArt Styles group, click the **Text Fill arrow**, click the **Black, Text 1** color, and then click any cell in the table. The text in the first row changes to black.

Tip

You can also change the font color of table text using the Font Color button in the Font group on the Home tab.

Teréza doesn't like the changes you made. She wants you to try formatting the table with a style. When you apply a style to a table, you can specify whether the header and total rows and the first and last columns are formatted differently from the other rows and columns in the table. You can also specify whether to use banded rows or columns, which fills alternating rows or columns with different shading.

To apply a style to the table:

1. Click the **Table Design** tab, if necessary. In the Table Styles group, the second style, Medium Style 2 – Accent 1, is selected. In the Table Style Options group, the Header Row and Banded Rows check boxes are selected, which means that the header row will be formatted differently than the rest of the rows and that every other row will be filled with shading. See Figure 2–19.

Figure 2–19 Current style and options applied to the table

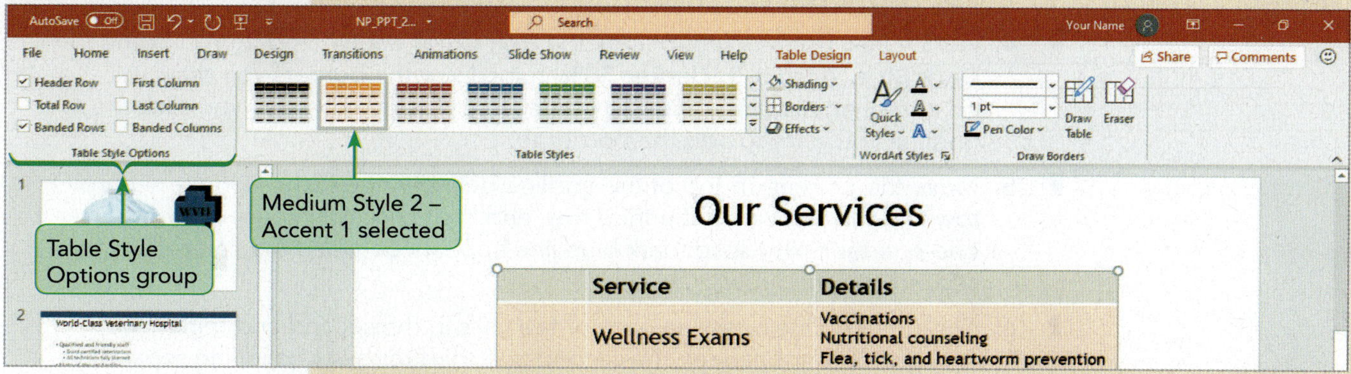

Javier Brosch/Shutterstock.com

2. In the Table Styles group, click the **More** button. The Table Styles gallery opens.

Tip

Select the View Gridlines button on the Layout tab to make the gridlines visible; deselect it to hide the gridlines.

3. Click the **Medium Style 3 – Accent 3** style (in the third row in the Medium section), and then click a blank area of the slide to deselect the table. This style adds borders above and below the top row in the table and below the bottom row. Because the Header Row check box in the Table Style Options group was selected, the first row is formatted differently from the rest of the rows. And because the Banded Rows check box was selected, every other row below the header row is filled with light blue.

Teréza wants you to change the borders between the rows to dark blue instead of white. Borders are different than gridlines. Gridlines are the lines that form the structure of a table. **Borders** are drawn on top of the gridlines. To add borders, you use the buttons in the Draw Borders group on the Table Design tab. Before you change them, the settings are solid-line borders, 1 point wide, and black. See Figure 2–20.

Figure 2–20 Current settings for borders

Javier Brosch/Shutterstock.com

To modify the borders of the table:

1. Click the table, and then on the Table Design tab, in the Draw Borders group, click the **Pen Style arrow**. A menu of line styles appears, including the No Border option. Teréza wants a solid line border, so you will not change the selection.
2. On the menu, click the solid line. The menu closes, the pointer changes to the pencil pointer, and the Draw Table button in the Draw Borders group is selected.

3. In the Draw Borders group, click the **Pen Weight arrow** [1 pt], and then click **¼ pt**.
4. In the Draw Borders group, click the **Pen Color arrow**, and then click the **Dark Blue, Accent 3, Darker 50%** color. Now the borders you draw will be one-quarter point, solid, dark blue lines. To add a border, you click the gridline you want to add the border to.
5. Move the pointer on top of the gridline between the first cell in the second row and the first cell in the third row, and then click the mouse button. A one-quarter point, solid, dark blue line appears between the first cells in the second and third rows.
6. Click the gridline between each of the cells in the second and third rows until the border between the second and third rows is a solid line separating the rows.
7. Create a border line between the third and fourth rows, between the fourth and fifth rows, and between the fifth and sixth rows. You are finished adding borders to the table.
8. In the Draw Borders group, click the **Draw Table** button to deselect it. The pointer changes back to its usual shape. Now that you added the borders, Teréza wants you to remove the shading from every other row.
9. In the Table Style Options group, click the **Banded Rows** check box to deselect it. All of the rows in the table are now filled with white.

Tip

You can also click the Borders arrow in the Table Styles group and use commands on that menu to apply or remove borders. The borders will be the style, weight, and color specified by the buttons in the Draw Borders group.

Filling Cells with Pictures

Just as you can fill a shape with a picture, you can do the same with cells. Note that many of the table styles include shaded cells as part of the style definition, so if you want to fill table cells with pictures and apply a table style, you need to apply the table style first. Otherwise, the shading that is part of the table style definition will replace the pictures in the cells.

Teréza wants you to add a picture to each row to make the table more interesting.

To fill the cells in the first column with pictures:

1. In the table, click in the first cell in the second row, and then click the **Table Design** tab, if necessary.
2. In the Table Styles group, click the **Shading arrow**, and then click **Picture**. The Insert Pictures window opens. See Figure 2–21.

Figure 2-21 **Insert Pictures window**

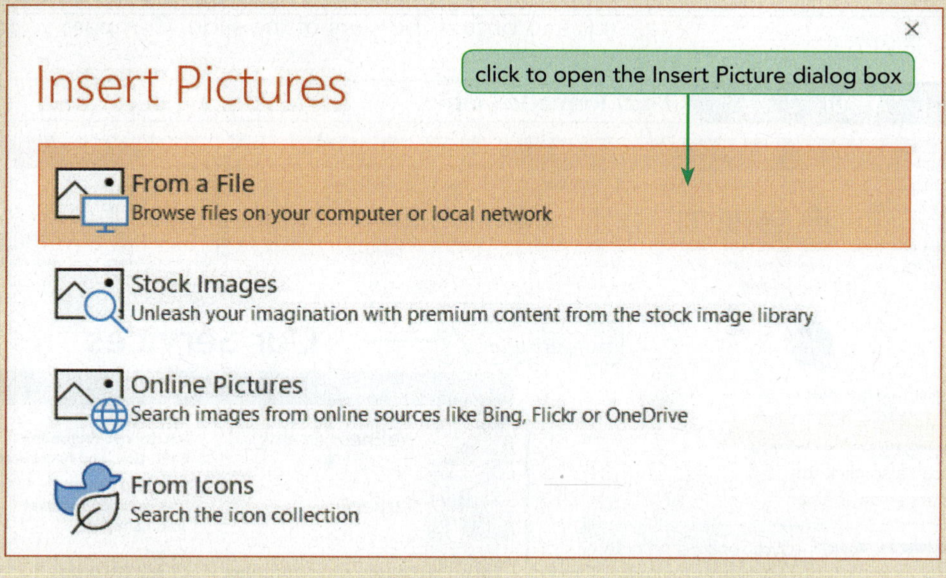

3. Click **From a File**. The Insert Picture dialog box opens.
4. Navigate to the **PowerPoint2 > Module folder**, click **Support_PPT_2_VetDog.jpg**, and then click **Insert**. The photo fills the cell.
5. Fill the first cells in the next four rows with the following pictures, all located in the **PowerPoint2 > Module** folder: **Support_PPT_2_OR.jpg**, **Support_PPT_2_MRI.jpg**, **Support_PPT_2_Chip.jpg**, and **Support_PPT_2_Teeth.jpg**.

The photos in the last two rows are too small, and they are distorted because they are stretched horizontally to fill the cells. To fix both of these problems, you'll increase the height of these rows.

To change row heights in the table:

1. Click in any cell in the second row in the table, and then click the **Layout** tab. In the Height box in the Cell Size group, 1" appears. The second, third, and fourth rows are each one-inch high.
2. Position the pointer to the left of the second to last row in the table so that it changes to the row selection pointer ➡, press and hold the mouse button, drag down until the pointer is to the left of the bottom row in the table, and then release the mouse button. The last two rows in the table are selected.
3. On the Layout tab, in the Cell Size group, click in the **Height** box, type **1**, and then press **ENTER**. The height of the selected rows increases to one inch. Now you will adjust the table's placement on the slide again. This time, you will use the Align commands instead of the smart guides.
4. Click in any cell to deselect the last two rows, and then in the Arrange group, click the **Align** button. A menu with commands for aligning the objects on the slide appears. Because only one object—the table—is selected, selecting a command will align the object to the borders of the slide.
5. Click **Align Center**. The table is horizontally aligned so that it is centered between the left and right borders of the slide.

6. In the Arrange group, click the **Align** button, and then on the menu, click **Align Middle**. The table is vertically aligned so that it is centered between the top and bottom borders of the slide. Compare your screen to Figure 2–22.

Figure 2–22 Final formatted table

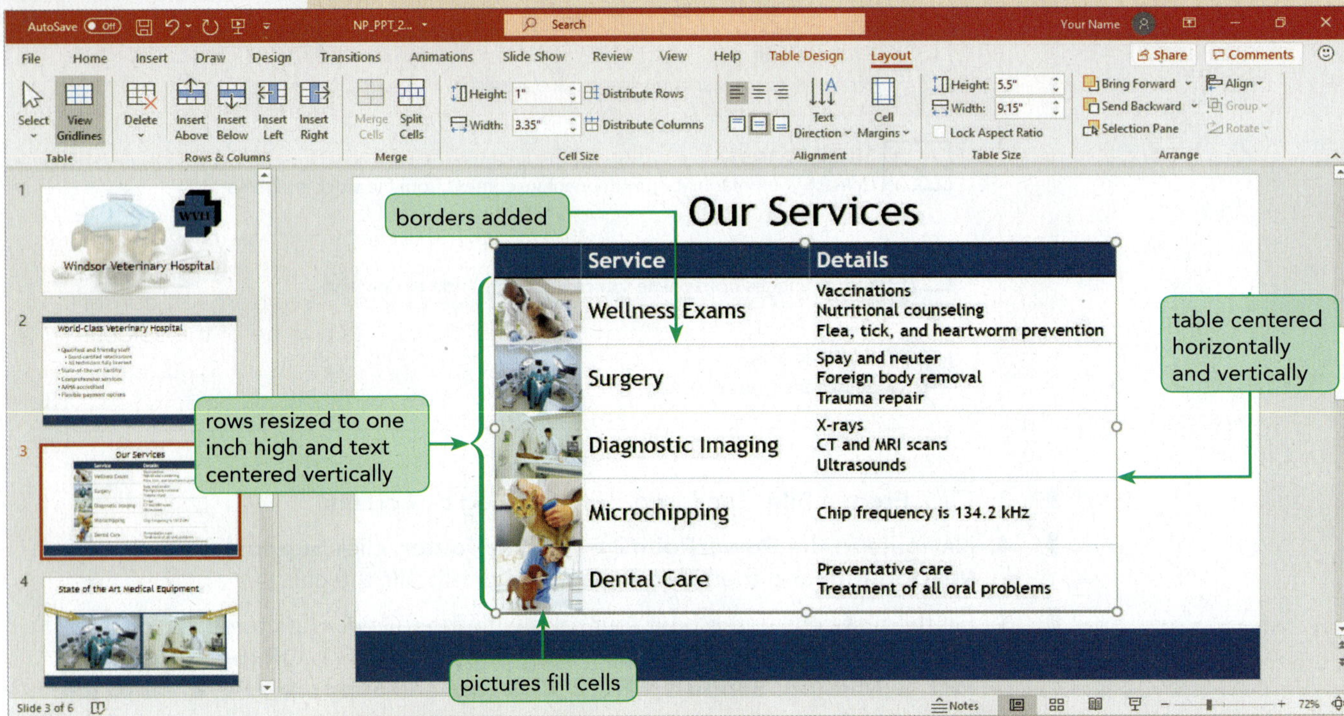

JPC-PROD/Shutterstock.com; nimon/Shutterstock.com; Ivonne Wierink/Shutterstock.com; Africa Studio/Shutterstock.com; Javier Brosch/Shutterstock.com

7. Save the changes to the presentation.

Inserting Symbols

You can insert some symbols, such as the trademark symbol, the registered trademark symbol, and the copyright symbol, by typing letters between parentheses and letting AutoCorrect change the characters to a symbol. You can insert all symbols, including letters from another alphabet, by using the Symbol button in the Symbols group on the Insert tab.

The hospital's slogan—"The only person who loves your pets more than we do is you."—is trademarked. Teréza wants you to add the trademark symbol ™ after the slogan on Slide 5.

To insert the trademark symbol:

1. Display Slide 5 ("We Treat All Small Animals"), and then click in the title text box immediately after "Animals."
2. Type **(tm** in the title text box.
3. Type **)** (close parenthesis). The text "(tm)" changes to the trademark symbol, which is ™. Teréza points out that the trademark symbol should appear after the slogan, not after the slide title.
4. Press **BACKSPACE**. The symbol changes to the characters you typed.

Tip

To insert the copyright symbol ©, type (c). To insert the registered trademark symbol ®, type (r).

5. Press **BACKSPACE** four times to delete the four characters, and then click in the text box containing the italicized slogan, immediately after the period after "you."
6. Type **(tm)** after "you." This time, the characters you typed did not change to the trademark symbol. If this happens, you need to use the symbol dialog box to insert the symbol.
7. Press **BACKSPACE** four times to delete the four characters, click the **Insert** tab, and then in the Symbols group, click the **Symbol** button. The Symbol dialog box opens.
8. If "(normal text)" does not appear in the Font box, click the **Font arrow**, and then click **(normal text)**.
9. Click the **Subset arrow**, scroll down, click **Letterlike Symbols**, and then click the trademark symbol (™) as shown in Figure 2–23. (The symbol might be in a different row and column on your screen.) In the bottom-left corner of the Symbol dialog box below "Unicode name," the name of the selected character is "Trade Mark Sign."

Figure 2–23 Symbol dialog box with the trademark symbol selected

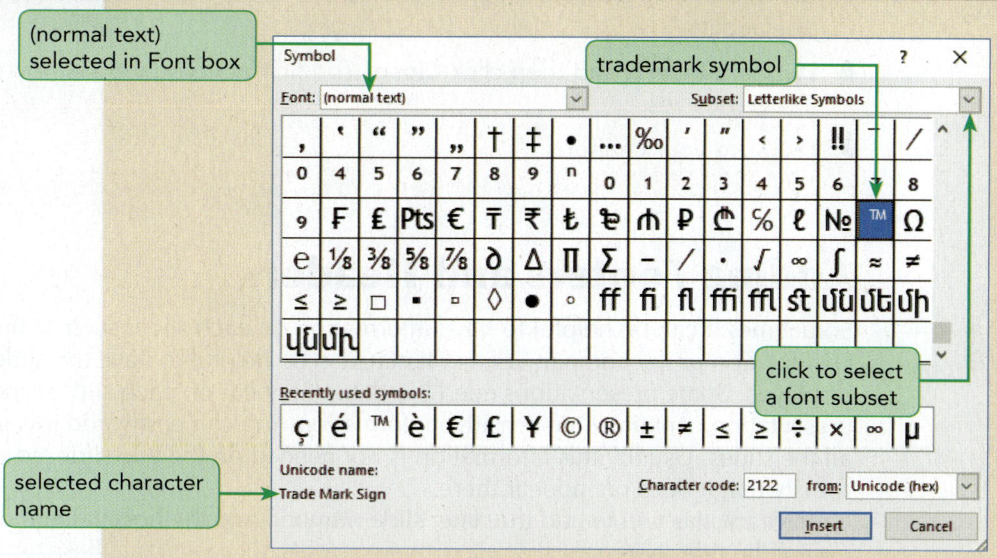

10. Click **Insert**. In the text box containing the slogan, the trademark symbol is inserted.
11. In the dialog box, click **Close**. The dialog box closes.

Teréza's first and last names contain two letters that are not in the English alphabet. You need to correct the spelling of Teréza's first and last names on Slide 6.

To insert special characters:

1. Display Slide 6 ("Contact Us for Assistance Traveling Abroad With Your Pet").
2. In the first bulleted item, click after the second "e" in "Tereza," and then press **BACKSPACE**. The second "e" in "Tereza" is deleted.

3. On the Insert tab, in the Symbols group, click the **Symbol** button. The Symbol dialog box opens.
4. At the top of the dialog box, click the **Subset arrow**, scroll the menu up, and then click **Latin-1 Supplement**. The list of symbols in the dialog box scrolls up to display the Latin-1 Supplement section.
5. Click **é**. In the bottom-left corner of the Symbol dialog box, the name of the selected character is "Latin Small Letter E With Acute."

   Trouble? If you don't see the letter é, click the down scroll arrow two times and look in the next two rows.
6. Click **Insert**. The letter "é" is inserted on the slide at the insertion point.
7. Click **Close**. The first word in the first bulleted item is now "Teréza."
8. In the first bulleted item, click after the "c" in "Goncalves," and then press **BACKSPACE** to delete the "c."
9. On the Insert tab, in the Symbols group, click the **Symbol** button to open the Symbols dialog box. The first row contains the é that you just inserted. You need to insert ç, which appears two boxes to the left of é.
10. In the dialog box, click **ç**, which has the name "Latin Small Letter C With Cedilla."
11. Click **Insert**, and then click **Close**. The first bulleted item is now "Teréza Gonçalves."
12. Save your changes.

Adding Footers and Headers

Sometimes it can be helpful to have information on each slide, such as the title of the presentation or the company name. It can also be helpful to have the slide number displayed. Some presentations need the date to appear on each slide, especially if the presentation contains time-sensitive information. You can easily add this information to all the slides. Usually this information is not needed on the title slide, so you can also specify that it does not appear there.

Teréza wants you to add the date, slide number, and the hospital name to each slide except the title slide.

Tip

Click the Insert Slide Number button on the Insert tab to insert the slide number on all of the slides. Click the Date & Time button to open a dialog box listing the current date and time in various formats that you can choose from.

To add a footer, slide numbers, and the date to slides:

1. On the Insert tab, in the Text group, click the **Header & Footer** button. The Header and Footer dialog box opens with the Slide tab selected.
2. Click the **Footer** check box to select it, and then click in the **Footer** box. In the Preview box on the right, the middle placeholder on the bottom is filled with black to indicate where the footer will appear on slides. See Figure 2–24. Note that the position of the footer, slide number, and date changes in different themes.

Figure 2–24 Slide tab in the Header and Footer dialog box

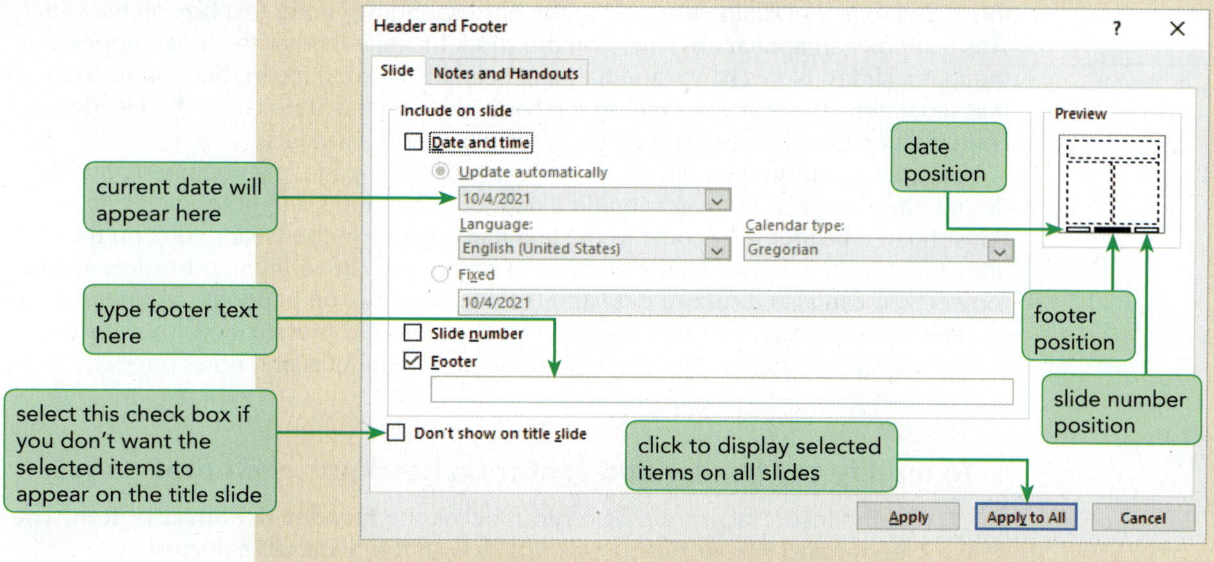

3. Type **Windsor Veterinary Hospital** in the Footer box.
4. Click the **Slide number** check box to select it. In the Preview box, the box in the bottom-right is filled with black.
5. Click the **Date and time** check box to select it. The options under this check box are no longer dimmed, indicating that you can use them, and in the Preview box, the box in the bottom-left is filled with black. You don't want the date in the presentation to update automatically each time the presentation is opened. You want it to show today's date so people will know that the information is current as of that date.
6. Click the **Fixed** option button, if necessary. Now you want to prevent the footer, slide number, and date from appearing on the title slide.
7. Click the **Don't show on title slide** check box to select it, and then click **Apply to All**. On Slide 6 the footer, date, and slide number are displayed. See Figure 2–25.

Figure 2–25 Date, footer, and slide number on Slide 6

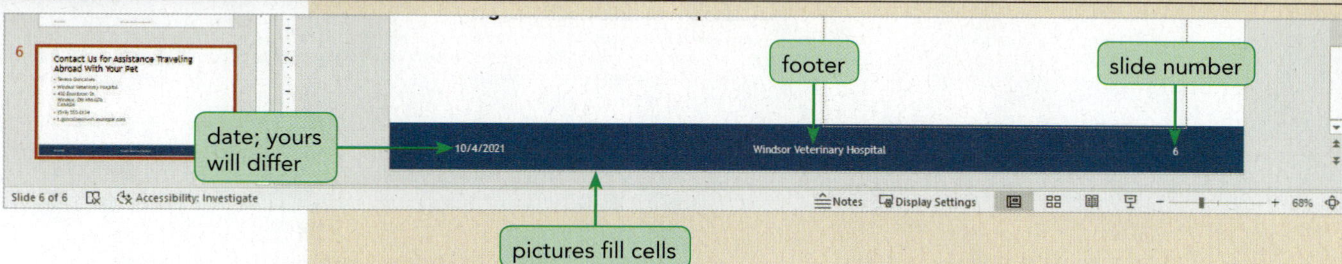

8. Display **Slide 1** (the title slide). Notice the footer, date, and slide number do not appear on the title slide.

Typically, a footer is any text that appears at the bottom of every page in a document. As you saw when you added the footer in the Header and Footer dialog box, in PowerPoint a **footer** is specifically the text that appears in the Footer box on the Slide tab in that dialog box and in the corresponding Footer text box on the slides. This text box can appear anywhere on the slide. In some themes the footer appears at the top of slides. Notes pages and handouts can also have a footer, but you need to add that separately. The text you enter in the Footer box on the Slide tab in the Header and Footer dialog box does not appear on notes pages and handouts.

A header is information displayed at the top of every page in a document. Slides do not have headers, but you can add a header to handouts and notes pages. In PowerPoint a **header** refers only to the text that appears in the Header box on the Notes and Handouts tab in the Header and Footer dialog box. In addition to headers and footers, you can also display a date and the page number on handouts and notes pages.

Teréza plans to distribute handouts when she gives her presentation, so she wants you to add information in the header and footer on handouts and notes pages.

To modify the header and footer on handouts and notes pages:

1. On the Insert tab, in the Text group, click the **Header & Footer** button. The Header and Footer dialog box opens with the Slide tab selected.
2. Click the **Notes and Handouts** tab. The Page number check box is selected by default, and in the Preview, the lower-right rectangle is bold to indicate that this is where the page number will appear.
3. Click the **Header** check box to select it, click in the **Header** box, and then type **Windsor Veterinary Hospital**.
4. Click the **Footer** check box to select it, click in the **Footer** box, and then type your name.
5. Click the **Apply to All** button. To see the effect of modifying the handouts and notes pages, you need to look at the print preview.
6. Click the **File** tab to open Backstage view, and then in the navigation pane, click **Print**.
7. Under Settings, click the **Full Page Slides** button, and then click **Notes Pages**. The preview shows Slide 1 as a notes page. The header and footer you typed appear, along with the page number. See Figure 2–26.

Figure 2–26 **Header and footer on the Slide 1 notes page**

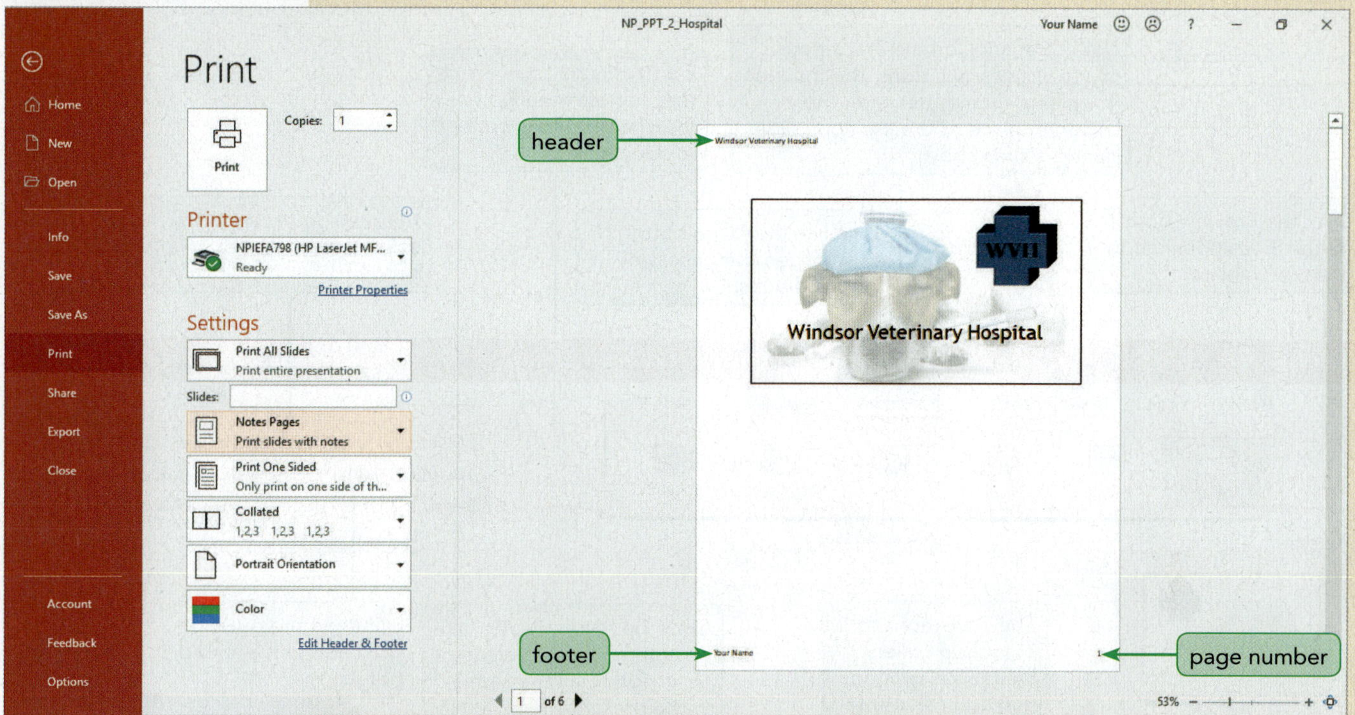

Javier Brosch/Shutterstock.com

8. At the top of the navigation bar, click the **Back** button to return to Normal view.
9. Save your changes.

You have modified a presentation by applying a theme used in another presentation; inserting, formatting, and duplicating pictures and shapes; and inserting a table and characters that are not on your keyboard. You also added footer and header information to slides and handouts. In the next session, you will continue modifying the presentation by applying and modifying transitions and animations, and adding and modifying videos.

Review

Session 2.1 Quick Check

1. Which contextual tab appears on the ribbon when you select a shape?
2. What is a style?
3. What is the fill of a shape?
4. In a table, what is the intersection of a row and column called?
5. How do you know if an entire table is selected and not just active?
6. How do you insert characters that are not on your keyboard?
7. In PowerPoint, what is a footer?

Session 2.2 Visual Overview:

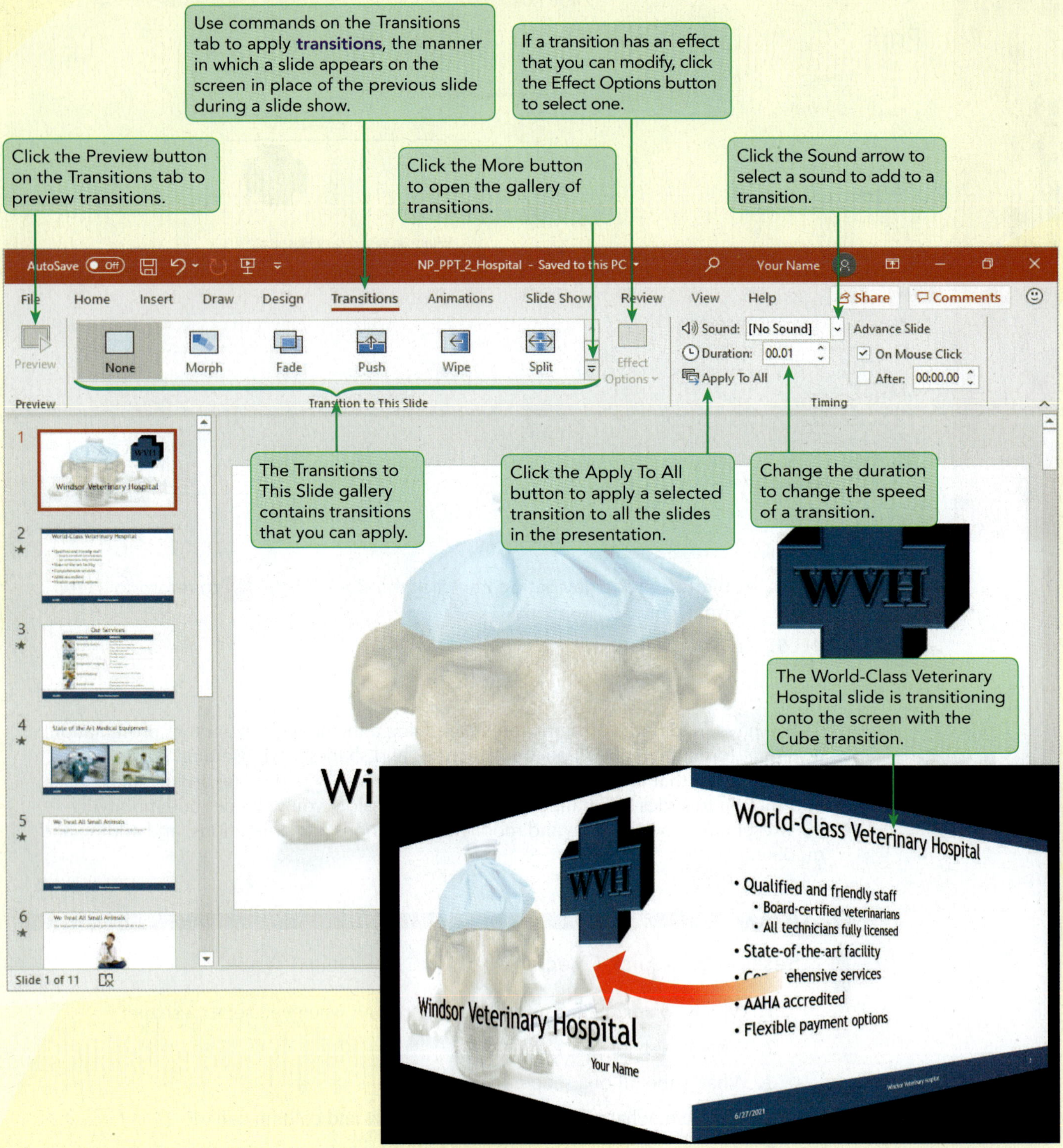

Javier Brosch/Shutterstock.com; JPC-PROD/Shutterstock.com; nimon/Shutterstock.com; Ivonne Wierink/Shutterstock.com; Africa Studio/Shutterstock.com; Veronica Louro/Shutterstock.com

Using Animations and Transitions

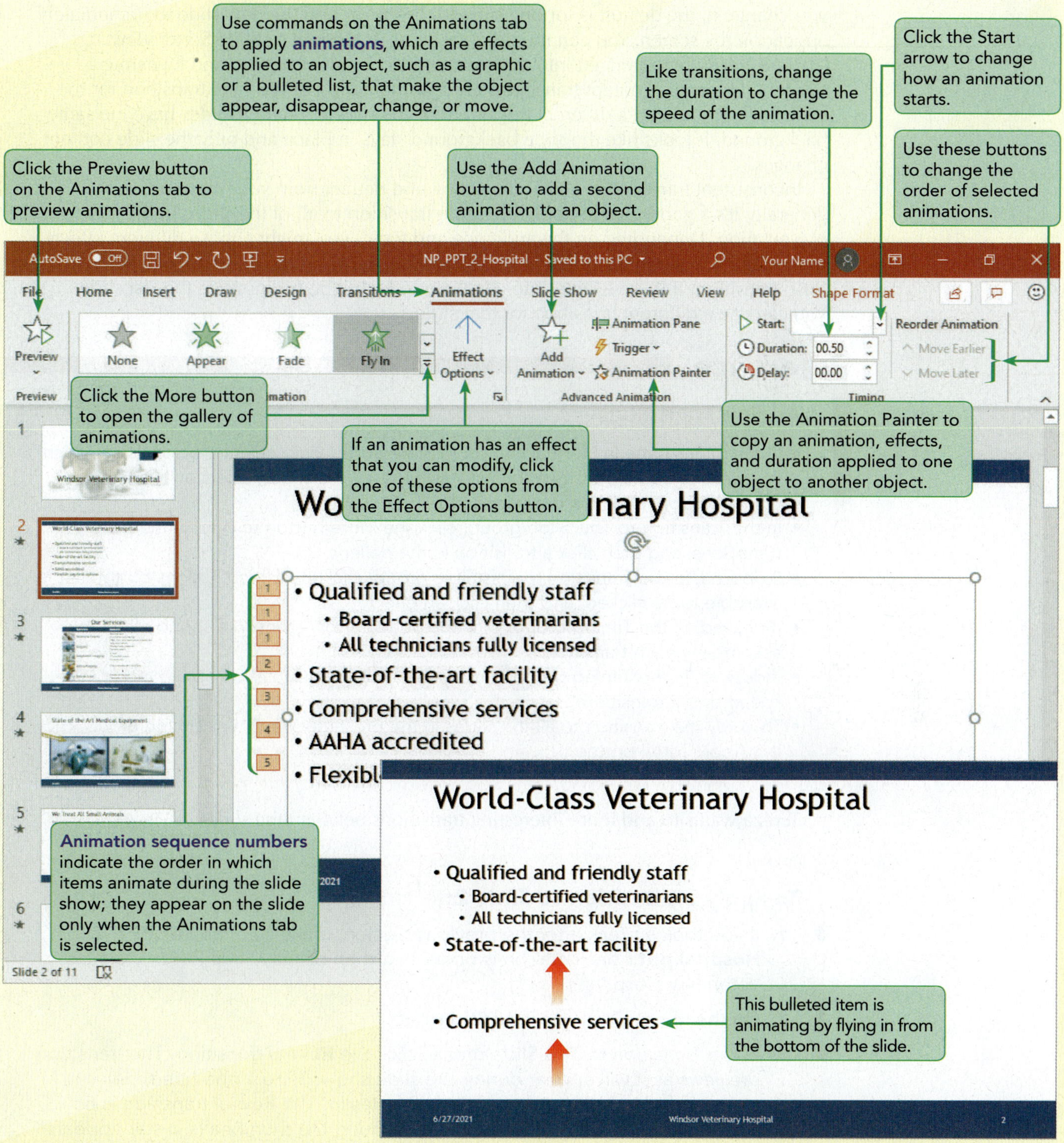

Javier Brosch/Shutterstock.com; JPC-PROD/Shutterstock.com; nimon/Shutterstock.com; Ivonne Wierink/Shutterstock.com; Africa Studio/Shutterstock.com; Veronica Louro/Shutterstock.com

Applying Transitions

The Transitions tab contains commands for changing the transitions between slides. Refer to the Session 2.2 Visual Overview for more information about transitions. Unless you change it, the default is for one slide to disappear and the next slide to immediately appear on the screen. You can modify transitions in Normal or Slide Sorter view.

Transitions are organized into three categories: Subtle, Exciting, and Dynamic Content. Dynamic Content transitions are a combination of the Fade transition for the slide background and a different transition for the slide content. If slides have the same background, it looks like the slide background stays in place and only the slide content changes.

Inconsistent transitions can be distracting and detract from your message, so generally it's a good idea to apply the same transition to all of the slides in the presentation. Depending on the audience and topic, you might choose different effects of the same transition for different slides, such as changing the direction of a Wipe or Push transition. If there is one slide you want to highlight, for instance the last slide, you can use a different transition for that slide.

Reference

Adding Transitions

- In the Slides pane in Normal view or in Slide Sorter view, select the slide(s) to which you want to add a transition, or, if applying to all the slides, select any slide.
- On the ribbon, click the Transitions tab.
- In the Transition to This Slide group, click the More button to display the gallery of transitions, and then click a transition in the gallery.
- If desired, in the Transition to This Slide group, click the Effect Options button if it is available to be clicked, and then click an effect.
- If desired, in the Timing group, click the Sound arrow to insert a sound effect to accompany each transition.
- If desired, in the Timing group, modify the time in the Duration box to modify the speed of the transition.
- To apply the transition to all the slides in the presentation, in the Timing group, click the Apply To All button.

Teréza wants to add more interesting transitions between the slides.

To apply a transition to Slide 2:

1. If you took a break after the previous session, make sure the **NP_PPT_2_Hospital.pptx** presentation is open, and then display Slide 2 ("World-Class Veterinary Hospital").
2. On the ribbon, click the **Transitions** tab.
3. In the Transition to This Slide group, click the **Reveal** transition. The transition previews as it will appear during the slide show: Slide 1 (the title slide) appears, fades away, and then Slide 2 fades in. The Reveal transition is now selected in the gallery. In the pane containing the thumbnails, a star appears next to the Slide 2 thumbnail. If you missed the preview, you can see it again.
4. In the Preview group, click the **Preview** button. The transition previews again.
5. In the Transition to This Slide group, click the **More** button. The gallery opens listing all the transitions. See Figure 2–27.

Figure 2–27 Transition to This Slide gallery

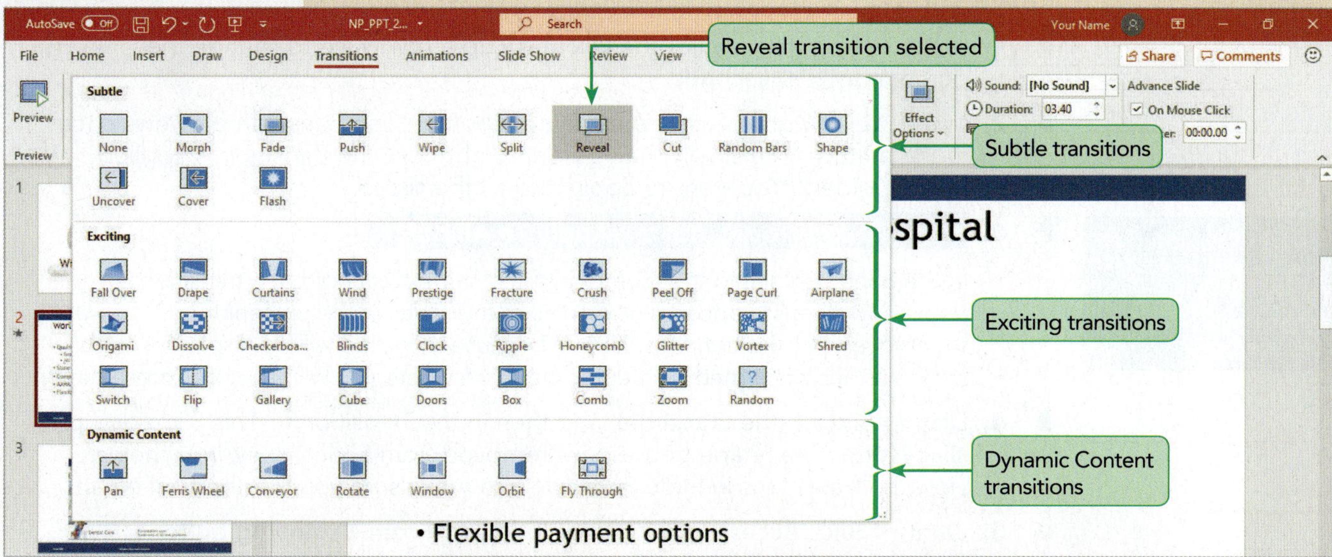

nimon/Shutterstock.com

6. Click the **Push** transition. The preview shows Slide 2 slide up from the bottom and push Slide 1 up and out of view.

Most transitions have effects that you can modify. For example, the Peel Off transition can peel from the bottom-left or the bottom-right corner, and the Wipe transition can wipe from any direction. You'll modify the effect of the transition applied to Slide 2.

To modify the transition effect for Slide 2:

1. In the Transition to This Slide group, click the **Effect Options** button. The effects that you can modify for the Push transition are listed on the menu.
2. Click **From Right**. The Push transition previews again, but this time Slide 2 slides from the right to push Slide 1 left. The available effects change depending on the transition selected.
3. In the Transition to This Slide group, click the **Shape** transition. The transition previews with a brief view of Slide 1, before Slide 2 appears in the center of Slide 1 and enlarges in a circular shape to fill the slide.
4. Click the **Effect Options** button. The effects that you can modify for the Shape transition are listed.
5. Click **Out**. The preview of the transition with this effect displays Slide 2 in the center of Slide 1 that grows in a rectangular shape to fill the slide.

Finally, you can also change the duration of a transition. The duration is the length of time, or the speed, from the beginning to the end of the transition. To make the transition faster, decrease the duration. To slow the transition down, increase the duration. The duration is measured in seconds.

Teréza likes the Shape transition, but she thinks it is a little fast, so you will increase the duration. Then you can apply the modified transition to all the slides.

To change the duration of the transition and apply it to all the slides:

1. In the Timing group, click the **Duration** up arrow twice to change the duration to 1.50 seconds.
2. In the Preview group, click the **Preview** button. The transition previews once more, a little more slowly than before. Right now, the transition is applied only to Slide 2. You want to apply it to all the slides.
3. In the Timing group, click the **Apply To All** button.

   In the pane containing the thumbnails, the star indicating that a transition is applied to the slide appears next to all of the slides in the presentation. You want to remove the transition from Slide 1 because that slide will be displayed on the screen as audience members enter the room where you will give your presentation.
4. Display Slide 1 (the title slide), and then in the Transition to This Slide group, click **None**. The Shape transition is removed from Slide 1 only. You should view the transitions in Slide Show view to make sure you like the final effect.
5. On the Quick Access Toolbar, click the **Start From Beginning** button. Slide 1 (the title slide) appears in Slide Show view.
6. Press **SPACEBAR** or **ENTER** to advance through the slide show. The transitions look fine.
7. End the presentation, and then save your changes.

Make sure you click the Apply To All button or the transition is applied only to the currently selected slide or slides.

Applying Animations

Animations add interest to a slide show and draw attention to the text or object being animated. For example, you can animate a slide title to fly in from the side or spin around like a pinwheel to draw the audience's attention to that title. Refer to the Session 2.2 Visual Overview for more information about animations.

Animation effects are grouped into four types:

- **Entrance**—Text and objects do not appear on the slide until the animation occurs. This is one of the most commonly used animation types.
- **Emphasis**—Text and objects on the slide change in appearance or move.
- **Exit**—Text and objects leave the screen before the slide show advances to the next slide.
- **Motion Paths**—Text and objects follow a path on the slide.

Animating Objects

You can animate any object on a slide, including pictures, shapes, and text boxes. To animate an object you click it, and then select an animation in the Animation group on the Animations tab.

Reference

Applying Animations

- On the slide displayed in Normal view, select the object you want to animate.
- On the ribbon, click the Animations tab.
- In the Animation group, click the More button to display the gallery of animations, and then click an animation in the gallery.
- If desired, in the Animation group, click the Effect Options button, and then click a direction effect. If the object is a text box, click a sequence effect.
- If desired, in the Timing group, modify the time in the Duration box to modify the speed of the animation.
- If desired, in the Timing group, click the Start arrow, and then click a different setting.

Slide 4 contains two pictures. Teréza wants you to add an animation to the title text on this slide.

To animate the title on Slide 4:

1. Display Slide 4 ("State of the Art Medical Equipment"), and then click the **Animations** tab on the ribbon. Because nothing is selected on the slide, the animations in the Animation group are gray.
2. Click the **State of the Art Medical Equipment** title text. The animations in the Animation group are green to indicate that they are now available. All of the animations currently visible in the Animation group are entrance animations.
3. In the Animation group, click the **Fly In** animation. The animation previews on the slide, showing the title text fly in from the bottom. In the Timing group, the Start box displays On Click, which indicates that this animation will occur when you advance the slide show by clicking the mouse or pressing SPACEBAR or ENTER. The animation sequence number 1 in the box to the left of the title text box indicates that this is the first animation that will occur on the slide when you advance the slide show. You can preview the animation again if you missed it.
4. In the Preview group, click the **Preview** button. The animation previews again.
5. In the Animation group, click the **More** button. The Animation gallery opens. The animation commands are listed by category, and each category appears in a different color. At the bottom are four commands, each of which opens a dialog box listing all the effects in that category. See Figure 2–28. You will try an emphasis animation.

Figure 2–28 Animation gallery

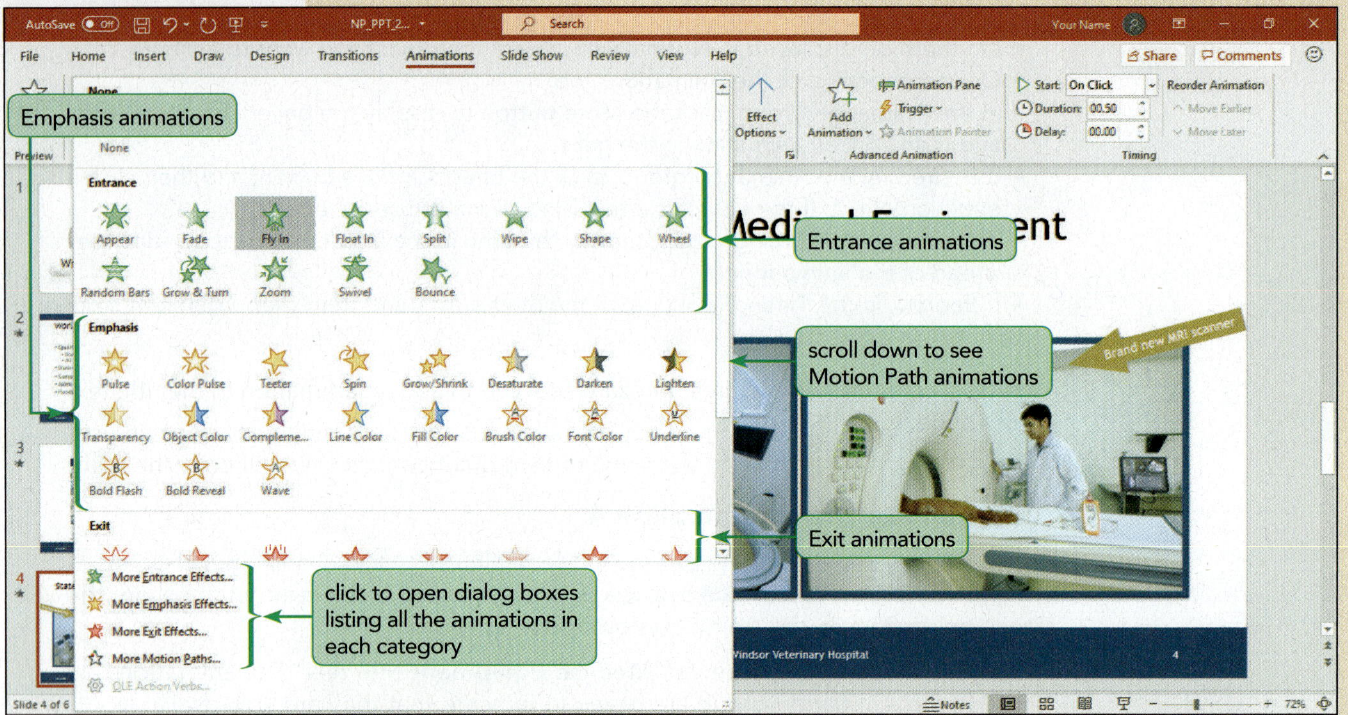

nimon/Shutterstock.com

6. Under Emphasis, click the **Underline** animation. The Underline animation replaces the Fly In animation, and the slide title is underlined in the preview.

The Underline animation you applied to the slide title is an example of an emphasis animation you can apply only to text boxes. You cannot apply this animation to other types of objects, such as pictures or tables.

Slide 4 contains two photos. To focus the audience's attention on one photo at time, you will apply an entrance animation to the photos so that they appear one at a time during the slide show.

To apply an entrance animation to a photo on Slide 4:

1. On Slide 4 ("State of the Art Medical Equipment"), click the picture on the right.
2. In the Animation group, click the **More** button. Notice that in the Emphasis section, six of the animations, including the Underline animation you just applied to the slide title, are gray, which means they are not available for this object. These six animations are available only for text.
3. In the Entrance section, click the **Split** animation. The picture appears starting from the left and right edges. In the Timing group, On Click appears in the Start box, indicating that this animation will occur when you advance the slide show. The animation sequence number to the left of the selected picture is 2, which indicates that this is the second animation that will occur on the slide when you advance the slide show.

You need to change the direction from which this animation appears, and you want to slow it down.

To change the effect and duration of an animation:

1. In the Animation group, click the **Effect Options** button. This menu contains Direction options.
2. Click **Vertical Out**. The preview shows the picture appearing, starting from the center and building out to the left and right edges.
3. In the Timing group, click the **Duration** up arrow once. The duration changes from 0.50 seconds to 0.75 seconds.

After you have applied and customized the animation for one object, you can use the Animation Painter to copy that animation to other objects. You will copy the Split entrance animation to the other photo on Slide 4.

To use the Animation Painter to copy the animation on Slide 4:

1. Click the photo on the right.
2. In the Advanced Animation group, click the **Animation Painter** button, and then move the pointer onto the slide. The pointer changes to the Animation Painter pointer.
3. Click the photo on the left. The Split animation with the Vertical Out effect and a duration of 0.75 seconds is copied to the photo on the left, and the animation previews.

After you apply animations, you should watch them in Slide Show view to see what they will look like during a slide show. Remember that On Click appeared in the Start box for each animation that you applied, which means that to see the animation during the slide show, you need to advance the slide show.

To view the animations on Slide 4 in Slide Show view:

1. Make sure Slide 4 ("State of the Art Medical Equipment") is displayed.
2. On the status bar, click the **Slide Show** button. When you click this button to start a slide show, the slide show starts from the current slide instead of from the beginning. Slide 4 appears in Slide Show view. Only the title, the arrow shapes, and the footer appear on the slide.
3. Press **SPACEBAR** to advance the slide show. The first animation, the emphasis animation that underlines the title, occurs.
4. Press **SPACEBAR** again. The photo on the right appears starting at the center of the photo and building out to the left and right edges.
5. Click anywhere on the screen. The photo on the left appears with the same animation as the photo on the right.
6. Press **ESC**. The slide show ends and Slide 4 appears in Normal view.

Teréza doesn't like the emphasis animation applied to the slide title. It's distracting because the photos are the focus of the slide, not the title. Also, she thinks it would be better if the photo on the left appeared before the photo on the right. Finally, Teréza wants the arrows to animate after each photo appears. To fix these issues, you will remove the animation applied to the title, add entrance animations to the arrows, and change the order of the animations so that the photo on the left animates first, followed by its arrow, then the photo on the right animates followed by its arrow.

To remove the title animation, animate the arrows, and change the order of the animations:

1. Click the **State of the Art Medical Equipment** title text. In the Animation group, the yellow emphasis animation Underline is selected.
2. In the Animation group, click the **More** button, and then at the top of the gallery, click **None**. The animation that was applied to the title is removed, the animation sequence icon no longer appears next to the title text box, and the other two animation sequence icons on the slide are renumbered 1 and 2. Next you will apply animation to the two arrows.
3. Apply the entrance **Wipe** animation to the "Recently updated OR" arrow, and then change its effect option to **From Left**.
4. Apply the entrance **Wipe** animation to the "Brand new MRI scanner" arrow, and then change its effect option to **From Right**. Now you need to select the animation applied to the photo on the left and change it so that it occurs first. You can select the object or the animation sequence icon to modify an animation.
5. Next to the left photo, click the **2** animation sequence icon. In the Animation group, the green Split entrance animation is selected. See Figure 2–29.

Tip

You can also click the animation sequence icon, and then press DELETE to remove an animation.

Figure 2–29 Animation selected to change its order

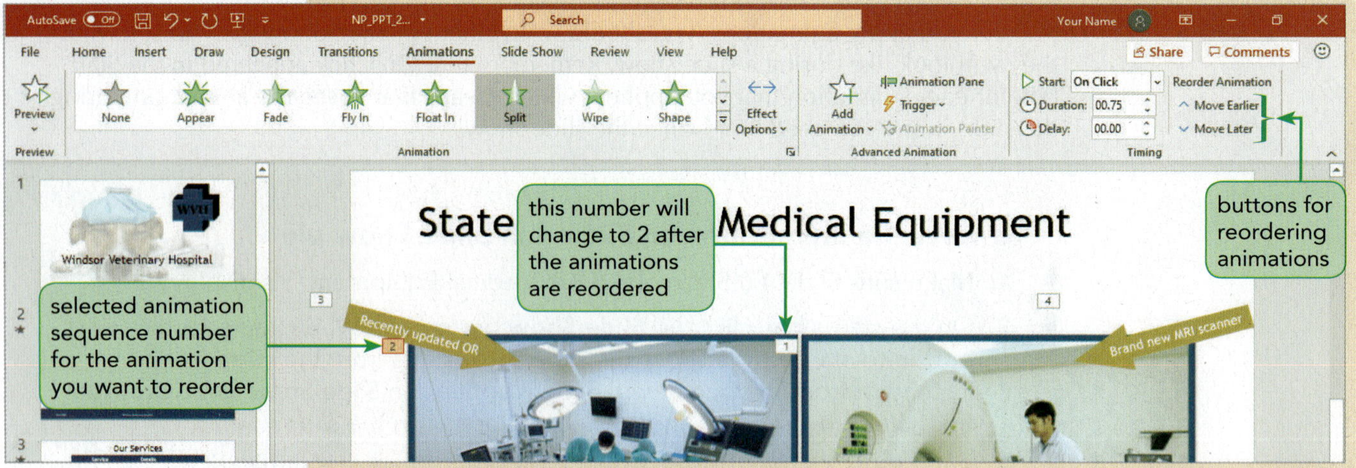

nimon/Shutterstock.com; Javier Brosch/Shutterstock.com

6. In the Timing group, click the **Move Earlier** button. The animation sequence icon next to the photo on the left changes from 2 to 1, and the animation sequence icon next to the photo on the right changes from 1 to 2. Now you need to reorder the animations so that the "Recently updated OR" arrow animates after the picture on the left.
7. Next to the "Recently updated OR" arrow, click the **3** animation sequence icon, and then in the Timing group, click the **Move Earlier** button.

8. In the Preview group, click the **Preview** button. The photo on the left appears, then the "Recently updated OR" arrow, then the photo on the right, and then the "Brand new MRI scanner" arrow.

Changing How an Animation Starts

Remember that when you apply an animation, the default is for the object to animate On Click, which means when you advance through the slide show. You can change this so that an animation happens automatically, either at the same time as another animation or when the slide transitions, or after another animation or the transition.

Teréza wants the arrows to appear automatically after each photo without the presenter needing to advance the slide show.

To change how the animation for the arrows start:

1. On Slide 4 ("State of the Art Medical Equipment"), click the **Recently updated OR** arrow. The Wipe entrance animation is selected in the Animation group, and in the Timing group, On Click appears in the Start box.
2. In the Timing group, click the **Start** arrow. The menu lists three choices for starting an animation: On Click, With Previous, and After Previous.
3. Click **After Previous**. Now this arrow will appear automatically after the photo on the left appears. Notice that the animation sequence number next to the arrow changed to 1, the same number as the animation sequence number next to the photo on the left. This is because you will not need to advance the slide show to start this animation.
4. Change the way the animation applied to the "Brand new MRI scanner" arrow starts to **After Previous**.

When you preview an animation, it plays automatically on the slide in Normal view, even if the timing setting for the animation is On Click. To make sure the timing settings are correct, you need to watch the animation in a slide show.

To view and test the animations:

1. On the status bar, click the **Slide Show** button. Slide 4 appears in Slide Show view.
2. Press **SPACEBAR**. The photo on the left appears, followed by the "Recently updated OR" arrow.
3. Press **SPACEBAR**. The photo on the right appears, followed by the "Brand new MRI scanner" arrow.
4. Press **ESC** to end the slide show.

When you set an animation to occur automatically during the slide show, it happens immediately after the previous action. You can add a pause before the animation so that there is time between automatic animations. To do this, you increase the time in the Delay box in the Timing group. Like the Duration time, Delay times are measured in seconds.

To give the audience time to look at the first photo before the second photo appears on Slide 4, you will add a delay to the animation that is applied to the photo on the right.

To add a delay to the animations applied to the arrows:

1. On Slide 4 ("State of the Art Medical Equipment"), click the "Brand new MRI scanner" arrow to select it, if necessary. In the Timing group, 00.00 appears in the Delay box.
2. In the Timing group, click the **Delay** up arrow four times to change the time to one second. After the photo on the right appears (the previous animation), the "Brand new MRI scanner" arrow will appear after a delay of one second.
3. Apply a one-second delay to the animation applied to the "Recently updated OR" arrow.
4. On the status bar, click the **Slide Show** button. Slide 4 appears in Slide Show view.
5. Press **SPACEBAR**. The photo on the left appears, and then after a one-second delay, the "Recently updated OR" arrow appears.
6. Press **SPACEBAR**. The photo on the right appears, and then after a one-second delay, the "Brand new MRI scanner" arrow appears.
7. Press **ESC** to end the slide show, and then save your changes.

Animating Lists

If you animate a list, the default is for each of the first-level items to animate On Click. This type of animation focuses your audience's attention on each item, without the distraction of items that you haven't discussed yet.

Teréza wants you to add an Entrance animation to the bulleted list on Slide 2. She wants each first-level bulleted item to appear on the slide one at a time so that the audience won't be able to read ahead while she is discussing each point.

To animate the bulleted list on Slide 2:

1. Display Slide 2 ("World-Class Veterinary Hospital"), and then click anywhere in the bulleted list to make the text box active.
2. On the Animations tab, in the Animation group, click the **Fly In** animation. The animation previews on the slide as the bulleted items fly in from the bottom. When the "Qualified and friendly staff" item flies in, its subitems fly in with it. After the preview is finished, the numbers 1 through 5 appear next to the bulleted items. Notice that the subitems have the same animation sequence number as their first-level item. This means that the subitems are set to start With Previous or After Previous. See Figure 2–30.

Figure 2–30 Fly In entrance animation applied to a bulleted list with subitems

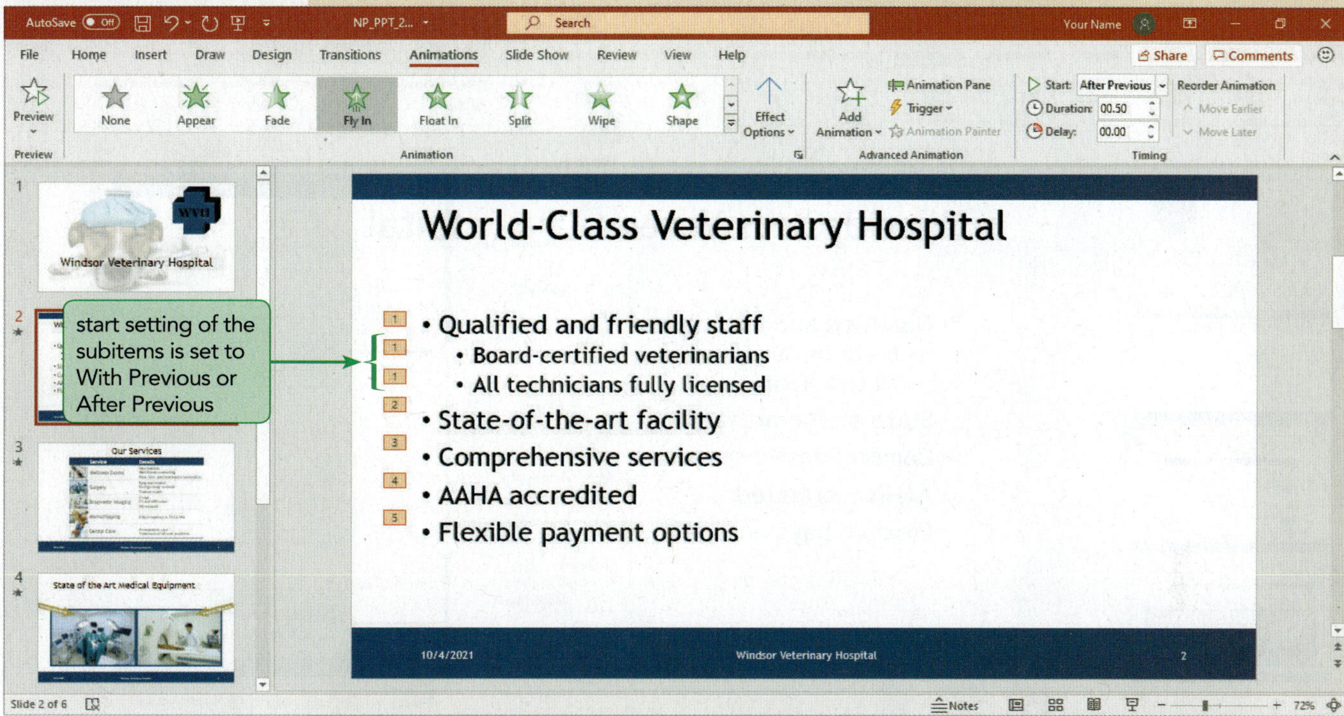

Javier Brosch/Shutterstock.com; JPC-PROD/Shutterstock.com; nimon/Shutterstock.com; Ivonne Wierink/Shutterstock.com; Africa Studio/Shutterstock.com

3. Next to the "Qualified and friendly staff" bulleted item, click the **1** animation sequence icon to select it. In the Timing group, On Click appears in the Start box.
4. Next to the subitem "Board-certified veterinarians," click the **1** animation sequence icon. In the Timing group, With Previous appears in the Start box.

If you wanted to change how the items in the list animate during the slide show, you could change the Start setting of each item, or you could change the sequence effect. Sequence effects appear on the Effect Options menu in addition to the Direction options when you apply an animation to a text box. The default is for the items to appear By Paragraph. This means each first-level item animates one at a time—with its subitems, if there are any—when you advance the slide show. You can change this setting so that the entire list animates at once as one object, or so that each first-level item animates at the same time but as separate objects.

To examine the Sequence options for the animated list:

1. Click in the bulleted list, and then in the Animation group, click the **Effect Options** button. The Sequence options appear at the bottom of the menu, below the Direction options, and By Paragraph is selected. See Figure 2–31.

Figure 2–31 Animation effect options for a bulleted list

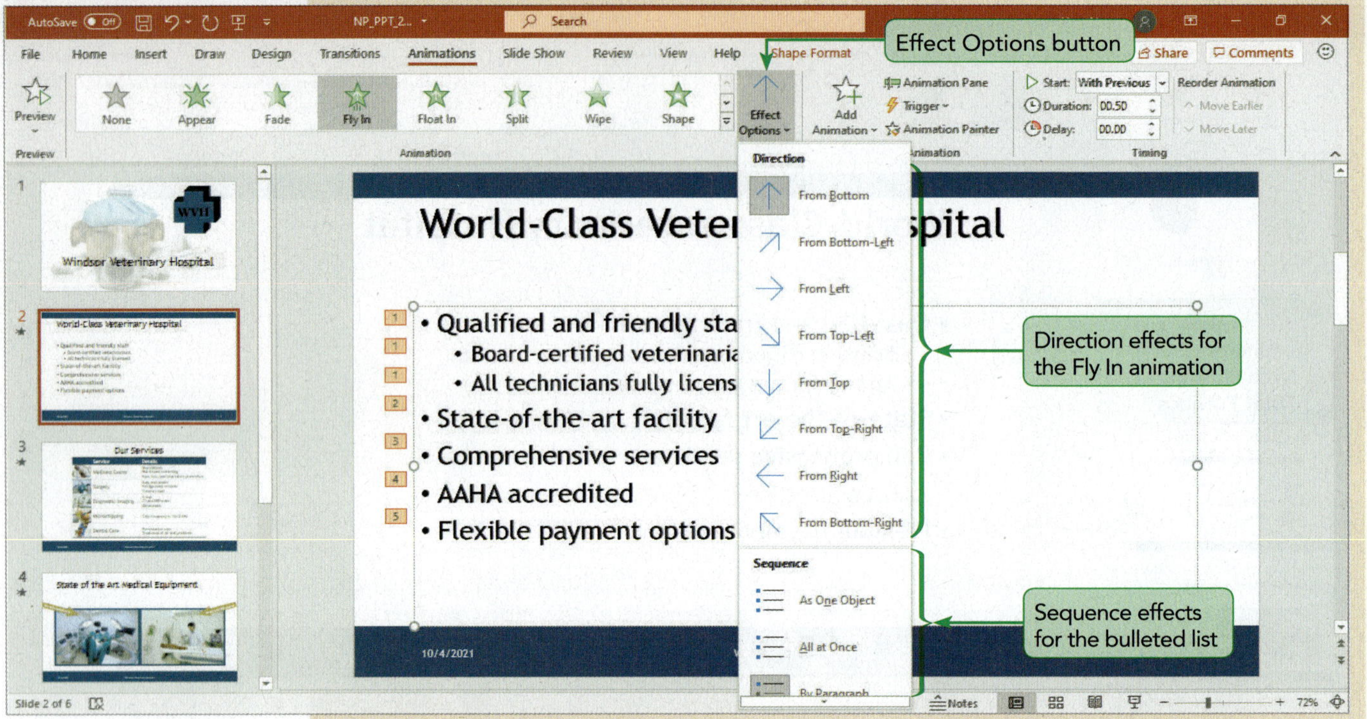

Javier Brosch/Shutterstock.com; JPC-PROD/Shutterstock.com; nimon/Shutterstock.com; Ivonne Wierink/Shutterstock.com; Africa Studio/Shutterstock.com

2. Click **As One Object**. The animation preview shows the entire text box fly in. After the preview, only one animation sequence icon appears next to the text box, indicating that the entire text box will animate as a single object. In the Timing group, On Click appears in the Start box.

Tip

It is easier to see the difference between the As One Object and All at Once sequence effect options when the Wheel or Grow & Turn animations are applied.

3. In the Animation group, click the **Effect Options** button, and then under Sequence, click **All at Once**. The animation previews again, but this time each of the first-level items fly in as separate objects, although they all fly in at the same time. Visually, there is not much of a difference between this option and the As One Object option for the Fly In animation. After the preview, animation sequence icons, all numbered 1, appear next to each bulleted item, indicating that each item will animate separately but you only need to advance the slide show once.
4. Next to the first bulleted item, click the **1** animation sequence icon. In the Timing group, On Click appears in the Start box.
5. Next to the second first-level item ("State-of-the-art facility"), click the **1** animation sequence icon. In the Timing group, With Previous appears in the Start box.
6. In the Animation group, click the **Effect Options** button, and then click **By Paragraph**. The sequence effect changes back to its original setting.
7. Save your changes.

Proskills

Decision Making: Just Because You Can Doesn't Mean You Should

PowerPoint provides you with many tools that enable you to create interesting and creative slide shows. Just because a tool is available doesn't mean you should use it. You need to give careful thought before deciding to use a tool to enhance the content of your presentation. One example of a tool to use sparingly is sound effects with transitions. Most of the time you do not need to use sound to highlight the fact that one slide is leaving the screen while another appears. Many people find sound transitions annoying or distracting.

You will also want to avoid using too many or frivolous animations. It is easy to go overboard with animations, and they can quickly become distracting and make your presentation seem less professional. Before you apply an animation, you should know what you want to emphasize and why you want to use an animation. Animations should enhance your message. When you are finished giving your presentation, you want your audience to remember your message, not your animations.

Using the Morph Transition

The Morph transition is a special transition that essentially combines a transition with an animation. With the Morph transition, you can move an object to a new location on a slide; change the size, shape, and color of an object; and zoom into or out from an object.

To use the Morph transition, you need to follow these steps:

1. Create a slide that contains all of the items you want to appear to change size or position during the slide show.
2. Duplicate that slide or create a second slide with at least one object in common with the first slide.
3. On the duplicate slide, move the object or objects to the new position or make other changes to the objects, such as changing their size or color.
4. Apply the Morph transition to the duplicate slide.

When you use the Morph transition, you might need to place objects in the area outside the actual slide. The area outside of the slide is part of the PowerPoint workspace, but anything positioned in this area will not be visible in Slide Show or Presenter view. To use the workspace, you may need to zoom out.

To drag objects off Slide 5:

1. Display Slide 5 ("We Treat All Small Animals"). This slide contains four pictures. During the slide show, each picture needs to appear in the center of the slide and then move out of the way to make space for the next picture. First, you will move all of the pictures off of the slide to the workspace, and then you will zoom out to see more of the workspace.
2. On the status bar, click the **Zoom Out** button [-] as many times as needed to change the zoom percentage to 40%.
3. Drag the first picture (the man sitting with several animals on him) to the left of the slide, using the smart guides to keep it aligned with the other pictures.
4. Drag the next picture (hands around a yellow bird) off the slide and position it to the left of the first picture.
5. Drag the next picture (a woman patting a bearded dragon) to the right of the slide, and then drag the last picture (closeup of a dog) to the right of the picture of the woman. See Figure 2–32. This is the starting slide for the Morph transition.

Figure 2–32 **Pictures moved off of Slide 5**

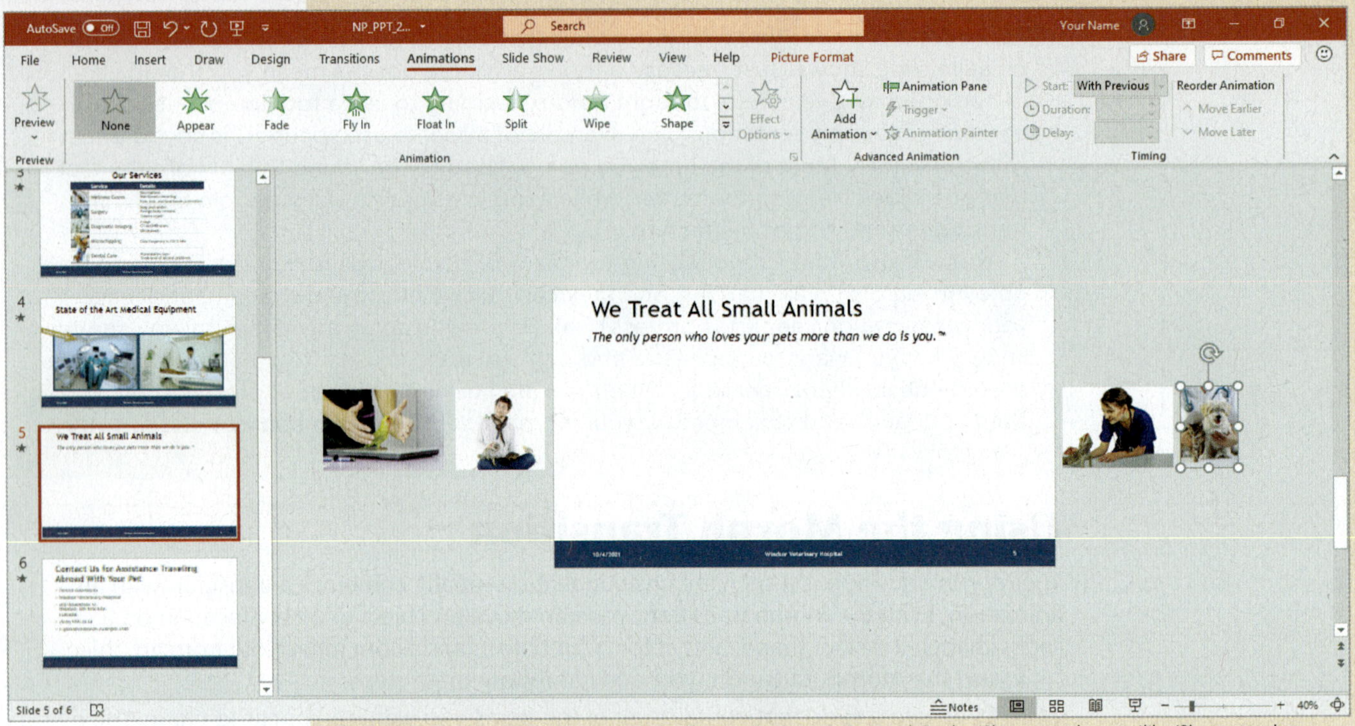

santypan/Shutterstock.com; Veronica Louro/Shutterstock.com; Rommel Canlas/Shutterstock.com; Ilike/Shutterstock.com

The steps in this section instruct you to place the objects at very precise locations. The instructions are specific so that your final file matches the official solution file. If you were creating this for your own use, the placement of the objects off the slide would not need to be so precise. After you place objects in your own files, preview the transition or watch it in Slide Show view, and then decide for yourself if you like the way the objects appear to move or if you want to reposition them for a better effect.

You have created the starting slide for the Morph transition. Next, you need to duplicate the slide and move and change at least one object.

To duplicate Slide 5 and resize and reposition a photo on Slide 6:

1. In the pane that contains the slide thumbnails, right-click the **Slide 5** thumbnail, and then click **Duplicate Slide**. The new Slide 6 is selected.
2. To the left of Slide 6, click the picture of the man sitting with several animals on him, and then click the **Picture Format** tab.
3. In the Size group, click in the **Shape Height** box, type **4**, and then press **ENTER**.
4. Drag the picture of the man to the center of the slide so that the smart guides show that it is centered both horizontally and vertically.

   Trouble? If you have difficulty making the correct smart guides appear, use the Align Center and Align Middle commands in the Arrange group.
5. Click the **Transitions** tab, and then in the Transition to This Slide group, click the **Morph** transition. The Morph transition is applied to Slide 6, and the picture of the man sitting moves onto the slide and resizes as the transition previews.

6. Display Slide 5, and then on the status bar, click the **Slide Show** button. Slide 5 appears in Slide Show view.
7. Press **SPACEBAR**. Slide 6 appears, and the picture of the seated man slides onto the slide and gets larger.
8. Press **ESC** to end the slide show.

Tip

If you want the objects to move more quickly or more slowly, change the duration of the Morph transition.

The Morph transition made it look like you had applied both the Fly In animation and the Zoom animation to the picture. Now that you have seen how the Morph transition works, you will repeat the process until the final slide shows all the photos correctly positioned and sized.

To complete the Morph transition effect for the pictures originally on Slide 5:

1. Duplicate Slide 6. The new Slide 7 is selected. On the Transitions tab, the Morph transition is selected. When you duplicated Slide 6, the transition was copied as well.
2. On Slide 7, change the height of the picture of the seated man to **3.2"**.
3. Drag the picture of the seated man to the lower-right corner of the slide so that the smart guides show that there is the same amount of space below the picture and above the title text box, and so that the right edge of the picture aligns with the right edge of the slide.
4. To the right of the slide, change the height of the picture of the woman patting the bearded dragon to **4"**, and then drag the picture of the woman to the center of the slide.
5. Duplicate Slide 7.
6. On the new Slide 8, change the height of the picture of the woman to **2.3"** and then drag the picture to the left so that the smart guides show that the center of the picture aligns with the top of the picture of the seated man, and so that there is the same amount of space between the right edge of the picture of the woman and the center of the slide as there is between the left edge of the picture of the seated man and the center of the slide.
7. To the left of the slide, change the height of the picture of the yellow bird to **4"**, and then drag the picture of the bird to the center of the slide.
8. Duplicate Slide 8.
9. On the new Slide 9, change the height of the picture of the bird to **2.1"** and then drag it to approximately one-quarter of an inch to the left of the seated man so one smart guide shows that its bottom aligns with the bottom of the picture of the woman and another smart guide appears vertically through the center of the picture of the bird. (This vertical smart guide is indicating that the center of the picture is aligned with the right edge of the text box containing the footer.)
10. To the right of the slide, change the height of the picture of the kitten and puppy to **4"** and then drag it to the center of the slide.
11. Duplicate Slide 9.
12. On the new Slide 10, change the height of the picture of the kitten and puppy to **3.5"** and then position it to the left of the picture of the bird so that the

middle of the picture of the kitten and puppy aligns with the bottom of the picture of the woman and so that there is the same amount of space between the picture of the kitten and puppy and the photos on either side of it.

13. On the status bar, click the **Fit slide to current window** button. Compare your screen to Figure 2–33.

Figure 2–33 Final positions of the pictures on Slide 10

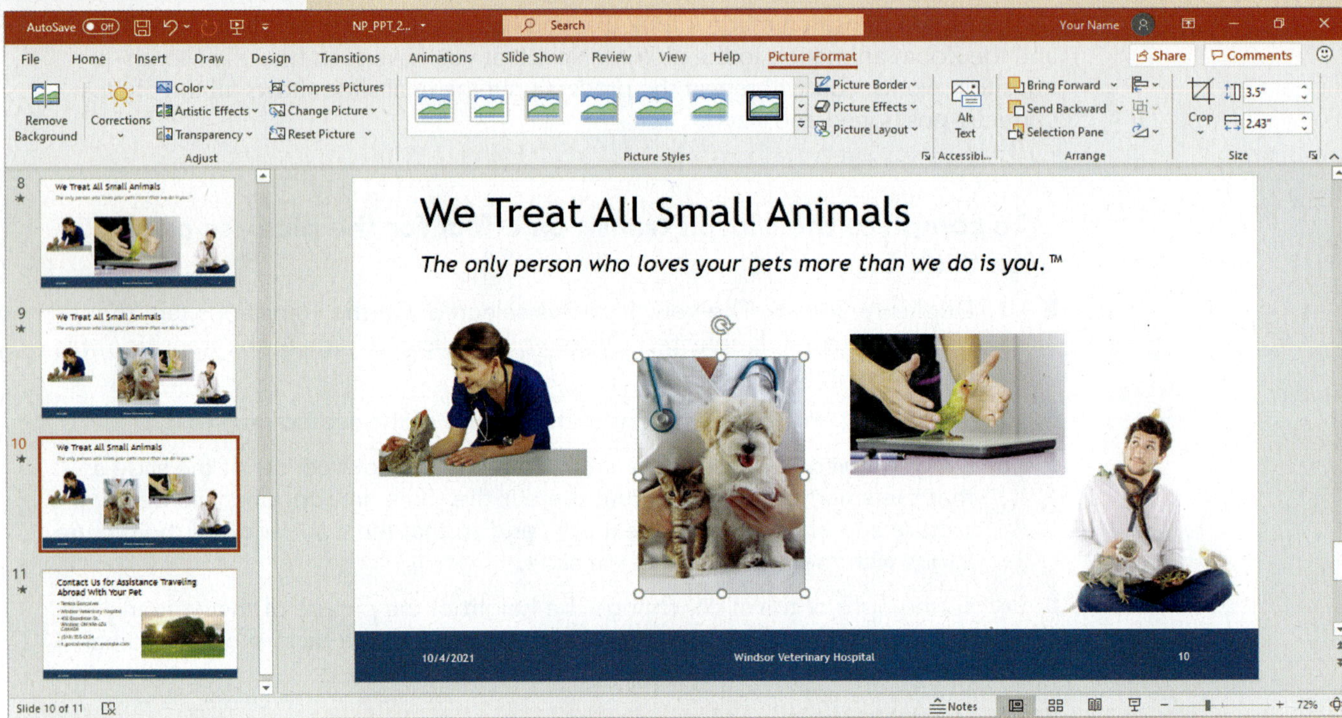

Rommel Canlas/Shutterstock.com; Ilike/Shutterstock.com; santypan/Shutterstock.com; Veronica Louro/Shutterstock.com

Now that you have created all the necessary slides, you can view the slides in Slide Show view to see the effect of the Morph transition.

To view Slides 5 through 10 in Slide Show view:

1. Display Slide 5 (the first "We Treat All Small Animals" slide), and then on the status bar, click the **Slide Show** button. Slide 5 appears in Slide Show view. The pictures that you positioned to the left and right of the slide are not visible. In the lower-right corner of the screen, the slide number 5 appears.
2. Press **SPACEBAR**. The picture of the seated man appears from the left, moves to the slide, and grows larger. In the lower-right corner of the screen, the slide number changes to 6.
3. Press **SPACEBAR**. The picture of the seated person shrinks and moves to the lower right corner of the slide while the picture of the person leaning over a table appears from the right, moves to the center of the slide, and grows in size. Again, the slide number changes.
4. Press **SPACEBAR** three more times. The other two pictures move onto the slide and are repositioned in their final locations. The changing slide numbers distract from the effect you are trying to create with the Morph transition.

5. Press **ESC** to end the slide show, and then click the **Insert** tab.
6. In the Text group, click the **Header & Footer** button, click the **Slide number** check box to deselect it, and then click **Apply to All**. Now the changing slide number will not distract the viewer from the Morph transition effect.

You can also use the Morph transition on slides that contain text. You will apply the Morph transition to Slide 2 so that the title on Slide 1 looks like it moves into the footer on Slide 2.

To apply the Morph transition to Slide 2:

1. Display Slide 1. The title text box contains the text "Windsor Veterinary Hospital."
2. Display Slide 2. The footer contains the same text as in the title text box on Slide 1—"Windsor Veterinary Hospital."
3. On the ribbon, click the **Transitions** tab, and then click the **Morph** transition. The Morph transition is applied to Slide 2 and previews.
4. On the Quick Access Toolbar, click the **Start From Beginning** button. Slide 1 appears in Slide Show view.
5. Press **SPACEBAR**. Slide 2 appears in Slide Show view, and as it does, the title text from Slide 1 moves down into the footer on Slide 2.
6. Press **SPACEBAR**. The first bulleted item flies onto the screen.
7. Press **ESC** to end the slide show, and then save the changes to the presentation.

Adding and Modifying Video

You can add video to slides to play during your presentation. PowerPoint supports various file formats, including the MPEG-4 format, the Windows Media Audio/Video format, and the QuickTime movie format. After you insert a video, you can modify it by changing playback options, changing the length of time the video plays, and applying formats and styles to the video.

Adding Video to Slides

To insert a video stored on your computer or network, click the Insert Video button in a content placeholder to open the Insert Video dialog box. You can also click the Video button in the Media group on the Insert tab, and then click This Device to open the same Insert Video dialog box.

Reference

Adding Videos Stored on Your Computer or Network

- In a content placeholder, click the Insert Video button to open the Insert Video dialog box, or click the Insert tab on the ribbon, and then in the Media group, click the Video button, and then click This Device to open the Insert Video dialog box.
- Click the video you want to use, and then click the Insert button.
- Choose how the video starts by clicking the Playback tab, and then in the Video Options group:
  - In the Start box, leave the setting as In Click Sequence to have the video start playing when you advance the slide show, when you click anywhere on the video, or when you click the Play button on the video toolbar.
  - Click the Start arrow, and then click Automatically to have the video start automatically when the slide appears in Slide Show view.
  - Click the Start arrow, and then click When Clicked On to have the video start when you click anywhere on the video or when you click the Play button on the video toolbar.
- Click the Play Full Screen check box to select it to have the video fill the screen.
- Click the Rewind after Playing check box to select it to have the poster frame display after the video plays.
- Click the Volume button, and then click a volume level or click Mute.

Teréza gave you a video that she wants you to add to Slide 11. The video shows a happy dog running towards the camera in slow motion.

To add a video to Slide 11 and play it:

1. Display Slide 11 ("Contact Us for Assistance Traveling Abroad With Your Pet"), and then in the content placeholder, click the **Insert Video** button. The Insert Video dialog box opens.
2. In the **PowerPoint2 > Module** folder, click **Support_PPT_2_Running.mov**, and then click **Insert**. The video is inserted on the slide in place of the content placeholder. The first frame of the video is displayed, and a video toolbar with controls for playing the video appears below it. The video contextual tabs appear on the ribbon. See Figure 2–34.

Tip

To link a video to a slide, in the Insert Video dialog box, click the Insert arrow, and then click Link to File.

Figure 2–34 Video added to Slide 11

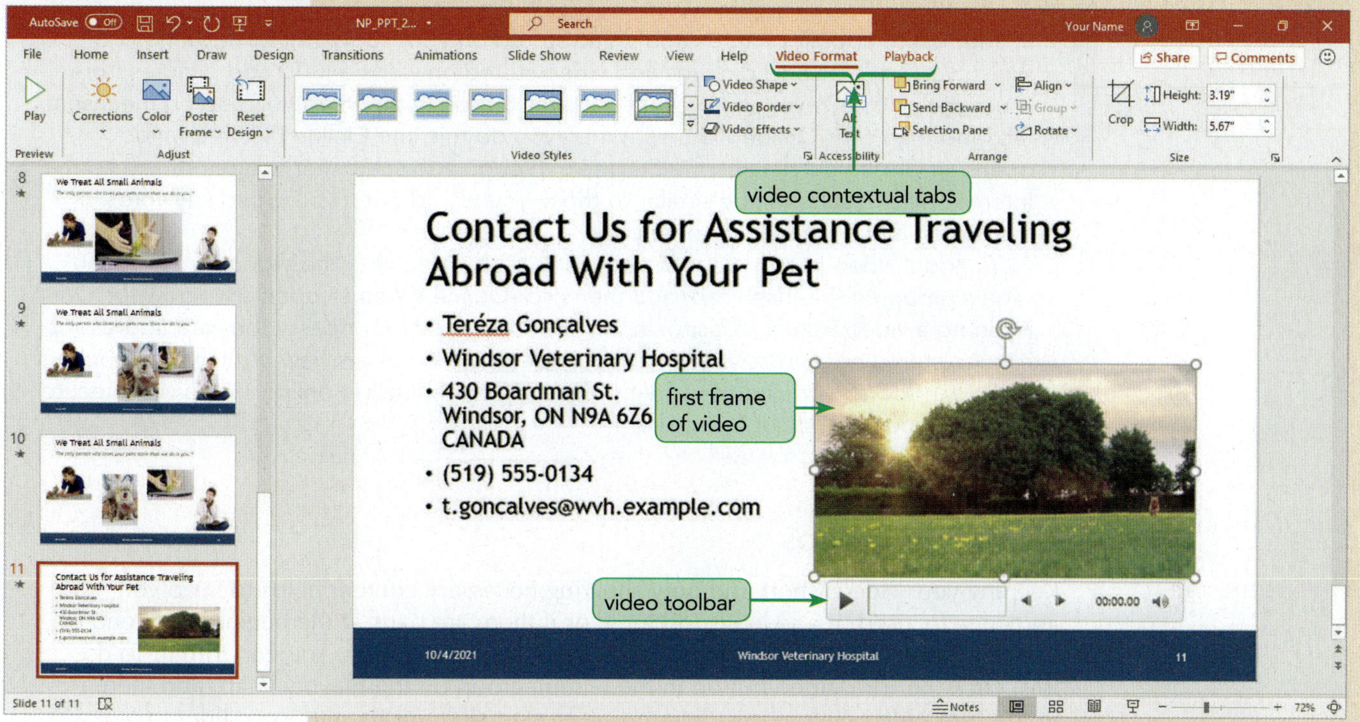

Multifocus/Shutterstock.com; Rommel Canlas/Shutterstock.com; Ilike/Shutterstock.com; santypan/Shutterstock.com; Veronica Louro/Shutterstock.com

4. On the video toolbar, click the **Play** button. The Play button changes to the Pause button and the video plays. Watch the 11-second video (note that this video does not have any sound).

5. Click the **Playback** tab. In the Start box, In Click Sequence appears. This means that the video will start playing during a slide show when you advance the slide show or when you click the video or the Play button on the video toolbar. Next, you'll watch the video in Slide Show view.

6. On the status bar, click the **Slide Show** button. Slide 11 appears in Slide Show view.

7. Press **SPACEBAR**. The video starts playing because you advanced the slide show.

8. Before the video finishes playing, move the pointer to make it visible, and then click the video. The video pauses. To stop the video from playing, you can click it, or you can move the pointer on top of the video and then click the Pause button on the video toolbar.

   Because you already started playing the video once, if you advance the slide show, the next slide will appear. If you want to start the video playing again, you need to click it or click the Play button on the video toolbar,

9. Move the pointer on top of the video. The video toolbar appears, and the pointer changes to the pointing finger pointer.

10. Click anywhere on the video. The video continues playing from the point it left off.

11. Press **SPACEBAR**. The black slide that indicates the end of the slide show appears.

12. Press **SPACEBAR** again to return to Normal view.

Insight

Inserting Pictures and Videos You Find Online

In addition to adding pictures and video stored on your computer or network to slides, you can also add pictures and video stored on websites. To add pictures from a website or OneDrive, you click the Pictures button in the Images group on the Insert tab, and then click Online Pictures. When you do this, the Online Pictures window opens, in which you can use the Bing search engine to search for images stored on the Internet. Your results will be similar to those you would get if you typed keywords in the Search box on the Bing home page in your browser.

To add a video from a website such as YouTube, you click the Video button in the Media group on the Insert tab, and then click Online Video to open a window for inserting a video from a website. In this window, you type or paste the web address of a video stored on a website such as YouTube or Vimeo. A preview of the video appears in the window so you can confirm it. Keep in mind that using online media is subject to each provider's Terms of Use policy.

Trimming Videos

Keeping your videos short and only showing necessary content helps to keep your audience focused. If a video is too long, or if there are parts at the beginning or end of the video that you don't want to show during the presentation, you can trim it. To do this, click the Trim Video button in the Editing group on the Playback tab, and then, in the Trim Video dialog box, drag the green start slider or the red stop slider to a new position to mark where the video will start and stop.

Teréza wants the video to end right after the dog runs off screen, so she wants you to trim it.

To trim the video on Slide 11:

1. On Slide 11 ("Contact Us for Assistance Traveling Abroad With Your Pet"), click the video to select it, and then click the **Playback** tab, if necessary.
2. In the Editing group, click the **Trim Video** button. The Trim Video dialog box opens. See Figure 2–35.

Figure 2–35 **Trim Video dialog box**

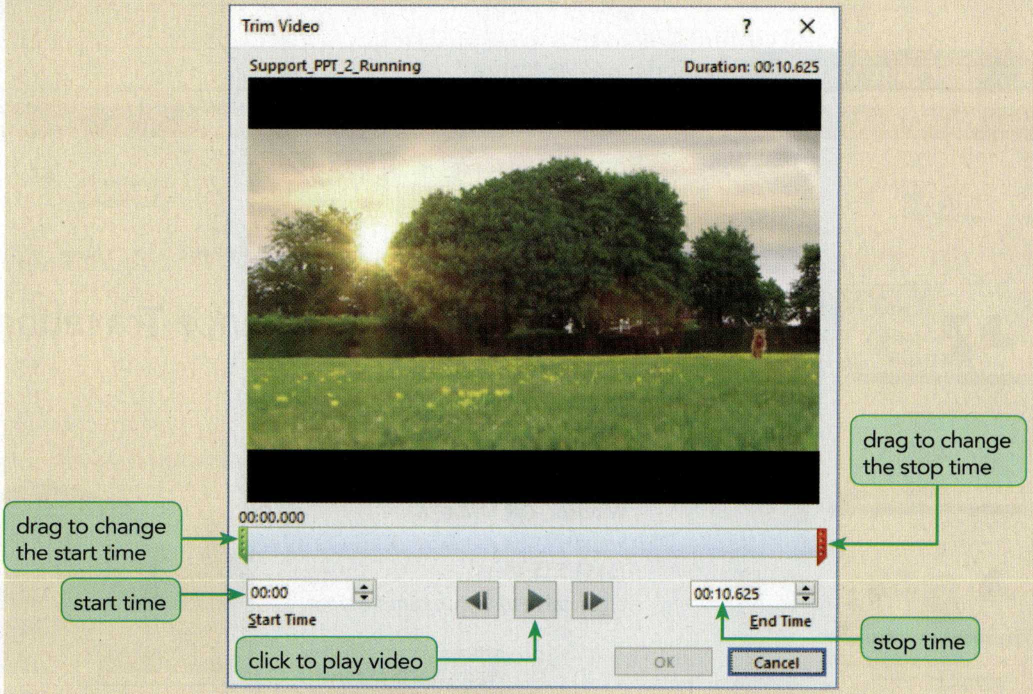

Multifocus/Shutterstock.com

Trouble? If the video appears black in the dialog box, click the Play button in the dialog box, and then click the Pause button to stop the playback. The video should appear.

Tip

Click a point on the video toolbar, click the Add Bookmark button in the Bookmarks group on the Playback tab to add a bookmark, then add the Seek media animation to the video. When you advance the slide show, the video will start from the bookmark.

3. Drag the red **Stop** tab to the left until the time in the End Time box is approximately 9.5 seconds.
4. If the number in the End Time box is not 00:09.500, click in the End Time box, click after the last number, edit the time so it is **00:09.500**, and then click **OK**.
5. On the video toolbar, click the **Play** button ▶. The video plays from the beginning but stops playing after 9.5 seconds. The last 1.5 seconds of the video do not play.
6. Save your changes.

Setting a Poster Frame

The frame that appears on the video object when the video is not playing is called the **poster frame**. The default poster frame for a video is the first frame of the video. You can select any frame from the video or any image stored in a file as the poster frame. If the video is set to rewind, the poster frame will reappear after playing.

Teréza wants you to select a poster frame for the video on Slide 11.

To set a poster frame for the video on Slide 11:

1. On Slide 11 ("Contact Us for Assistance Traveling Abroad With Your Pet"), click the video to select it, if necessary, and then click the **Video Format** tab.

2. Point to the toolbar below the video. A ScreenTip appears identifying the time of the video at that point. See Figure 2–36.

Figure 2–36 Setting a poster frame

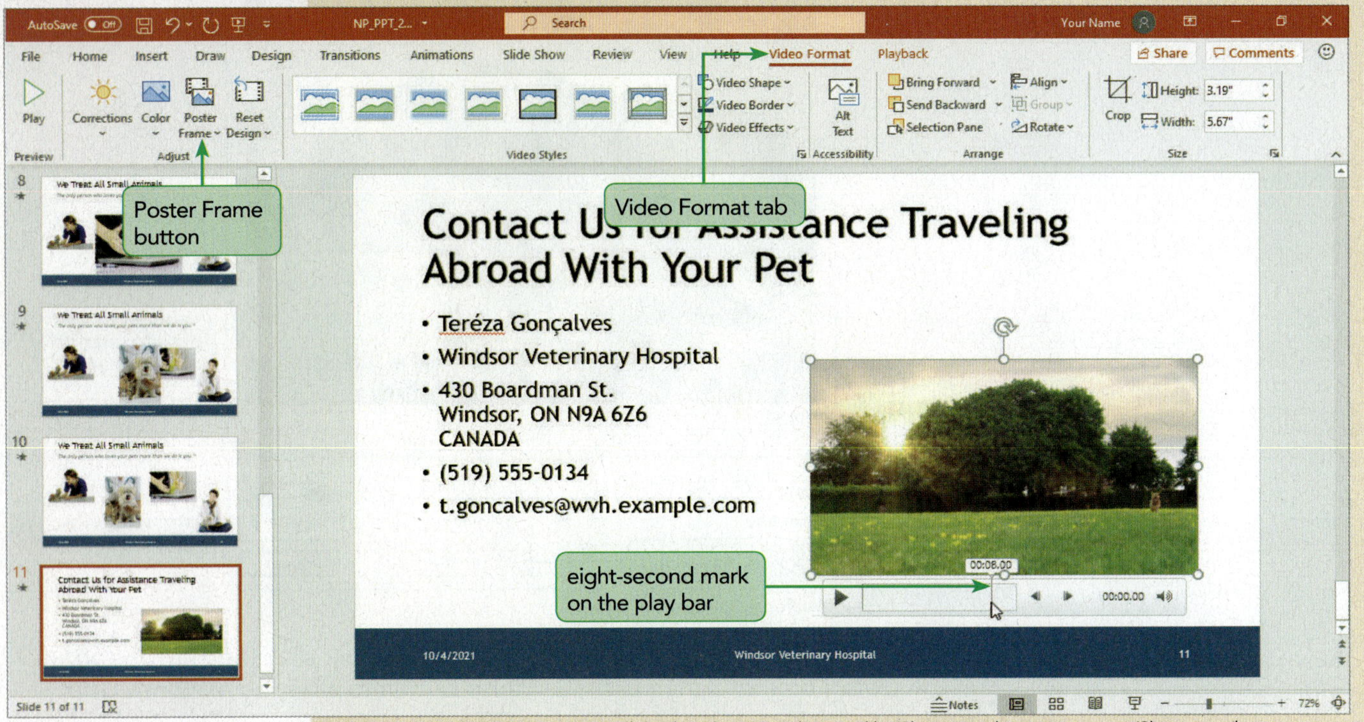

Multifocus/Shutterstock.com; Rommel Canlas/Shutterstock.com; Ilike/Shutterstock.com; santypan/Shutterstock.com; Veronica Louro/Shutterstock.com

3. On the video toolbar, click at approximately the 8.00-second mark. The frame at the 8.00-second mark shows the dog in the center of the video object.

   Trouble? You might not be able to click at exactly the 8.00-second mark. Click as close to it as you can (for example, 7.99 or 8.05).

4. In the Adjust group, click the **Poster Frame** button. The Poster Frame menu opens.
5. Click **Current Frame**. The message "Poster Frame Set" appears in the video's play bar, and the frame currently visible in the video object is set as the poster frame.
6. On the status bar, click the **Slide Show** button. Slide 11 appears in Slide Show view. The poster frame shows the dog in the center of the video object.
7. Click the video. The video plays. When it is finished, the video object shows the empty field that is at the end of the video.
8. Press **ESC** to end the slide show.

Tip

Like pictures, you can change the brightness and contrast of a video or recolor it using the buttons in the Adjust group. To reset a video, click the Reset Design button in the Adjust group.

Modifying Video Playback Options

You can change several options for how a video plays. The video playback options are listed in Figure 2–37.

Figure 2–37 Video playback options

Video Option	Function
Fade Duration	Set the number of seconds to fade the video in at the beginning of the video or out at the end of the video.
Volume	Change the volume of the video from high to medium or low or mute it.
Start	Change how the video starts: • In Click Sequence means that the presenter can start the video by advancing the slide show, clicking the video object, or clicking the Play button on the video toolbar. • Automatically means that the video will start automatically after the slide appears on the screen during the slide show. • When Clicked On means that the video starts when the presenter clicks the video object or clicks the Play button on the video toolbar.
Play Full Screen	The video fills the screen during the slide show.
Hide While Not Playing	The video does not appear on the slide when it is not playing; make sure the video is set to play automatically if this option is selected.
Loop until Stopped	The video plays until the next slide appears during the slide show.
Rewind after Playing	The video rewinds after it plays so that the first frame or the poster frame appears again.

As you have seen, when you insert a video, its Start setting is set to In Click Sequence. In Click Sequence for a video means the same thing that On Click means for an animation. Anything you do to advance the slide show causes the video to start. If you want to start the video by clicking the video object or the Play button on the video toolbar, set the Start setting to On Click. When On Click is selected, if you click somewhere else on the screen or do anything else to advance the slide show, the video will not play. You can also modify the Start setting so that the video plays automatically when the slide appears during the slide show. The Start setting is on the Playback tab.

In addition to changing the Start setting, you can set a video to fill the screen when it plays during the slide show. If you set the option to play full screen, the video will fill the screen when it plays, covering the slide title and anything else on the slide. You can also set a video to rewind so that it displays the poster frame after it plays.

Teréza wants you to change several playback options of the video on Slide 11. She wants the video to start automatically when Slide 11 appears during a slide show, and she wants it to fill the screen while it plays. When it is finished playing, she wants it to rewind so that the poster frame is on screen again.

To modify the playback options of the video:

1. On Slide 11 ("Contact Us for Assistance Traveling Abroad With Your Pet"), click the video to select it, if necessary, and then click the **Playback** tab. In the Video Options group, In Click Sequence appears in the Start box. See Figure 2–38.

Figure 2–38 Options on the Playback tab

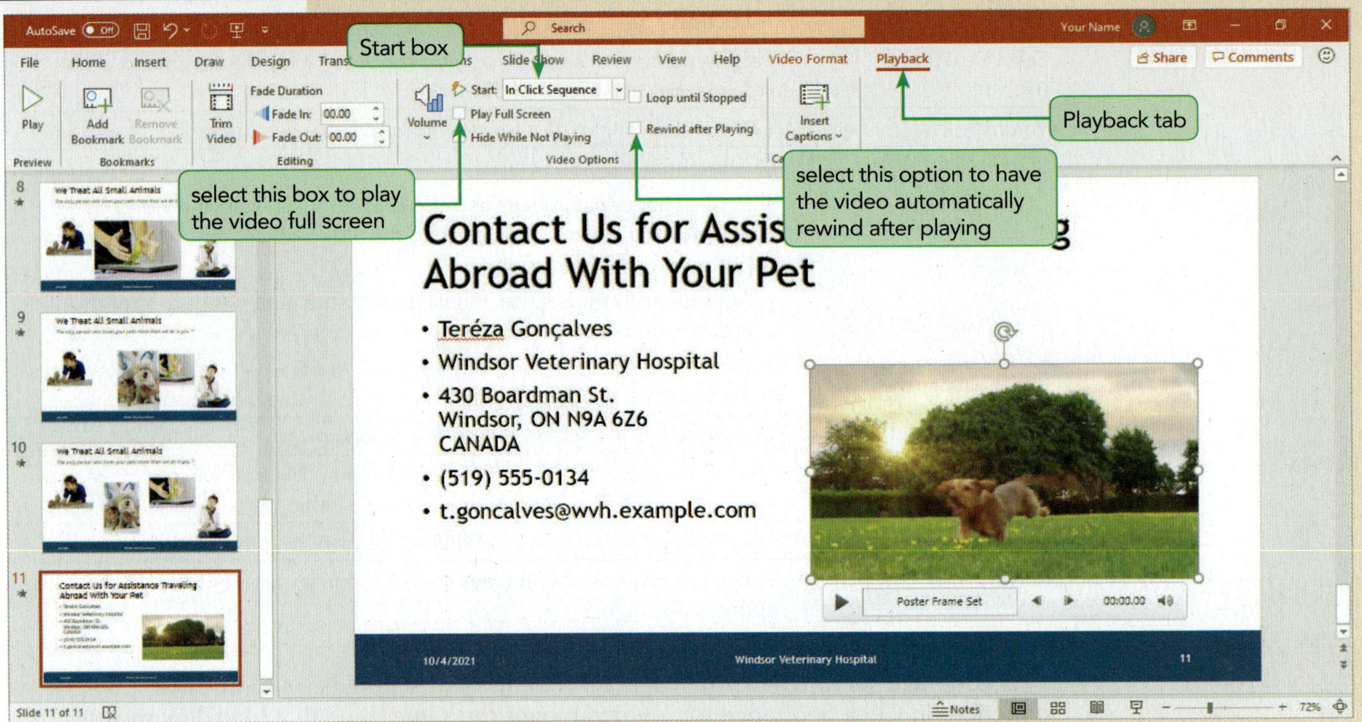

Multifocus/Shutterstock.com; Rommel Canlas/Shutterstock.com; Ilike/Shutterstock.com; santypan/Shutterstock.com; Veronica Louro/Shutterstock.com

Tip

You can adjust the volume of a video while it plays, or you can set the default volume by clicking the Volume button in the Video Options group on the Playback tab and then clicking an option on the menu.

2. In the Video Options group, click the **Start** arrow, and then click **Automatically**. Now the video will start automatically when the slide appears during the slide show.
3. In the Video Options group, click the **Play Full Screen** check box to select it. The video will fill the screen while it plays.
4. In the Video Options group, click the **Rewind after Playing** check box to select it. The video will reset to the poster frame after it plays.
5. On the status bar, click the **Slide Show** button. Slide 11 appears briefly in Slide Show view, and then the video fills the screen and plays. After the video finishes playing, Slide 11 reappears, and the poster frame appears in the video object.
6. Press **ESC** to end the slide show, and then save your changes.

Understanding Animation Effects Applied to Videos

When you insert a video (or audio) object, two animations are automatically applied to the video or audio object. The first animation is the Play animation. The Play animation is set to On Click. This means that when you advance the slide show, the video will start playing.

The second animation is the Pause animation. This animation has a special setting applied to it called a trigger so that you can click anywhere on the video to play it (or "unpause" it) and click the video again to pause it.

Both the Play and the Pause animations are Media animations. The Media animation category appears in the Animation gallery only when a media object—either video or audio—is selected on a slide.

If you change the Start setting of the video to Automatically, the Start setting of the Play animation is set to After Previous. If there are no other objects on the slide set to animate before the video, the Play animation has an animation sequence number of zero, which means that it will play immediately after the slide transition.

If you change the Start setting of a video on the Playback tab to When Clicked On, the Play animation is removed from the video and only the Pause animation is applied.

To see these animations, click the Animations tab on the ribbon, and then select a video object on a slide. The Pause and Play animations appear in the Animation gallery in the Media category.

You'll examine the video animations now.

To examine the Media animations applied to the video:

1. On Slide 11 ("Contact Us for Assistance Traveling Abroad With Your Pet"), click the video to select it, if necessary, and then click the **Animations** tab. Because you set this video to start automatically, two animation sequence icons appear next to it, one containing a zero and one containing a lightning bolt. In the Animation group, Multiple is selected because two animations are applied to this video. See Figure 2–39.

Figure 2–39 **Two animations applied to a video**

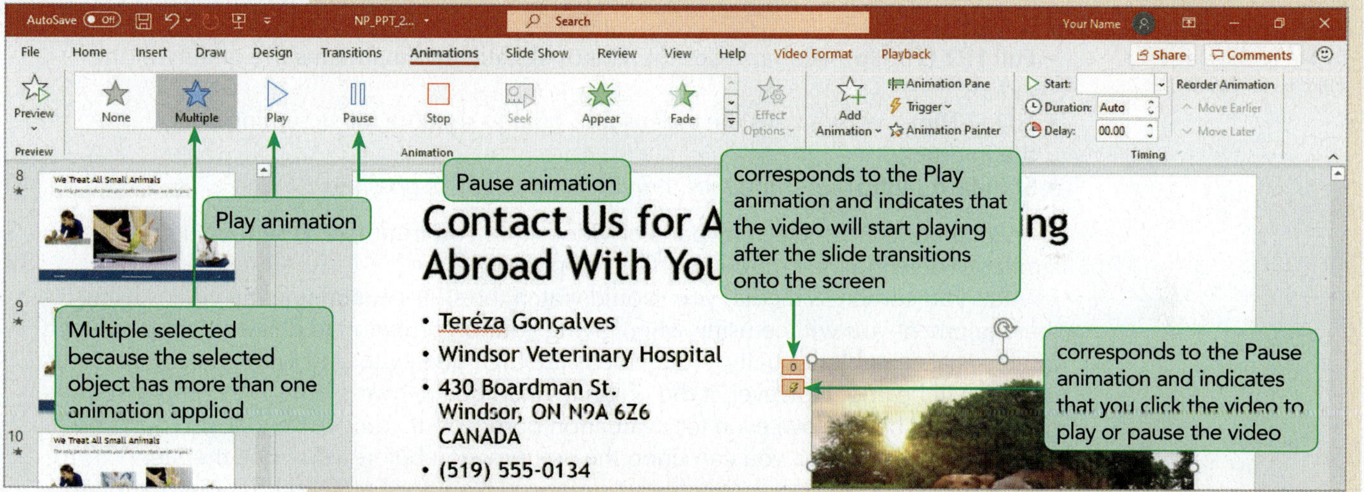

Multifocus/Shutterstock.com; Rommel Canlas/Shutterstock.com; Ilike/Shutterstock.com; santypan/Shutterstock.com; Veronica Louro/Shutterstock.com

2. In the Animation group, click the **More** button. The Media category appears at the top of the Animation gallery because a media object is selected.
3. Press **ESC**. The gallery closes without you making a selection.

   When more than one animation is applied to any object, you need to click each animation sequence icon to see which animation is associated with each icon.
4. Click the **0** animation sequence icon. In the Animation group, Play is selected, and in the Timing group, After Previous appears in the Start box. This start setting of the Play animation was changed to After Previous when you selected Automatically in the Start box on the Playback tab.
5. Click the **lightning bolt** animation sequence icon. In the Animation group, the Pause animation is selected, and in the Timing group, On Click appears in the Start box. This animation is applied automatically to all videos when you add them to slides. It is because of this animation that you can click anywhere on the video object during a slide show to play or pause it.

6. Click the **Playback** tab.
7. In the Video Options group, click the **Start arrow**, click **In Click Sequence**, click the **Animations** tab, and then click the **1** animation sequence icon. In the Animation group, Play is selected, but now On Click appears in the Start box.
8. Click the video, and then click the **Playback** tab.
9. In the Video Options group, click the **Start arrow**, click **When Clicked On**, and then click the **Animations** tab. There is only one animation applied to the video now. In the Animation group, Pause is selected, and On Click appears in the Start box.
10. Change the Start setting of the video back to **Automatically**.

Compressing Media

Tip

If you might want to show the presentation using a projector capable of high-quality display, save a copy of the presentation before you compress the media.

As with pictures, you can compress media files. If you need to send a file via email or you need to upload it, you should compress media files to make the final PowerPoint file smaller. When you compress files, you make the final presentation file smaller, but you also lower the quality of the video. You can compress videos using the following settings:

- **Full HD (1080p)**—compresses the videos slightly and maintains the quality of the videos
- **HD (720p)**—compresses the videos to a quality suitable for streaming over the Internet
- **Standard (480p)**—compresses the videos as small as possible

With all of the settings, any parts of videos that you trimmed off will be deleted, similar to deleting the cropped portions of photos.

After you compress media, you should watch the slides containing the videos using the equipment you will be using when giving your presentation to make sure the reduced quality is acceptable. Usually, if the videos are high quality to start with, the compressed quality will be fine. However, if the original video quality was grainy, the compressed quality might be too low, even for evaluation purposes. If you decide that you don't like the compressed quality, you can undo the compression before you close the file.

You will compress the media file you inserted. You need to send the presentation to Teréza via email, so you will compress the media as much as possible.

To compress the video in the presentation:

1. With Slide 11 ("Contact Us for Assistance Traveling Abroad With Your Pet") displayed, click the **File** tab. Backstage view appears displaying the Info screen.
2. Click the **Compress Media** button. A menu opens listing compression choices. See Figure 2–40.

Figure 2–40 **Compression options on the Info screen in Backstage view**

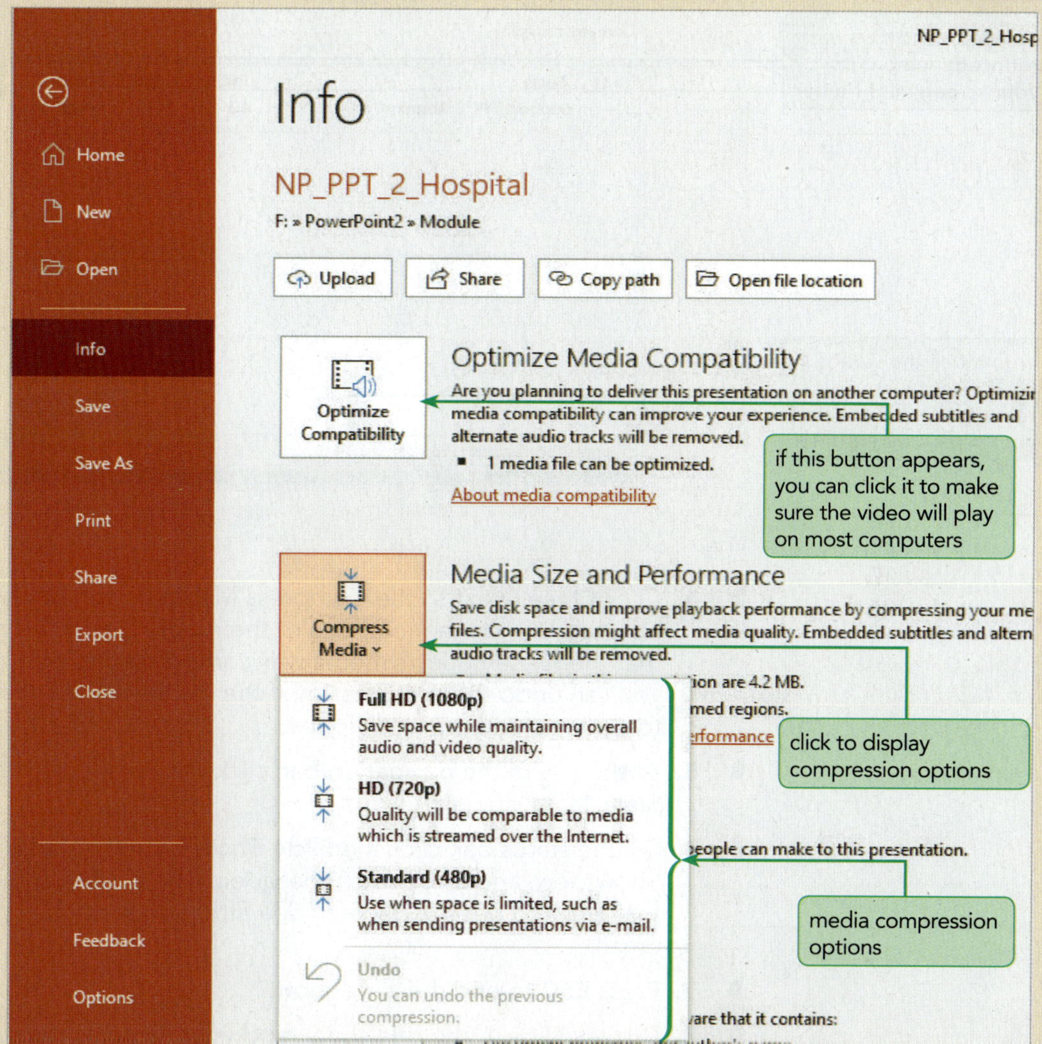

3. Click **Standard (480p)**. The Compress Media dialog box opens listing the video file in the presentation with a progress bar to show you the progress of the compression. After the file is compressed, a message appears in the Status column indicating that compression for the file is complete and stating how much the video file size was reduced. A message also appears at the bottom of the dialog box stating that the compression is complete and indicating how much the file size of the presentation was reduced. Because there is only one video in this presentation, the amount the video was reduced and the amount the presentation was reduced is the same. See Figure 2–41.

Figure 2–41 Compress Media dialog box

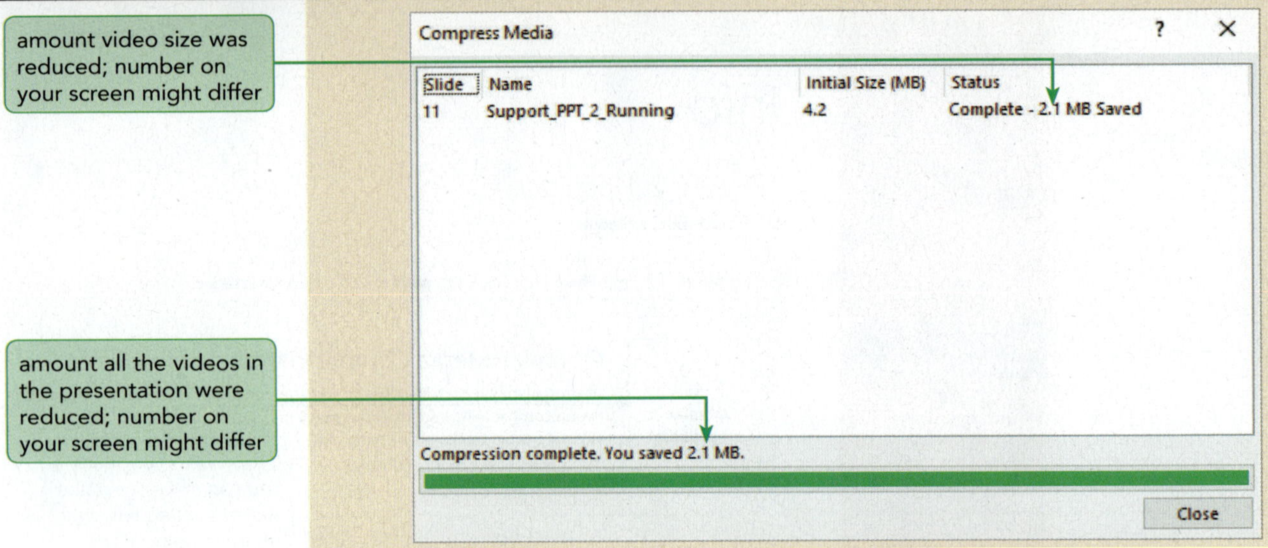

4. Click **Close**. Next to the Compress Media button on the Info screen, the bulleted list lists the total size of the media files in the presentation, states that the presentation's media was compressed to Standard (480p), and that you can undo the compression if the results are unsatisfactory. Now you need to view the compressed videos.
5. At the top of the navigation bar, click the **Back** button to display Slide 11.
6. On the status bar, click the **Slide Show** button to display the slide in Slide Show view, and then watch the video. The quality is lower, but it is sufficient for Teréza to get the general idea after you send the presentation to her via email.
7. Press **ESC** to end the slide show.
8. Display Slide 1 (the title slide), add your name as the subtitle, and then save your changes.

Now that you have finished working on the presentation, you should view the completed presentation as a slide show.

To view the completed presentation in Slide Show view:

1. On the Quick Access Toolbar, click the **Start From Beginning** button. Slide 1 appears in Slide Show view.
2. Press **SPACEBAR**. Slide 2 ("World-Class Veterinary Hospital") appears in Slide Show view with the Morph transition so the title on Slide 1 moves down to the footer.
3. Press **SPACEBAR** five times to display all the bulleted items, and then press **SPACEBAR** again to display Slide 3 ("Our Services").
4. Press **SPACEBAR** to display Slide 4 ("State of the Art Medical Equipment").
5. Press **SPACEBAR**. The photo on the left appears with the Split animation, and then after a one-second delay, the "Recently updated OR" arrow appears with the Wipe animation.

6. Press **SPACEBAR**. The photo on the right appears, and then after a one-second delay, the "Brand new MRI scanner" arrow appears.
7. Press **SPACEBAR**. Slide 5 ("We Treat All Small Animals") appears with only the title, the slogan, and the footer information displayed.
8. Press **SPACEBAR** five times, watching the pictures move on the screen with the Morph transition.
9. Press **SPACEBAR**. Slide 11 briefly appears, and then the video fills the screen and plays automatically. When the video is finished, Slide 11 appears again with the poster frame you selected displayed in the video object.
10. Press **SPACEBAR** to display the black slide that appears at the end of a slide show, and then press **SPACEBAR** once more to return to Normal view.
11. sam Close the presentation file.

The final presentation file with transitions, animations, and video is interesting and should enhance Teréza's presentation.

Review

Session 2.2 Quick Check

1. What is a transition?
2. What are animations?
3. How do you change the speed of a transition or an animation?
4. When you apply an animation to a bulleted list with subitems, how do the first-level items animate? How do the second-level items animate?
5. What is the Morph transition?
6. What is a poster frame?
7. For a video, what is the difference between the Start setting "On Click" and "In Click Sequence"?
8. What animation is applied to every video that you add to a slide no matter what the Start setting is?

Practice

Review Assignments

Data Files needed for the Review Assignments: NP_PPT_2-2.pptx, Support_PPT_2_Bath.jpg, Support_PPT_2_NewTheme.pptx, Support_PPT_2_Plate.jpg, Support_PPT_2_Sign.jpg, Support_PPT_2_Writing.mov

The practice manager at Windsor Veterinary Hospital, Brian Sarkar, organizes the hospital's Give Back volunteer program. Through Give Back, hospital employees can participate as volunteers at different events throughout the year. Teréza Gonçalves offered to help Brian run this program. Brian asked Teréza to help him prepare a presentation that he will use to describe the program to new employees. Teréza created the text of the presentation and asked you to find graphics to include. She also wants you to add animations and transitions to make the presentation more interesting. Complete the following steps:

1. Open the presentation **NP_PPT_2-2.pptx**, located in the PowerPoint2 > Review folder included with your Data Files, add your name as the subtitle, and then save it as **NP_PPT_2_Volunteer** to the drive and folder where you are storing your files.
2. Apply the theme from the presentation **Support_PPT_2_NewTheme.pptx**, located in the PowerPoint2 > Review folder.
3. Apply the Uncover transition to any slide. Change the Effect Options to From Bottom, and then change the duration to 0.50 seconds. Apply this transition to all of the slides, and then remove it from Slide 1 (the title slide).
4. On Slide 2 ("What Is Operation Give Back?"), add the trademark sign after "Give Back" and before the question mark.
5. On Slide 2, animate the bulleted list with the Fly In entrance animation, and then change the effect so the items fly in from the left.
6. On Slide 2, animate the slide title with the Float In animation, and then change the effect so that the title floats down from the top. Change the duration of the animation applied to the title to 0.50 seconds, and then change the way it starts so that the animation happens automatically after the previous action.
7. On Slide 2, change the order of the animations so that the title animates first.
8. Change the layout of Slide 3 ("2021 Give Back Days") to the custom Title and Table layout.
9. On Slide 3, insert a 3×3 table. Refer to Figure 2–42 to add the rest of the data to the table. Add a row if needed.

Figure 2–42 Data for table on Slide 3

Description	Date	Requirements
Groom animals at city animal shelter	Saturday, April 24	
Clean up city dog parks	Saturday, June 19	
Annual fundraiser dinner for city animal shelter	Sunday, September 12	

10. In the table, delete the third column (with "Requirements" in the first cell).
11. Apply the Light Style 2 – Accent 6 table style.
12. Add a new first column (to the left of the "Description" column). Fill each cell in the new column (except the first cell) with the following pictures, all located in the PowerPoint2 > Review folder, in order from the second row to the bottom row: **Support_PPT_2_Bath.jpg**, **Support_PPT_2_Sign.jpg**, and **Support_PPT_2_Plate.jpg**.
13. On Slide 3, format the table as follows:
    - Change the font size of all of the text in the table to 24 points. Then change the font size of the text in the top row to 28 points.
    - Change the fill of the first row to Tan, Accent 6, Darker 50%.

- Change the width of the first column to 2". Change the width of the second column to 4.25". And change the width of the third column so it is just wide enough to fit its widest entry (which is 3.6").
- Change the height of rows 2 through 4 to 1.4".
- Align the text in rows 2 through 4 so it is centered vertically.
- Change the border between rows 2 and 3 and the border between rows 3 and 4 to a three-point, solid line border using the Tan, Accent 6, Darker 50% color.

14. Reposition the table so it is centered horizontally on the slide and so the smart guides indicate that there is the same amount of space between the bottom of the table and the bottom of the slide as there is between the top of the title text box and the top of the slide.
15. On Slide 4, move the picture of the man serving the couple above the slide and the picture of the dog and the boy below the slide, using the smart guides to position them so the centers of the pictures align with the center of the slide. Then change the layout to the Section Header layout, and type **Scenes from Last Year** as the title.
16. Duplicate Slide 4. On the new Slide 5, delete the title text, and then change the layout to the Blank layout. Resize the picture of the man serving the couple so it is 7.5 inches high, and then position it on the slide so it is centered both horizontally and vertically on the slide. Apply the Rotated, White style to the picture on the slide, then change the color of the border to Dark Blue, Accent 3, Darker 50%.
17. On Slide 5, insert the Arrow: Right shape. Change the fill to Dark Green, Accent 4, Darker 25%, and change the outline to No Outline.
18. Resize the arrow so it is 1.5 inches high and 5.7 inches wide.
19. With the arrow selected, change the font size to 16 points. Then type **Ben Kim, veterinary technician, waiting tables at last year's fundraiser** in the arrow.
20. Drag the adjustment handle at the base of the arrowhead about one-quarter inch to the left to make the arrowhead larger. (The base of the arrowhead will be between the "e" and the "s" in "tables.")
21. Position the arrow to the left of the man serving the seated couple so the left edge of the arrow aligns with the left edge of the slide and the top of the border around the shape is about one-half inch below the top edge of the slide.
22. Apply the Wipe entrance animation to the arrow, and then change the effect so that it wipes from the left. Change the way the animation starts so that it starts after the previous action. Set a delay of one second.
23. Duplicate Slide 5. On the new Slide 6, reset the picture to remove the style. Then resize the picture so it is 3.75 inches high and center it vertically and horizontally on the slide.
24. On Slide 6, move the picture of the dog and boy onto the slide (it will be on top of the other picture and the arrow will still be visible). Resize the picture of the dog and the boy so it is 7.5 inches high, and then center it horizontally and vertically on the slide.
25. Copy the formatting applied to the picture on Slide 5 to the picture of the dog and boy on Slide 6.
26. Replace the text in the arrow with **Randy, son of Kathy Turner, HR Director, enjoying the dog park after the clean-up last year** on Slide 6.
27. On Slide 6, flip the arrow horizontally, and then position it to the right of the boy so the right edge of the arrow aligns with the right edge of the slide and the bottom of the border around the shape aligns with the horizontal smart guide that appears (the smart guide indicates the top of the picture underneath the picture of the dog and the boy).
28. On Slide 6, change the effect of the animation applied to the arrow so it wipes in from the right.
29. Duplicate Slide 6. On the new Slide 7, reset the picture of the dog and the boy, then resize that picture so it is 3.75 inches high. Delete the arrow. Change the layout to Title Only.
30. On Slide 7, position the photo of the man serving the couple on the left side of the slide, about one inch below the shading under the title text placeholder and so that the left edge of the photo aligns with the left edge of the title text placeholder. Position the photo of the dog and boy to the

right of the other photo so that its right edge aligns with the right edge of the title text placeholder and so its top and bottom align with the photo on the left. Add **Join the Gang!** as the slide title.

31. Apply the Morph transition to Slides 5, 6, and 7.
32. On Slide 8, use the Video button in the Media group on the Insert tab to insert the video **Support_PPT_2_Writing.mov** located in the PowerPoint2 > Review folder. Resize the video so it is 7.5 inches high, and then center it horizontally and vertically on the slide. Trim a bit from the end of the video so the number in the End box is 8.600. Set the poster frame by clicking about one-quarter of an inch from the end of the play bar. It will be approximately the 7.9-second mark. Finally, set the playback options so that the video starts playing automatically and rewinds after playing.
33. On Slide 9 ("Sign Up Today!"), replace the second "e" in "Tereza" with "é" and the "c" in "Goncalves" with "ç."
34. On Slide 9, delete the empty content placeholder. Insert the Arrow: Pentagon shape, and then resize it so that it is two inches high and five inches wide. Type **This way to feel great and help others!** in the shape. Change the font of this text to Bradley Hand ITC, change the font size to 32 points, and then format this text as bold.
35. Fill the shape with the Red, Accent 2 color. Then apply the Linear Down gradient in the Dark Variations section.
36. Format the shape with the Oblique: Bottom Left 3-D effect. Change the Depth of the 3-D format to 40 points. Change the Depth shading color to Red, Accent 2, Darker 50%.
37. Position the shape so that its middle aligns with the horizontal smart guide that indicates the middle of the slide and its left edge aligns with the left edge of the title text box. Then drag the rotate handle on the shape to the left so that the rotate handle is below the "p" in "Up" in the title.
38. Open the Format Shape pane to the Shape Options tab with the Size & Properties button selected and the Size section expanded. If the value in the Rotation box is not 345°, change it to 345°.
39. Add **Give Back Days at WVH** as the footer on all the slides except the title slide, and display the current date (fixed) on all the slides except the title slide. On the notes and handouts, add **Operation Give Back** as the header and your name as the footer, and show page numbers.
40. Compress all the photos in the presentation to E-mail (96 ppi), and then compress the media to Standard (480p).
41. Save your changes, view the slide show, and then close the presentation.

Apply

Case Problem 1

Data Files needed for this Case Problem: NP_PPT_2-3.pptx, Support_PPT_2_Calendar.jpg, Support_PPT_2_Cornucopia.jpg, Support_PPT_2_Fourth.jpg, Support_PPT_2_Labor.png, Support_PPT_2_Logo.pptx, Support_PPT_2_Memorial.jpg, Support_PPT_2_NewYear.jpg, Support_PPT_2_Sayings.mp4, Support_PPT_2_Sixty.png

Worldwide Phone Systems Ibrahim Khan is the director of human resources for Worldwide Phone Systems, a national telecommunications company headquartered in San Jose, California. He recently proposed a new system of paid holidays to the Board of Directors so that all of the employees in the company's diverse workforce will be able to request paid time off to celebrate their own religious or cultural holidays. The Board of Directors approved his plan, and now Ibrahim needs to present the details of the plans to department managers via a webinar. He asks you to help him finish the presentation, which will include photos, a video, and a table to communicate the new policy. Complete the following steps:

1. Open the file named **NP_PPT_2-3.pptx**, located in the PowerPoint2 > Case1 folder included with your Data Files, add your name as the subtitle on Slide 1, and then save it as **NP_PPT_2_Holidays** to the drive and folder where you are storing your files.
2. Apply the theme from the presentation **Support_PPT_2_Logo.pptx**, located in the PowerPoint2 > Case1 folder.
3. Apply the Cut transition to all of the slides in the presentation, then remove the transition from Slide 1 (the title slide).

4. Add **Worldwide Phone Systems** as the footer text. Display the footer text, the slide number, and the current date (using the Fixed option) on all of the slides including the title slide.
5. On Slide 1, draw a rectangle that is 11.7 inches wide and 0.2 inches high. Position the rectangle so it is on top of the date, footer, and slide number at the bottom of the slide. Remove the shape outline, and fill the rectangle with White, Background 1. (Note: You are doing this because you are going to duplicate this slide and apply the Morph transition to the new Slide 2, and this prevents the footer information from appearing on the new Slide 2.)
6. On Slide 1, insert the picture **Support_PPT_2_Calendar.jpg**, located in the PowerPoint2 > Case1 folder. Resize the picture so it is 4.3 inches high. Rotate the picture left by 90 degrees. Position the rotated picture to the left of the slide so that the top of the picture aligns with the top of the slide and so that there is about one-quarter of an inch between the picture and the slide.
7. Duplicate Slide 1. On the new Slide 2, delete your name, and then apply the Title 2 layout.
8. On Slide 2, rotate the picture of the calendar right by 90 degrees so that it is right-side-up. Apply the picture style Thick Matte, Black to the calendar picture, and then change the border color to the Red, Accent 2, Darker 25% color.
9. Position the picture in the upper-left corner of the slide so that the outside of the red border on the top and left side of the picture align with the top and left borders of the white part of the slide.
10. On the picture of the calendar, drag the rotate handle to the left until the top-left corner of the picture border is just touching the outside of the blue border around the slide. Note that when you release the mouse button, the picture will slightly increase in size so that the top-left corner of the picture will overlap the slide border.
11. Confirm that the picture of the calendar is rotated to 345°. If it is not, change the rotation so that it is.
12. Apply the Morph transition to Slide 2. Change the duration of this transition to one second.
13. On Slide 3, animate the bulleted list using the entrance Float In animation with the Float Down effect, and change the duration to 0.50 seconds. Animate the bulleted lists on Slides 5 and 6 using the same animation. On Slide 5, make sure you animate the list on the left first, and then animate the list on the right. Then on Slide 5, change the effect for both lists to All at Once.
14. On Slide 4 ("Five Fixed Holidays"), create a table with three columns and five rows. In the first row, type **Name** in the first cell, **Description** in the second cell, and **Date** in the third cell.
15. In the table, in the "Name" column, starting in the second row, type the following entries: **New Year's Day**, **Memorial Day**, **Labor Day**, and **Thanksgiving Day**. Then in the "Date" column, type the following entries: **January 1**, **Last Monday in May**, **First Monday in September**, and **4th Thursday in November**.
16. In the table, insert a new row between the Memorial Day row and the Labor Day row. In the new row in the "Name" column, type **Independence Day**, and in the "Date" column, type **July 4**.
17. In the table, delete the second column (with the label "Description" in the first row). Then add a new column to the left of the first column.
18. Change the table style to Medium Style 3 – Accent 4. Change the font size of all the text in the table to 24 points, and then align the text so it is centered vertically.
19. In the first column, starting in the second row, fill the cells with the following pictures: **Support_PPT_2_NewYear.jpg, Support_PPT_2_Memorial.jpg, Support_PPT_2_Fourth.jpg, Support_PPT_2_Labor.png**, and **Support_PPT_2_Cornucopia.jpg**.
20. Resize the first column in the table so it is 1.8" wide. Resize the second and third columns to fit their widest entries (2.83" and 4.03", respectively). Resize all the rows except the first row so that they are 0.95" high.
21. Align the table so that its left edge aligns with the left edge of the title text box and its top edge appears below the text in the title text box.
22. Draw one-quarter point black line in the table on the border between the last two cells in the first column. Draw another one-quarter point black line on the border between the first and second cells in the fifth row.

23. On Slide 5 ("Choose Five Floating Holidays"), draw a Rectangle: Rounded Corners shape that is 6.2 inches wide and 0.5 inches high, and then position it so its left edge aligns with the left edge of the title text box and its bottom edge aligns with the smart guide that indicates the top of the footer area. Type **More dates might be added depending on employee needs.** in the shape. Italicize the text in the shape. Change the fill of the shape to Gray, Accent 6, and remove the outline.
24. Change the Start setting of the animation applied to the first bulleted item in each list to With Previous.
25. On Slide 6, insert the picture **Support_PPT_2_Sixty.png** in the empty content placeholder. Add **Image of the number sixty** as alt text. Apply the Grow & Turn entrance animation.
26. Change the order of the animations on Slide 6 so that the picture of "60" animates first. Next, click the animation sequence icon next to "Floating holiday requests," and then move that animation earlier. Finally, change the Start setting of the animation applied to the picture of "60" so that it starts with the previous animation. The end result is that the first bulleted item will animate when you advance the slide show, and its subitems and the picture of "60" will animate with it.
27. Set the duration of the animation applied to the picture of "60" to 0.50 seconds, and then set a delay of 0.50 seconds.
28. On Slide 7, insert the video **Support_PPT_2_Sayings.mp4**, located in the PowerPoint2 > Case1 folder. Set the movie to play automatically and rewind after playing. Set the poster frame to the frame at approximately the 1-second mark.
29. Select the image of the red number sixty on Slide 6, and then compress all the pictures to E-mail (96 ppi). Compress the media to Standard (480p).
30. Save your changes, view the slide show in Slide Show view, and then close the presentation.

Create

Case Problem 2

Data Files needed for this Case Problem: NP_PPT_2-4.pptx, Support_PPT_2_Corporate.jpg, Support_PPT_2_Hospital.jpg, Support_PPT_2_Residential.jpg, Support_PPT_2_School.jpg

Abonza Food Services Maura Mitchell is the National Food Service Manager for Abonza Food Services, a food service and facilities management company that is contracted to run cafeterias and kitchens for a wide range of industries across the United States and Canada. Because they hire local food service managers frequently, monthly orientation and certification seminars are held in each region to train them. Maura created a presentation to help her with this training. She asks you to finish the presentation. Complete the following steps:

1. Open the presentation **NP_PPT_2-4.pptx**, located in the PowerPoint2 > Case2 folder included with your Data Files, add your name as the subtitle, and then save the presentation as **NP_PPT_2_Manager** to the drive and folder where you are storing your files.
2. Apply the Cube transition to all of the slides in the presentation. Remove the transition from Slide 1.
3. Add as a footer **Updated:** and then type today's date. Show the footer on all the slides except the title slide.

Explore 4. On Slide 1 (the title slide), apply the Appear entrance animation to the title, change the Start setting to After Previous, and then modify the animation so that the letters appear one by one. (*Hint*: Use the Animation group Dialog Box Launcher, and then change the setting in the Animate text box on the Effect tab.) Speed up the effect by changing the delay between letters to 0.1 seconds.

Explore 5. On Slide 1, add the Typewriter sound to the animation applied to the title. (*Hint*: Use the Animate text box again.)

Explore 6. On Slide 1, apply the entrance Flip animation to the reddish-orange shape in the upper-left corner of the slide. (*Hint*: Click More Entrance Effects on the Animations menu.) Change the Start setting of this animation to After Previous.

7. On Slide 1, copy the reddish-orange shape in the upper-left corner of the slide. Paste the copied shape onto Slide 2 ("Industries We Serve"), then remove the animation from the shape on Slide 2. Copy the shape on Slide 2, and then paste it onto the rest of the slides in the presentation.
8. Duplicate Slide 2. On the new Slide 3, change the title to **Schools**.
9. On Slide 3 ("Schools"), move the three photos on the right off the slide to the right, positioned so that they are still aligned with the remaining picture on the slide. (*Hint*: Select all three photos, and then drag them all together as a group.) Keep the photos in the same order as on Slide 2. Resize the picture of the children eating at a cafeteria table so it is five inches high. Position the picture so it is centered horizontally and so the bottom of the photo aligns with the smart guide that indicates the top of the footer text box.
10. Duplicate Slide 3. On the new Slide 4, change the title to **Residential Living**.
11. On Slide 4 ("Residential Living"), drag the picture of the children eating at a cafeteria table off the slide anywhere to the left. Then drag the picture of the group of adults onto the slide, resize it so that it is five inches high. Position the picture so it is centered horizontally and so the bottom of the photo aligns with the smart guide that indicates the top of the footer text box.
12. Duplicate Slide 4. On the new Slide 5, change the title to **Hospitals**.
13. On Slide 5 ("Hospitals"), drag the picture of the adults off the slide anywhere to the left (it doesn't matter if it is on top of the picture of the children). Drag the picture of the person in pink scrubs handing a tray of food to a patient onto the slide, and then resize it so that it is five inches high. Position the picture so it is centered vertically and so the bottom of the photo aligns with the smart guide that indicates the top of the footer text box.
14. Duplicate Slide 5. On the new Slide 6, change the title to **Corporate**.
15. On Slide 6 ("Corporate"), drag the picture of the person in pink scrubs handing a tray of food to a patient off the slide anywhere to the left. Drag the last picture on the right of the slide onto the slide (people standing in line in a cafeteria), and then resize it so that it is five inches high. Position the picture so it is centered horizontally and so the bottom of the photo aligns with the smart guide that indicates the top of the footer text box.
16. Apply the Morph transition to Slides 3 through 6, and then change the transition duration to 1.50 seconds.

Explore 17. Change the effect option on the slides that have the Morph transition applied so that each of the characters in the slide titles morph also.

18. On Slide 7 ("Our Clients"), insert a 2×4 table. Remove the formatting for the Header Row and Banded Rows, and then change the shading for all of the cells to No Fill. Enter the data shown in Figure 2–43 in the table.

Figure 2–43 **Data for the table on Slide 7**

Schools	Colleges High schools Middle schools Elementary schools
Residential Living	Assisted living Retirement homes
Hospitals	Patient meals Cafeterias
Corporate	Cafeterias Catered events

19. Insert a new column to the left of the first column. In the new first column, fill the cells with the following pictures, all located in the PowerPoint2 > Case4 folder: **Support_PPT_2_School.jpg**, **Support_PPT_2_Residential.jpg**, **Support_PPT_2_Hospital.jpg**, **Support_PPT_2_Corporate.jpg**.
20. Change the width of the first column to 2". Change the widths of the second and third columns to 2.5" each. Change the height of all of the rows in the table to 1.3". Center-align the table horizontally on the slide and then position it so that the bottom of the table aligns with the top of the footer text box.

21. Format the text in the second column as 24 points and bold. Center the text in the second and third columns vertically in the cells.
22. Select the table, and then remove the table borders. (*Hint*: Use the Borders button in the Table Styles group on the Table Design tab.) You might still see the table gridlines.
23. On Slide 7, insert a rectangle 1.3 inches high and 7 inches wide, and position it on top of the first row in the table so that the text and picture are covered. Use the smart guides to make sure that the top of the rectangle aligns with the top of the table and the sides of the rectangle are aligned with the sides of the table.
24. Apply the Wipe exit animation with the From Left effect to the rectangle. (*Hint*: Make sure you use the Wipe animation in the Exit category, not the Entrance category.)
25. Use the Duplicate command to duplicate the rectangle. Position the duplicated rectangle on top of the second row in the table, using the smart guides to make sure that the top of the duplicate rectangle aligns with the bottom of the first rectangle and the sides of the rectangle are aligned with the sides of the table. Then, duplicate the rectangle covering the second row in the table twice. If needed, position the third and fourth rectangles on top of the last two rows in the table.

Explore 26. Change the fill of each rectangle to the same color as the slide background. (*Hint*: Use the Eyedropper tool on the Shape Fill menu.) Remove the outline from the rectangles.

27. If you still see small lines above or below any rows in the table, click the rectangle covering that row, change its height to 1.35", and then reposition it so all of the row is covered.
28. On Slide 8 ("Health & Safety"), animate the bulleted list with the entrance Split animation. Change the effect to Horizontal In. Apply the same animation to the bulleted list on Slide 9 ("ServSafe Certification").
29. On Slide 9 ("ServSafe Certification"), add the registered trademark symbol ® after "ServSafe" in both the title and in the first bulleted item.
30. Compress all the pictures in the presentation to E-mail (96 ppi).
31. Save your changes, run the slide show, and then close the presentation.

INDEX

Note: **Boldfaced** page numbers indicate key terms

A

D

G

H

N

Q

R

T

Y

Z